POLICY MAKING
AND EXECUTIVE ACTION

McGRAW-HILL SERIES IN MANAGEMENT

KEITH DAVIS, Consulting Editor

MCDONOUGH   Information Economics and Management Systems
MCNICHOLS   Policy Making and Executive Action
MAIER   Problem-solving Discussions and Conferences: Leadership Methods and Skills
MARGULIES AND RAIA   Organizational Development: Values, Process, and Technology
MAYER   Production Management
MUNDEL   A Conceptual Framework for the Management Sciences
PETIT   The Moral Crisis in Management
PETROF, CARUSONE, AND MCDAVID   Small Business Management: Concepts and Techniques for Improving Decisions
PIGORS AND PIGORS   Case Method in Human Relations
PRASOW AND PETERS   Arbitration and Collective Bargaining: Conflict Resolution in Labor Relations
READY   The Administrator's Job
REDDIN   Managerial Effectiveness
SALTONSTALL   Human Relations in Administration
SARTAIN AND BAKER   The Supervisor and His Job
SCHRIEBER, JOHNSON, MEIER, FISCHER, AND NEWELL   Cases in Manufacturing Management
SHULL, DELBECQ, AND CUMMINGS   Organizational Decision Making
STEINER   Managerial Long-range Planning
SUTERMEISTER   People and Productivity
TANNENBAUM   Control in Organizations
TANNENBAUM, WESCHLER, AND MASSARIK   Leadership and Organization
VANCE   Industrial Administration
VANCE   Management Decision Simulation

POLICY MAKING AND EXECUTIVE ACTION

CASES ON BUSINESS POLICY

Fourth Edition

THOMAS J. McNICHOLS
Graduate School of Management
Northwestern University

Assisted in Case Preparation by

William L. Dejon
Graduate School of Management
Northwestern University

McGraw-Hill Book Company

New York St. Louis San Francisco Düsseldorf Johannesburg
Kuala Lumpur London Mexico Montreal New Delhi Panama
Rio de Janeiro Singapore Sydney Toronto

POLICY MAKING AND EXECUTIVE ACTION

Library of Congress Catalog Card Number 77-174621

07-045688-7

4 5 6 7 8 9 0 K P K P 7 9 8 7 6 5 4 3

The Northwestern University cases which appear
in this book are reproduced by permission of the
dean and faculty of the School of Business.
The cases represent reports of concrete events
and behavior prepared for class discussion.
They are not intended as examples of "good"
or "bad" administrative or technical practices.

CONTENTS

**PART EIGHT   THE REFORMULATION PHASE: RECYCLING AND
                        REAPPRAISING COURSES OF ACTION**

* Name of company, all individuals, and organizational designations have been disguised.

† International Policy Issues.

PREFACE

The fourth edition of *Policy Making and Executive Action,* like the previous three editions, is designed to provide a basic format and collection of cases for the teaching of business policy. The recognition and growing importance of business policy as a field of study and its importance as an integrating course in the final stages of study in business schools and schools of management have created a special demand for text material to delineate the field and for cases which present the problems and opportunities which confront the top-level administrators, the policy makers, in their efforts to guide and manage the total enterprise.

The new cases in this edition were selected with a view toward the significant trends and environmental changes with which the corporate executive must contend in our rapidly advancing technological society. The recent emphasis on mergers and acquisitions and the demand for the pressing of the financial and economic objectives of the firm have placed more stringent demands upon the financial acumen of the policy maker. The need to maintain a favorable earnings per share and an attractive growth pattern in attempting to "maximize shareholders' wealth" has once again given rise to "profit maximization" as the single most important corporate objective. We have passed through a decade where we have witnessed a wave of acquisitions and combinations and the advent of a new form of corporate enterprise, the conglomerate. The pattern of these developments is given recognition here in the addition of cases which present the problems, challenges, and opportunities faced by the policy maker in his quest for profitability, growth, and survival.

The development of our corporate technological society has created new social and environmental problems and has not readily solved many of the prevailing social ills. Today the policy maker is essentially faced with the dilemma of maximizing profits and simultaneously fulfilling the managerial responsibilities associated with corporate citizenship as he reacts to the problems of a changing environment. Public indignation over ecological problems, social stress, and, in the view of some, the failure of our industrial complex to satisfy the human needs of society have created new challenges for the policy maker. New cases have been added to this edition to reflect these significant issues and the role the policy maker must assume in a changing socially conscious environment. International cases stressing the complex problem of policy making on a global scale continue to be a feature of this book. New international cases have been added to this edition.

In this book efforts have been made to recognize possible variations in the purposes of teaching business policy as a subject area in the undergraduate curriculum, in graduate schools of business and management, and in executive development programs. It is assumed that despite varied approaches to the teaching of policy there is a common core that is apparent. In practically all instances the major purpose of the course is to develop facility in the analysis of business problems from the viewpoint of the chief executive or policy-making group, to provide a framework for decision making and policy formulation, and to guide the commitment of the firm.

A somewhat basic approach for developing the conceptual skill of policy making was used in selecting and arranging the cases in this book. This arrangement, however, is very flexible. It was not intended as an absolute guide, and changes in the sequence of the cases can readily be made to adapt the material to particular teaching techniques. With the exception of some of the cases in Parts Six and Seven, practically all the cases have a sufficient variety of policy issues to permit their effective use under two or more of the topical headings.

Part One includes introductory cases intended to provide direction and a framework for the analysis of business situations. The various functions and levels of the executive group should become apparent to the student in his initial exposure to policy cases, and in this phase of case analysis he should also begin to cultivate a "feel" or "way of thinking" about the management job from the standpoint of top-level administration. The importance of the role of the chief executive in shaping the corporate image and in charting the course of the business operation should become increasingly apparent as the student progresses from the simpler to the more complex cases.

The need for policy making—the "think" aspect of the administrator's job, which leads to the setting of guiding principles for courses of action—should also become apparent to the student at this stage. The case materials indicate that in actual business situations policy making may be a series of either formal or perhaps decidedly informal and unplanned acts or procedures. In some cases it may be quite evident that there is a serious lack of clear-cut policies to guide and direct the company's activities in strategic areas.

The student's ability to recognize the interrelationship of business functions in these early cases should mark the first step in a gradual development of a unique conceptual skill—the ability to see the business enterprise as a whole and the awareness that the various functions of the business organization are interdependent and must be coordinated for successful operation. As he progresses through the sequence of cases, it is not expected that he will perceive any abrupt change in the nature of the cases. His experiences with each distinct business situation are more likely to meld together in easy stages, eventually completing the whole structure of administrative skill.

The cases contained in Parts Two, Three, Four, Five, and Eight are integral blocks in the development of the overall administrative skill. In these sections the student is presented with diverse business situations of increasing complexity which serve as the raw materials for strengthening his analytical ability and for developing a conceptual and action-oriented approach to the problems of business policy. The cases in this grouping overflow from one topical heading into the next, and can, for the most part, be shifted readily from one section to another. The topical headings are used only to indicate the basic sequential processes of administration which define the executive functions.

This conceptual model of the administrative process outlined in the Contents may be briefly described as follows:

1. Diagnosis and Analysis: Viewing the firm as a system
2. The Decision-making Process: Developing the strategic design
3. The Strategy of Acquisitions, Mergers, and Expansion
4. The Implementation Phase: Developing organizational and control strategies.
5. The Reformulation Phase: Recycling and reappraising courses of action.

This conceptual framework is described in greater detail in the Introduction under the heading "Introduction to Business Policy."

Although the cases in Part Six represent a logical extension of the framework developed in the preceding sections, they are somewhat special in nature. They provide the student with an opportunity to examine the external, environmental problems of decision making associated with antitrust, minority groups, consumer pressures, and pollution. While the cases stressing these topics are not readily interchangeable with those of other sections, they can be effectively used in sequence with cases in other sections, particularly Parts Two, Three, and Four.

The cases in Part Seven stress the significance of the human factor and interpersonal relationships in executive administration. This phase of the administrator's job cannot, of course, be neatly separated from the total business situation and studied in a vacuum. It is constantly present in all business situations and consequently is also clearly evident in all business policy cases. The effective utilization of human resources is unquestionably the most important function of the executive. The role of the executive as a leader, the problems of delegation of authority, and communication problems within the organization are highlighted in the cases included in this section.

The suggested approach to case analysis and business policy described in the Introduction is intended as a sketch or background which might prove helpful to students in their initial encounter with business policy cases. The analytical scheme and the conceptual framework presented are somewhat basic in nature, and the student may find them useful in preparing cases for classroom discussion or in preparing case reports. Students may also find it profitable to supplement the case materials with books and selected articles in journals magazines, and newspapers in the field of business administration and business policy. Those students who are encountering the case method of instruction for the first time may also be interested in reading some of the current literature describing this method of teaching.

The student will, of course, look to the instructor for guidance and direction in the use of the introductory material of this book and in the use and selection of outside reading materials. The individual instructors are the best judges of the approach the student should take to the course. The utilization and sequence of the case materials and the explanation of the common pitfalls students are likely to discover in case discussions of business policy can be most effectively determined and explained by those who conduct the course.

ACKNOWLEDGMENTS

The collection of cases in this book was made possible by the cooperation of many business executives who provided the opportunity to write business policy cases about their companies and who generously shared their business experiences with the author and the case writers. I wish to thank Dean John A. Barr, Associate Dean Ralph L. Westfall, and the faculty of the Graduate School of Management for permission to use the Northwestern University cases which appear in this volume.

I wish to acknowledge my appreciation to the late Professor Richard Donham, former Dean of the School of Business of Northwestern University. He developed the original business policy course at Northwestern and initiated the case development program of the school.

The author is deeply grateful to the faculty members associated with the department of Policy and Environment and the Institute for Management of the Graduate School of Management of Northwestern who helped mold and develop the basic concepts of the teaching of business policy at the school. Professors who used the first three editions of *Policy Making and Executive Action* have generously reviewed the book and have made significant suggestions which have been incorporated into this fourth edition. There are a great number to whom I am indebted, and I wish to thank each of them for his contribution.

While many of the cases which appear in this edition were written by the author, a number have been prepared by present and former members of the faculty and staff of the Graduate School of Management of Northwestern. Present members who have written cases in their present or revised form include Professors Richard W. Barsness, Howard F. Bennett, and Edward T. P. Watson. Staff members include William L. Dejon, Miss Frances Sheridan, Robert C. Shirley, and Gerald A. Rolph. Former faculty and staff members include Professors Garret L. Bergen, Harper W. Boyd, Jr., Floyd S. Brandt, Dominic Parisi, and research associates Arne Benneborn, Joseph Connally, and Miss Martha Ottinger. I also wish to thank Thomas G. Newton for his contributions.

I wish to express my appreciation to Mrs. Verna Kummer, secretary of the case research department, for her immeasurable aid in the preparation of the cases that went into the four editions of this book, and to Mrs. Joyce Larsen for her assistance in the preparation of this edition. I also wish to thank Mrs. Perle Hill and Mrs. Gretel Murphy for their secretarial assistance. I am especially indebted to my wife, Willelene McNichols, for her editorial assistance, encouragement, and help.

THOMAS J. MCNICHOLS

POLICY MAKING
AND EXECUTIVE ACTION

INTRODUCTION TO BUSINESS POLICY

Defining the concept and meaning of the term *business policy* is not an easy task because of the many connotations associated with the word *policy,* which range from that of rules or procedures to be followed as general operating guidelines, to the significant management process of decision making. We are concerned with business policy as a specialized field of study, within the framework of business administration, which endeavors to incorporate the functions of the chief executive officer of the firm and his counterparts who define the mission, purpose, and major goals which direct and guide the total enterprise over a long-time horizon. Our major concern is with the sophisticated contemplative action of the top-level decision makers rather than the repetitive routinized actions which may be programmed or committed to decision rules. This type of administrative action, although significant and important within the operations of the functional areas of the enterprise, is not the province of the policy maker but rather the result of the generalized experience of the firm reflected in the performance of lower-echelon executives seeking to implement the policies of the top management group.

In addition to the cognitive aspects of the policy maker and his role as the architect and designer of the firm's blueprint for action, the field of business policy encompasses major elements of the management function beyond the formulation of basic economic and business objectives. It also includes the study and appraisal of the implementation and action decisions, the structuring and design of the organization,

1

and the development of an interpretative mechanism to provide the information and control necessary to insure the attainment of the basic objectives of the enterprise.

The development of business policy as a specialized field of study can be traced back to the early advances in scientific management. Over fifty years ago the writings and ideas of Frederick W. Taylor began to emerge and gain notice in the business world. Taylor's approach, although frequently criticized today as a "production, or machine concept" which avoided the human factor, laid the groundwork for a calculated organized response to problems encountered in the day-to-day operations of the firm. While Taylor did concentrate mainly on the production process, he provided the basis for the development of the functional specialists as an integral part of the management group. Taylor's theory of the separation of tasks on the assembly line as part of the production function was in effect expanded to other functions as business developed specialists in accounting, marketing, and finance and in more recent years in such areas as industrial engineering, industrial relations, public relations, and other allied areas which were added to commonly recognized staff requirements.

Executives with highly specialized training staffed these traditional departments which formed the "modern corporation." Personnel requirements were generally stated in terms of functional areas, and management training was developed along functional lines. Business schools, which were in their embryonic stages when Taylor began his writings, were quick to adopt the functional approach in their curriculums. There is no doubt that the development of specialists in each management function caused a minor management revolution. The intuitive "seat-of-the-pants" approach gave way, at least in the more advanced business operations, to the reasoned deliberations of trained executives. Although the application of expertise was (and perhaps to a great extent, still is today) at the operating level rather than the policy-making level, and was not spectacularly apparent, the results it produced on the business scene are manifest.

The specialist has been able to provide significant basic data to aid in determining weaknesses or strong points of the business operations. Information systems have been developed to supply management with data which gives a picture of the over-all operations of the business. The application of mathematical concepts, and the advances made in operations research and the behavioral sciences have added to the tools of decision making as important reinforcements to the work of the functional specialists.

While the division of business activities created experts that promoted and effected efficiency, it also complicated and increased the difficulty of developing top managers who could view the firm as a single coordinated entity. The policy makers were confronted with a complex organization of specialized functions and departments. How could they possibly be an expert in each functional field? How could they understand the operations of the multiple departments and staff positions of the large corporate enterprise? How could each department manager, divisional head, and vice president see his own position and responsibilities in relation to the goals and operations of the total business enterprise?

The policy makers had the advantage of looking down on the entire operation, but what kind of a view did they get? Were they looking at it through the eyes of specialists—each through the viewpoint of his own specialty? Top management were probably all specialists in one function or another. They most likely had received recognition for performing their particular role exceptionally well and thus had earned the opportunity to direct the corporate effort from the higher echelons of their new executive positions as part of the policy-making group. The skills and abilities they brought to their new positions were generally developed along specific functional lines, but as part of the policy-making team they were required to adapt their specialized knowledge to the entire business effort, not to just a subfunction of its operations. Except in a small number of companies, which provided a measure of executive development through an over-all look at the entire corporate effort through job rotation, the average executive entering the policy-making position brought little knowledge of directing, co-ordinating, and guiding the business as an integrated unit. In many instances the very factor which had projected him into the top management position—his expert knowledge and performance as a director of a specific function—frequently proved to be one of the greatest handicaps to him in his adaptation to the over-all viewpoint so necessary to the policy maker. Many policy makers suffered from functional emotionalism (and no doubt many are still afflicted with this malady today). The financial executive tended to see many corporate problems as essential manifestations of poor financial policy; the marketing manager, as part of the top management team, was inclined to think that all management problems could be solved by applying the "marketing concept"; the production-oriented executive attacked his dilemmas initially through the production line; others trained and experienced in different specialties tended to approach the decision-making process through their own familiar channels.

There is no doubt that qualified executives, despite their lack of background in the policy-making process, eventually learned through experience that the firm had to be viewed as a whole, that it was impossible to separate business problems into neat little compartments and proceed to solve them one at a time. The principle of *functional dynamics* soon became apparent. A decision to change a basic policy affected all departments and functions to a greater or lesser degree; significant changes in the marketing function, the additions to or deletions from the product line directly affected the production function. The interrelatedness of the operations of the firm had to be taken into account in all policy deliberations. Certain decisions might also affect the community, might make the corporation vulnerable to governmental action, or might disrupt labor relations.

The logical questions were asked. What can the executive do when he is continually faced with nonprogrammed complex business decisions? Is there any order of analysis, any administrative process which he can follow that will enable him to grasp the totality of the situation at any given time? Are there any specific "tools" which will aid the policy maker in effecting a combination of multiple functional activities and establish effective guidelines for action? These significant questions have been posed in the past and are constantly being asked by policy-making executives. They form the basis for a continuing search for a general management theory or concept which provides an approach to the management of the total enterprise. The study of business policy as a specialized field is in response to these questions and to attempts to provide a systematic methodology which will serve as a framework for the analysis of general management problems and opportunities of the business enterprise.

ANALYTICAL PHASE—IDENTIFICATION OF PROBLEM AREAS AND DETERMINATION OF ROOT CAUSES

A significant part of an executive's time is spent in problem identification or situational analysis. He is constantly engaged in a diagnostic procedure, probing, analyzing, and interpreting the significant internal and external events which affect the progress of the firm toward its preconceived goals. The key to analysis of major business problems is found in continued recognition of the function of the policy maker, that of establishing the enterprise goals and guiding the organization to the accomplishment of its mission objectives. In this context the firm must be viewed as a single system functioning as a whole unit through the interaction of its parts or subsystems. The basic concepts of the systems approach can be adapted to analyze the firm and evaluate its performance if we recognize some of the limitations of applying this technique to the nonstatic business enterprise which must remain flexible and dynamic if it is to cope with its competitive environment.

The first step in problem identification involves the fundamental process of examining all the facts and data available in a given situation. Before any action can be taken or any decision can be made, the policy maker must have as full an understanding as possible of the company's position and of the extent and nature of its problems. The dynamics of business and the changing economic scene make this analytical procedure a never-ending task. Each situation represents a particular complex of events at a point in time—subject to change and all the uncertainties and vagaries of a competitive business society.

The analytical approach designed to accomplish this phase of administration may vary to a great extent among executives. However, there are in each case basic factors to be considered and common questions to be asked:

What facts, figures, and data are available to give as complete a picture of the company as possible?

What additional information is needed to complete the picture?

What information is available concerning external conditions which can affect company operations?

Is this information sufficient to analyze the situation? If not, what additional information is needed and from what sources can it be gathered?

The gathering, sorting, and assessing of information will lead to more specific questions, which can be conveniently divided into two categories:

Internal factors within control of the company.

External or environmental factors considered to be beyond the control of the company.

Internal considerations may include:

How well is the company doing?

Is the company faring better or worse than its competitors?

Is it making or losing money?

What is its financial position?

What is its rate of return? Growth rate? Cost of capital?

Are there information and feedback problems?

What is the situation in marketing and sales?

Are there production problems?

Are there specific problems in allied functional areas?

What is the nature and extent of personnel or labor problems?

Are there problems of organizational design and structure?

Is there evidence of interpersonal-relations problems? Between executives and the employee group? Within the employee group? Factors of delegation, motivation, etc.?

External factors that may bear scrutiny are:

What is the state of the economy?

What do forecasts seem to indicate about the immediate and longer-run economic future?

What is the nature of the company's industry?

What is the pattern of competition in the industry?

Are there large companies in the industry that hold a great percentage of the market, or many small companies, each with a relatively small share of the market?

What is the state of technology relative to the firm's products? Potential competitive products?

How attractive is the company to the investing public?

How and to what extent does government regulation influence the industry?

What is the political and social environment in which the company operates?

This list of questions which the policy maker might logically consider in his analysis of internal and external factors affecting the company by no means exhausts the important and pertinent queries which may be made. They are merely suggestive of a line of reasoning which will direct attention to significant problem areas.

An appraisal of the firm's skills and resources will aid in further defining the analytical process and will tend to integrate the internal and external factors which may affect the company's position. An inventory of the specific assets, both tangible and intangible, which will enable the company to compete favorably and profitably may raise such questions as:

What property, plant, and equipment does the company own or lease?

What is the condition of these assets? Age?

Are there any special or unique features about these assets which give the company competitive advantages?

Is the company's location particularly advantageous? (For raw materials? Distribution? Labor?)

What about the company's product line? Marketing mix? Is it special? Unique? High quality? Diversified?

Is the distribution system of the company good? Exceptional?

What financial resources does the firm have which will enable it to maintain its position or acquire additional needed skills and resources?

Does it have ample working capital? Line of credit?

What prospects does it have for selling securities? Debt financing? Equity financing?

What personnel resources does the company have? An exceptional executive leader? President or chairman of the board? Executive group? Middle-management group? Skilled labor?

Does the company have good labor relations?

What intangible assets does the company possess? Does the public have a good image of the firm?

What is the state of its product development? Technological skills? Research and development capability?

Does the firm have a good brand name? Trademark? Patent? Copyright?

These questions, and many more which the student will be likely to raise when he appraises the skills and resources of the firm in a particular business situation, will lead to a consideration of the basic processes of policy making. What objectives have been set? How are these objectives to be attained? What plans has the company made? And most important, are the firm's objectives compatible with its skills and resources?

Engaging in the analytical process of appraising the functional areas of the business, examining the internal and external factors, and inventorying the skills and resources of the firm will afford an insight into the situation from several angles. While there will be overlapping in the procedures, multiple sightings from different vantage points will aid in putting the problems in perspective and in assessing the information gathered. The process of evaluating the mass of data obtained, separating the relevant from the irrelevant, and distinguishing between fact and assumption is a constant one which must be engaged in throughout the analysis of the business situation. Out of this sifting and refining of the raw data the significant problems of the company will begin to emerge.

Focus on the Policy-making Process. The next important step in the policy-making process involves the selection of the root cause of major problem areas of the firm—the focal points for action. What should be done? Where should we begin? There may be distinct evidence of problems in marketing, production, finance, and other allied areas. These problems represent a collection of matters that need attention; separately they do not provide a clue to the order of needed executive action. The problems cannot be attacked in a piecemeal fashion because of the interrelationship of the functional areas. Putting out the "fire" in the sales area may only cause a new fire to flare up in production. The major problems of the firm cut across departmental lines, and cannot be treated as separate self-contained distress areas.

Functional and departmental problems are really symptoms or manifestations of a more deep-rooted difficulty that lies within the spectrum of the policy-making process and in the area of responsibility of top management. The analysis and judgment of the top management group, the policy makers of the firm, must therefore transcend functional and departmental lines and conceive of the entity as a single unit directed toward predetermined goals and guided by planned courses of action. They must direct their attention to the underlying problems of the firm and not the surface indications.

exhibit 1

Analytical Phase

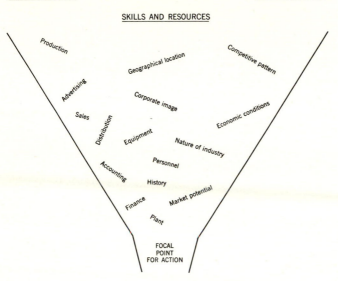

Formulation Phase—Review of Basic Objectives
and Reformulation of Root Strategy
Implementation Phase—Redesign of Operational Strategy
Organizational Phase—Redesign of Organizational Strategy
Interpretative Phase—Redesign of Control Strategy

The evidence of specific problems can, however, be translated into terms of basic processes of policy formulation. A more generalized diagnostic approach can then be applied to relate the symptoms to possible failures in one of the four basic areas of the policy-making process— the *formulation phase, implementation phase, organizational phase,* and *interpretative phase.* In the final analysis, the initial symptoms will point to one of the major problem areas, where the administrator can initiate action. Exhibit 1 illustrates this phase of the policy maker's task. He considers and analyzes all the facts and data available about the particular business situation and places them in the "analytical hopper," where they are sifted and refined until the core or the crux of the firm's problems is released from the bottom of the hopper.

The four basic steps in the policy-making process are difficult to isolate in the going concern. They are interdependent and meld to-

gether to form an over-all program. However, in most instances it is
possible to analyze them separately against the background of the significant problems and difficulties of the firm in each particular business
situation. Exhibit 2 illustrates this continuous "flow" of the policy-
making process and the interdependence of each basic step in decision
making and policy formulation.

Formulation Phase—Developing the Root Strategy. The administrator begins his diagnosis with an appraisal of the corporate basic objectives. Many of the problems and difficulties that are revealed in the
analysis of a business situation may be symptomatic of a failure to set
well-defined and realistic objectives. The lack of clear-cut goals will
lead to uncertainty in planning, in structuring and staffing the organization, and in setting up controls to measure the effectiveness and check
the results of administrative action. The objectives of the enterprise
serve as the continuing guiding force for all the company's activities,
the goal of all its planning, and the base from which the strategic
policies of the firm emerge. It is in this phase of the policy-making
process that management forms the root strategy of the firm.

Many attempts have been made to describe the process of developing
the "character" of a business or an "image" of the enterprise—as the
marketing or advertising group might prefer to name this abstraction.
The primary multifaceted state of the policy-making process is undoubtedly more difficult to describe than the successive steps of policy
making and lends itself more to conceptualization than the pragmatic
decision areas of implementation, organizing, and interpreting results.
In the formulation stage the enterprise establishes its basic business
objectives and predetermines its general course of action. The kind and
type of business the organization will engage in and the extent of the
commitment of its skills and resources are outlined in terms of goals
and broad policies intended to guide the enterprise.

In determining the root strategy of a company it must be assumed
that the elementary objectives of profitability growth and survival are
paramount and supersede basic business objectives which outline and
delineate the company's strategy. Businesses operating in a competitive
environment must be profitable in order to survive; thus the profit
objective is taken for granted and is cnly subjected to scrutiny in
relation to what the profit goals should be in terms of specific measures such as total profits; profits as a percentage of sales by divisions,
product lines, or geographical areas; and profits measured in terms of

exhibit 2
Conceptual Model of the Policy-Making Process

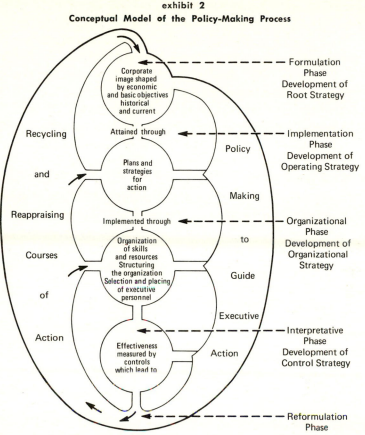

return on invested capital. If the management of a firm does not consider survival as an elementary objective, then their whole strategic pattern will be directed toward terminal goals such as a limited venture in terms of time with foreseeable liquidation or sale, or "conditioning" of the company for a potential merger or acquisition by another firm. A going business can only sell or be merged one time. Once management has determined a terminal objective, the course of executive action will be directed toward that end and not the normal competitive strategy dictated by the survival objective.

The elementary objective of growth must follow from profitability and is necessary to insure survival. While the old cliché that "no business can stand still—it must either grow or perish" has been frequently contested, the argument has been only in terms of degrees. In today's competitive business society, growth over time is essential to survival.

It is just a question of how much growth is necessary and manageable to maintain a dynamic business.

The root strategy of a business organization is determined over time and is a composite of basic business objectives expressed in terms of the specific allocation of the firm's skills and resources in the marketplace. In the initial stages of development of the firm the root strategy is usually easily discernible. For example, the Polaroid Land Camera Company, which enjoys international success, was organized to exploit the invention of Dr. Land. He had created a camera which not only took photographs but also developed the pictures in a matter of seconds. This product was, of course, unique, and it created a distinct niche in the camera market for the company. The major skills and resources of the company at its inception were based on the invention of Dr. Land and the obvious potential demand which existed in the marketplace for such a product. To be successful with its product, the Polaroid company had to develop operational strategies in terms of production, marketing, and financing to support its root strategy. An organization had to be formed and structured to accomplish the expressed goals of the newly formed company. While the root strategy of Polaroid was firmly determined by the nature of its innovative product, operational strategy had to be developed through time and experience in the marketplace. Other industrial giants which are part of our economy today stemmed from a scientific method or discovery, or clearly discernible skills or resources.

While a comprehensive plan may not be formalized and committed to paper in the initial stages of development of the business enterprise, the originators of any business must conceive of a basic niche they intend to occupy in the marketplace, whether it be for goods or services. The start of most small business endeavors is based on specific skills and resources of the entrepreneurs, either real or imagined. In most instances considerable thought is given to the economic need or function the embryonic enterprise will provide for society. The strength and viability of the need is the major external determining factor for the survival of the firm. The degree of "uniqueness," or extent of innovation present, in the goods or services offered by a business in the initial stages of its life cycle will be readily apparent and will provide the foundation for successful operation of the enterprise.

The necessity of defining the purpose and nature of a beginning business is evident. However, when the policy maker or student of business policy attempts to delineate the root strategy or basic characteristics of the going concern, the problems become more complex and difficult. The size and maturity of the firm in many cases tend to obscure its original intent and purpose for entering the competitive scene. The multiple stages of growth, the shifts in strategy and direction of the enterprise necessitated by the changing economic environment, complicate tracing the origin of specific strategies and differentiating between the various stages of the policy-making process. Acquisitions, mergers, diversification attempts, and product proliferation engaged in over a period of time blur and confuse the corporate image. Attempts to describe and trace the root strategy of the large, multiproduct, multidivisional, and conglomerate-type corporations sometimes defy conventional analysis and necessitate reverting to basic economic objectives to find a unifying link for the varied entrepreneurial efforts. Efforts to define root strategies and operational efforts are frequently restricted to the separate companies, divisions, or product-lines which make up the enterprise.

In the determination and analysis of the firm's basic objectives and root strategy, management must constantly keep in mind such questions as:

What place will the firm fill in the social order?
What need or service will it supply to society?
What market niche or industry position does the firm seek to attain?
What specific products or services is the firm going to make and sell?
Does the firm have a single-product line? Multiproduct line?
What decisions have been made about the size of the firm?
What share of the market does it seek?
How will it attempt to integrate? Horizontally? Vertically?
Are the firm's objectives compatible with its skills and resources?
What skills and resources does the firm have, and need, to accomplish its predetermined goals?
What are the strengths and limitations of its skills and resources?
Can it accomplish the stated goals with its financial resources? With its skills and resources in production and marketing? With its organization and personnel?

There are many other factors that are important in shaping the corporate image and guiding the direction of a company. The root strategy established over time develops a certain character and creates an image of the firm in the minds of its customers and competitors. Some firms are characterized as progressive, the forerunners in the industry, the ones most likely to develop new products. They seek and create new opportunities and assume the consequent risks attached to the innovating process. Others have a reputation for being conservative and steady. These companies are content to make changes and adaptations only when the "groundwork has been laid" and the element of risk in "plowing new ground" has been reasonably reduced by the action of other firms.

The personal objectives of individuals in management may also be a major factor in shaping the image of a company. For example, a desire to maintain ownership control may restrict the size and activities of a business by confining it to its own capital resources. Dominant individuals in management, even in large corporations, may be personally responsible for molding a particular reputation which a firm may enjoy or find a handicap.

The shaping of the corporate image is also inextricably tied in with the firm's relations with external groups. The manner and method it employs to attain its desired place in industry will have a profound effect on its employees, customers, competitors, and the general public. The business entity develops an institutional social philosophy which guides its actions in personnel relations, in community relations, and in relations with business associates, competitors, the government, and stockholders.

The basic objectives of a firm are not confined to a single-purpose goal but comprise a combination of tangible concrete goals and intangible guides which shape the business personality and create an image reflected in all the firm's operations.

Implementation Phase—Developing the Operating Strategy. Executive action follows from the formulation phase; the firm as a whole must commit itself to a plan of action calculated to attain the basic business objectives. Operating strategy defines the general and specific action which the company intends to execute in the marketplace. Of necessity, operating strategy must be more flexible and subject to more rapid and frequent change than the root strategy of the firm. Most companies engaging in competitive business are primarily concerned with operating strategy. The basic root strategy has been conceived and designed for all the firm's operations and in many instances represents an "institutionalization" of various developments and shifts in strategy which have been nurtured in the marketplace over a period of time. Once the basic objectives have been determined and reviewed, management must chart a course of action to direct the firm toward is predetermined goals through maximum utilization of its skills and resources.

The policies of the company, which constitute the guides for executive action, emerge from the root strategy of the organization and form the backbone of planning. The plans should consistently reflect the root strategy, and their efficacy must be constantly reappraised according to the established objectives of the firm.

The operating plans of a dynamic business organization at any given time may be difficult to identify and reduce to a list. Most firms have a variety of operating plans in various stages of completion—long-range plans, short-range plans, special programs, and specific plans relating to subfunctions of the firm. In attempting to evaluate the operating strategy it is convenient to think in terms of a master plan supplemented by detailed plans. The master plan should provide the over-all blueprint or coordinating factor for the entire company program of action and should be the directing or guiding force for detailed functional planning.

In any business venture there are no obvious courses of operating action that will lead the firm to assured success. The master plan, which outlines the principal steps the company will take in attempting to attain its objectives, will in all likelihood be subject to numerous changes because of the uncertainties of the marketplace. Long-range plans which outline action expected to be taken over a period of years, usually considered to be three to five years or longer, are subject to the greatest uncertainties and possibilities of change. Short-range plans, which are usually considered to run from three months to a year or three years, depending upon the nature of the company, are less likely to be changed. All plans, however, must be flexible and should be backed by alternative plans. The ability to keep pace with trends in the market is a necessary element in the planning function. The shifting and adjusting of plans as part of the operating strategy, may be required in order to cope with unanticipated moves by competitors or shifts in the economic scene. This ability to meet the demands of particular situations and to provide the necessary flexibility to cope with change is a vital part of day-to-day planning.

Capturing and maintaining market position is one of the most important elements of the implementation phase. In each stage of the company's development and progress toward attaining its objectives, particular functions may need attention. The emphasis may shift from marketing and sales to production or other functional areas that require special consideration at a particular time. The master plan should be designed to balance the company's skills and resources and to utilize them to the best possible advantage. All the functions and departments of the business unit must be coordinated, and conflicts of purpose between them must be resolved. The master plan must outline the comprehensive program and the timing of the principal steps in carrying this program into action.

In reviewing the plans and strategies of the firm the following specific questions may serve as guides in diagnosing problems in this area:

Has a range of alternative plans been considered?

Have well-defined alternative plans been drafted for use if needed?

Which plan best suits the company's skills and resources? Financial resources? Marketing skills and resources? Production skills and resources? Personnel and labor skills?

Have the external factors been considered in the selection of a master plan? Economic conditions? Competitive pattern? Industry factors?

Has the adopted plan been projected to determine extent of skill and resource utilization? Additional skills and resources needed? Possible effects of the plan on competitors? Potential customers and size of market?

Have the long-range and short-range plans been coordinated in the master plan?

Have divisional and departmental plans been coordinated in the over-all program?

Has a time schedule been worked out for each step in the planned program of action?

Has economic forecasting been employed to aid in determining for each product line the market potential? Share of the market expected? Sales goals?

Have a master and detailed budget been prepared?

Have quantitative data been used and evaluated to determine for each product line the costs? Selling prices? Profit margins? Inventory requirements? Cash requirements? Profit goals? Expected return on investments? Break-even point? Pay-out periods for capital investments?

Has an adequate research and development program been set up?

Have specific and detailed programs been developed for each product line in the functional areas and departments to carry out the master plan?

Are the company's operating plans and policies flexible enough to allow for changes, adaptations, and strategic action to cope with unanticipated changes in the marketplace?

Organizational Phase—Developing Organizational Strategy. Once the objective function has been determined and reviewed and the criteria function defined, the action stage is set and the operations must be carried out by executive and operating personnel. The execution of the long-range, short-range, and day-to-day actions of the firm's personnel are going to account for the success or failure of the business enterprise. The way the firm is organized, its structure, design, interrelationships, formal and informal, are effectively determined by the architects of the firm and the basic premise for their design is found in the formulation and implementation phases of the policy-making process.

From the viewpoint of the policy maker at the organizational phase, we have defined the goals of the system and have outlined the major operating strategies to attain these goals. If we examine specific companies we can easily trace the effect of redefinition of goals and objectives on the organization. To illustrate, a few simple examples—the firm which chooses to sell through agents or wholesalers rather than develop a complete sales force of its own will have a different composition and structure to its organization than a firm which has chosen to sell through its own sales group at all levels. If the automobile industry had initially chosen to sell their product through their own retail units, their organization would have been significantly different than it is at present under the conceived strategy of selling through franchised dealers who operate their retail sales and service establishments under "guided independence." Not only would the structure of General Motors, Ford, Chrysler, and American Motors be substantially different in shape and size but there would also be significant differences in organizational relationships. The functional dynamics vis-à-vis production-marketing would be more direct and pointed; the authority relationship would be direct; communication would be direct; and no doubt greater control would be exercised over selling policies, customer relations, and repair policies.

If we examine the product policies of companies we can readily see significant organization structure and strategy differences between single-line product firms and multiproduct firms. The proliferation of product lines both horizontally and vertically has introduced product managers and brand managers. The tendency to give operating independence to divisional, product managers, and brand managers has significantly altered the authority-control relations of many organizations. These shifts in operating strategy not only change the formal structure but also create a new informal structure and new organizational relationships. Frequently the patterns of development which follow a strategy shift or change are difficult to trace in the initial stages. After an operational strategy takes hold the organizational strategy develops.

The transition from policy making and operational planning to executive action is accomplished through the essential step of developing the organizational strategy. In the initial steps of organizational planning the firm attempts to develop an "ideal" structure which will provide the best possible grouping of projected activities. This "custombuilt" organization structure is designed to cover each phase and function of the firm's operations. It is intended to provide the most effective medium for harnessing and utilizing available skills and resources and for reflecting the firm's objectives and managerial philosophy.

The basic framework for decision making and action must establish the relationships between each level of the management job and clearly define authority links, spans, and limitations to permit executives and subordinates to understand the nature and extent of their responsibilities. In structuring a practical working organization, management will be confronted with many of the following problems:

How should operational activities be divided? By functional departments? By processes of production? By geographical location? Territories? Districts? Divisions? Product lines?

How should the lines of authority and responsibility be drawn?

Have relationships between units been clearly charted to fix responsibilities and allow for delegation of authority?

What limits should be considered for the span of management control and the length of lines of communication?

To what extent should operations and lines of authority be centralized? Decentralized?

Does the structure allow for the use of specialized functional skills?

How should the relationships between line and staff be defined?
Does the structure provide for balance and flexibility?

While an efficient organization structure will be a major factor in
determining successful operations, it still represents only the vehicle or
means through which executive action is channeled. The most important and difficult task is the selection and placement of a working management team which will effectively guide the firm along the lines
charted in the planning stages. While the organization structure should
be initially based on an ideal framework, invariably it must be adapted
for the human factor. In the final step of filling out the structure,
modifications of the ideal organizational form will be necessary to fit
the capabilities and limitations of available executive personnel.

Despite necessary and inevitable deviations from initially drafted
ideal structures, organizational planning will provide the firm with a
standard which will afford sounder evaluation of personnel, control
over organizational changes, and greater flexibility to adapt to environmental changes.

Executive personnel are charged with the responsibility of translat-
ing policies and plans into action and developing a smoothly functioning team out of the people within the organization. The personnel of
many and varied skills must be properly administered in a great variety
of functional activities on a day-to-day basis; their tasks and programs
must be arranged and their activities coordinated and directed toward
predetermined goals. The type and quality of executives required to
perform these managerial functions may vary to a great extent according to the nature, objectives, and policies of the firm. Despite titles,
management positions are not standardized. Similarly, management requirements within a firm are not static. Shifts and changes in objectives and plans, and the consequent demand for new and different
skills, may require a remolding of the organization structure.

Corporate expansion, in addition to creating a need for increased
executive personnel, will also undoubtedly cause shifts in management
levels. Problems of line and staff, decentralization, and management
training and development will become important factors in organizational planning. Adapting the organization to the dynamics of the business scene demands constant reappraisal of the interrelationship of the
multitude of factors affecting the human forces guiding the destiny of
the firm. Organizational design and structure should determine the flow

of the decision-making process. When organizations are ill-designed and lag behind the conceived strategies of the firm, their ineffectiveness is quickly felt and usually results in frequent by-passing and reliance upon the informal organization structure. There is always a search for the optimum organizational model which is a fleeting goal seldom if ever attained. It's a virtual certainty that the organizational design of all growing business enterprises lag behind their operating strategies.

Interpretative Phase—Developing the Control Strategy. Control strategies must be designed to constantly reflect the firm's operations as a total system. The performance measures designed for divisions, departments, and various other subunits should stem from the over-all objectives of the total enterprise and should measure the progress toward corporate objectives determined through the root and operating strategies of the business enterprise. The salient factors of communication, motivation, and delegation are an integral part of the control strategy. The quantitative and qualitative control measures are usually designed to reflect performance toward preconceived standards or objectives. While they will reveal deviations from stated goals they do not indicate individual behavioral characteristics which may result in inadequate performance. Goal conflict is more likely to be present than goal congruence. Managers of subunits may and do frequently have personal objectives which conflict with the over-all objectives of the firm. Their interpretation of the strategic design and goal set of the enterprise may not be in accord with that of the policy makers.

However, once the organization has put into action the plans and strategies designed to attain the firm's objectives, management is confronted with the problem of controlling and appraising day-to-day operations. It must assess the soundness of its plans and measure the performance of subordinates entrusted with the responsibility of putting specific programs into action. The review of the firm's operations requires a continuous flow of pertinent information through organization channels to enable management to make significant judgments regarding such questions as:

How well is the firm doing in relation to its economic objectives? Basic business objectives? In relation to competition? In relation to industry trends?

What is the relationship of progress to plan in the over-all program? In the timing and execution of specific programs?

How effectively are subordinates performing specific administrative functions in the execution of the firm's plans and strategies?

The ability of management to answer important questions of this nature depends upon the adequacy of its system of controls. Ideally, control measures are based upon the objectives, plans, and strategies of the firm and are designed to reflect the action, efficiency, and progress the organization has made toward attaining its predetermined goals. It is difficult, however, to examine the control function in isolation because it is so distinctly dependent upon and tied to the other phases of the policy-making process. Efficient controls are dependent, first of all, upon good planning, sound administrative policies, and a clearly defined organization structure. The firm's objectives and plans may thus serve as control standards to measure and judge the efficiency of operations. Control measures may indicate that changes or refinements are necessary in these basic objectives, plans, and strategies.

Despite the fact that the control function is so enmeshed with the other processes of administration, it is necessary for management to analyze this function independently to determine whether it meets the requirements of the firm's operations. A well-conceived control system will reflect the organization structure and tie the control standards to individual responsibility. In essence, control always reflects individual performance since specific functions are assigned, and authority and responsibility are delegated to particular persons within the organizational unit. A clearly defined organization structure aids in focusing attention on the individual or individuals responsible for meeting specific goals or standards of performance. The organization thus provides the vehicle not only for directing and coordinating action, but also for maintaining control and appraising individual performance.

The following policy questions will aid in further testing the efficacy of a control system:

Have strategic control points been selected which will most accurately reflect the progress of the firm and the performance of management?

What measures will best reflect the progress toward over-all company objectives? Toward the goals of particular subunits? Divisions? Departments?

Can the controls be readily comprehended by the management personnel who will be expected to utilize them in the day-to-day operations?

Are the controls forward-looking so that deviations from the charted course can be detected in sufficient time to apply corrective action?

Are the controls flexible enough to allow for necessary sudden shifts in planning and strategy?

Does the control system, in addition to detecting deviations from plan, provide the means to initiate corrective action?

For control measures to be effective in determining the adequacy of the firm's strategic design they must be conceived as a system and developed as a coordinated unit. It is useful to examine the control strategy in three phases:

1. Precontrol Phase. In this phase the root strategy of the firm is analyzed in relation to the firm's capabilities—its skills and resources. Is the firm capable of attaining a specific niche in the market place? Is its product line or service competitive enough to assure a specified market share? Is it unique? Innovative? Or obsolete? Does the firm have the financial and personnel resources needed to attain its objectives of market penetration, profitability and growth?

The determination of basic economic and business objectives must begin with an assessment of the skills and resources of the enterprise. Setting objectives or goals beyond the capabilities of the firm renders a control system ineffective from the start. Profitability and budgetary goals, which form the backbone of most business control systems, are frequently overstated and sometimes unrealistic in terms of the capabilities of the enterprise and the economic environment. To assure goal congruence, the root strategy and objectives of the organization must be realistically determined and measured against the inventory of skills and resources of the enterprise.

2. Continuing-control Phase. The appraisal of the capabilities of the management group and operating personnel must be a continuous process and not relegated to infrequent reappraisals triggered by crisis situations. Management development and training are essential ingredients of a control system. Delegating authority and responsibility to managers not ready or incapable of the tasks assigned them virtually assures that the enterprise objectives will not be attained. Continuing control suggests that a "pro-forma" organization chart be maintained to indicate the specific kinds and types of management skills required to attain long-run and short-run objectives. Unless the management group is subject to continued evaluation and development, maintaining the firm's position—or reaching new goals in terms of profitability, growth, and expansion—becomes a difficult if not impossible task.

3. Postcontrol Phase. This phase of the control system usually receives the most attention and review on the part of management. While recording and interpreting results is an essential and important executive function, it is still based on past performance and the effectiveness of the information system. The objective of control measures is to provide the information to assess progress toward predetermined goals and to aid the policy maker in problem identification. It must be remembered that the most elaborate control systems will not correct the mistakes of the past but only aid in providing for more effective executive action in the future.

Interpretation of results is a demanding on-going task of the policy maker. Failure to correctly interpret internal and external signs provided through the control system has led many a firm to failure, or slow profitless readjustment periods. Many business analysts maintain that the famed Packard Motor Car disappeared from the market because declining sales and profits in the depression period were interpreted as a need to market a lower priced automobile, rather than a need to reduce costs and upgrade its engineering and design, and to change marketing strategy. We can also find numerous examples of firms which operate on "strategy by drift" rather than utilizing planned strategy changes to correct and alter the course of the enterprise. The lack of an intelligent and decisive review of past control information may lead to a do-nothing policy and permit the corporate ship to drift with the economic tide until a crisis situation arises.

Reformulation Phase—Reappraisal and Recycling of the Policy-making Process. Exhibit 2 indicates the "closing of the system" in the reformulation phase. The information provided through the control system may indicate that the firm is performing according to expectations and the organization is functioning smoothly and according to plan. Almost invariably, however, an organization attempting to execute a complex program of plans and strategies subject to internal and external forces will deviate from its charted course. In our dynamic business society of today, corporate strategies and operating plans can be easily rendered obsolete by innovations, technological developments, environmental influences, and sudden changes in the marketplace.

When the control system indicates significant weaknesses in the root strategy, operating strategy, or organizational strategy and design, the whole cycle of the policy-making process is repeated or recycled.

In the day-to-day operations of the firm many shifts in strategy are necessary to cope with changes in the marketplace. However, drastic changes and reshaping of the strategy set are not usually dictated by the information system. It is possible that the external monitoring system may indicate a need for a change in root strategy which would require a recycling of the policy-making process. This action, however, usually occurs over a long-time period and is a complicated demanding task. A prominent example in recent business history is the reformulation of the root strategy and recycling of the policy-making process of American Motors by George Romney. The combination of Hudson and Nash, two financially distressed companies (misery loves company), to form American Motors put the new company in direct competition with the Big Three (General Motors, Ford, and Chrysler), which had significantly more skills and resources than American Motors. Romney decided to seek a special niche in the automobile market with a compact car—thus avoiding head-on competition with the Big Three. The concentration on the Rambler car redirected the skills and resources of American Motors from the production and marketing of a range of models in the lower-medium, medium to higher-medium price range, to a small low-priced automobile. This action necessitated significant changes in the company's strategic design affecting their mission within the automotive industry, their operating plans, organization structure, and control system. Relations with dealers were changed; the advertising strategy dictated a new theme stressing price, size, "compactness," and economy of operation. According to management it took seven years before the Rambler "caught on" and sales increased. While the reformulation of American Motors saved the company and gave it a short-term measure of success, it required a long-time span to revitalize the organization and effect the new strategic design.

The Ford Motor Company offers another situation where drastic action was necessary to revitalize an industry giant which entered the post-World War II period unprepared for an expanding market and severe industry competition. The policies of Henry Ford built the company into an industry leader; but in Ford's declining years his leadership lagged, efficient operating policies were lacking, and the organization was ill-suited to cope with the demands of the marketplace. Mr.

Ernest Breech, a General Motors executive, assumed a role of executive leadership at Ford in 1946. Mr. Breech is credited with revitalizing the company through the introduction of the successful management and financial techniques of General Motors. The emphasis of Mr. Breech was in the area of operating strategy and organizational strategy rather than a significant change in root strategy such as American Motors required. Production control and financial control received the greatest attention. Changes in the operating strategy necessitated a restructuring of the organization and a reappraisal of the organizational relationships. Unlike American Motors, Ford had a good market position, and while it had incurred financial losses it was not in a last-ditch fight for survival. A complete reformulation was not necessary to protect the company's position. The recycling process "closed the loop" and initiated action at the operating strategy level.

We can find many examples of reappraisal of company operations which lead to initiating action at the organizational phase, or the interpretative phase, which required changes in the control strategy. The corporate control system should provide a continuous information flow to permit "constant surveillance" of the policy-making process. When this occurs, except for unanticipated dramatic events, the firm should be able to make on-going adjustments and not be pressed into management by crisis.

Financial measures as essential parts of a control system may signal a declining profit trend and possible impending crises. We find frequent references in the business literature to a need not only for reformulation under these conditions but also an admonition to get out of the business and reinvest in more profitable industries. The railroads, steel producers, coal producers, and others in industries which appear stagnant or retrogressive often are placed in this category. Their declining position is frequently compared to the growth or glamour companies in the field of electronics, pharmaceuticals, computers, and office copiers. However, the difficulty or impossibility of industry change or rapid diversification for many of the lumbering giants in the so-called "stagnant industries" is frequently overlooked. Companies with billions of dollars invested in steel making, which have predicated their past success on knowing the "art of the steel business," whose executive group "think steel," cannot shift their skills and resources to the electronics or other glamour industries without painful or disastrous results.

The railroads are in a similar position with billions invested in rolling stock and right-of-way. To change their root strategy to that of a transportation company covering all facets of the field provides material for a lively discussion of the marketing concept but ignores the implications of a regulated industry, the anti-trust laws, and the virtual impossibility of an easy and orderly conversion of specialized assets. Recycling of the policy-making process in these industries is for the most part forced into the implementation phase dictating the need for significant changes in operating strategy rather than drastic action involving abrupt shifts of resources into new businesses. The "steel and railroad minds," so expert in their own fields, frequently are not capable of coping with the demands for changes in managerial concepts and techniques required by the new ventures. The Penn Central Railroad, in its merger and wide diversification moves, developed a severe cash crisis and managerial problems which led to receivership under Chapter 77 of the Bankruptcy Act. The railroad was placed under the management of four court-appointed trustees. Under their direction the freight service and operating efficiency improved dramatically. The railroad's position was also improved through a sale of nontransportation assets. Other railroads were able to improve their position by stressing operating efficiency and engaging in orderly diversification moves. The coal industry, long considered a declining and dying business, was revitalized by improving operating efficiency through mechanization and the use of new mining techniques.

Reformulation may be dictated by external environmental factors outside of the control of management. The cigarette industry in United States is now in the process of an "orderly retreat" from the sole reliance on cigarette production because of the link of cigarette smoking with lung cancer. Most of the producers in this industry are conducting diversification programs through the acquisition of producers of consumer products such as convenience foods, soft drinks, and liquors. Acquisitions and mergers in these areas, the cigarette manufacturers contend, provide them with an opportunity to utilize their experience, skills, and resources in the marketing of consumer products.

The external monitoring system of the business enterprise should provide inputs to appraise the realism and potential of the root strategy and to signal the need to reformulate to meet the new challenges of the opportunities and problems found in the external environment or "State of Nature." Internal controls coupled with inputs from the environment should aid in determining the effectiveness of operating strategies. The organizational structure and design should also be tested against performance measures as the agent for executing the operating strategies and providing the basis for the functioning of the control strategies. Interpretation and judgment of the effectiveness of organizational performance are dependent upon the quality and significance of the information system and will determine the extent of executive action needed in the recycling process.

PART ONE
THE
ROLE OF
THE
POLICY MAKER

1

SCANDIA
RADIO AB

Mr. Nels Pearson, president of Scandia Radio AB of Malmö, Sweden, had announced to the board of directors that, for personal reasons, he had decided to take an early retirement at age 60 and sever all of his connections with the company. The board had asked Mr. Pearson to remain for another year to give the company time to find a suitable successor who would be able to carry on Mr. Pearson's responsibilities, but Mr. Pearson agreed to remain for only six months. His leaving presented the Scandia board with the problem of replacing him with an executive skilled in the management of an international business.

Mr. Pearson had been with Scandia since the inception of the business. His schooling had been meager. As a youth, he learned radio technology in a home workshop. He joined the young Scandia organization as a vocational electrician. At Scandia young Pearson impressed Mr. Per Holm, then president, with his engaging personality and his knowledge of radio technology. Mr. Holm took him out of the shop and made him his office assistant. Mr. Pearson, over the years, took on many of Mr. Holm's administrative duties and in time became a senior executive with many responsibilities, including the direction of sales, both domestic and export.

In 1960, in recognition of his performance, Mr. Pearson was named executive vice president. In 1965 he became president, and Mr. Per Holm became chairman of the board. The export business, which he had started, remained one of Mr. Pearson's responsibilities. Mr. Pearson eventually became the sole director of the foreign business, which had grown from a simple operation of selling finished radios on the Continent to an intricate complex which covered the globe and included wholly owned plants and subsidiary companies, partnership arrangements, trading agents, wholesaling arrangements, royalty and licensing contracts, selling components to local assemblers, and the custom manufacture of parts for competitive manufacturers. Mr. Pearson managed this business with the help of only three assistants, who had never assumed much authority.

The Scandia management had never looked upon its international business as being a separate entity. The foreign business had been treated as an arm of the domestic business without a separate division, although over two-thirds of Scandia's income came from international sales.

THE COMPANY'S HISTORY AND POSITION

Scandia Radio Aktiebolaget of Malmö, Sweden (SRA), had been organized in 1917 to manufacture Edison-type phonographs under license for the Scandinavian market. In 1926 it dropped phonograph production in favor of manufacturing a quality radio of its own design, which was so well received in Sweden, Norway, and Denmark that SRA became the leading radio manufacturer in Scandinavia. During the 1930's Scandia began an export program, and at the start of World War II over half of Scandia's production was sold in markets outside of Scandinavia. After 1945 Scandia added some phonographs to its product line and later some television sets, and it continued to expand its foreign radio trade.

Scandia was recognized as the largest radio producer in Sweden and one of the leading radio producers in Europe. It was also a leader in the world radio trade, with 70% of its total production being sold abroad. Its emphasis had always been on high-quality table radios, which constituted 85% of its total sales volume. Approximately 90% of Scandia's radios were being sold in foreign markets. Almost all of its television sets, phonographs, and console combinations were sold within Scandinavia.

During the decade of the 1950's, the company experienced a major shift in its business. Its radio sales within Scandinavia dropped below the 1950 level. The management attributed the decline to two causes: (1) the advent of television, which competed directly with radios, and (2) the fast-rising general prosperity of Sweden, which provided Swedish consumers with the means to buy items previously beyond their reach. Scandia's radios now competed for the Swedish consumer's kroner with such items as automobiles, refrigerators, motorcycles, and washing machines. By 1960, radio sets were commonplace and unexciting in Sweden; many other products had more attraction.

At the same time that Scandia's home market was declining, its European markets were undergoing a similar decline, and for similar reasons. In the Common Market area the decline was accelerated by the new competition of Grundig in Germany and Philips of the Netherlands, both of which made excellent radios, had much wider product lines, and had the advantage of being EEC members.

Outside of Europe, the various market area potentials presented a mixed picture. In the United States, which was by far the largest and most prosperous market, national competition, mainly on a price basis, was intense. Everywhere in the world competition from other exporting manufacturers was growing, especially from the Japanese, who sold at prices too low for Scandia to meet.

While radios were a mature or declining product in most industrialized countries, there was a growing market for them in undeveloped areas of the world, where many people had yet to buy their first radio set. However, the standard of living in these areas was usually so low that many people could not afford to buy even the cheapest radio set, much less a Scandia. The potential in these areas was not clear, but it could be enormous. The situation was further complicated by the threat of nationalization in some of the developing countries.

SEARCH FOR A NEW PRESIDENT

"Mr. Pearson grew up with our company," said Mr. Holm, "and as our company grew, he grew with it. This made it possible for him to handle our foreign affairs with his left hand, so to speak, while with his right hand he handled many other matters. He still does that today, despite our large volume of overseas business. Now we will need a man who will devote practically all of his time to directing our international activities. The man will need to have many skills and talents. At this stage of our history, it is hard to say just what these skills and talents should be."

The board of directors,[1] at the request of Per Holm, (chairman of the board) had studied the problem of replacing Mr. Pearson and had

[1] See Exhibit 1 at the end of case.

come to three preliminary conclusions. First, that a formal search should be made, using management consultants, to find a new president; second, that the new president should be a man of proven performance in managing an international business; third, that consideration should be given to consolidating all of Scandia's international business in a newly created International Division, headed by a senior executive with appropriate staff support.

With the help of personnel consultants, the search had been narrowed down to three men, all of whom happened to be Scandia senior executives. The consultants advised that any one of the three was capable of holding the office, and they recommended that the board make the final selection, basing its choice upon the needs of Scandia. The board then decided that it would interview each of the three candidates personally before making its decision. Dr. Curt Scheer was the first candidate to be interviewed by the board. He was followed by Herr Heinrich Diederich and Mr. George Boyd.

Vita
Dr. Curt Scheer
Director of Finance and Administration, Scandia Radio AB
Age: 48
Place of Birth: Basel, Switzerland
Nationality: Swiss
Citizenship: Swiss
Religion: Roman Catholic
Parentage: Father—Swiss
                    Mother—Austrian
Height: 1 meter, 75 (5 ft. 9 inches)
Weight: 77.2 kilos (170 lbs.)
General health: Average good. Eyesight corrected by bifocals. Major impairment in hearing in the left ear.
Residence in childhood and youth: Basel, Switzerland
                                                        Mannheim, Germany
                                                        Geneva, Switzerland
Education: Volksschule, Gymnasium (public grade and high school), Basel, Switzerland
                 Wirtschafts Hochschule (Vocational Business College), Mannheim, Germany
                 University of Geneva, Geneva, Switzerland
Diplomas, Degrees: Vereidigter Buchprüfer (Chartered Accountant), Wirtschafts Hochschule, Mannheim
                               Dr. Rer. Oec. (Doctorate in Economics), University of Geneva (Majored in International Finance and Trade)

Dr. Rer. Pol. (Honorary; Doctorate in Political
Science), University of Upsala, Sweden

Experience:

2 years with Swiss-American Chamber of Commerce, New York
City, U.S.A.

2 years with Schweizerbank (Swiss Bank), Bern, Switzerland (as
Economist, International Dept.)

Scandia, 21 years:

Geneva Office, as financial executive and tax adviser, 3 years
Scandia headquarters, Malmö, Finance Dept., 5 years
Director of Finance, 5 years
Director of Finance and Administration, 8 years

Languages:

Switzer-Deutsch and German (native tongues)
French (learned in school)
English (learned during two years in New York, U.S.A.)
Swedish (learned while with Scandia)
Some Danish (learned from Danish-born wife)

Marital Status: Married

Nationality of Spouse: Danish born, of Swedish parentage. Long-time
resident of Malmö

Citizenship of Spouse: Swedish

Family: 4 children, ages 13 to 18

Business and Professional Associations:

International Association for Research into Income and Wealth
Fellow: Econometric Society
International Institute of Administrative Societies
European Union of Accountants
Member: International Committee for Historical Sciences
Associate Member, Scandinavian Historical Society, Malmö

Outside Interests:

Member, Malmö Civic Symphony Orchestra Board
Amateur musician (violoncello)
Sailing (yacht)
Author of numerous scholarly articles on international trade, world
political trends, international finance, the free trade areas, international corporate taxation, Swiss cantons as tax havens, the
Hanseatic League in Europe, the Viking Period in Scandinavian
history, the coming of the Free Trade Era, and Sweden's capitalistic social-welfare state.

PER HOLM'S REMARKS ABOUT DR. SCHEER:

"Dr. Scheer is our scholar. He is exceptionally able in statistical and
financial analysis. People are apt to describe him as 'figure-minded.' He

has a long memory for precise data, and without referring to records he can quote significant financial data ten years old. That once made me nervous; however, I've never found his figures to be far off.

"People usually see Curt Scheer as just an informed accountant, but that is really a surface impression. He is responsible for all of the company's money management, accounting and paperwork, and many other administrative matters. As our treasurer, I rely on him as the final authority in financial matters. He is Scandia's economist, and makes up our annual general economic forecasts by world areas. He oversees all our domestic and international tax matters. He is not a lawyer, but somewhere along the line he acquired a good deal of corporate legal knowledge, and so he has become our liaison with our company's attorneys. Curt also oversees all of our company's insurance matters, including the employees' group insurance and pension plan. He is also our link with the government on such things as import and export duties and restrictions, social welfare insurance, labor legislation, and income tax.

"Curt knows as much about Scandia in general as any one of us. He still supervises the costing system which he installed in our plants, and this has given him a good knowledge of our factory operations. He personally works with George Boyd on finalizing sales forecasts—in fact, he furnishes Boyd with the forecasts. He and Boyd jointly work out our pricing programs. And being the company's de facto legal officer has gotten him into anything and everything that the company does. What I'm saying, I guess, is that Curt Sheer is an economic and financial specialist who is really a broad-gauge generalist.

"Curt looks mild-mannered and easygoing, but underneath he's as tough as leather—a thorough workman who can handle a multitude of problems. He can have a dozen things going at once—union problems, court trials, insurance claims, new bond issues, tax appeals—like a juggler with a dozen balls in the air at the same time—and it doesn't seem to confuse him a bit, or to hurry his pace.

"People don't dislike Curt, but he's not likely to be the most popular one in a group. I've heard snide remarks about his being the company's efficiency expert, a typical auditor, always looking at the financial data. Actually, he's not unfriendly, but he's cool and reserved by nature. Maybe that goes with being an intellectual—what the Americans call an 'egghead.' They don't usually win popularity contests.

"Curt is definitely an international executive. He does a lot of reading, keeps up with world events, and travels a lot. Any installation we have, anywhere, he's been there, knows it first hand. He's more of a linguist than any of us, too. In fact, we look upon him as being *the* linguist for our headquarters office.

"For recreation, Curt plays a violin in an amateur symphony orchestra, and he also sails a yacht. Strange combination. His yacht is a big one—sleeps six. On his vacations he cruises the Mediterranean.

"Curt isn't a Swede, you know. He's Swiss, and he's kept his Swiss citizenship. His wife is Swedish, and the Scheer family seems to be Swedish in every way. I tend to think of him as being a Swede—he's been here so long and he fits in so well.

"Now, let's call him in so you can talk to him yourselves."

Dr. Scheer enters. Quietly smiling, he casually greets each director in turn. His dress has a slightly rumpled appearance. His soft bow tie and his gnarled thornbriar pipe, which he puffs at with deliberation, add to his casual effect. He wears bifocal eyeglasses. At times, he absently fingers the hearing aid in his left ear, as though he is preoccupied in searching for an answer, but most of his replies are prompt and incisive. His manner is relaxed, and his replies give the impression of complete candor. Mr. Holm leads the discussion:

HOLM: Dr. Scheer—you know of course, that you are being considered for the presidency of our company. This means general management of our international business. Would that have appeal to you?

SCHEER: I would have no objection to the appointment. I am already heavily involved in our international business.

HOLM: You are aware that we are being advised by consultants in our search. Our consultants have asked that each of the candidates answer certain questions to the board. Is this agreeable to you?

SCHEER: Certainly.

HOLM: Tell us about your career—as you have seen it.

SCHEER: You already have my vita, so I take it you want my view of my career. My father was Oberstudierot (educational counselor) at a Basel gymnasium. Before that he had taught economics. My mother was also a bookish kind of person. I was an only child, and I wasn't robust and spent a good deal of my childhood at home. As far back as I can remember I was among the literati, the cognoscenti, and the intelligentsia. As a boy I got it from both sides, from my father and mother, and so it couldn't help but rub off on me. It was always assumed that I would go the full route through university studies. I passed my Abitur without difficulty. My parents didn't have a lot of money, and from there on I went just about all the way through university on scholarships. My father was an economist, and at one time he taught political economy, as it was called in those days. I had intended to become a teacher—had hopes of becoming a professor of economics—but would even have been satisfied to live out my life as a humble docent. Working at something economic, you enjoy the fruits of the economy more than if you teach economics to others. I liked the fruits. It wasn't long before I connected with SRA, and from then on my life seems to have been Scandia Radio, all the way. I'm satisfied with the way it's gone.

HOLM: We all know that you have contributed greatly to Scandia. What do you see as your contribution?

SCHEER: Inaugurating a "systems" approach to our international financing. Scandia, like many other international companies, drifted into making investments abroad. You might say it even backed into that position, because it was compelled by competitive forces. Our investments were sporadic; there was no master plan. By the time I came to Scandia, our foreign commitment was so large that a continuation of such a policy would have been intolerable. The sheer size of our foreign operations demanded that we rationalize our financial systems.

HOLM: Could you be more specific? Give us examples?

SCHEER: Yes, several. During the last twenty years Scandia has increased its operations abroad tenfold. Considering the vagaries of foreign political actions, equity investments would have been perilous. It was obvious to me that foreign lenders would often be willing to provide us with a very high percentage of debt capital in proportion to our equity, and so that became our policy in new ventures: a limited amount of equity and a generous proportion of debt.

Now I know that Banker Andersson at this very moment is thinking of the high interest costs. But we have deliberately used our multiple foreign subsidiaries to keep down our money costs, by taking advantage of the low interest rates in one country to supply the capital needs of operations in high-interest areas. This is simple if the money can be freely shifted between countries. If it is restricted by local governments, then we simply delay or accelerate the payment on the intersubsidiary sale of raw materials, components, or finished goods between the companies within the Scandia family. For example: One of our Danish subsidiaries had a cash surplus, which it lent to another Danish subsidiary which was receiving goods from one of our Swedish subsidiaries. The Danish company prepaid its account with the Swedish subsidiary, and this money financed the movement of Swedish products into our Finnish subsidiary. Now here is what we accomplished:

If Finland had been required to pay for the goods, it would have had to borrow at the high going Finnish rate. If the Swedish subsidiary had financed the sale, it would have had to borrow at about 9%. But cash in Denmark was worth only 5%. Moreover, Danish currency was weak compared to the Swedish. By speeding up payments to Sweden, we not only obtained the money cheaper, but we hedged our position in Danish kroner at the same time.

Being as international as we are, we have also found it possible to adjust prices on intracompany sales according to a deliberate plan. If a country is in foreign exchange difficulties, it may earmark the scarce exchange for imports and not permit dividends to be remitted abroad. But in Scandia's case, I found it possible to take out our dividends, so to speak, by raising prices on intracompany sales proportionately.

Transfer prices are also a useful device for keeping down the overall corporate tax liability. We have found it possible to instruct our subsidiaries to set high prices on intracorporate shipments to high-tax countries and low prices on those low-cost countries.

I think that we ought to similarly systematize exchange-rate planning. We were well prepared when the English pound was devalued, by deferring payments and switching purchases to other countries. But we ought to set up a system of continuing studies which will scan all of our markets for fluctuations in exchange rate and for impending devaluations, so that we can take full advantage of them whenever and wherever they occur.

HOLM: What are your strong points as an executive?

SCHEER: I think that I have more respect for facts than most executives. Most situations that call for decisions lend themselves to quantification. I think of decision making as a syllogism. If you take the pains to do so, you can almost always spell out the major and minor premises in terms of concrete data. The conclusion then usually becomes obvious. You have only to calculate it, as you would in solving an equation. People may not always like it, when faced with these kinds of calculated consequences. But they can hardly argue. The results are self-evident.

HOLM: Do you feel deficient in any way?

SCHEER: (smiling wryly) The more I learn, the more I come to realize how little I know. That's not my pearl of wisdom, of course—I'm quoting. But as far as Scandia is concerned, I feel pretty well equipped. I say this in all due modesty.

HOLM: What do you think of Scandia's past performance?

SCHEER: Scandia has generally been considered a highly successful company, and so its past history has been chronicled as a success story. But what is success in an economic enterprise? Is it what the balance sheets and the income statements show? Can you measure it by any objective standards? I think that success is a relative thing, and I'm not sure to what you could definitely attribute the source. It might be the management, but management is a compound of the artful and the scientific and subject to good or bad fortune. For Scandia, fortune has been mostly good. As to our management, I think it's been good but primitive—competent in its rudimentary way, and effective, but rugged and unrefined. We've been like the old salt of a sea captain who roared at his young mate: "To hell with your barometers and weather gauges! When my bunions ache, there's a storm brewing, and we trim sail!"

HOLM: What do you think of Scandia as it is today?

SCHEER: I can give you three answers to that question. By any popular measure, Scandia is "prima"—in the money markets, in engineering circles and in the marketplace. That's what the public thinks. I don't think we can afford the luxury of basking in that glow. Which brings me to my second answer. If we take an introspective look at ourselves, we can hardly agree with the public's "prima" opinion. I'd say that the "prima" opinion is actually a "prima facie" opinion—one taken at face value. If we could only stand aside and take a detached look at ourselves, we'd see that our way of management is an anachronism—outmoded and outdated. If we continue to use present techniques, then we have reached our zenith. My third answer is that we are now at a stage in our history in which we have arrived at a point of divergence. We must conscientiously address ourselves to the question of choosing what we wish Scandia to be in the era of our posterity. If we resolve to determine that now, we probably can choose among a number of options still available to us at this time. If we ignore the dilemma, we will lose the initiative and thereafter experience stagnation.

HOLM: Which leads right into my next question. What do you see as the company's future?

SCHEER: We have our problems of the moment, but I see these as being eclipsed by the opportunities. Our future depends upon the attitude with which we face it. We can be reactionary, or conservative, or progressive. We are fortunate. We have many options.

HOLM: Could you be more explicit?

SCHEER: Some think that we have pushed too far, too fast, abroad, and that even in Scandinavia we will never again use our full capacity. We could retrench—cut back to our home market, survive there by eliminating ourselves of every last inefficiency, practicing Spartan economy to meet price competition. That would be reactionary. Taking that course, we would resign ourselves to remaining forever a relatively large producer in a market which is relatively small and might become smaller. No one could accuse us of being rashly ambitious, but no one could guarantee that it would be a sinecure. The conservative route would call for holding our present position, rationalizing, and consolidating as much as possible. In my opinion, our present position in untenable—we are beset by so many forces which are beyond our control, such as changes in consumers' preferences, or the shifting world economy. There are many self-seeking governments with narrow perspectives. And always, the whimsical, the unpredictable vicissitudes of politics. In our blind campaign for more sales, we have pushed ahead wherever we found an opening, and now our most advanced positions have weak lifelines. As conservatives, we would often find ourselves fighting rear-guard actions.

As progressives, we would have a number of attractive choices. It would depend on how we wished to be—what stance we chose.

HOLM: Along which of the three routes would you lead the company?

SCHEER: (curtly) That kind of decision should be reserved to the board of directors.

HOLM: Are you in agreement with the plan to set up an International Division?

SCHEER: There will be organizational difficulties. Henceforth, we will have a chief of the International Division, and a president. Over three-quarters of our business is now international. Who will actually be the chief executive?

HOLM: Do you want the office of president?

SCHEER: I am already so heavily involved in company-wide foreign affairs that international business takes up most of my time. Therefore, it might make things easier to handle if I had full direction of our business. I, of course, would be honored to accept the office if it is offered to me. I am enthusiastic about expanding our international business.

HOLM: Where will you live when you retire?

SCHEER: Right here, in all likelihood. My Swedish family won't let me move, and I don't care to move, either. I guess I've become Swedish by marriage. (*facetiously*) I thought we were talking about a promotion. Am I being fired? (*laughter*)

HOLM: Thank you very much for cooperating, Dr. Scheer.

Vita

Herr Heinrich Diederich

Director of Manufacturing, Scandia Radio AB

Age: 51

Place of Birth: Braunschweig, West Germany

Citizenship: German

Religion: Lutheran

Nationality of parents: Father: German

Mother: Polish/German (Danzig)

General health: Good—vision corrected by reading glasses

Height: 1 meter, 90 (6 feet 3 inches)

Weight: 99.9 kilos (220 lbs.)

Residence in childhood and youth: Braunschweig, Germany

Education: Volksschule, Braunschweig

Gymnasium, Braunschweig

University, Braunschweig Technische Hochschule

Diplomas, Degrees: Degree in Electrical Engineering

Experience:

Blaupunkt Radio, Braunschweig—8 years

Design Engineer, electronics—2 years

Production Engineer, car radios (for Volkswagens)—4 years

Assistant Production Superintendent, radios—2 years

Scandia Radio—22 years

Assistant Plant Superintendent, Denmark—2 years

Plant Manager, Austria—3 years

Assistant Plant Manager, Malmö—3 years

        Plant Manager, Malmö—4 years
        Director of Manufacturing, Scandia Radio—10 years
Languages: German—native tongue
            English—learned in school
            Swedish—learned while with Scandia
Marital Status: Married
Nationality of Spouse: German
Citizenship of Spouse: German
Family: 8 children, ages 8 to 22
         4 grandchildren
Business and Professional Organizations:
    Vice President: International Scientific Radio Union
    Chairman: Nordic Association of Radio Manufacturers
    Council of Nordic Master Craftsmen
    International Council of Societies of Industrial Design
    International Electronics Association
    International Esperantist Chess League
Outside Interests:
    Amateur radio operator
    Malmö Civic Men's Choral Society
    Home gardening
    Chess

PER HOLM'S REMARKS ABOUT HEINRICH (HEINZ) DIEDERICH:

"Heinz Diederich is our technical man. I believe that he knows as much about radio technology and audio amplification as anyone in the world today. He's lived close to radios since his early boyhood. We have Diederich to thank for a number of our patents.

"Heinrich looks like the old Prussian ramrod type of plant manager, and sometimes I believe that he is. But for assistants, he chooses modern youngsters who are college-bred technicians. They are as much organization men as engineers. Two of his present staff are engineers who have American Master of Business Administration degrees. Sometimes I wonder if these youngsters are accountants, or finance men, or production engineers.

"It caused a ruffle of ill will when we made Diederich, who is German, production chief of Scandia. There were some career Swedes in the Malmö plant who felt that they had prior rights. We are an international company now, and our people are going to have to learn to forget their Swedish origins, or any other kind of origins, for that matter. You could look at it another way: I didn't choose Diederich because he was non-Swedish. I chose him because he knows radio design and he knows how to turn out radios.

"Heinz will give you the impression of being slow-moving. He *is* slow-moving; but when he does move into something, you can be pretty sure that he's thought about it. I've heard that no one in Malmö has ever beaten him at chess. That's not because of his brilliant moves. He simply takes his time and wears out his opponent.

"Diederich acts like a growly old bear—sometimes he even roars a little—but that is a surface impression and a cover. He actually is a kind man. He treats people fairly, without any grinning or back-slapping. His people like him. Even the Swedes who were jealous of him didn't quit, and they are loyal to him now.

"Diederich has been a ham radio operator since he was eight years old. I'm told that the antenna for his home broadcasting outfit is the tallest and longest in Malmö. But radios aren't all of his life. At home he's all wrapped up in his kids, and by this time there are a few grand-kids. In summer he spends his evenings weeding his roses and ruta-bagas. Heinrich doesn't travel much. He'd rather be at home than any-where else—except in the plant.

"Diederich is a shirt-sleeved shop man. (*ruefully*) I sometimes wish he were more of the executive type. I don't think he spends a fourth of his time at his desk. At most any time I'll find him hunched over a drawing board with some young draftsman, or he'll be out patrolling the plant. He likes to feel the thump of the punch presses or hear the sputtering of the soldering irons and the whine of the circle saws. That races his pulse; that's life to him. Once when I almost choked on the smell of acid fumes in our electroplating shop he laughed and called it the perfume of production. It smelled as sweet to him as his begonias.

"Now let's have Heinrich in and talk to him."

Heinrich Diederich enters and nods to the group of directors. He is a big, portly man. His steel-gray hair is a stiff, crew-cut bristle. His manner is stolid, impassive.

HOLM: Herr Diederich, you know that you are being considered to head our company. Would the office of president have appeal to you?
DIEDERICH: Yes, if the board determined that I was best man for the job at this time.
(*Pause*)
HOLM: Would you explain, please?

DIEDERICH: As you know, I find my present job very challenging. However, if it is the decision of you gentlemen (*nodding toward the board*) that I can better serve the company as the chief executive officer, I would exert every effort to move the company forward.

HOLM: Our consultants have proposed certain questions which we would like to ask you.

DIEDERICH: Feel free.

HOLM: Please tell us about your career—as you have seen it.

DIEDERICH: My father was a tool and diemaker by vocation. When I was a little boy he told me that he was making the dies which punched out the condenser plates for the radios being made by an early Braunschweig radio manufacturer. I found that exciting. Radio was the rage in those days, in the early twenties. As a ten-year-old I built my first headphone set out of a few wires and a cardboard oatmeal carton, and I was proud to get reception from Hanover, which was over 30 kilometers away. I have always found technical and scientific things interesting. While the other boys were playing soccer, I was in my home workshop tinkering with the new neutrodyne and superheterodyne tube radios. When the other boys were fascinated with athletic and military heroes, my heroes were Ferdinand Porsche and Thomas Edison, Marconi, Morse, and Alexander Graham Bell. We were not poor—my father earned good wages, and he determined that I would do better than he had done. There was no tradition of schooling in our family, but he and my mother encouraged me and helped me. I am the first one in our family to achieve a university education. I liked the natural sciences best. They came easy to me. If I had been allowed to do so, I would have studied only science—I would never have opened a book on history, or economics, or government, or anthropology. I took my degree just in time to become a soldier. I didn't do much soldiering. I was assigned to a specialist post at an army headquarters unit as a radio technician. I never saw any heavy action. After the war, I was lucky again. I got a job with a radio company right in my home city of Braunschweig. I did well there, and then Scandia offered me a better job in Denmark. I had married early—before the war—and there were getting to be quite a few little Diederichs about. I couldn't afford to turn down raises. Besides, Scandia's excellent technology appealed to me. So I came to Scandia. I have not regretted it. I think that for an electronics engineer, I have had an ideal career.

HOLM: We all know that you have contributed a great deal to Scandia. What do you see as your contribution?

DIEDERICH: Three things. First, maintaining the high quality of our product line.

(*Pause*)

HOLM: How, specifically?

DIEDERICH: It is related to my other two points. My second point was the establishment of a spread of plants which virtually blanket the globe. My third point was the firm adoption of a policy of centralization of product planning, standardization of products, and quality control, with decentralization of production but with the overall production still directed centrally.

HOLM: Would you explain, please?

DIEDERICH: As our sales abroad increased, the pressure to establish local plants became strong. For example, our distributor in Canada, where we had a ten-week delivery schedule, didn't like predicting sales maybe six months in advance and maintaining a three-month supply in inventory. He wanted to draw from a plant in Montreal from which he could get deliveries within a week. So we built a small plant in Montreal. There are offsetting disadvantages to building small plants abroad. You lose the efficiencies of truly mass production that you get in a centralized home plant, which might more than offset duties and freight. And plants in developing countries might be very inefficient. For example, the radio which we produce in Colombia at $41 might be produced in Mexico for $32, and it might be produced in Malmö for only $18! But nevertheless, we have gone the route of building small plants abroad to give better service and to satisfy the demands for nationalization of production.

Now, along with the pressure to build plants abroad comes pressure to modify our products to suit the tastes and preferences of the local market. The pressure comes not only from our salespeople; it comes from our engineers abroad, too. I have resisted this pressure, and insisted on uniformity, on standardization of our products, and even of our production processes, everywhere. This is the only way we can maintain quality and cost control. Now, while we have decentralized production in the sense of spreading it to dozens of plants abroad and giving local plant managers a free hand when it comes to labor relations and working conditions and many other things, we still are working at achieving a co-ordinated centralization of production planning. Scheer is much more advanced with his centralized financial planning than we are in production planning. We are just beginning to shape up. It does not make sense to try to produce our total product at each location. This is obvious. Many of our plants are located in countries which don't have the basic raw materials, such as wood, or aluminum, or steel, or copper, yet they insist, for purposes of nationalizing production, on making as much of the product as possible. Therefore, we find ourselves making cabinets, or at least the veneers, in Arkansas and Canada and Sweden; in stamping chassis in Sweden, Germany, Holland, and the U.S.; in making tubes in Paris; and so on with other components. Often only assembly is done locally. Now, when you have this kind of operation, it must necessarily be integrated and co-ordinated by centralization of production planning, which we do here at Malmö. We don't yet have as smooth an operation here as I would like it to be, but I have some sharp young American industrial engineers who are studying the possibility of computerizing production schedules. But we have no intention of trying to run our individual plants on a day-to-day basis.

HOLM: Do you feel deficient in any way?

DIEDERICH: I have been a technical man, and in my end of the business I feel very confident. I am sure, however, that I would need to broaden my perspective in the president's role.

HOLM: What do you think of Scandia's past performance?

DIEDERICH: It has been excellent. SRA has always made as fine a radio as anyone in the world. We deserve our good reputation.

HOLM: What do you think of Scandia as it is today?

DIEDERICH: I think we are in excellent condition, as least as far as our Malmö production and our Continental plants are concerned. I am not that proud about what is coming out of our plants in Calcutta, or Zanzibar, or Buenos Aires. (*Pause*)

HOLM: Why not?

DIEDERICH: I should think that if developing nations want to get into production, they ought to begin with simple products—like shoes or furniture. A radio is a complex instrument. People cannot be cow herders today and radio makers tomorrow.

HOLM: What do you see as Scandia's future?

DIEDERICH: Well, I know that most people don't get very excited about radios any more. They are "old hat," as the English say. To my teen-age daughters, radios are as outdated as stereoscopes. I see it differently. There are great opportunities ahead for us. With our superior know-how, there are great areas that we have not even tried to exploit: the specialized kind of equipment needed by armies, air forces, and in seagoing vessels; the highly refined equipment needed by commercial aircraft; and the use of radio in many industrial and commercial applications, where radio might be much more practical than the telephones and telegraphy that we use today. The world today is so flooded with cheap radios that compete on a price basis that I think Scandia would do well to stay away from the general market. We ought to be doing what only *we* can do—making the superior-quality commercial sets that require superior talent in the making. It would mean cutting down on volume production, but we would then be in a field where we would have few competitors and where price, of course, would be a secondary consideration. It would be the answer to most of our world marketing problems. Products that are clearly superior —in the technical sense—vault right over the trade walls—the duties, the quotas, the nationalistic restrictions. Look at Swedish steel, or the Volkswagen, or Leica cameras, or Scotch whisky, or Wilkinson Sword razor blades, or Swiss watches, or Danish pottery.

HOLM: (*laughing*) You've made your point. Are you in agreement with the plan to set up an international division?

DIEDERICH: I am not sure how the International Division would work, but I cannot see that it would affect my end of the business very much. We already have full exchange of technical information, internationally. We also exchange personnel between all our foreign plants, as much as it is practical to do so. Our research and development will go right on as it is now, regardless of how you change the management. The new International Division might make quite a difference to Scheer and Boyd, but not to me.

HOLM: Do you want the office of president?

DIEDERICH: I would be honored, of course. While I am well situated in my present position, I still enjoy a challenge. I am interested in what is best for the company. I definitely would like the chance to be president.

HOLM: Where will you live when you retire?

DIEDERICH: I'm still a long way from retirement and hadn't really given it much thought. I assumed I would stay here until I retire, and maybe even stay here beyond 65, if it might be permitted. Most foreigners newly abroad tend to assume that their stay is temporary and that they will sooner or later go "home." But the longer you stay abroad, the more you get to be at home away from home. If I went home at age 65, I probably wouldn't feel at home there. I honestly cannot answer that question. Perhaps my wife can answer it.

Vita

Mr. George Boyd

Director of Marketing, Scandia Radio AB

Age: 47

Place of Birth: Blue Earth, Minnesota, U.S.A.

Nationality: American

Citizenship: U.S.A.

Religion: Protestant (nondenominational)

Parentage: Father: John Boyd, third-generation American of English-Irish ancestry

Mother: Elise Schmidt, fourth-generation American of German ancestry

General Health: Good. No physical infirmities.

Height: 5 ft. 10 inches (1 meter, 78)

Weight: 175 lbs. (72.5 kilos)

Residence in childhood and youth: State of Minnesota, U.S.A.

World War II: England, France, Germany

Postwar years: Chicago, Illinois, U.S.A.

Education: P.S. #4, Blue Earth, Minnesota

Blue Earth Public High School

Two years at Winona State College

Night School in Chicago—selected subjects in salesmanship, advertising, merchandising, retailing, market research, sales supervision, etc.

Diplomas, Degrees: 4-year High School Diploma

60-hour Business Diploma, Northwestern University Evening Division

Experience:

3 years U.S. Army, Infantry, Honorable Discharge; Rank, 1st Lieut.

 2 years Salesman, Home Beautiful Furniture Co., Chicago, Ill., U.S.A.

 3 years Lyric Radio Company, Chicago Area Sales Supervisor

 18 years Scandia Radio:

  6 years Lyric-Scandia, Midwest Sales Manager

  5 years Scandia Radio, Inc., Sales Manager, United States and Canada.

  2 years Assistant General Sales Manager, Scandia Radio AB, Malmö

  5 years Director of Sales, Scandia Radio AB, Malmö

Languages: English—Native tongue

     Swedish—Learned since 1965 with Scandia

Marital Status: Married

Nationality of Spouse: American, of English-Irish parentage

Citizenship of Spouse: U.S.A.

Family: No children

Business and Professional Associations: Delegate: International Marketing Federation.

Outside Interests: Spectator sports

      Reading

      World travel

PER HOLM'S REMARKS ABOUT GEORGE BOYD:

"I once heard a man who disliked George Boyd describe him, nevertheless, as the world's greatest salesman. That might be a little overdone, but not much. You may not believe it when you first see him, because he's not the glad-handing type. George can melt ice when he wants to turn on the charm, but he's not by nature a gusher. He doesn't even do much smiling. He plays his own personality straight. I think of him as being aggressive, first of all, and second, I think of him as a maker of deals.

"George is always out to capture something, or to talk somebody into some kind of a horse trade. He is an honest trader, but when he charges after something he gets it, just about every time. What he goes after, he brings home.

"Boyd drives himself hard. Even when he is relaxing, he's probably planning the next coup he's going to make. He drives his subordinates hard, too. Maybe too hard. He expects them to dedicate their total lives to Scandia, just as he does. I know that some of his people don't like him, but he gets things done.

"The Boyds have no children. He and his wife Ruth are a devoted couple. I sometimes think that Ruth works as hard at George's job as he does, and she enjoys it as much, too. She knows everyone who ever had anything to do with Scandia, and its competitors, and she knows their cousins and their uncles and their aunts. She's a living directory, and she helps George immensely. They are an excellent married working team.

"The Boyds are well off financially. Both of them had inheritances from their parents. They could live in style on income from investments if they cared to do so. Instead, they both work hard at George's job and live modestly in a seaside apartment near Malmö. You'd think that as sales chief he would have to do a lot of wining and dining, but they live quietly and only entertain when they need to do so.

"George is a talker. He can hold forth on most any subject, and he does—at length. He'll tell you—in no uncertain terms—what's wrong in the world and how to straighten it out. He'll tell you where world Christendom is heading, and what should be done about Apartheid in South Africa. And when George has the floor, he holds it. He's pretty dogmatic.

"As you will see for yourselves. Let's have him in and talk to him."

George Boyd strides purposefully into the board room, nods unsmilingly in the direction of the directors, and says, simply, "Gentlemen." He makes a trim, well-tailored impression. Boyd has dark, piercing eyes and black hair and looks younger than his age. He declines a proffered chair, says that he would prefer to stand, and addresses the group:

BOYD: I understand that you wish me to answer certain questions. I will be pleased to do so. In fact, I have been looking forward to this session.

HOLM: Would the office of president have appeal to you—especially in view of the fact that we are heavily international?

BOYD: It certainly would. Our international activities need unified direction. Our international business needs leadership—strong leadership—and I believe I can supply it.

HOLM: Please tell us about your life—from your own viewpoint.

BOYD: My father was a small-town merchant. He had the largest general store in Blue Earth, Minnesota, which was a prosperous farming community, and he did very well. My father was born on a farm in Minnesota. His parents came from England and Ireland.

My mother was American-born of German ancestry. Her parents were born in the United States and were proud of their ancestry in the United States dating back to the early 1800's.

My mother wanted me to become a teacher. She thought of that as a proud profession, and so I was sent to the State College. I really wasn't much interested in becoming a teacher. I had been helping my father in his store since I was a little boy, and I thought that the traveling salesmen who called on him led much more interesting lives than schoolteachers. There was one especially, who drove an old Dusenberg automobile, who was my boyhood hero. He sold underwear.

At State College I met my wife. We were married during the war period. Ruth and I have never regretted it. She has been a great help to me in my positions.

My parents were well off financially. They could easily have afforded to finance all of my schooling, but both of them believed in industry and thrift, and so they paid only for my tuition and board. If I wanted any spending money, I would have to earn that myself. At first I did odd jobs. They didn't pay well. Then I heard of a fraternity that wanted to buy new dishes and silver for its dining room. I got a special deal through a salesman who sold to my father, and I made the sale to the fraternity at a neat profit. Next I got the staple-food accounts for two fraternities, and later a laundry concession for the entire college. By my second year I was doing all kinds of business and earning big money for a young boy. I even sold the college itself a big order of furniture, and that "big-ticket" item was what led me into the furniture business in later years. My business dealings didn't do my grades any good, but they earned a lot of money, and inadvertently they became the most vital part of the education I received at that college. It saddened my mother, but my father was proud of me. Also, I got a taste for money early in life, and that was not good for a boy who was supposed to become a schoolteacher.

In World War II, I volunteered for service in the infantry at the end of my second year in college. After the war I didn't go back to school. A friend of mine got a job for me as a salesman in his father's wholesale business in Chicago. After a few months I was put in charge of radio sales. Three years later I accepted an offer to become Chicago sales manager of Lyric Radio, which was later bought by Scandia as a sales outlet. Scandia reorganized Lyric and made it a distributor, and I became North American sales manager. After a while I was invited to Malmö, and after a few years there, I became sales chief.

During my Chicago years, I had the opportunity to go to night school at a leading university, where I absorbed all the textbook knowledge I could find about selling and sales management. I already knew how to bargain—that seemed to be an inborn talent. I think I've led a charmed life. Except for the war years, I've always been doing what I like and what I'm best at—managing a sales operation.

HOLM: We all know that our sales have increased substantially in the years that you have directed our marketing. What do you see as your contribution to Scandia?

BOYD: Often when companies get into foreign operations, they do so rather aimlessly, without any real knowledge of their markets, which are quite likely to be very different in advanced countries versus developing countries or undeveloped areas. They lack sales sophistication.

I think this was especially true of Scandia. It sold abroad on the basis of old-established connections which it had developed haphazardly, on a sort of homespun who-knew-who basis.

I think I've modernized our sales tactics. Sales promotions abroad are now made on the basis of the most solid research which is available in each area, rather than according to "Who is our friend there?" Hunches have now been replaced with statistics, which we get not only from market researchers, but from economists, sociologists, and even political analysts. Sometimes our future in a country will depend upon an economic decision made by a politician, and then we even zero our investigations in on him personally, to try to get "inside" him to anticipate which way his thinking is going. Our marketing decisions are now worked out systematically, where before they were based on "gut" feeling.

HOLM: What do you think of the company's past performances?

BOYD: The rest of the world thinks that our company has performed superbly. I think that it has done very well, too, but I think that we have patches on the seat of our pants. We are still operating as though we were a Swedish company which is selling some of its radios abroad. This—at a time when only one in four of our products is sold in Scandinavia. Actually, we are an international company, or a transnational company, as some call it. We are not a truly "multinational" company. That name is usually reserved for companies that are truly global in production, sales, financing, and management. We haven't reached that stage yet. We sell in some markets; we have some production abroad; we have more debt financing abroad than we have equity investments; our top management is an international mix, but from that level down it's still mostly Swedes at home and locals abroad. And what's more significant, I think, is that our board is mostly Swedish and most of our thinking and our policies have a Scandinavian flavor.

HOLM: What do you think of the company's present position?

BOYD: I think that we have reached the proverbial fork in the road, and at this time we must be decisive. In the beginning Scandia looked upon its foreign sales as something it did with its left hand when both hands weren't needed to work on the home business. Exporting was a sideshow; the main act was in Sweden. The export sales went well and they earned money. But Scandia treated these earnings as something it did on the side, like a man who bets a few idle kroner on the racehorses and when he wins says, well, I'll bet it all again, and if I'm lucky, I may double my money once more.

It did this without much regard to alternative opportunities abroad elsewhere on the international scene which might have been more profitable. And Scandia is now almost a global corporation.

HOLM: What do you see as the company's future?

BOYD: Scandia has a very promising future. It is already an excellent company, but its present position could be merely the platform from which it steps into true global greatness. It could do that if we properly exploit the vast untapped potential for our products that lies waiting in the world market.

HOLM: Could you expand on that?

BOYD: We are already an international company, not a Swedish company selling in foreign markets; but we have never formulated a definitely defined strategy that would make the best use of our competitive advantages. And we have advantages—in technology, in reputation, in our brand name, in competent management, and in an established customer following.

We ought to face the fact that we are on the threshold of becoming a truly global company, and we ought to act like one. We ought to establish our production deliberately in areas where the costs are lowest, and that would mean shifting it away from Sweden, where the level of the economy is very high, resulting in high costs. We should shift production to areas such as the Far East, where labor is plentiful and wages are low. Many U.S. electronics manufacturers are now doing this and selling their products in the high-price United States market. We ought to build up sales where the market has the most potential and is most rewarding in profits. This would mean adding cheaper-quality products to our present line, ones that could be sold to the vast masses who still live in darkness and are just emerging into the light of civilization and are hungry for radios but cannot afford our expensive ones. If we were to operate as a true global corporation should, we could find a glittering array of opportunities to buy cheap and sell dear, what with our many differing markets, varying labor conditions, market demands, political influences, and money markets—provided that we can properly co-ordinate the total into an integrated and smoothly functioning operation. We are not operating that way today. Today we still treat overseas business on a sort of happenstance basis, as though it was a side issue.

HOLM: What are your strong points as an executive?

BOYD: I've heard, via the grapevine, that I'm a tiger in the jungle, and I'm proud of that criticism. Until lately Scandia subscribed to the philososphy of building the better mousetrap, and some of the world did actually beat a path to its door, but this won't work any longer in today's world market. You must drive hard, and you must wheel and deal.

HOLM: Wheel and deal?

BOYD: Yes. Get trading advantages wherever and however we can. Through natural economic advantages, or political influence, or systematically using the power structure that exists in every country. For example: We can make cabinets economically in lumber-rich Sweden or the United States; we can make radio and phono components more economically in Taiwan or Ireland, where labor rates are low. It might even be to our advantage, in some countries, to have competitors make some of our parts and components for us. We might do all that and assemble them in England for sale in the U.K. and Commonwealth markets. These intercountry exports and imports often amount to a significant percentage of these countries' foreign trade and give us a good deal of political influence.

HOLM: Do you feel deficient in any way?

BOYD: Not especially, except that I play the game to win, which means I play the game for blood, not for fun, and that's left a trail of people in my wake who aren't especially fond of me. Oddly enough, while many of these don't like me personally, they are still quite willing to do business with me because I make deals on the basis of having something that they want, and I'm willing to bargain.

HOLM: How do you rate the other contenders for the job?

BOYD: They are all competent executives. I wouldn't care to make any other public appraisal of the men whose help and loyalty I would expect to enlist if I were to become chief.

HOLM: Why do you want the job of president?

BOYD: Because I believe that Scandia's future lies in the direction of continued expansion of sales globally, and doing so profitably, and I would lead it to that goal.

HOLM: Where will you live when you retire, and what do you intend to do?

BOYD: (after a blank pause) Frankly, your question puzzles me. I have never given any serious thought to retiring. I guess that means that I feel I will go right on doing what I'm doing now, and die with my boots on, as they say in the States. As to where I'll live, that will be wherever my work takes me.

HOLM: Thank you very much. You have been very candid and most helpful.

PER HOLM: Well, gentlemen, that concludes our interviews. What do you think?

JAN ASTRÖM (lawyer): Gentlemen, in view of our line of questioning, I wonder if we have aproached this in the wrong way. What are we really looking for? What talents should our new president have? What special qualifications? How should he be different from our other executives? Do you think we would know a good international executive if we saw one?

STURE ANDERSSON (banker): I don't think our man needs to be an experienced internationalist. Any good broad-gauge executive could be competent in the job, even if he speaks only Swedish and has never been outside of Malmö.

INGEMAR HOLMLIND (department stores): How can he make major decisions about Scandia's world trade if he hasn't had experience as a world trader?

STURE ANDERSSON: I make decisions every day about fisheries and flour mills—and (looking pointedly at Holmlind) even department stores—and I am neither a fisherman nor a miller or a merchant.

INGEMAR HOLMLIND: But your decisions are financial ones.

STURE ANDERSSON: Scandia is a commercial enterprise. It certainly isn't nonfinancial.

PER HOLM: Well, gentlemen, we have had a busy day. I would suggest that we now adjourn and meet again a month from now. We must choose our new chief executive at our next meeting.

exhibit 1   **THE MEMBERS OF THE BOARD OF DIRECTORS**

Per Holm, Chairman, Scandia Radio (Swedish)
Nels Pearson, President, Scandia Radio (Swedish)
Sture Andersson (banker) (Swiss)
Jan Aström (lawyer) (Stockholm) (Swedish)
Francois DuBois (advertising agency executive) (Canadian)
Rune Gylling (President, International Paper Products Company) (Norwegian)
Lars Hägglund (executive vice president, international pharmaceutical manufacturer)
   (Swedish)
Ingemar Holmlind (President, Stockholm Department Stores) (Swedish)
Gunnar Swenson (international shipping firm) (Swedish)
Rolf Deinlund (president, machine tool company) (Danish)

exhibit 2

Organization Chart of Scandia Radio AB, Malmo, Sweden

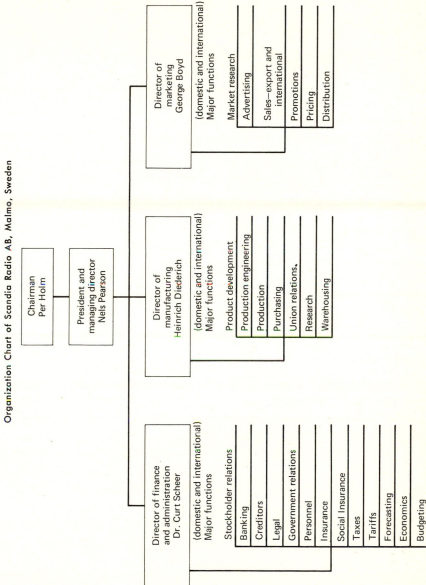

Chairman
Per Holm

President and
managing director
Nels Pearson

Director of finance
and administration
Dr. Curt Scheer

(domestic and international)
Major functions

- Stockholder relations
- Banking
- Creditors
- Legal
- Government relations
- Personnel
- Insurance
- Social Insurance
- Taxes
- Tariffs
- Forecasting
- Economics
- Budgeting

Director of
manufacturing
Heinrich Diederich

(domestic and international)
Major functions

- Product development
- Production engineering
- Production
- Purchasing
- Union relations.
- Research
- Warehousing

Director of
marketing
George Boyd

(domestic and international)
Major functions

- Market research
- Advertising
- Sales—export and
  international
- Promotions
- Pricing
- Distribution

2

ASTRA-LITE
CORPORATION

HISTORICAL DEVELOPMENT

The Astra-Lite Corporation was a medium-sized producer of industrial and commercial lighting fixtures located in Brooklyn, New York. The company was founded by John Cutter in 1920 to manufacture general electrical supplies for the building trade. Through specialization in light shields and light reflectors Astra-Lite gradually developed a relatively wide variety of commercial and industrial lighting fixtures. By 1930 the company had established a reputation as a producer of a quality line that was well accepted in a highly competitive industry. Many of the company's fixtures were of an exclusive design which permitted them to charge a higher price for their products than their competitors.

The building boom of the 1920's provided a ready market for Astra-Lite's products and the company grew from a small-sized operation to one with sales of over one million dollars.[1] The depression severely curtailed the construction of new commercial and industrial buildings and the remodeling of old ones. Astra-Lite suffered serious losses from 1931 to 1936 because of this drop in building activity, and did not recover until 1937 when the company showed a small profit from operations. With the increase in construction activity in the 1937–1941 period, Astra-Lite managed to show a profit each year.

In 1942 the company received a contract for lighting fixtures for military installations. By virtue of such contracts and the subcontracts received for the manufacture of airplane parts, the firm operated at full capacity throughout the war period.

[1] The sales of the company reached an all-time high of $4.5 million in 1952, and in 1956 amounted to $3.9 million. See Exhibit 3.

POSTWAR PROBLEMS

In 1946 Astra-Lite found itself in a postwar boom so great that it could not provide the lighting fixtures to keep pace with the demands of the building contractors. It was during this period, however, that many new manufacturers came into the field to take advantage of the unprecedented demand for lighting fixtures, chiefly of the fluorescent type. Astra-Lite managed to hold its position in the industry, despite the advent of new competition, mainly because of the backlog of new designs the company had held over from the war period. The intensity of the competition after 1950, however, created a serious problem for the company. The number of manufacturers in the field caused an over-supply of fixtures and allowed the building contractors to squeeze the suppliers for lower prices. This practice became very common when the contractors were faced with the rising labor and operating costs of the postwar period. The costs of producing fluorescent lighting fixtures were also constantly increasing in this period, mainly because of the rising raw material cost of steel, aluminum, and ballast. These materials accounted for over 50 per cent of the cost of the fluorescent fixture. Because of the intense competition in the fluorescent lighting field, Astra-Lite could not raise its prices to pass on the added costs of manufacture to the contractors. As a result their profit margin and the margins of producers in the same category were reduced substantially.

Astra-Lite was able to incorporate rising material costs only when it introduced new designs in fluorescent fixtures to the market. But because of the lack of any secure protection on new designs, other companies soon copied the design or introduced a similar one and the same competitive pattern of price competition again prevailed. The company, however, continued its policy of stressing quality and attempting to be an innovator in the lighting field. Despite changes in the management in this period of market difficulties, no thought had been given to lowering the quality or specialty design on which the company had built its reputation.

ORGANIZATION AND PERSONNEL

John Cutter, the founder of the company, had been responsible for the initial success of Astra-Lite. He had personally designed many of the fixtures that had established the company's reputation in the field. It was mainly through his efforts that the company gained a foothold in the fluorescent market. He served as president and general manager of the company from its inception in 1920 until his death in 1945.

Mr. Ronald Johnson became general manager of the company upon the death of Mr. Cutter. In 1946 he was appointed president of Astra-Lite at a special meeting of the stockholders. Mr. Johnson had been the general manager of the company's branch plant in Los Angeles, which served as a shipping point and performed some sub-assembly work. In addition to his duties in this capacity, he acted as the sales manager of the entire west coast area. Mr. Johnson was 52 years old, a graduate of New York University, and had been with the company for 15 years. Prior to joining Astra-Lite, Mr. Johnson had been employed by a public accounting firm and as an auditor for General Electric. During the war period he spent two years as a naval supply officer. He returned from service in 1944 and resumed his duties as general manager of the Los Angeles plant and sales district.

Mr. Robert Caswell was vice-president in charge of sales. He was 59 years old and had been with the company for 20 years. Prior to joining Astra-Lite he had served in various capacities as salesman, district sales manager, and assistant sales manager of a medium-sized electrical supply house. He was generally considered to have been John Cutter's right-hand man and had served as the acting general manager of the company during the frequent illnesses of Mr. Cutter from 1942–1945.

In 1953 the company suffered a loss of $44,000 and a special meeting of the stockholders was called. George Cutter, the brother of the founder of the firm, acting as the executor of the Cutter estate which still represented over 60 per cent of the outstanding stock, conducted the meeting. He accused Mr. Johnson of poor business tactics and failure to keep abreast of the current market situation. George Cutter maintained that Astra-Lite would be at the top of the heap if his brother were alive. Mr. Johnson attempted to explain the problems of selling lighting fixtures in the present changing and shifting market which was overrun with small manufacturers who stole designs and engaged in price cutting, often to their own detriment. He also pointed out that the business had changed considerably since the death of John Cutter, and the intensity of the competition prevented any of the medium-sized companies from showing much, if any, profit. Mr. Cutter was not satisfied with this explanation and demanded Mr. Johnson's resignation. Mr. Johnson agreed to resign but only if the company would honor the remaining year of his contract. A settlement was agreed upon and Mr. Robert Caswell was appointed acting president.

Mr. Cutter called a series of meetings of the Board of Directors, which had served only in a perfunctory capacity up to this time. Prior to the death of Mr. John Cutter a five-man board served the company. It was composed of John Cutter, George Cutter, Robert Caswell, Randolph Worth, a bank president, and Mrs. John Cutter. As a result of George Cutter's insistence, the Board was increased to seven members and Mrs. John Cutter, who never attended meetings, was dropped from the board by mutual agreement. The new directors included George Cutter's son, Frank Cutter, 31 years of age, a partner of a prominent New York law firm; Mr. Thomas Rand, the head of the industrial engineering department of Astra-Lite, who was promoted to vice-president at the time of his appointment; Warren Clifford, the president of a steel warehousing firm and a long-time business associate of the late John Cutter; and Frank Lochley, one of the largest minority stockholders, who had recently retired as an officer of a small Brooklyn bank. Mr. Lochley had personally handled the Astra-Lite account in the early stages of the company's development.

PERSONNEL CHANGES

After serving as acting president for one year, Mr. Caswell requested that he be relieved of his assignment and returned to his position as sales manager. He maintained that the duties of the president were too much of a strain on him, particularly because of his recent illness. Caswell also complained of the interference and lack of cooperation of Mr. Rand, the head of the industrial engineering department. At a special meeting of the Board of Directors in February of 1955, Mr. Frank Cutter was appointed president of the firm, and Mr. Rand was made executive vice-president in charge of industrial engineering.

Six months after Frank Cutter took over as president, drastic personnel changes were made and the firm's organization structure was changed. Mr. Caswell, who had become increasingly dissatisfied with Mr. Rand's operations, retired. His assistant, Andrew Sandage, 35 years of age, was appointed sales manager.

John Nelson, vice-president in charge of manufacturing and plant engineering, was dismissed, mainly on the recommendations of Mr. Rand, who maintained that he had not followed recommended cost-cutting techniques that were so necessary to increase the company's declining margin. Nelson insisted that such cuts would be at the sacrifice of quality and he openly stated that he saw little or no value in the procedures recommended by Rand's department. Nelson had joined the company in 1946 at the time of the postwar expansion. He took over a newly created position and assumed charge of the function previously performed under two departments, manufacturing and engineering. On the recommendation of Mr. Rand the functions of Nelson's department were again divided into two areas, engineering and manufacturing. The manufacturing operations were placed under a newly hired works manager, Mr. Leslie Butler, who formerly worked for Western Electric as an engineer and assistant works manager. Because of the importance of research and development in the lighting industry, Frank Cutter and Mr. Rand were both of the opinion that a top-flight man should be placed in charge of an engineering and product development department. Mr. Dennis Reed, who had twenty years' experience in engineering and development in a radio and television manufacturing firm, was chosen for the position and was given the title of vice-president in charge of engineering and product development. Mr. Reed left his former position to accept the Astra-Lite offer because of difficulties encountered when his firm, a medium-sized producer, was purchased by one of the largest manufacturers of radios, television sets and household appliances. Mr. Reed also assumed the position on the Board of Directors left vacant by Mr. Caswell's retirement.

As a result of Nelson's dismissal, the chief production and tool engineer, Clifford Wall, who had 20 years' experience with the company, resigned and later accepted a similar position with a New Jersey aircraft producer. Elliott Howe, the assistant chief engineer, who had been with the company for fifteen years, took over the position.

Harold Ramsey, the general purchasing agent, left in late 1954 over a salary dispute with Frank Cutter. Robert Sears, who had been the assistant purchasing agent of a competing company, was hired to replace Ramsey.

John Hill, the controller, resigned. He was 63 years of age. In submitting his resignation he stated: "I am not going to spend the last years of my working life being subjected to the whims of a nincompoop efficiency expert and the wild hallucinations of a boy still wet behind the ears." Hill's position was not filled. Frank Cutter stated that the department would be run by Hill's assistant, Raymond Cowden, and he,

Cutter, would personally assume the executive direction until Cowden proved his ability or they hired a competent man.

John Sima, in charge of sales promotion and advertising, left, mainly because he had expected to replace Mr. Caswell upon his retirement. In informing Frank Cutter of his intention to leave, he bluntly stated that the only reason Sandage was assistant sales manager prior to his

exhibit 1
ASTRA-LITE CORPORATION
Organization Chart, 1954

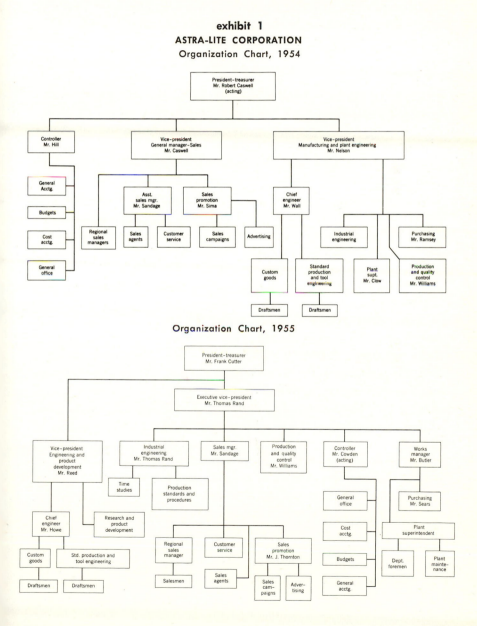

Organization Chart, 1955

promotion was because he was not capable of handling the important end of the business, pushing sales, and he could be trusted only with the administrative details of handling salesmen's accounts and customer services. Sima was replaced by Sandage's assistant, John Thornton, who had been with the company for three months. Thornton had ten years' experience in advertising and sales.

The changes in the organization of Astra-Lite between 1954 and 1955, when Frank Cutter became president, are indicated in Exhibit 1.

DEPARTMENTAL OPERATIONS

In July of 1955 Mr. Edward Williams, the head of production and quality control, who had joined the company in November 1953, submitted a proposal to control scrap in the manufacturing process. A procedure had been worked out with the accounting department to provide the needed information and reports that would indicate where the scrap was originating. These reports would then be submitted to the proper production departments to originate corrective action. Mr. Rand opposed this method and maintained that his department could eventually work out a more practical method of controlling scrap. The president concurred in this opinion and rejected Williams' plan.

In late 1955 no formal scrap control procedure had been instituted. The quality control department, without the necessary reports to indicate where the scrap was originating, attempted to control scrap through the inspection of the incoming fabricated parts and through sample checking of parts produced in the punch press department.

The industrial engineering department, under Mr. Rand, reported to the vice-president of manufacturing until Rand was appointed executive vice-president. Industrial engineering was responsible for time study, the development of standards and the issuing of standard manufacturing layouts. Because of short-staffing and the overlapping of functions with the production control department, industrial engineering had been an organizational problem since its inception. Because of this situation and the friction between the plant manager and the head of the production control department over the scheduling of orders to be manufactured, six men had held the position of production control manager in the period 1950 to 1955.

Thomas Rand, prior to his appointment as executive vice-president, had served as the firm's industrial engineer for a period of two years. He had been hired upon the recommendation of Mr. Lochley, the largest

minority stockholder. Mr. Rand was 45 years of age, a graduate industrial engineer, with twenty years' experience in his field. When hired by
Astra-Lite he was on the staff of Graybar, a former subsidiary of American Telephone and Telegraph. Several inducements unusual to Astra-
Lite's general executive employment policy were made to acquire the
services of Mr. Rand. His salary at the time he was hired was exceeded
only by that of the president. In addition, he was promised an opportunity to advance to the vice-president level if his work proved satisfactory to the president and Board of Directors.

In the first two years of his employment with Astra-Lite, Rand was
confronted with the problem of establishing an industrial engineering
department, which was formerly a function of general engineering. He
encountered much opposition from the vice-president of engineering,
the chief engineer, and the plant superintendent. Rand became particularly incensed when the engineering department refused to accept a
somewhat revolutionary plan he had devised to speed up the assembly
of fluorescent fixtures. Rand submitted this plan in article form to a
monthly industrial engineering magazine which featured it as a lead article. It attracted much interest in the lighting industry and was incorporated into the assembly lines of several medium-sized producers.

Shortly after being appointed executive vice-president, Rand added
five men to his staff to prepare manufacturing layouts of all standard
fixtures. When possible, standards on new parts and fixtures were to be
determined from similar parts manufactured in the past. On new parts
that could not be compared to those previously manufactured, a pilot
run was to be made to determine initial standards. Rand also received
the president's approval to install his own system for manufacturing
layouts and production orders. Many of the foremen in manufacturing
complained of the newly installed standards and contended that they
were highly inaccurate. In addition, they stated that the manufacturing
layouts contained very little information about how to perform the actual operations.

The layouts prepared prior to Rand's reorganization of the department contained detailed instructions for the most complex operations;
for example, the final assembly and pack on Ex-Lite fixtures required
16 detailed steps, and each of these steps was explained and the standard time for each was outlined. Under the new system the layouts for
Ex-Lite contained only the assembly-pack information and a total of
standard hours required for the whole operation.

Five months after the new system had been in operation, returns and allowances for fixtures improperly wired increased greatly. The works manager contended that if it had not been for the assembly department foreman and the sub-assembly foreman, with twenty and thirty years' experience, respectively, the returns would have been much greater. Because of the low efficiency rating of the assembly department, Mr. Rand transferred the foreman who had the job for the past fifteen years and hired a new man from another company that manufactured lighting fixtures. This foreman resigned within one month, stating that he could not raise production under the present system of layouts and standards. The works manager and the chief engineer concurred in this opinion. In a special report to the president they stated that it was not possible to assemble fixtures in the present allowable standard time and without detailed instructions being furnished the women assemblers.

Mr. Butler, the works manager, stated that he had little chance of solving the problem unless he had the opportunity of sitting down with the president and showing him in black and white just how the new system was working. He felt that there was no opportunity for this since Rand authorized the plan and he was likely to sidetrack any report or effort to get such information to the president.

The controller, chief cost accountant, and the head of the payroll section all complained of the difficulties created by the new system. They contended that the payroll section and cost department were not getting the necessary information from the producing departments to allow them to process the payroll on time and to record cost data for the budget analysis.

Mr. Rand also introduced a cost-saving program in the factory and office. Each department was given a stated quota to save out of their normal budget during the fiscal year. The controller considered this plan in direct competition with the annual budget, which was put into effect at the beginning of each fiscal year.

MARKETING

Astra-Lite sold its products through distributors who in turn sold to the contractor. In addition to distributors, Astra-Lite employed sales agents and salesmen. These men called on distributors to aid them in selling Astra-Lite fixtures. All distributors handled more than one line of lighting fixtures. In addition to calling on distributors, these salesmen contacted contractors and architects in an effort to get them to specify Astra-Lite fixtures in their proposals and specifications for new buildings and remodeling contracts.

The sales promotion was done by a small amount of advertising in trade publications, heavy expenditures for exhibits at building and association shows, and by intensive catalog promotion. Illustrated price catalogs were sent out to a mailing list of distributors, contractors, architects, and electrical consultants. Astra-Lite encouraged cooperative advertising by bearing approximately one-half of the expense of distributors' catalogs.

The company revised its catalog in July 1955 with a new illustrated edition, at an expense of $75,000. It was expected that the new catalog would not need to be replaced for several years. However, between July 1955 and July 1956, the company introduced more new products than during any comparable period in its history. To cover these products a new illustrated price list and catalog would have to be issued, which would cost approximately $40,000 to $50,000.

Prior to 1950 Astra-Lite employed a large number of sales agents who handled other electrical lines and were paid on commission. Since it was difficult to control the agents, the company started a program to replace them with salesmen. The replacement was rapid and the sales organization soon became a centralized function. But in the eyes of management it did not produce satisfactory results. In the spring of 1952 a reorganization of the sales department was instigated and a regional sales management plan was adopted. The salesmen were paid a high monthly salary, expenses were reimbursed, quotas were established for each salesman, and a commission was paid on all sales over the quota. The remaining sales agents, however, were still paid on a straight commission basis.

A regional sales manager was appointed for three geographic sections, the East, the Middle West and the West. This plan, after functioning for two and one-half years, was deemed unsatisfactory by the new president, Frank Cutter. He ordered a complete revamping of the entire sales program. The framework of the regional plan was retained, however, and in late 1955 a new sales plan calling for a scaled commission on all sales, a small salary and no reimbursement of expenses was instituted. This plan met with resistance from the salesmen. A few who had sold over their quota the previous year accepted the new basis of compensation. But the majority of the salesmen resisted and were eventually granted a salary scale that would work them into the new plan over a period of six months. Seven of the sales staff resigned rather than accept the new payment plan.

GENERAL

In July 1956 Frank Cutter told stockholders that, "a plant modernization program, with new facilities, new products, redesign and improvement of existing products, a new catalog and illustrated price list, more aggressive sales promotion, and the addition of key personnel on the managerial level . . . had a serious effect upon current operations. Consequently, the company experienced a net loss of $185,000 for the fiscal year. . . . Astra-Lite's raw material cost increased $40,000. However, the increase in sales volume and the beneficial effect of the mentioned major changes are expected to produce a more favorable profit picture in the current fiscal year."

Frank Cutter also informed the stockholders that the company was three years behind in development of products when he became president. But a concentrated effort was being made to remedy this situation.

He also stated that the company was considering setting up a complete assembly operation in its branch plant on the west coast. This, he stated, was necessary to get business in California where a firm needed a "Made in California" label on its products, and to reduce the high shipping costs of fixtures to that market area.

One month following the stockholders meeting a private consulting firm submitted a report on the feasibility of complete assembly of Astra-Lite products on the west coast. The report, based mainly on the confidential operations of another lighting manufacturer, indicated that it was cheaper to ship complete fixtures to the west coast rather than to assemble them out there. The logical place for an assembly plant on the west coast, according to the report, was in the San Francisco Bay area and not in Los Angeles.

In September 1956 Frank Cutter signed the contract to provide for the assembly of Astra-Lite fixtures in the Los Angeles plant. The vice-president of engineering and product development was of the opinion that the company should spend the money on research and development rather than expand their operations on the west coast.

exhibit 2 ASTRA-LITE CORPORATION
Balance sheet, 1946–1956, fiscal years ending June 30 (rounded to thousands of dollars)

	1956	1955	1954	1953	1952	1951	1950	1949	1948	1947	1946
Current assets											
Cash	$ 160	$ 79	$ 94	$ 225	$ 480	$ 410	$ 490	$ 451	$ 251	$ 240	$ 250
Accounts receivable	361	308	310	350	390	346	380	342	374	360	361
Inventories:											
Finished goods and work in process	342	345	340	360	410	340	361	240	220	180	200
Raw materials	370	352	350	348	377	293	313	280	270	300	180
Prepaid expenses	6	8	9	11	10	6	9	10	4	2	5
Total current assets	$1,239	$1,092	$1,103	$1,294	$1,667	$1,395	$1,553	$1,323	$1,119	$1,082	$ 996
Fixed assets											
Plant, property and equipment, net	1,140*	680	740	770	790	702	740	773	830	780	720
Deferred charges	8	6	8	9	10	8	9	6	7	7	6
Total assets	$2,387	$1,778	$1,851	$2,073	$2,467	$2,105	$2,302	$2,102	$1,956	$1,869	$1,722
Current liabilities											
Accounts payable	$ 167	$ 136	$ 165	$ 175	$ 197	$ 123	$ 182	$ 134	$ 130	$ 122	$ 110
Notes payable	75										10
Employees' withholding tax	18	12	16	14	18	12	14	10	6	8	7
Accrued wages	140	108	110	125	145	115	137	110	82	85	75
Accrued Federal income taxes	—	—	—	—	248	67	189	187	195	235	200
Total current liabilities	$ 400	$ 256	$ 291	$ 314	$ 608	$ 317	$ 522	$ 441	$ 413	$ 450	$ 402
Fixed liabilities and capital accounts											
Long-term debt	650										
Common stock	560	560	560	560	560	560	560	560	560	560	560
Paid-in surplus	100	100	100	100	100	100	100	100	100	100	100
Earnings retained in business	677	862	900	1,099	1,199	1,128	1,120	1,001	883	759	660
Total liabilities and capital	$2,387	$1,778	$1,851	$2,073	$2,467	$2,105	$2,302	$2,102	$1,956	$1,869	$1,722

* Mortgaged for debt of $650,000.

exhibit 3 **ASTRA-LITE CORPORATION**
Statement of profit and loss, 1946–1956, fiscal years ending June 30 (rounded to thousands of dollars)

	1956	1955	1954	1953	1952	1951	1950	1949	1948	1947	1946
Net sales	$3,900	$3,800	$2,700	$1,500	$4,500	$2,400	$4,100	$3,720	$3,300	$3,100	$3,000
Less cost of goods sold	2,960	2,850	1,970	1,100	3,000	1,590	2,580	2,350	1,980	2,015	1,950
Gross profit	940	950	730	400	1,500	810	1,520	1,370	1,320	1,085	1,050
Less expenses:											
Selling and engineering	970	798	648	300	750	480	820	740	726	465	450
General administrative	195	228	210	120	250	170	307	245	200	170	180
	$1,165	1,026	858	420	1,000	650	1,127	985	926	635	630
Operating profit	$ 225*	$ 76*	$ 128*	$ 20*	$ 500	$ 160	$ 393	$ 385	$ 394	$ 450	$ 420
Add other income	40										
	185*										
Deduct:											
Other expense			43	24	25	30	29	25	19	60	45
Federal income taxes					248	67	189	187	195	235	200
			43	24	273	97	218	212	214	295	245
Net income after taxes	$ 185*	$ 76*	$ 171*	$ 44*	$ 227	$ 63	$ 175	$ 173	$ 180	$ 155	$ 175
Dividends paid			$ 28	$ 56	$ 56	$ 56	$ 56	$ 56	$ 56	$ 56	$ 56
Retained earnings	$(185)	$ (76)	$(199)	$(100)	$ 171	$ 7	$ 119	$ 117	$ 124	$ 99	$ 119

* = loss.
( ) = reduction in retained earnings.

3

SUBURBAN
BANK AND TRUST
COMPANY

HISTORY

The Suburban Bank and Trust Company was chartered in the state of Indiana in 1916 and was incorporated in 1920. The bank was located in an outlying area of Indianapolis and was generally considered to be a specialized institution, catering mainly to local businessmen of the area. Suburban, however, ranked as one of the larger outlying banks in the Indianapolis section. At the end of 1955 deposits totaled about $120 million.

The special services and aggressive management of the bank resulted in rapid growth and established an excellent reputation for the institution. In the late 1920's many new banks were organized throughout the Indianapolis area. The competition for deposits became intense and Suburban soon found itself in direct competition with six new neighborhood banks which had opened during this boom. Suburban lost ground steadily to these institutions, because its ultra-conservative loan policy had alienated many business depositors, who withdrew their funds from the bank. "Why should I keep my money here?" was the general question. "I need a loan. Your bank won't grant it, but the new bank will. I'm going to put my money in one of the new, more progressive banks." This story was heard many times by loan officers at Suburban.

Henry Davidson, the chief loan officer, was determined to maintain a strict loan policy despite pressure from other bank officers and influential depositors. The name of "No Loan Davidson" was soon well known among the hard-pressed business depositors. As a result of Davidson's attitude there was constant bickering between him and the other bank officers. This period of disagreement was short-lived, however.

The stock market crash and the ensuing depression of the 1930's resulted in a period of moratorium for banks. Many of the "easy loan banks" never reopened.

Suburban reopened, the only one of the seven in the area to do so. The depositors who had left Suburban suffered severe monetary losses when the other banks in the area failed to reopen, while those depositors who had stayed with Suburban suffered no losses. Because of Davidson's determination to maintain high standards and a strict loan policy despite the pressure from members of his own staff, the bank survived. This firmly established the bank's reputation for soundness and subsequently was one of the chief factors responsible for its steady growth.

ORGANIZATION

Henry Davidson, the strong-willed force which kept the bank from "going under," was made president in 1949 at the age of 54. In fact, however, he had been directing the bank's operations since 1928 in his capacity as chief loan officer. He was considered by bankers throughout the state to be an exceptionally able administrator. One of his close friends in the banking fraternity remarked:

> He works just as hard today as he did thirty years ago when the bank was in its infancy. He is a man of boundless energy with the ability to make quick decisions. There is little doubt about his being the hardest-working person at Suburban. Banking hours are from 9:00 A.M. until 2:00 P.M. You'll always find Davidson at his desk opening the daily mail at 7:00 A.M., and he rarely leaves before 5:00 P.M.

Every department came under the personal supervision of Mr. Davidson. Very few decisions, whether important or merely routine, were made without his approval. Edward Frey, head of banking and deposits, stated:

> We have the utmost confidence in Mr. Davidson, but on many occasions he appears to try to show his authority by reversing decisions of others. A perfect example is the time I refused to authorize a check presented by a woman customer who had forgotten to have her husband en-

dorse the check as required. It was a clear-cut case. I'm sure that Mr. Davidson would have refused to cash the check had he been approached originally. However, even after I had refused to cash this check, which was in line with a policy he had established, he went right ahead and approved it anyway. It made me look foolish.

It's getting to the point where even the girls who work in my department go to him directly—they don't even bother with me. I'm supposed to be in charge, but you'd never know it. Other department heads will tell you the same thing, so it can't be that I'm always making the wrong decisions. Just take a look at him during banking hours; he has a long line of employees behind him and a long line of customers in front of him. He just has to have his say about everything.

Mr. Randall, executive vice-president, was sixty years old. He had been with the bank since its second year of operation. Most of the bank's customers preferred to talk to him. In contrast with Davidson, whose answers were abrupt and sometimes blunt, Randall was more discreet and had a milder manner of speaking. One of the larger accounts stated, "He has a wonderful personality and takes an honest interest in each one of his customers." Randall was considered by the other officers and employees of the bank as a good administrator capable of handling the bank's affairs in Mr. Davidson's absence. However, he was usually so busy with customers during banking hours that he was often unaware of the bank's management problems unless he stayed after banking hours and discussed them with subordinates.

Harper Young, the assistant vice-president, was forty-three years old. After twenty-five years in the real estate loan department, he was made manager. He had little to do with the bank's general management and policy decisions.

Dennis Tanner had the title of assistant cashier; however, he was more of a replacement officer and trouble-shooter. One day he worked in the commercial department; the next day he helped out in the real estate, the savings, or credit departments. He knew the general operations of the bank very well, but he had never had the opportunity to learn much about such special areas as investments, duties of a loan officer, or policy administration.

The board of directors was composed of seven members. They had monthly meetings but were dependent on Mr. Davidson for most of their information. In addition to Davidson and Randall, the board consisted of two real estate operators, an attorney, a president of a manufacturing firm, and Mr. Reynolds, the largest stockholder, who was the president and owner of a small chain of hardware stores. Mr. Reynolds summed up the board's operation in these words: "We have faith in Mr. Davidson so we usually follow his recommendations. There isn't much sense in trying to upset his apple cart. He's here every day; we meet only once a month."

Suburban had 290 stockholders. Many of them were local business-men, employees, or demised employees' families. The largest stock-holder, Mr. Reynolds, owned only 8 per cent of the total. The board members owned a total of about 40 per cent of the stock, which assured them of continuous control. The board members had served for the past sixteen years.

FINANCIAL

Earnings had risen steadily for the past ten years. Dividends had been modest—most of the earnings had been plowed back into the capital account.

EARNINGS AND DIVIDENDS PER SHARE, 1951–1955*

	1951	*1952*	*1953*	*1954*	*1955*
Earnings	$23.50	$22.00	$40.00	$46.00	$37.00
Dividends	7.00	7.00	7.00	7.00	7.00 †

* Based on number of shares outstanding each year end.
† Plus stock dividend: 50% declared at year end.

Deposit growth had been moderate but steady. Deposit growth for the nation had been increasing at a rate of about 4 per cent per year. Suburban's annual growth rate had been about 3.5 per cent for the past five years. Savings deposits made up the greater share of Suburban's deposit total. Savings deposits were also growing at a faster rate than demand deposits (checking accounts). Statistical data for selected years follow:

DEPOSIT DATA FOR 1953–1955 (IN MILLIONS)

	1953	*1954*	*% change*	*1955*	*% change*
Savings	$70.0	$73.5	Plus 5.0	$76.0	Plus 3.42
Checking	42.0	42.6	Plus 1.5	44.0	Plus 3.30
	$112.0	$116.1	Plus 3.7	$120.0	Plus 3.36

Although Suburban was not keeping pace with the national growth average for deposits, the management of the bank had not expressed concern. They refused to actively seek new business.

Davidson stated: "If a customer walks through the door we're glad to serve him, but we're definitely not going outside to try to get him in here."

The bank did not have a new business department. No effort was made to visit businessmen at their establishments and give them information concerning the various services offered by the bank. This method of solicitation was practiced by most of Suburban's competitors. George Daniels, president of the Exmoor National Bank, one of Suburban's chief competitors, made the following statement:

> We went out and hustled a million dollars' worth of new accounts last year. New business departments are as important as loan departments these days. Competition for the deposit dollar is intense. Besides competing with banks for commercial business, we're faced with a new threat for the savings dollar. Savings and Loan Associations are hurting our savings business, because they pay a higher rate of interest. So we just have to get new commercial accounts to pick up the slack.

Suburban, however, had one distinct advantage over most of the outlying banks. It had a trust department that was comparable to those of large mid-city banks. In describing the importance of the trust department Mr. Randall stated:

> A lot of our new commercial and savings business arises indirectly as a result of our trust department. We have the only bank trust department available to people who prefer to do business outside of the downtown area. Most people like to do all of their banking in one place, so when we get their trust business we usually get their checking and savings business as well.

INVESTMENT POLICIES

Investment policies were formulated by Mr. Davidson. Short-term and intermediate-term government securities comprised the bulk of the investment portfolio. Municipal bonds and equipment trust certificates also represented sizable holdings. Statutes permitted the holding of only certain types of high-grade securities. To this extent all banks were somewhat limited in what they could do investmentwise.

Mr. Davidson displayed unusual skill in selecting investments which provided a relatively high yield from a restricted group of high-grade securities. The bond account of Suburban had always shown better than average results. Mr. Davidson's record compared very favorably with that of the professional staffs of larger banks.

LOAN POLICIES

All loan policies were formulated by Mr. Davidson. He believed that the bank should not make a loan unless it was sure, beyond a reasonable doubt, that all principal and interest would be repaid as scheduled. He refused to take borderline risks. The criteria which he set up were considered to be very rigid by the members of the staff. Davidson had frequently stated: "We're in business to loan money, not to give it away and then hope for default and foreclosure or legal action." The bank's policy limited maximum loanable funds to about 25 per cent of deposits, or about $30 million. In 1955 the bank had $26 million outstanding in loans. The average bank in Suburban's class usually set its maximum loan limit at about 35 to 40 per cent of its total deposits.

PROMOTION POLICIES

The bank's stated policy was to promote from within. In recent years, however, two key positions had been filled from outside the organization. This was considered necessary because the two positions required experienced men and no one within the organization was considered qualified to take over.

Suburban did not have an active formal training program. From time to time an effort had been made to hire "trainees," but because of a personnel shortage they were rapidly placed in a particular job and usually left there.

The bank operated with a minimum of personnel. However, salaries were generally higher than for most banks the size of Suburban. This seemed to be the main factor in maintaining a stable work force. There had been a very low turnover rate among the male employees of the bank. Recently, however, two young men of recognized potential left the bank for other jobs. One of them explained:

> I'll have to go to work for less money, but at least I'll have a chance to learn and to progress accordingly. They're so busy and have so little help

at the bank that it's practically impossible to learn anything except what a person's particular job calls for. As a result, when a better job does "open up," it's necessary to bring in someone from the outside. There are plenty of good people here, but they can't get experience toward better jobs unless they are given the chance.

A veteran of twenty years said:

I'm stuck here. I can't afford to go somewhere else and take a salary cut. I have to think of my family. Most of us get promoted in order as jobs open up. But they pass all of us up on the big jobs in favor of an "experienced outsider." Sure I'm disgusted, but what can I do?

4

NORTHERN LUMBER DEALERS SUPPLY COMPANY

As he drove to the offices of the Northern Lumber Dealers Supply Company, Roy Freemont mentally reviewed the information contained in a folder in his brief case. Since his promotion in July to the position of district sales manager for Arnett-Townson, a large manufacturer of builders' supplies, Freemont had called upon almost all of the wholesalers in his district.

During the first week in September, Freemont had scheduled a meeting for early in October with Jerry Perkins, general manager of the Northern Lumber Dealers Supply Company. From the notes left in the file by his predecessor, Freemont recalled that Jerry Perkins shared the management of Northern with his cousin, James Hayward. Perkins worked as office manager, purchasing agent, warehouse manager, and bookkeeper, and his cousin Hayward performed similar duties in addition to acting as sales manager.

During the depression of the 1930's, the fathers of the two cousins started the Northern Supply Company with a very limited amount of capital. In 1939, the ill health of the senior Hayward forced him to leave the business. Both Jim Hayward and Jerry Perkins joined the firm after they got out of the service following World War II. The senior Perkins died in 1949, and that year the two cousins took over complete management of the firm.

Freemont noted that Northern was the only Arnett-Townson wholesaler in that urban area; Capital Supply, the other A-T wholesaler, went bankrupt in 1969. He also noted that during the last five years Northern had experienced a slight decline in sales (see Exhibit 1, 1966 to 1971 income statements). The folder also contained a note explaining that Northern owned its own land and buildings and borrowed sparingly from the bank (see Exhibit 2, 1966 to 1971 balance sheets).

In addition to Perkins and Hayward, the company employed one woman in the office who worked full-time as a bookkeeper, another woman who worked three days each week, a warehouse foreman, one truck driver, a part-time summer warehouseman and one salesman who spent almost all of his time on the road calling on accounts. Hayward divided his time between the office and selling on the road.

After he parked his car, Freemont went into the offices of the Northern Lumber Dealers Supply Company and met Jerry Perkins. After some introductory comments, Freemont asked Perkins if he would tell him a little more about Northern Supply. Perkins agreed, and after he finished taking care of a customer at the counter, they walked to a small private office and began to talk.

COMPETITION

Jerry began by commenting that the best way to characterize Northern Supply management was by their cautious waiting to see what was going to happen to their competitors. "This is about the most competitive town in the country. I don't think there is any such thing as a really intelligent competitor in this town. All they know is price competition, and they have sold that way for so long that they have educated the customer to shop for the best price. The results have been pretty drastic, because so many wholesalers around here have gone bankrupt, including Capital Supply, that there are only three of us left who are in direct competition. To give you an example, Central City is one half as large as this city but it supports 10 wholesalers. In effect, the local wholesalers cut their margins so low and waged such vicious fights over price that they just put themselves out of business."

Jerry went on to explain that both of Northern's competitors, each with sales of approximately $500,000 per year, were operating at a loss. In spite of losses, one continued to deliver almost everything to his customers at carload prices regardless of the quantities ordered. Jerry related a story about one of his competitors who offered to sell his business to an out-of-town buyer for $5,000 provided the buyer would take over receivables and payables. After a brief analysis of the books, the buyer allegedly refused to even consider the offer.

"One change that has occurred during the last few years," Perkins continued, "has been the drop in direct sales or direct billings. A few years ago we were doing almost half a million dollars a year in direct sales and now our direct sales are down to about $80,000 per year." He attributed most of the change to the increasing number of manufacturers who were willing to sell directly to the customer rather than bill the goods through the wholesaler. He indicated that two large cash-and-carry lumber and supply yards had obtained a sizable amount of business, but that most of the lumber yards in the area were either just getting by or actually operating at a loss. "Frankly, we lost a lot of customers who just could not make a profit, so they folded up."

SALES AND PROFITS

Before Jerry could answer Freemont's question about how Northern was performing in its market, he answered several telephone calls and waited on two more customers at the counter. When he returned he said, "We are getting by. Because we are flexible and willing to work hard, we have been able to hold out in this market. We have two trucks, for example, and on any given day or evening you may find me, Jim, or our salesman driving a truck making deliveries. We got into the delivery business in 1968, and this may help some. We are careful not to make unprofitable deliveries—the trucks don't go out of here with one little bundle on the back. By keeping our overhead low, working nights, and everybody working hard, we have been able to stay out of the red."

Jerry explained that because of the shift away from direct sales to more warehouse sales Northern had to increase its inventory and its product-handling activities. The net result was an increased gross profit but a decreased net profit as costs tended to increase. He attributed the 1968 drop in profits to the advent of a delivery service for the company and the 1969 and 1970 experiences to a wave of business failures which produced losses in excess of $10,000 in bad debts for Northern. He estimated, however, that Northern's net profit would probably rise from $8,000 to $10,000 in 1971.

Northern supplied goods to about 165 accounts, mostly lumber yards and building specialty accounts. The largest account purchased about $22,000 worth of goods per year and the next largest about $17,000. The remainder of the accounts were relatively small. He stated that an average month would yield sales divided roughly as follows:

Products	Sales	Approximate gross margins %
Ceiling panels	$ 8,200	11–18
Insulated board	2,700	4–10
Masonite products	21,000	15
Marlite	4,000	20–25
Roofing material	10,000	12
Asbestos	1,300	16–20
Gypsum	1,600	10
Finishes	600	20–25
Floor tile	2,400	20
Metal products	3,300	20
Cedar products	7,100	20
Insulation	4,400	10
Direct sales	6,600	5

Another factor that influenced Northern's profit experience was the institution in 1968 of an insurance and profit-sharing plan, which cost almost $7,000 per year. Jerry commented that the cash value of the insurance was beginning to increase and would begin to improve the appearance of the balance sheet within the next few years.

SOME PROPOSALS

Jerry stated that he and his cousin did not know which way to go. "We don't know whether to get larger or smaller. Right now we are just watching our competitors and waiting to see what happens to them. It looks like they may go out of business, and if they do, we may be able to get a bigger share of the local market, which we estimate to total about $2 million per year."

Jerry explained that Northern would like to increase its profits but that neither he nor his cousin were sure how to do it. He stated that he listened to every salesman who came in, hoping that he could find another good line which would require no more than a $35,000 to $45,000 investment in inventory but would improve sales and profits.

"We do not want to go into hardware, because that is a little out of our line, but we would like to take on some more sheet goods lines, which are what we are best equipped to handle. We have been thinking about taking on a line of plywood, because it is a high-volume, high-turnover item, but its profits are a little unpredictable.

"One thing that we are trying to do," Jerry continued, "is to increase our margins on sales to individuals who are either sent here by a retailer or who just walk in off the street. We have two price lists, a retail and a wholesale price, and any individual who comes in to buy something pays cash and pays the retail price. The dealers were sending customers to us for goods which they did not have. In effect, we were expected to perform all the services and do all the work for the very low markup we realize on most of our products. In July we did about $3,000 worth of retail business, and it is increasing every month. The dealers don't like it, but we almost have to do it to stay alive."

Jerry continued his discussion of direct selling to individuals by stating that both he and his cousin had been looking for a retail outlet of some kind for their products. They envisioned a cash-and-carry type store, but one which provided more services than are normally provided by cash-and-carrys. He predicted that they would probably have to put up their own buildings, because they had not been able to find a structure which exactly suited their idea of what the store should look like.

The conversation between the two men closed with Jerry's mentioning that he had a lot of questions about the wholesale type of business in that particular area and in the country as a whole. He commented that he was not sure that the traditional wholesalers had much of a future unless they were willing to adopt new and somewhat revolutionary means of doing business. He expressed the idea that more and more of the wholesale function was being performed by large retail outlets that served as wholesalers and retailers.

Just before the two men said good-by, Jerry said, "Well, Roy, I have told you quite a bit about our business, since you have a real interest in how well we do because we do buy about 20% of our merchandise from Arnett-Townson. What's your opinion? Do you have any solutions for our problems?"

exhibit 1 NORTHERN LUMBER DEALERS SUPPLY COMPANY

Income statements, 1966–1971 (in thousands)

	(9 months) Sept. 30, 1971		Dec. 31, 1970		Dec. 31, 1969		Dec. 31, 1968		Dec. 31, 1967		Dec. 31, 1966	
	Amount	Per cent	Amount	Per cent	Amount	Per cent	Amount	Per cent	Amount	Per cent	Amount	Per cent
Sales	$654.9	100	$933.5	100	$1029.1	100	$935.0	100	$1032.4	100	$1055.3	100
Cost of goods	568.4		811.1		901.5		833.1		913.3		937.8	
Gross profit	$ 86.5	13.2	$122.4	13.1	$ 127.6	12.4	$101.9	12.7	$ 119.1	11.8	$ 117.5	11.1
Expenses:												
Executive salaries	$ 30.0	4.6	$ 44.1	4.8	$ 42.8	4.2	$ 41.6	4.3	$ 38.1	3.8	$ 36.3	3.4
Other salaries and wages	14.9	2.2	23.0	2.5	20.7	2.0	17.5	1.9	16.0	1.5	15.0	1.4
Traveling expenses	1.8		2.0		3.3		3.2		4.7		5.0	
Stationery and postage	1.7		1.6		2.1		2.0		1.8		1.6	
Telephone and telegraph									1.6			
Utilities	2.1		3.1		2.8		2.4		2.0		2.1	
Social security and unemployment insurance	1.7		1.8		1.6		1.3		1.3		1.3	
Professional services	1.2		.6		.9		1.9		1.3		1.1	
Real estate and property taxes	2.9		7.3		7.5		5.9		6.5		5.3	
Depreciation	6.5		9.5		11.5		10.7		8.3		7.6	
General insurance	1.6		2.5		2.1		2.1		2.0		1.7	
Hospital insurance	1.2											
Executive insurance	3.5		.6		2.2		1.9		1.3		2.1	
Auto expense	.3		.5		.6		.8		.9		.7	
Provision for bad debts	2.0		5.4		6.0				.5			
Freight	1.1		1.3		1.7		1.9		2.5		2.7	
Pension trust	3.7		4.8		4.9		4.6		4.3			
Lift truck and expenses	2.2		3.2		3.1		2.3					
Miscellaneous	1.6		3.8		3.8		2.8		2.3		2.8	

exhibit 1 NORTHERN LUMBER DEALERS SUPPLY COMPANY

Income statements, 1966–1971 (in thousands)

	(9 months) Sept. 30, 1971 Amount	Per cent	Dec. 31, 1970 Amount	Per cent	Dec. 31, 1969 Amount	Per cent	Dec. 31, 1968 Amount	Per cent	Dec. 31, 1967 Amount	Per cent	Dec. 31, 1966 Amount	Per cent
Advertising	.1		.6		.7		.5		.5		.7	
Profit-sharing trust	......		.6		.6		1.1		1.2			
Donations	......		.3		.3		.5		.8		.8	
Total expenses	$ 80.1	12.2	$116.6	12.5	$119.2	11.6	$105.0	10.7	$ 96.9	9.7	$ 86.8	8.2
Net operating profit	6.4	1.0	5.8	.6	8.4	.8	14.9	1.6	22.2	2.1	30.7	2.9
Other income (expense)	(2.3)		(2.2)		(3.8)		(3.1)		(3.4)		(3.9)	
Profit before taxes	$ 4.1	.6	$ 3.6	.4	$ 4.6	.4	$ 11.8	1.2	$ 18.8	1.8	$ 26.8	2.8
Estimated income tax	$ 1.4		$ 1.2		$ 2.5		$ 4.5		$ 6.9		$ 9.8	
Net income	$ 2.7	.4	$ 2.4	.3	$ 2.1	.2	$ 7.3	.8	$ 11.9	1.2	$ 17.0	1.6

exhibit 2   **NORTHERN LUMBER DEALERS SUPPLY COMPANY**
Balance sheets, 1966—1971 (in thousands)

	Sept. 30, 1966 (9 months)	Dec. 31, 1965	Dec. 31, 1964	Dec. 31, 1963	Dec. 31, 1962	Dec. 31, 1961
Assets						
Current assets:						
Cash	$ 8.7	$ 5.9	$ 11.0	$ 16.0	$ 1.0	$ 4.6
Accounts receivable (less bad debt reserve)	77.5	92.5	98.1	101.9	107.3	114.1
Inventories	108.0	91.0	99.0	128.1	96.8	95.0
Unexpired insurance	5.6	3.2	2.6	3.0	3.6	2.5
Real estate tax deposit					1.3	1.2
Total current assets	$199.8	$192.6	$210.7	$249.0	$210.0	$217.4
Fixed assets:						
Land at cost	22.3	22.3	22.3	22.3	22.3	22.3
Buildings and equipment (less depreciation)	76.5	82.7	83.0	92.1	94.1	90.5
Cash surrender value life insurance	17.9	17.9	12.5	9.3	6.4	3.9
Total assets	$316.5	$315.5	$328.5	$372.7	$332.8	$334.1
Liabilities						
Current:						
Notes payable (bank)	$ 11.0	$ 11.0	$	$ 16.5	$ 16.5	$ 16.5
Stockholders' notes payable		3.3	3.3	7.7	7.7	7.7
Accounts payable	42.3	31.1	57.7	77.4	53.6	63.5
Mortgage payments (1 year)	4.9	3.8	3.5	3.3	3.5	3.1
Accruals	5.4	13.2	9.4	11.5	13.8	15.8
Total current liabilities	63.6	62.4	73.9	116.4	95.1	106.6
Fixed:						
Mortgage loan	29.4	32.4	36.3	38.1	28.8	30.3
Common stock	44.0	44.0	44.0	44.0	44.0	44.0
Preferred stock	114.4	114.4	114.4	114.4	114.4	46.1
Retained earnings	65.1	62.3	59.9	59.8	50.5	107.1
Total liabilities and capital	$316.5	$315.5	$328.5	$372.7	$332.8	$334.1

5

SOONER
DISTRIBUTING
COMPANY

Early in July, 1966, Mr. Richard Taylor, president of the Sooner Distributing Company, reviewed the results of his firm's business during the first six months of 1966. Sales for the Gordon Taylor Company, a Sooner Company subsidiary distributing floor products, were about $60,000 below the company's sales during the first six months of 1965. If the sales trend continued during the second half of the year, the consolidated operating statements for both companies would show a small loss during 1966 or, at best, only break even on a sales volume of about $4 million. His initial comment was "Ridiculous!" as he reviewed again both companies' profits for the preceding year. For the three years 1962 to 1965, the two companies earned a profit of less than 1% of sales. It seemed apparent to Dick Taylor that the impending decline in the Taylor Company sales for 1966 would make it almost impossible for the combined companies to show a profit. (See Exhibits 2 to 6 for operating statements. Exhibit 7 contains a study of 28 firms conducted by Western Rubber and Tile Company.)

Taylor's concern about the profits of his companies and the existing levels of sales prompted him once again to review the history, strategy, and effectiveness of his organizations in a search for weaknesses and possible opportunities.

BACKGROUND INFORMATION

In the increasing automobile population of the early 1900's, Gordon Taylor saw an opportunity for a new business in his home town of

Tulsa. In 1919 he opened the Sooner Distributing Company, a small wholesaling firm organized to distribute auto parts to the eastern and central Oklahoma territory. After World War I Mr. Taylor added a line of appliances. As appliance sales increased, the auto parts business declined and within a few years was eliminated completely. Except for the Depression years, the company grew steadily through its first 46 years of existence.

In 1939 Mr. Taylor accepted a franchise from the Western Rubber and Tile Company to sell their line of floor tile and linoleum. During World War II the Sooner Company distributed an extensive line of gas and electrical appliances, along with the new line of floor coverings.

Richard ("Dick") Taylor, the only child of Gordon Taylor, graduated from college in 1944. He began with the Sooner Company as a clerk and during the years that followed worked in almost every job in the organization. He became president of the company when his father died in 1955.

In 1946 the Sooner Distributing Company organized the Gordon Taylor Company as a wholly owned subsidiary. The Gordon Taylor Company distributed Western Rubber and Tile flooring products; the Sooner Company continued as an appliance distributor (see the organization chart in Exhibit 1). In 1966 Sooner was distributing TV and hi-fi sets, washing machines, refrigerators, and air conditioners, together with parts for each line.

ADMINISTRATIVE ORGANIZATION

When Dick Taylor took over as president of the Sooner Distributing Company, he owned well over 50% of the stock of the corporation. As president of the Sooner Company, he felt he could do his company the most good as an administrator and consequently directed most of his energy toward the administrative, organizational, personnel, and financial activities of the corporations. He stated that, in the position of top executive of his company, he did not feel he should contact dealers on a regular schedule or travel with the salesmen. He tried, however, to see every dealer who came into the offices. He attended as many dealer meetings as possible, although he stayed in the background. He knew many dealers, especially in the appliance field, on a personal basis and when a large promotion was on offered to have the salesmen bring their major accounts to his office for a conference.

Because of his background in the appliance business, Dick Taylor spent most of his time on matters pertaining to the Sooner Company. In 1964 he began to take a more active role in the Taylor Company as Burl Kavens, the president of the Gordon Taylor Company, approached retirement age. In 1965 Dick received $9,000 in salary from each company plus 10% of the total profits.

Although he was president of the Sooner Distributing Company, Dick Taylor assumed almost all of the financial and administrative responsibilities of the Gordon Taylor Company. The two companies operated with a single manager, controller, and clerical staff under the supervision of Dick Taylor.

In 1966, at the age of 69, Burl Kavens finished his 45th year with the company. He had played a major role in the decision to accept the Western Rubber and Tile line of products in 1939. From 1939 until the Gordon Taylor Company was organized in 1946, he functioned as the sales manager for the floor products. When the Gordon Taylor Company was organized, he was appointed president by Mr. Gordon Taylor. He had innumerable friends throughout the industry in both retailing and manufacturing circles. His relationships with dealers were described as being exceptionally close and cordial. Although he was president of the Gordon Taylor Company, his primary duties were those of sales manager, because most of the other administrative and financial aspects of the company were handled by Dick Taylor. Burl received $13,000 per year and 8% of the combined companies' profits.

In 1957 when the Tulsa branch was opened, Burl Kavens and Dick Taylor selected Neal Nelson to operate the branch and to begin training for the position of sales manager when Burl retired. His official title was that of sales manager; however, he actually functioned as branch manager. In 1965 Neal's salary was increased to $10,000 per year plus 2% of the profits, and he was given the position of vice president.

Only the sales organizations of the two companies were completely separate; salesmen in the Gordon Taylor Company did not sell appliances, or Sooner salesmen flooring products. Selling costs were recorded separately, but all other operating and administrative costs were combined and then divided between the two companies at the end of the year on the basis of sales volume (see Exhibit 5).

SALES AND COMPETITION

The sales organization of the Gordon Taylor Company included Burl Kavens, president of the Gordon Taylor Company; Neal Nelson, vice president; and seven salesmen divided between the Oklahoma City and Tulsa offices. The Sooner Distributing Company also employed seven salesmen in the two offices. The two company presidents, Taylor and Kavens, had their offices in Tulsa, while the two vice presidents, Neal Nelson (Gordon Taylor Company) and Carl Harrison (Sooner Company—appliances), were located in Oklahoma City.

In 1956 the Western Rubber and Tile Company granted permission to Sooner to open a branch in Oklahoma City. At that time Western flooring products were being distributed by the Oklahoma City Furniture and Supply Company, an old firm that distributed a large number of furniture and hardware products. Because floor coverings was only one of many lines which Oklahoma City Supply handled and thus was viewed as a minor activity for the company, Western decided to allow the Taylor Company to open a branch in the same city. The Taylor Company wished to open a branch not only because they realized the potential of the area, but because they knew of internal dissension within the Oklahoma City Furniture Company management and the possibility of that firm's discontinuing business.

The Sooner Distributing Company and the Taylor Company rented a warehouse which they stocked with both floor coverings and appliances. The Taylor Company assigned three salesmen to the warehouse early in 1957 to begin calling on accounts. The annual sales of flooring materials during the ensuing years were as follows:

Oklahoma City

1957	$260,000	1962	$772,000
1958	380,000	1963	884,000
1959	608,000	1964	890,000
1960	635,000	1965	925,000
1961	678,000	1966	815,000 (estimated)

Each of the salesmen received a monthly payment of $750 out of which he paid his expenses. In addition, each salesman was eligible for a bonus which had ranged from $2,000 to $3,000 per year during the period 1963 to 1965. The drop in sales during the first half of 1966 would probably have the effect of greatly reducing or eliminating 1966 bonuses. The present method of making a monthly payment to each salesman that included both salary and expense allowances was introduced in January, 1966. The new compensation program for the Gordon Taylor salesmen was inaugurated because of the steady increases in the size of salesmen's expense accounts. The program was already in effect for Sooner's salesmen. Many of the salesmen did not like the new plan, although there was no indication that it would reduce their actual monthly income. Dick Taylor thought that the company might lose one or possibly two salesmen at the end of 1966, particularly if there was no year-end bonus.

The Gordon Taylor Company had 825 to 875 active flooring accounts, which were serviced by seven salesmen. Of the total active accounts, 500 accounts signed a seasonal contract to buy a designated amount of goods from the Taylor Company. The 20 largest dealers were responsible for 60 to 70% of the Taylor Company's sales, and about one-third of the accounts that signed seasonal contracts purchased $2,000 worth or more of flooring materials each year.

The average salesman for the Taylor Company called on slightly more than 100 accounts, plus calls on potential customers. The territories were so structured that it took approximately three weeks for a salesman to call on all of his accounts. Dick Taylor commented that he did not believe that his salesmen were able to spend the time necessary to dig out new accounts because of the size of their territories. In an attempt to motivate salesmen to make more intensive selling efforts and spend extra hours, the company began a campaign to increase the number of orders of $25 or more and the number of salesman calls.

The Taylor Company estimated that an average salesman would have to produce a sales volume of about $300,000 per year in order to meet all costs involved and provide a small profit. The 1965 sales volume for each of Taylor's salesmen was as follows:

1. $303,000
2.   384,000
3.   457,000
4.   228,000
5.   295,000
6.   274,000
7.   254,000

The combined territories of the Taylor salesmen included almost all the counties in Oklahoma and a few adjacent counties in Kansas, Missouri, Arkansas, and Texas. The population of the counties totaled about 3.1 million, according to the 1960 census. Because the area was primarily agricultural, the population was undergoing some distinct changes. During the last few decades the average size of farms had increased fivefold, thus greatly reducing the number of farm homes in the territory. One county in the state had over 1,000 fewer farms than in 1940. Although there had been a 2 to 3% increase in population during the last decade, the rate of increase was one of the lowest for any state in the United States.

The geographical scattering of the population within the state tended to limit the effectiveness of the salesmen. The company estimated that their average salesman could make only about eight calls per day, because at least one third of his time was spent traveling.

Many of Taylor's customers were mechanics who left their jobs as floor tile layers in order to start a business of their own. For example, eight out of ten specialty floor tile stores within the city limits of Tulsa were owned by former floor tile layers. Although some of the tile layers became good businessmen, many of them were poorly trained and inept. Therefore, it was imperative that the sales force and management spend a certain amount of time in teaching their dealers simple and sound business principles.

Within the state of Oklahoma there were five Western Rubber and Tile distributors, including Taylor's two branches. In addition to the five distributors within the state, there were nine other Western distributors in adjoining states that sold some goods within Taylor's territory, particularly in the border counties.

Dick Taylor observed that competition had become much tougher as his competitors, both within the state and outside the state, had grown and become more aggressive. He attributed some of the increased competitiveness to the acceptance by his competitors of the specialty salesman concept. Most of his major competitors restructured their sales forces about 1960 to 1961 by designating and training their salesmen as specialty salesmen. As he reflected on the competitive situation within the state, Dick stated, "As the enemy deploys more and better-trained troops in the field, we have to meet them with more and better-trained troops." Because of increased competition, Taylor wanted to add an additional salesman but did not believe that either the existing sales level or sales potential would justify the increased costs. Dick was also afraid he would demoralize the sales force if he suggested dividing the area into more sales territories. Although competition was more intense, the Taylor Company had succeeded in holding 50% or more of the Western Rubber and Tile Company sales in Oklahoma (see Exhibit 8).

Both Taylor and Kavens believed that the most frustrated salesmen on the Taylor sales force were those working in and around Oklahoma

City, because of the competition they encountered there. Three years after Taylor opened its branch in Oklahoma City, the Oklahoma City Furniture and Supply Company sold its floor products business to the Rand Company, a carpeting wholesaler. The Rand Company deployed three salesmen in the area to match the three employed by Taylor. Dick Taylor estimated that the Rand Company's sales of hard-surface flooring products were only about half those of Taylor's Oklahoma City branch, yet they employed as many salesmen. He claimed that there were too many salesmen in the area for the amount of business and that the salesmen were actually only playing ring-around-a-rosy with each other as they chased the major accounts.

WAREHOUSING AND INVENTORY CONTROL

The Sooner Distributing Company owned a three-story building in Tulsa which housed the two companies' offices, appliance showrooms, service department, and some appliance warehouse space. The company had about $50,000 invested in the building, which was constructed some time before the turn of the century. The two floors and the basement of the building contained about 10,000 square feet of floor space. The top floor housed the executive and clerical offices, a display room, and some appliance storage area. The main floor housed the parts and repair division and some storage. The basement contained a small parts–storage area.

The company rented 13,000 square feet of space in a building immediately behind and adjoining the Sooner building. Flooring tile was stored in a basement room containing 4,500 square feet. A second-floor area containing 15,000 square feet was used as storage space for large appliances.

A small one-story building containing 10,000 square feet, some 50 feet behind the other rented building, was rented as a storage area for flooring sheet goods. A short railroad spur ran between the two buildings. One section of the sheet goods building was used for a small display room and provided office space for two women who processed orders and purchases.

All of the warehousing activities were performed by the warehouse manager, four full-time warehousemen, and one half-time worker. Three of the men were assigned to flooring materials, one was assigned to appliances, and the part-time worker divided his time between the two companies. The rental on each building averaged about 25¢ per square foot.

When an order for flooring materials was presented by a salesman or issued over the telephone, the warehouse manager or one of the girls in that office accepted the order. A four-copy work order was prepared immediately for use in filling the order. The order was numbered by a stamping machine when the processing of the order began. The original was a work copy; the second copy went to the customer; the third copy was called an office guard copy and was retained in the office for reference until the order had been processed and shipped; and the fourth copy served as a packing slip. The work copies were filed in numerical order, including any voided copies, which provided a check against misplaced orders.

A partial physical inventory of some goods was conducted almost every day. Thus, a complete inventory was conducted every two weeks. The results of the daily checks were compared with the inventory records kept in the main office. The company had no recorded pilferage losses of any significance.

Early in 1966 the Taylor Company began to search for another warehouse building in Oklahoma City. The established warehouse location contained 24,000 square feet of space, which was not adequate to meet the floor space requirements of the branch warehouse.

In July, 1966, the company rented a building which was located a few blocks from the old location. The building consisted of two floors and a basement, a railroad siding, and truck docks on both sides of the building. Like the Tulsa buildings, the Oklahoma City building had a lagre freight elevator. The building contained 47,000 square feet of floor space, enough to allow the companies to handle up to 50% more than their 1963 to 1966 volume of sales. For this additional space the two companies paid $1,000 per year more than the rental on the old location.

Dick Taylor was pleased with the warehouse operations of the two companies; eight full-time warehouse employees and one part-time employee handled a volume of sales exceeding $4 million per year. As well as he could determine, his warehousing costs were about equal to or lower than that of his competition. He favored multifloor warehousing because normally the rent per square foot was much lower than in new, single-floor warehouses. He explained that there would be few, if any, savings in labor cost, because a warehouse required a certain number of workers to take care of orders and to cover for each other during lunch periods and vacations. Since the size of the crew was fixed at some number larger than the number actually required to handle incoming and outgoing goods, they might as well be employed moving goods to upper floors. He speculated that even with the most modern and efficient storage area his companies would still require about the same number of warehouse employees. But the rent on modern warehouses was three to four times the figure he was paying for multistory warehousing facilities.

As Dick Taylor prepared to close his office for the day he wondered what he could do during the remaining months of 1966 to increase sales and profits. What should he do in 1967? He wondered specifically what he could do about the problem of selling costs and the area's limited potential for sales.

exhibit 1

SOONER DISTRIBUTION COMPANY AND GORDON TAYLOR COMPANY

Organization Chart

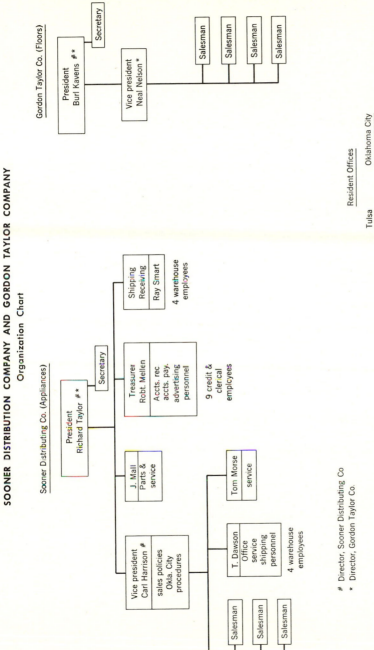

Director, Sooner Distributing Co
* Director, Gordon Taylor Co.

Resident Offices

Tulsa	Oklahoma City
Richard Taylor	Carl Harrison
Burl Kavens	Neal Nelson
Robt. Mellen	T. Dawson
Ray Smart	Tom Morse
J. Mall	

93

exhibit 2 GORDON TAYLOR (FLOORING)
Income statement, 1961–1965 (000's)

	1965		1964		1963		1962		1961	
	Amount	Per cent	Amount	Per cent	Amount	Per cent	Amount	Per cent	Amount	Per cent
Sales	$2195	100	$2100	100	$2240	100	$2120	100	$1912	100
Cost of sales	1812	82.6	1727	82.2	1879	83.8	1753	82.0	1568	82.0
Gross profit	383	17.4	373	17.8	361	16.2	367	18.0	344	18.0
Selling expense*	124	5.7	128	6.1	128	5.7	124	5.8	122	5.9
Selling profit	$ 259	11.7	$ 245	11.7	$ 233	10.5	$ 243	12.2	$ 222	12.1
Operating expenses:										
General and administrative*	40		40		49		55		53	
Personnel expense	2		2		1		1		1	
Intercompany charges for service, buildings, personnel, and internal expenses	171		168		143		131		127	
Total operating expenses	$ 213	9.6	$ 210	10.0	$ 193	8.5	$ 187	8.8	$ 181	9.6
Operating income	46		35		40		56		51	
Nonoperating income (expense)					9		(3)		(5)	
Income before contributions to profit sharing or taxes	46		35		49		53		46	
Contributions to profit-sharing trust	6	.3	5	.3	5	.2	6	.3	4	.3
Income before taxes	40		30		44		47		42	
Income taxes	14	.6	9	.4	17	.6	18	.8	16	.8
Net income	$ 26	1.2	$ 21	1.0	$ 27	1.2	$ 29	1.4	$ 26	1.4

* Selling and warehouse expenses are presented in detail in Exhibit 4.

exhibit 3 SOONER DISTRIBUTING COMPANY AND GORDON TAYLOR COMPANY

Consolidated income statement, 1961–1965 (000's)

	1965		1964		1963		1962		1961	
	Amount	Per cent	Amount	Per cent	Amount	Per cent	Amount	Per cent	Amount	Per cent
Sales	$4090	100	$4142	100	$4212	100	$3886	100	$3528	100
Cost of sales	3430	83.8	3450	83.3	3564	84.6	3246	83.6	2902	82.3
Gross profit	660	16.2	692	16.7	648	15.4	640	16.4	626	17.7
Selling expenses	234	5.7	259	6.3	242	5.7	244	6.3	241	6.7
Selling profit	426	10.5	433	10.6	406	9.6	406	10.5	385	10.9
Operating expenses:										
Warehouse expense	61	1.6	65	1.6	53	1.3	51	1.3	52	1.5
Service department	16	.4	21	.5	19	.5	15	.4	13	.4
Building expenses	57	1.4	59	1.4	59	1.4	58	1.5	51	1.4
General and administrative expenses	197	4.8	189	4.6	182	4.3	179	4.6	174	4.9
Personnel expenses	14	.3	14	.3	12	.3	11	.3	12	.3
Total operating expenses	$ 345	8.5	$ 348	8.4	$ 325	7.7	$ 314	8.1	$ 302	8.5
Operating income	81	2.0	85	2.2	108	2.6	113	2.9	83	2.3
Other income (expense)	(12)	(.3)	(18)	(.4)	(16)	(.4)	(7)	(.2)	6	.2
Income before contributions to profit sharing and taxes	69	1.7	67	1.8	92	2.2	106	2.7	89	2.5
Contributions to profit-sharing trust*	15	.4	15	.4	15	.4	15	.4	6	.2
Income before taxes	54	1.3	52	1.4	77		91	2.3	83	2.3
Income taxes	19	.5	15	.4	29	.7	29	.7	25	.6
Net income	$ 35	.9	$ 37	.9	$ 48	.9	$ 62	1.1	$ 58	1.5

NOTE: Some variation due to rounding.

* In 1948 Dick Taylor instituted a retirement trust plan; no contributions were made by employees. The original plan called for a specific company contribution only after a fixed percentage of profit arrived at by a government-approved formula was set aside for stockholders. However, because of a decline in operating profits during the early 1950's, no contributions were made. Government regulations regarding company profit-sharing trusts changed; therefore, amendments were made to the original trust providing that the directors of the company could use their discretion in determining the amount of the company's contribution to the employees' profit-sharing trust. Dick Taylor believed the employees should receive some contribution to the profit-sharing trust as long as the company showed some profit. In 1966, through company contributions and investment earnings, the trust's assets totaled approximately $150,000.

exhibit 4   GORDON TAYLOR COMPANY (FLOORING)
Balance sheets, 1961–1965 (000's)

	1965	1964	1963	1962	1961
Cash	$ 9.0	$ 13.0	$ 1.5	$ 47.8	$ 55.1
Receivables	248.0	264.1	201.0	167.8	132.2
Less collected loss reserve	(29.4)	(27.2)	(18.4)	(15.9)	(12.3)
Net receivables	219.6	233.9	182.6	151.9	119.9
Inventories—lower of cost or market	295.0	262.1	295.0	285.0	266.0
Total current assets	$523.6	$508.0	$479.1	$484.7	$441.0
Fixed assets—depreciation	3.5	3.9	3.5	5.3	1.0
Total assets	$527.1	$511.9	$482.6	$490.0	$442.0
Notes payable			$ 8.4		
Accounts payable	$ 65.3	$ 80.3	49.4	$ 81.7	$ 23.8
Estimated taxes	14.0	9.3	16.6	18.7	16.3
Accrued liabilities	20.8	19.3	27.0	34.6	18.1
Total liabilities	$100.1	$108.9	$101.4	$135.0	$ 58.2
Preferred stock	$117.0	$117.0	$117.0	$117.0	$117.0
Common stock surplus					
Donated					
Earned	310.0	286.0	264.2	238.0	266.8
Stockholders equity	$427.0	$403.0	$381.2	$355.0	$383.8
Total liabilities and equity	$527.1	$511.9	$482.6	$490.0	$442.0

exhibit 5 **SOONER DISTRIBUTING COMPANY AND GORDON TAYLOR COMPANY**
Sales and warehouse expense detail, 1961–1965 (000's)

Direct sales costs	1965				1964			
	Gordon Taylor		Consolidated		Gordon Taylor		Consolidated	
	Amount	Per cent	Amount	Per cent	Amount	Per cent	Amount	Per cent
Sales managers:								
Salaries	$ 26	1.2	$ 44	1.0	$ 26	1.1	$ 38	.9
Travel	6	.3	10	.2	6	.3	10	.2
Auto depreciation	....	.0	1	.2	1	.1	2	...
Intercompany administration	3	.2	0	...	4	.2	0	...
Services	....	...	....	...	....	...	....	...
Salesmen:								
Salaries and commissions	54	2.5	99	2.4	52	2.5	108	2.5
Travel	28	1.2	52	1.3	28	1.4	59	1.4
Depreciation—cars	1	.1	2	.5	1	.1	2	...
Total direct selling expenses	119	5.4	211	5.1	119	5.6	219	5.0
Advertising	6	.3	12	.3	10	.5	29	.7
Postage	....	...	5	.1	....	...	5	.1
Collection expenses	....	...	6	.1	....	...	6	.1
Total selling expenses	124	5.7	234	5.7	128	6.4	259	6.0
Warehouse expenses:								
Salaries	....	...	48	...	....	...	45	
Drayage and storage	....	...	9	...	....	...	13	
Shipping supplies	....	...	1	...	....	...	2	...
Parcel post	....	...	2	...	....	...	4	...
Truck repairs and depreciation	....	...	1	...	....	...	1	...
Total warehouse expenses	....	...	61	...	....	...	65	...

exhibit 5 (continued)

	1963				1962				1961			
	Gordon Taylor		Consolidated		Gordon Taylor		Consolidated		Gordon Taylor		Consolidated	
	Amount	Per cent	Amount	Per cent	Amount	Per cent	Amount	Per cent	Amount	Per cent	Amount	Per cent
	$ 25	1.1	$ 47	1.1	$ 23	1.1	$ 42	1.1	$ 21	1.1	$ 40	1.1
	4	.2	9	.2	4	.2	8	.2	3	.2	7	.2
	1	.1	2	...	1	.1	2	...	....	...	1	
	3	.2	0	...	4	.2	0					
	54	2.4	105	2.4	51	2.4	95	2.3	51	2.6	108	2.9
	31	1.4	57	1.3	33	1.5	64	1.5	29	1.5	59	1.6
	2	.1	3	.1	1	.1	4	.1	1	.1	2	.1
	120	5.4	222	5.3	118	5.5	215	5.1	104	5.5	218	6.2
	8	.4	8	.2	7	.4	19	.5	7	.4	14	.4
	....	...	5	.1	....	...	5	.1	....	...	5	.1
	....	...	6	.1	....	...	5	.1	....	...	5	.1
	128	5.7	242	5.7	124	5.8	244	5.6	112	5.9	241	6.7
	....	...	38	...	....	...	37	...	....	...	39	
	....	...	8	...	....	...	8	...	....	...	8	
	....	...	3	...	....	...	2	...	....	...	2	
	....	...	3	...	....	...	3	...	....	...	2	
	....	...	1	...	....	...	1	...	....	...	1	
	....	...	53	...	....	...	57	...	....	...	52	

exhibit 6   **SOONER DISTRIBUTING COMPANY AND GORDON TAYLOR**
Consolidated balance sheets, 1961–1965 (000's)

	1965	*1964*	*1963*	*1962*	*1961*
Cash	$ 41.6	$ 71.9	$ 14.2	$ 186.0	$ 184.0
Receivables	508.0	619.4	563.0	470.0	391.0
Less collection loss reserve	66.5	48.5	36.1	40.2	32.0
Net receivables	$ 441.5	$ 570.9	$ 526.9	$ 429.8	$ 359.0
Inventory—lower of cost or market	712.3	768.0	772.0	675.0	576.5
Total current assets	$1195.4	$1410.8	$1313.1	$1290.8	$1119.5
Bonds and insurance (cash value)	2.5	2.6	2.6	2.8	3.1
Fixed assets—depreciation value	24.1	27.6	23.4	29.9	28.2
Total assets	$1222.0	$1441.0	$1339.1	$1323.5	$1150.8
Total notes payable	137.5	269.2	126.4	9.8	11.7
Trade acceptances	. . . .	16.1	72.4	172.5	180.0
Accounts payable	76.5	106.0	83.6	118.8	28.6
Estimated taxes	19.5	17.5	29.8	29.2	25.4
Accrued liabilities	52.4	57.6	71.0	69.2	44.0
Total current liabilities	$ 285.9	$ 466.4	$ 383.2	$ 399.5	$ 289.7
Long-term notes (7%) stockholders	110.3	154.8	154.8	147.9	108.0
Total liabilities	$ 396.2	$ 621.2	$ 538.0	$ 547.4	$ 397.7
Preferred stock	$ 117.0	$ 117.0	$ 117.0	$ 117.0	$ 117.0
Common	77.5	77.5	77.5	77.5	77.5
Surplus					
Donated	77.5	77.5	77.5	77.5	77.5
Earned	575.0	568.0	543.0	518.0	496.0
Total capital stock and surplus	$ 847.0	$ 840.0	$ 815.0	$ 790.0	$ 767.0
Less stock reacquired for treasury	20.2	20.2	13.9	13.9	13.9
Stockholders equity	$ 826.8	$ 819.8	$ 801.1	$ 776.1	$ 753.1
Total liabilities and equity	$1222.0	$1441.0	$1339.1	$1323.5	$1150.8

exhibit 7   COMPARISON OF 28 WHOLESALE FIRMS

	Weighted Averages			
	Eight firms with annual sales of $1,800,000 or more	Seven firms with sales of $1,100,000 to $1,800,000	Eight firms with annual sales up to $1,000,000	All firms
Net sales:	100.00	100.00	100.00	100.00
Cost of goods sold	82.65	82.69	82.62	82.65
Gross margin	17.35	17.31	17.38	17.35
Selling expenses:				
Salesmen's salaries, commissions, and travel expenses	4.45	4.26	4.27	4.32
Showroom rent	.08	.13	.02	.08
Miscellaneous sales expenses	.31	.33	.27	.31
Total	4.84	4.72	4.56	4.71
Warehouse expenses:				
Wages of warehouse labor	1.10	1.43	1.45	1.25
Warehouse rent	.49	.60	.57	.53
Outbound freight, cartage, et cetera	.34	.34	.04	.39
Upkeep depreciation	.26	.10	.22	.21
Warehouse supplies and miscellaneous expenses	.07	.14	.19	.11
Total	2.26	2.61	2.47	2.49
Administrative and general expenses:				
Executive salaries	1.44	1.49	1.83	1.52
Officer salaries and wages	1.67	1.69	1.62	1.67
Utilities	.34	.53	.46	.41
Office rent	.13	.09	.05	.11
Insurance and taxes	.76	.71	.97	.79
Interest on mortgages and borrowed money	.19	.37	.33	.27
Repairs and depreciation of office equipment	.09	.11	.08	.10
Miscellaneous	.59	.46	.77	.59
Total	5.21	5.45	6.11	5.46
Losses from bad departments	.35	.40	.22	.34
Grand total expense	12.72	13.22	13.38	12.97
Other income	.12	.01	.21	.11
Profit before taxes	4.74	4.10	4.19	4.47

exhibit 8   WESTERN RUBBER AND TILE COMPANY AND THE GORDON TAYLOR COM-
PANY, 1963–1966
Oklahoma sales of floor covering

	Spring, 1963			Spring, 1964		
Product	Total Oklahoma Sales*	Taylor Company Sales	% of Busi-ness	Total Oklahoma Sales*	Taylor Company Sales	% of Busi-ness
Group 1—Linoleum and corlon, sq. yd	$ 417,000	$ 208,000	49.7	$ 392,600	$ 202,100	51.2
Group 2—Felt base and accolon, sq. yd	316,000	147,500	46.5	219,000	94,300	43.1
Group 3—Excelon and asphalt, sq. yd	2,785,000	1,493,000	53.6	3,070,000	1,725,000	58.8
Group 4—Luxury tile, sq. yd	317,000	182,000	46.7	186,500	73,500	45.9
Group 5—Wall cov-ering, sq. ft	29,300	13,600	46.3	30,200	14,800	49.0

exhibit 8 (continued)

Spring, 1965			Fall, 1965			Spring, 1966
Total Oklahoma Sales*	Taylor Company Sales	% of Business	Total Oklahoma Sales*	Taylor Company Sales	% of Business	Taylor's Estimated Sales Were About 15% Below 1961
$ 366,500	$ 179,000	48.9	$ 323,000	$ 185,000	54.5	
254,100	126,100	49.5	174,100	112,200	64.3	
3,500,000	2,095,000	60.1	2,710,000	1,790,000	66.0	
214,700	73,600	34.1	133,800	79,700	59.7	
30,650	15,900	51.7	26,600	18,300	68.7	

* Western Rubber and Tile Company sales in Oklahoma and a few counties in neighboring states.

PART TWO
BUSINESS AS A SYSTEM: DIAGNOSIS AND ANALYSIS

6

LEATHERCRAFT CORPORATION

EARLY HISTORY AND DEVELOPMENT

The Leathercraft Shoe Corporation was founded in Davenport, Iowa, in 1905 by George Meyer and Randolph Langford to engage in the jobbing of men's shoes and rubbers in Iowa, Nebraska, and northwestern Illinois. In 1909, after a series of profitable years, the partners decided to go into the manufacturing of men's shoes to assure a supply for their constantly increasing sales and to gain the profit advantages of a manufacturing operation. To accomplish this objective they purchased the machinery and equipment of a bankrupt Chicago shoe manufacturer and installed them in a warehouse near their sales office.

In 1912 the shoe manufacturing facilities were expanded and the sons of the founders, John Meyer and Kurt Langford, were brought into the business. John Meyer was 22 years of age. He had an engineering degree from Iowa State University and two years of experience in construction engineering. Kurt Langford was 21 years of age with two years of liberal arts education in a small Iowa college and one year of work experience.

In 1915 a new factory was built in Davenport to replace the original manufacturing facilities contained in the warehouse building. In the same year the company purchased a Davenport tannery to gain cost advantages and further integrate the firm's operations. The operation of a tannery by a shoe manufacturer was contrary to normal industry practice. Most manufacturers purchased their leather from independent tanneries.[1]

[1] This practice was still true in the industry in 1956.

In 1916 the original partnership of Meyer and Langford was dissolved and the firm was incorporated as the Leathercraft Corporation in the state of Iowa. At this time Kurt Langford was given the responsibility for shoe manufacturing and John Meyer took charge of tannery operations.

From the time he entered the company John Meyer conducted experiments in the tanning of horsehide in an effort to find a tough leather for bicycle shoes which would have advantages over cowhide. In 1917 he perfected a tanning process for horsehide and by 1918 the entire capacity of the tannery was utilized for the tanning of horsehide.

The use of horsehide as a leather for shoe manufacturing, instead of traditional cowhide, produced particular market advantages. Horsehide had a "tough shell" which gave the leather excellent wearing qualities, strong resistance to water, and the ability to dry soft. These advantages were incorporated into Leathercraft's main product line—a heavy-type work shoe. The characteristics of horsehide leather in a work shoe had strong appeal to farmers. As a result, within a few years after the conversion to horsehide, the company was concentrating its entire sales effort in rural areas. The company also found that the favorable characteristics of horsehide, which aided in selling its work shoes in rural markets, also applied to the Leathercraft line of work gloves which were produced from offal, the residue resulting from work shoe manufacture.

The concentration of the sale of Leathercraft's horsehide work shoes and work gloves in the rural markets proved to be successful. By 1930 the company was producing and selling over 1 million shoes annually. While Leathercraft experienced some losses in the early depression years of the 1930's, operations were profitable enough to allow the company to maintain its market position and to provide for the construction of a new plant. From 1941 to 1944 the company's main production effort was concentrated on manufacturing shoes for the armed services.

POSTWAR PROBLEMS AND MARKET CHANGES

The sales of Leathercraft Corporation increased substantially in the postwar period, rising from $5.4 million in 1945 to a peak of $12.1 million in 1951. Operating profit also showed a corresponding increase in this period, rising from $.5 million to $1.4 million. In 1952, however, the upward trend was halted and sales dropped to $10.2 million and continued to decline each year to a low of $8.7 million in 1955. Operating profits also decreased in this period from $.8 million to a deficit of $.3 million in 1955. (See Exhibit 12.)

The management of Leathercraft attributed the decline in sales and profits after 1952 to external factors beyond their control. They believed that a major reason for the decline was the dwindling farmer market caused by the shift of population from rural to urban areas. This shift, they pointed out, was decreasing the farm labor force and increasing the number of industrial and white-collar workers. There were also indications that the heavy-type work shoe produced by Leathercraft was not suitable for the average industrial worker who preferred a semi-dress type of work shoe. The company did not have a shoe in its line to meet this requirement.

In anticipation of the loss of sales in the work shoe and work glove markets the company introduced a line of dress shoes in 1950 and a line of dress gloves in 1953. In 1954 a semi-work shoe named the Lightweight was added to the product line in an effort to bolster sales in the industrial work shoe market. In a further effort to reverse the trend of declining sales the company placed a line of golf shoes, hunting boots, and other specialty shoes on the market.

In addition to the changing marketing conditions for its products, Leathercraft was also confronted with the rising price and diminishing supply of horsehide. At the same time farm population was decreasing, the nation's horse and mule population was also decreasing. The demand for horsehide, however, remained relatively constant in the face of a diminishing supply, which caused the price of horsehide to increase from $1.40 per butt in 1941 to $3.81 in 1954, representing an increase to the company of 171% in leather cost.

In an effort to cope with this situation Leathercraft gradually reduced its soaking of horsehide (the preliminary preparation of the hide for tanning) and looked for another type of hide as a substitute which would be low in cost and plentiful in supply.

MARKET CHANGES

Four main reasons were advanced by management for the shift in the company's market: (1) population shifts; (2) occupational shifts; (3) changing income patterns; (4) changes in the white-collar working group. They pointed out that the number of rural places, those under

2,500 in population, had declined 2% from 1930 to 1950, while the number of towns and cities (2,500 population and over) increased 16% in the same period.[2]

In addition, the farm population decreased 16.6% from 30 million to 25 million, from 1930 to 1950. In this same period the urban population increased 17% from 117 million to 137 million.[3]

The shift in population was accompanied by occupational changes. From 1940 to 1955 the farm labor force decreased 25%, from 8 million to 6 million. The industrial work force increased 56% in this period, from 14 million to 22 million.[4]

A study of national income statistics by management revealed that the median income of industrial workers increased from $1,000 annually in 1939 to $3,000 in 1952. In contrast, farm labor increased its median wage from $340 a year in 1939 to $675 in 1952.[5]

The white-collar group of salesmen, office workers, professional and technical men also fared better than the farm group in growth and income. In the period 1940–1955, urban white-collar workers increased from 12 million to 17 million, a 45% gain. Their median wage rose 150% in the period 1939–1952, from $1,500 to $3,750.[4]

RAW MATERIAL SUPPLY—INTRODUCTION OF PIGSKIN

Because of the diminishing supply and rising price of horsehide, Leathercraft gradually reduced its soaking of horsehide. In 1941 the company soaked 623,721 hides and in 1954 had reduced its soaking to 239,932. The percentage of Leathercraft's soakings to the national horsehide soakings declined from 56% of the total to 26% in 1954. Throughout this period the company was experimenting with other hides in an effort to relieve its dependence on a basic raw material which was high in price and low in supply.

Leathercraft's location in the heart of the hog-producing and pork-processing area of the nation directed the attention of management to pigskin as a possible answer to their leather problem. The supply of pigs was large and the price of pigskin was low, which seemed to offer the advantages formerly obtained with horsehide. In the period of

[2] *Statistical Abstract of the United States,* 1954, p. 29.

[3] *Ibid.,* p. 13.

[4] *Ibid.,* p. 208, and *Monthly Labor Review,* July, 1955.

[5] Data derived from the *Statistical Abstract of the United States,* 1940–1953.

1945–1948 pigskin averaged about 6.5¢ per pound as contrasted to 12.75¢ per pound for horsehide. In addition pigskin appeared attractive because Leathercraft had experience in processing the leather for work gloves.

The first tannery runs of pigskin which were made into work shoes in 1948 and 1949 were considered to be unsatisfactory. The leather proved to be too porous and did not have the quality of horsehide or cowhide leathers. As a result the company abandoned temporarily the use of pigskin in its line until it could produce a better product.

Upon investigation it was found that pigsides rather than bacon rinds, which the company used in its first attempts to tan pigskin, offered a more satisfactory hide for shoe manufacture. However, a problem of supply confronted the company because a large percentage of pigsides, as furnished by meat packers, were damaged by burning and knife cuts as a result of the skinning process.

In an attempt to improve the quality of pigsides the company developed a skinning machine. In 1950 Leathercraft was successful in getting three meat-packing firms to install its machine. In order to persuade the packers to accept the skinning machine, however, it was necessary to pay them a premium of 3.5¢ a pound over the market price of pigsides and guarantee to purchase the entire output of pigsides processed by the machines.

The packers who initially accepted the skinning machine and agreed to furnish pigsides to the company gave it up after a trial run. They felt the operation was too uncertain and they were not assured of a market for the pigsides if Leathercraft suddenly decided to abandon the idea. This action forced Leathercraft to seek other packers to install the machine. While the company was successful in finding others to use the machine, the supply of pigskin was not produced in uniform quality.

In 1951 Leathercraft resumed the tanning of both bacon rinds and pigsides and began the manufacture of both dress and work shoes out of this leather. During 1955 approximately 40% of the work shoe line was produced from pigskin. Although the leather had improved in quality, it had not reached a uniform quality which would make it entirely acceptable for use in shoes. The company, however, believed that the leather could be successfully tanned in the future to meet uniform quality requirements for shoe manufacture.

Leathercraft shoes produced from pigskin were reported to be acceptable in the market. However, members of the trade stated many objections that were raised by customers. The primary complaint concerned the inability of the leather to resist water and to hold its dye or color. The company stated that an improvement in tanning techniques made in 1955 would correct this fault.

PRODUCT LINES AND SALES POLICIES: WORK SHOES

Extent of Line. Leathercraft manufactured a broad line of work shoes in both horsehide and pigskin. In 1955 the company substantially increased the numbers carried in both the horsehide and pigskin lines to include 140 horsehide numbers and 90 different pigskin numbers, as indicated in Exhibit 1.

exhibit 1   LEATHERCRAFT SHOE LINE, 1955

Year	Horsehide Numbers	Pigskin Numbers	Average Price per Pair	
			Horsehide	Pigskin
1946	40	—	$5.40	—
1947	38	—	6.30	—
1948	40	3	6.40	$3.70
1949	28	3	6.00	3.70
1950	38	—	7.50	—
1951	40	15	7.25	5.40
1952	52	10	7.10	5.00
1953	37	30	7.80	5.90
1954	98	60	7.10	5.80
1955	140	90	7.30	5.50

Exhibit 2 shows Leathercraft's work shoe production in relation to production of the industry.

Sales Practices. In calling upon prospective customers the salesmen usually carried five or six sample cases for display. However, when they called on regular customers, usually only one case of samples was shown to the dealers. This case contained what the salesman considered his best sellers or basic numbers. The numbers usually found in this case would vary according to the sales representative's territory, but generally included many of the same numbers. In addition to carrying in the single sample case, several sales representatives carried one to four numbers in their hand which they hoped the dealer would add to his line. Usually these numbers were shown first to the dealer, followed

exhibit 2

Leathercraft and Industry Work Shoe Production,
Excluding Military, 1946–1954 (Thousands of Pairs)

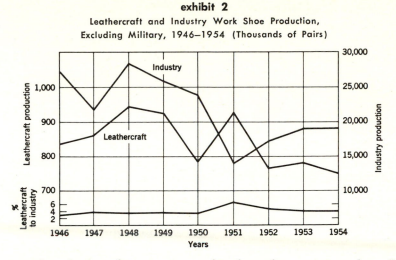

by opening the sample case on occasion for a few more numbers. In some instances as many as ten shoe samples were shown, but there were instances when the sample case was not opened at all. Occasionally a sales representative carried in a second sample case, or returned to his car for it when a special number was requested by the dealer or the salesman wished to impress the dealer with the size of the line.

Dealers in general expressed little interest in the Hunter styles, a line of hunting boots, the Sportsman line of golf and sports shoes, or the safety shoe line. Both dealers and sales representatives stated that there was little demand for two of these styles in their stores, since the Hunter styles and Sportsman were shoes which sold through sporting goods stores, particularly those stores in the larger cities. As a routine practice the salesmen did not make calls on sporting goods stores. Safety shoes, on the other hand, were generally either not in demand, or the dealer refused to handle them because of severe competition in this line from other sources.

The horsehide work shoe was generally acceptable as a line, although several dealers commented on the fact that farmers and industrial workers were demanding a lighter-weight shoe and were refusing to buy the heavy type of Leathercraft shoe. Although no specific objections were encountered concerning the pigskin line, some dealers expressed strong general prejudice against it. It was observed that the broadening of the work shoe line of horsehide and pigskin apparently failed to stimulate any interest on the part of the dealer to add additional numbers to his stock.

Pricing. The company believed that the rise in horsehide prices was gradually pricing its work shoes out of the market. One purpose of introducing the pigskin was to overcome this handicap and at the same time compete with cowhide. When the sales manager made field calls on dealers, he found that those located in the small towns and cross-road centers would usually sell a shoe at a lower gross profit than those located in the larger cities. The difference in gross profit averaged about 7%. Dealers in the less populated areas seemed satisfied with a lower profit because shoes generally represented a relatively small part of their business. In contrast, shoes represented the major or entire part of the city dealer's business. The city dealer found that when he marked up the price of Leathercraft shoes to obtain the gross profit he required, the price of any particular Leathercraft shoe would usually be considerably higher than competitive shoes of similar quality. He either was faced with reducing his margin on the Leathercraft shoe or pushing the sale of other competitive brands. The dealers usually chose to push the competitive brands since they could obtain a higher markup at a lower selling price. Exhibit 3, which follows, indicates the cost and price relationship of Leathercraft and two competing brands of shoes of similar or superior quality.

exhibit 3 COST-PRICE RELATIONSHIP PER PAIR OF SHOES OF
LEATHERCRAFT TO COMPETING BRANDS

	Cost to Dealer	Recommended Markup by City Dealer	Retail Selling Price
Leathercraft (horsehide)	$6.70	37%	$9.25
Brand A	5.70	40%	8.00
Brand B	6.05	30%	7.85

Country dealers, because of their lower markup, were not as reluctant to handle the Leathercraft shoe because the competition of price was not as severe and their low markup made the retail price of the shoes more acceptable to the customer.

Dealer markup practices affected pigskin shoe sales in the same manner. However, when dealers compared pigskin shoe prices with competitive cowhide shoe prices, they raised questions over price differentials. For example, it was pointed out that the features of one number of Brand A were so superior that they were unable to sell the competitive pigskin shoe at the same markup. In instances where smaller dealers handled Leathercraft exclusively, the pigskin line was used as the price leader over the horsehide. In larger stores where competitive work shoes were also handled, dealers pointed out that Leathercraft pigskin shoes competed with its own horsehide rather than good-quality cowhide shoes of competitors.

In the larger stores where price was the primary factor, the price leaders in cowhide shoes ranged from about $4.00 retail to $7.00. The most popular retail prices were $5.00 and $6.00. Dealers generally refused to consider Leathercraft's pigskin shoes, which cost them $5.00, as a strong competitor with cowhide shoes in the same price range.

Style. Style in work shoes did not change as often as in other types of shoes, and work shoes were frequently viewed as a staple product. Fit, comfort, and wear were stressed rather than style in the company's advertising. Many comments, however, were made about Leathercraft's style by dealers and sales representatives.

In an effort to determine the competitive standing of Leathercraft products, early in 1955 the company hired an independent marketing consulting firm to review the market with dealers, sales representatives, and other sources. The following summarizes the adverse comments obtained by the consultants about Leathercraft's styling of work shoes:

1. Customers want a lighter, trimmer-looking shoe. Leathercraft has never changed its basic, nineteenth-century style.

2. Although older customers still buy the same Leathercraft shoe year after year, younger men want a lighter, dressier work and safety shoe, something they can wear on the street.

3. Men in light industry want dressier and lighter safety and work shoes. Men in heavy industry are also asking more and more for a lighter shoe. Leathercraft shoes still look, feel and are heavy.

4. Horsehide and pigskin will not take a shine like cowhide.

5. White-collar people and foremen in the steel plants are urged to wear safety shoes. They need dressier safety oxfords for white-collar people and lighter, dressier safety shoes for foremen.

6. Leathercraft shoes are sloppy-fitting. Quarters are loose.

7. Leathercraft shoes are uniformly oversized and customers cannot get the same fit in the size they are wearing in a competitive shoe.

8. Competitive shoes in the same price range look like a neater shoe. Leathercraft shoes are not finished as well. Both the exteriors and interiors are rough.

Quality. Many comments were also made about the quality of the shoes. The reports of sales representatives and dealers indicated that, for all the quality its name once signified, Leathercraft shoes were generally below the quality standards of its competitors. Some common references to the quality of Leathercraft shoes were as follows:

1. Counters are made of paper.
2. Shanks are too light in weight.
3. Vamps are too soft.
4. Insoles are of inferior quality.
5. Welt strips on some shoes are too narrow and when the shoes are resoled they have to be rebuilt.
6. Welt stitching breaks or rots out is a typical comment from the dealers who sold to farmers.
7. Pigskin sponges water and cannot be worn where a man may run into bad weather.
8. Shoes do not meet the company's description. In one case the black sole of the wedge oxford was described as not marking the floor; however, it did. In another case the midsole of a safety shoe was described as being composed of rosin and cork; it was found to be made of rosin and sawdust upon analysis. Steel shanks had also been eliminated from shoes that were supposed to have them.
9. Typical dealer reaction to Leathercraft as compared with competitive shoes is found in this statement: "My Brand A selling at $8.00 looks better made than the comparable Leathercraft horsehide."

Workmanship. Workmanship had also received frequent adverse comments, such as:

1. Because of poor stitching, cork soles have come loose on some numbers.
2. Some shoes had poor heel seats.
3. Cemented cushions have come loose.
4. In one order of safety shoes the nails had not been cut off; the shoes had to be fixed before they were sold.
5. Quarters were sewn together wrong, resulting in a poor fit.
6. The leather in the toe of the soft-toe shoe is so poorly fitted that there were wrinkles in the toe.
7. The leather on some shoes is of noticeably different thicknesses.

Some of the samples sent to the salesmen were so poor that they had to be returned for new ones. Several dealers cited instances when they had to return shoes because of poor workmanship.

Deliveries. Another common complaint made by both salesmen and dealers concerned the slow delivery of work shoes. Sales representatives were reluctant to show new numbers for which future orders had to be placed. Several representatives did not display the new numbers at all or did so in only a few instances. One salesman said, "Why should I show the new shoes when I can't get good deliveries on current numbers?" Slow deliveries were reported on the basic fast sellers—often these took from three weeks to a month for delivery. Several salesmen reported that they often had to write special requests to get service in critical cases. Field trips by the consulting firm revealed the following common complaints:

1. Smith's Shoe Shop of Dubuque, Iowa, placed its 1954 fall order on September 28 for October or November delivery. The order was not shipped until February 25, 1955, at least a three-month delay. Seven days later the spring shipment arrived. The store returned the spring shipment to the factory at its own expense. This is typical of similar cases reported by salesmen where a slow delivery of an order for immediate shipment created an inventory problem for the dealer.

2. Williams Shoe Store, located in a small Illinois town, complained about the "lousy" deliveries, pointing out that deliveries had been "especially bad the last two months." The store's July order for fill-ins was delayed and then size 9½ was sent instead of 9. There were still outstanding two other orders which should have arrived by the time of the sales call. The manager commended two competing lines for their prompt deliveries and for their use of pre-printed cards on which fill-in orders could be written. This case is typical of slow deliveries on fill-ins.

3. Another dealer in southwestern Illinois ordered 12 pairs of work shoes in August, 1955, and waited three weeks for the shipment. Size 11 was not included and he was still waiting when the call was made in October for the filling of his special order for this one size.

4. A Wisconsin dealer ordered dress shoes and complained to the sales representative that he had not received them after two weeks.

5. A dealer in Ohio buys about four dozen Leathercraft shoes a year and a like amount of a competing brand. After commenting on how bad Leathercraft deliveries had been earlier, the dealer said the service still does not compare with competitive lines.

6. A general store in Indiana complained about Leathercraft deliveries for fill-ins. A chief competitor supplied a printed postcard to dealers for reorders and ships the shoes within three days after receiving the order.

7. A prospective Wisconsin dealer placed his first order in October for about $200; the order was almost canceled when the new dealer learned that the four pairs of field boots could not be delivered for six weeks. Only when the sales representative promised to make a special request for immediate shipment did the dealer reinstate the order.

Sales Territory Coverage. Leathercraft followed a sales program with work shoes of having sales representatives cover their territories by working one county at a time and completing it before moving to the next county. Each salesman was expected to make ten calls a day. Many of the sales representatives did not follow the company's program. However, the newer salesmen tended to adhere closely to the schedule set for their respective territories. The more experienced salesmen scheduled themselves on loop routes which enabled them to make calls in the territory going out and returning. Their routes were planned on a basis which provided time and frequency of calls in relation to the size and importance of the dealer or area. Considerable travel was necessary for all sales representatives regardless of whether they followed the company's program or not, since the majority of Leathercraft's dealers were located in rural areas and small towns.

Sales representatives considered it very difficult to sell industrial shoes because of the time involved in selling various key members of a plant before their product would be accepted. Many of the salesmen did not feel that the commissions justified the effort, compared with the commissions received from their sales to dealers.

Sales representatives also pointed out that specialized wagon jobbers with well-stocked trailers called regularly on plants where they sold and fitted shoes to employees on the spot. In several plants management made special arrangements with the jobber to absorb 10% to 20% of the shoe list price so that the employee could purchase work shoes at prices lower than the local dealer could offer them. In other plants certain employees acted as part-time agents of shoe manufacturers by conducting a mail-order business.

Leathercraft measured the sales performance of its sales representatives by the number of dealers sold in a territory and the volume sold to each dealer.

Exhibit 4 gives an analysis of the selling efforts of a sample of ten work shoe sales representatives by size of town. Exhibit 5 gives an indication of the company's sales per capita. Exhibit 6 provides an analysis of sales to work shoe dealers for 10 selected representatives covering 14 territories.

exhibit 4 **LEATHERCRAFT CORPORATION**

Work shoe dealers and sales by size of town, 1954—14 territories, 10 sales representatives

Size of Town	Dealer		Sales		Average Sales per Dealer
	Number	Per Cent of Total	Dollars	Per Cent of Total	
Urban					
1,000,000 or more	18	.5	$ 12,460	1.0	$692.22
500,000–999,999	24	.6	18,120	1.5	755.00
250,000–499,999	12	.3	4,460	.4	371.67
100,000–249,999	34	.9	15,360	1.2	451.76
50,000– 99,999	52	1.3	17,030	1.4	327.50
25,000– 49,999	71	1.8	25,800	2.1	363.38
10,000– 24,999	191	4.8	79,530	6.4	416.39
5,000– 9,999	217	5.5	95,750	7.7	441.24
2,500– 4,999	330	8.3	132,050	10.6	400.15
Rural					
1,000– 2,499	644	16.3	228,510	18.4	354.83
999 and under	2,363	59.7	611,840	49.3	258.92
Total	3,956	100.0	$1,240,910	100.0	$313.67

exhibit 5 **LEATHERCRAFT CORPORATION**

Work shoe sales per capita, 1954—14 territories, 10 sales representatives

Territory Numbers	County Population	Total City in County	Per Cent of Total	Total Work Shoe Sales	Work Shoe Sales per Capita
5	1,483,700	548,831	37.0	$ 69,440	$.05
10	2,565,600	1,392,811	54.3	138,370	.05
15	7,144,000	4,932,068	69.0	170,420	.02
20	117,800	49,324	41.9	21,810	.19
25	8,241,500	3,559,324	43.2	122,930	.01
30	2,781,000	1,290,627	46.4	83,360	.03
35	3,304,100	1,583,363	47.9	105,190	.03
40	1,311,300	357,801	27.3	78,850	.06
45	1,720,500	359,783	20.9	84,030	.05
50	4,674,800	2,084,966	44.6	207,840	.04
55	6,659,200	517,122	7.8	53,810	.01
60	5,041,600	2,303,647	45.7	22,900	.0045
65	2,312,000	685,900	29.7	17,590	.01
70	1,226,800	424,647	34.6	64,370	.05
Total	48,583,900	20,090,214	41.4	$1,240,910	$.026

exhibit 6 **LEATHERCRAFT CORPORATION**

Analysis of sales to work shoe dealers, 1954—14 territories, 10 sales representatives (number of dealers sold)

Territory Number	Total Work Shoe Dealers		Work Shoe Only		Work Shoes and Dress Shoes		Work Shoes and Gloves		Work Shoes, Dress Shoes, and Gloves	
	No.	Per Cent	No.	Per Cent	No.	Per Cent	No.	Per Cent	No.	Per Cent
5	291	100.0	139	47.8	26	8.9	95	32.6	31	10.7
10	430	100.0	173	40.2	60	14.0	131	30.5	66	15.3
15	437	100.0	180	41.2	44	10.1	153	35.0	60	13.7
20	56	100.0	28	50.0	8	14.3	18	32.1	2	3.6
25	357	100.0	118	33.1	125	35.0	48	13.4	66	18.5
30	372	100.0	196	52.7	30	8.1	93	25.0	53	14.2
35	372	100.0	222	59.7	35	9.4	89	23.9	26	7.0
40	222	100.0	81	36.5	18	8.1	80	36.0	43	19.4
45	275	100.0	132	48.0	37	13.5	74	26.9	32	11.6
50	538	100.0	248	46.1	128	23.8	98	18.2	64	11.9
55	245	100.0	118	48.2	36	14.7	72	29.4	19	7.7
60	102	100.0	62	60.8	9	8.8	24	23.5	7	6.9
65	71	100.0	42	59.2	8	11.3	16	22.5	5	7.0
70	188	100.0	75	39.9	13	6.9	78	41.5	22	11.7
Total	3,956	100.0	1,814	45.9	577	14.6	1,069	27.0	496	12.5

WORK GLOVES

Extent of Line. The number of work gloves offered to the dealer annually from 1946–1955 was as shown in Exhibit 7.

exhibit 7   LEATHERCRAFT'S LINE AND AVERAGE PRICE OF WORK GLOVES

Year	Numbers Horsehide	Numbers Pigskin	Average Price per Dozen	
			Horsehide	Pigskin
1946	40	Na	$13.00	Na
1947	90	40	13.75	$15.00
1948	70	50	19.10	15.10
1949	60	45	19.00	12.00
1950	55	90	21.00	14.90
1951	50	55	22.00	14.50
1952	52	85	20.00	15.00
1953	100	Na	17.40	Na
1954	60	100	18.50	16.00
1955	50	60	19.00	15.00

Na—not available.

In addition to the above lines the company offered 12 goatskin and buckskin gloves including two new dress buckskins.

Exhibit 8 shows Leathercraft's production of work gloves and the

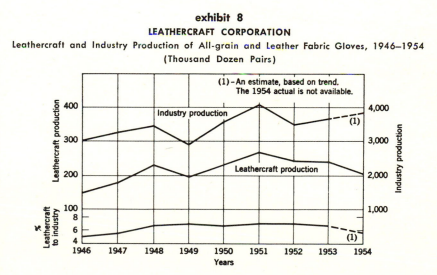

exhibit 8
LEATHERCRAFT CORPORATION
Leathercraft and Industry Production of All-grain and Leather Fabric Gloves, 1946–1954
(Thousand Dozen Pairs)

glove industry production of all-grain leather and leather-fabric gloves.

Sales Practices. In contrast to work shoes, work gloves were a point-of-purchase sale. The work gloves in most stores were usually displayed on small racks or on shelves, generally in small quantities. The glove racks were designed to hold a dozen numbers and were used by dealers for their entire line of work gloves, including their all-cloth numbers. These racks were generally located near the greatest movement, such as the cash register, wrapping counter, or other busy part of the store.

After checking on the present stock and getting reorders on the numbers the dealer was carrying, the sales representative usually showed about 6 or 8 numbers, infrequently as many as 10 numbers, from the 100 or so glove samples in his case. These were generally new numbers, numbers the dealer had not been carrying, or Leathercraft styles which could replace competitive styles the dealer was handling. The salesmen concentrated on showing two or three horsehide and pigskin drivers from the 18 numbers they carried in this line. They usually followed this style by showing the leather palm safety cuffs in one or two styles of horsehide and pigskin. The leather palm drivers in both horsehide and pigskin were usually shown, although some salesmen made no effort to push this line.

Additional lines were shown depending upon the store and the nature of its trade. Examples of the variation that the sales representative might show included:

Horsehide with knit wrist
Pigskin with knit wrist
Buckskin drivers
Goatskin drivers
Plastic-coated gloves

Generally sales representatives showed about 6 from 38 style numbers out of a total of 115 samples. Some of the sales representatives reported that they left as many as 15 to 20 style numbers at home.

Several salesmen expressed the view that some of the gloves designed for retail stores did not fit in with the stores they generally called on. Almost none of the dealers who were called upon in either urban or rural areas expressed interest in ski mittens, ladies' utility gloves, or dress buckskin gloves. The dealers usually stated that gloves of this nature were for sporting goods stores, department stores, or haberdashery stores.

Pricing. Price was not stressed in Leathercraft's promotion of its work glove line. The company placed the emphasis on the quality of the glove, pointing up such features as its durability, comfort, and ability to dry soft.

Dealers usually sold Leathercraft gloves at one-third gross margin. Aside from a few truck terminal stores where the markup was somewhat greater, no major differences in markup existed in either urban or rural areas. In the rural hardware or feed store where Leathercraft gloves were handled exclusively, the question of price was not usually raised. But in urban areas where competitive gloves were usually handled, the price question was of prime importance.

Field work by the sales manager uncovered the fact that in many truck terminals where Leathercraft's all-leather number had good acceptance, a competitive fabric-back glove was sold as a substitute. In other stores competitive gloves with cloth backs and split-cowhide palms were pushed by the dealer because they sold at $1.00 a pair and provided the dealer with a 50% markup. If the Leathercraft glove were to be sold for $1.00, the dealer's gross margin would amount to only 20%.

The proprietor of a large Army and Navy store, which was one of the best accounts in the area, stated that, "Customers will pick up anything for 95¢ but resist paying more. Leathercraft can't compete with the average glove." This dealer stated that he had hoped to feature Leathercraft as a quality item but could not because of the price. After handling the line five years he discontinued it, stating, "You can't sell quality, even at 10 or 15 cents more." This customer purchased $10,000 of Leathercraft gloves in 1951, and averaged about $6,000 in purchases annually in his five-year period as a customer.

Some sales representatives believed that competition had the advantage over all styles of Leathercraft gloves. Others believed that Leathercraft could compete favorably on the leather drivers but not on the leather palm line. Many salesmen felt that the pigskin glove competed with their own line rather than with the cowhide gloves of other producers.

Styling and Quality. Contrary to the reactions that work shoes appear too heavy and too rugged, dealers and sales representatives commented that work gloves had too much of a dress glove appearance.

A summary of the reactions of sales representatives and dealers to Leathercraft styling and quality obtained in the field work of the marketing consulting firm employed by the company is as follows:

1. A work glove must give the appearance of ruggedness and quality at a price. Leathercraft gloves look too dressy to take the abuse a work glove gets.

2. Industrial concerns refuse to buy Leathercraft gloves for their workers; not only are they too costly, but the gloves look and fit so much like dress gloves that workers pilfer them.

3. Leathercraft gloves are too good to be realistically competitive in industry. Plants buy cheap split cowhide gloves for their workers. These gloves are thrown away when they get greasy; the longer-wear feature of Leathercraft gloves does not count. In some cases Leathercraft gloves are purchased for plant foremen, as a prestige item for them.

4. In industrial areas, the traditional color of work gloves is gray. The Leathercraft yellow is hard to sell. One key dealer who refused to handle any more Leathercraft gloves reported that he had tried to feature Leathercraft gloves for five years but his customers preferred gray gloves.

5. Special gloves are often introduced too late in the season. As an example, the two dress buckskins were introduced July 15, 1955, after the customary time for the purchase of fall gloves by dealers.

6. Special gloves which have been added to the line do not fit into the line. As examples, the women's garden gloves, the ski mitten, and the two dress gloves. These special items were turned down by work glove dealers as items for other types of stores. It was frequently said of the two buckskin dress gloves, "They are beautiful, but we can't sell them. They belong in a haberdashery shop."

7. The buckskin dress gloves are not fully patterned after the usual dress glove. The shirred back runs counter to the open-cuff trend in dress gloves.

8. In industrial areas Leathercraft gloves appeal primarily to truck drivers. The truck driver who is reported to be a free spender buys the Leathercraft glove for driving because of the fit and softness. However, he buys a competitive, cheaper glove, either all fabric or fabric and split leather, for his heavy work.

9. The special quality of dry-soft has limited appeal in industry. Leathercraft gloves are bought by plants for the small percentage of workers who handle wet objects or chemicals.

10. The wearing quality of Leathercraft gloves was not universally accepted. Many dealers stated that cowhide split gloves wear better; some did believe that the Leathercraft glove outlasted cowhide.

11. At least in the urban communities, the intrinsic qualities of the Leathercraft gloves had not won customers. As one dealer said, "I have had no complaints, but not enough men who buy them come back for another pair."

12. In the rural market the buying habits of farmers have changed. They, too, are buying cheaper gloves, especially fabric. Now that they no longer use their hands for such jobs as corn shucking, they buy fabric gloves at 49 cents.

Workmanship. The complaints received by the sales representatives about the workmanship in Leathercraft's work gloves followed the same pattern as those on work shoes. The chief complaints were:

1. Some gloves are not properly sized. One company is returning an order because they are not properly sized.

2. Some gloves have poor seams. On several occasions, it was found that the pigskin seams, particularly, ripped out.

3. There were several instances where dealers complained that the glove fingers were too long.

4. The fact that the gloves in a pair were not matched was another fairly common criticism.

5. The leather is uneven.

6. The color is not uniform.

Deliveries. As in the case of work shoes, Leathercraft had improved its delivery of work gloves in 1955. Both the dealers and salesmen had noticed the improvements, and comments were generally favorable.

Many dealers stated that the speed of delivery was not too important in work gloves purchased from Leathercraft. Since the company did not use jobbers it was necessary for the dealers to place large orders well in advance of their need. The dealers also pointed out that they purchased most of the competitive lines from jobbers who provided almost continuous service and did not require large-quantity purchases.

Territory Coverage. The company sales program concerning territory coverage on work gloves generally followed the selling policy of the Work Shoe Division. In the field, sales representatives either followed the company program or scheduled loop routing as was found with work shoes. Many dealers who purchased Leathercraft work gloves also handled Leathercraft work shoes or dress shoes, or all three lines. (See Exhibit 6.)

Work glove representatives sold work gloves to dealers other than Leathercraft shoe accounts. These were gas stations, hardware stores, super markets, Army and Navy stores, grain and feed stores, implement dealers, clothing stores, and similar types of retail outlets. The sales representatives mentioned that it was practically impossible to sell more than three of these dealers in any one town due to the objections of dealers over others underselling them on the same Leathercraft brand glove. Competitive glove manufacturers, on the other hand, attained maximum dealer coverage by selling their own brand and unbranded gloves through jobbers, and private brand-name gloves through manufacturers of brand-name work clothes. A competitor of Leathercraft, for example, was able to sell five or six or more dealers in the same area or shopping center without creating dealer objections.

TERMS AND DISCOUNTS—WORK SHOES AND WORK GLOVES

The company believed that its terms to the trade were satisfactory on both work shoes and gloves. Most dealers believed them somewhat better than others in the trade. Some country and smaller dealers took advantage of the Leathercraft Term Plan which allowed a 5% discount on six dozen pairs of shoes. Competitors did not offer any discount on small orders. Small dealers were usually not too conscious of inventory turnover nor did they conduct their business on an inventory control basis. The larger dealers generally were not interested in the Term Plan because they claimed that they lost money when overstocked. Usually these dealers maintained strict inventory control. Some competitors offered larger dealers an annual rebate plan. For the first $1,000 of shoe purchases, the dealer received a 1% rebate, which increased 1% for each additional $1,000 of annual purchases up to $5,000.

In the case of work gloves, the discounts on volumes from 12 dozen pairs and up did not seem to appeal to most dealers, whether located in small or large towns.

Sales representatives were of the opinion that the volume discounts were satisfactory for larger-dealer accounts, but pointed out that their commission payments on net purchases made it unprofitable for them to go after volume accounts. They stated that they could sell three separate dealers 12 dozen pairs of gloves each and make more commission than selling one big account 48 pairs of gloves on one order. The sales representatives, in order to take advantage of maximum commissions, were calling on dealers only once a year rather than twice. This was done in order to write one order which carried a proportionately higher commission than the commission on two single smaller orders.

DRESS SHOES

The company had manufactured dress shoes for only five years and had never made a field analysis of its sales and retail outlets. From 1951, when the company started to produce dress shoes, through 1952, national production had an upward trend. Since 1952, national production and Leathercraft's output dropped. In 1952 Leathercraft produced 0.24% of the national production and in 1954 it produced 0.17%. (See Exhibit 9.)

exhibit 9
LEATHERCRAFT CORPORATION
Leathercraft and Industry Production of Men's Dress Shoes, 1951–1954
(Thousands of Pairs)

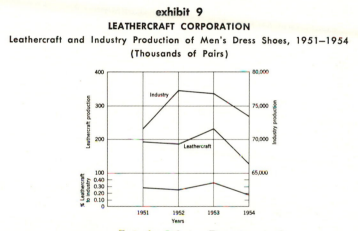

SOURCE: *Facts for Industry,* Department of Commerce, Series M68D and Leathercraft Records.

The work shoes and dress shoes were sold in the same manner with little, if any difference. Many of the work shoe dealers also carried the dress shoe line. (See Exhibit 6.) The dealers in larger towns and cities usually carried larger stocks of the semi-dress and dress shoes and less of the work shoe line. The more important the dealer, the larger was his dress shoe stock, and he often displayed his small stock of work shoes in the back room.

TURNOVER OF SALESMEN

A review of the 49 work shoe sales representatives covering the length of time each had been employed with the company as of August 1, 1955, revealed that one third of them had been with the company under one year, about another third between 1 and 5 years, and that the remaining third had been employed by the company over 5 years. The number of salesmen leaving in any one year varied between 5 and 24 and averaged 14.2 for the period 1948–1955. The average income of the 24 men who left the company in 1954 amounted to $4,164 compared to the industry's average annual earnings of $7,500 for footwear and clothing sales representatives.

When company sales representatives were questioned in the field concerning whether income was a possible reason for turnover, they thought that the 5% and 7% commission rates were fair and satisfactory. However, they felt that new men were unable to earn an adequate income because of the difficult task in selling sufficient volume against better competition and the more than usual resistance of many dealers to the Leathercraft line. They also mentioned the poor recruiting and selection and the fact that the position was oversold.

MANUFACTURING CAPACITY

The company operated a single plant at Davenport, Iowa, from 1903 to 1935. This plant had a production capacity of 1,050,000 pairs of shoes annually and was known as Plant 1. In 1935 Plant 2 was erected in Des Moines with an annual capacity of 210,000 pairs of shoes. Plant 3 was constructed in 1948 at Moline, Illinois, with an annual capacity of 375,000 pairs.

Shoe production capacity of Leathercraft by 1950 had increased from 1,050,000 pairs to 1,635,000. This production capacity was reduced to 1,425,000 pairs in late 1950 when Plant 2 was closed. Plant 4, however, was opened in 1951 at Rock Island, Illinois, with a capacity of 300,000 pairs of shoes, which was increased to 600,000 in 1954 to give the company a total capacity of 2,025,000 pairs of shoes. (Exhibit 2 indicates the annual production of Leathercraft and the shoe industry for the period 1946–1954.)

The company explained its decentralization of plants in the Tri-City area as a move to take advantage of the labor supply offered in each of the separate cities.

Prior to 1945 Leathercraft's tannery produced sufficient leather for the manufacture of 1,645,800 pairs of shoes annually. In 1950, in the expectation of pigside tanning, capacity was increased to provide leather for the production of 3,276,120 pairs of shoes. The cost of the new tannery building and the machinery and equipment amounted to $110,000.

INVENTORIES

Leathercraft employed a first-in-first-out (FIFO) method of inventory valuation. During the last ten years the company had gone through an upward trend in over-all material prices followed by a period of stabilization and in late 1955 a downward trend of over-all prices. The company's pricing policy reflected the changes in raw-material prices.

As indicated in Exhibit 12, Leathercraft's inventory turnover averaged 4.9 from 1946 to 1951. The average rate of inventory turnover for all shoe manufacturers in this period was 6.4. In 1953 and 1954 turnover dropped to an average of 3.5.

The relationship of inventory to working capital of Leathercraft and two of its chief competitors are indicated below in Exhibit 10.

exhibit 10   **INVENTORY TO WORKING CAPITAL RATIO**

Year	Leathercraft	Leathercraft (Excl. Hides Inv.)	Competitor A	Competitor B
1951	.74	.65	.64	.72
1952	.56	.51	.52	.56
1953	.85	.75	.66	.67
1954	.89	.79	.59	.59

Exhibit 11 shows the relationship of finished goods inventories in dozens of pairs (shoes and gloves) to production and shipment in dozens of pairs.

FINANCIAL POSITION

The trend of Leathercraft's operations are indicated in the following exhibits:

Exhibit 12. Financial and Operating Ratios
Exhibit 13. Detailed Listing of Manufacturing Expenses
Exhibit 14. Selling and Advertising Expenses
Exhibit 15. General and Administrative Expenses

exhibit 11 LEATHERCRAFT CORPORATION
Operating statistics, 1945–1954 (dozens of pairs)

	Work Shoes				Gloves				Dress Shoes			
	Shipments	Pro-duction (Packed)	Finished Goods Invent.	Invent. Pro-duction Ratio (%)	Shipments	Pro-duction (Packed)	Finished Goods Invent.	Invent. Pro-duction Ratio (%)	Shipments	Pro-duction (Packed)	Finished Goods Invent.	Invent. Pro-duction Ratio (%)
1945	75,922	77,585	9,115	.117	131,056	132,010	3,080	.023				
1946	71,550	69,823	7,680	.109	146,441	151,446	7,992	.053				
1947	72,435	71,917	7,476	.104	179,580	178,590	9,083	.051				
1948	77,642	78,859	9,213	.117	213,254	233,326	33,266	.143				
1949	76,850	78,094	16,239	.208	197,988	194,901	35,069	.180				
1950	70,107	65,162	6,733	.103	239,909	230,243	27,784	.121				
1951	73,997	77,621	11,649	.150	260,145	265,654	37,527	.141	18,008	15,910	3,165	.199
1952	66,890	64,738	10,510	.162	254,216	238,057	27,548	.116	15,899	15,328	2,903	.189
1953	64,504	65,945	15,923	.241	223,397	238,828	45,278	.190	17,111	19,494	5,908	.303
1954	61,241	66,266	22,639	.341	222,270	206,638	36,216	.175	13,184	11,043	3,933	.356

exhibit 12 LEATHERCRAFT CORPORATION
Financial and operating ratios, 1945–1955 (in millions of dollars)

	1945	1946	1947	1948	1949	1950	1951	1952	1953	1954	1955
Sales	$5.4	$5.8	$7.2	$8.5	$8.8	$9.8	$12.1	$10.2	$10.0	$9.0	$8.7
Operating profit	.5	.6	.9	1.2	.9	1.1	1.4	.8	.9	.3	(.3)
Net working capital	2.5	2.4	2.6	2.8	2.9	3.2	3.8	3.9	3.7	3.5	3.2
Balance sheet ratios											
Current ratio	4.6	4.7	3.9	3.2	3.2	3.0	3.5	4.2	3.8	4.1	4.3
Quick ratio	2.7	3.0	2.3	1.5	1.4	1.4	1.6	2.4	1.4	1.3	1.4
Inventory to net worth	39.5%	34.4%	39.9%	51.0%	52.6%	56.2%	58.2%	42.9%	61.4%	63.4%	72.9%
Fixed assets to net worth	13.9%	19.2%	22.9%	27.9%	26.1%	24.2%	23.7%	24.1%	26.2%	25.3%	27.0%
Total debt to net worth	21.7%	19.6%	24.2%	28.9%	31.4%	34.7%	42.1%	30.6%	30.0%	24.9%	39.4%
Operating ratios											
Cost of sales to fixed assets	9.0	6.9	6.8	5.6	6.2	6.7	7.5	6.4	5.5	5.5	5.5*
Net sales to avg. inventory	4.9	4.8	5.9	5.2	4.4	4.2	4.6	4.3	3.9	3.0	2.7*
Net profit to net sales	4.9%	5.4%	7.3%	7.5%	4.5%	4.8%	3.7%	3.4%	3.3%	1.4%	(2.2)%
Operating profit to net sales	9.1%	9.8%	12.5%	13.0%	9.1%	10.1%	11.0%	7.0%	7.7%	2.9%	(2.5)%
Inventory to working capital	51.2%	47.0%	56.2%	79.3%	79.9%	82.3%	73.8%	55.9%	85.4%	89.1%	89.1%

( ) indicates loss.

129

exhibit 13 LEATHERCRAFT CORPORATION
Analysis of manufacturing expenses, 1945–1954

	Total		Supervision		Other Salaries and Wages	Lasts, Dies, and Tools	Repair and Maintenance Materials	Heat, Light, Power and Water	Insurance	Provision for Depreciation	Rent
	Amount	% of Unadjusted Sales	Amount	% of Unadjusted Sales							
1945	$ 616,400	14.3%	$ 52,700	.0122%	$242,200	$10,300	$ 69,800	$ 51,200	$ 7,500	$ 31,700	$ 5,200
1946	731,900	15.2	76,600	.016	290,100	15,600	80,100	62,500	9,400	40,300	2,800
1947	945,500	15.1	48,100	.008	409,100	12,100	118,700	80,400	10,600	52,800	3,100
1948	1,131,900	14.6	87,800	.011	436,800	19,200	139,900	118,300	15,400	69,000	3,200
1949	1,233,000	14.7	101,600	.012	473,800	20,700	137,900	107,100	19,500	89,000	1,800
1950	1,311,000	14.4	98,800	.011	516,200	20,300	128,400	118,900	19,800	100,200	2,000
1951	1,564,500	14.1	113,500	.010	617,900	25,800	167,600	134,400	12,100	106,000	9,000
1952	1,539,200	16.0	121,600	.013	668,100	29,000	136,500	131,100	14,600	108,800	8,900
1953	1,696,000	17.9	142,100	.015	590,800	62,900	149,800	146,500	15,800	110,600	17,050
1954	1,628,200	18.2	144,500	.0162	582,400	42,400	120,700	139,600	15,800	123,000	17,300

	Freight, Express, and Cartage	Truck Expense	Supplies	Factory Office Supplies	Property Taxes	Telephone and Telegraph	Payroll Taxes	Travel	Engineering Services	Membership Dues and Subscriptions	Miscellaneous
1945	$ 7,500	$1,500	$29,900	$4,600	$17,500	$1,400	$27,900	$ 1,800	—	$ 700	—
1946	8,100	1,100	38,200	4,800	20,800	1,800	31,900	3,100	—	900	$ 4,200
1947	16,500	2,100	49,100	4,700	28,000	2,400	40,700	3,500	$2,000	1,500	4,900
1948	24,300	2,000	53,700	4,100	25,200	3,600	48,600	5,700	2,500	900	7,500
1949	29,800	900	43,700	4,900	30,500	4,500	51,400	4,900	300	1,900	11,100
1950	32,300	2,900	52,500	4,600	30,200	4,800	63,500	8,300	600	2,200	9,200
1951	39,400	2,600	76,400	8,500	39,100	5,800	74,800	10,000	600	2,900	14,300
1952	37,100	900	69,600	6,400	45,500	5,300	70,300	10,700	1,400	2,000	16,400
1953	52,900	100	78,400	6,000	48,600	6,400	77,800	16,600	9,900	2,100	21,800
1954	41,200	600	67,900	5,900	65,400	5,500	79,800	13,200	1,900	2,000	25,900

exhibit 14   LEATHERCRAFT CORPORATION

Analysis of shipping, advertising, and selling expenses by year, 1945–1954

Year	Total (Not Incl. Advertising)	Salaries and Wages	Commission	Repair and Maintenance	Heat, Light, Power, and Water	Insurance	Provision for Depreciation	Machine Rentals	Misc. Supplies	Stationery and Printing	Postage	Telephone and Telegraph	Payroll Taxes
1945	$439,758	$138,977	$206,916	$3,161	$2,132	$1,354	$5,221	—	$1,405	$2,634	5,079	$1,635	$5,259
1946	524,394	150,464	260,943	1,632	2,177	769	4,595	—	456	5,592	5,369	2,010	6,671
1947	701,685	188,411	369,821	2,776	2,623	901	5,981	—	1,425	11,396	7,894	1,926	6,607
1948	866,038	219,288	433,379	28,179	4,301	1,040	8,587	—	1,020	14,827	8,690	2,523	7,566
1949	1,038,341	270,746	481,414	4,163	5,042	809	11,928	—	5,143	18,367	11,158	2,873	9,602
1950	1,165,589	320,445	406,958	4,031	5,126	1,230	12,666	$11,159	8,082	23,071	11,358	4,498	13,314
1951	1,494,801	393,096	527,697	5,555	5,440	1,688	13,189	15,742	18,820	36,721	16,372	5,885	15,003
1952	1,414,278	410,794	438,066	8,520	7,359	1,775	13,931	22,257	12,467	19,511	20,098	5,782	16,182
1953	1,441,634	435,332	429,105	6,762	6,808	2,154	14,481	23,456	18,504	31,946	21,251	6,006	15,796
1954	1,446,363	427,693	401,978	4,641	7,809	1,777	15,733	23,924	16,718	29,711	20,417	6,168	16,969

Year	Provision for Doubtful Accounts	Salesmen's Traveling Expense	Credit Information Rating Books	Collection Expense	Salesmen's Samples	Salesmen's Educational Expense	Legal and Other Professional	Misc.	Advertising — Salary and Wages	Magazine Advertising	General Advertising	Dealer's Helps	Total Advertising
1945	$893	$49,891	$5,096	$890	$541	$8,094	—	$580	$6,729	$66,543	$3,499	$16,959	$95,701
1946	—	67,973	5,216	1,257	1,351	7,257	—	663	9,990	69,791	4,061	20,753	108,303
1947	7,594	77,477	6,975	1,677	2,610	5,336	—	255	13,638	105,501	4,930	19,498	148,050
1948	6,523	107,089	5,745	3,967	4,104	8,496	—	715	14,303	122,595	7,765	19,434	168,621
1949	17,065	162,228	7,395	7,189	2,947	19,481	—	790	18,797	146,365	13,036	23,859	209,449
1950	37,573	262,958	9,669	11,633	1,138	18,865	—	1,813	17,591	143,261	22,620	23,211	214,695
1951	46,216	337,152	12,963	14,416	7,657	22,896	—	1,192	28,638	220,108	30,058	41,685	331,619
1952	13,023	364,146	13,097	17,656	5,950	21,613	—	2,049	36,084	204,394	26,332	51,980	330,435
1953	3,073	360,100	13,055	18,302	3,478	27,257	$2,068	2,699	33,801	191,672	33,585	33,712	306,597
1954	10,326	390,625	14,204	15,703	10,285	28,514	95	3,075	28,387	188,403	26,636	31,672	290,315

SOURCE: Audit reports.

131

exhibit 15 LEATHER CORPORATION

Analysis of general administrative expenses, 1945–1954

	Total	% of Un-adjusted Sales	Salaries and Wages	Stationery and Printing	State Taxes	Telephone and Telegraph	Payroll Taxes	Group and Other Insurance	Legal and Audit	Travel, Postage, Gifts, Dues, Etc.	Miscel-laneous
1945	$32,348	.0075	$12,497	$ 803	$7,290	$1,519	$ 199	$ 837	$4,855	$1,498	$2,850
1946	43,760	.0091	27,471	202	7,114	1,730	298	18	4,012	1,892	1,035
1947	65,332	.0104	41,232	1,058	7,770	2,059	1,941	584	6,600	2,306	1,722
1948	75,984	.0098	52,818	1,431	8,509	1,970	2,047	696	2,578	3,827	2,108
1949	114,736	.0137	65,031	1,693	10,583	3,427	2,166	686	6,439	22,761	1,949
1950	127,801	.0141	96,456	1,410	10,867	3,700	4,378	1,889	4,174	2,491	2,435
1951	222,565	.0201	135,699	2,133	16,735	3,628	3,651	21,457	28,488	8,889	2,884
1952	249,866	.0260	138,765	2,355	19,926	3,456	3,792	30,096	32,473	17,469	5,489
1953	288,519	.0305	147,284	3,285	28,545	3,522	4,023	71,736	9,183	15,466	5,470
1954	315,544	.0353	139,580	3,397	29,435	3,122	4,879	76,915	42,411	8,209	7,537

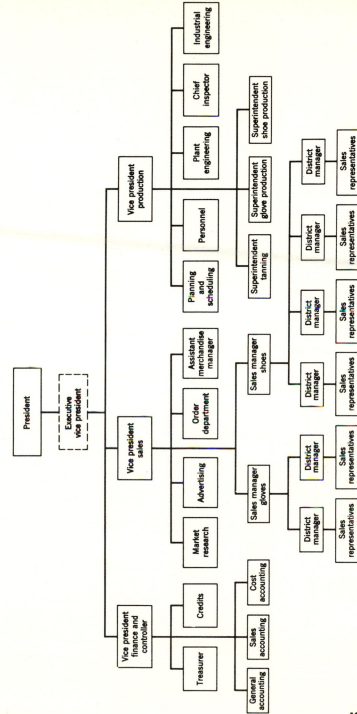

exhibit 16

LEATHERCRAFT CORPORATION

Proposed Organization

ORGANIZATION

Leathercraft's nine-man board of directors was composed of family members and employees. The informal executive committee was composed entirely of family members. This committee sometimes had difficulty in agreeing on company policy. The organization charts of the company, which were developed at considerable expense and effort, were not always used as guidelines. (See Exhibit 16.)

A great deal of money had been spent for gathering and recording accounting and statistical information to provide facts for formulating policy and making decisions. (See, for example, Exhibits 12–15.)

A comparison of base salaries with a normal salary curve, developed from the American Management Association Executive Compensation Survey, indicated that top executive salaries of the company were above those being paid in similar size companies. Contrariwise, a tendency to underpay the lower and middle management group was indicated.

7
LAURA LEE

"In a sense," said Bernard Fischer, chairman of Laura Lee, Inc., "we are a price operation. Our lines are definitely in the moderate budget category. We stay away from high fashion, even though we aim for a touch of high fashion. But we don't sell to the carriage trade. We leave that to Saks Fifth Avenue and Bonwit Teller. We're not 'shawl' trade either. We don't cater to the Slobovian housewife who wears a babushka and shops for junk. For a little less than we ask, the babushka shopper buys shoddy. For a little more, she could buy our garments, which would probably last her twice as long. We offer attractively moderate prices, but as fashion items our garments are definitely exceptional."

THE COMPANY IN 1971

Laura Lee, Inc., manufactured and sold to retailers a fairly wide line of women's garments, emphasizing knit garments and youthful lines. Through six subsidiaries it operated seven plants in the United States and one in Canada, which manufactured 90% of the merchandise it sold. It had its headquarters office in New York City, general offices in its main plant at Bridgeport, Connecticut, and sales offices and showrooms which covered the United States. It also had a sales office in Canada. It sold its garments through 15,000 independent retailers in the United States and Canada (see Exhibit 1). In 1971 it had sales of $32 million, total assets of $11.8 million, and a stockholders' equity of $6.6 million.

exhibit 1   LAURA LEE, INC.

Plants

Bridgeport, Connecticut	198M sq. ft.	Pop.	160,000
Bridgeport, Connecticut	57M		160,000
Shelbyville, Tennessee	64M		10,200
Saratoga Springs, New York	12M		15,300
Columbia, North Carolina	32M		1,600
Montreal, Canada	27M		1,600,000
Bristol, Vermont	20M		1,900
Warwick, Rhode Island	9M		43,000

Principal Sales Offices and Showrooms

1700 Broadway, N.Y.C.	Laura Lee
1700 Broadway, N.Y.C.	Cross Country
1700 Broadway, N.Y.C.	Lorraine
1700 Broadway, N.Y.C.	Cantigny
398 Seventh Avenue, N.Y.C.	Derby Day
404 Seventh Avenue, N.Y.C.	Calico Corner
8420 Dominion Blvd., Montreal	All lines
Memphis Sales Mart, Memphis, Tennessee	All lines
Houston Show Mart, Houston, Texas	All lines
Miami Exhibitors Mart, Miami, Florida	All lines
Pacific Apparel Mart, San Francisco	All lines
The Merchandise Mart, Chicago, Illinois	All lines

Bernard Fischer, age 67, was the majority stockholder. He began his career as a garment salesman. In 1934, when 30 years old, he formed a partnership to wholesale women's garments. In 1953 the business was incorporated and began to manufacture its own products. In the company's 1971 Annual Report, Bernard Fischer stated:

Until 1964 our business enjoyed a moderate and profitable internal growth by wholesaling a specialized line of moderate-priced women's fashion garments emphasizing the more youthful lines. We had developed a loyal retail dealer following through wholesaling. Counting on our strong position with retailers across the country, we resolved upon a five-point program which in concept was a turn around from our former policies.

First, we decided to sell directly to retailers to take advantage of the better opportunity for vigorous sales promotion which this would permit.

Second, our product line, which had been relatively limited, was to be widened by adding new categories of apparel and broadening the price range.

Third, we recognized the growing demand for knitted apparel, whose versatility and practicality appealed to modern women. New knitting yarns, especially the polyesters, made the production of knitted garments very attractive commercially. We decided to henceforth emphasize knitted budget dresses retailing between $20 and $30 until eventually we would become the national leader in this field.

Fourth, we had been a small manufacturer, and relatively inefficient. We decided upon a program of seeking out and acquiring other businesses within our field, which was a ready route available to us for swift and substantial growth. We had the finances to support such a program. Our intention was to grow large enough to enjoy the economies inherent in big business.

Fifth, we determined upon a program of establishing small branch plants in small towns, probably in the Central Southern states, where ample labor was available and union problems could be eliminated. Our ultimate aim was to have no more manufacturing operations in the New York garment district.

"Our sales have increased substantially through the years," said John Kaufman, treasurer, "and today we are in strong financial condition, but that isn't all that there is to our financial picture. Even by the erratic financial standards of New York City's garment district, Laura Lee has put together a pretty unstylish operating record. In spite of rising sales in the last five years, profits have bounced about, from 15¢ a share in fiscal 1967 to $2.19 in 1968, when net profit soared. We've added quickly to sales by broadening our product lines and by acquisitions, and that's resulted in some loose ends. We made money on most of our operations, but we also had one sizable inventory write-down, we had setbacks from the sale of two losing subsidiaries, and heavy start-up costs in new plants and in outerwear and rainwear. But the outlook for next year is good. We netted $2.31 a share in fiscal 1971, and we may reach $2.75 in fiscal 1972." (See Exhibits 2 and 3.)

THE ACRES OF DIAMONDS

Until 1964 Laura Lee sales had grown steadily but profits were faltering and Bernard Fischer was discouraged. That year, when he was showing the line in Kansas, he visited a luggage maker to shop for moderate-priced suitcases which Laura Lee salesmen could use for sample cases. In the luggage maker's display room Bernard Fischer noticed a large wall map on which the areas around cities like New York, Philadelphia, and Cleveland were studded with colored pins, but there were no pins on the smaller cities which he had been trying to develop. The luggage maker said that these were his retail dealers; that his line did not sell worth a darn in small cities and farm towns. "The

exhibit 2   LAURA LEE, INC.
Comparative consolidated balance sheets

	June 28, 1971	June 29, 1970	July 1, 1969	July 2, 1968	July 3, 1967
Assets					
Current assets:					
Cash	$ 665,185	$ 604,672	$ 495,571	$1,700,127	$1,386,135
Accounts receivable	3,575,139	3,847,719	4,171,833	189,088*	464,733*
Inventories:					
Finished goods	1,500,489	1,672,666	3,052,349	2,026,648	1,383,863
Work in process	1,307,398	892,398	1,044,904	1,202,066	1,037,829
Raw materials	2,800,065	2,418,059	2,078,198	1,901,138	976,624
Total inventories	$ 5,607,952	$ 4,983,123	$ 6,175,451	$5,129,852	$3,398,316
Prepaid expenses	98,499	127,286	100,200	116,571	144,798
Total current assets	$ 9,946,775	$ 9,562,800	$10,943,055	$7,135,638	$5,393,982
Property, plant & equipment:					
Land and buildings	585,306	552,074	522,207		
Machinery and equipment	1,935,136	1,627,714	1,550,097		
Leasehold improvements	686,040	568,174	429,751		
Total plant & equipment	3,206,482	2,747,962	2,502,055	2,136,268	1,990,677
Less depreciation	1,454,748	1,207,860	995,476	824,077	653,462
Net fixed assets:	1,751,734	1,540,102	1,506,579	1,312,191	1,337,215
Other assets	117,696	124,426	207,999	83,767	78,608
Total assets	$11,816,205	$11,227,228	$12,657,633	$8,531,596	$6,809,805
Liabilities					
Current liabilities:					
Notes payable to banks	$ 382,197	$ 2,456,132	$ 2,509,632	$	$
Accounts payable	2,448,047	2,016,192	2,480,382	1,506,357	1,873,895
Taxes	1,320,196	183,511	730,576	792,850	
Accrued expenses	319,002	316,305	625,398	552,086	388,271
Current payment on long-term debt	18,750	15,000	12,921	18,498	18,498
Dividends payable†	150,271	147,841			
Total current liabilities	$ 4,638,463	$ 5,134,981	$ 6,358,909	$2,869,791	$2,280,664
Long-term debt	541,257	559,920	578,756	591,696	610,212
Stockholders' equity:					
Common stock	1,001,806	985,605	981,000	981,000	981,000
Additional paid-in capital	140,656	59,431	36,406	36,406	36,406
Retained earnings	5,494,024	4,487,291	4,702,560	4,052,703	2,901,523
Total stockholders' equity	$ 6,636,486	$ 5,532,327	$ 5,719,966	$5,070,109	$3,918,929
Total	$11,816,206	$11,277,228	$12,657,633	$8,531,596	$6,809,805

* Accounts receivable were factored without recourse.
† Quarterly dividend.

realization hit me like a clap of thunder," said Bernard Fischer. "Where moderate-priced luggage would sell, so would the Laura Lee line. I had been a damn fool! I had been plowing all over the hinterland, while there were acres of diamonds right in my own back yard."

On his return to New York, Bernard Fischer switched his sales effort. The existing Laura Lee retailers in small cities and rural areas were retained, but the effort to obtain new retailers was now directed to metropolitan areas.

exhibit 3 LAURA LEE, INC.
Comparative consolidated statements of income

	June 28, 1971	June 29, 1970	July 1, 1969	July 2, 1968	July 3, 1967
Net sales	$32,251,908	$26,627,754	$25,732,516	$24,317,618	$19,804,149
Cost of sales	21,821,259	19,367,955	17,875,475	16,696,350	14,880,117
Gross profit	10,430,649	7,259,799	7,857,041	7,621,268	4,924,032
Selling and adminis- trative expense	6,944,178	6,414,011	6,057,327	5,295,912	4,704,471
Operating profit	$ 3,486,471	$ 845,788	$ 1,799,714	$ 2,325,356	$ 219,561
Interest	158,048	163,824	79,915	96,765	121,769
Income before taxes	3,328,423	681,964	1,719,799	2,228,591	97,792
Provision for taxes	1,726,500	346,500	637,500	195,000	00
Net income	$ 1,601,923	$ 335,464	$ 1,082,299	$ 1,433,591	$ 97,792
Net income per share	$2.31	$0.48	$1.65	$2.19	$0.15

Until 1964 Bernard Fischer had been his own designer, production superintendent, and sales manager. In 1964 he met Miss Noreen Mallory, a career fashion designer, whose designs so impressed Bernard that he persuaded her to come to Laura Lee as vice president, design, on a partial-stock-ownership basis. Later the same year Bernard Fischer engaged as vice president, manufacturing, Jacob Eisner, who had 12 years of production management experience in the needle trades. Until 1964 Laura Lee had grown significantly, but the growth had been entirely internal. In 1964 Laura Lee acquired the Derby Day line on an exchange-of-shares basis. This was the first of a series of acquisitions which were to follow.

"The pivotal year for our business was 1964," said Bernard Fischer. "It was our turning point. From then on sales shot up jet-propelled."

ACQUISITIONS AND EXPANSION

In May, 1966, Laura Lee acquired Cantigny, Inc., which manufactured and wholesaled moderately priced knitted garments retailing at $30 to $50, under the brand name "Cantigny." Cantigny was a well-established brand and for 18 years the company had operated its own plant at Saratoga Springs, New York.

The Derby Day knitted line which Laura Lee acquired in 1964 was manufactured by Dressmakers Limited in its modern plant in Montreal. Bernard Fischer decided to shift all knitwear manufacture to the more efficient Montreal plant, and during the summer of 1966 the Dressmakers plant was enlarged for that purpose. The Cantigny Saratoga Springs equipment was sold at auction and new equipment to produce the Cantigny line was installed in Montreal. From August to December the Saratoga plant was not producing, because of the move. In December the Saratoga plant began to produce some other Laura Lee lines, but these took only part of its capacity. "Immediately after we acquired Cantigny," said Mr. Bernard Fischer, "we switched its distribution from wholesalers to our direct-to-retailers system. Cantigny has fulfilled our every expectation. It was enthusiastically accepted for its styling and price as one of the finest lines in the country."

For the fiscal year 1966 Laura Lee had sales of $17 million, a net profit after taxes of $698,000, and net earnings of $1.02 per share. This represented the company's most profitable year up to that date.

For the year 1967, sales reached a new record high of $19.8 million, but net profits fell to $97,792 and earnings to 15¢ per share, which were the lowest earnings in a decade. Mr. Bernard Fischer explained that there were extraordinary charges of 51¢ per share, as a result of the reorganization of Cantigny and Dressmakers Ltd.; there had been heavy introductory expenses for entering Cantigny into Laura Lee's retail market; and there had been unexpected difficulties encountered in importing Dressmakers products into the United States. The Canadian government had charged an unforeseen high duty on knitting yarns shipped from Saratoga to Montreal. The United States Customs charged an arbitrarily high rate on the finished knitted garments shipped from Montreal into the U.S. and refused to make allowance for the fact that much of the content of the garments consisted of yarns which had been spun in the U.S. Laura Lee paid the extra charges and was appealing its case in Canadian and U.S. courts.

Early in 1967 Bernard Fischer decided to sell all of Laura Lee's lines in Canada through Dressmakers Ltd.'s established distribution system. Laura Lee garments received immediate acceptance in Canada, and sales were over $450,000 the first five months of operation. However, introductory expenses and further import-duty difficulties resulted in a loss of sales for the spring of 1967.

In June, 1967, Laura Lee acquired the Cross Country and Princess Juniors brands. Both of these lines were produced in rented loft quarters in the New York garment district. Cross Country manufactured casual dresses which its owners had sold in sportswear departments; Princess Juniors made dresses styled specifically for the mature woman who wore a junior size. "Princess," said Bernard Fischer, "will provide that look of youthfulness for our women's market that Laura Lee's 'Misses' lines provide for young ladies. It will widen our total line considerably." In 1968 sales of $24.3 million and profits of $1.4 million set new record highs. During 1968 Laura Lee acquired Buster Boy, which manufactured low-priced junior-size sportswear sold through specialty shops. It also acquired McLane, which made youthfully styled, highly sophisticated dresses specifically for women who wore sizes 8 to 16. Buster Boy became the bottom Laura Lee line, with retail prices of $7 to $12 for dresses; McLane became the top line, with $40 to $60 dresses. Both were manufactured in rented quarters.

During the year Bernard Fischer decided to enter the women's rainwear and outerwear business. He hired a sales manager and a plant superintendent who had experience in these lines, and Miss Mallory, working with these men, designed a line which was produced in the Bridgeport plant. The introduction went moderately well.

During 1968 Bernard Fischer also bought Loraine & Company and its "Loraine" brand name. Operating from a leased plant in Hartford, Connecticut, Loraine produced garments which duplicated a large sector of the Laura Lee brand line but gave Laura Lee added plant capacity and added significantly to its retail organization.

Sales increased in 1969 to $25.7 million, but net declined to $1.08 million and earnings per share to $1.65. Buster Boy continued to be manufactured under its former management, without any change in quality or price. Many Laura Lee retailers did not accept the "cheap" Buster Boy line, and many of those who did returned large portions of their purchases as being shoddy and not in keeping with Laura Lee standards. The McLane line was of excellent quality, but many Laura Lee dealers considered the prices to be above their range and did not take it on. After a year of effort, Bernard Fischer abruptly decided to discontinue both lines. The remaining inventories were sacrificed to jobbers and their production equipment was sold. Laura Lee wrote off $345,000 on the two lines.

During 1969 Mr. Bernard Fischer, following the advice of industrial engineering consultants, made a major revision of Laura Lee's cutting, sewing, and shipping operations. The company also made substantial capital expenditures to expand its manufacturing capacity, its warehouse space, and its New York City showrooms. The total expansion added 139,000 square feet to the company's operating capacity. Further additional capacity was obtained when Laura Lee bought the Pied Piper Company, which made misses' outerwear, and Calico Corner, which, in addition to dresses, made junior outerwear. With these companies Laura Lee acquired personnel experienced in the design, manufacture, and sale of outerwear and rainwear. Before the year ended, Laura Lee disposed of these companies' New York plants and moved their operations to a new plant which Laura Lee built for them in Columbia, North Carolina.

In 1970 sales increased again to $26.6 million, but net profit dropped to $335,464, or 48¢ per share; 1970 was a year of further expansion in capacity, with facilities at Shelbyville, Tennessee, expanded, a second plant built at Bridgeport, and new plants built at Bristol, Vermont, and Warwick, Rhode Island. Bernard Fischer attributed the decline in profits to disruptions caused by the expansions, to start-up costs at the new plants, and to temporary inefficiencies caused by the recent separation of the functions of cutting, sewing, and shipping, as well as uncertainty about the mini, midi, and maxi skirts and dresses.

THE CONVERSION TO FUNCTIONAL PRODUCTION

By 1968 Laura Lee was producing over 100 different garments at eight plants, and Mr. Samuel Fischer became convinced that the company was suffering from difficulties in co-ordinating production schedules and in integrating shipments. Following a study made by a national firm of industrial engineering consultants, Bernard Fischer consented to a major revision of all Laura Lee operations. During 1968 all cutting operations (except those of Dressmakers Ltd.) were concentrated in the Bridgeport plants. All leased plants were disposed of, and all sewing operations were parceled out to Laura Lee's owned plants, with each plant specializing in one or several of the brand lines. All shipping was concentrated in the new Bridgeport plant. All operations were computerized to co-ordinate production, inventories, manufacturing schedules, warehouse, and plant loads. Purchasing, shipping, billing, and accounts receivable were also computerized.

The combined and co-ordinated total operations were made possible by the use of a fleet of semi-trailer trucks, each capable of carrying a 12-ton load. Using alternating crews, these trucks operated 24 hours a day, picking up palletted loads of cut fabrics at Bridgeport and distributing them to the other plants, which sewed the garments. The trucks then hauled the finished garments back to Bridgeport, which became Laura Lee's centralized shipping center for all orders. Each truck averaged a fully loaded round-trip haul every two days. Samuel Fischer was convinced that the new system would minimize inventories, cut distribution costs, and give retailers much faster service.

ORGANIZATIONAL RELATIONSHIPS

"Until we became big in manufacturing," said Bernard Fischer, "I didn't give much thought to organization. I hired people as employees. Some were especially talented and just naturally took over supervision of some areas. I was boss, but I was on the road a great deal. If something important came up while I was away, it just had to wait."

The presidents of all Laura Lee subsidiaries answered to Bernard Fischer. Mr. Fischer asserted that the subsidiaries operated independently, but Noreen Mallory now had the final word in designing and Jacob Eisner co-ordinated the manufacturing activities in all plants, David Rose directed their merchandising programs, and Bernard Fischer integrated the sales of all units (see Exhibit 4).

Jacob Eisner was the first of the management staff personnel hired by Bernard Fischer. An operating manual written in 1965, a year after Eisner was hired, showed his duties included the supervision of all employees except those engaged in sales activities and in finance and accounting. At that time 24 managers and foremen reported to Jacob Eisner, including those responsible for purchasing, order filling, billing, and mailings to retailers. Jacob Eisner had authority to hire and fire most employees, and so he became the company's de facto personnel manager. Until Samuel Fischer came into the company, Jacob Eisner acted as president of the company in the absence of Bernard Fischer. Describing his duties in early 1971, Jacob Eisner said: "I'm theoretically cut back to a defined set of operations now, but that doesn't mean too much. I'm in charge of production, and that includes over 85% of the employees in the company. There aren't exactly neat lines around the jobs here. Even things like accounting and receivables tie into my area so directly that I still have a lot to say about them. I'm particularly inclined to get out of line, I guess, because until just lately everything was in my line." Bernard Fischer commented: "Some people think

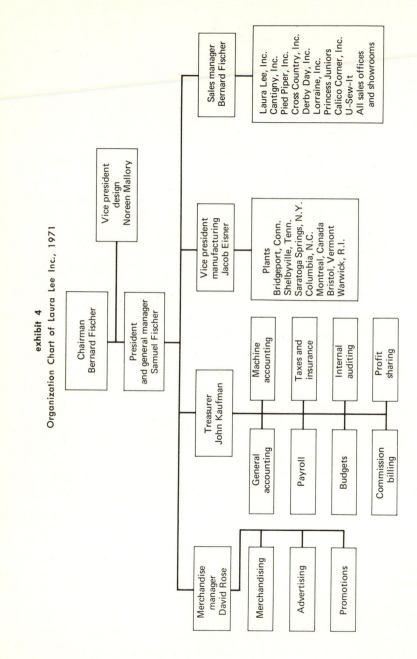

exhibit 4

Organization Chart of Laura Lee Inc., 1971

Chairman
Bernard Fischer

Vice president
design
Noreen Mallory

President
and general manager
Samuel Fischer

Merchandise
manager
David Rose

Treasurer
John Kaufman

Vice president
manufacturing
Jacob Eisner

Sales manager
Bernard Fischer

Merchandising

Advertising

Promotions

Machine
accounting

General
accounting

Taxes and
insurance

Payroll

Internal
auditing

Budgets

Profit
sharing

Commission
billing

Plants
Bridgeport, Conn.
Shelbyville, Tenn.
Saratoga Springs, N.Y.
Columbia, N.C.
Montreal, Canada
Bristol, Vermont
Warwick, R.I.

Laura Lee, Inc.
Cantigny, Inc.
Pied Piper, Inc.
Cross Country, Inc.
Derby Day, Inc.
Lorraine, Inc.
Princess Juniors
Calico Corner, Inc.
U-Sew-It
All sales offices
and showrooms

144

Jake is rough-hewn and old-fashioned, but I can say this for him: he's a first-rate production man. He gets those boxes out of the back door, even when it's a real battle to do so."

Noreen Mallory, as vice president, design, reported directly to Bernard Fischer. Miss Mallory supervised designing, and in this connection she worked closely with designers in Laura Lee's subsidiaries. While she had no authority over people in other activities; it was generally recognized that she was coming to have increasing influence upon Bernard Fischer, who was consulting her more and more on other matters. She was already considered one of the top management group.

Samuel Fischer was not a blood relative of Bernard Fischer, but he was the husband of Bernard Fischer's eldest daughter, Laura Lee Fischer. Samuel Fischer had been a successful corporate attorney when Bernard Fischer invited him to join Laura Lee. Samuel Fischer came to Laura Lee as vice president, administration, a position in which his duties were loosely defined as including everything except manufacturing and sales. Not long afterward he was named executive vice president, and when Bernard Fischer became chairman, Samuel became president and general manager. Bernard permitted him to direct the business generally, except for sales functions.

John Kaufman joined the company shortly after Samuel Fischer became vice president, administration. A CPA, he had eight years of public accounting practice. Hired as chief accountant, within two years he became, successively, controller and treasurer. Kaufman was responsible for all accounting, money management, and internal systems.

David Rose was the only new management staff member who had previous garment trade experience. A nephew of Bernard Fischer, he had joined Laura Lee at age 31 with 10 years' experience with the chain department stores operated by Aldens, the national mail-order house. David Rose started at a salary which was higher than that of any of the new management personnel except Samuel Fischer, and he was consulted in many general management matters.

SALES POLICIES AND PROBLEMS

Bernard Fischer had always concentrated his attention on the sales effort. In 1967, when Bernard became chairman and named Samuel

Fischer president and general manager of the company, Bernard Fischer remained, in name and in fact, the sales manager of the company.

Bernard Fischer remunerated his salesmen on the basis of a small salary and a liberal system of commissions paid on a graduated scale to a cut-off point. Commissions on sales over the cut-off point were made on a declining scale. The system resulted in exceptionally high earnings for most salesmen. A sales position with Laura Lee was considered to be attractive by most garment salesmen, and there was competition for the job. Bernard Fischer was selective in choosing salesmen and considered his sales force to be definitely superior. The majority of Laura Lee salesmen had been with the company for years, but there was a constant turnover among 5% of the group. Salesmen paid their own traveling expenses. Sales supervisors were paid an override on the sales of the men in their group. "Those of our sales people who enjoy very high earnings," said Bernard Fischer, "don't act like employees; they show a lot of independence. This has made problems for us. You can't boss these people around."

Laura Lee always had two seasonal sales slumps: one at Christmas and the other in midsummer. David Rose started a series of sales contests to combat the summer lull. High-scoring salesmen were offered prizes such as all-expense tours to Europe or Hawaii, mink stoles, home air conditioners, color TV consoles, diamond earrings, and sterling silver sets. There was a range of values in prizes, so that even a low achiever received at least $50 worth.

The contests went very well in every area except that of Pierre Armand, sales manager of Laura Lee in Canada. Mr. Armand had been sales manager of Dressmakers Ltd. of Montreal and had been retained by Bernard Fischer after that business was acquired in 1964. Mr. Armand received an override on all Laura Lee sales made in Canada, which resulted in giving him an income which was one of the highest in the Laura Lee organization. Mr. Armand let it be known that he was not interested in spending his summer conducting a sales contest. His earnings during the regular sales seasons already placed him in a high tax bracket. No amount of persuasion had been successful in getting him to change his mind.

Another problem concerning salesmen was brought to light when Robert Kearney came to Laura Lee as systems manager. He studied every Laura Lee operation to adapt it to computers. His studies included an analysis of the cost of filling orders, from which Kearney concluded that Laura Lee was losing money on small orders. The compiled statistics indicated that Laura Lee was losing $7 on every $20 order it filled. His figures showed the company's break-even point to be about $60. On an order of $400, the company made a net profit of $78. In the spring of 1970, 37% of all orders had been in amounts under $400, 26% had been under $60, and 20% had been under $20. The study showed that many of the small orders were fill-in orders mailed by retailers directly to Laura Lee sales offices; they were not orders written by salesmen at the time they called on retailers.

Samuel Fischer was seriously concerned about Kearney's findings and called a meeting of his management staff group to find a solution. Some thought that there were salesmen who were chronic small-order-writers, and that these salesmen ought to be fired. Others were for persuading these salesmen to stop writing small orders; they suggested putting the salesmen on probation before letting them go. Others blamed the retailers and suggested that retailers should be required to accumulate small orders until they had $150 worth. Setting a minimum-order size was also considered. It was the feeling of the group that no hasty action should be taken, that the matter should be studied over an extended period—perhaps for a full year. Bernard Fischer said he knew of no competitor who had such a minimum-order rule, and he feared that setting such a rule would cause Laura Lee retailers to switch to competitors.

LAURA LEE'S PRODUCT LINES

"The names of our lines sound like a strange collection," said Bernard Fischer, "but they are very valuable to us. Every one of them is well known to retailers and to the women who are our retail customers. We paid a lot of money to buy those well-established names, and now we are beginning to cash in on them."

Laura Lee was the name of Bernard Fischer's first-born daughter. The Cantigny line had been so named by its former owner, who, as a soldier in the First World War, had fought in a battle there. The Pied Piper line had once featured bright solid colors, but it had long since phased these out in favor of popular hues. Calico Corner had originated as a low-price line, but over the years it had traded up to moderate prices. The Princess Juniors and U-Sew-It lines were the only ones whose names presently had descriptive utility. The reason for the names of the rest of the Laura Lee lines had been lost with time.

"What's in a name?" said David Rose. "In all my years in the business I have yet to learn of any way to choose a name that will be a sure winner. But I am sure that if you promote a line enough, you can be certain that the line will sell—regardless of what you call it."

"Our line has grown," said Noreen Mallory, "and it is still growing, but there is a limit to how much we can expand it, and we are already straining against that limit. Now we are even beginning to get into the quality brackets—like the 'good, better, best' categories of the mail-order houses. The fuller the line, the more sales we get; but the more we add to the line, the more problems we have in inventories and manufacturing and in working capital and in the cost of salesmen's samples." The Laura Lee 1970 catalog had 122 items in it; the 1971 catalog had 143.

The garments which Noreen Mallory designed for the Laura Lee line consisted mainly of shifts, two- and three-piece ensembles, dresses, sleepwear, some lingerie, and a few items of outerwear and rainwear. In the last two years Miss Mallory had added a very limited line of midi and maxi skirts and dresses. However, no effort was made to "push" these lines. Both Miss Mallory and Bernard Fischer felt they should put emphasis on their very popular line of pant suits which had matching skirts. Bernard Fischer said, "I don't think our kind of customer is going to go for these 'turn-of-the-century' styles. We'll wait and see. If necessary, we can easily add to our line." David Rose, who had come to have a good deal of voice in "balancing" the Laura Lee lines, said: "We need to have one conservative line; several for youth that have 'swing' in them; and one sophisticated line that has 'schmaltz' in it." (See Exhibit 5.)

Some of the help which David Rose gave Miss Mallory had to do with giving each section of the line balanced representation. "Noreen might put in eight jerseys," said David Rose, "just because every one of them was an appealing design; you just cannot have eight jerseys in a line as short as ours. I'd have to talk her out of two or three of them." Mr. Rose said that part of his job was to "quantify" Miss Mallory's ideas, because "she isn't very good at that herself." He explained that the line was limited in several ways. "We begin by estimating how much our total sales for the year will be. Next we decide how many designs we are going to have in each section of our total line. We

exhibit 5
LAURA LEE FASHIONS

exhibit 5   (continued)

might decide, for example, that we are going to sell $1.8 million in teenwear, $450,000 in sleepwear, $1.2 million in shifts, and so on, down the line. Noreen tends to be carried away by her own attractive designing. She'll put in one of her charming creations at 9,000 units, and I might be forced to agree with her that it will be a top seller, but I might also be forced to tell her that we must cut it down to 6,000 units —that there just isn't any more room in the line."

In 1969 Laura Lee added matching hats and costume jewelry to its line. The hats were often made of the same material as the garment to be matched, and the jewelry, most of which sold for $2 to $5, featured the color combination which was considered to be important. The aim was to give the customer that "total" look. The Laura Lee line did not include, however, such accessories as handbags, gloves, or leather belts, although it did include beltings made of other materials. David Rose told Bernard Fischer he had learned that a direct competitor of Laura Lee was doing an annual leather and plastic belt business of over $2 million. Noreen Mallory said it would help her designing if she had more belts to work with. Bernard Fischer was reluctant to get into leather belts. "We'd have to buy them," he said, "and then we'd just be wholesalers, depending upon somebody else's design talent and manufacture. I doubt that we make any profit at all on the accessories we now sell."

"People think of us as producers of fashion garments," said Noreen Mallory, "but that's not really what we sell. We sell fabrics. Fabrics are the key to our success." Miss Mallory explained her remark in this way: There were many fabrics which were "standards," such as wool, cotton, linen, nylon, rayon, silk, and, more recently, the polyesters. Any housewife who was at all familiar with fabrics would easily recognize a garment made from one of these, and she could estimate pretty well what a garment made from that fabric ought to cost. She could also estimate what the garment would cost if she sewed it herself.

For the Laura Lee group, Noreen Mallory chose fabrics which had what was known in the textile trade as a "blind" look. These blind fabrics were made from a combination of several fibers or yarns, or they were made by weaving techniques which were unique and nonstandard. Therefore, it was difficult for a housewife to recognize such fabrics and to know their value. A housewife would not be able to guess what a fabric cost by the yard. If she were able to identify the fabric, she would find that in retail yard goods shops it sold for $2.50 a yard. Laura Lee was able to buy it, in quantity, at $1.85 a yard or less.

Miss Mallory exhibited several folders which had in them assorted swatches of fabrics and a variety of yarns. "This is the beginning of our next season's line," she said. "Here, for example, is a houndstooth fabric woven from a combination of nylon acrylic and rayon. Each of these yarns will pick up only certain dyes while repelling others. The dyes are applied successively and the result is a fabric that will look as though it is woven of different-colored yarns and the finished cloth will have the appearance of being wool. Out of a fabric like this one we will make a suit that will look as though it is at least a $50 garment. But Laura Lee will sell it to retail for $30."

The Laura Lee organization took pains to give all of its garments an air of elegance. "Our customers," said Bernard Fischer, "are typically small-town people who have seldom been far from home. Even those who live in metropolitan areas tend to be quite provincial. Our garments are designed to have about them the air of sophistication of Paris, London, or New York, and to our kind of customer, that spells glamour. But we are also careful not to give our customers the impression that we are all-out high-style. That might scare them. Some of our customers are the kind who might like the offerings of classy shops like Bergdorf's or Lord and Taylor, but they would hesitate to go into those shops for fear that the garments they liked might be too high-priced for them, and then they would be embarrassed at having to leave without having made a purchase."

In keeping with this general theme of elegance, the Laura Lee catalog was printed in full color on heavy enamel stock paper and the garments, modeled by professional models, were displayed photographically against romantic backgrounds. The photographic backgrounds were selected to give the garments an aura of distinction. Thus a catalog might feature New York settings and the models would be photographed in prominent Manhattan scenes, such as Fifth Avenue, the Brooklyn Bridge, or Central Park. A catalog with the Paris theme subtly wove in landmarks like the Eiffel Tower, Notre Dame, and the Arc de Triomphe. The customer reading the catalog was taken on a capsule tour of a romantic and legendary city.

"This elegance theme is not just an empty sham," said Bernard Fischer. "We insist that our salesmen impress upon our retailers that their attitude toward customers should be one of service. We try to persuade our retailers that they should dote just as much on the $10 customer as on the $100 one. That's not the way the mail-order houses and chains operate these days. Most of them seem to have the motto: Have clothes; will sell; try and find a clerk!"

PRICE AND QUALITY

"I usually design garments that are very simple in line and in design," said Miss Mallory. "That saves money in manufacturing. Every additional cut and every extra inch of sewing adds to the cost of the garment. And if you jazz it up with frills, that adds a lot to your factory cost.

"When we buy our fabrics from selected mills, they are woven for us on a contract basis. Occasionally we buy a stock fabric from a mill. When we do, we buy in quantity and stipulate that the mill withdraw the fabric from its regular line," stated Miss Mallory.

As a matter of rigid policy, Laura Lee did not deal with whole-salers. "That eliminates the layers of markup that go to the middle-man," said Bernard Fischer, "and presumably gives our retailer mer-chandise at lower cost. We have to do that to sell at our moderate prices." Laura Lee skirts were priced as low as $5; blouses started at $6 and few were higher than $8; dresses sold from $10 to $14; shells (or tops) were as low as $4.50; most suits were between $15 and $30. The only item over $50 in the 1971 brochure was a skirt-and-pant suit combination which was priced at $65.

"Until the spring of 1968," said Bernard Fischer, "I did the setting of prices. My magic formula was simple: Our price was set at two and one-half times the factory cost of the garment. If the factory cost of an item was $4, it went into our catalog at $10. We try to take competition into account, but the trouble is that we don't know what competition is charging until our show is already on the road, and by then it's too late. Our catalogs are already printed and the word is out; we can't change. Two years ago David Rose and I had been riding the circuit for about ten days when we discovered that we had underpriced our line badly. That mistake cost Laura Lee at least a quarter of a million dollars. In the future we will try to inch up on our two-and-one-half formula; we'll try to get $10 on a $3.75 factory cost. The difference will not be in the cost of the garments. That is already at bedrock, and we could only work that down by cutting quality. The wider margin will come from jogging up our retail prices a little."

In recent years Bernard Fischer was no longer doing the pricing alone. David Rose, as merchandising manager, had a significant influence on pricing; so did Mr. Kaufman and Mr. Eisner.

Mr. Bernard Fischer insisted that the Laura Lee emphasis on moderate price did not mean that they sold cheap merchandise. "Our garments are cut full and are well tailored," said Mr. Bernard Fischer. "Anyone who knows anything about sewing has only to look at the seams, the tailoring, and the workmanship, and they can see that our garments are not cheap stuff. We choose quality fabrics and we cut to full specifications, and that in itself is a sign to any knowing customer that ours are 'quality' garments. Our typical customer is a matron, and while she doesn't like to admit it, even to herself, over the years her personal cargo has probably shifted somewhat. If she normally wears size 10, she will find that she can wear a size 8 in our garments. That flatters her, of course; all women like to feel that they are slimmer than they really are. But even if she knows that she is being kidded, she will recognize this as the benchmark of a quality garment. All quality garment makers cut their sizes full."

"Back orders," said Mr. David Rose, "are our largest single source of complaint from our retailers. Others in the garment business suffer just as much as we do from unpredictable good and poor sales seasons and from unexpected shortages of supply, but we mean to do something about it."

It had been Noreen Mallory's practice to try to judge which of her fashion designs would be the big sellers. Most of the time her judgment proved true, but in spite of her considerable talent there were times when an undistinguished garment would skyrocket in popularity. "When a single item suddenly sells like wildfire," said Mr. Rose, "we are very likely to run out of fabric. When that happens we are usually unable to get the mill to gear up for a rerun in a big hurry, and so we run into back orders and delays. In 1970 we had one single garment which unexpectedly sold in a volume of almost $700,000."

Mr. Rose, with Mr. Bernard Fischer's approval, decided to poll all of Laura Lee's retailers, asking them to choose the 10 items in the new catalog which they thought would be best sellers. His thinking was, he said, that the garments which appealed to retailers would also appeal to Laura Lee customers. If this proved true, Jacob Eisner could alert the fabric mills concerned so that they could be prepared to process supplementary orders on short notice.

In the fall of 1970, Laura Lee polled its retailers. Ninety per cent of them responded, and Mr. Rose was surprised at the consistency of their selections. Out of 143 items in the line two items, a shift and a pant suit line, were the most popular choices. In almost every dealer's return they were included among the top 10. There were six other garments which received the votes of more than 75% of Laura Lee's retailers.

QUALITY CONTROL

"One of our fundamental principles at Laura Lee," said Mr. Jacob Eisner, vice president, manufacturing, "is that our garments must be duplicated exactly, without any variation. If a woman buys a blouse at Penney's and the blouse so impresses the woman's neighbor that she wants one like it, the neighbor will go looking at Penney's. If it happens that the blouse was an especially good seller, Penney's may have placed several supplementary orders with manufacturers for it. Maybe the manufacturers were the ones who made the original lot; maybe they were not. After a few reorders, the original fabric may no longer be available, and attempts at duplication are not precise. Colors might drift away from the original, and buttons and ornamentation may have undergone substitutions. By that time the blouse might be a far cry from the original."

When Jacob Eisner came to Laura Lee, the company had 143 sources of supply for its fabrics. By 1971 Mr. Eisner had cut the list down to less than 30, and 10 of these supplied the bulk of Laura Lee's requirements.

As a result of a program which Mr. Eisner had worked out, there were five textile mills which produced 75% of Laura Lee's fabrics. Mr. Eisner required of these that each one have a man who would work very closely with Noreen Mallory to keep her informed of market trends, new fibers, new weaves, new fabrics, and ideas. He also required that each of these mills have a liaison man who would keep in touch with Mr. Eisner on a weekly-visit basis. The contact man was to be a top official of the mill. Through these men Mr. Eisner aimed to get immediate attention to Laura Lee requirements. Mr. Eisner had not chosen small mills because Laura Lee would overtax their capacities.

He had not chosen large mills because Laura Lee's business was not big enough to impress the biggest mills. Those he chose did an annual volume of $10 million to $15 million. Mr. Eisner said his plan was his own innovation. As far as he knew, no other garment maker had such an arrangement.

CATALOGS, ADVERTISING, AND PROMOTION

When Samuel Fischer joined Laura Lee, the company did not publish a catalog but printed a simple black-and-white price list several pages long. About 100,000 of these were used per year and the total cost, which was borne by Laura Lee, was less than $5,000 a year.

There had been mounting pressure from the sales organization for the company to print an illustrated catalog which salesmen and retailers could use as a sales tool. Some competitors did this. Bernard Fischer had allowed Samuel Fischer to print illustrated catalogs on the consideration that the retailers pay only a part of the cost. He insisted that any catalog had to be a quality production, in keeping with the high-quality standards of Laura Lee. The original catalog was 14 pages long, illustrated in full color, cost about 15¢, and was sold to those retailers who wanted it at 7¢.

As the Laura Lee line expanded, the catalog was enlarged to 40 pages. Professionals now did the art work, modeling, and the layout, and studio costs alone were over $60,000 a year. The retailers, who believed that the catalogs helped them, used them liberally. About 4 million catalogs were printed each year. The cost of the books was estimated to be 21¢ apiece; the price to retailers had been raised to 10¢.

Samuel Fischer made up figures which indicated that catalog production had cost the company over $400,000 in 1969. He proposed that the price of the books be raised to at least 20¢. He would even be willing, he said, to charge the retailers 25¢, which he believed to be the true cost of the catalogs. His thinking was that the retailers would not object to paying 25¢ for a book that was such a big help to them in selling. He also pointed out that if the company could recover part of the $400,000 cost of the books each year, this would add to Laura Lee's annual profit. Bernard Fischer was very reluctant to raise the price of the books. He pointed out that Laura Lee had been in a good profit position throughout the period in which the catalogs had been upgraded.

In addition to the catalogs, which were a necessary part of the garment business, Laura Lee did a modest amount of advertising. The only medium which had been used in the past was a few magazines of limited circulation, and the advertising had been aimed more at recruiting new retailers than at selling merchandise. Since coming to Laura Lee, Samuel Fischer had been under mounting pressure from salesmen and retailers for some expanded program of advertising. Samuel Fischer had considered numerous enlarged advertising plans, including shared-expense plans in which the company would furnish copy and mats free to retailers, with the company sharing the cost of advertising placed by the retailers, probably on a 50:50 basis. There was a reluctance to go into national advertising because Laura Lee sales territories did not yet extend to all parts of the country.

In November, 1970, Samuel Fischer announced that management had decided upon a considerably enlarged program of advertising with a theme which would emphasize the fashion appeal of Laura Lee garments. A $350,000 advertising expenditure had been budgeted for the coming year; the company was going to go national in advertising, to bring the Laura Lee message to tens of millions of potential customers. Page-size magazine ads in full color were to appear in such periodicals as *McCalls, Mademoiselle, Harper's Bazaar, Vanity Fair, The New Yorker, Life, Family Circle,* and *Woman's Day*. Samuel Fischer said that he had deliberately chosen a few sophisticated magazines, like *Vanity Fair* and *The New Yorker,* which he realized were not ordinarily read by Laura Lee customers. To stretch his advertising expenditure he intended to place a limited number of ads in this type of magazine; the ads would be reprinted and identified as to source and used in showcard form in dealers' shops and display windows, in direct mailings, and in Laura Lee catalogs. Mr. Fischer felt that this use of these magazines would lend an aura of sophistication which would impress Laura Lee customers.

To aid in promotion of Laura Lee's line, David Rose proposed to Bernard Fischer that he be allowed to experiment with putting on traveling fashion shows at airports. To do this he intended to lease a large plane, perhaps even the new Lockheed Hercules cargo-carrying "air-truck," capable of carrying a full entourage of models and the total line of Laura Lee garments. Using berthing accommodations for the personnel, including twin alternating flying crews, a single airplane flying westward could show the combined Laura Lee lines to retailers assembled at as many as four airports across the country in a single day. David Rose was ecstatic at the prospect of the novelty value of the airport fashion shows, which, as far as he knew, had never before been attempted. Samuel Fischer was skeptical, saying that he had heard that the operating cost of such an aircraft was $15 a minute while on the ground and $30 a minute when aloft. Bernard Fischer was inclined to give the idea a limited tryout but had not yet consented to do so.

NEW DEVELOPMENTS—U-SEW-IT

The concentration of all Laura Lee cutting operations in Bridgeport gave Mr. Bernard Fischer an idea. "In recent years there has been a rebirth of interest in home sewing," he said. "With our new efficient cutting operation at Bridgeport, we are in an excellent position to capitalize on it." The result was Laura Lee's U-Sew-It operation.

The new U-Sew-It Division offered the customer cut pieces of any Laura Lee garment (except knits) in her size, together with a pattern and directions for sewing. Customers were informed of the U-Sew-It plan through a full page in the Laura Lee catalog and by poster-sized showcards in Laura Lee retail shops. Each retailer was asked to buy a book of fabric swatches from which the customer could choose her preferred material. Retailers were supplied with order forms, which were mailed to the Bridgeport plant. A separate unit at Bridgeport filled each order singly and mailed it directly, on a C.O.D. basis, to the customer. Each order included buttons, thread, and bindings. Retailers received a percentage on every order. Billing, shipping, and retailer commissions were computerized.

"Our U-Sew-It Division," said Mr. Fischer, "will bring us a whole new segment of sales from women who do all their own sewing and would not buy our finished garments anyway. They will be attracted by our stylish garments and our offerings of fabrics, many of which they would not find in yard goods shops. U-Sew-It will relieve them of the task of cutting the pieces of the garment, which is perhaps the biggest job in home sewing. Our cuttings will be ample in size, so that the housewife has leeway to make individual adjustments. She will duplicate our finished garments exactly, at a lower price, have a perfect fit, and have the proud satisfaction which comes with being able to say that she sewed the garment herself." Bernard Fischer had planned prices which would be enough below finished-garment prices to be attractive and would still be high enough to sustain profit margins. "If this system works," he said, "we will earn just as much profit on a U-Sew-It dress as on one of our finished garments."

U-Sew-It was introduced in the Summer 1968 Laura Lee catalog. Although retailers were assured that they would earn as much on a U-Sew-It sale as on the sale of a finished garment, many of them did not believe this and feared that U-Sew-It would encourage the trend toward home sewing and cut into their sales. Only about half of them were willing to buy the sample books and place the showcard posters in their shops, and protests to the salesmen and to Bridgeport forced Mr. Fischer to remove the page from future Laura Lee catalogs. Sales for the latter half of 1968 met Mr. Fischer's expectation, but cost figures indicated a net operating loss.

In 1969 Mr. Fischer advertised U-Sew-It widely in national magazines. The ads invited women to send in a coupon requesting a brochure on the U-Sew-It plan and the Laura Lee catalog. The ads also invited women to stop in at any Laura Lee retail shop to see Laura Lee garments and to ask the retailer about U-Sew-It. This resulted in increased U-Sew-It sales for those retailers who had sample books and went along with the plan, but it was resented by those retailers who objected to U-Sew-It. During the year frictions developed in the Bridgeport plant. The U-Sew-It employees complained that the "regular" cutting employees tended to monopolize the cutting schedules, pushing U-Sew-It aside as being small and unimportant compared to the big orders processed for Laura Lee finished garments.

In 1970 Bernard Fischer opened company-owned U-Sew-It stores in Ames, Iowa; Lancaster, Pennsylvania; South Bend, Indiana; Wheeling, West Virginia; Ironton, Ohio; and Paducah, Kentucky. These cities had been carefully selected as being in areas where U-Sew-It would have appeal.

U-Sew-It sales volume in 1969–1970 was $327,000 and showed a net loss of $83,000. Sales in 1971 were $684,000 and showed a net loss of $37,000. During 1971, seventeen Laura Lee retailers dropped the entire Laura Lee line because they objected to the U-Sew-It operation. "We're bleeding a little," said Mr. Bernard Fischer, "and we're going to bleed a little more, but it isn't going to kill us. Some day U-Sew-It is going to be big business. It's just taking a little longer to catch on than I expected. I tell the doubters to look at the unpainted furniture business. That didn't skyrocket overnight either, but today it's a big deal, and it's here to stay."

8

BARTL'S
BREWERY

On January 1, 1965, control of Bartl's Brewery, of Dayton, Ohio, was turned over to Mr. Royce Chandler and his associates. The management of Bartl's had been in turmoil for several years, and during the preceding two years the company had been operated by a court-appointed receiver. Mr. Chandler's acquisition of the company climaxed protracted negotiations which eliminated the old stockholders and management, and a reorganized company emerged. Publicly, Mr. Chandler voiced enthusiasm about the prospects for Bartl's future. "We will see to it," he said, "that this fine old firm, which has weathered many a storm in its hundred-year history, will maintain its rightful place in Dayton industry." Privately, he and his associates in the new management were still trying to settle upon a definite course of action.

HISTORY

Bartl's, the oldest brewery in Ohio, was founded in 1862 by Bernhard Bartl, who learned brewing in Germany and emigrated to America in 1855. After working as a brewer in St. Louis and Milwaukee, he leased the plant of a defunct brewery on the site of the present Bartl's Brewery and began his own business. Success came quickly; when Bernhard Bartl died in 1898, he was reputed to be wealthy, and Bartl's was a thriving concern.

Bernhard Bartl, Jr., nicknamed "Judge" Bartl because he had studied law, followed his father as manager of the brewery. He preferred the brewing business to the practice of law and spent two years in Cincinnati studying "modern and scientific brewing techniques," then joined his father. Judge Bartl's management of the brewery was thrifty, conservative, and prudent. He added a chain of taverns which Bartl's began operating in 1900, introduced a limited line of bottled beer in 1913, switched to near beer during Prohibition, and enlarged the plant to double its capacity when Prohibition was repealed.

In 1935, Judge Bartl was joined by Bartl Koerner, the only son of the Judge's only sister, who had shared equally with the Judge in the inheritance of the brewery. Bartl started as a salesman and subsequently held a number of offices in sales and operations. After five years he was sharing the management of the brewery with his uncle. The Judge supervised production; Bartl Koerner managed everything else. The joint management went smoothly for 11 years. During this period Bartl's was making a profit and continued to expand. Bartl Koerner extended sales into the periphery of the Dayton market, added canned beer, and in a single spectacular crash promotion entered Bartl's in the Indianapolis market, which eventually grew to be as large as Bartl's home market in Dayton.

Before World War II the large national brewers had operated from single central breweries because the lack of a uniform water supply would have caused beers brewed at other points to be "off flavor." Their strategy had been to produce beers which were presumably premium in quality and could command the higher prices which warranted the expense of shipping them to distant points. After the war new technologies solved the water problem, and national breweries proceeded to establish branch plants, brew locally, and sell at local prices. Canned beer became popular, and a myriad of competitive innovations were introduced by the nationals: "pop-tops," "rack-packs," "zip-caps," and "cold-packs." A wide variety of shapes and sizes appeared in cans, bottles, and widemouthed "mug-jugs." The total consumption of beer increased substantially, but the increase was in home consumption, while there was a trend away from tavern drinking (see Exhibits 7 to 9). Throughout its history Bartl's had featured draught beer sold to the bar trade. Company profits declined from $1.7 million net in 1947 to $92,000 in 1951.

In 1952, Judge Bartl, then 81, became chairman of the board, and Bartl Koerner, who had been executive vice president for 11 years, was elected president. Judge Bartl brought in James Randall, a furniture executive, whom he made executive vice president and general manager. Bartl Koerner succeeded in ousting Mr. Randall and voiding his 10 year contract, publicly charging his uncle with senility and saying that "he never knew anything more than how to make beer—the way it was made 60 years ago. . . ." Thereupon, the Judge forced Bartl Koerner from the presidency, stating that he had developed megalomania and believed himself capable of succeeding at anything, even converting Bartl's into a national brewery. For 15 months—January, 1953, through March, 1954,—Koerner was in a state of psychic depression, the presidency remained vacant, and the company was managed by the sales manager. Backed by his mother and his wife, who was independently wealthy, Bartl Koerner appointed six board members who re-elected him president. The first thing Bartl Koerner did was to fire the sales manager. The Judge tried again to oust Bartl, charging him with wasteful and extravagant management. Failing in this attempt, the Judge resigned from the board in 1956, leaving control of the company to Bartl Koerner. In 1957 Judge Bartl died.

Sales and profits continued to decline in the period from 1956 to 1962. Local retailers were not sure that Bartl's would survive the effects of the previous infighting for control. Within a year of Koerner's return in 1956, sales volume fell 45%. Koerner blamed his uncle, who, he said, had put all the company's capital into bricks and mortar. He launched a huge sales drive with little result, and after another five years of losses—January, 1958, to December, 1962—the company went into voluntary receivership (Exhibits 1 and 2). The first official act of the trustee was to dismiss Bartl Koerner

In January, 1965, the reorganized company emerged, the trustee asserting: "We released many employees, cut salaries and wages, cut many expenses, and insisted on a general austerity program. Within a year we were no longer operating on a hand-to-mouth basis. We were able to make ends meet, were earning a profit, and didn't have to borrow additional funds from the banks." (Exhibits 1 to 3. See also Exhibits 11 and 12 for comparable national figures.) On January 1, 1965, the reorganized company was turned over to the group headed by Royce Chandler.

THE REORGANIZATION

Royce Chandler, who played the leading role in the reorganization, had been operating a Dayton advertising firm called Chandler and

Associates. Bartl's Brewery was one of his clients. Mr. Chandler was described as "a warm and enthusiastic man, always buoyant and with an ever-hopeful disposition." His agency had a reputation for creativity and had launched numerous successful advertising campaigns which were said to have made Mr. Chandler a millionaire. At the end of 1964, Bartl's owed Mr. Chandler a total of $70,000, an accumulation of approximately two years of fees (Exhibit 2).

Under the Chandler reorganization plan effected January 1, 1965, holders of the old preferred stock received, on a share-for-share basis, new preferred stock in the reorganized company. Holders of the old common stock received nothing. Five hundred thousand dollars in new common stock ($1 par) was subscribed and paid for. All delinquent accounts were paid in full; all other accounts were carried forward to the reorganized company.

Mr. Chandler called his plan the "Chandler–Dayton-Businessmen and Bartl's Brewery Employees' Reorganization Plan." "This is not just an ordinary business reorganization," said Mr. Chandler, "this is the fulfillment of an ideal."

"Raising capita was not our prime objective," said Mr. Chandler, "we were more interested in people than in money. We wanted to make Bartl's Brewery a 'people's brewery' operated by Dayton businessmen, with every employee and every stockholder a part owner of the business. We eliminated the 'beer baron' concept, under which one man dominates a brewery. We have selected carefully the business leaders we have permitted to join us, and we have limited their subscriptions to 20,000 shares each. Thus, no one individual will dominate the board and dictate policy. We are especially proud of the fact that every employee and key executive of Bartl's has become a co-owner of the brewery. I could have bought the brewery myself. Several of my friends offered to buy all of the common stock. We rejected all these offers and have selected instead a plan whereby the investors will work together as a team of coequals."

Upon the request of Chandler, all active employees subscribed to the minimum of 100 shares of the new issue of common stock; some bought more. Mr. Chandler, with undisclosed associates whom he represented, subscribed to 100,000 shares and became president of the brewery at a salary of $2,500 a month. He brought into the company two of his agency associates: Selden Spears, who was made vice president of operations, at $1,500 a month; and Elbert Holbrook, vice president of sales, at $1,300 a month. The brewmaster, treasurer, controller, and purchasing agent were each invited to subscribe 10,000 shares, which they did, and they were continued in their offices (Exhibit 6). "Our group recognizes and commends the loyalty and the willing efforts of the supervisory and management personnel," said Mr. Chandler. "Each of them will be given job security and the opportunity for advancement."

The Dayton businessmen who subscribed were vendors and other creditors of Bartl's. A strong advocate of the plan had been Jacob Pardisi, regional agent for the United Brotherhood of Brewers, which represented the Bartl employees.

THE TAX LIEN

Mr. Chandler's reorganization had been based upon the assumption that Bartl's would be exonerated from a pending Federal claim for taxes. The claim arose from four years under Bartl Koerner's management during which, the revenue bureau claimed, Koerner and his friends had charged lavish Bahama winter vacations to company expense when these trips actually had nothing to do with the brewery. The original claim was for an additional $390,000. In a preliminary decision which ruled out fraudulent intent, the claim was cut to $272,800. From this action Mr. Chandler had assumed that the entire claim would eventually be dropped.

On January 14, 1965, two weeks after the reorganization date, the courts declared $125,600 of the $272,800 government claim valid, payable by the end of 1965. The new Chandler management was shocked at the realization that this would cut into the $500,000 additional capital it had raised. After take-over expenses and the payment of delinquent claims, working capital amounted to about $245,000. However, management was considering borrowing the money from two Dayton banks where Chandler had established lines of credit for Bartl's as part of the reorganization process. The banks had extended the credit on the understanding that they would receive a first mortgage on all of the brewery's real estate, plant, and equipment if the credit were used.

COMPETITION AND PACKAGING

When Mr. Chandler took over, he estimated that only 40% of Bartl's volume was in packaged form (15% canned and 25% bottled) and that the remaining 60% was sold as draught beer. He realized that in 1963 over 80% of national beer consumption was in packaged[1] form (see Exhibit 9).

Bartl's had always produced premium beer and sold it in draught form. It had been slow to get into packaging and when it did tended to favor bottles. Its market was mostly local, confined to Dayton, Indianapolis, and other areas of Ohio and Indiana. In recent years all of its markets had been invaded by the nationals, whose brands were backed by strong national advertising and promotion programs.

Mr. Chandler saw Bartl's competition as (1) Henkel's, a Dayton brewery smaller than Bartl's whose output was 50% draught and 50% packaged; (2) the Superb Brewery of Fort Wayne, larger than Bartl's, which sold mostly packaged beers, marketed in several states and in Chicago, and was a direct competitor in Indianapolis; (3) several national breweries, which sold mostly canned beers. Bartl's was the only one featuring a superior brew.

Bartl's had always been an advocate of draught beer. Beer drinkers of discriminating taste considered draught beer to be superior in flavor to packaged beer, and brewmasters generally agreed with them. August Burg, Bartl's brewmaster, was also strongly of this conviction. "Packaged beers taste as differently from draught beer," he said, "as cabbage tastes from sauerkraut. Can or bottle it and it is no longer the real thing. People don't seem to care about taste anymore, though. They'll even drink bottled beer at a bar that serves the same beer on tap."

Initially Bartl's produced draught beer only; it added bottles in 1913. In 1946, the industry turned to canned beer and found immediate consumer acceptance. Judge Bartl had waited until every competitor was selling canned beer before he reluctantly joined the trend in 1951, and then he permitted only the canning of Bartl's standard-grade, lower-priced brew, Bartl's Bonus Brew (Triple B brand). Later a beer between the standard and premium grades was added which was sold only in cans. The cans were sold in selected non-tavern areas through grocers. Bartl's Premium was sold only in kegs and as recently as 1958 had been delivered in central Dayton on a wagon drawn by a team of elegantly-harnessed Clydesdales. It had been an axiom of Judge Bartl that "the brewery that makes the best brew and has the biggest horses and the fanciest brass ornaments makes the most sales." When Mr. Chandler

---

[1] Packaged beer is beer sold in cans and bottles. All other beer is draught beer sold in kegs or barrels.

took over, Bartl's was still canning only its two bread-and-butter brands on two canning machines which were over 10 years old and turned out only one third as many cans per minute as modern equipment.

Mr. Holbrook, sales vice president, was in favor of switching all brands to cans and placing heavy promotion behind the move, concentrating on retail grocery outlets and packaged-liquor stores. He had statistics showing that over half of all packaged beer was sold in grocery stores, and that women purchased 50% of this, even though they drank only about 30% of it. "They don't buy for taste," he said. "Even the men don't care about flavor anymore. After the first glassful, they don't care what they're drinking" Mr. Burg, the brewmaster, argued against the idea. He pointed out that this would require the purchase of modern canning machines; that more plant space would have to be built; and that draught beer wholesaled for less, yet brought higher margins to both brewers and distributors.

Bartl's had six draught beer salesmen calling on the local tavern trade to take orders for beer, which was delivered to them once a week. Four draught beer salesmen traveled in the rural areas of Ohio and Indiana. Sales of bottled and canned beer were handled as house accounts. Packaged liquor stores' and grocers' orders were taken by two sales assistants. Draught deliveries were made in Bartl's trucks; package deliveries were farmed out to a cartage company except for Bartl's own taverns (see Exhibit 5 and 9).

Taverns selling Bartl's draught beer were not sold bottled beer. Mr. Chandler proposed to sell them any and all forms. Grocery stores preferred cans to bottles, because cans took less shelf space and eliminated the nuisance of handling return bottles. Canned national brands which were coming into local markets were heavily advertised. Mr. Chandler was not convinced that the quality of any brew was of first importance. "The housewife who buys in a grocery store will choose whatever name first pops into her head," said Mr. Chandler. "If we advertise enough, that name will be Bartl's."

MARKET RESEARCH

In 1957, Bartl Koerner had for the first time used market consultants to make studies of the local markets. Mr. Chandler held that this had been done out of desperation and at exorbitant expense, and he questioned Bartl Koerner's ability to interpret the findings. Mr. Chandler stated that his long experience in advertising gave him ample knowledge of the market and he had no intention of using consultants. He would use only *Brewer's Almanac* data and surveys made by local newspapers (see Exhibit 13).

THE UNIONS AND PROFIT SHARING

In the third week of January, Mr. Chandler met with the employees to discuss a profit-sharing plan which he had devised. He wished to do this before meeting with the union leaders on April 1 to negotiate the annual union contract. Mr. Chandler handled this himself because the company no longer had a personnel manager. "We might hire a personnel director again when we have need for one," said Mr. Chandler. "Now that our employees are co-owners of the brewery we may never again need one." Mr. Chandler emphasized to the employees that he was now talking to them in their new role, in which they were co-owners and co-managers of the brewery. In his profit-sharing plan he proposed that the first 10% of net profit after taxes be reserved as a base return for stockholders. Above that, each worker would receive an additional 1/2 of 1% of his gross pay for each additional 1% of net profit earned. Above 15% net earnings each employee would receive a 1% bonus for each 1% addition to net profit. Sales, production and financial figures were to be given to each employee monthly. The profit-sharing plan was to take the place of any current increase in wage and salary rates, but only for the present.

The initial employee reaction to the plan was cool, but when 59% of them voted for it, unanimous agreement was obtained. Included in the majority group were office employees, who were not union members. When they learned of the employees' decision, the union leaders objected strongly and had several discussions with the employees and with Mr. Chandler, but the employees held to the plan.

The bonuses were to be paid out after each monthly accounting period. January and February both resulted in losses. In mid-March, at a time when the company was short of working capital, a canning machine was shut down for repairs and 24 employees were laid off for two weeks. March figures again showed a loss.

When Mr. Chandler met with the union for contract negotiations, the union leaders, claiming unanimous employee backing, asked for a cancellation of the profit-sharing plan and a straight 35¢ per hour increase. Negotiations were conducted in an atmosphere which Mr. Chandler described as "belligerent and hostile and altogether unrealistic." At times during the bargaining the union threatened to call a strike. It also threatened to publish advertisements in the Dayton papers challenging Mr. Chandler to make good his boast that Bartl's was now managed by its employees who were co-owners, a threat which Mr. Chandler called blackmail.

The bargaining ended in the dropping of the profit-sharing plan, and the company settled for a wage rate that was no higher than wages generally in Dayton, but that placed Bartl's wages 32¢ above the national brewing industry average. The office employees, who were nonunion, retained the profit-sharing plan. "One of these months," said Mr. Chandler, "we will be earning substantial profits and will be sharing them with our office staff. It will be interesting then to see the reaction of the union members."

PRICING

In April, 1965, Mr. Chandler announced his intention of raising Bartl's prices to retailers. "Dayton," said Mr. Chandler, "is the cheapest beer market in the United States. The retail price of beer here is just about the same as the wholesale price in other areas." The new schedule of prices included a 23¢ increase to retailers on a case of twenty-four 12-ounce bottles, raising the price from $2.60 to $2.83 a case. Henkel's, a Dayton competitor, announced that it also intended to raise prices. The Superb Brewery of Fort Wayne, another competitor did not raise prices but publicly stated that increased costs justified a raise in prices.

Bartl-owned taverns, which featured draught beer, did not raise the bottle price. Other taverns in Dayton and Indianapolis raised their prices from 30¢ to 35¢ a bottle. Contrary to expectations, the competitive breweries did not raise their Dayton and Indianapolis prices but did raise their prices in other markets where prices in general were higher. To make the new price more acceptable to customers, Mr. Chandler ran a series of ads in local papers, featuring the theme "the 30¢ bottle of beer, like the 5¢ cigar, is on its way out."

Three weeks later, after suffering a substantial loss in volume, Mr. Chandler rescinded the price increase. "We had assumed," said Mr. Chandler, "that the general level of local prices would go up. It is incredible that our competitors raised prices in other places but not in Dayton and Indianapolis. We hope that most of our old customers will return to Bartl's beer and sell it again for 30¢ a bottle" (see Exhibit 4).

VELVET GOLD

In May, 1965, a faulty canning machine left too much air in the cans, allowing the beer to continue to ferment inside them and resulting in a beer that brewers termed "skunky" because its strong flavor gave the drinker "beer breath." In eliminating the trouble the Bartl brewers did two things: first, they adjustd the vacuum controls, and in doing so they inadvertently overcompensated; second, they removed the light brown crust of foam which appeared as a normal thing on the surface of all fermenting beer in the open fermentation process. To their surprise, they found that they had brewed a beer that was excepitonally light and pale, comparable to the highest quality premium beers. Also, the new brew seemed to leave absolutely no aftertaste.

Mr. Chandler believed that they had chanced upon a revolutionary improvement in the age-old brewing process. In presenting their discovery to the board of directors, Mr. Chandler said, "Elimination of 'beer breath' will put us leagues ahead of anyone in the industry, including the nationals."

Mr. Chandler proposed that Bartl's introduce the new brew as a fourth item in its line. He named it Velvet Gold and planned to market it in golden cans and gold-foil–sheathed bottles. The introduction was to be launched by heavy promotion and advertising on radio and television and in the regional editions of national magazines. His ad theme featured the slogan "Smooth as Velvet, Rich as Gold." Canned and bottled Velvet Gold was to be sold as a super-quality brew at prices which were higher than those of most premium beers.[2] It was to be distributed through all channels, with heavy emphasis on grocery stores.

Mr. Chandler had the brewers condense the crust of foam which they had removed and put it in pill-sized bottles labeled "Slurge." These bottles were mounted on a placard which explained that the nauseous-looking moldy liquid in the little bottle was the dregs which other brewers left in their beers, giving the drinker "beer breath," and that only Bartl's was purified of "slurge." These exhibits were presented to taverns to be placed on bars.

[2] Premium beers are considered lighter, smoother, and in general easier to drink.

DISTRIBUTORSHIPS

Mr. Chandler believed that operating the brewery at full capacity would be the only means of achieving low-cost production; that high volume would help to absorb overhead expenses; and that rising sales would have an immeasurably stimulating effect on Bartl's employees and customers alike and relieve Bartl's of its tarnished public image.

In June, Mr. Chandler and Mr. Holbrook proceeded to expand Bartl's regional territory by taking on additional distributorships in neighboring areas. At first distributors were to cover Ohio and southern Indiana; later southern Michigan, western Pennsylvania, and West Virginia were to be added. A third campaign would take in all of Kentucky, where beer sales were regulated by counties.

Mr. Chandler thought that Bartl's premium quality beer could compete favorably with the nationals and that his personal skill in advertising would enable him to match the national advertising of the national brands. As an initial inducement, prices to new distributors were shaded by as much as 11¢ in the expectation that strong consumer acceptance would later enable prices to be raised. Quick delivery in Bartl's trucks in LCL lots would be at lower cost than the carload shipments of the national brewers.

After two months Mr. Chandler considered the first phase to be successful. Sales volume had increased substantially, but costs had risen disproportionately, resulting in a slight loss on the new business. Some national brands had resorted to a strategy of selling at local prices, which caused Mr. Chandler to delay raising prices in the new territories. He also hesitated to enter Kentucky without further investigation.

BARTL'S TAVERNS

In 1965, Bartl's was still operating nine taverns in Dayton, the remnant of a chain of twenty-eight which Judge Bartl had viewed as a means of selling draught beer. The Judge had called them rathskellers or *Bierstubes;* the public called them saloons.

There was a growing realization in the brewing industry that local barrooms were passing out of the American scene. "The old-fashioned neighborhood tavern," said a brewery executive, "was once a comfortable haven where work-sore husbands and fathers could take refuge and relax . . . but it is now slowly but surely heading for oblivion. Brewers' eyes have to be on the supermarket, on back-yard patios, and on picnic grounds. That's where you sell beer today." Mr. Chandler was undecided about keeping Bartl's nine remaining taverns in operation.

One tavern on the suburban edge of the city was known as "The Garden" because it had attached to it an open-air beer garden so popular that it gave promise of becoming a Dayton tradition. When the weather permitted, the beer garden, where only draught beer was served, was filled to overcapacity. In the barroom, which had the atmosphere of a cocktail lounge, considerably more liquor than beer was served. The Garden did a big business at cocktail hours all year round, and the beer garden did an overflow business weekends and holidays, weather permitting. It served food only in the evenings and offered a limited and unchanging menu of plate suppers: roast beef or pork, a fish item, and steaks. Portions were hearty, the cooking was plain but excellent, and a meal cost from $1.50 to $2.

A second tavern, located in an old industrial section and dubbed "The Gashouse," served cold sandwiches of hearty proportions to local factory workers. Its offerings were limited to ham, salami, swiss cheese, hardboiled eggs, pickled herrings, and kippers, which were served only at lunch hours. Beer was the main beverage served to men only.

The largest of the Bartl taverns, known simply as "Clark Street," was situated in downtown Dayton between the shopping and office section and the railroad depots. Clark Street was open from 10 A.M. until 2 A.M. It served a fairly wide variety of cold sandwiches, hot sandwiches of beef, pork, corned beef, and baked thüringer, and plates of hot corned beef or roast beef hash. It was the only Bartl tavern that served food at all hours. It was renowned in Dayton for the size of its sandwiches—four slices of ham or almost an inch of swiss cheese was normal—and the price was only 50¢. A very mixed clientele was served, and the sales of beer and liquor were about equal.

A fourth tavern, the University Pub, situated adjacent to a branch of a large university, did a sizable volume that was almost entirely draught beer. The Pub had no cooking facilities but served snack items such as potato chips and pretzels. It was heavily patronized by students, both men and coeds.

Every tavern required union grill men, and some of them required bus boys and dishwashers. The Garden and Clark Street required full-time chefs. Bartenders and food service employees belonged to different unions, and each refused to share the others' work. Headquarters had constant union and personnel problems with the food taverns. The small staffs made any absenteeism a critical problem. Day help was used to fill vacancies, there were frequent jurisdictional disputes, and most of the food-service help remained only a short time.

The Garden regularly incurred sizable losses in its food business which were offset by the profits it made on cocktails and liquors. Clark Street made a regular profit on beer and liquor sales and a modest but steady profit on its large volume of food sales. The Gashouse broke even on food sales, and made a profit on its large draught beer volume.

According to the income statements (Mr. Chandler questioned the accuracy of the accounting data) the whole chain of taverns was operating at a profit, but in some years the final net profit of the chain was less than $1,000. Some taverns were profitable; some were not. The profits and losses, however, had averaged less than $1,000 for the past five years. The controller wanted to close them; the brewmaster, however, was in favor of keeping them and proposed starting a few in Indianapolis. Mr. Chandler felt that he ought to give his attention to regional and national marketing.

There were 178 independently owned taverns in Dayton, and most tavern operators resented the Bartl-owned taverns, believing that Bartl's Brewery subsidized the taverns and operated them at losses for the public-relations benefits involved. Only 48 independently owned taverns handled Bartl's draught beer. No other brewery operated its own taverns. No Bartl-owned tavern sold competing packaged liquors. Virtually every independently owned tavern did.

The taverns were a constant subject of argument among the Bartl management. Some claimed the effort was not worth the small profit. Tavern managers claimed the actual net was larger; that too much headquarters overhead was charged to them although headquarters gave them no service. All the taverns managers claimed the taverns generated business for Bartl's everywhere.

Some believed that the cocktail-lounge atmosphere of the Garden barroom was not in keeping with the Bartl image. Others charged that Clark Street and Gashouse sandwiches were too large and their prices too low. The managers claimed that the outsized sandwiches drew trade from a six-block radius and that changing prices or portions would kill their business. The Gashouse manager insisted that it was the large sandwiches which supported his profitable beer trade. Some criticized the taverns for being just as simple and austere as they had been 40 years ago. There was no entertainment, no dancing, and a minimum of decor. Even the Garden did not use linens for table service.

DIRECT DISTRIBUTION

By September, 1965, sales volume had exceeded expectations and was continuing to rise, but profits had not improved. Mr. Chandler and Mr. Holbrook were discussing the possibility of converting to direct distribution in the new territories. This would mean tripling the sales force and adding a sales supervisor. It would involve inventories, credit, bad-debt losses, smaller trucks, and more frequent deliveries. Canned beer would be featured, saving 1/3 of the shipping space, but more canning machines would be needed. Mr. Chandler hesitated to make the move because of the capital requirements involved—one fully automated line of canning equipment would cost from $275,000 to $400,000.[3] "We prefer to be a self-sustaining operation," he said, "and not get involved with the banks."

VELVET GOLD

Velvet Gold had produced an initial spurt of volume, but by October, 1965, sales were steadily declining. Unexpected developments had occurred. The "slurge" sales theme was resented by all competitors, who used paid advertisements to refute it, saying that there was a normal amount of residue in all brewing processes. The National Brewers' Association deplored the publicity being given to the possible impurity of all beers and censured Bartl's sales tactic as "unorthodox, if not unethical, and certainly not in good taste." It asked Mr. Chandler to desist from using the "slurge" bottles. At the height of the publicity a competing tavern operator derisively nicknamed Velvet Gold "Vicious Gook," a name that caught on and spread through tavern circles and through the trade.

In mid-October, Mr. Chandler offered Velvet Gold in draught form to local tavern operators at regular beer prices. Every one of them turned it down. Thereafter, Mr. Chandler wondered if he should quietly withdraw Velvet Gold from the Bartl line. He was reluctant to do so because sizable expenditures had been incurred in promoting it, and he felt it might catch on in the future.

---

[3] Included in the line would be a canner, a sealer, filling equipment, packers, and required conveyors.

BARTL'S BAVARIAN

Mr. Chandler was still convinced that there was a place in the Bartl line for a super-quality, premium-priced beer. Imported beers such as Dortmund DAB and other pilsner beers were gaining rapidly in popularity and sold at high prices. Recognizing this, some national breweries had undertaken to produce pseudo-foreign beers which they marketed under names that gave the impression that they were actually foreign. Mr. Burg, the brewmaster, thought that this would be a good strategy for Bartl's and assured Mr. Chandler that he would have no difficulty brewing a beer that was genuinely "German import" in character. Mr. Holbrook thought that the idea had merit. In December, 1965, Bartl's Bavarian was introduced in draught form to the tavern trade in Dayton at regular prices, and it met with a good reception. If consumer acceptance proved good enough, it was planned to extend its sales in bottle form, but there was no intention to sell it in cans.

SHIPMENTS CROSS-COUNTRY

The initial response of Bartl's Bavarian was good, but it was followed by a sales slump. Mr. Chandler interpreted this as the normal pattern for a newly introduced product and felt sure that the new brew had good potential. He proposed that it be sold in draught and in bottle form on a national basis, beginning in markets which were far from Bartl's home territory. His thinking, said Mr. Chandler, was in keeping with the Biblical saying that "a prophet is not without honor except in his own country." Mr. Chandler and Mr. Holbrook traveled to Arkansas and Texas to secure distributorships. In mid-January one carload was shipped to Little Rock and another to Dallas, each carload covered with huge decorative signs announcing the arrival of Bartl's Bavarian in the new territory. Mr. Chandler also arranged extensive advertising to launch the newly introduced Bavarian entirely at Bartl's expense. If results in the next two months were satisfactory, he was considering extending sales into Oklahoma and other parts of Texas.

MERGER RUMORS

In January, 1966, Mr. Chandler met with the press to deny rumors that Bartl's was in financial difficulty and was seeking to sell out.[4]

---

[4] The $125,600 tax lien had not yet been paid.

"Bartl's Brewery is now operating profitably," he said, "and we do not intend to cheapen the value of its properties by putting them on the auction block. I did not become president of this respected and long-prosperous institution to preside over its liquidation. The brewing industry is going through a period of trial. Since repeal over 600 breweries have gone out of business. Of the 200 that remain, less than half will survive the coming decade. Cutthroat competition from national breweries, price cutting, rising wages, and taxes will bankrupt many more small breweries. Only the strong regional or semi-regional breweries will survive. Bartl's Brewery will definitely be one of the survivors."

exhibit 1 BARTL'S BREWERY
Statement of consolidated income (years ending December 31)

	1959	1960	1961	1962	1963	1964
Sales	$3,502,108	$3,141,244	$2,782,824	$2,422,401	$2,871,264	$3,500,367
Less federal and state excise taxes	990,941	877,525	771,111	672,526	1,012,159	1,200,814
Net sales	$2,511,167	$2,263,719	$2,011,713	$1,749,875	$1,859,105	$2,299,553
Cost of goods sold	1,767,240	1,572,652	1,383,584	1,180,044	1,270,044	1,672,267
Gross profit	$ 743,927	$ 691,067	$ 628,129	$ 569,831	$ 589,061	$ 627,286
Selling and delivery expenses	572,636	514,574	509,253	478,745	411,991	420,034
Administrative and general expenses	269,447	214,206	209,777	193,427	125,207	137,207
Total	$ 742,083	$ 728,780	$ 719,030	$ 672,172	$ 537,198	$ 557,241
Profit from operations	1,844	(37,713)	(90,901)	(102,341)	51,863	70,045
Other income	14,466	22,583	19,512	16,154		
Gross income	$ 16,310	$ (15,130)	$ (71,389)	$ (86,187)	$ 51,863	$ 70,045
Income charges:						
Interest	10,800	7,528	7,805	16,154	12,837	13,569
Other	21,700	11,291	7,791	12,116	17,116	19,046
Total	$ 32,500	$ 18,819	$ 15,596	$ 28,270	$ 29,953	$ 32,615
Income before provision for taxes	(16,190)	(33,949)	(86,985)	(114,457)	21,910	37,430
Provision for income taxes						
Net income for the year	$ (16,190)	$ (33,949)	$ (86,985)	$ (114,457)	$ 21,910	$ 37,430

Balance sheet, 1959–1965

Assets	1959	1960	1961	1962	1963	1964	Jan. 30, 1965*
Current assets:							
Cash	$ 74,261	$ 63,763	$ 31,767	$ 28,928	$ 34,071	$ 31,601	$ 365,924
Revenue stamps	18,569	15,569	14,931	10,284	12,412	13,987	30,791
Trade accounts receivable	265,690	302,360	354,326	328,884	339,301	341,944	343,640
Other receivables	31,426	27,512	16,966	14,791	14,439	13,038	13,068
Total	$ 389,946	$ 409,204	$ 417,990	$ 382,887	$ 400,223	$ 399,670	$ 753,423
Less allowance for bad debt	8,714	9,856	12,132	19,577	12,877	13,695	13,781
Total	$ 381,232	$ 399,348	$ 405,858	$ 363,310	$ 387,346	$ 385,975	$ 739,642
Inventories:							
Finished goods	67,134	54,413	49,990	44,794	47,895	64,127	65,533
Materials and supplies	41,420	39,176	41,176	47,432	41,717	42,770	41,111
Total inventories	$ 108,554	$ 93,589	$ 91,166	$ 92,226	$ 89,612	$ 106,897	$ 106,644
Prepaid expenses	8,413	9,169	19,700	8,178	12,717	13,905	13,905
Total current assets	$ 498,199	$ 502,106	$ 516,724	$ 463,714	$ 489,675	$ 506,777	$ 860,191
Miscellaneous investments	8,571	27,512	28,145	26,008	31,359	28,811	28,811
Property—at cost:							
Land	82,850	82,850	82,850	82,850	82,850	82,850	82,850
Buildings, machinery and equipment	1,696,943	1,684,294	1,907,177	1,918,903	1,886,917	2,040,280	2,040,280
Cooperage and bottles	217,123	203,151	181,560	164,107	200,191	248,614	251,739
Total	$1,996,916	$1,970,295	$2,171,587	$2,165,860	$2,169,958	$2,371,744	$2,374,869
Less reserve for depreciation	868,492	959,856	1,075,619	1,162,941	1,184,587	1,275,900	1,283,421
Net of depreciation	$1,128,424	$1,010,439	$1,095,968	$1,002,919	$ 985,371	$1,095,844	1,091,448
Leasehold improvements (unamortized)	77,136	73,365	67,862	89,171	82,316	20,579	18,364
Total property	$1,205,560	$1,083,804	$1,163,830	$1,092,090	$1,067,687	$1,116,423	$1,109,812
Deferred charges	14,284	6,114	20,359	20,146	7,840	16,363	15,887
Total assets	$1,726,614	$1,619,536	$1,729,058	$1,601,958	$1,596,561	$1,668,374	$2,014,701

exhibit 2 (continued)

Liabilities	1959	1960	1961	1962	1963	1964	Jan. 30, 1965*
Current liabilities:							
Accounts payable and accruals	$ 485,264	$ 535,939	$ 524,346	$ 524,116	$ 499,925	$ 498,654	$ 437,331
Notes payable—due in one year	28,600	27,800	37,300	37,100	35,300	35,300	35,300
Federal taxes payable	14,100						134,873†
Other taxes payable	35,000						7,294
Total current liabilities	$ 562,964	$ 563,739	$ 561,646	$ 561,216	$ 535,225	$ 533,954	$ 614,798
Deposits on containers	34,385	27,931	27,146	37,210	39,191	49,390	46,303
Notes payable: 5% due 1975‡	328,500	305,600	536,100	512,200	483,400	454,600	454,600
4% 4½% due 1970†	91,400	91,400	88,200	81,700	75,200	68,700	68,700
3¾%	17,100	12,200	6,700				
Total notes payable	$ 437,000	$ 409,200	$ 631,000	$ 593,900	$ 558,600	$ 523,300	$ 523,300
Consulting fees owed				32,000	32,000	70,000	
Capital stock and surplus:							
Preferred stock	377,540	354,540	330,300	330,300	330,300	330,300	330,300
Common stock	119,999	113,943	115,366	118,895	119,743	119,743	500,000
Surplus: paid in	142,310	131,716	132,118	133,412	133,412	133,412	
Surplus: earned	52,416	18,467	(68,518)	(172,975)	(151,910)	(91,725)	
Total capital stock and surplus	$ 692,265	$ 618,666	$ 509,266	$ 409,632	$ 431,545	$ 491,730	$ 830,300
Total liabilities	$1,726,614	$1,619,536	$1,729,058	$1,601,958	$1,596,561	$1,668,374	$2,014,701

* After reorganization.
† Inclues the tax lien of $125,600.
‡ Maturity dates renegotiated at a time of reorganization.

exhibit 3 BARTL'S BREWERY

A six-year comparison

	1959	1960	1961	1962	1963	1964
Barrels sold	106,813	95,930	85,714	74,522	78,081	95,975
Net sales	$2,511,167	$2,263,719	$2,011,713	$1,749,875	$1,859,105	$2,299,553
Earnings before income taxes	....	....	....	....	21,910	37,430
Net earnings	(16,190)	(33,949)	(86,985)	(114,457)	21,910	37,430
Per cent of net earnings to net sales	....	....	....	....	1.2	1.6
Amount earned on common stock	....	....	....	....	21,910	37,430
Earnings per share	....	....	....	....	.004	.075
Plant property and equipment	911,301	807,288	944,890	838,812	785,180	1,080,604
Current assets	481,199	502,106	516,724	463,714	524,675	571,777
Current liabilities	562,964	563,739	561,646	561,216	444,860	533,954
Working capital	(81,765)	(61,633)	(44,922)	(97,502)	79,815	37,823
Long-term debt	437,000	409,200	631,000	593,900	558,600	523,300
Wages, salaries, benefits per barrel	5.46	5.54	5.68	5.75	5.90	5.92
Revenue per barrel after taxes	23.51	23.61	23.47	23.48	23.81	23.96
Retained earnings	....	....	....	....	21,910	37,430
Taxes (excise)	990,941	877,525	771,111	672,526	1,012,159	1,200,814

exhibit 4 BARTL'S BREWERY

Stated approximate retail beer prices, January 1, 1965

Brand	12 Oz. No return		12 Oz. Return		32 Oz. No return		32 Oz. Return		12 Oz. Can		16 Oz. Can	
	Six Pack	Case of 24	Six Pack	Case of 24	1 Bottle	Case of 12	1 Bottle	Case of 12	Six Pack	Case of 24	Six Pack	Case of 24
Bartl's Standard	$ .99	$3.85	$ .97	$3.79	$ .43	$5.00	$ .40	$4.70	$1.09	$4.20	$1.29	$4.90
Bartl's Premium	1.25	4.85	1.15	4.50	.52	6.20	.48	5.65	1.15	4.50	1.45	5.65
Brand A	1.29	4.90	1.19	4.60	.53	6.26	.48	5.66	1.19	4.60	1.50	5.80
Brand B	.99	3.86	.99	3.86	.45	5.30	.40	4.70	1.19	4.60	1.50	5.80
Brand C	1.24	4.30	1.19	4.60	.52	6.20	.48	5.65	1.19	4.60	1.50	5.80
Brand D	1.29	4.90	1.19	4.50	.51	6.10	.48	5.65	1.19	4.60	1.50	5.80
Brand E	.99	3.80	.93	3.65	3/1.10	4.35	3/1.00	4.00	1.09	4.20	1.30	5.00
Brand F	1.29	4.90	1.19	4.60	.53	6.26	.48	5.66	1.19	4.60	1.50	5.80
Brand G	1.26	4.85	1.17	4.50	.43	5.00	.39	4.60	1.17	4.50	1.35	5.20
Brand H	1.09	4.20	.99	3.80	.43	5.00	.39	4.60	1.09	4.20	1.29	4.90
Brand I	1.29	4.90	1.19	4.65	.52	6.20	.48	5.65	1.39	5.30	1.50	5.80
Brand J	1.24	4.30	1.19	4.60	.53	6.26	.48	5.65	1.19	4.60	1.29	4.90
Brand K	1.09	3.80	.99	3.45	.43	5.00	.39	4.60	.99	3.85	.99	3.80
Brand L	.99	3.80	.89	3.80	3/1.10	4.30	3/1.00	4.00			1.29	4.90
Brand M	.99	3.80	.99	3.80	.42	4.95	.39	4.60	.99	3.80	1.29	4.60
Brand N	1.00	3.90	.90	3.50	3/1.10	4.30	3/1.00	4.00	.92	3.45	1.19	4.60
Brand O	.75	2.85	.65	2.45	.31	3.60	.29	3.35	.75	2.85	.95	3.65

* Obtained locally; does not include special promotions or sales.

Includes prices of Schlitz, Pabst, Budweiser, Millers, Blatz, Old Style, Black Label, Drewry's, Ballantine, Hamm's, Peter Hand, Champagne Velvet, Tavern Pale, Van Merritt, and Canadian Ace.

exhibit 5 BARTL'S BREWERY
Shipments by months for Bartl's breweries, 1965

Month	Barrels Shipped	Per cent Change over Previous Year
January	6,478	1.7
February	6,321	7.3
March	8,187	5.7
April	8,345	−5.7
May	9,397	7.7
June	10,904	2.9
July	9,013	−7.5
August	9,201	5.6
September	7,323	−9.6
October	6,750	−6.3
November	6,391	4.6
December	7,665	1.0
Total	95,975	Net 0.3

exhibit 6
BARTL'S BREWERY
Organization Chart, January; 1965

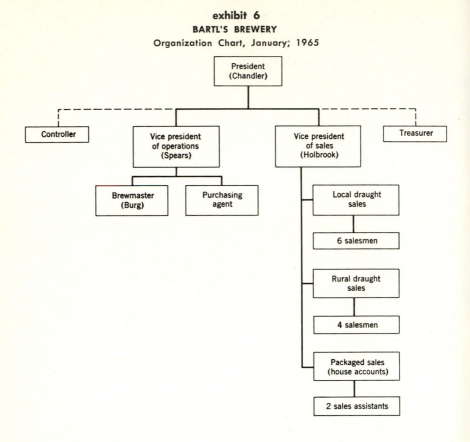

exhibit 7   INDUSTRY WITHDRAWALS AND PER CAPITA
CONSUMPTION OF MALT BEVERAGES
Fiscal years ending June 30, 1934–1963

Year	Estimated or Actual Population	Total Taxpaid Withdrawals (Barrels)	Per Capita Consumption (Gallons)
1934	126,373,773	32,266,039	7.9
1935	126,250,232	42,228,831	10.3
1936	126,053,180	48,759,840	11.8
1937	128,824,829	55,391,960	13.3
1938	129,824,939	53,926,018	12.9
1939	130,979,718	51,816,874	12.3
1940	131,669,275	53,014,230	12.5
1941	133,121,000	52,799,181	12.3
1942	133,920,000	60,856,219	14.1
1943	134,245,000	68,636,434	15.8
1944	132,885,000	76,969,764	18.0
1945	132,481,000	79,590,598	18.6
1946	140,054,000	81,286,821	18.0
1947	143,446,000	82,629,441	17.9
1948	146,093,000	86,992,795	18.5
1949	148,665,000	85,809,068	17.9
1950	150,697,361	83,511,994	17.2
1951	153,383,000	83,246,162	16.8
1952	155,761,000	84,293,646	16.8
1953	158,312,000	84,559,162	16.6
1954	161,190,000	85,747,439	16.5
1955	164,302,000	84,456,627	15.9
1956	167,262,000	85,537,307	15.9
1957	170,295,000	84,321,156	15.3
1958	173,452,000	83,948,536	15.0
1959	177,135,000	85,638,382	15.0
1960	179,323,175	88,928,883	15.4
1961	183,057,000	87,925,801	14.9
1962	185,822,000	90,693,253	15.1
1963	188,531,000	91,493,577	15.0

SOURCE: *Brewer's Almanac*, 1964 (United States Treasury Department, Internal Revenue Service, Alcohol and Tobacco Tax Division, and Bureau of Census), p. 12.

exhibit 8 TAXPAID PACKAGED WITHDRAWALS OF MALT BEVERAGES BY TYPE OF CONTAINER (Industry)
Calendar years 1959–1963 (based on a standard 12-ounce bottle or can)

Type of Container	1959		1960		1961		1962		1963	
	Barrels	% of Total	Barrels	% of Total	Barrels	% of Total	Barrels	% of Total	Barrels	% of Total
Metal cans	28,069,945	39.9	26,879,524	37.9	26,494,948	36.9	27,501,674*	37.1	29,622,697	38.8
One-way bottles	4,324,007	6.2	5,884,812	8.3	8,436,364	11.7	10,347,305	14.0	11,681,115	15.3
Returnable bottles	37,914,510	53.9	38,191,259	53.8	36,979,445	51.4	36,279,520*	48.9	35,043,346†	45.9
Total packaged withdrawals	70,308,462	100.0	70,955,595	100.0	71,910,757	100.0	74,128,498	100.0	76,347,158†	100.0

* Revised.
† Last six months unaudited.
SOURCE: Brewer's Almanac, 1964 (United States Treasury Department, Internal Revenue Service, Alcohol and Tobacco Tax Division), p. 25.

exhibit 9 INDUSTRY PRODUCTION, DRAUGHT AND PACKAGED SALES, AND TOTAL
TAXPAID WITHDRAWALS OF MALT BEVERAGES
Calendar years 1933–1963 (quantities in 31-gallon barrels)

Calendar Year	Production	Packaged Sales	% of Total	Draught Sales	% of Total	Total Taxpaid* Withdrawals
1933†	24,501,678	6,467,400	31.6	14,002,241	68.4	20,469,641
1934	43,155,146	10,022,344	25.0	30,012,563	75.0	40,034,907
1935	48,013,218	13,311,837	29.5	31,831,195	70.5	45,143,032
1936	56,134,316	20,218,406	38.1	32,791,610	61.9	53,010,016
1937	58,259,570	24,431,399	43.8	31,300,794	56.2	55,732,193
1938	53,630,463	23,734,562	46.2	27,668,571	53.8	51,403,133
1939	55,222,501	26,043,002	49.3	26,744,031	50.7	52,787,033
1940	53,863,734	26,761,946	51.7	25,049,151	48.3	51,811,097
1941	60,636,547	32,199,010	56.1	25,204,362	43.9	57,403,372
1942	68,271,501	37,917,179	58.7	26,666,939	41.3	64,584,118
1943	75,624,489	44,248,184	60.9	28,444,754	39.1	72,692,938
1944	85,779,934	49,534,252	62.3	29,970,952	37.7	79,514,204
1945	88,205,537	52,664,148	64.3	29,177,247	35.7	81,841,395
1946	83,312,516	53,010,253	66.6	26,530,243	33.4	79,540,496
1947	91,742,212	58,899,447	67.6	28,272,887	32.4	87,172,334
1948	88,125,320	58,699,355	69.0	26,367,959	31.0	85,067,314
1949	88,618,322	59,443,805	70.3	25,113,802	29.7	84,557,607
1950	88,178,356	59,487,521	71.8	23,342,616	28.2	82,830,137
1951	89,742,138	61,706,743	73.6	22,116,893	26.4	83,823,636
1952	90,489,824	63,359,469	74.7	21,477,011	25.3	84,836,480
1953	92,104,063	65,830,505	76.5	20,214,611	23.5	86,045,116
1954	88,940,268	63,927,035	76.7	19,377,986	23.3	83,305,021
1955	90,285,488	66,179,019	77.9	18,798,255	22.1	84,977,274
1956	90,338,445	67,087,002	78.9	17,921,154	21.1	85,008,156
1957	89,465,986	66,982,200	79.4	17,388,825	20.6	84,371,025
1958	90,120,512	67,168,341	79.6	17,256,368	20.4	84,424,709
1959	93,127,427	70,308,462	80.2	17,313,897	19.8	87,622,359
1960	93,415,363	70,955,595	80.7	16,957,244	19.3	87,912,839
1961	95,030,031	71,910,757	80.8	17,117,674	19.2	89,028,431
1962	96,831,989	74,128,498	81.3	17,068,659	18.7	91,197,157
1963‡	100,576,505	76,347,158	81.4	17,446,815	18.6	93,793,973

* Withdrawn from production for selling purpose.
† April through December.
‡ Figures for last six months unaudited.
SOURCE: *Brewer's Almanac*, 1964 (United States Treasury Department, Internal Revenue
Service, Alcohol and Tobacco Tax Division), p. 19.

exhibit 10   MALT BEVERAGE INDUSTRY—FEDERAL SPECIAL-TAX PAPERS*
Post-Prohibition—fiscal years ending June 30, 1933–1963

Fiscal Year	Brewers	Wholesale Dealers	Retail Dealers	Retail Dealers at Large†	Temporary Dealers‡
1933	331	14,135	262,639		
1934	756	17,630	230,322		
1935	766	15,300	181,770		
1936	739	14,640	186,282		
1937	754	13,813	177,834	11	13,850
1938	700	12,727	166,615	2,566	19,535
1939	672	11,472	157,985	144	22,834
1940	683	13,068	150,952	161	21,600
1941	587	10,820	145,447	191	20,476
1942	523	10,105	141,327	179	17,864
1943	491	8,885	121,100	158	10,010
1944	480	8,902	113,625	40	7,973
1945	476	9,062	118,815	29	9,146
1946	471	10,145	125,716	40	11,070
1947	485	12,374	140,213	98	11,104
1948	475	13,617	160,970	71	13,533
1949	444	14,038	167,434	56	13,090
1950	407	14,015	177,203	83	13,060
1951	390	13,735	175,448	96	12,812
1952	359	13,226	175,147	63	11,861
1953	333	12,190	183,175	67	11,568
1954	334	12,015	182,080	92	10,856
1955	299	11,792	178,163	90	11,122
1956	274	11,537	172,924	102	9,866
1957	278	11,320	168,394	97	9,603
1958	255	11,088	161,041	169	8,875
1959	260	10,879	158,712	173	8,867
1960	240	8,685	153,541	186	8,783
1961	230	8,174	147,933	182	9,172
1962	224	8,046	145,865	183	9,050
1963	217	7,783	144,116	214	8,078

* These figures show the total number in each category purchasing special-tax stamps at any time during the fiscal year.
† All permanent retail establishments selling beer.
‡ Those dealers which are of a seasonal nature such as concession stands at ball parks and race tracks.
SOURCE: *Brewer's Almanac*, 1964 (United States Treasury Department, Internal Revenue Service, Alcohol and Tobacco Tax Division), p. 92.

exhibit 11 ESTIMATED PERCENTAGE PROFIT AND LOSS STATEMENTS FOR ENTIRE BREWING INDUSTRY
Calendar years 1962–1964

	1962		1963		1964	
	Returns with Net Income	Returns with No Net Income	Returns with Net Income	Returns with No Net Income	Returns with Net Income	Returns with No Net Income
Gross sales*	90.8	99.2	99.4	99.5	99.1	99.2
Interest, rents, royalties, etc.	2.0	.2	.2	.2	.3	.3
Other receipts	6.9	.6	.4	.3	.6	.5
Total receipts	100.0	100.0	100.0	100.0	100.0	100.0
Cost of goods sold †	46.0	37.2	48.3	40.6	44.6	41.9
Compensation of officers	.6	.8	.6	.9	.5	1.0
Rents paid on business property	.2	.4	.3	.3	.3	.2
Repairs	.9	1.2	1.0	1.3	1.1	.6
Bad debts	.1	.2	.1	.2	.1	.4
Interest paid	.3	.4	.3	.5	.3	.0
Contributions or gifts	.1	.0	.2	.0	.1	.0
Depreciation, depletion, and amortization	2.5	3.4	2.8	2.8	2.6	2.4
Advertising	7.0	6.8	6.5	6.8	6.7	7.0
Contributions under pension plans, etc.	1.0	.0	1.0	1.3	1.0	1.4
Loss (net) on sales of other than capital assets	.0	.0	.1	.5	.1	.6
Taxes other than Federal income taxes‡	24.3	31.7	23.1	27.6	25.2	31.0
Other deductions	10.4	21.1	10.3	20.1	11.3	16.4
Total deductions	93.4	103.2	94.6	102.9	93.9	102.9
Net profit (or loss) before Federal income taxes	6.6	(3.2)	5.4	(2.9)	6.1	(2.9)
Federal income taxes	3.3		2.7		3.1	
Net profit (or loss) after taxes	3.3	(3.2)	2.7	(2.9)	3.0	(2.9)

* "Gross sales" consists of amounts received for goods, less returns and allowances, in transactions where inventories are an income-determining factor. Beginning with the year 1958 "Gross sales" and "Gross receipts from operations" have been combined under the term "Business Receipts."

† "Cost of goods sold" and cost of operations exclude indemnifiable amounts of taxes, depreciation, depletion, amortization, advertising, and contributions under pension plans and other employee benefit plans included therein.

‡ This item excludes (1) Federal income and excess profits taxes, (2) estate, inheritance, legacy, succession and gift taxes, (3) income taxes paid to a foreign country or possession of the United States if any portion is claimed as a tax receipt, (4) taxes assessed against local benefits, (5) Federal taxes paid on tax-free covenant bonds, and (6) taxes reported under "Cost of goods sold."

exhibit 12   ESTIMATED PERCENTAGE BALANCE SHEET FOR ENTIRE BREWING INDUSTRY
Calendar years 1962–1964

	1962		1963		1964	
	Returns with Net Income	*Returns with No Net Income*	*Returns with Net Income*	*Returns with No Net Income*	*Returns with Net Income*	*Returns with No Net Income*
Assets:						
Cash	9.2	7.3	8.3	9.7	8.2	7.6
Notes and accounts receivable	11.0	10.5	10.2	10.7	10.0	16.3
Less: reserve for bad debts	.3	.6	.3	.6	.3	.9
Inventories	12.8	13.2	14.6	15.1	13.6	10.7
Government securities	5.3	3.3	7.8	3.9	7.8	1.6
Other investments	4.8	3.8	4.0	3.7	5.4	11.6
Gross capital assets (except land)	80.3	105.0	81.8	103.3	85.5	96.5
Less: reserves	30.4	49.4	33.6	52.9	37.0	53.1
Land	2.7	3.9	2.7	3.3	2.8	3.9
Other assets	4.6	3.0	4.5	3.8	4.0	5.8
Total assets	100.0	100.0	100.0	100.0	100.0	100.0
Liabilities:						
Accounts payable	6.3	6.4	6.2	6.8	5.5	8.0
Bonds, notes, mortgages payable:						
Maturity less than 1 year	.9	3.8	1.8	2.9	1.7	6.9
Maturity more 1 year	8.5	11.8	8.4	12.9	.9	17.3
Other liabilities	9.4	4.8	11.0	5.5	9.6	9.1
Capital stock preferred	3.4	2.2	2.2	2.0	1.8	3.4
Capital stock common	15.0	20.9	14.8	16.8	16.0	15.7
Surplus reserves	1.3	2.6	.6	2.3	.7	.6
Surplus and undivided profits	55.2*	47.5*	55.0*	50.8*	56.8*	39.0*
Total liabilities	100.0	100.0	100.0	100.0	100.0	100.0

* Deficit. Amounts shown as "Deficit" consist of negative amounts of earned surplus and undivided profits. Note that both groups had negative earned surpluses.

exhibit **13** **EXTRACTS FROM SURVEY OF LOCAL NEWSPAPERS**

1. Why use fancy-dressed people in beer advertising when beer is not a prestige product?

2. The upper-class man does not drink beer; he drinks hard liquor. The middle-class, everyday man serves beer before, during and after dinner, whereas the upper-class man serves cocktails, wines, and highballs.

3. The consumer couldn't care less if an advertisement shows a member of high society, a celebrity, or a movie star, drinking beer. He feels that the individual wouldn't ever drink the beer and is only being paid for his endorsement.

4. The average consumer does not want to drink in the same establishment as the man from the upper class, as a beer will cost a minimum of 50¢, and it doesn't taste any better than when purchased at the local beer hall.

5. Beer is a drink for sociable people; it allows people to relax. The fact is accepted that beer puts everyone on the same social level. When drinking beer, the president of the company becomes "one of the boys."

6. Beer drinkers are particular about the taste of their beer. The average consumer may not understand the words the beer drinker uses; he applies terms such as "smooth," "light," and "refreshing" to the beers he likes, and to those he dislikes, he applies terms such as "bitter," "biting," "smelly," and "sickening."

7. The average man prefers beer advertising which conveys the impressions of "relaxation," "wholesomeness" and "pleasure." He detests "sexiness" in beer advertising. If the former "attitudes" or "images" can be applied to a brand of beer, the consumer will like and drink the beer.

8. The average consumer cares little about how beer is processed, its place of production or the type of water used. All he is concerned with is taste.

9. Beer is found at ball parks, at picnics, at home, and at other informal gatherings where friendliness and fellowship is sought. Beer is a social refreshment along with soft drinks as contrasted to the more formal hard liquors or "mixed drinks."

10. An individual can enjoy the leisurely drinking of beer, through an evening and not "overdo it." No constant counting of intake is needed. The consumer is even able to participate properly in sporting events without his abilities being handicapped.

11. Women, previously considered non-consumers, are becoming more important to the sale of beer though they still drink only when their male companions do, and then usually drink the same brand they do.

9

ELECTRIC
STEEL
CORPORATION

The Electric Steel Corporation was organized in New Albany, Indiana, in 1949 for the purpose of producing and selling high-quality steel using the Dornin process.[1]

Mr. John Chambers, a prominent Indiana industrialist, formed the original group which formulated the plans for Electric Steel and engaged in the promotion and financing of the company by public subscription.

At the first stockholders' meeting, held in early 1950, Mr. Chambers was elected President and Chairman of the Board of the newly formed corporation. At the same meeting four of the founding group who held large blocks of the outstanding stock were elected, along with Mr. Chambers, to three-year terms as Directors of the company.

The original plans of the company contemplated financing and expenditures as shown in Exhibit 1.

Late in 1951 it became apparent to management that the estimates of financial requirements necessary to place the company in operation were inaccurate. The actual costs of construction and preparation of

---

[1] After the steel is melted in an electric furnace the specially formed ingots are worked in a forging press to give a grain structure which insures an unusually high quality of steel. The Dornin ingots weigh 3.9 tons in contrast with conventional ingots which weigh from 6 to 16 tons. The specially designed ingot and the press shop are the heart of the Dornin process. The other facilities are largely conventional for the production of electric furnace steel.

exhibit 1 **ELECTRIC STEEL CORPORATION**
Original financing plan

Financing

Funds provided by common stock (400,000 shares)	$ 88,825
3½% debentures due 1961 (subordinate)	4,000,000
Reconstruction Finance Corporation loan	8,556,126
Total	$12,644,951

Expenditures

Acquisition of land and construction of steel plant	$ 9,035,657
Electric power transmission facilities	491,000
Preliminary expenses	100,000
Interest on debentures through June 15, 1956	700,000
Estimated interest on RFC loan	75,000
Financing cost	250,000
Working capital	1,993,294
Total	$12,644,951

the plant and equipment for production proved to be substantially in excess of estimated costs. The plant was built on a 130-acre tract of land, four miles from New Albany, Indiana, along the Ohio River.

Difficulties and delays encountered in the construction of this plant, which was originally planned as a highly efficient electric-furnace producing unit containing the most modern and efficient equipment avail-

exhibit 2 **ELECTRIC STEEL CORPORATION**
Comparative income statements and selected ratios for the years ended July 31, 1956–1954

	1956 Amount	Per Cent	1955 Amount	Per Cent	1954 Amount	Per Cent
Net sales	$17,273,275	100.00	$10,788,114	100.00	$5,413,155	100.00
Cost of goods sold	15,110,763	87.50	9,473,617	88.00	5,940,094	109.70
Gross profit or (loss)	$ 2,162,512	12.50	$ 1,314,497	12.00	($ 526,939)	(9.70)
Selling, general and administrative expenses	$ 743,866	4.30	$ 719,649	6.70	$ 621,239	11.50
Other expense (income)—net	76,891	.40	40,452	.40	24,098	.40
	$ 820,757	4.70	$ 760,101	7.10	$ 645,337	11.90
Net profit (loss) before interest, depreciation and taxes	$ 1,341,755	7.80	$ 554,396	5.10	($1,172,276)	(21.60)
Depreciation	$ 516,019	3.00	$ 507,345	4.70	$ 430,753	8.00
Interest	621,897	3.60	621,188	5.70	582,606	10.70
	$ 1,137,916	6.60	$ 1,128,533	10.40	$1,013,359	18.70
Net profit (loss) before income taxes	$ 203,839	1.20	($ 574,137)	(5.30)	($2,185,635)	(40.30)
State and Federal income taxes	–0–	–0–	–0–	–0–	–0–	–0–
Net profit (loss) for period	$ 203,839	1.20	($ 574,137)	(5.30)	($2,185,635)	(40.30)
Net profit before interest charges	$ 825,736		$ 47,051		($1,603,029)	
Cost of sales to fixed assets		1.50		.94		.62
Inventory turnover		13.00		12.00		9.00

able in the industry, were mainly responsible for the increase in costs over the estimated expenditures.

After several unsuccessful attempts to acquire additional financing the Board of Directors decided to drastically revise their original plans for the mills in an effort to conserve the company's rapidly dwindling working capital. As a result, less efficient equipment than originally contemplated was substituted in many parts of the plant, and certain equip-

exhibit 3   **ELECTRIC STEEL CORPORATION**
Comparative balance sheets, July 31, 1956–1953

Assets	1956	1955	1954	1953
Current assets:				
Cash	$ 295,691	$ 284,198	$ 85,663	$ 1,521,672
Receivables—net	1,870,046	974,021	852,061	1,113
Inventories	1,351,680	956,147	625,325	691,385
Other current	70,000	87,500	114,978	–0–
Total current assets	$ 3,587,417	$ 2,301,866	$ 1,678,027	$ 2,214,170
Other assets:				
Restricted funds	–0–	$ 122,500	$ 262,500	$ 480,535
Cash surrender value insurance	–0–	11,480	8,089	4,760
	–0–	$ 133,980	$ 270,589	$ 485,295
Plant and equipment:				
Cost	$10,591,627	$10,258,701	$10,149,118	$ 9,500,823
Reserve	1,462,573	951,036	443,692	–0–
	$ 9,129,054	$ 9,307,665	$ 9,705,426	$ 9,500,823
Deferred charges:				
Preoperating expenses	–0–	$ 1,033,885	$ 1,033,885	$ 1,033,885
Other	$ 296,943	325,754	365,628	407,871
	$ 296,943	$ 1,359,639	$ 1,399,513	$ 1,441,756
Total assets	$13,013,414	$13,103,150	$13,053,555	$13,642,044
Liabilities				
Current liabilities:				
Notes payable	$ 5,081,453	$ 2,966,876	$ 2,214,276	$ 700,000
Accounts payable	1,402,916	1,226,167	1,073,750	989,407
Accrued expenses and interest	1,177,164	743,906	375,112	87,041
Total current liabilities	$ 7,661,533	$ 4,936,949	$ 3,663,148	$ 1,776,448
Long-term debt	$ 8,898,522	$10,837,148	$11,487,217	$11,776,771
Capital and deficit:				
Capital stock	$ 6,625	$ 6,625	$ 6,625	$ 6,625
Capital surplus	82,200	82,200	82,200	82,200
Deficit	(3,635,466)	(2,759,772)	(2,185,635)	–0–
	($ 3,546,641)	($ 2,670,947)	($ 2,096,810)	$ 88,825
Total liabilities	$13,013,414	$13,103,150	$13,053,555	$13,642,044
Working capital	($ 4,074,116)	($ 2,635,083)	($ 1,985,121)	$ 437,723
Increase (decrease) in working capital over prior year	($ 1,439,033)	($ 649,962)	($ 2,422,844)	$ –0–

ment included in management's plans to obtain maximum operating efficiency was eliminated.

The company did not produce steel until the fall of 1953 and the first shipments were made in December of 1953. The unanticipated delay in starting production and the operating difficulties encountered resulted in substantial losses in the first two years of operation. In the third year of operation the company made a profit. The financial results for this period are shown in Exhibits 2 and 3.

INDUSTRY TRENDS AND THE POSITION OF ELECTRIC FURNACE STEEL

As indicated in Exhibit 4, steel production has fluctuated greatly over the past 20 years, ranging from a low of 31,752,000 net tons in 1938 to

exhibit 4   ELECTRIC STEEL CORPORATION
Steel industry production by furnace type, years 1936–1955 (thousands of net tons)

Year	Total Production in U.S.	Open-hearth		Bessemer		Electric	
		Production, Tons	Per Cent of Total	Production, Tons	Per Cent of Total	Production, Tons	Per Cent of Total
1936	53,500	48,761	91.2	3,873	7.2	866	1.6
1937	56,637	51,825	91.5	3,864	6.8	948	1.7
1938	31,752	29,080	91.6	2,106	6.6	566	1.8
1939	52,799	48,410	91.7	3,359	6.4	1,030	1.9
1940	66,983	61,573	91.9	3,709	5.6	1,701	2.5
1941	82,839	74,390	89.7	5,577	6.8	2,872	3.5
1942	86,032	76,502	89.0	5,553	6.4	3,977	4.6
1943	88,837	78,622	88.6	5,626	6.3	4,589	5.1
1944	89,642	80,364	89.7	5,040	5.6	4,238	4.7
1945	79,702	71,940	90.3	4,305	5.4	3,456	4.3
1946	66,603	60,712	91.2	3,328	5.0	2,563	3.8
1947	84,894	76,874	90.5	4,233	5.0	3,788	4.5
1948	88,640	79,340	89.5	4,243	4.8	5,057	5.7
1949	77,978	70,249	90.1	3,946	5.1	3,783	4.8
1950	96,836	86,263	89.1	4,535	4.7	6,039	6.2
1951	105,200	93,167	88.6	4,891	4.6	7,142	6.8
1952	93,168	82,846	88.9	3,524	3.8	6,798	7.3
1953	111,610	100,474	90.0	3,856	3.5	7,280	6.5
1954	88,312	80,328	91.0	2,548	2.9	5,436	6.1
1955	117,036	105,359	90.0	3,320	2.8	8,357	7.2

SOURCE: American Iron and Steel Institute.
NOTE: Crucible steel production included with electric steel. All production of steel for ingots and castings included.

a high of 117,036,000 net tons in 1955. Both open-hearth and electric-furnace steel production reached a peak in 1955. Electric-furnace steel production in that year amounted to 8,357,000 net tons, or 7.2% of total production. This figure was double the average electric-furnace steel tonnage of the 1947–1949 period. The year 1955 was an exceptionally good year for the steel industry in general and market conditions for all types of steel were more favorable than they had been in any previous period, including the war years.

exhibit 5 OPERATING RATES IN STEEL INDUSTRY PRO-
DUCTION AS PERCENTAGE OF CAPACITY

Year	Total All Types of Furnaces, %	Electric Furnaces, %
1946	72.5	46.6
1947	93.0	74.6
1948	94.1	93.7
1949	81.1	61.9
1950	96.9	87.9
1951	100.0	94.5
1952	85.8	82.6
1953	94.9	71.2
1954	71.0	52.0
1955	93.0	77.3

SOURCE: American Iron and Steel Institute.

The market for high-quality steels for which the electric steel plant was designed constituted a relatively small part of the total market for all grades and types of steel. This market, however, had shown a much more rapid growth than the industry as a whole. The trend in the industry pointed toward a continued expansion of the market for a great variety of high-quality steels which can be produced only in electric furnaces.

Despite its more rapid growth, electric steel production has been subject to greater fluctuations than the industry in general. As indicated in Exhibit 5, the operating rates for electric furnaces are significantly lower than the total indusry.

During periods of low demand for high-quality steels it is possible, although not always economically feasible, to use excess capacity of electric furnaces to melt carbon and low grades of alloy steel normally produced by the open-hearth process. However, electric steel producers seek to melt only higher grades of alloy and stainless steels for which their furnaces were designed. The costs of producing low-quality steels in electric furnaces far exceed the costs of melting these steels in open-hearth furnaces.

As shown in Exhibit 6, approximately 90% of all steel produced from

exhibit 6   FIVE-YEAR ANNUAL AVERAGES OF GRADES OF STEEL (IN THOUSANDS OF TONS)

Average	Total	Carbon	Alloy	Stainless
1941–1945	85,410	74,978	9,994	438
1946–1950	82,990	75,700	6,695	595
1951–1955	103,065	93,577	8,488	1,000

SOURCE: American Iron and Steel Institute.

1941 to 1955 was of the carbon variety. High-grade alloy and stainless steels, however, showed growth throughout this period. From 1946 to 1955 the production of stainless steel increased at a rate of approximately 8.6% annually while that of alloy increased approximately 2.7% per year.

Because of the wide fluctuations in annual production and the frequent low-capacity operations of electric furnaces, successful producers in this area of the industry are required to have special skills and resources. Their product line must provide an adequate profit in a normal market and their sales organizations must be capable of competitively securing and maintaining profitable accounts for their specialized products. It is necessary to establish a sound reputation in the trade as a quality producer with a prime rather than secondary source of steel. Production facilities are of paramount importance and must be capable of producing the quality, grades, types and quantities of steel that permit an adequate return on investment.

PLANT FACILITIES

The main plant of Electric Steel consisted of five connected buildings with a total area of 150,000 square feet, as indicated in the following exhibit.

Exhibit 7   PLANT AREA OF ELECTRIC STEEL

Buildings	*Area in Square Feet*
Melt shop	20,500
Teeming or pouring shop	21,000
Soaking pit and press shop	23,000
Rolling mill, finishing and shipping	67,000
Change house and motor room	18,500
Total	150,000

In addition to the main plant the company had the following auxiliary structures on the plant site:

Electric sub-station

Open crane runway extension to melt shop and part of scrap yard

Laboratory

Plant office, storeroom and first-aid station

Acetylene generator station

Oxygen storage facility

In addition to the main plant and auxiliary structures, the company had storage areas for scrap, ingot molds, refractories, and other necessary operating supplies. There were overhead cranes in all of the main plant buildings except the change house and the motor room. There was no maintenance or machine shop; however, there was one general-purpose lathe and one roll lathe.

The 130-acre plant site was close to barge facilities of the Ohio River and had a direct connection with a railroad. The property was not fenced and losses from pilferage frequently occurred.

OPERATING EQUIPMENT AND THE PRODUCING PROCESS

The company had five major producing departments. The operations and the facilities of these departments were as follows (see Glossary of Terms on page 340).

The *melt shop* operation included the loading of scrap and charging to furnaces, melting, pouring ingots and stripping ingots out of molds. Two basic types of arc electric furnaces were used for melting the steel. Each furnace had a rated capacity of 60 tons per heat and actual heat weights averaged about 62 tons. The combined annual capacity of the furnaces was 242,000 tons. The capacity of the furnaces varied, however, with different product mix and with the various tap-to-tap heat times for the different analyses of the steels produced. Electric Steel produced as much as 180,000 tons of ingots annually. On a 6-day, 18-turn basis, producing high-quality steels only, the plant capacity was rated at 135,-000 tons of ingots annually.

The ingots were poured in Dornin molds and in conventional molds. The conventional ingots weighed from 6 to 16 tons and the Dornin ingots weighed only 3.9 tons. The conventional ingots, because of their weight, had to be stripped from the molds by a 75-ton pouring crane. A 10-ton crane was used for stripping the lighter Dornin ingots. Because of the lack of space in the plant, however, there was interference between the pouring operation and the stripping of Dornin ingots. This sometimes resulted in a loss of ingot heat and required additional soaking pit time.

The *soaking pits* of Electric Steel were arranged in two batteries, each with four pits and one stack. The soaking pits were used twice in the processing of Dornin steel, first to heat the ingots prior to the forging operation and second to heat the forged blooms for the rolling operation. The heating time required in each case was dependent upon the steel analysis and also on the heat retained in the entering ingot or bloom.

Two 10-ton cranes serviced the soaking pits and the press shop. The cranes were not of the stiff-necked variety specified for the soaking pit operation and consequently slowed operations and increased the time during which it was necessary to have the soaking pit covers opened. The building which housed the soaking pits, press shop, and hot scarfing operation was too short to allow more than one crane to reach the soaking pit and the scarfing operation at one time.

There was only one damper for each battery of soaking pits, which made it difficult to maintain the degree of heating practice control necessary for high-quality steel. There were no recuperators to provide preheated air. The recapturing of heat through recuperators would have reduced fuel costs. One of the eight soaking pits was usually out of service for routine maintenance.

The *press shop* consisted primarily of a 2,500-ton hydraulic upsetting press and a 1,500-ton forging press. In addition there were manipulators for the forging press, a transfer car, and a hot scarfing station.

The Dornin ingot was pressed into a pear shape on the upsetting press, with a small cylindrical projection left at the top in which nonmetallic inclusions were concentrated. The ingot was then forged into a 16-inch-square bloom on the forging press, after which it was hot-scarfed to remove the entire skin in most cases. After this process the steel was returned to the soaking pits for reheating prior to rolling.

The *rolling mills* consisted of a single-stand 24-inch, 2-high reversing blooming mill and a 24-inch billet and bar mill. The billet and bar mill had a 3-high stand and a 2-high stand driven off the same shaft. In addition the mill was equipped with a bloom shear, a transfer table between the two mills, and a cooling bed.

It was found after the early operations that the blooming mill manipulators were not conventional and as a result the roughing operation was slowed down. This factor also made it difficult to roll slabs.

The mills were only capable of reducing blooms, billets, and rounds (and some sizes of slabs) down to $3\frac{7}{8}$ inches. It was not possible to produce sheets or bars in smaller dimensions. This limitation prevented the company from reaching the major portion of the high-quality steel market.

The finishing and shipping facilities were located in an extension of the mill building. These facilities included pickle and wash tanks, grinders, power hack saws, chipping hammers, a billet straightener, three annealing pits, and three car-type annealing furnaces. The annealing equipment was used principally to control the rate at which alloy, high carbon, and large-section, lower-carbon billets and blooms cooled. This operation was necessary to obtain the desired qualities of strength and ductility in the steel.

The company made shipments mainly by rail and truck, with a minimum of shipments by water. The shipping and finishing areas were overcrowded and caused extra handling of most of the finished goods.

Production Problems. The specially designed Dornin ingot and the press shop are the most important factors in the Dornin process of producing steel. Without these distinct features the other facilities are largely conventional for the production of electric furnace steel. The pressing of the Dornin ingot into a forged bloom introduces a cost into the processing of steel that is not present in conventional production. This additional cost is offset partially by a higher yield from the ingot to the finished product. However, to be profitable it is generally conceded in the steel industry that the Dornin process must be applied to the maximum extent possible to high-priced, high-profit alloy steels.

The production of high-grade steel through this process requires that a high proportion of the volume produced be control-cooled after roll-ing. This requires that there be a proper balance between forging and rolling facilities and the finishing and controlled cooling facilities in or-der to produce a profitable product mix.

The conservation of heat in ingots and forged blooms is an important production factor which reduces the soaking pit heating time. The maximum travel distances of hot steel between melt shop, soaking pits, and press shop should not exceed 100 feet.

Retention of heat is important because if alloy steel ingots are allowed to cool unduly, they will crack. These ingots cannot be "banked" with-out slow cooling. The slow-cooling process requires that once an alloy melt has started, subsequent processing must follow in regular se-quence. Consequently, each process must be accurately timed and scheduled to allow for a relatively precise assembly-line-type of opera-tion. This requires a correlation of the capacities of all the production processes.

In consideration of its production difficulties Electric Steel Corpora-tion hired a firm of engineering consultants in the fall of 1956 to make an analysis of its technical operations and particularly its capacity lim-itations. The analysis of the consulting firm is shown in Exhibit 8. The capacity analysis indicated that the slow-cooling facilities constituted the company's primary bottleneck in its attempt to produce high-priced, high-profit alloy steels. Only 29% of Electric Steel's melting capacity could be slow-cooled. The soaking pits were the cause of the secondary bottleneck. The capacity of the pits was only 84% of melting capacity. The excess of melting capacity over soaking capacity amounted to 2,392 ingot tons. The excess of soaking pit capacity over slow-cooling capacity was estimated at 6,412 tons per month.

It was estimated by the consulting firm that it would require approxi-mately $3.5 million to correct the unbalanced production facilities. This figure did not include supplementary finishing and shipping facili-ties, which would also be required.

SALES AND PRODUCT MIX

Exhibit 9 shows the sales of Electric Steel Corporation by dollar vol-ume and grades from 1954 to 1956. The company substantially in-creased sales volume in this period to where approximately 12,500 tons were shipped monthly. This was accomplished only by running on a

exhibit 8   **ELECTRIC STEEL CORPORATION**
Summary of analysis of Present facility capacity

Capacities	Tons Shipped per Month
Slow-cooling:	
Aircraft steel	1,500
Alloy steel	1,820
Total	3,320
Soaking pits:	
Aircraft steel	1,500
Alloy steel:	
Slow-cooled	1,820
Air-cooled	607*
Carbon and shell steel	5,805
Total	9,732
Press shop	9,732†
Mill	9,732†
Melt shop:	
Aircraft steel	1,500
Alloy steel	2,427
Carbon and shell steel	5,805
Excess	1,888‡
Total	11,620

Potential Product Mix at Capacity Operation		Tons Shipped per Month	Tons Shipped per Year
Product:			
Finished products			
Aircraft steel		1,500	18,000
Alloy steel			
Slow-cooled	1,820		
Air-cooled	607		
		2,427	29,124
Carbon and shell steel		5,805	69,660
Total		9,732	116,784
Ingots		2,392§	28,704
Total		12,124	145,488
Capacity ratios:			
Slow-cooling capacity to melt shop capacity		29.5%	
Soaking pit capacity to melt shop capacity		83.7%	

* Assumption that 75% of total alloy volume would be slow-cooled and that 25% would be air-cooled.
† Based on present operation of 14 turns per week. Could be increased materially with up to 21 turns per week.
‡ This is an excess melting capacity in terms of finished tons, including processing yields.
§ Excess melt shop tonnage converted to ingot tons.

exhibit 9 ELECTRIC STEEL CORPORATION

Net sales by grades of steel, 1954–1956 (in thousands of tons and millions of dollars)

Year / Period	Gross Sales (Less Freight)		Ingots		Total Finished		Commercial Carbon		Shell		Alloy*		Aircraft	
	Tons	Dollars	Tons	Dollars	Tons	Dollars	Tons	Dollars	Tons	Dollars	Tons	Dollars	Tons	Dollars
Total 1954 fiscal	53.1	$ 5.7	-0-	-0-	53.1	$ 5.7	N.A.	N.A.	N.A.	N.A.	N.A.	N.A.	N.A.	N.A.
Total 1955 fiscal	105.0	10.9	5.0	$ .3	100.0	10.6	25.0	$2.4	59.0	$5.8	16.0	$2.4	†	†
1956 1st quarter	35.8	3.8	8.7	.6	27.1	3.2	7.0	.7	11.7	1.3	7.4	1.0	1.0	$ .2
1956 2nd quarter	37.7	4.3	11.7	.9	26.0	3.4	14.1	1.5	2.4	.3	7.5	1.1	2.0	.5
1956 3rd quarter	38.0	4.5	8.0	.7	30.0	3.8	15.7	1.7	5.0	.6	7.2	1.1	2.1	.5
1956 4th quarter	39.0	4.7	10.2	.9	28.8	3.8	9.4	1.12	10.4	1.2	6.9	1.0	2.1	.5
Total 1956 fiscal	150.5	17.3	38.6	3.1	111.9	14.3	46.2	5.0	29.5	3.4	29.0	4.2	7.2	1.7

N.A. = Not Available.

* Includes a small amount of miscellaneous sales.

† Included in alloy sales.

7-day, 21-turn basis. The increase in sales for the fiscal year 1956 was largely due to increases in carbon and ingot sales.

Ingots were first offered for sale by Electric Steel in June of 1955 in an effort to use excess melting capacity over that required for finished production. In 1956, 25.6% of the tonnage and 17.6% of the dollar volume of total sales were obtained from sales of ingots. All of the ingots that were sold were shipped to other mills for conversion to finished products.

While the Electric Steel plant was not designed to produce commercial carbon steel, the company produced as much as 40% of its total output in this grade in one quarter of 1956 and averaged over 30% of total output in the fiscal year. Because of strong market conditions in the second half of 1955 which carried over into 1956, Electric Steel was able to raise its price on carbon steel $9 a ton over the former going market price and add $7 per ton for freight charges which the company previously absorbed. These two factors enabled the company to realize in 1956 approximately $705,000 more than would have been possible in a normal steel market.

The sale of commercial carbon steel, however, proved to be the least profitable of all the grades sold. Exhibit 10 shows the gross profit per

exhibit 10 ELECTRIC STEEL CORPO-
RATION
Gross profits by grade of steel, 1956

Grade of Steel	Gross Profit per Ton
Carbon	($ 1.33)
Shell	10.63
Alloy	14.36
Aircraft	49.21
( ) Denotes loss.	

ton for the grades produced based on the company's standard cost system.

The production of shell steel by Electric Steel Corporation varied from nothing to 6,846 tons monthly. The average monthly sales in 1956 amounted to 2,460 tons. The company did not anticipate increased sales of shell steel in the next year of operation because of the closing of a number of ordnance plants and the reduction in the production schedule of others. The demand for this type of steel fluctuated greatly, since it was dependent upon the placement of government contracts.

The 1956 sales of high-quality steels for which the Electric Steel plant was designed accounted for 36,000 tons, or 25% of the total output. This amounted to 34% of the total dollar volume. In 1956 the company sold alloy steel, other than aircraft, for an average net price of $145 per ton. This price compared with the going market price for open-hearth quality steel, and was $20 a ton less than competitive electric furnace steel.

The equipment of Electric Steel Corporation limited it to the production of semi-finished products such as blooms, slabs, and billets. While these grades and forms of steel represented the most profitable products of the company, in the industry as a whole they accounted for only 10% of the alloy steel market. In 1956 there was no indication of the trend toward increased industry sales of alloy steel in these forms. In the preceding years blooms, slabs, and billets accounted for less than 10% of total alloy steel sales. Generally these forms of alloy steel were subject to greater fluctuations in sales than the industry as a whole. Specialty steels, particularly stainless steel and heat-resistant alloys, provided the most profitable and growing market. Up to 1956 Electric Steel had not entered this market.

The company sold all of its commercial products through 9 commission sales agents, with the exception of ingots which were sold by the Vice President of Operations, Mr. Dietrich. Shell steel was considered as a direct sale by the company since agents were not paid a commission for the sale of this grade and the bulk of the sales were made by company representatives. The agents had offices located in the following principal cities: Chicago, Illinois; Indianapolis, Indiana; Cleveland, Columbus, and Cincinnati, Ohio; New York; Philadelphia and Pittsburgh, Pennsylvania; New Haven, Connecticut; Tulsa, Oklahoma; Houston, Texas; and Los Angeles, California.

The remainder of the country not covered by agents, including the Detroit area, was covered by two employees of the sales department. The company formerly had contracts with agents covering Alabama, Detroit, Wisconsin, and St. Louis but canceled them in 1955 because management considered their performance unsatisfactory.

In 1956 a small number of agents accounted for the bulk of commercial sales. Sales were made to 123 customers and 65% of sales were made to 13% of the customer list. Two of the customers accounted for approximately 22% of total sales. The sales of the other 8 agents ranged from 0.2 to 9% of commercial sales, excluding ingots. Electric

Steel representatives made sales direct amounting to approximately 5.5% of sales, excluding ingots and shell steel. Shell steel sales accounted for 21% of commercial sales, excluding ingots.

The sales expenses of Electric Steel, as shown in the following exhibit, have been a small and declining part of total expenses of finished steel sales.

exhibit 11 **ELECTRIC STEEL CORPORATION**
Distribution of sales expense as a percentage of finished steel sales, fiscal years
1954–1956

	1954	1955	1956
Total selling expense	$ 142,988	$ 252,621	$ 320,199
Finished product sales	5,685,304	10,410,941	14,320,000
Expense as % of sales	2.426%	2.426%	2.236%
Breakdown of selling expenses:			
Salaries	19.22%	6.47%	7.47%
Travel and entertainment	14.80	5.01	5.11
Advertising	2.19	.02	.03
Payroll tax and insurance	.93	.27	.44
Commissions	62.58	87.83	86.86
Other	.28	.40	.09
Total	100.00%	100.00%	100.00%

As indicated in Exhibit 11 the agents' commissions constituted the principal part of selling expenses. They received commissions of 3% on alloy sales, 2½% on carbon bar, and 2% on all semi-finished carbon steel, but were not paid for any sales of shell steel.

ORGANIZATION

The organization chart of Electric Steel Corporation is shown in Exhibit 12. Mr. Chambers, one of the company's founders, was President and Chairman of the Board. Mr. Chambers was 65 years of age and had some 30 years of experience as an executive of one of the country's largest steel producers and was a member of the Board of Directors of several companies located in Indiana. Through several years of experimentation, Mr. Chambers developed what he considered to be satisfactory working relationships with his executive group. All department managers, with the exception of plant personnel, reported directly to him.

Mr. Chambers spent a good part of his time in attempting to establish the reputation of the company as a producer of high-quality specialty alloy steels employing the Dornin process. Because of initial difficulties

exhibit 12
ELECTRIC STEEL CORPORATION
Organization Chart, 1956

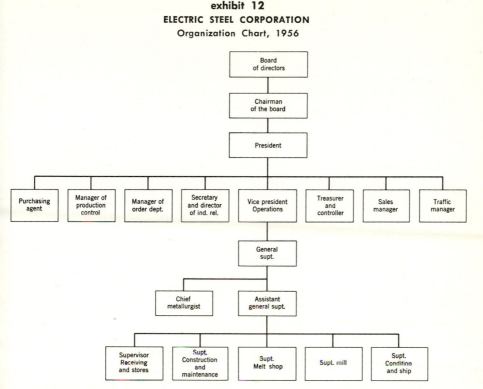

in getting the organization under way, he also found it necessary to spend much of his time on financial matters. The problem of utilization of plant capacity he considered necessary to the company's survival and as a result he felt that he frequently was forced to be "a peddler of steel in all its forms."

Because of the pressure of what Mr. Chambers termed "keeping the ship afloat," he found that he did not have the opportunity to spend as much time with his executive group as he thought was necessary. Mr. Dietrich, the Vice President of Operations, usually acted as the chief executive during Mr. Chambers' absence.

Mr. Chambers felt that his operating executives were very competent and resourceful individuals. He also expressed his confidence in his middle management group and department heads. He stated that they had frequently proved their competence by maximum utilization of the company's incomplete production facilities. He also frequently referred to the report of a personnel appraisal made by a management consulting firm which stated that the company "had been able to attract and retain higher-caliber personnel than could be reasonably expected under the circumstances." The report also stated that "the manufacturing organization had done a good job with the available equipment and facilities and had displayed considerable imagination in maintaining a schedule with the limited funds available for facilities and replacements."

Mr. Davis, the General Sales Manager, was 46 years of age. He had been brought into the company by Mr. Chambers to organize and develop a sales organization along the lines of a prominent specialty steel producer which had employed Mr. Davis as an Assistant Sales Manager. In addition to Mr. Davis, the sales organization was made up of an Assistant Sales Manager, a Traffic Manager, and nine commission sales agents.

Mr. Simmers was the Treasurer and Controller. He was 52 years of age and had previously worked for a large public accounting firm as well as a large steel producer as a head of an auditing section. Mr. Simmers installed a cost system, a sales and financial control system along the lines of the steel firm where he was formerly employed. His systems and handling of the Treasurer-Controller's function were frequently praised by both Mr. Chambers and Mr. Dietrich.

Mr. Dietrich occupied the important position of Vice President of Operations. He had 20 years' experience in various capacities with a producer of electric furnace steel. He was General Plant Superintendent when he left his previous company to come to the Electric Steel Corporation. Mr. Dietrich was 58 years old, and was considered in the industry to be a capable production man.

The other members of the executive group ranged from 34 to 57 years of age with an average age of 46. With the exception of the Purchasing Agent, who was with the company at the beginning of operations, the service of the other members averaged approximately 2 years.

FINANCIAL POSITION

Early in 1957 Mr. Chambers and Mr. Simmers expressed concern about the working capital problems of Electric Steel. They pointed out that companies similar to theirs in the industry considered minimum working capital requirements to be 15% of current sales. In 1956 six of the more successful electric furnace producers of specialty steels had from 15 to 38% of current sales in working capital and the average of the 6 producers was 24%. Mr. Chambers was of the opinion that if sufficient working capital could be obtained the day-to-day operations would eventually take care of themselves. He frequently pointed out that the original financing of the company placed it in a strained position from which it had never fully recovered. However, he felt that progress was being made and cited the 1956 profit figures as evidence of the company's potential.

The financial results for the first 3 full years of operation of the company are shown in Exhibit 2. Comparative balance sheets from 1953 to 1956 are shown in Exhibit 3.

GLOSSARY OF TERMS[2]

Annealing Heating steel and holding it at a suitable temperature followed by cooling at a suitable rate, with the object of improving machinability and coldworking properties.

Banked A charged furnace which is allowed to cool at a slowly diminishing rate until cold.

Billet A semi-finished product of a blooming or billet mill, either square or rectangular in section, and having a maximum cross-sectional area of 25 sq. inches.

Bloom Semi-finished products hot rolled from ingots and rectangular in shape with a minimum cross-sectional area of 25 sq. inches.

Heat One complete operation of a furnace from charging to tapping.

Pickling The process of chemically cleaning the surface of a metal object in preparation for further working.

Rolling mill In its simplest form a rolling mill consists of two rollers, one above the other, turning at the same speed, but in opposite directions so that the metal is drawn into them. Its purpose is to flatten metal objects.

Roughing The first phase of rolling or hammering a white hot ingot into blooms or slabs.

Scarfing The process of cutting out thin defective surface areas of ingots usually by the use of the oxy-acetylene method.

Skin A thin surface different from the main mass of a metal ingot.

Slab A semi-finished hot rolled product worked down from the ingot following the stage of the bloom but distinguished from the billet by its flat section. It has a minimum thickness of 1½ inches and a width generally more than twice the thickness.

Soaking pit A vertical reheating furnace for uniformly heating ingots to the temperature required for rolling.

Teeming The pouring of molten steel from the ladle into ingot moulds.

Turn A term denoting the amount of equipment utilization; i.e., a 7 day, 21 turn is necessary for maximum equipment utilization.

[2] *An Encyclopedia of the Iron and Steel Industry,* The Technical Press, London, 1956.

10

THE
MOHAWK
RUBBER
COMPANY

ORIGIN OF THE COMPANY

"When the Mohawk Rubber Company started in Akron forty-eight years ago," said Mr. William T. Ernst, treasurer of the company, "it was at a time when it was as much the fashion to organize an automobile or a tire company as it is today to go into electronics. Since that time over five hundred companies started out to make tires. Today, there are only thirteen left."

In 1913 Mr. Samuel Miller, an executive of the Goodyear Tire and Rubber Company, formed the Mohawk Rubber Company by purchasing the assets of the Stein Double Cushion Tire Company, a producer of solid and pneumatic tires. At that time the major companies (Goodyear, Goodrich, Firestone, and U.S. Rubber—known as "the Big Four") had been in existence for only about a dozen years. Mohawk enjoyed profitable operations until 1930. In the early 1930's, however, sales decreased sharply causing sizable operating losses. In 1934 Mr. Ray E. Bloch, then credit manager of the company, worked out a financial arrangement with the company's banks and creditors who were threatening it with bankruptcy. As part of the deal Mr. Bloch was made president and general manager of the company. He immediately set out to rehabilitate the company. By 1937 the company had earned a modest profit and although sales remained between two and three million dollars per year until World War II, operations were profitable each year.

After World War II sales increased steadily from $8 million to nearly $21 million in 1951. Profits in this period more than quadrupled, amounting to more than $1 million in 1951. Both sales and profits declined precipitously during the next three years and in 1954 the company sustained a loss of more than $600,000 when sales dropped

exhibit 1

THE MOHAWK RUBBER COMPANY

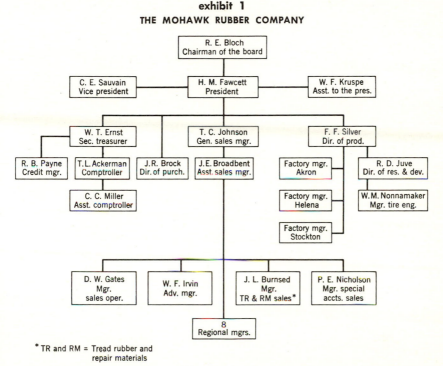

* TR and RM = Tread rubber and
  repair materials

to $8.8 million. The company's loss in 1954 resulted from the termination of government contracts, and also from the writing off of certain fixed assets no longer required. From 1950–1953 government contracts accounted for average annual sales of approximately $9.2 million, representing approximately half of the company's sales during that period.

In 1956 Mr. Bloch became chairman of the Board and Henry Fawcett, then thirty-six years old, became president and executive officer of the company. Sales rose steadily from 1955 to 1961, reaching a peak of $36 million in 1961 with net income of $1.75 million. (See Exhibit 2.)

In 1961 the company was engaged in the manufacture and sale of

exhibit 2 **MOHAWK RUBBER COMPANY**
Statement of income, years ending December 31st (in thousands of dollars)

	1961	1960	1959	1958	1957	1956	1955	1954	1953	1952	1951	1950	1949
Net sales	$36,379	$32,326	$31,657	$25,513	$20,842	$15,127	$14,330	$8,865	$16,264	$19,190	$20,884	$11,551	$8,360
Cost of products sold	28,739	25,749	25,543	20,526	17,807	13,012	12,709	9,104	14,969	16,347	16,486	9,724	7,284
	7,640	6,577	6,114	4,987	3,035	2,115	1,621	(239)	1,295	2,843	4,398	1,827	1,076
Selling, administrative & general expenses	3,603	3,910	3,406	2,673	1,755	1,287	1,009	830	1,021	1,096	1,047	775	628
	4,037	2,667	2,708	2,314	1,280	828	612	(1,069)	274	1,747	3,351	1,052	448
Other income	49	34	112	95	26	16	54	21	16	30	23	13	39
	4,086	2,701	2,820	2,409	1,305	844	666	(1,048)	290	1,777	3,374	1,065	487
Other deductions	475	430	259	191	136	72	25	293	28	1	19	4	9
Income before taxes	3,611	2,271	2,561	2,218	1,169	772	641	(1,341)	262	1,776	3,355	1,061	478
Federal taxes	1,860	1,203	1,342	1,153	606	402	320	(cr)694	(cr)365	1,092	2,283	465	182
Net income	$1,751	$1,068	$1,219	$1,065	$563	$370	$321	$(647)	$627	$684	$1,072	$596	$296

exhibit 3   **MOHAWK RUBBER COMPANY**
Balance sheet, years ending December 31st (in thousands of dollars)

	_1961_	_1960_	_1959_	_1958_	_1957_
Assets					
Cash	$ 833	$ 906	$ 686	$ 835	$ 368
U. S. tax notes	—	—	—	—	
Less amount applied on taxes					
Receivables (net)	9,900	7,346	6,648	5,378	3,787
Tax refund due	—	—	—	—	
Inventories	6,564	5,793	5,958	4,469	3,827
Total current assets	17,297	14,045	13,292	10,682	7,982
Other assets	341	149	385	443	102
Plant and equipment	11,369	9,899	8,552	6,023	5,867
Depreciation	3,999	3,329	2,572	2,271	2,219
Net plant and equipment	7,370	6,570	5,980	3,752	3,648
Deferred charges	—	193	259	189	124
Total assets	$25,008	$20,957	$19,916	$15,066	$11,857
Liabilities					
Bank loans	$ —	$ 1,000	$ 750	$ —	$ 550
Accounts payable	5,059	3,743	3,733	$ 4,031	2,816
Current part of term debt	—	128	—	—	323
Accrued expenses	1,723	1,278	1,369	192	188
Advances	—	—	—	—	—
Taxes	1,357	833	812	970	481
Total current liabilities	8,139	6,982	6,664	5,193	4,358
Long term debt	5,500	4,106	4,000	2,500	1,524
Common stock	636	516	492	225	144
Capital surplus	4,544	4,316	3,858	3,075	606
Earned surplus	6,189	5,037	4,902	4,073	5,225
	11,369	9,869	9,252	7,373	5,975
Total liabilities	$25,008	$20,957	$19,916	$15,066	$11,857

rubber and rubber products used in the transportation field. It manufactured passenger and truck tires in the popular sizes for the replacement market which it sold through dealers and distributors, principally in the Middle West and South. Its inner tubes were produced by another manufacturer. Mohawk's sales divided into two major product groups—automobile tires and tubes which accounted for approximately 75% of 1961 sales, and tread rubber and repair materials which constituted 25% of sales. In 1961 Mohawk produced more than 1,400,000 tires, approximating 1.8% of the industry replacement tire

exhibit 3   (continued)

1956	1955	1954	1953	1952	1951	1950	1949
$ 489	$ 564	$ 109	$ 320	$ 400	$1,269	$ 323	$ 609
—	—	—	—	—	—	—	402
							(176)
2,297	1,680	1,222	1,057	1,431	1,919	1,762	923
—	—	701	192	—	—	—	—
3,703	2,580	1,906	2,542	3,595	3,654	2,480	1,451
6,489	4,824	3,938	4,111	5,426	6,842	4,565	3,209
100	100	97	95	93	92	90	88
5,353	3,835	3,765	4,155	3,939	3,261	2,656	2,115
1,964	1,804	1,634	1,538	1,324	1,207	1,062	959
3,389	2,031	2,131	2,617	2,615	2,054	1,594	1,156
75	39	52	68	39	45	32	30
$10,053	$6,994	$6,218	$6,891	$8,173	$9,033	$6,281	$4,483
$ 300	—	$ 350	—	—	—	—	—
1,873	$1,205	749	$ 842	$1,238	$1,292	$1,421	$ 269
249	—	—	—	—	—	—	—
80	88	73	124	74	72	36	15
—	—	—	—	—	—	—	14
347	376	7	89	1,092	2,290	222	0
2,849	1,669	1,179	1,055	2,404	3,654	1,679	288
1,650	—	—	—	—	—	—	—
142	142	142	142	142	142	142	142
557	557	557	557	557	557	557	557
4,855	4,626	4,340	5,137	5,070	4,680	3,903	3,486
5,554	5,325	5,039	5,836	5,769	5,379	4,602	4,185
$10,053	$6,994	$6,218	$6,891	$8,173	$9,033	$6,281	$4,483

volume, and some 40,000,000 pounds of tread rubber and repair materials, which approximated 8% of the industry volume. In tread rubber and repair materials used in recapping and repairing tires, the company had been the country's largest producer for many years.

Manufacturing operations were conducted in the company's own plants in Akron, Ohio, and West Helena, Arkansas, and at a leased plant in Stockton, California. The company had 1,180 employees, most of whom were hourly rated production workers. The Akron plant had a capacity of 2,000 tires per day while the Helena plant had a daily capacity of 7,800 tires. In addition, the two plants each had a capacity of 75,000 pounds of tread rubber and repair materials daily. A small amount of tread rubber was produced in the Stockton plant by its subsidiary, the Mohawk Corporation. Service to the company's 1,500 dealers and distributors was provided from four warehouses in Ohio, Arkansas, Georgia, and California. The company's home office was in Akron.

THE RUBBER INDUSTRY

The rubber industry was dominated by four large producers known as "the Big Four" or the "Majors." Each had annual sales of over a half billion dollars. The industry also included a number of small producers, known as "independents," whose sales were generally between $15 million and $100 million a year. General Tire, which was also classed as an independent, was an exception, and had sales of over $500 million. (See Industry Notes.)

The Majors manufactured synthetic rubber for their own use and for resale to the independents. Their supply of crude natural rubber was obtained partly from plantations they operated themselves and partly by purchase on the open market. The Majors also manufactured materials allied to rubber, such as plastics and chemicals, both for their own use and for resale to others.

The Big Four sold a full line of tires and tubes under their own brand names to the original equipment market and in the replacement field. These large producers considered original equipment tires (called first-line tires) to be good business, even though it yielded a relatively low profit. They believed that this large volume production paid a considerable portion of their overhead expenses; that it enhanced their reputation for prestige; and, probably most important, they believed that the motorists would be inclined to continue to buy the brand of tires which came with the car. Only the Big Four and General Tire and Rubber shared the original equipment market.

In the replacement field the Big Four sold their tires through independent dealers, or through company-owned retail stores. They also produced private brand tires for mail order houses and for the large oil companies. Both the number of private brands and the total volume of this type of business had been showing a sharp rising trend. A recent survey showed Sears Roebuck & Company's Allstate brand to be ranking third, behind Goodyear and Firestone, as national sales leaders. Department stores and chain stores were becoming an increasingly popular outlet for tires. In addition to tires, the Big Four fabricated numerous other rubber products, such as hose, belting, and rubber footwear. The Big Four engaged in extensive research, both pure and applied.

The independents generally sold their tires in the replacement market through independent dealers. This market had considerably more potential, since there were 80 million replacement tires sold annually, while new car production seldom exceeded 25 million tires per year. (See Exhibit 4.) Some independents manufactured private brands for mail order houses and oil companies.

Within each quality grade the raw materials used by the various tire manufacturers were generally the same, and so was the design and the construction of the various types of tires. Manufacturing methods and processes were almost uniform throughout the industry. In fact, most tire makers secured their rubber mixing mills, their tire building equipment, and their molds from the same equipment manufacturers. The result was that the quality of the tires of each of the leading manufacturers was comparable at the same quality grade, and their prices within quality brackets were fairly uniform.

The rubber industry was traditionally affected by new automobile sales. To offset this in the postwar period all of the majors had diversified to the extent that only about half of their production was in tires. (See Exhibit 5.)

SOME SPECIAL ASPECTS OF SELLING TIRES

Historically, the tire business was highly competitive. All members of the industry, including the Big Four and the small producers alike, strove to increase their share of the market by high pressure advertising and price competition. The advertising copy in their newspaper and national magazine advertisements at one point became so filled with wild and exaggerated claims that the industry leaders agreed with the Federal Trade Commission to restrain their excesses in copywriting. The superlatives and boasts continued, however, and companies publicly accused each other of publishing misleading claims for their products.

Although most producers continued to emphasize advertising, it

exhibit 4

(a) Sales of Motor Vehicles and Production of Automobile Tires, 1929–1939; 1947–1960.
(b) Indexes of Shipments of Replacement and Original Equipment Tires, 1929–1939;
1947–1960

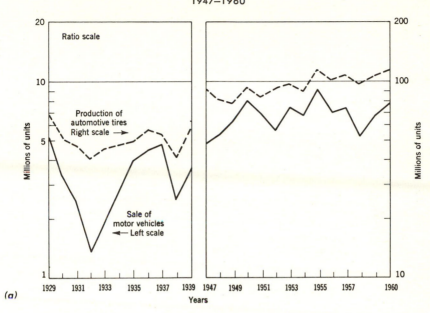

(a)

SOURCE: *Rubber Products Industry—A Statistical Compendium*, N.I.C.B., New York, 1959, and Bureau of the Census, 1960.

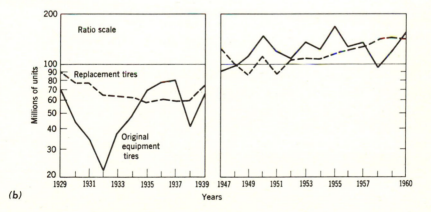

(b)

SOURCE: *Rubber Products Industry—A Statistical Compendium*, N.I.C.B., New York, 1959, and Bureau of the Census, 1960.

exhibit 5

Employment in subindustries of the Rubber Products Industry, 1929–1939; 1947–1960

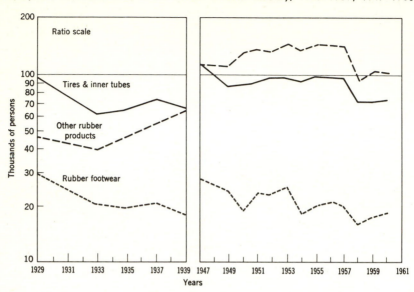

SOURCE: *Rubber Products Industry—A Statistical Compendium, N.I.C.B.,* New York, 1959, and Bureau of the Census, 1960.

was generally recognized that price was the most powerful factor in achieving tire sales. The major producers, by virtue of their predominance in size, took the lead in setting general price levels. No small producer was in a position to set his prices above those of the Big Four; in fact, it was typical of the small producer to shade his prices to a level slightly below that of the Majors.

Selling tires was distinctly different from the selling of most other products in that it was virtually impossible to generate additional demand for tires. "People simply do not want to buy tires," said a sales executive of a competitive company. "They buy tires only when they are forced to do so. There is no impulse factor; there is only the emergency factor." For this reason it was the strategy of the major producers to have a widespread distribution network, intensively covering the country geographically. The major producers were undertaking a program of building their own outlet stores, which handled their tires, and, in addition, many other types of merchandise. The volume of tires sold by large department stores such as Macy's in New York and Wieboldt's in Chicago was rising rapidly; many chain stores of all kinds were adding tires to their lines; variety chains, such as Neisner's; food supermarkets, and even drug chains; and a few enterprising wholesalers were having tires manufactured under their own brand names, which they marketed through any and all of these types of outlets.

The Mohawk management was in general agreement with the industry trend toward more widespread outlets. "To sell tires," said Mr. Fawcett, "you have to knock on doors. In our case, it is the dealer's door."

SALES

"In tread rubber," said Mr. William T. Ernst, "we have been a leader in the industry for many years. In tire sales, however, our largest competitors—Goodyear and Firestone—each do more business every two weeks than we do in a year. But despite the great and almost overwhelming advantages which rightfully belong to the Big Four, 25.3% of the replacement tires bought in 1960 were brands that did not belong to the Big Four, to Sears, Montgomery Ward or Standard Oil. A Look Magazine survey the same year showed that 33.4% of the people asked said they would buy tires not made by the large companies, or that they didn't know what make they would buy. Certainly if one-third of the replacement market is open to all tire manufacturers, there is plenty of room for more Mohawk growth."

In 1961 passenger car tires accounted for about $18,000,000 of Mohawk's sales volume; truck and farm tractor tires about $9,000,000; and tread rubber and repair materials about $9,400,000. Of the $27,000,000 tire sales, the premium grade tubeless Golden Arrow represented nearly 25%; the tubeless Arrow Chief 17%; Arrow Chief, tube, 33%; and Braves, tube, 25%.

When Henry Fawcett became president of the company in 1956, Mr. Charles Sauvain, a veteran of over thirty years' service with Mohawk, was the company's general sales manager. For many years Mr. Sauvain had been in the financial end of the business, principally as credit manager under Mr. Bloch, and when the sales manager left rather suddenly in 1952 Mr. Sauvain, feeling that this would be in the nature of a promotion, asked for the position and received it. One of Mr. Fawcett's first major objectives, when he became head of the company, was to stimulate a more aggressive attitude toward sales. Before the end of 1956 Mr. Sauvain had been promoted to treasurer, and Mr. Fawcett brought into the company Mr. Thomas Johnson to direct the sales function. Mr. Johnson had had considerable experience in the tire business as a tire adjuster, doing general field service work, traveling as a salesman in a territory, and finally as a district sales manager.

Until Mr. Johnson became sales manager, salesmen had been paid on a straight commission basis, drove their own cars, and paid their own expenses. In his first nine months Mr. Johnson dismissed nine of the company's thirteen salesmen, and then he proceeded to build a new sales force. The company sought college men, but accepted high school graduates. Previous tire sales experience was required, and preference was given to those having major rubber company experience. The aim was to hire men in their middle thirties or younger, but exceptions were made. Salesmen were paid a base salary plus a liberal bonus after they reached a certain quota. On this basis the average salesman earned from $8,500 to $11,000 a year.

Each salesman was furnished with a new car every fifteen months and had an expense account which ran around $400 a month. At the end of Mr. Johnson's first year in office, the company had a sales force of 48 men.

With the new sales force, a methodical campaign of developing the dealer organization in one limited territory at a time was undertaken. The first objective was the southeastern states, where the Mohawk management believed buyers were less brand conscious. The Big Four had done extensive national advertising in this region but it was believed that this advertising did not reach the southern rural population effectively, since they were not regular readers of the national magazines. Management also believed that the lower prices of Mohawk tires would have appeal. The first campaign—twelve weeks of television and radio advertising (Grand Ol' Opry)—was aimed at Florida and Alabama, and gave away 50 sets of tires every two weeks to holders of the "lucky license" numbers posted in Mohawk dealers' stores. The company also began to use regional advertising that was available in such magazines as *Life*. The advertising program cost about $50,000 and the give-away tires another $24,000.

In 1956 the company had about 750 dealer accounts. During 1957 fifty new dealer accounts were being opened each month, and by the middle of 1961 the company was adding an average of 100 dealers a month to its distribution system and had approximately 1,500 active dealers and distributors.

The company's next campaign was aimed at developing Georgia and South Carolina and a warehouse was built at Atlanta to service the territory. In addition, serious consideration was being given to the market in the East where the company hoped to establish a new automated plant by 1963.

The company had eight regional sales managers directing forty-eight salesmen. The sales volume in each territory was between $240,000 and $1,000,000. The practice was to have the regional manager in each new territory sign up enough accounts to reach the $240,000 break-even point, whereupon the territory was turned over to a salesman. If a salesman developed over $1,000,000 volume in his territory, the area would be divided to form two sales territories.

Mr. Fawcett believed that the Majors sold their tires principally on a brand preference basis through national advertising, but that Mohawk tires could best be sold on the basis of dealer-customer relationships. Therefore the initial sales effort was aimed at attracting new dealers and building a loyal dealer organization.

To attract new dealers the company offered exclusive territory franchises. The guarantee of a protected territory was a concession which none of the Majors granted, and the Mohawk management considered it their most important sales point. The salesmen emphasized this by pointing out to prospective dealers that the Big Four had opened many of their own retail stores in areas of high potential and that this was a constant threat to independent dealers. Mohawk also offered a price differential which was thought to be approximately 8% to 11% below the Majors for tires of like quality. (See Exhibit 6.)

exhibit 6   PRICE COMPARISON OF MOHAWK
TIRES AND "BIG FOUR" TIRES

	Mohawk	Big four
Golden Arrow	$14.75	$16.17
Arrow Chief	13.98	15.32
Brave	9.63 (nylon)	9.63 (rayon)

The company also assured its customers that its tires conformed to industry standards of quality at each grade. Mohawk also offered its retail customers an unconditional road hazard guarantee which no other manufacturer granted. Adjustments on defective tires cost

Mohawk about ½% to ¾% of its sales dollar; the road hazard guarantee raised this expense to about 2%.

Salesmen called on their dealers about every ten days. They took carload orders themselves, and the dealers sent in fill-in orders. The salesmen spent their time seeking new accounts, giving the dealer sales and merchandising help, aiding him in planning advertising, seeing that he was properly identified as a Mohawk dealer, and keeping his relations with Akron smooth.

Any dealer buying over $100,000 per quarter received a 3% quantity weight discount on all carload orders, 2% on truckloads and on fill-in orders. To qualify for the discount he had to take another carload every three months. Distributors, who usually received this discount, operated on a very narrow markup, sometimes as little as 75¢ to $1 a tire. Oil companies usually used a markup of 15%.

The company paid the freight on each shipment of 200 pounds or more to a single destination. It cost 25¢ to ship a tire from Akron to New York City, $1 to ship it from Akron to Texas, and $3 to $4 to ship it to California. Because of the freight expense, a higher price per tire had to be charged at distant points, and promotions on a cut-price basis could not be extended to the West Coast.

To overcome this disadvantage the company established what it called "dealer-warehousemen." Dealer-warehousemen were distributors to whom the company shipped in carload lots to get the benefit of the low freight rate. The dealer-warehouseman acted as the company's warehouseman and local shipper. These distributors were paid 5% over cost on the first $65,000 annual volume, and 3½% on any volume over $65,000. When Mr. Fawcett became president of the company he believed that lack of an adequate warehouse system and insufficient stocks of tires in the field had been one of the company's major problems. In 1959 the company had warehouses at Akron, Ohio; Helena, Arkansas; Atlanta, Georgia; and Stockton, California. It planned eventually to have additional warehouses at Minneapolis, Minnesota; Portland, Oregon; Memphis, Tennessee; and Dallas, Texas.

The company did no forecasting, nor did it do any market research. Management assumed that there was enough potential in every territory to warrant its sales effort. In estimating the extent of its overall volume, it considered that replacement tire sales were definitely keyed to new car production; that good new car years were followed two years later by good tire replacement years. Also, in especially poor new car years, the rise in replacement tire sales came the same year, due to buyers switching from new to used car purchases and replacing the tires. Management, however, was beginning to follow car registrations more closely, and breaking them down according to salesmen's territories.

The management considered it important to limit its line to the 72 most popular sizes and types of tires, compared to 120 to 135 sizes offered by other companies. This simplified production and limited inventory, but there was a higher profit margin in the odd sizes and the salesmen were feeling pressure from their dealers to expand the line in this direction.

"The rubber industry," said Mr. Fawcett, "has become a vast complex in the American economy. It involves chemicals, industrial rubber goods, miscellaneous rubber products, as well as the familiar automobile tire. Although we have no genuinely reliable yardstick to measure by, it is probable that seventy-five percent of the rubber industry is still concerned with tires. In the tire field there are three principal categories: tires sold as original equipment on new vehicles; tires sold in the replacement market; and rubber materials sold to recap and repair tires. Barely 1% of our sales are in the original equipment field. This is because the auto manufacturers buy in such substantial quantities that it would take a far greater percentage of our capacity than we can afford to spare. Also, the margin of profit on such business is too small to justify the large percentage of over-all production capacity that would be committed. We believe that it will be in our interest to build solidly for the long-range future by establishing a loyal dealer organization. At present no single Mohawk customer, including the government, accounts for as much as ten percent of our sales."

As a matter of policy, the company did not manufacture tires for new equipment, nor did it accept contracts from mail order or chain stores, considering that this business was too uncertain to permit it to monopolize production facilities. Management thought this type of business might disrupt the normal flow of production destined for the company's retail dealers.

"There are certain advantages in being a small company," said Mr. Bloch, chairman of the Board. "We can turn on a dime. The big companies are too ponderous and slow moving to be able to do that."

Until 1959 Mohawk produced both nylon and rayon cord tires. Management believed that this raised production costs considerably. It meant twice as much cord purchasing, more complex production schedules, shorter production runs, and additional inventories. Management also believed that the rayon manufacturers had been opportunists in their price policies. In the summer of 1959 there had been a price spread of only about 7% between nylon and rayon tires. When Mohawk dropped rayon in 1959 it was the only major tire manufacturer to do so. (See Exhibit 7.)

TREAD RUBBER AND REPAIR MATERIALS

Mohawk had for many years been a leading producer of tread rubber and repair materials used in the recapping of tires. Prior to World War II it had been known in the industry as being principally a producer of "camelback" (the trade name for rubber used in recapping), and the management had treated tires as a secondary product line. In 1961 the company was still a factor in the camelback industry, supplying approximately 8% of the national production, which represented 25% of its total sales. In addition, tire sales, which comprised 75% of Mohawk's sales, accounted for 1.8% of the national production.

The Mohawk management believed that the retread business had a great future potential. Research had produced improved materials and application processes that had largely eliminated most of the former disadvantages of recapping. Recapping had become the accepted practice for trucks, taxis, and commercial fleets. Industry shipments of tread rubber had grown from 95 million pounds in 1947 to more than 500 million pounds in 1961. During that period Mohawk's tread rubber production had increased from 6 million to more than 30 million pounds a year.

In spite of heavy emphasis on the expansion of tire sales, the Mohawk management expressed determination to remain a factor in the tread rubber industry. "We are still the largest producer of camelback and repair material in the country," said Mr. Fawcett, "and the recapping business is growing. Today there are 105 million new tires made a year; but each year 60 million tires are recapped. Recapping has become the accepted standard practice of taxis and trucks. Even the commercial airlines are now experimenting with recapping their tires. The growing popularity of nylon casings will make many more sound casings available which will be suitable for recapping. The day will come when there will be a tire recapped for every new tire made."

Mohawk sold retread rubber to independent recappers and distributors on a technical specification basis, with standards set according to the performance required for usage on either taxis, light or heavy duty trucks, passenger cars, or other vehicles. Mohawk served about 600 of the 10,000 tread rubber dealers in the country. Sales were through 24 tread rubber distributors. It also did special compounding on a "prescription" basis and, through its close connections with major manufacturers, it was able to provide tire recappers with technical advice on compounds and on processing methods. Profit margins were lower on retread materials but overhead and selling expense were also lower. Price competition in tread rubber was keen—½¢ to 1¢ a pound might switch a customer from one product to another. Mohawk's prices were average for the industry, and in its advertising it featured the quality factor. The general theme was usually expressed as follows:

"Why buy cheap retread rubber? Is
your reputation worth 1¢ a pound?"

LABOR AND LABOR RELATIONS

At the Akron plant some 600 hourly and 160 administrative employees turned out nearly 1,500 passenger and truck tires a day. It took about ten days to train an employee for most jobs, and about a month to six weeks for an employee to develop skill on the most exacting job—that of tire building. In keeping with a gentleman's agreement with the other rubber manufacturers of Akron, the Mohawk plant did not hire anyone in the employ of another rubbermaker, even if he voluntarily asked Mohawk for a job. Neither did the Mohawk employment manager advertise in Akron papers, but used the Cleveland and Canton papers instead. The Mohawk personnel director believed that most of his employees had less than average education, came from lower-than-average income families which lived in the poorer residential districts. Rubbermaking, with comparatively high pay, was attractive to them in spite of the fact that much of the work was hot, heavy, and dirty. The personnel director also believed that the work situation created problems; management believed the employees were easily led by their union leaders, and were typically suspicious of anything coming from the company.

Exhibit 7

THE WALL STREET JOURNAL, Monday, September 14, 1959

Mohawk Rubber Drops Rayon Cord Tire Lines For All-Nylon Output

President Says Move Is Caused By 'Rising Public Preference' For Nylon Replacement Tires

By a WALL STREET JOURNAL *Staff Reporter*

AKRON, Ohio—Mohawk Rubber Co. has discontinued using rayon cord in passenger car tire production and converted entirely to nylon.

H. M. Fawcett, president of Mohawk, said, "Our move to nylon reflects our research findings which show nylon cord tires to be superior in all performance characteristics. It also reflects the rising public preference for nylon in the replacement tire market."

Mohawk's move follows by less than a month a general round of price cuts by makers of nylon tire cord, led by Du Pont Co. The reductions, which ran from 8% to 11%, cut sharply the differential between nylon and the best grades of rayon, or rayon-derived, tire cords. Following the reduction, an official of one big tire maker said it made the price difference between the two types of cords "very thin, if any at all."

Mohawk officials, however, did not specify the price cut as a reason for their move. They indicated that the increasing proportion of nylon tire production was the primary reason for their action.

Mohawk's total production goes to the replacement tire market. In 1956, nylon cord tires accounted for 22% of Mohawk's sales. This year, prior to discontinuance of the rayon line, nylon tires accounted for 70% of the company's production, according to Thomas Johnson, sales manager.

Mr. Fawcett gave as an additional reason for the changeover, the simplification of dealer inventory problems. "By offering only nylon cord tires," he said, "Mohawk dealers across the country will be able to simplify and standardize their inventories. This will enable them to offer their customers better service than ever before."

Mr. Fawcett also said the line simplification should eliminate much confusion among buyers about the many types and kinds of tires available.

Nylon cord tires now account for about 40% of the total passenger car replacement market, up from 10% of the market in 1955.

In 1936 Goodyear adopted a modified Bedaux incentive system in connection with a six-hour work day as a share-the-work proposition to spread employment during the depression. Under this system a man was able to produce in six hours as much as he would normally put out in eight, and the two hours saved were added to his wages as a bonus. The original plan allowed no lunch or relief period and called for six hours of continuous production. The employees liked the short work day and later the unions came out strongly in favor of it. The rubber companies were unable to eliminate it so that the six-hour day became industry practice in Akron.

Plants operated around the clock, with shifts changing at noon, 6 p.m., midnight, and 6 a.m. Each shift had an 18-minute rest period and a lunch period which totaled about an hour per shift.

Typical wages were about $2.90 an hour plus fringe benefits of approximately 75¢ per hour. Piece rates were such that the average employee was able to produce his daily quota in 4½ to 5 hours ("capping out," in employee jargon), after which he would remain idle rather than earn an additional bonus. Under a general tacit agreement among themselves, employees would not exceed their quotas.

Because of the six-hour shifts, most of the employees found time to work at another job outside of the plant. Some held a second full-time job, while many operated small service businesses from their homes, such as auto repairs, saw sharpening, gardening, house painting, or farming. The Mohawk personnel management believed that since most employees had a second source of earnings, their annual incomes were relatively high for their station in life. As a result it was difficult to deal with many of the employees because they had achieved some degree of financial independence. Supported by their secondary source of income, employees could take a strike without much suffering. The result was a strong union which constantly and vigorously sparred with management. By 1957, when grievances regarding wage rates, work methods, departmental jurisdiction, and working conditions multiplied to what management considered a "prohibitive degree," the company decided to take a "hard nosed" attitude toward the union. Thereafter they met with the union an average of seven hours each week on grievances, and in a two-year period took 88 of them to arbitration, winning 80% of them. During the same period two other tiremakers took 2 and 7 grievances to arbitration and most of these were compromised.

After experiencing four illegal work stoppages in 1958 management announced that the next wildcat strike would result in an automatic seven-day suspension. Later in that year when a fifth stoppage occurred, management held firm and invoked the rule, closing the plant for seven days. This was the last work stoppage. The Mohawk management, nevertheless, professed that its attitude toward the union was one of respect and cooperation. It believed that the rubber unions were entirely honest and free from scandal, and had never been known to indulge in any double-dealing or "sweethearting." Management stated that it believed the rubber unions were here to stay, and that it was willing to continue to deal with them in spite of the daily sparring.

In June 1961 a new 2-year contract, matching the pattern set by the rubber tire industry, was negotiated with the United Rubber Workers increasing hourly workers' wages $7\frac{1}{2}¢$ an hour the first year and $7¢$ an hour the second year. In addition, supplementary unemployment benefits were extended from 26 to 39 weeks and the weekly maximum benefit was raised $5 a week. Other fringe benefits negotiated included an eighth paid holiday, four weeks vacation for employees with 22 years' service (formerly 25 years' service) and three weeks vacation for employees with 10 years' service (formerly 11 years' service).

PRODUCTION PROCESS

The process of tiremaking used by all manufacturers was virtually identical. The crude rubber, both natural and synthetic, was mixed with carbon black, oil, and sulphur in specific proportions to produce a desired grade. Initially mixed in a "Banbury" mill, whose beater blades speedily achieved a uniformly smooth blending of the ingredients, the rubber was then kneaded by "warm-up" roller mills till it reached the desired temperature to give it the plasticity required for forming. The batch was then extruded through dies into the shape and size of the tread to be formed. Concurrently the fabric for the cord which formed the carcass was impregnated with rubber by a "Z" calender train, in which the fabric was coated with rubber as it passed through a highly precise series of cylindrical rollers somewhat like a newsprint roller press. The bead, the rubber-coated wire cable reinforced band which held the tire rim to the wheel, was fabricated separately.

The various components of the tire—the tread and sidewall rubber, the cord material for the plies, the beads, flipper strips and chafing strips—were then brought together to the tirebuilder, who assembled the parts on a tirebuilding machine, an ingenious apparatus whose central cylinder expanded to form the tire and collapsed to permit it to be removed. The crude tire then went to the curing mold where it was inserted in a die of the desired dimensions and tread. Here it was heated by steam, under pressure, for the time required to vulcanize the rubber. After curing, the tire was shaved smooth of mold-marks, painted, powdered, inspected, and wrapped for shipment.

Calender tolerances were as close as plus or minus 1/1,000th of an inch. In a twenty-pound tire, which used twelve pounds of tread rubber, no more variation than 3/10ths of a pound of rubber was permitted. All materials were bought by the pound, while tires were sold on a per-unit basis. The assembly operation performed by the tirebuilder required a high degree of accuracy.

PLANTS AND FACILITIES

Mohawk's Akron plant had been built in 1898 by another manufacturer and it was acquired by Mohawk in 1913. It was situated literally within the shadow of the original and principal plant of Goodyear, whose huge complex of multi-storied buildings, separated from Mohawk only by a railroad track, surrounded and dwarfed the little Mohawk factory. The Akron plant consisted of four units: a compounding plant, where the crude was milled; a tire-building plant, where the tire parts were assembled and cured; a warehouse and service garage; and the executive office building. The compounding building was across the street and separated from the other buildings.

At the time Mr. Fawcett became president in 1955 he believed that lack of local plants and warehouses was one of Mohawk's major problems. In 1956 the company bought a plant in West Helena, Arkansas, which had been built in 1948 by the Chrysler Corporation for the production of wooden frame station wagon bodies. The plant had been idle since Chrysler switched to metal bodies. The facility, which had been built at a cost of over $1 million by Chrysler, was purchased by Mohawk for $300,000. The purchase was financed by an $800,000 bond issue made by the Arkansas Development Corporation, with guarantee by Mohawk. The funds were used to pay for the plant, to buy six new Bag-o-matic presses, and to furnish working capital.

Since there were no rubber workers in the Arkansas labor market, the management undertook to train a work force. For this purpose nine Akron supervisors were chosen, one for each of the principal production operations, such as tread tubing, curing, Banbury milling, tire building, etc. Each man was chosen for having shown exceptional competence in his operation and, in an attempt to avoid carrying over to West Helena the bad work habits and practices which had been built up at Akron, only men who were known to be good "company men" were chosen.

Believing that younger men would better lend themselves to being trained, the management at West Helena gave preference to the hiring of men in their twenties. Almost none of them had had any previous factory experience similar to that at Mohawk; most of them had worked in Arkansas hardwood lumbering mills, or on farms. No requirements as to education or previous experience were set, but employee applications were screened for ability through a series of tests such as a physical test, manual dexterity tests and intelligence tests. Most of the new employees lived within a radius of twenty miles of West Helena, because they had local family connections. Trained and skilled personnel, such as motion and time study men or maintenance mechanics, were recruited from cities as far away as Memphis.

The West Helena plant was single storied, high ceilinged, with a long rectangular floor pattern, and lent itself well, the Mohawk management believed, to the laying out of an efficient production flow. Where the Akron production process was complicated by the multi-storied buildings and by the fact that it was housed in several buildings, necessitating considerable in-plant transportation, the Helena operation was designed to bring in the raw materials at one end of the plant and transport them within the plant automatically by belts, chutes, and conveyors through a production system that flowed from the raw materials at one end of the plant to the finished tires at the other end.

Most of the tire makers, including Mohawk at its Akron plant, still cured their tires on "pot heaters" or "watch-case" molds—split section molds in which the tire had to be inserted and withdrawn by hand, limiting one man to the servicing of only two molds. In 1949 the bag-o-matic process was introduced. Under this process an insert, a heavy rubber inner tube, was inflated inside the uncured tire to mold it. The bag-o-matics were entirely automated, being served by conveyors which inserted the uncured tires into the mold and carried away the cured tires. One man attended a battery of 24 machines. West Helena was the only tire plant in the industry using bag-o-matics exclusively.

West Helena employees belonged to Local #539 of the United Rubber Workers. Being a newly organized local, management was able, it believed, to write into the contract the best phases of its Akron experience, and to eliminate the items which had caused its difficulties. Where the piecework rates at Akron had made substantial allowances for sub-standard buildings, work methods, and working conditions, the West Helena rates were considerably tighter; they also allowed less fringe benefits and contained considerably stricter disciplinary rules. In its first three years of operation the Helena plant averaged two grievance meetings a month, each of which lasted about two hours. No grievance had ever been carried to arbitration. Where the Akron management had considerable difficulty with certain vices, such as excessive drinking, the West Helena plant had no such experience.

The West Helena superintendent found, however, that his employees required close supervision and that he was short of competent supervisors and of employees who were of supervisory caliber; he considered absenteeism his major employee problem.

The supervisors who had been trained from the employee group tended to lack initiative and as a result they themselves needed constant direction. It was common for a supervisor to be on close friendly terms with his employees and often they were blood relatives, a situation which bred familiarity, lack of discipline, and disrespect. Two attitudes, both extremes, appeared among these foremen—one group was too easy-going; the other quite autocratic.

The Helena plant, contrary to the industry practice, worked an eight-hour day, three shifts a day, six days a week. Although wage levels were below those of Akron and in the rubber industry generally, they were high compared to other wages in the area. Employees were generally eager to turn out high production, but only during their standard eight-hour day. They were so eager, in fact, that the management found it necessary to put a ceiling of 25% over normal on incentives in order to keep a smooth and undisrupted flow of production. Most employees were unaccustomed to earning much money, a circumstance which caused them to work hard until their weekly earnings reached, say, $100, beyond which the employee would not be interested in higher earnings. It was difficult to get employees to work overtime, almost impossible to get them to work on Sundays, and the rate of absenteeism on Mondays was exceptionally high. The West Helena plant management nevertheless considered their employees' morale to be high, for the employees appeared to be appreciative of their high wages; they made an effort to conform; and most of them were receptive to company problems.

At West Helena the average plantwide wage rate was substantially below the rate paid by Mohawk at Akron. Mohawk's wage rates were about 7¢ higher than those of the Big Four. About 30% of the cost of a finished tire was made up of labor costs. In 1959 the per unit cost of direct labor and overhead at West Helena was running about 75% of that at Akron. The West Helena superintendent believed these savings resulted from lower wage rates, more efficient machinery and plant layout, higher employee morale, and higher per employee production at the lower wage rates.

The Akron plant obtained the bulk of its raw materials from one of the major rubber companies. The Helena plant obtained its raw material requirements independently, and directly from producers. Latex, refined from "wild" rubber, coming from abroad, was purchased from brokers at New Orleans, the port of entry. Synthetic rubber was bought from chemical concerns, whose principal refineries were located at Texas gulf ports. Both sources were only a short distance from West Helena.

The West Helena plant opened in September 1956 with a production of 600 tires a day plus 20,000 pounds of tread rubber; in June 1957, the rate was stepped up to 1,500 tires a day; in September 1958, to 3,000 tires a day; and in June 1959, to 4,200 tires a day. In the fall of 1959 an addition was built which added 50% to the floor area of the plant and a new $750,000 Z-calender train was installed. The original battery of six bag-o-matic presses was increased to 34. By mid-1961 there were 350 hourly workers and 50 staff personnel, and production increased to 5,700 tires a day plus 60,000 pounds of tread rubber.

"In the years following 1961," said Mr. Ernst, "we must rely on the crystal ball. We do know, however, that there will be more cars on the road and more people driving them. The Interstate Highway System will enable people to drive faster at safer speeds. Tires for compact cars might cost less, but it is doubtful whether they will wear any longer than regular tires. They have less weight to carry, but they revolve faster. In our opinion, both the tire market and the recapping industry will expand as they did in the fifties. . . . Mohawk should be able to increase its sales by the mid-sixties to the $40 to $45 million range, and by the late sixties to the $45 to $55 million range . . . earning on a consistent basis $1,700,000 to $2,000,000 annually."

U.S. TIRE INDUSTRY NOTES

Goodyear, the world's largest rubber fabricator, derives approximately 60% of its total sales from tire lines, which is fairly evenly divided between original equipment and replacement. Other products include: synthetic rubbers, plastic resins, plastic films, adhesives, aviation products, film cushioning, and vinyl flooring. Foreign operations, mainly tire lines made outside the U.S., account for over 20% of sales. Defense work averaged ⅛ of the total sales in 1950–54 and has continued important.

Daily tire capacity approximates 130,000 units with Chrysler its main original equipment outlet, and lesser amounts being supplied to Ford, American Motors, and General Motors. Replacement sales are handled through an estimated 70,000 dealers, oil companies, and some 600 company stores.

Firestone Tire & Rubber Co. is the nation's second largest tire producer and obtains nearly ⅔ of its sales from tires. The rest comes from about 770 company stores, natural and synthetic rubber, mechanical rubber goods, foam rubber, plastic and chemical products, metal items, and military items. Approximately 1,000 different sizes and types of pneumatic tires are manufactured, as well as more than 12,000 products in other fields. Daily tire capacity approximates 130,000 units. Original equipment normally accounts for about half of the unit tire volume, with Ford and General Motors the main outlets. In addition, the company also supplies a majority of the original equipment tires used by Studebaker-Packard. Replacement tire business in the U.S. and Canada is handled through approximately 60,000 independent dealers, oil companies, and company stores.

United States Rubber Company is the third largest rubber fabricator and derives about half of its sales from its tire division. The
rest comes from the mechanical rubber goods, footwear and general
products, textile, and chemical divisions. Military work is relatively
small. Foreign business accounts for slightly more than 20% of sales.

Daily tire capacity approximates 113,000 units. Nearly ⅔ of the
tire volume is replacement. General Motors is by far the largest
customer for the company's original equipment tires with smaller
amounts being supplied to Studebaker-Packard. The company owned
11 retail stores in 1959 and by 1961 it had more than 140, reflecting
the acquisition of two tire store chains and the opening of additional
units.

B. F. Goodrich Co. is the fourth largest rubber company and is
the most diversified of the "Big Four," deriving about 55% of its
revenue from nontire lines. The balance comes from an extensive line
of industrial rubber products, flooring and footwear, chemical and
plastic products, foamed and sponge rubber products, aviation and
missile components, and textile items.

Daily tire capacity approximates 65,000 units, with General Motors
its main equipment outlet, and lesser amounts being supplied to
Ford, American Motors, and Chrysler. Replacement sales, which are
more important volume-wise than original equipment sales, are
handled through several thousand independent dealers, through
more than 600 company-owned stores, and through the sale of private
brand tires to oil companies and a large mass merchandiser.

Armstrong Rubber Company ranks fifth in the tire industry on the
basis of unit volume, having a daily tire capacity of 47,000. Roughly
95% of sales is attributable to tires, solely for the replacement market,
with Sears Roebuck taking about 67% of the tires produced (about
70% of Sears' total requirements). Miscellaneous rubber products
account for approximately 5% of total sales.

Distribution of tires is made through 1,200 independent distributors
who sell to dealers throughout the country. Export sales to 70 foreign
countries are handled by 125 foreign distributors.

General Tire & Rubber Company is fifth in size among domestic
rubber fabricators. However, less than 50% of its volume and net
income in 1961 was derived from tires, plastics, chemicals, and other
miscellaneous products. Wholly-owned RKO General accounted for
approximately 14% of net income. About 36% of its consolidated net

income came from 84%-owned Aero jet-General Corporation (a leader in rockets and propellants and related atomic energy products).

Daily tire production approximates 26,000 units, supplied mainly to the replacement and fleet markets.

Lee Rubber & Tire Corporation derives an estimated ⅔ of total sales from tire lines, including replacement passenger car, truck, and bus tires, camelback, and various tire sundries. The other ⅓ comes from more than 1,000 items of mechanical rubber goods, including

FINANCIAL DATA OF THE BIG FOUR AND LEADING INDEPENDENT TIRE MANUFACTURERS*

Income statistics (in millions of dollars)

Goodyear Tire & Rubber

Year Ended Dec. 31	Net Sales	% Oper. Inc. of Sales	Maint. & Repairs	Deprec.	Net Bef. Taxes	Income Taxes	Net Inc.
1961	1,473.4	14.6	....	52.67	154.48	77.14	76.19
1960	1,550.9	12.3	40.1	49.82	138.38	66.52	71.02
1959	1,579.3	12.3	41.2	49.70	141.59	64.68	76.01
1958	1,367.6	13.7	34.7	47.41	135.04	66.49	65.74
1957	1,421.9	12.9	37.0	43.27	135.58	67.73	64.83
1956	1,358.8	12.8	36.6	38.14	130.49	66.30	62.46
1955	1,372.2	12.0	36.7	32.88	126.64	66.97	59.67
1954	1,090.1	11.7	30.4	33.83	91.43	43.37	48.06
1953	1,210.6	12.7	34.0	30.19	117.77	68.45	49.32
1952	1,138.4	12.6	30.6	25.94	108.11	69.10	39.01

Firestone Tire & Rubber

Year Ended Oct. 31	Net Sales	% Op. Inc. of Sales	Oper. Inc.	Maint. & Repairs	Deprec.	Net Bef. Taxes	Net Inc.
1961	1,182.7	14.6	171.7	....	49.1	124.2	63.63
1960	1,207.2	14.1	170.6	40.5	45.7	126.6	65.03
1959	1,187.8	14.4	171.2	34.9	40.7	129.0	64.60
1958	1,061.6	14.3	151.6	33.0	41.4	107.2	53.75
1957	1,158.9	13.9	161.4	37.5	39.0	119.8	61.69
1956	1,115.2	14.2	158.0	35.3	36.9	119.8	60.54
1955	1,114.9	13.3	148.6	23.2	32.0	114.3	55.38
1954	916.0	12.2	111.8	19.9	27.9	81.5	40.51
1953	1,029.4	11.8	121.7	22.1	24.7	94.2	46.75
1952	965.4	12.0	115.8	19.5	20.7	84.0	43.08

packing and conveyor belting, hose for the automotive, mining, steel and petroleum industries, and accessories for the automotive industry.

Tire sales are normally confined to the replacement and fleet markets. Distribution is nationwide, through 51 factory branches in principal cities east of the Mississippi, and in Dallas and Fort Worth, Texas, through Phillips Petroleum and Signal Oil. Daily tire capacity approximates 7,500 units.

The company also sells batteries under the Lee name.

FINANCIAL DATA OF THE BIG FOUR AND LEADING INDEPENDENT TIRE MANUFACTURERS (continued)*

Pertinent balance sheet statistics (in millions of dollars)

Goodyear Tire & Rubber (continued)

Gross Prop.	Capital Expend.	Cash Items	Inven- tories	Receiv- ables	Cur. Assets	Cur. Liabs.	Net Workg. Cap.	Cur. Ratio Assets to Liabs.	Long- term Debt
908.8	82.64	75.7	349.8	262.4	687.9	147.9	540.1	4.7–1	230.98
844.1	74.55	72.4	342.0	234.8	649.2	127.7	521.5	5.1–1	227.14
789.0	55.64	46.8	348.1	236.9	631.8	121.4	510.4	5.2–1	231.02
747.2	53.35	49.1	309.4	225.7	584.2	107.1	477.1	5.5–1	236.35
708.5	82.95	44.3	341.4	198.6	584.3	135.1	499.2	4.3–1	241.09
638.4	88.85	50.6	317.1	196.9	564.6	113.3	451.3	5.0–1	243.03
561.6	70.96	67.3	303.2	177.4	547.9	87.4	460.6	6.3–1	240.21
501.5	33.08	51.1	249.4	168.4	468.9	106.8	362.1	4.4–1	191.44
476.9	50.37	68.0	246.0	149.9	463.9	62.5	401.5	7.4–1	195.44
435.6	52.76	44.8	275.4	160.4	480.7	83.5	397.2	5.8–1	200.00

Firestone Tire & Rubber (continued)

Gross Prop.	Capital Expend.	Cash Items	Inven- tories	Receiv- ables	Cur. Assets	Cur. Liabs.	Net Workg. Cap.	Cur. Ratio Assets to Liabs.	Long- term Debt
604.0	70.87	45.5	287.7	233.6	566.8	183.1	383.7	3.1–1	76.0
555.9	82.81	43.9	283.6	226.6	554.1	173.5	380.6	3.2–1	76.9
501.5	48.48	69.5	250.1	227.7	547.4	152.9	394.5	3.6–1	91.8
472.5	37.77	45.7	245.3	197.3	488.3	128.3	360.0	3.5–1	96.5
456.2	73.72	45.3	268.6	199.6	513.5	184.4	329.1	3.8–1	101.2
399.2	58.57	45.3	241.7	195.0	482.0	160.7	321.3	3.0–1	105.7
358.9	55.72	53.1	211.5	169.1	433.7	125.5	308.2	3.5–1	110.2
320.7	43.69	65.1	199.7	128.3	393.1	92.4	300.7	4.3–1	114.5
292.9	43.68	67.1	192.2	132.7	392.7	98.6	293.3	4.0–1	118.8
266.1	42.95	74.8	185.3	123.7	383.7	95.5	288.2	4.0–1	121.5

FINANCIAL DATA OF THE BIG FOUR AND LEADING
INDEPENDENT TIRE MANUFACTURERS (continued)*

Income statistics (in millions of dollars) (continued)

United States Rubber

Year Ended Dec. 31	Net Sales	% Op. Inc. of Sales	Maint. & Repairs	Depr. & Obsol.	Net Bef. Taxes	Net Inc.	$8 Pfd. Earns.
1961	940.4	8.6	....	25.7	52.79	27.10	41.97
1960	966.8	9.4	31.36	24.2	67.31	30.74	47.21
1959	976.8	10.7	31.27	24.4	78.02	35.58	54.65
1958	870.6	9.2	26.00	24.7	50.15	22.67	34.82
1957	873.6	8.9	26.80	22.7	57.13	29.70	45.61
1956	901.3	9.5	28.70	21.8	61.83	31.87	48.95
1955	926.2	11.3	27.19	19.6	76.91	33.56	51.54
1954	782.5	9.6	23.73	17.6	54.53	27.96	42.94
1953	839.9	10.4	26.57	16.0	72.61	32.73	50.27
1952	851.1	12.4	24.57	14.4	88.56	28.17	43.27

Armstrong Rubber (continued)

Year Ended Sept. 30	Net Sales	% Oper. Inc. of Sales	Maint. & Repairs	Depr., Depl. & Amort.	Net Bef. Taxes	Inc. Taxes	Net Inc.
1961	119.39	13.2	1.88	4.55	9.58	4.73	4.85
1960	116.78	12.8	3.59	4.02	9.72	4.75	4.96
1959	117.16	13.8	....	3.43	11.92	6.02	5.90
1958	81.32	12.4	1.87	2.71	6.44	3.21	3.23
1957	76.14	12.0	1.87	2.47	5.84	2.89	2.95
1956	71.31	11.9	2.25	2.15	5.49	2.69	2.80
1955	68.98	12.0	1.38	1.96	5.32	2.59	2.73
1954	55.38	10.8	1.01	1.69	3.41	1.74	1.67
1953	62.29	9.8	1.11	1.31	4.14	2.42	1.72
1952	55.44	8.9	0.86	0.96	3.76	2.11	1.65

**FINANCIAL DATA OF THE BIG FOUR AND LEADING
INDEPENDENT TIRE MANUFACTURERS (continued)***

Pertinent balance sheet statistics (in millions of dollars) (continued)

United States Rubber (continued)

Gross Prop.	Capital Expend.	Cash Items	Inventories	Receivables	Cur. Assets	Cur. Liabs.	Net Workg. Cap.	Cur. Ratio Assets to Liabs.	Long-term Debt
556.77	36.09	54.0	240.7	150.8	445.5	134.0	311.5	3.3–1	149.70
529.25	26.51	57.6	243.5	138.3	439.4	121.1	318.3	3.6–1	154.67
526.95	25.00	56.8	252.8	144.8	454.5	142.2	312.3	3.2–1	159.92
507.87	27.58	54.8	226.6	143.4	424.8	129.0	295.8	3.3–1	164.66
461.51	36.11	39.4	234.9	120.0	394.2	112.1	282.1	3.1–1	169.03
449.19	32.51	33.3	252.2	138.3	423.9	138.1	285.8	3.1–1	174.48
417.71	35.28	51.4	225.0	130.3	406.8	147.0	259.8	2.8–1	155.50
389.26	31.69	53.1	189.6	112.4	355.1	122.7	232.4	2.9–1	120.90
365.43	26.03	70.5	192.9	96.2	359.6	128.3	231.3	2.8–1	120.90
346.69	26.26	73.0	193.7	95.1	361.8	155.5	206.3	2.3–1	102.72

Armstrong Rubber

Gross Prop.	Capital Expend.	Cash Items	Inventories	Receivables	Cur. Assets	Cur. Liabs.	Net Workg. Cap.	Cur. Ratio Assets to Liabs.	Long-term Debt
62.22	9.55	21.65	31.38	15.68	68.76	21.59	47.17	4.5–1	34.95
53.54	10.09	6.07	40.84	16.75	63.74	31.57	32.17	2.0–1	17.67
44.57	6.92	5.95	35.94	11.65	53.64	24.56	29.08	2.2–1	10.90
29.39	2.32	4.52	23.19	10.55	38.32	17.22	21.10	2.2–1	8.17
27.42	3.40	4.15	22.23	9.91	36.33	19.52	16.81	1.9–1	6.04
24.45	1.97	3.77	21.46	9.77	35.03	19.69	15.34	1.8–1	5.09
23.14	2.71	2.88	17.42	8.50	28.84	14.52	14.32	1.9–1	7.39
21.22	2.56	3.67	12.39	7.62	23.68	9.08	14.60	2.6–1	10.37
19.12	3.32	2.52	14.63	6.00	23.15	15.00	8.15	1.5–1	3.79
16.14	2.31	4.00	13.21	6.89	24.09	14.48	9.61	1.7–1	4.19

FINANCIAL DATA OF THE BIG FOUR AND LEADING INDEPENDENT TIRE MANUFACTURERS (continued)*

Income statistics (in millions of dollars) (continued)

Lee Rubber & Tire

Year Ended Oct. 31	*Net Sales*	*% Oper. Inc. of Sales*	*Maint. & Repairs*	*Depr. & Depl.*	*Net Bef. Taxes*	*Inc. Taxes*	*Net Inc.*
1961	44.68	2.2	. . . .	0.83	0.45	0.17	0.28
1960	44.30	2.1	1.18	0.82	0.52	0.19	0.33
1959	52.16	7.9	1.28	0.72	3.37	1.85	1.52
1958	46.56	9.4	0.99	0.63	3.81	2.01	1.80
1957	48.60	8.6	1.05	0.60	3.65	1.88	1.77
1956	46.58	8.5	1.19	0.58	3.40	1.79	1.61
1955	45.91	9.2	1.10	0.54	3.73	1.98	1.75
1954	39.39	8.4	0.77	0.54	2.92	1.52	1.40
1953	46.30	9.2	0.76	0.74	3.63	1.96	1.67
1952	45.34	7.3	0.83	0.47	3.11	1.34	1.77

B. F. Goodrich

Year Ended Dec. 31	*Net Sales*	*% Oper. Inc. of Sales*	*Maint. & Repairs*	*Deprec. & Amort.*	*Net Bef. Taxes*	*Income Taxes*	*Net Inc.*
1961	757.8	10.7	. . . .	25.10	59.78	28.75	31.03
1960	764.7	10.2	30.18	23.78	57.51	27.49	30.02
1959	771.6	11.5	28.37	21.77	73.38	35.80	37.58
1958	697.3	12.7	26.12	21.34	70.64	35.18	35.46
1957	734.7	12.4	29.93	21.13	75.91	36.54	39.37
1956	724.2	14.1	27.89	19.47	86.85	43.08	43.77
1955	755.0	14.8	20.94	19.68	94.99	48.33	46.66
1954	630.7	14.4	20.30	16.12	75.29	36.47	38.82
1953	674.6	15.1	20.70	13.44	88.09	53.86	34.23
1952	624.1	16.2	17.24	11.27	89.44	57.08	32.36

FINANCIAL DATA OF THE BIG FOUR AND LEADING
INDEPENDENT TIRE MANUFACTURERS (continued)*

Pertinent balance sheet statistics (in millions of dollars) (continued)

Lee Rubber & Tire (continued)

Gross Prop.	Capital Expend.	Cash Items	Inven-tories	Receiv-ables	Cur. Assets	Cur. Liabs.	Net Workg. Cap.	Cur. Ratio Assets to Liabs.	Long-term Debt
19.80	1.02	3.78	10.06	7.39	21.67	3.39	18.28	6.4–1	Nil
19.05	0.80	3.89	11.92	5.97	22.12	3.11	19.01	7.1–1	Nil
18.44	1.60	4.14	11.72	7.57	23.64	4.01	19.63	5.9–1	Nil
17.05	1.28	4.80	11.29	6.97	23.15	3.57	19.58	6.5–1	Nil
15.97	0.66	6.70	9.84	6.48	23.11	3.72	19.39	6.2–1	Nil
15.50	0.49	5.64	10.93	6.00	22.67	3.79	18.88	6.0–1	Nil
15.25	1.41	5.75	10.68	5.29	21.80	3.68	18.12	5.9–1	Nil
13.95	0.21	8.42	8.90	4.19	21.56	3.67	17.89	5.9–1	Nil
13.79	1.10	6.90	8.46	4.42	20.00	3.12	16.88	6.4–1	Nil
13.09	2.07	6.13	8.89	3.99	19.40	3.23	16.17	6.0–1	Nil

B. F. Goodrich (continued)

Gross Prop.	Capital Expend.	Cash Items	Inven-tories	Receiv-ables	Cur. Assets	Cur. Liabs.	Net Workg. Cap.	Cur. Ratio Assets to Liabs.	Long-term Debt
419.8	56.17	61.2	169.5	155.7	386.4	95.7	290.7	4.0–1	98.56
378.4	41.38	66.9	160.5	131.2	358.5	78.0	280.5	4.6–1	98.52
357.3	34.28	24.3	177.7	140.6	342.6	90.9	251.7	3.8–1	41.31
347.4	27.62	59.7	154.1	132.6	346.4	94.0	252.4	3.7–1	43.80
331.1	38.87	45.4	168.7	119.2	333.3	89.3	244.0	3.7–1	45.75
302.9	37.01	73.4	147.3	123.0	343.6	98.5	245.1	3.5–1	46.99
277.6	30.29	85.6	147.3	117.7	350.6	109.5	241.1	3.2–1	49.65
264.6	28.03	92.1	121.6	105.3	319.0	93.4	225.6	3.4–1	51.66
227.1	23.42	93.1	128.3	94.5	316.0	105.6	210.4	3.0–1	54.60
210.0	21.92	82.3	131.2	95.2	308.8	111.7	197.1	2.8–1	56.56

FINANCIAL DATA OF THE BIG FOUR AND LEADING
INDEPENDENT TIRE MANUFACTURERS (continued)*

Income statistics (in millions of dollars) (continued)

General Tire & Rubber

Year Ended Nov. 30	Net Sales	% Oper. Inc. of Sales	Maint. & Repairs	Deprec. & Amort.	Net. Bef. Taxes	Net Inc.
1961	809.02	8.6	. . . .	17.37	53.93	27.34
1960	753.95	7.3	24.14	14.61	44.81	22.79
1959	676.94	8.6	23.42	13.62	50.32	26.62
1958	469.78	8.0	18.00	11.38	24.69	11.28
1957	421.17	6.8	13.74	10.48	19.68	11.30
1956	390.47	7.3	11.54	7.95	22.09	10.86
1955	295.73	8.6	9.05	5.77	21.63	11.60
1954	216.99	5.3	7.22	4.68	6.92	4.50
1953	205.37	6.0	5.67	3.84	9.74	6.28
1952	185.91	7.4	4.66	3.13	12.08	6.15

**FINANCIAL DATA OF THE BIG FOUR AND LEADING
INDEPENDENT TIRE MANUFACTURERS (continued)***

Pertinent balance sheet statistics (in millions of dollars) (continued)

General Tire & Rubber (continued)

Gross Prop.	Capital Expend.	Cash Items	Inventories	Receivables	Cur. Assets	Cur. Liabs.	Net Workg. Cap.	Cur. Ratio Assets to Liabs.	Long-term Debt
206.38	....	14.36	78.95	153.47	246.78	122.74	124.04	2.0–1	102.28
179.02	25.91	11.04	73.48	151.81	236.34	129.74	106.60	1.8–1	82.57
157.03	28.63	13.18	72.93	106.86	193.14	80.42	112.72	2.4–1	87.67
134.59	16.12	13.11	60.06	95.04	168.22	92.03	76.19	1.8–1	66.96
121.61	24.70	10.20	62.23	77.05	149.50	70.05	79.45	2.1–1	71.01
98.07	21.85	10.71	59.47	75.01	145.20	77.99	67.21	1.9–1	53.61
79.59	10.84	10.79	48.26	63.75	122.80	70.40	52.40	1.7–1	21.08
70.15	7.17	9.93	43.31	47.16	100.41	55.68	44.73	1.8–1	22.05
52.03	6.26	6.66	39.48	34.38	80.53	35.81	44.72	2.2–1	23.02
44.78	4.57	8.28	33.30	35.40	77.00	38.81	38.19	2.0–1	18.99

* *Standard Listed Stock Reports, 1962.* Standard and Poor's Corporation, Ephrata, Pa.

PART THREE
THE
DECISION-MAKING
PROCESS:
DEVELOPING
THE
STRATEGIC DESIGN

11
VOLKSWAGENWERK

"This medal," said the chairman of the Sperry Award Committee, "is awarded to the developers of the Volkswagen, which, in concept, engineering design, and production has made available to the world an automobile of small size for multiple uses; with unique attributes of universality; of low initial and operating costs; of simplicity of design and having ease of maintenance; comfort with adequate performance; and suitable for rural and urban use."

It was the first time that the Sperry Award, whose selection committee consisted of representatives of four leading American engineering associations, had been bestowed upon members of the automobile industry. It was the first time that the award had been granted to a non-American.

VOLKSWAGENWERK

In 1971 Volkswagenwerk was the fourth largest automaker in the world and the biggest in Europe, and was surpassed in the world only by General Motors, Ford, and Chrysler. It was by far the largest exporter of autos in the world. In less than twenty years Volkswagenwerk had grown to be the largest industrial firm in Germany. It ranked fourth in size among European manufacturers, surpassed only by Royal Dutch Shell, Unilever, and Philips Gloeilampenfabrieken. It had 190,000 employees in its six plants in Germany and its twelve subsidiaries, five of which had production plants. Its Wolfsburg plant covered 2,127 acres. (See Exhibit 1.)

exhibit 1   SELECTED DATA OF VOLKSWAGENWERK AG
             AND ITS SUBSIDIARIES AND AFFILIATES

		1970	1969	Increase (Decrease)	%
Sales (DM)					
Volkswagenwerk AG and its subsidiaries and affiliates	in million DM	15,791	13,934	1,857	13
	domestic sales—%	31	29		
	export sales—%	69	71		
	per employee DM	87,467	84,826	2,641	3
Volkswagenwerk AG	in million DM	9,913	9,238	675	7
	domestic sales—%	38	34		
	export sales—%	62	66		
	per employee DM	83,336	84,763	−1,427	−2
Sales (units)					
Volkswagenwerk AG and its subsidiaries and affiliates	number of vehicles	2,206,921	2,087,109	119,812	6
Volkswagenwerk AG	number of vehicles	1,625,885	1,633,625	−7,740	
Production					
Volkswagenwerk AG and its subsidiaries and affiliates	number of vehicles	2,214,937	2,094,438	120,499	6
Volkswagenwerk AG	number of vehicles	1,621,197	1,639,630	−18,433	−1
Labor force					
Volkswagenwerk AG and its subsidiaries and affiliates	at year-end	190,306	168,469	21,837	13
Volkswagenwerk AG	at year-end	124,792	112,454	12,338	11
Investments					
Volkswagenwerk AG and its subsidiaries and affiliates	in million DM	1,536	1,076	460	43
Volkswagenwerk AG	in million DM	1,131	740	391	53
Depreciation					
Volkswagenwerk AG and its subsidiaries and affiliates	in million DM	836	691	145	21
Volkswagenwerk AG	in million DM	579	536	43	8
Net earnings					
Volkswagenwerk AG	in million DM	190	330	−140	−42
Dividends proposed	in million DM	166.5	166.5	—	—

Volkswagenwerk had over 9,000 sales and service agencies in 136 foreign countries. They were supplied with completed cars, components for assembly, and replacement parts by a charter fleet of about 80 ocean-going ships, some of them capable of carrying 2,650 vehicles on one sailing.

Volkswagenwerk manufactured only one product line—motor vehicles. During most of its history 70% or more of its production had consisted of one single model—the Volkswagen Beetle. Since 1967 the percentage of Beetles produced had declined; during the 1960's management added many other models to the line. However, at the beginning of 1971 approximately 55% of daily output still consisted of Beetles.

ORIGIN AND HISTORY OF THE COMPANY

The history of the Volkswagen began with Ferdinand Porsche, a self-educated Austrian engineer, who was a world-famous pioneer designer of high-powered racing cars. Porsche wished to demonstrate his versatility by designing a low-cost, sturdy utility automobile for the man of limited means. Unable to interest German industrialists, Porsche's pioneering work came to the attention of Adolph Hitler. Hitler immediately recognized the demagogic appeal that might be realized in producing a "people's car."

Hitler decreed that Porsche was to develop a Volkswagen (a folkswagon) for which Hitler set the specifications. It was to be a four-seat "family" auto, with a two-cylinder, air-cooled, 14-horsepower engine. It was to cruise at 65 miles per hour (100 kilometers per hour) and travel 32 miles on a gallon of gasoline (about 15 kilometers per liter). It was to be sturdy enough to need no repairs for 80,000 kilometers (50,000 miles) and it was to sell for DM 1,000 ($250). Porsche became convinced that Hitler's specifications were impractical and eventually designed an antomobile that was close to his original concept. He considered the 1,000-mark price unattainable and ignored it.

The original Volkswagen plant was built at Wolfsburg, between Hanover and Berlin. Only 210 of the original models were built, and none of these were ever sold to the public. One day after construction of the plant began, the Wehrmacht marched into Czechoslovakia and Hitler ordered the Volkswagenwerk converted into war production. During the war the plant produced 70,000 cars for the German army.

During the war Allied bombers destroyed 65% of the Wolfsburg plant. Later the British took over the plant. It was their plan to reactivate it to produce staff cars for a few years for their occupation forces, and then to dismantle and appropriate the production equipment. Production lagged. Only 1,785 cars were produced in 1945. Output was 10,020 in 1946; 8,973 in 1947. The British authorities came to the conclusion that the Volkswagen was not practical as a motor vehicle and that the production machinery was in such poor condition that it was not worth dismantling.

The British Occupation Forces concluded from their assessment that if the Volkswagen were returned to the Germans, "no undue competition on the world market against British products" was to be expected. Allied auto manufacturers, including the Americans and Russians, also turned down offers to take over the plant. In 1947 Allied occupation policy shifted from dismantling to reindustrializing West Germany. The British then invited Heinz Nordhoff to take over direction of the Wolfsburg plant and to convert it to making cars for the German people.

Heinz Nordhoff was a German automotive engineer who had been an executive of General Motors' Opel Brandenburg organization, which had produced military trucks for the Wehrmacht. Nordhoff became unemployed at the end of the war because American occupation laws forbade German executives to work at anything but manual labor. Destitute, he crossed into the British Zone, where he was suddenly offered full authority to manage the faltering Volkswagen plant.

In Herr Nordhoff's first six months production tripled; it totaled 19,244 for 1948 and 46,154 for 1949. In the following years sales and production rose steadily: 1950, 90,038; 1951, 105,712; 1952, 136,013; 1953, 179,740; 1954, 242,373. In 1955 the one-millionth Volkswagen was produced. The second-millionth was reached in 1959; the third-millionth, in 1960; the fifth-millionth, in 1961; and the ten-millionth, in 1964. Exporting had begun early and, as a matter of policy, export sales had been given priority. By 1957 over half of the company's production was sold abroad and the Volkswagen was outselling all other cars in Germany, Belgium, Denmark, Holland, Sweden, Switzerland, Austria, and Portugal.

TRANSITION AND FINANCING

In 1948 Volkswagenwerk was theoretically ownerless. The previous owner had been the German Labor Front, an arm of the Nazi organization, which no longer existed. The British occupation authorities had turned the works over to the West German Federal Government in 1949, and since that time the Volkswagenwerk GmbH had been administered by the State of Lower Saxony on behalf of the Federal government. The chairman of the board was Dr. Hans Busch, State Secretary in the Ministry of Economic Affairs for the Bonn government.

During the 12-year period following 1949 the Volkswagenwerk was neither a state nor a capitalistic enterprise. The State of Lower Saxony was not entitled to any profits from the Volkswagenwerk, and the state government did not participate actively in directing its activities beyond appointing the members of the Aufsichtstrat (the board of directors), who were mostly civil servants who did not take a personal interest in operational matters.

The original rehabilitation of the Volkswagenwerk had been financed by soliciting advances from prospective dealers. Thereafter, expansion had been financed out of earnings, all of which were retained by the theoretically ownerless organization.

The Bonn government was a reluctant title-holder. Under Konrad Adenauer the Christian Democratic Party was pledged to free enterprise and was resisting pressure from the Socialists for a continued nationalization of major production facilities. The Adenauer government had become heir to vast property holdings, some inherited from the Nazi government and some dating back to the time of the Kaiser. The Bonn government controlled 314 German industrial firms, worth over DM 4 billion ($1 billion). These firms controlled 50% of Germany's iron-ore mining, 20% of hard coal mining, 70% of aluminum production, 42% of lead production, 28% of zinc, 18% of oil, and 5% of steel. The Federal government also owned in full the German railway, telephone, and telegraph systems. Ludwig Erhard felt that these widespread holdings placed him in the untenable position of preaching laissez-faire economy while actually practicing socialism. Furthermore, the public had come to look upon Volkswagenwerk as being government-owned.

THE PUBLIC STOCK SALE

In May, 1960, the Bundestag enacted a statute defining the legal position of Volkswagenwerk GmbH, and in July, 1960, it enacted a statute permitting the transfer into private possession of the shares of Volkswagenwerk. In the ensuing stock sale Volkswagenwerk acquired 1,500,000 shareholders and became the second largest joint-stock venture in the world, second only to American Telephone and Telegraph. Capitalization was at DM 600 million ($150 million) divided into 6 million bearer shares of DM 100 ($25). Twenty per cent of the stock went to the Federal Republic, 20% to the State of Lower Saxony, and the 60% balance was allocated to German residents. The shares were offered at DM 350 ($87.50) and there were discounts of 10% to 25%, graded according to income and family status of the purchaser.

The average initial price was DM 280 ($70). Employees of Volkswagenwerk were given a cash grant to buy one share and an option to buy another nine; they bought an average of five shares. The proceeds of the stock sale and future dividends on the shares held by the Federal Republic and Lower Saxony went to the Volkswagen Foundation, a philanthropic trust organized for scientific research and the teaching of science.

EVOLUTION OF THE PRODUCT LINE

When Herr Nordhoff took charge of Volkswagenwerk, he said, "The Volkswagen is a good auto. Therefore let us improve it." This became a basic Volkswagen policy. Another Nordhoff maxim had been: "Let us continue with only one model, which we will constantly improve."

When critics were warning that Volkswagen was making the same mistake that Ford had made when he stayed with the Model T too long, Volkswagenwerk management pointed out that there was a basic difference: Henry Ford had produced the same automobile, without any significant changes, year after year. The Volkswagen, however, was constantly being improved. During the course of its history, hundreds of technical improvements were made in the Volkswagen; only the exterior body lines remained unchanged.

In the early 1960's Volkswagenwerk was meeting pressure from its dealers to increase the line of models. Management refused to change, pointing out the tremendous cost-price advantage inherent in the one-car, one-model strategy. Other auto makers made heavy capital expenditures for production equipment for their new models, with the result that the price of their 1½-liter cars rose by DM 400 ($100). During the same period the price of the Volkswagen was reduced by the same amount.

Volkswagen management pointed out that the early changes in styling in pioneer automobiles had been introduced to accommodate technical developments. Later, fashion became dominant because of strong sales competition. All cars had come to be good and most of them were equally good, in the sense that not one of them stood out clearly from the rest in regard to price, economy, and comfort. For this reason the secondary consideration of appearance began to decide the fate of the product. The customer who was offered a number of cars, all with the same performance, and all at about the same price, chose the one which his wife found attractive.

In 1949 Volkswagen introduced the De Luxe Sedan, a slightly more elegant version of the standard Beetle. Later the horsepower was increased. In 1950 the Volkswagen Commercial appeared. This was the basic Volkswagen power plant with a "Micro-Bus" body and "Mini-Van" bodies of many types. In 1955 the Karmann-Ghia was added to the line. This was a sleek-lined two-seat coupé on the basic Beetle frame.

In 1961, when the Volkswagen rate of growth had begun to decline, Volkswagen introduced the VW 1500, which had slimmer lines than the 1200, a 53-hp engine, and deluxe features. It was priced 50% over the Beetle. The next year Volkswagen brought out the Variant (known elsewhere as the Squareback), a small, sleek station wagon. Public reaction to this car was mixed, reception was slow, and the rate of growth continued to decline. In 1965 Volkswagen brought out the 1300 line, which had the same basic styling as previous Beetle models but had a 50-hp engine. The same year VW introduced 1600 versions of the Squareback and its companion, the Fastback, which had 65-hp engines.

In 1968 the VW 411 appeared in Europe. This was a sedan with sleek lines and was made available in both two- and four-door models. It had a four-cylinder air-cooled 80-hp engine, cruised at 90 mph, and had deluxe appointments. It was replaced in 1969 by the 411 E, a more powerful car with an 85-hp electronic fuel-injection engine. The company simultaneously introduced a station wagon version.

In August of 1970 Volkswagen announced a revolutionary new version of the celebrated Beetle, which it called the Super Beetle. In outward styling the new model appeared to be the same as the Beetle, but it was three inches longer and had almost twice the luggage space, a 60-hp engine, a larger fuel tank, a blower-equipped ventilating system, and more elegant inside appointments than the Beetle. It was announced as being in 89 different ways different from the Beetle. It was priced at about DM 400 more than the conventional Beetle (VW 1600). (See Exhibit 2.)

exhibit 2   DEVELOPMENT OF THE VOLKSWAGEN LINE

Volkswagen Beetle (Sedan and Convertible)

1945   Volkswagen 1200 Standard 25 bhp DIN; 1954 36 bhp SAE; 1965 (VW 1200 A)
41.5 bhp SAE.

1949   Volkswagen 1200 De Luxe Sedan and 4-seater Convertible 25 bhp DIN; 1954
36 bhp SAE; 1960 41.5 bhp SAE; 1965 (as VW 1300) 50 bhp SAE; 1966 (as VW
1500) 53 bhp SAE;

1970   VW 1300 53 bhp SAE, VW 1302 53 bhp SAE, VW 1302 S 60 bhp SAE.

VW-Karmann Ghia

1955   Coupé, 1952 Convertible 36 bhp SAE; further development as for De Luxe
Sedan.

Volkswagen 1600

1961   VW 1500 Sedan, VW 1500 Karmann Ghia Coupé 54 bhp SAE;
1962   VW Variant 54 bhp SAE;
1963   VW Sedan, Variant and Coupé 1500 S 65 SAE;
1965   VW 1600 TL Fastback (new), other models as VW 1600;
1966   VW 1600 L Notchback Sedan;
1969   VW 1600 L Karmann Ghia Coupé went out of production.

VW 411

1968   2- and 4-door Sedan (Normal and L) 76 bhp SAE;
1969   Sedan and Variant 411 E and LE 85 bhp SAE;

VW Commercial

1950   VW Commercial 25 bhp DIN; 1954 36 bhp SAE; 1960 41.5 bhp SAE; 1963 51
bhp SAE (One Tonner); 1965 53 bhp SAE;
1967   1968 VW Commercial 52 bhp SAE; 1970 60 bhp SAE.

VW Micro Van

1965   introduction; body by Westfalia, Wiedenbrück.

VW 181

1969   introduced as multipurpose vehicle; 53 bhp SAE.

VW K 70

1970   VW K 70 and VW K 70 L; 4-door Sedan, front-wheel drive, water-cooled;
optionally 88 (SAE) bhp or 105 (SAE) bhp engine.

THE BASIC MODEL

The basic Volkswagen model accounted for the bulk of the company's production. Over the period of the company's history almost
70% of its production consisted of the 1200, or slight variations of it—
the 1300 and the 1500. It was said that Volkswagenwerk was virtually

a one-product company; that no other major company in the world depended upon a single model of a single product to produce such a high volume of sales.

Over the years the Volkswagen had become, the world over, a popular subject for good-natured humor. In the English-speaking world its standard pseudonym was "The Beetle." A dictionary of Modern American English listed: "Beetle; a Volkswagen automobile; from its appearance." Typical of the whimsical humorous treatment given the Beetle by the press was this introduction to a feature article in an American magazine:

> It's an inelegant, squatty, lumpy-looking piece of machinery that is not very big, does not go very fast, has very little chrome, and makes too much noise. It has a dinky little engine in back, and a pouty, hurt-feelings look in front. In the United States, where cars are bought largely on styling, Volkswagens have been laughed at, mocked, slandered, abused and insulted . . . but the Volkswagen is seen in the best circles. Belgium's King Bodouin tools around Europe in a sun-roof sedan. The Volkswagen agents in Bangkok are two Thailand princes, cousins of the King of Siam. Princess Margaret drives a station wagon . . . .

The basic Volkswagen had remained virtually unchanged since it was designed by Ferdinand Porsche in the 1930's (see Exhibits 3 and 4). It had a four-cylinder air-cooled rear "boxer-type" engine which developed 36 horsepower. It had minimum passing power—68 miles per hour (110 km) (with a favorable tail wind). It traveled over 12 kilometers on a liter of gasoline (30 miles on a gallon). It had torsion bars instead of coil springs at a considerable savings in space and weight. The basic Volkswagen had no fuel gauge. The complete engine weighed less than 100 kilograms (198 pounds), a replacement engine cost only DM 860 ($237), and changing engines took only half an hour. It had a four-speed floor shift. There was a minimum of luggage space under the front bonnet (the hood) and behind the rear seat. It seated four passengers. Tires frequently lasted over 40,000 miles. The Volkswagen was unique in that it did not have a beamed chassis; the entire car was built upon a platform frame which provided a watertight underside for the body.

Herr Nordhoff had been confident that so long as motorists were interested in basic transportation, the Beetle would remain a dominant force in the world market. "For a while," he said, "we felt uncertain

exhibit 3
THE BASIC MODEL

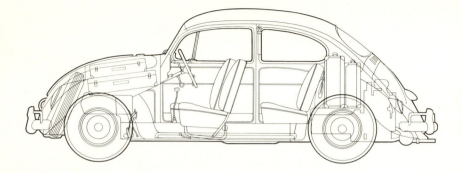

about the direction of the market. The wish for something more luxurious was there. But the large majority still wanted low-cost driving, and so long as they wanted that, they would want the Volkswagen. The Beetle will always remain the ideal automobile for people in many regions of the world."

CHANGING OBJECTIVES

In its 1969 report to shareholders, the Volkswagenwerk management stated:

Volkswagenwerk AG and its subsidiary and affiliated companies, with sales of DM 13,900 million in 1969, attained a magnitude which required, to a certain extent, a realignment of its objectives and organization. During the past year, therefore, the following significant steps were taken in this direction:

1. The Beetle, which has been the basis of VW's success for more than twenty years and which remains the most successful automobile in the world, will continue to be produced with a daily output of approximately of 5,000 units. However, the position of Volkswagenwerk in a growing automobile market can be maintained only with an expanded product line which will appeal to a wider range of consumers. In 1967 daily production of 6,000 cars included about 4,400 Beetles, or 68% of daily production. This ratio, however, has changed considerably since then. At the beginning of 1970 some 9,000 cars, including more than 5,000 Beetles, were produced daily by Volkswagenwerk AG and its subsidiaries and affiliates. However, while the production of this model increased more than 17%, its proportionate share of the daily output decreased to 58%. This trend will continue

exhibit 4
THE BEETLE

in future years as a result of further growth, particularly since several new technical concepts are now available.

2. Experience has shown that an automotive enterprise with such an extensive production program, once it reaches a certain size, can no longer maintain and expand its market position with only one product line and one sales organization. After the acquisition of Auto Union GmbH in 1965 and with the introduction of the newly developed medium-sized car, we had to decide whether the company's objective was to produce primarily Volkswagens or whether a new product line should be marketed in addition to the Volkswagen. After careful evaluation of all the facts, the decision was made in favor of the second alternative in 1968 with the introduction of the Audi 100. Another important step toward diversification of our product line was the formation in 1969 of AUDI NSU AUTO UNION AKTIENGESELLSCHAFT by merging Auto Union GmbH with NSU Motorenwerke AG. The diversified product line of the newly organized company now made it feasible to establish a sales organization independent of Volkswagenwerk for the purpose of selling these products. The competition between the VW and AUDI NSU product lines, although managed by different, autonomous groups within the same company, is expected to provide additional stimulation for product development and sales for the whole company.

In addition to AUDI NSU AUTO UNION, VW-Porsche Vertriebsgesellschaft mbh was established in 1969 to market sports cars manufactured by both Porsche and Volkswagen. The unique characteristics of this business also make it necessary for this company to operate, to a great extent, on its own initiative and responsibility.

3. The orientation of the company toward product groups which are in competition with each other also requires reorganization of the management of Volkswagenwerk AG. On the one hand, the development, production, and marketing of the VW product line must continue unchanged, whereas the business policy of the entire company must be determined by corporate management, and at the same time the policies of the different groups must be coordinated. In 1969 organizational changes were initiated toward separating the two areas of responsibility within Volkswagenwerk AG, since a separation into two companies is presently not feasible. In addition to the competition within the enterprise, these measures will insure that maximum integration is achieved in those areas where cost savings can be realized or other business opportunities can be pursued advantageously.

AUTOMATION

Automated equipment required huge capital investments. United States auto makers often found automation economically impractical because of their annual model changes. With only a single model, produced in increasing quantities year after year for more than a decade, Volkswagen was able to carry automation further than any other car maker.

In an impressive display of automation, Volkswagen fabricated, assembled, and welded roof, front, and rear body sections of the Beetle in what was virtually a single mechanical operation (see Exhibit 5). An operation of forming front hoods, which had formerly required 52 men, now used 12 men and automated equipment at a labor savings of 77%. In another operation, the manufacture of horns for bumpers had been reduced from 108 men to 18 men at a labor savings of 83%.

Volkswagenwerk also automated its office operations: inventory controls, bookkeeping, procurement records, component and parts records, and the distribution of the finished automobiles. The Wolfsburg payroll operation was computerized, with the result that a single machine turned out the paychecks for 40,000 employees in 12 hours, an operation that had required a week of work by 200 payroll bookkeepers.

exhibit 5

THE AUTOMATED "MERRY-GO-ROUND"

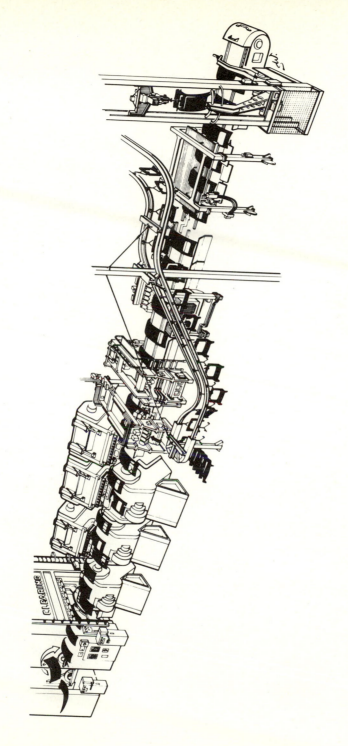

(A)

exhibit 5   (continued)

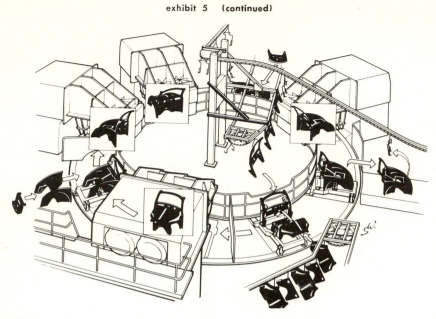

(B)

(C)

exhibit 5 (continued)

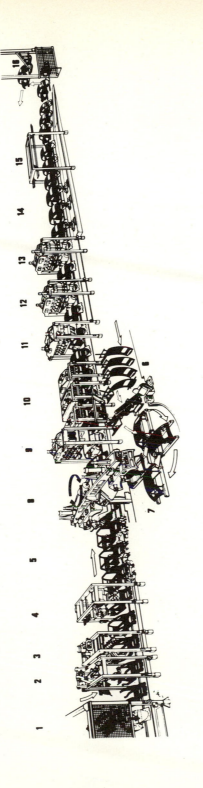

THE LABOR FORCE

Volkswagen's continuing increase in production necessitated a considerable expansion of its labor force and the increased utilization of the labor force both by working overtime and by adding extra work shifts. A basic reason for the company's establishment of branch plants in Germany was the fact that it had exhausted the local supply of labor at Wolfsburg. The shortage of labor in Germany, coupled with the general inflationary trend in the German economy, caused VW's labor costs to rise sharply, as indicated in Exhibit 6.

exhibit 6   LABOR FORCE—VOLKSWAGENWERK AG AND SUBSIDIARIES

	12/31/1970	12/31/1969	Increase	%
Volkswagenwerk AG				
Wolfsburg	59,200	55,603	3,597	6
Hanover	27,447	26,817	630	2
Kassel	17,533	16,140	1,393	9
Emden	8,123	7,002	1,121	16
Brunswick	7,381	6,845	536	8
Salzgitter	5,108	47	5,061	—
	124,792	112,454	12,338	11
AUDI NSU AUTO UNION	29,147	26,595	2,552	10
Other domestic subsidiaries	946	761	185	24
Volkswagenwerk AG and its domestic subsidiaries	154,885	139,810	15,075	11
Foreign production and assembling companies	32,773	26,330	6,443	24
Foreign distributing companies	2,648	2,329	319	14
Foreign subsidiaries and affiliates	35,421	28,659	6,762	24
Total labor force of Volkswagenwerk AG and its subsidiaries and affiliates	190,306	168,469	21,837	13

To satisfy its personnel requirements Volkswagen found it necessary to employ an increasing number of workers from foreign countries. During 1969 the ratio of foreign workers to the total labor force of VW AG rose from 8.9% to 11.5%. In January 1971, 14.4 thousand foreign workers, of whom 8 thousand were from Italy, were working for VW, almost all of them at the Wolfsburg plant, where a separate village, known locally as "the Italian Village," had been built for them on the outskirts of Wolfsburg. Cooperation between the German and Italian employees was good during working hours, but the Italians had some feeling that they were discriminated against in the social life of the town. The remainder of the foreign employees were mainly Greek, Spanish, Turkish and, since 1970, Tunisian nationals. The wage scales and working conditions of all VW employees were uniform, regardless of nationality, but the expense of recruiting foreign employees increased VW's total labor costs.

The company's labor costs were also increased because wage rates in Germany were rising faster than the rate of productivity; social insurance costs were rising, and the company had a substantial investment in apartments for its employees. In accordance with a previous agreement with its unions, the company granted a wage increase of 3.75% on January 1, 1969, and another increase of 10% on October 1, 1969. In December, 1970, the company agreed to a 12% wage increase, longer holidays, payments for savings schemes, and a subsidy for sickness insurance premiums. During 1969, 1,281 apartments and private homes for employees were completed, and an additional 752 were constructed in 1970. In 1971, 1,705 homes were under construction. Wages and salaries paid by Wolkswagenwerk AG for 1970 amounted to DM 2.3 million compared with DM 1.8 million in 1969. The cost to VW of compulsory, contractual, and voluntary social contributions and benefits increased to DM 1.1 million in 1970 from DM .8 million in 1969.

INNOVATIONS IN ENGINES

In 1966 the NSU Spider, a small sports-type car, adopted the Wankel engine. Twelve companies in the United States, Britain, France, Italy, and Japan were experimenting with the engine. The Wankel engine, developed in 1954 by Felix Wankel, a German automotive engineer, replaced conventional cylinders and pistons with a triangular rotor. It had only two major moving parts and weighed considerably less than conventional engines. In France, Renault, in a joint research contract with American Motors Corporation in the United States, was developing a rotary engine similar to the Wankel, but neither Renault nor American Motors had put their engine into production.

In the United States General Motors, Ford, and Chrysler had long been doing extensive research on new types of engines. One of these was the gas turbine engine, a rotary engine which could use any one of several common fuels, such as diesel oil, fuel oil, kerosene, or alcohol.

The 1960's saw a sharp rise in interest in electric autos. All major United States auto makers were actively developing experimental models, and some of these were so advanced that they were being road-tested under practical driving conditions. None, however, had yet reached the stage of becoming a commercial reality.

The Volkswagen engine had been one of the critical items in Ferdinand Porsche's original design of the automobile. The basic Porche-designed engine had been used in over 16 million Volkswagen vehicles of all body types, and it had achieved renown for its superior performance. From the beginning in 1948 it had been subjected to constant continuous research. During its 20-year history more research had been expended upon it than on any other engine in the entire history of the auto-making world. The engine remained virtually unchanged, however, the only changes being in technical refinements and increases in horsepower.

Notable among Volkswagen "firsts" in technological advances was an electronic fuel-injection system developed in 1968 for use on the Fastback and Squareback sedans. This electronic unit controlled the amount of fuel to be injected according to engine speed, engine load, intake manifold pressure, and engine temperature. Another major advance was the introduction of Volkswagen's Electronic Engine Diagnosis program. This featured a VW-developed Electronic Diagnosis Stall, in which a Volkswagen of any age could be put through some 96 different tests. The diagnosis equipment included an electronic console complete with oscilloscope, voltmeter, ammeter, tachometer, battery load tester, dwell and advance meter, stroboscopic timing light, and ohmmeter. It also included wheel alignment and headlight testing units. The Volkswagen management described the hour-long electronic engine examination as being "much like a medical doctor's electrocardiogram." During its first year, over three million VW owners availed themselves of the VW Diagnosis.

RESEARCH AND DEVELOPMENT

Historically Volkswagenwerk had always subscribed to a policy of extensive research activities. In earlier years these efforts had been beamed largely at technical improvements in the Beetle. During the 1960's the objective of the research and development activity was shifted. In 1971 Volkswagen's scientists and engineers were still pursuing the development of futuristic engineering principles, but were also adapting the current product line continuously to changing market conditions.

The research activity included experimenting with novel propulsion methods. The principles of gas dynamics were used to determine the optimum of carbon oxide mixtures and other harmful mixtures such as hydrocarbons and nitrous oxides.

To conduct its exhaustive research efforts effectively, new techniques were applied, using modern measuring and testing devices. Program-controlled simulators were used to simulate in the laboratory the dynamics to which the automobile was subjected on the road. Cold, climate, and altitude chambers were used to test the operational safety of the vehicles under varying environmental conditions.

Efforts to improve safety features were intensified. For example, in order to enlarge the crushing zone, the front end of the VW 1600 was lengthened and the front frame was strengthened for greater collision resistance. The development program also centered around the development of novel systems, such as air cushions, which would minimize the harmful effects of accidents.

The development activities within the Volkswagen organization were not restricted to Volkswagenwerk AG. Recently acquired subsidiaries still retained their specialized programs. NSU at Neckarsulm still had the primary responsibility for the development of the rotary engine; the Audi 100 coupé was developed at Ingolstadt; another VW 1600 Squareback sedan was developed in Brazil. However, all research and development activities were centrally controlled and co-ordinated from Wolfsburg.

THE WORLD AUTO INDUSTRY

In 1970 there were six countries which produced most of the world's record output of 28.9 million autos (see Exhibit 7). All of these, except Japan, were in North America and Europe. World production had risen steadily during the 1960's except for a decline during 1967. Gains in 1969–1970 more than offset the 1967 decline.

The United States was by far the largest producer and consumer of automobiles. It alone produced 8.4 million units in 1970; this was 29% of the world production. Its 1969 production was a decrease of 6% from its 10.8 million total for 1968. The United States exported only a

exhibit 7

Worldwide Automobile Production and Output of Major Automobile-producing Countries
and of Volkswagenwerk AG and Its Subsidiaries and Affiliates in Millions of Units
(Logarithmic Scale)

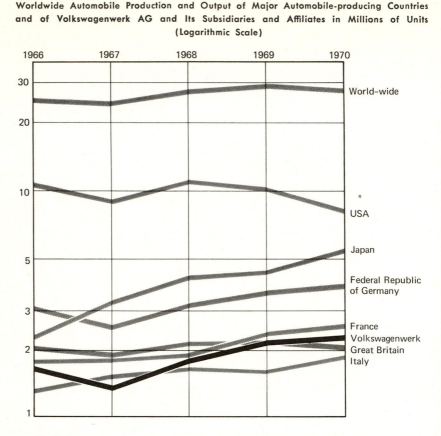

negligible proportion of its production—less than 1.5%. However, the
U.S. companies, through subsidiaries abroad, accounted for a large
share of non-U.S. production: 20% in France; 50% in Britain; 40%
in Germany.

In 1967 Japan became the second largest auto producer in the world.
Japan had achieved its standing from an insignificant position in 1950
(see Exhibit 7). In 1963 Japan had produced 1.3 million vehicles; in
1970 it turned out 5.2 million. Japan was striving to export, and its
shipments abroad had been rising sharply. In 1971 Japanese cars were
competing vigorously with Volkswagen in the U.S. Japan had also cut
into Volkswagen's markets in the East, such as the Australian market.

The German auto industry produced 3.8 million vehicles in 1970.
Except for the recession of 1967 its output had risen throughout the

1960's. Since 1967 the German auto industry had made larger gains than that of France, Italy, or the United Kingdom.

The European auto manufacturers were not, in every sense, free enterprisers. Volkswagen was partly government-owned and Renault was wholly government-owned. Citroen was a subsidiary of Michelin Tire and sold its Citroens in competition with other French or European car makers, who were at the same time major buyers of Michelin tires. Peugeot was owned by the Peugeot family and its activities were said to be influenced by the many commercial activities of the Peugeot family. Fiat was a major factor in the industrial life of Italy, and its interests were carefully guarded by the Italian government. In Germany, France, and England the American Big Three—General Motors, Ford, and Chrysler—had major producing subsidiaries which were backed by the enormous resources of their American parents. The operations of all European auto makers were directly affected by the actions of their governments in regulating their national economies.

The European automotive industry did not have an automotive components industry to support it, such as the United States auto industry had. Therefore, a European auto maker short of production capacity could not freely shift to buying components from vendors. All of the European auto makers were short of an adequate labor supply.

It was predicted that during the 1960's the European auto industry, which had over forty firms, would go through a period of consolidations, culminating in the absorption or failure of most of the small firms and the survival of five or six large producers. Some analysts predicted a realignment which would parallel the American experience: from 3,000 original auto makers the United States industry had narrowed down to the Big Three and a relatively few small firms.

During the 1960's there were some mergers of European auto makers, particularly in England, but there was a more pronounced trend toward associations and cooperative working arrangements. Citroen arranged to have some of its components produced by Simca (Chrysler) at Simca's Nanterre plant. Alfa-Romeo assembled and distributed Renault's Dauphines in Italy. Renault, in turn, distributed Alpha-Romeo's Giulios in France. Pininfarina, the Italian body-builder, made a variety of bodies for Peugeot. British Motors sold in the Common Market by having the Italian firm Innocenti assemble its Austin A-40, the Spyder sports car, and the Morris 1100.

At one time the major European auto makers had proposed that they arrange a cooperative agreement whereby competition in the smaller-class autos would be regulated and largely eliminated, but the coopera-tive arrangement never materialized. In another move in 1966 Volks-wagenwerk and Daimler-Benz set up a joint company for research work.

THE WEST GERMAN AUTOMOTIVE INDUSTRY

Volkswagen, Opel, and Ford dominated the German industry. Most of the German producers specialized in certain size and price classes of autos, none of them made a complete line of vehicles, and many of the very small producers were very specialized, limiting their produc-tion to a certain model of a single vehicle.

The growth of the German industry had been phenomenal. The 1970 production of 3.8 million vehicles compared with 306,000 pro-duced in 1950. In 1965 production had been 3 million, a growth of 875% from 1950. From 1960 to 1965 the growth was 45%.

West Germany's production of motor vehicles was equivalent to 12% of the world total. For many years Germany had been the largest exporter of vehicles in the world. The gain in exports, however, like the growth in production, was declining. In addition to the domestic production of completed vehicles and complete "knocked-down" ve-hicles, German vehicles were also produced outside of Germany in a number of other countries, in many cases using parts and major com-ponents supplied by the German factories. During 1965 the "ausland" (foreign) production of Volkswagens totaled 132,721. In 1970 it amounted to 324,745 vehicles. (See Exhibits 8 and 9.)

THE EUROPEAN INDUSTRY OUTLOOK

During the 1960's European auto sales had been increasing at an average annual rate of about 15% in the industrial countries—over twice the growth rate of the United States. In 1970 Europe produced over 11 million cars, an increase of over 66% in 4 years, while United States production rose only 25%. During the decade the number of cars per capita in many countries in Europe increased fivefold. In 1969, for the first time, the total European output of cars exceeded that of the United States.

During the 1950's every conceivable means of locomotion was seen on Europe's streets and roads, from bicycles to scooters, motorbikes,

exhibit 8   VOLKSWAGEN

	Total Production						U. S. Registrations			
Year	Total	Cars	Trucks & Station Wagons*	Total Inside Germany	Total Outside Germany	Total Exported from Germany	Cars	Trucks†	Total	Year
1945	1,785	1,785	—	1,785	—	—	—	—	—	1945
1946	10,020	10,020	—	10,020	—	—	—	—	—	1946
1947	8,987	8,987	—	8,987	—	1,656	—	—	—	1947
1948	19,244	19,244	—	19,244	—	4,464	2	—	2	1948
1949	46,154	46,146	8	46,154	—	7,128	157	—	157	1949
1950	90,038	81,979	8,059	90,038	—	29,387	390	—	390	1950
1951	105,712	93,709	12,003	105,712	—	35,742	601	10	611	1951
1952	136,013	114,348	21,665	136,013	—	46,881	980	33	1,013	1952
1953	179,740	151,323	28,417	179,740	—	68,754	6,343	271	6,614	1953
1954	242,373	202,174	40,199	242,373	—	108,839	28,907	2,021	30,928	1954
1955	329,893	279,986	49,907	329,893	—	177,657	50,457	5,233	55,690	1955
1956	395,690	333,190	62,500	395,690	—	217,683	64,803	14,721	79,524	1956
1957	472,554	380,561	91,993	472,554	—	270,987	79,038	25,268	104,306	1957
1958	553,399	451,526	101,873	549,710	3,689	315,717	120,442	30,159	150,601	1958
1959	696,860	575,407	121,453	688,477	8,383	404,185	159,995	31,377	191,372	1959
1960	865,858	725,939	139,919	841,043	24,815	489,272	177,308	26,555	203,863	1960
1961	1,007,113	838,513	168,600	959,773	47,340	533,420	192,570	30,170	222,740	1961
1962	1,184,675	1,004,338	180,337	1,112,424	72,251	627,613	240,143	36,865	277,008	1962
1963	1,209,591	1,020,297	189,294	1,132,080	77,511	685,763	307,173	36,090	343,263	1963
1964	1,410,715	1,210,390	200,325	1,276,135	134,580	797,468	383,978	4,614†	388,592	1964
1965	1,542,654	1,352,778	189,876	1,409,933	132,721	851,114	420,018	3,627†	423,645	1965
1966	1,583,239	1,391,866	191,373	1,431,114	152,125	964,576	452,937	3,294†	456,231	1966
1967	1,290,328	1,127,587	162,741	1,115,426	174,902	812,959	563,522	4,453†	567,975	1967
1968	1,707,402	1,453,483	253,919	1,489,281	218,121	1,104,752	537,933	2,690†	540,623	1968
1969	1,830,018	1,556,884	273,134	1,579,654	250,364	1,098,893	569,182	2,259	571,441	1969
1970	1,898,422	1,610,411	288,011	1,573,677	324,745	1,060,042				1970
Totals	18,818,477	16,042,871	2,775,606	17,196,930	1,621,547	10,710,952	4,256,881	259,710	4,616,599	Totals

* Box-shaped station wagons known in Europe as Microbuses.
† Volkswagen bus-like station wagons which were included in truck registrations through 1964 have been included in passenger car statistics since then and accounted for 51,389 of the 537,933 VW passenger cars registered during 1969.

exhibit 9 **TOTAL PRODUCTION OF VOLKSWAGEN AND SUBSIDIARIES
1969–1970**

	1970	*1969*	*Increase (Decrease) Units*	*%*
Volkswagenwerk AG	1,625,885	1,633,625	−7,740	
AUDI NSU AUTO UNION	309,560	264,714	44,846	17
	1,935,445	1,898,339	37,106	2
Less sales to subsidiaries and affiliates	695,542	685,626	9,916	1
	1,239,903	1,212,713	27,190	2
Volkswagen do Brasil	234,837	176,266	58,571	33
Volkswagen of South Africa	39,571	33,724	5,847	17
Volkswagen de Mexico	35,488	25,798	9,690	38
Motor Producers	17,320	14,678	2,642	18
Volkswagen of America*	565,838	558,880	6,958	1
Volkswagen Canada	38,255	39,116	−861	−2
Volkswagen France	31,223	25,484	5,739	23
Other subsidiaries or affiliates	4,486	450	4,036	
Total sales	2,206,921	2,087,109	119,812	6
Sales of passenger cars including squareback sedans	1,919,748	1,816,487	103,261	6
Sales of trucks and station wagons	287,173	270,622	16,551	6

* Together with its subsidiaries.

motorcycles, mopeds, and three-wheeled quasi-automobiles. By 1971,. factory bicycle racks were standing largely empty and employees were clamoring for more parking space for their automobiles. Congestion and traffic jams were increasing to serious proportions. London police estimated that over 200,000 cars streamed into central London daily. During holiday weekends there were back-ups fifteen kilometers (9 miles) long on Germany's autobahns.

The increase in automobiles was the result of growing affluence. The growth rate of the European economy in the 1960's was almost 5%. The growth of the European auto industry was expected to remain between 10% and 15% in the years immediately ahead. Demand for cars in Europe was expected to be over 11 million in 1971, and production capacity, which had increased significantly during the 1960's, was expected to rise to over 12 million. European buyers had long been accustomed to waiting long periods for delivery. With production capacity overtaking demand, waiting lists were vanishing, and the

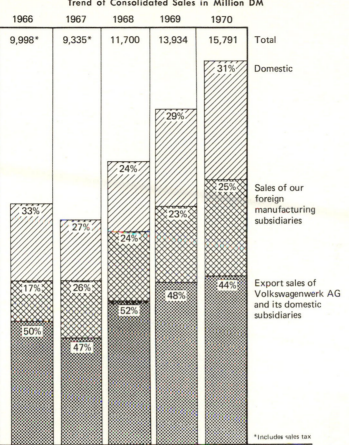

exhibit 9

Trend of Consolidated Sales in Million DM

1966	1967	1968	1969	1970	
9,998*	9,335*	11,700	13,934	15,791	Total
				31%	Domestic
			29%		
		24%			
33%				25%	Sales of our foreign manufacturing subsidiaries
	27%		23%		
		24%			
17%	26%			44%	Export sales of Volkswagenwerk AG and its domestic subsidiaries
		52%	48%		
50%					
	47%				

*Includes sales tax

seller's market was becoming a buyer's market. Auto purchasers' attitudes were changing. They were becoming more discriminating and more demanding.

Two trends were evident; first, the public was passing up motorized bicycles in favor of autos, and motorists were trading up to bigger and more elegant autos; second, there was a trend toward faster cars. Auto makers generally recognized the changing conditions.

European auto makers had believed it to be axiomatic that production should always be at full plant capacity and, having until recently been chronically oversold, they were not inclined to risk overexpansion.

Sources of capital for expansion were limited, and Europe did not have the sources of capital formation available to the United States producers. Expansion and modernization in Europe were customarily financed out of plowed-back earnings because there was no broad market for automobile securities. Also, in recent years price competition and rising costs had been depressing earnings.

Roads and driving facilities in Europe were generally inadequate. The majority of roads were outmoded. Almost 90% of France's rural roads were less than 7 meters (21 feet) wide. Italy had made progress on its program of building a network of autostrada, but England lacked the funds needed to expand its system of Dual Carriageways. Congestion had brought paralysis to many English cities, and authorities were resorting to declaring inner cities autoless malls. A discouraged motorist said, "We are beginning to wonder whether owning a car is worth the brain fag."

THE AMERICAN BIG THREE IN EUROPE

American auto makers owned or controlled five of the thirteen major European auto companies. These were Adam Opel AG (GM, Germany); Ford Werke (Ford Motors, Germany); Vauxhall (GM, England); Ford of England (Ford Motors, England); and Simca (Chrysler, France). The European assets of these United States subsidiaries totaled over $2 billion, and they had at their disposal the immense capital reserves and research and engineering facilities of their Detroit parents. In 1971 General Motors and Ford produced about one out of every three German cars. Ford Werke had 14.6% of the German market; Opel had 19.7% and Chrysler-Simca had 3.6%. (See Exhibit 10.)

Over the years the Detroit headquarters managements of the American Big Three had concentrated their efforts on the high-potential United States market and allowed themselves to be displaced in international trade by their European competitors, who were more export-minded and had the small, economy cars which appealed to motorists in less developed countries.

Following the booming growth of the European auto market, General Motors Opel and Ford Werke had introduced economy models of their own design in the 1963 market—the Kadett and the Taunus 12 M (now the German Ford). These achieved immediate consumer acceptance, and both companies planned expansion programs. It appeared that the Detroit managements had decided to seriously contend not only for a share of the European market, but for a position in the

exhibit 10
New Vehicle Registrations of Passenger Cars (Including Dual-purpose Vehicles) in the
Federal Republic of Germany and West Berlin in 1969 and 1970

Volkswagenwerk AG and its subsidiaries and affiliates	1970	631,765	30.7%
	1969	568,779	31.7%
Opel	1970	405,824	19.7%
	1969	349,959	19.5%
Ford	1970	301,075	14.6%
	1969	280,112	15.6%
Renault	1970	148,615	7.2%
	1969	113,377	6.3%
Daimler–Benz	1970	145,882	7.1%
	1969	127,624	7.1%
The Fiat Group	1970	141,378	6.9%
	1969	137,043	7.6%
BMW	1970	86,674	4.2%
	1969	77,348	4.3%
Simca	1970	74,019	3.6%
	1969	53,855	3.0%
Peugeot	1970	37,488	1.8%
	1969	26,836	1.5%
Citroën	1970	31,326	1.5%
	1969	21,812	1.2%
Others	1970	53,781	2.7%
	1969	40,131	2.2%

world market as well, mounting their campaign from their European subsidiaries. Within a five-year period the total production capacity of the Big Three in Europe was doubled. Together, they had an aggregate capacity approaching 3 million vehicles annually.

It was expected that a world-wide competition for shares of the world market was impending and that in it the contestants would use forceful tactics. Postwar Europe had been a seller's market in which the European auto makers had found low-pressure sales promotion sufficient to their needs. The Detroit managements had long experience in fighting for market share in the fiercely competitive United States market, and it was expected that they would introduce their aggressive tactics into their campaigns for the world market. It was not clear how aggressive they might dare to be before encountering the opposition of the national governments of the European auto makers.

THE KADETT AND THE TAUNUS (THE GERMAN FORD)

The new Opel Kadett was a 46-horsepower, four-seat sedan with the engine in front and rear-wheel drive. Compared with other European small cars, it had graceful body lines. The Kadett's factory list price in Germany was DM 5,076 ($1,370), compared with the 40-horsepower Volkswagen at DM 5,150 ($1,400). Although the Kadett had a wheelbase of only 91.5 inches versus Volkswagen's 94.5, the Kadett looked as though it was longer than the Beetle. To produce the Kadett, Opel built a new DM 1,000 million ($270 million) plant at Bochum, Germany, with an annual capacity of 250,000 units, representing an increase of 60% in the company's production capacity.

The German Ford had long been in the development stage. It replaced a larger car of the same name—the Taunus—and it was slightly larger and more powerful than either the Volkswagen or the Kadett. The Ford had a front engine and a front-wheel drive, and it seated five. Like the Kadett, it featured relatively graceful body styling. Its factory list price in Germany was DM 5,480 ($1,480). Production began in 1962 in the big Ford Werke plant at Cologne. Shortly thereafter a newly built plant at Genk, Belgium, went into production, raising capacity 30%, or 120,000 units.

In the German postwar market each auto maker had offered a line that was limited to a relatively narrow price and horsepower range. Ford Werke and Opel broke with tradition. Each offered a range of cars to the growing affluent market which was becoming susceptible to the "trade-up" psychology. Old-line German auto makers were appalled at the prospect that the Americans in Germany might introduce the United States custom of annual model changes.

JAPANESE COMPETITION

In 1967 Japan became the second largest automobile producer in the world, surpassing Germany for the first time. In 1969 VW sales in the United States slumped for the first time, and commentators asserted that this was the result of competition, not from Detroit, but from two Japanese cars, the Toyota and the Datsun. Actually, VW sales declined from 1968 as the result of an East and Gulf Coast dock strike which halted deliveries of new VWs to about three-fourths of the country's

VW dealers for nearly 100 days. By the time 1969 ended, however, U.S. sales had climbed back to within about 18,000 units of the 569,292 sold in 1968. Volkswagen remained by far the most popular imported car in the United States, outselling Toyota over four to one, but for the first time VW captured less than 50% of the U.S. foreign car market. In 1965 VW had 65% of the market; in 1968 it had 58%; in 1969 it had less than 50%. Toyota's U.S. sales doubled in 1969 to achieve 11% of the U.S. import market. In 1970 Japan had 18% of the world automobile market, and West Germany had 13%. (See Exhibit 7.)

While the VW remained utilitarian in appearance, the Japanese cars were stylishly designed. A number of years ago Toyota had attempted to enter the U.S. market and failed. Following this experience, the company sent a team of automotive engineers to the States to make an exhaustive study of U.S. car preferences and road conditions. When the new Toyotas were entered into the U.S. market, they seemed to mimic Detroit. The Toyotas had relatively high horsepower (90 to 115 hp), which appealed to Americans; Toyota offered six models to choose from; luxury appointments, such as floor carpeting, tinted glass, and whitewall tires, were standard equipment. Many American buyers ordered expensive extras: air conditioning, for example, at $295.

The 1970 basic price of most Toyotas and Datsuns was about the same as that of the Volkswagen 113, which was $1,839 at the East Coast. However, price was not the only attraction of the Japanese cars. The Japanese cars offered many options. The four-door models seemed to have great appeal.

Some United States Volkswagen dealers would have liked to see four-door Volkswagens imported. Most, however, wanted to stay with the short line. "The Beetle is the biggest thing we have going," said a U.S. dealer. "Seventy per cent of our sales are the bug. Volkswagen is already selling too many models in the United States. I personally wouldn't want to see the line complicated any more."

THE PRICE RISE OF 1962

On March 21, 1962, Herr Erhard, then Minister of Economics, appealed to West Germans to exercise restraints in raising prices and wages. Wage and salary levels had risen 12.8% in 1961 while production increased only 5.9%. On March 28, Volkswagenwerk announced that the home price of the Beetle would be raised by DM 240 ($60).

A spirited debate ensued. Herr Erhard rebuked the auto makers for "behaving just as irresponsibly as the trade unions" and tried to persuade them to rescind their price increases. The Volkswagen management declined, pointing out that VW workers had been receiving wage increases since 1957, and the VW automobile had been improved, but its price had not been raised. Herr Erhard then persuaded the Bundestag to reduce the German duties on imported cars by 50%. However, imports accounted for only 9% of German auto sales. Most duties were reduced from 10% to 5%. However, Renault, Fiat, and Simca reacted by cutting their prices only 2% to 3%. The result was that the Volkswagen management expressed no concern over their tariff "punishment."

The incident had widespread repercussions within Germany. Considerable displeasure was voiced throughout West German industry at the Adenauer regime for its unilateral manipulation of import duties for domestic economic regulatory purposes without reciprocal favors from the foreign beneficiaries concerned.

THE FREE TRADE AREAS

It was believed that the European auto makers were reluctant to enlarge their plants or engage in combinations—either at home or abroad—until the direction of the Common Market and the European Free Trade Area was more predictable. Europe had a population of 350 million, but only 180 million were in the EEC area, where most of the autos were manufactured. British Motors Leyland was the only sizable producer in EFTA. The production of Sweden was relatively small.

The Common Market had two objectives respecting tariffs: (1) the reduction of tariffs between member nations, and (2) equalization—the adjustment of taxes—so that autos imported from other member countries would bear no greater tax burden than autos produced by the member country itself. In 1971 Common Market tariffs on automobiles had been eliminated.

It was the opinion of the Volkswagenwerk management that the German membership in the Common Market had brought new international trade barriers to Volkswagen. Barred by restrictions and taxes, Volkswagen set up a sales subsidiary in France, but had sold an aggregate of only about 140,000 vehicles there throughout its entire history.

In Italy, Volkswagen had set up a service organization, mainly for European Volkswagen-driving tourists, which so impressed the Italian public that the Italian government, concerned for the protection of Fiat, had threatened to raise duties against German imports despite EEC regulations. Volkswagen had sold only about 200,000 vehicles in Italy up to the end of 1969.

THE VOLKSWAGEN IN THE UNITED STATES

By 1971 Volkswagen had become the most sensational sales success ever achieved in the United States by a foreign industrial product. In 1970, 569,696 Volkswagens were delivered to customers in the U.S. In addition, 21,344 Porsche and Audi models were also delivered to U.S. customers.

During the first few years of its history the Volkswagen management had not found it difficult to develop export markets in European countries, especially those which did not have comparable auto production facilities. Sales in the United States, however, did not go well. A few hundred cars were shipped to the United States in 1953 and 1954, and these went begging for want of buyers. The United States sales representative was convinced that it would be possible to sell only about 800 cars a year in the U.S. Nevertheless, Volkswagenwerk decided to enter the American market. It founded a subsidiary called Volkswagen of America, Inc., which was to be the U.S. importing organization.

In 1954, 8,895 Volkswagens were sold in the United States. In 1955 Volkswagenwerk estimated that it would sell 20,000, but by midsummer sales were at the rate of 2,500 a month. In August, 1955, Volkswagen purchased the Studebaker assembly plant in New Brunswick, New Jersey, with the intention of assembling Beetles there, using United States-made parts, such as body stampings and wheels, and engines made in West Germany. At the time it was explained that Volkswagen needed more production capacity to meet the fast-rising United States demand; Wolfsburg was already overburdened; North Atlantic shipping was costly and in short supply. Production was scheduled to begin in October, 1956, but six months after the Studebaker plant purchase Volkswagen sold the plant and the American production plans were abandoned. It was said that the Volkswagen management had come to the conclusion that preliminary cost estimates had been too low and it became clear that the venture would cause Volkswagenwerk to lose money. Others believed that American buyers of Volkswagens were strongly influenced by the fact that the car was made in Germany, by German craftsmen, an appeal which would be lost if the cars were made in the United States. Others attributed the reversal to the high cost of American labor and to the labor union climate in the American auto industry.

In 1955, 35,851 Volkswagens were sold in the United States, and every year thereafter sales in the U.S. increased regardless of the fluctuations in sales of American automobiles. "In the United States we serve a distinct and separate market," said Herr Nordhoff. "We do not compete with American companies. This puts us completely outside the problems of the United States auto industry."

In 1964, Volkswagenwerk built a 2-million-square-foot assembly plant at Emden, West Germany, a seaport on the North Sea coast. The plant was adjacent to the shiploading docks, employed about 8,000 workers in 1971, and assembled West German-produced parts into Volkswagens made specifically for shipment to the United States and Canada via Volkswagenwerk's charter fleet of ocean-going automobile freighters.

COMPETITION PRESENTED TO VOLKSWAGEN BY U.S. SMALL CARS

Detroit did not seem concerned about foreign cars imported into the United States until the late 1950's. Then it responded to rising imports by producing a wide line of "compact" models, such as the Ford Falcon, the Chevrolet Corvair, and the Plymouth Valiant. All of them were bigger, heavier, more luxurious, and about $250 higher in price than most imports. They did not match the imports in economy of operation. With the introduction of compacts, foreign imports dropped to about 340,000 in 1962, about half of the 1959 volume. It was thought that this was the result of the poor quality of many of the imports and of their incompetent marketing and service organizations, rather than of competition from American compacts.

Volkswagen had set up a strong sales and service organization before it entered the U.S. market, and it offered a quality product. Its sales rose 60% during the period when its foreign competitors were losing ground. After the 1962 slump, Toyota, Renault, and Fiat redesigned their cars and returned to the U.S. with improved products and better service organizations. Imported car sales reached a low in 1962, but rose 224% to 1.1 million in sales in 1969. They reached 1.2 million units during 1970 while Detroit's sales dropped about 7%.

Within a few years a $500 gap had developed between the lowest-priced U.S. small cars and imports. Detroit then began to import its own captive foreign models—Ford's Cortina, the GM Opel, and Chrysler's Sunbeam. They also reduced the prices of their compacts by about $200. Ford and American Motors brought out new, smaller, lower-priced compact models—the Maverick at $1,995 and the Hornet at $1,994, which was still $155 above the basic Beetle price of $1,839 in 1970. Foreign car sales continued to rise. It was generally conceded that higher material and labor costs made it impossible for the U.S. companies to make money on a U.S.-built Volkswagen-sized car.

In 1971 foreign autos accounted for an unprecedented 15% of the U.S. market. Some Detroit analysts predicted that over-all imported and domestic small-car sales (everything from compacts on down) would expand from their current 29% share of the total U.S. market to as much as 50% by 1980. For Detroit this posed a formidable challenge. Cutting costs to arrive at a selling price competitive with imports meant that Detroit would have to design both an entirely new car and new manufacturing techniques.

General Motors responded by spending $100 million to introduce four models of its new Chevrolet Vega 2300 at a basic price of $1,950 plus tax and dealer preparation for a delivered price of $2,091 for the two-door sedan (see Exhibit 11 specifications). Models included two-

exhibit 11   HOW THE MINIS LINE UP

	Super-Volkswagen Beetle	Chevrolet Vega 2300	Ford Pinto	American Motors Gremlin
Length, inches	159	170	163	161
Wheelbase, inches	95	97	94	96
Height, inches	59	51	50	52
Width, inches	61	65	69	71
Weight, pounds	1807	2190	2029	2640
Engine size, horsepower	60	90	75	145
Miles per gallon	26	25	26	24
Top speed, miles per hour	81	90	85	100

SOURCE: *U. S. News & World Report*, August 17, 1970.

door sedans, coupés, station wagons, and trucks. Extras, such as auto-matic transmission ($111), deluxe interior ($125.95), and power steering ($95), could raise the price to over $2,500. All models other than the two-door were higher in price. Volkswagen's basic Beetle (Model 113) sold for a basic list price of $1,839 at port of entry. (See Exhibit 12.)

The Vega went on sale September 10. On September 11, Ford intro-duced its Pinto, a two-door sedan, offered at $1,994 including federal tax plus dealer preparation. Chrysler was known to be developing a competitive "R" car which would not be ready until 1972. American Motors had entered its comparable Gremlin on April 1, and it was the only American company to sell more cars in the first half of 1970, but it suffered a loss of $14.1 million on that volume.

American auto makers were confident that the new mini-cars would sell, but they were afraid that the little cars would steal business from their companies' bigger models. To compete in price and quality, Chevrolet built the most automated auto plant in the United States for the Vega, which came off a computer-controlled assembly line at the rate of 100 an hour, which was two-thirds faster than the average

exhibit 12   SUGGESTED RETAIL LIST PRICES FOR VOLKSWAGEN BEETLE
AT U.S. EAST COAST PORTS OF ENTRY

Effective Date	Model Year	Price
August 1, 1955	1956	$1,495
August 1, 1957	1958	1,545
August 1, 1959	1960	1,565
March 9, 1961	1961	1,595 (DM revaluation)
June 22, 1965	1965	1,563 (tax decrease)
August 1, 1965	1966	1,585
January 1, 1966	1966	1,574 (tax decrease)
March 16, 1966	1966	1,585 (tax increase)
August 1, 1966	1967	1,639
August 1, 1967	1968	1,695
October 25, 1967	1968	1,699
August 1, 1968	1969	1,749
December 1, 1968	1969	1,799 (imposition of German export tax)
August 1, 1969	1970	1,839 (unofficial mark revaluation)
August 1, 1970	1971	1,780
December 16, 1970	1971	$1,845 *

* Price is for all U. S. ports of entry.

American assembly-line rate. To cut costs, Ford made its Pinto in only one model. The Pinto's 75-hp engine was built in England; its optional 90-hp engine was made in Germany; England and Germany supplied Pinto fuel pumps, steering gear, four-speed transmissions, and distributors. Carburetors were imported from Ireland and bearings from Japan.

All of the mini-car makers abandoned the annual model change. Ford and Chevrolet planned to keep their model style constant for five years. American Motors had always been slow to change its styling.

With its new mini-cars Detroit hoped to discover whether the allure of imports was really bound up with the foreign origins of the car and "old-world craftsmanship" or whether the determinant was simply low price. One market research executive stated: "It's a combination of low original cost, low operating and maintenance cost, and a reputation for durability."

For 1971 Detroit planned to offer many new compacts which were just a little bigger than the minis. Lincoln-Mercury planned to offer the Comet, a model similar to the Ford Maverick but with a V-8 engine; American Motors, the Sportabout, a compact station wagon; Chrysler, the Dodge Demon, a price leader; Ford, a four-door version of the Maverick; Pontiac, its first compact, the Cirrus.

Ford expected to sell 400,000 mini-cars in 1971; GM predicted sales of 400,000; Volkswagen looked for an increase of about 5% over 1970 and sales of 600,000; Toyota and Datsun predicted a combined total of 250,000. The aggregate was considerably greater than total small-car sales had ever been in the United States. "What we are going to see is a lot bigger market for small cars in the United States," said a Volkswagen executive, "and it's up to us to get our share." President Perkins of Volkswagen of America thought that Detroit had completely missed on styling. "They should have come up with some interesting engineering," he said. "A car distinguishable from other cars—but what they have produced is a car so similar that it blends right into the scenery."

Herr Nordhoff had believed that Volkswagen sales in the United States would peak at about 400,000 but would not go much beyond that. Competitors in the auto industry believed that he had consistently underestimated the potential. (See Exhibits 8 and 13.)

In 1970 Volkswagen accounted for approximately 43.3% of imported car registrations in the U.S. (47.4% in 1969).

exhibit 13   **VOLKSWAGEN DEALER RETAIL SALES IN THE UNITED STATES**

1955	35,851
1956	49,550
1957	72,555
1958	85,985
1959	129,315
1960	162,037
1961	191,584
1962	217,236
1963	270,788
1964	313,426
1965	357,144
1966	411,956
1967	443,510
1968	569,292
1969	551,366
1970	569,696

THE SUCCESSION IN MANAGEMENT

In January, 1967, Herr Nordhoff, then 68, said, "It is not only customary, but compelling, to think in time about one's successor." Herr Nordhoff planned to retire at the end of 1968. The Volkswagenwerk board chose to succeed him, Herr Kurt Lotz, 54, who had been a Luftwaffe general staff major in his early career, assigned to assessing war needs, which Herr Lotz described as his "first strong contact with industrial planning." At the end of the war he took a job as a clerk in Mannheim with the German subsidiary of Brown, Boveri & Cie, which manufactured all kinds of electrical equipment from home appliances to locomotives. Within 12 years he rose to chairman. In April, 1967, he accepted the offer of the Volkswagenwerk board to succeed Herr Nordhoff. Because, as he put it, he was "long on organization and diplomacy and short on knowledge of automaking," it was planned that he would work with Herr Nordhoff until Nordhoff retired. Herr Nordhoff passed away in April, 1968, and Herr Lotz became managing director of Volkswagenwerk. (See Exhibit 14.)

Herr Lotz summarized the traditional policy position of Volkswagen and the problems the firm was likely to encounter in the 1970's in an address to the stockholders on July 3, 1969:

> Our production facilities are now again being fully utilized. The great demand for Volkswagens all over the world made it necessary to incur a great deal of overtime and extra shifts last year. . . .

In view of our exceptionally high earnings in 1968, many stockholders wish for higher dividends. Higher dividends would not please all of our stockholders. One year is too short a time period on which to base dividend payments. In 1967 our domestic production fell 22%. Our plants were closed for 33 working days. Our workers lost a great deal of income. We paid out our regular 20% dividend in those trying times; in our contrasting better situation in 1968 we should feel it our duty to do vice versa to strengthen our organization. We have plans for substantial capital investments in 1970 and 1971. . . .

The times in which one can consider the competitive ability of a company in terms of a nation or of Europe have long since passed. Imported cars have achieved a market share of 23% in Germany. The subsidiaries of American companies are in a very strong position throughout Europe. During the past year they grew faster than any of their competitors. Seen from the opposite viewpoint there does not exist in the United States a single branch plant of a European automobile manufacturer. The market share of imported cars in the United States grew last year—and Volkswagen is still the largest foreign competitor—but competition in the U.S. will be considerably sharpened by the appearance of new small American cars.

. . . we must consider the Volkswagenwerk relative to its larger competitors with respect to size and its production capacity. Volkswagen has followed the policy of producing a car of good value which would appeal to the largest market share. This requires mass production to enjoy the economies of scale. Then one must aim one's endeavors at the most capable competitors in the world market. These are considerably larger than we are. To cite a few figures: From its beginning until today Volkswagen has achieved an aggregate volume of about 90 billion marks. This is roughly the same as the volume which the world's largest automobile company did in 1968 alone. The total sales volume of Volkswagenwerk in 1968 is roughly about the same amount as the growth in sales of our largest competitor in the year 1968 alone.

What concerns us more than our small size is our relatively small equity capital and the unfavorable ratio of our base capital to our reserves. This is especially true in comparison with our principal American competitors. The reserves of the consolidated Volkswagenwerk companies for 1968 were about three times the company's base capital. The reserves of our three largest American competitors, by comparison, are seven, twelve, and eighteen times the amount of their present capital.

The reserves of our parent company, Volkswagenwerk AG, do not even double the amount of its base capital. If we wished to reach the same strength as our larger competitors, we would have to increase the reserves of our consolidated corporation by about 7 billion marks. In doing this, we would not have reached the absolute level of the reserves of our American competitors, but only the *ratio* between base capital and reserves.

exhibit 14
The Organizational Structure of Volkswagenwerk AG and Its Domestic and Foreign Subsidiaries and Affiliates

Corporate Management

Chairman of the Board of Management	Research and Development	Production and Quality Control	Marketing

Groups

Volkswagen

Plant Locations   Wolfsburg
Hanover
Kassel
Emden
Brunswick
Salzgitter (under construction)

Distributing Companies

Volkswagen of America, Inc.
Englewood Cliffs, N.J.
Capital Stock US$5,000,000
100.0%

Subsidiaries and Affiliates
Volkswagen Southeastern Distr., Inc.
US$ 250,000   100.0%
Volkswagen Northeastern Distr., Inc.
US$ 250,000   100.0%
Volkswagen North Central Distr., Inc.
US$ 250,000   100.0%
Volkswagen South Atlantic Distr., Inc.
US$ 250,000   100.0%
Volkswagen South Central Distr., Inc.
US$ 250,000   100.0%
VICO Corporation
US$2,602,864   48.5%
Sylvan Avenue Corporation
US$ 400,000   100.0%
Volkswagen Products Corporation
US$ 1,000   100.0%

Volkswagen France S.A.
Villers–Cotterêts
Capital Stock   FF 7,000,000
100.0%

Subsidiaries and Affiliates
Société Volkswagen
de Financement S.A.
FF   7,500,00   99.0%
Service d'Assurance Volkswagen S.A.
FF   100,000   51.0%

Volkswagen Canada Ltd.
Toronto, Ontario
Capital Stock   can$500,000
100.0%

Subsidiaries and Affiliates
Vorelco Ltd.
can$2,000,000   100.0%

Svenska Volkswagen AB
Södertalje
Capital Stock   skr 42,000,000
33.3%

**Weser–Ems–
Vertriebsgesellschaft m.b.H.)**

Bremen
Capital Stock   DM 3,000,000
50.0%

Subsidiaries and Affiliates

Volkswagen do Brasil S.A.
São Bernardo do Campo
Capital Stock   NCr$364,493,920
80.0%

Subsidiaries and Affiliates
Cia VVD de Crédito
NCr$ 7,592,000   100.0%
Distrivolks S.A.
NCr$ 1,000,000   100.0%
Forjaria São Bernardo S.A.
NCr$ 5,575,620   33.3%
VEMAG S.A.
NCr$ 54,988,979   49.6%
10.4% AUDI NSU
       AUTO UNION AG

Volkswagen of South Africa Ltd.
Uitenhage, C.P.
Capital Stock   R 800,000
64.9%

Subsidiaries and Affiliates
South African Motor Acceptance
Corporation (PTY) Ltd. (SAMAC)
R 1,000,000   50.0%
50.0% Volkswagen
       of America, Inc.

Volkswagen de Mexico, S.A. de C.V.
Puebla/Pue
Capital Stock   mex$467,121,000
100.0%

Subsidiaries and Affiliates
Volkswagen Comercial, S.A. de C.V.*)
mex$5,000,000   100.0%

Producing Companies

Motor Producers Ltd.
Melbourne, Australia
Capital Stock $A 10,000,000
100.0%

*) Formed or acquired
   in 1970.

exhibit 14 (continued)

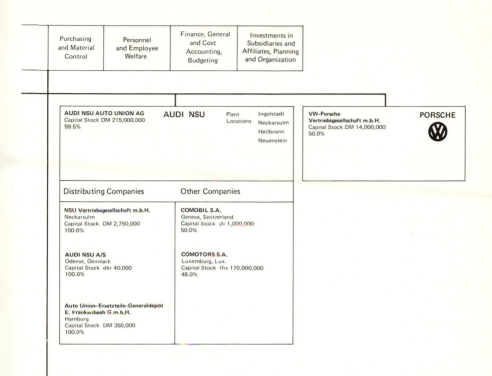

We must think in terms of the much larger order of things which will exist in a very few years. The European auto industry has been in a period of reorientation which is beamed at the world market. Because of this, we in Europe must achieve a much stronger cooperation. If, in this, we see painted on the wall a horror picture of the mighty powers which are growing mightier, and who are bent on strangling world competition, then I say to you: the truth looks different than that! We have the responsibility for the maintenance of employment and for the optimum use of invested capital. If the European automobile industry strives today more strongly than in earlier days for more productive unities, this does not occur because of a hunger for might, but rather because of these responsibilities. I do not wish to be misunderstood. A merger of companies in the automobile industry is not a patent medicine. There is a place for small companies, and their place will remain in the future. Where, however, a merger gives promise of assuring continued employment and at the same time strengthens competitive position, then the social value of the merger should not be overlooked.

The model policies of the Volkswagenwerk have been a much discussed theme for many years. I have been told that the proposal to substitute another model for the Beetle has been around for as many years as this model has enjoyed success. If one were to reduce our model policies to a short formula, one might say:

1. Our organization should produce an automobile which will sell on the market, and at a sufficient rate of profit. Over the years Volkswagenwerk has unquestionably achieved both of these goals. This conclusion does not change the fact that not all of our models have been equally well accepted. The VW 411, for example, has not yet fulfilled our expectations, but this may still change. . . .

2. The development engineers in an automobile plant must concern themselves with advances in automobile technology; changes in buyers' habits; keeping the product capable of competing. This assignment must be undertaken behind closed doors and without talking about it openly. I would nevertheless like to talk about the direction of our work. The founding of the Volkswagen-Porsche organization might be the first indication of the new direction. . . . In the future sports cars developed by both firms will appear in the market under the name Volkswagen-Porsche. . . . The Volkswagenwerk development potential has grown so large that it has room for every technical concept. . . .

. . . discussions about the balance of payments and the revaluation of the D-Mark have brought about a general rise in interest in the subject of German capital investments abroad. There is generally widespread agreement that foreign investments are a suitable means to strengthen the position of an organization in the current market, to lessen our excess export balance, and thereby influence the rate of exchange.

A stronger engagement of German industry abroad is in fact a pressing necessity. The Volkswagenwerk was one of the earliest to act in this regard. But we are not satisfied with our successes and our activities abroad. We must establish plants in industrially developed countries. German investment abroad has lagged far behind.

Speaking of only the automobile industry, a comparison between the United States and West Germany in this respect is very enlightening. Of all of the automobiles which the United States sells outside the United States, less than one-quarter are exported from the United States. Considerably more than three-quarters of the American cars sold abroad are made by subsidiaries of American companies abroad. If one considers the aggregate of the cars which German firms sell abroad, the figures are exactly reversed: more than three-quarters of the German cars sold abroad are made in Germany and exported; only one-quarter of the German cars sold abroad are made by foreign subsidiaries of German companies. We can reduce this to a short formula—the U.S.A. produces abroad; West Germany exports to foreign markets.

Certainly in all such considerations one must keep in mind that German industry abroad has suffered two severe setbacks in two world wars. For this very reason there is the necessity that we should again strive to produce more abroad. Comparative figures indicate that in the period after 1950 we have remained considerably behind in international development.

One cannot, of course, disregard the risks involved in building up a production facility abroad. In spite of this, we must risk investments abroad to decrease the proportion of our domestic production which we export, but above all, through plants in other lands, to better exploit the markets there. . . .

BUSINESS TRENDS AND DEVELOPMENTS OF VOLKSWAGENWERK AG AND ITS SUBSIDIARIES AND AFFILIATES DURING 1970

In the 1970 report to the shareholders, the Volkswagen management stated:

The 1970 business year for the Volkswagenwerk AG and its subsidiaries and affiliates was characterized by continuing growth and receding profits. With an increasing demand it was not possible, despite extra production shifts, to produce enough vehicles to enable all market possibilities to be exploited. Even the completion of the sixth VW plant at Salzgitter did not enable the bottleneck in production to be overcome on a short-term basis. If the company and its subsidiaries and affiliates were able to increase sales in 1970 by 13.3% to DM 15,800 million, this can be attributed primarily to the sales success of the producing subsidiaries, apart from additional profits due to price increases and the increased proportion of models giving bigger profit margins. In addition the good development of sales was favorably influenced by the continued lively demand for vehicles on the domestic market. Thus domestic sales increased by 21.2% to DM 4,900 million while the sales achieved by foreign subsidiaries increased by 23.6% to DM 3,900 million. On the other hand the export sales of the domestic companies only rose by 3.7% to DM 7,000 million.

Altogether 2.2 million vehicles were sold by Volkswagenwerk AG and its subsidiaries and affiliates in 1970, around 6% more than in the previous year. In the Federal Republic the volume of sales rose by 8.3% to 725,055 vehicles, and in countries where the Volkswagenwerk has its own production plants it rose by 30.6% to 327,216 vehicles. On the other hand, the Volkswagenwerk's and its domestic subsidiaries' export sales were down slightly by 1.6%. This drop in exports can mainly be ascribed to the inability of the domestic producing companies to cope with the demand and to losses of sales in some countries following the revaluation of the Deutsche mark.

The sales range was once again expanded in 1970. In the second half of the year the new VW 1302 and VW K 70 models were introduced and were well received by the market. At AUDI NSU work started on production of the Audi 100 Coupé, while Volkswagen do Brasil commenced production of the VW 1600 TL (Fastback), the VW 1500 "Beetle," and the Karmann Ghia TC.

In the year under review the Volkswagenwerk AG acquired the Selbstfahrer Union group of Hamburg, the largest car hire company in the Federal Republic. The Volkswagenwerk AG also owns 50% of the stock of the Weser-Ems-Vertriebsgesellschaft m.b.H. of Bremen, founded in 1970.

The considerable rise in material and labor costs made price increases on the part of the Volkswagenwerk AG and AUDI NSU inevitable during the year under review. These price increases had to be carefully calculated so that they correspond to market conditions and did not endanger the full use of production capacity, and thus the jobs of workers. The additional proceeds resulting from the price increases and from cost savings due to rationalization measures, were not, however, sufficient in 1970 to prevent a considerable drop in profits. In 1970 the net earnings of the Volkswagenwerk AG dropped to DM 190 million (1969 DM 330 million). Despite this considerable drop in profits, the management and the board of directors propose to distribute to the stockholders DM 166.5 million out of the 1970 net earnings. This dividend is equivalent to a distribution of 18.5% on the capital stock increased in the previous year from the company's own funds, or DM 9.25 on DM 50 par value of capital stock.

(See Exhibits 15 to 20, financial statements and selected data.)

exhibit 15   **VOLKSWAGEN AG**
Statement of earnings for year ended December 31, 1970

	1970	1970	1969
	DM	DM	Thousand DM
Sales (excluding sales tax)	9,912,843,888		9,237,876
Increase in inventories	115,670,116		74,964
		10,028,514,004	9,312,840
Material, wages and overhead capitalized as additions to plant and equipment		109,819,716	76,472
Gross output		10,138,333,720	9,389,312
Expenditures for raw materials, supplies and other materials		5,812,246,211	5,118,598
Excess of gross output over expenditures for raw materials, etc.		4,326,087,509	4,270,714
Income from profit assumption agreements	660,372		501
Income from investments in subsidiaries and affiliates	78,819,690		87,087
Income from other financial investments	18,363,979		5,540
Other interest and similar income	99,006,290		81,081
Gain on disposal of property, plant, equipment and investments	3,756,619		2,395
Elimination of reserves for undetermined liabilities no longer required	98,853,956		43,744
Other income	106,467,104		110,878
including extraordinary income of DM 11,418,286			
		405,928,010	331,226
		4,732,015,519	4,601,940
Wages and salaries	2,286,907,710		1,816,145
Social expenditures—compulsory	253,384,815		204,516
Pension expenditures and voluntary payments	94,065,185		81,547
Provision for depreciation of physical plant	535,514,558		432,219
Write-down of financial investments	43,073,171		103,773
Write-down of other current assets and provision for doubtful trade acceptances and accounts	9,395,041		15,207
Loss on disposal of property, plant, equipment and investments	1,767,744		1,564
Interest expense and similar charges	41,245,027		22,270
Taxes			
a) on income, earnings and property DM 262,192,270			551,037
b) other DM 2,391,940			167,761
	264,584,210		
Share-the-Burden Property Levy	2,756,086		2,756
Expenditures under loss assumption agreements	7,444,303		8,160
Additions to reserves for special purposes	4,042,235		43,422
Other expenses	997,346,127		821,321
		4,541,526,212	4,271,698
Net earnings		190,489,307	330,242
Net earnings brought forward from previous year		415,932	—
Transfer from the reserve for the Share-the-Burden Property Levy		1,875,000	1,795
		192,780,239	332,037
Transfer to other reserves from net earnings		26,000,000	165,121
Net earnings after reserve transfers		166,780,239	166,916

During 1970, pension payments amounted to DM 7,066,724;
payments during the next five years will approximate
120, 136, 156, 184, 210% of this amount.

exhibit 16 VOLKSWAGENWERK AKTIENGESELLSCHAFT
Balance sheet, December 31, 1970

Assets	Jan. 1, 1970 DM	Additions DM	Deductions DM	Transfers DM	Accumulation of Discount DM	Provision for Depreciation DM	Dec. 31, 1970 DM	Dec. 31, 1969 Thousand DM
Property, plant, equipment and investments								
A. Property, plant and equipment								
Real estate and land rights								
with office, factory and other buildings	1,131,821,128	171,900,278	6,093,470	118,393,520		112,907,969	1,303,113,487	1,131,821
with residential buildings	14,301,754	383,948	86,774	7,240		1,058,941	13,547,227	14,302
without buildings	37,493,691	2,874,200	535,949	−3,932,972		157,395	35,741,575	37,494
Buildings on leased real estate	20,331,740	1,180,854	41,224	570,453		2,515,917	19,525,906	20,332
Machinery and fixtures	520,644,972	365,084,543	4,437,022	59,082,835		245,731,041	694,644,287	520,645
Plant and office equipment	141,088,368	153,003,584	2,476,369	49,485,505		151,643,295	189,457,793	141,088
Construction in progress	240,994,462	209,278,535	25,865,877	−188,689,143		19,800,000	215,917,977	240,994
Advance payments to vendors and contractors	40,264,546	30,803,178	2,321,973	−34,917,438		1,700,000	32,128,313	40,264
	2,146,940,661	934,509,120	41,858,658			535,514,558	2,504,076,565	2,146,940
B. Investments								
Investments in subsidiaries and affiliates	240,074,786	196,239,528	2,206,250			17,248,473	419,065,841	240,075
Other investment securities	15,443,751						13,237,501	15,444
Long-term loans receivable with an initial term of four years or longer	154,704,129	133,386,638	5,642,220		3,277,495	25,824,698	259,901,344	154,704
Face value at 12/31/70 DM 432,852,187								
including secured by mortgages DM 223,966,094								
subsidiaries and affiliates DM 187,696,892								
loans in accordance with section 89 AktG DM 11,121,205								
	410,222,666	329,626,166	7,848,470		3,277,495	43,073,171	692,204,686	410,223
	2,557,163,327	1,264,135,286	49,707,128		3,277,495	578,587,729	3,196,281,251	2,557,163
Current assets				DM	DM	DM	DM	
A. Inventories								
Raw materials and supplies					416,575,834			336,334
Work in progress					344,826,005			236,868
Finished products					257,904,526			196,460
						1,019,306,365		769,662
B. Other current assets								
Advance payments to suppliers					2,721,716			1,818
Trade accounts receivable					100,356,996			72,950
including amounts due in more than one year DM 6,281,148								
Trade acceptances					2,698,872			8,367
Cash on hand, including post office checking account balances					675,126			627
Cash in banks					529,218,364			746,482
Securities					41,772,424			8,769
Receivables from subsidiaries and affiliates					115,091,962			187,813
including amounts for goods and services rendered DM 43,288,999								
Miscellaneous other current assets					256,199,397			238,266
						1,048,734,857		1,265,092
							2,068,041,222	2,034,754
Prepaid and deferred expenses							75,244	124
							5,264,397,717	4,592,041

Liabilities			Dec. 31, 1970	Dec. 31, 1969
	DM	DM	DM	Thousand DM
Capital stock			900,000,000	750,000
Reserves				
Legal reserve		233,799,000		233,799
Reserve for the Share-the-Burden Property Levy				
Jan. 1, 1970	20,943,000			
Transfer to earnings	1,875,000	19,068,000		20,943
Other reserves				
Jan. 1, 1970	1,335,125,578			
Transfer for increase of capital stock	150,000,000			
Transfer from 1970 earnings	26,000,000	1,211,125,578		1,335,126
			1,463,992,578	1,589,868
Reserves for special purposes				
Reserve for investments in developing countries in accordance with section 1 of the tax law		105,134,663		102,813
Reserve for price increases in accordance with section 74 of EStDV		8,896,338	114,031,001	7,176
				109,989
Allowance for doubtful trade acceptances and accounts			5,153,000	4,133
Undetermined liabilities				
Old-age pensions		475,318,570		397,078
Other undetermined liabilities				
Maintenance not performed during current year		7,000,000		15,000
Warranties without legal obligation		3,166,000		3,774
Other		683,809,455		621,766
			1,169,294,025	1,037,618
Liabilities with an initial term of four years or longer				
Due to banks		22,200,000		29,600
Other liabilities		92,773,195		100,650
including amounts due within four years DM 63,509,774			114,973,195	130,250
Other liabilities				
Trade accounts payable		761,697,208		546,766
Due to banks		32,877,000		—
Prepayments by customers		15,990,025		9,345
Accounts payable to subsidiaries and affiliates		140,744,671		22,338
including trade accounts payable DM 10,065,298				
advance payments received DM 114,390,012				
Miscellaneous other liabilities		378,457,016	1,329,765,920	224,463
Deferred income			407,759	802,912
Net earnings after reserve transfers (available for distribution)			166,780,239	355
Share-the-Burden Property Levy				166,916
Present discounted amount DM 19,667,283				
Quarterly installment DM 689,021				
			5,264,397,717	4,592,041
Contingent liabilities with respect to trade acceptances DM 228,319,569				

exhibit 17 VOLKSWAGENWERK AKTIENGESELLSCHAFT AND ITS DOMESTIC SUBSIDIARIES

Consolidated balance sheet, December 31, 1970

Assets	Jan. 1, 1970 DM	Jan. 1, 1970 Companies Included for the First Time DM	Additions DM	Deductions DM	Transfers DM	Provision for Depreciation DM	Dec. 31, 1970 DM	Dec. 31, 1969 Thousand DM
Property, plant, equipment and investments								
A. Property, plant, equipment and trademarks								
Real estate and land rights								
with office, factory and other buildings	1,281,665,199	15,170	232,497,857	6,244,011	140,079,921	120,392,613	1,527,621,523	1,281,665
with residential buildings	312,422,447		31,717,780	271,154	1,889,224	10,708,363	335,049,934	312,423
without buildings	60,773,267		14,260,271	2,578,875	4,532,476	157,394	67,764,793	60,773
Buildings on leased real estate	22,610,550		2,676,901	399,035	— 540,235	2,858,158	22,579,493	22,611
Machinery and fixtures	625,147,852	18,983,626	41,455,874	4,222,744	72,919,098	285,591,600	819,708,480	625,148
Plant and office equipment	217,994,311		280,869,195	20,051,911	59,672,173	229,330,860	328,136,534	217,994
Construction in progress and advance payments to vendors and contractors	339,754,224	21,333	313,586,160	28,264,046	—270,568,175	21,500,000	333,008,163	339,754
Deviative assets	2					16,133		
Trademarks						1	5,200	
	2,866,367,852	19,020,129	1,287,064,038	62,022,776		670,555,122	3,433,874,121	2,866,368
B. Investments								
Investments in subsidiaries and affiliates	66,583,546	59,282	21,413,341	1,000	182,975	17,262,263	70,975,881	66,584
Other investment securities	15,443,751			2,206,250			13,237,501	15,444
Long-term loans receivable with an initial term of four years or longer	130,504,392	313,523	104,010,632	4,633,358	—	748,438*	229,264,776	130,504
Face value at 12/31/70 DM 266,005,366 including secured by mortgages DM 72,335,295 subsidiaries and affiliates DM 15,677,738 loans in accordance with section 89 of AktG DM 11,208,206 loans in accordance with section 115 of AktG DM 12,600								
	212,531,689	372,805	125,423,973	6,839,608	182,975	18,010,701*	313,478,158	212,532
	3,072,899,541	19,392,934	1,412,488,011	68,862,384		688,565,823*	3,747,352,279	3,072,900

	DM	DM
Current assets		
A. Inventories	1,307,460,310	985,801
B. Other current assets		
Advance payments to suppliers	3,862,273	3,483
Trade accounts receivable	181,318,960	133,100
including amounts due in more than one year DM 8,035,240		
Trade acceptances	4,788,848	12,679
including acceptances discountable at German Federal Bank DM 612,045		
acceptances due from subsidiaries and affiliates DM 66,780		
Checks on hand	259,152	20
Cash on hand, including German Federal Bank and post office checking account balances	1,400,786	946
Cash in banks	612,701,787	840,498
Securities	41,772,424	8,769
Receivables from subsidiaries and affiliates	129,348,733	165,569
including amounts for goods and services rendered DM 48,477,699		
Loans receivable in accordance with section 89 of AktG	33,175	33
Loans receivable in accordance with section 115 of AktG	13,092	
Miscellaneous other current assets	545,283,903	512,631
	2,828,243,443	2,663,529
Prepaid and deferred expenses		
Discount on loans payable	4,613,779	3,160
Other	6,791,232	4,089
	11,405,011	7,249
	6,587,000,733	5,743,678

exhibit 17 (continued)

Liabilities		Dec. 31, 1970	Dec. 31, 1969
	DM	DM	Thousand DM
Capital stock		900,000,000	750,000
Reserves			
Legal reserve	233,799,000		233,799
Reserve for the Share-the-Burden Property Levy	19,068,000		20,943
Other reserves	1,211,125,578		1,335,126
		1,465,992,578	1,589,868
Adjustment items arising from consolidation			
Capital consolidation	–81,378,196		52,572
Other adjustment items	190,409,709		159,256
		109,031,513	211,828
Minority interest in AUDI NSU AUTO UNION AG			
including minority interest in net earnings thereof DM 4,141,200		87,652,672	144,794
Minority interest of unconsolidated subsidiaries in consolidated subsidiaries			
including minority interest in net earnings thereof DM 4,718,681		4,768,681	5,461
Reserves for special purposes			
Reserve for investments in developing countries in accordance with section 1 of the tax law	106,554,663		104,233
Reserve for price increases in accordance with section 74 of EStDV	8,896,338		7,176
Reserve for replacements in accordance with paragraph 35 of EStR			485
		115,451,001	111,894
Allowance for doubtful trade acceptances and accounts		9,640,110	8,236
Undetermined liabilities			
Old-age pensions	519,279,248		432,874
Other undetermined liabilities			
Maintenance not performed during current year	7,000,000		17,077
Warranties without legal obligations	6,766,000		6,060
Other	823,530,163		705,312
		1,356,575,411	1,161,323
Liabilities with an initial term of four years or longer			
Due to banks	207,994,569		206,314
including secured by mortgages DM 185,766,643			
Other liabilities	202,845,213		202,370
including secured by mortgages DM 108,045,345			
including amounts due within four years DM 110,948,838		410,839,782	408,684
Other liabilities			
Trade accounts payable	962,548,067		685,352
Due to banks	426,812,902		198,251
Prepayments by customers	20,974,853		12,203
Accounts payable to subsidiaries and affiliates	119,850,321		8,916
including trade accounts payable DM 8,108			
advance payments received DM 114,244,843			
Miscellaneous other liabilities	439,952,542		264,622
		1,970,138,685	1,169,344
Deferred income		3,026,336	4,146
Net earnings after reserve transfers and minority interests		155,883,964	178,100
		6,587,000,733	5,743,678
Contingent liabilities with respect to trade acceptances	DM 165,850,325		
Contingent liabilities with respect to guarantees	DM 1,438,464		

* Reduced by Accumulation of Discount of DM 1,834,847

exhibit 18 **VOLKSWAGENWERK AKTIENGESELLSCHAFT
AND ITS DOMESTIC SUBSIDIARIES**

Consolidated statement of earnings for year ended December 31, 1970

	1970		1969
	DM	DM	Thousand DM
Sales (excluding sales tax)	11,853,681,854		10,755,392
Increase in inventories	147,297,529		80,055
		12,000,979,383	10,835,447
Material, wages and overhead capitalized as additions to plant and equipment		169,975,005	117,547
Gross output		12,170,954,388	10,952,994
Expenditures for raw materials, supplies and other materials		7,197,732,065	6,233,961
Excess of gross output over expenditures for raw materials, etc.		4,973,222,323	4,719,033
Income from investments in unconsolidated subsidiaries and affiliates	24,661,273		41,859
Income from other financial investments	16,919,891		4,005
Other interest and similar income	134,847,910		109,981
Gain on disposal of property, plant, equipment and investments	8,216,194		6,147
Elimination of reserves for undetermined liabilities no longer required	101,218,547		46,592
Elimination of reserves for special purposes no longer required	485,000		—
Other income including extraordinary income DM 17,762,836	142,168,974		143,452
		428,517,789	352,036
		5,401,740,112	5,071,069
Wages and salaries	2,773,184,246		2,189,061
Social expenditures—compulsory	310,415,102		249,378
Pension expenditures and voluntary payments	105,318,568		89,506
Provision for depreciation of physical plant	670,555,122		536,977
Write-down of financial investments	19,845,548		104,144
Write-down of other current assets and provision for doubtful trade acceptances and accounts	15,108,539		19,955
Loss on disposal of property, plant, equipment and investments	3,950,536		2,862
Interest expense and similar charges	80,354,962		49,594
Taxes a) on income, earnings and property DM 286,849,278			583,002
b) other DM 6,478,658			180,573
	293,327,936		
Share-the-Burden Property Levy	3,324,088		3,324
Expenditures under loss assumption agreements	3,078,609		5,090
Additions to reserves for special purposes	4,042,235		44,588
Other expenses	916,036,422		674,281
		5,198,541,913	4,732,335
Net earnings		203,198,199	338,734
Balance carried forward		203,198,199	338,734
Net earnings brought forward from the previous year		4,714,652	12,152
		207,912,851	350,886
Transfer from the reserve for the Share-the-Burden Property Levy		1,875,000	1,795
		209,787,851	352,681
Transfer to other reserves		26,000,000	165,121
		183,787,851	187,560
Transfer from adjustment items arising from consolidation Capital consolidation	3,125,600		—
Other adjustment items	—		3,558
		3,125,600	
		186,913,451	191,118
Transfer to adjustment items arising from consolidation Capital consolidation			1,131
Other adjustment items	22,169,606		—
		22,169,606	
Minority interest in net earnings of AUDI NSU AUTO UNION AG		4,141,200	6,476
consolidated subsidiaries		4,718,681	5,411
Net earnings after reserve transfers and minority interests		155,883,964	178,100

292

exhibit 19 VOLKSWAGENWERK AND ITS SUBSIDIARIES AND AFFILIATES

Comparative summary of selected financial data 1966–1970*

	Consolidated Total†					Volkswagenwerk AG				
	1966	1967	1968	1969	1970	1966	1967	1968	1969	1970
Assets (in million DM)										
Property, plant, equipment and investments (as at Dec. 31)	2,981	3,237	3,289	3,869	4,521	2,129	2,343	2,277	2,557	3,196
Additions during the year	872	787	708	1,076	1,536	703	615	508	740	1,131
Depreciation during the year‡	651	496	619	691	836	567	386	530	536	579
Current assets (as at Dec, 31)§	2,758	2,381	3,130	3,839	4,447	1,333	1,163	1,718	2,031	2,663
including inventories of	1,512	1,229	1,352	1,710	2,128	650	576	640	770	1,019
Liabilities										
Stockholders' equity	2,539	2,738	3,100	3,610	3,624	1,837	2,021	2,191	2,386	2,412
including reserves and retained earnings¶	1,704	1,886	2,237	2,588	2,486	1,087	1,271	1,441	1,636	1,512
minority interest	85	102	113	272	238					
Liabilities	3,200	2,880	3,319	4,098	5,334	1,625	1,485	1,804	2,202	2,847
payable within more than four years	657	631	644	725	943	366	362	426	455	651
Balance sheet total§	5,739	5,618	6,419	7,708	8,948	3,462	3,506	3,995	4,588	5,259
Balance sheet ratios (in percent)										
Property, plant, equipment and investments as a percentage of balance sheet total	52	58	51	50	51	62	67	57	56	61
Property, plant, equipment and investments as a percentage of current assets	108	136	105	101	102	160	201	133	126	155
Current assets as a percentage of short-term liabilities	125	123	138	138	118	120	119	147	150	116
Stockholders' equity as a percentage of balance sheet total	44	49	48	47	40	53	58	55	52	46
Stockholders' equity as a percentage of liabilities	79	95	93	88	68	113	136	122	108	85
Stockholders' equity as a percentage of property, plant, equipment and investments	85	85	94	93	80	86	86	96	93	75
Stockholders' equity and long-term liabilities as a percentage of property, plant, equipment and investments	107	104	114	112	101	103	102	115	111	96

* Amounts for 1966 were adjusted to conform to AktG 1965.
† Consolidated figures for 1966, 1967, 1968 and 1969 were adjusted to the new basis for comparison in 1970.
‡ Amounts for the years 1967, 1968, 1969 and 1970 are not exactly comparable with those for 1966 because of the valuation requirements of the new stock corporation law.
§ For the years 1968, 1969 and 1970, current assets and balance sheet totals were decreased by the amount shown under liabilities as allowance for doubtful trade acceptances and accounts.
¶ Includes reserves for special purposes consisting of equity capital.

exhibit **20**   **SUBSIDIARIES AND AFFILIATES**
Selected data of major VW subsidiaries and affiliates

	Sales in Million DM		Number of Employees at Year End	
	1970	Percentage Change As Compared to Previous Year	1970	Percentage Change As Compared to Previous Year
Manufacturing companies				
AUDI NSU AUTO UNION AG, Neckarsulm	2,079	26	29,147	10
Volkswagen do Brasil S. A., São Bernardo do Campo*	2,376	31	23,946	26
Volkswagen of South Africa Ltd., Uitenhage, C. P.*†	382	14	4,115	17
Volkswagen de Mexico, S. A. de C. V., Puebla/Pue.*	297	29	3,631	30
Motor Producers Ltd., Melbourne	121	13	1,081	1
Distributing companies				
Volkswagen of America, Inc., Englewood Cliffs, N. J.*†	4,323	7	1,722	10
Volkswagen Canada Ltd., Toronto, Ontario	329	−2	449	−5
Volkswagen France S. A., Villers-Cotterêts*	151	15	391	33

* Includes the employees of its subsidiaries.
† Sales consolidated with its subsidiaries.
Note: Sales converted to DM based on the yearly average rates of exchange. Sales of Volkswagen do Brasil were converted to DM based on monthly average rates of exchange.

12

BUCYRUS-ERIE

For the Bucyrus-Erie Company of South Milwaukee, Wisconsin, 1961 was a year of return to profitable operations. Shipments during the year totaled over $75 million, an increase of 18% over the 1960 volume of $63 million, and backlog of orders at the end of the year was $32 million, up 17% from 1960. The year's operations had returned net earnings of $1.12 per share, and further improvements in earnings were expected. Management, nevertheless, in the interests of prudence, decided to forgo any distribution of dividends. They stated that this was for the purpose of strengthening the financial position of the company and providing working capital to finance the increased volume of orders which was expected in the coming years.

The favorable operations of 1961 followed three years of losses which were unprecedented for B-E. Prior to these years, the company had been able to point to an almost unbroken record of profitable operations. During the loss years management drastically contracted its operations, sold plants and facilities, and pared down costs. This retrenchment was a direct reversal of the tactics of the first half of the fifties when management expanded its production capacity to meet the increase which was generally expected in the construction industry, particularly in road building, but which had failed to materialize.

In his letter to the stockholders which accompanied the 1961 Annual Report, Mr. R. G. Allen, who joined the company in 1957 and became chief executive officer in 1958, was cautiously optimistic. "Moderately higher sales of the company's small machines," he said, "should follow the U.S. and Canadian recovery and increased spending on highway and building construction. Large machine business should remain excellent both here and abroad." Then, Mr. Allen added a word of admonition: "It becomes imperatively critical to recognize," he warned, "that future profits and wages can be assured only if our costs and productivity can match those of manufacturers at home and abroad who are becoming increasingly competent, productive, and eager for orders."

EARLY COMPANY HISTORY

The Bucyrus-Erie Company was formed on December 31, 1927, as a consolidation of the Bucyrus Company of South Milwaukee and the Erie Steam Shovel Company of Erie, Pennsylvania, both of which had been founded in the 1880's. The former was the world's largest producer of small power shovels. Although the product lines were somewhat related, there were considerable differences in the two companies. The customer groups, buying habits, channels of distribution, problems of engineering design, manufacturing techniques, and physical location of plants all differed. The consolidated company was organized to fit the centralized pattern of the Bucyrus Company. This meant that there were manufacturing, sales, and engineering departments—each separate and responsible for its function. Within each major department, product divisions were developed. With the exception of one brief experiment in decentralization in a plant at Richmond, Indiana, which the company owned for only a few years in the latter 1950's, the organization structure of the company was always centralized.

Throughout its history B-E had been headed by men who had spent their business careers in the earth-moving industry. Mr. W. W. Coleman, who became head of the combined companies in 1927, had been president of the Bucyrus Company since 1912. Mr. George A. Morrison, the senior vice president, had risen through the ranks from his first job in South Milwaukee as a machinist apprentice. Together they set the company's policies and directed its affairs. When Mr. N. Rulison Knox became president in 1943, Mr. Coleman continued as chairman of the board of directors, and Mr. Morrison became vice chairman of the executive committee. When Mr. William Litle became president in 1952, Mr. Coleman and Mr. Morrison were still active in management. These men, together with a few other senior executives, made the critical decisions.

PLANTS, PRODUCTS, AND COMPANY POSITION

With gross assets of over $77 million and a payroll of four thousand employees, Bucyrus was one of the four largest firms in the construction and mining machinery industry. The company's products enjoyed a reputation for high quality and premium price. About 25% of its production was exported, and export sales had been increasing. About 75% of shipments was original equipment, and the remainder replacement parts. Major products (see Exhibit 5) were classified in the following categories:

Large Excavators (35% of total sales). These were power shovels and draglines, most of which were 2½ to 36 cubic yards capacity, and a few whose capacity was over 100 cubic yards. (See Exhibit 8.) Bucyrus was the leading manufacturer in the large excavator field. Its broad line of power shovels and draglines, which were used for stripping, quarry, and mine excavating, accounted for about 50% of the industry's sales. Bucyrus had only one competitor in the stripping excavator field (Universal Marion), and four competitors who produced quarry and mine excavators. Sales of stripping machinery typically accounted for about 25% of the company's sales, quarry and mining machinery 10% to 15%. The sales of these products were increasing in relation to total company sales. Quarry and mine excavators sold for $200,000 to $500,000 each; walking draglines for $200,000 to $800,000; most stripping excavators sold for about $1 million, with a few very large ones priced over $2 million. In walking draglines Bucyrus had only two competitors and supplied about 30% of the total market demand.

General Purpose Excavators (55% of total sales). These were power shovels, cranes, and draglines of ⅜ to 4 cubic yards capacity. There were over twenty companies in the general excavator field; over forty companies, if cross-competitors manufacturing other types of earthmovers were taken into account. Bucyrus-Erie manufactured the most complete line in the industry, and usually supplied 10% to 15% of the industry demand. Prices ranged from $15,000 to $175,000.

Drills (about 5% of total sales). This category included cable-type water well, oil well, and blast hole drills. Bucyrus-Erie was the world's largest producer of cable-type drills, most of which were water well drills, and supplied over 70% of the market demand. There were less than half a dozen manufacturers of this type of drilling equipment. Bucyrus' production of small size blast hole drills (about 6 inches) was insignificant, but the company was a factor in the production of large size blast hole drills (9 inches and over), supplying well over 50% of the market demand. Prices of most cable-type drills were from $1,000 to $30,000; blast hole drills ranged as high as $175,000.

Special Products (about 5% of total sales). Included in this category was a newly developed tower crane used in the construction of large multi-storied buildings, whose long boom had a reach of over twenty stories in height. Also included were hydro cranes, whose hydraulically powered booms delivered great power with ultimate precision, and flame piercing drills, capable of blast hole drilling into solid rock at tremendous speed.

Plants. In 1962 the company had three plants: South Milwaukee, Wisconsin, where it manufactured strippers, large excavators, walking draglines, quarry and mine shovels, railway cranes and drills; Evansville, Indiana, which produced general purpose excavators, cranes, hydrocranes and drills; and Erie, Pennsylvania, which produced general purpose excavators and cranes.

EARLY PRODUCT LINE POLICIES

Prior to the consolidation, the Bucyrus Company had not actively sought opportunities for product diversification. Although it had added material loaders, gasoline tractors, and trenching machines to its line during World War I, it had not continued their manufacture after the war. For the most part, this policy was carried over to the consolidated Bucyrus-Erie Company. The new company's management and its engineers devoted their efforts to building larger and more efficient power cranes, shovels, and draglines. In those few instances in which the company added other machinery to its line, management purchased the manufacturing rights from smaller companies.

In the depression years of 1931 to 1935, in an effort to sustain its sales volume, B-E acquired three new products which could be manufactured and distributed through the company's existing facilities. These products—walking draglines (a type of large excavator), drills of the cable churn type, and tractor equipment (scrapers, bulldozers) soon developed substantial volume, and by 1939 accounted for 39% of the company's total sales of new equipment, and over 50% of its profits.

THE WAR PERIOD—1941 TO 1946

During the war years Bucyrus-Erie maintained high levels of production but management deliberately chose to undertake only a limited amount of special war work. Over 90% of the company's wartime production was of its regular lines of equipment for highway and construction projects at home and abroad. There were no additions to plant facilities or product lines. Expenditures for maintenance slightly exceeded depreciation allowances, and the company emerged from the war with its equipment in good condition and in strong financial condition. It was equally well prepared for either a boom or a depression.

At the beginning of 1946 management believed that the market potential for its products was excellent, and that it had ample finances to undertake an expansion program. It was reluctant to do so, however, because of its concern over the possible saturation of postwar markets. At the end of the war industry production of excavators was running at three times the normal rate and about 85% of this was in general purpose excavators. B-E management was aware that many of these would be offered for sale secondhand after the war and it feared that this might undermine the sale of new equipment for years to come.

Immediately following the end of the war B-E received a flood of orders. Even though it was generally recognized that this swollen demand was temporary, management felt itself caught upon the horns of a dilemma. Operations were now at capacity level and two years would be required to expand facilities, by which time management felt sure the boom market would decline. At the same time it feared that failure to expand would result in a permanent loss of a substantial share of the market. Those B-E customers who had been obliged to turn to other suppliers for their equipment during the boom would probably continue to look to their new suppliers for service, parts, and additional equipment.

After weighing these factors, the executive committee in August of 1946 approved a modest expansion of the South Milwaukee and Evansville plants. The expansion was to be limited to the estimated supply of available labor and as much work as possible was to be subcontracted, even at above normal cost if necessary. In making this decision the company was aware that the expansion would fall short of allowing it to maintain its "normal" share of demand.

POSTWAR EXPANSION PROGRAMS

Bucyrus-Erie undertook three expansion programs in the ten-year period between 1946 and 1956. By 1956 the company had expected to double its World War II capacity and all of its production facilities were expected to be completely modern and better coordinated than ever before.

The first expansion took place during 1946 and 1947 and involved an expenditure of $3.8 million. This program doubled erecting and plate shop capacity at Evansville and increased erecting and casting capacity at South Milwaukee. Nothing was done at Erie. During these years, however, subcontracting rose from its wartime peak of $3.8 million to $4.8 million in 1946 and $7.2 million in 1947. Shipments in 1946, nevertheless, were only 65% of the wartime peak and in 1947 rose only to 88%. During 1946 and 1947 the company had experienced shortages of steel and electrical equipment and had suffered from strikes, friction in labor relations, and high employee turnover.

The sales department compiled a new ten-year forecast for the period beginning January 1, 1948. This predicted a "normal" annual volume of $48 million, and projected an $8.4 million, four-year program of replacements, improvements, and additions which was to achieve the "normal" volume by 1951 and eliminate the necessity for subcontracting. By 1951 the company's over-all capacity had been increased by 20%. Of the capital expenditures involved, South Milwaukee's heavy shovel plants had received 61%; Evansville's general purpose excavator shops received 34%; and the Erie shops, 5%. Production in 1950 was, however, 20% below that of 1947, backlogs fluctuated from a peak of $75 million in early 1948 to $15 million in late 1949, and substantial subcontracting continued.

During the postwar years significant industry changes took place. Demand for large excavators and blast hole drills declined, while the demand for general purpose excavators, tractor equipment, and other types of drills continued relatively high. Industry capacity expanded and keen competition appeared in some areas. The growing strength of competition was a source of particularly serious concern to the Bucyrus-Erie management. Mr. Coleman, chairman of the board, emphasized to the executive committee in March, 1951, the growing financial strength and productive capacity of the company's competitors, as well as the "continued increase in the demand for the company's products." He then called for a new study of the market and concluded: "No time should be lost in making this study, as it is most essential that the position of our company in the industry be maintained." It was as a result of this request that the company undertook its third long-range forecast of the postwar period. This third forecast resulted in the May, 1951, decision of management to further expand by purchasing existing plant capacity to increase general purpose excavator production.

In this third expansion B-E spent $3.7 million to buy $97\frac{1}{2}\%$ of the capital stock of the National Erie Corporation of Erie, Pennsylvania, a commercial steel foundry and machine shop. This increased B-E's foundry capacity by 50%, its machining capacity by 25%, and while the added facilities were not modern and efficient, management considered that high-cost production would still not be as costly as subcontracting. Volume, however, was still only at what the management called "normal" and 50% short of anticipated peak requirements. In planning for future sales the company set as a goal a 50% increase in general purpose excavator capacity over the 1952 production facilities. The planning provided for an expenditure of $2.8 million for improvement of the production facilities at Erie Plant No. 1, and $1.1 million to increase by 50% the casting capacity of the National Erie plant. In the expansion program plans were made to make 70% of the floor space at the Evansville plant available for the production of general purpose excavators.

In the aggregate, these expansion programs increased the company's investment in plants and equipment 400% from $4.7 million in 1945 to $18.5 million in 1954. Shipments rose from $32 million in 1945 to $66 million in 1954. Backlog of unfilled orders which had fluctuated during the ten-year period amounted to $3.8 million at December 31, 1953.

Management recognized that any expansion program would be complicated by the company's multiple-product line. It would be necessary to decide upon the priority and the extent of the expansion of each item since the manufacturing facilities varied substantially both in character and in location. Also, large excavators required casting facilities, machine tools, and erecting equipment of such large size that there were few opportunities for subcontracting. On the other hand, general purpose excavators, drills, and tractor equipment lent themselves more readily to subcontracting, a factor affecting the decision for any expansion of facilities.

During this period the senior B-E officials were brought under heavy pressure by mining officials, with whom they dealt directly, to increase their production of large excavators. Although a strong demand existed for general purpose excavators, management felt less pressure here because of the impersonal nature of marketing these machines through distributor channels. Tractor sales were also at peak demand and B-E felt obliged to fulfill its obligation as the chief tractor equipment supplier for International Harvester dealers. The demand for all types of drills was also heavy, and management felt compelled to maintain its leading position in each field of drilling.

BUCYRUS-ERIE AND THE TRACTOR EQUIPMENT BUSINESS

In the early 1950's a number of major machinery manufacturers expanded their lines to include excavating, earth-moving, and road construction equipment. Leading companies such as Caterpillar Tractor, Allis-Chalmers, Westinghouse, and General Motors added tractor-drawn and tractor-mounted earth-moving equipment to their product lines. Some of these companies also diversified into allied lines, adding such construction equipment as ready-mixers, tampers, road graders, road pavers, pile drivers, and cranes.

These moves, in the opinion of industry observers, indicated that intense interest had been aroused in the enormous road-building program that was to take place during the coming decade. The actions of many firms, particularly the tractor manufacturers, reflected their thinking that a broad line of equipment would help them to expand their market share. Of these, Caterpillar, International Harvester, Allis-Chalmers, Oliver, Euclid (General Motors), and LeTourneau (Westinghouse) accounted for almost all of the tractor business, as well as for most of the desirable distributors.

Bucyrus-Erie had added tractor attachments (bulldozers, scrapers, graders, rollers—see Exhibit 6) to its product line in the depression years of the early thirties when the sale of power shovels was at low ebb and the company needed a product line to keep its shops busy, even on a partial basis. At that time, when the development of modern tractor prime earth-movers was still in the pioneering stage, B-E undertook the design and production of a line of tractor-mounted earth-moving accessories designed to fit the track-type heavy duty tractors made by International Harvester Company (IHC). The result was a joint cooperative undertaking in which both companies exchanged every modification in design and planning, and coordinated their sales and production schedules. IHC made the tractors; B-E made the attachments; both were marketed through IHC's established organization of industrial equipment dealers, who presented B-E equipment as the IHC approved attachments for IHC tractors.

From 1936 through 1946 tractor equipment was the fastest growing segment of the company's products, both in respect to sales and profits. From 1946 to 1952 tractor equipment represented 25% of the company's sales volume of new machinery. Forecasts indicated that this volume was not temporary and in the postwar expansion program top priority was given to tractor equipment facilities.

By 1950 many of the major objectives of the tractor equipment program had been achieved. The most significant part of the program that was not realized concerned the amount of manufacturing capacity which B-E provided for the production of tractor equipment. The company had aimed to maintain an 80% parity with IHC's crawler output, but had been unable to do so because postwar demand exceeded B-E's capacity, and lengthy strikes had reduced output. Furthermore, Bucyrus-Erie management had consistently been reluctant to commit additional manufacturing capacity to tractor equipment because of the uncertainty of IHC's plans. IHC had been unwilling from the beginning to commit itself exclusively to Bucyrus-Erie equipment.

International Harvester, determined to compete for Caterpillar's position as leader of the industry, strongly desired to have an integrated tractor and equipment operation. Caterpillar built and had full control over the design, manufacture, and distribution of its tractors and tractor equipment. IHC, in contrast, controlled only its crawler tractor line and its distributors had to deal with some twenty manufacturers who supplied the allied tractor equipment. This put IHC at a twofold disadvantage: coordination of manufacture and distribution was difficult, and IHC's entire marketing expenses had to be absorbed by its tractor line alone.

Since there was no assurance that IHC would continue the cooperative arrangement, B-E was reluctant to commit more production facilities to tractor equipment without an offsetting agreement by IHC. With this in mind, the B-E management, in its various postwar plant expansions, had designed its additions to the tractor equipment plants to permit easy conversion to the production of the company's other products.

In May, 1952, the senior executives of International Harvester invited the B-E management to a top-level meeting of the executives of both companies. The discussion at this meeting was entirely amicable with both parties exhibiting an appreciation of the differing implications to each of their mutual problem and with both agreed that some major change in the existing arrangement was imperative. As a result of this meeting the International Harvester management proposed to the B-E management that IHC would, beginning in November, 1953, design, produce, sell, and service its own line of tractor equipment. This proposal was acceptable to the Bucyrus-Erie management, which agreed to retire from the tractor equipment field. The transition was to be programmed over a period of three years. The Bucyrus-Erie management stated that it felt its facilities used in the production of tractor attachments could best be utilized in the production of its traditional product lines—cranes and excavators.

PLANNING FOR THE FEDERAL HIGHWAY
PROGRAM AND ITS AFTERMATH

In the mid-50's management felt that the outlook for the company as a whole was very promising. Its 1955 Annual Report stated: "For the longer term, forecasts generally indicate that the next decade may be one of unprecedented growth." In its planning, the Bucyrus-Erie management leaned heavily on expectations that the Federal Aid Highway Act of 1956 would set in motion the biggest construction job in history. The Bucyrus-Erie management believed that, of the estimated total of fifty billion dollars to be spent on roads, a considerable part would be spent for the earth-moving and materials handling equipment. Accordingly, the company prepared for greatly increased sales volume in the years immediately ahead. It expected sales volume to approach $150 million annually by 1960. Most of the increase they anticipated would come from small and medium-sized commercial cranes and excavators.

At Evansville, Indiana, an expansion and modernization program costing $2 million was completed in 1957. At the same time, the company built a new $12 million plant at Richmond, Indiana, for the manufacture of drilling machines and drill tools. The Richmond plant, completed early in 1958, released facilities at South Milwaukee and Evansville to be used for the expansion of small excavator production. Expenditures for property, plant, and equipment in 1957 amounted to $13.6 million.

The year 1958 was a year of depression for the mining industry. The market for construction equipment also went into a severe decline. The company's entire line of shovels and cranes, from the smallest to the largest, was affected by the recession. There was a sharp reduction of Bucyrus-Erie shipments in 1958. The year ended a decade of expansion during which the company's property account more than quadrupled. (See Exhibit 7.)

exhibit 7   SELECTED STATISTICS ON BUCYRUS-ERIE SHIPMENTS (IN MILLIONS)

Year	Pounds Shipped	Property Account	Dollar Volume Shipped
1948	175	$ 9.1	$65
1955	135	20.4	75
1957	132	33.3	87
1958	100	37.6	58

Commenting in later years on this performance Mr. Allen said: "If we interpret boom period growth rates as normal, and project these rates progressively into five-year sales forecasts, disaster is bound to follow. It appears from the record that that is precisely what happened in the past." The decline in tonnage, Mr. Allen thought, could be traced to several causes: the liquidation of the tractor equipment division, which had yielded as much as $17 million in sales; the disposal of the dredge division; the growing popularity of front-end loaders for earth-moving, which cut into small excavator sales; the demand for cranes designed specifically for lifting alone was competing with B-E's dual-purpose equipment; and lastly, the sharp recession of 1958. The great expectations of the road program never materialized, and the entire construction industry suffered.

Mr. Allen's first major official act as president was to shut down the Richmond plant to stop the heavy losses from that operation, to offer the plant for sale, and to move the production of drills back to South Milwaukee and Evansville. Concurrently, a program was undertaken to reduce the heavy investment in fixed and working assets in order to reestablish an acceptable profit to capital invested ratio.

Plant capacity was designed to allow for prescheduling to 85%, leaving 15% available for emergency work. Formalized monthly progress reports were instituted showing direct labor and cost variances from budgets. To stress the profit objective the controller had set up seven profit centers: large excavators, commercial crane excavators, blast hole drills, well drills, hydrocranes, subcontracting, and the Canadian operation. Emphasis was placed on the return on investment employed as the most valuable yardstick. According to Mr. Birk, the new controller, there was an increasing awareness within the company of the relationship of turnover to profits.

"I am fully aware," said Mr. Allen, "that there is a limit to shrinking assets, to consolidations and to the mothballing of existing facilities. This can hardly be called a growth policy. Our former strength, however, has been sapped to the point where retrenchment is essential to preserve our corporate health. We are retreating temporarily from an extended front which we could not hold. By so doing, we gather our strength and then we move forward."

DOMESTIC MARKETS IN 1962

"Today, with at least 85 direct competitors bidding for customers' dollars throughout the world," said Mr. Lewis C. Black, vice president, domestic sales, "our company is facing the most highly competitive conditions in its 82-year history." Mr. Black was convinced that a keen awareness of market desires and needs was imperative and that the ability to produce designs rapidly in order to capitalize on changing market trends was more important now than at any time in the history of the earth-moving equipment industry. Mr. Black felt that it would be highly desirable if the company could find some way of diversifying into other areas to avoid its heavy dependence upon the fluctuations of the construction and mining industries.

Bucyrus-Erie marketed machinery and equipment to four major groups of customers. Arranged in the order of their total purchases they were: (1) construction contractors; (2) pit, quarry, and mine operators; (3) oil and gas field drillers; and (4) water well drillers. The principal customers for Bucyrus-Erie's general-purpose excavators were construction contractors. Their business was usually based on subcontracting and was often specialized. Therefore, despite the fact that there were more than 400,000 building contractors in the country, a relatively small number of them accounted for the major portion of Bucyrus-Erie's shipments to the construction market.

It was estimated that over 50% of the construction industry's top executives were engineers, and in selling to them all cost elements were usually reduced to a common denominator, such as cents per cubic yard. Most of the selling to these contractors was done by distributors with the assistance of manufacturers. Typically, distributors stocked, sold, and rented all classes of construction equipment, maintained spare parts inventories, repaired and rebuilt equipment. Usually a contractor could buy or rent from a local distributor all the equipment necessary for any construction job. Distributors also often financed their customers. Generally a distributor carried anywhere from 20 to 150 noncompeting lines of products to meet the varied needs of his customers. His salesmen knew every equipment user in the territory.

Bucyrus-Erie reached the construction contractors' market through approximately 65 construction machinery distributors, and Mr. Black felt that his set of distributors were the best in the country. He considered them to be a vital link in his sales effort because of their intimate knowledge of local conditions and customers and because they were better equipped to handle the intricate trade-in business.

Nearly half of the company's distributors carried a line of tractors and tractor equipment, usually of one of the four major producers—Caterpillar, International Harvester, Allis-Chalmers or Euclid. Some B-E executives considered this to be a subject of major concern, because tractor equipment gave the distributor a higher gross profit (27%) than Bucyrus-Erie shovels (15%), which certain company executives felt would influence the dealer to give priority to his line of tractors in his sales efforts. Caterpillar and IHC both painted their equipment a brilliant yellow, and often a Bucyrus-Erie salesman, returning from a call on a distributor, would make wry jokes about having found "yellow paint all over the place." Mr. Allen felt that this was a matter of major importance that ought to be corrected as soon as possible. "We cannot," he said, "continue to tolerate being in a secondary position with our distributors. We must insist that ours be their first line." Mr. Black agreed. "Of course you must insist on your fair share of your distributor's time," he said, "but it might often happen that the best distributor for us is one who also handles a major tractor line, and the two might go very well hand-in-hand. Some of our best distributors today also represent major tractor manufacturers. These are usually the distributors who have the financial strength, the good organization, and the shop facilities that are important to Bucyrus-Erie."

LARGE EQUIPMENT

"Heavy" or "engineering" construction—such projects as highways, dams, bridges, and industrial construction—was a principal market for Bucyrus-Erie general-purpose equipment.

Large excavating equipment, such as that used in open-pit mining, was usually custom-built to the customer's specifications, and it might take several years to open and develop the mine, and plan and fabricate the excavator. Final decisions regarding the purchase of large equipment were usually made by the top executives of the mining firm upon the advice of the engineering and operating management. Because almost all of these large machines were custom-built, their sales were supervised directly by the general sales manager and they were sold directly from the company's home office.

Mr. Black felt that customers were better informed today than ever before, and that perhaps because of this they had become, as he put it, "very nickel and dime conscious." For many years B-E had been able to maintain its prices at a level 5% to 15% higher than competition, a premium the company attributed to its long-standing reputation for high quality, performance, and service. "More and more," said Mr. Black, "we are finding that our prices must be set to meet competition. Old customers tend to be loyal, but the new ones need to be convinced that they are getting something additional in return for the higher price." Bucyrus-Erie had a long-standing policy of keeping its prices firm, with only minor adjustments in recessions.

"There isn't a single manufacturer in the excavating machinery and drill industry today," said Mr. Black, "who even comes close to matching Bucyrus-Erie in the range of models available. Our salesmen can meet any customer demand with our line of over forty models." In recent years efforts had been made to fill out and broaden the line, and numerous new models had been introduced.

In the post World War II years, Bucyrus-Erie had been reluctant to concede to the growing demand for cranes for building construction. This stemmed from management's thinking that cranes which were designed for lifting only would not produce as much of the profitable parts business as would dual-purpose machines and excavators, and furthermore, these were years in which most of the company's plants had been operating at full capacity. In the late 1950's, however, management deferred to market demands and introduced a tower crane especially designed for high-rise building projects, and also a line of mobile truck-mounted cranes. (See Exhibit 5.)

Mr. Black saw a mixed future for the company's various product lines. "I expect the large stripping machinery business to be good for the next five years," he said, "in fact, it will probably be a growth market. The demand for medium-size excavators will be somewhat static. Larger cranes and excavators will probably also be static or, at best, show modest growth. The market for smaller cranes and excavators will continue to fall off, while sales of hydrocranes might show some upward trend. The picture for water and oil well drills is muddled and we really don't know what to expect."

The market for the larger machines, according to Mr. Black, was showing promise now because the development of the very large stripping machines (100 cubic yards) had made it possible to further exploit played-out coal mines where thin veins of remaining coal had been buried so deep under overburden that mining it had been uneconomical. The market for medium-size pit and quarry shovels was static because the industry was currently well supplied with shovels that had a life expectancy of over twenty years. The small excavator market continued to dwindle because of the inroads made into it by front-end loaders and tractors.

ADVERTISING AND SALES PROMOTION

"There has been a drastic change in our approach to advertising, sales promotion, and public relations over the past few years," said Mr. Frank T. House, manager of public relations and sales promotion. "The new management is convinced of the importance of these tools."

Mr. House mentioned in particular in-plant training schools for sales-men; weekly mailings to 800 distributor salesmen; monthly field reports of on-the-job machine performances; sales training films to train distributor salesmen; and a new approach to advertising, featuring a large photo, a captive headline, and small copy.

"We have a new concept in our public relations theme," remarked Mr. House, "where we center around three things: (1) we see ourselves as the spokesman for the industry; (2) we are the oldest and most reputable firm in the field; (3) we are a company on the move (new ideas, new products, up to date, aggressive, and progressive)."

The advertising theme for 1962 was "the longest line on earth" stressing the company's ability to fill every need within their field. In institutional films, the company was featuring its production facilities and technical know-how and skills in designing new and larger excavators. "I think these films are adding prestige to our company," said Mr. House. "They show something spectacular, the biggest excavators on the earth. Of course, a small buyer is not in the market for these machines, but it gets him to think about Bucyrus-Erie. If we can make the big machines, we can certainly make the small ones."

FOREIGN MARKETS

Export sales had long been an important segment of Bucyrus-Erie's business. The first steps initiating foreign sales were taken by Mr. Coleman as early as 1913. Mr. Coleman devoted much of his time during his long career as president to the development of a global system of distribution. In 1913, 6% of the company's production was exported. By 1927 the export share of sales had risen to about 25% of the company's total volume, and it had remained at about that percentage ever since.

During the period 1913–1927 machines were shipped to nearly one hundred countries, although a few major purchasing areas such as Chile, India, Japan, Manchuria, Mexico, Russia, and Sweden accounted for the bulk of sales. Most of the company's exports were of large machines to be used in major expansion programs affecting a nation's transportation system, its mining facilities, or its agricultural resources (irrigation and reclamation). For this reason the company's sales to particular countries fluctuated widely from year to year as major programs were initiated or completed.

Ruston-Bucyrus Ltd., Bucyrus-Erie's English affiliate, was formed in 1930 to take over the entire business of Ruston & Hornsby Ltd., B-E's principal competitor in the world market. B-E management thought this move was necessary to compete on favorable terms in foreign markets. For example, Ruston & Bucyrus had been able to offer its ½-cubic-yard shovel in France for 35% less than the comparable B-E model, with delivery time of five days compared to five weeks for the American machine. As part of the affiliation agreement Bucyrus-Erie and Ruston-Bucyrus arranged to act as distributors of each other's products in the various world markets. Also, Ruston-Bucyrus was given access to Bucyrus-Erie designs and production methods. Ruston-Bucyrus personnel continued to be British, but the company's policies and procedures were to follow patterns prescribed by Bucyrus-Erie.

In 1962 Bucyrus-Erie had an Export Sales Department of 35 people headed by Mr. Jorge A. Rossi, director of the International Division. Under him were two regional sales managers, one responsible for the Bucyrus-Erie sales in Ruston-Bucyrus territory. Figures compiled by the American Power Shovel Association indicated that in 1961 Bucyrus-Erie accounted for about 20% to 30% of the total United States exports of excavators.

"There is a world-wide trend," said Mr. Rossi, "toward the use of more excavators to develop underdeveloped countries. I would estimate the world market potential to be $50 to $60 million a year in addition to the total business now being done. It is in this area that our company has its greatest potential in years to come." The problem, said Mr. Rossi, was not to develop demand, but to find a means of financing the sales. In most of the foreign projects in which Bucyrus equipment might be used, the foreign government was involved in some way in the project. The prospective buyers in most underdeveloped countries were short of dollars, and so were their governments. This presented B-E with two different problems in financing: one to the contractor; the other to the country. Often there was no solution. "If financing were available," said Mr. Rossi, "we could double our export sales volume."

The source of a large part of Bucyrus-Erie's business abroad was the foreign aid program of the United States. Sales were also made possible by the World Bank. In former years Bucyrus-Erie had been able to make use of the Export-Import Bank in Washington which had furnished financing and assumed all of the credit risk. Bucyrus-Erie had also made use of the Export-Import Bank in Washington in financing project sales to foreign governments or sales sponsored by foreign governments. Under such arrangements the Export-Import Bank assumed all of the credit risks. With the decline of project sales and the increase in commercial sales in foreign markets, Bucyrus-Erie found it increasingly difficult to arrange for financing. In addition to the problem of financing, B-E management felt import restrictions presented formidable barriers.

B-E's major competition in the world market came from other American manufacturers. With overcapacity in the American market, the domestic competitors of B-E made every effort to find prospective customers abroad. The Germans also presented some competition, but their capacity was so limited that they were hardly able to supply their own demand and that of Western Europe. Their lower labor rates, however, gave them a strong competitive advantage, and they had an advantageous position within the Common Market. If England joined the Common Market, Bucyrus-Erie felt that through Ruston it would be able to compete in the Common Market area on equal terms.

Bucyrus-Erie, as well as Ruston-Bucyrus, worked through local distributors in all foreign markets. These intermediaries were deemed most important as sales outlets because of their knowledge of the languages, local customers, and governments. They supported Bucyrus-Erie in getting import licenses, helped with financing, and took care of the necessary service. Many of these distributors also represented a major American tractor account which sometimes caused a problem. With a 27% discount on tractors compared to 15% on Bucyrus-Erie products, the distributors tended to put their money and effort behind the higher discount lines. "This is a problem we have to live with," said Mr. Rossi. "We try to overcome it through persuasion, friendship, credit help, and a constant training of their salesmen."

"To sell excavators abroad requires quite a different approach than to sell them in the U.S.," said Mr. Rossi. "The foreigners are less sophisticated in this field. Their lack of knowledge is evident, but as a seller, you have to be careful in not showing them that you feel this way about them. Operating costs which are considered so important in the U.S. mean very little to a foreigner. What he is concerned about is the initial price and the expected lifetime of the equipment." Mr.

Rossi said that Bucyrus-Erie faced a problem in getting qualified salesmen to their export organization. The turnover was high. High salaries could not offset this. A high caliber Bucyrus-Erie man was a family man and he would not like to stay away from home more than 4 to 6 weeks. In addition, after a couple of trips around the world, he had no desire whatsoever to continue traveling.

"The world is becoming more nationalistic," said Mr. Rossi. "In drills, we do very little business abroad today. Selling expenses are too high and local manufacturers have grown up in most countries. Many of them are copying our models. Even in excavators, we have seen in some areas attempts made toward local manufacturing. It is easy to make a cheap shovel, but difficult to make one which will last. Therefore, most of them have failed. But, the nationalistic trend and problem of financing export sales have forced us to seriously consider if we should not open joint production facilities with local people in some of the most promising foreign countries." In such a venture, said Mr. Rossi, Bucyrus-Erie would primarily export its technical know-how and skills and teach the foreigners to make a quality excavator. The higher production costs through smaller volume was expected to be offset by savings in labor costs. The protection given a local industry would give it a good start, and it was felt that it would not take away any of Bucyrus-Erie's present export business because such a venture would primarily capture the market share the company could not get anyway under prevailing conditions.

"One day, we might see Bucyrus-Erie and Ruston-Bucyrus as one big international company with a centralized sales and service organization for the entire world market with production facilities placed at strategic points around the globe," concluded Mr. Rossi.

RESEARCH AND DEVELOPMENT

Bucyrus-Erie had always regarded the continuing improvement of its product lines as being basic to the success of the company. Because of the keen competition in the industry, management felt that no effort should be spared in "the continuing development of excavators that will move more material faster and at lower cost, and drilling equipment that will drill water wells, oil wells, and blast holes even more rapidly and economically."

In 1962, the company had an engineering department of 200 people.

a modern laboratory, and extensive testing grounds. The department was headed by Mr. George Y. Anderson, vice president of engineering, a veteran of many years of service with the company. The engineering department was organized into the following divisions:

1. Commercial cranes and excavators from ⅜ to 5 cubic yards.
2. Large excavators from 5 cubic yards and up
3. Special products (tower cranes; hydrocranes; jet-piercing drills)
4. Drills
5. Dragbuckets and dippers
6. Administration (day-to-day operational procedures, records, assignments, etc.)

Mr. Anderson felt that it was only in rare instances that a man might be found who had both creative design ability and administrative skill, and therefore technical work was separated from routine clerical work. Each chief engineer in the technical product divisions had an administrative assistant assigned to him, and this assistant reported, in a staff relationship, to a man in charge of over-all engineering administration. Dragbuckets and dippers were placed in a separate division because they were stock items of a replacement nature, which were interchangeable on many shovel models. Lumped together in the Special Products Division were those products which were too small in sales volume themselves to support a specialized engineering staff.

Although the engineering department was organized in product divisions to obtain the benefits of specialization, engineers were shifted from one product to another. There were decided differences in the engineering required for the various product lines. The large machines, it was thought, required the most skilled engineers. The engineering of drills was quite different from the engineering of excavators. To design drills required a practical "drill ability" on the part of the designer—an intimate knowledge of how well-drillers operated in the field, and so a typical senior engineer in drills spent half of his time traveling to observe well-drillers in action. There was close daily contact between the sales and engineering departments for all product lines, and product specialists from both the sales and engineering departments often visited distributors and customers.

"We don't put all our brains and effort behind the development of large excavators," said Mr. Anderson, "but there has been a continuous market trend toward larger and larger machines, and especially today, there is a terrific demand for the very large ones." As an example, Mr. Anderson pointed out the development of Model 3850-B for the Peabody Coal Company. This machine would be the world's largest mobile land machine, with a dipper capacity of 115 cubic yards, and priced well above $5 million. This size was required to remove an overburden with a depth of 150 feet before the coal was reached. Through long-term sales contracts of coal, the Peabody Coal Company for the first time had been able to finance such an investment. Financing, and not engineering, had hampered the development of this machine in the past.

"To develop, for example, four new models of large machines over a four-year period," remarked Mr. Anderson, "requires 60,000–70,000 man-hours of engineering. With a fluctuating demand, we can't keep a fulltime staff of such a size that we can take care of the peaks ourselves which might, from time to time, require a 50% increase of capacity. In these situations we have found it very helpful to turn to outside consultants for help. The men brought in temporarily need the guidance of strong internal leadership."

"We are engaged in an active search for new opportunities outside our present product lines comparable to our skills, knowledge, and facilities," he continued, "but, so far, we haven't been able to find anything worthwhile." He felt that the mechanical principles of machines designed for lifting and digging were essentially the same today as always. No new concepts had cropped up. Improvements made over the years had to do more with details than basics. New manufacturing techniques and lighter and stronger materials had made it possible to substantially reduce the weights of the machines. A 1-cubic-yard excavator weighed 75,000 pounds in 1930. Today the same shovel weighs 55,000 pounds. Electrical controls had made the operations of a machine speedier and safer. Auto safeguards were used for acceleration and deceleration. Air controls had shortened cycle times. There were fewer patents in the excavating industry today than ever before. Many details invented by Bucyrus-Erie were now standard. In the small machine area, copying among competitors was very common. "No one in the industry has ever come up with anything really revolutionary," said Mr. Anderson. "The basic concepts of our products have always remained the same, and our research and development have been limited to making refinements. We have never tried to come up with something of a 'Buck Rogers' science-fiction nature—something, say, like a method of disintegrating or vaporizing earth instantly, on the spot."

The most revolutionary earth-moving machine that had ever been introduced into the industry was the recently developed giant wheel excavator. The idea had not been originated by Bucyrus-Erie, but came from Germany where the wheels were used for mining brown coal, an extremely soft, low-grade form of coal. Bucyrus-Erie, which was the only maker of wheel excavators in the United States, had made only a few of them. These had been very large ones, designed to strip overburden from coal deposits. Reaction to these machines within the company was mixed. Some engineers felt that use of these wheels in American mines would be limited because of the large rock deposits encountered. They pointed out that every wheel so far sold had since been transferred by the purchaser to other uses. Others in the company, especially among the sales personnel, were enthusiastic about the prospects of the wheel.

The largest machines were usually designed to be used for specific purposes and under specific operating conditions. These could never be entirely copied for another customer. Although Bucyrus-Erie was willing to accommodate the specific requests of customers for minor design changes, a studied effort was being made to eliminate these small accommodation requests. Toward this end, the company produced the broadest line of machines in the industry, and tried in every way to standardize component parts. The power plants, for example, lent themselves to the design of interchangeable units.

ORGANIZATION

In the early 1950's a program of promoting younger men to positions in middle management was undertaken, but by that time serious gaps had appeared in the middle and top management ranks. It was for this reason that Mr. Allen was brought into the company to become chief executive; both Mr. Litle and the company's bankers were of the opinion that there was no one within the company who had the broad gauge executive talents required to head the company. Mr. Allen recognized this deficiency in management personnel. When he came to the company and sought someone who could be groomed to succeed him on his retirement, he found no one whom he thought young enough and with enough perspective. He brought Mr. Berg into the company as executive vice president. Because it was felt that staff specialists were also lacking at the top level, Mr. Chantry was hired as treasurer and Mr. Birk was invited to join the company as controller.

In 1962 Mr. Allen and Mr. Berg shared the top management responsibilities. Mr. Allen was clearly the head of the company, decided major policy matters, strove to give the company a sense of direction, acted as the general administrator of the business, and personally supervised sales, distribution, finance, banking, and the Bucyrus-Ruston affiliate; Mr. Berg, who worked closely with Mr. Allen, gave his attention to manufacturing, engineering, and certain areas of finance and control.

When the Richmond plant came into operation, Mr. Litle, seeking to revamp the company and make it a decentralized operation, set up a management organization at Richmond. This unit was intended to be autonomous, a pilot-run experiment that was intended to be duplicated at other units of the company. With the sale of the Richmond plant, however, and the retrenchments which followed, the plan was abandoned, and the trend was reversed. To cut overhead expenses staff positions were eliminated wherever possible, and so were some management levels, such as the coordinating office of vice president, finance, which had formerly joined the activities of the treasurer, the controller, and the corporate secretary. General managers at each of the company's three plants were also eliminated—all functions at each plant reported to Mr. Berg.

Mr. Allen intended to concentrate on matters of organization. "Now that we have taken care of most of our crises," he said, "I can turn my attention to getting the company into better shape as an organization." Mr. Allen intended to make divisions more autonomous, and to concentrate on bringing up additional younger people. He was especially interested in seeking out people with administrative ability. "In the past," he said, "the management would promote the brilliant design engineer who had seniority. I think this was a mistake and might waste the talents of a good man. I would prefer to reward the brilliant design engineer in his paycheck, and give the administrative job to the man who has shown that he has management talent."

FUTURE PROSPECTS

"For years our company was like a great old ship riding at its moorings and collecting barnacles," said Mr. Allen. "We were falling behind the competitor parade because our predecessors had their feet too firmly planted in tradition." Mr. Allen characterized the present management as one of progressive conservatism. "Present executives are better informed than the old ones who never traveled in the field to see customers and distributors," he remarked. A product planning committee had been formed consisting of Mr. Berg, Mr. Anderson and Mr. Black. They were working on five-year plans for the company. The aim was to make the plans fairly stable but not rigid. Any program changes had to be signed by either Mr. Allen or Mr. Berg. "We are actively looking for mergers to broaden our product lines," continued Mr. Allen. "Two years ago we hired an outside consultant, a specialist in acquisitions, to look around for us. I must admit, however, that we so far haven't taken any steps in this direction. Our cash position and deflated stock have, up to now, prevented any action."

"Our main objective is a profitable growth," he said, "but I would like to stress that in the light of our past experience no brick will be laid or any money spent on expansion unless an analysis can clearly show us that the additional investment will give us a reasonable return at all times—even in down swings of the economy."

He felt the growth would come primarily from four sources: (1) cranes for lifting, (2) foreign markets, (3) subcontracting, and (4) acquisitions. The company had been late in entering the crane business but had made rapid progress over the past three years. He considered tower cranes and climbing cranes as the most promising of the company's new designs. The expansion abroad would be directed toward joint ventures with local manufacturers in foreign countries. No financial commitments were intended. Bucyrus-Erie would export its technical know-how and skill. "Of course this will not put any smoke up our own chimneys but it will add to our profits," said Mr. Allen. "I think we Americans are living in a fools' paradise. In our striving for higher living standards we let our manufacturing costs grow higher and higher . . . continuously diluting our ability to export our goods. In the excavator business we will see a dynamic growth in underdeveloped countries for years to come. Bucyrus-Erie would very much like to compete for this business but I am afraid we will not be able to do so because of our high costs. The Germans and the Japanese are today still producing for their own domestic markets. When they have the capacity to export, Bucyrus-Erie's foreign markets could very well dry up over night." A policy of the old management had been that a government contract should be avoided. This was reversed under Mr. Allen and the company was now engaged in making heavy components for transportation of missiles. It was felt that government contracting would provide excellent opportunities in the future.

A new staff department to engage in market research and economic planning was to be formed, and it was to report directly to Mr. Allen, who emphasized that he intended to take a close personal interest in its activities. "Too often in the past," said Mr. Allen, "it was discovered, when it was too late, that the thing we had stubbed our toe on was a golden nugget. I want to be very sure that from here on we don't kick aside any more of those golden nuggets." Mr. Allen cited as an example the front end loaders which had drastically cut into Bucyrus-Erie's sales of small excavators. It was ironic, he said, that an engineer at Bucyrus-Erie had first developed this equipment principle, and when he took his design to his superior, he was rudely rebuffed. The engineer quit on the spot, took his designs to a competitor, who hired him, accepted his designs, and went into production. "We missed a golden opportunity there," said Mr. Allen, "and now it's too late. We could still go into production of them now, but we wouldn't be able to find any distribution outlets. They are all tied up by our competitors."

Mr. Allen was concerned that Bucyrus-Erie was in a secondary position to the major tractor manufacturers with the distributors. He felt an objective of the company should be to become a prime account to all of its distributors. How this could be done was not solved yet. "We have to broaden our line," said Mr. Allen. "However, I don't think we are in a position to reenter the manufacturing of tractor equipment. Purchased parts would be too great. We would have to acquire an engine manufacturer. Instead it might be possible for us to work out a marketing combination deal with a major tractor manufacturer to approach the distributors with a package."

"In summary, it is my confident belief that we can build back toward the strong and enviable position which Bucyrus-Erie once held and I think 1961 marked the turning point," he concluded.

exhibit 1   **BUCYRUS-ERIE COMPANY**
Balance sheet trends and ratios 1955–1961 (in thousands of dollars)

	1961	1960	1959	1958	1957	1956	1955
Net assets							
Cash & equiv.	$ 4,065	$ 5,216	$5,387	$ 3,177	$ 2,054	$12,735	$10,353
Receivables, etc.	14,399	15,807	11,183	10,925	8,928	10,876	8,045
Inventories	32,055	35,020	36,318	36,117	41,241	36,276	26,256
Total current assets	50,519	56,043	52,888	50,219	52,223	59,887	44,654
Total current liabilities	19,244	20,840	15,843	13,408	17,559	15,121	13,476
Working capital	31,275	35,203	37,045	36,811	34,664	44,766	31,178
Net fixed assets*	25,058	26,512	35,202	37,620	33,349	22,382	20,430
Other tang. assets	1,873	2,211	2,133	2,201	2,199	2,126	2,279
Total net tang. assets	$58,206	$63,926	$74,380	$76,632	$70,212	$69,274	$53,887
(*Gross fixed assets)	42,549	42,755	52,378	51,745	46,211	33,492	30,709
Debt and equity							
Long term debt[1]	10,200	18,000	18,500	19,000	9,500	10,000	10,000
Pfd.Stock							
Common stock †	9,331	9,331	9,331	9,331	9,331	9,331	7,776
Surplus (less intang.)	38,675	36,595	46,549	48,301	51,381	49,943	36,111
Reserves & approp. surpl.	—	—	—	—	—	—	—
Total capitalization	$58,206	$63,926	$74,380	$76,632	$70,212	$69,274	$53,887
(†Outstanding com. shs.)	1,866	1,866	1,866	1,866	1,866	1,866	1,555
Balance sheet ratios							
Current ratio	2.63	2.68	3.34	3.74	2.97	3.95	3.32
Quick ratio	.21	.25	.34	.24	.11	.84	.77
% L.T. debt to capitalization	17.50	28.20	24.90	24.80	13.51	14.43	18.56

NOTE: Fiscal year ends December 31.   [1] Includes insurance Reserves.

exhibit 1 (continued)
Balance sheet trends and ratios 1947–1954 (in thousands of dollars)

1954	1953	1952	1951	1950	1949	1948	1947
$13,642	$12,119	$12,172	$ 8,167	$ 7,858	$12,978	$ 6,226	$ 7,103
4,253	3,808	6,120	8,735	8,260	5,630	8,198	6,016
22,546	27,734	28,549	25,926	19,301	16,341	21,982	17,535
40,441	43,661	46,841	42,828	35,419	34,949	36,406	30,654
10,019	14,151	17,671	20,102	11,720	11,207	12,699	12,752
30,422	29,510	29,170	22,726	23,699	23,742	23,707	17,902
18,548	18,188	16,560	16,457	13,440	12,270	9,114	7,098
2,342	2,181	2,242	2,349	2,084	1,971	1,985	1,744
$51,312	$49,879	$47,972	$41,532	$39,223	$37,983	$34,806	$26,744
28,366	27,279	24,900	24,092	19,506	18,090	14,681	12,723
10,365	10,365	10,365	339	313	310	347	298
—	—	—	4,445	4,445	4,445	4,445	4,445
7,776	7,776	7,776	7,776	7,776	7,776	7,776	6,176
31,921	30,488	28,581	27,722	25,439	24,202	20,616	15,825
1,250	1,250	1,250	1,250	1,250	1,250	1,622	—
$51,312	$49,879	$47,972	$41,532	$39,223	$37,983	$34,806	$26,744
[a]1,555	[a]1,555	[a]1,555	[a]1,555	[a]1,555	[a]1,555	[a]1,555	[a]1,271
4.04	3.09	2.65	2.13	3.02	3.12	2.87	2.40
1.36	.86	.69	.41	.67	1.16	.49	.56
20.20	20.78	21.61	.82	.80	.82	1.00	1.11

[a] Adjusted common shares.

exhibit **2** **BUCYRUS-ERIE COMPANY**
Operating trends and ratios 1955–1961 (in thousands of dollars)

	1961	*1960*	*1959*	*1958*	*1957*	*1956*	*1955*
Income statement							
Net sales	$75,166	$63,629	$75,362	$58,272	$87,510	$86,586	$71,737
Cost of sales	70,084	62,743	70,750	58,848	73,435	70,491	57,031
Depreciation	2,702	2,736	2,915	2,500	2,580	2,369	2,137
Operating profit	$ 2,380	$(1,850)	$ 1,697	$(3,076)	$11,495	$13,726	$12,569
Other income,							
chgs. net	990	739	982	798	742	1,185	1,268
Interest chgs.	778	1,150	1,083	830	363	397	375
Income taxes	510	(990)	887	(1,428)	6,703	7,716	6,945
Net income	$ 2,082	$(1,271)	$ 709	$(1,680)	$ 5,171	$ 6,798	$ 6,517
*Special charge		8,684	2,465				
Net income to surpl.		($9,955)	($1,756)				
Ratio analysis							
Cost of sales as a % of sales	93.2	98.5	94.0	101.0	83.8	81.5	79.6
Oper. profit as a % of sales	03.18	(02.9)	02.3	(05.3)	13.1	15.9	17.5
Net income as a % of sales	02.78	(02.0)	00.9	(02.9)	05.9	07.8	09.1
Sales as a % of net fixed assets	300	240	214	155	263	388	350

* 1960: Losses and expenses in realigning, closing, and disposing of plants and equipment (after $1,230 refundable income taxes) $3,394; adjustment and losses on disposal of obsolete and excess inventories (less $1,717 allocated refundable income taxes) $550; total: $8,684.

1959: Provision for possible losses on future disposal of idle facilities and related deactivation costs ($1,710), less gain from disposal of other facilities sold during the year ($95,000), $1,615; provision for inventory adjustments $850; total: $2,465 (after applicable income taxes $2,898).

exhibit **2** (continued)
Operating trends and ratios 1947–1954 (in thousands of dollars)

_1954_	_1953_	_1952_	_1951_	_1950_	_1949_	_1948_	_1947_
$65,990	$78,582	$78,554	$78,886	$49,587	$58,055	$69,133	$56,538
54,779	65,029	64,081	61,890	40,822	46,519	58,457	46,872
1,928	1,733	1,670	1,481	1,123	966	940	748
$ 9,283	$11,820	$12,803	$15,515	$ 7,642	$10,570	$ 9,736	$ 8,918
836	718	533	430	527	438	217	269
352	364	132	—	—	—	—	—
5,225	7,157	8,115	9,930	3,510	4,373	4,129	3,732
$ 4,542	$ 5,017	$ 5,089	$ 6,015	$ 4,659	$ 6,635	$ 5,824	$ 5,455
—	—	233	311	311	311	311	311
$ 4,542	$ 5,017	$ 4,856	$ 5,704	$ 4,348	$ 6,324	$ 5,513	$ 5,144
83.0	82.8	81.6	78.5	82.3	80.1	84.6	82.9
14.1	15.0	16.3	19.6	15.4	18.2	14.0	15.8
06.9	06.4	06.5	07.6	09.4	11.4	08.4	10.3
356	432	474	479	369	473	759	79

exhibit 3
BUCYRUS-ERIE COMPANY
Organization Chart, March 1, 1962

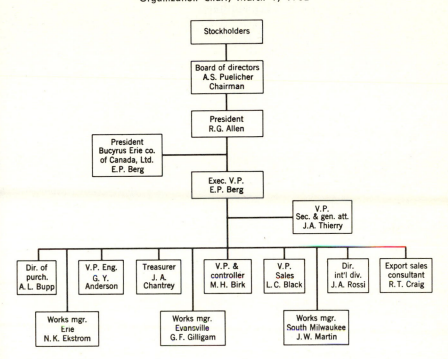

exhibit 4   SOME COMPETITORS TO BUCYRUS-ERIE AND THEIR PRODUCT LINES
IN 1960

Thew: Total net sales in 1960—$24.9 million.
> Material handling and excavating machinery including diesel, gas and electric power shovels, light portable cranes, clamshells, draglines, skimmer scoops, back diggers, motor truck cranes, shovels, locomotive cranes and moto-loaders.

Northwest: Total net sales in 1960—$11.1 million.
> Excavating machinery, power shovels, cranes and other excavating and material handling equipment of the crawler type, draglines, clamshells, trench digging machinery.

Koehring: Total net sales in 1960—$57.2 million.
> A varied line of heavy construction equipment for roads, general construction etc., including power shovels, cranes and draglines, pavers, mixers, finishers, trenchers, rollers and compactors, also hydraulic presses.

Caterpillar Tractor: Total net sales in 1960—$716.0 million.
> Crawler tractors, heavy-duty off-highway wheel tractors, motor graders and other earth-moving equipment. Machines are used principally for road building and maintenance, heavy construction, earthmoving, logging, snow removal, oil field work, quarrying, freighting, material handling and agriculture operations.

Clark Equipment: Total net sales in 1960—$196.8 million.
> Transmissions, driving and steering axles, axle housings, tractor drives, lift trucks, towing tractors, Ross carriers, powered hand trucks, excavator cranes, tractor shovels, tractor dozers, tractor scrapers, electric steel castings, gears, hydraulic pumps, forgings and material handling equipment.

Gardner-Denver: Total net sales in 1960—$84.8 million.
> Patented rock drills, equipment and accessories, air tools, air motors, portable drill mountings, steam and electric driven pumps, compressors, electric and air hoists, steam drilling engines and mechanical loaders, air powered drills, screw drivers, nut setters, hoists, grinders and chipping and riveting hammers, seismograph and geophysical drilling equipment for the oil industry, and light oil well drilling rigs and rotary drilling equipment for construction and mining industries.

Ingersoll-Rand: Total net sales in 1960—$185.8 million.
> Air and gas compressors, rock drills, oil and gas engines, pumps, condensers, pneumatic tools, air conditioning and refrigeration machinery, general mining, tunneling and quarrying machinery.

SOURCE: Standard and Poor's, *Industry Surveys,* 1961. Moody's *Manual of Industrials,* 1961.

exhibit 5
Bucyrus-Erie Product Lines

GENERAL PURPOSE EXCAVATORS — ⅜ to 4 cubic yard shovels, cranes, draglines and hoes.

TRUCK CRANES — 10 to 45 ton capacity truck-mounted crane-excavators.

QUARRY AND MINING MACHINES — 2½ to 18 cubic yard electric shovels and draglines.

HYDROCRANES — 5 and 12 ton capacity.

BUCYRUS ERIE
PRODUCTS

BUCYRUS-ERIE COMPANY, with its Canadian subsidiary and British affiliate, is the world's largest manufacturer of power cranes and excavators. The Company is also a large producer of drilling machinery.

Other lines manufactured by Bucyrus-Erie are railway cranes to 250 ton capacity, dragline buckets from ⅜ to 34 cubic yards, drilling tools, and specialty items for use with excavating and drilling machinery.

DRILLS — Rotary, flame piercing and cable tool drilling machines for blast holes. Cable tool and rotary drilling machines for water wells, oil wells and seismograph prospecting.

STRIPPING SHOVELS — 2 to 115 cubic yard capacity.

WALKING DRAGLINES — 4 to 34 cubic yard capacity.

WHEEL EXCAVATORS — 850 to 2500 cubic yards per hour normal capacity.

BUCYRUS-ERIE COMPANY
OFFICES AND PLANTS

GENERAL OFFICES — SOUTH MILWAUKEE, WISCONSIN

PLANTS

SOUTH MILWAUKEE, WISCONSIN — Excavators; walking draglines; railway cranes; drills

EVANSVILLE, INDIANA — Excavators; cranes; Hydrocranes; drills

ERIE, PENNSYLVANIA — Excavators and cranes

REGIONAL OFFICES

NEW YORK, NEW YORK — 30 Rockefeller Plaza*

CHICAGO, ILLINOIS — 105 West Adams Street

ATLANTA, GEORGIA — 32 Peachtree Street, N. E.

SOUTH SAN FRANCISCO, CALIFORNIA — 120 Freeway Street

*9 Rockefeller Plaza after April 15, 1960.

SUBSIDIARY

BUCYRUS-ERIE COMPANY OF CANADA, LIMITED
GENERAL OFFICE AND PLANT — GUELPH, ONTARIO
SALES OFFICE — TORONTO, ONTARIO, 2489 Bloor Street West

AFFILIATE

RUSTON-BUCYRUS, LIMITED
GENERAL OFFICES AND PLANT — LINCOLN, ENGLAND
SALES OFFICES:
LONDON, ENGLAND — Crompton House
GLASGOW, SCOTLAND — 223 St. Vincent Street

Representatives and distributors throughout the United States and in other principal countries of the world.

exhibit 6
Bucyrus-Erie Tractor-Mounted Equipment

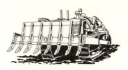

exhibit 8
The Bucyrus-Erie 3850-B Stripping Shovel

The Model 3850-B now being built by Bucyrus-Erie for Peabody Coal Company will be the world's largest stripping shovel.

This earthmoving giant will:

... Tower as high as the deck of the Golden Gate Bridge.

... Stand 56 feet higher than the Statue of Liberty and 45 feet higher than Niagara Falls.

... Have a working reach of 1/12th of a mile.

... Be more than twice the size of any shovel now in operation.

... Consume power equal to the requirements of a city of 12,000 population.

... Require 250 railroad cars for delivery to the erection site.

◀ **ONE DAY'S PRODUCTION** of the 3850-B, the world's largest earthmoving machine with its 115 cu. yd. dipper, would fill 1,700 railroad cars in a train nearly 15½ miles long.

13
OLYMPIA WERKE

HISTORY

Olympia Werke began its existence as the Union Typewriter Company, which was organized in 1903 by the AEG, the Allgemeine Elektrisches Gesellschalt (the General Electric Company of Germany). It had been the intention of the parent company to produce an electrically operated machine, but by the time production plans materialized it had been decided that it would be more practical to make a manual machine. The acceptance of the original machine prompted the company to expand its factory in Erfurt (now a part of East Germany). The company's progress was interrupted by World War I; after the war the company changed its name to the Europa Typewriter Company, and the brand name Olympia was adopted. In 1942, the company produced its millionth typewriter.

In April of 1945 the Erfurt plant was heavily damaged by bombing, and the Russians confiscated what production facilities remained. The Olympia top management group, however, remained intact and quietly proceeded to search for a new location in West Germany. This was found in the abandoned German Navy barracks on the harbor at Wilhelmshaven. During the summer of 1946 a new production facility was arranged there, based upon a complete set of microfilmed plans and blueprints of the company's products, plants, and facilities, which had been daringly smuggled across the East German border in a single suitcase by three company officials.

The stay in the Navy barracks was temporary. Soon a new and modern plant was built a few miles inland in Wilhelmshaven. Shortly thereafter a second new factory was built in the neighboring city of Leer to undertake the production of a new lightweight portable typewriter. During the early 1950's Olympia developed a four-function calculating machine, and the management was considering building a plant to manufacture the new machine. Instead of building, it merged with Brunsviga Werke of Brunswick, which had two plants, 1,200 experienced employees, and long experience in making calculating machines. The emergent company was called Olympia Werke AG. In the ensuing years, Olympia added to its line a variety of adding and calculating machines, bookkeeping machines, and a limited line of data-processing equipment, but typewriters continued to dominate its operations. During the period from 1951 to 1963, Olympia's sales increased tenfold, and it extended its market to include all of the globe. By 1963, it had produced over 5 million office machines.

From its inception Olympia had operated fairly independently of the AEG, which continued to own all of Olympia's invested capital in 1963 of 68 million DM ($17 million). From time to time, at critical junctures, the AEG made major policy decisions directly affecting Olympia's future, and in some instances these were not in keeping with the thinking of the Olympia management.

Throutgout its history, Olympia had been a successful and profitable operation.

OLYMPIA WERKE IN 1964

In 1964, the bulk of Olympia's production was concentrated in its huge plant at Wilhelmshaven, which produced mainly typewriters. The branch plant at Leer manufactured small portable typewriters; Brunsviga Werke produced other office machines. Its labor force in Germany approximated 16,000 employees. Olympia's only other manufacturing facilities were assembly operations in Chile and in Canada which were relatively insignificant in size.

The typewriter line of Olympia included standard manuals, standard electrics, regular portables, and flat portables. To complement the typewriter line the company also manufactured transistor dictation machines and transcribers. Its line of office machines included manual and electric four-function machines, automatic bookkeeping machines, hand-operated and electric calculating machines, and a limited line of programming equipment.

THE GERMAN MARKET

Roughly 40% of Olympia's production was sold in Germany, where it supplied approximately 50% of the domestic requirement of typewriters. Its only significant competitors in Germany were Adler and Triumph, both of which, Olympia officials conceded, had maintained their share of the market by making a good product, by good management, and by their well-established reputations. American typewriter producers tended to concentrate their efforts on the United States market, which was the largest in the world. Some competition was experienced from Olivetti of Italy and from the subsidiaries of American companies which operated production facilities in the Netherlands, where labor costs were lower than in the United States or Germany. Even in Germany, Olympia did not compete on a price basis. As elsewhere, its policy was to compete on the basis of high quality and dependable service and to sell at prices which were moderately high.

Olympia distributed in Germany through branch houses and subsidiaries which were 100% company-owned sales and service operations. Its branch house operations were limited to the home market, where the company had an installation in every principal German city. All of the branches were staffed by Germans who had been trained by Olympia at Wilhelmshaven. Branch house operations were tightly controlled by the inland sales department of the sales division at Wilhelmshaven, which virtually dictated all policies with respect to personnel, pricing, retailer standards, service, advertising, and branch house operations. In Germany the wholesaling function was handled by Olympia. However, in all other parts of the world Olympia sold to wholesalers. Outside of Germany Olympia sold strictly for cash at wholesale prices, which were fairly uniform, on a world-wide basis. In Germany its terms of sale varied a great deal and were the subject of negotiations between the Olympia branches and the retailers. In Germany there was a single fixed retail price established for every Olympia machine, and strict controls by the branch houses permitted no deviation from this price.

Olympia believed that the German share of world consumption would increase during the coming years because of Germany's continually expanding economy and the growing popularity of portable typewriters (which were often used by business concerns as office machines). Olympia also expected its share of the German market to increase with the introduction of new models: electric, flat, and electric portable machines.

MANUFACTURING

The concentration of Olympia's production in its Wilhelmshaven plant permitted long, uninterrupted runs of single models with a minimum of setup changes and changes in tooling. The production process was highly mechanized, and wherever possible, it was automated. The plant management aimed at the ultimate in smooth work flows, using highly efficient mechanized, belted, or conveyorized carriers.

The Olympia headquarters management looked upon its efficient mass production methods as being integrally linked to its policy of producing typewriters which were high in quality. High-quality standards added heavily to production costs in the use of materials of premium technical specifications; in the use of many high precision instruments; in numerous inspections against tight tolerances; and in performance tests that allowed margins far beyond the requirements encountered in normal usage. The management aimed to have its low-cost, efficient production more than offset the high costs of producing a premium-quality product.

One of the advantages which had attracted the Olympia management to Wilhelmshaven was the fact that this sector of Lower Saxony in northern Germany was largely a rural area which, in the immediate post-World War II period, had a surplus of labor of the type used by Olympia. Only a small percentage of the employees were veterans from the Erfurt plant, and most of these were in supervisory capacities. About half of the work force were women. Within a few years the Wilhelmshaven plant had exhausted the local labor supply, drawing from a radius of 50 kilometers (30 miles). Thereafter refugees were attracted from Eastern Europe. On 1964 over 80% of the Olympia work force consisted of local residents, and approximately 20% were refugees.

Most of Olympia's work force were young people; the average man was 33, the average woman 29. Many who were from peasant homes and those who were refugees and had suffered difficult times considered themselves to be fortunate to be working under such favorable conditions. Their attitude generally was appreciative. Union conflicts were negligible, and occasional grievances of employees were settled in a friendly manner in negotiations between the management and the

Workers' Council. The management took pride in the good spirit of the work force and their high productivity.

DISTRIBUTION

Olympia divided its sales into domestic, European, and export. The management stated that it had organized these sales divisions because (1) it believed that the whole sales function was too large for a single administration; (2) the approach to the European market was different, Europe being more uniform and more like a single market; (3) the documents involved in overseas business varied a great deal in nature; and (4) European transactions tended to be more refined and more stable. "Overseas business," said Mr. Heinz A. Krueger, director of overseas sales, "is rougher. Sometimes it is actually volatile."

In Germany, Olympia sold to retailers through its own chain of wholly owned branches. In Paris, Milan, Brussels, Stockholm, London, Zurich, Luxembourg, Bogota, and Santiago, Olympia wholesaled its machines through wholly owned subsidiaries. Europe was looked upon as an extended German market. The European subsidiaries were operated on the same basis as the German branches and were staffed by German nationals trained at Wilhelmshaven. The company had no partnership arrangements anywhere. In all other territories outside of Europe sales were made through wholesalers which were independently owned agencies of the company. Olympia did not have any administrative offices between the headquarters level at Wilhelmshaven and the wholesalers. "We feel no need for any embassies abroad," said Mr. Krueger. "We might need them some day, but not yet."

The subsidiaries had been established in some instances because the management felt that it would be dangerous to entrust a very large market to an independent agent. In other instances it did so because no one with enough capital was found to finance a large agency. "The typewriter business is neither exciting nor romantic," said Mr. Krueger. "No fabulous quick fortunes are made selling typewriters. It takes substantial capital to finance a large agency . . . sometimes several million dollars . . . and since we make no flowery promises to potential agents, venture capital tends to find other activities more attractive."

PRICING

"Ten years ago," said Mr. Krueger, "when the reborn company was still young, out first agents had a lot to say about pricing. Now headquarters virtually dictates price levels, especially in the large markets. In fact, all marketing policy making has swung to Wilhelmshaven."

In the open market there were six firms selling on a world-wide basis which informally established the world price level. On low-price models, a field in which Olympia did not participate, costs were a factor in setting prices. Olympia's prices were moderately higher than those of most competitors.

In the open market prices did not generally fluctuate much in the short run. There was no need to guarantee agents against losses from price reductions, which simply did not occur. Prices abroad were intended to be competitive, and the Olympia management stated that its agents were reliable and had little inclination to cut prices. Retail margins were not large enough to permit much deviation from the normal price structure. No agent would cut prices as a matter of routine strategy, and in those rare instances in which one did temporarily drop prices, he would do so only after consulting headquarters. Wilhelmshaven suggested the retail price on newly introduced models and sometimes urged agents to raise their prices on going models. Agents regularly reported to Wilhelmshaven their prices and the prices of their competitors. Olympia machines were never permitted to get into the hands of discount houses. "Violations of our pricing policies simply do not happen," said Mr. Krueger. "No agent would be inclined to be headstrong and go his own way. Our relations with our agents are friendly and helpful. They consider themselves to be part of the 'Olympia family.' "

The f.o.b. price was fairly uniform on a world-wide basis, with a few exceptions to meet competition. Consumer prices varied widely, however, because of the costs over f.o.b., such as freight, licenses, and duties. In exceptional instances Olympia made allowances for this to keep agents alive in particularly distant and competitive markets, but this rarely occurred. Markups were f.o.b. plus 6 to 7% for cif,[1] plus duties, taxes, and licenses, which varied widely. Landed cost to the agent was marked up 40 to 60%, depending upon local competition. Thus the typical pricing structure would be:

F.o.b.	100
Cif	6
Duties, fees, etc.	34
Landed price	140
50% markup	70
Final price	210

[1] cost, insurance, freight

Markups were the same in each territory for all competitors. They varied widely, however, from one territory to another, generally varying inversely with the volume sold in that market; in high-volume territories markup tended to be lower. Sales costs, such as advertising and the local level of salesmen's salaries, also affected the final price.

Olympia's wholesale prices in the open market tended to be fairly uniform, but in the government market, where thousands of typewriters were bought on a single purchase contract, prices tended to fluctuate. Government business was looked upon in the industry as prestige business, which was jealously sought after for its advertising value. Prices were tendered in sealed bids, and to the government purchaser, price tended to be the determining factor, with quality playing a secondary role. School and institutional business tended to follow the government pattern.

Olympia did not, as a matter of policy, engage in promotional price deals. Olympia was established in most markets, and management felt no need to cut prices to gain entrance into any new market, except possibly such markets as Spain and parts of Africa. If this expedient were to be used, it would be a very temporary thing. The only other instance in which headquarters cut prices was, in case of distressed stocks or outmoded models, and these were sold off quietly in the home market through the branch house organization. This rarely happened, however.

"We have seriously considered," said Mr. Krueger, "the possibility of charging higher prices. We came to the conclusion that charging the highest price possible would be shortsighted. Volume in individual markets fluctuates widely from year to year, but aggregate sales do not fluctuate greatly and show a steady increase. We decided that our best strategy would be to charge a moderately high price and push ahead on all fronts equally."

ADVERTISING

Olympia machines were advertised in practically every type of medium all over the world. On national advertising within a sales territory the local Olympia agent handled the program. Olympia took little part in these programs unless Wilhelmshaven contributed to a local campaign; in these instances it retained the right of approval on all advertising matters. International advertising costs were paid for by Olympia, national costs by the agents. The bulk of Olympia advertising was centered on typewriters in local and national campaigns, and national advertising costs were typically 4 to 5% of the retail sales dollar. Wilhelmshaven provided many promotional materials, such as leaflets, slides, school calendars, and posters, without charge. The advertising appropriation varied only with the over-all trend in sales volume. The advertising effort varied widely from country to country. In general the free markets, where all competitors met on a par, required more advertising than the restricted markets.

Olympia advertising was beamed mainly at consumers, and, since only a very small percentage of any population used typewriters, perhaps as little as 5%, the ad campaigns were designed to meet this segmented market. Advertising themes emphasized quality, reliability, and the availability of service. All advertising was low-pressure. In Germany, Olympia headquarters took the initiative in originating ad themes, and some of these proved suitable for export to other markets. It was the management's experience, however, that no single ad theme was suitable in all markets, because of language and cultural differences. Two popular slogans were: "Olympia typewriters don't cost—they pay" (Australia) and "Olympia writes best of all—because Olympia is best of all" (United States).

Advertising agencies were used extensively by Olympia agents abroad, but not in all territories. The headquarters management believed that they proved particularly helpful in Anglo-Saxon areas. Ad agencies did market research, selected media, created mottoes, slogans, and themes, and wrote copy. They also did consumer sampling, in which Olympia usually rated well.

MARKET RESEARCH

Olympia's overseas agents sometimes used consultants for market research at their own volition and at their own expense. The Olympia headquarters never did so. In its early years at Wilhelmshaven it had used consultants occasionally before entering new overseas markets, but when the company attained world coverage it discontinued this practice. Olympia's market research was conducted by a staff group at Wilhelmshaven which did all of the data collecting for the entire company. There were also four men in the overseas department who did "desk work," analyzing the data collected by the research group.

The main objective of the research group was to collect figures on world market movements. For the overseas department it gathered import figures on every country in the world, even very small ones. On typewriters the company aimed to know what every country had imported and from whom, by models. These data were collected from Olympia's own organization and from government statistics. The data on its own sales were gathered by its sales and service representatives from a standard questionnaire designed by Olympia headquarters. Government information was obtained through the German Federal Statistical Office, which had information on virtually every area of the world. It was the company's experience that sufficient statistical data were available on most areas. Even countries which were underdeveloped economically often had good statistical information because of the efficient government services that had been developed for them in their colonial days.

Based upon the data Olympia collected it made forecasts, one per country per year. These forecasts became the basis for all company planning, including production. "Our Wilhelmshaven operation was once definitely production-minded," said a sales executive. "That was understandable, since in our early years here we were rebuilding our production facility from nothing, and that took all of our attention. Lately, however, more and more attention is being paid to sales, even though we have been oversold for a number of years."

The Olympia research staff felt that it was not difficult for them to make accurate forecasts. The over-all volume of typewriter sales in most markets was stable and sudden market shifts were rare. The Olympia management felt that it had its finger on the market pulse much better than most of its competitors.

SALES

In 1963 about 60% of the Olympia unit volume was sold in the export market. World production of typewriters had been about 5 million units in 1963. The United States produced 27% of this total, West Germany 22%, Italy 15%, and the Netherlands 10% (which included production by subsidiaries of United States manufacturers). Out of the total production, 2.4 million were sold in export markets. In 1962 the German consumption was about 6% of world consumption, whereas its share of the typewriter export market (which was largely the Olympia share) was 25%. In 1963 it was 27%. This 2% rise represented an 8% increase in the amount of Olympia's export sales. By comparison

Italy's (Olivetti's) share had increased from 21 to 22%. Olympia's typical market share in most established areas of the world market was 20% or more. Its principal competitors for overseas business were Remington, Royal, Underwood, Smith-Corona, and Olivetti. The largest single market was the United States, which consumed about 40% of total world production, or 2 million machines, but United States producers usually confined their sales efforts to the American market and did not play any significant role in the export field. Germany consumed about 500,000 units, the rest of Europe 1.3 million, and the rest of the world 1.2 million.

Olympia believed that not only its volume of export sales but its percentage share of the total export market would continue to rise. The world typewriter market had been growing lately, at the rate of 12 to 15% every two years, and the German share of the market had been keeping pace. Olympia's typewriter exports had been rising faster than other German exports, and the Olympia management believed that the introduction of new models in the near future, such as the electric, the flat, and the electric portable, would increase its market share. The management was confident that the world demand for typewriters would accelerate, especially the demand for portables. Portables were increasingly in demand for home use, and in some markets were used both in homes and in offices. Electrics were also increasing in popularity.

In the export market it was the aim of the Olympia management to compete on the basis of high quality, which it considered basic and fundamental; on the basis of thorough and dependable service; and on the basis of prices which were moderately high rather than low. "We are the Mercedes of the typewriter industry," said an Olympia executive, "but where the Mercedes price is twice or more than that of a Volkswagen, our prices are only about 15 to 20% above those of our competitors."

In the German market Olympia's terms of sale varied considerably, but its terms for export sales were fairly uniform. In general, it sold on some basis in which no credit risk was involved: letters of credit, advance payments, or documents against acceptance, and certain exporting companies in the free cities of Hamburg and Bremen handled payment of Olympia's bills on presentation. Olympia's overseas receivables averaged about 30 days.

Olympia concentrated on selling its typewriters, mostly the manual ones, in the export markets, other office machinery and equipment being considered secondary products. Its grand market strategy was to push ahead uniformly on all fronts at the same time rather than to concentrate on selected markets. World typewriter sales followed general economic trends, with few cyclical swings that were significant. Neither were there seasonal variations, even in the Christmas period. Olympia planned a future hard push of the sale of newly designed electric typewriters in the high-potential and well-developed areas, such as the United States and England.

THE OVERSEAS SALES STAFF

The overseas division of Olympia was headed by Mr. Heinz Krueger, director of overseas sales, who held the title of *Prokurist,* which was just below the level of board member. He had formerly answered directly to the board, but in 1963 the AEG had approved a change in the headquarters organization, as a result of which a new office of general sales manager was created. Herr Mossner was appointed to it and made a *Vertriebsdirektor* and a member of the board. Although the overseas division accounted for two-thirds of Olympia's sales volume and demanded much attention because of fluctuations in individual markets, distances, and its lack of homogeneity, the entire division had less than 50 people. Of these, only four people, including Herr Hubert Fleige, reported directly to Mr. Krueger (see Exhibit 3).

The link between Wilhelmshaven and its agents abroad was Olympia's sales and service representatives. A typical representative joined the company at about the age of 20. He would spend about two years in the headquarters office as a clerk, learning in general the operations of an overseas territory. This would be followed by a period of six months of technical training in the plant, after which he would spend some time working for one of the German branches. He would then represent Olympia in one of its overseas areas. The representative traveled a circuit, regularly visiting Olympia agents. His duty was to assist agents in every way, along Olympia policy lines, in achieving their share of the market. "It is our belief at Olympia," said Mr. Krueger, "that an agent should not need to experiment. Therefore we give our agents, through our sales and service representatives, methods and practices which have already been tried and proven elsewhere." The representatives were prepared to handle service questions, advertising plans, credit policies, the management of agent inventories, training of agency personnel, the layout and decor of showrooms, and any matter at all in the whole-saling operation. Sales and service representatives were well paid in comparison with Olympia representatives in Germany. Olympia usually had five or six such representatives on its staff. In 1964, however, there were only two.

It was Olympia policy to leave most of the sales activities in the hands of its agents. In keeping with this policy, the company's sales and service representatives, after a few years of traveling their circuit and a short refresher course at Wilhelmshaven, would leave the employment of Olympia and join one of the company's agents as a sales and service representative. The agency employing the representative would be chosen by Olympia headquarters and he would work for it on a contract basis, the terms of the contract and his remuneration being suggested by Wilhelmshaven. At the agency the representative would carry on the same activities he had formerly performed for Olympia, concentrating on his particular agency and carrying his help further down toward the retailer level. In 1964 there were over 20 such Olympia-trained representatives at various overseas agencies. In addition to these there were innumerable sales representatives who were nationals employed by the agents and trained by Olympia's sales and service representatives or in classes conducted by headquarters at Wilhelmshaven.

In addition to these sales and service men, there were four group leaders at headquarters who had general responsibility for the sales activities in their respective territories (see Exhibit 3). Their responsibilities were limited, however, to the administrative handling of sales. They were not charged with generating sales volume. Generating sales volume was considered to be the responsibility of the agent.

AGENCIES

For purposes of distribution Olympia divided the world into over 100 market areas. In over 80% of these areas Olympia sold through agencies. In most of the world, agencies were Olympia's liaison between Wilhelmshaven retailers and the ultimate consumers.

It was the responsibility of the agencies to generate sales through advertising and through promotion. Agencies performed the wholesale function, selling mostly to retail dealers, but occasionally to consumers. They imported stocks and maintained inventories. They granted short-term credit to retailers. They sold to several types of customers: to retailers, to consumers, to governments and governmental institutions, and to schools. Agencies did repair work, cleaning, and maintenance work and performed guarantee work on behalf of Olympia, in which case they acted in the name of Olympia in making good Olympia's guarantees.

In large-volume markets, where large capital investment was required to establish an agency (perhaps several million dollars), agencies were usually corporations; in middle-sized markets they were often partnerships and sometimes proprietorships; and in small markets most of them were proprietorships. Most of the capital investment in an agency would be used to finance inventories. The requirement of Wilhelmshaven was that an agency have on hand at all times a three-month stock, plus one month on order, one month in transit ("on the water"), and the accounts receivables of its retail dealers.

The character of the concerns which *wholesaled* Olympia machines varied. Most of them were wholesalers of office equipment and supplies, but where these were not available Olympia might use trading firms, which handled many products and operated somewhat in the manner of a mail-order house. The Wilhelmshaven management was selective in its choice of agencies and was only interested in agencies which would actively promote the sale of Olympia products. In most parts of the world it could afford to be selective, for the internationally advertised Olympia line was considered to be attractive, and many wholesalers were eager to secure a franchise. Olympia would not do business with the 'agency-hunter', the trading company which was always eager to add either items or sources to its catalogue. Olympia used trading houses only in such areas as parts of Africa and Asia, where, as an Olympia executive put it, "the geography is big, but the sales potential is small."

In general, Olympia had one agent in each market area, and in most instances a market area consisted of one country, but there were some exceptions. A country like Saudi Arabia was large in area but contained two trading areas which were distinct and far removed from each other, in which case two agencies were granted franchises. In any event, each agent was strictly limited to doing business only in his own market area, and his contract with Olympia guaranteed him exclusivity in his territory. Olympia itself was not permitted to sell directly in that territory. At the same time, agencies were not required to be exclusively Olympia agencies. They usually handled many other products, including the office equipment and machinery of other manufacturers. They were not permitted, however, to handle lines of typewriters and calculating machines which were directly competitive with Olympia.

The agencies were not compensated directly by Olympia in the sense of being paid a commission on sales. They were independent businesses which purchased and resold Olympia products and they received their compensation in the form of markups. It was a stated policy of the Wilhelmshaven headquarters that Olympia would take a direct interest in fostering the profitability of its agencies. Wilhelmshaven furnished them with advertising advice and materials, sometimes at no cost, and at times on a shared-cost basis. International advertising was done by Olympia at no cost to the agencies. Olympia often deliberately set manufacturer's prices at a level which would enable the agents to earn a reasonable profit; it gave them technical assistance; and at times it lent them people from headquarters, in which case the agency assumed the salary expense involved.

Wilhelmshaven trained the agency's marketing men, in most instances at no cost to the agency. This was done in two ways: (1) Olympia's sales and service representatives did on-the-spot training in the course of their routine calls upon agencies; (2) for longer and more intensive training programs the personnel of the agency were sent to Wilhelmshaven at the expense of the agency. Once there, Olympia provided the training free of charge.

Olympia did not have any capital invested in its agencies. None of them were joint ventures. Occasionally Olympia might provide an agency with short-term credit in the form of bills of exchange or extended credit terms, but this was limited to agencies which were young and was only a temporary expedient. Extended credit was never granted to an established agency.

The pattern of distribution in each agent's marketing area evolved out of the circumstances existing in the territory. In a territory like Australia, which covered a vast area, there were several city-centered trading areas, each separated from the other, in which the agent might operate from branches of his own. Again, a market like Burma meant only Rangoon, the port city, and was virtually a single-city operation. Agents were free to determine their own best method of distribution. If an agent were new and green and did not have an insight into the typewriter business, Olympia would instruct and advise him, in which case Olympia would expect that the agent follow its advice.

Retailers might be granted a local franchise by their agency. If they were, they would normally be required by the agent to carry a minimum inventory of machines in stock. Sometimes agencies granted retail dealers consigned stock arrangements. Exclusiveness at the retail level was not common; most retailers carried several brands of office machinery. Agencies were free to make whatever inventory arrangements they wished with their retailers. They also set their own credit terms and sometimes even supplied long-term capital to a promising new retailer. In general, the burden of financing, including the carrying of inventories, was on the agency.

All agency relationships were governed by a legal contract between Olympia and the agency, and the contract specified that any dispute arising from the contractual agreement would be settled according to German law in the Court of Wilhelmshaven. The Olympia management stated that such disputes were virtually nonexistent. The management at Wilhelmshaven extended itself to cultivate the friendship of its agents, and it claimed that it had been so successful in that its sales organization had come to be known as "the Olympia family."

EXPORTING PROBLEMS

In selling in the export market Olympia faced several obstacles: there were other large producers who sold in the world market, whose production costs were lower and who sold at lower prices; there were large producers who operated branch plants in local markets; there were import duties which ranged from 0 to as much as 40%; there were preferential duties; there were preferential quotas and preferential treatment; there were those nations which were nationalizing production; there were free trade areas; and there were nonquality machines being sold on a very low-price basis.

Remington, Royal, Underwood, Smith-Corona, Olivetti, and certain Japanese producers all had large-scale production facilities. All except the latter two produced quality machines which they sold at normal price levels. While American producers tended to concentrate upon the American market, some were now operating branch plants abroad.

Since Germany consumed less than 10% of the world typewriter requirement, the Olympia management believed that any large producer had to look to the world market to obtain enough volume to make possible mass production of a quality machine at reasonably low cost. Furthermore, Olympia believed that its own production should be concentrated in its one huge plant at Wilhelmshaven. It reasoned that this enabled the production management to make the fullest use of its expert engineering talents, which it thought would be weakened if spread to other locations. It made possible the strict policing of quality controls. The labor force at Wilhelmshaven was experienced and stable, and there was good morale. Long runs of single models were practical, using the ultimate in cost-saving equipment. The Olympia management did not believe that any typewriter factory producing less than 50,000 machines a year could operate efficiently and turn out a satisfactory machine.

The Olympia management believed itself to be strongly handicapped in the Commonwealth areas because of their system of preferential duties. In countries like Australia, Canada, New Zealand, and Rhodesia the preferential difference ranged from $7\frac{1}{2}$ to 22%. In Australia, Underwood was able to sell its machines for £70, and Olympia, despite its higher costs and duties, was forced to match this price. There was a tendency, however, toward equalization in recent years. Brazil, for example, had reduced its duty from $17\frac{1}{2}$ to $7\frac{1}{2}\%$. New Zealand, on the other hand, still maintained a duty of 25%.

Quotas were also tending to disappear from year to year, but in 1964 Olympia still had to contend with many. The French had a system which gave preferential treatment to certain countries, such as Algeria. Imports into these countries would typically favor France, giving the French perhaps 40% of the total allotment and parceling out the remaining 60% to all others.

Another allotment system which restricted Olympia was the "oldest established importer" system. This system aimed to maintain the status quo, preference being given to imports from companies which were already established in the market. This worked strongly against Olympia which was a relative newcomer in almost all world markets, dating to the post-World War II period. Olympia's serious exporting effort was even more recent, having begun only in the late 1950's.

Some countries set quotas which were intended to protect and to foster national production. These countries took either of two means to implement their resetrictive policies: (1) they assessed import duties at restrictive or sometimes prohibitively high levels; or (2) they simply forbade imports. Argentina, for example, permitted no imports at all. Brazil, Mexico, and India were severely restrictive. "Some countries," said an Olympia executive, "are so unrealistic that they prefer to produce within their own borders at any cost no matter how high. Others blindly shut out all imports. We do not believe that any country can maintain this exclusion policy permanently. Others, like the Australians, have policies which are more refined, but are nevertheless rather impractical. The Australians have invited us to set up a plant in Australia. They would require, however, that our Australian-produced typewriter be restricted to a factory cost which we would guarantee would not be over 20% higher than the cost of comparable imported machines. How can we possibly guarantee this? We don't see the economies of setting up factories in the various world markets at the present time."

In Canada and the United States Olympia believed that it faced the hurdle of high duties and other restrictions. "I cannot understand," said Mr. Krueger, "what our price in Germany has to do with our price in the United States and Canada. The end effect of these duties and restrictions is the hampering of free trade, and this is generally not in keeping with American foreign trade policies. Olympia is one of the few foreign companies which has been successful in selling in these markets, but we have done so at the cost of profits. In Canada our price must have added to it all the expenses to land our machines in Canada, plus duties of $17\frac{1}{2}\%$." The major competitors of Olympia in the Canadian market, Underwood, Remington, and Olivetti, all manufactured within the Commonwealth. Olympia did not. This factor, maintained Olympia's management, placed the company at a distinct disadvantage.

In the Philippines, the United States was given preferential treatment. Olympia had been charged a duty as high as 20% on its machines, whereas the United States producers paid no duty. In turn, the United States reciprocated by buying up the cane sugar production of the Philippines. The Philippines had lately been leveling their duties, reducing them by stages from 20 to 15 to 10%. In doing so they were torn between their wish to get away from their colonial status and their wish to maintain the income which accrued to their government from the import duties. Olympia, following its policy of covering all markets, even the low-profit ones, kept its foothold in the Philippines.

Foreign aid programs tended to work against Olympia. Those countries which received substantial United States aid tended to give preference to United States-produced goods. In Egypt, which had close trade ties with the Russians, Nasser did business on a bartering basis, trading Egyptian cotton for Russian Bloc radios, refrigerators, typewriters, or canned milk. This preferential treatment to others resulted in a landed cost to Olympia that was prohibitive. "It would have cost us a loss of 25

DM per typewriter to sell our machines in Egypt," said Mr. Krueger, "therefore in this instance we abandoned our policy of pushing ahead on all fronts, and we gave up the Egyptian market."

The Olympia management believed that there were some slight advantages accruing to it in the operation of the Common Market. French and Italian duties, which had been high compared to those of Germany, were now leveling. Olympia had once paid 40% duty to export to Italy, whereas the Italians could export to Germany at 15%. Olympia saw distribution and costs as being a second Common Market advantage. Europe would become an extended German market. Selling in Paris, Rome, or Amsterdam would become the same as selling in Bremen, Frankfurt, or Munich. In the European Free Trade Area, however, Olympia believed the outlook was somewhat different. "It has been our experience," said an Olympia executive, "that England thinks England first, and Commonwealth second, and then EFTA." Mr. Krueger said that some knowledgeable authorities believed that the totally free trade era was as far as 30 years away. He himself believed that it would be realized within 10 years.

The free trade areas which were developing in other parts of the world affected Olympia. Argentina had closed its borders to the importation of typewriters entirely, and Brazil had imposed strong restrictions on imports. Together, Argentina and Brazil had enough manufacturing capacity to supply all of Latin America. The end result, according to Olympia, was high-cost production that resulted in a low-quality machine which was sold at a high price. "A typewriter," said Mr. Krueger, "is not the kind of product with which a developing nation should start its manufacturing. A typewriter is highly technical, has about 3,000 precision parts, requires skilled industrial labor, and a high degree of organization in the flow of materials and the assembly process. Neither do these countries have a large enough mass market for typewriters to enable them to manufacture in mass at low cost. The Indians are turning out typewriters today, but they are definitely shoddy products. They would be better off if they had chosen products which are relatively simple to make . . . like furniture or shoes."

Every major producer of typewriters which competed with Olympia in the world market had branch plants and local assembly facilities at strategic points abroad. Olympia had none, except for token assembly operations it had established in Chile and Canada, nor was there any inclination to shift production to foreign locations. Olympia's AEG parent company had committed Olympia to a one-large-plant policy, the thinking of the parent management being that Olympia had a huge manufacturing facility at Wilhelmshaven now, and it had consistently had a backlog of orders which kept the huge facility operating at capacity. Since typewriters were postponable purchases, AEG did not wish to have any general economic recession, with the accompanying accelerated slump in typewriter sales resulting in idle plant capacity and high overhead costs. Furthermore, in terms of AEG policies, although Olympia was doing very well on the present basis, it had enough current problems to deal with to keep it fully occupied, and it had neither the time nor the manpower to establish facilities abroad.

In general, the Olympia management agreed with the thinking of its AEG parent. However, Olympia management believed that at times it was faced with a choice of (1) dominating a market or (2) abandoning it totally. They also expected that the coming free trade era would tend to emphasize this kind of choice. There was a chronic labor shortage in Germany. Olympia had pressed for further expansion of the Wilhelmshaven plant to work off its chronic backlog, but the AEG had not approved, citing that it was easy to add bricks and mortar but impossible to secure more workers. Olympia had never resorted to the expedient used by other labor-hungry plant operators in Europe, who sent missions abroad to import workers on a contract basis from such places as Portugal, Morocco, Malta, and Turkey.

The Olympia management had from time to time made studies of the possibilities of establishing plants in South America, Central America, and the Far East. On the basis of these studies it had prepared detailed plans which would enable it to start construction of plants in any of these areas on very short notice. The management of Olympia often debated the advisability of establishing plants abroad. The question frequently asked was "when and where?"

OTHER CONSIDERATIONS

"I think that our major problem," said Mr. Krueger, "is one faced by the entire typewriter industry. It is the same situation which faced the American automobile industry an era ago, and from which the present auto industry evolved. During the 1920's there was a great shake-out process going on in the auto industry, and in the end there remained only a few large producers. The typewriter industry today is a mixture of many large, small, and intermediate companies. There are big swings in production . . . occasional dumping . . . some producing largely for export . . . some not interested in exporting at all. All of this would have regulated itself except for Olivetti, which had its own unique policy. This policy seemed to be: dominate the world market; Olivetti-ize the world. In carrying out this policy Olivetti sold machines at half its factory cost to get into some markets. The Olivetti American manager said, 'Put an Olivetti in every butcher and baker shop . . . and don't worry about whether it's ever paid for . . .'

"The fights, the slashing, are gradually disappearing. Little producers are selling out before they go broke. The business which remains is conducted on a fairly reasonable basis. If in the end only five large producers remain, and each is satisfied with his market share, the entire business will be more orderly. Then we can still be strong competitors, but within economic limits. Olympia selling is low-pressure, dignified. We do not believe in hard selling at any level, nor in using credit as an inducement. Olympia does not mean to monopolize the world. We have been consistently oversold, but we are not expanding production. Olympia wants only its fair share of the market. It means to let others live. We set goals which are reasonably attainable, and we attain them.

"I often wonder whether we are not too preoccupied with our policy of high quality. People are becoming less interested in products which last a long time. Our machines have an average life of 15 years. Our machines have cast and pressed parts, like the frame, which are machined, drilled, tapped, and threaded and are screwed together. This permits precision, and the resulting typewriter is highly accurate and durable. Now the Japanese have commenced to make a typewriter which has a plastic frame which is so designed that it can simply be clipped together by hand . . . no drilling, tapping, screwing involved. Their machine is produced at very low cost, it sells for a very low price, and there is no intention that it give quality performance. It is sold with a three-year free service guarantee, and after that length of time the consumer can dispose of it.

"This leads me to wonder whether there might be some much simpler means of writing mechanically than the conventional typewriter. A typewriter performs a fairly simple function—it translates writing by hand into a mechanical means of writing. In the form that current typewriters take, this means producing a precision machine which has over 3,000 parts, making it so that it will perform precisely, making it so that it will last, and making it so that it can be sold for about $100. I should think that mechanical writing could be done by some device that would be much simpler, less precise, and less costly. But there has been no change in the basic idea of the typewriter since its invention. No one has come up with any revolutionary new principle. There has been some experimentation with photoelectric and chemical-reaction writing, but nothing useful has emerged. And we at Olympia are continuing on the assumption that there is not going to be any radical change in the current method of mechanical writing.

"I think that Olympia now has certain advantages over its competitors in the export market. We have an established, accepted line of high-quality machines. We have a reputation for giving good service. We are loyal to our agents and have their loyalty. Our agents know they will receive fair treatment from us. They also know that our policies and our prices change only very slowly. The 'Made in Germany' label still has the connotation of high quality abroad, although others are now catching up to us. And our associates in business know that we believe in conducting our business systematically, that we believe in knowing our limits, and that we do not believe in trying to overdo.

"Our long-range objectives are to increase and consolidate our market share; to achieve more co-ordination of manufacturing and sales and more sales orientation; to produce machines in the most rationalized way for profitability; to do more research to keep pace with developments; to reliably determine what our optimum program ought to be. . . .

"Perhaps we ought to be thinking more about other office machines. Olympia is now, in a sense, the primitive in the industry, and this segment represents a small part of our business. We have chosen to concentrate on what we call consumer items . . . principally mechanically operated office machines and mainly typewriters, which we produce in mass volumes. Office machinery ranges all the way from flat portable typewriters ($40) to computers ($250,000). The whole product line includes calculating machines, check writers, bookkeeping machines, adding machines, dictating machines, comptometers, data-processing equipment, and photocopy machines. Olympia now makes most of these, in a limited way, and we are expanding our line. All of these are within the sphere of our interest, but we cannot make all of these on a volume basis. Where should we draw the line? Electric and electronic machines are becoming popular, but we have no such department worth speaking of. Should Olympia follow the trend? Should we copy IBM or Remington?"

Balance sheet, 1954–1963 (in thousands of dollars)

Assets	1954	1955	1956	1957	1958	1959	1960	1961	1962	1963
Current assets:										
Cash	$ 589	$ 84	$ 102	$ 78	$ 509	$ 738	$ 1,008	$ 808	$ 924	$ 1,022
Accounts receivable	4,561	4,732	5,722	6,290	9,617	9,972	4,153	4,774	7,660	8,067
Realized payments on account	15	11			16	4	12	7	20	26
Received from subsidiaries		163	278	192	116	382	859	1,010	1,680	942
Demands from payments on account							2,989	2,497		
Other receivables	315	465	528	730	1,129	869	915	1,020	903	804
Inventory:										
Raw, auxiliary, and working materials	964	1,405	1,732		2,638	2,241	3,089	3,694	3,139	2,566
Work in process	1,903	2,588	3,334		5,921	6,045	6,708	6,388	6,104	5,707
Finished goods	616	903	1,081	6,776	3,011	2,145	2,515	3,342	4,253	4,244
Other	8	33	90	127	221	262	135	259		
Total current assets	$ 8,971	$10,384	$12,867	$14,193	$23,178	$22,658	$22,483	$23,799	$24,683	$23,378
Fixed assets:										
Improved property										
Business buildings	44	74	71	212	537	519	504	453	425	420
Factory buildings	3,067	5,606	7,152	8,104	11,312	10,790	10,435	10,204	11,240	10,900
Unimproved property	47		27	13	9	9	4	54	247	512
Buildings under construction	231	750	149	607	841	450	536	1,499	877	524
Payments on account	47	151	127	258	139	53	163	246		
Machines	3,285	3,410	3,998	4,775	6,806	6,133	5,809	6,281	6,722	5,992
Tools, factory, and business equipment, vehicles	855	1,412	1,463	1,669	2,083	2,000	1,866	1,874	1,810	1,848
Shares, patents, and valuable papers	129	174	962	3,430	1,077	1,029	2,184	2,184	2,940	3,010
Total fixed assets	$ 7,605	$11,577	$13,949	$19,068	$22,804	$20,983	$21,501	$22,795	$24,261	$23,206
Total assets	$16,577	$21,959	$26,816	$33,260	$45,984	$43,642	$43,987	$46,597	$48,946	$46,584

exhibit 1 (continued)

Liabilities

	1954	1955	1956	1957	1958	1959	1960	1961	1962	1963
Current liabilities:										
Installment credits	1,690	1,750	1,750	1,750	3,931	4,277				
Liabilities for export							6,815	7,987	16,507	13,392
Bills of exchange	661	1,147	1,866	2,498	3,125	3,125				
Other short-term bank liabilities	1,711	219	957	715	4,237	2,846				
Accounts payable	871	1,114	766	1,258	1,249	837	1,106	1,320	1,080	835
Liabilities through acceptance of bills	804	1,995	2,378	3,628	3,542	2,545	3,707	3,361	2,750	2,378
Down payments from customers	34	26	69	55	48	113	70	57	109	42
Liabilities to subsidiaries		1,250	1,250	157	966	178	151	183	455	375
Other short-term liabilities	592	712	949	1,097	1,535	1,578	1,821	1,887	1,903	2,162
Total current	$6,363	$6,963	$9,985	$11,158	$18,633	$15,499	$13,670	$14,795	$22,804	$19,184
Long-term notes and credits from banks	4,081	5,297	5,951	7,561	9,219	8,645	8,998	9,534	2,275	1,949
Allocated reserves	1,203	2,162	3,066	3,669	4,349	5,631	7,565	7,945	7,594	9,451
Items that limit-restrictions					15	15	25	24		
Capital:										
Required reserve funds	400	625	625	875	1,250	1,250	1,375	1,375	1,375	1,375
Optional reserve funds	250	250	375	375						
Supply										500
Basic capital	4,000	6,250	6,250	8,750	11,250	11,250	11,250	13,750	13,750	13,750
Total capital	$4,650	$7,125	$7,250	$10,000	$12,500	$12,500	$12,625	$15,125	$15,125	$15,625
Net profit for the year	280	410	562	854	1,262	1,350	1,575	1,575	1,146	1,375
Total liabilities	$16,577	$21,959	$26,816	$33,260	$45,984	$43,642	$43,987	$46,507	$48,946	$46,584

exhibit 2 OLYMPIA WERKE

Profit and loss statements, 1954–1963 (in thousands of dollars)

	1954	1955	1956	1957	1958	1959	1960	1961	1962	1963
Proceeds from manufacturing activities (Net of CGS)	$11,446	$14,564	$18,862	$22,131	$26,629	$29,158	$34,247	$35,902	$36,734	$37,956
Proceeds from non-manufacturing activities	30	36	245	487	798	347	722	1,336	1,389	672
Gross yield	$11,476	$14,600	$19,107	$22,618	$27,427	$29,505	$34,969	$37,238	$38,123	$38,628
Less:										
Salaries and wages	6,456	8,358	11,087	12,663	15,889	17,001	19,175	22,183	23,823	23,327
Social dues	606	857	1,092	1,467	1,861	2,090	2,331	2,661	2,841	2,773
Other social expenditures	3	3	6	9	8	8	697	655	781	762
Depreciation:										
Fixed capital	1,774	2,517	3,644	4,717	4,656	4,824	4,336	4,515	4,405	4,113
Floating capital	.....	.....	.....	.....	.....	654	409	58	5	171
Maintenance expenditures	195	410	408	474	534	.....	.....	.....	.....	.....
Interest expense	653	713	1,029	1,000	1,439	1,597	1,653	1,343	1,463	1,287
Taxes:										
On profits	950	1,104	1,134	1,258	1,374	1,964	2,219	1,820	1,311	1,719
Other taxes	.....	.....	.....	.....	.....	.....	1,069	1,000	1,123	1,045
Property adjustment for refugees-capital levy	.....	.....	.....	.....	.....	.....	395	30	29	28
Correction for interest-free loan	160	.....	18	21	27	15	.....	.....	.....	.....
Other expenditures	.....	.....	.....	.....	.....	.....	1,109	1,271	1,194	1,529
Annual profit	$ 679	$ 638	$ 691	$ 1,009	$ 1,634	$ 1,352	$ 1,576	$ 1,702	$ 1,148	$ 1,874
Allotment to required reserve	.....	225	.....	153	375	.....	.....	125	.....	500
Allotment to free reserve	400	.....	125	.....	.....	.....	.....	.....	.....	.....
Net profit	$ 280	$ 410	$ 562	$ 854	$ 1,262	$ 1,352	$ 1,575	$ 1,575	$ 1,148	$ 1,375

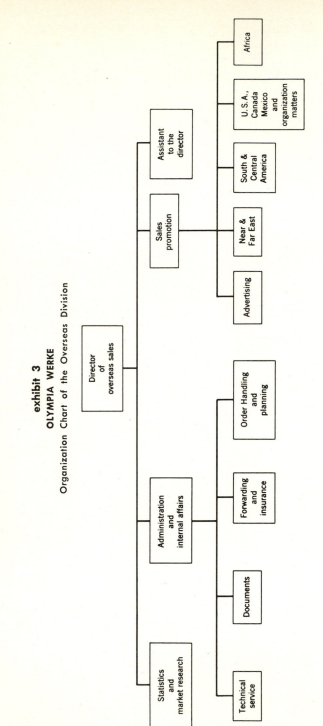

exhibit 3
OLYMPIA WERKE
Organization Chart of the Overseas Division

352

14

THE
TRUST
COMPANY

In January, 1967, the press announced that Mr. Howard Stokes had been elected chairman of the board of the Falls City Bank and Trust Company of Louisville, Kentucky. Mr. Stokes' election was the culmination of events which began in February, 1965, when Mrs. Beatrice Beaumont, the major stockholder in the bank, died. Inheritance tax demands made it necessary for her husband, Mr. John Jay Beaumont, to sell either his wife's stock or some of his substantial plantation properties. He chose to sell the stock. Shortly thereafter Mr. Beaumont, at the age of 68 and in ill health, resigned as president of the bank, an office he had held for 30 years. Following these events the bank's stock dropped to less than its book value. Ten months later Stokes Enterprises, headed by Howard Stokes, announced that it owned the controlling stock interest in the bank.

Howard Stokes, aged 58 and a native of Milwaukee, Wisconsin, was a self-made entrepreneur with widely varied interests. He had started his business career as a proprietor of a dry goods store which he expanded into a department store which also did a mail-order business. Finding his strongest mail-order customer following was in Kentucky, Tennessee, and Missouri, he moved his business to Louisville in 1945. By 1966 he had a thriving mail-order business in the South Central states, had 14 small department stores in Kentucky, and kept up side interests in supermarkets, motels, a catering service, a vending service, several real estate ventures, and an accident insurance company.

Mr. Stokes' immediate interest in the Falls City Bank stemmed from his accident insurance company, which sold policies via mail-order catalog and also from booths in each of his stores. The insurance company generated substantial funds for investment. Mr. Stokes had in mind annexing branch banking offices to each of his five department stores in Jefferson County, which he believed would be a ready-made vehicle for attracting depositors. He also had plans for granting consumer credit. In the first years of his ownership numerous changes took place in the Falls City Bank and Trust Company.

ORIGIN AND EARLY HISTORY OF THE BANK

The Falls City Bank and Trust Company was organized by a number of prominent Kentucky families in 1862 to engage in the trust business. These Kentuckians, realizing their tenuous position as a border state, deeded their properties to the Trust Company and made it the depository for their wills. Louisville, originally known as Falls City,[1] was a Union stores depot during the Civil War, an activity which brought it commercial prosperity.

Kentucky was a Union state, but many Kentuckians were Southern in culture and sympathies. The original Falls City Trust Company was owned and staffed by Louisvillians of Southern family backgrounds. Throughout the Confederacy there were Southerners who feared that a Northern victory would mean confiscation of their properties, and during the war they liquidated their wealth and deposited the proceeds in banks in Liverpool and Birmingham. In 1868, when the confiscation hazard had passed, the Falls City Trust Company amended its charter to become the Falls City Bank and Trust Company to enable it to accept the deposits of the substantial funds which were flowing back from England.

During the first years of its existence the bank attracted the trust patronage of the leading families of Kentucky. Its banking services were largely an offshoot of its trust connections and were rendered as an accommodation to its trust clientele. In later years its reputation as a trust company became so eminent that when Louisvillians said "the Trust Company" they meant the Falls City Bank and Trust Company.

---

[1] Louisville was originally called Falls City because it was located near a series of falls on the Ohio River which required boat traffic to be portaged. The transferring of passengers and freight gave birth to the city.

From its founding until 1966 the Trust Company was managed by members of its founding families.

THE LOUISVILLE COMMUNITY

Louisville was the largest city in Kentucky and the seat of government for Jefferson County. It had a population of 382,400, and Jefferson County had a population of 683,300. The metropolitan Louisville population was estimated to be over 800,000. Louisville was situated on the southern bank of the Ohio River and was the largest city close to southern Indiana and Illinois. By virtue of this it was the main wholesale and retail center for a trading area of 47 counties with a population of 1,575,300 and effective buying income of close to $4 billion.

The economy of Louisville was diversified and included industry, agriculture, commerce, and finance. Louisville was 50 miles from Frankfort, capital of the state, and was the regional headquarters for a number of federal agencies. Louisville was an educational center; it had 11 colleges and universities and was a regional center for the performing arts.

Agricultural activities in the area included tobacco raising, the breeding of beef cattle, and the siring and training of thoroughbred race horses. Churchill Downs, seat of the world-renowned Kentucky Derby, was in Louisville.

Louisville was the United States' largest producer of synthetic rubber, paint, varnish, and whisky. It ranked second in cigarettes, home appliances, and aluminum for home use, and it was a large producer of farm tractors, household appliances, trucks, chemicals, furniture, printing, textiles, tools and dies, and food processing. In 1971 it had over 300,000 people employed in 850 manufacturing plants.

LOUISVILLE BANKING STRUCTURE

At the year-end in 1967 there were six banks in Jefferson County (see Exhibit 1). Three were considerably larger than the Trust Company. The Southland Bank and Trust Company was the youngest, founded in 1920, and it was the largest, with deposits of $517 million. The oldest, the Kentucky State Bank, was established in 1851 and had

exhibit 1   MAJOR LOUISVILLE BANKS, 1967

	Date Founded	Deposits (in millions)	Loans (in millions)	Branches
Southland Bank and Trust Company	1920	$517	$248	23
The Kentucky State Bank	1851	453	212	26
The Jefferson County Bank	1862	358	194	17
The Falls City Bank and Trust Company	1862	150	52	0
The Bluegrass Trust Company	1900	30	n.a.	0
The Stockman's Bank	1900	20	11	0

deposits of $453 million. The third, The Jefferson County Bank, a commercial bank since its origin, with deposits of $358 million, dated from 1862, as did the Trust Company. There were two small banks, both founded in 1900: the Bluegrass Trust Company, with $30 million in deposits, which did mainly trust business and was located in the affluent suburb of Saint Joan; and the Stockman's Bank, with deposits of $20 million, located at the thriving Louisville stockyards. The Trust Company, with deposits of $150 million, was ranked in size between the two small banks and the three large ones.

The larger banks were full-service banks and had numerous branches; the Trust Company did not have any branches. The larger banks offered extensive correspondent banking services to country banks in Kentucky and adjacent states. They had drive-in facilities and competed for consumer credit business. The larger banks were heavily oriented toward wholesale banking activities and extended sizable lines of credit to major corporations. All of them had divisions which offered full international banking services.

The Louisville banks had grown with the postwar boom in Jefferson County, especially the "young" Southland Bank and Trust Company, which was known to have aggressive management. The Trust Company had also grown during the postwar period, but at a considerably slower rate. Among the banks of Louisville, the Southland was said to have the largest share of large corporate accounts; the Jefferson County Bank was said to be the most liberal loan-maker and did the largest volume of consumer financing; the Kentucky State Bank was said to do a heavy mortgage loan business; and the Trust Company was said to have the most elegant and antiquated banking house and the most exclusive clientele.

THE TRUST COMPANY BUILDING

In 1892 the Trust Company had built a Greek Ionic banking edifice in Jefferson Shores, a prestige neighborhood, in the style which was in vogue for banks at that time. It was opposite the Jefferson County Courthouse. In 1971 the Trust Company, 10 times its 1892 size, was still housed in the same building. The original main banking floor, a showpiece of Victorian elegance at the time the bank was built, still had the same unchanged decor: the marble rails and columns, the plush upholstered furniture, heavy velvet portieres, an abundance of brass ornamentation, and deep-piled carpetings.

In 1938 the Trust Company had built a plain, functional building to the west of its main building to house its enlarged clerical operations. It had three floors aboveground and 12 times the area of the original building, and was connected to the front building by runways at the basement and second-floor levels. The public was admitted only to the front building.

In 1950 the Kentucky State Turnpike was built, crossing the Ohio River via the new Daniel Boone Bridge. The turnpike bisected Jefferson Shores, crossing the city in a way which cut off the Trust Company from central Louisville. This made Jefferson Shores difficult to reach. The area also showed signs of deteriorating.

JOHN JAY BEAUMONT

John Jay Beaumont, who had been president of the Trust Company for three decades, had been described by a friend as "A Southern gentleman of wealth and good breeding, a patrician of cultured tastes —and an anachronism in the modern Kentucky scene of today." Mr. Beaumont was acquainted with every "old-line" family in northern Kentucky. He owned several thousand acres of bluegrass plantation land on which he bred Aberdeen Angus cattle and thoroughbred race horses. His wife had inherited the largest single block of stock in the Trust Company. At age 38 John Jay became president and he held the office for 30 years. The most important clients of the Trust Company did business with Mr. Beaumont on a personal-friendship basis. Mr. Beaumont came to be known as an authority on trust estates in Kentucky.

The Board of Directors and Staff under John Jay Beaumont. In Mr. Beaumont's day the chairman of the board had been Mr. Julian Johnstone, head of a chain of Kentucky supermarkets. Mr. Johnstone spent a considerable portion of his time on Trust Company business. He had been described as "a real working chairman, not just a figurehead." The Johnstone board had 17 members, whose average age was 63. Eight members seldom attended meetings; nine members attended every meeting. Among the nine were three senior officers of the bank.

Under Mr. Beaumont it had been the officers of the trust division who were looked upon as having higher status. Four-fifths of them were attorneys by profession; a number of them were considered wealthy. The officers in the banking department were a relatively smaller group and were varied in age and years of service with the Trust Company, as well as in personal backgrounds. Many had come to the Trust Company after learning their specialized functions in other banks. As a group, the Trust Company's officers were paid salaries which were 20% higher than those of the larger Louisville banks. Their caliber was considered to be excellent, but during the 1960's the Trust Company's high-pay policy was repeatedly being criticized by minority stockholders.

Until 1967 Mr. John Jay Beaumont had been president, chief executive officer, and chairman of the executive committee. He was active in banking matters but spent most of his time on trust activities, which he and Mr. William Shermington administered jointly. Mr. Beaumont had approved all lines of credit and loans and had passed on all personnel appointments.

Mr. Shermington, 64, an attorney, was a cousin of Mrs. Beaumont's. He had been with the Trust Company for 35 years and had headed the trust division since 1940. Under Mr. Shermington were six full vice presidents, each of whom was responsible for one or more types of trust accounts. When Mr. Shermington was absent from the bank, Mr. Beaumont assumed his duties as head of the trust division.

Mr. Reuben Daniels, 54, vice president, cashier, and a director, was a graduate of the Stonier Graduate School of Banking. He had come to the Trust Company at the age of 40 with extensive previous banking experience. Mr. Daniels supervised all banking operations but took almost no part in trust activities. He was seldom absent from the bank, he rarely traveled, and his outside activities were limited.

Since 1950 the Trust Company was managed by Messrs. Beaumont, Shermington, and Daniels as an executive team. The trust officers were sometimes consulted. So was Malcolm Pinney, the chief loan officer, who was the only commercial banker other than Mr. Daniels who was considered to have senior status. (See Exhibit 2.)

By virtue of its association with many influential Kentucky families, the Trust Company attracted to it employees of high caliber at all levels. Young men from old Southern families came to it; many of them had independent means. As a result, there was also a steady departure of the Trust Company's young men, who left to take more responsible jobs with other banks. The bank also experienced a high rate of turnover among its female employees, who usually worked there only a few years, until marriage. Mr. Beaumont had been proud to point out that the Trust Company had trained more trust officers than any other bank in Kentucky; he asserted that this gave it friendly and loyal connections with scores of other banks.

Savings. Over the years demand deposits had constituted a large part of the total deposits of the Trust Company, but after World War II time deposits had increased in importance. In 1954, savings made up 37% of the Trust Company's total deposits.

During the postwar period savings and loan associations, which paid higher interest rates, had become popular. Other Louisville banks countered by mounting aggressive advertising campaigns directed at attracting savers. The Trust Company did not advertise, and at no time did it aggressively seek time deposits. After the new Kentucky Turnpike cut off the Trust Company from the traffic flow in the Louisville city center, its savings desposits declined.

Commercial Business. Throughout its history the inclinations of its owners, financial limitations, and lack of specialized personnel had prevented the Trust Company from offering comprehensive banking services with the same depth and breadth as competitive banks. Trust activities had always been considered primary. The Trust Company had developed few correspondent bank relationships. Its staff of savings and banking officers was capable but was much smaller than the staff in its trust division. Lack of branches and limited automation of operations had further restricted its banking activities.

"The Trust Company under Mr. Beaumont has not developed its commercial banking in keeping with the economic development of the region," said Mr. Reuben Daniels. "We have no intention of trying to

exhibit 2
Organization Chart of the Falls City Bank and Trust Company, 1966

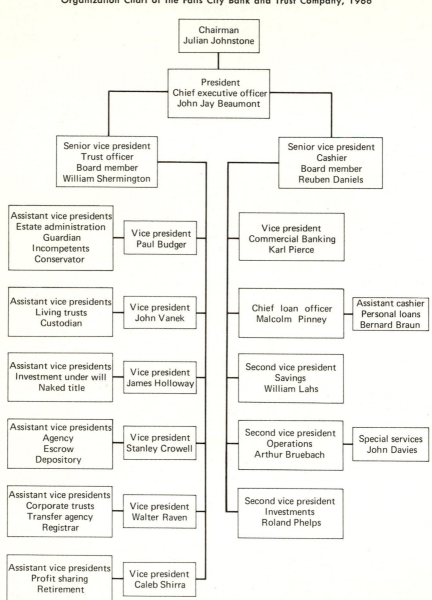

become Louisville's largest bank. Every year we turned away enough business to keep a moderate-sized bank going. We turned them away because these accounts might require loan accommodations which we would not consider." Mr. Daniels said that there were whole categories of businesses whose patronage the Trust Company did not care to have at all because, as he put it, they were too "volatile." He cited as examples jewelers, taverns, night clubs, and furriers.

The Trust Company under Mr. Beaumont did not have a new-business department. Mr. Pinney, the chief loan officer, had a second vice president who assisted him and who spent about half of his time calling on prospective customers.

Personal Banking. Under Mr. Beaumont's management the Trust Company tended to discourage personal checking accounts. Accommodation accounts were granted to trust clients and the principals in its major commercial accounts. Others were required to make an initial deposit of $1,000 and to maintain minimum average balances of $500.

Personal loans were usually made only to important customers, and also on an accommodation basis. Most of these were collateralized by marketable securities. No consumer financing was done until 1950, when a Ford Motor Company regional truck dealer near Louisville requested some dealer financing. Retail financing was then extended to other auto agency accounts, and later to a large local International Harvester tractor dealer. Other commercial customers who did retail business were allowed to discount their customers' installment notes, but no customer loans were made directly to individuals. During Mr. Beaumont's day the Trust Company did not operate a consumer credit department.

Special Service. For many years the Trust Company had operated a special service department to perform accommodation services, such as clipping bond coupons, buying government bonds, and cashing matured securities. Under Mr. Beaumont these services had been expanded considerably and customers were using it to purchase out-of-town theater tickets, to make hotel reservations, to anonymously purchase racehorse blood stock, and to purchase travel accommodations. All special services rendered had to be approved by a senior officer. All were gratis to customers of the Trust Company. The department had five employees.

Progress under Mr. Beaumont. During Mr. Beaumont's tenure the Trust Company's personal trust business grew, and corporate trust operations had an even larger growth. The Trust Company had also added a foreign department, which had become well established; most of its transactions were finalized through its correspondent connections in New York, Chicago, or San Francisco. Savings and commercial deposits had grown, but not in keeping with national growth rates. Greater Metropolitan Louisville had seen the most rapid growth in its history in the post-World War II period, and the larger Louisville banks had growth which had exceeded the national averages.

It was during Mr. Beaumont's administration that the clerical operations building had been built and some commercial and savings operations had been computerized. A parking lot had been added, and at the time of Mr. Beaumont's retirement a drive-in banking facility was being considered. A night depository had been installed in 1945. A Women's Finance Forum had been organized in 1952, and a Collective Investment Trust for Qualified Employees (mostly officers) had been started in 1958.

ORGANIZATIONAL CHANGES AFTER THE STOKES PURCHASE

"My interest in the Trust Company," said Mr. Stokes at the time of the purchase announcement, "stemmed primarily from the exceptional fund of talent it has in its staff of officers and employees. With these fine people we mean to make the Falls City Bank the leading Louisville bank, offering every modern banking service to its community." During the months which followed, there were many changes in the organization of the Trust Company.

The board of directors was reduced in size by the resignation of five members, including the chairman. Howard Stokes became the new chairman. Carsten Scheer, financial vice president of Stokes Enterprises, was made vice chairman, with the understanding that he would still continue to occupy his time as general financial director of Mr. Stokes' numerous business operations, spending about one day a week at the Trust Company. (See Exhibit 3.)

Reuben Daniels was elected president and chief executive officer of the bank with jurisdiction over both trust and banking activities. Upon announcement of this, Mr. Shermington took an early retirement. Byron Holowell, a young trust attorney, was advanced over the heads of several trust officers to become a senior vice president and head of the trust department, whereupon two trust officers resigned.

exhibit 3

Organization Chart of the Falls City Bank and Trust Company, 1971

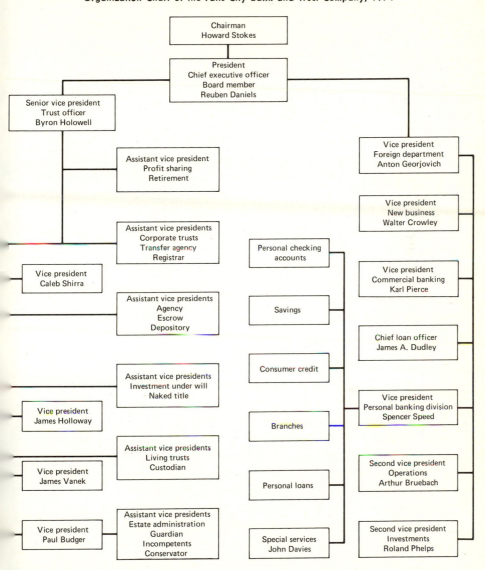

Reuben Daniels continued to direct banking activities while Byron Holowell managed the trust department.

Frederick Gardiner, a junior vice president of the Home Acceptance Corporation, was brought into the bank to organize a consumer credit department. Spencer Speed, a 30-year-old assistant cashier, whom Mr. Beaumont had described as a "precocious youngster, brimming with ideas and smoldering in frustration," was made a vice president and placed in charge of a newly created unit called the Personal Banking Division, which included personal checking accounts, savings, consumer credit, and branches. Walter Crowley, who was junior vice president and assistant manager of the new-business department of the Southland Bank and Trust Company, was brought into the Trust Company as a vice president to organize a new-business department. It was rumored that he had been attracted by a high salary.

Under the new administration Mr. Daniels, who had only a passing knowledge of trust matters, tended to give prior attention to banking business and left the trust operations to Byron Holowell. Within the Trust Division there were indications that the vice presidents in charge of the sections—living trusts, corporate trusts, and so forth— were having little to do with Byron Holowell. No new vice presidents were named to replace those who had resigned; their previous assistants acted in their places.

Howard Stokes came to the bank only to officiate at board meetings; he seldom contacted any of the officers personally. Carsten Scheer appeared early every Friday morning, and after visiting with Byron Holowell for about a half-hour he spent the next hour or two with Reuben Daniels, reviewing what had been done in the banking division, studying loans and loan applications, looking over new accounts, and conveying to Mr. Daniels any new suggestions coming from Mr. Stokes. He then made his way through the bank, talking to officers in many departments. "It was a trying experience," said Mr. Daniels. "I was a career banker and I was being subjected to the advice of two men who had never had any banking experience. Often they suggested actions which were nonprofessional. Mr. Scheer's practice of talking to junior officers directly was highly unsettling."

During the period the Trust Company underwent what Mr. Daniels described as "an unreasonable series of audits by the bank examiners which were so severe that they amounted to harassment." [2] The third examination that year was in progress when Mr. Pinney, the chief loan officer, resigned. Two months later Mr. James Dudley, chief bank examiner of the District of Tennessee (which included all of Kentucky), resigned from his office and was elected vice president and chief loan officer of the Trust Company. Thereafter the Trust Company was managed by a triumvirate of Scheer, Daniels, and Dudley.

[2] The expenses of bank examinations are borne by the bank being examined.

OPERATION OF THE TRUST COMPANY UNDER
STOKES' MANAGEMENT

Two months after Stokes became chairman the Trust Company opened its drive-in banking service. Three tellers' windows had been built as an annex to the operations building. During the first six months of their operation, two were usually in use. There was no significant change in deposits held.

In July, 1967, the Trust Company announced the opening of a consumer credit department as part of its personal banking service. Extensive advertising in the Louisville trading area invited the public to use the bank for its credit needs—"auto, furniture, signature loans—$25 to $5,000." Automatic credit arrangements were also made available.

During the postwar period Louisville had experienced a strong trend toward the suburbs. Suburban shopping centers mushroomed. During the first half of the 1960's five such centers, ranging from 12 to 70 acres, were built—The Mall, Westland, Roseland, Pleasure Ridge, and Oxmoor. Stokes Enterprises had one of its chain stores (called Bargains Unlimited) in each of these plazas, plus two stores in the city. By the end of 1967 the Trust Company was prepared to open branches in annexes added to each of the Bargains Unlimited stores.

In April of 1967 word passed through the community that the Beaumont family trust accounts had been transferred to the Bluegrass Trust Company. During the following months a number of Louisville old-family estates—the John Hunt Morgans, the Breckenridges, the Mc-Daniels, and the Hardins—followed suit. Howard Stokes remarked, "This does not cause us any concern. The Trust Company has been operated as though it was an exclusive social club. But the dues it collected were low-income trust fees. We mean to earn high income from commercial banking."

During the spring and summer of 1967 a new advertising campaign was launched introducing "the new Trust Company *Bank*." The ads emphasized the banking, savings, loan, and branch services of the Trust Company and said little about its trust division. It was the first time in its history that the Trust Company had done such advertising, and the campaign used all available media—billboards, newspapers, radio, television, and direct mailings. Its printed ad themes featured "A

Complete Banking Service—Where Parking Is No Problem—Checking Accounts, Time Deposits, Savings Accounts, Auto Loans, Consolidation Loans, Business, Collateral, and Real Estate Loans. Drive-In Banking Hours, 9 A.M. to 6 P.M., Monday through Friday."

During 1967 the number of savings accounts increased by 21% but total savings deposits increased by only 7%. The number of personal checking accounts increased by 32%. "That was not really an impressive gain," said Mr. Scheer, "when you consider that we started from a very low base." Trust business declined. There was no appreciable change in demand deposits, despite vigorous solicitations made by the new five-man new-business department. "The banking business is slow-moving," said Mr. Scheer. "You don't have any spectaculars to bring the public rushing in, the way they do when we have give-away sales at our Bargains Unlimited stores."

While the number of commercial accounts had increased by 6%, total demand deposits had declined by 1½%. During the year Stokes Enterprises' deposits had added substantially to the Trust Company's assets. These gains were more than offset by the loss of local government deposits, due, Mr. Scheer said, "to the inordinate attention that was being paid to our affairs by the bank examiners."

For the year 1967 the Trust Company showed only a nominal profit and a drop from its long record of moderate but steady earnings. Mr. Scheer attributed the drop to reorganization expenses, the cost of new facilities (drive-in and branches), and the start-up expenses for the bank's new activities.

BANK LOCATION AND FUTURE FACILITIES

During the spring months of 1968 Mr. Scheer investigated the possibility of moving the Trust Company to a city-center location. There was a bank building in downtown Louisville which he thought was ideally located, quite central and close to the larger banks. Mr. Scheer came to the conclusion that it was too old and too small and it had no parking or drive-in possibilities. It was occupied by a finance company. Consideration was given to using it for a downtown branch, but projections indicated that a split operation would probably be at high cost.

A second possibility considered was an old department store in the city center. Built in 1933, the building was 12 stories in height and almost half a block square. The trend toward suburban shopping had caused its sales to decline to such an extent that it was known to be seeking a buyer. The store building required considerable remodeling to transform it into a banking facility, and the Trust Company would not use more than the lower five floors, leaving the question of how the upper floors might be used profitably. It was suggested that they might be used for a Bargains Unlimited store, but Mr. Stokes took a dim view of operating a department store which had no ground-floor level, even if the display windows would remain available. "That fine old store is dying from downtown-itis," said Mr. Stokes. "Our store would probably suffer from the same disease. We find the suburbs healthier."

The possibility of building a new structure had also been considered. No suitable vacant land was available, nor were desirable improved sites, and a new structure, it was conjectured, might cost approximately $6 to $7 million.

In their letter to shareholders which accompanied the year-end annual report for 1970, Messrs. Stokes and Scheer stated:

> For the year 1970 your bank enjoyed a continuing improving trend. Operating income was up from 1969, reflecting more commercial lending and higher lending rates. Consumer loans contributed significant earnings but larger operating expenses, and a 27% increase in interest expense held down the final net earnings. Last year's gain in net profits was achieved despite the surtax, which reduced net per share by 14¢.
>
> New accounting regulations require banks to restate year-end results to include provisions for loan losses and profits and losses on securities tranactions. This did not affect your bank's earnings significantly. Loan-loss experience and charge-offs were modest. There were virtually no changes in your bank's investment portfolio.
>
> Throughout its history your bank has been heavily engaged in Trust business. Your new management intends to reorient your bank toward a major participation in wholesale banking activities. Recently your bank has been competing successfully with other large regional banks to participate in extending sizable lines of credit for major corporations. The opportunity was available to us because during the current period of money stringency, money center banks have been compelled by lack of funds or federal policy to turn away prospective borrowers. Loan-to-deposit ratios in many regional banks have been pushed to 80% or higher. Your bank's ratio has been about 50% or less for many years. Because regional banks have been experiencing a heavy runoff of commercial certificates of deposit, they have had to resort to other sources of high-cost funds, along with many money-market banks.

During most of the past decade demand deposits were trending toward a higher percentage of your bank's total deposits while the percentage of time deposits declined. Due to the promotional efforts of your new management this trend has been reversed. At the close of 1970, on average balances, time deposits accounted for 40% of your bank's total deposits; by contrast, three years ago they represented less than 20%. Certificates of deposit account for much of the gain.

OPERATIONAL CHANGES

Early in 1971 the Trust Company entered the retail charge field with the initiation of the South Central Bankamericard Service, which was also available to other banks throughout the South. Mr. Stokes had seen this move as a very promising supplemental means of granting credit in his chain of stores, which already had their own established credit-card system. At the year-end the Trust Company had generated only 7,500 accounts with receivables of $157,000 outstanding. In contrast, the largest Louisville bank, which had extensive correspondent connections with country banks, had 200,000 accounts with $6 million outstanding.

The charge-card start-up program involved large promotional expenses which caused the program to show a loss for the year. "We had anticipated a much larger acceptance," said Mr. Scheer. "Apparently the typical Trust Company client does not feel the need for a credit card, and the typical customer of our Bargains Unlimited stores is not a customer of the Trust Company." The credit card department was later made a part of the newly formed travel service department. Mr. Scheer remarked, "The huge start-up costs are now over. We believe that by 1972 we will generate enough volume to reach the break-even point." He also pointed out that while credit-per-card had been small compared with national averages, so had the Trust Company's bad-debt losses.

A major event in 1971 was the expansion of the Trust Company's data processing operations, which, Mr. Scheer said, "offered significant growth potential." Up to this date the Trust Company had only a limited application of data processing applied to its banking operations. A data processing services department was now organized. All possible banking, savings, credit-card, and trust activities were tabulated, and the service was offered to the Trust Company's country bank correspondents. The latter were offered a wide range of services, including the processing of demand and savings deposits and installment loans.

During 1971 the Trust Company mounted a vigorous campaign to enlarge its correspondent banking connections, and the computer service was offered as a sales point. The project was only moderately successful; only a few new correspondents were acquired, and in no month did the services for outside customers increase by more than 2%. At the year-end the Trust Company's data processing services had three outside customers. A leading Louisville bank had 31 such customers. Mr. Scheer attributed this to the fact that the larger bank had a much larger correspondent following and more sophisticated, high-capacity equipment. He thought that it would only require a higher volume to make the computer operation pay, and he was considering installing larger equipment and also processing the operations of the Bargains Unlimited stores.

In 1964 figures published by *The American Banker* had indicated that the Trust Company's Trust Division was the largest in the State of Kentucky from the standpoint of trust income. Since 1967 this trust business had been declining, both in terms of number of accounts and in terms of net income. "It isn't hard to see why," said Mr. Weldon, an old trust officer. "The new owners of the bank seem to be deliberately phasing out our fine trust business." He pointed out an ad theme, attributed to Mr. Scheer, which had been published widely:

You Know Us As
THE TRUST COMPANY
We would like you to think of us as
THE FALLS CITY BANK
A Full-Service Bank

At the end of 1971 trust accounts declined for the fifth straight year. "I don't think that the computers did us any good," said Mr. Weldon. "Some of our ads trumpeted that we now have a fully computerized trust service. I'm sure that many of our old customers didn't like to feel that they were fully computerized." In 1971 trust income fell to about 8% of total earnings. Since 1967 nine of the Trust Division's managerial personnel had left; they had been replaced by the promotion of juniors, and no additions had been made.

Historically, many of the Trust Company's influential clientele had also held political office, and the Trust Company had become the obvious depository for the government funds which they controlled. In 1971 its total deposits of the State of Kentucky and political subdivisions constituted a much higher proportion of its demand deposits than any other Louisville bank. "It has become a tradition in Kentucky," said Mr. Reuben Daniels, "that the Trust Company is the leading depository of government funds."

During the 1960's the three largest Louisville banks had mounted aggressive campaigns to capture government accounts. One of the larger banks had engaged as a vice president a man who had formerly been Treasurer of the State of Kentucky. "This could hurt us," said Mr. Daniels. "That man knows where every vein of government gold lies. He also has connections which can open the right doors in the Capitol and in many a county courthouse and many a city hall."

FUTURE PROSPECTS

In the 1971 annual report Mr. Scheer said:

> Recently your bank has been working to improve its competitive position in the international banking arena. Our Foreign Department, established forty years ago, has now been enlarged to become our International Department, offering full international services. Previously voluntary restraint guidelines imposed by the Federal Government and our dependence upon our Chicago and New York correspondents placed a limit upon our ability to lend to foreign borrowers. A recent venture with leading regional banks across the country has led to the formation of Allied Bank International, which will make us fully competitive in international services with any other bank in our area.

In 1971 there were significant gains in consumer credit accounts. While operating income increased, net income showed a slight decline.

Mr. Scheer had been heavily occupied with Mr. Stokes' other interests, which were flourishing, and had not always been able to spend his usual Friday at the bank. In major matters none of the other officers acted without direction, and this had brought an increasing amount of banking questions to Mr. Stokes for decision. This was a development he had not anticipated and did not desire.

At the end of 1971 Mr. Stokes and Mr. Scheer were, themselves, still referring to the bank as The Trust Company. (See Exhibits 4 and 5.)

exhibit 4 FALLS CITY BANK AND TRUST COMPANY
Comparative income statements, 1967–1971 (in thousands)

	Years Ending December 31				
	1967	*1968*	*1969*	*1970*	*1971*
Operating Income:					
Interest on loans and fees	$3,615	$4,065	$5,093	$ 5,212	$ 6,339
Interest on securities	1,800	1,840	1,035	2,567	2,889
Interest—political subdivisions	80	77	69	64	58
Trust department income	1,220	1,212	1,111	1,013	981
Other income	300	380	1,241	1,278	1,959
Total income	$7,015	$7,574	$8,549	$10,134	$12,226
Operating Expenses:					
Salaries and wages	$1,479	$1,579	$1,778	$ 1,905	$ 2,369
Employee benefits (pension, etc.)	370	395	445	476	547
Interest on deposits	1,792	2,070	2,821	3,385	4,070
Provision for loan losses	60	44	24	46	60
Interest on borrowed money	30	17	20	34	51
Occupancy rentals (branches)	00	00	17	54	57
Other operating expenses	1,650	1,773	1,781	2,528	3,213
Total operating expenses	$5,381	$5,878	$6,886	$ 8,428	$10,367
Income taxes	374	520	442	418	600
Net securities gains (losses)	(2)	3	28	(6)	3
Net income	$1,258	$1,179	$1,249	$ 1,282	$ 1,262

exhibit 5   FALLS CITY BANK AND TRUST COMPANY
Comparative balance sheets, 1967–1971 (in thousands)

	Years Ending December 31				
	1967	*1968*	*1969*	*1970*	*1971*
Resources:					
Cash and due from banks	$ 24,380	$ 26,050	$ 32,780	$ 41,902	$ 46,289
United States Government obligations	43,508	39,820	44,702	53,172	61,289
Federal funds sold	4,000	7,000	3,000	4,000	4,000
Government institution obligations	740	813	895	984	1,083
Municipal obligations	18,119	16,730	16,503	15,454	13,599
Federal Reserve Bank stock	300	300	300	300	300
Other investment securities	1,079	1,187	1,306	1,437	980
Loans and discounts	72,484	75,732	83,505	83,855	93,440
Building and equipment	999	1,099	1,209	1,330	1,463
Interest receivable	653	719	791	870	956
Other assets	422	464	510	561	617
Total	$166,684	$168,914	$185,501	$203,865	$224,016
Liabilities:					
Demand deposits	$120,471	$114,145	$116,491	$109,793	$118,146
Time deposits	29,940	37,548	50,225	73,662	83,630
Total deposits	$150,411	$151,693	$166,716	$183,455	$201,776
Interest collected but not earned	2,133	1,852	2,100	2,369	2,640
Other liabilities	612	673	740	814	902
Dividends payable	190	190	190	190	190
Capital stock	3,400	3,400	3,400	3,400	3,400
Surplus	6,200	6,200	6,200	6,200	7,194
Undivided profits	1,474	2,416	3,465	4,698	4,902
Reserves for loan losses and contingencies	2,264	2,490	2,690	2,739	3,012
Total	$166,684	$168,914	$185,501	$203,865	$224,016

15

RALEIGH
INDUSTRIES

Raleigh Industries started in business in 1888 under the ownership and direction of Frank Bowden, a young man of means, who had become a cycling enthusiast because he believed that cycling had so improved his health that it had saved his life. His venture coincided with the great cycling boom of the late 1800's, and by the beginning of the twentieth century his plant in Nottingham was turning out 30,000 cycles a year. Bowden adopted Dunlop tires, which made cycling more comfortable; the Shurmey-Archer variable three-speed gear, which made riding less strenuous; and the lightweight English-style frame. Over the years he acquired the rights to such famous cycle names as BSA, Humber, Rudge-Whitworth, Triumph, Sunbeam, and Brooks Saddles. Raleigh achieved such a reputation for its dependable and fashionable cycles that by 1950 its Nottingham plant had grown to be the largest cycle factory in the world, and Raleigh was selling in every world market.

During the period from 1950 to 1959 both domestic and export demand fell so drastically that production was reduced from 4 million to 2 million cycles a year. Describing the situation in his 1959 report to shareholders, Chairman George Wilson said:

> The prospects for the bicycle are difficult to foresee. For the past three years sales in both our home and export markets have continued to decline. There are several reasons for this, and the reasons which apply in the case of the home market differ from those which apply in our export markets.
>
> In the home market it is a fact that never since the war has the sale

of pedicycles in this country ever equalled pre-war levels. There are many factors to which this development can be traced. Foremost among them is the improved standards of living of the population, which has given rise to an enormous increase in motorized transport on the roads of this country. You have only to be outside the gates of any large factory at closing time to have ample evidence of this. The incidence of purchase tax, the restrictions on hire-purchase and the competition the bicycle is facing from the recent introduction of so many forms of heavily advertised domestic appliances, are all further factors. For these reasons I do not expect to see the demand for pedal cycles in this country ever again achieve post-war levels.

In the case of our export markets, however, I see the position very differently. In many of our large overseas markets there has been an inevitable, albeit sporadic, rise in the standard of living which is introducing into the range of potential cycle purchasers many thousands of people who are for the first time in their lives able to acquire a personal means of transport. It is a fact that in the large native territories a bicycle is one of the most sought-after and prized possessions. However, on the export side, we are meeting increasing embargoes on imports into some of our principal markets.

ACQUISITION BY TUBE INVESTMENTS

Tube Investments Limited was a major British industrial company which controlled numerous iron, steel, and aluminum producing and manufacturing subsidiaries (see Exhibit 1). It was a large producer of tubing, an activity which led it into the manufacturing of cycles. Its cycle division, the British Cycle Corporation, operated plants in Birmingham, close to Nottingham, and produced such well-known brands as the Phillips, Hercules, Sun, Armstrong, and Norman. British Cycle was second in size only to Raleigh, and both companies competed actively in both home and foreign markets.

There had always been close cooperation between Raleigh and Tube Investments. Tube Investments supplied Raleigh with its requirements for tubing for cycle frames and brought many of its own components from Raleigh. Both firms looked on it as an economically natural relationship that had been built up over the years. The coordination of the two operations was so close that for many years the managements had entertained the thought of combining them.

When Raleigh was experiencing the drastic decline in sales during the latter fifties, Tube Investments was having the same experience. Both companies found themselves vying for the potential which remained.

exhibit 1   TUBE INVESTMENTS LTD.

History: Registered in England in 1919.

Business: Manufactures precision tube, cycles and components, aluminum electrical engineering and iron and steel products. Company and subsidiaries operate following divisions: Steel Tube, Cycle, Aluminum, Electrical, Engineering and Iron and Steel, General and overseas.

Subsidiaries: British Aluminum Co. Ltd. (appended statement—51% owned by company and 49% by Reynolds Metals Co.—see general index) which in turn controls Canadian British Aluminum Co. Ltd. (appended statement). Also has a number of subsidiaries and affiliates in England, Argentina, Australia, Canada, New Zealand, Pakistan, So. Africa, Eire, India, Italy, Kenya, Norway, Southern Rhodesia, U. S. A., France, Germany and Holland.

Also Raleigh Industries Ltd., (100%).

Board of Directors: Lord Plowden, Chmn.; Sir I. A. R. Stedeford, Pres.; Lord Clitheroe, Vice-Chmn.; Sir William Strath, L. Dobson, Man. Dir.; Sir David C. Watherson, E. D. E. Andrews, W. Hackett, Jr., A. J. S. Aston, L. L. Roberts, E. L. Burton, C. H. T. Williams, E. G. Plucknett, R. G. Soothill, Lord Normanbrook, M. L. G. Boughton, B. S. Kellett, J. W. Menter.

Secretary: H. A. Woodroffe.

Annual Meeting: In December.

No. of Stockholders: July 31, 1964, 7% preference, 1,455; 4½% preference stock, 3,964; ordinary, 48,213.

No. of Employees: July 31, 1964, 60,600 (incl. British Aluminum).

Head Office: T. L. House, Five Ways, Birmingham 16.

Consolidated income account, years ended July 31

	1965	1964
Sales (net)	£215,800,000	£194,100,000
Trading profit	22,817,843	20,279,539
Dividends and interest income	1,116,728	1,125,554
British Aluminum Co.	3,633,829	2,982,630
Total	27,568,400	24,387,723
Depreciation	7,112,203	6,369,182
Taxation, net	5,936,767	5,068,825
Minority interest	1,369,437	929,837
Loan interest	1,361,302	1,065,923
*Extraordinary expenses	1,293,836	2,595,645
Net profit	10,494,854	8,358,311
Preference dividends	168,618	173,334
Ordinary dividends	3,325,216	3,250,046
Retained by subsidiaries	1,141,414	1,661,556
Balance for year	6,859,606	3,272,375

* Concentration of production, pre-production and commissioning of new steelworks (Park Gate).

exhibit 1   (continued)

Consolidated balance sheet, as of July 31

Assets	1965	1964
Inventory	£ 60,496,000	£ 56,514,806
Debtors	54,443,000	46,928,953
Other current	1,386,000	1,635,632
Total current	£116,325,000	£105,079,391
*Plant machinery, etc.	93,272,000	92,736,176
Trade investment	9,122,000	8,745,695
Subsidiary advances	4,394,000	5,569,592
Shares subsidiaries not consolidated	7,908,000	7,907,576
†Other assets	7,272,000	7,481,945
Total	£238,293,000	£227,520,375
Liabilities		
Creditors	£ 28,650,000	£ 23,094,943
Tax payable	4,887,000	6,473,120
Banks	3,327,000	3,035,008
Other current	2,766,000	5,478,518
Total current	£ 39,630,000	£ 38,081,589
7% preference stock	828,000	828,487
4½ preference stock	5,000,000	5,000,000
Ordinary stock	35,375,000	35,374,646
5¼% loan stock	7,500,000	7,500,000
Capital reserves	33,262,000	33,108,786
Revenue reserves	51,546,000	46,524,508
Subsidiary debentures	15,007,000	15,254,317
Future tax	7,438,000	5,572,570
Minority interest	26,710,000	25,660,870
Profit and loss	15,997,000	14,614,602
Total	£238,293,000	£227,520,375

* Net after depreciation.

† Difference between cost of subsidiary shares and book values of net assets attributable to such shares, less writeoffs.

SOURCE: *Moody's Manual of Industrials, 1966.*

This situation brought to a head the merger which had long been under consideration. Tube Investments and Raleigh each had subsidiaries which operated factories in Ireland and South Africa. In 1959 these were merged and their production and distribution facilities amalgamated. It was generally recognized that this was a pilot run which contemplated a later merger of the full-scale cycle interests of both companies.

In 1960 the cycle interests of Tube Investments and Raleigh were combined by an exchange of ordinary shares. Tube Investments became the emergent parent company, with Raleigh Industries Limited a subsidiary operating as a division. At the same time, the board of directors of Tube Investments asked the board of Raleigh Industries, enlarged by the addition of two Tube Investment executives, to assume responsibility for the combined cycle, component, and motorized divisions of the group, with Mr. Wilson continuing as chairman of Raleigh. As a result of the merger, Raleigh Industries came into control of 80% of the total cycle production capacity of the United Kingdom, with its only competition a few small producers. During the next several years the Raleigh management rationalized the combined production and distribution facilities of the group; it diversified by adding wheeled toys and a reeled safety belt to its product line; it revitalized its motorized cycle activities by developing new mopeds and scooters; it developed a new small-wheeled bicycle of revolutionary design; and it devised new strategies in a determined effort to hold its substantial export markets which were being pre-empted by foreign competitors.

ORGANIZATIONAL CHANGES

Mr. George Wilson had been managing director and chairman for 20 of his 40 years with Raleigh, having succeeded Sir Harold Bowden, the son of the founder, Sir Frank Bowden, in 1955. Mr. Wilson was nearing retirement age at the time of the merger, and although he was still very active and well-liked wihtin the company, he felt that the new challenges facing Raleigh might better be met by a man who was younger and more vigorous. Mr. Wilson continued to serve as chairman until his death in 1963; in January, 1962, he retired as managing director to be succceded by Mr. Leslie Roberts, who had been brought into the company to head the production activities. During the next several years there were numerous changes in the Raleigh personnel.

The board was increased from seven to eight members, six of whom were new as executives of the company and as members of the board. The new board acted in two roles: it met as a main board for policy-making purposes once a month; and acting as an executive committee it met weekly to act upon operating matters (see Exhibit 2).

In 1965 Mr. T. E. Barnsley, formerly a financial executive with Tube Investments, was brought into Raleigh as deputy managing director, a newly created position. Most of the former managing directors of small subsidiary units which had been liquidated as a result of the merger were worked into the new organization. Of the middle and top management staffs of the combined group, 38 out of 50 people were replaced.

exhibit 2
RALEIGH INDUSTRIES
Organization Chart

Chairman managing director
L. L. Roberts

Deputy managing director
T. E. Barnsley

Director of administration. Company secretary B. L. C. Dodsworth
- Registrar: Asst. company secretary S. C. Hearn
- Raleigh Industries Gradual payments Ltd. T. G. Hicks
- Purchasing director C. W. Fellows
- Computer unit D. Dixon
- Overseas dev. L. C. Clarkson
- Solicitor

Group finance director A. M. A. McLarty
- Deputy – R. W. Williams
- Chief financial accountant J. A. Byford
- Chief works accountant
- Budget officer H. C. Edge

Motorized division director T. J. Taylor
- Technical manager J. G. Toplis
- Production man. G. A. Fryer
- Sales manager J. M. Larcomba

Head of consultancy services C. N. Millidge

Personnel executive director R. G. Allen
- Training manager D. C. Taylor
- Staff manager
- Management services manager R. G. Farnworth
- Works engineering manager D. C. Redfern
- Works personnel manager F. Blackwell

Director of factories L. S. F. Charles
- Cycle production director J. Ward
- Toy production manager M. Pound
- Components contract Prod. director M. S. M. Smith
- Technical services director J. F. Harriman
- Contract sales director H. T. Shepherd

Sales and marketing director A. A. Hutchison
- Distribution transport man. R. G. Battesworth
- Home sales man. F. Donnelly
- Marketing man. P. C. Seales
- General export sales manager R. A. L. Roberts
- Export J. Cumming
- Carlton cycles K. R. O'Donegan

RALEIGH—THE WORLD'S LARGEST CYCLE MANUFACTURER AND EXPORTER

In 1966 the British cycle industry was the largest in the world and sold about 65% of its production abroad. Raleigh commanded a leading position in the industry, exporting over 70% of its total production, which comprised nearly all of the cycle exports from the United Kingdom and represented nearly half of all of the total bicycle exports of the whole world. Raleigh exported cycles to 140 different markets. Its closest competitors, the Japanese, sold in only about half as many export markets. (See Exhibits 7 and 8 for statement of financial condition.)

exhibit 3 **SPREAD OF BICYCLE EXPORT MARKETS 1962–1964**

Exporting Country	Number of Markets Served*		
	1962	1963	1964
United Kingdom (Raleigh)	138	140	140
Japan	31	83	77
France	39	35	34
Western Germany	24	18	22
Austria	19	21	22
Netherlands	8	11	11
Poland	17	25	n.a.

* Minor markets are not shown.
SOURCE: Company's records.

Of Raleigh's manufactured products of bicycles, bicycle components, mopeds, wheeled toys, and a reeled safety belt, the export sales of bicycles and bicycle components consistently formed over 70% of the company's turnover. In the period from 1951 to 1965 there had been shifts of great magnitude in the whole bicycle trade, and the world export market had been declining, but Raleigh's share of world exports had been increasing, as shown by the most recent figures available:

exhibit 4 **NUMBER OF BICYCLES**

Year	Raleigh Exports	World Exports	Raleigh Exports % World Exports
1961	1,322,000	3,006,000	44.0
1962	1,343,000	2,796,000	48.0
1963	1,542,000	2,981,000	51.7

SOURCE: Company's records.

Raleigh accounted for nearly all of the United Kingdom exports of bicycles:

exhibit 5   EXPORTS OF BICYCLES, UNITED KINGDOM, 1962–1964

Year	Raleigh Exports	U.K. Cycle Industry	Raleigh % of U.K. Cycle Exports
1962	£10,956,000	£11,405,000	96.1
1963	12,786,000	12,816,000	99.8
1964	9,338,000	9,523,000	98.1

SOURCE: Company's records.

exhibit 6   EXPORTS OF BICYCLES TO THE U. S. A., 1962–1964

Year	Raleigh Exports	U.K. Industry Exports	Raleigh % U.K. Industry	Raleigh U.S. Cycle Exports % Total Raleigh Cycle Exports
		By Value		
1962	£4,881,000	£4,577,000	100.0 +*	44.6
1963	5,299,000	5,740,000	92.3	41.4
1964	3,200,000	3,365,000	95.1	34.3
		By Units		
1962	636,000	596,000	100.0 +*	47.4
1963	695,000	753,000	92.3	45.0
1964	395,000	415,000	95.2	35.0

* The Raleigh figures are of goods involved; the United Kingdom figures are of goods shipped. This accounts for the anomaly of 1962.
SOURCE: Company's records.

Since 1951 there had been a rapid and steady decline in the world trade in bicycles, as import duties and restrictions had their effect and as developing nations nationalized their production. In 1951, the all-time year for bicycle production, the total British output was some 4 million machines. In 1965 it was 1,740,000 of which 1,128,000 were exported.

exhibit 7 RALEIGH INDUSTRIES LIMITED AND ITS SUBSIDIARIES

Consolidated balance sheet, 31st July, 1965

	£	£	31st July, 1964 £	31st July, 1964 £
Share capital (Note 3)	5,722,505		5,722,505	
Capital reserves (Note 4)	7,395,249		7,339,500	
Revenue reserve				
Unappropriated profit	987,529		543,311	
	14,105,283		13,596,316	
Future income tax				
1965–1966 assessment	31,500		549,500	
Overseas tax 1966–1967	39,000		39,000	
Corporation tax				
Payable 1st January 1967	860,500			
6% debenture stock 1978–1983 (Note 5)	3,283,857		3,332,618	
Loan from tube investments limited	3,771,013		4,934,668	
Total capital employed	£22,052,153		£22,434,102	

L. L. ROBERTS
B. C. DODSWORTH } *Directors*

	£	£	31st July, 1964 £	31st July, 1964 £
Fixed assets (Note 6)				
Freehold land and buildings	4,179,571		4,324,335	
Leasehold land and buildings	153,777		166,644	
Plant and machinery	1,324,102		1,631,127	
Other equipment	430,993	6,088,443	421,281	6,543,387
Goodwill (Note 7)		1,817,237		1,817,237
Investment in associated companies (at cost)		376,024		376,024
Current assets				
Stocks (Note 8)	6,259,665		6,421,611	
Debtors	10,674,563		10,153,737	
Current accounts with fellow subsidiaries	82,659		86,782	
Quoted investments (market value £26,231 (£28,580))	25,068		25,068	
Cash in banks and in hand	742,243	17,784,198	587,168	17,274,366
Deduct:				
Liabilities and provisions				
Trade creditors and accrued charges (Note 9)	2,598,442		2,658,400	
Current accounts with fellow subsidiaries	84,254		111,174	
Current taxation	726,610		607,706	
Preference dividend accrued	4,443		4,632	
Proposed ordinary dividend	600,000	4,013,749	195,000	3,576,912
Net current assets		13,770,449		13,697,454
Total net assets		£22,052,153		£22,434,102

381

exhibit **7A   RALEIGH INDUSTRIES LIMITED AND ITS SUBSIDIARIES**
Notes on accounts

1. Directors' emoluments

The emoluments of the Directors of Raleigh Industries Limited were as follows:

	1965 £	1964 £
Fees	500	333
Other emoluments	57,259	61,916
Payment on cessation of employment	8,500	10,000
	£66,259	£72,249

	1965 £	1964 £
2. Taxation		
Based on the profit of the year:		
Income tax	(105,290)	446,138
Corporation tax	860,500	
Profits tax		177,132
Overseas tax	98,979	67,145
Exceptional items:		
Additional income tax 1965–1966	34,000	
Prior years' overprovisions	(17,944)	(70,826)
	£870,245	£619,589

Taxation is stated after estimated relief of £27,000 (£56,000) from investment allowances. Corporation tax has been calculated at 40%.

	At 31st July, 1965	
	Authorized £	Issued and Fully Paid £
3. Share capital		
6 per cent cumulative preference shares of £1 each	1,000,000	1,000,000
Ordinary shares of £1 each	6,500,000	4,722,505
	£7,500,000	£5,722,505

There has been no change during the year.

4. Capital reserves	£	£
Share premium account		
At 31st July, 1964 and 1965		77,838
Debenture redemption reserve		
At 31st July, 1964	167,382	
Appropriation from profit and loss account	48,761	
At 31st July, 1965		216,143
Surplus on realization of fixed assets		
At 31st July, 1964	597,122	
Surplus on sale of land and buildings	15,988	
At 31st July, 1965		613,110
Surplus on revaluation of buildings in 1948		
At 31st July, 1964 and 1965		160,926
General reserve		
At 31st July, 1964 and 1965 (being the total other reserves of Raleigh Industries Limited at the date		

exhibit **7A**   (continued)

of acquisition in 1960 by Tube Investments Limited)	6,306,496
Total capital reserves of Raleigh Industries Limited at 31st July, 1965	7,374,513
Total capital reserves at Raleigh Industries Limited at 31st July, 1964	*7,309,764*
General reserve—subsidiary companies	
At 31st July, 1964 and 1965 (being the total other reserves of subsidiary companies at the date of acquisition in 1960 by Tube Investments Limited)	20,736
Total capital reserves of the group at 31st July, 1965	£7,395,249
Total capital reserves of the group at 31st July, 1964	*£7,330,500*

5. 6 per cent debenture stock 1978–1983

£3,500,000 6 per cent debenture stock 1978–1983 was issued at £97 per cent during 1957–1958 and is repayable at par on 31st July, 1983, or at the option of the company after 31st July, 1978. There are provisions for annual sinking fund payments, commencing in the year ended 31st July, 1961, designed to secure the repayment of one-half of the principal amount of the stock at par by 31st July, 1983, through annual drawings or purchases by the company in the market. The sinking fund payment this year amounted to £47,281 and this has been used to redeem £48,761 of stock. The relative sum has been transferred from profit and loss account to debenture redemption reserve.

6. Fixed assets

Italic figures relate to the previous year.

	Valuation or Cost at 31st July, 1964, £	Acquisitions, £	Disposals, £	Valuation or Cost at 31st July, 1965, £	Accumulated Depreciation, £	Net Book Value, £
Freehold land and buildings	5,604,446	28,707	177,155	5,455,998	1,276,427	4,179,571
	6,106,750	*48,439*	*550,743*	*5,604,446*	*1,280,111*	*4,324,335*
Leasehold land and buildings	241,964	3,280	31,508	213,736	59,959	153,777
	252,941	....	*10,977*	*241,964*	*75,320*	*166,644*
Plant and machinery	6,233,525	86,738	197,161	6,123,102	4,799,000	1,324,102
	6,290,983	*266,587*	*324,045*	*6,233,525*	*4,602,398*	*1,631,127*
Other equipment	1,301,097	137,577	85,871	1,352,803	921,810	430,993
	1,237,040	*148,392*	*84,335*	*1,301,097*	*879,816*	*421,281*
Group totals	£13,381,032	256,302	491,695	13,145,639	7,057,196	6,088,443
	£13,887,714	*463,418*	*970,100*	*13,381,032*	*6,837,645*	*6,543,387*
Raleigh Industires Ltd. totals	£13,093,583	242,706	485,875	12,850,414	6,878,874	5,971,540
	£13,592,044	*460,423*	*958,884*	*13,093,583*	*6,667,676*	*6,425,907*

exhibit **7A** (continued)

The detailed figures for Raleigh Industries Limited do not differ materially from those shown above for the group.

The net book value at 31st July, 1965, includes £182,284 for assets which were independently valued on 1st July 1948. Otherwise fixed assets are stated at original cost to the companies now forming the group.

Depreciation is calculated separately for each fixed asset (excluding freehold land) on the straight line basis to amortize the cost of the asset by the end of its useful life.

The accumulated depreciation includes provisions made by certain companies before they joined the group.

7. Goodwill

This comprises the cost of goodwill, trade-marks, etc., purchased together with the excess of the purchase consideration of shares in subsidiary companies over the book value of their tangible assets at the date of acquisition.

8. Stocks

Stocks, comprising raw materials, work in progress, finished goods and stores, are stated, consistently with previous years, at the lower of:

(a) Cost (including an appropriate proportion of overhead expenditure), and

(b) Net realizable value.

9. Outside shareholders' interest

Outside shareholders' interest in the share capital and reserves of subsidiary companies, £555 (£555) has been included in trade creditors. Such shareholders' interest in the profit of the year £35 (£35) has been excluded from the account on page 6.

10. Contracts for capital expenditure

There were commitments for capital expenditure at 31st July, 1965, of approximately £142,000 (£50,000) not provided for in these accounts.

11. Foreign currencies

Assets and liabilities have been converted at rates of exchange ruling at the date of the balance sheet.

MANUFACTURING

In 1952 the Raleigh management had expected sales to continue to rise, and Raleigh made a £1.5 million ($4,260,000) addition to its plants. In 1957 it built another 20-acre, £5 million ($14,200,000) addition, which had been planned in 1953, but by the time this addition was completed sales had fallen sharply. In 1957, for the first time in 20 years, Raleigh was constrained to reduce the work week for three months. In 1958 it introduced a four-day week.

In 1959 Mr. Wilson, chairman, brought into the company as head of factories Mr. Leslie Roberts, a dynamic manager, who had been a manufacturing executive with Rootes Motors. Later Mr. Roberts became managing director. Mr. Roberts' first major objective was to rationalize manufacturing. The new combined group employed 14,500

exhibit 8   **RALEIGH INDUSTRIES LIMITED AND ITS SUBSIDIARIES**
Consolidated profit and loss and appropriation accounts, year ended 31st July, 1965

	£	£	31st July, 1964 £	£
Profit of the group	2,742,515		2,189,111	
Deduct: depreciation of fixed assets	568,035		601,234	
		2,174,480		1,587,877
Other income				
From associated companies	19,591		748	
From quoted investments	1,995		1,746	
		21,586		2,494
		2,196,066		1,590,371
Interest payable				
On debenture stock	197,031		200,695	
On loan from parent company			11,228	
		197,031		211,923
		1,999,035		1,378,448
Exceptional items				176,470
Profit before taxation		1,999,035		1,201,978
Taxation (Note 2)		870,245		619,589
Net profit of the group for the year				
carried forward (Note 9)		1,128,790		582,389
Net profit of the group for the year of which £1,059,356 (£500,732) is dealt with in the accounts of Raleigh Industries Limited)		1,128,790		582,389
Unappropriated profit brought forward from previous years				
Raleigh Industries Limited	248,241		24,206	
Subsidiary companies	295,070		231,413	
		543,311		237,619
Profit available for appropriation		1,672,101		820,008
Appropriations				
Capital reserves (Note 4)	48,761		44,947	
Dividends (*less* income tax)				
On 6 per cent preference shares	35,811		36,750	
Proposed on ordinary shares	600,000		195,000	
		684,572		276,697
Unappropriated profit carried forward				
Raleigh Industries Limited	623,025		248,241	
Subsidiary companies	364,504		295,070	
Total unappropriated profit of the group as shown in the consolidated balance sheet		£987,529		£543,311

people in nine widely separated factories, each with its own management, with a total floor area of 4.5 million square feet.

During the years which followed the merger, the number of plants was reduced from nine to five by disposing of those Birmingham plants which duplicated Raleigh's Nottingham operations. All tubing, saddle, and replacement parts manufacture was concentrated in the remaining Birmingham plants. All cycle manufacture (intermingled with toy production) was concentrated in the 60-acre Nottingham plant complex, which remained intact. The number of employees was reduced to 9,000.

Mr. Roberts' rationalization program was continued by Mr. L. S. F. Charles, whom Mr. Roberts brought into the company. Mr. Charles introduced more automatic processing in plating transportation, in heat treatment, and in enameling. On the premise that bicycle costs consisted of about 50% materials and 15% labor, Mr. Charles scrutinized intensely those processes which tended to be wasteful of materials. He introduced electrostatic spraying; brazing of tubing joints; scintering moulding; the use of plastic where possible; and cold instead of hot forging. Time study and piece rates were critically reviewed; factory layout and material handling were under constant study; and design engineers focused their attention on economies in product designs. As a result, the over-all consumption of material per unit was reduced by 10%.

In 1966 production was still at such a low level that there was 20% excess plant capacity at Nottingham. The excess was spread throughout many departments of the plant and therefore could not be sold or leased. To utilize the excess capacity the company sought custom manufacturing jobs. These consisted of straight machine work for some leading auto makers, forming tubing for a perambulator manufacturer, and a variety of small jobs. In 1966 contract work accounted for about 10% of the company's total turnover.

COSTS AND PRICES

Raleigh prices were determined by a factory-cost formula, and the resulting price was shaded to meet competitive prices, aiming to earn a minimum 10% net profit. The Raleigh management had statistics which indicated that in a three-year period the retail price index showed a rise of 14%, and wage rates in the engineering industry increased 22%. Abroad, pricing policies tended to be dictated by distributor competition, and United Kingdom cost increases could not be passed off to foreign customers via raised prices in countries where no cost-price rise had taken place. Although Raleigh's long line of models included several price categories, all Raleigh cycles were high quality, and its prices tended to be 8 to 10% above competitors'. As the company's sales turnover fell from year to year, it was observed that the fall was greatest in those products which had the highest margins.

Raleigh had statistical data which indicated that bicycle prices on an index basis in Great Britain (1954 = 100) were standing at 131.4 in 1963. This compared with 119.8 for all manufactured products, 70.9 for refrigerators, 97.4 for washing machines, and 112.6 for vacuum cleaners. Although these products were not directly competitive, they were a call on the consumer's disposable income, and they possibly had more attraction than a bicycle. Research indicated that children were eager to buy bicycles, and most objections to buying came from parents, mainly on price.

Purchase tax in England constituted 14.8% of the retail price. This meant that in every £20 ($56.80) the customer paid about £3 ($8.52) in purchase tax.

THE UNITED STATES MARKET FOR BICYCLES

The United States was by far the largest single bicycle market in the world. It had been Raleigh's largest export market for years. In the United States Raleigh had popularized the lightweight, "sport," English-style bicycles so successfully that these models took the market away from the old-style, heavy-framed American cycles.

Between 1950 and 1956 the Raleigh share of cycles imported into the United States decreased by over 60% and Raleigh's sales there declined every year thereafter, in spite of the fact that total cycle sales in the United States rose steadily throughout the period from 2.5 million in 1960 to 5 million in 1965.

The United States was essentially a "price" market, and Raleigh's major customers were mail-order houses and chain stores which bought in mass quantities on a price basis. Raleigh's declining sales resulted from a sharp increase in the activity of America's own cycle makers, who were now contesting the market Raleigh had pioneered there for lightweight cycles. Most of Raleigh's mass-volume customers had switched their purchases to local producers or to other importers who were making cycles to the customers' specifications under their private labels and doing it for prices which were sometimes below Raleigh's factory cost. To Raleigh, with its premium-priced line, this was marginal business, but nevertheless valuable. As recently as 1954 Raleigh had sold about 1 million cycles in the United States.

The United States duty was $22\frac{1}{2}\%$ for a cycle with less than 26 inch wheels and weighing less than 36 pounds. For larger cycles the duty was $11\frac{1}{4}\%$. This meant that Raleigh typically paid a duty of $11\frac{1}{4}\%$ plus about 5% for freight costs, giving the local manufacturer making the same cycle an advantage of $16\frac{1}{4}\%$.

In 1966 Raleigh management made a policy decision to limit its volume in the general United States market and to concentrate on the sale of its Raleigh-labeled cycles and the premium-branded lines, which were to be sold through the retail dealer trade. Raleigh also planned to continue to sell to the smaller chain stores and the minor mail-order houses. In doing this, Raleigh realized that it would be cutting in half its potential United States dollar sales volume.

Raleigh had always sold substantial quantities of components in the United States. Increasing emphasis was to be placed on this component business.

THE EUROPEAN MARKET FOR BICYCLES

A major market area of the world in which Raleigh bicycle sales had been minimal was western Europe, particularly in the countries of the Common Market. The recent sharp drop in bicycle sales had been in the United Kingdom, but not in Europe generally. In 1966 it was estimated that Germany had a sales potential of 1.5 million cycles versus 600,000 for the United Kingdom. Raleigh's lack of sales in western Europe was due partly to tariff barriers, which were generally about 20%, and partly, the management admitted, to sheer neglect.

In 1965 Raleigh had a market survey of western Europe made by international consultants, and it followed this with a survey made by its own staff. Based upon its findings, a European sales promotion tour was undertaken, featuring the slogan, "Go Gold Medal Cycling." The tour covered Belgium, Holland, Germany, Switzerland, Denmark, and Sweden, and promoted the RSW 16 and the Compact (see following sections of the case).

Raleigh did not now have a plant in the Common Market, and the management looked upon Europe as a whole as an unexploited territory. The failure of the Common Market negotiations had been a disappointment to the Raleigh management. Pending the possible entrance of the United Kingdom into the ECC, Raleigh planned to make every effort to become established in the Common Market as soon as possible, in spite of the 20% tariff hurdle. The thinking of the management was that if this could be done, then if England did join the Common Market, Raleigh would already be established and have a 20% advantage. There were also long-range plans to establish a plant in Germany, but the plans were still in the discussion stage.

THE MOULTON

There had been no change in the basic design of the bicycle since the turn of the century. The lightweight English sports model had become the predominant design in the bicycle market. Its large-size wheels were considered to be an engineering necessity, since large wheels took up road shocks.

Alex Moulton was a British Motors Corporation design engineer who had developed the famous BMC Hydrolastic Suspension shock absorbers. In about 1960 it occurred to Mr. Moulton that there would be many advantages in a small-wheeled bicycle if it were not for the shocks due to the small wheels. Moulton designed a short-based, 16-inch-wheel bicycle with unique rubber suspension shock absorbers in both forks and with handle bars and seat which were adjustable to accommodate riders of all sizes.

Moulton brought his design to Raleigh, which saw possibilities in it and permitted Moulton to use their design laboratory to do further developmental work. Raleigh finally decided against producing it; Moulton took his cycle to his employers at British Motors and persuaded them to manufacture it.

Moulton Cycles Limited's first cycle to be marketed appeared in 1963 bearing the brand name Moulton (see Exhibit 9). It found immediate consumer acceptance and was hailed by the industry as the first new bicycle design in 70 years. Selling in only a limited area around London, the Moulton achieved an estimated turnover of 40,000 units in its first year, and volume increased each year thereafter. In succeeding years Moulton added several other models to his line, including one model

exhibit 9

constructed largely of aluminum alloy, another with a six-speed gear-shift, another which was collapsible for stowing in a car trunk, and another with an automatic gearshift.

It was expected that Moulton's sales in the 1965 cycle year would be about 75,000 units.

RALEIGH'S MARKET RESEARCH ON BICYCLES

In 1963 Raleigh commissioned a study of basic motivation and attitudes towards bicycles. The profile of the English cyclist which emerged characterized him as associated with poverty, low social status, and hard times. The bicycle was seen as the poor man's useful and valuable friend. Bikes were usually pictured as old and worn, and their dilapidated condition did not matter to the owner.

In 1964 Raleigh carried out the most comprehensive product research regarding bicycles that had ever been undertaken in the United Kingdom. The project included product testing of both 16- and 20-inch models.

From this research project it was found that 75% of all bicycles were bought for children under 15, whereas 62% of Moulton owners were over 25 years of age. Only 25% of Moulton owners were children in the 8 to 15 age group. Some 58% of Moulton owners came from car-owning families and 13% from families owning two cars. Prior to the introduction of the Moulton, only 55% of the Moulton owners had wanted a bicycle, yet 95% of the owners were pleased that they had bought one.

Commenting on the research findings, Mr. Peter Seales, Raleigh's marketing manager said, "For years the two people who rang the bell on the bicycle shop most have been the school child and the working-class adult. They wanted something just to take them to school and work. The profile of today's cyclist is quite different: highly educated, with sophisticated ideas concerning dress, style of living, and careers. We believe we have discovered a market segment heretofore uncatered for."

THE RSW 16 AND THE COMPACT BICYCLES

Based upon its research findings, Raleigh developed what it described as an entirely new concept in cycling, the RSW 16—from Raleigh Small Wheel 16. (The names Elite and Citizen had been considered but discarded because it was thought that they might eventually lose their identification with Raleigh.) (See Exhibit 10.)

The RSW 16 was extremely compact, being 4 to 6 inches (10 to 15 centimeters) lower in height and 11 inches (28 centimeters) shorter in over-all length than the typical standard cycle. This greatly enhanced handling, maneuverability, and storage characteristics. The same design was equally suitable for men or women, boys or girls. The handle bar and saddle bar positions were adjusted to permit use by children of eight or nine years, and adults up to 6 feet 4 inches (1 meter 93 centimeters) in height. This made it a cycle which could be used by the entire family.

The RSW 16 had specially designed 16-inch (41 centimeters) balloon tires of 35# pounds per square inch (2.44 kilos per square centimeter) to give a smooth, comfortable ride. It was equipped with a three-speed Sturmey-Archer gearshift, dyno hub-operated lighting, a prop-stand, carrier, and a large detachable carrier-bag, yet was considerably lighter than any standard cycle. Brake and lighting cables were almost entirely concealed.

exhibit **10**

Along with the RSW 16 the company developed the Raleigh Compact, a folding bicycle with no loose components, whose folding actions required only 10 seconds (see Exhibit 11). The main frame member folded in the shotgun manner, providing instant locking and perfect rigidity. It was necessary to press only one lever to release the mechanism and fold the bicycle. The specifications of the Compact were identical to that of the RSW 16, except that the cables did not pass through the frame, and lighting was not included as standard equipment. When folded, the size of the cycle was 38 × 30 × 15 inches (97 × 77 × 38 centimeters), permitting it to be easily fitted into the average car trunk.

PROMOTION OF THE RSW 16 AND RALEIGH CYCLES

Mr. Peter Seales had proposed that Raleigh exploit the developing leisure market, pointing out that camping, caravaning, boating, and other leisure sports were collecting an increasing amount of consumer

exhibit 11

spending each year. Raleigh salesmen and retail dealers were puzzled at the thought of projecting their cycles, with their old-fashioned image, into this leisure-society spending picture (see Exhibit 12).

It was believed that the bicycle was underpublicized as a product and that it was meeting progressively more skillful competition from other consumer items such as tape recorders, transistor radios, and record players. Raleigh had information which indicated that producers of these products were spending up to 8% of their sales dollar on advertising. Raleigh was spending 4%. The United Kingdom cycle industry spent less than 1%.

With the launching of the RSW 16 in 1965, the leisure-market theme was revived. "To help place our bicycles in the leisure-society picture," said Mr. Seales, "we need the assistance of the trend-setters, the people who already have four-stroke motor mowers, the *Sunday Times* readers, the people who have had movie cameras for years. These are the people who can set the lead with the RSW 16, and tens of thousands of people will be willing to follow. All of our RSW 16 marketing launch is aimed at people who would not normally be in the market for a cycle. We

exhibit 12
THE NEW PROMOTION THEME
"All sorts and sizes of people can ride a horse; so it is with the Raleigh RSW 16."

mean to increase our business, and not merely provide a substitute shape which would still limit the number of bicycles sold each year in this country."

Mr. Seales asserted that his own usage of advertising was not intuitive but was on an actuarial basis. Raleigh's future advertising was to use "glamour" themes to combat the social inferiority of the bicycle. Pictorial advertisement featured beauty queens, stage and screen celebrities, equestrians in riding costume, golfers, hunters, and airline hostesses, all riding the RSW 16. Typical of these celebrities were Leslie Langley,

Miss World; Peter Thompson, 1965 British Open Golf Champion; Uffa Fox, world-famous yachtsman; Graham Hill, noted racing driver; and Mary Quant, the "darling of the smart fashion set."

The question of the price of the RSW 16 was strongly influenced by the research findings, which indicated that Moulton owners had been willing to pay a high price. Since Raleigh was aiming its new promotions at the upper-income groups, it believed that it could raise the price considerably above conventional bike prices. The RSW 16 was introduced at £30 9s ($86.46). The Moulton price was £30 ($85.20).

The projected sale of the RSW 16 was 75,000 for the first year. At the end of an eight-month period in 1965–1966, 80% of the quota had been achieved.

MOTORIZED PRODUCTS

The Raleigh management had been observing the moped (motorized pedicycle) market with interest for a number of years, because motorized cycle sales in the United Kingdom had been very small in comparison with the business on the Continent, where sales were flourishing. In 1958 Raleigh entered the field with a low-priced utility vehicle which raised the United Kingdom industry sales from 46,000 in 1958 to 115,000 in 1959 (see Exhibit 13). Pleased with this initial success, the management stated that it saw a bright future for mopeds and that eventually the production of mopeds might become just as essential to the company's economy as the production of pedicycles. It also envisioned the growing demand spreading to Africa and Asia.

In 1960 Raleigh's moped sales fell sharply. Technical difficulties had developed in a crankshaft in the engine, which was purchased from a French manufacturer. Furthermore, the government had reinstituted credit restrictions in the form of tighter hire-purchase requirements. "There can be no doubt," said Mr. George Hamilton Wilson, then chairman of Raleigh, "that the moped has yet to be accepted in this country as it has been on the Continent, for a number of reasons. For one thing, until recently, no United Kingdom manufacturer has produced a moped to a quality specification and price capable of competing with the machines produced on the Continent. We have restrictive legislation governing licensing, driving tests, and the minimum age at which the tests may be taken. In recent years our government has pursued a "stop-and-go" policy with respect to hire-purchase terms. Finally, we have

exhibit 13

Automatic MkII

A more powerful version of the RUNABOUT.
Engine power output is increased by 30% (1.7
B.H.P. at 5,000 R.P.M.) and a telescopic front
fork is fitted to provide extra comfort; Automatic clutch; Adjustable handlebar and saddle;
Double dipping headlamp; Full width hub
brakes, front and rear; 1⅜ imp. gallon (6.2 litre)
fuel tank with reserve tap; Electric horn.
Colour finish: Pearl grey and charcoal grey
enamel. Bright chromium plated fittings.

Supermatic

This is the high performance
machine in the range. Engine output is increased to 2.66 B.H.P. at
5,500 R.P.M.; Automatic clutch;
Automatic transmission; Swing-
ing arm front and rear suspension;
Adjustable handlebars; Dual seat
and pillion foot rests. Electric
horn. Colour finish: Carmine Red
enamel, bright chromium plated
fittings.

RUNABOUT

An elegant machine, fitted with the 1.39 B.H.P.
version of the basic two-stroke engine; Automatic clutch; Adjustable handlebar and saddle;
Sturdy, bicycle type front forks; 1⅜ imp. gallon
(6.2 litre) fuel tank fitted with reserve tap;
Single beam headlamp; Calliper front brakes
with full width hub brakes at the rear. Colour
finish: Pearl grey and Raleigh green enamel.
Bright chromium plated fittings.

RALEIGH

MOPEDS

exhibit 13 (continued)

RM6
Runabout

RM8
Automatic MKII

RALEIGH ™.

a highly efficient and co-ordinated public transport system in this country."

Although United Kingdom industry sales in general had fallen, regardless of make, Raleigh's sales had not dropped as much as others, and Raleigh continued to gain in market share. Mr. Wilson was convinced that mopeds and scooters would remain relatively unpopular in the United Kingdom, because Continental competitors were far ahead in development and design. To match Continental standards Raleigh entered into agreements with the Société des Ateliers de la Motobecane to manufacture under license the Mobylette type of moped, a leading world seller, and with the Società per Azioni Edoardo Bianchi to make a Bianchi-type scooter, one of the most attractively styled. Both were to sell in the popular price category.

Total industry demand in the United Kingdom fell to 42,000 in 1962. At this time Raleigh was nearing completion of a moped design and development project on which its engineers had worked for several years. In 1963 Raleigh re-entered the moped market with a range of four new machines, designed for specialized applications suitable for post-office, police, and other service duties. Only two major components, the engine and frame pressings, were imported from France; the wheels, brakes, lighting equipment, and all other components were designed and manufactured in Nottingham and Birmingham. The new Raleigh moped, called the Runabout, was low-priced, and with it Raleigh again proceeded to lead the field in the United Kingdom. In 1965 the United Kingdom industry consisted of a number of small assemblers of imported components and Raleigh, who was the only major producer. Raleigh was turning out over 40,000 mopeds a year, which was 66% of the industry turnover.

In 1964 Raleigh exported about 1,500 mopeds; in 1965 about 3,000. This was at a time when a single major European manufacturer was exporting 140,000 mopeds a year. Early in 1966 Raleigh launched a full-scale sales drive aimed at capturing the untapped markets in Britain's Commonwealth countries, the Americas, and certain European markets. It was expected that a greatly increased output would go to those markets where, through the cycle side of its business, Raleigh had long-established distribution outlets. Some dealers were not convinced that this strategy was sound, believing that it was a mistake to mix bicycles and powered machines under the same roof. The thinking was that if bicycles predominated, moped customers would not be attracted; if powered cycles predominated, bicycle sales would suffer.

In 1966 the United Kingdom license age for motor bikes was still 16, versus 14 in Europe generally. Stiff driver tests were compulsory. Licensing costs were high enough to discourage low-income customers. Hire-purchase regulations continued to fluctuate, with the required deposit seesawing between 10 and 20% of the purchase price. Abroad, many developing nations, whose people found cycles attractive, were nationalizing manufacture.

In 1966 mopeds and toys accounted for about 10% of the company's turnover.

TOYS

Raleigh's first major departure from cycle manufacture came in 1960 with the introduction, under the Sunbeam label, of a line of wheeled toys (see Exhibit 14). The line included tricycles, bicycles, toy wheelbarrows, scooters, gocarts, and roller skates. There were sizes to accom-

exhibit 14

TODDLERS TO TEN-YEAR-OLDS

THEY ALL WANT A

RALEIGH made SUNBEAM

Says Dr. Sunbeam

modate children of all ages. Additions to the toy range were constantly being studied. In doing so Raleigh worked with nurseries, where new toys were "play-value" measured. These practical tests showed, for example, that the coaster feature on a chain-driven tricycle frustrated small children, who would drive up to an obstruction and then find themselves unable to reverse. Elimination of the coaster and substitution of a direct drive allowed the child to back up. It also lowered the cost of the tricycle.

For many years Lines Brothers had been the major producer of toys in the United Kingdom. Lines made complete ranges of all kinds of toys. It was believed that many retailers welcomed the entrance of Raleigh into the toy field, for they resented the dominance of Lines. Raleigh toys received good initial acceptance from toy dealers.

The Raleigh management eventually came to believe that their original toys had too much built-in quality. The high-quality features had been deliberate as an introductory strategy: ball and roller bearings, chromium and nickel finishes, high-quality paints and finishes. "Our tactic," said a Raleigh sales executive, "was to build 8 shillings worth ($1.12) of extra quality into each toy and sell it for a price that was 3 shillings (42¢) higher." From year to year the company retreated from that policy. By 1966 its quality was still somewhat better than that of competition, and its prices were only slightly higher. Retail dealers were still of the opinion that Raleigh's high-quality toys lasted too long.

In the United Kingdom, Sunbeam toys were sold through the same retailers who handled Raleigh cycles. The attempt was made to use cycle distribution channels abroad, but the toys proved too bulky for their relatively low value to permit shipment to be made economically over long distances. Consideration was given to shipping them completely knocked down, which would permit the nesting of parts compactly. This, however, would require design changes, such as substituting nuts and bolts for many rivet applications to permit their reassembly abroad by simple means. This meant adding to production costs at home. "To gain 9,000 unit sales in Nigeria," said a Raleigh export executive, "might cost us our profit on the sale of 90,000 units in the United Kingdom."

THE BROOKS SAFETY BELT

In August of 1962 Raleigh's subsidiary, the Brooks Saddle Company, entered into an agreement with Teleflex Products Limited to produce and market under the Brooks trade name a safety harness on the inertia reel principle for motorists. During the war the Brooks firm had produced substantial quantities of harnesses for parachutists, and the new belt was a modified version of the inertia harnesses used by military air crews and commercial pilots. The unique feature of the new belt was an inertia reel which permitted freedom of movement yet locked and secured its wearer into the seat upon impact or violent deceleration. By virtue of the reel principle, the belt automatically adjusted itself to persons of any size; there was no feeling of being "trussed up," to which many motorists objected, but the belt would lock securely under any sudden forward movement. When uncoupled, the surplus belt would automatically rewind into the reel (see Exhibit 15).

After considerable developmental work, Raleigh agreed to produce the belt. Research among auto and accessory dealers had indicated that there was a demand for such an accessory. The Minister of Transport had indicated his intention of making safety belts standard required fittings on all new motor cars, although he had no authority to compel motorists to wear them.

The Brooks Company did not market its belts through Raleigh cycle channels; the entire output was sold to a distributor who wholesaled both auto and bike accessories. Attempts to get new car manufacturers to adopt the belt were unsuccessful. British Motors had been on the verge of adopting them but had finally decided not to do so. In 1966 the only sale of the belts was to individual consumers, who bought them through auto accessory retailers and had to have them fitted to their cars.

The Brooks belt retailed for £6 15s. ($19.14). Its chief competitors were the Romack at £4 7s. 6d. ($12.43) and the Raydyot at £4 4s. ($11.93). The Raleigh management conceded that the Brooks belt had not made much of an impact upon the market but had given the Raleigh management some experience in diversification.

CYCLE COMPONENTS

A bicycle could be divided into two basic kinds of parts: (1) parts which were technically simple to make, involved little engineering, and were relatively low in cost, such as frames, fenders, spokes, handle bars, and carriers; and (2) intricate parts, which required sophisticated product engineering, exacting metallurgy specifications, and precision manu-

EXHIBIT 15

A FTER a period of great secrecy extending over several years, a revolutionary type of car safety belt incorporating an inertia reel which permits complete freedom of movement, yet which locks and secures its wearer safely into the seat upon impact or violent deceleration, was demonstrated in public for the first time on August 13th.

The new belt, introduced by J. B. Brooks Ltd., can be used in every type of road vehicle ranging from family saloon and sports car to high speed touring coaches and heavy commercial vehicles.

Mr. Ernest Marples, Minister of Transport, has indicated his intention to make safety belts standard fittings for new motor cars, but also that he has no power to compel motorists to wear them. Because it allows complete freedom of movement, the Brooks belt will be welcomed by many people who have previously been averse to wearing safety belts because of a feeling of restriction.

BROOKS INTRODUCE CAR SAFETY BELT

This new belt is a modified version of the well known inertia harness currently used by the military air crews and pilots of leading airlines, such as BEA and BOAC. The patent inertia reel is the product of Teleflex—a firm which has had a vast amount of experience in the aircraft equipment field. Research on the car inertia reel included tests up to 26 G retardation.

Brooks have also had experience in the exacting aircraft equipment field, for during the war they were responsible for supplying the harness of thousands of parachutes.

One of the outstanding characteristics of the Brooks Reel Safety Belt is the freedom of movement allowed. There is no feeling of being 'trussed up', all controls can be easily reached and the driver can lean forward (at halt signs, for example) without restriction. But under impact or violent deceleration, the reel immediately locks.

A feature of the belt is the two-way buckle which is completely foolproof, being fully operative whichever way it is fastened and which is easily released by a flick of the finger.

exhibit 15   (continued)

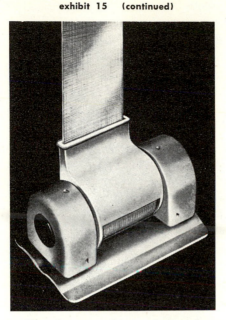

The other great advantage is that when
not in use the reel automatically winds the
surplus webbing away, but keeps it always
ready to hand, and also avoids entangling
the feet or trapping the harness in the door
thereby keeping the webbing clean and free
from 'scuffing'. Due to its flexibility, it does
not crease clothing and it is immediately
adjustable to any man, woman or youngster.
In fact, 'Brooks take Reel care of you!'

facturing, such as gears, hubs, generators, brakes, gearshifts, sprockets,
and wheel rims. A single cycle had well over 1,000 individual parts,
which could be combined into some 8,000 differentiations in the completed cycle. Most components were standardized and interchangeable.

For decades Raleigh had sold not only completed cycles but also component parts to other cycle manufacturers. In a period of fifty years,
this business had grown to such proportions that by 1960 almost every
country in the world which had local cycle manufacture imported Raleigh components. In the course of the growth of its components business, Raleigh had developed solid and friendly relationships with virtually every manufacturer of bicycles in the world. Raleigh completed-
cycle sales had been declining, partly because many emerging nations
were building their own cycle plants and partly because importers in developed countries were discovering that they could produce Raleigh-type

cycles of their own manufacture at lower cost. In each of these instances the new cycle manufacturers looked to Raleigh to supply them with at least a portion of their component parts.

The simple components were typically large in bulk, heavy in weight, and relatively low in value, making them economically unsuited for shipment over long distance. The intricate components, on the other hand, were small in size, light in weight, and high in value. Local manufacturers found it easy to make the simple components. The intricate components, however, required a large investment in product engineering, machinery, and equipment. Furthermore, Raleigh, with its huge production, was able to utilize mass production techniques to turn out its quality components at costs which small producers could not match.

Threatened with the permanent loss of overseas completed-cycle sales, Raleigh decided to put concentrated effort behind the sale of components. Its objective was to have every cycle manufacturer in the world use components manufactured by Raleigh. This was to be achieved by (1) a considerable advertising expenditure allocated to advertising components; (2) a royalty agreement with the local manufacturer giving him the right to use the Raleigh names and trademarks on his completed cycles, conditional upon certain specific components and a certain percentage of the total components per cycle being Raleigh components made in the United Kingdom; and (3) Raleigh, where necessary, engaging in local manufacture itself, drawing supplies of components from the United Kingdom to the extent that this was allowed by the local government. Raleigh believed that by this strategy it could permanently sustain production in its United Kingdom plants. Especially promising were certain components which were already world-famous, such as the Sturmey-Archer range of gears, brakes, and lighting equipment (see Exhibit 16). The percentage of profit was also higher on these types of components than on the simple low-value parts.

The Raleigh management was aware that component sales and completed cycle sales might become competitive with each other. A local producer might assemble a cycle largely from Raleigh components and market it, using the Raleigh brand names, in the same markets where Raleigh was itself selling its completed cycles manufactured in Nottingham. Sometimes foreign competitors sought deliberately to capitalize on the Raleigh brand names. A Malaysian distributor, for example, assembled cycles from components bought from many companies. He used

exhibit 16

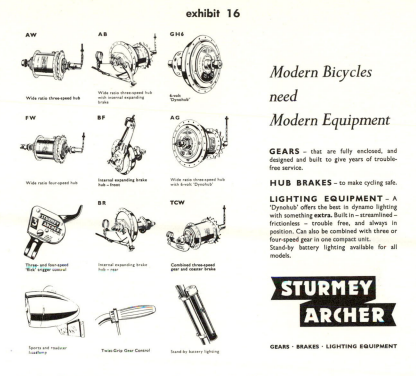

AW
Wide ratio three-speed hub

AB
Wide ratio three-speed hub with internal expanding brake

GH6
6-volt 'Dynohub'

FW
Wide ratio four-speed hub

BF
Internal expanding brake hub – front

AG
Wide ratio three-speed hub with 6-volt 'Dynohub'

Three- and four-speed 'flick' trigger control

BR
Internal expanding brake hub – rear

TCW
Combined three-speed gear and coaster brake

Sports and roadster headlamp

Twist-Grip Gear Control

Stand-by battery lighting

Modern Bicycles

need

Modern Equipment

GEARS – that are fully enclosed, and designed and built to give years of trouble-free service.

HUB BRAKES – to make cycling safe.

LIGHTING EQUIPMENT – A 'Dynohub' offers the best in dynamo lighting with something **extra**. Built in – streamlined – frictionless – trouble free, and always in position. Can also be combined with three or four-speed gear in one compact unit.
Stand-by battery lighting available for all models.

STURMEY ARCHER

GEARS · BRAKES · LIGHTING EQUIPMENT

only the Raleigh frame, but he used the Raleigh nameplate. Through legal action Raleigh stopped him from doing so.

Although Raleigh knew of no means of completely eliminating the danger of intracompetitive conflicts, it attempted some measure of control by regulating the use of its brand names. On all Raleigh-produced assembled cycles the components were Raleigh brand-name labeled. Its Phillips subsidiary had long been engaged in the production of components under the Phillips name, which was continued, and the Phillips name was also permitted on Raleigh-produced cycles. Sturmey-Archer parts and Brooks saddles everywhere bore their brand names, whether on Raleigh cycles or competitors' cycles, but all other components sold to competitors bore no labels at all. Neither would Raleigh put another cycle maker's name on Raleigh-made parts, but under pressure from very large customers, Raleigh was beginning to make exceptions to this rule.

The production of completed cycles made up the majority of Raleigh's turnover, but its sale of components in the export market was growing steadily. Raleigh produced components and accessories for its own com-

pleted cycles, for the replacement market, and for sale to other manufacturers. Of those components which were not made for use on Raleigh
completed cycles, the ratio of production was one part for replacements
to three parts produced for other manufacturers.

DISTRIBUTION CHANNELS

Raleigh sold its products in the world markets through independent
wholesale distributors, and in some instances through its own selling
companies or agents. Occasionally it sold directly from its Nottingham
headquarters to mail-order houses, chain stores, or department stores,
but this was exceptional; most Raleigh sales in the world markets were
made through wholesalers.

Distributors were usually of necessity fairly large-sized trading firms,
since they were required to carry costly inventories of cycles and components and had to finance extensions of credit to their retail customers,
often for a year at a time in those export markets where the economy
depended upon a single farm crop. In Mauretia a whole year's sales
might depend on whether there was a good sugar crop; in another area
it might be maize. Many distributors in Africa, the Far East, and the
East Indies were old, established trading companies which handled general merchandise. Distributors were permitted to sell to anyone. Since
historically individual brands had come to be well-established and identified with certain distributors, the same retailer might buy Phillips from
one wholesaler, Raleigh from another, and BSA from a third, a practice
which Raleigh Industries believed to be to its advantage. In the United
Kingdom and in Europe generally, wholesalers handled bicycles only, or
bicycles were their main product line. In Europe Raleigh had a much
closer relationship with its distributors, every one of whom it knew in-
timately. In some export areas it knew no more about its distributors
than the knowledge it gained by doing business on a mail-order basis.

In many areas, even where Raleigh had distribution channels, components were sold through separate channels. Motorized equipment was
commonly sold through cycle wholesalers but often to separate retail
outlets. Sunbeam toys were sold by all Raleigh cycle dealers and were
also sold through other channels which handled only toys.

Raleigh believed that a major current problem was to change the
attitude of its distributors, to arouse them to enthusiasm in the new
Raleigh sales methods, and to persuade them that it was to their interest

to generate the same kind of excitement in their retail dealers. Until 1960 there had been no innovation in the industry. There had been no research, and distributors were ignorant of their own market potentials. They tended to be conventional-minded about the bicycle as a product, about its uses, about their retail dealers, about advertising, and about their markets. This was especially true of many old, established trading firms which handled a wide variety of merchandise. Many distributors did little to generate sales to retailers and were satisfied to take what business came their way.

RETAILERS

Raleigh believed that its retailers in the United Kingdom could be classified in four categories.

One-man shops were very prevalent. These often had their own unique and highly individualistic ways of doing business. Raleigh thought the best of them to be very good, but most of them led a doubtful existence.

There was the Limited Company type of retail shop, often a solid family business, employing three to ten people and sometimes more. Here individuals tended to specialize, customers were better served, and the business was conducted more efficiently.

Still another class was represented by the "multiples," typically chain specialty stores or chain department stores, which operated anywhere from ten to several hundred stores. These outlets sold huge volumes of accessories, but Raleigh believed that they could sell a much greater volume of cycles if they had more sales drive. They bought ahead, maintained good stocks, had well-informed sales personnel, and maintained high standards of store cleanliness, all traits which Raleigh believed educated nearby small retailers and "kept them on their toes."

Last, there were what Raleigh called the "big boys." These supermarket-style retailers were a postwar phenomenon. They were well capitalized, were shrewd traders, and set up huge retailing establishments in population centers, with plenty of room for well-lit displays of merchandise in mass quantities.

In the character of its retail dealers, Raleigh recognized a chronic problem. Many individual cycle dealers had gotten into the business by starting a home repair shop, later getting into the selling of cycles. They tended to forever remain service-oriented. "The Depression spawned a whole generation of cycle retailers who were good at repairing but not good at selling," said a Raleigh sales executive. "They are not sales-minded and not merchandise-minded, and in today's modern marketing world, they are an anachronism. They are not good business managers and are often just hanging on. Most of them have been pushed off the high streets onto the back streets, into shabby shops with old-fashioned fronts where they have an odd cycle or two lying about. Many of them will be quick to tell you that the cycle business is a dying trade, that everyone wants cars."

Before the merger British Cycle Company retailers and Raleigh retailers competed across the street from one another. Raleigh and British Cycle vied with each other for the dealer's loyalty, standards for dealerships degenerated, and there was little attention given to the ultimate customer. Retailers handled cycles from both companies, and since most dealers were usually short of money, they bought consecutively from one manufacturer after another, in round-robin fashion, until they had accumulated enough money to pay the overdue bill of the first supplier, whereupon they would proceed to make the rounds again. When Raleigh and British Cycle merged, most small dealers suddenly found themselves owing all their bills to the new Raleigh Industries. With their accounts past due, their only remaining source of supply consisted of small local cycle makers, whose offerings were not as attractive. As a result of this incident Raleigh lost sales volume and also lost dealers who switched to small manufacturers. Dealer ill will for Raleigh was generated in such proportion that the retail dealers' association came to carry on a virtual vendetta against Raleigh.

In 1962 Raleigh had 12,000 retailers in the United Kingdom, served by 14 distribution centers. In 1964 the number of distribution centers was reduced to 6, and the number of retailers was reduced to 7,500. Retailers were guaranteed once-a-week deliveries, with fully assembled cycles delivered to them by trucks.

The number of outlets for retail sales of cycles in the United Kingdom declined 35.97% between 1950 and 1961, compared to a decline of 0.51% for retail outlets for all types of trade. During the same period retail outlets for household goods increased 12.0% and radio and electrical outlets increased 59.42%. The number of retail outlets for cycles continued to decline after 1961, but at a less drastic rate.

At the time when Raleigh was reducing the number of its retail dealerships, it also decided to sell to chain stores and mail-order houses. These outlets had been difficult to serve because of a general problem: there were so many bicycle variations needed to suit each individual customer's needs. There were men's and women's bicycles; sizes from 19½ to 23 inches; gears or no gears; lights; accessories; colors. There were 28 basic models, and in all there might be some 18 possible combinations of a single model. Mass retailers balked at carrying the inventories required to support such an operation. Individual retailers stocked only the fast-moving models and depended on fast delivery service from Raleigh to obtain variations, but chain merchandisers were geared only for forward buying.

In the RSW 16 Raleigh was now able to offer mass retailers a single, unvarying product suitable to buyers of either sex and all sizes: an all-purpose cycle which was fully equipped. The prospect had attraction for the chains as well as for Raleigh.

SALES TRAINING

"Training in the two-wheeler trade," said a Raleigh sales executive, "is either nonexistent or haphazard. Each new entrant muddles along until he learns how they do it in the particular firm where they joined the business. Since our trade is characterized by widely differing forms of outlets, the employee 'trained' with one firm might be astonished at how differently another firm operates, even though both are in the same town."

Until the early 1960's Raleigh had provided no training within or outside of the company. With the reorganization of the home sales market, a training manager was introduced into the home sales department. His function was to teach Raleigh salesmen who called upon retailers how to conduct their sales calls more efficiently. No training was provided by Raleigh for retailers or distributors. If retailers received any training from distributors, it was at the volition and expense of the distributor, but this seldom occurred. Occasionally a nearby overseas distributor might bring a group of his retailers to Nottingham, at their own expense, for a visit of a day or two. There they might view the plant but not do much of anything else.

PROBLEMS OF EXPORT

"The export potential for bicycles is best," said Mr. R. A. L. Roberts, Raleigh's export sales manager, "in those underdeveloped regions of the

exhibit 17   GROUP BICYCLES AND TRICYCLES*

Calendar Year	Basis	Total Production		Production for Home Market		Exports	
		Units	Value £	Units	Value £	Units	Value £
1963	Actual	1,723,805	15,597,000	314,932	3,947,000	1,408,873	11,650,000
1964	Actual	1,415,406	12,872,450	321,865	3,689,450	1,093,541	9,183,000
1965	Estimated sum of firm's present expectations	1,329,143	12,167,566	327,600	3,754,296	1,001,543	8,413,270
1966	Estimated	1,257,972	11,581,151	332,200	3,807,012	925,772	7,774,139
1967	Estimated	1,238,400	11,418,064	338,400	3,878,064	900,000	7,549,000
1970	Estimated	1,258,800	11,606,848	358,800	4,111,848	900,000	7,495,000
1970	National plan	1,769,258	16,090,563	402,331	4,611,813	1,366,926	11,478,750

* Bicycles with frames not less than 15 inches and tricycles with wheels not smaller than 14 inches.

SOURCE: Company's records.

world where the standard of living is still comparatively low. There, most people would be eager to buy a bicycle, but the irony of it is that most of them cannot even afford shoes. There would be many good export markets in countries which would like to import bicycles, but which cannot afford to do so. But the current general world prosperity is reaching even these people." (See Exhibits 17 and 18.)

exhibit 18   RALEIGH PROJECTED BICYCLE EXPORTS BY UNITS

Sales Areas	Raleigh Actual Sales, 1964	Raleigh Projected Sales, 1967	Raleigh Projected Sales, 1970
Europe	107,082	107,000	107,000
Africa	216,718	178,000	108,000
North America	450,415	400,000	490,000
Central America	42,346	40,000	42,000
South America	69,998	35,000	35,000
Pacific	21,850	20,000	21,000
Asia	194,180	120,000	97,000
Miscellaneous	140		
Total	1,102,729	900,000	900,000

SOURCE: Company's records.

In exporting, Raleigh had tended to do better in the East, where there were vast underdeveloped areas of population, than in the West, which was more industrialized. Mr. Roberts felt that Raleigh had a hard core of export business which tended to stay with it, but the cream of the export business was in those markets which tended to fluctuate. In many of these the bicycle business depended on short-term agricultural prosperity and whether the current major national crop matured well. Farmers were especially good potential in many emerging nations, where they were, for the first time, earning enough cash to afford a bike. In some, like Nigeria, there were government boards which controlled agricultural marketing, and in these the bicycle business depended directly on governmental regulations.

There were great differences in the level of import duties in the various world markets. The duty to Raleigh ranged from zero in EFTA (European Free Trade Area) countries to 200% in some Latin American countries.

There was a growing tendency for many of Raleigh's traditional African, Middle Eastern, and Asian export outlets to prohibit or to greatly restrict their imports because of a shortage of sterling or of foreign exchange of any kind. Many of these would have continued to be desirable export markets if they could only have found a means of paying for their imports.

Nationalization of production, dictated by either economic or political pressure, was making severe incursions into Raleigh's export trade, with countries often closing their borders completely to imports. Nottingham could no longer ship to many regions which had formerly been prime Raleigh markets but now had their own production facilities: Indonesia, India, South Africa, Eire, Brazil, Argentina, and Mexico. As a general practice, if Raleigh saw such a threat in time, it tried to work up enough volume in the market on an export basis to make it feasible to locate a plant within the market (see Exhibit 18).

Raleigh was losing some markets to producers behind the Iron Curtain and in the Far East. Russia and Eastern Bloc countries were selling British-type lightweight bicycles in world markets at what appeared to be artificial prices. Japan and China were taking over mass-volume "price" markets, where their low wage and cost levels permitted them to sell at prices which Raleigh could not match.

Wherever it could do so, Raleigh intended to continue to export from Nottingham. If this proved impossible, Raleigh would consider overseas production. Failing either of these alternatives, Raleigh would try to insure that overseas manufacturers obtained their components from Raleigh's United Kingdom plants.

16

SEALED-FRESH COMPANY

"In my opinion, our main problem today is getting consistency of earning power," said Mr. John A. Drake, president of Sealed-Fresh Company, in September of 1961. His company produced and sold fresh chilled orange juice to a 9-state midwestern area with the Detroit area as the major market.

"We are as conscious as anyone of the value of long-term goals," he went on. "Yet again and again we have consciously chosen courses of action which have had long-term detrimental effects to achieve short-term advantages. We have done so because at the time our reserves were so thin that we could not have taken the short-term disadvantage and survived as a corporation. This has been partly because of the industry we're in and partly because of our financial position. Important long-range objectives have on occasion received lower priority than the long-range goal of corporate survival."

With fresh chilled orange juice as its main product the company was vulnerable to crop failures and the subsequent price fluctuations for fresh oranges. For example, the freeze in Florida during the winter of 1957 had a profound effect on fruit prices of the orange crop of 1958–59 with prices increasing more than 400%.

Mr. Drake felt that as a practical matter, it was impossible to pass on all of the increased cost of raw material due to hurricanes and freezes in the selling price. He noted that products of inferior quality, including orange drinks and orangeades, were produced and sold at prices equal to or below their price before such events occurred. "It is apparent to us," Mr. Drake continued, "that the consumer is confused. What are these orange products in the dairy display case? Are they juice or drinks? Are they diluted? Are they freshly-squeezed oranges, or reconstituted frozen concentrate? This confusion and ignorance make it difficult for us to get the premium price to which we are entitled for our high quality product."

He remarked that the company management was working under constant pressure due to limited financial resources. Management believed that continued diversification into other food product lines would ease its problems and stabilize profits. "Our primary niche in the food industry will be the production and distribution of refrigerated (approx. 35°F) food products," Mr. Drake stated. Orange juice, he said, is basically a commodity, facing the intense competition and low profit margins common to such products. Sealed-Fresh intended to diversify into high quality, high priced "recipe" products which gave the consumer the benefits of labor saving plus skillful and exclusive seasoning, blending, cooking, etc. "I am convinced," said Mr. Drake, "that our management skill will make it possible for us to do a better job than our competitors in this area."

The company's first step in the diversification program was the acquisition in May of 1960 of Nitti Frozen Foods, a producer of frozen pizzas and hamburgers, and it was in the process of investigating the possibilities of acquiring other food companies. Sealed-Fresh produced other refrigerated products such as grapefruit juice, lemonade, two kinds of orange drink, pineapple-grapefruit drink, fruit salad, gelatin salad, potato salad, cole slaw, and bulk orange juice. However, the sales volume of these products amounted to less than 10% of the total sales and the contribution to profit was negligible. (See Exhibit 1.)

COMPANY BACKGROUND

Sealed-Fresh Company was formed on October 15, 1956, by consolidation of three interlocking chilled juice operations. The three predecessor companies, jointly managed by the same people, had encountered financial difficulties. The former president, who had a reputation for being a very competent salesman, had demonstrated little financial and organizational ability. Consequently, despite sales growth to approximately $1.1 million, the 1956 operations were unprofitable. The sizeable operating losses which the former management incurred resulted in part from heavy overhead and the lack of financial controls.

exhibit 1   SEALED-FRESH COMPANY
Sales analysis by type of product for typical summer week

Type of Product	Cases	Amount
Sealed-Fresh orange juice	14,430	$51,484
Private brand orange juice	235	815
Total Orange Juice	14,665	$52,299
Grapefruit juice	124	399
Sealed-Fresh lemonade	581	1,354
Private brand orange drink	285	699
Private brand lemonade	204	738
Sealed-Fresh fruit salad (quarts & pints)	52	283
Sealed-Fresh gelatin salad	177	528
Sealed-Fresh potato salad	170	499
Sealed-Fresh cole slaw	67	199
Nitti pizza (11", 12", & 14")	172	2,344
Private brand herring	70	376
Private brand bulk orange juice (in gallons)	300	303
Private brand (dairy) orange drink deliveries	18	11
Total		$59,932

As financial problems increased, the former president was able to raise small amounts of funds from friends and associates, including suppliers. In addition, loans approximating $500,000 were made from several banks, the major participant being a state bank in a neighboring state. When bankruptcy appeared certain, the creditors turned to several investment bankers for assistance in raising funds through the flotation of a stock issue. However, most investment bankers were not interested because of the poor financial condition of the three companies. Finally, Sealed-Fresh turned to the Daniel L. Taylor Company, a Detroit investment banking house, for help. At first the Taylor Company was not interested, but when the state bank asked the Taylor group to try to work out a solution, it reluctantly agreed to attempt to reorganize the company.

Under the refinancing arranged by Mr. Taylor and the group of investors he represented the following arrangements were made:

1. Certain creditors, holding claims of $48,500 and $51,000 respectively, modified their claims and agreed to receive payment at the specified rate of ¼¢ or ½¢ on each quart of orange juice sold by the company; other creditors, with claims aggregating $535,000, agreed to accept contingent certificates having no rights other than to participate in the earnings of the company to the extent of 50% of the net income in excess of $100,000 per fiscal year.

2. In exchange for the sum of $258,000, Sealed-Fresh on February 19, 1957, transferred to the Reiter Company, owned by Mr. Taylor and the group of investors he represented, substantially all of the real estate, machinery and equipment owned by Sealed-Fresh in Florida and Detroit, Michigan.

3. The Reiter Company immediately leased back the facilities to Sealed-Fresh for a term of ten years, at a monthly rental of $3,300 for the first sixty months, and $1,400 a month for the remaining sixty months.

4. Sealed-Fresh issued and transferred to the Reiter Company new common stock amounting to 51% of the total outstanding Sealed-Fresh common stock, for a cash payment of $22,500.

In order to protect its investment, the Taylor group immediately brought in Mr. John A. Drake as president of Sealed-Fresh. Mr. Drake, who was in his early thirties, had been a co-partner in an investment brokerage business with Mr. Taylor for several years. Mr. Drake had also successfully operated his own furniture and gift store in a suburban community of Detroit.

From the period of consolidation, October 15, 1956, through March 31, 1957, the company incurred an operating loss of $141,500, the bulk of which was sustained prior to February 1, 1957, the date when the new management took over. For the balance of the fiscal year ending September 28, 1957, the improvement in operations reduced the operating loss to $112,000. (See Exhibit 2.)

On December 4, 1959, a group of investors loaned Sealed-Fresh $65,000, receiving in exchange 8% subordinated convertible debentures due in 1964. This enabled the company to settle the contingent certificates by issuing 11,000 shares of common stock making a cash payment of $47,000, and issuing a promissory note for $165,000 due February 4, 1961. At the end of January, 1961, Sealed-Fresh issued an additional $65,000 of 8% convertible debentures due in 1965 and obtained a commitment for a loan of $100,000 from a Detroit bank, contingent upon the acquisition of the Reiter Company. On January 27, 1961, Sealed-Fresh purchased the Reiter Company by issuing 25,800 shares of $10 par, 8½% convertible preferred stock. The bank made the $100,000 loan and the $165,000 due the holders of the former contingent certificates was paid in full on February 4th.

With the acquisition of the Reiter Company Sealed-Fresh replaced an annual lease charge of $39,600 with a preferred dividend requirement of $21,950. The dividend requirement, although cumulative, was payable only if earned and, under the bank agreement, had to be earned better than four times on an annual basis before being paid. (See Exhibit 3.)

exhibit 2   SEALED-FRESH COMPANY
Income statements, 1957–1961, fiscal years ending September 30 (in thousands of dollars)

	1957	1958	1959	1960	1961
Net sales	$1,873	$3,021	$3,292	$2,978	$3,557
Cost of goods sold	1,392	2,104	2,394	2,095	2,451
Gross profit	$ 481	$ 917	$ 898	$ 883	$1,106
Selling, administrative and distribution expenses	593	801	893	973	1,048
Operating profit (loss)	$ (112)	$ 116	$ 5	$ (90)	$ 58
Other income	111*	6	1	24	15
Other expenses	27	23	—	18	55
Net earnings (loss)	$ (28)	$ 99	$ 6	$ (84)	$ 18
Special item:					
Provision for payments due creditors of predecessor corporations under deferred payment agreements	7	20	22	16	11
Net increase (decrease) to surplus	$ (35)	$ 79	$ (16)	$ (100)	$ 7

* Includes gain on sale of fixed assets of $103.

exhibit 3   SEALED-FRESH COMPANY

Balance sheets, 1957–1961, fiscal years ending September 30 (in thousands of dollars)

	1957	*1958*	*1959*	*1960*	*1961*
Current assets					
Cash	$ 19	$ 37	$ 19	$ 5	$ 44
Accounts receivable—net[1]	107	141	164	180	200
Inventories	69	120	68	107	106
Prepaid expenses	31	23	34	47	69
Total current assets	$226	$321	$285	$339	$ 419
Fixed assets—at cost					
Land, building, trucks and equipment	270	336	408	479	820
Less accumulated depreciation[1]	95	128	168	210	236
	175	208	240	269	584
Leasehold improvements—less amortization	56	59	63	56	8
Total fixed assets	$231	$267	$303	$325	$ 592
Other assets					
Deferred charges	36	36	25	42	48
Goodwill purchased	—	—	—	14	14
	36	36	25	56	62
Total assets	$493	$624	$613	$720	$1073
Current liabilities					
Notes payable to bank[1]	—	—	15	54	111
Current maturities of notes and obligations payable	100	137	63	202	77
Accounts payable—trade	39	52	106	171	199
Accrued liabilities	41	30	34	43	29
Total current liabilities	$180	$219	$218	$470	$ 416
Noncurrent liabilities					
Notes payable (collateralized by certain equipment)[1]	27	40	46	37	76
Notes payable to bank	—	—	—	—	45
8% convertible debentures due 1964[2]	—	—	—	65	65
8% convertible debentures due 1965[2]	—	—	—	—	65
4% subordinated note due 1964	—	—	—	22	22
Obligations payable to former contingent creditors—less current maturities	—	—	—	17	10
Total noncurrent liabilities	$ 27	$ 40	$ 46	$141	$ 283

[1] Notes Payable to Bank. Accounts receivable and inventories together with a chattel mortgage on certain assets in Florida are pledged as collateral for loans in the amount of $155,300 under an agreement dated January 27, 1961. At September 30, 1960, accounts receivable of $75,100 were pledged as collateral.

[2] 8% Convertible Debentures. At the option of the holders, the 8% convertible debenture bonds may be exchanged for common stock of the Company at any time prior to maturity on the basis of one share of common stock for each $1 of par value of the bonds.

exhibit **3** (continued)

	1957	1958	1959	1960	1961
Stockholders' equity					
8½ % cumulative convertible pref. stock[3]	—	—	—	—	258
Common stock	61	61	61	70	70
Additional contributed capital	260	256	256	107	107
Retained earnings (deficit)	(35)	48	32	(68)	(61)
	286	365	349	109	374
Total liabilities and capital	$493	$624	$613	$720	$1073

[3] 8½ % Cumulative Convertible Preferred Stock. The certificate of incorporation was amended to include the authorization of 50,000 shares of $10 par value preferred stock. This stock shall receive preferential cumulative dividends and is convertible to the common stock of the company at one share for each $1 of par value of the 25,800 shares of preferred stock issued and outstanding.

DIVERSIFICATION

"The chilled orange juice industry is a fairly new industry. It can be traced back only to 1952," said Mr. Drake, "but still it has passed the stage in its growth curve when the demand was skyrocketing, and it has now appeared to level off. It requires very little capital and skill to enter this field."

He went on to say that many people saw a chance to make quick money. The industry in 1961 was over-crowded with companies. Several of them had already been forced to go out of business and many of those which were left were on the verge of bankruptcy. It was the goal of Sealed-Fresh to become one of the survivors. Management strongly believed this aim could be achieved through a constant improvement of its merchandising and distribution skill. "We are now in a position to pick up those who fail," Mr. Drake continued. "The pressure on profit margins is severe and several of the companies I have talked to are considering selling out. Most of the owners, however, are still hopeful and want to wait and see." Mr. Drake was convinced it was only a question of time before some of them would have to sell.

Despite management's confidence in the future of the orange juice division in the long run, it did not want to put all its eggs in one basket. Violent price fluctuations of the raw material due to hurricanes and freezes could probably never be avoided. Management was constantly looking around for other companies with related product lines with which to merge. "Our financial position," said Mr. Drake, "is such that we cannot at the present time buy any good successful company. We have to search for 'sick' companies where we believe our better management skill can improve their earning power."

Three criteria had to be fulfilled before Sealed-Fresh would consider a merger with another company:

1. If possible, there should be an economic overlap in marketing and/or production with its present operation.

2. It had to be a food product, but a refrigerated recipe product rather than a commodity.

3. The product should move in reasonably good tonnage.

Several companies had been turned down because their product lines, such as fish and artificial cream, did not have enough tonnage. Sealed-Fresh preferred to seek a small specialized share of a big market rather than to fight for a large share of a small market. In this respect, further penetration of the egg and potato market was considered to be attractive with annual sales of $400 million, but Sealed-Fresh had not been able to find any suitable prospects in this area.

The acquisition of Nitti Frozen Foods in the spring of 1960 followed after an aggressive search. Nitti Frozen Foods produced and sold frozen pizzas and hamburgers in the Detroit market and had an annual sales volume of $400,000. The Sealed-Fresh management realized that any immediate economic overlap between the two companies would be of minor importance. Management felt, however, that many of the problems facing the pizza market were similar to those in the juice market and that the merchandising skill they had developed in their own business could be of value in reshaping Nitti into a profitable operation.

THE MARKET FOR CHILLED ORANGE JUICE AND ORANGE DRINKS

The Detroit area was the company's major market. Since its product was highly perishable, Sealed-Fresh aimed for a 500-mile radius of the Detroit area. Delivery had to be limited to one or two days of the product's expected shelf-life of about 14 days. Consumption of orange juice and drinks was highest in urban areas. The competition within Detroit was intense. Differences in price and quality between various brands were significant. The Sealed-Fresh product was the highest priced brand in the market, selling at retail for 43¢ a quart. In the summer of 1960 a major chain outlet introduced its own private brand, which sold at 29¢ per quart. The competitor who packaged this private brand also produced another brand which retailed at 25¢ per quart in a second chain. In addition, the A&P brand was priced at 29¢ per quart, and the remainder of Sealed-Fresh's competition in the Detroit area included at least six other brands, most of which sold from 25¢ to 35¢ per quart. Sealed-Fresh also had to meet competition at the consumer level from various brands of frozen concentrated orange juice and orange drinks.

Concentrated juice accounted for 75% of the total orange juice and orange drink consumption in Detroit. It was priced at retail at about 20¢ per can. A reconstituted can of concentrated juice provided 1/4 less juice than a quart of fresh chilled orange juice. Fresh orange juice accounted for 16% of the total market while orange drinks had the remaining 9%. There was a larger price spread between various brands of chilled juice in the Detroit area than in the rest of the country. It was recognized in the trade that large quantities of juice were marketed in Detroit. According to figures compiled by Market Research Corporation of America, the average price for the whole country in August, 1961, for fresh chilled orange juice was 41.5¢ a quart. (See Exhibit 4.)

A Detroit newspaper maintained a panel of families in the metropolitan area who kept diaries of their purchases of various food and drug items. A study of these records was undertaken by Sealed-Fresh's advertising agency. (The highlights of the findings are shown in Exhibit 7.)

Market information similar to this about regional markets was not available. According to Mr. Reynolds, director of marketing, the study in itself did not reveal much new information, but primarily confirmed previous general estimates of management. He admitted, however, that he was surprised at the small population base for consumption of chilled orange juice. Also, the high turnover among people who tried chilled orange juice and then went out of the market disturbed him. He felt this might be due to special price offers in various stores during the year, making people switch on a temporary basis from tomato juice, grape juice, etc., or other forms of orange juice, and when the price offer was over they went back to their original consumption patterns. He believed that those few families

exhibit 4
CHILLED ORANGE JUICE
Consumer Purchases and Prices Paid

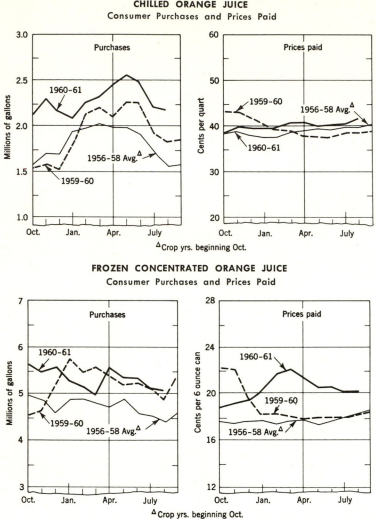

△Crop yrs. beginning Oct.

FROZEN CONCENTRATED ORANGE JUICE
Consumer Purchases and Prices Paid

△Crop yrs. beginning Oct.

SOURCE: U.S. Department of Agriculture, Economic Research Service.

who were regular users of chilled orange juice did so for the sake
of convenience more than any other reason. A carton could be always
at hand in the refrigerator and the housewife did not have to bother
about opening a can and diluting the contents. The better taste of the
chilled juice would also be a factor of importance, he felt, among
more discriminating consumers.

SALES PATTERNS

Sales climbed to $3.3 million in fiscal 1959 from $3.0 million in fiscal 1958. Profits, however, dropped from $99,000 to $5,700, due primarily to higher fruit prices. The company lost approximately $50,500 during the first quarter of fiscal 1959, and earned approximately $56,000 during the last nine months of the fiscal year.

In the fall of 1959, management was optimistic about the near future. The new crop was being harvested at lower prices and it was quite evident that the total crop for the coming year would be considerably larger. The citrus concentrate industry had on hand the highest inventory in its history. Operations were expected to prove very profitable. More aggressive competition was expected, however, especially from competitors who would enter the company's marketing area for the first time.

The expected profitable operations failed to materialize. Sales dropped back to $2.9 million in fiscal 1960 and resulted in a loss of $84,000, of which the frozen food operation accounted for $14,900. The loss sustained by the parent company took place primarily over an 8-week period in May and June as a result of an increase in the price of oranges of more than 100%. In addition, several companies entered the industry during 1959 and attempted to secure a share of the market on the basis of low prices. To compound the problem, the principal competitors of Sealed-Fresh reduced their prices. By August, 1960, as some competitors went out of business and others withdrew from the midwestern market, the company again started to earn money. Sealed-Fresh increased prices on three occasions in the fall of 1960. Sales totaled $3.6 million in fiscal 1961, and profits amounted to $18,000. (See Exhibit 5 for an analysis of sales for a typical summer week during fiscal 1961.)

The company's share of the chilled orange juice market in Detroit had slipped from 60% in 1958 to 25% in 1961, due to the many brands introduced by competitors during the 4-year period. On the other hand, the company made substantial gains in sales to regional markets outside Detroit in 1960 and 1961.

"Of course, we will try to reverse the trend in Detroit," said Mr. Reynolds, "but I do not think our primary goal should be to recapture all of our lost market share in Detroit. In our type of business, with an easy entry and increasing acceptance of the product category by the trade, it is probably uneconomic to attempt to retain a 60% market share in a major market. Although we are always working to convert users of other chilled juice brands to our product, thus increasing our market share, absolute volume is more important than percentage of the market." Management was of the opinion that the major source of added consumption (i.e., extra sales) would be found in converting a small portion of the users of frozen concentrate. If promotions and advertising with this objective helped competitive chilled juice brands to some extent, Sealed-Fresh was confident that it would get more than its normal share of the new business.

The chilled orange juice industry, in the opinion of Sealed-Fresh officials, had done a very poor job of merchandising, advertising, and sales promotion in the past. They maintained that the consumer was confused. She was not fully aware of the differences in quality, quantity, etc., received for the higher price paid. Sealed-Fresh considered that it was its responsibility to inform and educate the public within the financial resources the company had available. "Sometimes, even if it sounds contradictory," said Mr. Reynolds, "I wish we had another high-grade competitor in the market, promoting broader usage of quality chilled orange juice as we try to do."

The Detroit City Sales Force. By September, 1961, the company had 18 trucks on the streets in Detroit handling store delivery. Each truck was operated by a driver-salesman. The system was similar to that used by major soft drink companies. The duties of a driver-salesman included: (1) soliciting accounts, (2) delivery, (3) collecting, (4) arranging displays, (5) rotating the stock, (6) fighting for cooler display space.

"Our route sales force has a reputation of being one of the best in the city," said Mr. Reynolds. "We need more routes, but the present profit margins do not permit this. To keep ahead of competition and maximize sales it is desirable to service most stores at least twice a week. City traffic and the number of accounts have grown to such an extent that this has become difficult with the existing number of routes. In addition, the introduction of the pizza line and the push we have given it has left less time for the driver-salesman to solicit new juice accounts. The driver-salesmen are members of the Teamsters' union, and are paid a union base salary plus 10¢ for each case of juice sold. They are guaranteed a minimum salary but there is no maximum."

Mr. Reynolds also stated, "The question of store delivery is a chronic problem in the industry. Many chains prefer warehouse delivery, while the union favors store-door delivery. Most dry shelf and frozen items are handled through the chain warehouses. On perishables such as orange juice, warehouse delivery gives lower initial costs to the supplier, but the store-door method affords better opportunity for in-store merchandising of the product and careful control of stock rotation. Sealed-Fresh has been generally successful in selling chain headquarters on the net advantage of store-door service, although the issue is always cropping up." (See Exhibit 5.)

exhibit 5   SALES ANALYSIS BY TYPE OF OUTLET FOR TYPICAL SUMMER WEEK

Area and Outlet	Orange Juice, %	Other, %
Detroit		
Corporate chains	14.7	16.9
Voluntary chains (cooperatives)	4.9	14.3
Independent stores	20.9	67.5
Dairies	25.9	—
Institutions	0.2	—
Total Detroit	66.6	98.7
Regional		
Total Regional	33.4	1.3
Grand Total	100.0	100.0

The Regional Sales Managers. "Soon after joining the company in January, 1960," said Mr. Reynolds, "I became convinced that our best growth potential was in the regional markets within a 500-mile radius of Detroit. These markets had been less developed for chilled juice than Detroit or major eastern metropolitan markets. Competition is primarily from Florida packagers, but is by no means as fierce as in Detroit. More than 500 miles west the population density becomes too low for profitable distribution of a perishable product, and on the east coast Florida producers with excess capacity and a large stake in holding the markets would fight back with the lowest possible prices."

In 1960 the Detroit area accounted for 76% of the company's total sales and the regional markets for 24%. Mr. Reynolds stated that the company's goal was to have more than 50% of total sales from its regional markets. In Mr. Reynolds' opinion the somewhat lower mark-up required by regional market retailers and the lower wage levels would more than offset the added freight cost to these areas. Sales in the regional markets were made through dairies which in turn delivered the juice to retail stores and direct to homes.

In fiscal 1961 the sales outside Detroit accounted for 32% of the company's total sales and Mr. Reynolds expected it to be 40% in fiscal 1962.

exhibit 6   COMPARISON OF SALES BETWEEN DETROIT AND REGIONAL MARKETS
(FOR FISCAL YEARS 1960, 1961, AND 1962)

	1960	1961	1962*
Detroit	76%	68%	60%*
Regional	24%	32%	40%*

* Estimated.

"We constantly look for more imaginative merchandising methods," said Mr. Reynolds. "Our toughest marketing problem is to work effectively through a typical dairy organization and reach the consumer. A dairy wholesale route driver can earn as much as $15,000 a year. Orange juice to him is a secondary product to milk and can add little to his commission income. Yet, good store display is important to our sales, and it is highly desirable to keep track of juice which is about to exceed its expiration date and pull it from the stores. A consumer who gets old juice probably will not touch the product again for a long time. To get dairy drivers' cooperation in these tasks is difficult. The home delivery drivers are not so highly paid, but are generally moving too fast to cover their routes to be effective face-to-face salesmen for an individual item in their line."

"One step that helped us a little," continued Mr. Reynolds, "was to move the regional sales managers out of Detroit to live in their territories. Two of the regional sales managers were moved from Detroit and stationed in Pittsburgh and Indianapolis, and a new man was hired for northern Ohio. The dairies were pleased over having company representatives in their local areas. Six months after the moves were made a significant increase in sales was noticed in each of the districts affected."

Mr. Reynolds was very pleased with the regional sales force. He thought they were highly motivated men. He did not need to push them. "As a matter of fact," he remarked, "they are pushing us constantly, asking the home office for more and better working tools to be able to do a better job."

The Pittsburgh Market. In an effort to expand its sales the company entered the Pittsburgh area which was approximately one-third the size of the Detroit market. It had no entrenched competition and its potential appeared large enough to support a company route sales force similar to the one in Detroit. Most people in the industry felt it was impossible to take away the store delivery from the dairies and still get their cooperation in home delivery. They were convinced that Sealed-Fresh would not succeed in such an attempt. However, after one year of preselling the dairies on the idea, the latter agreed to let in the company's own route sales force and they agreed to continue to handle the home delivery for the company.

By October of 1961 Sealed-Fresh had five trucks on the streets in Pittsburgh handling orange juice and pizzas. After four months of operation it was still in the red. Mr. Reynolds expected it would take an additional six months before the company started to make money in the area. Sealed-Fresh had attained fair distribution but sales per store were low compared to Detroit. Ideally, the metropolitan area covered would require at least eight trucks instead of five to give proper service. The initial surveys undertaken indicated a promising outlook because of a lack of orange juice in the stores. But it was not fully realized until later the extent to which poor service by the dairies had ruined the store market. The consumers and the grocery trade had lost confidence in the product.

Marketing Proposal for Fiscal Year 1961–62. In his budget for the fiscal year 1961–62 Mr. Reynolds set forth as a major objective:

> to arrest and reverse the long-term sales decline of Sealed-Fresh brand orange juice in the Detroit market, by (1) increasing Sealed-Fresh's share of the chilled orange juice market, and (2) broadening the consumption base and volume of chilled orange juice.

The proposed plan called for an over-all increase in sales of 28% (from 790,000 cases in 1960–61, to 1,015,000 cases in 1961–62; each case contained 12 quarts). Sealed-Fresh's share of the chilled orange juice market was to be restored to over 30%. The objectives were to be accomplished through a combination of lower retail prices and increased advertising and promotion expenditures. A key element in the proposed budget was the assumption of a large, hurricane-free, freeze-free, Florida crop which would result in significantly lowered product cost.

Although management could not predict the danger point, it was certain that it had to reverse the sales trend in Detroit before it lost its dominant position in that market. Management further believed that if the Detroit market declined far enough it would become more attractive to a Florida producer for another invasion. Another reason for the recommendation was that Sealed-Fresh had never really tested what could be done by an effective 12-month campaign.

According to the marketing plan, the retail price would be reduced on October 1, 1961, from 43¢ per quart to 39¢. Past experience had shown that a retail price below 40¢ per quart could cause a significant increase in the company's sales volume. During the fall of 1960 Sealed-Fresh had been able to keep a retail price of 39¢ per quart, supported by extensive advertising and promotion. A substantial gain in sales was noticed. Unfortunately, the cost situation resulting from hurricane damage to the fruit crop forced Sealed-Fresh to increase the price to 43¢ per quart. In spite of the fact that the advertising and promotion program was carried on for an additional two months after the price increase, the sales volume dropped immediately about 15%. Furthermore, in one chain outlet where the price of competitors' products had been kept at 25¢ per quart, the differences in volume between chilled orange juice and concentrated orange juice were noticeably smaller than in other stores. "The present cost and profit situation does not actually justify a price reduction," said Mr. Reynolds, "but it has to go along with the proposed advertising program in hope that increased volume will make up the difference."

Estimated total advertising and promotion expenditures amounted to $263,000, or 7.8% of projected orange juice dollar volume of $3,360,000. This was substantially greater than the 6.6% rate spent in fiscal 1961 and the 6.4% and 4.3% spent in fiscal years 1960 and 1959 respectively.

RAW MATERIAL SUPPLY

Three sources of supply of freshly extracted orange juice were available to Sealed-Fresh. The supply could be drawn from Florida, California, or Texas. The Florida market was the most important, accounting for 70% to 80% of all oranges grown in the U.S.; California and Arizona accounted for 15% to 20%, Texas and Louisiana for the rest. The company had made it a policy to get its juice primarily from Florida and California. The Texas market was not used unless a shortage of fruit occurred in the other markets.

In Florida three principal crops could be distinguished. The early season started in mid-September and ended in November; the mid-season started in December and ended in mid-February, and the Valencia season lasted from mid-March to mid-June. Over this period of time the supply of oranges varied substantially. The peaks came normally during two six-week periods in January and May when 4 to 5 million boxes of oranges were moved per week as compared to the low in March when only 400 to 500 thousand boxes were moved per week. About 20 large producers of frozen concentrated orange juice usually did their buying during the two six-week peaks, when the fruit had its highest quality. They accounted for more than 65% of all purchases made and had a strong influence upon the market price. Sealed-Fresh and other chilled orange juice producers did their Florida buying over a 39- to 42-week period.

During the California Valencia season—which started in mid-May, reached its peak in August, and ended in October—Sealed-Fresh bought freshly extracted juice from California. However, since California oranges at this time of the season had a much higher acid content, the Florida oranges with low acid content were blended with the California oranges during the summer periods.

A very large percentage of all oranges from Florida were handled by grower-owned cooperatives, with the growers getting 75% of the price on delivery and the rest at the end of the season. The remaining "free market" fruit could be bought under three different contracts:

1. A spot cash price
2. A bulk contract (on a fixed date in the future the buyer agreed to buy all fruit produced by a certain orchard at a fixed price, regard-

less of quantity of fruit. The buyer took all the risks for freezes, hurricanes, etc.)

3. A future price contract (on a fixed date in the future the buyer agreed to buy a certain number of boxes at a fixed price per box)

In trying to avoid speculative profits or losses the Sealed-Fresh management had decided to buy on a day-by-day spot-price basis. It hoped to average out during a 5-year period. Only 10% of the orange crop in the state was sold on the free cash market. The company had so far been buying from broker-dealers (so called "bird-dogs") who moved about 12 million boxes a year. Sealed-Fresh was in this market for approximately 280,000 boxes per year.

The company faced three difficult periods during each year in the months of March, June, and September, when the fresh Florida fruit was immature and in short supply. In these periods it became vital to have concentrate at hand for blending. Concentrate had to be purchased during the peaks of the season. A decision about buying had to be made 3 to 6 months ahead, taking into account the expected future price, the start of the season which could vary from year to year, and the anticipated future sales volume of Sealed-Fresh. Management felt this to be the most important decision to be made in the company and very risky. "We can be the best managed company in the industry," said Mr. Haines, who together with Mr. Drake handled the buying of raw material, "but still lose money on a large scale depending upon how we choose to buy." The effect of a concentrate buying decision could be several times the normal operating profit for a year—for better or worse.

PRODUCTION AND PLANTS

The company operated two plants—one in Detroit from which it distributed its product to grocers and dairies, and one in Florida, where the juice was extracted and readied for shipment to Detroit.

The Florida plant operated 40 weeks of the year and employed 10 people, 2 of whom worked for the company the year around. The others were seasonal workers, mainly local housewives, who were glad to get an extra job at $1.25 per hour. The working hours varied between 8 hours per week early in the season to 60 hours per week during the peak season. The work involved was fairly simple. The oranges were carefully selected and passed through a series of cleansing processes before the machinery processed them. A perforated tube entered the orange from the bottom and a squeezing device came down from above. The juice was forced into the tube and drained away. It passed through a pulp remover and then, before it was chilled, it was subjected to six seconds of 186° temperature which arrested chemical change without disturbing the flavor.

Immediately thereafter it was chilled to about 28° to 30°F. and shipped in special trucks or rail tank cars which brought it to Detroit with a gain of not more than 5 degrees in temperature. There it was blended, packaged, and trucked out to stores and dairies. The Detroit plant employed 19 people, 8 of whom were involved in packaging, 5 in the warehouse, 4 in maintenance and sanitation, and 2 in quality control.

The Detroit plant could at most keep a "half a day" inventory which made proper delivery scheduling important. The company leased seven rail tank cars and two trucks for the shipments between Florida and Detroit. The trucks were more flexible but also more expensive than the rail cars. One problem that had been facing management was to find a reliable railroad. After several switches between various companies they finally felt they had found the "right" railroad. Despite the fact that the juice was transported 300 miles out of the way to get to Detroit from Florida, the delivery was faster than ever before.

NITTI FROZEN FOODS

Mr. Nitti started his business in 1954 and was one of the earliest producers of frozen pizzas in the Detroit market. By 1960, because of easy entry, the market was overcrowded with producers. Around 300 pizzerias of one kind or another, most of them restaurants, were competing for the consumer dollar in Detroit. Many were also supplying neighborhood grocery outlets, competing on a price basis selling frozen pizzas for 39¢ to 69¢ at retail. The profit margins were low and there was an average of one bankruptcy every month. Because of consumer taste preferences, there was much switching between brands. Most producers operated locally. The total market for pizzas in the U.S. was estimated at $50 million a year in 1960.

On May 1, 1960, Sealed-Fresh purchased Nitti Frozen Foods. The purchase price consisted of $15,500 in cash, Sealed-Fresh's $22,000 4%

subordinated four-year note, and 66,667 shares of Sealed-Fresh common stock. In addition, Mr. Nitti was given a two-year employment contract with Sealed-Fresh.

Prior to the purchase by Sealed-Fresh, Nitti frozen pizzas were sold from 39¢ to 49¢ at retail and the business was dependent primarily on two chain accounts and one large distributor. After the deal was closed it was found that since the fall of 1959 Mr. Nitti had been losing accounts, among them the National Foods account. In addition, in several stores where his product had been the only brand, there were now three or four other brands. Until October 29 of 1960, Nitti Frozen Foods was conducted as a division of the parent company and thereafter as a wholly-owned subsidiary company. Mr. Nitti had difficulty adjusting to the new philosophy of the Sealed-Fresh management and resigned from the business in June, 1961. Mr. Drake took over as general manager for the pizza division and assigned Mr. Haines as sales manager and Mr. Wayne as production manager, both from the parent company.

The Sealed-Fresh management soon became convinced that it was impossible to make a good tasting pizza selling from 39¢ to 69¢ at retail. At this price the cost of the crust and package became significant and left little room for good ingredients and a profit. It believed in an entirely different approach to the market which would avoid direct competition from low-priced items. Consumers had the opportunity of ordering good-tasting pizzas from restaurants at a price of $2 and up. "We see ourselves as the 'Sara Lee' of the pizza business," said Mr. Haines, "marketing a good tasting, high quality, high priced product, sold through grocery stores."

A market test was made in the summer of 1960 to find out what kind of pizza the public wanted with respect to price, size, and taste. Six items were introduced: two sizes, 14 and 12 inches in diameter, each either with cheese only, cheese and sausage, or cheese, sausage, and mushrooms (deluxe). From sales experience the number of items were cut down and in September of 1961 only two items were marketed —a 14-inch deluxe combination pizza and a 12-inch sausage and cheese pizza.

The high expectations placed by the food industry upon frozen foods in the early 1950's had not materialized. It had been forecast that by 1960 the frozen food business' share of the total food market would be 10%. The figure realized was closer to 5%, which had an effect upon the traffic passing the frozen foods displays in the stores. Sealed-Fresh intended to introduce and concentrate its operations on refrigerated pizza instead of the frozen variety. Management contended that refrigerated pizza could be placed in the dairy display in the store together with such items as eggs and milk, which were not impulse items and thereby avoid direct competition from other frozen food specialties.

The refrigerated line of pizzas accounted for more than 50% of the total Sealed-Fresh pizza business in September of 1961. The 14-inch deluxe pizza was sold at retail for $1.59 and the 12-inch sausage and cheese for $1.09. At the end of the summer of 1961 the company decided to expand pizza sales from local distribution within Detroit to a regional market including the same states as their market for chilled orange juice. The refrigerated pizza had a shelf-life of only six days, which required a fast turnover to keep down returns. Furthermore the large pizza, which accounted for a big share of the total sales, appealed particularly to lower-middle income families to whom it represented a complete meal. This had taught Sealed-Fresh to hand pick stores for distribution; the Nitti pizza was sold only in half of the stores of the major food chain in the Detroit area.

By September of 1961 the sales force of the pizza division consisted of Mr. Haines who handled the one major chain account in Detroit and was soliciting the others. Sealed-Fresh's largest account for pizzas had to be cleared through the central offices of the food chain for all 1,400 stores supervised by its midwest division. Mr. Haines intended to market frozen items in smaller cities and the refrigerated ones in larger cities. In addition, Mr. Haines was soliciting frozen food brokers outside Detroit, and Mr. Saxon, vice president, special sales, handled a certain number of major pizza accounts in Detroit along with his key orange juice accounts.

When Sealed-Fresh entered the Pittsburgh market it expected the pizza business to be secondary to chilled orange juice. Up to October of 1961 the reverse was true. At that time, management was also aiming for store-door distribution in the Chicago market with their refrigerated pizza. This market was twice the size of the Detroit market and had similar characteristics from a social-economic point of view. No refrigerated pizza was marketed in the area. Because of many failures the chains and the distributors were reluctant to try a new brand. Mr. Haines, however, was hopeful that he could offer them something new and get their cooperation. The company would then use its own trucks for delivery, and he estimated sales of $300,000 to $500,000 annually in the Chicago area.

When the large pizza first was introduced in the Detroit market it was sold at $1.40 retail; it became a success and the management raised the price to $1.59, which had no noticeable effect on sales. Management planned to enter the Chicago market with a $1.69 retail price for their deluxe pizza, which included an allowance for merchandising.

In promotion and advertising the company used mainly in-store promotion and price specials. Sales had been very responsive to the latter. For example, in July, with 20¢ off, sales increased 31% above the average for the preceding time period, and again in September with 10¢ off, sales showed an increase of 208%. This led Mr. Haines to suggest that a "10¢ off" promotion on the 14-inch pizza and "7¢ off" on the 12-inch pizza should be scheduled once during each six-week period commencing October 23, 1961, subject to an analysis of the results.

When Sealed-Fresh took over Nitti Frozen Foods, management realized that rigid quality control in production would be a key factor. Most complaints from consumers concerned the taste. With the high quality, high priced items that the new management intended to market, this control became even more important. This was an area of disagreement between Mr. Nitti and the new owners, and one of the reasons that led to the former's resignation from the business. The new man put in charge of production of pizzas was a graduate food technologist who had supervised the quality control of the juice division.

Pizza production consisted mainly of hand operations primarily performed by a work crew of 40 women and 3 male supervisors. Because of limited plant capacity, proper production scheduling was of significant importance. In October of 1960 an extra night shift had to be added to keep pace with production demand.

In October, 1961, Mr. Haines in commenting upon the operation, remarked that "sales had doubled since the same period last year and should approximate $560,000 for the 1961 fiscal year." He went on to say that "despite this good showing, we did not make any profit this year. Our present operation requires an average sales volume of $11,000 per week to break even. Sales have slacked off the past few months, but this is customary in this kind of business in the summer months." He stated further that he expected sales to grow to $1 million in 1962 and that he was confident that the business would become profitable from then on. He also pointed out that the company was seeking to buy other pizza producers in order to get their trade accounts. In addition, the company was searching for other recipe food products selling above $1 at retail to extend its product line. As an example, Mr. Haines mentioned fresh fruit pies. "Originally five producers of fruit pies had operated in Detroit," he said. "Today, only two are operating."

CORPORATE DEVELOPMENT

"To fill a vacancy," said Mr. Drake, "I would prefer to have a man with both brains and experience. If, for any reason, I cannot fill a job with a man possessing both, I would much rather choose a man with brains. Given time, the man with the brains will gain the experience." By 1961 Mr. Drake felt that he had gathered around himself a management team which, as a group, was comparable in quality to that of any company the same size. The average age of the management group was approximately 35 years.

In October, 1961, Mr. Drake, in addition to being the president of Sealed-Fresh, was in charge of production and acted as general manager for Nitti Frozen Foods. When Sealed-Fresh bought the latter company it was assumed that it could be run as a division and use a minimum of existing management's time. After Mr. Nitti resigned, management decided there was no longer any need to run the pizza operation as a subsidiary and it was brought back as a division of the Sealed-Fresh Company.

Mr. Drake strongly believed in giving as much freedom of action as possible to his management team. The officers met every two or three weeks to get away from day-to-day operations and discuss the long-term prospects of the company. Mr. Drake tried to schedule his activities in advance but found this difficult to do. In his opinion the need for a general manager for Nitti Frozen Foods had diminished after he had brought in his own people to take charge of production and sales, but on the other hand he realized the need for a man in charge of production of the orange juice division. Despite his belief in giving his subordinates independence of action, he found himself involved, because of the weak working capital position of the business, in assignments that preferably should have been carried out by others.

FUTURE PROSPECTS

Sealed-Fresh officials expected the orange juice business to continue to be competitive. They considered the long-term outlook for success to be enhanced by the fact that the major component of cost—oranges —was showing a downward trend. Many young orange trees had been planted in Florida in the past few years. In time the trees would contribute to an ever-expanding crop. Examination of the available data indicated that projected crops were increasing at a faster rate than population. Barring freezes or hurricanes, management expected this would lead to considerably larger orange juice sales because lower orange prices would lead to lower retail prices of orange juice. They expected the retail price to come down to 27¢ to 35¢ per quart by 1964, reducing the price spread between frozen and chilled juice to about 5¢ per quart on an adjusted quantity basis.

Mr. Drake contended that the expansion of the orange division would come primarily from consolidation with other orange juice companies and less from internal growth. Mr. Reynolds expected that the future distribution system would include company route sales forces in four to six key metropolitan areas within a 500-mile radius of Detroit. In those areas the company would probably keep branch warehouses for distribution to the dairies in the surrounding territory. This arrangement had been tried in Pittsburgh and found to be more profitable than the older method of having semi-trailers leave from Detroit to visit each dairy in the rural areas. Locations considered next in line for company route sales forces were Indianapolis and Cleveland. Sealed-Fresh also had plans to reach outside the 500-mile radius of Detroit by selling through dairies in New Orleans, Memphis, Houston, Fort Worth, and Dallas. Initially, the company planned to make shipments to these areas out of Detroit.

Sealed-Fresh also expected very rapid expansion in the pizza division through enlarged consumer acceptance and better coverage of distribution outlets within the Detroit area. The pizza division, according to Mr. Drake, had a larger potential than the juice division. He pointed out that steps had been taken to streamline pizza production. "With the introduction of automated equipment," said Mr. Drake, "we foresee the possibilities of increased productivity significantly greater than what can be accomplished in the production of orange juice."

Another company official remarked that the heavy returns from stores during the first year had substantially reduced profit margins, but that great strides had been made to standardize the quality of the product. In addition, efforts had been made to increase the shelf-life of the pizzas to 10 days or more. He emphasized that in view of the bright expectations for the pizza business, taste surveys were constantly being undertaken to find out consumer preferences, and that the management had decided to concentrate on this product in the immediate future.

exhibit 7   ORANGE JUICE CONSUMPTION PATTERNS AMONG THE FAMILIES IN A
DETROIT CONSUMER PANEL
Highlights from a study undertaken by Sealed-Fresh's advertising agency

A. *Consumption of Orange Juice and Drink*
   1. Usage of orange juice and drink is almost universal among families in Detroit. Of the 258 families, 86% bought some orange juice and drink during the two year period.
   2. Incidence of purchase is higher among upper income and larger families but is over 70% in every population subgroup.
   3. While incidence of purchase is high in all groups, the rate of consumption varies markedly by group. The highest consumption rate occurs among upper income families ($8,000 and over) and larger families (five persons and over). Upper income families are 27% of the panel and consume 39% of all orange juice and drink. Larger families are 26% of the panel, and they account for 40% of all orange juice and drink consumption.
   4. As is the case with many products, a small segment of the population accounts for the bulk of the orange juice and drink consumed. Heavy users (those who used more than 6.5 quarts a month on the average) make up 9% of the panel and account for 44% of all orange juice and drink consumed. Medium users (2.6–6.5 quarts a month) make up 19% of the population and account for 36% of total consumption. Together, these two groups are 28% of the population and account for 80% of all consumption.
   5. Heavy and medium users of all orange juice and drink account for the bulk of each of the types of orange juice. They account for 72% of all Sealed-Fresh consumed, 72% of all chilled juice, 82% of all concentrated juice, and 79% of all chilled drink.
   6. Heavy users tend to be large, upper income, native white families.
   7. Concentrated juice is the dominant type of juice both in the incidence of use and in the heaviness of use:

exhibit **7** (continued)

> 73% of panel families tried concentrated juice in the two year period and they consumed an average of 54 quarts per family. Concentrated juice accounted for 75% of total orange juice and drink consumption.

8. Chilled juice ranks far behind concentrated juice in importance. While 48% of families tried chilled juice they consumed an average of only 17 quarts per user family in the two year period. Chilled juice accounted for only 16% of all orange juice and drink consumption.

9. Chilled orange drinks were tried by 25% of families who used an average of 18 quarts per user family in the two year period. Chilled drinks accounted for 9% of all orange juice and drink consumption.

B. *Changes in Usage of Orange Juice and Drink Between 1959 and 1960*

1. There was a total increase in the consumption of orange juice and drink between 1959 (September 1958–August 1959) and 1960 (September 1959–August 1960). Total quarts consumed rose 20%.

2. The expansion of the total market for orange juice and drink was due exclusively to an increase in the consumption of concentrated juice which rose 27% while chilled juice increased only 3% and chilled drink decreased 4%.

3. While total consumption of chilled juice did not change sharply between 1959 and 1960, the market was not a static one. While 34% of families used chilled juice in 1959, 12% dropped out of the market in 1960. These were counterbalanced by 14% who began to use chilled juice in 1960, making a total of 36% of users in 1960.

4. The monthly consumption of chilled juice was higher in the summer months than in the winter months in 1959 but the gap was eliminated in 1960.

C. *Usage of Chilled Juice*

1. Chilled juice constitutes a relatively small percentage of the total orange juice and drink market. While 48% of all panel families tried some chilled juice in the two year period, chilled juice accounted for only 16% of all orange juice and drink consumed.

2. The key group of heaviest users of chilled juice (consumers of 64 quarts or more) make up only 3.4% of all panel families but account for 57% of all the chilled juice used. An additional 3.4% accounted for an additional 18% of all chilled juice. Thus, 6.8% of families consumed 75% of all chilled juice.

3. Heavy users of chilled juice tend to use chilled juice rather than other types. Among families that consumed 63 quarts or more in the two year period, 80% of all their orange juice and drink consumption was chilled juice. Among fairly heavy users of chilled juice (17–63 quarts) chilled juice accounted for more than half their consumption. These findings indicate that chilled juice is directly competitive with other types of juice (particularly concentrated).

exhibit **7** (continued)

4. The heaviest users of chilled juice also tend to be heavy users of all orange juice and drink. These families tend to be larger families with higher incomes. They are of particular importance in the chilled juice market because their heavy use accounts for a high percentage of total consumption of chilled juice.

5. Home delivery was not very important among families that were the heaviest users of chilled juice who accounted for 57% of total consumption. Among these families, only 15% of all chilled juice consumed was home delivered.

D. *Usage of Sealed-Fresh*

1. Usage of Sealed-Fresh shows the same pattern as usage of all chilled juice. While 32% of families tried the brand, Sealed-Fresh accounted for only 6.5% of all orange juice and drink consumed.

2. Although Sealed-Fresh plays a relatively minor role in the total market for orange juice and drink, it plays a major role in the chilled juice market. Two thirds of all chilled juice users tried Sealed-Fresh in the two year period and Sealed-Fresh accounted for 40% of all chilled juice consumed.

3. Families that tried Sealed-Fresh generally had a high level of experience with other types during the two year period; 64% used other brands of chilled juice, 81% used concentrated, and 36% used chilled drink.

4. Sealed-Fresh has a higher share of market among heaviest users of chilled juice than among people who use less chilled juice.

5. A small group of families—2.1%—accounted for 57% of all Sealed-Fresh consumption.

6. Upper and middle income families account for a disproportionately high proportion of Sealed-Fresh consumption.

17

WILKINSON SWORD LIMITED (A)

Early in 1966 the financial press in London reported:

> Wilkinson Sword is one of the great success stories of British industry in recent years. Within ten years the profits of this family-owned firm have gone up a hundred fold. In 1954 they amounted to £20,451 ($57.3 thousand) before taxes. In 1963, having expanded from earnings alone, profits were £2,048,076 ($5.7 million). The directors estimated that profits for 1964 would be £3,250,000 ($9.1 million); actual profits earned in 1964 were £3,534,520 ($9.7 million); in 1965 the company earned £2.2 million ($6.1 million) before taxes. (See Exhibits 1 through 4.)

The company, which manufactured swords, garden tools, and fire protection devices, had introduced a newly developed razor blade in 1956. In the years which followed, the number of its employees quadrupled, it built numerous new plants in the United Kingdom and other parts of the world, and it entered its products in more than 50 world markets. In 1966 the Randolph and Latham families, which had been in control of the company for almost 100 years, continued to own 70% of the capital stock (see Exhibit 5).

COMPANY HISTORY AND DEVELOPMENT

The Wilkinson Sword Company Limited traced its origins to Henry Nock, a gunsmith who established one of the largest gun and bayonet factories in the city of London in 1772. Nock had an enterprising apprentice named James Wilkinson, who married his daughter and became his partner. When Nock died in 1804 Wilkinson took over and in 1820 added swordmaking for Navy and Army officers to his gunmaking activities. His son Henry, who succeeded him, moved the business to Pall Mall in central London, close to the Admiralty and War offices in Whitehall. James Wilkinson had secured an appointment as gunmaker to King George III, the first of nine royal appointments to British sovereigns which were to follow. Sword production was at its peak during the latter decades of the nineteenth century, when the Wilkinson firm supplied arms for the Crimean and Boer Wars and for the vast British armies throughout the Empire. In addition to making swords, cutlasses, sabers, and boarding pikes, the company also made lances. By the close of the century cavalry-sword production alone was between 30,000 and 60,000 a year, and it was estimated that at any time Queen Victoria's armed forces had in use about half a million Wilkinson weapons.

The reign of Edward VII was peaceful and production dropped sharply. Under George V during World War I, the Wilkinson factory, moved to larger quarters in the Acton area of London, converted to emergency production and turned out 2.5 million bayonets in addition to capacity production of swords. After the war, production virtually ceased, and the company reverted to the making of a hollow-ground straight-edged razor which it had been producing in modest quantities since 1890. At the turn of the century the company had developed a safety razor which could be stropped automatically. In 1920 it began to make pruning shears, and it soon became the leader in the British Isles. During the 1930's it also had fleeting experiences in the making of nail clippers, scissors, table cutlery, and other cutting tools. At one time it manufactured the Wilkinson Touring Autocycle and the Pall Mall Bicycle. The company began, in 1938, the manufacture of fire detection and protection equipment for aircraft, a joint venture with the Graviner Manufacturing Company Limited.

During World War II Wilkinson again converted entirely to war work, producing for the Allied armies millions of bayonets, swords, commando knives, armor-piercing shot, flak suits, and bullet-proof waistcoats. During the war the Graviner Company installed its fire-fighting equipment in a vast fleet of Allied aircraft.

With the cessation of hostilities the Wilkinson plants were again abruptly idled. Safety-razor production was later resumed, but was slowed up by the postwar shortage of brass. There was some activity in Graviner fire protection equipment, which was adopted for use by the commercial airlines, then a fledgling industry. Garden tools became a major product, with the line expanded to include all garden tools with cutting edges, both clippers and cultivating tools. Sword production slowly picked up with the change of the army to its peacetime role.

In 1956 Wilkinson brought out its first stainless steel razor blade. In 1961 it introduced its historic Teflon-coated Wilkinson Sword Blade.

ORGANIZATIONAL STRUCTURE AND POLICY

"Ten years ago," said Mr. Denys Randolph, assistant managing director, "we were a little company with a total employee strength of 750, and we were owner-managed. Direct control of all sides of the business was possible by the chairman and the managing director."

With the rapid expansion of the business in the decade which followed, the management undertook a series of organizational moves to effect more decentralization. As a result the company was divided into six operating divisions: shaving, hand tools, fire protection, swords, research and international (see Exhibit 6, organization 1965).

Until 1964 razor blades and garden tools had been handled on a joint basis throughout the world. Overseas subsidiaries had handled both products, and originally even the United Kingdom sales force had done the same. In 1964 two separate divisions were established and their activities clearly separated.

Wilkinson Sword (West End) Limited controlled the Pall Mall office and showroom. It dealt mainly with sword activities and armored waistcoats, but it also provided a public-relations function for the group as a whole.

Wilkinson Sword (Research) Limited dealt with research on a group basis, with its managing director answering to the parent board.

Wilkinson Sword (International) Limited provided a service to the parent board and the several divisions on financial, legal, planning, and property matters.

The parent board met monthly and controlled over-all policy, but the day-to-day business of the group was managed by the international board, which acted as a management committee. The international board was comprised of H. B. Randolph, chairman; Peter Randolph, deputy chairman; Roy Randolph, managing director; Denys Randolph, assistant managing director; R. Griffiths, assistant managing director; and Bernard Hansom, managing director of the international and research divisions. The international board met every two weeks and made the operating decisions, which the parent board usually approved at its monthly meetings (see Exhibit 7).

The Randolph family held about 65% of the non-public capital stock, and a further 35% was held by the Latham family. Mr. H. B. Randolph, the chairman, was past 70. He officiated at board meetings, acted as titular head of the company, and represented it in public affairs.

Since the majority of the company's turnover (sales) was now from overseas operations, one or the other of the top executives was abroad at almost any time. Therefore it was arranged that the deputy chairman and the managing director share the executive responsibility for operating activities. Except for occasional misunderstandings, the arrangement seemed to work well. Peter, the oldest Randolph son, was clearly conceded to be the top authority. He was the principal planner, coordinated the groups, made the most critical decisions, and delegated to the division heads. It was observed that he was acting more and more in the role of chairman of the group. Roy Randolph, the second son, was considered the company's marketing man. In Peter's absence he acted as chief executive. Denys Randolph, the youngest of the brothers, was seen as the "project" man, because he had exhibited a talent for launching special programs and seeing trying problems to successful conclusions.

For marketing purposes the world was divided into four areas: (1) Europe, including the United Kingdom; (2) the Americas, North and South; (3) the Far East, Australia, and New Zealand; and (4) the Middle East and Africa. The pattern of operations in each of these areas varied according to the nature of the activities involved (see Exhibit 7).

In the course of the reorganization each of the major activities of the group had been incorporated as a separate corporation. Some of these incorporations were said to be for the purpose of providing director status to a man who had formerly exercised extensive authority but was in title only a department manager. Each of the subsidiary companies had its own board. Many of the boards were interlocking, with some individual directors sitting on many boards. All the subsidiary companies were wholly owned except Graviner and Wilkinson Sword G.m.b.H. in which Wilkinson held a $66\frac{2}{3}\%$ interest.

"The reorganization of our company," commented a Wilkinson official, "seemed to follow more along personality lines than along the lines of organizational objectives. We seem to have accommodated the place and the personalities of people now in the management, rather than

to structure the organization according to the needs of the various divisions." A case in point was the Graviner organization. Prior to the merger
of Graviner and Wilkinson, Mr. N. G. Bennett had directed the activities
of the Graviner organization, which handled the sales of Graviner products. In Wilkinson, Mr. D. R. Gatley had been in charge of Graviner
technical matters and manufacturing. In the reorganization each of these
men was made joint managing director of Graviner (Colnbrook) Limited, with equal authority. Thereafter Bennett handled all sales and
promotional activities. He had spent 15 years in Graviner sales activities,
was considered an excellent sales director, and had shown a disinclina-
tion to become involved in production matters. Gatley, who had been in
charge of Wilkinson fire protection activities for eight years, took charge
of all Graviner inside activities, including design, engineering, production, finance, and personnel.

PRODUCT DIVISIONS

Shaving Division. Wilkinson Sword dated its entry into the razor business back to 1890. In 1898 the company introduced its first safety razor.
Wilkinson became a factor in the razor blade industry in Great Britain;
the company was only moderately successful, however, in this venture.
Production of razor blades was suspended in World Wars I and II.
In the post-World War II period Wilkinson Sword decided to become
a major re-entry in the razor blade market. In pursuing this policy it
developed a somewhat revolutionary coated stainless steel blade which
was introduced in 1961. The new blade proved to be successful almost
instantaneously and catapulted the firm into a position of market leadership rivaling the international giant, Gillette of the United States.

Blade production between 1961 and 1965 increased over 500%. Wilkinson Sword's market share in Great Britain increased from 20% in
1962 to 45% in early 1966. In the United States market the company's
position increased from a 2 to 3% share to 15% of stainless blades in the
same period. In the early part of 1966 Wilkinson was exporting over 60%
of its razor blade production and had established itself as a major factor
in the industry on an international basis.

Gillette filed a patent-infringement suit against Wilkinson in West
Germany in 1963. The suit stated that Gillette had filed a patent application on a Teflon-coated stainless steel blade three months prior to Wilkinson's patent application for the same process. This action resulted in

an agreement by Wilkinson to pay Gillette one fifth of a cent on each 15¢ blade sold in the United States and slightly more on each blade sold in other international markets. Despite this handicap, Wilkinson's sales continued to increase, mainly at the expense of Gillette.

Garden Tools. Wilkinson Sword had actively participated in the garden tool market since 1920. In 1948 the company initiated an attempt to develop a complete line of implements and in 1958 and 1962 redesigned the line to keep pace with the British market. The company made 17 varieties of garden tools and was engaged in the manufacture of lawn mowers as a result of the acquisition of the Flexa Lawn Mower Company in 1964. Approximately 30% of the garden tool sales were exports, mainly to the United States, which accounted for one half of the export sales. The remaining half were distributed in Europe, South Africa, Australia and New Zealand.

The sale of garden tools in the United States was initiated in 1960. The promotion and development of distributors for the garden tool line were tied to the introduction of the company's Teflon-coated stainless steel blade introduced in 1961. The popular and somewhat revolutionary razor blades were offered as an incentive to the garden tool dealers, who soon became engrossed in selling the limited supply of razor blades they could obtain and relegated the garden tool line of Wilkinson Sword to a secondary position. The razor blades were withdrawn from the garden shops in 1963 and 1964 and distributed through the conventional channels of drug-stores and supermarkets. In 1964 the garden tool line was separated from the company's other products in both manufacturing and sales.

In the first few years after World War II heavy emphasis was placed on garden tools. This gradually gave way to a heightened interest in Graviner products, which in turn was eclipsed by the booming razor blade business. The garden tools were not deliberately neglected, but the other activities of the company tended to receive priority. Garden tools had always been profitable but at a rate which was unattractively low. In 1965 it was the lowest in profitability of the company's several product lines, accounting for approximately 8% of the total sales. Management expected an increase in sales in future years of about 30% per year. The company's sales in garden tools had shown an increase of approximately 7% per year in the period from 1960 to 1965.

Graviner Division. In 1964 the Graviner Division was made a separate operation with Wilkinson Sword owning two thirds of the stock and Graviner one third. The Graviner operation was considered by management to be autonomous except for capital expenditures, personnel matters, and plant location. By company policy Graviner's products were limited to safety and control equipment, mainly in the area of fire protection and control. The Graviner equipment had gained a world-wide reputation in the field of highly sophisticated fire protection equipment used in aircraft, ships, boats, industrial plants, and stationary engine rooms. Military use accounted for 40% of the division's sales; the remainder was for civilian use. Graviner produced about 19% of the total sales of Wilkinson Sword and accounted for a substantial portion of the company's total profit. Prior to the introduction of the new razor blade and its corresponding increase in sales, Graviner accounted for approximately 60% of the total company sales.

The manufacturing of Graviner products was mainly on a job-shop basis. About 400 products were in production at any given time and only a few orders were for 1,000 pieces or more. The company's reputation and product line were based on engineering skill and the development of highly technical products. The management of the Graviner Division felt there was great potential for their products throughout the world and mainly in the highly developed countries of Europe and the United States.

Sword Division. "In understanding our company position," an executive of Wilkinson Sword remarked, "you must be aware of the important role the sword has played throughout our development. I think it is fair to say that the sword image and craftmanship have been key factors in our marketing policy through the years and explain a good deal about our company's approach."

In an article describing Wilkinson's activities, a popular news magazine reported:

> Contrasted with its automated razor blade factory and assembly lines, Wilkinson's highly skilled swordmakers ply their craft in dingy corners, using tongs and hammers as much as five hundred years old to forge, grind and polish ribbons of high-tensile steel.
> The company pridefully recalls that its blades were bloodied in the Battle of Waterloo; that its heavy curved sabers were used in one of history's last cavalry charges, the Sudan Uprising, in which a then young officer named Winston Churchill took part. . . .

Commenting on this, Major John Latham, director of the Wilkinson Sword Division and a member of one of the company's owning families, explained: "It is the variety of patterns in swords which has prevented the craft of swordmaking from adopting modern manufacturing techniques. Each and every country has different designs, no two regiments have exactly identical swords, and most customers require special embossing on the blades of their names and ranks. True, the blade is now forged from bar steel by pneumatic hammers instead of the smith's brawny arm, and mechanical stamping and acid etching have largely done away with hand engraving. But the craft is about the only remaining one in which the basic methods of manufacture have not changed since the Bronze Age."

Over the thousands of years of sword history there had come to be an endless variety of swords, and Wilkinson took pride in the claim that it could make any sword in the world. There were blades with cutting edges on both sides, single-edged blades, straight blades, curved blades, and blades purely for thrusting. Hilts varied from simple grip and cross-guard to complicated basket hilts. The parts might be fine-plated with gold, silver, nickel, or rhodium, and handles might be set with jewels. Scabbards were of steel, leather, or wood covered with leather or velvet. "It was not until 1908," said Major Latham, "that a British War Office committee, which had sat intermittently since 1884, produced the 1908 pattern British Cavalry Trooper's Sword, which is reputed to be the best sword ever designed. It was a great triumph, but unfortunately it came at a time when the sword, as a weapon of war, was completely outmoded. It is also a bit of an anomaly," reflected the major, "that the swords Wilkinson turns out today, thanks to modern metallurgy and forging techniques, are better fighting weapons than the swords it made in the days when its swords were actually used as fighting weapons."

In 1966 the Wilkinson Sword Division had about 50 employees, production amounted to about ½ of 1% of the company's total turnover. Of the 4,000 swords it produced each year, only about 20 were alike, and its catalogue listed over 1,000 types which had been codified. Of the 4,000 swords it made in 1965, 25% were "cheap" swords—Masonic, cadet, lodge, and dancing swords—which were made of quality materials, but not subjected to the most rigorous tests. These sold for about $20 to $25. Sixty per cent were regulation swords for armies, navies and air forces. These sold for $60 to $110. Some 15% were custom-built. These were literally hand-crafted, and might cost $500 to $10,000, depending on finishes and jeweling. In this category were the sword of honor presented to General Eisenhower after V-E Day, the Sword of Stalingrad presented to Stalin by Winston Churchill, the NATO sword presented to General Lauris Norstad, and the Traveling Sword of the

Lord Mayor of London. The most costly sword Wilkinson had ever made was one presented by an Indian raja to Edward VII on his coronation. The hilt was embossed with jewels, and the sword was valued at about $30,000.

The heyday of the sword had been in the latter part of the nineteenth century when it served as a fighting weapon, was a regulation part of army and navy dress, and was also a part of a fashionable man's clothing, as the umbrella today is part of the proper attire of a London City man. Although the sword was largely an anachronism in 1966, there was, nevertheless, still a world sword industry, with competing producers in England, Germany, Spain, France, and Japan. The greatest demand was for low-priced cadet, ceremonial, and stage swords, in which Wilkinson found itself unable to compete with the low prices offered by foreign producers, even the high-quality producers in Solingen and Toledo. As a matter of policy Wilkinson declined to lower its quality standards, and so an increasing part of the world sword trade was pre-empted by the Spaniards and the Japanese. The swords which Wilkinson once made for the American cadets at West Point, Annapolis, and Quantico now came mostly from Germany and Japan. Traditionally, the Commonwealth countries had maintained in England buying agents known as crown agents, who had always favored Wilkinson with their sword purchases and continued to order in substantial quantities.

Wilkinson considered itself to be a factor in the world sword business. It regularly received orders from some 60 countries and was looked upon in the industry as the most eminent sword manufacturer in the world. The sword division had no salesmen, did no advertising, took only what business came to it, and in 1966 had a backlog of nine months of orders. "Competitors have an advantage over us," said Major Latham, "in that they can deliver promptly. If our order book ever gets down to a month or two, we will go out and sell swords."

Wilkinson believed that swords would continue to be in demand and that the potential would grow. "As long as there are wars," said Major Latham, "there will be swords . . . even if they are used only for recruiting purposes. Furthermore," he said, "everybody loves a military parade. But modern scientific weaponry and functional combat uniforms are not very thrilling, and all of the glamour would be gone if it were not for swords."

Major Latham said that sword demand had increased almost 50% in recent years, the chief demand coming from the emerging nations in Africa and Asia. "These nations are newly sovereign," said the Major, "and they place a high premium on ceremony. What can be more cere-monious than flourishing a hand-tooled sword? There is a growing de-mand for them from African and Asian government officials who wear them with their ornate ceremonial dress uniforms. Wilkinson had on hand orders from Sudan, the Hashimite Kingdom of Jordan, Kuwait, Israel, Ghana, Canada, Australia, Singapore, Bahrein, and Venezuela.

There was also evident a budding fashion in the use of specially de-signed swords as a corporate status symbol. American industrial com-panies were beginning to use decorative swords to add a touch of Old World color to their corporate board rooms. Lodges, orders, and fraterni-ties were beginning to use them for the same purpose.

For decades Wilkinson had been refurbishing old swords—hereditary swords which had been handed down from fathers to sons who were entering military service. The restoration activities had grown to be a brisk business. Incidental to it Wilkinson had come to operate an antique weapon-trading business in which it bought and sold historic weapons from all over the world. These activities had come into being sponta-neously and had grown to such volume that they interfered with the production of new swords. Wilkinson also operated a museum of weaponry and a showroom on London's prestigious Pall Mall. These were open to the public without charge.

"In the old days," said Major Latham, "our company relied mainly on swords for its bread and butter. Today, even though swords are less than 1% of our company's business, we still do considerably better than breaking even. The Sword Division has always paid its way, and if it were a completely separate unit and relieved of the Pall Mall show-rooms, we would make a very tidy profit. But swords are the traditional product of our company, and as a prestige item they mean much more to us than their profitability. The public-relations aspect of our swords is fantastic, and we look upon our sword business as having far greater value to us than its monetary value. It has given Wilkinson world-wide publicity. Our competitors in any of our lines have nothing like it."

The Wilkinson razor blade was called the Wilkinson Sword Blade, and behind the words were pictured crossed swords. Garden tool adver-tising featured such themes as "Swordsmanship in Shears," and tools were given such names as the Saber Pruner or the Super-Sword Pruner. Some Graviner advertising also carried the theme. One Graviner bro-chure announced: "The Swordsman Fire Extinguisher—Extinguishant: Bromochlorodifluoromethane."

Research Division and Product Policies. "In recent years," said Mr. H. B. Randolph, chairman of Wilkinson, "we have built new factories in England, Canada, America, Germany, and Australia. Our name has been prominent in exhibitions of British industrial design in Malta, Moscow, Tokyo, Sweden, Spain, Belgium, and Holland. We sell our products in more than 50 territories throughout the world. These are vital activities now, but the real future of our company lies in new products and developments. The key to our prosperity 20 years from now is labeled "Research."

Mr. Randolph said that this meant an investment in men as well as in facilities. Wilkinson believed that no less than 10% of its work force should be engaged in some form of research, and it now had over 300 people engaged in research activities. The company provided university scholarships for postgraduate research students, retained senior faculty members of leading universities as consultants, and also used professional consultants.

"As a matter of policy," said Mr. B. S. Hansom, director of research, "we always choose high-priced professional consultants. We try to ensure that we are buying good advice by paying high fees to consultants who have established reputations."

Mr. Hansom pointed out that until a few years ago most of the company's research had been in Graviner activities. Graviner had been steeped in short-term projects, and no one was doing genuine research. For research in depth Graviner had depended upon the government-sponsored Farnborough Aircraft Research.

Mr. Hansom saw the distinction between research and engineering as being threefold. First, the time scale was different, research being directed to the activities of future years rather than to the urgent problems of manufacture today. Second, the emphasis on equipment was different, enabling research to investigate much more radical changes than would be feasible in the engineering departments. Third, some projects involved such depth of scientific investigation that specialist teams had to be recruited and provided with elaborate apparatus. By integrating a number of such teams Wilkinson believed that a proper continuity of interest and utilization of equipment could be maintained, which was especially important in a company with a diversity of products.

In 1959 research was separated from engineering and development and formed into a new division. Five years later, having grown to ten times its original size, it was incorporated as Wilkinson Sword (Research) Limited to give it equal status with other companies in the group and to prevent operating managers from imposing their daily problems upon the research people. The research group was provided with its own new building at Colnbrook, equipped with offices, laboratories, work shops, and a technical library. Project teams were supported by service groups on matters such as information searching, library, patents, analytical laboratories, and statistical surveys. Their findings were available to any section of the company.

"It is surprising," said Mr. Hansom, "how often the knowledge gained in one field can later be applied to quite a different area." Mr. Hansom cited as a dramatic example the Teflon stainless steel razor blade coating. Wilkinson's original stainless blade developed at Solingen was not a remarkable success and posed production problems. The indicated solution seemed to be some kind of coating which would make the blade more honable and stroppable and protect the cutting edge from corrosion. This project was deliberately taken away from the Solingen firm, which had vast experience in cutting edges, and was assigned to the Graviner research group, which knew nothing about razor edges. "This was on the basis," said Mr. Hansom, "of the old joke that runs, 'He didn't know it couldn't be done, so he went ahead and did it.' But we were not joking. The Solingen people would often have looked back to research data of 10 years ago to find that the process they were about to test had already been tested and had been found worthless. But science has moved ahead very rapidly, and during those 10 years changes in technologies might have made that worthless process entirely adequate. Our Graviner people had had experience with Teflon, which they used to coat some of their high-performance components, and they knew it to be an extremely tough coating. They may not have known that it does not do well under the 400° temperature at which carbon steel blades are tempered—which the Solingen people would have known—but stainless blades do not require such tempering. At any rate, the Graviner people successfully developed our present coated stainless steel blade.

"We need to do more scientific investigation in depth," Mr. Hansom said. "We suddenly find ourselves with a large business, and we are compelled to defend it. To find out what a razor actually does, we think we should investigate the whole process of shaving. What is hair? Why is young hair different from old hair, thin, thick, live, dead hair? How is hair cut? What happens when any kind of blade cuts any kind of material? Does the edge go between the molecules? Does the edge go through individual molecules? The tip of a razor blade edge is one millionth of an inch wide. Viewing it requires an electronic microscope, which is laboratory equipment. Engineers can't handle that small a dimension, can only work to thousandths. Wilkinson now has blades that cut very well. If they did not do so tomorrow, would we know why?

"Seven years ago we had no shortage of research problems. We listed them, weighted them roughly for priorities. Now we have a research planning team which formulates research policies and makes recommendations to the board. We now have three research groups—Graviner, shaving and hand tools—and we are thinking of forming a fourth group for developing new product lines which would not necessarily be related in any way to our present ones.

"We may be in danger of overdoing on innovation and neglecting sales aspects. Our Graviner people are aircraft-oriented, accustomed to selling to governments, but not too skillful in selling in the civilian markets. Take Graviner's hand-held fire extinguishers, which are high-quality and expensive. Most people don't have fires, but laws and insurance regulations require some people to keep on hand fire extinguishers. Therefore, if you don't have a fire problem, but you do have a fire insurance problem, then don't buy our expensive extinguishers. This means that Graviner's market is only those people who do have fires. Graviner ought to find that there is a great deal more potential in fire extinguishers."

As to patent protection, the Wilkinson management expressed an attitude of cynicism. "The question of patenting," said Mr. Hansom, "often catches us in a dilemma. Only truly new ideas can be patented. Obvious ideas—like Columbus balancing an egg on its tip by denting the shell—cannot be patented. If an idea is thought by its inventor to be obvious and is not patented, the inventor has no protection at all. But if the obvious idea is patented, it can be contested for infringement."

Wilkinson was deeply involved in patenting in its Graviner operation, which, as a normal routine, carried on extensive research and development programs involving the ultimate in intricate engineering. "Patents play a significant role in our Graviner business," said D. R. Gatley joint managing director. "Graviner holds many good master patents which cover very wide areas, some of which are almost principles. But we do not depend upon patent protection. Competitors are quick to make Chinese copies of our innovations, and patents only serve to delay them. But they do delay them. And by that time we mean to be ahead of them again with something new."

exhibit 1 **WILKINSON SWORD LIMITED AND ITS SUBSIDIARY COMPANIES**
Consolidated balance sheet, 31st December, 1965

	1965, £	1964, £
Issued share capital of Wilkinson Sword Limited	2,000,000	2,000,000
Capital reserve (Note 1)	703,093	723,796
Revenue reserves and retained profit (Note 2)	2,932,144	2,218,706
Total interest of Wilkinson Sword Limited shareholders	5,635,207	4,942,502
Future taxation:		
Income tax 1965–1966		938,715
Taxation equalization reserve (Note 3)	288,000	247,000
	288,000	1,185,715
Interest of outside shareholders in subsidiary companies	274,214	257,109
Current liabilities:		
Creditors and accrued expenses	1,154,390	1,624,609
United Kingdom and Overseas taxation, including corporation tax £902,770 (Note 4)	2,165,911	1,317,205
Proposed dividend of Wilkinson Sword Limited	500,000	293,750
	3,820,301	3,235,564
	£10,017,722	£9,620,890

	1965, £	1964, £
Fixed assets (Note 5):		
Land and buildings	1,207,745	879,137
Machinery and equipment	1,658,369	1,324,115
Motor vehicles	128,516	75,954
Capital work in progress	308,941	503,344
	3,303,571	2,782,550
Current assets:		
Stocks and work in progress (Note 7)	2,487,314	1,857,143
Debtors and prepayments	2,282,370	2,617,313
Quoted investments		62,207
Bank deposits	1,150,000	1,500,000
Cash and bank balances	794,467	801,677
	6,714,151	6,838,340

On behalf of the Board

H. B. RANDOLPH ⎱
P. RANDOLPH   ⎰ *Directors*

	£10,017,722	£9,620,890

exhibit 2   **WILKINSON SWORD LIMITED**
Balance sheet, 31st December, 1965

	1965, £		*1964, £*
		Issued and	
	Authorized	*fully paid*	
Share capital:			
Ordinary shares of 4/- each, fully paid	500,000	500,000	*500,000*
Non-voting 'A' ordinary shares of 4/- each,			
fully paid	2,000,000	1,500,000	*1,500,000*
	£2,500,000	2,000,000	*2,000,000*
Capital reserve (Note 1)		827,573	*827,573*
Revenue reserves and retained profit (Note 2)		2,156,749	*1,528,785*
Total capital and reserves		4,984,322	*4,356,358*
Future taxation:			
Income tax 1965–1966			*937,615*
Taxation equalization reserve (Note 3)		288,000	*247,000*
		288,000	*1,184,615*
Current liabilities:			
Creditors and accrued expenses		732,433	*1,076,742*
Provision for unrealised profits on stocks of			
subsidiary companies		277,460	*277,460*
United Kingdom taxation, including corporation tax			
£670,000 (Note 4)		1,672,160	*780,047*
Proposed dividend		500,000	*293,750*
		3,182,053	*2,427,999*
		£8,454,375	*£7,968,972*
Fixed assets (Note 5):			
Land and buildings		1,033,907	*829,262*
Machinery and equipment		1,188,752	*917,971*
Motor vehicles		75,060	*47,625*
Capital work in progress		304,640	*412,836*
		2,602,359	*2,207,694*
Shares in, and amounts owing, by subsidiary companies			
(Note 6)		2,187,157	*1,548,057*
Current assets:			
Stocks and work in progress (Note 7)		1,340,329	*935,983*
Debtors and prepayments		908,075	*1,251,156*
Bank deposits		1,150,000	*1,500,000*
Cash and bank balances		266,455	*526,082*
		3,664,859	*4,213,221*

On behalf of the Board

H. B. RANDOLPH ⎱ *Directors*
P. RANDOLPH   ⎰

	£8,454,375	£7,968,972

exhibit 3   NOTES ON THE ACCOUNTS

1. CAPITAL RESERVE

	£
Balance at 31st December including share premium £484,681	827,573
Deduct: Goodwill arising on consolidation	124,480
	£703,093

2. REVENUE RESERVES AND RETAINED PROFIT
Wilkinson Sword Limited

	General Reserve £	Fixed Asset Replacement Reserve £	Retained Profit £	Total £
Balance at 31st December 1964	100,000	240,500	1,188,285	1,528,785
Transfers	(100,000)	(240,500)	340,500	
Transfers from subsidiaries			38,327	38,327
Profit for year retained by Wilkinson Sword Limited			589,637	589,637
			£2,156,749	£2,156,749

The Group	£
Retained profit of Wilkinson Sword Limited	2,156,749
Add: Profits attributable to Wilkinson Sword Limited retained by subsidiary companies	775,365
	£2,932,114

3. TAXATION EQUALIZATION RESERVE

The taxation equalization reserve represents the taxation benefits arising from accelerated depreciation of fixed assets allowed for taxation purposes in the form of capital allowances.

4. CORPORATION TAX

Corporation tax on 1965 United Kingdom profits has been provided at the rate of 40% and is payable on 1st January, 1967.

exhibit 3 (Continued)

5. FIXED ASSETS

	Wilkinson Sword Limited			The Group		
	Cost or Valuation £	Accumulated Depreciation £	£	Cost or Valuation £	Accumulated Depreciation £	£
Land and buildings	1,080,935	47,028	1,033,907	1,265,677	57,932	1,207,745
Machinery and equipment	1,687,902	499,150	1,188,752	2,422,422	764,053	1,658,369
Motor vehicles	105,223	30,163	75,060	183,100	54,584	128,516
Capital work in progress	304,640		304,640	308,941		308,941
	£3,178,700	£576,341	£2,602,359	£4,180,140	£876,569	£3,303,571
Increase in 1965	£600,954	£206,289	£394,665	£842,903	£321,882	£521,021

Depreciation of fixed assets is calculated at rates sufficient to write off the assets during their expected normal lives.

6. SHARES IN AND AMOUNTS OWING BY SUBSIDIARY COMPANIES

	1965, £	1964, £
Shares held in subsidiary companies at cost	434,337	434,238
Amounts owing by subsidiary companies	1,774,903	1,125,665
	2,209,240	1,559,903
Less: Amounts owing to subsidiary companies	22,083	11,846
	£2,187,157	£1,548,057

7. STOCKS AND WORK IN PROGRESS

Stocks and work in progress have been valued at the lower of cost and net realizable value. The cost of work in progress and finished stocks includes an appropriate proportion of manufacturing overhead costs.

8. CAPITAL COMMITMENTS

Contracts for capital expenditure for which no provision has been made in the accounts are estimated to amount to £136,000 (1964 £360,000).

9. FOREIGN CURRENCY

Assets and liabilities of overseas subsidiary companies have been converted into sterling at rates of exchange ruling at the balance sheet date.

exhibit 4   **WILKINSON SWORD LIMITED AND ITS SUBSIDIARY COMPANIES**
Consolidated profit and loss account for the year ended 31st December, 1965

	1965, £	1964, £
Group trading profit for the year, before taxation, and after deducting and adding the items set out below	2,194,516	3,534,520

After deducting:		
Directors' remuneration		
Fees	3,500	2,600
Other emoluments	106,091	92,035
	109,591	94,635
Auditors' remuneration	22,559	16,508
Depreciation	337,437	196,646
	469,587	307,789
And after adding:		
Interest received (gross)	78,338	68,952

Taxation on the profit of the year:		
United Kingdom taxation		
Corporation tax (Note 4)	902,770	
Profits tax		352,000
Income tax	16,895	842,309
Taxation equalization reserve	41,000	167,000
	960,665	1,361,309
Overseas taxation	99,580	572,096
	1,060,245	1,933,405
Less:		
Overprovision for taxation	292,444	
(including overseas recoveries of £178,684)		
	767,801	1,933,405
Group profit after taxation	1,426,715	1,601,115
Outside shareholders' interest after taxation in subsidiary companies	105,357	118,203
Group profit after taxation attributable to Wilkinson Sword Limited	£1,321,358	£1,482,912

exhibit 4 continued

	1965, £	1964, £
Group profit after taxation attributable to		
Wilkinson Sword Limited	1,321,358	1,482,912
Deduct:		
Profit retained by subsidiary companies	114,221	345,929
	1,207,137	1,136,983
Deduct:		
Interim dividend paid: 10%	200,000	200,000
Final dividend proposed: 25%	500,000	500,000
	700,000	700,000
Less:		
Income tax deducted from dividends and retained	82,500	283,750
	617,500	416,250
Retained profit of Wilkinson Sword Limited:		
Remaining from the year 1965	589,637	720,733
Brought forward from previous years	1,188,285	467,552
Transfers from reserves (Note 2)	378,827	
Retained profit of Wilkinson Sword Limited		
at 31st December, 1965, carried to balance sheet	£2,156,749	£1,188,285

exhibit 5

DEVELOPMENT OF WILKINSON SWORD LIMITED

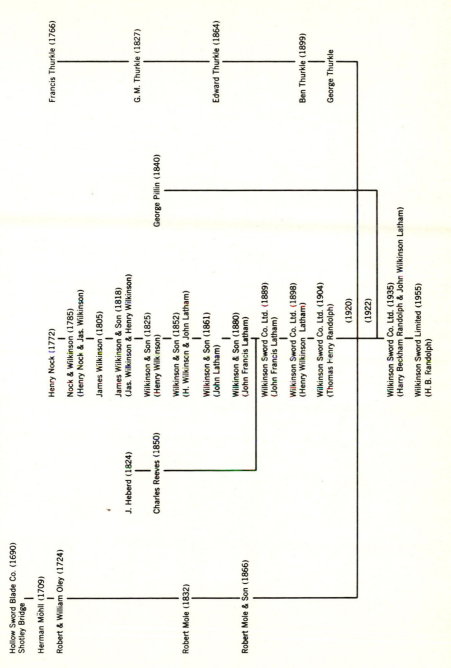

exhibit 6
WILKINSON SWORD LIMITED AND MEMBER COMPANIES
Organization 1965

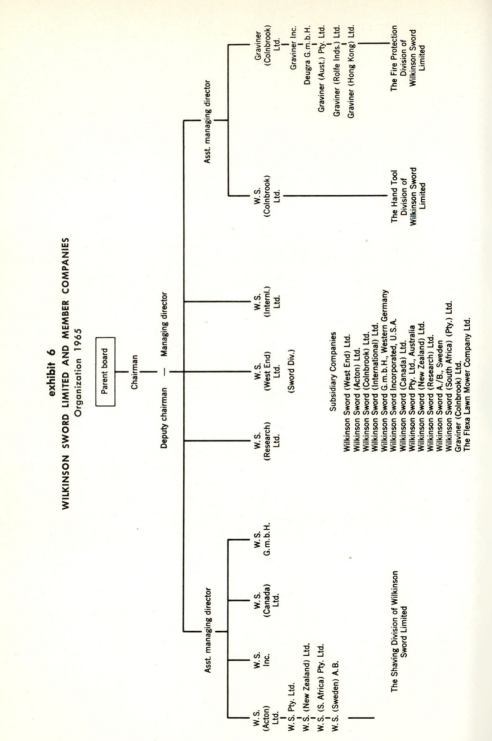

Parent board

Chairman — Managing director

Deputy chairman

Asst. managing director

Asst. managing director

W.S. (Acton) Ltd.
W.S. Pty. Ltd.
W.S. (New Zealand) Ltd.
W.S. (S. Africa) Pty. Ltd.
W.S. (Sweden) A.B.

W.S. Inc.

W.S. (Canada) Ltd.

W.S. G.m.b.H.

The Shaving Division of Wilkinson Sword Limited

W.S. (Research) Ltd.

W.S. (West End) Ltd.
(Sword Div.)

W.S. (Interntl.) Ltd.

W.S. (Colnbrook) Ltd.

The Hand Tool Division of Wilkinson Sword Limited

Graviner (Colnbrook) Ltd.
Graviner Inc.
Deugra G.m.b.H.
Graviner (Aust.) Pty. Ltd.
Graviner (Rolfe Inds.) Ltd.
Graviner (Hong Kong) Ltd.

The Fire Protection Division of Wilkinson Sword Limited

Subsidiary Companies

Wilkinson Sword (West End) Ltd.
Wilkinson Sword (Acton) Ltd.
Wilkinson Sword (Colnbrook) Ltd.
Wilkinson Sword (International) Ltd.
Wilkinson Sword G.m.b.H., Western Germany
Wilkinson Sword Incorporated, U.S.A.
Wilkinson Sword (Canada) Ltd.
Wilkinson Sword Pty. Ltd., Australia
Wilkinson Sword (New Zealand) Ltd.
Wilkinson Sword (Research) Ltd.
Wilkinson Sword A./B., Sweden
Wilkinson Sword (South Africa) (Pty.) Ltd.
Graviner (Colnbrook) Ltd.
The Flexa Lawn Mower Company Ltd.

exhibit **7**

WILKINSON SWORD THROUGHOUT THE WORLD

For many years now we have considered the world to be our market and do not think in terms of the Home Market and Exports.

For Management purposes, we are divided into six Operating Divisions: the Shaving Division; the Hand Tool Division; the Graviner Division; the Sword Division; the Research Division; the International Division, which co-ordinates all plans.

For marketing purposes we have divided the world into four areas:

Area 1 Europe, including the United Kingdom.

Area 2 The Americas, North and South.

Area 3 The Far East, Australia and New Zealand.

Area 4 The Middle East and Africa.

Area 1 Europe

Acton (manufacture of swords, razor blades, garden tools, management headquarters).

Colnbrook (manufacture of Graviner fire and hazard protection and detection systems, group research and development).

Brentford (warehouse and distribution; headquarters for U.K. and International marketing).

Slough (plastic moulding, classified projects).

Cramlington (manufacture of razor blades).

Staines (manufacture of industrial fire and explosion detection equipment and marketing).

Solingen (West Germany) (manufacture of razor blades; marketing, distribution and sales promotion of both razor blades and garden tools).

Dusseldorf (part assembly Graviner products and marketing).

Paris (Graviner sales and service).

Area 2 U.S.A. and Canada

Mountainside, New Jersey (part manufacture of razor blades, sales and marketing, including garden tools).

Toronto (part manufacture of razor blades, sales and marketing, including garden tools).

Washington D.C. (Graviner—sales and service).

Area 3 Far East, Australia and New Zealand

Australia (part manufacture of razor blades, sales, exports and Graviner sales and service).

New Zealand (sales and distribution and Graviner sales and service).

Hong Kong (Graviner sales and service).

Area 4 Middle East and Africa

Wilkinson Sword (South Africa) (Pty.) Limited, Marketing Company established in 1964.

Throughout the world, razor blades are now sold in 50 countries and garden tools in 26.

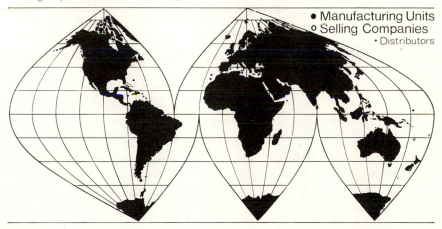

● Manufacturing Units
○ Selling Companies
· Distributors

WILKINSON
SWORD
LIMITED (B)

THE SHAVING DIVISION

Wilkinson's first experience with making cutting implements other than swords came in 1890 when it initiated the manufacture of a straight-edged (cutthroat) razor. The razor gained a reputation for being superior to German razors, which until then were considered the best ones made. In 1898 Wilkinson developed the first safety razor with a hollow-ground, single-edged blade. In 1920 it produced the Empire Safety Stropping Razor, which was so designed that its blade could be stropped automatically while in the razor.

In 1954 Mr. H. B Randolph, Wilkinson's chairman, made the acquaintance of Rud Osberghaus, of Solingen, Germany, which was world-renowned as the center of the high-quality German cutlery industry. Rud Osberghaus made excellent razors, but the firm was chronically short of capital. Mr. Randolph first licensed production from Osberghaus, and eventually Wilkinson bought a majority interest in the business.

At the end of World War II, Wilkinson, which had been fully occupied with war work, decided to return to the razor business, this time as a serious contender. Contrary to later press reports, which indicated that Wilkinson had unwittingly stumbled into the discovery of its dramatically successful stainless steel blade, the venture into stainless steel was the result of deliberate and methodical planning. Wilkinson had decided to re-enter the razor blade business, but not as a marginal producer. Its decision was to withhold its re-entrance until it had developed a strong blade which was clearly exceptional and which would allow the company to achieve a position in the world blade industry.

Stainless steel had long been known to razor blade manufacturers, who had shied away from it because it posed technical and commercial problems. The Wilkinson management was aware of these problems, but it believed that there were possibilities in stainless which the industry had not explored. It started discussions with a company in Solingen which was soon to become Wilkinson's affiliate. After years of development Solingen produced a blade which Wilkinson adopted for production in 1956. Consumer reaction indicated that it was looked upon as a high-quality blade, but it had some features that were questionable. The "first-shave" quality of the blade was not much better than that of high-quality carbon steel blades.

Believing that a friction-free protective coating was the solution, Wilkinson relieved Solingen of further development responsibility and assigned the project to its own U.K. research group, which had extensive experience with highly durable preservative coatings for metals but no experience with razor blades. As a result, after several years of research, Wilkinson, in 1961, introduced its phenomenally keen and long-lasting stainless steel blade, which was clearly an advance over any existing competitive blade.

News of the new blade's remarkable sharpness and durability spread rapidly by word of mouth as one shaver told another of its wonderful qualities. One London barrister commented, in a widely publicized quotation: "It doesn't just shave off your whiskers. It *breathes* them off." As the whispering campaign gained momentum, demand soared far beyond the company's capacity to produce. "We were swamped with orders," said Mr. Peter Randolph, the managing director. "But we were not going to permit ourselves to be stampeded into wild expansion. Increasing production capacity at great speed and maintaining quality do not always go together, and we were determined that in our case they should do so."

The company quickly stopped advertising, but the blades continued to gain publicity from newspapers and periodicals, which carried their remarkable story as news. By the end of 1961 Wilkinson had 6% of the total United Kingdom blade market (previously dominated by Gillette, 75% share), and stores distributing Wilkinson blades were constantly out of stock. Retailers began a self-imposed rationing system, selling the blades singly, or selling them only to favored customers. Many retailers reported that their supply would be exhausted within 15 minutes of its receipt by customers who had been waiting in line to capture a few blades.

Plans were drafted to increase production by 100% in 1962 and 300% in 1963. Production was carried on in portions of the Acton sword and hand tool plant, to which additions were made. The German factory at Solingen was enlarged to meet the demand from the Common Market, and in 1964 a new plant devoted to razor blade production alone was erected at Cramlington in northeast England. In the home market there was a functioning distribution organization and Wilkinson had obtained 20% market share by the end of 1962, and 31% by the end of 1963. In spite of the massive and mounting competition, Wilkinson's United Kingdom market share at the end of 1964 had risen to 36%. During 1964 advertising had been resumed, and in early 1966 Wilkinson had a reported 47% share of the United Kingdom razor blade market. In the United States, during 1964, when major competitors were introducing similar stainless steel blades with extravagant introductory campaigns, Wilkinson switched its blade retailing away from its garden tool dealers to chemists, grocers, newsagents and tobacconists. In early 1966 Wilkinson had 15% of the United States market for stainless blades.[1]

In 1963 the company was already selling abroad to such an extent that Mr. Randolph was saying "The world is our market." Within three years new plants had been built in Germany, the United States, Canada, and Australia. Fifty export markets had been opened and the company was aggressively establishing itself "in every part of the world which shaves the modern way" (there were parts of the world where

---

[1] There are different ways in which market share can be expressed. For razor blades there are four possible categories in any national market:
  1) All adult males of shaving age;
  2) All wet shaves (double edge and single edge);
  3) All double-edge blade shavers;
  4) All stainless double-edge blade shavers;
In the United Kingdom (4) is 90% of (2). In the United States, (4) is 75% of (3) and 60% of (2).

To add yet another complication, market shares are sometimes expressed in percentages of blade units and here it must be remembered that one stainless unit equals three carbon units in terms of life. Hence, the conflict in claims made by Wilkinson Sword and Gillette where both may correctly claim to be market leaders in a particular area. Wilkinson Sword, being exclusively stainless, is talking of share of users; Gillette, being manufacturers of both stainless and carbon units, can simultaneously claim leadership in share of units.

primitive people shaved with broken glass). In 1966 over 60% of Wilkinson's production was exported.

Early in June, 1964, the press made known to the public that Wilkinson was paying the Gillette Company a royalty of about $\frac{1}{5}$ of a cent on every 15¢ blade Wilkinson sold in the United States and slightly more for each blade sold elsewhere in the world. The royalties, explained Mr. Randolph, stemmed from a patent infringement suit which Gillette had brought against Wilkinson in West Germany in 1963. Wilkinson and Gillette had developed the same Teflon razor blade coating simultaneously, but the Gillette patent filing had preceded that of Wilkinson by about three months.

At the time of the announcement both firms made statements giving as their reason the wish to avoid protracted litigation. The consent decree came as a surprise, for Gillette attorneys were known to have prepared a vigorous prosecution of their claim. Wilkinson, in turn, had asserted that it had a clear right to the patent and that it intended to carry its defense to the highest court. Observers noted that shortly after the royalty agreement Wilkinson floated a public stock issue. That Wilkinson intended to "go public" had not been known to the Gillette management. When Wilkinson and Gillette first started negotiations for a royalty agreement, Wilkinson had not planned to go public. This was a separate decision taken during the course of the negotiations which lasted about one year. Shortly after the agreement Gillette launched its new Silver Stainless Blade with a tremendous fanfare of advertising. Wilkinson had been long awaiting Gillette's introduction of a competitive product.

While sales continued to increase, profits were declining largely because Wilkinson now needed to advertise. "We made certain forecasts and we geared our output to them," said Mr. Randolph. "But we underestimated the marketing resources of our competitors, our blue friends. Well, it has proved more difficult than we expected. Believe me, though, we don't intend to stand still"

THE RAZOR BLADE MARKET

Until Wilkinson became a major producer, the world razor blade industry had consisted of (1) three large American producers which had international plants and markets; and (2) numerous small producers who manufactured and sold nationally or regionally.

The big three were Gillette, which produced the Blue Blade and the Super Blue Blade (the Randolphs always referred to Gillette as "our blue friends") and later produced the Silver Stainless; the American Safety Razor Company Division of Philip Morris, which made the Gem (carbon) and later the Personna (stainless); and the Schick Safety Razor Company Division of Eversharp, Inc., which made the Pal (carbon) and later the Krona-Plus (stainless). Each of the big three had long experience in the razor blade business.

Wilkinson, like most others in the industry looked upon Gillette as its principal competition. Gillette dominated the world market. Until Wilkinson produced its coated blade, Gillette claimed 70% of the $175 million United States blade market, 75% of the United Kingdom market, and an estimated 50% of the total world market. While Wilkinson sold in 50 world markets, Gillette sold in 100.

Gillette's main plant was a new 10-acre factory in Boston, where all its American razor blade production was concentrated, and it had sizable foreign plants to which it exported its expert technical knowledge. In a typical year Gillette produced 10 million razors and $2\frac{1}{2}$ billion blades in the United States and an additional 4 billion blades abroad.

In 1962, Gillette's peak year, it earned a record profit of $45 million, which represented a margin of 16% on sales volume. In 1960 Gillette had introduced its Super Blue Blade, which was priced 40% higher than its regular Blue Blade. It was estimated that the Super Blue accounted for 25% of Gillette's total sales and returned one third of the company's net profit.[2]

Although Gillette had been paying out 75% of its earnings in dividends, it had accumulated a substantial surplus. Its recent statement showed assets of about $200 million, of which about one third were in cash and marketable securities. Carl Gilbert, Gillette's chairman, spoke of his reserves as "artificial courage." "Companies that have to worry about cash sometimes get pushed," said Mr. Gilbert. "Sometimes they try to do in twelve months what can't be done in twelve months, but could be done in eighteen. With Gillette, if something requires five years, we'll take five years."[3]

RAZOR BLADE PROMOTION

Wilkinson accompanied its introduction of the coated stainless steel blade in 1961 by a modest program of advertising. When the unprece-

[2] Company Annual Reports, 1962–1965.

[3] Walter Guzzardi, Jr., "Gillette Faces the Stainless-Steel Dragon," *Fortune*, July, 1963, p. 160.

dented word-of-mouth campaign quickly created a wave of demand far
beyond the company's ability to produce, the company decided to cease
all advertising. "We didn't think it was a good idea to advertise something people couldn't readily obtain," said a Wilkinson sales executive.
"It leaves a nasty taste."

Wherever possible, advertising contracts were canceled, but there
were some instances in which agencies had made commitments to others.
Rather than pay out fees and get nothing in return, the Wilkinson management sought to put the time and space to some good use. The management decided to apologize to the public for being unable to furnish
them with blades. The result was a fresh wave of demand from people
who were now hearing about the blades for the first time.

For three years Wilkinson did virtually no advertising. During the
period its share in every market area it entered rose rapidly, the rise
generated only by the spoken testimonials of satisfied customers.

In 1964, faced with massive and mounting competition, Wilkinson
resumed advertising, now on a national and international scale. "The
company's pre-eminence as a craftsman in steel and cutting edges was
reflected in our advertising," said Mr. Randolph. "The sword image,
which is unique to our company alone, was powerfully exploited. The
Wilkinson Sword has become a byword for the best in British craftsmanship and engineering. We believe that quality products supported by
quality advertising make an unbeatable combination" (see Exhibit 1).

In 1964 Wilkinson used television for the first time in the United
States. Its allocation for the year's advertising approached $3 million.
In 1963 Gillette had launched its new Silver Stainless Blade with $4
million worth of television and radio commercials. It was estimated that
Gillette had been spending over $30 million per year on world-wide
razor blade advertising. In 1965[4] it increased this expenditure significantly (see Exhibit 2).

RAZOR BLADE MANUFACTURE

A razor blade was a highly engineered product, mass produced on
automated machinery at the rate of 700 blades a minute, yet precise
to tolerances of a millionth of an inch. The ultra-high precision requirements, when combined with high-speed mass production, presented continuing problems in quality control.

A carbon steel blade was made of steel containing 1.2% carbon, a

[4] *Ibid.*, p. 247.

tractable material which was subject to corrosion but which took a good edge. Stainless steel contained 11.5% chrome, was resistant to corrosion, and kept its edge longer. But stainless was tough, hard to grind and hone, and took a poor edge. It required a chemical coating to insure good shaveability. Stainless steel as a raw material cost three times as much as carbon steel. Wilkinson, like all other producers, bought its stainless steel from Uddeholms A/B of Sweden.

In manufacturing there were nine main processes: perforating, hardening, normalizing, polishing, cleaning and drying, etching, grinding and honing, stropping, and coating. There were numerous detailed inspections during production, including the use of microscopes and blue lights. Over 20% of the razor blade work force was engaged in quality control. "If a man happens to get a bad blade," said a production executive, "he remembers it." In its early experiences, Wilkinson had critical manufacturing problems, sometimes scrapping over 20% of production.

Research findings, according to company officers, showed that men's beards differed, as did their standards for a good shave. The age of the shaver made a difference, and hair thickness varied from person to person. The technique of shaving had a decided effect: the heat of the shaving water, the soap used, and the time allowed for the soap to soften the beard were all factors that influenced blade performance. Because of this, Wilkinson was not satisfied that razor blades lent themselves entirely to objective testing. Therefore it subjected its daily production of blades to an actual shaving test. In a test-shaving room at the plant numerous staff members shaved every day, using soaps or creams of their own choice and their own personal techniques of shaving. Their opinions were recorded and the blades checked microscopically after use. Only after these final user-tests was any batch of blades released for sale.

Initially Wilkinson had concentrated its attention on the edge of the blade. In 1966 it was giving attention to the body of the blade and to its packaging.

Wilkinson kept a statistical record of letters of complaint, which, in 1966, were running about four-tenths of a letter per million blades. The management attempted to answer every letter.

FACTORS IN RAZOR BLADE COMPETITION

When Wilkinson made its re-entrance into the razor blade business, it made only its coated stainless steel blade. Gillette had no stainless steel blade in its line but placed heavy emphasis on its highly profitable Super Blue Blade. For three years Wilkinson and others, with their new stainless steel blades, cut deeply into Gillette's market share. Gillette had earned record profits in 1962, but its profits fell 8% in 1963 despite higher sales volume and dropped another 11.5% in 1964. During these years, as one commentator put it, Gillette literally sat back and thought. Factors considered by razor blade manufacturers were: stainless steel cost three times as much as carbon, production costs were higher, but there were no additional expenses. All told, stainless blades did not cost three times as much as carbon blades, while the price of the stainless blade would be about 15¢ versus 6.7¢ for the Super Blue Blade.

How long a stainless steel blade would last was an open question, and both shavers and blade makers indulged in playing the "numbers game" of counting shaves per blade. Wilkinson believed its blades gave ten good shaves, and it advertised at least seven. Analysts reasoned that the industry now had stainless blades which lasted three times as long as the best carbon blades, cost less than three times as much to make, but sold for more than twice the price. But the shaves-per-blade estimates might prove inaccurate, and as technology improved, stainless blades might give three or four times as many shaves as a good carbon blade, which would give stainless blades an overwhelming advantage over competitive carbon blades.

What type of shaver would be drawn to the stainless blades was uncertain. Wilkinson's initial experiences indicated that they attracted the high-price, quality buyers and prudent buyers as well, since they resulted in a lower cost per shave. If this proved true in the long run, it held the prospect of the entire industry becoming largely a one-blade industry, with a cut to one third of its present unit production. Such a cut would have drastic consequences for the big producers of carbon blades and might result in mass dismissals of employees and idle plant capacities.

By the end of 1965, in terms of total blade markets, stainless steel blades had taken over 85% of the United Kingdom market, 40% of the German market, and 25% of the American market.

exhibit 1

exhibit 2 HOW THE RAZOR-BLADE MANUFACTURERS ALLOCATE THEIR AD DOLLARS (U.S. MARKET)
(Figures are in thousands of dollars and are gross time or space billings)

	Network TV		Spot TV		Magazines (general and farm)		Newspapers (incl. supplements)		Radio Spot	Network
	1963	1964	1963	1964	1963	1964	1963	1964	1964	1964
Gillette										
Razors and blades	$1,971.2	$ 45.6	$1,000.5	$ 888.1	$······	$······	$ 434.4	$······	$ 137.0	$ 220.0
Razor blades	11.4									
Razors, blades and Right Guard	474.2	······	······	······			98.9	487.2		
Razors, blades and Foamy	2,237.9	1,174.9								
Razor blades and Sun Up	89.2	181.7					······			
Razor blades and Right Guard	1,097.2									
Stainless-steel blades and Foamy	424.7	2,896.3								
Stainless-steel blades	873.6	2,136.7								
Men's gift sets	320.4	331.7								
Lady Gillette razors and blades	451.3	······	······	······	18.0	156.9				
Shaving kits	······	942.4								
Total	7,951.1	7,709.3	1,000.5	888.1	18.0	156.9	533.3	487.2	137.0	220.0

	1	2	3	4	5	6	7	8	9	10
Schick										
Razor blades	615.0	63.4			553.3	37.0			392.0	1,370.0
Razors and blades			2,685.6	1,530.7	36.0	11.5	1,379.2			
Razors, blades and shave cream								873.0		
Stainless-steel blades and Hot Lather		147.0								
Stainless-steel blades		493.4						22.5		
Stainless-steel blades and shave cream		441.9								
Injector razor		96.8			88.9					
Lady Eversharp										
Total	615.0	1,242.5	2,685.6	1,530.7	678.2	48.5	1,379.2	895.5	392.0	1,370.0
Pal										
Stainless-steel blades	0.4	25.9								
Stainless-steel razors and blades	35.3	260.8	113.4	28.4						
Razors and blades	555.6	84.7								
Injector razor and blades	173.2				238.8	28.7				
Total	764.5	371.4	113.4	28.4	238.8	28.7				
Personna	1,396.8	3,178.0	531.4	39.6	1.8	162.6				
Wilkinson		74.6		682.7						

SOURCES: Publishers Information Bureau; Bureau of Advertising, ANPA; TvB-Rorabaugh; Leading National Advertisers/Broadcast Advertisers Reports, Radio Advertising Bureau.

Table reproduced from *Printers' Ink*, June 11, 1965, p. 50.

WILKINSON
SWORD
LIMITED (C)

GARDEN TOOLS

"We believe," said Mr. Denys Randolph, managing director of the hand tool division, "that the best way to get into any line is to make the best quality products in the world. There weren't any quality garden tools in England until we introduced our line. Now customers are demanding quality tools. In pruners, shears, and cultivators we have creamed 80 to 90% of the top price market in England. Furthermore, we now have about 25% of the total garden tool market."

Wilkinson had first introduced a line of pruning shears in 1920 to combat the post-World War I depression. Moderately successful, the garden tool activities were virtually discontinued during World War II, only to be revived again in 1948 when Wilkinson concentrated seriously on making a fairly complete line. "The Wilkinson management keeps in mind," said Mr. Denys Randolph, "that garden tools tided the company over after each world war."

In 1958 and again in 1962 the company undertook a complete design alteration of its hand tool line. The redesign was based upon findings from research the company had done covering garden tool users and dealers in the United Kingdom. Price groups were studied, as were their social characteristics, sizes of gardens, the plants grown in them, the tools used, the types of retail shops, their size, the tools they handled, and the variations by areas. As a result the company proceeded to make seventeen varieties of tools, including seven pruners, four cultivators, five shears, and a lawn-edging knife. On every tool specific attention was given to the geometry of cutting edges, styling, strength, lightness, and durability. Floating bearings were made for shearing tools, and a myriad of patterns were tried to perfect a streamline styling in tune with modern taste. The company's first public annual report to stockholders announced that on May 8, 1964, Mr. S. A. Randolph had the privilege of receiving from H.R.H. Prince Philip, the Duke of Edinburgh, a design award for the company's hand shears.

Garden tools were originally manufactured in the Acton plant, where swords and razor blades were also produced, and production was somewhat intermingled. The low volume did not permit mass-production economies. There were numerous hand operations, and many components, such as wooden handles, were bought. Wilkinson considered that its special talents lay in design and in the processing of the cutting edges. Prices were based upon a cost formula and were shaded somewhat to make them competitive. The resulting prices and gross profit were high, but the final net return was low.

Exports of garden tools had increased in the post-World War II period and at the end of 1964 accounted for 30% of garden tool sales. Half of the exports went to the United States, with Europe, South Africa, New Zealand, and Australia making up the remainder. The United States was believed to have a high export potential, followed by Australia. South Africa was believed to have promise because of the high standard of living of a segment of the white population. Europe as a whole was a large market, but there were many competitive producers on the Continent, and Wilkinson had made little headway there.

In 1964 Wilkinson bought the Flexa Lawn Mower Company, Ltd. which manufactured a lawn mower on a new principle, with flexible steel blades and a flexible cutter bar which adjusted to each other. It was a small company which had sold about 1,000 mowers a year. The Wilkinson management bought Flexa with the thought of entering the lawn mower market as a whole, later adding other models. Mr. Randolph pointed out that in the United Kingdom one competitor, Qualcast, had 90% of the mower market; it also had 40% of the German market. "Qualcast might at this time," said Mr. Randolph, "be in just as vulnerable a position as Gillette was. Who knows?"

In 1960 Wilkinson had decided to launch the sale of its garden tools in the United States market, where it believed that there was huge potential for a line of super-high-quality garden implements. Mr. Charles

Coe was engaged as Wilkinson's United States representative, and from an office in Manhattan he set out to invade the New England market.

Wilkinson garden tools were priced to retail at two to three times the price of comparable American tools. Meeting strong price resistance, Mr. Coe resorted to placing his tools with garden shops and hardware stores on a consignment basis, and he tried aggressively to convince his dealers that while Wilkinson tools might provide only 15% of the retailer's sales volume they would provide 30% of his profit. Mr. Coe provided his dealers with attractive placards and display stands. A typical stand displayed Wilkinson's self-developed Swoe (sword-hoe), which was described as the first significant improvement on the common garden hoe in 2,000 years. The stand displayed the three-edged Swoe, an implement which had the appearance of a long-handled golf putter with a twisted shaft. A placard described it as "The wonderful, wonderful Swoe," adding, "To Swoe is a pleasure" (see Exhibit 1).

Mr. Coe was meeting only frustration when, in November, 1961, he received a sample shipment of the new stainless steel razor blades from London. Stories had drifted back to him of their skyrocketing success in England. Mr. Coe made passing reference to the blades in a promotional letter to his garden tool dealers, and he received an immediate and positive reply. He distributed his limited supply, and within days his dealers were begging him for more.

Mr. Coe then hit upon the thought of using the blades to promote the sale of garden tools. Thereafter he supplied the blades to his dealers, rationing his limited supply. Dealers were told that they were to offer the blades as an inducement to each customer to buy a garden tool. Dealers found that their scant supply of blades was quickly exhausted and that their customers returned promptly, not for more garden tools, but for more blades. By the spring of 1962 it was discovered that a black market had developed, with dealers selling them one blade at a time and only to those customers who were willing to pay premium prices.

Mr. Coe then modified his distribution policy. The blades, he announced, would be available only to "authorized dealers." A retailer became an authorized dealer by purchasing from Wilkinson one each of its line of garden tools, which entitled the dealer to also purchase two cartons of razor blades. In return for the order Wilkinson would supply the dealer with a handsome floor display for the garden tools and would mail to 400 of the dealer's customers a free razor blade together with a brochure promoting the tools. Customers tried the new blades and about a third of them immediately wanted more; some dealers reported conversions of over 75%. To get more blades the customers were drawn into the garden shops—the only place where more blades were available. There the customers were to be sold on the garden tools. Since only rarely were drugstores and supermarkets willing to stock expensive imported pruning shears and garden hoes, the policy limited Wilkinson blade distribution to hardware stores, garden shops, and greenhouses. Under pressure because of the limited availability of the blades, Mr. Coe explained: "Actually, we are trying to restrain our dealers from advertising our blades."

The blades moved into distribution, and as word of their qualities spread Mr. Coe's New York office was flooded with orders. Wholesalers of sundries and druggists' supply houses besieged him. Macy's asked for six cartons a week. People traveled in from the suburbs to try to wheedle a few packages from Mr. Coe personally. With supplies grossly inadequate, wild rumors sprang up, all of them unfounded. It was said that Wilkinson's plant in England had been mysteriously burned out; that the company had been bought up by Gillette; that Wilkinson's production machinery had been sabotaged; that desperate competitors had cornered the world supply of stainless steel. "We have three girls here answering phone calls and writing letters explaining that our blades are rationed," said Mr. Coe. One frustrated American wrote an open letter to the *Daily Telegraph* criticizing the British for failing to supply the demand and ending: "Wake up, Britain!" Wilkinson replied that it was awake, but it was having production problems.

In England, where the blade shortage was just as drastic, the company was marketing its blades through chemists and chain stores and it was meeting problems parallel to those in the States. At length, Mr. H. B. Randolph, the chairman, decided to reverse the marketing policy. "The garden-tool side of our activities has now been settled," he announced. "Distributors have been informed that garden tools henceforth will be sold through hardware stores and garden shops, and the blades will be sold through druggists and food stores."

Wilkinson then stepped up its advertising, added more salesmen, and undertook expensive promotions of garden tools (see Exhibits 2 and 3).

While this was occurring, razor blade sales continued to soar, but the blades were constantly in short supply. "Until supply catches up to demand," said Mr. Coe in New York, "if people like our razor blades, we hope that they might try our garden tools. . . ."

In 1964, to revitalize the garden tool activities, Mr. Denys Randolph, who was reputed to be the company's "trouble shooter," was made managing director of the hand tool division. In an early move he separated garden tool activities from other products in manufacture, sales, and distribution. "Wilkinson, as a whole, has smarted under the 'one-product' criticism," said Mr. Randolph. "We mean to correct this image. Recreational spending is growing, but gardening seems to be diminishing because people are tending toward recreation which takes them away from home. Nevertheless, there is today a £50 million English gardening market. We already have the distribution. We should be able to capture more of that market. Our annual growth has been 7%. We mean to aim for a progressive advancement of about 30% per annum." The garden tool line accounted for approximately 8% of the company's turnover and had the lowest profit return in the product line.

exhibit 1

exhibit 1 (continued)

W 461   W 469

W 470

W 470
SWOE 60/-. Combines the principles of the dutch and draw hoe.
New stainless steel blade has
three cutting edges and is hollow
forged to prevent even damp
soil sticking and impairing its
efficiency. Aerates the soil, creates
tilth, hoes fast and safely between plants. Maroon plastic
sleeve to aluminium tube handle
(58″ long). Shock-absorbing,
comfort-shaped grip. Design
Centre Award Winner.

W 461
Wrake 60/-. Cultivates as it
rakes. Rustproof aluminium
bronze head, very hard wearing,
resists abrasion. Swept back
head rakes safely between plants,
prevents overspill of soil at sides.
Handle (57½″ long) as SWOE.

W 463
Standard Hoe 45/-. A conventional hoe of unconventional
quality. Sword steel blade
chromed for protection against
rust, hardened and tempered to
withstand heavy and constant
use, even in the heaviest soil.
Edge retains its sharpness far
longer than similar types. Over-
all length 58½″. Handle as SWOE.

W 469
Long-Handled Fork 45/-. Three-
pronged forged carbon steel
head, chromed for protection
against rust. Light and strong, it
gives a long, effortless reach—
ideal for wide flower beds.
Overall length 56½″. Handle as
SWOE.

W 468
New Edging Knife 60/-. Stainless steel blade, slightly pointed
to cut effortlessly into hard turf.
Permanently sharp, it stands up to
the hardest wear, even in stony
ground. Maroon plastic sleeve to
light, strong aluminium shaft.
Aluminium handle, covered in
grey nylon. Overall length 39″.

exhibit 2

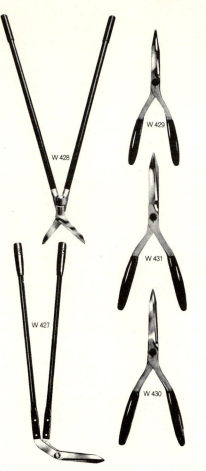

W 431

Notched Shear 70/-. For heavier hedges, such as beech and yew. Unique serrated cutting notch grips thicker branches and slices through cleanly and effortlessly. Floating bearing ensures smooth action, never tightens or slackens. Double cushion stop prevents arms getting tired. $8\frac{1}{4}''$ blades.

W 430

Sword Shear 65/-. For grass and light hedges: perfect for privet. Floating bearing ensures effortless action, never tightens or slackens. Double cushion stop eliminates arm fatigue. Light and beautifully balanced, can be used continuously with great comfort and little effort. $8\frac{1}{4}''$ blades.

W 429

Ladies Shear 60/-. Weighs less than 24 ozs. Though so light it adds great strength to a lady's arm. She will specially appreciate how the floating bearing ensures smooth, effortless action: how the double cushion prevents her arms tiring: how its beautiful balance makes it so comfortable to use. 7″ blades.

All the above shears have won Design Centre Awards.

W 427

Edging Shear 75/-. Tapered, hollow—forged, rust—resisting sword steel blades and long, light, tubular steel handles (with shock-absorbing rubber grips) make light work of trimming edges. Floating bearing maintains correct tension along the entire cutting edges. 8″ blades.

W 428

Lawn Shear 100/-. Designed to cut grass no mower can reach. New, push-button, *detachable handles* in tough aluminium alloy with maroon plastic sleeves. New bolt assembly includes stainless heel plate and unique pivot spring to ensure smooth cutting action. $8\frac{1}{2}''$ blades.

exhibit 3

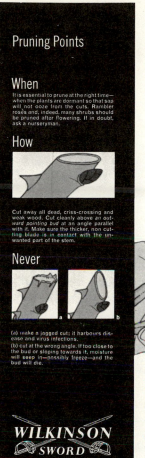

Pruning Points

When

It is essential to prune at the right time—when the plants are dormant so that sap will not ooze from the cuts. Rambler roses and, indeed, many shrubs should be pruned after flowering. If in doubt, ask a nurseryman.

How

Cut away all dead, criss-crossing and weak wood. Cut cleanly above *an outward pointing bud* at an angle parallel with it. Make sure the thicker, non cutting blade is in contact with the unwanted part of the stem.

Never

(a) make a jagged cut; it harbours disease and virus infections.
(b) cut at the wrong angle. If too close to the bud or sloping towards it, moisture will seep in—possibly freeze—and the bud will die.

WILKINSON SWORD

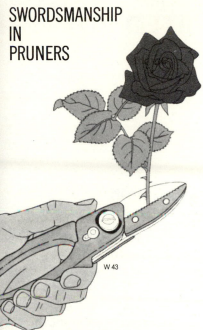

SWORDSMANSHIP IN PRUNERS

W 43

All Wilkinson Sword Pruners are designed on a tried and proved principle—that of the pruning knife. Thus, the holding blade steadies the stem, while the cutting blade slices through with surgical precision, making a perfectly clean cut without bruising—whether it be the tender sprig of a rose bush or the sturdy branch of a tree. The rust-resisting blades stay sharper far longer. The aluminium alloy handles combine lightness with strength, fit snugly into the hand. The nylon bearings ensure smooth action, less wear, never have to be adjusted or oiled. And the range provides for every pruning need the amateur—or professional—gardener is likely to meet.

WILKINSON SWORD LIMITED (D)

GRAVINER DIVISION

Early in the 1930's a retired officer, Captain Salmon, invented an inertia switch which triggered automatically to extinguish crash fires in automobiles. The switch was developed by an engineer named Mathison who later adapted it to aircraft. Mathison's switch proved to be reliable and was in demand, but he lacked sufficient funds and so was embarrassed by sizable orders tendered to him by the British government. Mutual acquaintances introduced him to Mr. H. B. Randolph, and an arrangement was made whereby Mathison's Graviner Company (gravity-inertia) did the selling and Wilkinson did the developing and manufacturing.

Graviner production began in the sword factory at Acton. In 1939, when it became evident that Graviner equipment would become vital in the war effort, a new plant was erected at Colnbrook adjacent to the London International Airport.

Expansion of the Graviner business continued steadily, and Graviner equipment became increasingly complex. In 1958, working in cooperation with the Royal Aeronautical Establishment at Farnborough, Graviner developed an explosion suppression system designed to prevent explosions of the fuel tanks in case of an incendiary strike on bombers. Graviner now supplied protective equipment for most British military aircraft. Its equipment was also fitted to all British civil aircraft, including the Comet, Britannia, Viscount, and Vanguard. The company also developed adaptations of its equipment for other types of fighting vehicles and for railroad equipment and ocean-going ships.

482

Prior to 1964 Graviner and Wilkinson had been separate, privately owned companies, each operating from the site at Colnbrook. The relationship was harmonious, but there were problems of communications between the two companies and occasionally conflict of opinion over product development and investment. In July, 1964, it was decided to eliminate these difficulties by merging the two companies. A new company, Graviner (Colnbrook) Limited was formed, with Wilkinson Sword owning two-thirds of the stock and Graviner one-third. This operation was designated as the Graviner division and was independent in operations except for capital expenditures, personnel policies, legal matters, and building and site locations (see Exhibit 1). It followed very wide policy guidelines laid down by the headquarters management. For example, its products were to be limited to safety and control equipment.

Since the Graviner facilities were geographically separate from the others in the Wilkinson group, most of which were ten miles away at Acton, the Graviner Division tended to be especially autonomous. The Graviner Division made capital equipment, whereas the other Wilkinson divisions made consumer products.

In 1966 Graviner had a world reputation for its special skills and technologies associated with protection of aircraft and missiles, and its equipment was being increasingly adapted to railroad locomotives and cars, armored fighting vehicles, ocean-going freighters, tankers and passenger ships, small boats, hover craft, industrial plants, and stationary engine rooms. It was also producing general-purpose hand-held fire extinguishers. Its product line included (see Exhibits 2, 3 and 4):

Fire protection equipment for military aircraft
Fire protection equipment for commercial aircraft
Explosion suppression equipment for military aircraft
Explosion suppression equipment for industrial purposes
Fire protection for power boats and auxiliary yachts
Gas turbine temperature-monitoring systems
Dual-purpose fire extinguishers
Temperature control switches
Indicating thermistor controllers
Oil mist detectors
Marine diesel scavage-duct fire detectors
Explosion protection systems for industry
Centralized temperature monitoring

In 1965 the approximate split among the total Wilkinson turnover (sales) was shaving 73%, hand tools and swords, 8% and Graviner 19%. The turnover split for 1966 was expected to be the same. Prior to the recent growth of the shaving business, Graviner turnover had represented 60% of the total Wilkinson volume. Graviner produced 19% of the company's total turnover, and it produced a substantial portion of the company's total profit. It had consistently earned more profit than the sword or the hand tool divisions; 40% of its sales were military, 60% were civilian, and 30% of its total sales were exported. The military portion of its business was subjected to costing by governmental bureaus on a labor, materials, and overhead formula which allowed a 5% profit. Civilian sales were priced out according to a formula which resulted in prices that were high but were considered competitive. Of the company's 3,000-plus employees, 850 worked in the Graviner division.

Since there was a growing tendency for the British government and others to buy American airplanes or American air frames in which were installed home-manufactured engines, Graviner had formed a subsidiary company to represent it in Washington, D.C. Since Graviner equipment was being used increasingly in German military equipment, Graviner formed a German company, Deugra Gmbh, to exploit Germany and the Common Market, and it was acquiring a German plant site in expectation of the entrance of England into the Common Market or to be used in the event that England failed to gain entrance. A policy decision was made to manufacture in Australia to circumvent the 30% Australian import duty. Subsidiaries were also formed in New Zealand and Hong Kong, and consideration was being given to establishing a Graviner subsidiary in France. Some of these subsidiaries had been the outgrowth of representatives of the company who for years had been performing after-sale services for Graviner, such as holding spares, undertaking systems overhauls, and doing maintenance and repair work. It was intended that the new companies would continue these services but would henceforth also expand the Graviner markets in their areas.

The Graviner manufacturing processes tended to be job-shop in nature, with some 400 products in production at almost any time, and only a few in batches of 1,000 or more on a single order. There was a great amount of product design and development engineering, which required a high order of engineering skill. Eighty per cent of materials were purchased on a "released" basis, which required strict conformance and certified compliance with mechanical specifications. Graviner equipment included many micro-miniaturized electrical and electronic components, many of which had been in existence for only a few years. Graviner had, for example, been using transistors long before they were popularly used in radios.

Graviner production involved very close controls on manufacturing processes and the ultimate in inspections. The management felt that it had a moral obligation to produce an ultrareliable product, since safety and human lives were at stake, and costs and prices were secondary. Therefore it sought high-grade employees, paid premium wages, and as a matter of policy would permit no wage-incentive scheme of any kind. Wilkinson felt that in an industry in which quality was generally high, its Graviner quality was the highest; that its production efficiency was low compared to that of manufacturers generally, but high compared to that of others in the industry.

The Graviner management felt that there was a great unexploited potential for the future expansion of its business. "Most marine engine-room systems," said Mr. D. R. Gatley, joint managing director of Graviner (Colnbrook) Limited, "are archaic, primitive. During the next three or four years most ships will probably have remote engine-room controls, not only for temperature control, but also for pressure, flow of fuel, level of fuel, and many other parameters. By way of strategy for expanding our business, we are always looking for new products, mostly via the research and development route. The world population of airplanes is not increasing, and it may even diminish, with the trend toward larger airplanes. But there is a vast unexploited market for automated industrial processes and marine engine rooms. We also have a large potential for geographic expansion. The United States market is ripe for geographic expansion, even based upon our now-existing line of Graviner products."

exhibit 1
GRAVINER (COLNBROOK) LIMITED

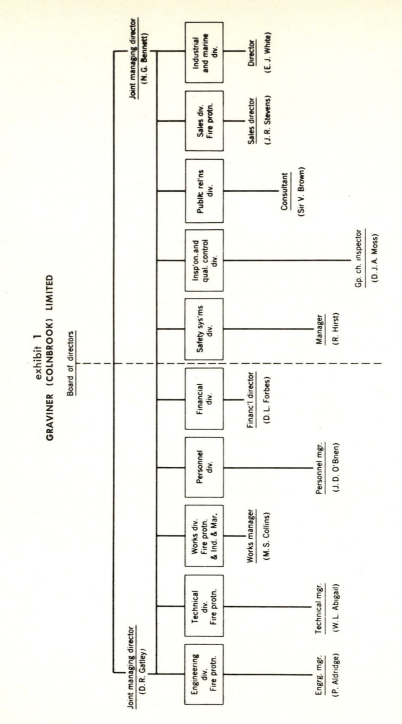

Board of directors

Joint managing director (D. R. Gatley)

Joint managing director (N. G. Bennett)

Engineering div. Fire protn. — Engrg. mgr. (P. Aldridge)

Technical div. Fire protn. — Technical mgr. (W. L. Abigail)

Works div. Fire protn. & Ind. & Mar. — Works manager (M. S. Collins)

Personnel div. — Personnel mgr. (J. D. O'Brien)

Financial div. — Financ'l director (D. L. Forbes)

Safety sys'ms div. — Manager (R. Hirst)

Insp'on. and qual. control div. — Gp. ch. inspector (D. J. A. Moss)

Public rel'ns div. — Consultant (Sir V. Brown)

Sales div. Fire protn. — Sales director (J. R. Stevens)

Industrial and marine div. — Director (E. J. White)

exhibit 2

A TYPICAL 1000 GALLON TANK

IGNITION COMMENCING
Time: 0 Milliseconds
Pressure: 0·00 p.s.i.

DETECTOR OPERATES
Time: 35 Milliseconds
Pressure: 0·20 p.s.i.

SUPPRESSION COMMENCES
Time: 40 Milliseconds
Pressure: 0·55 p.s.i.

Time: 45 Milliseconds
Pressure: 0·9 p.s.i.

Time: 50 Milliseconds
Pressure: 1·30 p.s.i.

Time: 55 Milliseconds
Pressure: 1·65 p.s.i.

SUPPRESSION COMPLETE
Time: 60 Milliseconds
Pressure: 2·00 p.s.i.

How does it work?

An EXPLOSION PROTECTION SYSTEM reacts instantly to sense the explosion and render it harmless.

There is a measurable time between the ignition of a combustible mixture and the build-up of pressure to destructive proportions. Although this time may be only a few milliseconds, it allows in fact, plenty of time for the EXPLOSION PROTECTION SYSTEM to operate. These diagrams show pressure time relationships in the suppression of a typical explosion.

A system of such rapidity offered a new safety tool to industry and GRAVINER has developed this for combating DUST AND GASEOUS EXPLOSIONS.

An Explosion Protection System detects an incipient explosion and actuates devices that suppress, vent or initiate other action to prevent the spread and effects of the explosion. The patented system is based on the discovery that an explosion is not an instantaneous occurrence but requires a definite time for the development of destructive pressure.

During this time, it is possible to take whatever protective action the application requires.

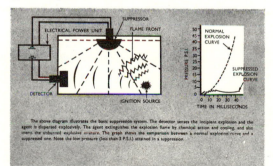

The above diagram illustrates the basic suppression system. The detector senses the incipient explosion and the agent is dispersed explosively. The agent extinguishes the explosion flame by chemical action and cooling, and also inerts the unburned explosive mixture. The graph shows the comparison between a normal explosion curve and a suppressed one. Note the low pressure (less than 3 P.S.I.) attained in a suppression.

exhibit 2 (continued)

Where can an Explosion Protection System be used?

The Factories Act requires steps to be taken that will limit the effects and spread of an explosion should a plant be handling materials which can explode.

It is not possible in a brochure of this size to cover all possible applications, but a study of the typical examples described here will show the flexibility of the system and suggest how it may be adapted to different problems. An experienced engineer can visit you to discuss how these and other techniques can be related to your particular problem.

Whilst these methods were originally developed for the more severe gaseous or fuel/air mixture type of explosion, the majority of applications have so far been in the dust explosion field.

In all the following illustrated applications, the plant is automatically shut down when the explosion occurs.

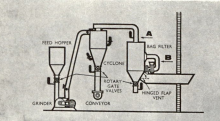

PROTECTION SYSTEM FOR A TYPICAL GRINDING PLANT
Explosion is detected at mill or cyclone. Cyclone suppressed.
Filter advance inerted and vented. Inlet and outlet
via Rotary Gate Valves inerted. Mill not shown suppressed
but can be if necessary.

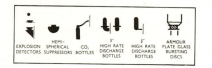

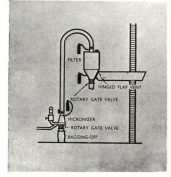

PROTECTION SYSTEM FOR A FLUID ENERGY MILL
Mill itself usually able to withstand the explosion pressure
and is allowed to vent itself into filter. Filter is vented.
Explosion is detected at micronizer exit and filter inlet. CO_2
injected in micronizer extinguishes following fire, and
additional CO_2 Bottles advance inert filter.

exhibit 4

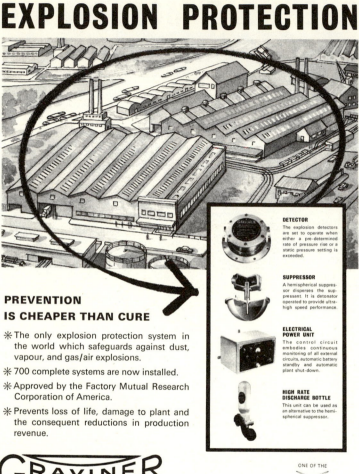

WILKINSON SWORD LIMITED (E)

On December 14, 1965, the *Guardian,* Manchester and London, reported:

> Wilkinson Sword's non-voting shares dropped to 17s (shilling = 14¢) 6d (penny = .01¢) at one time yesterday. Earlier this year they stood at 39s. In April, 1964 they had come to the market at 54s. This is, in many respects, a classic case. . . .

> Wilkinson Sword, a company first registered in 1889, came in the market after several years of spectacular success. This is nothing unusual. Many private firms succumb to the temptation to cash in when the going is good. Like others, Wilkinson went along to a top City merchant banker and asked for help. The banker—Lazards—made one of its rare mistakes. It marketed the shares at what was widely regarded as much too fanciful a price. The issue, which had initially promised to be one of the most successful ever, was barely subscribed and Wilkinson got off to an unfortunate start.

Mr. Peter Randolph, the company's deputy chairman, told financial reporters that the decision to go public had not been made without a certain amount of regret, but that the board had been forced to decide whether to control the company back to a level rate of progress, which might be as low as 10% yearly, or really go ahead progressively by raising extra capital. Mr. Denys Randolph, assistant managing director of the hand tool division, explained:

> Many people claimed that our issue was a failure, and certainly in retrospect it appears that it should have been handled differently. In

the early stages of 1961 it became obvious that the company had found a winner. It was apparent that demand would soon far outstrip production, and the question was how to gear ourselves to supply the demand. For many years the company had engaged in long, medium and short range planning. The long term plan stated that the aim should be to expand at a rate of approximately 12.5% per annum of assets employed—but not more than 20%. It was felt that to expand faster than this would be to stretch management, personnel and finances too far. However, it became evident toward the end of 1961 and the beginning of 1962 that expansion rates on the razor blade side far exceeding this could be achieved. This was particularly so as the return of capital investment was extremely fast, and the only problem was: could management and personnel react and accept this very rapid expansion? It was felt that, although we were first in the field, the competitors, all American, who are always quick to follow new innovations, would overtake us unless we took full advantage of our product lead and established ourselves in fair proportion in the world market. Therefore plans were laid to increase production by 100% in 1962 and by 300% in 1963. This meant new factories and a large plant-building operation. . . .

The marketing had been arranged by Lazard Brothers, described by the London Times as "a suitably long-established firm of merchant bankers, with the assistance of Panmure Gordon, one of the City's bluest-blooded brokers. . . ."

exhibit 1   EXCERPTS FROM LAZARD BROTHERS & CO., LIMITED, OFFER FOR SALE BY TENDER APRIL 20, 1964

Lazard Brothers & Co., Limited offer for sale by tender 700,000 Ordinary Shares of 4s each and 1,050,000 Non-Voting "A" Ordinary Shares of 4s each in 350,000 units comprising two Ordinary Shares and three Non-Voting "A" Ordinary Shares of 4s each at a minimum price of £13 10s per unit. The shares now offered rank in full for all dividends hereafter declared.

Procedure on Application: Applications must be for five units or multiples thereof (except in the case of applications from employees) . . . and must be made at a minimum price of £13 10s per unit.

Basis of Acceptance: Notwithstanding that applications may be received at different prices all units for which applications are accepted . . . will be sold at the same price. This price and the basis of acceptance . . . will be determined as follows:

1. The sale price will in principle be the highest price at which sufficient applications . . . are received to cover the total number of units offered. Nevertheless regard will be paid to the desirability of spreading the

shares and establishing a proper market and in order to achieve this a lower sale price may be fixed. . . . All applications below the sale price will be rejected.

2. Preferential consideration will be given, in respect to a total of not more than 10,000 units, to applications from employees of the company . . . at the minimum price of £13 10s per unit. . . .

[The following extracts were taken from a letter from Mr. H. B. Randolph reproduced in the Offer for Sale:]

Working Capital: The company has hitherto found from its own resources substantially the whole of the funds which it has required. The Directors have decided, however, that new capital should now be raised from outside the company to finance the rapid expansion of its business at home and overseas. For this reason the company has agreed to allot to you for cash 500,000 ordinary and 155,775 Non-Voting "A" Ordinary Shares, all of 4s. each, being part of the shares comprised in your Offer for Sale. The net proceeds of this issue, based on the minimum price at which the units are being offered for sale, will amount to approximately £1,687,000, which with depreciation and retained profits will, in the opinion of the Directors, ensure that the company will have sufficient resources for its present needs. In order to provide sufficient shares to obtain quotation and to establish an adequate market, shareholders of the company have in addition agreed to sell 200,000 ordinary and 894,225 Non-Voting "A" Ordinary Shares which you have agreed to purchase.

Profits Prospects and Dividends: Taking all known factors into account and subject to any unforeseen circumstances, the Directors expect that the combined profits before tax (calculated on the same basis as that used in the Accountants Report) for the year to 31st. December, 1964 will be not less than £3,250,000 as compared with £2,048,076 for 1963; turnover is expected to increase at an even greater rate. On profits of this order the Directors would expect to recommend total dividends for the year on the Ordinary and Non-Voting "A" Ordinary shares of 35%, less income tax, of which 10% would be declared as an interim in about December, 1964, and 25% would be payable as a final dividend in May or June, 1965. The net cost of such dividends (£428,750) would be covered 3.5 times by net profits of £1,503,125, this figure being arrived at by deducting United Kingdom income tax of 7s 9d in the £ and profits tax at 15% from the profits, before tax, of £3,250,000 referred to above. . . . Dividends totaling 35% would show a gross return of nearly 2.6% at the minimum price at which you are proposing the shares for sale. Looking further ahead we expect sales to increase in volume but profit margins on razor blades to be reduced, particularly as the Directors are determined to maintain the lead the company has already achieved which will entail increasing expenditure on advertising and on research and development. . . . In general, therefore, the Directors expect that from 1965 onwards profits should continue to increase although not at the same rate as in the period 1962 to 1964.

Financial commentators were unanimous in the view that the indicated dividend yield of 2.6% had "left little to go for." Opinions were voiced in various financial journals:

> Wilkinson Sword had the unenviable distinction of being one of the few issue flops of 1964. In fairness to the company's financial advisers, they were confronted with formidable problems last April. The public appetite for straightforward issues "with something to go for" threatened to reach South Sea Bubble proportions. The spectacle of offers being subscribed 100, 150 and 175 times over had aroused a storm of criticism.
>
> Wilkinson admitted that it had rejected "well over one thousand attempts to combine with, associate with, or take us over" before it went public last April. . . .

Commenting on the issue in January, 1966, Mr. Randolph said: "The group turnover in 1965 increased by 16.9%, and the profit was 2.2 million against 3.5 million for 1964—still a very large profit for a company our size. To say that things had gone as we had expected would be foolish and false. We underestimated to some extent the competition's marketing resources, which enabled them to exploit the world markets more quickly than we had expected, and their financial resources, which enabled them to pour money into advertising. Despite this, in January to November, 1965, our share of the double-edged users in the United Kingdom has increased from 37 to 43% and our share of the stainless blade market in the USA has increased from 10 to 15%. All other markets have increased, albeit not as fast as we had hoped. Also, there are still large areas of the world which have not been tapped, and it is felt that our forecast for a further 100% increase in turnover could be achieved by opening up in these new markets."

PROSPECTS IN 1966

In 1966 the Labor Government had under consideration a Finance Act which would introduce a corporation tax. The Act was not yet complete, and the rate and terms of the tax were not yet fixed, but the expectation was that full relief for overseas taxation would not be obtained in all cases on overseas profits brought into the United Kingdom.

"It would be premature," said Mr. H. B. Randolph, "before the passing of the Finance Act to prophesy the future, but a company such as ours, which obtains nearly 60% of its turnover and profits from overseas operations, cannot but be concerned about the effect of present thinking on its trading. It has been our policy slowly but surely to place more of our assets in terms of men, money, plants, and buildings overseas, and almost without fail we have found that, although the road is hard, the journey is worthwhile in terms of ultimate volume of turnover, and in terms of stability of operations, and in terms of local government support, which is so important. We wish to continue this progress and hope that we shall be allowed to do so."

Management weighed the prospects for the future. In 1965 it found itself deeply involved in the razor blade business, which accounted for 73% of sales. Garden tools and swords accounted for 8% of sales, and the company was adding to this line on the basis of attractive prospects. Sword sales were negligible in amount (approximately 1% of sales), but the management was convinced that the sword image was invaluable in advertising and public relations. The Graviner Division accounted for 19% of sales and represented, in the mind of management, a venture into the important and growing area of scientific research and development, coupled with highly developed and complex product lines. It was felt that the divisional shares of turnover would be approximately the same in 1966 as in 1965.

PART FOUR
THE
STRATEGY OF
ACQUISITIONS,
MERGERS,
AND EXPANSION

18
LAUREL
FOODS

"We had two alternatives," said Mr. Allan C. Prior, chairman and treasurer of Laurel Foods, Inc. "We could have continued to operate as we had been doing, to expand by internal growth by adding to our product line and expanding our volume. This would have left us in danger of being bought up—probably by some larger competitor—and at less than our value. The second alternative was to expand rapidly in a manner which would enhance the value of our company.

"We chose to expand by making acquisitions. This was not an easy thing to do. At most times we could not trade our stock without taking a loss. This meant we had to use cash. We had ample cash for working capital, but not enough to finance a large-scale acquisitions program. Therefore we had to borrow, and to make deals.

"We don't want to be bought up. We have a good organization, and a valuable pool of skills and talents. We would rather develop our potentials ourselves. Besides, we think that anyone who would pay a high acquisition price for us at this time would be a damn fool. We are not so naïve that we would be flattered at being acquired by any company which had such foolish management."

When Mr. Prior bought Laurel Foods in 1952, its sales volume was approximately $3 million a year. During the next 20 years, under his direction, sales volume and earnings per share increased steadily. When the acquisitions program began in 1967, annual sales were $10,569,457 and earnings per share $2.37. Sales volume for 1970 was $28,978,000 and earnings per share $2.45. Projected sales for 1971 were

$34,500,000 and earnings per share for 1971 were expected to be $2.78. (See Exhibits 3 to 6, pp. 526–528)

"Our acquisitions program did not roll off according to plan at all," said Mr. Prior, "but we think it was successful nevertheless. The trouble is that today we are more vulnerable to being acquired than we were before we began. Hardly a month goes by, lately, but that we find ourselves fending off some corporate suitor."

ORIGIN AND DEVELOPMENT OF THE COMPANY

Laurel Foods had its origin in Gourmand Foods, a business begun by a Dr. James Patrick Gorman, a medical doctor, who chose the company name because it had a "gourmet" sound, and because it was a play upon his own name. Dr. Gorman was a health food faddist, and through Gourmand Foods he intended to sell meat sauces containing barley malt and soya derivatives he had developed in his home laboratory. He also produced a rose hip jelly (flavored with rosebuds); a jam made from ground ripe olives and cashew nuts; dandelion and honey nectar; and canned vegetables grown on hydroponic farms. When Gourmand Foods began to keep Dr. Gorman away from his prospering medical practice, he sold the business to Jason Ruggers.

Jason Ruggers was a patient of Dr. Gorman and had contracted a terminal disease which the doctor told him would run its course in three years. Ruggers had been very successful in sales management positions in several food processing firms, and he decided to go into business for himself despite his illness.

Ruggers had the idea that he might capitalize on the use of monosodium glutamate (MSG), a flavor enhancer which had been developed by the Japanese. MSG had the property of opening more fully the taste buds in the mouths of humans, thereby enhancing the flavors in the foods to which it was applied. Chicken fat had long been a worthless commodity on the food market in the United States. Jason Ruggers made a soup stock from it, added MSG, and reduced it to a heavy paste form by dehydration. This paste, called "chicken base," would reconstitute into flavorsome soup by the simple addition of hot water. Ruggers then developed a similar beef base. He packed his bases in large-size containers and sold them exclusively to the institutional food industry. Jason Ruggers' bases were the first concentrated soups offered to the institutional food market to eliminate the stock kettle in which the chef had boiled meat scraps and bones to make soup. Ruggers then developed a line of gravies and sauces, which he marketed under the name "Laurel Label." Jason Ruggers passed away eight years after buying Gourmand Foods.

Following Jason Ruggers' death, ownership of the company was vested in a Cleveland bank which was the executor of Mr. Ruggers' will. The bank placed one of its trust officers on the Gourmand board and through him directed the company. The sales manager and the plant superintendent acted as co-chief executives. When no relatives offered to become interested in the business, the bank decided to sell the company.

Allan C. Prior was president and owner of the Home Yeast Company of Cleveland, a family business begun by his grandfather. His company made packaged yeast for home baking. Home baking had been declining for some time, and Mr. Prior felt sure that the trend would not reverse. "The handwriting was clearly on the wall," said Mr. Prior. "I had not intended to buy a going business, but when I heard about Gourmand Foods, it impressed me." Mr. Prior arranged with the bank to merge Gourmand with Home Yeast by an exchange of shares. The combined enterprise was named Laurel Foods. Mr. Prior was president, treasurer, and the largest stockholder.

THE TRANSITION PERIOD

Jason Ruggers had owned 75% of the Gourmand common stock. At the time he took over the business it had sales of a little less than $200,000. At the time of his passing it had 70 employees and sales of $3 million.

"There was a period to begin with," said Mr. Prior, "when we didn't do much of anything with our newly acquired business. For about a year we let it go on just as it had been doing while we watched and studied to learn all about it."

Gourmand Foods had been doing its processing in two small rented loft locations in central Cleveland, not far from the Home Yeast plant. Mr. Prior moved the production lines into the Home Yeast plant and dropped the leases on the lofts. Some old employees resigned, but with sales volume rising, the total organization became larger. In 1956 Mr. Prior sold the remaining yeast business to Amalgamated Grocers and had plans blueprinted for a new plant to be built in the suburb of

Lakewood. The same year he hired Donald Spencer as a salesman and Edgar Sandhill as an accountant. Eventually these men were to become, respectively, president and financial vice president and, together with Mr. Prior, were to form the top management trio of the company.

Donald P. Spencer considered himself a native Virginian because he had grown up in Virginia. Mr. Prior met Donald Spencer in 1956, when Spencer was general manager of a Southern chain of restaurants which was a customer of Laurel's. He liked Spencer's management style and persuaded Spencer to come to Laurel as a salesman. He successively promoted him to sales manager of the Eastern Division; vice president and general sales manager of the company; and, in 1965, first vice president, with general managerial responsibilities.

"As to personalities," said Mr. Prior, "Donald Spencer and I are cut out of entirely different cloths, but the combination has worked out very well. I sit at my desk and smoke my pipe and read reports and work them over with my slide rule. Spencer has always been the dynamo, the innovator, the instigator, the salesman, the vendor contact man, the operator. He travels ten times as much as I do, and he knows everything that's going on outside. By the time Spencer had been with us a few years he was the quarterback who was calling the signals on most things that went on at Laurel."

In 1964 Mr. Prior and Mr. Spencer agreed that Laurel ought to have a second plant somewhere in the South. The next year Donald Spencer found a suitable plant site in Richmond, Virginia, where he had been living and from which he directed sales activities. The new plant was a duplication of the Lakewood plant on a one-third scale, producing Gourmand and Laurel label foods. To manage it, Mr. Spencer hired Karl M. Brunner, a furniture sales manager, who was Mr. Spencer's next-door neighbor.

In 1966 and 1967 Mr. Spencer and Mr. Brunner concentrated their attention on the Richmond plant and on increasing sales in the South. Their efforts were successful and Mr. Spencer persuaded Mr. Prior that a second new plant to serve the Southwest would be practical. An existing plant building in New Orleans, about the size of the Richmond plant, was purchased for this purpose in January, 1967, and Mr. Brunner was made general manager. To replace Mr. Brunner as manager of the Richmond plant Mr. Spencer hired Mr. Royal Bentley, a salesman for the Container & Packaging Corporation, which had sold the new Richmond plant tin cans and corrugated cartons. Mr. Bentley was a lifelong resident of Richmond and had long been a personal friend of Mr. Spencer.

In July, 1967, Mr. Prior was elected chairman of the board and chief executive of the company. In that office he continued to act as treasurer. Mr. Spencer was elected president and general manager of the company. Since Mr. Spencer was the company's de facto general sales manager and was at this time concentrating on expanding the company's sales in the South and Southwest, he chose to continue to operate from his office in Richmond. Mr. Brunner was made vice president of the Richmond Division; Mr. Bentley was made vice president of the New Orleans Division. Mr. Edgar Sandhill, who had previously been promoted to controller and secretary, was elected financial vice president and worked very closely with Mr. Prior on money matters.

"One of the most astute things Jason Ruggers had done," said Mr. Prior, "was to specialize in selling to the institutional food trade. He foresaw the changes which were coming in the food industry. Our first decade in our new plants was taken up with gradual growth and with solidifying our position as suppliers to the institutional food industry."

THE INSTITUTIONAL MARKET

An executive in the food industry described the institutional food industry as "a real bastardized, polyglot, adulterated, hodgepodge conglomeration." It included anyone who was a mass preparer of food for the final consumer, in the form of meals, sandwiches, or snacks. The industry's customers included restaurants, hotels, cafeterias, caterers, schools, prisons, jails, night clubs, orphanages, resorts, the military services, chain stores with lunchrooms, commercial airlines, in-plant eating facilities, country clubs, ocean liners, automated food vendors, and railroads.

All of the institutional buyers wished to buy their foods in gross quantities, but these gross quantities varied a great deal in size. A small restaurant would buy soup base in the one-pound jar size and might even buy in split-case lots. A military unit would buy it by the carload, in 40-pound steel drums.

Different types of institutional buyers tended to look for different attributes in the foods they bought. Most, but not all of them, were interested in buying foods which were as fully prepared as possible, so that a minimum of labor was required to bring them to the serving stage, because chefs were expensive and kitchen help was in short supply. Most, but not all, welcomed any soup base which required only the addition of hot water before serving. Some, however, figured that if they needed to keep enough kitchen help on hand full-time to take care of the peak periods when meals were being served, they might as well keep them busy by having them do time-consuming jobs in the interim periods, and this might include cooking soup from the natural ingredients. They might do this even though it cost a little more than using a convenience soup base.

All institutional buyers were interested in the elimination of waste. Cooking from raw ingredients, a chef would cook only a single batch. This meant estimating in advance how much would be required for the day. To a chef who had a fixed number of people to serve, such as in a prison, this caused no problem, but it was always a problem in a public restaurant or an operation like a commercial airline, where the quantity requirements might vary widely in a very short space of time. Food in convenience form permitted preparing an original batch and making additions to it with a minimum of labor and on very short notice, and with the virtual elimination of leftovers.

Governmental institutions, such as county homes and orphanages, were interested in foods which were plain, wholesome, and economical. A soup base was attractive to them because one pound made five gallons of broth at a cost of 1.3¢ per cup. Consumers, such as public restaurants and plant cafeterias, were also interested in economical servings, but they were more interested in serving foods which were attractive in appearance, appetizing, and flavorsome. High-class restaurants, night clubs, and country clubs were first of all interested in high-quality foods and gourmet and connoisseur foods; to them the cost per serving was not of great consequence.

Laurel Foods made several quality grades of some of its products, but it discovered that it was difficult to correlate any class of institutional customer with the specific quality level the customer purchased. Laurel sold to prisons which might operate on a budget limit of less than 50¢ in total food cost per prisoner per day; it also sold to the most elegant supper clubs in New York City, which commonly calculated their cost of food per meal served at over $20. "The perplexing thing," said Mr. Prior, "is that we often find the prison buying our highest-quality soup stock, while the luxury restaurant might be buying the lowest grade."

"Some see the food industry as being mature," said Mr. Prior. "We see it as being a growth field, both in the retail and the institutional sectors. Today, there are more people, people are eating more and eating better, and many more people are eating outside of their homes —and doing so much more often. The institutional food market is growing fast. Look at the great growth in recent years of people eating in schools, colleges, hospitals, and company cafeterias. Look at the spectacular growth of the food-vending business. We intend to remain in the institutional field, and we intend to remain specialists in that field, offering products that are high-quality, that help the chef cut down on labor, equipment, and costs, and specializing in those products that require personal selling and service."

LAUREL'S GROWTH PERIOD

"Laurel Foods has gone through three phases while I've been with it," said Mr. Prior. "First there was a five-year period of transition, reorganization, and shakeout. Then came a ten-year period when we settled down to the hard job of improving our products and production methods, adding to our product line, expanding our sales volume, and building up our reputation with institutional wholesalers and institutional buyers. The third phase was the five-year period from 1967 through 1971—the acquisition years. Looking back over our history, I think that our present business really began, in a sense, when we moved into our new Lakewood plant in 1957. We had a new plant, we had a revamped organization, we had streamlined our product line, and we were ready to work up to an ever higher cruising speed."

Gourmand had originally used many "raw" raw materials. Chicken was bought as eviscerated carcasses, which were deskinned and deboned by hand. Beef was bought raw and ground into hamburger or diced into cubes. Smoked hams were trimmed of rind and fat and the meat diced for use in bean soup. Many vegetables were bought raw in season. Women stood in long lines at moving belts separating off-colored peas from fresh sugar peas.

There were still some hand operations when the new Lakewood plant began production, but they were eliminated within the first few years by searching the market for new materials which were in as finished a state as possible. This effort was continued until eventually Laurel bought only raw materials that required mixing, blending, cooking, and packing (see Exhibit 1). "The people who do the primary processing of foods as they come from the farm have terrific headaches in production problems," said Mr. Prior. "A year's tomato harvest might be only three weeks long, so people like Campbell's reduce the whole crop to dehydrated paste in 50-gallon drums that go into inventory for further processing later. We buy the paste, and start from there. Fresh fruits are so highly perishable, we couldn't possibly handle them. Besides, there are excellent imitation flavors available that are much simpler to use. We use items like pre-processed mushrooms, because the fresh ones can go off flavor overnight and ruin your production. In general, we aim to use as little labor as possible in our plants. Therefore, we lean hard on our purchasing agent. It's up to him to search out raw materials that are as finished as possible."

Systematic processing lines were installed, automated equipment was used wherever possible, and conveyors were used to eliminate in-plant transport. However, it proved impossible to automate and mechanize entirely. There were too many items in the product line, and volume was not large enough to permit uninterrupted production runs. "A company like Quaker Oats has such large volume that an oatmeal line will literally never shut down," said Mr. Prior. "With that kind of mass production they can develop highly specialized machinery of their own which automatically does everything, from taking the raw oats out of the bin to sealing the packages of rolled oats in cartons and shunting them into a box car. We don't have the mass volume. We are largely limited to standardized food-processing equipment."

Many of Gourmand's old recipes and formulations were dropped and replaced by new ones. The product line was increased from 40 items to 80. Expansion of the product line and the refinement of formulas brought on problems in inventory control and scheduling. "We found ourselves scheduling ever-changing short runs of products that had a high multiple of ingredients," said Mr. Prior. "At the same time, we had to hold down inventories, because we didn't have much money, and still we wanted to promise any customer immediate delivery on any item. The scheduling problem became so complicated that it almost whipped us. Fortunately, computers came into common use and saved the day for us."

exhibit 1 **LAUREL FOODS**
Some typical raw materials used by Laurel Foods in 1971

Armola
Ascorbic Acid
Adipic Acid
Asparagus Cuts—Frozen
Bacon ends—$\frac{3}{16}$",
  Smoked
Barley, Pearl
Beans, Baby Lima, Dried
Beans, Frozen, Green
Beans, Green Lima,
  Frozen
Beans, Navy
Beans, Small, Red
Beef Extract
Dehydrated Beef Extract
Powdered Cooked Beef
Imitation Beef Flavor
Beef Chuck, $\frac{1}{2}$", Ground
Corned Beef, Canned
Beef, Ground, Raw, $\frac{3}{16}$"
Cured Chipped Beef
Beef Leg Bones
Beef Flanks, Ground, $\frac{1}{8}$"
Beef Navels, Ground, $\frac{1}{8}$"
Beef Trimmings, Raw, $\frac{1}{8}$"
Beef Heart Meat, Ground,
  $\frac{1}{8}$"
Beef Bones, Crushed
Beef, Diced, Raw, $\frac{3}{4}$"
Beef Tripe, Scalded, $\frac{3}{16}$"
Butter, 93 Score, Salted
Dicalcium Phosphate
Cabbage Powder
Cabbage Dices
Cabbage Granules
Carotenes, Conc., 5%
  Natural
Carrot Chips, Frozen
Carrot Dices, $\frac{3}{8}$" Cubes
Carrots, Frozen, Crinkle
Carrots, Crinkle Cross-Cut
Carrot Powder
Calcium Sulphate
Celery, Dehyd., Diced
Celery Stalk, Frozen
Celery Leaves, Dehyd.
Cheddar Cheese, Dehyd.

Cheese, Parmesan, Grated
Chicken, Cooked, Ground,
  Frozen
Chicken, with Skins, Frzn.
Chicken, with Giblets
Chicken, Dehyd., Pulv.
Chicken, Cooked,
  Chopped
Chicken, Cooked, Diced
Chicken Gizzards &
  Hearts
Chicken Fat—Rendered
Chicken Livers, Frozen
Citric Acid, Anhydrous
Clams, Frozen, Minced
Cocoa, American
Coconut, Desiccated
Black Cherry Shade
Butterscotch, Undried
Caramel Color
Caramel, Powdered
Chocolate Shade
Lemon Shade
Lime Shade
Corn, Frozen
Vegetable Oil
Cream, Raw
Cream, Sour
Dextrine
Custard, Imitation
Lemon Juice
Loganberry Florasynth
Orange Flavor
Peppermint Oil
Raspberry Nodes
Strawberry Flavoring
Vanilla, Pure
Vanilla, Imitation
Flour, Potato, Fine
Flour, Potato, Gran.
Soy Protein
Fumaric Acid
Garlic Powder
Gelatin, 275 Bloom
Gelatin, 240 Bloom
Gum Acacia
Ham, Chopped

Ham, Ground
Lactic Acid
Lactose
Leek, Discs
Leek, Powder
Lentils
Lobster Meat, Frzn., Pink
Macroni, Ditali
Macroni Shells
Milk, Fresh
Milk, Whole, Powder
Milk, Solid, Dry
Monosodium Glutamate
Mushrooms
Egg Noodles
Olive Oil
Okra, Sliced, Canned
Strawberries, Frzn., Dried
Black Pepper, Superesin
Celery, Superesin
Soluble Oleo Paprika
Soluble Turmeric
Onion Flavor
Onion Flakes, Toasted
Onions, Minced
Onions, Granulated
Onions, Powdered
Onions, Sliced, Dehyd.
Peas, Frozen
Peas, Green Split
Peppers, Green Bell,
  Diced
Peppers, Red, Canned,
  Diced
Pimentos, Canned
Potatoes, Dehy., Diced
Potatoes, Dehyd., Crushed
Potato Flakes
Potassium Citrate
Rice, Long-Grain
Salt, Fine-Flake
Sodium Benzoate
Anise Seeds, Whole
Allspice, Ground
Sweet Basil, Rubbed
Bay Leaves, Ground
Caraway, Ground

During its early Lakewood years, Laurel decided upon a long-range program of developing strong wholesaler loyalties. "We decided that our sales were always going to be two-way mutual benefit programs," said Mr. Prior. "We weren't satisfied if we only made money ourselves. Our jobber had to make money, too. We wanted steady business. We didn't want any one-shot deals. Suppose we asked a jobber to promote a new soup. We would send a Laurel man to show the jobber how to sell it. We would give him promotional materials, ask him to share program costs and advertising expenses with us. We would have our salesman demonstrate the product to the jobber's leading institutional customers. Ours isn't the kind of business where you nod your head or scratch your ear and you've made a deal. Our kind of selling can't be done in five minutes. It takes years of cultivation to develop the strong kind of bond we want. We don't sell on a lackadaisical basis; we don't care for catch-as-catch-can salesmanship. Our kind of selling is hard work, but it has worked out for us. In our first years at Lakewood, we fortified our special position in the food business, and we built a loyal customer following that competitors will find pretty hard to raid."

THE PLANNED ACQUISITION PROGRAM

During the decade 1957 to 1967 Laurel had consistent growth in sales and earnings per share and paid regular dividends every year. It was in strong financial condition with assets in 1967 of $6,994,968, including $2,117,563 in cash and securities. The strong financial position of Laurel prompted management to plan an acquisition program. Mr. Prior made the following comments about the criteria the company decided upon as guidelines for acquisitions:

Any company which makes money is of interest to somebody, and we were in that position. I held the largest block of stock, but it wasn't a majority and the rest was scattered. We were unlisted, shares traded were few, and traders in the over-the-counter market didn't know Laurel. Our market value was above book value, but because of all these other things our stock sold at a low multiple of earnings. In a situation like that you can become the victim of some financial sleight-of-hand. Somebody whose stock is selling at $30 to $1 of earnings can buy somebody whose stock is $9 to $1 of earnings by an exchange of stock at $15 for the $9 stock and still up their earnings.

We decided to improve our earnings per share by making acquisitions, but our low multiple didn't put us in a good position to do so. Nevertheless we decided to try, and we set certain standards for acquisitions.

Any prospective company to be acquired had to have sales of $1 million, be profitable, its margins and its income per share about the same as Laurel's. If these factors did not all coincide, profit ratio to equity was to be the overriding determinant.

It would be preferable if the prospect was in the food business and sold to institutional customers. It would be helpful if it used raw materials similar to Laurel's; these could probably be processed on Laurel's equipment.

Location was not thought to be important. Laurel's main plant was in a North Central state. We thought that with our expansion on a national basis acquisitions far removed from Lakewood might improve Laurel's distribution system. Perhaps the farther away, the better.

Laurel was not seeking any specialized skills and talents to remedy any lack in its own organization. Any acquisition should be self-sufficient as to management, able to operate on its own, without drawing on Lakewood personnel.

Equipment and production facilities were not to be a determinant. Machinery, we believed, was easy to acquire. There was no need to buy a business just to acquire equipment.

We thought it desirable for the prospect's distribution pattern to parallel Laurel's. This would permit Laurel to weave the new sales organization into its own.

We thought the prospect should have shown good growth. Its outlook for continued growth should have been as good as Laurel's.

We sought equity investment of about $500,000. Later it was thought Laurel might use specialists to seek out prospects, but initially it did its own searching.

The dominating consideration was to be sales and profitability. There isn't too much difference in processing food products that are different. The important questions to us were: Could we sell the product? Would it make money for us?

GOLDEN BATTER FOODS

"It seems that the first thing we did in our acquisitions program," said Mr. Prior, "was to scrap the guideline plans we had made. Our first acquisition was Golden Batter Foods, which didn't fit the specifications at all."

The Laurel management had not seriously considered any acquisition prospect until Donald Spencer proposed buying Golden Batter Foods, which had been his customer in his salesman days. In late 1967

Laurel Foods purchased 98% of the outstanding shares of Golden Batter Foods. The total cost of the acquisition was $4.9 million, which was financed by a term loan of $1.4 million from a bank payable in four equal installments at 5% interest and $3.5 million obtained from an insurance company at a 5.75% rate payable in 10 annual installments starting in 1972.

Golden Batter, located in Baltimore, Maryland, originally a producer of pancakes and waffle flours, was owned by the Lazano brothers: Carmen, Dominic, and Bruno. The brothers had gradually expanded their line to include potato chips, mayonnaise, salad dressings, pancake and waffle syrups, and condiments. They also developed and patented a semiautomatic machine which baked and froze waffles, and then proceeded 'to sell frozen waffles in the Delaware, Maryland, and Virginia area. Their sales had been mainly to retail grocers, and through the past decade the brothers had developed a wholesale grocery trade, selling these retailers the customary line of "dry" groceries. The brothers had developed a profitable business which had 300 employees, a sales volume of $12 million, and a net equity of over $3 million. At the time of the acquisition, 5% of Golden Batter's sales volume was in frozen waffles, 50% in the wholesale groceries, 25% in mayonnaise, 10% in potato chips and snack foods, and 10% in various other products, including condiments.

The Golden Batter organization and operation were originally retained intact except for the transfer of Karl Brunner from Laurel's Richmond plant to Golden Batter's Baltimore plant to learn the business. Carmen Lazano remained as president on a five-year employment contract at $30,000 base salary plus a minimum annual incentive bonus of $7,500. Dominic and Bruno received similar contracts. Carmen had always been active in sales, personally entertaining buyers from leading chain stores. Dominic managed production and Bruno was in charge of the warehouse and the truck fleet.

To produce its frozen waffles, which were the only round, 9-inch, home-sized waffles on the commercial market, Dominic Lazano had invented a "merry-go-round" waffle-baking machine. Golden Batter flour was mixed with cream of tartar, milk powder, and trace flavor ingredients. Oil, water, canned eggs, and butter flavor were mixed separately and then stirred into the dry mix. The resulting batter was poured into a dispenser, which blew the batter into twin round waffle grids. The grids closed automatically and baked while traveling around the carousel, which took 80 seconds. The grids then opened automatically, and an operator flipped out the baked waffles. The waffles then traveled by belt through a cooler room, and then went into a 20°-below-zero blast freezer room, and then were automatically packaged and packed in corrugated cartons.

In Mr. Spencer's opinion the Golden Batter waffles were the most appetizing waffles he had ever tasted. He decided to double the number of carousels and put the waffles into distribution through Laurel's East Coast institutional wholesalers. Some of these wholesalers also sold to retail grocers, and, to Mr. Spencer's surprise, there suddenly developed a strong retail demand for the waffles. Housewives liked their flavor and crispness and their "homemade" shape and size. Before the year-end, carousel capacity was again increased to triple Golden Batter's original capacity.

In early 1968, Karl Brunner took over the management of Golden Batter. Carmen Lazano remained as president, but he was to spend all of his time making sales calls. Dominic and Bruno continued to act in their previous capacities.

Golden Batter processed potato chips. Some were sold to wholesalers, but most of them were sold to retailers in the East Coast states by 17 truck salesmen, who also sold "bar-snack" items such as smoked kippers, pickled herring, and packaged shelled nuts. Some routes were over 300 miles long. Mr. Brunner decided to add corn chips, pretzels, and pretzel sticks to the truckers' line, which added moderately to volume. Mr. Brunner, with Donald Spencer's approval, decided to try frozen French fried potatoes, which could be processed on the company's present potato chip equipment and sold to Golden Batter's present customers. This project was planned while Golden Batter was expanding its sales of potato chips by selling them at wholesale through Laurel's institutional jobbers all along the East Coast. The Laurel potato chip venture was successful beyond expectations and overburdened Golden's potato chip production capacity, leaving no room for the frozen French fries. Mr. Brunner obtained a short-term lease on an existing plant and began production. It soon became apparent that the frozen French fries were not going to sell at a volume that would justify the investment required. Mr. Prior announced that the leased facility was being closed down. Management calculated that the loss on the venture reduced Laurel's 1968 net income about 30¢ per share.

Golden Batter mayonnaise and condiments (Thousand Island and French dressing, ketchup, and chili sauce) had been selling in a volume of about $1 million a year at the time Laurel took over. Since Laurel had put them into its institutional jobber distribution system, volume had increased to $2,650,000. "I don't think those products are in keeping with our Laurel and Gourmand lines. I'm sure we would never have chosen to add mayonnaise and ketchup to our line. They are low-margin, but they are making some profit, and so I guess we'll keep them," said Mr. Prior.

"When we got a close look at the Golden Batter wholesale grocery business, we came to the conclusion that it was a pretty lame operation. The brothers had patched together a piecemeal product line that totaled about 1,000 products. A full line should have 15,000. There were whole categories—like paper products, matches, toothpicks, and soaps—that they didn't have at all. They had some Heinz and Campbell's products, and a lot of fruits and vegetables packed under their Golden Batter label, which struck us as being inappropriate on foods like canned green beans. The Golden Batter wholesale business generated about 50% of Golden's sales volume, but less than 25% of Golden's net profit."

Mr. Prior offered to sell the wholesale business to every wholesaler Laurel knew, but none were interested. Finally, Mr. Spencer negotiated a deal with a wholesaler who took over the entire inventory at cost, and Laurel in exchange received promotional preference from the wholesaler on Laurel and Gourmand products. As a result of disposing of Golden Batter's wholesale grocery business, Laurel's consolidated sales volume for 1970 was reduced by approximately $4 million.

During 1970 Golden Batter waffles had been expanded into the North Central and New England states, where they found immediate acceptance. They also continued to grow in popularity among retailers, and several chain stores approached Golden Batter with private-label proposals, which Mr. Brunner declined. The Golden Batter waffle plant went from two to three shifts. The waffles were distributed throughout the eastern half of the country and in some of the Western and Southwestern states. The demand from wholesalers who sold to retailers and chains surpassed that of institutional buyers. The Baltimore plant had no more room for additional carousels; therefore, operations were extended to three shifts six days a week, and in some instances the plant worked on Sundays.

The Laurel management was finding the potato chip and snack business to be intensely competitive. "For our high-quality Gourmand and Laurel foods," said Mr. Prior, "we had always made it a policy that we obtain a premium price in keeping with our premium quality. We are finding that we can't do that with potato chips and corn chips. Chips are chips—there's not a lot of difference—and we have big competitors who are mass producers and turn them out at low cost. Also, the potato market is very mercurial." During 1970, Laurel's sales of potato chips increased because they were added to Laurel's institutional distribution system. Two regional and two national chip producers had retaliated against the Laurel expansion by price cutting. "We had to meet their prices," said Mr. Prior. "I don't know what the final figures will show, but I have a notion that we are trading dollars on that big potato chip and snack business we are developing."

COASTAL FOODS

In February of 1970, Mr. Spencer called upon an old friend, John Dorsey, the owner of Coastal Foods, of Boston, Massachusetts, to discuss with him another food company which Mr. Spencer wanted to acquire. He found that Coastal Foods itself was for sale. Mr. Dorsey had taken a substantial credit loss on a customer who had falsified his financial statements and was having other difficulties. Mr. Spencer found very little that was of interest to him in Coastal Foods until Mr. Dorsey told him that Coastal had a contract to act as the world-wide marketing arm of Chapro SA, of Transkenya,[1] Africa, a lobster and shrimp-producing venture which was slated to go into operation in the near future. Mr. Spencer felt that the prospects of Chapro were fascinating. At this time, the Chapro company was only a corporate shell with a plan; it was seeking an American company which might buy half its shares and supply it with managerial talent. Mr. Spencer became interested in Coastal Foods; its marketing contract with Chapro, which was transferable, would allow Laurel to buy into Chapro.

Coastal Foods was an export-import trading operation which did not produce or process foods. Its six-man staff was engaged in importing seafoods, mostly lobster tails, from New Zealand, Formosa, Japan, and Australia and selling them in the United States and Europe. About an equal portion of its sales volume came from selling United States' fish, canned fruits, and vegetables in Europe. Coastal's entire organiza-

---

[1] Transkenya was an east-coast African nation (name disguised).

tion, including Mr. Dorsey, consisted of six "traders" in Australia, Japan, the United States, and Europe. They generated a sales volume of $6 million in 1969. Coastal Foods owned no real estate, and its only fixed assets consisted of some office furniture. In 1969 it operated at a loss.

In May, 1970, Laurel Foods made a subordinated loan of $150,000 to Coastal Foods and received an option to buy all of its outstanding stock. Laurel then exercised its option, acquiring all of Coastal's common in exchange for 5,000 shares of Laurel (which had a market value of about $120,000). At the time, Coastal Foods had a small deficit in equity. In taking over Coastal, Laurel became contingently liable for a certain indebtedness of Coastal in the amount of $420,000. In the months which followed, Mr. Spencer disposed of Coastal's canned fruit and vegetable business, but he retained a small import business Coastal did in canned fish. Three "traders" were released and the rented offices in Europe, Formosa, and Japan were closed; however, the seafood trading business was carried on as before. Mr. Spencer believed that Coastal's connections would be of great value to Laurel when the Chapro venture went into operation. In the meantime, he thought that Laurel might use Coastal as a source for some of the seafood which Gourmand used in its seafood soups.

CHAPRO SA

Mr. Spencer was eager to acquire Chapro because he felt that Laurel needed more pre-portioned meat and fish items, and the 6-ounce and 7-ounce lobster tails which Chapro would produce would be ideal. Mr. Spencer had considered frying chickens, halved or quartered, but they were too competitive. Laurel wanted only products which were high-margin. "We already used lobster in some of our Gourmand foods," said Mr. Spencer, "but secondary processors don't make any money on lobsters. The prime producer does. The catchers and prime processors who de-tail and clean them have been in a seller's market for a long time. They can just about call their own shots. Buying into Chapro, we'd have a source for both pre-portioned frozen lobsters and those that would go into Gourmand lobster bisque."

For many years, fishermen had known that there were rich deposits of rock lobster off the coast of Transkenya, and there was every reason to believe that there were also shrimp and other edible shellfish. The

beds had remained unfished because the Transkenians were Mohammedans who did not eat shellfish, and until recent years there had
been no way to ship any catch to foreign buyers, because Transkenya's
1,150 miles of coastline did not include a single seaport which could
accommodate ocean-going vessels. Transkenya was a new republic
which had become a sovereign state in 1962. Through AID funds from
the United States, it had built its first port facility at Konora. The port
included a sheltered seaplane harbor, and Laurel meant to ship out its
catches by air freight. The Transkenians who had incorporated Chapro
were not Mohammedans. They had a 12-year concession from the new
government to fish a 10-mile strip, and they had rounded up crews of
non-Mohammedan fishermen. Chapro had no assets and its organizers
had no money. They did have good connections with the Transkenian
government officials. They were fluent in English. In July, 1970, Laurel
Foods purchased a 49% equity interest in Chapro for a nominal consideration. Transkenian law limited foreign ownership to less than
50%. As part of the deal, it was agreed that Laurel would manage
Chapro, for which it would receive a management fee; that Laurel
would have exclusive marketing rights to all Chapro products; that
Laurel would receive a sales commission of 10% off the gross sales of
all Chapro production; and that the initial capital required to finance
Chapro's trawlers, processing plant, and transport facilities—as well as
working capital—was to be supplied by Laurel in the form of loans
to the company.

Late in September, 1970, shipment was made from Baltimore of a
prefabricated plant building, together with all required processing and
freezing equipment. The same freighter carried two large trawlers and
a smaller service launch. Fishing and processing were expected to begin
by the year-end, but an unforeseen delay was encountered when it was
discovered that the new port of Konora had no facility to provide fuel
for ships. The Transkenian organizers of Chapro obtained a concession
from their government to build an oil depot at the port on land owned
by the government, the depot to be financed by Laurel and operated
under contract by Red Sea Shell, Ltd. At the end of 1970, Laurel Foods
had advanced a total of $900,000 to Chapro in the form of loans. "It
was a speculative business," said Mr. Prior. "The Office of Foreign
Direct Investments of the Department of Commerce limited foreign
investments by U.S. companies and might tighten its restrictions in the
future. It also required annual repatriation of foreign earnings, and

it might at any time require the repatriation of short-term assets held abroad. We were subject to all of the risks of starting a new business in a young, foreign country, and the nature and depth of the resources in our concession area had as yet been untested. We might also be affected by further governmental actions—both of our government and of that of Transkenya."

ARCTIC MEATS, INC.

In early 1970, the Laurel management decided that they ought to look for more frozen items to sell with Golden Batter waffles. The trend toward those frozen foods which were just one step removed from being ready-to-serve was very strong, in both the institutional and the retail fields. Frozen meat cuts such as chops, steaks, and cutlets showed no signs of becoming popular with housewives, but institutional buyers were becoming very much interested in frozen meats cut in fixed-weight proportions; they saved butchering time for the chef, and the fixed proportions helped him to control his costs.

Arctic Meats, Inc., of Houston, Texas, was a business owned and operated by a Mr. John Jones, whom Mr. Spencer met through Mr. Dorsey of Coastal Foods. Mr. Jones imported commercial-grade veal and beef from Argentina, New Zealand, and Australia, cut it into chops, steaks, and cutlets and sold them, frozen, to institutional wholesalers for use in restaurants, plant cafeterias, and institutions. Mr. Jones also made meatballs and hamburger patties. Most of his sales had been in the South and Southwestern states. Mr. Jones was having health problems, and his was a one-man management. During 1970, the costs of meat from his sources had risen sharply, and at the same time prices of his finished products had been forced down by competition, causing operating losses for 1968 and 1969. Mr. Jones also wished to take an early retirement.

In March, 1970, Laurel Foods purchased all of the stock of Arctic Meats for $1.6 million, payable in four equal installments, one at the time of purchase and the remainder over a three-year period from July, 1971 to July, 1974 at a rate of 7.5% interest. At the time of the purchase the equity in the business was about $500,000. Sales had been about $4 million in recent years, and this figure included other frozen prepared foods not produced by Arctic which Mr. Jones sold through his institutional distributors. Laurel immediately dropped these extra items, which reduced volume to about $2 million. Mr. Spencer thought that in the short run Laurel could use Arctic to supply the ground and diced meats which were used in some Laurel products. Mr. Jones was retained to manage the business on an indefinite basis until firm plans were made.

SETTLER FOODS

In August of 1970 a Laurel salesman happened to introduce Mr. Spencer to Ephraim Shaw, proprietor of Settler Foods, of Jefferson, Kentucky. Three days later Mr. Spencer bought Settler Foods for Laurel. Settler Foods' six-man organization produced frozen noodles, which they sold directly to restaurants and retailers in the Louisville area. Their sales volume was very small; housewives had not found their better flavor and texture attractive enough to justify their considerably higher price. Mr. Spencer thought the better flavor and texture would decidedly improve Laurel and Gourmand soups. Freezing had the effect of case-hardening the noodles at their surfaces, eliminating shrinkage. Laurel used many frozen meat, fish, and vegetable ingredients in its products, and it used dry noodles, which had to be added separately because they took longer to reconstitute and allowance had to be made for the fact that they swelled and absorbed broth in the process. Mr. Shaw assured Mr. Spencer that the frozen noodles could be added right along with the other frozen ingredients at a savings in time and labor and would result in a more flavorsome product.

Mr. Shaw had not been planning on selling his business, but he was having difficulty paying the wages of his five employees. A deal was struck when Mr. Spencer offered him 3,000 shares of Laurel common stock (market value, about $75,000) in exchange for his equipment, which was in rented quarters. Mr. Shaw was not offered employment with Laurel, and his employees were released. His customers were notified that the business was being liquidated, and the equipment was shipped to the Lakewood plant of Laurel. "Actually," said Mr. Prior, "the only thing that we bought on that deal was the machinery and a few simple formulas."

CHAPRO PROBLEMS

With the acquisition of an amphibious airplane late in November, 1970, the Chapro operation was completed and fishing operations were started. Three shipments of frozen lobsters had been processed successfully and production was rising fast when the entire operation was stopped by a political coup in Transkenya. Before investing in Chapro, Laurel had obtained a contract from the Agency for International Development insuring 80% of the equity investment in Chapro against expropriation and war. However, war had not been officially declared and no one had expropriated Chapro's assets, except for the radios in the trawlers and the airplane. The Chapro operation never made a remittance to Laurel Foods. While the three shipments it made were profitable in themselves, Chapro was expected to show a loss on the operation.

GOURMAND PRODUCTS

"We don't care what products we make," quipped Mr. Prior, "as long as they are legal, ethical, and profitable—and as long as they please our institutional buyers."

In 1971 there were over 100 items in the Gourmand line, and less than 10 of these had been in the line in their present form five years ago. One-third of Gourmand's competitors had longer lines, but two-thirds had shorter, and since Laurel insisted on quality in its Gourmand foods, and offered personal sales service and swift delivery, Mr. Prior believed Gourmand could compete with anyone.

Among convenience foods, there were some foods which were considered by the industry to be accepted and some which were as yet unaccepted. Among the accepted foods were canned soups, fruits, and vegetables; puddings, pie fillings, gelatins, and ice cream; portion-controlled raw chops, breaded cutlets, breaded fish fillets, and turkey rolls. Among the unaccepted items were bread and rice puddings; precooked meat and fish; precooked potatoes in most any form; and meat stews. Until it went into its expansion program, Laurel produced only convenience foods which were well accepted, but lately it had been doing some pioneering.

Gourmand products were designed for the institutional chef. Basically, they offered him convenience, quality, and the elimination of labor and waste. Some items, like vichyssoise and sauce Hollandaise, had appeal because many chefs did not know how to make them. Jason Ruggers had used the Laurel label on common soup items which were a grade below his top quality. Over the years the Laurel label had been phased out altogether in favor of the Gourmand label, and all Gourmand foods were of top-quality grade except the chicken and beef bases, which were offered in four grades of quality.

During the 1960's the chicken and beef bases, which had always been basic to the product line, were still the largest sales-volume items in Laurel's business. Eventually these had been supplemented by a ham-style base, designed to give a smoked-ham flavor to such soups as bean, pea, or lentil. Closely related to these bases were chicken gravy base and beef gravy base.

The elementary line of soups had been expanded into two categories, each of which included a wide variety. There were meat soups, which included bean with bacon, chicken gumbo, and split pea with smoked pork. The meatless soups included all of the traditional vegetable soups, clam chowder and turtle soup, and cheddar cheese soup.

In its early stages the company made gelatin desserts in several flavors. These had been expanded into several categories of desserts in a wide variety of flavors. In addition to Gourmand Gelatin in ten flavors, there was Special-Jel, which had the unique property of requiring no refrigeration after preparation without loss of shape or texture. Recent additions to the dessert line had been Bavarians in a variety of flavors and two lines of puddings and pie fillings, one of which was instant, requiring only the addition of milk and mixing.

In earlier years the company had tried a few canned stews, which had not been particularly successful. With the acquisition of Arctic Meats, Gourmand added an entire line of Heat & Serve convenience foods of commercial-grade quality. This line included Sloppy Joe beef and sauce, chili con carne, corned beef hash, sliced beef in gravy, chicken meat in gravy, turkey in gravy, and barbecue and spaghetti sauce. In these lines Gourmand could not command its usual premium price for extra quality. This field was highly competitive, competition was on a price basis, and margins were low.

At about the same time that Gourmand introduced its Heat & Serve line it introduced two other lines which were in the luxury food class. One, called Gourmand Potage Imperial, had only four items: jellied consommé, consommé Madrilene, vichyssoise, and lobster bisque. The other, called Gourmand Imperial Sauces, included Sauce Stroganoff, Sauce, Newburg, Hollandaise, Italienne, Aux Champignons, and Sauce Creole. These soups and sauces were the highest-priced and highest-margin items in the Gourmand line. Sophisticated chefs were attracted to them because they could not generally duplicate their delicate nuances in flavor, and because they did not care to take the time to make these complicated preparations themselves. The Imperial lines were well accepted and were profitable but did not develop a large volume of sales.

Until 1970 the Gourmand line was the only Laurel line which had national distribution. During the 1960's its dollar sales volume had tripled. In 1971 it generated 45% of the consolidated sales of Laurel and contributed 70% of total profits. Golden Batter's sales were 40% of the total and its profit was 30% of total. Arctic Meats and Coastal Foods contributed 15% of the sales volume; both had been loss operations.

ORGANIZATION

"We aren't as formal as a larger organization would be," said Mr. Prior. "There's a great deal more of cutting across lines. Also, we're growing very fast and getting a lot more complicated and we're very spread out. I used to be able to walk down the hall to see if a large expenditure was O.K. Now at this moment our president is in Richmond, our purchasing agent is in Hong Kong, our director of manufacturing is in Houston, and we have a trouble shooter in Africa."

Mr. Allan Prior, as chairman of the board and chief executive officer, handled financial matters, accounting, employee relations, and stockholder relations. He described his job as "the tedious task of watching what is going on and keeping people informed." Mr. Prior was especially watchful of the profit performance of divisions. He did not ordinarily contact people throughout the company, but worked through division managers. Mr. Prior handled any attempted take-overs of Laurel.

Mr. Donald Spencer, the president, was described as the company's operating man who got into everything—acquisitions, sales, sources of supply, manufacturing, and personnel—but he was most active in sales and was looked upon as the company's general sales manager. He left financial matters to Mr. Prior and Mr. Sandhill. Mr. Spencer traveled constantly, and any executive wishing to talk to him personally traveled to wherever he was at the moment. Mr. Spencer spent one or two days a month in the Lakewood office.

Mr. Edgar Sandhill, the third member of the top management trio, had the title "Financial Vice President." Mr. Sandhill worked very closely with Mr. Prior on financial and general policy matters. In 1965 Mr. Prior had hired a certified public accountant who had relieved Mr. Sandhill of most of his controllership duties. Mr. Sandhill's office was adjacent to Mr. Prior's, and they often consulted.

In early 1971, at Mr. Prior's suggestion, the Laurel organization had been divisionalized into five operating divisions: Gourmand, Golden Batter, Arctic Meats, Coastal Foods, and Chapro. (See Exhibit 2.) Each of the divisions had a general manager who had profit responsibility and who answered to Mr. Spencer. The general managers were responsible for all phases of their division's operations. If they felt they needed headquarters approval for anything, they contacted Mr. Spencer, wherever he was, or they brought it up at a general meeting of the top management of the company. These meetings, which included all line and staff executives from headquarters and the divisions, were held once a month or as needed in Lakewood.

At Golden Batter Karl Brunner, the general manager, felt the Lazano brothers added nothing to his management and he let it be known in Lakewood and Baltimore that he was not in favor of renewing their contracts.

Mr. Brunner was in charge of Golden Batter waffle production, wherever it was. He had no authority over John Rude, who had been appointed general manager, frozen food sales, and who operated from Golden Batter's Baltimore office. Mr. Rude was in charge of selling any frozen food produced by any division of Laurel. He answered to Mr. Spencer. Frozen foods were the fastest-growing product category in Laurel, and frozen waffles was the fastest-growing item. The Lazanos had sold $250,000 worth a year; in 1971 sales were expected to be over $3 million. Mr. Rude spent much of his time on waffle sales. In doing so, he ignored Mr. Brunner and took his proposals directly to Mr. Spencer. He launched major promotions in new territories at times when Mr. Brunner had no more production capacity. He decided to change the packaging of the waffles without letting Mr. Brunner know. He decided on the "Instant Griddle Breakfast"[2] pack without consulting Mr. Brunner. Mr. Brunner had been brought into the company as a close friend of Mr. Spencer. So had Mr. Rude, who, it now appeared, was a closer friend to Mr. Spencer than was Mr. Brunner.

[2] Instant Griddle Breakfast consisted of a Golden waffle on a tray, sausages, and syrup, which required only brief oven heating to be served.

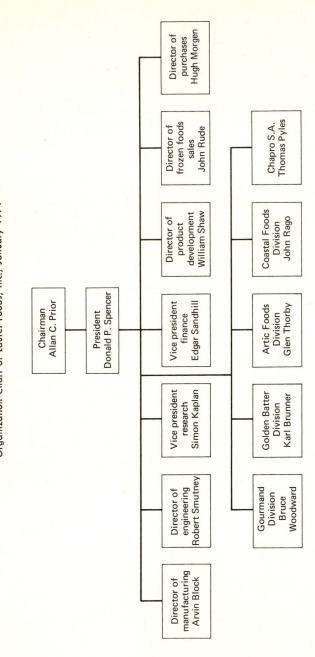

exhibit 2

Organization Chart of Laurel Foods, Inc., January 1971

Chairman
Allan C. Prior

President
Donald P. Spencer

Director of manufacturing
Arvin Block

Director of engineering
Robert Smutney

Vice president research
Simon Kaplan

Vice president finance
Edgar Sandhill

Director of product development
William Shaw

Director of frozen foods sales
John Rude

Director of purchases
Hugh Morgen

Gourmand Division
Bruce Woodward

Golden Batter Division
Karl Brunner

Artic Foods Division
Glen Thorby

Coastal Foods Division
John Rago

Chapro S.A.
Thomas Pyles

During the acquisition period the Laurel executive staff had been enlarged. The staff was expanded to include a director of manufacturing, a chief engineer, a manager of product development, a chief purchasing agent, a director of research, and a controller. "An organization doesn't grow evenly," said Mr. Prior. "Sometimes we found ourselves overstaffed in some spots and thin in others. As a general thing, talented people are our greatest need. Therefore, if we find two equally promising candidates for a job, we will hire both and find some spot to keep one of them occupied until we can make full use of his talents." Mr. Bruce Woodward had been hired in this fashion as one of two equally good candidates when Laurel was looking for an additional regional sales manager. Mr. Woodward had temporarily been in the number two position. At present he was vice president and general manager of the Gourmand Division, the company's largest. The man who had been given preference when they were hired had long since left the company.

Of the nine top executives of Laurel, four had their office in Lakewood and the other five were variously located. At Lakewood were Messrs. Prior, Sandhill, and Kaplan and the controller. Mr. Spencer had no office at Lakewood and used a spare office at Richmond at times when he was there. The director of manufacturing had found it necessary to travel a good deal because of new plant construction and to phase new acquisitions into the organization. There were times when he would spend several months at one new plant. The duties of the chief engineer largely paralleled those of the director of manufacturing, and they worked on a cooperative basis. Actual manufacturing operations were the responsibility of the general manager of each division, and each plant had a superintendent.

"I know that we are spread out too much," said Mr. Prior, "and that accounts for a lot of traveling and some communications problems, but this isn't a permanent situation; some day we'll all be together. In the meantime we use the telex a lot between plants. We give our people all the information they need to do a job; we also give them a lot of latitude in decision making."

In 1971 Laurel's finances, accounting, employee relations, legal matters, insurance, product development, and research were centralized at Lakewood. All cash collected was forwarded to Lakewood, and all bills were paid from there. However, the preponderance of Laurel operations were trending toward the Baltimore-Richmond area, and

Mr. Spencer spent more time there than anywhere else. Since his home was in Richmond, there were rumors that Laurel might move its headquarters there.

DEVELOPMENTS AND PROSPECTS

On November 30, 1970 Laurel, through an underwriting group, sold 100,000 shares of its $3.50 par value common stock at an average price of $23.60 per share, netting $2.3 million to the company. Of this amount, $700,000 was used to retire the bank term loan, $900,000 was allocated to cover the advances made to Chapro, and the remainder of the proceeds were used to increase working capital.

At their last meeting in December of 1970 the Laurel board of directors decided to ask the stockholders to authorize the issuance of 150,000 cumulative preferred shares, stating that while there were no further acquisition negotiations in progress at that time, the board felt that it would be wise to be in a position to act promptly whenever an opportunity might present itself. At the same meeting the board discussed a proposal to build a new plant on the West Coast, probably in San Francisco. Mr. Spencer wanted it to be a Golden Batter plant; Mr. Prior favored an additional Laurel plant. The board members saw no reason why it should not be a dual facility, and they took it under advisement. One board member suggested that it might be in order to add a wing to the Lakewood plant to house a Golden Batter waffle operation to serve the North Central states. Throughout 1970 the company had difficulty in keeping up with the rising demand for waffles, and two major chain stores had undertaken to produce their own, which were a duplicate of Golden Batter's.

In his 1970 Annual Report Mr. Prior stated that sales and earnings for the year had been depressed by unusually poor potato crop conditions and by the elimination of substantial amounts of the product mixes of Coastal Foods and Arctic Meats; also, the sale of additional stock diluted earnings per share. During the year the company had spent $500,000 to enlarge and improve its domestic facilities. The expenditure included the building of a small waffle plant, less than half the size of the Baltimore plant, adjacent to the new Laurel plant at New Orleans.

In late 1970 Golden Batter was extended to full national distribution. Golden Batter sales continued to increase, and the increase was almost entirely in sales to retail distributors. In February of 1971 the directors voted to build another waffle plant at San Francisco. Laurel was also making market tests of Settler frozen noodles and Instant Griddle Breakfasts in supermarkets in the Chicago area.

In March of 1971 Laurel made capital investments of over $2 million, most of which was for the San Francisco plant and a major addition to the Lakewood plant. The future prospects of the Lakewood plant were clouded by a condemnation suit brought by the city of Lakewood to appropriate virtually all of the remaining vacant property Laurel owned at Lakewood, which would prevent any further expansion. Laurel was appealing the case, but the issue was in doubt.

"We are an in-between-size company at the moment," said Mr. Prior. "We are not big enough to have momentum, and we are too big to have some of the advantages of small companies—like quick and easy communications, and the avoidance of a lot of red tape and paperwork. We produce as many—and maybe more—varieties in our line as a big operator like Heinz. But the big operator wouldn't have as streamlined an organization as we have. They would probably require a soup division, and a gelatin division, and a sauce division, and maybe even a Sloppy Joe division.

"We will continue to grow, both internally and by acquisitions. Right now we are in a digestive situation, in a consolidation stage. We have gone as far as it is sound to go in borrowings and in selling stock. We must now reduce our debt and build our earnings. Our future expansion would be via equity means.

"Laurel now has more shares outstanding. More investment bankers have become familiar with our company. Our last stock flotation was sold in small quantities, and we picked up 400 additional shareholders. This has given us a better basis for regular trading in our stock. The day is coming when Laurel will have a sound basis for becoming listed—not on the big board but on a smaller exchange. You must have people recognize your stock, and then the market value of it will be a more accurate reflection of its actual value. You must also have a proven record of performance—and that means earning money.

"The year 1970 was not an especially profitable year, and so at this time in 1971 our stock is down and we are more vulnerable to being acquired than we ever were. Our goal now is to push up the market value of our stock to where we can use it to make acquisitions. We are going to do that by expanding and by following the institutional market wherever that leads us. We are not going to do it by pumping out a lot of high-powered publicity. We are not going to try to pull rabbits out of a hat.

"We have purchased 15 acres adjacent to our Richmond plant for possible future expansion of the Laurel plant. In terms of an acquisition program we have gotten pretty far from our original guidelines, but every company we have bought has strengthened our position with our institutional wholesalers. Soon we'll be able to offer them as full a line as any big food processor."

exhibit 3   LAUREL FOODS, INC.
Comparative consolidated statements of income and retained earnings

	1970	1969	1968	1967	1966
Net Sales	$28,978,233	$21,147,408	$23,251,377	$10,569,457	$9,919,159
Costs and Expenses:					
Cost of goods sold	18,884,262	13,094,798	15,329,943	8,641,141	8,403,732
Selling and administrative expense	7,080,593	5,333,353	5,294,955	Incl. in CGS	Incl. in CGS
Depreciation and amortization	556,948	582,984	616,628	240,358	226,872
Interest	270,997	271,374	298,056	00	
Income before Income Taxes:	$ 2,185,432	$ 1,864,899	$ 1,711,795	$ 1,687,957	$1,515,427
Provision for Fed. & state income taxes	1,131,600	900,000	878,247	817,104	722,100
Net income	$ 1,053,832	$ 964,899	$ 833,548	$ 870,853	$ 793,327
Retained earnings, beginning of year	4,381,273	3,747,360	3,243,159	2,661,781	2,211,855
	$ 5,435,105	$ 4,712,259	$ 4,076,707	$ 3,532,635	$ 3,005,182
Cash dividends declared	(401,545)	(330,985)	(329,348)	(289,476)	(343,401)
Retained earnings, end of year	$ 5,033,560	$ 4,381,274	$ 3,747,360	$ 3,243,159	$2,661,781

exhibit 4   LAUREL FOODS, INC.
Consolidated financial position (years ending December 31)

	1970	1969	1968	1967	1966
Current Assets:					
Cash	$ 866,443	$ 416,691	$ 1,379,242	$ 782,094	$ 368,508
Marketable securities	298,560	00	147,952	1,335,469	1,634,346
Accts. receivable (net)	2,458,389	1,500,128	1,475,410	666,532	636,467
(less allowances for bad debts)	(101,850)	(28,650)	(65,537)	(8,178)	(7,335)
Inventories, at cost (first-in, first-out, or mkt, whichever is lower)	3,437,148	2,661,244	2,232,056	1,411,250	1,319,998
Prepaid expenses	154,894	130,169	99,758	37,965	34,518
Total Current Assets	$ 7,215,435	$ 4,708,232	$ 5,334,418	$4,233,310	$3,993,837
Properties—at cost:					
Bldgs. and equipment	9,435,683	9,008,035	8,891,011	3,767,302	3,550,498
Accumulated deprec.	4,412,221	4,211,655	3,818,517	1,656,759	1,487,685
Net bldgs. & equipment	5,023,462	4,796,380	5,072,495	2,110,543	2,062,813
Construction in progress			47,917	81,000	
Land	2,062,603	1,880,717	1,428,681	507,894	327,894
Total net properties	$ 7,086,065	$ 6,677,097	$ 6,549,092	$2,699,437	$2,390,707
Other Assets:					
Intangibles, at cost less depreciation	2,070,042	845,559	839,101		
Investments & advances made to Chapro and subsidiaries	905,400	682,539	00		
Surrender value, life insurance	120,112	92,858	75,105	41,480	56,401
Prepaid Fed. income taxes	66,341	64,991	00		
Total Net Assets	$17,463,395	$13,071,276	$12,797,717	$6,994,968	$6,440,946
Current Liabilities:					
Bank notes payable	$ 400,643				
Current payment—long-term debt		$ 349,999	$ 349,999		
Accounts payable	859,653	623,444	540,028	$ 338,232	$ 528,682
Accrued expenses	1,341,472	1,012,126	1,077,074	798,687	506,102
Federal and state taxes	578,750	345,406	425,034	482,041	542,519
Dividends payable	106,573	82,543	82,002	82,551	205,459
Total Current Liabilities	$ 3,287,091	$ 2,413,518	$ 2,474,137	$1,701,511	$1,782,762
Other Liabilities:					
Long-term debt	$ 4,624,999	$ 4,200,001	$ 4,550,000		
Reserve—deferred compensation	172,152	139,341	108,983	$ 108,910	$ 95,121
Minority equity in subsidiary			40,200		
Total Other Liabilities	$ 4,797,151	$ 4,339,342	$ 4,699,183	$ 108,910	95,121
Stockholders' Equity:					
Common stock	$ 1,776,233	$ 1,382,482	$ 1,382,482	1,382,482	1,382,482
Capital surplus	2,569,360	601,962	615,316	608,430	608,430
Retained earnings	5,033,560	4,381,273	3,747,361	3,243,159	2,661,781
Total	$ 9,379,153	$ 6,365,717	$ 5,745,159	$5,234,071	$4,652,693
Less: Treasury Stock (at cost)	000	41,302	120,761	49,525	89,631
Net Stockholders' Equity	9,379,153	6,318,414	5,624,398	5,184,546	4,563,062
Totals	$17,463,395	$13,071,276	$12,797,717	$6,994,968	$6,440,946

exhibit 5   **LAUREL FOODS, INC.**
Five-year financial review

	1970	1969	1968	1967	1966
Earnings Results:					
Net sales	$28,978,233	$21,147,408	$23,251,377	$10,569,457	$9,919,952
Income before tax	2,185,432	1,864,899	1,711,795	1,687,957	1,515,427
Tax on income	1,131,600	900,000	878,247	817,104	722,100
Net income	1,053,832	964,899	833,548	870,853	793,327
Avg. per-share earnings	$ 2.45	$ 2.63	$ 2.28	$ 2.37	$ 2.16
Dividends declared	401,546	330,985	329,348	289,476	343,401
Per share	$ .90	$ .90	$ .90	$ .80	$ .93
Depreciation and amortization	556,948	582,984	616,628	240,358	226,872
Financial Position:					
Working capital	3,928,344	2,294,714	2,820,081	2,531,799	2,211,075
Working capital ratio	2.2	2.0	2.1	2.5	2.2
Properties, net	7,086,065	6,677,097	6,549,092	2,699,437	2,390,707
Total assets	17,463,395	13,071,276	12,797,717	6,994,968	6,440,946
Long-term debt	4,625,000	4,200,002	4,550,001	00	00
Shareholders' equity	9,379,154	6,318,414	5,624,397	5,184,546	4,563,063
Avg. per-share value	$19.80	$17.22	$15.44	$14.13	$12.53

exhibit 6   **LAUREL FOODS, INC.**
Summary of sales and income by years

Year	Net Sales	Net Income	Dividends
1957	$ 4,329,954	$ 263,062	24¢
1958	4,894,116	249,571	24
1959	5,080,987	257,625	24
1960	5,196,478	217,900	24
1961	6,041,628	416,896	40
1962	7,283,085	535,584	50
1963	8,510,418	569,667	55
1964	8,278,231	526,347	55
1965	9,151,089	663,771	72
1966	9,919,159	793,327	93
1967	10,569,457	870,853	80
1968	23,251,377	833,548	90
1969	21,147,408	964,899	90
1970	28,978,233	1,053,832	90
1971 (est.)	34,500,000	1,200,000	

19

MARCOR, INC. —A MERGER

On October 31, 1968, the stockholders of Montgomery Ward and Container Corporation of America voted to combine the assets and managements of the two companies into Marcor, Inc. This merger resulted in a marketing-oriented, diversified, multi-billion-dollar company composed of leaders in the merchandising and packaging industries.

MONTGOMERY WARD

For the fiscal year ending January 31, 1970, Wards had over $2 billion in sales, making it the third largest general merchandising operation in the United States. Sales outlets were comprised of retail department stores (approximately 500) and catalog sales agencies or departments. Approximately 95 per cent of all merchandise was sold under the company's private label; credit sales contributed about one-half of total sales.

Products and Services. Wards' larger retail department stores carried a full line of products:

1. Soft goods—apparel and accessories, piece goods, notions, linen, and bedding.

2. Home furnishings—furniture, draperies, floor coverings, housewares, and table appliances.

3. Major household appliances—stereo phonographs, television sets, air conditioners, refrigerators, freezers, and laundry equipment.

529

4. Automotive equipment—tires, batteries, and accessories.

5. Miscellaneous hard goods—hardware, power tools, sporting goods, toys, building supplies, and lawn, garden, and farm equipment and supplies.

In addition to the above products, most stores provided services for delivery, installation, and repair of merchandise sold. Many of the larger stores contained departments such as beauty salons, optical and hearing aid centers, and "boutique" shops designed to serve customers by carrying full families of products, such as the Ski Chalet, Golf Pro Shop, International Gourmet Shop, Fur Salon, and Television Salon. Wards also provided professional advice in planning and remodeling kitchens and bathrooms and in installing central heating and air conditioning. Accommodation centers were available to customers (for paying utility bills, cashing checks, and photocopying), as were cafeterias, home decorating and sewing courses, and self-development programs for young girls.

Subsidiaries. Wards operated the following subsidiaries:

1. Standard T Chemical Company, Inc., developed, manufactured, and sold consumer and commercial paints, household detergents, industrial coatings, floor maintenance products, paper coatings, and resins. Sales were made to Wards' merchandise departments, as well as to other companies.

2. The Ajax Manufacturing Division, formerly a manufacturer of fence and farm products, was acquired in 1924. It produced camper and utility trailers and tool stands. All the products were sold through Wards' retail and catalog outlets under the private brand names "Riverside," "Western Field," and "Powr-Kraft."

3. Wards organized Montgomery Ward Life Insurance Company in 1966. In less than two years of operation, life insurance in force had exceeded $665 million, including a $300 million group policy covering Wards' employees and $200 million in credit accounts. Life insurance in force had increased to over $1 billion by 1970.

4. A 98 per cent interest in Pioneer Trust and Savings Bank, Chicago, was acquired by Wards in 1966.

5. Associated Sand and Gravel Company, a producer of concrete pipe, concrete products, and paving materials was acquired early in 1968. This acquisition complemented Wards' ownership of Hydro Conduit Corporation and its affiliates (the latter company has since been sold by Wards to Marcor). Associated Sand and Gravel was also

engaged in the installation of asphalt paving and the extraction, processing, and sale of sand and gravel.

Company History. Wards was founded in 1872 by Aaron Montgomery Ward and his brother-in-law, George R. Thorne. The company was exclusively a mail-order sales firm until 1926, when it opened the first of its chain of retail stores in Marysville, Kansas. Until 1958, Wards retail stores were located in a large number of separate markets, most of which were rural. Since 1958, Wards had been engaged in a program designed to shift the focus of its operations from the rural and single-store urban markets to multiple-store metropolitan markets.

Much of the company's early sales difficulty was attributed to Sewell L. Avery, chief executive officer of Wards from 1931 to 1955. Known as a strict disciplinarian, Avery kept the company basically sound during the Depression and in the late 1930's developed a program for opening new retail stores and closing old ones. From 1941 to 1955, however, Avery hoarded funds in anticipation of a second great depression and refused to open any new stores. At the time of Avery's departure in 1955, the company had (1) accumulated $327 million in cash and securities, (2) become known as a "bank with a store front," and (3) remained a rural-oriented mail-order business with an outmoded store organization concentrated in small towns in the Midwest.

Avery's successor was John Barr, former legal counsel to Wards. Barr spent $154 million for expansion and modernization of facilities between 1957 and 1961, opening a total of 58 new stores; several old stores were closed during the same period. Robert Brooker, former vice president in charge of manufacturing at Sears, Roebuck and Co. and president of Whirlpool, accepted the post as president and chief operating officer of Wards in 1961.

Brooker's Strategy. One of Brooker's first moves was to recruit key executives experienced in mass merchandising—many of whom came from Sears. Around 30 key individuals made a commitment to join and stay with Wards in the attempt to implement a new concept of mass distribution. Working with these key people, along with some talented hold-overs from Wards, Brooker developed a plan for expansion which could be implemented while maintaining a degree of profitability.

Brooker conceived that, externally, Wards' strategic situation was the opposite of Sears'. Historically, Wards had been in small towns and had not moved into the new urban markets. On the other hand, Sears originally had big-city markets and had also expanded into most of the major new markets. In addition, many other competitors had moved into the newer urban markets, including J. C. Penney, some department stores, and various discount houses. Consequently, Wards was at a strategic disadvantage in almost every market because of the advantages accruing to established retailers in the form of customer loyalty, higher volume, and greater exposure.

The basic strategy developed for retail store location revolved around three key points of action: closing of smaller unprofitable stores, relocation of smaller stores, and opening of new stores in the major urban markets. The basic objective was to make the transition from small stores to large stores without having costs jeopardize earnings. Two elements of cost were present: start-up costs for new stores and closing costs for old stores. The latter cost items (employee transfers, uncollected accounts which must be forfeited, and so forth) were estimated to total $30,000 to $40,000 for each store closed.

Operating within the cost constraint, Brooker worked out a plan for relocation, closing, and expansion with two Wards executives, Harold Dysart and Howard Green. The programming of store relocations in areas where the company already had acceptance was a key element of the plan, as was the opening of new stores based on the "metro district" concept—the latter term referred to the establishment of a central management team for each major metropolitan market to co-ordinate buying, promoting, and selling activities of all stores within the district.

Brooker also implemented a new procurement and inventory control system, cut the number of supply sources in half, initiated computer applications in various operations, and developed new policies and modes of operations for catalog and credit sales. The net result of these changes was an increase in profitability up through 1965.

1966: A Setback. In the plan developed by Brooker, it was anticipated that earnings per share would grow by roughly 15 per cent a year after 1962. The projection turned out to be fairly accurate up through 1965, but instead of realizing the projected $2.30 a share in 1966, earnings fell to $1.24. Two major reasons for the setback given by Brooker were overconfidence in operations and a credit squeeze.

The plan had gone reasonably well in the relocation of stores and in the development of some major metro markets. The trouble came, according to Brooker, "in metro markets where we were the invaders." Major losses were incurred in the Los Angeles and Chicago markets where the "basic mistake . . . was in deciding that since we were doing so well on the schedule we'd set up, we could add more on—and it was just too much for us to digest." There were not enough people trained in the metro organization concept, and the net result was a deficiency of managerial skills. The credit squeeze problem resulted from too great a reliance on short-term borrowing in the immediately preceding years. Brooker had to choose whether to maintain receivables and borrow more money or to tighten credit terms to customers and lose sales. The final decision was to cut back on credit terms to customers, and, according to Brooker, "that subsequently hurt our sales and profits. . . . we were a little too conservative, but at least we were prudent."

Financial Position. Exhibit 1 presents a five-year summary of financial information for Wards as of January 31, 1968; the data indicate Wards' financial position prior to the beginning of merger negotiations with Container Corporation.

CONTAINER CORPORATION OF AMERICA

Container Corporation was founded in 1926 by Walter P. Paepcke, who served as chief executive officer for more than 30 years. To form the company, Mr. Paepcke combined the paperboard packaging facilities of Chicago Mill and Lumber Company with the plants and facilities of several other paperboard-fabricating firms.

In 1970 the company was the largest manufacturer of paperboard packaging (shipping containers and folding cartons) in the United States, and the second largest manufacturer of paperboard. Container and its subsidiaries manufactured and sold corrugated and solid-fiber shipping containers, folding cartons, fiber cans and drums, paper bags, plastic packaging, and paperboard in the form of containerboard and boxboard. The company's domestic shipments of shipping containers and folding cartons represented approximately 6 and 9 per cent, respectively, of the totals of these industries; its domestic production of paperboard represented approximately 6 per cent of the total production of that industry in 1970.

Container's products were used extensively in the packaging and shipping of food products, canned goods, clothing, soaps, beverages, furniture, automotive products and accessories, petroleum products, electrical equipment, household items, textiles, drugs, tobacco, and

exhibit 1   WARDS AND SUBSIDIARIES
Statistical summary (in thousands) *

Operations:	1963	1964	1965	1966	1967
Net sales	$1,500,112	$1,697,390	$1,748,360	$1,894,123	$1,879,009
Net earnings	20,967	21,865	23,963	16,528	17,425
Federal income taxes	17,353	17,300	17,748	10,939	13,357
Dividends	13,880	13,550	13,555	13,556	13,555
Earnings reinvested from previous years	7,087	8,316	10,408	2,972	3,870
Additions to properties and equipment	74,093	73,023	68,203	57,866	26,654
Depreciation and amortization	13,347	17,143	19,152	22,058	23,906
Number of retail stores	512	502	502	493	475
Number of catalog stores	737	818	864	793	719
Number of catalog sales agencies	...	108	287	569	632
Average number of employees	83	94	98	105	101
Financial Position:					
Working capital	$ 566,831	$ 588,516	$ 702,628	$ 651,017	$ 704,525
Accounts receivable	573,363	717,379	834,953	832,599	848,908
Inventories	328,564	349,867	400,206	408,433	401,043
Net investment in properties & equipment	216,757	269,146	311,576	344,212	338,409
Long-term debt	128,652	200,288	349,383	350,599	414,665
Stockholders' interest:					
Capital stock & earnings reinvested	637,936	646,250	656,733	659,818	662,073
Investment per common share	49.63	50.27	51.09	51.32	51.61
Earnings per common share	1.57	1.66	1.83	1.24	1.31
Dividends per common share	1.00	1.00	1.00	1.00	1.00
Shares outstanding:					
Class A	141	139	139	139	125
Common	12,569	12,579	12,581	12,586	12,586
Number of stockholders	97	92	87	88	85

* Except for figures on number of retail stores, catalog stores, and catalog sales agencies; and on investment, earnings, and dividends-per-common-share items.

many other products. The increased use of packaging in recent years had been attributed to factors such as low cost, light weight, design techniques, improved protection and display characteristics, and the adaptability of products to mechanical packaging machinery and methods of industrial customers.

Manufacturing. In 1970 manufacturing operations were carried out in 83 packaging plants and mills in the United States and in 52 plants overseas. In the United States, there were 14 paperboard mills, 30 shipping containers, 14 folding cartons, 10 fiber cans, and 6 plastic packaging plants. Production operations were highly integrated. Overseas, Container's facilities consisted of 6 paperboard mills and the following fabricating plants: 13 shipping containers, 5 folding cartons, 3 fiber cans, 1 plastic packaging, and 2 paper bag plants.

As the company continued to expand its end-use markets, the packaging plants created a growing demand for the paperboard produced in company mills, which, in turn, drew upon substantial timber holdings owned by Container. In 1970 the company owned, leased, or had cutting rights on 779,000 acres of timberland. It also had a 49 per cent equity in the T.R. Miller Mill Company, which owned an additional 194,000 acres.

Financial Position. Exhibit 2 presents a five-year summary of financial information for Container Corporation as of December 31, 1967; the data indicate Container's financial position prior to the beginning of merger negotiations with Wards.

Earnings increased more than 70 per cent from 1963 through 1967. Profits (after taxes) for 1968 were anticipated, at the time of negotiations, to be about 2 per cent off from 1967. Dividends had kept pace with earnings over the 1963–1967 period, increasing from 92.5¢ per

exhibit 2   **CONTAINER AND SUBSIDIARIES**
Statistical summary (in thousands of dollars) *

	1963	1964	1965	1966	1967
Net sales	$356,814	$390,575	$405,689	$460,365	$463,135
Net earnings	19,125	23,140	27,301	34,231	32,906
Earnings per share	$ 1.71	$ 2.06	$ 2.42	$ 3.06	$ 2.95
Per cent return on shareholders' equity	11.4	12.9	14.2	16.8	14.7
Common stock dividends	$ 10,003	$ 11,055	$ 12,848	$ 13,996	$ 14,555
Property additions and improvements	36,545	30,373	36,540	44,032	50,060
Depreciation & depletion	15,831	17,353	18,454	19,593	20,752
Current assets	103,226	118,478	114,279	133,214	125,230
Current liabilities	47,577	45,357	48,583	67,971	53,725
Working capital	55,649	73,121	65,696	65,243	71,505
Current ratio	2.17:1	2.61:1	2.35:1	1.96:1	2.33:1
Property, less reserve	$183,678	$192,661	$211,866	$236,251	$247,401
Deferred income taxes and other liabilities	8,661	8,823	12,850	17,421	19,660
Long-term debt	62,487	63,343	59,832	69,484	71,882
Shareholders' equity	179,926	191,943	203,717	223,417	241,105
Book value per share	15.79	16.89	18.19	19.95	21.64

*Except for figures on earnings per share, % returns, book value per share, and current ratio items.

share in 1963 to $1.30 in 1967. Sales had grown 35 per cent in the same period, with over $463 million in net sales realized during 1967. Return on shareholders' equity improved from 11.4 per cent in 1963 to 14.7 per cent in 1967. This return on equity measure had traditionally been used by Container in the measurement of performance of individual plant managers; managers were given considerable autonomy in developing local markets and in gearing production to meet local needs under the "profit center" concept.

Container's recent growth was almost entirely internal and a result of "business as usual." According to Leo Schoenhofen, then the president of Container: "All we did was concentrate on manufacturing quality paperboard and plastic packaging products—on developing outstanding creative services for our customers—doing what we know how to do best—analyzing the needs of a market and finding a way to meet those needs—at a profit!" Schoenhofen also noted at the time, "Container has had an extremely successful modernization and expansion program—which has been financed primarily through retained earnings. And if this program continues as planned, we can look forward to continued growth in sales and earnings in the next five to ten years and beyond."

REASONS FOR THE MERGER

"We wanted to make a whale too big to get through the door." This was the explanation given by a Wards executive as to why the giant retailer and Container Corporation decided to merge into a holding company named Marcor, Inc., in November of 1968. Both companies felt vulnerable to a take-over, and, in large part, the merger was designed as a defense against this threat. Circumstances peculiar to each company, however, have also been cited as reasons for the merger.

Montgomery Ward. The following reasons have been given by Wards' management as justification for the merger in 1968:

1. The slump of Wards in 1966 resulted in depressed stock prices, and rumors began to circulate that the company was a prime candidate for a take-over. When queried about such a threat, Brooker replied: ". . . It was impossible to avoid recognizing that we were exposed. It is true that we were behind our planned level of progress, the price of our stock was down, and there were some rumors. Every so often we'd hear that someone was going to make a pass at us, though there was

never anyone who approached us directly. This was a problem throughout the business community, and we were no exception. You know when you take charge of a company that is in trouble, you may have this problem somewhere along the line. You become most vulnerable when raiders see that you have solved your basic problems and are about to turn around. . . . As I thought about it then, I could see that some conglomerates, Litton and Gulf & Western, for example, were successful—they convinced managements that it was good to join them. A number of conglomerators—Ling, for example—had a sense of timing, had paper, and could buy almost anything. They could borrow to pay cash. But some failed at take-over because they didn't have management in their corner. A raider—as I use the term—tries to divide a company by moving without consulting its management or board."

On the subject of whether some powerful acquisitor could have accomplished a take-over, Brooker stated: ". . . We were an inviting prospect, but the management of Montgomery Ward in 1966 and 1967 was not easy prey to anyone. We would have been willing to talk to anyone legitimate if it would have been good for the stockholders. But it would also have to have been good for the management team, because they were under no obligation to stay if the top structure changed. All of them—the twenty or thirty key men—were basically independent people. They didn't have to work at Montgomery Ward. It wasn't a captive management. The people weren't chattels of the company. They were people who had come here, taken the risk, and done well. . . . It was to the shareholders' advantage to have these men running the company . . . Most people who are interested in making a take-over want to get the management, too. Legitimate people want to arrange an acquisition on a basis that will get management support. If I had been faced with someone who sought management's agreement for a take-over, I would have had to go back to the people I had brought in and see what they wanted to do. That goes back to the commitments I made to them and they made to me at the beginning of my administration. That doesn't mean a tender offer couldn't have won, but if one had come along, we'd have fought it." Management also felt that Wards was about ready to turn the corner—a feeling apparently shared by outside financial analysts. Thus the combination with Container was consummated, in part, to gain the defensive value of increased size.

2. "One of the things that made this deal," said Gordon R. Worley, financial vice president of both Wards and Marcor, "was the tax deferral available to Montgomery Ward. Our earnings were not sufficient to utilize our full tax deferral. With this combination, we'll be in a position to bring the Container earnings under this tax-deferral umbrella, and, in effect, we will be able to defer the federal income tax on Container's earnings for a considerable period of time." The tax deferrals were a result of the federal tax laws as they applied to Wards' credit business; credit sales were reported, but the gross income on them did not have to be reported until collection was completed. "Since we are in the consumer-credit business and our receivables are constantly turning over," Worley explained, "as we collect $1 million we generate another $1 million to replace it. As long as we continue to stay in business and as long as our receivables continue to exist, we have what amounts to a permanent deferral of this gross income." In January, 1970, total tax deferrals available to Marcor from 1970 through 1973 were projected at $210 million. This source of funds could be used by Marcor in any way—to expand Container's operations, to expand Wards' operations, or to make acquisitions.

3. As stated by Brooker, "The combination of Container talents will bring to Wards a new look at the way we handle retailing and the way we handle the catalog. . . . If you bring in individuals who are competent and have ideas in other fields, they challenge your ways of doing business." Also, Brooker noted, "They have some skills in direct mail that I have been very interested in. We have a strong feeling that there is an opportunity in direct mail." Container's expertise in graphics was expected to play a major role in improving this and other forms of advertising. The fact that both companies were strongly marketing-oriented also contributed, in management's opinion, to a degree of "fit" between the two companies, and management expected it would produce synergistic effects. Some synergism was also anticipated management-wise, in that top managers in manufacturing, distribution, and sales could be brought together as a creative management team.

4. Another major attraction to Wards' management was the gaining of an experienced top management man of good age (54) in Leo Schoenhofen, then the chief executive officer of Container, who later became chairman of Marcor (upon Brooker's retirement from that position in May, 1970). Also, Wards was basically only one-deep in men with top management experience, as was Container. It was

believed that the merger would result in two-deep at the Marcor level —a buying of time in order to further develop the human resources in each organization.

5. Finally, the fact that both Container and Wards were Chicago-based companies meant that no Wards or Container people would have to be moved around to different geographical areas.

Container Corporation. Container also had a number of reasons for merging with Wards:

1. Schoenhofen stated, "To be very plain, the basic advantage to Container Corporation from the stockholders' standpoint is that it enables us to extend our activity. There was some question in our mind in looking over the next ten years as to whether we would be able to finance our expansion just to keep our market position, not necessarily to increase it." The additional cash flow, emanating from Wards' tax deferral benefits, would thus enable Container to maintain and improve its market position.

2. Because Wall Street had always lumped Container with the bulk of the paper industry (incorrectly so, in the opinion of management), the company had a low price/earnings ratio of 10. Container's management felt that its creativity in design and marketing warranted a better evaluation—one which could be achieved with the merger. Also, the low price/earnings ratio made Container vulnerable to a take-over.

3. Container had been seeking ways to diversify into other areas of packaging and related fields that seemed to offer profit potential. The company had found, however, that it generally could not afford to acquire the kinds of companies which appeared attractive. In the early part of 1968, Container's management was also approached by a half-dozen acquisition-minded companies and had extensive exploratory conversations with them. As stated by Schoenhofen, "These were all situations in which one and one added up to two—or two and two added up to four—but no more. We felt we needed some synergism— a situation that we could contribute to and benefit from. We think we found this in the marketing orientation that is common to the Marcor companies."

4. Container's management was also reluctant to merge with another company for fear that the company would lose its identity—and perhaps even lose control of its organization. By joining with Wards in the formation of Marcor, Container had the opportunity to keep its own organization intact and to maintain its identity. The merger was made with the understanding that the Marcor management would

maintain and strengthen the identity of each of the Marcor subsidiaries. Associated with this advantage was the feeling that Container
would have a much better chance of pursuing and achieving its individual corporate objectives than ever before.

5. Another stated advantage of the merger to Container was that
the deal was consummated with the understanding that Schoenhofen
would move up to be chief executive officer of Marcor when Robert
Brooker retired in 1970. This fact further assured Container's management that the company's aspirations would not be neglected even
though it was expected that Wards would account for approximately
80 per cent of Marcor's total sales in the near future. Also, Wards and
Container agreed that the two firms would be equals in policy making
via membership on a joint committee composed of senior executives
divorced from line responsibilities.

6. As in the case of Wards, Container was also only one-deep in top
management experience at the policy level.

FINANCIAL ANALYSIS AND TERMS OF THE MERGER

When asked how Container and Wards reached agreement on the
exchange of stock for the merger, Brooker replied: "Obviously, during
the period of talking you establish certain criteria that enable you to
make an agreeable offer. We wanted to buy at the best price we could
and at a ratio that would appeal to Container. But we didn't really
have to bargain in the usual sense. We worked out a ratio that they
thought was very fair, so there wasn't anything to bargain in it. They
tried it out on Al Gordon, their financial adviser and a member of
their board. He gave some practical advice that involved adjusting
some of the relationships of the securities but not the ultimate value.
In a tax-free merger, more than half of the exchange has to be for
equity. For some technical reason, it's not good to have fifty-fifty, so
what we wanted was to get no more than 49 per cent of the Container
stock tendered for debentures. Actually we got between 41 and 42 per
cent." The accounting for Marcor was on the basis of a partial pooling
of interests.[1] Since all of Wards' shares of common stock were ex-

---

[1] "Pooling of interests" purchase agreement enables the parent corporation to treat
new acquisitions as if they have always been a part of the parent insofar as reporting
of earnings is concerned; the alternative, "purchase accounting," allows the parent
to take credit for an acquired company's profits only from the date of the acquisition.

changed for shares of Marcor (one for one), all of Wards' earnings could be pooled into Marcor. Because, however, only 59 per cent of Container's shares were exchanged for preferred shares of Marcor (one for one), only 59 per cent of Container's earnings could be pooled by Marcor. The remaining 41 per cent of Container's shares were purchased through the issuance of Marcor 6.5 per cent subordinated debentures. Accordingly, these earnings were not available to Marcor prior to November 1, 1968, the effective date of the merger; thus 41 per cent of Container's earnings through October 31, 1968, could not be included in Marcor's 1968 reported earnings.

Prior to the actual merger, financial analysts at Wards performed several analyses to indicate the potential benefits of the merger. Using 1968 earnings projections, and assuming that the merger had occurred at the beginning of fiscal 1967, analysts prepared the statement of pro forma earnings shown in Exhibit 3.

exhibit 3   PRO FORMA EARNINGS
(In thousands)

	Pro Forma		Partial Pooling to Be Reported	
	1967	*1968*	*1967*	*1968*
Wards and subsidiaries	$17,425	30,000	$17,425	30,000
Container Corporation	33,971	32,400	20,017	22,716
Total	51,396	62,400	37,442	52,716
Less: Interest (after taxes) on 6.5% subordinated debentures	9,115	8,273	—	2,082
Net earnings	$42,281	54,127	$37,442	50,634
Less: Dividends—				
$2 convertible preferred	13,186	13,166	13,186	13,166
Wards' Class A Stock	—	—	968	643
Net earnings available to common stock	$29,095	$40,961	$23,288	$36,825
Earnings per share	$2.31	$3.25	$1.85	$2.93
Earnings per share assuming full conversion of convertible preferred	$2.20	$2.82	$1.90	$2.61

Analysts also prepared a pro forma consolidated balance sheet (Exhibit 4) for the end of fiscal 1968. One of the more important indications of the pro forma balance sheet was a projected borrowing base of $1,072 million. This compared with senior long-term debt of $551 million (the remainder of the long-term debt was subordinated) plus short-term debt of $413 million for a total debt of $964 million—a debt-to-equity-plus-subordinated-debt ratio of slightly better than one to one. Eliminating Montgomery Ward Credit Corporation (the financing vehicle for credit sales) would result in a total senior debt of $321 million and equity and subordinated debt of $819 million—better than a 2.5 to 1 ratio (debt to equity plus subordinated debt). This was considered a most satisfactory ratio by management, who felt that it should enable Marcor and its subsidiaries to leverage their business still further with substantial amounts of additional debt.

exhibit 4   PRO FORMA BALANCE SHEET
(In thousands)

Assets:		Liabilities:	
Cash	$ 65,000	Notes payable	$ 413,000
Receivables	1,008,000	Accounts payable	162,000
Inventories	444,000	Accrued expenses	86,000
Prepaid & other	54,000	Federal taxes:	
Total current assets	1,571,000	Currently payable	10,000
Investment in subsidiaries	91,000	Deferred	106,000
Properties & equip. (net)	648,000	Total current liabilities	$ 777,000
Deferred charges	9,000	Deferred federal taxes	13,000
Excess cost of subsidiaries		Long-term debt	846,000
over book value at date of		Minority interest	12,000
acquisition	$ 148,000	Equity	819,000
	$2,467,000		$2,467,000

Looking at the cash flow and deferred taxes available to Marcor, it was projected that $170 million would be generated from earnings, depreciation and amortization, and deferred federal income taxes in fiscal 1969. The pro forma cash flow statement (Exhibit 5) was developed:

exhibit 5   PRO FORMA CASH FLOW STATEMENT—FISCAL 1969
(In thousands)

Net earnings before dividends	$ 60,000
Depreciation and amortization	53,000
Federal taxes (deferrable)	57,000
Total funds from operations	$170,000
Deduct:	
Capital expenditures	95,000
Dividends	26,000
Total funds required	$121,000
Funds available after operating requirements	$ 49,000

The $49 million represented estimated excess cash flow before consideration of any increase in customer receivables. Since Wards elected the installment basis for paying its federal taxes in 1963 and also elected to file a consolidated tax return in 1965, it was able to defer the payment of federal income taxes on the gross profit contained in uncollected customer receivables at the end of each tax year. It was also predicted that Wards would have $945 million of customer receivables as of January 31, 1969 (the company actually had $990 million of receivables at that date); the receivables was estimated to be 40 per cent—which meant that Marcor could defer for tax purposes $370 million of taxable income, representing $184 million of taxes which would normally be payable. Wards' earnings through October 31, 1968, and Marcor earnings through January 31, 1969 (the end of fiscal 1968), were projected to utilize $210 million of the tax deferral, permitting the deferral of $106 million for fiscal 1968. The balance of $78 million (Exhibit 6) would be available for use by the combined companies of Marcor, since Container and its earnings would be included in the consolidated tax return of Marcor beginning November 1, 1968. Exhibit 6 summarizes the tax deferral position estimated for fiscal 1968 and through fiscal 1973:

exhibit 6   TAX DEFERRAL—FISCAL 1968–1973
(In thousands)

	Fiscal 1968	Through Fiscal 1973
Customer receivable balances	$945,000	$1,500,000
Deferred gross profit on credit sales	370,000	600,000
Total tax liability deferrable	184,000	300,000
Utilization in reduction of taxes payable	106,000	300,000
Available to offset future taxes payable	$ 78,000	—
Estimated net increase in deferred taxes in the five-year period		$ 194,000

The projections indicated that Marcor would be able to defer upward of $60 million a year in federal income taxes through 1971, at which time the excess deferral would probably be fully used. The amount of the annual tax deferral was expected to rise thereafter, however, based on the estimated growth in Wards' outstanding receivables. As indicated in the previous exhibit, the annual tax deferrals were expected to total $300 million at the end of the five-year period.

The foregoing data indicated to both Wards and Container that each would be able to finance a greater rate of growth, as a result of the merger, than was possible to either company on an individual basis. Wards' earnings had not been sufficient to fully utilize the tax deferral in the past, and such a benefit had not been available to Container.

MARCOR: OBJECTIVES, ORGANIZATION, AND RESULTS

When Marcor came into existence in November, 1968, its basic objective was to "achieve growth through marketing concepts." It was anticipated that the holding company would finance the growth and provide coordinating plans for its subsidiaries. No basic changes in the name, administration, or operation of Montgomery Ward and Container were anticipated. Each of the companies would continue to have its own board of directors, officers, administrative staffs, and service functions; also, each was to continue its own programs of growth and expansion in merchandising, marketing, and manufacturing.

Objectives. Marcor's objectives, as stated in January, 1970, were to:

1. Provide a financial structure which would make possible the physical investment needed to achieve sales and profit objectives.

2. Help all segments achieve their objectives by providing financial control and accountability in all company operations and in the measuring of performance at all levels.

3. Further develop personnel resources within the corporation with programs which would assure a successful future management, and to maintain a balance of programs for systems research and product development.

4. Diversity through internal development and acquisition into related and compatible areas in which Marcor's marketing capabilities, technical competence, and management skills could make significant contributions to sales and profit growth greater than established corporate norms.

5. Achieve an average annual sales growth of 8.5 per cent and average annual net earnings growth of 14 per cent through 1974. Container's goal was to achieve an average annual increase of 10 per cent in both sales and earnings through 1974, while Montgomery Ward expected an average increase in sales of 9.5 per cent per year over the same period.

Top Management Organization. The co-ordination of planning and management of Wards and Container was accomplished primarily through overlapping boards of directors. The board of directors for

Wards included the president of Container; similarly, Wards' president sat on the board of directors for Container. The board of directors for Marcor included five of Wards' top officers and four of Container's, in addition to the normal representation of outside individuals.

The top operating executive officers for Marcor as of October, 1970, were:

1. Leo Schoenhofen, Chairman of the Board and Chief Executive Officer of Marcor.

2. Robert Brooker, Chairman of the Executive Committee.

3. Gordon Worley, Vice President of Finance for both Marcor and Wards.

4. Daniel Walker, Vice President and General Counsel of both Marcor and Wards; Secretary of Wards.

5. Richard Kelly, Secretary of Marcor; Assistant General Counsel of both Marcor and Container.

Brooker, upon his retirement as chairman of Marcor in May, 1970, assumed the chairmanship of the executive committee of both Marcor and Wards. The executive committee determined matters of policy between the quarterly board meetings and was influential in all major capital investment decisions. In addition to Brooker, the executive committee included Schoenhofen, Edward Donnell (Ward's president), and Henry Van der Eb (Container's president). Exhibit 7 presents the top organizational relationships as of January, 1971.

Role of Top Management. The role of Marcor's operating executives in the operation of Wards and Container was to be a blend of "outside counselor and parent." The executives expected to preserve what was best at each of the companies, but they also believed that they could introduce a new degree of objectivity and independent scrutiny, permitting a fresh look at both operations.

Marcor's management expected to remain small and flexible so that it could respond quickly and effectively to new problems. It planned to draw freely on the management capabilities of both Wards and Container from time to time, assembling task forces to tackle particular projects and disbanding or reshaping the force as each problem was solved or redefined. The top executives also expected that Marcor would experience almost continuous restructuring and augmentation as its role evolved.

One of the most direct and immediate benefits seen by the Marcor management was the infusion of many of the specialized management skills and techniques of each company into the other's management

exhibit 7
Marcor Organization As of January 1971

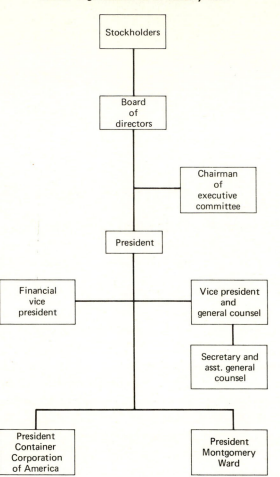

force. Available management talent would be directed into critical areas first while additional opportunities in all parts of both operations were evaluated. This process, it was hoped, would involve the introduction of new management techniques and the temporary or permanent shifting of personnel within and between the two operations.

Marcor executives also saw, as one of their major tasks, the combining of development programs of each company to provide "cross-training" of the managements of Wards and Container. It was anticipated that Marcor could strengthen its continuing-development program for management personnel in this way.

Administrative Functions. Except for the policy-level decisions, the primary functions of Marcor were performed by personnel from both Wards and Container. Wards personnel prepared the analyses and reports necessary for the co-ordination of financial planning, budgetary administration, accounting, and investor relations for Marcor. Wards people also performed the public relations function at the Marcor level, although Container handled all advertising. No administrative services were performed at the Marcor level for either Wards or Container. Both companies continued to perform their own legal, accounting, personnel, public relations, and other staff functions independently. Some thought had been given to centralizing these types of services (not only for Wards and Container, but also for their individual subsidiaries), but no action had been taken as of January, 1971. The major reason given for the lack of centralization was the desire to maintain the autonomy of Wards and Container; both companies preferred to move slowly toward establishing formal intercompany ties as opposed to informal working relationships and sharing of expertise.

Joint Task Forces. Very few joint operating forces were established to achieve the synergistic effects anticipated in the combination. One task force composed of Container's carton and packaging experts and Wards personnel was established to work on the protective packing of products received from Wards' suppliers. The project was expected to result in a substantial reduction in product damage and, consequently, in increased customer satisfaction.

Another task force was appointed to study how the retirement plans of the two companies might be integrated. This problem, as a part of the larger question of equalization of total compensation structures, revealed basic differences in industry practices which mitigated against common compensatory arrangements. The major result after nine months of study indicated that control should not emphasize equalization between similar positions in the two companies; rather, control should seek to ensure that each company remained competitive in salary, retirement plans, and other benefits with firms in the particular industry in which it operated.

Although few formal task forces had been assembled, informal sharing of ideas and expertise was encouraged by top management.

Planning staffs from the two companies held meetings to discuss new approaches and common denominators in planning. Similarly, purchasing, traffic, and personnel department heads informally discussed common problems. This approach emanated from the emphasis on retention of autonomy and the desire of top management to avoid conflict at an early stage in the merged firm's life cycle; Marcor officials preferred to move slowly to ensure cross-fertilization of ideas and techniques in a conflict-free environment.

Personnel Transfers. In the first two years after the merger, only one incident occurred where personnel were formally transferred from one company to the other. At the time of the merger, Wards operated four IBM 360s in its computer processing center, while Container had only one 360 computer. The computing facilities were physically combined, although Wards and Container continued to perform systems analysis and programming independently. All keypunch and other operations were performed by Wards for both companies; this involved the transferring of around 20 keypunch operators and clerks from Container's payroll to Wards'. One systems analyst was transferred from Wards to Container at the same time.

Financial Results. Exhibit 8 presents a five-year statistical summary for Marcor, and assumes that the merger occurred before fiscal 1965. The actual post-merger results for a complete year of operation are reflected in the fiscal 1969 column.

Marcor net sales rose to $2.7 billion in 1969, an increase of 8.6 per cent over 1968. Both Wards and Container posted record sales during the year; Wards' sales improved 8.5 per cent from $1.99 billion to $2.16 billion, and Container increased sales 8.6 per cent from $469 million in 1968 to $510 million in 1969.

During the five years, consolidated net sales of Marcor increased at a compound annual rate of 5.4 per cent. During the same period, sales of Wards increased at a compound annual rate of 4.9 per cent, while sales of Container increased at a rate of 5.5 per cent.

Earnings for 1969 were $67 million, up 24.4 per cent over $53.8 million in 1968, on a partial pooling basis. Had the merger occurred on February 1, 1968 (the beginning of fiscal 1968), Marcor 1969 earnings would show a 16.1 per cent rise from $57.7 million in 1968, on a comparable pro forma basis. Earnings per share for 1969 would be up 19.7 per cent from $3.50 in 1968; fully diluted 1969 earnings were $3.43, against $2.95 in 1968 on a comparable pro forma basis.

exhibit 8 MARCOR, INCORPORATED
Five-year statistical summary (in thousands)

	1969	1968	1967	1966	1965
Operations:					
Net sales	$ 2,715,150	$ 2,500,705	$ 2,352,293	$ 2,354,488	$ 2,154,049
Net earnings*	66,950	53,810	37,443	36,699	40,050
Taxes on income (including all subsidiaries)*	58,417	49,920	27,582	26,527	30,685
Dividends*	25,701	25,265	22,131	21,803	21,215
Additions to properties and equipment	136,328	99,722	95,945	101,898	104,743
Depreciation and amortization	50,226	47,432	45,417	41,651	37,606
Financial Position:					
Working capital	$ 869,574	$ 842,784	$ 778,639	$ 711,842	$ 765,108
Accounts receivable	1,176,410	1,047,823	900,348	879,475	875,792
Inventories	530,819	499,448	447,955	457,120	445,173
Net investment in properties and equipment	750,372	706,491	602,279	580,463	523,442
Long-term debt—Senior	630,788	603,734	469,898	395,082	384,215
—Subordinated	295,472	299,181	29,950	25,000	25,000
Stockholders' Interest:					
Stockholders' equity*	$ 859,347	$ 817,615	$ 791,675	$ 777,544	$ 762,851
Investment per common share (book value of shares outstanding at end of year)	44.13	41.23	39.42	38.19	37.03
Earnings per common share and common equivalent share	4.19	3.14	1.85	1.79	2.04
Earnings per common share assuming full dilution	3.43	2.72	1.85	1.79	2.03
Shares outstanding:					
Preferred (pro forma prior to 1968)	6,558,072	6,612,352	6,566,049	6,597,704	6,598,680
Common	12,751,264	12,613,392	12,586,557	12,586,557	12,581,422
Number of stockholders	80,862	88,248	104,661	104,456	102,902

* Amounts prior to November 1, 1968, have been reduced by the portions applicable to Container Corporation shares exchanged for debentures at that date.

FUTURE GROWTH PHILOSOPHY

"We have no reluctance to achieve growth through acquisition. But growth through acquisition is not essential . . . we should concentrate on accelerating the growth of our present business to achieve the greatest profitability within the company and the maximum benefit for shareholders." These words by Brooker summarized Marcor's basic growth philosophy. The company would acquire another on-going concern if two major conditions were met. First and foremost, a company would not be acquired unless it provided a degree of "fit" with Marcor's operations. Secondly, the potential acquisition should be undervalued in terms of current market price.

Wards and Container each had manpower designated to evaluate potential acquisitions. Prospects were generally identified informally —by top corporate officers, by "marriage" brokers who contacted the companies, or by a multitude of other personal or published sources. Once a potential acquisition had been identified, evaluations were conducted to determine degree of fit, future earnings prospects, and management capabilities. No formal criteria were employed; individual cases were judged according to different standards, as appropriate. In addition to the "degree of fit" criterion, however, much emphasis was to be placed on good management, as it was expected that any acquired companies would continue to operate rather autonomously. Neither Wards nor Container had any desire to be a conglomerate.

20

TANDY
CORPORATION

ACQUISITION PROPOSAL

In July of 1967, Charles D. Tandy, chairman of the board and chief executive officer of Tandy Corporation, learned that Leonards Department Store, a privately held department store complex in Fort Worth, Texas, might be for sale. Four years earlier, Charles Tandy had approached Leonards' owners with an offer to purchase the Leonard Company in order to have an immediate profit offset to a sizable tax loss carryover from the then recently acquired Radio Shack Corporation. No deal was made at that time because of a very high asking price on the part of Leonards' owners ($20 to $21 million cash) and the reluctance of Tandy Corporation bankers to finance an acquisition of that size.

Charles Tandy, however, retained an interest in acquiring Leonards, and in order to maintain a close contact with the company, Paul Leonard, president of Leonards and son of one of the founders of the company, was asked in 1965 to become a director of the Tandy Corporation. In July of 1967, Paul Leonard informed Charles Tandy that there had been some discussion by members of the Leonard families of the desirability of selling the company because of anticipated future estate problems. This discussion was precipitated by concern for the health of Mr. O. P. Leonard (age 70), one of the co-founders and principal owner of Leonards. Subsequent discussion with Paul Leonard indicated to Charles Tandy that an acquisition might be feasible, and

551

he then requested that financial information be prepared by Leonards for evaluation by Tandy Corporation personnel.

THE TANDY CORPORATION: HISTORY AND DEVELOPMENT

The Tandy Leather Company, a predecessor company of the Tandy Corporation, was co-founded in 1919 by Dave L. Tandy to supply shoe findings to the boot and shoe repair industry. During World War II, Dave Tandy became aware of the acute need by veterans' rehabilitation centers for materials which, with elementary skills and tools, could be assembled into useful and attractive items. Knowing from experience how difficult leathercrafters found it to obtain leather, supplies, and tools, he offered a specialized range of products to meet this need. When Charles Tandy, Dave Tandy's son, returned home from the Navy in 1947 at the age of 29, he joined the family firm and concentrated his efforts on the sale of leather-working materials. While in Hawaii, Charles Tandy had observed the large quantities of leathercraft supplies being used in the hospitals and recreation centers and envisioned a national chain of leathercraft stores to meet the needs of leathercraft users.

In 1947, Charles Tandy opened two small retail stores specializing exclusively in leathercraft supplied in El Paso and San Antonio, Texas, to develop and test sales and operation concepts for the proposed specialty leathercraft store chain. Both these ventures netted over a 100% return on investment in their first year of operation. According to Charles Tandy, three key concepts of store management and control were tested and proven successful in the operation of the first two stores:

1. *Catalog Support of a Specialty Product Line.* To increase a store's sales range and to bring customers back to the store, a leathercraft catalog was prepared and mailed out in response to inquiries derived from small classified advertisements placed in national magazines. These inquiries were found to be primary source of new business for the company. Each store specialized only in leathercraft, and their personnel became experts in this product line.

2. *Employee Participation.* Charles Tandy and his management group believed that developing competent people was as vital to an organization as a good product line, and that without incentives, neither the people nor the company could grow. A profit-sharing plan was imple-

mented which allowed each store manager to receive a share of the pre-tax profits of his store. Also, employees of the company were allowed to buy into each new operation in the initial stages and to share in its growth.

3. *Control.* To meet the needs of the profit-sharing program and for management information and control, the "profit center" (or control center) accounting technique was implemented, where each store was treated as a separate and distinct business operation, with all expenses and material purchases charged to that center at actual cost. This control system, although developed by necessity for the stores, was also implemented for internal control and overhead operations (accounting, advertising, etc.). The manager of each center was treated as an entrepreneur in the real sense: he was held responsible for maximization of profits. To accomplish this, he had to strive to maximize income by providing satisfactory service at a competitive price and to control expenses to a minimum acceptable level. A complete monthly profit and loss statement was prepared and made available to the manager no later than the fourteenth of the following month, showing the success or lack of success of his activities. Included on this statement were total income, itemized expenses by natural categories, and net profit. Consolidated results were prepared for each management level.

Through the use of the control center concept, each divisional unit and each subunit level was held accountable for the profit it earned and the loss it sustained. In this way, the burden of relating revenue and costs was shifted downward from top management to the lowest control unit.

The basic control procedures, merchandising concepts, and management methods developed in the first two Tandy stores were applied to all expansion areas in the ensuing years and the plan was rated by Charles Tandy as the main reason for the success of the corporation.

The initial success of the first two stores encouraged Charles Tandy to open an additional 13 leathercraft stores by 1949, all of which were successful. A central warehouse was added. Additional items extending the product line included the "U-Do-It" line, which consisted of a kit containing complete material for a leather project. Factories were established to produce the products sold. Tandy management then evaluated other product lines which could be adapted to its type of marketing and operating procedures. In 1950, the Tandy organization acquired the American Handicraft Company of East Orange, New Jersey, a company with an excellent line of do-it-yourself handicraft products, two established retail stores in the New York market, and useful knowledge of school and institutional markets.

In the period 1950 to 1955, sales increased to approximately $8 million with after-tax earnings of $523,000. The company had leased stores in 75 cities.

In 1955, because of possible estate problems of David L. Tandy, who had been ill during the preceding year, the Tandy management sold the Tandy Leather Company to the American Hide and Leather Company of Boston, Massachusetts.

AMERICAN HIDE AND LEATHER COMPANY

The American Hide and Leather Company was incorporated in 1899 under the laws of the state of New Jersey. Its principal business was the tanning, finishing, and sale of calf leather and cattle-side upper leather. In 1955, after several years of substantial losses and at a time when the tanning industry in general was in a depressed condition, its directors decided that diversification was essential for the survival of the company. In mid-1955, it acquired all the outstanding stock of Tandy Leather Company of Fort Worth, Texas, and certain associated corporations. The Tandy group received $230,000 cash, fixed notes totaling $2 million, and options to purchase 500,000 shares of American Hide and Leather Company stock at $4 a share distributed over a four-year period.

On June 30, 1956, the company included two operating units: Tandy Industries, Inc., of Fort Worth, Texas, and a large tannery operation in Lowell, Massachusetts. The Lowell tannery was not profitable, and with the excess of productive capacity, the intense competition prevailing in the industry, and unsatisfactory labor relations, company management stated that they could see little likelihood that its operation could be greatly improved. During the latter part of 1956 the company disposed of the inventories and all physical assets pertaining to the tanning operation. The funds received were used to retire debt, to increase working capital, and to acquire new companies.

Three new companies were acquired in fields wholly unrelated to the leather industry. On July 1, 1956, the Musgrove Petroleum Corporation, Inc., of Wichita, Kansas, became a wholly owned subsidiary through the exchange of 196,028 shares of the company's common stock for all the outstanding stock of Musgrove. On September 21, 1956, the company purchased for cash the assets and name of Shain & Company, Inc., of Boston, Massachusetts, a leading converter and distributor of fabrics and meshes for the shoe industry. On October 1, 1956, Dunbar Kapple, Inc., of Geneva, Illinois, became a wholly owned subsidiary through the exchange of 294,342 shares of the company's common stock for all of their outstanding stock. On December 31, 1956, the assets and name of Tex Tan of Yoakum, Texas, was acquired for cash and notes.

In December of 1956, following approval by the stockholders, the name of the company was changed from American Hide and Leather Company to General American Industries, Inc., to more clearly reflect the activities of the company and the expected pattern for its future.

PROBLEMS OF THE 1955–1959 PERIOD

The period from 1955 to 1959 was a troubled one for General American Industries. Musgrove Petroleum experienced a decline in profits as excessive domestic inventories and imports of foreign oil drastically reduced both the demand for domestic oil and its selling price. The low selling price in turn made it uneconomical to continue development and exploration work on sites which were not conveniently located in relation to pipelines and refineries. Thus, both the production and drilling divisions of Musgrove Petroleum Corporation were faced with substantially reduced demand for their products and services. As a result, the original development and exploration program had to be substantially curtailed.

During this same period, an abrupt change in military policy regarding expenditures for aircraft and missiles (which occurred in the fall of 1957), combined with the economic recession, seriously disrupted the Dunbar Kapple production and delivery schedules. Since Dunbar Kapple engineered and tested most of the items which it made for the aircraft industry and for missiles, a process which required several months before production could be started, the sudden change in military policy reduced production schedules below profitable levels. As a result, the Dunbar Kapple sales and earnings were well below the levels anticipated at the beginning of that year.

In Shain & Company, gross profit margins were reduced because of intensive competition and profits were adversely affected by some unusual expenses inherent in the building and promoting of new lines. Only the Tandy and Tex Tan groups were profitable.

It became apparent to the Tandy management that further dilution of the Tandy group interests would take place unless immediate corrective action was taken. This triggered a successful take-over bid of the parent corporation by the Tandy-Tex Tan groups, and in November, 1959, a new board of directors composed of Tandy supporters replaced the previous board (see Exhibit 1). The new board immediately implemented a study of the past history and the future prospects of the various divisions of the company. This study revealed that only two of the five divisions of General American Industries had a record of constant growth. After consideration of these facts, the board of directors authorized the company to sell the remaining three divisions. The two divisions retained were Tandy Industries and Tex Tan of Yoakum, Texas. The divisions sold were Musgrove Petroleum Corporation, Dunbar Kapple, Inc., and Shain & Company. The sale of these three divisions was accomplished during the first six months of 1960. A substantial loss was incurred on the sale of these divisions. The Tandy and Tex Tan Companies' net sales and income over the preceding 10 years had shown substantial growth and profitability.

exhibit 1   **GENERAL AMERICAN INDUSTRIES**
Board of directors

1958–1959 Board of Directors
Charles D. Tandy
   Chairman of the Board and President, Tandy Industries
Stanley M. Rowland
   President and Treasurer of the Company
John B. Collier, Jr.
   President, Fort Worth Poultry & Egg Company
James H. Dunbar, Jr.
   President, Dunbar Kapple, Inc.

Philip A. Russell
   Stone & Webster Securities Corporation
John Slezak
   Chairman, Kable Printing Company
Pierce C. Musgrove
   President, Musgrove Petroleum Corporation, Inc.

1959–1960 Board of Directors
Charles D. Tandy
   Chairman of the Board and President of the Company
Carl C. Welhausen
   Vice President of the Company and General Manager, Tex Tan
John B. Collier, Jr.
   President, Fort Worth Poultry & Egg Company
A. H. Hauser
   Vice President, Chemical Bank New York Trust Company
J. S. Nye
   Partner, Nye & Whitehead

J. L. West
   President, Tandy Leather Company
L. A. Henderson
   Secretary-Treasurer of the Company, Vice President of Tandy Leather Company

Charles Tandy, the new chairman of the board and president of General American Industries, stated that "while the operations, customer service, and sales programs of the two divisions were entirely independent, the Tandy and Tex Tan Companies supplemented each other in production facilities, distribution methods, and coverage of markets, and this favorable combination lent itself to a sound, integrated expansion program."

ACQUISITIONS AND EXPANSIONS, 1959–1967

During the 1960–1961 fiscal year the name of the corporation was changed from General American Industries to Tandy Corporation to reflect, according to Charles Tandy, the new direction of the company and to allow the company to benefit from identification with the many Tandy stores throughout the country.

At the end of 1961, 125 leathercraft stores were operating in 105 cities of the United States and Canada. The acquisition of Clarke and Clarke, a leathercraft supplier in Ontario, Canada, provided the company an entry into the Canadian market. It was apparent to Charles Tandy, however, that cash flow was in excess of the expansion requirements of the corporation and that the company would need to acquire additional operations in order to maximize growth. In late 1962, this search resulted in three acquisitions, each of which was related to and/or supported existing company operations. Sturdy Die and Machine, Inc., of South Gate, California (a manufacturer of leathercraft tools); Corral Sportswear Company, of Ardmore, Oklahoma, a manufacturer of leather sport and casual clothing; and Cleveland Crafts, Inc., a retailer and manufacturer of arts and crafts material and supplies, were all acquired for cash.

Two growth opportunities were developed during the 1962–1963 fiscal year through negotiations with Cost Plus, Inc., of San Francisco and with Radio Shack Corporation of Boston, Massachusetts. According to Charles Tandy, "the agreements reached enabled the Tandy Corporation to measure the earning ability of both companies prior to making an equity investment in them and in their marketing fields." Options held by Tandy Corporation, if exercised, would give it a 38% interest in Cost Plus, Inc., and a 62% interest in Radio Shack Corporation.

COST PLUS IMPORTS

Cost Plus, Inc., was an importer and retailer of home furnishings, decorations, housewares, and gifts. Its overseas buyers made merchandise selections in many of the established and remote producing centers of the world, and sales were made to the public from one retail location in San Francisco. This importer-direct-to-consumer marketing plan offered the attraction of extremely low selling prices for tastefully chosen merchandise of a unique and handcrafted character which could not be readily duplicated. Annual sales volume at the San Francisco Fisherman's Wharf location had grown from $650,000 in 1958 to more than $3 million in 1963.

In September of 1962, Tandy, through a financial and distribution agreement, obtained an option to acquire an equity in Cost Plus, Inc., and the rights to establish additional Cost Plus stores in other cities. Stores were opened in early 1963 in San Mateo and Richmond, California, and in Fort Worth, Dallas, and San Antonio, Texas. With the opening of stores in Houston, Texas, and San Leandro and San Jose, California, a total of eight Cost Plus stores were in operation in late 1963.

RADIO SHACK CORPORATION

As early as 1961, Charles Tandy felt that the consumer electronics business might lend itself to the marketing techniques, control methods, and merchandising skills that had been developed in the other specialty businesses operated by Tandy. Late in 1961 Tandy Corporation acquired the consumer inventory of the Sweico Corporation, a small electronic supplier located in Fort Worth, to use as a pilot operation to learn the business. It became obvious to management, however, that to move forward in this area, a greater variety of merchandise and manpower talent was needed. This was made available in April of 1963, when Tandy Corporation acquired an option to purchase a majority interest at book value in Radio Shack Corporation, of Boston, Massachusetts.

Radio Shack Corporation was a distributor of consumer and industrial electronic components, equipment, and parts with sales in 12 New England stores, a mail-order division, and an industrial division, with sales of approximately $15 million in fiscal 1963. In April of

1963, Tandy Corporation concluded an agreement which granted it immediate management control and options to acquire a majority interest in the company. Radio Shack in the years immediately preceding 1963 experienced rapid growth but recorded substantial operating losses, and immediate corrective action was needed to save the company from imminent bankruptcy.

Because of the potential importance of this acquisition to the future growth of Tandy Corporation, Charles Tandy personally assumed responsibility for its operations. At the same time he remained the chief executive officer of Tandy Corporation. Charles Tandy confided at that time that he considered this new job one of the biggest and most difficult challenges of his career up to that date. He had to recast every aspect of the company: the distribution system, the advertising, and the merchandising program. In addition, he had to solve the problem of a very large consumer accounts receivable. His objective was to develop a prototype store and merchandising program that could be expanded across the nation. In two years the Radio Shack division began to show profits. By 1967, sales had climed to $29,702,000 and profits to $860,000 with 156 stores in operation nation-wide (see Exhibit 2).

exhibit 2   STORES IN OPERATION BY DIVISION

	1967	1966	1965	1964	1963	1962	1961	1960
Tandy Leather Company	120	117	114	115	124	108	102	97
American Handicraft Company	42	35	27	26	24	23	18	18
Western Saddlery	—	—	—	—	6	5	5	5
Meribee Needle Arts	1	1	1	8	3	—	—	—
Cost Plus Imports	—	—	15	9	4	—	—	—
Tandy Electronic Stores	—	—	—	—	5	1	—	—
Radio Shack Stores	156	87	59	36	12	—	—	—
Wolfe Nursery	1	—	—	—	—	—	—	—
Total	320	240	216	189	183	140	125	118

During fiscal 1965, 96,000 shares of Tandy Corporation common stock were issued to State Mutual Life Assurance Company in exchange for the outstanding preferred stock of Radio Shack Corporation. Conversion of the preferred stock in June of 1965, together with the exercise of a stock purchase option during that month, brought Tandy Corporation's holdings of Radio Shack Corporation common stock to 85% of the outstanding shares. A series of financial moves and reorganizations increased their percentage ownership, and in June, 1967, Tandy Corporation acquired the remaining outstanding stock of Radio Shack Corporation (3.8%) for 32,172 shares of the common stock of Tandy Corporation, thus becoming the owners of 100% of the outstanding shares. This company was then merged into Tandy Corporation and the corporate structure was dissolved.

During fiscal 1967, Tandy Corporation acquired Wolfe Nursery, Inc., which put the Tandy Corporation in the garden supply and household plantings business. The corporation hoped to expand this operation into a store chain.

Early in 1967, in a speech given before a group of security analysts, Charles Tandy stated that his personal goal for Tandy Corporation was to increase its sales threefold every five years, as he had done in the past years. When asked if this would still be possible with the company sales now in the multi-million-dollar range, Charles Tandy replied that this same question was raised many times over the past years when sales were at lower levels and he could not then or now see where size could affect the ability to achieve his objective. (See Exhibits 5 to 8.)

TANDY CORPORATION OPERATING DIVISIONS 1967

The annual report of 1967 described the divisions as follows:

Tandy Corporation is presently composed of eight divisions whose operations include manufacturing and distribution, integrated retailing, and direct-mail sales of products keyed to educational and recreational markets.

Each operating division serves the needs of a distinctive and fast-growing area of modern educational and recreational activity, and each is benefiting from increased leisure time, higher income and broadening public interest in the production and creative use of non-working hours.

The growth experienced by Tandy Corporation in its operation during the uncertain economic climate of 1966 is evidence of the continued dramatic expansion in the educational and recreational requirements of our modern society.

Tandy Corporation's eight operating divisions currently are:

Tandy Leather Company. The Tandy Leather Company subsidiary markets materials, equipment, and kits used in producing artistic and functional items of genuine leather through its 120 company-owned retail and mail-order stores in the United States and Canada. Primary lines of merchandise are footwear kits, handbag and wallet projects, parts and materials for the assembly and finishing of personal accesories, specialized tools, leathers, and hardware. More than half of the product mix is manufactured or assembled in its own integrated factories in Fort Worth, thus assuring a controlled supply of proprietary merchandise designed especially for the needs of schools, hospitals, recreational organizations, and other institutional establishments. Sales to semiprofessional and hobbyist leather craftsmen make up a significant and growing portion of the business of the division.

Wolfe Nursery, Inc. The acquisition of Wolfe Nursery, Inc., of Stephenville, Texas, in the fall of 1966 introduced Tandy Corporation into still another major recreational and leisure-time market. The care and maintenance of garden and household plantings and grounds is a popular activity for men and women of all ages, particularly in suburban residential areas. The increasing number of garden clubs, flower shows, and neighborhood beautification programs is ample evidence of this trend. Wolfe Nursery, with its 40 years of experience in supplying live nursery plants, fruit trees, insecticides, fertilizers, garden equipment, and related items at wholesale and by mail order, is now increasing its retail garden centers, with eight in operation in Texas at the year-end. Nursery-farming operations in Stephenville and production contracts with other growers assure an adequate supply system for the anticipated retail expansion.

Tex Tan Welhausen Company. The Tex Tan Welhausen division manufactures distinctive leather accessories and markets them through a growing dealer organization now consisting of more than 12,000 retail outlets in the United States and seven foreign countries. At its plant in Yoakum, Texas, Tex Tan Welhausen produces wallets, travel kits, and belts of the highest quality through a combination of imaginative design, use of the finest leathers, and the maintenance of a traditional pride of workmanship dating back many years. The division's products are sold in leading department stores, men's stores, and gift shops and are featured in popular men's magazines. A co-operative advertising program with dealers makes extensive seasonal use of metropolitan newspaper and television media.

Tex Tan Western Leather Company. The Tex Tan Western Leather Company division is considered to be the largest manufacturer of saddlery and riding equipment in the United States marketing under its own brand names. The division distributes its products through more than 8,000 ranch supply, outdoor stores, and "Western" outfitters throughout the country. From its origin as a supplier to ranchers and stockmen, Tex Tan Western Leather Company has expanded its markets to include riding clubs, boarding stables, and camping and other modern outdoor recreational activities. The product line has been expanded further with the addition of personal accessories of Western design manufactured with the same care and skill developed over many years of saddlery production in the company plant in Yoakum.

Radio Shack Division. The Radio Shack division now operates 156 company-owned consumer electronic supply stores in the United States. This was an increase of 69 retail outlets during the past 12 months. The Radio Shack product line includes parts and circuitry components used extensively in educational and experimental work; audio system components for entertainment; communications equipment for commercial and recreational use; and associated supplies and equipment. Sales emphasis is placed upon the division's private brands and trademark items which are engineered by Radio Shack and produced under contract by manufacturing firms both domestically and abroad. The technological instruction given by schools, industry, and the military services has created an interest in and an understanding of electronics and its practical everyday applications among a rapidly increasing portion of the population. Considerably more than one million individual names appear on the Radio Shack customer list, in addition to thousands of commercial and institutional accounts.

Corral Sportswear Company. The Corral Sportswear Company subsidiary manufactures and distributes fine leather sportswear designed to serve the markets for both traditional and contemporary fashions in leather garments. Suedes, "roughout," and other specialty leathers are worked into attractively styled jackets for men, women, and children and are sold through the more than 4,000 outlets which now carry the "Jo-O-Kay" brand. During the year a second production facility was added to the company plant in Ardmore, Oklahoma, and a line of women's leather handbags and accessories was introduced, resulting in a sharp increase in the number and type of sales outlets which the company may now serve. Continuous emphasis on the use of genuine fine leathers has assured the Corral Sportswear Company a distinctive place in the very competitive outerwear industry.

American Handicrafts Company. The American Handicrafts Company subsidiary serves educational and recreational institutions and hundreds of thousands of individuals who perform creative crafts work for pleasure or profit through its 42 retail and mail-order stores operated nationally. The division markets materials and equipment, in bulk as well as in kit form, for use in over 30 fields of handcraft and art work other than leathercraft. Craft supplies are assembled in the Fort Worth facility from sources all over the world and are processed or packaged for distribution through the store system and by mail order. Basketry materials from Malaysia, mosaic tile from the Orient and Southern Europe, art metals from Scandinavia, and artist supplies from the United States and Europe are typical of the merchandise lines in which this division specializes.

Merribee Company. The Merribee Company division sells needlecraft materials, kits, and supplies to individual and institutional customers nationally, distributing solely by mail order from its warehouse and assembly rooms in Fort Worth. Domestic and imported yarns for knitting, Irish linen for embroidery work, garment kits, instructions, patterns, and sewing and weaving equipment make up the essential merchandise lines. Needlework, in its various forms, is one of the oldest of handicraft activities and continues to rank among the highest in popular interest, year after year. The Merribee consumer catalog and other direct-mail sales literature reach and serve thousands of customers, mostly women, who live in suburban and rural areas where a full selection of needlework materials is not readily available. The Merribee division fills the needs of one of the many specialized fields of recreational and educational interest.

LEONARD'S DEPARTMENT STORE

In July of 1967, at the request of Charles Tandy, financial information was furnished by Leonard Brothers for evaluation as a possible acquisition. In subsequent conversations with the Leonard family, they indicated that they would be flexible in working out a formula which the Tandy Corporation could accept for the purchase of Leonard operations. It was stated that the Leonard family might consider reducing the capital investment required if they were able to retain ownership of the buildings used by the department store. Leonards would then rent the properties to the purchaser of the business. To further reduce capital requirements and provide a more adequate return on investment to the Tandy Corporation, Charles Tandy also discussed the possibility of the selling of the accounts receivable of Leonards to a financial institution.

In 1967 Leonard's Department Store was the largest retailer in the Greater Fort Worth trading area. Leonards was founded in 1918 by J. Marvin Leonard in a small, rustic one-room store 20 feet wide with about 1,500 square feet of space. Counters were boards on barrels; display cases were wash tubs. Two years later, Marvin's brother, Obadiah P. Leonard, joined him in the venture. Both men were in their early twenties. The first store was outgrown within two years and the Leonards added the 15 feet next door, then the next 25 feet, then a two-story building. The products sold included groceries, meats, fruits, vegetables, auto accessories, hardware, notions, and seeds at wholesale and retail. In 1967 Leonard's Department Store operated over 500,000 square feet of sales area covering a six-block area in downtown Fort Worth. With over 2,000 employees, it was one of the 10 largest employers in Fort Worth. (See Exhibits 9 to 12 for financial data.) Leonards retained its sales volume despite a general trend toward decreasing sales volume in most inner cities. This was due primarily to a convenient 29-acre 5,000-car parking lot located on the outskirts of the central business district which provided essential free parking for Leonard customers. The parking area was connected to the retail store by a private subway system, the only subway owned and operated by a private corporation in the world. This subway operated early in the morning to provide persons working in downtown Fort Worth with free parking. As the only downtown terminal for the subway system was the Leonard Department Store, there was subtle encouragement for the subway patrons to shop at Leonard's. Over 7 million riders used this subway each year (see Exhibit 3).

Leonard's 108 separate merchandising departments offered products ranging from huge farm tractors to exquisite mink coats. In addition to traditional department store product lines, Leonard's operated a food supermarket, a complete farm and ranch store, a service station, and an auto service center. The Leonard's customer base was made up primarily of middle-class, lower middle-class, and low-class population groups for apparel merchandise; however, all income classes were considered as potential purchasers of their hard goods lines. Leonard's had the reputation for being an in-depth merchandiser, offering the

exhibit 3
Layout of Leonards in 1967

Leonards

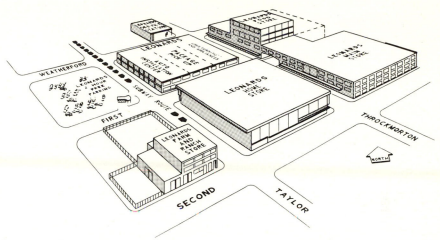

widest selection of merchandise of all retailers in the trading area. In recent years, Leonard's had moved to upgrade its over-all image in order to increase its sales to the upper middle-class population.

Leonard's organizational structure was typical of most department stores. The company's operations were divided into two divisions; the merchandise division, responsible for sales and inventories, and the operating division, responsible for all other functions, including the physical store plant, customer service, credit, maintenance, subway, parking lots, etc. The accounting control system was also typical of department stores. Department managers were responsible for and received feedback information on sales, returns, gross margins, salary expense, miscellaneous selling expense, and the net contribution to corporate overhead and administrative expenses (defined as Net Sales less Total Expenses). Primary emphasis was placed on net sales and gross sales margins.

Paul Leonard, the president of Leonard's, at 42 years of age was recognized by the industry as one of the top retailers in the United States. Mr. Leonard expressed an interest in remaining with Leonard's as president if the Tandy Corporation decided to acquire the company. The other members of the Leonard management team were also considered competent retailers and experts in their respective fields.

To maximize sales opportunity and protect existing sales levels in the Fort Worth trading area, Leonard's management felt that expansion into the suburbs was essential. With this objective, an option to purchase land in northeast Fort Worth was pending and another potential location in Arlington, Texas, was under negotiation. Arlington was a community to the southeast of Fort Worth but within the Fort Worth trading area (located approximately halfway between Fort Worth and Dallas). It was contemplated that these new operations would be full-line stores and would be designed to appeal to the middle high-income groups as well as to the traditional customers of Leonard's, thus upgrading the over-all image of the company in the trading area. It was expected that both stores together would have approximately 250,000 square feet of floor space.

FORT WORTH, TEXAS, TRADING AREA

Leonard's Department Store sales were closely linked to the economy of the Fort Worth, Texas, retail trading area. In 1967, Fort Worth, with a population of approximately 745,000 in the two-county metropolitan area, was the mercantile, commercial, and industrial headquarters for much of West Texas.

Fort Worth prided itself on being the city "where the West begins." It was established as a frontier army post in 1849 by Major Ripley Arnold and named for General Jenkins Worth, who distinguished himself in the Mexican War. The outpost became a stopping place on the storied Old Chisholm Trail and a shipping point for the great herds of Longhorn cattle being sent to Northern markets. Progressive city leadership brought the first of nine railroads to Fort Worth in 1876 and, with the subsequent West Texas oil boom, made the city an important metropolitan entity. (See Exhibit 4.)

Historically, Fort Worth's economy had been based on agriculture-oriented industries with major livestock marketing facilities, grain, manufacturing firms, and services. In 1967 the Fort Worth employment base was well diversified with strong representation in the aircraft industry. General Dynamics, Fort Worth Division, manufactured the F-111 jet for the Defense Department and the Bell Helicopter Company built helicopters for both military and civilian use. A total of 25 major manufacturing firms were located in the area, including producers of food and beverages, mobile homes, automobiles, and medical supplies. Fort Worth was also a center for higher education: the seven

exhibit 4 FORT WORTH METROPOLITAN AREA

City of Fort Worth, Incorporated Area . . . .   212 square miles
Tarrant County . . . .   860 square miles
Standard Metropolitan Statistical Area . . . .   1600 square miles

(The U. S. Bureau of the Budget has defined the Fort Worth Standard Metropolitan Statistical Area to include Tarrant and Johnson Counties—an area covering 1,600 square miles. Cleburne is the county seat of Johnson County.)

Population

Year	Fort Worth	Tarrant County	SMSA
1967	375,000*	700,000*	745,000*
1960	356,268	538,495	573,215
1950	277,047	361,253	392,643
1940	177,662	255,521	255,905

* Estimated.

Employment

	1957	1967	% Increase
Total Civilian Labor Force	222,140	316,200	42.3
Employment Total	212,840	307,500	44.5
Agricultural	3,900	3,150	−19.2
Nonagricultural	208,940	304,350	45.6
Manufacturing	55,215	93,350	69.1
Mining	3,535	2,020	−42.9
Construction	13,250	15,270	15.3
Transp., Comm., & Utilities	16,620	16,190	− 2.6
Trades	52,630	73,600	39.8
Finance, Ins., & R.E.	9,290	13,350	43.7
Services & Misc.	34,940	55,200	57.9
Government	23,260	34,980	50.4

local college and university campuses had an enrollment in excess of 33,000 students. The Fort Worth area was also the location of 16 state government offices, 14 federal government offices, and 8 military installations.

CONSIDERATION OF THE ACQUISITION

The Tandy Corporation management gave serious consideration to the proposed acquisition of Leonard's Department Store. In an effort to reach a conclusion, several lengthy discussions were carried on with the top management group of Leonard's. Both parties hoped to reach a conclusion about the acquisition as soon as possible. Mr. James L. West, president of Tandy Corporation, pointed out several factors concerning the proposed acquisition that needed to be considered, especially the matters of price, adaptability, and organizational relationship.

exhibit 5 **TANDY CORPORATION**
Seven-year statistical summary, year ended June 30

	1967	1966*	1965†	1964	1963	1962	1961
Net Sales	$60,703,805	$49,875,701	$42,784,605	$23,853,039	$20,310,127	$17,693,507	$15,961,250
Earnings before Federal Income Tax	3,542,277	3,225,029	2,261,962	1,498,818	1,117,522	1,226,259	964,603
Federal Income Tax	930,779	929,887	760,540	555,631	409,089	245,794	245,051
Net Earnings	2,611,498	2,295,142	1,501,422	943,187	708,433	980,465	719,552
Net Earnings as Per Cent of Sales	4.3%	4.6%	3.5%	4%	3.5%	5.5%	4.5%
Net Earnings as Per Cent of Stock-holders' Equity at beginning of year	28%	33%	36%	30%	12%	20%	16%
Current Assets	22,039,768	18,635,429	17,505,413	9,130,686	8,409,197	7,343,739	6,883,451
Current Liabilities	4,938,411	4,869,522	4,838,228	2,036,025	2,330,573	1,212,656	1,656,126
Current Ratio	4.5 to 1	3.8 to 1	3.7 to 1	4.5 to 1	3.6 to 1	6.1 to 1	4.2 to 1
Net Working Capital	17,101,357	13,765,907	12,667,185	7,094,661	6,078,624	6,131,083	5,227,325
Long-term Liabilities	10,906,691	8,429,027	8,590,011	5,188,125	5,450,484†	2,133,280	2,372,473
Net Property and Equipment	3,617,741	2,130,992	1,670,695	674,118	753,259	698,917	588,307
Earnings per Common Share	2.06	1.80	1.21	.89	.67	.63	.46
Common Shares Outstanding	1,267,858	1,272,462	1,243,376	1,060,938	1,060,938‡	1,561,061	1,527,398
Stockholders' Equity	11,982,359	9,359,778	7,058,428	4,112,958	3,169,771‡	5,962,199	4,744,838
Net Worth per Common Share	9.45	7.36	5.68	3.88	2.99	3.82	3.11
Retained Earnings	9,858,938	7,247,440	5,091,395	3,633,115	2,689,928	1,981,495	990,153
Stockholders and Nominees	2,231	2,472	2,465	2,297	2,479	3,004	2,666

* Restated to reflect pooling of interests resulting from merger of Radio Shack Corporation.
† Includes Radio Shack Corporation subsidiary which was consolidated effective July 1, 1964.
‡ Reflects issuance of $3,500,000 of debentures in exchange for 500,123 shares of outstanding common stock in 1963.

exhibit **6**   **TANDY CORPORATION AND SUBSIDIARIES**
Consolidated statement of income and retained earnings

	Year ended June 30,	
	1967	*1966*
		(Restated, see Note 1)
Net sales............................	$60,703,805	$49,875,701
Other income.......................	370,532	407,249
	61,074,337	50,282,950
Costs and expenses:		
Cost of products sold................	33,835,258	28,262,875
Selling and administrative............	22,772,766	18,070,717
Depreciation.......................	339,160	263,927
Interest on debentures...............	226,756	227,253
Other interest charges, less interest income.........................	357,018	158,067
	57,530,958	46,982,839
Income before federal income tax and minority interest..........	3,543,379	3,300,111
Provision for federal income tax (Note 4)..	930,779	929,887
Net income before minority interest......	2,612,600	2,370,224
Minority interest in net income.........	1,102	75,082
Net income....................	2,611,498	2,295,142
Retained earnings—beginning of year (Note 1).........................	7,247,440	4,952,298
Retained earnings—end of year.........	$ 9,858,938	$ 7,247,440
Net income per share of common stock:		
Average outstanding shares........	$2.06	$1.80
Pro forma, assuming conversion of warrants (Note 7).............	$1.78	$1.55

exhibit 7   TANDY CORPORATION AND SUBSIDIARIES
Consolidated balance sheet

Assets

June 30,

	1967	1966
Current assets:		
Cash...............................	$ 3,221,220	$ 1,171,461
Accounts and notes receivable:		
Trade, less allowance for doubtful		
accounts........................	4,202,751	5,084,148
Other...........................	236,924	81,659
Inventories, at lower of approximate cost		
(substantially on a first-in, first-out		
basis) or market:		
Finished merchandise.............	12,678,552	10,388,261
Raw materials and work in process.	1,322,943	1,531,707
Other current assets................	377,378	378,193
Total current assets...........	22,039,768	18,635,429
Property and equipment, at cost less		
accumulated depreciation (Note 2)....	3,617,741	2,130,992
Other assets, including deferred charges..	707,901	769,992
Unamortized excess cost of investment		
(Note 3)........................	1,462,051	1,391,780
	$27 827,461	$22,928,193

exhibit **7** (continued)

Liabilities and Stockholders' Equity

June 30,

	1967	1966
		(Restated, see Note 1)
Current liabilities:		
Notes payable to banks (Note 5)......	$ 332,202	$ 466,145
Purchase obligations due within one year	121,281	150,660
Accounts payable.................	1,562,732	1,407,616
Accrued expenses..................	2,086,487	1,708,084
Federal income tax (Note 4).........	835,709	1,137,017
Total current liabilities........	4,938,411	4,869,522
Other liabilities:		
Notes payable to banks (Note 5)......	6,553,267	4,149,155
Purchase obligations due after one year (Note 5)........................	760,508	444,650
6½% Subordinated debentures, due 1978 (Note 6)....................	3,482,900	3,494,500
Other noncurrent liabilities..........	110,016	340,723
	10,906,691	8,429,028
Equity of minority stockholders in Radio Shack Corporation (Note 1)..........		269,865
Stockholders' equity (Notes 1, 7, 8 and 9):		
Common stock, $1 par value:		
2,000,000 shares authorized		
1,696,574 shares issued.............	1,696,574	1,696,574
Capital surplus....................	3,651,473	3,306,293
Retained earnings.................	9,858,938	7,247,440
	15,206,985	12,250,307
Less—Common stock in treasury at cost—428,716 shares (1967) and 424,112 shares (1966).........	3,224,626	2,890,529
	11,982,359	9,359,778
Commitments (Note 10)		
	$27,827,461	$22,928,193

exhibit 8   TANDY CORPORATION AND SUBSIDIARIES
Notes to financial statements June 30, 1967

Note 1—Principles of consolidation and merger of Radio Shack Corporation

The accompanying consolidated financial statements include the accounts of the parent company, Tandy Corporation, and its subsidiaries.

As of June 30, 1966, Tandy Corporation owned 269,357 shares (85.47%) of the outstanding common stock of Radio Shack Corporation. In fiscal 1967, Radio Shack issued to all its stockholders rights to purchase at $8 per share three new shares of common stock for each share previously owned. Tandy exercised its rights and purchased 808,071 Radio Shack shares. As authorized by Radio Shack stockholders, Tandy also purchased at $8 per share 133,755 additional shares under rights granted to, but not exercised by, other stockholders. Furthermore, during the year Tandy purchased 1,090 Radio Shack shares directly from a stockholder. The foregoing transactions brought Tandy's ownership interest in Radio Shack to 96.2%, comprising 1,212,273 common shares.

Effective June 30, 1967, Tandy acquired the remaining minority interest (3.8%) in Radio Shack through a statutory merger of the latter company into Tandy, in connection with which Radio Shack minority stockholders received two Tandy shares for each three Radio Shack shares previously owned. This transaction was treated as a pooling of interests for financial accounting purposes and the accompanying financial statements give effect to the pooling on a retroactive basis.

As a result of giving retroactive effect to the pooling transaction, the consolidated financial statements for the year ended June 30, 1966 have been restated as follows:

	Amount of Restatement (Debit) Credit
Minority interest in Radio Shack	($ 96,596)
Treasury stock (32,172 shares issued)	241,933
Capital surplus	(33,116)
Retained earnings:	
Balance at July 1, 1965	(139,097)
1966 net income	26,875

Note 2—Property and equipment

	June 30, 1967	1966
Buildings	$ 539,262	$ 522,570
Machinery, equipment, furniture and fixtures	4,785,820	3,434,520
	5,325,082	3,957,090
Less accumulated depreciation	2,062,643	1,853,900
	3,262,439	2,103,190
Land	355,302	27,802
	$3,617,741	$2,130,992

Certain of the purchase obligations referred to in Note 5 with unpaid balances aggregating $570,589 are secured by the mortgage of property and equipment carried in the consolidated balance sheet at a net amount of approximately $762,556.

Note 3—Unamortized excess cost of investment

exhibit 8   (continued)

During the fiscal year ended June 30, 1960, $1,000,000 was paid in final settlement of the purchase price of certain subsidiaries acquired in 1955. This final settlement was capitalized as goodwill, the excess cost of the subsidiaries arising from prior purchase payments having been amortized during the period from acquisition through June 30, 1960.

Tandy Corporation's aggregate cost of investment in Radio Shack Corporation exceeded its aggregate equity in book value of net assets at dates of acquisition by $376,896. As stated in Note 1, Radio Shack was merged into Tandy Corporation as of June 30, 1967.

In connection with the tax settlement described in Note 4, an amount of $85,155 was transferred during 1967 from property and equipment accounts to excess cost. Such amount arose in connection with several acquisitions of businesses during the early 1960's.

The Board of Directors has adopted the policy of reviewing these excess costs annually and the full amount will continue to be carried as an asset unless the Board determines that there has been a decline or a limitation in the value, at which time an appropriate amortization policy will be adopted.

Note 4—Federal income tax

Federal income tax has been provided on the basis of separate returns to be filed for each corporation.

In fiscal 1967 and 1966, Radio Shack Corporation's net income was not subject to federal income tax due to the application of loss carry-overs. Had such loss carry-overs not been available, consolidated net income would have been reduced by approximately $400,000 in 1967 and $300,000 in 1966. As stated in Note 1, Radio Shack was merged into Tandy Corporation as of June 30, 1967. At that date Radio Shack had loss carry-overs for federal income tax purposes aggregating approximately $4,000,000, which in the opinion of the company's legal counsel may be applied against the taxable income of the parent company over the next two years.

A settlement of certain prior years' income tax disputes was effected and the resulting adjustments were recorded during 1967. The effect of these adjustments upon the accompanying consolidated financial statements was immaterial.

exhibit 8   (continued)

Note 5—Purchase obligations and bank loans

Purchase obligations:

	Portion Due Within One Year	Portion Due After One Year
Note payable to profit-sharing trusts of Tex Tan Division, 5½%, payable in eight instalments, secured (Note 2)	$ 24,200	$ 169,400
Notes payable in connection with purchase of building, 6%, payable in monthly instalments until January, 1985, secured (Note 2)	2,381	66,608
Note payable in connection with acquisition of assets in 1965, 6%, payable in three instalments	35,200	76,000
Note payable in connection with purchase of assets in 1967, 6¼%, first principal payment in 1973, secured (Note 2)		232,000
Note payable in connection with purchase of building by Radio Shack, 5%, payable in eight instalments, secured (Note 2)	9,500	66,500
Note payable in connection with acquisition of a company in 1967, payable in four instalments	50,000	150,000
Total purchase obligations	$121,281	$ 760,508

Notes payable to banks:

5% note	$300,000	$3,850,000
5½% note due December 26, 1968 (Paid in August, 1967 from proceeds of new financing described in second succeeding paragraph) ..		2,700,000
Others	32,202	3,267
Total notes payable to banks	$332,202	$6,553,267

The 5% bank loan ($4,150,000) is payable in four annual instalments of $300,000 and a final instalment of $2,950,000 in 1972.

In August, 1967, Tandy arranged for $6,000,000 in additional long-term financing of which $3,000,000 was received in August with the remaining $3,000,000 to be received in January, 1968. The loan is payable over 14 years with the first payment due in January, 1971 and bears interest at the rate of 6%.

Note 6—6½% Subordinated debentures

The debentures are subordinate to all "senior indebtedness" (as defined in the indenture), including purchase and borrowed money obligations, and may be redeemed by the company in whole or in part at any time at principal amount and accrued interest or surrendered by the holders at any time until December 31, 1969 in payment for common stock purchased upon exercise of warrants described in Note 7.

Note 7—Common stock

Warrants for the purchase of 219,677 shares of common stock were outstanding at June 30, 1967. These warrants were issued in connection with the 6½% subordinated

exhibit 8   (continued)

debentures and entitle the holder to purchase common stock at $7.50 per share until December 31, 1967 or $9.00 per share from January 1, 1968 through December 31, 1969. Warrants were exercised for the purchase of 19,996 shares of stock during the year. The pro forma per share data in the statement of income is based on the assumption that all such warrants were exercised as of July 1, 1965 and the related proceeds applied against outstanding debt.

Changes in treasury stock during the year ended June 30, 1967 consisted of the following:

	Number of Shares	Cost or Average Cost
Purchased on the open market......................	39,600	$586,035
Issued upon acquisition of net assets of Wolfe Nursery Co.	(15,000)	(102,150)
Issued upon exercise of stock purchase warrants........	(19,996)	(149,788)
Net increase during fiscal 1967....................	4,604	$334,097

Note 8—Capital surplus

The increase of $345,180 in capital surplus during the year ended June 30, 1967 is comprised of:

Excess of proceeds from exercise of warrants for purchase of 19,996 shares of capital stock over average cost of treasury shares issued..............	$ 182
Excess of market value over average cost of treasury shares issued in connection with the Wolfe Nursery acquisition............................	78,553
1967 increase in capital surplus resulting from pooling of Radio Shack....	266,445
	$345,180

Note 9—Dividend and other restrictions

The indenture covering the company's debenture issue and the 5% bank loan agreement impose, under certain conditions, requirements or restrictions relating to minimum working capital, net worth, payment of dividends (other than dividends payable in capital stock of the company), and purchase, redemption, or other retirement by the company of any shares of its capital stock. Under the most restrictive provisions such payments are limited to approximately $2,200,000 as of June 30, 1967.

Note 10—Commitments

The company leases property, which includes stores, administrative offices, and warehouses, under leases expiring between 1968 and 1983. Approximate minimum annual rentals under such leases are summarized below:

Fiscal Year	Amount
1968..............	$1,950,000
1969..............	1,750,000
1970..............	1,500,000
1971..............	1,200,000
1972–75...........	1,050,000
1976–79...........	900,000
1980–83...........	50,000

exhibit 9 LEONARD'S INC.
Consolidated statement of income

	Nine Months Ended		Years Ended				
	October 28, 1967	October 30, 1966 (Unaudited)	January 29, 1967	January 30, 1966	January 31, 1965 (Unaudited)	December 29, 1963 (Unaudited)	December 29, 1962 (Unaudited)
Revenues:							
Net sales (exclusive of sales of leased departments)	$26,082,770	$24,178,549	$34,353,272	$31,433,938	$31,086,829	$30,129,633	$32,272,503
Carrying and service charges	974,832	724,692	1,080,193	885,712	785,775	737,352	664,543
Commissions—leased departments	201,872	171,934	243,425	239,012	187,198	145,765	118,344
Interest income (principally from stockholders and affiliates)	26,425	6,127	8,169	55,353	153,238	108,710	39,133
Other income	35,959	39,283	47,419	110,593	67,970	13,590	40,160
	27,321,858	25,120,585	35,732,478	32,724,608	32,281,010	31,135,050	33,134,683
Costs and expenses:							
Cost of goods sold (Notes 2&8)	17,535,547	16,590,622	23,337,039	21,494,892	21,336,052	20,916,476	23,063,031
Selling, general, and administrative expenses (b)	7,565,218	7,118,574	9,658,406	9,077,338	9,068,228	8,574,558	8,737,380
Depreciation	251,757	264,465	340,614	354,658	392,585	375,933	223,596
Provision for doubtful accounts	218,964	133,849	382,325	424,241	—	372,965	500,471
Interest:							
Long-term debt	50,471	57,040	76,053	69,904	—	308	5,363
Other	200,094	146,520	205,174	92,799	221,155	348,456	184,663
Minority interest in net income (loss) subsidiary	20,207	7,849	14,699	9,922	13,787	8,272	(691)
Provisions for income taxes (c)(d):							
Current	2,163,442	133,853	275,411	(390,196)	589,050	221,985	179,445
Deferred	(1,485,884)	273,757	535,981	949,903			
	677,558	407,610	811,392	559,707	589,050	221,985	179,445
	26,519,816	24,726,529	34,825,702	32,083,461	31,620,857	30,818,953	32,893,258
Income before extraordinary items	802,042	394,056	906,776	641,147	660,153	316,097	241,425
Extraordinary items:							
Moving and temporary relocation expense, less applicable income tax reduction of $64,779							(59,796)

Loss on sale of accounts receivable in connection with discontinuance of department store operations of Everybodys, less applicable income tax reduction of $72,296							(66,735)
Gain on sale of real estate, less applicable income tax of $36,585						109,756	
Discount on sale of accounts receivable, less applicable income tax reduction of $100,806					(100,807)		
Loss on sale of marketable securities, with no income tax effect			(478,882)				
Provision for loss on sale of accounts receivable, less applicable income tax reduction of $112,362 (c)		(121,725)					
Gain on sale of assets and business, less applicable income tax of $162,861 (a)	171,411						
Net income	$ 851,728	$ 394,056	$ 906,776	$ 162,265	$ 559,346	$ 425,853	$ 114,894

NOTES TO CONSOLIDATED STATEMENT OF INCOME

(a) During the year ended January 30, 1966, Leonard's issued 352,946 shares of its common stock in exchange for all the outstanding shares of Everybodys. This transaction has been accounted for as a "pooling of interests," and accordingly the operations of Everybodys have been included in the above statement for the entire period to September 22, 1967, when Everybodys was merged into the Company. In the year ended December 29, 1962, Everybodys had sales of approximately $2,300,000 prior to discontinuing department store operations; subsequent revenues, principally from investments, have not been material.

At February 2, 1964 Leonard's changed its fiscal year from the 52–53 weeks ending nearest December 31 to the corresponding period ending nearest January 31. As a result, operations, including sales and net income of $2,174,887 and $5,514, respectively, for the period December 30, 1963 to February 2, 1964, have been omitted from the above statement.

The consolidated statement of income for the year ended January 30, 1966 has been restated, principally to include the loss on sale of marketable securities, as recommended by opinion No. 9 of the Accounting Principles Board.

(b) See Note 6 to financial statements for lease obligations.

(c) Beginning with the year ended January 30, 1966, Leonard's has reported income from certain sales on the installment method for federal income tax purposes and has provided deferred income taxes on the difference between income reported for financial statement purposes and that reported for income tax purposes. As a result of a change in policy relating to option and contract accounts receivable (see Note 3 to financial statements), the deferred federal income tax became payable currently.

(d) Leonard's deducts investment tax credits from the current federal income tax provision in the years in which it is applied to reduce taxes otherwise payable. The amount of such credits applied was: 1962—$28,042; 1963—$31,067; 1965—$11,933; 1966—$1,612; 1967—$18,483 and the nine months ended October 28, 1966 and October 28, 1967—$17,083 and none, respectively.

exhibit 10   **LEONARD'S INC.**
Balance sheet, October 28, 1967

Assets

Current assets:

Cash...		$ 1,078,247
U. S. Treasury bills, at cost which approximates market value.....................................		494,388
Inventory (Note 2).............................		7,042,244
Accounts receivable, less allowance for losses of $870,034		9,251,885
Due from stockholders, affiliates, and others..........		3,137,924
Prepaid expenses and other assets....................		151,932
Total current assets.........................		21,156,620
Property and equipment, at cost (Note 3):		
Buildings and improvements......................	$ 3,731,192	
Furniture, fixtures, and equipment.................	36,358	
	3,767,550	
Less accumulated depreciation and amortization......	1,595,072	
	2,172,478	
Land..	589,559	
Net property and equipment..................		2,762,037
		$23,918,657

Liabilities and Stockholders' Equity

Current liabilities:

Accounts payable..............................		$ 1,299,332
Accrued expenses..............................		576,074
Federal income tax (Note 4).....................		2,126,957
Long-term debt due within one year...............		121,484
Total current liabilities......................		4,123,847
Long-term debt due after one year (Note 5)...........		8,150,886
Commitments (Note 6)		
Stockholders' equity:		
Common stock: $1 par value, 2,500,000 shares authorized and issued, including shares in treasury........	$ 2,500,000	
Capital in excess of par value (Note 7)..............	200,537	
Retained earnings..............................	12,331,589	
	15,032,126	
Less cost of common stock held in treasury—870,329 shares (Note 7)..............................	3,388,202	
Total stockholders' equity....................		11,643,924
		$23,918,657

See accompanying notes.

exhibit 11   LEONARD'S INC.
Consolidated statement of retained earnings (Note 1)

	Year Ended			Nine Months Ended
	January 31, 1965	*January 30, 1966*	*January 29, 1967*	*October 28, 1967*
	(Unaudited)			
Balance at beginning of period................	$11,970,066	$12,413,237	$10,656,694	$11,479,861
Net income...............	559,346	162,265	906,776	851,728
Retained earnings of Everybodys applicable to 293,484 shares of common stock acquired for its treasury (Note 7)........		(877,601)		
Excess of cost over par value of 352,946 shares of treasury stock issued in exchange for all of the outstanding stock of Everybodys (Note 7).....		(1,020,349)		
Dividends paid:				
1965 and 1966—$.01 per share...............	(25,000)	(20,858)		
1967—$.05 per share.....			(83,609)	
Everybodys, prior to pooling of interests........	(91,175)			
Balance at end of period....	$12,413,237	$10,656,694	$11,479,861	$12,331,589

See accompanying notes.

exhibit **12   LEONARD'S INC.**
Notes to financial statements, October 28, 1967

1. Basis of consolidated statements of income and of retained earnings

The consolidated statements of income and of retained earnings include the accounts of the Company, its wholly owned subsidiary, Everybodys (see Note (a) to consolidated statement of income), to September 22, 1967, when it was merged into the Company, and its majority-owned subsidiary, Mitchells of Fort Worth, Inc. Intercompany accounts and transactions have been eliminated.

2. Inventories

Inventories were valued principally at the lower of average cost or market determined by the retail inventory method. The amounts of inventories used in the computation of cost of goods sold for the three years and nine months ended October 28, 1967 were as follows:

February 3, 1964	$5,615,434
January 31, 1965	5,289,516
January 30, 1966	5,413,387
January 29, 1967	5,645,795
October 28, 1967	7,042,244

3. Property and equipment

Depreciation has been provided on the straight-line or declining-balance methods at annual rates based on the estimated remaining useful lives of the depreciable assets as follows:

Buildings and building improvements	4–50 years
Furniture and fixtures	5–12½ years
Automotive equipment	3– 6 years
Subway and tunnel	5–17 years

Maintenance, repairs, and renewals of a minor nature have been charged to expense as incurred. Betterments and major renewals which extend the useful life of fixed assets have been capitalized.

Upon sale of property and equipment, the cost and accumulated depreciation applicable thereto have been removed from the accounts and any resulting profit or loss reflected in income.

4. Federal income tax

See Notes (c) and (d) to consolidated statement of income.

5. Long-term debt

Long-term debt at October 28, 1967 consisted of:

5½% secured promissory note due April 15, 1975	$7,042,250
5½% unsecured promissory notes due in annual installments of $100,260 including interest to April 15, 1975	640,576
5½% unsecured promissory notes due in annual installments of $92,272 including interest to April 15, 1975	468,066

exhibit 12   (continued)

The aggregate amount of maturities for each of the five years subsequent to October 28, 1967 were: 1968—$121,484; 1969—$131,742; 1970—$138,988; 1971—$146,632; 1972—$154,697. These notes have subsequently been paid in full.

6. Lease obligations

The Company was obligated for minimum annual rentals of approximately $524,000, plus additional rents contingent on sales volume, under long-term leases with affiliated organizations.

7. Stockholders' equity

There were no changes in capital in excess of par value during the three years and nine months ended October 28, 1967.

On April 15, 1965 the Company acquired 414,167 shares of its common stock for $1,597,581, of which 352,946 shares costing $1,373,295 were later used in the acquisition of Everybodys (see Note (a) to consolidated statement of income). On the same date Everybodys acquired 293,484 shares of its common stock for $1,207,703. Everybodys also acquired, at the same date, 766,608 shares of the Company's common stock for $2,982,833, which shares are held in the treasury.

During the year ended January 29, 1967, the Company acquired an additional 42,500 shares for $169,219 and, during the nine months ended October 28, 1967, incurred additional costs of $11,864 in connection with shares previously acquired.

8. Supplementary information

All of the following were charged to profit and loss accounts other than cost of goods sold:

	Year Ended			Nine Months Ended
	January 31, 1965	January 30, 1966	January 29, 1967	October 28, 1967
	(Unaudited)			
Maintenance and repairs......	$110,900	$124,509	$162,774	$ 94,988
Depreciation and amortization of property and equipment...	$392,585	$354,658	$340,614	$251,757
Taxes other than income taxes:				
Payroll.................	$216,812	$232,485	$275,522	$220,239
Ad valorem and other.....	105,188	107,572	108,901	96,038
Franchise..............	50,684	42,424	34,009	36,185
	$372,684	$382,481	$418,432	$352,462
Rents....................	$720,378	$724,547	$747,142	$558,416

No management and service contract fees or royalties were incurred.

PART FIVE
THE IMPLEMENTATION PHASE: DEVELOPING THE ORGANIZATIONAL AND CONTROL STRATEGIES

21
BOSSART'S

In reviewing Bossart's position at the year end, Mr. James Johnson, the executive vice president noted several factors. Located in a large eastern city, Bossart's had opened its fifth retail store in the city the previous fall. Mr. Johnson was particularly interested in the overall effects of the firm's new department store on the company's operations. He noted that Bossart's net sales had increased appreciably and that the new store was more than achieving its predicted volume. While this performance was gratifying, Mr. Johnson was nevertheless concerned with two major problems which he felt the new store had created.

We expected the D store [the symbol used by management to identify its new store located in a recently constructed shopping center called People's Plaza] to take some business from the First Street and A stores because they are located within the same general shopping area. However, D has been so successful that both the First Street and A stores are experiencing a squeeze on their profit margins. These reductions in volume are making it hard for the First Street and A store managers to keep costs in line.

The D store has created another problem because our longstanding policy of the same store hours for all outlets had to be changed. The D store broke the established tradition by setting hours more suited to the shopping habits of its customers. Then the C store wanted to open and close at still another set of times. In the case of the D store, the different time schedule was necessary and has undoubtedly helped the store's volume. The new hours at the C store haven't materially affected their volume and have created some operating and personnel difficulties. Attracting and retaining competent sales people who have to work at least two evenings is difficult.

EARLY HISTORY AND DEVELOPMENT

In the early 1880's, when the city's population was about 250,000, Daniel Bossart arrived in America from Switzerland. After one year's work in a small dry goods store, he joined with a friend, Leslie Scherer, in a retail business venture called Bossart's. The store's location in a resi-

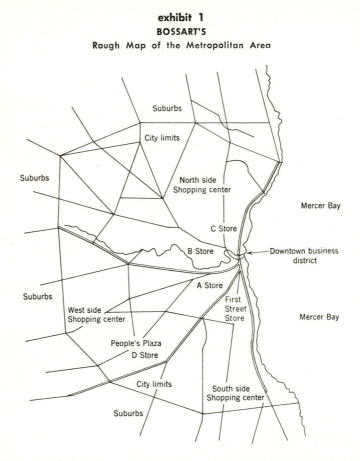

exhibit 1
BOSSART'S
Rough Map of the Metropolitan Area

dential area of the city outside of the downtown business district was regarded as a key factor in the company's early success. When new stores were added over a fifty year period, management continued to choose neighborhood areas located between the center of the city and the suburbs. (See Exhibit 1.)

The first and second Bossart stores (called First Street and A by the management) were located on the south side of the city. They were both about two miles south of the center of the downtown business section and separated by approximately a half mile. The third store opened by Bossart's (called B) was located about two miles west of the center of the downtown business district, and the C store was a mile north of the downtown center. The D store, (People's Plaza), was located in the southwest section of the city on the edge of the suburbs. It was about five miles southwest of the First Street and A stores. The city's population at that time was about 750,000 and the metropolitan area had well over a million people.

When the first four Bossart stores were established, each of their neighborhoods was considered to be on the outskirts of the city. However, as the city grew and the suburbs became more mature, the stores became surrounded by the growing populations, and neighborhood shopping areas developed at each location. Bossart's sales volume climbed as the city's residents found Bossart's stores conveniently located and competitive with the large downtown stores with respect to price, service and quality of merchandise.

As the four stores grew with their neighborhoods, Bossart's management endeavored to keep the four units operating essentially as one store. It was their thought that if Bossart's had uniform stores, the company would derive many advantages of a centralized (one-store) operation. Furthermore, the public would have one, not four, images of what a Bossart store was.

On the occasion of Bossart's 50th anniversary, the firm's president, Mr. Leslie Scherer, explained the company's major characteristics as follows.

> Few department stores in America are like Bossart's. Some are single stores in a central part of the city or the district. Others have a parent store with branches. Others are organized like a chain group. Bossart's four stores are organized on yet a different plan. They are under one ownership and control, have certain functions in common, and yet are managed as four distinct stores. Each store has its own manager, who is responsible for the unit's operation, yet the Bossart name is one; the reputation and good will are one; Bossart's contact with the market in buying merchandise is one. In advertising, which is done from a central bureau, the same items are offered at the same time in the four stores. Each Bossart store is a community store, having its entire stake in the community it serves. Yet in spirit, in policies, in reputation, and in operating methods, the four Bossart stores constitute one merchandising activity.

EXPANSION PERIOD

During the postwar period management carried out a program of expansion and modernization of all existing facilities. Each of the four stores and the warehouse building were improved, as Bossart's sought to maintain its position as the city's leading retailer both in terms of volume and quality.

Keen competition was felt from several sources within the trading area served by the Bossart stores. (See Exhibit 1.) There were two large department stores and several specialty stores in the downtown business district. One of the large department stores was a unit of a large national chain of department stores, while the other was part of a large eastern retailing organization. Three Sears stores, seven Penney's stores, several specialty stores and numerous variety stores were also affecting Bossart's share of the retail business in the city. Of particular concern to Bossart's management was the opening of the large North Side Shopping Center, three miles from Bossart's C store. A unit of one of the large downtown stores (the national chain) was the major retail outlet at the North Side Shopping Center. Two large variety stores and several specialty stores were also located there. In view of the changing competitive picture, Bossart's undertook plans for further expansion. Originally, the firm's directors had in mind a single outlying store located near the growing suburbs; but as time passed and they observed the country-wide interest in shopping centers, the directors found more and more attractive the notion of developing a complete shopping center with the Bossart unit as the dominant store.

The ground-breaking ceremonies took place for Bossart's new shopping center plaza on the far southwest side of the city. People's Plaza, as the center was called, was planned as the city's largest and most modern shopping center.

Bossart's failed in its efforts to negotiate a deal with a major downtown department store to have it establish an outlet at People's Plaza. Bossart's did manage, however, to get Penney's and one of the city's leading specialty stores to join the complex at the new center. The center was opened with total building area of nearly one million square feet, parking facilities for 7,000 automobiles, and a complete range of stores and service organizations.

Bossart's annual sales volume was approximately $60 million. It had more than 5000 employees and the floor area in the five stores totaled over a million square feet. The A, B, C, and D stores had equal floor areas and accounted for three-quarters of the company's total floor space.

While management felt that Bossart's competitive position in the city had been strengthened due to the new D store in People's Plaza they were concerned about recent announcements made by the two large downtown stores. The eastern firm had announced its plan to lease a store in an established shopping center in a suburb immediately south of the city. The store would be about five miles south of Bossart's First Street and A stores and four miles southeast of the new D store. Prior to this announcement, Sears had been the only major retailer at the South Side Shopping Center, which was considerably smaller than both People's Plaza and the North Side center.

The national chain also announced plans to develop another shopping center on the west side of the city. It revealed that a well-known Philadelphia retailing concern had already agreed to lease one large retail unit while the national chain would occupy the other area. This new center, which would not be completed for a few years, was to be located about three miles from People's Plaza in a west side suburb. In size and style, it was planned to be at least on a par with People's Plaza.

GENERAL ORGANIZATION

Throughout Bossart's history, a member of the Bossart family had been president of the firm. When Daniel Bossart passed away, his partner and son-in-law, Leslie Scherer, became president and general manager of the store. When Leslie Scherer died, his son, Leslie Jr., succeeded to the presidency. After Leslie Jr. died, his younger brother, Steven, became president.

The Bossart organization was largely a mixture of two distinct service groups: those with over twenty-five years of service with the company and those who had joined the firm within the past twelve years. Reporting to Mr. Steven Scherer, the president, were two men, each a representative of one of the above-mentioned groups.

Mr. Harry Gargill, who had been with Bossart's for more than 40 years, was a vice president and treasurer. He was principally interested in the financial aspects of the company. In recent years he had concerned himself largely with the financial planning for the construction and leasing at People's Plaza.

Mr. James Johnson, on the other hand, had been with Bossart's less than twelve years. He had joined the firm as a vice president following successful retail experiences with an eastern retailing concern and a well-known department store in the West. As the executive vice presi-

exhibit 2
BOSSART'S
General Organization Chart

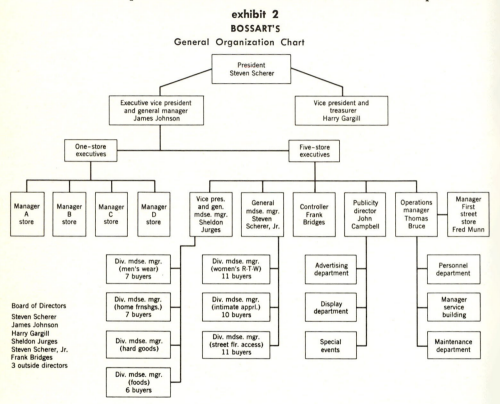

dent and general manager of Bossart's, he was primarily responsible for all the operations affecting the company's retail business. Mr. Johnson had eight people who reported directly to him. As shown in Exhibit 2, these eight men were divided into two groups—the A, B, C, and D store managers and the heads of the functional divisions (merchandise, control, publicity, and operations). The store managers were usually referred to among the Bossart management as "one-store executives," while the heads of the functional divisions were called "five-store executives."

The responsibilities of the First Street store manager were consider-ably different from those of the managers of the other stores. In the latter stores, each manager was responsible for both the selling and the oper-ating phases of the store. Each of these stores had a superintendent who handled the operating problems and five divisional supervisors who had charge of the selling floors. These relationships are shown in Ex-hibit 3. The A, B, C and D store managers reported directly to Mr. Johnson.

exhibit 3
BOSSART'S
A, B, C, and D Stores, Organization Chart

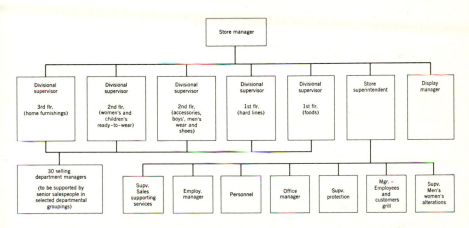

The First Street store manager, on the other hand, reported to the operations manager and was directly responsible for only the operating aspects of his store. The buying organization under the two general merchandise managers was responsible for the selling function in the First Street store. Each division merchandise manager acted as a divi-sional supervisor at the First Street store and was responsible for a num-ber of selling departments. The buyers under each division merchandise manager acted as department managers at the First Street store. Mr. Johnson summed up their dual roles in saying, "The buyers have line responsibilities at the First Street store and staff relationships with the other four stores." The executive offices and the buying organization were all located at the First Street store.

Mr. Munn had been the superintendent at the First Street store for a period of years. When the new position of store manager was created he was selected for the job. No one was appointed to fill the position Mr. Munn vacated. Mr. Munn continued to report to the operations manager, whose office was next to Mr. Munn's.

Each store manager received regular reports from the controller's office on the operations of his store. Copies of the operating reports of each store were also sent to Mr. Johnson and the "five-store executives."

THE "FIVE-STORE EXECUTIVES"

There were two general merchandise managers who reported directly to Mr. Johnson. Mr. Sheldon Jurges, a vice president of over forty years' experience with the company, was the general merchandise manager in charge of four major classifications of merchandise. These lines were men's wear, home furnishings, hard goods, and foods. Under Mr. Jurges were four division merchandise managers and 30 buyers. Mr. Steven Scherer, Jr., a son of the president, was the general merchandise manager in charge of the remaining "soft" goods. These were women's ready-to-wear, intimate apparel, and street floor accessories. Mr. Scherer had three division merchandise managers and 32 buyers under him. Mr. Scherer, who was under 40 years of age, had been with the company approximately ten years.

The merchandise divisions had the buying responsibility for the five Bossart stores. Each buyer specialized in a line of merchandise such as women's hosiery and was in constant contact with the manufacturers of these products. This often involved considerable traveling to trade shows and manufacturers' showrooms. Each buyer operated within the limits of a predetermined budget and Bossart's established merchandising policies of price and quality. Still he was allowed considerable flexibility in his buying program and his personal income depended to a great extent on the success he had in purchasing the "right" merchandise.

Each buyer's performance was measured with respect to his sales, gross profit margin, and inventory composition and amount. The buyer was also responsible for the supervision of the selling force at the First Street store.

With their offices in the First Street store, the buyers tried to visit each of the other Bossart stores once a week. During these visits a buyer attempted to work out any problems that related to his particular line of merchandise. At the A, B, C, and D stores the buyer set prices, ordered markdowns, determined assortments and planned promotions, and in these matters he had direct authority. In such things as the location or arrangement of merchandise displays, however, he would make suggestions, and his suggestions were generally but not always accepted by the department manager in charge of the department which sold the buyer's merchandise.

At the First Street store, where the buyer was responsible jointly with the store manager for the selling function, it was much easier for the buyer to put his ideas into immediate practice. The sales people reported directly to him, and as department manager he always knew the status of the department's budget.

Each buyer also spent a great deal of time each week controlling the inventory of his merchandise. In many departments this required a trip once a week to the service building (warehouse) and a detailed review each week of reports showing the sales and inventory by product classifications for each store.

The publicity division was under the direction of Mr. John Campbell. Under his supervision were the advertising department and the display and special events department. Advertising for the five stores was handled by a centralized staff at the First Street store location. Advertisements were run in the local papers under the Bossart name and carried a message that applied equally to all stores. It was a rare occasion when one of the Bossart stores advertised independently in the local papers. Sales promotion and display were handled in the A, B, C, and D stores by a person at each location who reported directly to the store manager. The First Street store's sales promotion and display were handled by an individual who reported to a five-store display director, who, in turn, reported to Mr. Campbell.

The operations division, which was managed by Mr. Thomas Bruce, was responsible for all merchandise-handling functions, store services, and personnel. The company had a service building where all the merchandise was received, marked, stored, and eventually shipped to the five Bossart stores. The maintenance department was responsible for maintaining the interiors and exteriors of all Bossart stores at the high levels always associated with the company's reputation.

Each of the stores had a personnel office which hired the line employees, such as sales people, for that store. The First Street store also hired the five-store maintenance and warehouse employees. Buyers were hired by the general merchandise managers, and five-store staff personnel were hired by the five-store executives, who also supervised executive training programs.

Mr. Bruce's main function was the determining of the amounts and types of operating assistance that should be administered to each store. He worked closely with the store superintendents at the A, B, C, and D stores and the store manager at the First Street store on the operating problems of each unit. He was also in daily contact with Mr. Johnson, to whom he reported directly.

The controller's office was under the direction of Mr. Frank Bridges. Mr. Bridges had been with the firm for over forty years and was a member of the board of directors. He had been promoted to his present position from assistant controller several years previously. His office gathered and distributed the accounting and statistical information relative to the stores' operations. For instance, sales and inventory records of each store were consolidated by lines of merchandise and reports were sent to each buyer relative to his line.

COMMITTEES

"Bossart's was not managed by committees," said Mr. Johnson, the executive vice president and general manager, "but we use them as a means of focusing attention on management problems, co-ordinating thinking and action, and as a means of top-level communication." The company had four committees: the General Management Committee (GMC), the Expense Control Committee, the Division Merchandise Managers' Committee, and the Wage Committee.

The General Management Committee had 18 members, which included five functional division heads, the five store managers, and the seven merchandise division managers. Mr. Johnson regarded this committee as a "communications get-together." The group met whenever Mr. Johnson felt the need to discuss general policy matters. He often used these meetings to present major policy decisions that top management had reached.

The Expense Control Committee was composed of the five functional division managers and the five store managers. This group met once a month with Mr. Johnson. At these meetings budgets were determined and later reviewed. Current trends affecting the stores' operations and any problems relating to expense control were also discussed.

The Wage Committee was made up of five store managers. This group was originally brought together to establish wage programs that could be administered uniformly in all Bossart stores. However, it developed that the store managers found it convenient to discuss at these meetings any common problems they wished brought to Mr. Johnson's attention. One store manager said, "I like these meetings because each store has an equal vote on problems facing a manager. When a decision is reached, even if I am opposed to the idea, I don't mind going along with the group. We all respect the judgment of each other on the store manager's problems, which are many."

The Division Merchandise Managers' Committee was made up of the two general merchandise managers, the seven merchandise division managers, the five store managers and the publicity director. Their meetings were concerned mainly with the merchandising and publicity problems of the company.

Decisions reached at the merchandising, store managers, and expense control meetings were often announced at the General Management Committee meetings.

In addition to the use of committees, Mr. Johnson kept in close contact with all Bossart operations by means of personal observation and direct contact with the management personnel. He tried to visit the A, B, C, and D stores at least every two weeks and met with their store managers about as often. He also exercised control of management activity through a system of operating reports that came to his desk regularly. "I follow these reports closely because it gives me the opportunity to raise key questions. When something seems out of line I contact the person responsible and expect to get a reasonable explanation," said Mr. Johnson.

"A great deal of my control problems," he went on, "are simplified by our unique organizational set-up. We have both five-store and one-store executives. Therefore, if there is some difficulty relating to a certain line of merchandise at a particular store, I can contact the merchandise people right in this office or I can get in touch with the appropriate store manager."

INTERSELLING

Mr. Johnson explained that "the internal organization of the Bossart stores is in a state of transition because we are adopting a plan of interselling.' Until now the organization of each store paralleled the traditional merchandising organization in that each department manager and his salespeople were responsible for selling a line of merchandise which had been procured by one buyer. Recent steps have been taken, however, to establish fewer selling units within each store."

"Interselling" meant that several units formerly classed as departments were grouped together as one selling unit under one department manager. Sales people assigned to the selling group might sell at any sales area within the selling unit. The department manager shifted the personnel to the selling areas where the sales efforts were most needed at particular times. Prior to interselling a salesperson was assigned to a certain station and sold only the products at that station. These items of sportswear were a typical example: Better sportswear, better blouses, and better casual dresses were each a separate line, and each was bought by a different buyer. Although in each store their stations were adjacent, each line had its own salesperson who sold only the items at her station. The buyers had often helped instruct the sales people assigned to the stations where their merchandise was sold.

Interselling did not originate at the D store; Bossart's had tried the plan elsewhere on a trial basis, and while results had shown promise, the management found that some resistance was encountered from buyers and sales people who were reluctant to change their ways. When the D store was opened, however, its entire organization was based on interselling and its success there was helping to break down the resistance of the merchandising organization at the other stores.

Mr. Johnson observed after a year of profitable operations at the D store that organizational performance was satisfactory, and that he hoped to follow the same basic pattern of interselling at the other stores. "We've already begun forming new selling groups at the A, B, and C stores, and before long we will have interselling in full swing at all of these stores. It will take longer to put this principle into practice at the First Street store because the buyers are still very much in the picture at that location."

THE FIRST STREET STORE

The First Street Store was the first Bossart store opened and was traditionally the leader in sales volume. For several years it had contributed a larger share of sales than the other Bossart stores. Although this percentage dropped significantly with the opening of the new D store, it was still the largest volume unit. In terms of net sales, the D store ranked a close second, while A, C, and B followed in that order.

The First Street store was unlike the other stores in that there were no department managers directly responsible to the store manager. The buyers acted as department managers for their respective lines of merchandise, or in many cases delegated this responsibility to the assistant buyer.

One of the division merchandise managers expressed the opinion that most of the 62 Bossart buyers regarded the selling responsibilities of the merchandise organization at the First Street store as an essential aid to them in their merchandising function.

> Every buyer tries to spend some of his time each day on the selling floor. He uses this time to instruct the salespeople in his department, and to make a few sales himself. In that way our buyers get close to the customer. They find out just what the customer wants and how he can best be sold.
>
> There are other reasons why this arrangement is valued by our buyers. A buyer has full authority at all the stores in setting prices, ordering markdowns, planning advertising and promotions. But only at the First Street store can he order such details as the location and arrangement of merchandise.
>
> The buyers also feel that control of the selling responsibility at the First Street store helps their overall showing. The buyers feel that at the First Street store, where they have full authority over the selling function, they have an opportunity to test their ideas, and those which prove out at the First Street store, they feel, should be equally successful at all of the other stores. Thus the buyer's supervision of his selling department at the First Street store becomes a proving ground that he feels will enable him to increase his sales volume at all the stores, and thereby increase his income, too.

THE B STORE

Mr. Mason, the manager of the B store said that his time was divided as follows: 50% acting as a liaison for his store's organization in its relations with people located at the First Street store, 40% on exclusively B store problems, and 10% on general company business.

> I probably should spend more time on B store problems exclusively. There are enough of them. The new D store has hurt our volume, our

neighborhood has gotten old and is declining, and our expenses have been increasing all the time.

The changeover to interselling should help to get our expenses back in line. However, I wonder if it will increase our problems in dealing with the buyers.

22

THE ARCHER-DANIELS-MIDLAND COMPANY

The Archer-Daniels-Midland Company had its origin in a firm founded in 1902 by George Archer and John Daniels to "manufacture flax and other oil producing seeds and cereals into their natural products, and to sell the products so manufactured by it." In 1923, after a number of firms had been acquired by the parent company, the Archer-Daniels-Midland Company was organized to take over their combined assets. During its first ten years the company's investment in plant increased from $130,000 to $1 million; by 1923 its combined properties were carried on its books at $7 million. At that date the company had become the largest producer of linseed oil in the world.

In 1927 a grain division was formed to operate four terminal elevators. Two years later the company became a producer of foundry core oils and an importer and processor of foreign and marine oils. Soybeans were added to its crushing activities and the company expanded into extensive new lines of food, livestock feed, and chemical products. In the early 1930's it acquired the Commander-Larabee Corporation, the nation's third largest flour miller, which operated 14 flour mills.

By 1962 the company had developed hundreds of new products through refining and modifying raw linseed oil, crude soybean oil, and marine and whale oils. Its expanded operations covered the United States and extended into Latin America and Europe. (See Exhibit 1.) The company had reported earnings every year since its incorporation and had paid quarterly dividends without exception for more than a quarter of a century.

"Our business," said Mr. John Daniels, president of the company, "is best described in general terms as the processing of agricultural and chemical products. While we are primarily an agricultural processing company, we are growing in the chemical field. We are expanding overseas. Our objective is to achieve a more even balance of profits from agriculture, chemicals, and foreign operations. About 99% of our products go to other industries for further processing into finished goods. We have virtually no consumer products."

CORPORATE DEVELOPMENT

John Daniels and George Archer had been personal friends long before they became partners to organize the Archer-Daniels Linseed Company in 1902. In 1903 they hired Samuel Mairs, then twenty-four years old, as a bookkeeper and he was successively promoted to secretary and director. In 1909 he succeeded John Daniels as treasurer. Together this trio managed the business for over twenty years.

Mr. Daniels and Mr. Archer occupied facing roll-top desks in an office in the crushing mill. They gave close supervision to every detail of the business even to supervising such minute matters as the opening of the morning mail so that the envelopes could be saved to provide the day's scratch paper. Mr. Mairs supervised the bookkeeping, handled bank relations, and accumulated numerous small day-to-day administrative responsibilities. It was said of the partners that their personalities made a fortunate combination—Mr. Daniels was a bear, Mr. Archer was a bull, and Samuel Mairs acted as modifier.

In 1911 Shreve Archer, the twenty-three year old son of George Archer, joined the company. While he was given the title of treasurer, he was put to work at manual labor. In 1914 Thomas L. Daniels, the son of John Daniels, joined the company as treasurer and Shreve Archer became vice president. In November of 1924 Mr. John Daniels, then sixty-seven, became chairman of the board and turned the presidency over to Shreve Archer, who was thirty-six years old at the time. Samuel Mairs meanwhile had been made vice president, and under Shreve Archer became executive vice president.

Under the presidency of Shreve Archer the company went into a period of great expansion. Shreve was reputed to be a canny trader with an intuitive sense for recognizing a bargain. It was during his term in office that the company merged with other linseed crushers to become the nation's largest operator; it added soybeans to its line, and this grew to be a larger item than linseed; it bought and built terminal elevators; it purchased the Commander-Larabee Mills; and it added numerous smaller lines, such as core oils, foundry products, the flax fiber mill, and the alfalfa division.

Shreve Archer occupied a corner office next to Thomas Daniels, then a vice president, and Mr. Mairs. The doors of these offices were left open and the executives walked in and out of each other's offices freely. If one of them felt the need for discussion, he stepped into the next office. Some matters brought them all into Shreve Archer's office. After such a discussion a decision was usually made at once. Among the rank and file personnel in the company Mr. Mairs came to have the reputation of making most of the decisions. "Actually," said one of his contemporaries, "this was only because Mr. Mairs had little inclination to travel, was the one who could always be found at his desk, and therefore had gathered to himself the supervision of many small day-to-day operating details. Even as executive vice president he insisted that all capital expenditures over $25 be presented for his approval. Shreve Archer, Thomas Daniels, and Samuel Mairs generally agreed on policy issues and acted as a team. But it was Shreve who called the big turns, and he did that personally. He was a power in his own right."

In 1947 Shreve Archer died suddenly at the age of fifty-nine. Mr. Mairs, then sixty-eight, became chairman of the board, and Thomas Daniels, fifty-five, was elected president. In January of 1955 Mr. Mairs passed away, and with his passing Thomas Daniels, then sixty-two, was the only one of the old top-management trio who remained.

During the spring months of 1955 Mr. Thomas Daniels carried on alone all of the activities that had formerly been performed by Shreve Archer, Mr. Mairs, and himself. He became acutely aware of the organization problems that had developed over the years. There were few formally organized divisions. Management tended to be along product lines, and plants were the operating units. "The company," said an executive, "was literally one big pool. People worked in specialized areas, but often they weren't sure who their boss was, except at the very top."

There was an executive committee, but it was inactive. There was a central accounting department, which served most branches. Accounting staffs existed at only some of the outlying plants and divisions. There was no central engineering department to serve all of the mills, nor was there any central coordination of production. The mills had done most of their own buying under the supervision of the top management trio. Sales strategy was developed at the product level, and research, which had been no more than tolerated a generation ago, had become of critical and pressing importance. Purchasing, transportation, and quality control were not under the specific direction of any one executive in the home office. Warehousing and distribution were handled at the plant level. There was no systematic salary administration or job evaluation.

During his first year as president Mr. Thomas Daniels actively supervised financial matters and kept in close hourly touch with the grain markets. The executives in charge of the linseed and soybean business reported their activities to him daily. Eighteen senior executives, including the treasurer and the controller, reported directly to him. In a typical week he read between 50 and 60 detailed reports on markets and on operations. "Besides all this," said Mr. Thomas Daniels, "the business had become much more complicated. We were no longer simple producers of linseed oil. I felt I could no longer carry the burden alone." During the summer of 1955 the executive committee agreed upon the need for a reappraisal of the management, and for that purpose the services of a firm of management consultants, Richardson, Henry, Bellows and Company, were retained.

While the original study made by the consultants was intended to be primarily a personnel audit to evaluate the management resources of the company, the consultants reported that their comprehensive analysis of the company's operations definitely pointed to the need for improvement in certain areas of operations and organization. Therefore they were engaged to make a further study of all of the elements of the organizational structure, its planning, and staffing. There emerged definite recommendations regarding organizational structure, positions, and position relationships. The Archer-Daniels-Midland executive committee studied the recommendations and decided to adopt most of them.

A new office of administrative vice president was established. This office was to coordinate the service staff functions of purchasing, traffic, employee relations, warehousing, and quality control. Another new office with the title of assistant to the president was created for the purpose of relieving the president, as much as possible, of his routine duties. The office of director of marketing, originally established in 1953 for the purpose of coordinating all sales and merchandising activities of the company's numerous product lines, was reaffirmed and given new emphasis.

Until this time the executive committee had been composed of those men in the top management group who were considered to be important in directing the affairs of the company, and they had been chosen without regard to their particular positions or functions. In the reorganization the composition of the committee was changed to include both general and staff executives. Also, one young executive was appointed to the committee to act as its secretary for a six-month period on a rotating basis, for the benefit to be gained in observing the proceedings of the committee. The executive committee was again reactivated, it met weekly, and reviewed all matters of major importance.

The size of the board of directors was increased to nineteen members. Four of the younger executives were placed on the board for the experience it would afford them. The board included five outside directors whose detached viewpoint was considered valuable.

All jobs were evaluated and a system of salary administration was installed. A standard cost system was adopted and accounting figures were refined to give division managers more details of their operations. In production, each division appointed a production coordinator and the responsibility for manufacturing was shifted to the divisions. Commodity buyers, who formerly answered to top management in Minneapolis, reported to the managers of their divisions. Policy making on trading in commodities, formerly centralized in top management, was set daily by each division head.

"The effect of our reorganization," said Mr. Thomas Daniels, "was to shift the major responsibility out of my office and down the line. The division managers are now our key people, and they make the critical decisions."

In 1958 Mr. Thomas Daniels became chairman of the board and his son, John Daniels, then 37, became president, chief executive officer, and chairman of the executive committee.

RESEARCH AND PRODUCT DEVELOPMENT

"I believe," said Mr. Thomas Daniels, chairman of the board, in 1961, "that the major problem facing our company is clearly defined: many activities of former years no longer yield a profit. The crushing of oilseeds, which once gave our organization bread-and-butter income, must be replaced with the production of chemicals and other products which yield a higher profit. We hope to achieve this by skillful research."

Archer-Daniels had carried on research for many years, but until 1946 it had been only a limited effort. "Until a few years ago," said Mr. James Konen, vice president and director of research, "if any research project took more than six months, management had a tendency to get nervous and say, 'Look, this is costing a lot of money. How about quitting?' And if I ever presented a requisition for a new piece of laboratory equipment that cost over a thousand dollars, I knew that I'd better be prepared to explain exactly how that expenditure was going to pay off."

In the earlier days the entire cost of any research project had been charged to the division concerned. Accounting methods were not refined enough to reflect the benefits, and therefore, division managers often did not fully appreciate research. Efforts were made by division managers to maintain the profit position of their respective divisions and to keep expenditures under control in so far as possible. Management was also intensely interested in maintaining expense control but at the same time furthering product development and research in all of the divisions.

In general, the new tactic was to take the research effort one step further than the basic product stage. "We still have in mind that we expect practical results from our projects," said Mr. Konen. "Our approach is about half way between practical and pure research."

During the period following World War II Mr. Konen, head of research activities, had been promoting to management the idea of a development department which would take the results of the experimental research done by the laboratories and bring it closer to the market-production stage. He considered the idea as a possible way to aid research and sales. "There's more to research than just producing new products," he said. "New products have to be developed to the application stage. They have to be produced, and they have to be sold." On the consideration that these developmental activities were taking place anyway, and that it would be more efficient to perform them systematically under central direction, the executive committee approved the creation of a development department.

"My job," said Dr. George Nelson, who headed the department, "is to analyze any new product for commercial acceptance. We relate all items to a profitability base, measuring profitability as profit related to capital investment." It was intended that the department would have three general objectives:

The Evaluation of New Products. Determining the probable demand, the most lucrative markets, and the economic worth of products. The appraisal of similar products and the competitive position of ADM regarding manufacturing facilities and raw materials.

Market Research. Objective analysis of new products and the markets for them through market surveys. Market research activities were divided into three main groups: Industrial chemicals, resins and plastics, and agricultural products.

The Acquisition of New Companies. The investigation of any existing companies or processes which ADM had the opportunity of acquiring.

In working out the marketing of a new product, the development department tried to determine where the product might be useful. Then they approached leading manufacturers in that industry and presented it to them. If the prospect was interested, the development department worked closely with their engineering and production people until the new product was well under way to achieving consumer acceptance. At that point the funds to put it into full production would be allocated, and the production and sale of the product would be shifted to the division which would produce it.

THE SOYBEAN DIVISION

ADM made its entrance into the growing soy products industry in 1928 when it started to process soybeans by using the same hydraulic presses that it used for flaxseed. At that time the industry was in its infancy, having been born during the first World War when the demand for fats, oils, and proteins spurred the production of soybean products. The first large scale use of soybean oil was in such products as margarine, shortenings, and salad dressings. Consumer acceptance was so strong that during the decade of the thirties production increased sixfold, and by 1940, 80% of the half-billion-pound annual output went into these products. Livestock and poultry feed producers found that soybean oil meal served as an excellent high protein feed supplement in poultry mashes and hog feed supplements. In 1955 the bulk of the 6½-million-ton production of soybean oil meal was used in livestock feeds, and most of the balance went into soy flour which was used in bakery goods, pancake and waffle flours, and protein bread. Since 1940 ADM had been known as the largest and most efficient producer of soybean products in the world. During the fifties it added to its product lines edible soybean oils, which it sold to the producers of cooking and salad oils and to the canners of tuna and sardines.

"During World War II," said Mr. Thomas Daniels, chairman of the board, "the soybean industry was cradled in the lap of luxury by the demand for fats and oils. After the war life became real and earnest. Overexpansion plagued us. Every processor had excess capacity and tried to get his share of the market—and a little more. Add to this a good deal of speculation and the result was chaos in the market place." After the war, ADM's soybean plants had been operating at about 75% of capacity. During only 10% of the year did soybean oil and meal bring a better price than the soybeans themselves.

As a mater of company policy ADM did not process its basic products into ultimate consumer products. It did not engage in the manufacture of paints for fear of offending paint manufacturing customers. For the same reason it refrained from making salad oils, shortenings, and margarines. Management reasoned that the company's name was not known to the retail public; neither did the company have retail marketing skill or experience. The trend, however, was toward further refining of its products to bring them closer to the state of the ultimate consumer's products, but stopping just short of the finished commodity. Less than half of the company's volume was in basic products. The balance was refined and modified into what the management called "upgraded" products.

Mr. Thomas Daniels believed that the soybean industry could not match the petrochemical industry in resources for research; that industry was making competitive inroads into the ultimate soybean markets. Mr. Daniels also believed that the federal government should properly undertake the "pure" research into the basic nature of soybeans, their composition, component separation, and fundamental reactions. Thereafter private industry could avail itself of the findings and develop new products such as adhesives, binders, foaming agents, and emulsifiers. "A few million dollars spent by the government in such research," he said, "would forestall many millions presently spent for price supports in the soybean market."

Mr. Daniels was of the opinion that the industry should press expansion into foreign markets. In European markets generally soybean oil was discriminated against as an inferior product in favor of the scarcer olive oil, even in margarines. He also believed that the American market had not been fully exploited. "Americans are a value-conscious and diet-conscious people," he said, "and the soybean is our finest source of low-cost vegetable protein. Both home and abroad we have to do a good deal of old-fashioned American selling."

In 1961 soybean products amounted to 34% of ADM's aggregate sales. In the prewar period they had accounted for 14% of the company's volume.

CHEMICALS

George Archer, one of the founders of the company, had often said in his day that linseed oil was good enough as a vehicle for any paint, and that he was satisfied to produce high quality linseed oil, produce it at low cost, and sell it on a price basis. He had little use for chemists. In its early history the company had done no refining. It sold its basic linseed oil to refiners who processed it according to paint manufacturers' specifications. As late as 1923 ADM had offered a limited line of only 18 grades of linseed oil.

Over the years the demand for refined oils grew, while the use of crude linseed oil declined. Before the days of paint chemistry the average gallon of exterior house paint contained about five pounds of linseed oil. This was the standard unit of sale, and to compete the manufacturer could do one of two things: sell the same product at a lower price, or sell a superior product at the same price.

The extraction of linseed oil (or soybean oil) was a simple process which required little technical knowledge. "Beyond requiring a pretty good sense of market timing, which our people had," said an Archer-Daniels executive, "it was no trick at all to operate as a processor." The result was that many small marginal producers entered the field and competition between them forced all of the profit out of the conversion operation. Inferior oils added to the deterioration of the market. For as little as 4¢ a pound industrial users might switch from linseed oil to soybean oil.

Early paints had been simple products: an oxide or lead base, a pigment for color, and linseed oil for a vehicle. Competition forced manufacturers to seek new and superior ingredients. The trend was to odorless paints that were fast drying, had greater covering quality and more opacity. A gallon of typical modern paint contained three pounds of refined special-purpose linseed oil, and the remainder was in other ingredients.

Previously, a linseed salesman had been a salesman, not a technician, and he sold on a friendship basis and for price. With the transition to the vehicle business, selling was no longer on a "wining and dining" basis. Selling came to be strictly on a technical specification, low-pressure basis. Salesmen were technicians who could go into a customer's laboratory and discuss technical matters with purchasing agents who were generally paint chemists. The conversion operation also changed with the new technology. Common laborers were replaced by trained operators, and the modern mill foreman was a college graduate with a degree in chemistry.

ADM was first drawn into the field of industrial chemicals by its wish to sell a larger portion of its oil production as a refined, finished product, commanding a better margin than that derived from the sale of the basic crude oil. In a series of acquisitions, dating back to the early thirties, ADM acquired concerns which processed various types of oils, such as core oils, Chinawood (tung) oil, oiticica, perilla, menhaden, sardine, sperm, and herring oils.

In a foreign venture with Peruvian partners, ADM constructed a land-based whaling station near Lima, Peru, at a cost of $1.5 million. From this base three whaling ships killed about 2,000 whales a year, producing about 7,000 metric tons of sperm oil. ADM was the largest marketer of sperm oil in the U.S. Sperm oil was unique among all other oils in that its viscosity did not change with extreme changes in temperature. This property made it ideal for use in cosmetics, watch lubrication, and automatic transmissions.

In 1930 a subsidiary of ADM was organized to produce fatty acids, which led to the production of many new products not previously manufactured by the company. ADM also produced glycerides, glycerine, and saturated or fully hydrogenated oils, contrasted to partly hydrogenated products such as Crisco and Fluffo. Nineteen different grades were produced, many in the form of flakes, and they were used in a wide variety of products including rubber, leather, tin-plate, plastics, lubricating grease, cosmetics, and detergents.

Early in 1954 the ADM management decided upon a major expansion into the field of fatty alcohols, and for that purpose it built a plant which used the sodium reduction process, which produced either saturated or unsaturated alcohols. The expected volume for these products did not develop, and during its early years the plant never operated at more than 25% of its 12 million pound annual capacity, which resulted in substantial losses. After considering converting to other processes, or converting the plant to other uses, either of which would be costly expedients, the company finally sold the plant.

Although the total dollar volume of ADM's chemical production had multiplied several times during the postwar period, the operation had not been consistently profitable. The profit pattern tended to be similar to that of proprietary drugs: any new product which found acceptance would earn high profits until competition entered the field, when profits might disappear abruptly. Peak profits were not as high because chemical users balanced costs against performance, and because there was a high degree of substitutability in industrial chemicals.

RESINS AND PLASTICS

ADM's gradual movement toward plastics started in the early thirties when the company began to expand its limited facilities for the production of special and refined linseed oils. In 1931 the research laboratory developed a new product made from linseed oil which it called ADM 100 Oil. This product was marketed continuously from that time on as a nitrocellulose lacquer plasticizer. (A plasticizer is an ingredient that softens and lends flexibility to hard, resinous material.) ADM 100 Oil found a ready market among manufacturers who sought a permanent film-forming lacquer plasticizer for furniture finishes, metal lacquers, and automotive primers. Nitrocellulose, as a basic ingredient of all lacquer, is classified as a plastic, and with the production of ADM 100 Oil, Archer-Daniels entered the plasticizer industry. Since 1931 ADM had developed through research three additional lacquer plasticizers for specific uses and the company followed with active interest any developments in the lacquer industry.

In 1947 the research laboratory became interested in developing a plasticizer for the rapidly growing polyvinyl chloride or "vinyl" resins field.[1] From the company's research there emerged, in 1953, its first vinyl plasticizer, Admex 710, which found extensive applications in such products as raincoats, garden hose, wall coverings, shower curtains, and seat covers. During the period 1955–57 the company introduced five more vinyl plasticizers which were used in floor tile, electrical insulation, wall coverings, infants' wear, foam for cushions, footwear, rainwear, weatherstripping, and molded products.

The Resins and Plastics Division was generating an increasing share of ADM's annual total sales volume and contributing a relatively high percentage of the company's net profit. It had earned a net profit every year since its establishment and, next to the grain division, was the most stable operation in the company. It was, of all the divisions, the heaviest contributor to the company's research program. As much as 4% of its sales dollar was allocated to research activities. It was generally believed that most of the division's future expansion would be based on the results of continuing research.

Early in 1958 the division bought Crosby Aeromarine, a producer of fiberglass boats. "It was not our intention to get into the boat business in a big way," said Mr. Walter Andrews, head of the Plastics Division, "but we were interested in acquiring the molding facilities and manufacturing knowledge of the company so that we could apply it to other shapes and forms." Three years later ADM sold the boat company, stating as its reason that it did not provide the expected market for plastic resins, and that it was a drain on manpower and resources.

THE TERMINAL ELEVATORS

The Archer-Daniels Grain Division was formed in 1927 with the original intention of acquiring elevators to provide storage for flaxseed

---

[1] Polyvinyl chloride is a hard, brittle resin which has little value when used alone. However, when a plasticizer is added and the mixture is processed with heat, the result is a finished, flexible vinyl material which can be made into a variety of calendered, extruded, or molded consumer products.

and soybeans. During the next few years, by new construction and by additions to existing elevators, ADM expanded its elevator capacity at Minneapolis to 14 million bushels. During the next two decades there was considerable expansion into other parts of the country, particularly the Southwest, the Midwest, and the Pacific Northwest. At the start of World War II the grain division had a capacity of 37 million bushels. In 1962 it was operating 29 terminal and subterminal elevators, with a total capacity of 97 million bushels.

The grain division performed two principal operations: Storage of grain owned by others, and the merchandising of grain. As much as 30 million bushels of the elevator capacity had been used to store grain for the Commodity Credit Corporation. About 10 million bushels of the capacity was used by the Commander-Larabee Mills, about 12 million for other processing raw material storage, and most of the balance was used for the division's merchandising activities. These merchandising activities were extensive and were carried on in both national and international markets. Although wheat constituted about 70% of the grain handled, all kinds of grain were handled, including corn, barley, soybeans, oats, and flaxseed. To secure the highest practical grade the elevators were equipped to clean, dry, mix, and blend grains. Customers included flour mills, feed manufacturers, maltsters, and grain exporters. All grains purchased by the company were hedged.

In 1960, to improve its grain procurement facilities throughout the upper Midwest, Archer-Daniels bought the J & O Grain Company, which had 12 grain-buying offices in the North Central states, an office in Chicago, and a seat on the Chicago Board of Trade. Management believed that by this move it would enhance the efficiency of its grain merchandising activities by improving its grain buying and originating facilities. Early in 1962 it purchased the Norris Grain Terminals which operated 11 terminal elevators with 12 million bushels capacity in four midwestern states. The Norris terminals complemented the existing Archer-Daniels terminals.

Mr. Carl Farrington, vice president in charge of the grain division, reported directly to Mr. Thomas Daniels until 1958. About once a week Mr. Farrington called on Thomas Daniels in the president's office to discuss affairs, and occasionally Mr. Daniels phoned him to ask the reason for having taken some market position even though it was hedged. Mr. Farrington said that over the years there had been a trend toward giving him more and more independence due, he believed, to the satisfactory relationship he had established with top management and to the fact that his division was consistently one of the most profitable in the company. The grain division seldom posed problems of a critical nature to the executive committee or the board. During the decade of the 1950's it had earned a higher return on its investment than any other division in the company.

For many years grain storage had been a profitable activity. However, in recent years there had been a reduction in the storage fees paid by the Federal Government. In view of this trend management decided upon a program of reducing the storage part of its business. At the same time it mounted a campaign to intensify its merchandising activities and to expand its exportation of grain with the thought that this would maintain the over-all profitability of the grain division.

THE COMMANDER-LARABEE MILLS

Early in the 1930's Archer-Daniels bought, at a fraction of its face value, the defunct Commander-Larabee Corporation. The purchased company operated 14 mills which had a daily capacity of over 3 million pounds of flour, and owned over 5 million bushels of elevator capacity. Under ADM management the operation became profitable within a few years.

Since the beginning of the century the per capita consumption of flour in the United States in the form of bread had been declining, but total consumption had remained constant. Making up for the decline in bread consumption was an increase in the consumption of flour in what millers called "the more glamorous forms," such as crackers and cookies, spaghetti, macaroni, and noodles. There was a sharp rise in the popularity of macaroni products in their convenience food forms—canned spaghetti, ravioli, canned chicken and noodles, or tuna and noodles, and cheese mixes. All forms of macaroni (paste goods) were made from semolina flour which was milled from durum—a hard, high-protein wheat. Commander-Larabee's durum products department was one of the country's largest producers of semolina flour.

In the 1950's many flour millers and bakers had been converting to bulk flour systems. The bulk system abandoned bags in favor of transportation of flour in bulk trucks. The flour was conveyed within the mills by augers or pneumatic tubes. Bulk handling proved an efficient operation for the small mill whose customers were within trucking range, and it was especially advantageous to the large miller who happened to operate the only mill in a large metropolitan center. Commander-Larabee's mills were in neither situation, and in the middle 1950's their profits began to decline. The division then began to ship bulk flour in railroad cars, and the mills convenient to water transportation shipped sacked flour in barges. Despite this move many long-standing customers switched to mills which had converted to bulk handling at an earlier date.

Except for bulk handling there had been no revolutionary developments in flour milling. No better way of milling wheat flour had been discovered since the age-old method of pressing the grain between rollers. During the past few decades, however, there had been a constant succession of small improvements in processing and refining.

There had been little research in the industry on the basic chemistry of flour, but there had been a good deal of experimentation with the types of wheats and flours which could be used for special baking purposes, such as crackers, cookies, breads of various compositions, and cakes. Commercial bakers tended to produce more specialty breads and pastries, and their changing technology was forcing the milling industry to change its technology. There was more classifying of streams of grain particles and streams of flours, more nutrition tests, and an increased demand on commercial mills to do "prescription milling."

"The Commander-Larabee Division," said Mr. English, the division manager in 1957, "has been one of the most independent divisions in the company. Headquarters furnishes us with money and with borrowing power. We make monthly reports and are always available for consultation, but we consult on only the broadest of policy matters. The home office does not direct our operation. We have generally been profitable, and therefore they feel quite easy about it."

THE ALFALFA DIVISION

By the end of World War II Archer-Daniels' was a leading supplier of protein supplements to the livestock feed industry through its production of soybean oil meal, linseed oil meal, and mill by-products. An important ingredient it did not produce was dehydrated alfalfa meal. The company entered this field in 1951 by purchasing the Small Company of Neodesha, Kansas, the nation's leading producer of alfalfa meal.

The Small Company operated 55 dehydrating plants located in 10 of the plains states. Alfalfa was purchased from farmers within a radius of 10 miles of each mill. It was chopped and blown into wagons at the time it was mown, and it was transported to the mill where it was dehydrated by a hot-air process, ground into meal by hammer-mills, and bagged.

During the years immediately following the acquisition the ADM management reduced the number of Small plants to 36, modernized them to reduce production costs, and undertook to improve the product. The important ingredient in alfalfa meal was vitamin A, which was highly perishable under ordinary storage conditions, and for this reason the Small Company had stored its finished inventory in cold storage plants. The ADM management developed a new method of pelleting the meal which made for easier handling, and reduced the surface exposure subject to vitamin loss. These pellets were then stored in an inert gas in huge storage tanks, each having a capacity of over 10,000 tons, and also in standard concrete tanks of smaller size. This preserved 95% of the vitamin A content against 55% formerly saved.

FLAX FIBER

In 1939, Shreve Archer bought a flax fiber plant in Winona, Minnesota. Archer-Daniels had never owned any flax straw facilities of its own, and it was only a coincidence that the Winona mill which it acquired at this particular time processed straw from flax, and that Archer-Daniels was a major producer of linseed oil made from flaxseed.

Until 1940 the bulk of American cigarette papers were made principally from linen rags that were imported from Europe. When World War II halted foreign imports cigarette makers turned to improving American papers, which had previously been considered inferior. Until 1941 the Winona mill had never processed more than 7,400 tons a year. Under Archer-Daniels' management the method of processing was revised so that, by blending several grades of straw, it was able to produce a tow that made a satisfactory cigarette paper.

As a result production was increased several fold. The entire output of the plant was sold to a paper mill, which in turn sold the paper to the major American tobacco companies.

The Flax Fiber Division plant usually had 100 employees. Forty per cent of its product by weight was in tow, which was sold to the Ecusta Paper Company. The principal other products of the division were shives, the woody portion of the straw, which were sold to a maker of wallboard.

The investment in the fiber mill was carried on the company's books at a nominal figure. The paper mill which purchased most of the output maintained a close business relationship with the fiber mill management. Routine and special reports on the fiber mill operation were mailed to the ADM executives in Minneapolis. Under ADM's management the fiber mill had returned a profit every year. Since the operation was on a cost-plus contract basis, the risk of unprofitable operations was minimized.

CORPORATE CHANGES UNDER JOHN DANIELS

Prior to election as president in 1958 John Daniels had been one of 17 vice presidents. As such he had taken an active part in the reorganization activities and had earned a reputation for being deliberate and methodical. John Daniels was convinced that the narrowing margin between costs and prices and the resulting decline in profits was a trend that could be arrested only by drastic action. Therefore, in June, 1959, he announced the following program:

1. To determine the most efficient form of organization for ADM.
2. To set objectives and policies and communicate them effectively.
3. To appraise each operation for return on investment, and profit outlook.
4. To dispose of operations which did not meet profit standards.

In a second major reorganization within a decade, all operations were consolidated into two domestic groups: an Agricultural Division, and a Chemical Division. (See Exhibits 2, 3, and 4.) To this was added a third group: the Overseas Division. "You might say," said John Daniels, "that Archer-Daniels today is two entirely separate and decentralized businesses—an agricultural processor and a manufacturing chemist. The fact that they exist side by side is important because each strengthens the other."

"In the second step," said Mr. John Daniels, "we set objectives and formulated policies, and communicated them to all management personnel. These spelled out, among other things, areas of concentration, rate of growth, and standard return on investment."

In the third step, Mr. Daniels said, each individual operation was appraised in terms of objectives, taking into account promise of future growth and fitness with the long range objectives of the company. Return on investment studies were made for each profit center and a standard rate of return was established. New ventures were also evaluated on the basis of payout and projected return on investment. As a rule of thumb, any new venture to be considered had ultimately to produce at least 20% return before taxes.

Finally, those operations which were marginal, or showed little promise of future growth, or whose character was not considered to fit the pattern of ADM's business, were disposed of. Included in the various dispositions were several major divisions of the business.

For many years linseed products had been declining in relative volume, while soybean and chemical volume had been increasing. In 1941 linseed products had represented 36.38% of total sales volume; in 1961 it was only 8.92% of the total. In the most dramatic move in its program of dispositions, the company closed its last remaining linseed oil plant in 1961. Linseed oil, the product on which the company had been founded, was henceforth produced for ADM by others under toll contracts.

ADM entered the growing livestock feed business in 1930. Using linseed oil meal, soybean oil meal, and alfalfa meal (the principal ingredients of livestock feeds) which it produced in its other divisions, the company compounded a rounded line of poultry and livestock feeds which it sold under the brand name Archer Booster Feeds. In the early 1960's it was marketing about 100,000 tons of formula feeds a year, which was about 1/3 of 1% of the estimated national consumption of 35 million tons. At that time ADM also was the nation's largest producer of linseed oil meal, soybean oil meal, and alfalfa meal, of which it produced over a million tons a year. The latter it sold to the major livestock feed producers of the country.

"The feed business," said John Daniels, who had once been vice president in charge of the feed division, "had always been treated as an orphan child in our company. We had difficulty deciding to what extent we wanted to be in the business. We were afraid that if we got into it in a big way, we might offend major customers in the raw ingredients end of our business."

In 1960 management disposed of the feed business. "This had been our largest consumer business," said John Daniels, "and, in general, we would rather be suppliers of raw materials." He added that the business had been relatively unprofitable.

When ADM acquired the Commander-Larabee Flour Mills the acquisition included a chain of some 80 small country grain elevators. These elevators, located in the plains states, had acted as wheat collecting stations for the flour mills. When trucks replaced horse transportation, these elevators became obsolete as grain collection stations, and the company disposed of all but 40 of them. These 40 still collected grain, but they were largely converted into farm supply stores which sold a rounded line of seeds, feeds, fertilizers, insecticides, herbicides, fungicides, and light farm tools and equipment. The country elevators had always been profitable. Nevertheless, in the early 1960's, the company sold them. "The elevators," said John Daniels, "were poorly located for the type of grain merchandising we envisioned for the future."

When Archer-Daniels bought the Small Company (which became the Alfalfa Division) the purchase included a machine shop in which Small had designed and manufactured most of the equipment it used to harvest and process alfalfa. The Archer-Daniels management expanded the machine shop operation and placed its services at the disposal of all of the ADM divisions on a competitive basis. The intention was that the machine shop would fabricate and service for all of the company's mills such equipment as hammermills, pneumatic and mechanical conveying systems, dust collectors, and bulk flour and feed bins. In 1960, however, the management sold the machine shop. John Daniels announced that ". . . this operation did not fit into the pattern we had cut out for ADM. . . ."

In the period following World War II chlorophyll became an extremely popular product. Premium quality alfalfa was the richest source of chlorophyll and Archer-Daniels was the world's largest producer of high quality alfalfa meal. Impressed with the possibilities, Archer-Daniels bought, in 1952, two small concerns which produced chlorophyll, and management made plans to expand their capacity. However, the company's 1953 Annual Report stated that the expected demand for chlorophyll had failed to materialize. By the end of that year the company disposed of its chlorophyll plants, asserting that the operation had proved to be unprofitable, and showed no promise.

Some of the foregoing disposals were profitable. However, the company's 1960 report described in detail a $7 million net write-off of assets to cover losses anticipated from the disposal program.

In the same year, 1960, John Daniels announced that $40 million was being budgeted during the next three years for an expansion program. "We will pursue every justifiable growth route in our expansion," said Mr. John Daniels. "At this stage we are utilizing four such routes: Plant construction; plant lease; plant purchase, including acquisition of established businesses; and joint ventures."

In May of 1962, in one of the most spectacular moves in its expansion program, the first processing unit of the company's new Peoria Chemical Center went into production. This plant, which had been under construction for 18 months, was the first unit of a plant complex which would consolidate many of the company's far flung chemical operations. Included in the comprehensive plan was the moving of some plants, the closing of leased plants, and the sale of others. The Peoria Chemical Center had been conceived as a basic plant for industrial and specialty chemicals and plasticizers. It was designed to permit expansion as new products and technologies were developed by Archer-Daniels' research laboratories. The new plant covered 33 acres and consisted of 21 buildings and a 150-unit tank farm for storage of raw materials and finished products. The Peoria plant produced its own hydrogen, nitrogen, inert gas, and compressed air. It pumped and treated its own water from five wells, and had a complete waste purification and disposal system that eliminated pollution of nearby streams. Its network of processing equipment included chemical reactors, distillation units, a molecular still, high pressure splitting columns, automatic deionizers, pressure autoclaves and centrifuges.

exhibit 1
ARCHER-DANIELS-MIDLAND COMPANY

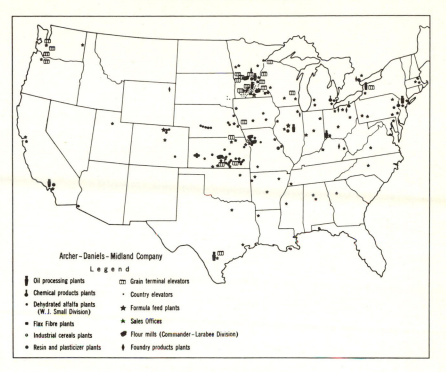

Archer – Daniels – Midland Company

Legend

▮ Oil processing plants	▥ Grain terminal elevators
⬦ Chemical products plants	· Country elevators
Dehydrated alfalfa plants (W. J. Small Division)	★ Formula feed plants
▪ Flax Fibre plants	☆ Sales Offices
○ Industrial cereals plants	◆ Flour mills (Commander–Larabee Division)
● Resin and plasticizer plants	◆ Foundry products plants

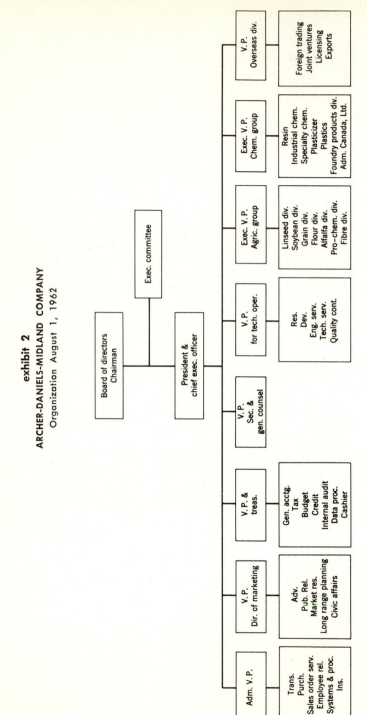

exhibit 2

ARCHER-DANIELS-MIDLAND COMPANY

Organization August 1, 1962

exhibit 3 ARCHER-DANIELS-MIDLANDS COMPANY
Major operating groups

CHEMICAL GROUP

Departments and Products	Principal Industries Served
Foundry products—Core oils, binders and washes, foundry supplies, bentonite	Foundry, oil well drilling, taconite
Industrial chemicals—Fatty acids, hydrogenated oils, sperm and marine oil products, spermaceti, glycerine, pitches	Protective coating, soap, rubber, lubricant, textile, leather, cosmetics, detergent, metal working
Specialty chemicals—Fatty nitrogens, fatty alcohols, olefins, hydrocarbons	Textile, detergent, cosmetics, petroleum, ore separation
Resin—Synthetic resins, resin solutions, specialty resins, esters	Industrial and architectural paints, varnish, ink, adhesives, gum bases
Plastics—Polyester and urethane resins, Freight Liner products	Reinforced plastics, marine, building materials, furniture, transportation
Vinyl plasticizers—Epoxy, polyester and monomeric plasticizers	Vinyl plastics for flooring, upholstery, films, coatings, extrusions, moldings
Coated chemicals—Coated plant food	Lawn, garden, commercial horticulture

Plants

Cleveland, Ohio; Colony, Wyoming; Decatur, Illinois; Elizabeth, New Jersey; Los Angeles, California; Newark, New Jersey; Pensacola, Florida; Peoria, Illinois; Valley Park, Missouri

AGRICULTURAL GROUP

Divisions and Products	Principal Industries Served
Grain—Wheat, barley, corn, grain, sorghums, oats, rye, flaxseed, soybeans	Milling, malting, distilling, oilseed processing, formula feeds
Flour—Wheat flour, durum flours, millfeeds	Bakery, macaroni, formula feeds
Alfalfa—Dehydrated alfalfa	Formula feeds
Linseed—Linseed oil, linseed oil meal	Paint, chemical, formula feeds
Soybean—Soybean oil, soy flours, soybean oil meal, lecithin	Margarine, salad oils, bakery, specialty food, formula feeds, adhesives, paper, paint, chemical and pharmaceutical
Flax fiber—Flax tow, shives	Fine paper, foundry, formula feeds
Prochem—Starches, isolated soy proteins, protein supplements	Paper, building materials, explosives, adhesives, foundry, ore separation, oil well drilling, paint, bakery, specialty foods

Plants

Soybean plants: Decatur, Illinois (2); Mankato, Minnesota; Fredonia, Kansas
Flour mills: Minneapolis, Minnesota (2); N. Kansas City, Missouri; St. Joseph, Missouri
Flax fiber plant: Winona, Minnesota
Prochem plants: Evendale, Ohio; St. Joseph, Missouri

exhibit 3 (continued)

Terminal elevators: Illinois—Chicago, Joliet, Morris, Ottawa, Peoria, Sheldon, Spring Valley; Iowa—Burlington, Council Bluffs; Kansas—Hutchinson, Wellington; Louisiana—*Destrehan; Minnesota—Minneapolis (6), St. Louis Park, St. Paul; Missouri—Clinton, St. Louis; Nebraska—Murray, Omaha; Oregon—Portland; Tennessee—Memphis; Texas—Kenedy; Washington—Tacoma, Vancouver; Wisconsin—Superior
* Under Construction

OVERSEAS DIVISION

Foreign Operations

Wholly-owned subsidiaries: Canada: Archer-Daniels-Midland, Ltd., Toronto—resins, foundry products, chemicals, isolated proteins, industrial cereals; Holland: N. V. Archer-Daniels-Midland, Verkoopmaatschappij, Rotterdam—commodity trading; Panama: Archer-Daniels-Midland, S.A., Panama City—overseas licensing
Affiliates and associates: Belgium: Oleochim, S.A., Brussels—fatty acids and derivatives; Colombia: Productos Quimicos Admicol, S.A., Bogota—resins, plasticizers, foundry products; Germany: Scado-Archer-Daniels GmbH & Co., Rühle—resins, plastics; Holland: Nederlandsche Castoroliefabriek Necof, N.V., Geertruidenberg —paint vehicles, castor oils; Scado-Archer-Daniels, N.V., Zwolle—resins, plastics; Alchemica, N.V., Schoonebeek—phthalic anhydride; Mexico: Productos Api Aba, S.A., Gomez Palacio, Guadalajara, Mexico City—formula feeds; Admex, S.A., Mexico City—resins, plasticizers; Peru: Cia. Ballenera del Norte, S.A., Lima—sperm whaling; Spain: Oleotecnica, S.A., Castro-Urdiales—resins, foundry products, fatty acids, soaps, margarine; Sweden: Scado-Archer-Daniels, A/V, Vallakra—resins, plasticizers; Australia: Jordan Chemical Works (A'sia) Pty., Ltd., Sydney—resins, paint vehicles, foundry products

exhibit 4   **ARCHER-DANIELS-MIDLAND COMPANY**
Organization, operations, plants and affiliations, 1962

PLANTS

ADM operated the following plants in 20 states and Canada. Processing plants were strategically located in raw material producing and importing areas and when practical close to their markets.

29 terminal elevators; total grain storage capacity of approximately 95 million bushels	3 chemical plants
	2 vinyl plasticizer plants
	3 foundry products plants
4 soybean processing plants	2 bentonite mining properties
5 vegetable and marine oil refineries	1 industrial cereals plant
4 flour mills	1 isolated soy protein plant
30 alfalfa dehydrating, blending, and storage plants	1 flax fiber plant
	4 pilot plants
5 resin and plastics plants	

exhibit 4 (continued)

RESEARCH AND SERVICE LABORATORIES

These were located at Minneapolis; Newark, New Jersey; Los Angeles; Wyandotte, Michigan; Cleveland and Evendale, Ohio; and Toronto, Canada, and assisted production and sales by finding new uses for existing materials and developing new products. A new Central Research Laboratory was under construction in suburban Minneapolis.

Pilot plants tested new products under actual plant conditions. Control laboratories were maintained at each major manufacturing plant to assure uniformity of products.

ORGANIZATION

The company's activities were organized into three marketing units—the Agricultural and Chemical Groups and the Overseas Division.

Agricultural Group

The Agricultural Group was engaged in the processing, storing and marketing of agricultural commodities.

1. *Linseed Division.* ADM was a major marketer of linseed oil which was produced from flaxseed and was used in the manufacture of paint, varnishes, and other products. After the linseed oil had been removed from the flaxseed, the remaining linseed oil meal became an excellent source of vegetable protein for livestock feed.

2. *Soybean Division.* ADM was one of the largest processors of soybeans, which yield soybean oil and soybean oil meal. The oil was widely used in the food industry as a salad and cooking oil and in margarine and vegetable shortening. It also had many industrial uses. Lecithin, a derivative of soybean oil, had applications in foods and pharmaceuticals. Soybean oil meal was a valuable livestock and poultry feed ingredient. ADM also was the largest producer of industrial and edible soy flours. Important industrial applications were plywood adhesives, boxboard, wallboard, paints, and pet foods. Edible uses included icings, meringues, baby foods, specialty foods, bread, pastries, and macaroni.

3. *Flour Division.* ADM was one of the largest flour millers in the United States, with a daily wheat flour capacity of 43,500 cwt which included 4,000 cwt semolina used in the manufacture of spaghetti and macaroni. Its products were sold primarily to the baking and macaroni industries.

4. *Grain Division.* One of the nation's largest grain merchandising companies, ADM bought and sold grain in all of the principal markets and carried on export trade throughout the world. It also purchased large amounts of grain for its own milling and processing operations. ADM operated 29 terminal elevators which cleaned, handled, and stored grain. The company's total grain storage capacity was approximately 95 million bushels. A new export terminal was being built at Destrehan, Louisiana.

5. *Dehydrated Alfalfa Division.* ADM was one of the largest producers of high quality dehydrated alfalfa, an important ingredient of many formula

exhibit 4 (continued)

feeds. It operated 30 plants located in Arizona, Colorado, Kansas, Missouri, Nebraska, and Utah.

6. *Flax Fiber Division.* ADM was a major processor of flax straw from which it produced flax fiber and shives. The fiber was used to make cigarette paper, air mail stationery, fine printing papers, and U.S. currency. Shives were used in wallboard, in livestock feeds, as fillers for agricultural fertilizers, and for other industrial purposes.

7. *Industrial Cereals Department.* These products derived from grain sorghums and corn were used in several segments of the paper industry, building materials, dynamite, wallboard adhesives, core binders, ore flotation and oil well drilling mud.

8. *Isolated Protein Department.* Isolated proteins extracted from soybeans were important ingredients of many industrial products. They had basic applications in the coating of fine printing papers, water dispersible paints, adhesives, and building products.

9. *Ardex Department.* Marketed Ardex 550, a protein supplement and milk solids replacement for use in spaghetti and macaroni products, bread, and other foods.

10. *Productos Api-Aba, S.A. ADM,* in partnership with a group of Mexico City industrialists, manufactured and marketed livestock and poultry feeds.

Chemical Group

The Chemical Group manufactured and marketed broad lines of resins for protective coatings and plastics, industrial chemicals, hydrogenated oils used as intermediates by many industries, and vinyl plasticizers for plastics. The group also refined and processed marine oils and sperm whale oil for protective coatings and special industrial uses.

1. *Resin Department.* Marketed more than 300 synthetic resins and resin solutions primarily for the protective coating and printing ink industries. Specialty resins also had been developed and were sold in volume to the chewing gum and adhesives industries. Products included chemically modified oils, alkyd resins, water reducible resins, rosin esters, modified esters, and pure and modified phenolics.

2. *Plastics Department.* Marketed laminating polyester and urethane resins for reinforced plastics, urethane foam and elastomers. These resins had many applications in the production of boats, corrugated plastic sheeting, lining of bulk storage tanks, seat cushions, automobile crash pads and insulation. Also marketed adhesives, calking compounds and protective coatings sold under the Freight Liner trade name for use in repair of freight cars and other equipment.

3. *Industrial Chemicals Department.* Marketed fatty acids, hydrogenated oils, sperm and marine oil products, spermaceti, glycerine and pitches. These had a variety of uses, including paints, soaps, printing inks, rubber, lubricants, textiles, leather, cosmetics, and detergents.

4. *Vinyl Plasticizer Department.* ADM's line of Admex epoxy plasticizers

exhibit 4 (continued)

was used by the plastics industry for such products as garden hose, vinyl fabrics, toys, shower curtains, foot wear, and floor tile.

5. *Specialty Chemicals Department*. Marketed a line of fatty nitrogen chemicals which find their principal applications in fabric softeners, detergents, petroleum additives, corrosion inhibitors, bactericides, printing inks, waterproofing formulations, and ore separation processes. In addition, offered a line of fatty alcohols and derivatives, including fatty olefins and hydrocarbons. Principal markets for alcohols were in detergent and viscosity index improvers for motor oils. Olefins were used as chemical intermediates, while hydrocarbons were used as functional fluids.

6. *Foundry Products Division*. Largest processor of core oils and other additives for the foundry industry, it offered a binder for every type of core practice. Made a line of parting compounds, air setting binders, shell molding and hollow core resins.

7. *Archer-Daniels-Midland (Canada) Ltd.* A wholly owned subsidiary, it processed core oils and binders, resins and special linseed, soybean and marine oil products that were distributed throughout Canada.

Overseas Division

ADM's foreign operations were handled by this division with the exception of the formula feed business in Mexico and diversified businesses in Canada. Overseas activities included export sales, fats and oils trading, licensing, and joint ventures.

1. *Export Sales*. Many ADM products were sold in nearly every country. Sales representatives were located in more than 35 markets abroad.

2. *Foreign Trading Department*. In addition to world-wide trading in vegetable and marine oils, fats, and meals, ADM also purchased commodities on world markets for its own domestic needs.

3. *Licensing*. ADM S.A. Panama, a wholly owned subsidiary of ADM, had entered into a number of licensing agreements on a royalty basis for the manufacture and sale of ADM products in specific foreign markets. Licensing agreements were in effect with the following companies:

> Scado-Archer-Daniels N V, Zwolle, Holland—for plasticizers, phenolic, alkyd, urea and other synthetic resins for the plastics and surface coatings industries.
>
> Scado-Archer-Daniels GmbH, Rühle, Germany—for plasticizers, phenolic, alkyd, urea and other synthetic resins for the plastics and surface coating industries.
>
> Nederlandsche Castoroliefabriek NECOF N V, Geertruidenberg, Holland—NECOF processed castor oil and produces paint vehicles, core binders and foundry specialties, as well as a full range of PVC stabilizers.
>
> Holtz & Willemsen, KG, Krefeld-Uerdingen, Germany—for soybean meals, flours, and specialties.
>
> Azienda Lavorazione Colori Resine e Affini, Milan, Italy (ALCREA)—for plasticizers, plastics, resins, copolymer oils, and foundry binders.

exhibit 4 (continued)

Bunge Corporation, New York City, New York—General exchange of know-how was provided for products manufactured by ADM and the Bunge Group in Argentina, Brazil, Paraguay, Peru, and Uruguay. Specific licensing agreements covered soybean flours, soy protein specialties and lecithin with Bunge's Brazilian associate, Samrig of Porto Alegre.

Jordan Chemical Works (PTY) Ltd., Sydney, Australia—for all types of resins, surface coating oils and materials for the plastic and foundry industries.

4. *Joint Ventures*. ADM had entered into partnership with a number of companies in foreign countries. Licensing agreements also exist with most of them.

Admex, S.A., near Mexico City, Mexico—Admex, S.A. distributed resins and plasticizers manufactured on a toll basis by Quimica Organica S.A.

Oleochim, S.A., Brussels, Belgium—This company operated a plant in Ertvelde which manufactured fatty acids and their derivatives. Oleochim S.A. was owned jointly by ADM and Palmafina, a Belgian company.

Nederlandsche Castoroliefabriek NECOF, N V, Geertruidenberg, Holland—The capital of this company was made up in majority of Netherland interests. ADM owned a small equity. In addition to the products manufactured under ADM S A licenses, NECOF processed linseed and castor oils.

Scado-Archer-Daniels, N V, Zwolle, Holland.

Scado-Archer-Daniels, GmbH, Rühle, Germany—In addition to licensing contracts, ADM had a capital investment in these two companies. They produced resins and plasticizers.

Alchemica, N V, Schoonebee, Holland—Owned by Scado-Archer-Daniels group, this company produced phthalic anhydride, an important raw material for coatings resins.

Scado-Archer-Daniels, Vollakra, Sweden—Owned by the Scado-Archer-Daniels group, this company manufactured resins and plasticizers.

Oleotecnica, S.A., Castro-Urdiales, Spain—Production included margarines, shortenings, soap, detergents, PVC stabilizers, wire drawing compounds, core binders, fatty acids, hydrogenated triglycerides, specialty oils, and other derivatives from fats and oils.

Cia Ballenera del Norte S.A., Lima, Peru (BALNOR)—This company operated a land based whaling station near Paita, Peru. BALNOR was owned generally by an ADM Peruvian subsidiary (Consorcio Peruano del Norte S.A.) and Peruvian interests (Sindicato de Inversiones Industriales S.A.).

Productos Quimicos Admicol, S.A., Bogota, Colombia—Admicol distributes resins, plasticizers and foundry products manufactured for it on a toll basis in Colombia.

exhibit 5   ARCHER-DANIELS-MIDLAND COMPANY
Statements of consolidated earnings and reinvested earnings, Archer-Daniels-Midland
Company and subsidiaries, years ended June 30

Earnings	1962	1961
Income:		
Net sales and other operating income	$245,896,523	$213,115,452
Dividends received and interest earned	426,664	399,178
Profit on sale of securities (less provision for possible loss on investments)	1,136,987	947,468
Other	257,318	288,059
	$247,717,492	$214,750,157
Costs and expenses (including provision for depreciation: 1962—$2,598,740; 1961—$2,497,307):		
Cost of products sold and other operating costs	$221,410,793	$191,228,627
Selling, general and administrative expenses	16,221,615	16,258,606
Interest expense	1,701,882	887,145
Other	165,883	107,581
	$239,500.173	$208.481.959
Earnings before taxes on income	$ 8,217,319	$ 6,268,198
Taxes on income	3,796,051	2,520,468
Net earnings for the year	$ 4,421,268	$ 3,747,730
Reinvested earnings		
Balance at beginning of year	$ 59,781,738	$ 59,209,598
Net earnings for the year	4,421,268	3,747,730
	$ 64,203,006	$ 62,957,328
Deduct cash dividends paid—$2 a share	3,195,208	3,175,590
Reinvested earnings at end of year	$ 61,007,798	$ 59,781,738

exhibit 5 (continued)
Consolidated statement of financial position, Archer-Daniels-Midland Company and subsidiaries, June 30

	1962	*1961*
Current assets:		
Cash	$ 5,326,593	$10,788,460
Receivables	20,662,401	18,294,983
Inventories	50,950,276	43,930,985
Prepaid expenses	1,098,282	1,380,839
Total current assets	$78,037,552	$74,395,267
Current liabilities:		
Notes payable	$11,000,000	$ —
Accounts payable and accrued expenses	15,133,546	23,459,685
Taxes on income	1,547,834	902,058
Anticipated replacement cost of inventories	242,000	344,000
Total current liabilities	$27,923,380	$24,705,743
Net current assets (working capital)	$50,114,172	$49,689,524
Investments and other assets	5,808,222	5,865,900
Property, plant and equipment	58,172,752	38,275,323
Term bank loans	(18,000,000	—
Deferred liabilities and credits	(1,636,452)	(2,404,170)
Net assets	$94,458,694	$91,426,577
Shareholders' equity		
Common stock	$33,382,734	$33,382,734
Additional paid-in capital	595,304	523,960
Reinvested earnings	61,007,798	59,781,738
Common stock in treasury	(527,142)	(2,261,855)
	$94,458,694	$91,426,577

exhibit 5 (continued)

Ten-year summary of financial and operating data (fiscal year ends June 30th) (in thousands of dollars except per share figures and others)

	1961	1960	1959	1958	1957	1956	1955	1954	1953	1952
Financial:										
Working capital	$ 49,690	$ 50,815	$ 50,978	$47,954	$ 46,737	$ 50,645	$ 48,380	$ 50,201	$ 47,610	$ 49,091
Per share	31.26	32.06	31.75	30.15	30.19	31.10	29.38	30.52	28.95	29.85
Inventories	43,931	33,312	39,084	33,320	36,668	41,368	26,506	31,283	39,634	44,164
Net property and plant	38,275	37,774	42,435	43,118	41,535	41,949	42,419	38,392	38,319	37,872
Net additions to property and plant	4,430	4,160	3,298	5,452	3,179	3,082	7,559	3,001	3,314	6,033
Total assets	118,536	107,644	115,226	111,716	108,803	111,550	105,350	105,261	100,146	102,969
Shareholders' equity	91,427	90,708	98,698	95,953	92,914	93,987	92,116	89,591	87,867	88,619
Per share	57.51	57.24	61.48	60.32	60.02	57.71	55.93	54.47	53.42	53.88
Operating:										
Net sales and other operating income	213,115	239,895	239,370	225,812	231,869	221,378	230,793	216,425	227,520	240,189
Payrolls	24,858	27,631	25,634	24,523	22,476	21,421	20,846	19,987	21,127	21,310
Depreciation	2,497	3,233	3,729	3,869	3,593	3,552	2,380	2,928	2,866	2,617
Provision for income taxes	2,520	2,878	5,750	3,607	5,353	6,061	6,317	5,044	2,365	6,368
Total taxes	4,626	5,181	7,840	5,548	7,125	7,842	8,000	6,549	3,784	7,774
Net income	3,748	3,665	5,435	3,904	5,204	5,872	5,750	5,013	3,853	7,413
Per share	2.35	2.31	3.38	2.45	3.36	3.60	3.49	3.05	2.34	4.51
Cash dividends	3,176	3,196	3,206	3,189	3,194	3,270	3,292	3,289	4,605	4,577
Per share	2.00	2.00	2.00	2.00	2.00	2.00	2.00	2.00	2.80	2.80
Retained in business	572	469	2,229	720	2,010	2,602	2,458	1,724	(752)	2,836
Other:										
Outstanding shares (in thousands)	1,590	1,585	1,605	1,591	1,548	1,629	1,647	1,645	1,645	1,645
Number of shareholders	9,196	8,598	7,787	6,837	6,315	6,197	5,449	5,102	4,941	4,764
Number of employees	3,706	4,661	5,038	4,903	4,652	4,674	4,651	4,940	4,930	5,424
Common stock:										
Price Range*	43–33	40–30	49–38	44–29	39–28	41–35	43–32	46–32	52–30	60–48

* Fractions omitted.

23

WESTERN SOAP PRODUCTS —NEWARK DIVISION

Western Soap Products was a large producer of soaps, detergents, edible oil products, and toilet articles such as shaving soap and tooth paste. There were six divisions of the company in separate geographical areas. Each division operated as a profit center and served as a geographical headquarters for all company operations in that area. The division manager was responsible for a variety of functions other than manufacturing, although the production function was considered his primary responsibility. For example, research and development at Newark was under the division manager mainly for administrative purposes, although from time to time the department would engage in specific applied research for the Newark Division. The Newark plant was the only installation other than the headquarters company which had a research laboratory. The sales function was administered by the division manager because the Newark plant provided the products for a nine-state area on the East Coast. Sales promotions, advertising, and national co-ordination were directed from national headquarters in Chicago. The accounting department was mainly concerned with cost accounting, systems, and maintaining records and information for profit center reporting to headquarters. The budgeting department was concerned with forward planning and with the necessary analysis and information gathering to maintain the Newark budget in accordance with company-wide budgeting procedures. The payroll and disbursements department handled the largest payroll in Western's operations, as well as making all cash disbursements associated with plant and division expenditures. All of these departments worked closely with their counterparts in national headquarters in Chicago. The Newark Division had the largest budget in the company, and the product line produced at the plant provided the greatest sales volume of all of Western's divisions.

For a period of ten years there had been a succession of division managers at the Newark Division. Jim Powell, president of Western, reminisced about this period:

We've been through a lot of changes at Newark. John Edwards, who became division manager in the early stages, held things together, but some major projects lagged. To some extent, he pushed what he was interested in, but he was overloaded with 12 department heads reporting to him. (See Exhibit 1.) Edwards was succeeded by Homer Jacks. Under Jacks the plant was expanded and the district was enlarged. The number of departments was increased to 14. (See Exhibit 2.) When the staff requirements became greater because of continued expansion, the number of departments was increased to 16. Under the burden of this type of organization Jacks allowed the organization to be redrafted to place the assistant manager in an operating position to whom six department heads reported directly while the others reported to the division manager. (See Exhibit 3.) The assistant division manager at Western Soap assumed various roles depending on the division manager. Some divisions used the assistant manager as Jacks intended (as indicated in Exhibit 3). Headquarters, however, envisioned the assistant manager's role as the slubstitute for the division manager in his absence.

Division managers made frequent trips to headquarters and were usually involved in many community affairs. The assistant managers frequently represented the Newark Division when the demands by the community became too numerous and time-consuming for the division manager to handle. The assistant manager's role was also considered as an opportunity for management development, and frequently promising executives were assigned this position as part of rotational training. In all cases, however, assistant division managers were considered as *assistants to* the division manager. Continued growth of Western Soap and the Newark Division put further strain on the division manager, since his office was a channel for a constant stream of communications from the headquarters office to the various departments of the plant. The pressure was partly relieved by direct communications between headquarters staff and plant staff on technical matters affecting individual departments. However, because of his position as the administrative and line manager of the Newark Division, Homer Jacks felt it was necessary to be kept informed of all matters pertaining to operations.

In an effort to relieve himself of continued pressures of meeting with

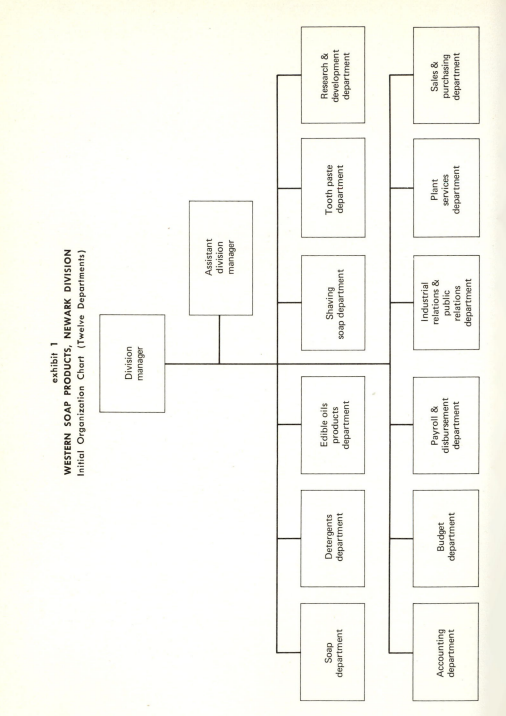

exhibit 1

WESTERN SOAP PRODUCTS, NEWARK DIVISION

Initial Organization Chart (Twelve Departments)

632

exhibit 2

WESTERN SOAP PRODUCTS, NEWARK DIVISION

Organization Chart under Jacks (Fourteen Departments)

exhibit 3
WESTERN SOAP PRODUCTS, NEWARK DIVISION
Organization Chart under Jacks

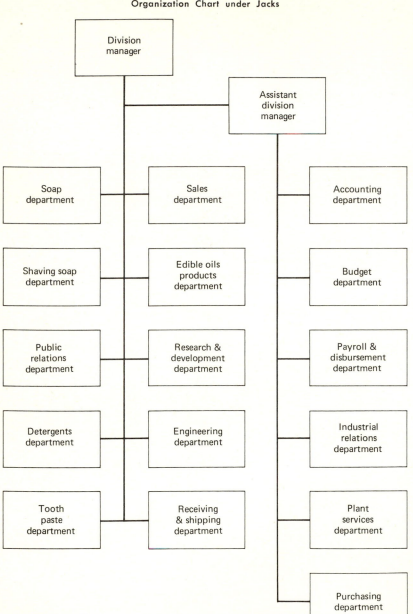

department heads Jacks consolidated some activities to simplify the organization. For example, accounting, budgeting, and payroll were placed under one man. This arrangement worked so well that Jacks later combined industrial relations and plant services. (See Exhibit 4.)

These changes helped, but didn't cure. Jacks found that he couldn't push many decisions down to department heads, which he wanted to do. Too many decisions were being thrown up to him, in part because he had a lot of new people who hadn't been seasoned in their jobs— also in part because a lot of projects needed co-ordination with numerous departments. Jacks just had to take first things first, and some department heads saw very little of him.

When Jacks moved up to a position at company headquarters, he was succeeded by Bob Stevens, who, as assistant division manager, had long felt that the organization needed an overhaul. He feared that he would be smothered by administrative detail while important projects would languish. As the new division manager, Bob Stevens discussed his ideas with management at the home office as well as with members of his own team. Briefly, Stevens thought that three administrative co-ordinators ought to be introduced into the line so that each administrator would have five or six department heads reporting to him. These three would take a big load off the shoulders of the division manager. (See Exhibit 5.) While there were mixed reactions to Stevens' proposal, he decided to give the system a try. Some of the views expressed in discussions about the problem were as follows:

CLIFF EDSON (*chief engineer*): Our present setup, with 13 men reporting to the manager, hasn't been working out. Some department heads hardly ever get a chance to see the boss.

ART JOHNSON (*vice president of industrial relations*): We could try introducing another level of management, but I'm not happy with that suggestion. I think the industrial relations department head of the division should be able to go directly to Bob Stevens on important matters.

BOB STEVENS: Your industrial relations man could still come to my office if he couldn't get satisfaction from his administrative co-ordinator. Of course, I would expect most problems to be ironed out at the administrative co-ordinator's level. If that didn't happen, there'd be no sense having an administrative co-ordinator.

ART JOHNSON: Will the theory really work out in practice? You say a department head can see the division manager, but won't a department head be reluctant to go topside and run the chance of alienating the administrative co-ordinator? Either the administrative co-ordinator is line or staff, and if he's line, he's going to be the boss. You are actually pushing department

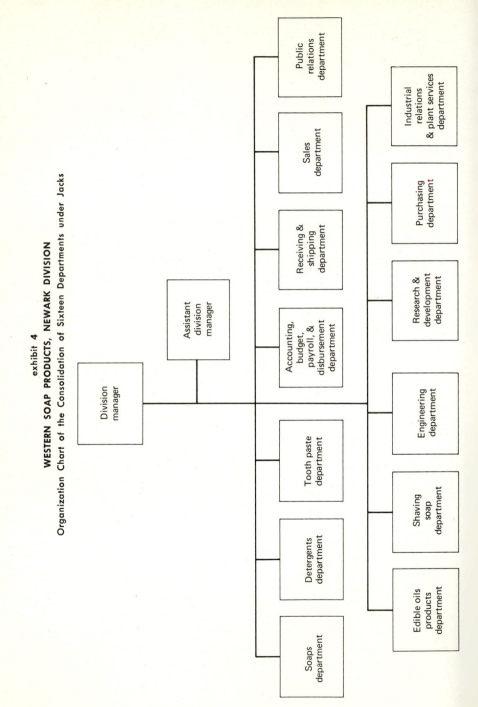

exhibit 4
WESTERN SOAP PRODUCTS, NEWARK DIVISION
Organization Chart of the Consolidation of Sixteen Departments under Jacks

exhibit 5
WESTERN SOAP PRODUCTS, NEWARK DIVISION
Organization Chart under Stevens

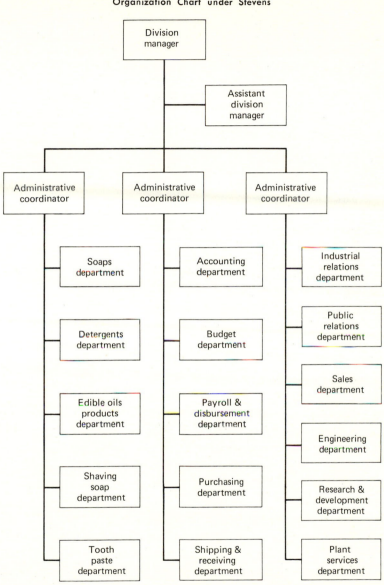

heads farther down the line with one more level in the channel of communication. Why not push more decisions down to department heads?

BOB STEVENS: Department heads already have the authority to clear with each
other on programs affecting more than one department. The number of
decisions that must be made after this preliminary clearance has been
taken care of is still so large that some screening is needed to relieve me.
These administrative co-ordinators will get to know my way of doing
things. I'm going to work very closely with them; we'll meet several times
a week. They'll be in a position to tell department heads whether to go
ahead, whether to drop a project, or whether a meeting with me is
necessary.

SAM SMITHERS (*vice president of production*): These co-ordinators will be
walking a tightrope. We're interested in decentralizing authority, but
the administrative co-ordinator will be tempted to keep the reins in his
hands. How can they keep from making decisions that we'd like the
department heads to make?

BOB STEVENS: At present the department heads are relatively new. If you
throw problems at them, they won't know what to do. They'll do nothing.
Some guidance is needed, but I can't handle them all.

Ultimately, the proposal for three administrative co-ordinators was
approved by top management, and the organization at the Newark
Division was changed accordingly. Stevens held a number of meetings
with department heads and the three administrative co-ordinators.
One of the most frequent questions that came up was this one: "If we
as department heads still have the right to take some matters up to
Mr. Stevens, how do we know what to bring up?" To this question, the
answer was as follows: "We can't spell out all the situations. The best
we can do is to give a general guide. Whatever you feel you can handle
yourself, go ahead and take care of it. All our department heads have
now had long experience in the company. It isn't like when many of
us were new. I think you'll have no trouble making decisions."

After a year of trial, Stevens made a study of how his organization
was working. On the plus side of the ledger, he felt that he had been
relieved of a lot of administrative detail. He felt department heads
had been doing a good job in planning a variety of projects. On the
minus side was the realization that too many plans were not being
translated into action. The administrative co-ordinators were sometimes holding up decisions. Instead of counseling, advising, and giving
a go-ahead or passing a tough decision up the line, they sometimes
acted as bottlenecks. If this continued, the initiative of department
heads would be killed. Stevens wondered whether he was responsible

for this result. Had he been too critical of his administrative co-ordinators, so that they were reluctant to make decisions? Perhaps some change in the organizational relationship would be necessary. Stevens noted that the administrative co-ordinators were presenting and explaining programs coming up from department heads. Very often the administrative co-ordinator was not as familiar with the details as the men who had worked them out. A number of times an administrative co-ordinator would make a poor showing because he lacked this knowledge. Perhaps the bottleneck was caused in part by the belief that an administrative co-ordinator should be an expert on all matters relating to his area of interest.

There seemed to be two alternatives that might help the situation. The administrative co-ordinators were in the main channel of communication and authority. Possibly the present arrangement put too much pressure on an administrative co-ordinator; he would find it almost impossible to stay in the background. If administrative co-ordinators were placed in an advisory position with direct lines of communication going to department heads, then the relationship between department heads and administrative co-ordinators would develop into a more consultative arrangement. At any rate, Stevens was concerned with the role the administrative co-ordinator was playing. One other explanation for the administrative co-ordinator's dominant role occurred to Stevens. He had picked men who had come up the ladder within one of the departments they'd supervised. Possibly from habit the administrative co-ordinators were getting into too much detail.

24

BLAW-KNOX

In 1961 the management of Blaw-Knox considered that they had finally integrated their numerous subsidiaries and divisions into a single corporate unit. "But," said Mr. Snyder, president of the company and chairman of the board, "only the initial objectives of our program have been accomplished so far. We've correlated the divisions, and succeeded in getting the people at the divisional and plant level to think as one company. We've re-asserted the staff functions and put new life into them. The big job now is to upgrade our profit picture. We're working at that by hammering away at costs and weeding out the poor earners in our product lines. We also need more long-range planning. We've got to learn to think years ahead. We've also got to be thinking about bringing up our younger people so that eventually we have better executive personnel."

Mr. Cordes Snyder Jr. was elected president of Blaw-Knox in 1951 following a working capital crisis which had resulted from the independent action of the company's subsidiaries and division managers. Mr. Snyder started his career with Blaw-Knox as a shop metallurgist and through a series of quick promotions became manager of a division which he operated profitably for nine years. Feeling that his opportunities with Blaw-Knox were limited, he left to become president of Continental Foundry and Machine Company. Later he accepted a position as vice president of Koppers Company. In 1951 Mr. Snyder was offered the presidency of Blaw-Knox. Knowing that the company needed, as he put it, "a helluva lot of attention," he deliberated a full month before accepting, considering what had to be done and discreetly exploring the management's attitude toward him, especially certain people whose cooperation he felt he would need. When he did accept, it was with the tacit understanding that he was to plan and execute a drastic and far-reaching reorganization of the entire company.

CORPORATE DEVELOPMENT

Blaw-Knox had its origins in a sewer contracting business started in 1906 by Jacob Blaw based on the use of collapsible steel forms. A few years later Luther Knox pioneered a business which produced pressed and welded foundry equipment. These businesses combined to form the Blaw-Knox Company in 1917. The operations of the newly formed company were consolidated in a new plant built at Pittsburgh. During the ensuing decades Blaw-Knox, by merger and purchases, entered into numerous other industries and added many new products to the company's line: foundry equipment, road-paving machinery, steel towers, gas cleaners, steel buildings, high-alloy castings, rolls for the metals industry, cast-steel plant equipment, and rolling mills and machinery. In addition, Blaw-Knox developed within its existing facilities such products as clamshell buckets, open steel grating for flooring, and numerous other steel and foundry products.

During World War II Blaw-Knox became an important producer of heavy armament. Its most significant wartime activity, however, was the establishment of a standard design for synthetic rubber plants for the Defense Plant Corporation. From this experience the company established one of its major divisions, the Chemical Plants Division.

Moses Lehman, the first president of Blaw-Knox, was a prosperous Pittsburgh shoe merchant who had supplied the newly founded company with financing and given it the benefit of his business acumen. He was followed by his son Albert, who was president until 1934. Three years of interim officeholders followed until William Witherow, who had been a board member for four years, was elected president. His administration was characterized by extreme, decentralization, diversification, and independent operation of the subsidiaries and divisions. During this era the function of headquarters was described as that of a holding company in which the divisional vice presidents acted with the independence of subsidiaries, and the president limited his activities to listening to their reports at the monthly meetings of the board of directors.

As Blaw-Knox had expanded through the years into new product lines and new industries, each unit added was allowed to operate as it did prior to acquisition. Since most acquisitions involved products which were different from anything the company had previously produced, individual plant operations were continued with little change and with a minimum of direction from the home office. The personnel acquired were also retained, including the executives. It was assumed that they had proven their competence by successful performance and they brought with them strong sales followings. The Blaw-Knox management saw no reason to change their method of operation as long as it was profitable.

The board of directors consisted of seventeen members, fourteen of whom were division managers, staff executives, or presidents of subsidiary companies, and the others represented banking connections. When Mr. Witherow was president, he was said to have looked upon his executive function as that of a coordinator, leaving the major decisions to be made by division managers, whom he saw only at board meetings. Each division manager acted as though he was the head of an independent company, and he made his own plans with the assurance that there would be little interference from the corporate executives at Pittsburgh. Operating authority rested with the division managers and the board usually approved whatever recommendations they made. "Controls were loose," said a division manager. "As long as you were in a profit position, nobody bothered you very much." The division managers, however, felt themselves to be in competition with each other, on a rivalry basis, and they measured their success by their sales volume, the spectacular contracts they captured, and the profits of their divisional operation.

After coming into the Blaw-Knox organization each unit continued to handle its own sales, production, industrial relations, and research. There was no central coordination of staff functions. The executives in the Pittsburgh office who carried on the staff activities had no authority over their corresponding staff functions at the division level, and the division staff personnel answered to the vice president in charge of their division.

The controller of the company, who had been a company lawyer, assumed the controller function because of the necessity for someone at headquarters to consolidate division reports. He did not exercise authority over division accounting staffs which operated independently and without uniformity. Accounting was on a completed contract basis, which meant that it was not taken into sales figures until the contract was completed. This was criticized as distorting sales figures, for it occasionally happened that several large contracts might be 90% completed at statement date, but would nevertheless be entirely excluded from sales figures.

Purchasing was done independently by each division. Each division had its own credit manager who was responsible to the division manager for credit granted and for the policing of accounts receivable. Accounts payable were also treated as a divisional responsibility, with each division setting its own standards and procedures.

Eleven different design groups were scattered throughout the company and these were concerned primarily with adjusting products to the needs of individual customers. Research efforts were entirely at the division level and each project was considered separately rather than as part of a company-wide program. Only two divisions had laboratory facilities for exploring new fields, and their efforts varied, requiring little more than one professional man per year.

The legal department reviewed all of the company's contracts, including sales and union contracts. While the substance of the contracts was determined by each division, there was criticism to the effect that business tended to be done on a legal basis.

Personal salesmanship had become a company tradition. Division heads cultivated the patronage of the top executives of the steel companies and other large organizations that presented a potential market for Blaw-Knox products. Much of the business was done on a reciprocity basis. Sales personnel were mainly engineers who directed most of their efforts toward obtaining big and spectacular contracts to satisfy the prevailing thinking among division managers that large and special orders were the key to a profitable operation.

The treasurer, who had been in office for many years, had accepted the pattern of the treasury department as it had developed. Elderly and due to retire soon, he showed no inclination to disturb the system which, until 1951, had functioned well enough. There was no coordination of the company's over-all finances, and the treasurer's staff performed such duties as compiling company reports for statement and tax purposes. The director of safety reported to the treasurer because his efforts had a direct effect upon insurance premiums, which were paid by the treasury department.

Financial planning was done at the division level with each manager arranging for his own requirements. Plant expenditures were not formally budgeted. Each division manager simply discussed his major projects with other division managers at the monthly board meetings. It was this practice which precipitated the change of management which took place in 1951. That summer a number of unusually large contracts had suddenly increased the company's bank credit requirements from the usual $10 million to $18 million. The banks finally consented to the full amount of the credit but imposed restrictions upon any further consolidations, acquisitions, and capital expenditures. Following this, those Blaw-Knox directors who represented its banks persuaded the board to seek new leadership for the company, an action which culminated in the election of Cordes Snyder in 1951. When Mr. Snyder became president, Mr. Witherow assumed the position of chairman of the board. At this date the Blaw-Knox organization consisted of the parent company and three principal subsidiary companies which operated ten plants through nine divisions and had foreign subsidiaries in London and Paris. The structure of the company had never been reduced to an organization chart.

REORGANIZATION UNDER CORDES SNYDER

By the time Mr. Snyder took office he had decided that, while his reorganization promised to be thorough and far-reaching, it would be a gradual and slow-moving process which might take years to accomplish. He stated that several reasons led him to this decision: he did not wish to alarm Blaw-Knox industrial customers by setting off an internal upheaval; he did not wish to antagonize the skilled employees, who were loyal to their managers and old systems; and finally, he wished to retain as many division managers as he could, for he valued their talents and wished to enlist their help.

One of Mr. Snyder's early moves was to change the size of the board of directors. The board had seventeen members, several of whom were in their seventies and five of whom were division managers. Mr. Snyder was convinced that the deliberations of a small board of younger men who were not company executives would be more constructive. "I want somebody who can beat me over the back," he said, and within a year he induced the board to reduce its membership to eleven. Three of those who left the board were division managers who had been requested to resign their directorships.

Mr. Snyder also merged the company into a single corporate unit. It had consisted of four corporations that operated eleven different businesses.

Mr. Snyder outlined the following objectives for the unified company:

> To establish a more centralized management system by a program of integration which would serve to effect better control.
>
> To make an engineering study of manufacturing facilities and management organization, looking to a strengthening of both.
>
> To make a marketing survey to determine which markets the company was in the best position to serve profitably.
>
> To make a technical study to serve as a guide in establishing a research and product development division or department, and a corresponding program.
>
> To prepare for increased participation in the national road-building program, and in the construction of public works.
>
> To increase the company's penetration and impact on the chemical and food processing markets. The aim would be to become a factor of substance in this field, not merely a fringe participant, and strive to make a real contribution.
>
> To lower production costs and increase the profit ratio. Any segment of the business not responding to upgrading and offering no promise of profitability was to be considered a subject for elimination.

During his first several years in office Mr. Snyder gradually proceeded to place controls upon the divisions. "My objective," he said, "was to re-establish a certain amount of centralized control and co-ordination of divisional activities while still remaining essentially a decentralized operation. This meant re-emphasizing certain staff functions, such as sales, production, industrial relations, accounting and finance, and making them uniform throughout the company. At the same time I wanted to allow the divisions to retain most of their independence."

Mr. Snyder replaced the staff executives in the finance, legal, and accounting departments, and he created four new staff offices: sales, production, development and research, and industrial relations. Most of the new staff executives were brought in from outside the company and were younger men, typically in their early forties. Each of them was made a vice president of the company, a point which Mr. Snyder considered to be of importance, for he felt that this would give them equal status in dealing with division managers.

To replace the treasurer, early in 1952, Mr. Snyder chose George Langreth, who had achieved a reputation for financial reorganizations. Reflecting the new status to be accorded the office, Mr. Langreth was elected vice president of finance and treasurer. In 1953 William Rodgers, who had previously conducted a successful business of his own, was brought into the company to fill the newly created position of vice president and general sales manager. Howard Winterson came into the company as vice president of industrial relations, and George Kopetz was promoted to another newly created position—vice president of production. In 1953 Mr. Snyder brought into the company a former commander of naval ordnance, Captain Eugene Rook. In 1955 Capt. Rook was appointed vice president of fabricated products operations. In 1956 Dr. D. F. Jurgensen was brought into the company as vice president of development and research, and in 1957 J. Sterling Davis joined the company as controller. (See Organization Chart, Exhibit 1.)

An early move under Mr. Snyder was the compilation of an organization manual, the writing of job descriptions, and a manual of procedures. Since the new formal organization structure was something new that many of the old executives would be meeting for the first time, Mr. Snyder set up a Control Section to coordinate the activities between the divisions and between the line and staff executives. Mr. David Tomer, an engineer who had extensive experience in organizational work, was placed in charge of the control section. Mr. Snyder brought Mr. Tomer, whom he had known at Koppers, into the company. Mr. Tomer was to counsel and advise executives on the initial phases of the new coordinated practices. He was given the title of assistant to the president.

In the course of changing operating procedures, Mr. Snyder took away from the division managers two authorities: the first was their authority over financial appropriations in two areas—capital additions and improvements in plant and equipment, and research. Requests for appropriations which were over $1,000 were now required to be submitted to an appropriations committee which analyzed them and either submitted them for approval to the operating committee or held them. The operating committee consisted of the heads of all the divisions and the staff executives. Major appropriations took a further step to the board of directors. All appropriations were coordinated by the financial executive of the company. In addition, control over the employment of management personnel and the setting of their salaries was taken away from the division managers and placed under the supervision of a salary committee which worked out a management compensation plan. All new personnel came under the plan, and the salaries and positions of all current personnel were systematically reviewed and realigned.

In his contacts with management personnel, Mr. Snyder constantly emphasized the importance of using the guidance of the staff people.

PRODUCT LINES AND PRODUCT DEVELOPMENT

In 1951 the list of products produced by the company was the largest in its history. (See Exhibit 2.) Diversification had become a well-established tradition within the company and division managers took pride in the widespread array of products and dissimilarity of the product lines turned out under the Blaw-Knox name. Mr. Snyder looked upon this as an item of concern that deserved his special attention.

"Long ago," he said, "we achieved a record for quantity in the matter of identifying products with our name. I am not implying criticism of past management policy in creating this complex picture. Definite gains were achieved by putting our eggs into many baskets. But this diversified activity led to a pride in mere numbers of products. I am proud of our product mix and happy that we are diversified, but there is a danger in depending too much on the variety of our activities. It is my judgment that we are at a crossroad in this company's history where the emphasis must be placed on the performance of each product line, rather than on pride in quantity, especially if the quantity does not add to our quality and profit performance. We may have to conclude that some of the company's present products no longer fit the future picture. We must be sure that we aren't keeping any 'sacred cows.' If any product no longer meets the full needs of our customer, or cannot be produced efficiently enough to return a profit, we must acknowledge that fact and agree that it is time to do something about it."

In examining the widespread array of sizes and models within each product line, Mr. Snyder noted that a single item like clamshell

exhibit 1

BLAW-KNOX COMPANY

Organization Chart, September 6, 1957

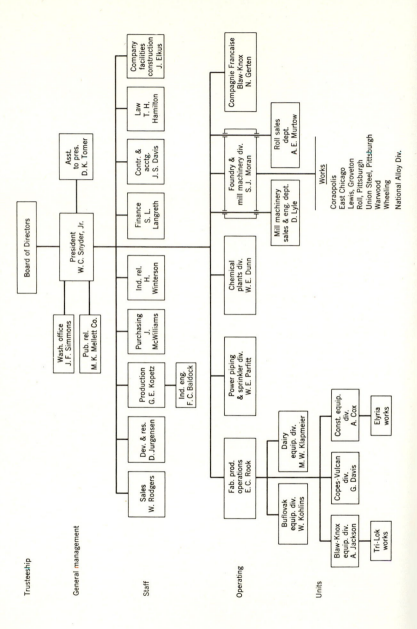

Trusteeship

Board of Directors

General management

Asst. to pres. D. K. Tomer

President W. C. Snyder, Jr.

Wash. office J. F. Simmons

Pub. rel. M. K. Mellett Co.

Finance S. L. Langreth

Contr. & acctg. J. S. Davis

Law T. H. Hamilton

Company facilities construction J. Elkus

Staff

Sales W. Rodgers

Dev. & res. D. Jurgensen

Production G. E. Kopetz

Ind. eng. F. C. Baldock

Purchasing J. McWilliams

Ind. rel. H. Winterson

Operating

Fab. prod. operations E. C. Rook

Power piping & sprinkler div. W. E. Parfitt

Chemical plants div. W. E. Dunn

Foundry & mill machinery div. S. J. Moran

Compagnie Francaise Blaw-Knox N. Gerten

Buflovak equip. div. W. Kohlins

Dairy equip. div. M. W. Klapmeier

Const. equip. div. A. Cox

Mill machinery sales & eng. dept. D. Lyle

Roll sales dept. A. E. Murtow

Blaw-Knox equip. div. A. Jackson

Copes-Vulcan div. G. Davis

Units

Tri-Lok works

Elyria works

Works

Coraopolis
East Chicago
Lewis, Groveton
Roll, Pittsburgh
Union Steel, Pittsburgh
Warwood
Wheeling
National Alloy Div.

648

buckets might include over a hundred models and sizes; a cement-mixing truck might be equipped with a costly device for adjusting the pouring chute; and if the stock sizes in the evaporator line included 45-gallon and 50-gallon models, and a customer tendered an order specifying that he required a 47-gallon model, he would probably be accommodated.

Mr. Snyder emphasized the need for standardization. "We should not only establish stable items," he said, "but we should develop

exhibit 2 **BLAW-KNOX COMPANY**
Divisions and subsidiary companies and partial list of products in 1951

Blaw-Knox Company
  Blaw-Knox Division
      (Blawnox, Pa.)
    Concrete finishing machines
    Concrete paving spreaders
    Clamshell buckets
    Truck mixers
    Concrete buckets
    Subgraders
    Steel bins
    Concrete-mixing plants
    Open steel flooring
    Transmission towers
    Radio and television towers
    Gas cleaners
    Steel forms for concrete
      construction
    Chemical and process equipment
    Water-cooled furnace equipment
      for high-temperature furnaces
  Buflovak Equipment Division
      (Buffalo, N.Y.)
    Vacuum rotary dryers
    Double-drum dryers
    Evaporators
    Pilot-plant equipment
    Gray iron castings
    Miscellaneous equipment for the
      food processing and chemical
      industries
  Lewis Foundry and Machine
      Division (Groveton, Pa.)

    Rolling mills and auxiliary machinery for rolling ferrous and nonferrous metals
    Rolls for steel and nonferrous rolling mills
  National Alloy Steel Division
      (Blawnox, Pa.)
    Alloy steel castings for highest resistance to extreme temperatures, abrasion and corrosion
  Pittsburgh Rolls Division
      (Pittsburgh, Pa.)
    Rolls for steel and nonferrous rolling mills
  Union Steel Castings Division
      (Pittsburgh, Pa.)
    Heavy alloy steel castings for general industrial use
Blaw-Knox Construction Co.
  Power Piping Division
      (Pittsburgh, Pa.)
    Prefabricated piping systems for high pressures and temperatures
  Blaw-Knox Sprinkler Division
      (Pittsburgh, Pa.)
    Automatic sprinkler systems, fog nozzles, water curtains and deluge systems for fire protection
  Chemical Plants Division
      (Pittsburgh, Pa.)

exhibit **2** (continued)

Complete plants for the chemical and process industries

The Foote Company, Inc.
(Nunda, N.Y.)
Black top road pavers
Concrete road pavers

Buflovak Midwest Co.
Buflovak Midwest Co. Division
(Mora, Minn.)
Specialized equipment for the dairy industry including dry milk elevators and flakers, pulverizers, dryers, evaporators, hotwells, etc.

Foreign Affiliates
Blaw-Knox Limited
(London, England)
Compagnie Française Blaw-Knox
(Paris, France)

standard sizes, standard designs, standard construction, standard sequences of repetitive production, and even standard costs. We should also develop standardization of parts and components, so that small inventories will serve wide categories of products on a company-wide basis."

In keeping with this aim, a group called the Fabricated Products Operations was organized. Any product which required burning or riveting, cutting or welding, or the fitting or assembling of components into finished products was considered a fabricated product. Fabricated products production had previously been carried on in six unrelated divisions, each of which produced several lines of fabricated products. One division, the Blaw-Knox Division, produced some 15 major product lines, most of them unrelated. The objective of the new department was to coordinate fabricated products operations and screen them for profitability. A production coordinator scheduled all orders and analyzed every product for its prospective profit. As a result, a number of lines were integrated, some lines were dropped, and emphasis was placed on those lines which were considered to have growth or profit potential.

The management of Blaw-Knox looked upon the over-all product mix which it had accumulated over the years as diversified strength against recessions. Management was aware that most of its products were capital goods and especially sensitive to fluctuation in the general economy, but it pointed out that short recessions would not affect business until one to three years later, except in new orders taken and backlog figures. Management felt that over the long run the completed-contract basis of accounting tended to level out cyclical fluctuations.

In the latter part of 1955 Mr. Snyder arranged to buy Continental Foundry and Machine Company, a large rival steel mill equipment producer with a more complete line of rolling mill machinery and facilities. It was a major acquisition, doubling the company's foundry production, which already represented the largest single segment of its sales.

In earlier years sales to steel makers had represented half of Blaw-Knox's volume, but experience with the cyclical nature of the steel business during the depression years had persuaded the Blaw-Knox management to lessen their dependence on steel and expand in other directions. In 1951 the Foundry and Mill Division contributed only 36% of B-K sales, and by 1955 the percentage was down to 25%. By that date, however, Mr. Snyder's management had come to look upon the steel industry as having growth possibilities, and it was this thinking that resulted in the purchase of Continental in November, 1955.

Ten years previously, in 1945, Mr. Snyder had been president of Continental for one year and consequently was well acquainted with the company's situation. Blaw-Knox foundry plants had been concentrated in the Pittsburgh area, and in Continental's huge East Chicago Works Mr. Snyder saw an opportunity for a strategic advance into the growing midwestern market. Continental also had the facilities to make a full range of rolling mill equipment, including the larger sizes. "During the war Blaw-Knox built a big mill for Kaiser," Mr. Snyder recalled, "but the castings were too big for our shops and we had to subcontract them." Continental also had ample facilities for making the largest size castings, which Blaw-Knox could not produce. "Now we can spread our production, and manufacture equipment at the plant nearest the customer," said Mr. Snyder, "and eventually there are certain to be economies through plant consolidations."

Blaw-Knox emerged from the Continental acquisition as the nation's second largest supplier of mill equipment. In 1956 the Blaw-Knox share represented one-third of the market available to the three largest producers and Mr. Snyder expected B-K's share to increase. Early in 1959 Mr. Snyder made the arrangements for Blaw-Knox to purchase the assets of the Aetna-Standard Engineering Company, which manufactured seamless and buttweld pipe mills, cold drawing equipment, and related auxiliaries for sheet, tinplate, and other flat mill products supplemental to Blaw-Knox rolling mill machinery and other lines.

Nearly $12 million was spent for this acquisition to acquire annual sales of approximately $20 million.

In 1960 total sales of all Blaw-Knox products reached $193 million, an all-time high, and of this amount nearly one-third came from the Continental and Aetna operations.

Mr. Snyder did not think that the steel industry's cyclical nature would pose a problem for Blaw-Knox for some years to come. "We are witnessing the most creative era of steel's development and growth," he said. "There is every reason to believe that for the next several years steel will continue to be one of the economy's fastest growing segments. The emphasis so far is on additional ingot tonnage. But eventually the industry is going to need new blooming and slabbing mill facilities, together with additional plate and structural mills to meet the increasing demand for finished products. Beyond that, in the coming years, there should be capacity for these steel products in new regions."

MARKETING AND SALES

It was intended in the reorganization that Mr. Rodgers, the new general sales manager, would establish broad general sales policies that would apply throughout the company. He was to assist the division sales managers in their appraisal of markets and in interpreting the performance of certain segments of their markets. This was to be accomplished from the feedback information he received from large accounts of Blaw-Knox and from other industry sources. From this information he was to advise and assist the divisions in establishing new areas for sales and to aid the divisions in the selection of sales personnel and in the selection of distributors and agents. Although it was intended that Mr. Rodgers would act mainly in an advisory capacity as a staff executive, the function proved to be flexible and at times Mr. Rodgers participated actively in helping the divisions obtain new customers.

During the postwar period a sizable portion of the company's volume each year had been comprised of government work. In 1954 defense work contributed 58% of net income. In 1955 less than 20% of net income derived from that source and a strong effort was made to further decrease defense work. By 1957 it contributed only about 10% to net income. Management was of the opinion that long-term defense contracts were not likely to be switched abruptly to other companies and therefore would become a stabilizing influence.

In the summer of 1959 the company entered into fixed price contracts with the U.S. Government covering construction of Atlas missile launching complexes and the manufacture of related equipment. Due to changes in specifications and mistakes in the original bids on the construction contracts, actual costs greatly exceeded anticipated costs. The total missile contract amounted to $31.9 million, with total direct costs amounting to $40.5 million, or nearly $8.6 million greater than contract receipts. Late in 1959 the company initiated and obtained some relief action with the Government. Other relief action was not obtained until 1961 when the Government agreed to an adjustment of nearly $7.9 million. The company adjusted its annual profit and loss statements by charging excess costs of $4.5 million in 1959, $4.1 million in 1960, and credits of $7.9 million in 1961, causing corresponding adjustments in the profit picture for each year.

Early in Mr. Snyder's administration he established annual company-wide sales conferences. "I am not surprised," said Mr. Snyder, addressing a sales conference, "that some of you have admitted that you learned about some of our products for the first time at these meetings. Many of our customers, too, identify us with just one line of goods. Very few people associate the name Blaw-Knox with all of the activities in which we are engaged. I guess we have to live with this matter of being unable to achieve an over-all product identity in people's minds. But there is a way of helping it. Know your company and its products. Know the big picture—and serve the *total* opportunity."

Salesmen were urged, regardless of division affiliation and primary responsibility, to interest themselves in uncovering sales leads for all products. They were urged to tip each other off to new sales possibilities and where such cooperative effort resulted in new business, they were assured that credit would be given to "the beagle who nosed it out."

The familiar Blaw-Knox diamond set against a rectangular background was adopted under Mr. Snyder as the official company emblem to provide a distinctive designation for the company and its products. On those products of acquired concerns which still used their original names, emphasis was gradually shifted to the Blaw-Knox name, and it was intended that eventually all products would bear the Blaw-Knox name alone.

It was Mr. Snyder's intention to continue defense work on a reduced scale and to keep the company in a position to operate on a much larger defense basis in the event of a national emergency. "We have no intention," said Mr. Snyder, "of becoming another General Dynamics." In 1961 less than 15% was government work.

The 1961 annual report indicated that income from foreign sales in 1961 amounted to $219,000 as contrasted to $275,000 the previous year. In commenting on the decline in foreign income, Mr. Snyder explained that the decrease was due principally to a reduction in the dividends received from Blaw-Knox Limited. In his letter to the stockholders in April, 1962, Mr. Snyder called attention to the problem of overseas operations and the probable growing importance of such operations. He stated:

> The rapid growth and increasing potency of overseas trading blocks, the most noted being the European Common Market, dictates continuing reappraisal and realignment of your company's foreign operations and marketing activities. Overseas business for Blaw-Knox has increased steadily with volume of export sales ranking second only to those of our largest domestic market area, namely the iron and steel industry. Maintaining this position in markets abroad, under the developing competitive circumstances, will probably require expansion in manufacturing arrangements as well as in marketing procedures.

Foreign subsidiaries and associates of Blaw-Knox included Blaw-Knox Chemical Engineering Company, Limited, London, England; Blaw-Knox Limited, London, England; Copes Regulators Limited, London, England; Compagnie Française Blaw-Knox, Paris, France; and Blawknox Japan Company Limited, Tokyo, Japan.

RESEARCH AND DEVELOPMENT

In 1954 Mr. Snyder engaged Arthur D. Little Company, industrial research consultants, to make a comprehensive survey of the research effort of Blaw-Knox. As a result of this survey Dr. Jurgensen was appointed staff vice president of research and development to build up and coordinate research programs in the divisions.

Dr. Jurgensen immediately established a central research and development group. He explained to the division managers that the function of this group was to impart an over-all understanding of the research activities to the operating units, emphasizing that the talents, abilities, and knowledge in one group were to be made available to all other groups so that units might mutually reinforce each other.

In reviewing the tradition of spontaneous initiative and imagination that had given Blaw-Knox an impressive record of invention, Dr. Jurgensen said:

> Industrial research is no longer a case where one fertile mind sits, thinks, and works in some obscure garret. It's a team effort—it's the combined, incessant pounding of many minds: the director of research; the research engineers; the technical experts in various fields; the designers and engineering department; the sales manager and his organization; the marketing and sales promotion specialists; the industrial engineers; the manufacturing people; the finance organization.

A central task force was organized to review projects and impart an over-all knowledge of research to the operating divisions. The group consisted of Dr. Jurgensen, a metallurgist, a mechanical engineer, and a chemical engineer. Projects reviewed by the committee included a pilot plant for gravel benefication; the design and construction of antennae structures for radio telescopes for astronomical and astralphysical exploration; an aluminum foil mill which would yield a thinner sheet in a width 50% greater than ever before accomplished at double the previous maximum speed; a basic research project on "temper brittleness" in metals; a pilot plant for disposing of waste pickle liquor; and a new technique for computing pipe stresses by electronic computer.

PRODUCTION AND PLANTS

"One of my most trying problems," said Mr. Snyder, "was to dilute the historical concept of full autonomy at the divisional level." This, he found, was specially true of plants whose managements had long been accustomed to thinking in terms of their own operations. Mr. Snyder was convinced that maximum efficiency in production could be achieved only by coordination of the production operations in all plants through a staff executive in charge of all production. Expecting to meet vigorous opposition from plant managers whose independence would be curbed, Mr. Snyder sought a man of strong convictions for the office. On January 1, 1956, George Kopetz was elected to the newly created post of vice president of production. Kopetz, who had been vice president in charge of the chemical plants division, had not had extensive manufacturing experience but Mr. Snyder thought that he had shown strong managerial judgment.

For the foundry and mill machinery group, a central planning department was established in the headquarters office in Pittsburgh. This department allocated jobs to plants, worked out the backlog of orders according to machine loads and plant capacities, and also allocated the work geographically. Over-all plant loads were assigned to plants from Pittsburgh, but particular details, such as machine assignments and scheduling, were left to the plant management. In other divisions this was done informally.

Purchases of components, supplies, and small quantities of steel, which had previously been made independently by each plant, were consolidated in the Pittsburgh office under the vice president of purchasing. Purchases of basic raw materials and large quantities of steel had always been made centrally. Inventories were also controlled. The over-all aim was to keep inventories at one-sixth of the sales volume of each line.

Kopetz was convinced that proper planning and scheduling were the most effective means of saving money and maintaining a stable work force. He believed that a good standard cost system was the only effective way to show up variances in such factors of production as inefficient machinery, defective materials, and bottlenecks. "My job, in a nutshell," said Mr. Kopetz, "is to see to it that the work gets done on time, and on budget."

The foundry and mill machinery plant managers generally went along with the new system without objection. They found that the central scheduling made for flexibility. By proper scheduling a large rush order could now be worked on simultaneously by several plants, making it possible to meet the customer's requirements. It made it possible also to take the large contracts which no single division previously could have accepted. Under the new system, however, these plant managers knew less about the orders they were producing. They knew the estimated costs they were expected to meet, but selling prices were deliberately withheld from the plants.

New technical developments turned up by one plant were thoroughly worked out and tested by that plant and then passed along to all other plants. The foundry plant managers and the fabricated products managers had meetings once a month to exchange technical information.

In 1955 Blaw-Knox invested $3.5 million in the construction of a new plant at Mattoon, Illinois, to consolidate all of the company's production of road-building equipment. This was the company's first new construction since Blaw-Knox had built its original facilities at Blawnox, Pennsylvania, in 1919. The remainder of its plants were those it had acquired from merged concerns.

When Blaw-Knox bought the All-Purpose Spreader Company of Elyria, Ohio, in 1954, it was already producing similar equipment at Nunda, New York, in the Foote Construction Division, and at Blawnox in the Blaw-Knox Equipment Division. In the new plant at Mattoon all production of road-building machinery was combined under one roof and the organizations of the three operations were combined in a newly-formed Construction Equipment Division.

INDUSTRIAL RELATIONS

Prior to 1951 each division of the company handled its own labor relations and each plant made its own labor settlements, with the result that the unions played one division against another, and also played Blaw-Knox against some of its steel customers which also contracted with the same unions. The latter situation was not only a source of embarrassment but at times lost customer good will.

When Mr. Howard Winterson was brought into the company as vice president of industrial relations in 1952, Mr. Snyder charged him with setting up a department which would operate effectively as a staff function. Under Mr. Winterson's direction a centralized industrial relations department was established which handled all union contract negotiations, including the authorization of all arbitration settlements. In addition, the department introduced a company-wide wage and salary administration plan in which all jobs were evaluated and the positions of all current personnel were systematically reviewed and realigned. A strict policy of promotion from within was inaugurated. Division managers were no longer free to hire new key management personnel or to make promotions. The addition of personnel, transfers, and promotions within the management group were screened by the office of Mr. Winterson, and division managers were expected to follow his recommendations unless they had serious objections. Mr.

Winterson was pleased with the results of the new promotion policy. "During one year," he said, "out of 214 promotions in the management group, 194 were from within the company. This is approximately nine out of ten."

FINANCE

When Mr. Langreth was appointed vice president of finance in 1952, working capital shortage was a critical problem. Mr. Langreth instituted a methodical program of financial controls aimed at increasing cash balances and reducing bank loans, inventories, and accounts payable.

All bills, which previously had been paid independently by divisions, were now paid by the central finance office in Pittsburgh. Accounts receivable were also centralized and supervised from the office of the treasurer. Commitments for all funds, including capital expenditures, were made subject to review and approval of the treasurer.

There was a tradition in the company of growth from retained earnings, rather than from the sale of capital stock, and Mr. Langreth intended to abide by the tradition. The company's stock had been selling at high prices and Mr. Langreth did not wish to generate a group of unhappy stockholders by selling them stock at the current high prices. To retain funds in the business, stock dividends were declared in all years from 1953 to 1961, except 1955.

In an effort to acquire substantial funds to carry out Mr. Snyder's planned capital expansion program to modernize the company's plants, and to take advantage of favorable conditions in the lending market, Mr. Langreth arranged to obtain a 3.5%, $15 million loan with a maturity date of 1975. Under the loan agreement $10 million was borrowed at the end of 1954, and the balance was required to be borrowed in 1955. Temporarily the borrowed funds were invested in U.S. Government securities. In 1954, when the loan agreement was executed, management believed that the funds acquired would be adequate to carry to completion all expansion plans then contemplated. One year later, in an attempt to further improve working capital and to accommodate new expansion plans, new lines of credit totaling $20 million were arranged with the Mellon Trust Company —$10 million for financing defense business and $10 million for commercial requirements. By the end of the year more than $7 million was borrowed for defense work. Despite sizable acquisitions, through the period 1955–1962 funds were acquired from retained earnings. Long-term debt in this period decreased from $21 million to $15.4 million. (See Exhibit 3.)

ACCOUNTING AND CONTROL

In April of 1957 Mr. J. Sterling Davis came to Blaw-Knox at the invitation of Mr. Snyder to fill the position of controller which had been vacant since the former controller had retired in mid-1955. For 30 years Mr. Davis had been an accounting and financial executive in utilities and in industry. He came to Blaw-Knox with the understanding that he was to revamp and unify the accounting procedures of the entire company.

"My primary job," said Mr. Davis, "is to collect data and report the facts of the operations to management in such form that management can make proper decisions. These facts must be reported quickly and must include past, present, and future operations. Decisions can be good only if they are based on accurate facts, and the accounting must be geared to collect those facts. Management cannot produce better decisions than the quality of the information it receives."

One of the first moves made by Mr. Davis was to establish what he called "true responsibility accounting," whereby results, whether good or bad, might be assessed against the responsible individual. "Whenever a profit went sour," said Mr. Davis, "we got two answers: the sales department claimed the manufacturing costs were too high, and the production department said that the sales department gave the material away." Under the previous accounting system, management could not be sure who was right.

Mr. Davis proceeded to install a standard cost system directed toward enabling management to measure individual responsibility. Manufacturing operations were judged on the extent of variance from standard cost and sales efforts were judged on the amount of profit above standard cost. The new system started in 1957 was still in the process of adjustment and correction in 1961.

Mr. Davis also established a system of budgetary controls. Previously sales forecasts had been based upon past performance. The emphasis was now shifted to sales potential. In 1956, before Mr. Davis was connected with the company, Blaw-Knox elected to adopt the last-in, first-out method of valuation of prime material inventories so that current costs would be matched against current revenues.

Accounting records were, as far as practical, reduced to standard forms. Invoicing had previously been done by each division independently, some of them using their divisional name rather than the name of the company. A standard invoice form featuring the name Blaw-Knox was now designed for use throughout the company. Company-wide policies were established governing the granting of credit, the collection of receivables and the payment of accounts payable. Accounts receivable and accounts payable were adapted to machine accounting methods so that data might be sorted and summarized to produce more detailed statistics.

MANAGEMENT CHANGES

In a message to management personnel on May 28, 1959, Mr. Snyder outlined his plans for strengthening the company organization through further integration of the company's operating units and through the establishment of group management and the realignment of top management positions of these groups. Effective June 1, 1959, all operating units were consolidated into two groups—the Foundry and Mill Machinery Group, and the Fabricating, Engineering and Construction Group—with the newly acquired Aetna-Standard Engineering Company listed as a Division and operating as a third group. Mr. A. E. Murton was appointed vice president and general manager of the Foundry and Mill Group; Mr. Kopetz, vice president and general manager of the Fabricated, Engineering and Construction Group, and Mr. Coffey, vice president and general manager of the Aetna-Standard Division.

On September 28, 1959, Dr. Jurgensen, who had headed the company's research and development department for three years, was named vice president and general manager of the Construction Equipment Division headquartered in Mattoon, Illinois. With this change, responsibility for research and development was transferred to the individual operating units. (See Exhibit 4.)

In a further effort to streamline the organization Mr. Snyder, on December 27, 1960, appointed Mr. Winterson to a newly established position of vice president-administration, with general supervision of the executive staff accounting, administrative and productive services, industrial relations and personnel, law, marketing, purchasing, and traffic departments.

In mid-July, 1961, when Mr. Kopetz, who had been vice president and general manager of the Fabricated Products and the Engineering and Construction Services Group, resigned, the direction of these two groups was added to Mr. Winterson's responsibilities.

Early in 1962 Mr. George Langreth died suddenly and the position of treasurer and vice president of finance remained vacant for more than six months. In discussing a replacement Mr. Tomer, assistant to the president, remarked, "Mr. Snyder believes in promoting from within where competent people are available. However the company does not have enough men trained to take over." Consequently, the company hired Mr. Charles Strange to fill the position.

In March, 1962, Mr. Snyder established a new central staff department—the marketing services department—and hired Mr. Frank Farnum, formerly of the Raytheon Company of Lexington, Massachusetts, as director. (See Organization Chart, Exhibit 4.) Duties of the newly established department included the conducting of studies to determine the most profitable markets for the company's products, the need for redesign of products and product lines to meet customer requirements. These functions were formerly performed by the staff sales department headed by Mr. Rodgers.

In discussing these changes Mr. Tomer remarked that the company had a good management training program in operation and that 26 college graduates were currently undergoing training. He also emphasized that most supervisory and management positions had been filled by qualified personnel promoted from within the company.

In summing up the operations, Mr. Tomer went on to say that, "As the company matures under the leadership of Mr. Snyder the managers become more adept at carrying out their functions according to Mr. Snyder's wishes. Thus, all our managers today have much more of the Blaw-Knox philosophy as espoused by Mr. Snyder than they had ten years ago."

exhibit 3 BLAW-KNOX COMPANY

Comparative statistics (in thousands of dollars, except share figures)

	1961	%	1960	%	1959	%	1958	%	1957	%
Operations:										
Net sales of products and services	$174,518	100.0	$192,810	100.0	$161,295	100.0	$167,709	100.0	$182,663	100.0
Costs and operating expenses	170,774	97.8	180,558	93.5	144,881	89.5	152,155	90.7	167,780	91.9
Operating income	$ 3,744	2.2	$ 12,252	6.5	$ 16,414	10.2	$ 15,554	9.3	$ 14,883	8.1
Missile contracts—excess costs (recoveries)	(7,892)	(4.5)	4,101	2.6	4,500	2.8	—	—	—	—
Non-operating income	1,741	1.0	1,580	.8	1,424	.8	1,248	0.6	1,279	0.7
Interest expense	775	.04	880	.4	742	.4	820	0.4	1,055	0.6
Income before taxes	$ 12,602	7.2	$ 8,851	4.6	$ 12,596	7.8	$ 15,982	9.5	$ 15,107	8.2
Provision for taxes on income and renegotiation	7,150	4.1	4,604	2.4	6,765	4.2	9,050	5.4	8,100	4.4
Net earnings	$ 5,452	3.1	$ 4,247	2.2	$ 5,831	3.6	$ 6,932	4.1	$ 7,907*	4.3
Depreciation and amortization included in costs	3,498	2.0	3,623	1.9	3,156	1.9	2,510	1.5	2,520	1.4
Repairs and maintenance included in costs	4,171	2.4	4,421	2.3	4,188	2.6	3,618	2.1	4,610	2.5

exhibit 3 (continued)

Financial position:

Cash and equivalent	$ 20,480	$ 12,537	$ 9,662	$ 25,278	$ 12,108
Total current assets	72,470	75,958	63,461	68,799	74,082
Total current liabilities	29,756	36,057	24,731	21,766	32,037
Net current assets (working capital)	42,714	39,901	38,730	47,033	42,045
Total assets	112,810	117,313	105,399	99,725	106,047
Long-term debt	15,450	16,625	17,800	18,725	19,650
Capital stock	19,768	19,211	18,671	18,056	17,546
Other capital	10,885	9,658	8,785	6,777	5,608
Retained earnings	36,951	35,762	35,412	34,401	31,206
Total capitalization	83,054	81,256	80,668	77,959	74,010

Property, plant and equipment:

Before depreciation and amortization	$ 66,630	$ 65,084	$ 63,709	$ 50,626	$ 49,812
After depreciation and amortization	38,427	39,391	40,586	29,888	30,926
Expenditures for property, plant and equipment	2,749	2,575	14,013	1,563	1,755

Dividends:

Amount paid in cash	$ 2,696	$ 2,620	$ 2,543	$ 2,196	$ 2,021
Per share outstanding at time of declaration	1.40	1.40	1.40	1.25	1.20
Stock dividend—percent	2½%	2½%	2½%	2½%	4%

* Includes non-recurring credit of $900,000.

exhibit 3 (continued)

Operations:

	1956	%	1955	%	1954	%	1953	%	1952	%
Net sales of products and services	$167,009	100.0	$109,161	100.0	$101,128	100.0	$120,068	100.0	$99,941	100.0
Costs and operating expenses	151,791	90.9	103,493	94.8	92,250	91.2	104,068	86.7	88,086	88.1
Operating income	$ 15,218	9.1	$ 5,668	5.2	$ 8,878	8.8	$ 16,000	13.3	$ 11,855	11.9
Missile contracts—Excess costs (recoveries)	—	—	—	—	—	—	—	—	—	—
Non-operating income	676	0.4	635	0.6	584	0.5	523	0.4	537	0.5
Interest expense	1,028	0.6	439	0.4	28	0.0	290	0.2	460	0.5
Income before taxes	$ 14,866	8.9	$ 5,864	5.4	$ 9,434	9.3	$ 16,233	13.5	$ 11,932	11.9
Provision for taxes on income and renegotiation	7,900	4.7	3,420	3.2	5,310	5.2	12,095	10.1	7,743	7.7
Net earnings	$ 6,966	4.2	$ 2,444	2.2	$ 4,124	4.1	$ 4,138	3.4	$ 4,189	4.2
Depreciation and amortization included in costs	2,601	1.5	1,975	1.8	1,691	1.6	1,474	1.2	1,363	1.3
Repairs and maintenance included in costs	4,730	2.8	2,198	2.0	2,100	2.1	2,705	2.7	2,631	2.7

exhibit 3 (continued)

Financial position:

Cash and equivalent	$ 12,768	$ 12,635	$ 24,471	$ 14,183	$ 9,928
Total current assets	71,323	56,046	50,126	46,120	45,615
Total current liabilities	35,754	26,282	16,077	26,123	28,613
Net current assets (working capital)	35,569	29,764	34,049	19,997	17,002
Total assets	104,571	89,872	68,105	63,986	64,032
Long-term debt	20,575	21,000	10,000	—	—
Capital stock	16,761	15,694	15,694	14,468	14,115
Other capital	4,474	2,010	2,010	784	537
Retained earnings	27,007	24,885	24,324	22,611	20,767
Total capitalization	68,817	63,589	52,028	37,863	35,419

Property, plant and equipment:

Before depreciation and amortization	$ 48,699	$ 47,715	$ 31,228	$ 29,375	$ 28,799
After depreciation and amortization	31,796	32,725	17,258	16,719	17,090
Expenditures for property, plant and equipment	3,580	17,597	2,269	1,162	1,088

Dividends:

Amount paid in cash	$ 1,891	$ 1,883	$ 1,831	$ 1,694	$ 1,764
Per share outstanding at time of declaration	1.20	1.20	1.20	1.20	1.25
Stock dividend—percent	5%	—	1½%	2½%	—

exhibit 4
BLAW-KNOX COMPANY
Organization Chart, April 2, 1962

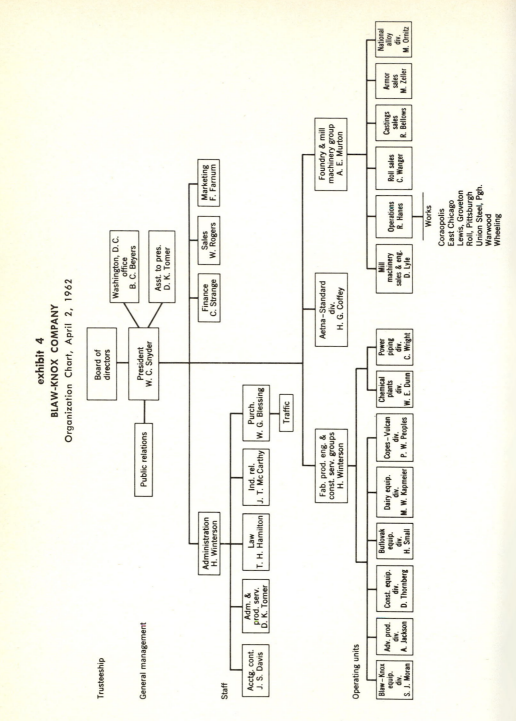

Trusteeship

General management

Staff

Operating units

Board of directors

President
W. C. Snyder

Public relations

Washington, D. C. office
B. C. Beyers

Asst. to pres.
D. K. Tomer

Finance
C. Strange

Sales
W. Rogers

Marketing
F. Farnum

Administration
H. Winterson

Acctg. cont.
J. S. Davis

Adm. & prod. serv.
D. K. Tomer

Law
T. H. Hamilton

Ind. rel.
J. T. McCarthy

Purch.
W. G. Blessing

Traffic

Fab. prod. eng. & const. serv. groups
H. Winterson

Aetna–Standard div.
H. G. Coffey

Foundry & mill machinery group
A. E. Murton

Blaw–Knox equip. div.
S. J. Moran

Adv. prod. div.
A. Jackson

Const. equip. div.
D. Thornberg

Buflovak equip. div.
H. Small

Dairy equip. div.
M. W. Kapmeier

Copes–Vulcan div.
P. W. Peoples

Chemical plants div.
W. E. Dunn

Power piping div.
C. Wright

Mill machinery sales & eng.
D. Lyle

Operations
R. Hanes

Roll sales
C. Wanger

Castings sales
R. Bellows

Armor sales
M. Zeller

National alloy div.
M. Ornitz

Works

Coraopolis
East Chicago
Lewis, Groveton
Roll, Pittsburgh
Union Steel, Pgh.
Warwood
Wheeling

666

exhibit 5 **BLAW-KNOX COMPANY**
Divisions and subsidiary companies and partial list of products in 1962

OPERATING GROUPS	MAJOR PRODUCTS BY INDUSTRY CATEGORIES

OPERATING GROUPS

Foundry, mill machinery and metal processing equipment
  Continental
  Lewis
  National Alloy
  Rolls
  Union
  Medart
  Aetna-Standard
  Plant Locations
  Blawnox, Pa.
  Coraopolis, Pa.
  East Chicago, Ind.
  Groveton, Pa.
  Pittsburgh, Pa.—2
  Wheeling, W. Va.—2
  Ellwood City, Pa.
  Warren, Ohio
Fabricated products
  Blaw-Knox Equipment
  Buflovak Equipment
  Copes-Vulcan
  Construction Equipment
  Dairy Equipment
  Plant Locations
  Blawnox, Pa.
  Buffalo, N. Y.
  Erie, Pa.
  Mattoon, Ill.
  Mora, Minn.
Engineering and construction services
  Chemical Plants
  Power Piping
  Engineering Locations
  Pittsburgh, Pa.—2
  Plant Locations
  Pittsburgh, Pa.
  Jackson, Miss.

MAJOR PRODUCTS BY INDUSTRY CATEGORIES

Metal processing and fabricating
  Rolling mills and accessory equipment, shears, tables, lathes, and straighteners
  Pipe and tube mills, cold drawing equipment; annealing, tinning, and galvanizing lines; sheet and strip finishing equipment
  Iron and steel rolls
  Water-cooled doors and frames, valves, charging boxes, ladles, slag pots, dolomite machines; heavy steel, armor, and high alloy castings
Highway, public works, and general construction
  Bituminous and concrete pavers, spreaders, finishers, subgraders, road forms, truck-mixers, and aggregate concrete mixing equipment
  Heavy forms for subways, tunnels, dams; clamshell buckets
Chemical, petroleum, and food process
  Design, procurement, and erection of plants for the chemical, food, gas, petroleum, petrochemical, nuclear, and other process industries
  Design and fabrication of evaporators, dryers, welded pressure vessels, digesters, mixers, and milk and food processing equipment
Public utilities and general
  Fabrication and erection of pressure piping and pipe hangers
  Metal grating, running boards, stairs, and walks
  Communication and transmission towers, radio telescopes, tracking and scatter antennas
  Steam boiler accessories and gas cleaners

exhibit 5 (continued)

FOREIGN INVESTMENTS

Blaw Knox Limited, London, England

Blaw Knox Chemical Engineering Company, Limited, London, England

Copes Regulators Limited, London, England

Compagnie Française Blaw-Knox, Paris, France

Blawknox Japan Company Limited, Tokyo, Japan

exhibit 6 **BLAW-KNOX COMPANY**
Statement of operation and retained earnings year ended December 31, 1961

	1961	*1960*
Revenues:		
Sales of products and services	$174,517,781	$192,809,582
Other income	1,741,188	1,579,653
	$176,258,969	$194,389,235
Costs and expenses:		
Cost of products and services	$141,954,566	$148,929,820
Selling and administrative	17,545,409	20,211,591
Repairs and maintenance	4,170,680	4,421,322
Depreciation and amortization	3,498,410	3,622,668
Retirement plans	3,605,557	3,371,549
Interest	774,779	880,039
	$171,549,401	$181,436,989
	$ 4,709,568	$ 12,952,246
Recoveries in 1961 of costs in excess of contract amounts—missile contracts Excess Costs in 1960 and 1959	(7,892,058)	4,100,828
	$ 12,601,626	$ 8,851,418
Taxes on income:		
Federal	6,708,000	4,278,000
Pennsylvania	442,000	326,000
	$ 7,150,000	$ 4,604,000
Net income for the year	$ 5,451,626	$ 4,247,418
Retained earnings at beginning of year	35,762,537	35,411,594
	$ 41,214,163	$ 39,659,012
Dividends:		
Cash—$1.40 per share	2,696,187	2,619,622
Stock—2½% each year		
1961—48,215 shares at $32.50	1,566,988	—
1960—46,857 shares at $27.25	—	1,276,853
1959—45,540 shares at $50.00	—	—
	$ 4,263,175	$ 3,896,475
Retained earnings at end of year	$ 36,950,988	$ 35,762,537

exhibit 6 (continued)
Statement of financial position December 31, 1961

	1961	1960
Current assets:		
Cash	$14,522,376	$12,536,858
U. S. Treasury bills	5,958,075	—
Receivables, less estimated doubtful accounts	28,715,738	36,331,879
Manufacturing inventories	20,779,191	21,970,621
Contracts in progress—costs less billings	1,541,089	4,456,855
Prepaid expenses	953,607	661,359
Total current assets	$72,470,076	$75,957,572
Current liabilities:		
Note payable to bank	$ —	$ 6,000,000
Accounts payable	11,128,620	16,443,550
Salaries, wages and other employee compensation	4,262,703	3,777,592
Federal taxes on income	4,714,268	2,093,515
Long-term debt payable within one year	1,175,000	1,175,000
Other current liabilities	8,475,061	6,567,162
Total current liabilities	$29,755,652	$36,056,819
Working capital	$42,714,424	$39,900,753
Property, plant and equipment (net)	38,427,417	39,390,936
Investment in foreign affiliates and other assets	1,912,624	1,964,742
Total assets less current liabilities	$83,054,465	$81,256,431
Long-term debt	15,450,000	16,625,000
Excess of assets over liabilities—stockholders' equity	$67,604,465	$64,631,431
Stockholders' equity:		
Capital stock—authorized 3,000,000 shares, $10 par value—issued 1,976,788 and 1,921,133 shares	$19,767,880	$19,211,330
Other capital	10,885,597	9,657,564
Retained earnings, excluding amounts transferred to other capital accounts	36,950,988	35,762,537
Total stockholders' equity	$67,604,465	$64,631,431

25

WESTERN LUMBER AND BUILDING SUPPLY CORPORATION (A)

Western Lumber and Building Supply Corporation, of Spokane, Washington, known throughout the building industry as "Western Lumber," was incorporated in 1906 as successor to several West Coast lumbering companies which operated in the northwestern United States. Spokane, which was centrally located for the company's 1906 timbering operations, continued to be the company's headquarters though in later years the company had plants and sales offices throughout the United States, Canada, and Europe.

For decades Western Lumber's activities consisted of felling timber in the Pacific Northwest and milling it into basic construction lumber, which was shipped to the growing cities of the East and Middle West. As wood technology became more sophisticated, Western extended its product line. Its first major fabrication undertaking was the manufacture of plywood, initially for sheathing to replace boards in building construction and later for furniture manufacturers. As the market for simple construction lumber became highly competitive, Western Lumber gave priority to the more refined plywood business, which yielded higher margins and lent itself to innovations. It added other fabricated building products to its line and gradually withdrew from the vast timbering operations of its early years, phased out many of its Pacific Coast sawmills, and built a number of plants in the United States, Canada, and Europe which manufactured high-quality fabricated building materials and certain industrial specialty items.

Western had been one of the first producers of prefinished hardwood floorings. Success in this field led it into the production of parquet flooring, and later it developed a rounded line of resilient floor coverings. Western Lumber achieved a reputation for the high quality of its floor coverings and became a leader in that field. It also produced a limited line of carpetings.

When the plywood business began to suffer from overcapacity, Western emphasized its production of fine veneers for furniture making. When furniture-makers took to producing their own veneers, Western shifted to making natural wood veneer prefinished wall sheathing, which was profitable at first but later suffered from intense competition, especially from cheap imports, such as Philippine mahogany. In 1971 Western Lumber's wall paneling line was limited to ultra-high-quality veneers, such as oak, birch, cherry, pecan, and walnut, and natural wood prefinished boards of the same woods, all of which were high-priced and catered to a very small segment of the market. Western did not produce woods which went into these products; it bought them from other lumbering companies. In 1971 Western Lumber's wall covering line accounted for a relatively minor portion of its total sales, and the company's promotional efforts were concentrated on its other product lines.

The establishment of the Ceilings Division was a natural sequel to the production of wall and floor coverings. The company's first ceiling tiles were made from pressed wood chips; later its tiles were made from lighter wood pulp, sugar cane, and other plant fibers. These materials were largely supplanted by mineral-fiber boards, which came into demand because of the increased tightening of fireproofing standards in building codes. Western initially bought mineral wool from mineral wool-blowing companies, but it later established its own plants. The company was an early entrant into the field of suspended ceilings, in which the ceiling tiles were laid without direct attachment into metal channels suspended from the ceiling.

Western Lumber had been an early supplier of sawdust as an insulating material for icehouses. The widespread acceptance of home refrigeration during the 1920's coincided with Western's expanding position in the field of linoleum, which used cork as a base. Cork was superior to wood as an insulant, and Western Lumber soon became a major importer of cork and a leading supplier of insulants to the refrigeration industry. Both wood and cork were later displaced by rubber compounds and plastic insulants, and Western moved to these materials as cork usage waned. When cork was at peak popularity, Western bought plantations and cork-processing factories in Spain, which it still operated in 1971.

Western Lumber's Precision Products Division was a result of its cork activities. Among the early products Western developed to use cork were rollers employed in paper processing and printing machinery. These high-precision rolls were first made from densely pressed ground cork, and later from rubber and ground cork in combination and from numerous other materials. Western also developed rubber composition beltings for use in light machinery where the application demanded precision and reliability in performance. In both of these lines Western achieved an eminent reputation for the quality of its product and for its service. Both these lines were high-margin lines in which the company had relatively few competitors. The major rubber companies had attempted to compete with Western in industrial products, but their effort was short-lived; they had been unable to match the service Western gave its industrial customers.

POSITION OF THE COMPANY

In 1971 Western Lumber produced and sold five main product lines: ceilings, wall coverings, floor coverings, insulation, and composition rollers and belts. It also made some bottle and flask stoppers (closures). During its history the company had ventured into the production of composition roofing, wallboard, and corrugated board for cartons, but in each of these fields it had failed to gain a foothold and had withdrawn. It had never attempted to achieve a full line of building products. It did not fabricate anything from metal; even the metal frames used in its suspended ceilings were manufactured by others.

Western Lumber owned 27 plants in the United States and 9 domestic subsidiaries, which were engaged in sales and distribution activities. Eight foreign subsidiaries operated 12 plants and 19 sales offices in Canada, Europe, and Australia. Western Lumber had total assets of almost $479 million, and 19,166 stockholders had an equity of over $374 million. It had 27,775 employees and a sales volume of $627 million. It had hundreds of items in its product lines, and it was heavily engaged in research to add new items to its line. Its international activities were substantial, but it had not, as yet, tried to enter all foreign markets. In 1971 it attempted to increase its penetration in certain selected foreign market areas. (See Exhibit 1.)

exhibit 1

Organization Chart of Western Lumber and Supply Company, Spokane, Washington

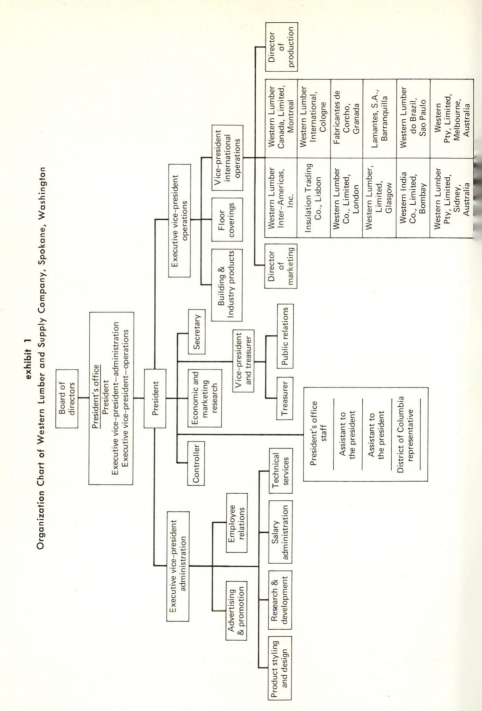

ORGANIZATION OF INTERNATIONAL OPERATIONS

In the early decades of its history, Western Lumber had limited its sales efforts to the United States. It drifted into doing an export business when it received unsolicited orders from Canada and, later, from Britain. When adverse exchange rates made exporting to Britain uneconomic in the 1930's, Mr. Homer Parsons, then Western Lumber president, prevailed upon the Canadian and British sales subsidiaries to build their own plants and undertake the production of floorings. After the formation of the European Economic Community, Western felt that a resilient floorings plant in Germany was justified; by that time it had developed a continental sales volume of $17 million, served mainly from British production.

"Until about twenty years ago," said a Western International Operations Division executive at Spokane, "Western Lumber was insular in its thinking. Export sales were just 'bothered with.' Top management people seldom visited a foreign unit. Foreign business was treated as a sort of 'plus' business, to be pushed when domestic sales were down. But the foreign business grew in spite of this inhibiting attitude. Several multiple changes occurred in the top management of Western which resulted in the appointment of a new chief executive, which changed the approach toward foreign business. The present management sees business opportunities as being business opportunities, no matter where they are. Foreign growth opportunities are looked upon as being at least as good as those in the United States. Neither is given priority. Promotional efforts are considered case by case. Investment, in the 1960's, in new plants was made at a considerably higher rate abroad than in the United States."

In the United States the Western Lumber Spokane management believed that in some product lines and market areas it had achieved a saturation level of 80% to 90%. In some of its most active foreign markets it had a penetration of only 25%, and in many areas it was not selling at all. In 1971 it was not the foreign subsidiaries which were pushing headquarters management for further expansion; rather, it was Spokane which was promoting more international business. Top management personnel regularly visited Western's foreign installations. "International and foreign executives," said a Spokane executive, "now rate the same status and prestige as United States executives. That was not true ten years ago."

Prior to January, 1959, there had been a Foreign Trade Division in Spokane which handled the sale and shipment of products abroad made by the parent company. Later an export operations department was organized in Spokane to act as liaison between the United States and England, Canada, and Spain. This group co-ordinated sales, controlled investments, made top management appointments, and regulated salaries of management personnel abroad. In time conflicts developed between the foreign trade and export operations departments, primarily as a result of competition between various manufacturing units for sales in overlapping market areas. For a period of time the Spokane president's office divided the world into spheres for marketing purposes. In January, 1959, the International Division was formed in Spokane, and it took over direction of all foreign operations. This included co-ordination of all production, emphasis on product uniformity, sales forecasts, control of investments, annual budgets, profit budgets, and managerial personnel.

The International Division in Spokane exercised both line (command) and staff (advisory) authority over foreign operations. All managing directors of foreign subsidiaries and the director of marketing and the general production manager reported directly to the vice president and general manager of the International Division. (See Exhibit 2.) The vice president had complete line authority over all foreign personnel, and had profit responsibility for the entire foreign operation. The directors of international marketing and production at Spokane did not have line authority over any personnel abroad, but they had strong advisory authority. "If I wanted to fire the English company's production manager," said Mr. William Schilling, the Spokane director of production, "I wouldn't have the authority to do so. The general manager of the Spokane International Division would be able to do it; so would the managing director of the English company. He's the man's line boss. But if I wanted that man fired, I'd see to it that the English managing director got rid of him. We exercise strong staff authority at the International Division. Our foreign subsidiaries listen respectfully to our advice. Our recommendations are followed."

In practice, the foreign units directed their own operations under the close observation of the International Division, which received daily, weekly, and monthly reports on activities. All subsidiary managing directors met at Spokane once a year for a week-long session in

exhibit 2
Organization Chart of the International Division

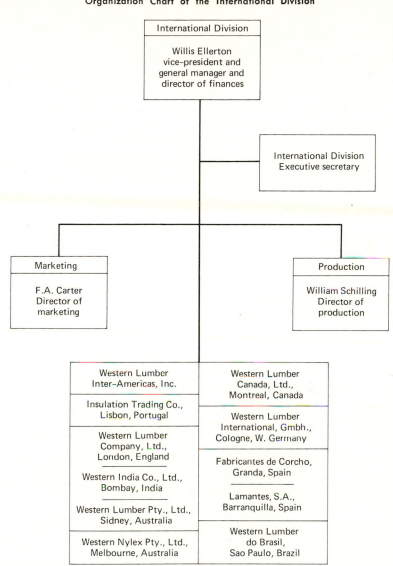

which they presented their programmed five-year plans to the Spokane executive committee and the president's office. On special major projects the International Division was consulted in advance. Thus when the English company was considering changing its ceiling tile formulations and expanding its ceilings plant, the English production manager spent three weeks in the United States consulting Spokane executives. "It was a very involved situation," said the Spokane international director of production. "The final decision, made by the English management, was to go ahead, on the premise that the possible loss of opportunity outweighed the risks involved. Spokane then approved a $250,000 addition to the English plant."

As to capital expenditures, international or foreign subsidiaries were authorized to spend up to $6,000 on their own authority. Expenditures over $6,000 were subject to later approval by the vice president of the International Division, who managed international finances, and expenditures of over $10,000 went to the president's office. None went beyond the president to the board of directors.

The managing directors of the foreign subsidiaries were chosen by the International Division, with the approval of the Spokane executive vice president and the president's office. The appointment of staff members at other levels was made by the subsidiaries themselves, in consultation and with the approval of Spokane. In this regard the opinion of the foreign subsidiary often prevailed. Thus the director of international production at Spokane on one occasion asked the managing director of the Spanish company to "lend" him his best young production man for a year. "Like hell I will," said the Spanish manager. "He'll be spoiled by his stay in the States, and I'd never get him back." The Spokane international director of production reluctantly conceded the point and looked elsewhere for a man.

Western Lumber executives in Spokane voiced the opinion that Western was trying to become a truly international company in every respect, rather than an American company with heavy international commitments. "With respect to managerial personnel," said a Spokane international executive, "we are already international, insofar as this is possible. We at Spokane would like to put the best man available into any position anywhere. Sometimes we have done so, and sometimes it has worked, but, sad to say, the world isn't ready for that yet. The management at Spokane is really the only true international group in the company. We can usually place an American man most anywhere. But there are certain foreign nationals who simply refuse to go to certain other countries. In some places international animosities are still strong."

For at least a decade Western Lumber had been considering establishing a semiautonomous European unit. The possibility was discussed every year at the annual meeting of the managing directors of the foreign subsidiaries, but for various reasons it was never done. The negative decision was usually based on the argument that every subsidiary drew heavily on American staff services in research and development, in marketing advice, in production, and in engineering services. Such staff services were not available in any European subsidiary. Also, with the rapid improvement and ease of travel and communications, management thought that the need for establishing such a subunit was diminishing.

THE INTERNATIONAL PRODUCT MANAGERS

In each of Western's foreign subsidiaries there were sales managers who had sales responsibility for a particular product line. "In the past," said a Spokane International executive, "many of these sales managers lived in fear. Many felt their own inadequacy in product knowledge, in sales, and in advertising skills, compared with Spokane and American marketing managers. Their line boss was the managing director of their subsidiary, and both of them tended to be defensive of their own weaknesses; and so they swept their shortcomings under the rug. Finally the rug became so bulgy that the president's office saw the lumps and acted by creating a group of international product managers."

In 1969 the International Division in Spokane appointed four international product line managers, each of whom was given the responsibility for promoting one or more of Western's main product lines. Each of the men chosen was an acknowledged expert in his product field and had advanced through the ranks of the sales department. (See Exhibit 3.)

The international product line manager was very different from the product line manager concept domestically. Domestic product line managers worked *for* their sales chief. International product line managers worked *with* their counterparts, who were the product managers in the subsidiary companies abroad. Where domestic men worked in

exhibit 3

Organization Chart for International Marketing

Marketing
Director of international marketing

Western Hemisphere

Marketing co-ordinator

Western Lumber Inter–Americas, Inc. General Manager Asst. general manager

Export order & shipping General manager Manager, orders Manager, shipping

Manager, Honolulu office Manager, New York office Manager, Puerto Rico office

Product manager Rubber products, packaging & closures

Product manager Carpet and wall coverings

Product manager Ceilings

Product manager Floor coverings

Service manager

Western Lumber Pty., Ltd. General Manager

Marketing function

Western Lumber Co., Ltd., London, England
Western India Co., Ltd., Bombay, India
Western Lumber Ltd., Kildare, Ireland
Western Lumber Canada Ltd., Montreal, Canada
Cooper Carpets Ltd., Canada
Western Lumber International, Gmbh., W. Germany
Fabricantes de Corcho, Granada, Spain
Lamantes, S.A., Barranquilla, Spain
Western Nylex Pty., Ltd., Australia

one large United States market, which was generally much the same everywhere, the international men worked in a world divided into six major marketing areas,[1] each of which was quite different.

If a domestic product manager conceived a project, he would work on it with the help of all of the American staff at his disposal—in product design, product testing, market research, manufacturing, advertising, and other functions. When the product was ready, he would have it approved by his superior and set launch dates, and the domestic district sales managers would then be told what to do.

If an international product manager conceived a promotional idea, he could not develop it independently as did the domestic managers. He would have to work with many staff specialists in each of the six major marketing areas, in each of which there were likely to be differences in cultures, tastes, preferences, economics, customs, climate, technical variations, etc. Of the six areas, four might accept the project, and each of the four might modify it to suit his region. These four would then fit it to their own production schedules, set their own launch dates, determine their own advertising themes, and fit the new product into their budgets. Most projects would involve the introduction of products which had already been introduced and were successful in the United States, but each foreign unit already had its own established set of product lines, and adjustments would be needed to fit in suggested additions.

An international product manager was responsible for the promotion of his product lines in all of the six major market areas, but only in a general way. His counterpart in each subsidiary had the direct responsibility, but the international product manager had no line authority over his international counterparts. The international director of marketing had line authority over the four product managers, but he did not have profit responsibility. Only the vice president, international operations, had profit responsibility for all foreign operations. "Our responsibilities are nebulous," said an international product manager, "and so is that of our chief. We are expected to push our product lines, and headquarters watches the performance of product lines closely. We have considerable authority, too, but it is all on the basis of developing rapport with our counterparts; we don't carry a club. And we always have to be careful to keep the chiefs of our

---

[1] Canada, Latin America, Europe, Africa, the Far East, and Japan.

counterparts informed of everything we are doing. Some subsidiary chiefs might be running scared, and these want everything to go through them. You have to be very careful that they don't get the idea that you are bossing their people. You've got to be purer than Caesar's wife."

During the 1930's each Western foreign subsidiary, as well as Western USA, had its own export department, and all of them tried to sell any of Western's products anywhere in the world. The export operations department in Spokane co-ordinated production but not sales, and as a result there was considerable overlapping in sales effort, with some markets missed and some double-covered. Thus the United States, Canadian, and English sales managers might all be trying to sell the same Western product in Jamaica at the same time. After World War II ended, the foreign subsidiaries were short of production and wished to import from the United States, which was not able to fill its own sales requirements. The United States typically exported far more of its production than any other Western unit. In 1971 it was still exporting more than all of the foreign subsidiaries combined, even after the rapid rise of overseas production with the building of numerous plants in the 1960's. A major function of every international product manager was to co-ordinate exports between the foreign subsidiaries and to allocate United States exports. The United States produced all Western products; no subsidiary produced the total product line; and the United States production supplemented the production of all international subsidiary plants.

Each international product manager had his own budget and paid for his own expenses when traveling to help a subsidiary, which pleased the foreign managers. This was determined by United States Internal Revenue regulations, which also required that the travel expenses of the top International executives, when they visited a subsidiary, be charged to the subsidiary—which was resented. The total expense of supporting the international product managers operation, which amounted to a moderate six-figure sum annually, was allocated to the subsidiaries. Their profit was measured both before and after the allocation of headquarters' expense.

SALES AND MARKETING

Of the total Western Lumber sales made outside of the United States, the U.S. supplied about 40% of the products, Canada supplied about

20%, and the balance was manufactured by Western Lumber subsidiaries outside of the United States. The Western Hemisphere imported virtually nothing from abroad. Sales abroad had tripled during the 1960's, and manufacturing abroad was expected to quadruple by the end of 1972, reflecting the increased output of the numerous plants which Western had built since 1965. Total foreign sales were over $90 million and were approaching 15% of Western's total sales volume in 1971, and were expected (in realistic budgets) to double and triple within the next several years.

In general, all subsidiaries were free to sell any of Western's products within their territories, subject to certain exceptions as to source of supply. While the sales manager of each subsidiary was free to determine his own product line and direct his own promotional programs, the sales executives at International headquarters at Spokane exerted a strong influence on a local manager's choices and were especially selective as to products promoted, favoring such lines as mineral ceilings, which were considered to have great long-range potential, and discouraging cork products, because of their declining potential. Any jobbed products[2] handled by a subsidiary required the prior approval of the director of marketing of the International Division, after sales and profit projections had been forecast, and after samples had been tested by the international director of production. Subsidiaries abroad were permitted to engage in research and development projects in keeping with their capabilities, but 95% of R&D was done by Western's large centralized research facilities in the United States.

In practice, nine out of ten foreign marketing programs originated in the field and were launched and aided by close co-operation with Spokane headquarters. Thus, if the floorings manager in Germany wished to try to sell carpetings in Italy, he would submit a draft of his plan to the product manager of carpet and wall coverings in the International Division at Spokane, who would try to help with counsel and advice. In a typical instance, the Australian company asked for floorings in blue, white, and rose colors, which Western did not have in its line. After counseling with Spokane, the Australian company agreed to try some of the lighter-colored shades which were a standard part of the Western line. The Australian company was gratified to discover that these standard Western colors soon were enthusiastically accepted by Australian customers. "We don't boss our subsidiary managers,"

[2] Any product manufactured by one Western unit and sold by another Western unit was termed a "jobbed" product.

said a Spokane international product manager. "Direct command is out. We advise, counsel, suggest, and in general try to be helpful. We are pleased to see that response to our Spokane suggestions has been improving greatly."

Each foreign subsidiary had its exclusive sales territory. In purchasing products from other Western units, however, they might have the option of choosing from any one of several Western plants as a source. Thus, the Australian company had four possible sources of vinyl asbestos tile: the United States, Canada, Britain, and Germany. In such instances a joint decision as to what source to use was made by the vice president of the International Division together with the International director of production. The decision was not made on the basis of price, but on the basis of plant capacities and loads and proximity to market.

Transfer prices [3] were often arranged by mutual agreement between the marketing managers of the subsidiaries involved in the transaction, but all such prices came under the close scrutiny and control of the International Division director of production. At the beginning of each year each subsidiary general manager would send his transfer price list to Spokane, where the director of production would pass upon it after relating the prices to factory costs and expected period expenses; after this procedure, the approved list was sent to all Western subsidiaries. "Transfer prices are closely controlled by my office," said the international director of production. "The subsidiary managers are much involved, and our transfer prices are subject to negotiation. Sometimes in hard bargaining cases provisional prices are set, and occasionally an arbitration will go all the way to the president's office. In the end, we in production mostly have the final say, because we think in terms of costs and capacities; the sales people tend to bargain too much."

Western's retail price policy was to hold its prices moderately high in all markets, compared with popular prices. In most markets this was justified by the high quality of Western products. In some markets Western found its products matched in quality by local products, and in these instances it strove to maintain its higher price levels by better promotions and by capitalizing on the Western Lumber name.

Being relatively new in the world market, Western Lumber had only

---

[3] "Transfer" prices were the prices of jobbed products charged by the producing unit to the selling units of Western.

fragmentary coverage. Even in Europe, where it was building a number of plants, it did not have coverage in depth in most countries. It sold virtually nothing in the emerging nations of Africa; there were heavy restrictions against imports in South Africa and India; Japan was a questionable market in which Western was considering selling jobbed products. Western was almost shut out of the Mexican market, as well as many other Latin American markets. Western sold a limited amount of products to Eastern Bloc countries through Swiss export houses, with the merchandise drop-shipped by the English or German companies to Germany, Poland, and Bulgaria. Western had no marketing activities in the Far Eastern Communist Bloc areas, but was aware that a trickle of its merchandise filtered into these areas through Hong Kong intermediaries.

INTERNATIONAL PRODUCTION

Western Lumber's international production was co-ordinated by Spokane headquarters, which co-ordinated the output of individual foreign plants with annual sales forecasts. Spokane also adjusted outputs for shorter periods when necessary and had the authority to allocate production to sales outlets in the event of emergencies. (See Exhibit 4.)

Western was developing fairly comprehensive production of all of its products in every major market area. Every subsidiary, however, even those which most closely duplicated the comprehensive Western pattern of plants and products in the United States, was unique and different in some respects. Each had different sources of supply; each had a different product line mix; there were significant differences in mechanization and efficiency; and almost every subsidiary had an employee and union relations situation which was unique to its own setting. The United States plants, for example, were considerably more mechanized than the foreign plants because labor costs in the United States were very high. United States labor costs were from 100% to 200% of German labor costs, even though German labor costs were considered high in world trade circles, and the German labor costs included 34% in social benefits.

Every effort was made to standardize technical specifications, material specifications, and quality control on a company-wide basis. Toward this end samples of foreign-source raw materials were sent to

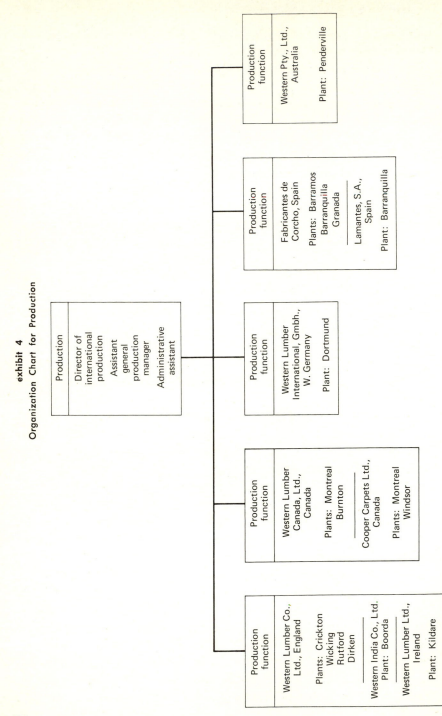

exhibit 4
Organization Chart for Production

Production

Director of international production

Assistant general production manager

Administrative assistant

Production function

Western Lumber Co., Ltd., England

Plants: Crickton
Wicking
Rutford
Dirken

Western India Co., Ltd.

Plant: Boorda

Western Lumber Ltd., Ireland

Plant: Kildare

Production function

Western Lumber Canada, Ltd., Canada

Plants: Montreal
Burnton

Cooper Carpets Ltd., Canada

Plants: Montreal
Windsor

Production function

Western Lumber International, Gmbh., W. Germany

Plant: Dortmund

Production function

Fabricantes de Corcho, Spain

Plants: Barramos
Barranquilla
Granada

Lamantes, S.A., Spain

Plant: Barranquilla

Production function

Western Pty., Ltd., Australia

Plant: Penderville

the Spokane research center for exhaustive testing. Periodically samples of foreign-produced products were also routinely inspected by Western's U.S. research and development department, which also supplied a great deal of technical information to all subsidiaries in daily letter form. There was a growing exchange of technical information between subsidiaries, which Spokane encouraged, and when any subsidiary achieved a major breakthrough it was transmitted to Spokane, which disseminated it to all Western subsidiaries.

Spokane headquarters also encouraged widespread and constant communications between all Western units. There were numerous weekly reports on production, sales, and technical performances, plus monthly summaries. There were telex communications daily between all units, and these were supplemented by the liberal use of long-distance telephone calls. Spokane believed that there was no substitute for inter-plant visiting, and so subsidiary executives, from middle-management level up, visited other units quarterly or semiannually. The four Spokane international product managers were constantly touring the globe.

In employee relations, Spokane sought to have its international subsidiaries follow its United States principles—to foster good communications between employees and management, and to cultivate good community relations. Spokane did not lay down definitive guides concerning union relations, preferring to allow these to follow local patterns. Wage and salary levels and policies were also suited to local patterns, even though this caused decided disparities between individual units in different countries.

INTERNATIONAL FINANCING

Mr. Willis Ellerton, Western's vice president and general manager, international operations, in addition to having profit responsibility for international operations, personally managed international financing. It was Western Lumber headquarters policy that its foreign subsidiaries, in general, should be self-sufficient financially. They were so until 1966, when the extensive building of plants in England and Germany proved to be beyond the means of those companies. During 1967 and 1968 the United States parent company made nonrepayable loans which totaled several million dollars to these companies, and it was expected that the programmed growth of these and some other overseas companies during the next few years might call for further similar advances. A ceilings plant was built in England in 1966, a rubber products plant in Germany in 1967, a rotovinyl plant in Canada in 1968, and a vinyl corlon plant in Australia in 1969. There were no lending-borrowing relationships between subsidiary companies, except for the payables and receivables resulting from intercompany product purchases. Most of the subsidiaries did not have excess cash, and were suffering from "growing pains."

Western Lumber did not take advantage of foreign tax havens, as some international companies did. Some companies regularly delayed payments on receivables between subsidiary companies to build up working capital where needed, and Western occasionally did this between Germany and France, and more between the United States and subsidiaries to alleviate temporary cash squeezes. It seldom engaged in the popular practice of juggling rates of exchange between countries of differing currencies. There were finance men in Spokane who tried to be alert to impending devaluations of currencies, but Western's subsidiaries were generally heavily financed in local currencies and paid back their loans in local currencies; therefore they were protected against major losses due to devaluation. Western Lumber did not make it a practice to borrow abroad in the country in which interest rates were currently the lowest, and then loan the funds to the subsidiary which needed them. It was a popular practice among multinational companies to charge subsidiaries for "services rendered" by the parent company to drain off profits which would otherwise be taxable as dividends. Western did this, "but we try to be realistic," said Mr. Willis Ellerton. "We follow United States Internal Revenue Service requirements and don't go beyond their standards. We relate the service charges to actual values for the services rendered."

"In an over-all way," said Mr. Ellerton, "Western is very operational-oriented and very service-oriented, but we are fairly naïve in the management of our international financing. We will eventually need expertise in our international money matters, and will need to develop more sophistication in this area.

"Western's policy with respect to remittances from foreign subsidiaries has changed," said Mr. Ellerton, "and it will change still further. The old traditional policy reflected a concern for cash flow to Spokane headquarters, in the form of dividends, fees, or royalties. It was a single-minded concentration on return on capital employed. This internal headquarters viewpoint has been de-emphasized in favor of earnings per share. We are now in a dynamic growth period and are much more interested in reinvestment of earnings than in remittances. We realize now that the 'return on capital employed' concept had been adhered to too religiously. We had given too much priority to the present, and had not made enough allowance for long-range prospects. We are quite willing to make loans from Spokane to subsidiaries who are temporarily in a deficit position. In fact, we are now investing— and reinvesting—substantially more than Western is earning from its total international operations. And in exceptional instances, such as our German company, we are satisfied because we feel that the potential is great."

It was believed that the Spokane headquarters' view of the profitability of foreign operations had been prejudiced by the "return on capital" concept. Western's "return on capital employed" concept was defined as "all capital employed" or *all* assets employed. Western's foreign subsidiaries were heavily leveraged, typically using more debt than the U.S. parent company and usually at a higher interest cost. "If the earnings of our foreign subsidiaries were measured in terms of return on stockholders' equity," said Mr. Ellerton, "it would show them in a much more favorable light. Until the decade of the 1960's, Western had made only modest investments in its foreign subsidiaries, and the subsidiaries did their own internal financing and grew from reinvested earnings. If earnings were measured against original investment, they would be extraordinarily high." Spokane's investment in its British company had been less than $1 million; in Canada it had been less than $50,000; in Spain it had been less than the latter. In the case of these investments the annual net earnings of each company regularly exceeded Spokane's total original investment. This was even true of Spain, whose earnings were generally considered to be too modest to be worthwhile.

THE FOREIGN SUBSIDIARIES

The Canadian company was one of the oldest and largest of the Western Lumber foreign subsidiaries. It manufactured almost all of the products made by the parent company, and it had recently absorbed a company which was a leading Canadian carpet manufacturer. The Canadian company was the only foreign subsidiary which had established a consumer identity comparable with that of the United States parent company, from which it was believed to obtain a significant amount of "spillover" benefit in advertising. The management of the Canadian company was considered to be stable, well-experienced, and competent. It was staffed almost entirely by Canadians, with only a few Americans, and it acted with a great deal of independence. Prospects for expansion of the Canadian company's business appeared to be very promising. The International Division in Spokane often looked upon the Canadian company as the bellwether of Western's foreign operations. It was usually the most profitable of Western's foreign subsidiaries.

The English company was only slightly smaller than the Canadian company, and had a history dating from the post-First World War era. It also made most of the products made in the United States, except for carpetings. During its relatively long history, its management had gone through several phases. The longest of these was a period under the direction of the company's founder, who, by hindsight, was seen as an independent personality, under whom the company "grew up" as more of an English company than an American one. Under the founder, the English company saw several decades of dynamic growth. Under his successor it experienced a period of consolidation and rationalization and more growth, but with a reorientation to its position as one of the several foreign subsidiaries of the American parent company. An American was now managing director. He had already done much to convert the English operation to Western Lumber's systematic "scientific" management, such as in planning, budgetary controls, co-ordination of production and sales, and profit planning.

The German company was the youngest of the Western Lumber foreign subsidiaries. "Germany has the biggest opportunity of any of our European operations," said a Western Spokane executive. "It has also had the roughest experience. For ten years it has been a marginal operation." The German company made rubber products and a limited line of floor tiles and sold ceilings made in England or the United States. It was scheduled to build a ceilings plant of its own which would be the largest in Europe. Its management was relatively inexperienced, and it had been disrupted by moves to new locations and by organizational changes. The Spokane management saw them as a mixed and uneven group; some were characterized as "old-time authoritarians," some as "the new liberal postwar young Germans."

exhibit 5   **WESTERN LUMBER AND BUILDING SUPPLY CORPORATION
AND SUBSIDIARIES**

Consolidated balance sheet, December 31, 1971, with comparative figures as of
December 31, 1970

	1971	1970
	(000)	(000)
Assets		
Current assets:		
Cash	$ 13,428	$ 14,960
U. S. Treasury and other securities	357	8,361
Accounts and notes receivable (less allowance for discounts and losses)	76,606	72,035
Inventories	110,305	91,480
Prepaid expenses	3,912	3,757
Total current assets	204,611	190,594
Sundry assets and investments, at cost or less	3,032	3,258
Property, plant, and equipment, at cost (less accumulated depreciation and amortization)	271,510	249,168
	$479,154	$443,021
Liabilities and Stockholders' Equity		
Current liabilities:		
Notes payable	23,082	12,446
Current installments on long-term debt	779	1,312
Accounts payable and accrued expenses	46,370	39,439
Federal and foreign income taxes	9,247	10,374
Total current liabilities	79,840	63,572
Long-term debt	8,063	8,369
Deferred income taxes	15,274	14,151
Deferred investment credit	2,074	2,420
Stockholders' equity	374,261	354,508
	$479,154	$443,021

There were more than the usual complement of foreigners—Americans, Canadians, and Englishmen. Headquarters did not attribute the losses incurred by the German company to its management, but to over-capacity in some industries and to unfortunate incidents which had occurred. The amount of the losses had been smaller each year, and 1971 was the company's first over-all profit year. Spokane had definite plans for further expansion of the German company.

The Spanish company was the oldest of Western's subsidiaries, dating from before the turn of the century. It had begun as a supplier of cork to the parent company, and was still largely a cork-fabricating operation, although cork was considered to be a dying product. The Spanish company was looked upon by Spokane executives as an anachronism and its future was thought to be questionable. It sold no

exhibit 6   WESTERN LUMBER AND BUILDING SUPPLY CORPORATION
AND SUBSIDIARIES

Statement of consolidated earnings, year ended December 31, 1971, with comparative figures for 1970

	1971 (000)	1970 (000)
Current Earnings		
Income:		
Net sales	$627,540	$587,440
Other income	3,776	2,998
	$631,316	$590,439
Costs and expenses:		
Cost of goods sold	416,627	398,500
Selling and administrative expense	109,630	100,166
Depreciation and amortization	26,310	24,107
Other charges	2,582	2,473
Earnings before income taxes	76,165	65,191
Federal and foreign income taxes	37,785	29,378
Net earnings	$ 38,380	$ 35,812
Earnings per share of common stock (based on average shares outstanding)	$ 2.70	$ 2.52
Retained Earnings		
Amount at beginning of year	$267,996	$251,498
Net earnings for the year	38,380	35,812
	$306,566	$287,311
Deduct dividends:		
Preferred stock	488	488
Voting preferred stock	216	—
Common stock	18,023	16,225
Common stock of pooled companies prior to combinations	2,070	2,631
	20,798	19,344
Amount at end of year	$285,767	$267,966

flooring, sold very little ceilings, and only a small amount of rubber products. Efforts had been made to sell the business, but no way had been found of getting the proceeds out of Spain. It did the smallest volume of any of the European companies, and while it had been profitable for the past twelve years, the profits were marginal. Spokane considered the quality of its management to be good, however, and its middle management was thought to be superior to that of most Spanish companies. The Spanish economy had been growing fast, and it was the consensus in Spokane that the future of the Spanish company, for the next few years at least, would be to grow with the economy.

exhibit **7   WESTERN LUMBER AND BUILDING SUPPLY CORPORATION
             AND SUBSIDIARIES**

Five-year financial summary (in thousands)

Year	1971	1970	1969	1968	1967
Net sales	$627,540	$587,440	$583,618	$562,561	$532,260
Earnings before income taxes	$ 76,165	$ 65,191	$ 80,820	$ 88,121	$ 85,417
Federal and foreign income taxes	$ 37,785	$ 29,378	$ 38,278	$ 41,419	$ 42,485
Net earnings	$ 38,380	$ 35,812	$ 42,543	$ 46,702	$ 42,932
Earnings per share of common stock	$ 2.70	$ 2.52	$ 3.01	$ 3.32	$ 3.07
Dividends per share of common stock	$ 1.45	$ 1.40	$ 1.40	$ 1.37½	$ 1.25
Average number of employees	27,775	29,175	28,433	27,614	26,654
Year-end Position					
Working capital	$125,130	$127,023	$132,389	$137,299	$122,685
Net property, plant, and equipment	$271,510	$249,168	$227,338	$197,584	$177,932
Total assets	$479,154	$443,022	$431,078	$406,685	$373,663
Stockholders' equity	$374,262	$354,508	$338,815	$315,922	$289,068
Book value per share of common stock	$ 27.99	$ 26.58	$ 25.34	$ 23.50	$ 21.24
Number of stockholders	19,166	20,414	21,507	21,919	19,533
Common shares outstanding	13,963	13,892	13,888	13,848	13,738

WESTERN LUMBER AND BUILDING SUPPLY CORPORATION (B)

Western Lumber's "English company" was the first venture of Western Lumber and Building Supply Company abroad. Western's Canadian company manager had been receiving an increasing volume of unsolicited floor covering orders from England, and in 1922 was permitted to launch a linoleum sales campaign in London, The fluctuating British economy in those years undercut the promotional effort, but by 1928 the venture was returning a modest profit. When the 20% devaluation of the English pound in 1930 made importing difficult, it was arranged to have the most popular Western linoleum patterns custom-manufactured under the Western label in England and sold by Western's own sales force. Cork items were later added to the product line.

The English company was only moderately successful until the early 1930's, when an enterprising linoleum production engineer developed a rubber compound underlay for leveling the steel decking of seagoing ships, permitting linoleum or cork tiling to be laid over the steel. This business was profitable, and the method was so advantageous that every major shipbuilder in Britain made extensive use of the product. World War II expanded sales and profits.

In 1935 a linoleum plant was built in Manchester to supply the shipbuilding trade and the British civilian market. The custom-manufacturing arrangement was terminated. Cork floor tiles and corkboards continued to be imported from Spain, but in 1937 a small plant was built in Crickton, a London suburb, to manufacture cork-lined

694

crown bottle caps and cork bottle stoppers. British sales of this product had grown to over a half-million dollars annually. In 1939 the Crickton plant began compression plastic molding, making bottle, vial, and container closures. During World War II specialized products were molded for the RAF, and the Crickton cork fabricators turned out cork products for the armed services, such as life preservers, floats for Navy cables, and rafts for bombing targets.

In 1944 Mr. Dudley Kenton, then general manager of the English company, spent four months in the United States making a comprehensive long-range plan for expansion of the English operations. As a result of this plan, Western disposed of its Manchester plant and built an expanded floorings plant in the northeastern coastal port town of Wicking. A plant to produce Western's low-temperature rubber and plastic compound insulants was built in Rutford on the outskirts of Liverpool. Ceiling tiles produced in the eastern United States were introduced into Britain, and several years later the size of the Wicking plant was doubled by the addition of a ceilings plant, and a mineral wool plant was built at Dirken (Birmingham) to manufacture mineral wool from steel mill slag. In 1969 Mr. Kenton was succeeded as general manager by Mr. James Steele, an American.

In the period 1970–1971 the English company generated the largest sales volume of any overseas Western Lumber unit. It had the largest complex of plants and produced the main lines of products made by the parent company.[1] It was earning an attractive profit, was selling throughout England and in the export market, and was planning to expand its operations.

FACILITIES

The first English headquarters office was established in the Crickton plant. In 1971 headquarters offices were still there, but of the top management (see Exhibit 1), only Mr. James Steele, the managing director, and Mr. Craig Luton, the director of manufacturing, had their offices at Crickton. Lack of space for its growing operations had forced the company to lease a building called Briargate Manor in the

---

[1] Product lines made in the United States but not made in England included lumber, prefinished wood flooring, parquet floorings, certain types of resilient floorings, plywood, wall panelings, and carpetings.

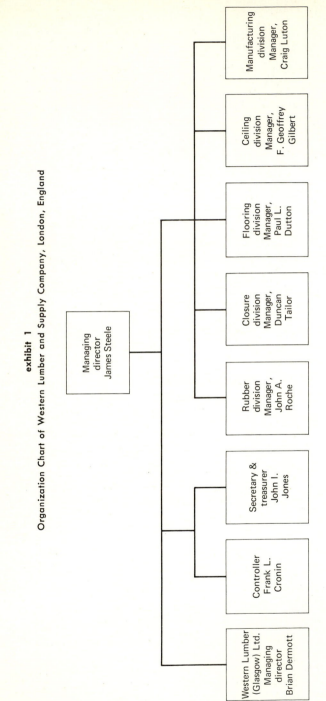

exhibit 1

Organization Chart of Western Lumber and Supply Company, London, England

Managing director James Steele

Western Lumber (Glasgow) Ltd. Managing director Brian Dermott

Controller Frank L. Cronin

Secretary & treasurer John I. Jones

Rubber division Manager, John A. Roche

Closure division Manager, Duncan Tailor

Flooring division Manager, Paul L. Dutton

Ceiling division Manager, F. Geoffrey Gilbert

Manufacturing division Manager, Craig Luton

town of Chipping, three miles away, and the managing directors of the Ceilings, Closures, and Rubber Products Divisions, together with their staffs, were domiciled at Briargate. Crickton and Chipping were 18 miles from central London. Mr. Dutton and his Floorings Division staff occupied a sizable rented office in Covent Mall, a building just off Regent Street in central London which had convenient travel and communications connections with the bulk of Mr. Dutton's customers, who were mostly in the London area.

The Wicking flooring and ceiling plant was an overnight rail journey from Crickton; not being on any dual carriageway, it was a full day's journey by car. The mineral wool-blowing plant had been situated at Dirken in the English Midlands in order to be adjacent to supplies of slag from the steel mills. The Rutford rubber plant had access to Liverpool's ample shipping facilities. Both of them were six hours from Crickton.

All of the English company managers spent a sizable portion of their time traveling between their offices and plants, especially the headquarters directors, who were away from their offices a third of the time. To give prompt service, 13 distribution warehouses were maintained, and shipments to these were made by lorries from Western's various plants. "We are pretty well scattered about on the map," said Mr. Steele, "but that is a problem that everyone in England must contend with—the shortage of buildings, and the government's regulation of the distribution of industry and the population."

FLOOR COVERINGS

"The reason for our weakness in the retail floor covering market," said Mr. Paul Dutton, manager of the English Flooring Division, "is the shortness of our line. Our Wicking plant has existed since 1948 making the same products. Western Lumber's reputation is not being justified by our operation in England. We need new facilities to make a new and broader line."

In 1971 the Wicking plant was producing asphalt, vinyl asbestos, and flexible vinyl asbestos flooring, all in tile form, and adhesives and mastic flooring underlayments. It did not produce sheet materials. It sold 85% of its output to flooring contractors, $6\frac{1}{2}$% to retailers, and $8\frac{1}{2}$% to the institutional market—public authorities, schools, and hospitals. In the housing tile market Western had a 31% share of the asphalt market and 17% of the flexible vinyl. Mr. Dutton expected his vinyl asbestos share to increase by 1% within a year and flexible asbestos to increase by 6%. Flexible vinyl was an especially supple material which the English company had developed from Western's standard vinyl asbestos by putting more vinyl in it; the flexible material was better suited to the cool climate in the British Isles. It also permitted brighter colors.

Mr. Dutton explained that in the United States there were retailers who specialized in the sale of floor coverings and who offered an installation service. In England, before World War II, most floor coverings had been linoleum in rug form, and it had been sold through department and furniture stores. During the war ladies' shoe styles ran to stiletto heels, which bit into soft linoleum. "It killed linoleum sales," said Mr. Dutton. "Vinyl had not yet come in, and English householders turned to woven carpeting. Department and furniture stores, however, did not want to bother with installing any kind of flooring, and they lost interest. This caused flooring contractors to come into being."

Wicking was on the extreme northeastern coast of England, about 250 miles from London, which was Western's principal market for floorings. The plant site had been set at Wicking at the persuasion of government authorities because it was close to the shipbuilding industries, and the government wished, when the wartime shipbuilding boom was over, to keep industries from gravitating away from the area. The English management had expected to import a sizable portion of its floorings from Western's Canadian company. It also expected to develop overseas markets and accepted the site because it had good shipping-line connections with Montreal and with the Continent. The plant was planned in 1944 but was not built until 1948. By that time ship decking sales had fallen off and linoleum had become unpopular. Therefore, the original plan to produce lineoleum was discarded and an asphalt tile facility was installed instead.

The Wicking plant was being built at the time that department stores and flooring contractors were taking over the market from furniture stores. "The new flooring craftsmen," said Mr. Dutton, "tended to be butchers or bakers one day and flooring contractors the next day. The problem is still with us. They lack technical skill and capital, and they are not good business managers." Since retailers were no longer taking on flooring lines, Western selected nine flooring contractors in the London area and offered them 15 patterns which English architects had selected from the Western United States pattern line. The management then concentrated all its sales efforts on securing orders from builders, and the effort was so successful that the plant was oversold. "We went to some trouble then," said Mr. Dutton, "to train our flooring contractors and their installers. Since then our problem has been to get the tile rather than the sales."

From this beginning, Western solidified its position with building contractors. The English company management believed that it could get the widest coverage by supporting them. "We have the highest-quality flooring products in the United Kingdom," said Mr. Dutton. "However, our extremely narrow line and our prices—which are the highest in the industry—do not appeal to retailers, who cater to the popular-price, do-it-yourself market. In the United States the name Western Lumber is known to everyone. Not so in England. Mrs. Smith, in England, would immediately recognize the name of our principal competitor—Gorby. But contractors and architects would recognize the name Western Lumber."

Western Lumber spent less than 2% of its flooring sales revenues on advertisements, which it placed only in builders' and architects' journals. It also staged a program of demonstrations of installation for architects. "The retail market segment is immense," said Mr. Dutton. "Out of a total resilient market of 140 million square yards, 100 million goes to retailers; but that still leaves 40 million which is sold through contractors, and selling through contractors, our 60-man sales force is supplemented by over 2,000 salesmen employed by our flooring contractors. We are weak in the retail field, but we are clearly the leader in the contract field. Contractors like us. We are the only flooring manufacturer in the UK which does not offer its own installation service. We are the only one which does not compete with installers." In England alone Western had six major competitors. "All of them have much broader lines than Western," said Mr. Dutton. "All of them sell much more at retail than we do. All of their prices are below ours, and every one of them offers a fixing service."

In 1970–1971 most of the English company's flooring sales were of the three flooring tiles manufactured at Wicking; its imports from the United States and Canada were small. Ninety-six per cent of the

Wicking production was sold within the United Kingdom, and 4% of it was sold overseas, mostly in the Republic of Ireland. "The Irish duty on carpeting is 26⅔%," said Mr. Dutton, "and on resilient flooring it is 12½%. Freight costs are almost prohibitive." A typical carton of tile weighed 50 pounds; a roll of sheet material might weigh a ton. Ireland had almost no resilient flooring production of its own, and Western of England estimated that it had a 60% share of the Irish market.

Under its industrialization program the Irish Government had recently granted £250,000 ($600,000) to a French manufacturer to build a plant in Ireland, stipulating that 80% of its production was to be exported. Fearing a price war, Western of England had countered by buying a small plant in Ireland to make floorings not produced at Wicking, to be sold both in Ireland and in the United Kingdom. The Irish Government contributed £30,000 ($72,000) to the venture. "It is only a small operation," said Mr. Dutton, "but it will give us expertise in operating a small plant." Aside from Ireland, the English company sold a very small quantity of floorings in Africa, the Near East, and Hong Kong. On the Continent it faced Common Market duties, and in EFTA countries it was not competitive in price.

"We are in the floor coverings business," said Mr. Dutton, "not just resilient floorings; and our greatest need is a broader line." Mr. Dutton estimated that there were 100 million square yards of carpeting being sold in the United Kingdom annually. Eighty-five per cent of this was sold at retail, leaving 15% available to the contract market. He hoped that the English company would soon add carpeting to its line, either on a make or a buy basis. Within recent years Western had acquired mills in the United States and Canada which produced carpeting, but there were obstacles to importing American production into England. English duties on synthetics were prohibitive, the English market was well supplied with wool carpetings by local manufacturers, and freight costs on shipments from America were extremely heavy.

Mr. Dutton saw the future for English floor coverings operations as being very bright. He had plans, in time, to import the full Western line from Canada, and when volume justified it, to manufacture the line in England in a new plant to be located somewhere more convenient than Wicking. The Flooring Division was the largest segment of the English company's operations. It had always been profitable, and in 1971 operations were exceptionally profitable. "We are exceeding our budget expectations very handsomely," said Mr. Dutton.

RUBBER PRODUCTS

The English company had at first imported the Western "rubber products"[2] from Western plants in the United States; later, it imported them from Western's Swiss and German plants. A bay had been added to the Wicking plant in 1961 to perform fabricating and finishing operations on rubber compounded in Switzerland, and in 1964 an integrated rubber plant was built at Rutford (Liverpool), and all rubber production was transferred there.

In the United States, Western Lumber sold its Tempack mainly for insulating refrigerator and air conditioning equipment. In England, where the climate was relatively cool, air conditioning had not yet become popular, and the bulk of the English output of Tempack was used for small-bore central heating applications. It was estimated that 13% of all English dwelling units had central heating. Whereas the United States Western Lumber parent company had six competitors which made comparable products, there was no comparable product manufactured from rubber in the United Kingdom. There were, however, about 15 manufacturers of urethane, which had about the same performance characteristics and cost only one-third as much as Tempack. Statistics indicated that forced-circulation hot air was becoming the most popular form of central heating in England. The English company was trying to develop a reinforced insulating material which would in itself form the ducting, eliminating the need for sheet metal, but the project was still in an early exploratory state.

Western Exactorol products were sold to the paper-processing and printing machinery industry. "The paper and printing industries," said Mr. John Roche, manager of the English company's Rubber Division, "are becoming world-wide. We try to hold down the size of our line, especially since individual orders are typically small, but the pressure to expand the line is always there. Thirty years ago Western had two original formulations of compounds. Today we have 38 and the line is still increasing."

The textile industry also was a large user of precision roller cover-

---

[2] *Tempack,* a light rubber compound resembling sponge rubber, used as an insulant to cover pipes and ducts, mostly in low-temperature applications and to a lesser degree in moderately high-temperature applications.
Exactorol, high-precision rubber compound rollers used in paper-processing and printing machinery; also, rubber beltings used in applications requiring precision.

ings. "We have deliberately stayed away from the textile industry," said Mr. Roche, "even though they are larger consumers of roller coverings than the paper and printing industries. For decades the English textile industry has been declining as more textile mills are being established on the Continent and in the States. The textile business also takes a bad dip about every third year. Furthermore, it is too traditional, too craft-oriented, and too loathe to change."

During the decade of the 1960's office duplicating machines had skyrocketed into popularity. The English company had become an early supplier of rollers to some of the leading duplicating machinery manufacturers, and it soon found itself custom-manufacturing specialized rollers for makers of lithographing, mimeographing, photocopying, and film-processing equipment. It supplied as much as 40% of the United Kingdom requirement in some machinery lines, and Mr. Roche was considering whether his division should make a serious attempt to enter the general office machinery field, which would include typewriters and calculating machines. He was already accepting small orders for custom-made rollers of any size, from $1/2$ inch to 18 inches in diameter, which weighed from a fraction of an ounce to $1/2$ ton. "We are the only Western Lumber rubber unit," said Mr. Roche, "which will supply rollers for anything that requires a roller cover. This custom trade is a small but rapidly growing field, and applications for new jobs are coming to us daily. While the volume is small, it has the highest profit margin in our line."

In 1971 the Rubber Division generated 9% of the money turnover of the English company. As recently as 1962 it had earned a return on capital employed which approached 30%; but it encountered sizable losses during the years following the transition to the new plant, and in 1971, while again earning a profit, its return on capital was well below the level considered acceptable by Western Lumber headquarters.

CLOSURES

"Closures," said Mr. Duncan Tailor, manager of the English company's Closure Division, "are what our American headquarters office calls de-emphasized products, and therefore we spend only $1/4$ of 1% of our sales dollar on advertising and promotion. All senior United

States Western Lumber executives came up through the building products end of the business. They think in terms of floorings or ceilings. Even accounting budgets and reports are designed in terms of board feet and square yards, which doesn't fit our packaging operations at all. Furthermore, Western Lumber's building products are homogeneous and are produced for inventory, whereas almost every single item in our packaging line is made to order for a specific customer. We get very little product guidance from headquarters. I think we know more about closures than they do."

Through one sales agent in the West Country and 10 salesmen who covered England, Scotland, and Ireland, the Closures Division sold crown corks, plastic screw caps, and stopper corks directly to bottlers in the United Kingdom. Other Western Lumber closure units also produced packaging items—bottles, flasks, vials, etc.—but the English company handled only closures. It was entirely a cork operation until 1935, when it began to develop products made from other materials. In 1971, its largest single item was its crown cork line, which generated a return on capital employed of almost 20%. It had 15% of the United Kingdom market in crown corks, a 45% share of the cork and stoppers market, 8% of the plastic cap business, but less than 1% of the total screwed-on closure potential. "Crown corks," Mr. Tailor concluded, "support the rest of our closures operations."

The English Company bought cork rods from which disks were sliced for its crown caps, but it no longer bought them from Western's Spanish cork-producing company. Its main supply was bought from Cork Imports, Limited, a wholly owned purchasing agency of Western Lumber, which supplied 90% of its cork requirements. Most of Cork Imports' purchases were made from non-Western Portuguese sources. Cork Imports considered the Portuguese cork industry to be more efficient, and since Portugal was in EFTA, these imports were without duty. Mr. Tailor pointed out that because Americans were not large consumers of wine, the United States company had de-emphasized its cork-stopper sales about a decade ago. "But the British," he said, "are now becoming a nation of wine-drinkers. Taxes on hard liquors are going up, and so Englishmen are drinking more wine."

In the screwed-on closure field, in which Western had less than 1% of the potential, aluminum screw-on caps had become very popular. "We own our plastic molding machines," said Mr. Tailor, "and on these we can give technical advice. But aluminum cap machines can only be leased, and therefore these would be out of our control."

Mr. Tailor felt that since closures were being de-emphasized, Western's headquarters management scrutinized requests for capital investment very carefully. "The Spokane people tend to think in terms of United States volume," said Mr. Tailor. "Where the American closures plant might make 50 million of a particular plastic cap, we in England might be able to sell only one-half million. It might require £10,000 ($24,000) worth of equipment to make it. Therefore we are required to import such plastic caps. Interoffice transfer price raises the price 15% above factory cost; import duty adds 15%. Therefore we are often unable to compete in price. Our plastic caps cost about 15% more than competitive aluminum caps."

On one occasion the English research staff had developed a resealable crown cap with a plastic liner. Resealable crowns were illegal in the United States, but they were permitted in the United Kingdom. Mr. Tailor emphasized to the Spokane executives the large potential involved: a single English brewery such as Watney's might have 20,000 retail pub outlets in which the bartenders could pour several drinks from the same bottle of ale. The purchase of the machine, which cost £12,000 ($28,000), required nine months of correspondence before receiving headquarters' approval. Within six months the machine was being operated 24 hours a day.

Spokane headquarters divided the world into marketing areas for the sale of building products such as floorings and wall panelings, but any Western closure plant was permitted to sell its products in any market. "The world is our market," said Mr. Tailor. "We can theoretically sell anywhere, but margins are so slim that exporting would not pay. Therefore we sell only in the United Kingdom and Ireland. We have almost no exports. But being an American company pays off in sales to the liquor, drug, and chemical industries. The big buyers in the Scotch trade are Americans: Seagrams and Hiram Walker. Also, Avon, Colgate Palmolive, Revlon, and Johnson and Johnson are big names in England, and, being American, we get a friendly reception from them."

For the year 1971 the Closures Division generated 27% of the sales volume of the English company, and sales were increasing. Its return on capital employed, however, was low compared to that of other Western operations.

CEILINGS

Western Lumber ceilings sales in the United Kingdom had returned only small profits in the first five years when products were imported from the United States. They were then profitable for three years, until the English company built its own plant in 1964. From 1964 to 1967 operations were unprofitable; however, from 1967 to 1971, operations were again profitable, at a gradually increasing rate.

Western had entered the ceiling business in the United Kingdom in 1955 with the importation of Cellulux, its wood fiber ceiling tile. This led to the importation of its mineral fiber ceilings, Stonex and Stoneboard. The mineral fiber lines had been introduced because Scandinavian imports (duty free) undersold Cellulux, and because the sale of all wood fiber tiles was being depressed by increasingly strict municipal fire codes. Western felt the need for new products to establish the Western Lumber image in the ceilings industry, and it hoped to achieve a position in the industry by organizing a network of specialist contractors who would use Western's unique ceilings and would give strong priority to Western Lumber products.

Stonex, a 12 by 12-inch board, was the first mineral fiber ceiling to be introduced. Its range of patterns did not appeal in the United Kingdom, and its price, which was far above that of Cellulux, favored sales of the wood fiber board. Later the price of Cellulux advanced, and, as fire regulations became more demanding, sales of Stonex improved. Stoneboard, a 24 by 48-inch board, was introduced nine months after the initial Stonex promotion. "In retrospect," said Mr. Geoffrey Gilbert, manager of the Ceilings Division, "we believed that this was poor timing, and to the disadvantage of both Stonex and Stoneboard. However, Stoneboard was a revolutionary step in the United Kingdom market, being a sophisticated concept of an exposed metal suspension ceiling." With the introduction of Stoneboard, Western launched a program in which technically proficient area representatives were appointed and charged with two specific tasks: (1) getting specifications from builders and (2) maintaining close co-operation with ceiling contractors. The program was successful, and the English company was able to set up an approved contractor system throughout the United Kingdom, with approved contractors agreeing to install only Western Lumber ceilings. To raise their standards, Western established a school to instruct contractors in technical matters and train them in profitable business practices.

The potential for Western ceiling products was difficult to gauge because there was no central source of information (see Exhibits 2 and 3). Government statistics grouped ceilings materials under the nebulous classification of "insulating boards," which included many materials outside the Western Lumber range, such as plasterboard, insulating underlinings, or polystyrene.

In 1971 there were restrictions on building in the United Kingdom which depressed the volume of new construction. Mr. Gilbert believed, however, that a large untapped market existed in the field of old-building remodeling and where fire-inert ceiling coverings were especially attractive. Since 1966 there had also been an accelerating growth in government-supported educational building.

In the wood fiber field, in which Western Lumber had an 8% share of the market, it faced nine major competitors: all but one imported their products. In the mineral fiber field Western had two-thirds of the market, with only two major competitors, each of which had a 10% share, and four other large companies collectively had a 15% share. As to competitive materials, Mr. Gilbert had estimates which showed that asbestos board had 39.3% of the market, metal tray and strip 31.5%, plaster tiles 10.3%, plasterboard (suspended) 15.7%, and luminous ceilings 3.2%.

Wood fiber tile was still losing ground in the contractual market, and the decline was especially apparent in the metropolitan area of London, where Western made the major portion of its sales. Wood fiber sales were growing, however, in the domestic and light commercial field, where the tiles were installed by tradesmen not wholly engaged in ceiling installation. Conversely, Mr. Gilbert was confident that mineral fiber board and tile sales would increase because the versatility of face designs in mineral tiles was appealing, their on-site handling and performance qualities were superior, and the thinking of both users and specifiers was shifting to suspended ceilings because of the advantages such ceilings offered.

Western Lumber of England sold ceilings through two broad groups. First, there were continuous users who were wholly engaged in ceiling installation, or firms which had departments which were so engaged. These were of two types: (a) those which promoted and installed only

Western ceilings; (b) those which supplied any type and make of ceiling. Second, there was a group of noncontinuous users, and this group included any purchasers of tile not included in the first group. Western served these customers through independent wholesalers which stocked and promoted Western ceilings. These wholesalers specialized in the sale of boards, tiles, and laminates. Most of Western's competitors, in both wood fiber and mineral fiber, distributed through wholesalers who maintained inventories.

All ceiling contractors preferred to purchase direct from the manufacturer, paying minimum prices; only two of Western's approved contractors maintained inventories; and all of the contractors expected orders to be delivered within 24 hours. There were only 10 competent ceiling salesmen among all of Western's approved contractors. The Ceilings Division spent about 1% of its sales revenues for advertising and promotion, most of which consisted of advertisements in architectural, engineering, and trade journals. In normal competitive work contractors aimed for a 10% profit before tax on the ceilings they installed, and where competition was limited they tried for 15%; often, because of their poor business management and poor on-site organization, they finished with considerably less than 10%. Western Lumber's management was of the opinion that ceiling contractors were becoming increasingly financially unstable as a result of their inefficient management. They lacked business knowledge and capital, demanded extended credit, and were poor payers with low credit ratings. Most of them completely ignored the 2½% cash discount for monthly settlement, and many of them required four months' credit.

Noncontinuous users of Western ceilings were required to purchase through one of Western's eight wholesale distributors. Selling direct to users would have involved thousands of occasional purchasers. Distributors preferred buying in bulk at advantageous terms so that they could resell to merchants at discount prices. Distributors maintained inventories and maintained sales staffs. All distributors did extensive advertising in local newspapers and national magazines. Western's competitors shared advertising expenses with their distributors; Western did not. The typical distributor worked on a 40% gross margin, from which he aimed to net 15% before taxes. If distributors sold to contractors (which Western discouraged), they worked on a 10% margin, which they found unsatisfactory. Most distributors had sound financial structures, collected their monthly cash discounts, and earned higher net profits than contractors, even though they carried many slow-paying user accounts which were expensive to administer. Distributors never sought extended credit.

The Ceiling Division management believed in the cultivation of personal customer relationships and good technical selling. To this end new salesmen underwent intensive training. The sales force numbered 12: one man in Ireland, one in Scotland, five in London, and five in the remainder of England. Their mission was to create a desire in specifiers to use suspended ceilings as an element in their buildings. The specifiers were architects and heating and ventilating engineers.

Western had two types of ceiling contractors. The first were the approved contractors, which handled Western ceilings exclusively, in consideration of which they were given the best discount structure. To these contractors the Western salesmen referred the bulk of their inquiries for quotation. Western provided training programs in sales and management for these contractors and ran joint promotions with them.

The second type of contractor was the ceiling contractor with no allegiance to any particular company. This group was kept fully informed of Western products through mailings and personal sales calls. The attempt was made to upgrade promising ones into the approved category if an available territory existed. By continuous contacts these contractors were encouraged to specify Western ceilings rather than those of competitors.

There were a number of differences between Western sales policies and those of its competitors. Western had the largest sales force engaged in selling ceilings direct to specifiers and servicing ceiling contractors. Its standard of training was superior. Its "approved contractors" policy embraced all of the leading suspended-ceiling contractors, and the Western management believed that this acted as a block to competitors. Western's sales effort was in depth, aimed at all specifiers, regardless of size, whereas competitors tended to scramble after large contracts. Western had a stable price list and avoided concessions; competitors often made deals to get large contracts. Western looked upon its approved contractors as an extension of its own operation. Competitors often had their own installation staffs, which antagonized contractors. Western did no installing.

In the suspended-ceilings market, the English company management believed that the final buying decision was made by the contractor, but that the contractor was generally strongly influenced by the specifier (the architect, designer, etc.). The specifier, however, was often influenced by his client—the user, the building owner. In the fixed-tile and do-it-yourself market, the buying decision seemed to rest with the distributor, who, in turn, was totally influenced by the popularity of the product with users, installers, or distributors (assuming satisfactory profit margins). Based upon these beliefs, the English company concluded that it was in the best interest of the manufacturer to advertise and promote to all categories of customers.

exhibit 2   WESTERN LUMBER AND SUPPLY COMPANY, LTD., LONDON, ENGLAND
The estimated market*—sales in 1969, 1970, and 1971

Wood Fibre Materials—including bagasse and flax-based materials:

	Sales in Sq. Ft. (Millions)		
	1969	*1970*	*1971*
Competitors:			
Home producers or home converters	12.5	13.0	13.0
Imported	13.0	13.5	13.5
Western Lumber:			
Imported	4.0	3.0	3.0
	29.5	29.5	29.5
Mineral Fibre Materials:			
Competitors:			
Home producers	1.5	2.5	4.0
Imported	4.0	4.0	3.0
Western Lumber:			
Home-produced	2.2	2.0	10.5
Imported	6.4	6.3	2.0
	14.1	14.8	19.5
Metal Tray and Tile Ceilings:			
Mainly home-produced	6.0	6.0	6.0
Other Ceilings:			
Asbestos board, plaster tiles, Fibreglass, plasterboard on exposed grid systems	12.0	12.5	13.0
Total:	61.6	62.8	68.0

* SOURCE: Company data.

exhibit **3**   **WESTERN LUMBER AND SUPPLY COMPANY, LTD., LONDON, ENGLAND**
Market shares*

Whole Market	*1969* *M Sq. Ft.*	*% of* *Market*	*1970* *M Sq. Ft.*	*% of* *Market*	*1971* *M Sq. Ft.*	*% of* *Market*
Wood Fibre	29.5	47.8	29.5	47.0	29.5	43.3
Mineral Fibre	14.1	22.0	14.8	23.5	19.5	28.6
Metal	6.0	9.8	6.0	9.5	6.0	8.8
Others	12.0	19.5	12.5	20.0	13.0	19.3
	61.6	100.0	62.8	100.0	68.0	100.0

Western *Lumber Share*	*1969* *M Sq. Ft.*	*% of* *Market*	*1970* *M Sq. Ft.*	*% of* *Market*	*1971* *M Sq. Ft.*	*% of* *Market*
Wood Fibre	4.0	13.5	3.0	10.1	3.0	10.1
Mineral Fibre	8.5	61.0	8.3	56.0	12.5	64.1
Metal	—	—	—	—	—	—
Others	—	—	—	—	—	—

* SOURCE: Company data.

WESTERN LUMBER AND BUILDING SUPPLY CORPORATION (C)

At the end of 1971, Mr. John A. Corkill, general manager of Western Lumber International, Gmbh., Cologne, Germany, wrote a report analyzing the situation of his company. His analysis ended with the following conclusions:

> Our gross profit margins in Germany are not satisfactory, but we have already taken steps to improve them. We are suffering from low profit margins because of what appears to have been unrealistic budgeting, particularly on jobbed products.[1]
>
> Our Rubber Products Division is recovering after initial losses due to planned projections which were based upon accounting assumptions which were too optimistic.
>
> We have a fine new floorings plant which was built for mass production at a time when the floorings industry in Germany suddenly expanded to such an extent that it developed extreme overcapacity.
>
> Our ceiling sales have been doing well, but we do not have our own manufacturing facility, and therefore we suffer the adverse effects that come with making volume sales of a product which we must import from distant sources.
>
> There have been many shifts in our top management personnel lately. That, and the moves from Basel, Switzerland, to Dortmund, Germany, and then to Cologne have disturbed some management loyalties which we hold to be valuable.
>
> On a total company basis, on the other hand, the substandard performance on the part of the German company has been offset by

[1] In Western Lumber terminology any product sold by a Western Lumber unit but manufactured by another Western unit was a "jobbed product."

increased margins in the parent company and in the associated companies which supply our German company.

We have excellent manufacturing facilities in Dortmund. We have capable supervisory employees. We have an inexperienced but willing work force. We have some of the problems and inefficiencies which go with starting a new set of plants, but these should soon be behind us. I am confident that 1972 will be a good year for our German company.

ORIGIN OF THE GERMAN COMPANY

In the period following World War II, Western Lumber Company U.S.A. and its subsidiary, Western Lumber Ltd. of England, developed a substantial market in Germany for floor tiles and other Western products. In 1955, Western, U.S.A. established two sales subsidiaries: Western Lumber International, S.A., in Basel, Switzerland, and Western Lumber Handelgesellschaft, Gmbh., Dortmund, Germany. The German company sold Western Lumber products in Western Germany. The Swiss company sold throughout the remainder of Europe, except in Spain, which was covered by Western's Spanish subsidiary, Fabricantes de Corcho, S.A., of Granada, Spain.

The Continental floor tile business grew, and in 1958 Western headquarters in Spokane decided to establish a tile plant on the Continent. The plant was built at Dortmund in 1960. Concurrently, a number of competitors, recognizing the potential in the growing Common Market, expanded production, resulting in gross overcapacity in the industry. Intense price competition ensued, in which the Dortmund company did not participate because of Western's world-wide policy of making its sales on the basis of high quality rather than low price. As a result, the Dortmund company was unable to generate enough volume to operate its plant efficiently. It experienced losses from the start, and these losses continued through 1971.

THE MOVE TO COLOGNE

Originally, Basel, Switzerland, and Dortmund, West Germany, were independent sales subsidiaries of Western of Spokane, Washington, U.S.A. They had no formal corporate connection, but since Dortmund sold only in the German market and the Swiss company sold in all of the rest of Europe, International headquarters at Spokane decided, in the beginning, that the Dortmund management should look to the

Swiss company management for direction so that the Swiss company could co-ordinate all Continental European activities.

As the years went by, it was Dortmund which developed the largest volume of business, and with this development the two managements tended to grow apart, with the German management looking less and less to Basel for direction. The building of a plant at Dortmund to supply all of the Continent augmented the independence of the German company. In 1965, a new general manager, Arthur Alder, an American, took over the Swiss company's management, and when he was unable to obtain a Swiss work permit, he established his office at Dortmund, from which he directed all Continental activities for 13 months. In 1966, Mr. Alder was replaced by John A. Corkill as chief of the Swiss company. Mr. Corkill decided to establish his headquarters office in Cologne rather than Dortmund. His reasoning was that Germany tended to dominate the European economy, and Cologne was close to Dortmund and had excellent travel and transport facilities. Following Mr. Corkill's recommendation, Western's Spokane International Division headquarters liquidated the Swiss company, changed the name of the German company to Western Lumber International, Gmbh., and designate Cologne as its headquarters office. (See Exhibit 1.)

For a year and a half the controller's office had been at the Dortmund plant. All accounting, billing, and order handling had been done there, and since Mr. Alder had his office there, the personnel had come to look upon Dortmund as the headquarters location. The move to Cologne was followed by a period of rivalry between personnel at Dortmund and Cologne, with some Dortmund people attempting to assert their independence. Mr. Corkill was aware that there had been six changes in senior executives in Switzerland and Germany during the past eight years. "This excessive turnover," said Mr. Corkill, "has certainly not fostered the development of any great loyalty to the company. One of my first major objectives was to remedy this, and to leave no doubt in anyone's mind that we were now an international operation, directed from Cologne." Mr. Corkill moved all executive, sales, and clerical offices to Cologne. In the course of this, some management personnel resigned and two Dortmund lower-level managers at first declined promotions to higher-level positions in Cologne and had to be persuaded to accept.

The Paris sales office, which had been an arm of the Basel company, had generated a sizable sales volume in France and was very profitable.

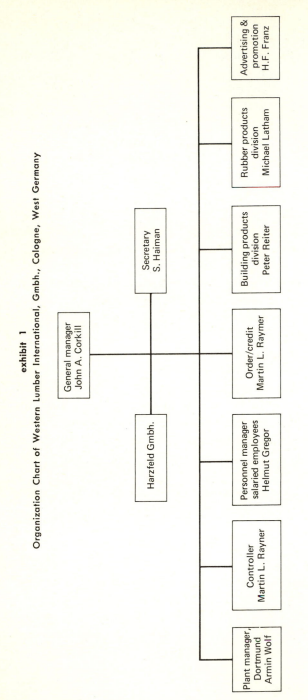

exhibit 1

Organization Chart of Western Lumber International, Gmbh., Cologne, West Germany

General manager
John A. Corkill

Secretary
S. Haiman

Harzfeld Gmbh.

Plant manager, Dortmund
Armin Wolf

Controller
Martin L. Rayner

Personnel manager
salaried employees
Helmut Gregor

Order/credit
Martin L. Raymer

Building products
division
Peter Reiter

Rubber products
division
Michael Latham

Advertising &
promotion
H.F. Franz

It was staffed entirely by Frenchmen, who operated with virtual autonomy. When the Spokane International headquarters designated Cologne as the seat of Continental European operations, it became a point of diplomacy to establish Cologne's image as an international company rather than a German company to aid in directing subsidiaries such as France.

RUBBER PRODUCTS IN EUROPE AND WORLD MARKETS

The Western Lumber Exactorol line consisted of covers for the rollers used in printing and paper-making machinery. These were made from synthetic rubber compositions, some of which included cork. Western had become a leader in this field internationally, having developed an eminent reputation for the quality of its products and for the excellence of its service.

Tempack was a foamed rubber material made in flexible tube form and in sheets, used for covering cold lines in refrigerated equipment and air conditioning units. Western Lumber had developed Tempack as a result of its search for improved insulating products. In the rubber industry, Tempack was classed as a specialty product. The major rubber companies had tried to compete in this field but withdrew when they found that they were unable to give the required exacting customer service.

In 1964, Western Lumber's largest production of Exactorols and Tempack tubes and sheets was in Bridgeport, Connecticut, U.S.A. In the United Kingdom it had two plants, operating on a co-operative basis, producing Exactorols and Tempack tubes, but they did not make Tempack sheets. The Basel, Switzerland, plant did final finishing work[2] on Exactorols and kept a warehouse inventory for sales outside the Commonwealth area, but it did not perform the primary operations, which were done either in England or in the United States. A plant in Barranquilla, Spain, did Exactorol finishing and kept a warehouse stock for the Spanish market. A Canadian plant made Tempack tubes, but made no sheets.

In 1964, the marketing of Western Lumber products in England, Continental Europe, Africa, and the Near East had been divided into four areas: Western Lumber Handelgesellschaft, Gmbh., of Dortmund

---

[2] Cutting the roller coverings to length and grinding them to precise diameter sizes within limits of tolerances.

was responsible for all sales in Western Germany. Western Lumber International, S.A., of Basel was responsible for the United Kingdom, Ireland, and the Commonwealth countries. Fabricantes de Corcho, S.A., of Granada, covered Spain.

In the United Kingdom, Western Lumber had a significant share of the industrial roller market served by Exactorols, and it had substantial penetration in Tempack for low-bore hot water heating services. The United Kingdom roller market was not growing, and the outlook indicated that it would probably decline. The Tempack market was growing and was believed to have considerable potential.

Western Lumber had an established reputation and a 20% share of the roller covering market in Germany, Switzerland, France, and Italy, and these markets were growing. Their potential was believed to be much larger than that in the United Kingdom. Western had entered Tempack into the German and Swiss markets in 1960, and its growth potential was considered substantial although the market had not been penetrated. In Spain, Western was the leading supplier of roller coverings, but it had no significant sales of Tempack. Exactorol volume in Spain was not expected to grow, but it was believed Tempack might have potential there in the future.

The European Free Trade Association consisted of the United Kingdom, Switzerland, Austria, Portugal, Norway, Sweden, and Denmark. In this area, duties charged on imports from nonmember nations (extra-EFTA duties) were significant.

The European Economic Community included Germany, France, Italy, Holland, Belgium, and Luxembourg. Extra-EEC duties were also significant here, but duties on imports from member nations (intra-EEC duties) expired at the end of 1967.

The Dortmund operation had incurred losses approaching DM 5 million ($1,375,000) in the years preceding 1964, and these could be carried forward for tax purposes to offset a portion of any capital investment which the company might decide to make in new plant and facilities in Germany.

PROBLEMS OF RATIONALIZATION

During the 1950's, Western Lumber developed a profitable volume of Exactorol and Tempack sales in continental Europe. The Dortmund company was supplied in part by Western Lumber, U.S.A., but mainly by Western's English company. It also bought Exactorols from the Swiss company.

Floor tile losses in Germany continued, while the profitable Exactorol sales grew. Also, a growing potential for Tempack became apparent. Considering these circumstances, the Western Lumber headquarters management at Spokane concluded that higher profits would be made if a rubber products plant were to be operated within the Common Market. It also felt that there ought to be a single source of supply for continental European sales. None of the plants supplying the Continent at that time were in the EEC. Complicating the situation was the outlook that the Common Market and the European Free Trade area would continue to be separate and competing trade areas. The Spokane management also felt that there was a need for long-range rationalization of all the company's rubber operations in Europe.

With this in mind, the Spokane headquarters organized a study team to analyze the situation. The team consisted of three senior executives from the Spokane International Operations Division: one in marketing, one in production, and one in finance.

After an initial appraisal of the European situation, the study team decided to analyze the long-range economics involved and to recommend a long-range plan based upon total Western Lumber Company interests. Initial considerations developed the following alternatives:

1. A single manufacturing plant in the United Kingdom to supply Europe, Africa, and the Near East.

2. A single manufacturing plant on the Continent, preferably in the European Economic Community, to supply all of Europe, Africa, and the Near East.

3. Two separate plants:
   (a) One in the United Kingdom to supply the United Kingdom, the Commonwealth countries, and the European Free Trade Association countries, except Switzerland and Austria.
   (b) One in the European Economic Community to supply the remainder of Europe, including Spain, and all of Africa and the Near East, except the British Commonwealth countries.

The Study Team Recommendation
(Interoffice communication)

To: Mr. Cedric Alderton, Vice-President, International Operations
From: Exactorol/Tempack Study Team

Having studied many combinations for the manufacture of Exactorols and Tempack in England and on the continent of Europe, this study team recommends:

1. A complete manufacturing unit in the United Kingdom to take care of the British market and the areas served from the United Kingdom.
2. Another complete manufacturing unit in West Germany to serve the European Economic Community, the rest of Europe, Africa, and the Middle East.

While this will have the short-term effect of lowering our return on capital invested, this decision is the wisest in the long run. Our reasoning follows:

1. Basel has built a substantial Exactorol/Tempack business in the area to be served by the German plant. Certainly prudence would require that we build upon this position for the future. Briefly:

   (a) Our present position is vulnerable. Any major competitor might build a plant in the Common Market.

   (b) Future product improvement in Exactorol will come in smaller increments. Competitive products will come to nearly match ours in quality. This places stress on (c).

   (c) Service, via technical advice and prompt delivery. Our Continental customers will feel more secure if Western has a sizable capital commitment in the Common Market.

   (d) So long as we rely on imports, we are wide open to the vagaries of governments, import restrictions, changes in duties, and other variables beyond our control. We have seen this happen all too often. A recent example was our ceilings business in Canada, where we enjoyed a favorable market position but lost it when a change in duty classification made it necessary for us to increase substantially our landed prices and we lost the market to local manufacturers.

2. Dortmund needs added manufacturing operations. We reviewed many possibilities; Exactorol production was clearly the most advantageous. The market is assured; we are already firmly entrenched and enjoy sales leadership. Exactorol is a high-margin line.

3. While the tax loss carryover of Dortmund will not be a continuing advantage, it will be a "plus" factor of considerable magnitude. It will represent about 80% of our proposed capital investment in fixed assets. The tax loss carryover is for five years.

4. Informed observers agree that for the next 15 years the Common Market will surpass England in the production and use of equipment employing roller coverings such as our Exactorols. Currently, the Common Market has four times the potential of the English market, and this ratio is expected to continue.

5. By 1968, the Common Market countries had a common exterior tariff barrier. Should the Labor Party prevail at the coming British

elections, the English government will probably impose import restrictions. Then the Common Market Community will probably retaliate with counter-restrictions. The proposed common European Economic Community external duty on Exactorols is 12% and on Tempack 18%. This situation re-emphasizes the dangers of relying on imports to service the Common Market.

(signed) (The Study Team)

THE NEW DORTMUND PLANT

The move from Basel to Dortmund was accomplished on time, but during 1966 and 1967 a series of events occurred which directly affected the German company's rubber operation. The Basel inventory had been moved to Dortmund without a prior evaluation, and on arrival it was discovered that about 60% of it consisted of slow-moving and obsolete items.

Western Lumber's Bridgeport, Connecticut, plant in the United States produced a larger volume than all other Western rubber plants combined, and it normally sold a major portion of its output on a jobbed-product basis to the subsidiaries abroad. In anticipation of the changes being made in the European plants, Bridgeport had built up reserve inventories. During 1966, Bridgeport met a totally unexpected surge of demand from the United States market which was so strong that its inventories were exhausted, and it suddenly found itself in an extremely oversold position. Its Exactorol shipments were then placed on allocation. The allotments were a percentage of normal 1965 sales, which left Dortmund's rapidly expanded 1966 and 1967 demand inadequately supplied.

Dortmund then turned for help to the English company, which normally supplied a substantial portion of Dortmund's rubber requirement. The English company had just built a new plant which was completed several months behind schedule, and when completed it experienced labor recruiting and training problems, resulting in low output. At this time, the demand in the United Kingdom market increased to such an extent that the English plant could barely supply the requirements of the United Kingdom. A joint decision was then made by executives of the English management, the German management, and a senior executive from the International Division at Spokane to the effect that the English company should serve, first, the domestic U.K. Market; second, the Commonwealth countries; third, others. This severely reduced the flow of rubber products to the Continent. In August of 1967, the Bridgeport plant encountered a strike which resulted in a four-month shutdown. Western's Canadian company encountered a similar strike which lasted five months. Both strikes aggravated the shortage of supply at Dortmund.

During this period Dortmund, instead of selling its own production, as had been planned, had to resort to jobbing stocks. Since it was important that Dortmund maintain Western Lumber's reputation for excellence in service, the German company, in desperation, was forced to air-freight stocks at high expense from any source available, including Western's company in India. On numerous occasions it also airfreighted deliveries to its customers.

THE RUBBER PRODUCTS MARKET IN 1971

It was the opinion of Western's Cologne management that the Germans, in the post-World War II period, had been very innovation-minded and that they welcomed any product which would help them sell internationally. "This gave Western a head start in Germany," said Mr. Michael Latham, the Englishman who was heading the Cologne's rubber products sales. "The manufacturers of the machines which use our Exactorols as components were crying for protection, but the government gave them only a minimum amount of protection, because exports were a major source of foreign currencies, and foreign currencies were needed to buy capital equipment. The Germans liked our Exactorols because they have a lot of respect for quality and precision. The German-made machines which use our Exactorols are exported widely. The buyers tend to buy replacement rollers which are the same make as the originals, and therefore we automatically developed a world-wide export market in which we get the pick of roller-covering distributors."

Mr. Latham said that he had tried all sorts of ways to measure the total potential of the German market for roller coverings, but could not be sure of his estimates. He believed that Western had about 35% to 40% of the present market. His sales in Germany represented only 40% of his total sales; 60% were export sales. The German domestic sales were growing, but export sales were growing even faster as replacement orders mounted. Mr. Latham believed that the Cologne company did not wholeheartedly sell all Western Lumber products in

Germany because of the prohibitive tariffs on some of them, but this did not hold true for Exactorols. Neither were German-made Exactorols barred from any foreign markets of importance by tariffs. Exceptions were Austria, which had high EFTA duties and was therefore sold Exactorols made in London by Western's English company; and Egypt, which had shut out English, United States, and German manufacturers and was now being supplied with Exactorols by Western's India company, a subsidiary of its English company.

Cologne's principal competition consisted of Detrol (Detroit Roller, U.S.A.), which built a plant in Scotland in 1967 and sold in the same markets as Western; Markus, a Swiss manufacturer, which sold in EFTA countries; and Cardosi, an Italian producer, which sold in the Common Market countries on the basis of price. The price of Exactorols in Germany had originally been based upon the price at which they were imported, which was a high price. It had been even higher than the price in the high-priced United States market. In 1971, German prices were still above U.S. prices, but were declining. "We have always sold our roller coverings on the basis of quality and service, and we still do," said Mr. Latham, "but competition is forcing our hand on prices more and more. Ten years ago our prices were 40% higher than competition and we didn't worry, even though our home-produced product costs are much less than our landed price of jobbed products used to be." Cologne based its prices upon the American company's price list, but its prices outside of Germany were lowered about 12%.

Mr. Latham believed that there was an unlimited potential in the German market for Tempack, since they had no direct competition. In 1971, the company had over 60% of the German market. In Germany, Tempack was used as a cool-application insulant, but it was also being used as an insulant in electrical applications. Herzog, a leading German manufacturer of household appliances and automotive electrical components, was using it on a trial basis to cover electrical conductors in appliances and in automotive ignition systems. "If applications like this prove out," said Mr. Latham, "our sales will boom. The Germans are ingenious. Technical developments in materials might make our Exactorols obsolete in time; but for our Tempack, German manufacturers are turning up new applications daily. We think that, for Tempack, the sky is the limit."

In 1971, Cologne's Rubber Products Division was considered by

Western's Spokane headquarters to be performing very well in comparison with rubber operations in other Western subsidiaries. Cologne's rubber products sales were considered to be very profitable.

FLOOR COVERINGS

"Our floorings operation in Germany is a bleak picture," said Mr. Peter Reiter, the American-born Building Products Division manager of the German company. "We in Germany recognize this. Looking back, it seems that the decision to put a plant in Germany was a mistake. We have less than 10% of the German vinyl asbestos market, where our share should be at least 20%, and our plant is geared to produce for more than a 20% market share. We have a fine floor tile plant, but it operates only at 1.5 shifts a day, and we don't have the sales volume to operate the plant three shifts a day to bring down costs. And so we are trying desperately to increase our sales in a total market which is decreasing. If we were to shut down our plant, we might have a 50:50 chance of succeeding in making our flooring operation here profitable, but we are not going to do that."

The Dortmund plant made vinyl asbestos tiles in residential patterns. It had also made asphalt tiles until early in 1969, when it dropped asphalt because of cutthroat price competition. "In most countries Western Lumber is strong in floorings because it has a broad line," said Mr. Reiter, "but in Germany, Western is on the outside looking in. Here our production is confined to vinyl asbestos, which is the very mature line. There is no trick in turning out good resilient flooring; all of our major competitors turn out quality products. What we need is more volume, and we could get it if we had more products to supplement our line."

In standard tiles, Mr. Reiter believed that Western Lumber was on a par with its competitors. On vinyl residential tiles, he thought that Western might have a superior product. This line was Cologne's lead line; it included the company's most popular patterns and it received the company's main promotional push, but it constituted only 20% of the Dortmund plant's output. "Vinyl asbestos is a waning product," said Mr. Reiter, "and so we feel compelled to supplement our line. We ought to import from our Canadian company. They make Corlon and printed rotovinyl in sheets and tufted carpeting. Our competitors are offering polyvinyl chloride tiles, which are very flexible, and are handling needlepunch and tufted carpetings and an abundant variety of sheet materials."

Western Lumber's competition in Germany and Europe consisted of Deutsche Linoleum, which dominated the German market and produced high-quality products; and Kromine in Holland, which was described by Mr. Reiter as "the giant of them all" and which sold in every export market. There were about six other major competitors, including rubber companies, such as Dunlop and Continental, which produced other floor coverings in addition to their rubber floor tiles. Mr. Reiter conceded that the major producers made quality floorings and were what he termed "first-rate competitors in every way." It was also common knowledge, he said, that there was considerable over-capacity in the industry, which resulted in extremely intense competition, and that the competition took the form of price cutting.

Vicious price cutting and dumping were common in the German and European floorings market, where many smaller firms were fighting for survival. Western Lumber had been forced to follow the price leaders. From the time the plant had begun to produce until 1971, its prices had been reduced by 40%. "As to pricing," said Mr. Reiter, "we follow headquarters policy. This means that we have been an extremely reluctant price-reducer. We are usually the last one to get on any downward spiral. It is Western Lumber's company-wide philosophy that we may meet competition head on, but we shouldn't ever take the lead in price cutting." Mr. Reiter was of the opinion that German floor tile prices were the lowest in the world—lower, even, than those of Japan.

Mr. Reiter said that a secondary effect of the desperate competition had been to make a shambles of distribution channels. "Before the deluge," he said, "most manufacturers sold through wholesalers or operated their own distribution systems. When the flood came, many middlemen just rolled over and died. Distribution became chaotic. Manufacturers sold anything to anyone, anywhere. They still sell through wholesalers if they can, but they sell direct to retailers, they sell to one-man installation contractors, and they even split cartons. The future of all flooring wholesalers in Europe is doubtful."

In most of its export markets Cologne continued to sell through local wholesalers, but in northern Germany it sold exclusively through one large wholesaling firm, Harzfeld, Gmbh. Harzfeld was the largest wholesaler of floor coverings in Germany. It had been a family business until 1965, when the principal owner died and Western Lumber bought the company. Harzfeld sold all kinds of floor coverings, including carpetings. It also sold wood floorings, parquet, and wood paneling, all of which were very popular in Germany. Before being acquired by Western, Harzfeld had been Western's wholesaler in northern Germany, where Harzfeld had a strong customer following. Members of the Harzfeld family still managed the business.

"Until a couple of years ago," said Mr. Reiter, "the Harzfelds felt that their mission in life was to be an outlet for our tile production. Profitability was incidental. We reversed their thinking on that. We convinced them that they must be profitable, and that they must be independent of us." Harzfeld produced a sizable volume of sales and continued to grow during the period of Western ownership, but from 1964 through 1968 Harzfeld had operated at a loss. In 1971, Cologne sold through Harzfeld in northern Germany and through wholesalers in southern Germany. The Cologne sales office did the advertising and promoting and was responsible for national account sales and large single projects. Harzfeld's line was being enlarged with a view to ultimately having a full line, and it was expanding into other parts of Germany. Within two years Harzfeld increased its volume by 55%, and in 1971 it earned a profit. As Harzfeld volume grew, Cologne's own sales force was reduced from 20 to 5 salesmen.

Cologne sold about 50% of the flooring it manufactured in Germany and exported 50%. There was a similar sharing in the sales of the floorings it imported from the U.S.A. and Canada. In Italy, natural terrazzos were available, and the Italians did not like the synthetic facsimiles which were popular elsewhere in vinyl; also, the natural terrazzo price was below the price of vinyl in Italy. Cologne believed that it was making good progress in France. "We have good rapport with the French," said Mr. Reiter, "and are well received there, but we must be careful to maintain our image as an international company, rather than as a German company." Cologne found its own production barred from Scandinavia by a 30% import duty, but it continued to sell there and had the floorings shipped from the English plant, which was within the EFTA area. For reasons which were not clear to the Cologne management, it had never been able to generate any worthwhile sales of resilient floorings in the Benelux countries despite the fact that it had conducted several strong promotional campaigns there.

In 1971, Cologne's floor coverings sales continued to incur losses.

The floor coverings industry in Germany continued to suffer from overcapacity, and no relief was expected within the foreseeable future.

CEILINGS

Western's German company did not have a ceilings plant, but it sold Western Lumber ceiling tiles and boards on a jobbed-product basis. It had previously imported most of its requirements from the United States. In 1968, it switched to England and thereafter obtained 90% of its stocks from that source.

Wood fiber tiles were popular in Europe, but this business was highly competitive, as a result of low-cost imports from manufacturers in Scandinavia, who had vast supplies of wood at their disposal. The Scandinavian tiles were thought to lack styling and quality. Cologne sold Western wood fiber tiles in competition with the Scandinavians at a 40% premium price, but this business was confined to the luxury sector of the market, which was estimated to be only about 10% of the total. Cologne had to import the wood fiber tiles at relatively high intercompany transfer prices and pay the heavy cost of shipment from the United States, since Western's English plant did not make wood fiber tiles.

Cologne placed its main sales emphasis on mineral fiber ceilings, which it believed had the greatest potential. Mineral ceilings had only about 20% of the European continental ceilings market in 1971; the remaining 80% was in plaster, gypsum, wood, or metal. The United States market had gone 80% to mineral coverings, and the German management believed that the European market would soon follow the U.S. trend. Cologne's largest market was France, where it was exceeding its sales forecast and held a 45% share of the market. Its next largest market was Germany, where it had a 15% market share, which was slightly less than the budgeted expectation. It also sold a modest volume in the Near East. The total sales of ceilings of Cologne were well above budget, and the management believed that within five years Western ceilings would dominate the Continental market.

Elsewhere in the world, and especially in the United States, Western Lumber had successfully promoted suspended ceilings in which the tiles or boards were placed, without any fixed attachment, in a metal grid suspended from the ceiling. These were of two types: the exposed grid, in which the tiles were simply laid into metal strips which supported them; and the concealed grid, in which the metal strips were concealed in the joints of the tiles. In the exposed-grid ceilings, it was possible to gain entrance into the plenum chamber above the suspended ceilings by simply lifting out some of the tiles. This was not possible in the concealed type, in which the tiles were relatively fixed in position once the ceiling had been installed. Elsewhere in the world it had been Western's experience that 75% of the market preferred the exposed grids, but in Europe the percentage was reversed—Europeans preferred the concealed grids. They considered the metal of the exposed grid to be unattractive. At the same time, they wanted easy access to the plenum chamber should maintenance or repair of underlying utilities be required.

In other markets boards (24 by 48 inches) outsold tiles (12 by 12 inches) in the ratio of two to one. In Europe, consumers preferred tiles and showed no inclination to change their preference. "Sometimes you just can't win the fight to get a U.S. item accepted abroad," said Mr. Reiter. "Perhaps it would be best to acknowledge that there are plenty of things about boards that could be improved. Maybe we should follow local preferences."

Western's mineral ceiling prices were 10% above its competitors'. To justify this, Western was pushing the sale of its suspended ceilings, in which it could show contractors that the installed cost of the ceiling was lower because of the simplicity of the installation method. Cologne sold to both wholesalers and contractors, and its promotional efforts were beamed at specifiers, who were architects or engineers.

The bulk of the English ceilings plant's production was in inch sizes. These were unacceptable in Germany and France. Germany was centered on the DIN module (Deutsche International Normal), which stemmed from bricklaying standards and measured 62.5 by 62.5 centimeters. The French used AFNOR, which was based upon 30-, 60-, 90-, or 120-centimeter graduations. In the early postwar period it had been possible to sell inch sizes on the Continent, which was then a seller's market, but buyers now rejected any sizes but their own. The English plant produced the DIN and AFNOR sizes when required to do so, but it added substantially to costs because of the changes in machine setup which were involved, and because it shortened production runs.

Cologne's sales management was trying hard to capitalize on the fire protection advantages of mineral tile. Fire codes had been common in the U.S. for decades, but in Europe they were just beginning to be used. Western's mineral ceilings retarded heat long enough to keep beams from sagging for four hours, and salesmen used this fact as a strong sales point. Fire retardation was used as a theme in Cologne's advertising, and Germany's sales managers did considerable behind-the-scenes work to encourage fire protection requirements with city officials, government authorities, insurance companies, and government testing laboratories.

Cologne had numerous local competitors for ceiling tiles in German, French, and Scandinavian firms, but its strongest competition came from several subsidiaries of United States companies, which had local production: Celotex had a plant in England; U.S. Gypsum had recently built a plant in Belgium; and Johns-Manville had a licensed production arrangement with a German manufacturer. Western's ceiling sales by Cologne were moderately profitable, and both in volume and profitability were increasing. Cologne management envisioned a complete ceilings production facility, to be built in Germany within the next five years.

WESTERN LUMBER AND BUILDING SUPPLY CORPORATION (D)

"When I first came to Spain," said Mr. Mark Kroll, general manager of Western Lumber's Spanish operations, "I was, in effect, a production manager. We had surplus employees, turned out too much scrap, had antiquated operations, costs were high, so were expenses, and we had too many plants.

"We didn't have a marketing problem; we sold all of our production —but we sold it at a loss. We still have some production problems, but now I am giving my attention to marketing. In effect, I am now a marketing manager.

"Actually, if I were acting as I should as General Manager, and Western Lumber was just coming into Spain for the first time, we probably would not operate plants. We would have a small sales force operating out of Madrid, and we would be selling a product line which would be quite different from our present one. But my management has inherited the remnants of Western Lumber's long cork history in Spain, and my job is to work out something from that base. What we do might be an evolution, a gradual change; or it might be a metamorphosis, a transformation to something entirely different."

WESTERN LUMBER IN THE CORK BUSINESS

In its sawmill operations in the United States in the early 1900's, Western Lumber produced massive quantities of sawdust, which it sold as an insulating material to icehouses and cold storage companies. During the 1920's home refrigerators came into popular use. Since cork was used as an insulant in the refrigerators, Western added cork insulation to its line. At this time Western also added linoleum (a cork product) to its prefinished wood flooring line (parquets, etc.). Linoleum and insulation sales rose rapidly. Seeking to control the source of its cork supply, Western bought cork plantations and cork-fabricating facilities in Spain, the world's leading source of cork. By 1930 Western Lumber had a spread of facilities in Spain and had become one of the largest producers of cork and basic cork products in the world.

Cork had long since passed the peak period of its popularity and was rapidly being supplanted by synthetic materials which had technical and economic advantages. During the post-World War II period, Western Lumber had been phasing out its Spanish operations, and by the 1960's its headquarters management was actively addressing itself to the question of what should be done with its remaining Spanish facilities. The question was complicated by the fact that Western's Spanish business was still moderately profitable. However, in quality cork production, Spain was being out-produced and underpriced by Portugal.

BACKGROUND OF THE SPANISH COMBINE OF PLANTS

In 1925, mainly to obtain control of its sources of supply, Western bought a cork-fabricating company in Granada. Later a cork insulating board plant was built at Malaga and new curing ovens were installed at Granada, which increased Western's insulating board capacity to 2.5 million board feet per month. At this time Granada and Malaga employed 1,500 people.

In 1929 Western Lumber acquired the Spanish firm of Fabricantes de Corcho, S.A., together with its subsidiaries, Cork Imports, Incorporated, of New York, and Cork Supply Ltd. of London. Fabricantes de Corcho had plants in the coastal towns of Barramos and Barranquilla and in Pagura and Cherone. Through this acquisition Western Lumber also acquired a 55% interest in Lamantes, S.A.; Lamantes operated a cork plant which was also in Barranquilla, close to the Fabricantes de Corcho factory. In 1931 Western consolidated all of its Spanish holdings in Fabricantes de Corcho, S.A., with headquarters in Granada. The 55% ownership interest in Lamantes was not changed and still existed in 1971. (See Exhibit 1.)

exhibit 1

Organization Chart of Fabricantes de Corcho, S.A.

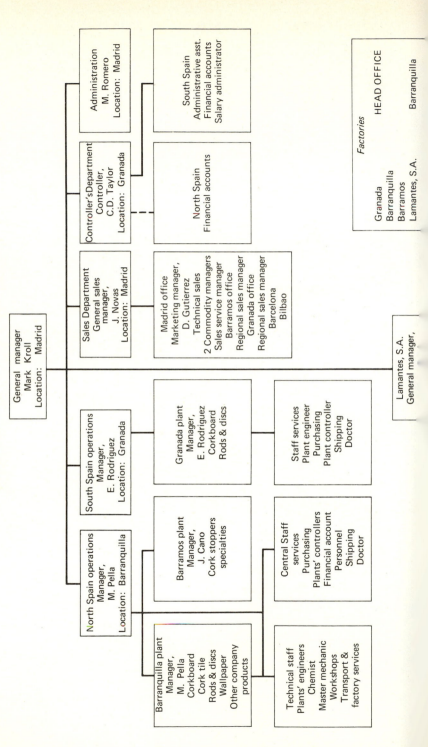

730

THE EFFECTS OF THE SPANISH CIVIL WAR
AND WORLD WAR II

The general economic depression of the 1930's caused Western's operations to suffer large losses. During the Spanish Civil War three Western plants (Granada, Malaga, and La Boca) were in Nationalist Franco territory, while four others (Barramos, Barranquilla, Pagura, and Cherone) were located in the Loyalist north. During the course of the war the northern plants came under fire and suffered 20 million pesetas ($280,000) in damage.

Fabricantes prepared and sold basic cork raw materials to Western Lumber in the United States and to its subsidiaries in England, Switzerland, and Germany. An even larger volume of its output consisted of manufactured products: corkboard, cigarette tipping, gaskets, roller coverings, seine floats, bottle stoppers, mooring buoys, crown cap liners, flooring, insoles for shoes, and handle grips for tools. Some of these products were sold in Spain, but most were exported, largely to the United States. The 1930 United States Tariff Act sharply depressed U.S. imports, and Fabricantes was forced to scale down its operations to the volume required for Spain and Europe.

World War II almost halted Spanish imports. It stopped exports to Germany, which had been a major buyer of wine and champagne stoppers and beer bottle crown discs. For six months no vessels were available for Spanish exports, and thereafter priorities favored United States and British requirements to the virtual exclusion of all other trade.

WESTERN'S CHANGING BUSINESS IN SPAIN

Mr. Mark Kroll, an American, had been managing director of Western Lumber's Spanish operations since 1950. Reminiscing about Western's experience in Spain he said:

> Until the war ended, cork was 100% of Western's business in Spain. Headquarters looked upon Spain as a source of raw and semiprocessed cork, mostly for shipment to the United States and England. During the postwar years, Spain operated with large losses.
>
> I came to Spain in 1950 to sell Fabricantes. Headquarters wanted to sell the whole show, but that never came to pass. We initiated some

drastic evolutionary measures, which kept me there much longer than I had expected. In 1958 the government revalued the peseta at 60 to the dollar. Losses in the Fabricantes program were suddenly converted to profits. There followed a ten-year period during which we disposed of our surplus facilities, and we initiated an all-out attack on expenses. Western Lumber once employed over 3,000 people in Spain and was prosperous, but later it got into perilous financial condition and was regularly into the banks for overdrafts up to 80 million pesetas (about $1,120,000). Now we are down to about 600 employees, but every factory is earning a modest profit, we have reduced our overdrafts to 20 million pesetas (about $280,000), and we are paying dividends to headquarters regularly. Since 1967 we have been backing three drives: a concentration on marketing; the improvement of our sales organization; and an importation program.

THE FABRICANTES MANAGEMENT [1]

In 1966 Mr. Kroll moved his office to Madrid, which was closer to the center of Spain. Fabricantes was then managed from Madrid, although some of the top management had offices at other locations. The company's legal seat remained at Granada, taxes and official company reports were filed from Granada, Fabricantes' comptroller had his office there, and Mr. Kroll flew to Granada when his presence was required at official functions, such as meetings of the board of directors.

Three of Fabricantes' board members were Spaniards; the other four were American, English, or Canadian. Sr. Vicente Robles was general manager of Lamantes Barranquilla; Sr. Pablo Cortes was a prominent Madrid businessman; and Sr. Carlos Cortez, Fabricantes' legal counsel, was a resident of Seville. Mr. Roger Hyatt, who was president of the board, had been the general manager of Fabricantes, but had returned to the United States for reasons of health. The remaining board members were: Mr. Kroll; Mr. Donald Mercer, vice president and general manager of Western Lumber International; and Mr. William Schilling, general manager of production, Western Lumber International. There was one substitute member, Dr. Pedro Allicante, who was director of personnel of Fabricantes.

The board met its legal responsibilities by meeting four times a year. All capital expenditures above 42,000 pesetas ($3,000) required board approval; so did major personnel action (which had already been

[1] See Exhibit 1.

cleared with Mr. Kroll and Spokane headquarters). Board approvals were automatic.

Mr. Kroll, chief executive of Fabricantes, had a capital expenditure approval authority up to $3,000 (42,000 pesetas). There were no control limits on inventories or current expenditures. Mr. Kroll had control of all salaries through his control of the annual budget, which included all salary changes. No specific limits had been placed upon Mr. Kroll's powers of appointment; however, he cleared major actions with Spokane.

CORK—MARKETS AND PRODUCTION

"Tourists say that Spain is different," said Sr. Mario Romero. "Cork is also different. It was used by the Greeks for flask stoppers over 2,000 years ago, and its technology and uses have not changed much since. And it seems that its usages have been exhausted—not much more can be developed from it." Sr. Romero, Mr. Kroll's administrative assistant, had long experience in the cork industry and was considered the company's cork expert.

Cork was the outer layer of the Cork oak tree, which was native to the Iberian Peninsula. Cork oaks were not cultivated in systematic plantations, but grew at random in open, park-like groves. They were usually grown in conjunction with hog feeding, the pigs being grazed in the cork forests, where they fattened on the acorns. The average oak tree had to reach 35 years in age before being stripped for the first time; thereafter it required nine years or more before it could be stripped again. Cork oaks had a life of 500 to 700 years. It was common practice that tracts of oak forest were owned by large landowners who leased the grazing rights to pig farmers but retained the cork harvesting to themselves. Cork harvesting and cork-acorn pig-feeding were both marginal-profit operations. There had been very little study of how the cork tree might be improved to produce more cork or cork of a higher quality, and therefore the wild-tree product was accepted as it came. Neither had much research been done to find uses for cork other than the traditional ones. The Confederated European Cork Association was said to be studying possible new products from cork, but no results had been published.

Sr. Romero admitted that the cork industry in Spain was experiencing a long period of decline. "Spain never was really the leader in the cork business," he said. "The Portuguese cultivate their forests better than the Spaniards, and so they produce higher-quality cork. They have always had a higher volume of production than Spain, and they are the number one producer in the world today. Portugal's largest export is Port wine; its second is cork. Cork is number eight in rank among Spain's exports."

Portuguese cork undersold Spanish cork in the world markets. Porguese wage rates were lower than the Spanish ones, its labor taxes were not as high, and Portugal being a small country, its producing forests were close to seaports, whereas Spanish cork areas were inland. From the port of Lisbon ships carried Portuguese cork to most every port in the world.

Western Lumber did not have any cork production or fabrication facilities in Portugal. However, its subsidiaries, Cork Imports Incorporated of New York and Cork Supply Limited of London, had agency offices in Lisbon which bought all kinds of cork for United States and United Kingdom usage. These agencies did not limit their buying to Portugal, but could buy from any source they preferred, regardless of whether the source was affiliated with Western Lumber or not, but in most instances the buyers made their purchases in Portugal.

"Western Lumber has lost interest in the cork business," said Mr. Kroll, "but our Spanish operation is now profitable. However, we don't know how much profitability is left in the present product mix. In some areas we are getting a larger share of a shrinking market because Fabricantes has become more aggressive, both in pricing and in service, where our competitors might be coasting."

Mr. Kroll cited cork liners for crown bottle caps as an example. Cork had long been the traditional material for these liners, and cork had technical advantages, being suitable for every known bottled material except mineral waters, which disintegrated the cork. Competition from plastic liners was now mounting and it was believed that in the long run varnished sealers would take over the market. In 1971 cork liners accounted for 40% of Fabricantes' total sales volume, and they were more profitable than most other products in its line. Start-up in plastic liner production was costly because the equipment—the dies and plastic ejection molders—were expensive. Therefore, the first cost of plastic liner production, usually at relatively low volume, was higher than that of cork. In the long run and at high volume, plastic was conceded to be lower in cost.

To discourage newcomers from entering into plastic production, Fabricantes resorted to (1) price competition, and (2) giving faster service. The price concessions were in the form of a progressive series of discounts from list price for several quantity brackets of liners purchased in a single business year, up to a discount of 15% for all purchases over a certain volume. As a result of these discounts the business of some customers doubled, but there were some customers who demanded that the maximum discount of 15% be made applicable retroactively to all of the liners which they had bought in the course of the year. To give better service, Fabricantes persuaded Western's Spokane management to permit it to invest ptas 1,500,000 (about $21,000) in this "mature" product to expand its disc-slicing capacity so that it could guarantee swift delivery to its major customers during the midsummer months, when demand was at its peak. In 1971 Fabricantes was making more profit on cork liners than on all other cork products combined.

Cork floor tiles were considered to be a declining-profit item. They had once been a popular international product, manufactured at several Western Lumber plants; now Fabricantes Barranquilla was the only plant which continued to produce them. When Fabricantes once sold cork tiles in a widespread world market, 85% of its production now went to the United Kingdom. Cork tiling presented technical problems. The tiles were not uniform in color. The color also changed with age and exposure to light, so that furniture or throw rugs, if moved, left behind an outline of their former position. Cork absorbed grease, and it did not readily accept varnish or wax finishes. It could not be dyed. It changed in dimension with age, and to allow for this, it had to "rest" in unfinished form in a warehouse and was finished to final dimensions only upon receipt of an order.

Cork tiles were sold in competition with vinyl tiles, which had technical and aesthetic advantages and were sold at a retail price which was below that of cork tile. The Fabricantes management was convinced that cork tiles could never be produced at as low a cost as vinyl, even at very high volume levels. Its export sales to England had been a loss operation for many years. Sr. Romero would have liked to change the image of cork flooring in the public mind by convincing them that cork was a luxury product, and that its varying shades of color were attractive (as had been done with knotty pine in the United States), but this would have required a sizable expenditure for missionary advertising for a product which Western Lumber headquarters considered to be on its way out.

Cork Imports Incorporated in the United States had once been a subsidiary of Fabricantes and had once sold a sizable volume of Fabricantes cork tiles in the United States. Later Cork Imports became a direct subsidiary of Western Lumber, U.S.A., after which it dropped the direct distribution of cork tiles from its line and sold Fabricantes cork tile only to wholesalers and contractors who did not compete with Western Lumber in other floor tilings. Mr. Kroll and Sr. Romero had tried to restimulate the interest of Cork Imports in tile floorings but had not succeeded.

"Our only remaining customers for cork flooring are the British," said Sr. Romero. "They are traditionalists and like to have cork flooring in their wood-paneled offices. They also use it in commercial areas and in public places, like schools and libraries. It's a good business, but our English sister company insists on prices that are so low that we regularly lose money on the operation. We would like to raise our prices to a point where we would earn a little profit, but our English friends tell us that if we do that, they will stop buying our cork tiles. They would rather sell vinyl anyway."

It was Western's policy to discount transfer prices, allowing the producing company only a modest profit. In the event of an intercompany disagreement on transfer price, a Western Lumber International Division executive, the director of production, acted as umpire and was authorized to set the price. Early in 1971 Fabricantes had appealed for such an arbitration with respect to the price paid by the English company for cork tiles, and as a result the price was increased 8%. The English company management accepted the ruling, but they pointed out that they would have to sell the cork tiles at higher prices, which might very well result in a fading away of their present cork tile sales. This was especially likely because competitors were selling Portuguese-made cork tiles of equal quality at lower prices. These lower-priced Portuguese cork tiles were also being sold in the United States market.

At Barranquilla Fabricantes also manufactured cork stoppers for wine, brandy, and cordial bottles. These were cut whole from the top grades of natural cork, the quality being determined mainly by the lesser incidence of pores, which meant that the high-quality cork had greater density. The scrap which remained after stoppers had been cut from the natural cork was ground and pressed into agglomerated cork, which went into lower-quality usages, such as corkboard or crown bottle-cap liners. Therefore the production of stoppers was interlinked with the production of other cork products, and all were interdependent.

There was a substantial demand for bottle stoppers for spirits and liquors in Europe, especially in Spain, Italy, France, Germany, and England. However, only quality wines and liquors used cork stoppers. Quality wines were aged in barrels for several years before being bottled. The cheaper everyday table wines were bottled and sold the same year, before the next grape crop was harvested. The cheap table wines were the big-volume item, and the trend was toward using plastic stoppers for these, or plastic-tipped cork stoppers. In 1971 bottle stoppers represented 24% of the total sales volume of Fabricantes, and the profit margin on them was fairly high. To cultivate this business, the Fabricantes management kept in close touch with wineries and distillers.

THE TREND AWAY FROM CORK

In the 1950's Western Lumber in the United States gradually began to move away from the use of agricultural raw materials, such as wood and cork. In the floor covering field vinyl, asphalt, and asbestos materials were proving to be more durable and were replacing linoleum. The insulation field was being pre-empted by synthetic products, such as Fiberglas, foam glass, and polystyrene. In the closure field a myriad of plastic materials had become available to replace cork for bottle stoppers. Gypsum, cement, and mineral fiberboards were competing with wood and corkboards. The eager public acceptance of the technical and economic advantages in many synthetic products was seen by Western Lumber's top management as a clear warning that a long-range decline in the use of all natural fibers was imminent, and it shifted its strategies accordingly. Some headquarters executives went so far as to predict that cork would eventually disappear from the Western line altogether.

In 1958 the Pagura plant, which had manufactured cork tips for cigarettes, was closed because of a shift in customer preferences to other types of filter tips. In 1959 the Cherone plant was closed because of the decline in the demand for corkwood. In 1963 the Malaga corkboard plant was sold. This reduced the number of Western Lumber plants in Spain from seven in 1957 to four in 1964. In 1957 there had been 3,200 employees; in 1971 there were 585.

In the early 1900's the price of cork had been low and stable. During World War II and the Korean conflict the price rose sharply, causing cork to be replaced by substitute materials. In 1971 the only regularly profitable items produced by Fabricantes were rods and discs (for crown bottle-cap liners), champagne bottle stoppers, and cork wallpaper. Corkboard, cork pipe covering, cork floor tile, and cork bottle stoppers (except champagne corks) were usually break-even items, and sometimes they lost money.

THE FABRICANTES BARRAMOS PLANT

The city of Barramos was located on the Costa Brava, the northern Mediterranean coast of Spain. It had one of the finest beaches in north Spain, and as a resort area it was outranked only by the French Riviera. European tourists flocked to Barramos. Numerous high-rise apartments had been built up all around the Fabricantes Barramos plant, and as a result the plant real estate value had increased significantly. The actual value of the Fabricantes Barramos real estate was a subject for speculation among Fabricantes executives. Optimists believed that in Spain's fast-rising economy Barramos land values would appreciate at an accelerating rate. Others pointed out that the value of such land was highly speculative and fluctuated sharply depending on current building programs, the total dwelling units in existence, occupancy percentages, and similar factors. Some realtors believed that the area was already saturated and that the time of peak price had already passed; there had been periods when there had been no buyers in the market at any price. The Barramos property was carried on the Fabricantes books at a value of about 2 million pesetas ($28,000); estimates of its actual value ranged as high as 20 million ($280,000), and even the most conservative estimates valued the parcel at triple its book value.

The Barramos plant produced cork bottle stoppers, and this had been a loss operation until 1964, when drastic cost reduction programs resulted in achieving the break-even point. Cork bottle stoppers were generally being displaced by plastic stoppers, which were cheaper. No one in Western Lumber believed that the cork stopper business had a promising future. Barramos also produced floor tiles; gasket materials; expansion joints for buildings, bridges, and airfields; antivibration pads for machinery; and wads for cartridges. The profit margin on these items was attractive, but the total sales volume was very small.

It had been suggested that the plant site be converted into a deluxe resort hotel, but the cost of remodeling appeared to be prohibitive. Moreover, the operation of a resort hotel was not within the stated operating policies of Western.

The Barramos and Barranquilla plants were only five miles apart and operated as separate companies before Western acquired them. In 1969 they were still separate operations. Barramos employed less than 100 people, and there had been problems in staffing the management. Barranquilla employed over 400 people, Mr. Kroll considered it to be well managed, and it was the most profitable of the Fabricantes plants. Mr. Kroll was very much interested in the possibility of shifting the Barramos production activities to Barranquilla. He believed that shifting the profitable products from Barramos to Barranquilla would cause Barramos to become a chronic loss operation, which would legitimately permit the permanent release of the remaining employees, at the same time enhancing the profitability of Barranquilla.

THE FABRICANTES BARRANQUILLA PLANT

Although Barranquilla was located five miles inland from Barramos, it was still considered to be within the coastal resort area. The land. the plant occupied had also appreciated in value, but not as much as at Barramos. It was carried on the Fabricantes books at 3 million pesetas ($42,000), and its actual value was subject to the same conjectures as that of the Barramos land.

Barranquilla produced corkboard, cork floor tile, cork gasketing, cork wallpaper, and cork rods. Its main activity at one time consisted of making cork cigarette tips, which had kept whole batteries of machines busy. Cork now had been displaced in the industry by plastic tips. The prices of all of the Barranquilla products were being driven down by synthetic substitutes. The single exception was cork wallpaper, which carried a good gross margin.

LAMANTES, BARRANQUILLA

Lamantes, S.A., was owned 55% by Western Lumber (USA) and 45% by the family of Sr. Vicente Robles, who managed the plant. The plant, which employed 32 people, was ten minutes' walking distance from the Fabricantes Barranquilla plant, but there was no interchange of any kind between the two operations. Lamantes manufactured only champagne corks, a business which was doing well in 1971. A decade ago the champagne cork business had been declining, because of the competition from plastic stoppers. Champagne producers, however, had come to believe that the plastic did not perform as well technically, and that the quality of the champagne was affected. High-quality champagnes underwent two bottlings. The first one used one grade of cork, the second one used a different grade of cork, and the second cork imparted a flavor to the aging champagne. Champagne bottlers believed that plastic stoppers affected the taste of the champagne; many were now reverting to cork. There was also a tradition that the opening of a champagne bottle should be accompanied by a resounding pop of the stopper, which corks provided but which was absent in plastic stoppers.

In 1964 a major program of improving the Lamantes product was undertaken, and this, together with a cost reduction program, had resulted in a sharp increase in sales. Lamantes' sales volume represented about 10% of the total sales volume of the Spanish group and accounted for about 20% of total profits. It was believed that the future of the champagne cork stopper business was very promising.

Sr. Robles, who was 73 years old in 1971, personally supervised every detail of the operation of the Lamantes plant. He reported regularly to Mr. Kroll and worked in harmony with him.

FABRICANTES IN GRANADA

"We must do something about our Granada plant," said Mr. Kroll, "and we would do it tomorrow if we could—but we are restricted by Spanish law. We would like to drop the production of unprofitable items in Granada. This would mean dropping 100 people from our payroll. But this over-all operation of our Granada plant is profitable, and as long as that is true, the government will not permit us to release employees."

Granada produced corkboard, which had been a losing operation for years; it also produced rods and discs, which were profitable enough to offset the corkboard losses and place the Granada plant in a borderline position.

One of the largest customers of Fabricantes Granada was the Western Lumber Contracting Corporation, U.S.A., a wholly owned subsidiary of the parent company. The Contracting Corporation was a building contractor, specializing in insulation, its specialty being the insulation of industrial and commercial buildings which require refrigeration. To obtain Contracting Corporation business, Fabricantes Granada had to meet the low prices of Portuguese competitors, where labor rates were lower, where there was a larger supply of natural cork, and where it was rumored that export business was subsidized by the Portuguese government. The Contracting Corporation did not restrict its usage of insulating material to cork. It used whatever material was most suitable to any specific job, whether the material was made by Western Lumber or not, and therefore it used such materials as Fiberglas, foam glass, and polystyrene. Fabricantes Granada therefore had to compete with these synthetics.

The immediate area in which the Granada plant was located had once been an industrial sector on the edge of the city. All of Fabricantes' industrial neighbors had sold their lands to residential developers; Fabricantes was the only factory which remained, and it was surrounded by modern housing developments. As a result, the value of Fabricantes' Granada had increased significantly. It was carried on the company books at 2 million pesetas ($28,000), but was variously estimated to have a market value of as much as 60 million pesetas ($840,000). During the past few years the company had received unsolicited bids in substantial amounts for the purchase of the parcel, but none had been seriously considered. "But the handwriting is clearly on the wall for all to see," said Mr. Kroll. "We know that we ought to take some kind of action before the city government forces us to do so. They could complicate our problems by appropriating the right-of-way for streets to run through our present plant area. They could also take over the whole plant site by eminent domain procedure. Then we would be in the uncomfortable position of having to contest an action by a city in which our company is well liked, especially by the people in our immediate area, many of whom are loyal Fabricantes employees."

Anticipating the need to move, Fabricantes Granada had bought a 14-acre tract of land outside of the City of Granada, and Mr. Kroll was considering several alternatives before drawing plans for a new plant. "I might propose," he said, "to end the murderous price competition that has always plagued the entire corkboard industry by holding to higher prices for our Granada production. This would probably price Fabricantes out of the market. We would lose our customers and be forced to reduce production. At the lower production volume employees would automatically go from incentive pay to their base wage rates. The employees to be dropped would then in all likelihood be willing to accept a termination bonus and resign. This would make the maneuver entirely legal."

"What we would like most, however," said Mr. Kroll, "would be to say to the City of Granada: 'We will move our rods and discs to a new plant on our new 14-acre site, but we would like to drop the corkboard.' But we are not really sure how our 'higher-price' strategy might work out. It might actually result in raising corkboard prices throughout the industry. We at Fabricantes might have more influence than we think."

CORKBOARD

Corkboard, which consisted of coarsely ground cork granules pressed and baked into board form, was the cork product which had originally led Western Lumber into the cork business. During the 1920's it had been considered superior to sawdust as an insulant, and in the 1960's many design engineers still considered it the best of all insulating materials. The closed-cell construction of cork made it an excellent nonconductor of heat; competing synthetic materials had cell structures which only approached, but did not match, those of cork. In many applications where vibration was a factor, such as in ships, trains, and trucks, cork had superior performance characteristics; where plastic insulants hardened and disintegrated in time, cork retained its resilience and elasticity and full shape indefinitely. In spite of severe competition which drove down the price, much demand for corkboard remained.

Cork was a dense material, weighing about one and one-half times as much as synthetic insulants, which placed it at a disadvantage in many applications where lighter materials were preferred. Corkboard was also dirtier and was more costly to handle in the installation stage. It had to be sawed and fitted and sealed with adhesives; many synthetics could be knife-cut. In the United States, Western Lumber had developed and was marketing a liquid plastic material which was blown into the space to be insulated, where it solidified as a lightweight, cream-colored foam, filling every crevice and requiring no shaping and no adhesive. Most plastic insulants cost only three-fourths as much as cork, or less.

Fabricantes manufactured corkboard at Granada and Barranquilla, and at both plants the manufacturing process was considered to be old-fashioned and inefficient. The Granada plant used the steam-baking process, by which the cork granules were baled into large blocks, steam-baked in retorts under high pressure, and later sawed to board dimensions. It was largely a hand process, and while it made a stronger coakboard, the production process was costly, resulting in an operation which had been losing money for many years. At Barran-quilla, Fabricantes made corkboard under licenses by the Garlati process, which was more automated and efficient and resulted in mod-est profits.

The Fabricantes management had decided against converting the Granada plant to the lower-cost Garlati process for three reasons: The owner of the Garlati process had already given license rights to a com-petitor in Granada, which meant that acquiring manufacturing rights would involve lengthy negotiations. The Western Lumber headquar-ters management considered corkboards to be a "mature" product—one which had already passed the peak of its sales potential—and therefore felt it too late to warrant the investment required. Finally, Fabricantes might soon move from its present residential location in Granada to its new plant site, and in moving, the management would prefer to phase out the corkboard operation altogether. While the Garlati process resulted in a profitable operation, all of the rest of the industry used the steam-baking process, which produced a stronger corkboard.

In 1971 cork products accounted for 81% of the sales volume of Fabricantes, and corkboard was the second largest-volume cork prod-uct, generating 24% of cork product sales and surpassed only by rods and discs; in some recent years its volume had equaled that of rods and discs. "Regardless of our present volume of production," said Mr. Kroll, "the world market for corkboard has shrunk, and will shrink further. And the Portuguese are selling corkboard at prices which are lower than we can produce it." Mr. Kroll was considering the possi-bility of Fabricantes having two separate corkboard operations in Spain: Granada, using the steam-baked process, would sell at higher prices; Barranquilla, using the Garlati process, would sell at lower prices. Each of these corkboards had different technical characteristics, and he thought that the two price levels might be maintained by having two product names. Also, the Granada and Barranquilla plants sold their output in relatively independent markets.

CORK WALLPAPER

Cork wallpaper consisted of highly porous cork sliced extremely thin ($\frac{1}{13}$ of a millimeter) by special machines and cut into small rectangles which were laid with an adhesive upon a painted paper. The poorest grades of cork were used to take advantage of the irregular porous openings, and through these openings the colors of the paint—usually luminous hues, such as chartreuse, shocking pink, copper, bronze, or gold—shone with a pleasing effect. The production process was largely a hand process; a skilled girl could lay the rectangles on about six to eight rolls a day. Cork wallpaper was exceptionally durable, but it had the disadvantage of fading and showing light areas where pictures had been hung. It was also expensive, retailing for about $10 for a 30-foot roll.

Despite its high price, cork wallpaper found immediate acceptance with interior decorators who catered to the luxury market. Fabricantes placed heavy promotional effort behind a drive to sell it to the Western companies in Germany, England, and the United States. The sales drive was successful, but Fabricantes, which manufactured the wallpaper only at Barranquilla, quickly found itself flooded with orders and badly oversold. Barranquilla made a strenuous effort to increase production, but since this involved training girls in the hand skill required to lay the rectangles accurately upon the paper, increasing production volume was a slow process. The oversold condition prevailed for many months, and while Barranquilla was struggling to increase its output, the associated companies decided that, although the profit margin on cork wallpaper was exceptionally high, the total potential volume of sales of this luxury product was so low that it was not worth fighting the battle of delayed deliveries, and they lost interest. Barranquilla meanwhile had geared up its production to serve a world market, and it overproduced an abundance of stock for inventory. In 1971 Fabricantes tried to re-enthuse the associated companies, which countered by asking Fabricantes to hold the inventory stocks, permitting associated companies to order as little as 50 rolls at a time. Sixty per cent of Fabricantes wallpaper sales were to a single distributor in the United States; the remaining 40% went to Germany, France, and the United Kingdom. The dollar-value sales volume of Fabricantes' cork wallpaper was approaching $300,000, which Western's Spokane headquarters did not consider impressive, except that Fabricantes sales were at a gross margin of 30%, in addition to which the Spanish company received a 20% tax rebate on the invoiced value, and other Western companies retailed the wallpaper at a high rate of profit. The volume of cork wallpaper sales was slowly growing. In terms of return on capital employed, wallpaper was the most profitable item in the Fabricantes product line.

IMPORTED PRODUCTS

In 1962 the Spanish government liberalized import restrictions. The following year Western embarked upon an importation program, concentrating upon (1) Western Lumber's Exactorol roller-covering line; (2) mineral fiber tile ceilings; (3) Western's Tempak pipe covering insulation.

The Spanish government classified all imported products in three categories:

a. Liberalized, which meant that they could be brought in in any quantity at any time, subject to duty.

b. Globalized, which meant that they could be brought in occasionally (usually twice a year). This made continuity of supply very difficult.

c. Bilateral, in which each shipment of the product had to be negotiated with the government, whose approval was required before it was permitted to be imported.

Most Western Lumber resilient floor coverings were in the globalized category, which had caused constant out-of-stock problems. The only item which lent itself to importation on a practical basis was asphalt tile, which was not popular in Spain. Importing resilient floor covering had been attempted without success and the project was abandoned. Needle-punch carpets were liberalized and Fabricantes was actively seeking a source for this product.

The Fabricantes management was of the opinion that Western's ceiling tiles encountered little competition in Spain. Substitutable products, however, such as plasterboard and other gypsum fabrications, provided strong competition. The low living standard in Spain caused Western Lumber's imported products to be out of reach of the majority of Spanish consumers. The Spanish economy, in 1970–1971, had one of the fastest growth rates in Europe, and the Fabricantes management believed that the growing prosperity of Spanish consumers held great promise for some Western Lumber products.

In 1971 the sale of three imported Western Lumber "jobbed" products accounted for 11% of Fabricantes' total sales volume and returned 47% of Fabricantes' net profit after taxes. Subject to unpredictable import restrictions in the future, the Fabricantes management estimated that within five years its sales of jobbed products would reach ptas 300 million (about $4.2 million). The company's total sales of all its products in 1971 was ptas 180 million ($2.5 million)—a return after taxes of about 10%, and a return on invested capital (at book value) of approximately 7%.

EXACTOROL IN SPAIN

Earlier in its history Fabricantes had produced precision cork-covered rollers, and these had been distributed in the world market through a Spanish distributor. When exports were resumed after World War II, cork as a roller covering was supplanted by rubber and compounds of rubber and cork, which Western manufactured in the United States, Germany, and England. When the Fabricantes management reassessed its product lines, cork roller coverings were dropped in favor of the technically superior rubber compounds, which could be sold at an attractive profit, whereas cork rollers were a losing operation. Cork roller coverings were still in demand in the price-conscious Spanish market, and some of Fabricantes' competitors were known to be importing them from abroad.

When stabilization came to Spain, rubber was globalized and, anticipating aggressive competition, Fabricantes made massive imports of Exactorols from Germany. Later rubber was liberalized, and Fabricantes mounted an intensive advertising campaign which was successful. In 1971 Fabricantes had 40% of the Spanish roll covering market, sales were still rising, and it believed that it would soon have a 70% market share. Exactorols accounted for 4% of Fabricantes' total sales volume in 1971, and were more profitable than most other products. Fabricantes wanted to manufacture its own Exactorols, but Western

Lumber headquarters did not wish to proliferate Exactorol manu-facture. Therefore the Spanish company continued to import from Western's German company.

TEMPAK

Tempak, Western Lumber's rubber insulating covering, had not been imported by Fabricantes until late in 1969. Mr. Kroll was aware that every other Western Lumber company in Europe was selling Tempak profitably. Refrigeration was not yet popular in Spain; air conditioning was found mainly in public buildings, and its use was growing. Since rubber was liberalized, Fabricantes set a sales goal of ptas 3 million (about $42,000) for 1971, and exceeded its sales goal. Management was pleased with this effort and decided to set up a crash sales program for 1972.

SALES OF CEILING PRODUCTS

Sales of imported ceilings, begun in 1968, made a promising start, and in 1971 represented 13% of the total sales volume of Fabricantes and provided an attractive return on capital employed, but without full allowance for organizational expenses.

The Fabricantes management believed that in Spain high quality was not a sales point, and that Spanish consumers bought largely for price. Mineral fiber tiles, which were the only ones which the Spanish company tried to sell, took about 20% of the total Spanish ceilings market, and Fabricantes had a 50% share of the mineral tile business. It faced strong competition from many cheaper types of tiles: cork compounds, gypsum, metal, and plastic.

Statistical data on building construction were scarce in Spain, but Fabricantes' ceilings sales manager had figures which showed that new dwelling units constructed had increased from 135,000 in 1962 to 268,000 in 1971; the upward trend was expected to continue, but at a slower rate. No statistics were available on other types of building con-struction, and so the Fabricantes sales staff kept alert for any known buildings being built, such as offices, stores, theaters, churches, and supermarkets.

Mr. Kroll believed that if Western Lumber's headquarters could miniaturize a ceiling tile line, Fabricantes could build its own plant. A ceiling plant, however, called for a substantial investment, which

Fabricantes' present business did not warrant. For the time being the intention was to import inventories whenever permitted, and to sell ceilings opportunistically whenever the market was good in Spain, Africa, or the Near East.

FLOORINGS

While floor tiles were a major item to every other Western Lumber associate company, there was no flooring activity in Spain. The only flooring which could be imported on a liberalized basis was asphalt tile. Fabricantes had sold some, but its softness made it vulnerable to impressions in the hot Spanish climate. Spanish consumers, who had bought it with the idea that any American-made product would be serviceable, were disappointed. Fabricantes eventually bought back almost all the asphalt tile it had sold, at a considerable loss.

In Spain's semi-Moorish culture, ceramic floor tiles were the most popular, and there were many firms producing these. Western Lumber did not make or sell ceramic tiles anywhere. Next in popularity were wooden tiles, similar to the parquet flooring, and these were made by a number of competitive Spanish firms. Fabricantes did not make either wood tiles or parquet, and while Western in the U.S. still made parquet, the Spokane management considered parquet to be a mature product which was not worth promoting in a competitive foreign market.

In 1971 Fabricantes did not sell any floor covering. It was investigating the potential for rotovinyl, a resilient floor covering, which it thought might sell on a superior-products approach, but it had doubts because it believed that Spaniards preferred low price to high quality. It was not clear whether rotovinyl would be classified by the Spanish authorities as liberalized, globalized, or bilateral. There was only one producer of rotovinyl in Spain, a subsidiary of a German firm, which had built a sizable plant for the purpose of supplying the Spanish market, and indications were that this firm was doing very well.

LABOR RELATIONS

"The Spanish labor authorities like Fabricantes," said Mr. Kroll. "Our union relations are excellent. We have never had a major labor disturbance."

Early in his administration, Mr. Kroll had begun to hold monthly meetings of the shop stewards. Factory managers and the company's personnel manager were required to attend these meetings. The company's personnel manager sat in on the meetings of the company's board of directors. Mr. Kroll attended the shop steward meetings twice a year or more and told the stewards in as much detail as possible what was presently occurring and the company's plans and prospects for the future.

All Spanish workers were united under government auspices in the Syndicate, a national amalgamation of craft unions. This was the labor arm of the Falangist Party. Fabricantes was a member of the Wood and Cork Syndicate.

Under Spanish law, a company could not dismiss an employee without government permission (which also involved making a partition payment to the employee), and such permission was not easy to obtain. Neither could a plant be shut down, or a production activity within a plant be eliminated, without government permission, and such permission would not be granted if the activity were profitable, even if its profitability was marginal.

Spanish wages were relatively low. Spanish law set the minimum rate at 98 pesetas (about $1.37) for a working day of 8 hours. The average hourly wage was 30 pesetas (42¢), which gave a worker 1,440 pesetas ($20.16) for the 48-hour work week. In addition the worker received Spanish social insurance, for which the employer paid, at the rate of 20 pesetas (28¢) an hour, and this rate was increasing. It was believed that the low wage levels and the high degree of job security fostered complacency.

To combat lethargy, Mr. Kroll introduced profit improvement programs, and in 1971 Fabricantes finished its third program. These consisted of substituting mechanization for manual operations; substituting modern equipment for that which was obsolete; introducing new techniques; encouraging suggestions from employees for higher efficiency; and reducing the number of employees on the company payroll by allowing attrition to take its course and by negotiations for indemnizations for employees whose jobs were eliminated by the improvement program.

FUTURE OF THE SPANISH OPERATION

The immediate profit prospects from the Spanish operations, according to a Western headquarters executive, hung from three threads:

(*a*) cork exports, (*b*) tax rebates on exports, and (*c*) imported non-cork products.

Cork and cork products were waning in popularity and faced competition from new plastic materials. Rods and discs, Fabricantes' most profitable export, were shipped largely to the United States, where they met with tariff charges of 40% of their f.o.b. value. Since Spain was not a member of the Common Market or the European Free Trade Area, it met tariff hurdles in most of Europe.

Tax rebates on exports were substantial; the rate was 12½% plus customs tariff on cork products, and 20% of the f.o.b. value of wallpaper. Wallpaper was the only product which seemed to have growth potential.

Importing non-cork products to be sold on a jobbed basis was described by a Fabricantes executive as an uphill fight all the way. These products were imported into Spain, with its low standard of living, from countries which had high-level economies. They could be sold only as luxury products or on the basis of their high quality, and Spain was a price market in which quality was secondary.

In its consideration of the future of the Spanish company, Western Lumber's Spokane headquarters had suggested three options which it proposed for consideration: (1) to seek new products which could be produced in Spain and marketed abroad through the associated Western Lumber companies as jobbed products; (2) to acquire Spanish manufacturing facilities which would put Fabricantes into non-cork businesses; (3) to convert Fabricantes' facilities to the manufacture of non-cork products.

Mr. Kroll thought that there might be some possibility for Fabricantes to get into the fabrication of partions of the movable metal type. There were ample supplies of steel in Spain, and manufacturing know-how and the licensing of designs could be had from major United States steel companies who were now producing and selling such partitionings, but not in Spain. There was also the possibility of making a co-operative arrangement to assemble farm equipment from some American manufacturer. No immediate move was expected to be made into these prospects; both were under study.

Mr. Kroll had serious reservations about the acquisition of Spanish manufacturing facilities. He would like to find some family-type business which was lacking capital for growth; it ought to be a business which Fabricantes could assist in a very real way; it could possibly be a foreign company which would like to enter a new product into the Spanish market and could use Fabricantes' established position. Mr. Kroll said that the investigations he had made to date indicated that the companies which were available were more a source of problems than a source of solutions.

Converting the present plants to non-cork production would mean using only the present building shells and using the present labor force, "with which we are stuck anyway," said Mr. Kroll. He thought that Western's Tempak line of rubber insulants might offer such a possibility for perhaps one Spanish plant. The raw rubber could be imported from Western's German company. Sale of Tempak in Spain and in Fabricantes' export markets would supplant the waning sales of cork insulants and help defray general overhead expenses. However, initial attempts to sell imported Tempak in Spain had stirred little interest. Refrigeration was scarce in Spain's low-level economy.

"Our ultimate aim," said Mr. Kroll, "is to try to develop enough sales volume to some day justify the establishment of production facilities in Spain for lines which have found consumer acceptance. The mere objective to manufacture is not enough. We must look at it in two ways: what reasonable profits might be expected from such a venture if it were to be successful; how to retreat from the new project if it were not to be successful. Mr. Kroll thought that the capital invested in any such project ought to be recovered in the form of retained earnings five years from the date on which the project was approved. "But we are not going to buy a problem tomorrow to solve a problem today," he said. "We are not going to put a mature product into production. A national disease in Spain seems to be the proliferation of anything that is good by everybody until it becomes no good for anybody. Cork was once a good product in Spain, but now the industry is hopelessly overcrowded. Metal bottle-cap crowns were once a good business; today there are 26 metal crown manufacturers in little Spain, where there are only 10 in the big United States. Even the infant Spanish automobile business is already reaching a state of overcapacity."

Liquidating the entire Spanish operation had been considered, but permission to do this would not be granted by the Spanish government as long as Fabricantes was profitable and created jobs for 600 Spaniards. "Western Lumber's headquarters has de-emphasized cork," said Mr. Kroll. "It has lost interest in it. It might not be interested in Spain at all—but it is stuck with it!"

APPENDIX A
SPAIN

Spain (195,000 square miles) together with Portugal (35,000 square miles) occupies the Iberian Peninsula, a land mass which is separated from Europe by the Pyrenees Mountains. Spain is arid and semitropical, and its geography is more like northern Africa than like Western Europe. There is a facetious saying among Europeans that Africa began at the Pyrenees. Culturally, politically, and in other ways, Spain is unique among European nations.

In land area Spain is the second largest country in western Europe (France, 213,000 square miles; Spain, 195,000 square miles). Its population of about 30 million was the fourth largest, and its population per square mile of 148 was relatively low (Holland, 819; England, 765; Belgium, 751; Germany, 552; France, 203). Its topography varies greatly from great mountain ranges in the north to high arid plains in the central area to lush river deltas in the south. Only 38% of the land is arable. The principal crops were cereals, olives, grapes, cork, nuts, sugar beets, oranges, fruits, and tobacco.

Spain had ample mineral resources: coal, iron ore, lime, copper, lead, zinc, tin, mercury, potash, and sulphur. Its principal manufactures were iron and steel, textiles, chemicals, pharmaceuticals, electrical equipment, shoes, leather products, cement, and canned fish. It had adequate hydro-electric power, railroads, and roads. Its principal cities were Madrid, with 2,260,000 population; Barcelona, with 1,900,000; Valencia, with 505,000; Seville, with 442,000; Zaragoza, with 326,000; Malaga, with 301,000; and Bilbao, with 298,000. It had world seaports in Barcelona and Valencia on the east, Seville on the south, and Bilbao on the north.

Prior to 1960 Spain was considered a developing country, but in 1962 the United States Internal Revenue Act classified Spain as a fully developed country. Forty per cent of her population was still employed in agriculture, but industrialization, fostered and aided by the government, was increasing rapidly. National income was $10.69 billion in 1962; $13.3 billion in 1964; and $21.6 billion in 1968. The aim of the government's Social and Economic Development Plan, started January 1, 1964, was to achieve a yearly growth rate in GNP of 6% based upon productivity and employment. In 1970–1971 Spain enjoyed the highest economic growth rate in Europe.

The weekly wages of skilled laborers ranged from $20 to $25; those of unskilled workers were considerably lower. In 1959 there was unemployment of 8%; in 1968 there was no unemployment. Per capita income increased from $311 in 1962 to $460 in 1967. Public and private investment was increasing at a rate of about 5% annually. The ownership of automobiles, telephones, television sets, and radios in Spain was still considerably lower than in most industrial nations.

Although they were united as a nation, the Spanish people nurtured strong regional feelings—stronger than in any other country in modern Europe. Its regions were separated by topographical differences and by climatic, cultural, language, and political differences. Galicia, in the northwest corner, was the "Ireland" of Spain, with verdant green mountains and hills, moist and warm enough to raise corn very successfully; Galicians spoke a language of their own rather than Castilian. The Basque Provinces at the western end of the Pyrenees were peopled by three million Basques, a distinct race, extremely proud of their background and history and differing from other Spaniards in their cuisine, their customs, and especially their unique language. Catalonia, the four provinces in northeast Spain, was peopled by the Catalans, considered to be the most energetic of Spaniards; much of Spain's industry and trade was centered there. The Levant in central eastern Spain is a region comparable in climate with Southern California in the United States. Great irrigation installations had been built there, and Valencia oranges and rice were produced in abundance. Andalucia was an agricultural region in the south which had ample sunshine and warmth, but rainfall only in winter. Despite this handicap it produced much of Spain's export crops: grapes, almonds, citrus fruits, dates, and olives. Castile, the largest of the regions, is the great central plateau area, and it is separated from the other regions by high mountain ranges through which only a few roads penetrated. Castile was largely agricultural, and, being semi-arid, its economy was based on sheep raising and the cultivation of wheat. Spain's Island Provinces consist of the Balearic Islands in the Mediterranean, where the natives insisted on speaking Catalan as their language, rather than Castilian (as also did the Catalonians). The second island group is the Canaries, off the coast of Morocco. Both island groups had distinct culture traits which made them an attraction for tourists from all over the world.

During their history the Spaniards had tried various forms of government, none of which endured, principally because of regional differences. Eventually they tried to establish a republican form of government—the Second Republic, which brought about a violent struggle between two groups: one favored a strong central government, the traditional social system, alliance with the Catholic Church, and control of all Spain from Madrid. The other wanted separation of Church and State, local autonomy, and a republic in which the Catalonian and Basque provinces would be dominant. This was the setting for the Spanish Civil War, with the Loyalists in the north and the Franco Nationalists in the south. The Nationalists were the victors, and after the war Spain became in theory a democratic monarchy but without any monarch, with Franco as Regent, Caudillo (Leader), Chief of State, Commander-in-Chief, Prime Minister, and head of the Falange Party. General Franco did not attempt to force integration upon the regions of Spain. The Spanish Parliament was called the Cortes Españolas, signifying the plural—the "Spanish Parliaments." It was said that many Catalonians (or Basques, or Galicians, or Castilians) continued to say, "I am a Catalan first, and a Spaniard second!"

Spain had no colonies upon which to draw. It had a long history of political instability. Its industrialization was begun late and carried forward spasmodically.

Spain had suffered from the depression of the 1930's and was devastated by the Civil War. When peace came, food, raw materials, and equipment were in short supply, domestic production could not be raised, and importations were barred by the lack of gold or foreign exchange reserves. World War II halted virtually all imports and stopped reconstruction efforts. During these years the government was forced to impose strict controls on most aspects of economic life. After World War II the Marshall Plan revived Europe, but Spain was not invited to participate, which accentuated the isolation of the Spanish economy.

In July, 1959, the government drew up a stabilization program in co-operation with the International Monetary Fund and the Organization of European Economic Cooperation. The peseta was devalued, restrictions were imposed upon both public and private spending, and a program of trade liberalization was adopted. This Stabilization Plan became the basis for Spain's national development program.

The Spanish Economic and Social Development Plan, started in 1964, encompassed the whole panorama of human activity in Spain. Its over-all objective was an annual 6% rise in gross national product.

This economic and social program used all of the instruments of persuasion and compulsion available to the government. The tax policy was designed to induce investment. Wage policies favored people of lower incomes to enable them to increase their standard of living and to increase consumption. Farm policy was designed to make the price of Spanish crops competitive with those of other European producers, which involved expensive programs of irrigation, fertilization, and farm mechanization. The plan included inducements to bring industry to underdeveloped regions, such as Burgos in the north and Seville in the south.

Spain was not a member of the European Common Market or the European Free Trade Area, a circumstance which hampered her in international trade. Spain had applied for associate membership in the EEC in February, 1962, and acceded to the General Agreement on Tariff and Trade on July 1, 1963. Her admission was actively being considered.

PART SIX
MANAGEMENT RESPONSIBILITIES AND THEIR LIMITS

26
MASON
CHEMICALS,
INC.

Early in February, 1965, U.S. Secretary of Health, Education, and Welfare, Anthony Celebrezze, called for a public conference to consider the problem of water pollution in the Chicago area. The conference, called under legislative authority granted in 1948 and amended in 1956, was to convene March 2 at McCormick Place, Chicago, and to run for four days.

A few days before Secretary Celebrezze's action, the U.S. Public Health Service had issued a special report stating that dangerous amounts of sewage and industrial wastes were being discharged into Lake Michigan and the Calumet River system in Indiana and Illinois.[1] Public Health Service officials, whose concern in the matter was based on the fact that the pollution moves across state boundaries, said that the Grand Calumet River and Indiana Harbor Canal were grossly polluted, and that the southern end of Lake Michigan was becoming seriously affected by pollutants.

Lake Michigan provides the water supply for nearly five million people in Chicago, its suburbs, and the Indiana cities of Gary, Hammond, Whiting, and East Chicago. The lake also is a source of water for industrial processes and cooling purposes in dozens of major industrial plants in the area, and is used for swimming, boating, water skiing, and fishing. The rivers and canals in the area are used primarily for shipping, but also somewhat for recreational boating.

Among the business firms called to appear at the anti-pollution con-

[1] See Exhibits 1 and 2.

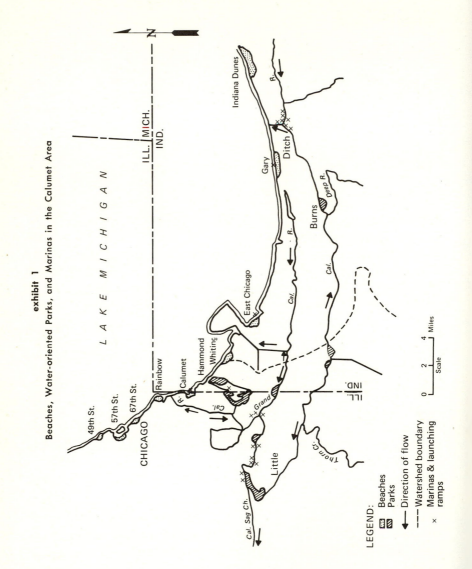

exhibit 1

Beaches, Water-oriented Parks, and Marinas in the Calumet Area

LEGEND:

Beaches

Parks

Direction of flow

Watershed boundary

× Marinas & launching ramps

Scale: 0 2 4 Miles

exhibit 2
Generalized Water Movement, January 21 to 24, 1963. Total Flow 19 Miles

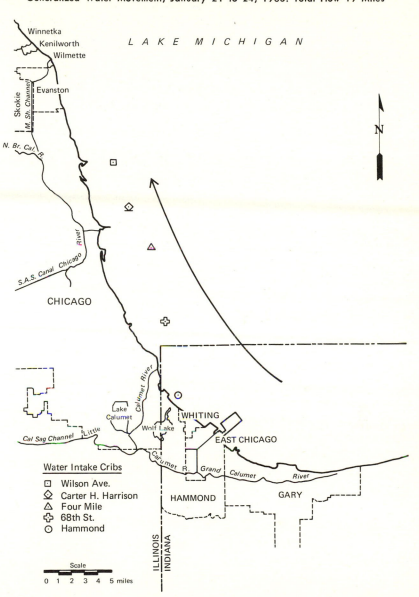

LAKE MICHIGAN

Winnetka
Kenilworth
Wilmette
Evanston

Skokie
N. Sh. Channel

N. Br. Cal. R.

River

S.A.S. Canal Chicago

CHICAGO

Calumet River

Lake
Calumet

WHITING

Wolf Lake

EAST CHICAGO

Cal Sag Channel   Little

Calumet R.   Grand   Calumet   River

HAMMOND   GARY

N

Water Intake Cribs

☐ Wilson Ave.
◇ Carter H. Harrison
△ Four Mile
✚ 68th St.
⊙ Hammond

ILLINOIS
INDIANA

Scale

0 1 2 3 4 5 miles

ference was Mason Chemicals, Inc., a medium-sized producer of heavy industrial chemicals. Its diversified line of specialty chemicals includes those used in petroleum refining, metal processing and coating, and the production of such diverse products as iron and steel, automotive and refrigeration equipment, and insulation and building materials. Over 80% of the company's production occurs at its large plant in East Chicago, Indiana, and most of its sales are made to other industrial firms located in Indiana, Illinois, Wisconsin, Ohio, and Michigan.

The firm's sales for the past five years have averaged about $120 million, and in fiscal 1965 the company had sales of $146.7 million and a net operating profit of $17,764,000. Sales and operating profits for 1965 were both about 6% higher than in 1964. Other income (from investments, real estate, patent royalties, etc.) totaled $1,931,000. As a result of certain business deductions and special tax credits, Mason Chemicals paid only $6,919,000 in federal and state income taxes on its total income of $19,695,000.

With a net income of $12,776,000, the company paid $4,373,000 in common share dividends (no preferred stock is outstanding) and added $8,403,000 to its retained earnings. The addition of this sum brought its retained earnings to a total of $50,834,000 at the end of fiscal 1965. The stockholders' equity in the company at the end of 1965 was approximately $90 million.

Property, plant, and equipment were valued at a cost of $120 million, less accumulated depreciation of $65 million. Annual depreciation charges have averaged $6 million. In recent years new capital expenditures by Mason Chemicals for plant and equipment have varied greatly but have averaged $8 million per year. Long-term debt at the end of 1965 stood at $25 million and is being reduced at a rate of from $3.5 million to $4 million per year.

FEDERAL CONCERN OVER WATER POLLUTION

The Public Health Service report issued in February, 1965, declared that large quantities of municipal sewage and industrial wastes, "treated to varying degrees," are discharged into the area's waters. As a result, the streams are discolored, often smelly, and marked by floating debris and oil. "Along the shores of Lake Michigan, in Indiana and the southern shore in Illinois, the waters are discolored by suspended and dissolved waste materials, in sharp contrast to the pleasing appearance of the rest of Lake Michigan," the agency said.

United States Steel Corporation, Youngstown Sheet and Tube Co., and Inland Steel Co. were cited by the report as the largest sources of waste in the river and canal, and three petroleum refineries (Cities Service Petroleum Co., Sinclair Refining Co., and Mobil Oil Co.) were listed as "lesser but still major sources of waste."

The principal sources of waste discharged directly into Lake Michigan were identified by the Public Health Service as Union Carbide Chemicals Co., American Oil Co., American Maize-Products Co., United States Steel Corporation, and Mason Chemicals, Inc.

Communities in the area, however, were equally at fault, the agency said. It cited ineffective disinfection in municipal waste disposal systems, the prevalence of combined storm-sanitary sewage systems that discharge untreated sewage during and after heavy rains, and the increasing number of small treatment plants that discharge into ditches and small streams.

The public conference called by Secretary Celebrezze involved sewage and industrial wastes from about 35 municipalities and 40 plants. Under federal law, the participants in a water pollution conference are expected to draw up a program to improve their local situation. If this fails, then the Secretary of Health, Education, and Welfare may convene a hearing at which sworn testimony is given, following which the hearing board makes recommendations and the Secretary orders specific action. If local governments and plants still do not co-operate, then the Secretary has authority to take the matter to court.

Use of this three-step enforcement machinery, with its emphasis on giving the contributors to water pollution ample opportunity to remedy the situation voluntarily, had accelerated considerably in recent years. And federal action seemed likely to continue to grow, since public concern over both air and water pollution had risen sharply in the past three years, and President Johnson had committed his administration to work toward effective remedies. The Chicago area conference represented probably the most complex water pollution problem that had been tackled thus far by the conference approach, and much depended, of course, on the attitude and degree of co-operation shown by the participating municipalities and companies.

BACKGROUND OF MASON CHEMICALS AND
THE PROBLEM OF WATER POLLUTION

The history of Mason Chemicals, Inc., in the matter of waste disposal is fairly typical of other firms in the industrial region at the south end of Lake Michigan. Prior to 1940, there were no sewage treatment facilities of any nature in this plant. The entire effluent was discharged into Lake Michigan, which the plant had access to by means of some large private sewers. In 1940, sanitary sewage facilities were made available to the plant by the East Chicago, Indiana, Sanitary Board. At that time, sanitary sewage was separated from the cooling waters that were being returned to Lake Michigan.

In 1944 an extensive six-month survey and study of all industrial wastes was initiated by the company for the following purposes:

1. To classify the pollution load of industrial wastes on the basis of individual sources.

2. To determine the basic characteristics and magnitude of waste from each source.

3. To determine seasonal fluctuations affecting each waste.

4. To develop methods to reduce and control the strength of these wastes.

On the basis of the findings obtained in this survey, Mason Chemicals, Inc., embarked on a waste abatement program which was completed in 1950. Through this program the daily plant sewer loadings to Lake Michigan were reduced from 61,148 pounds of BOD (biochemical oxygen demand, a measure of pollution) to 3,200 pounds. This was accomplished by the isolation of all waste-bearing waters, the re-use of process waters, the recovery of all solids possible, and the reduction of considerable volatile organic matter. To accomplish this reduction in pollution the company spent approximately $8 million.

In 1952 Mason Chemicals began a modernization and expansion program, the most important feature of which was the shift from a batch operation process to continuous-process production of most chemicals. This change resulted in more waste waters than could be handled by the existing waste abatement program. In order to cope with the larger volume of waste waters and provide a "permanent"-type system for controlling pollution, Mason Chemicals built a lagoon treatment system.

Chemical production capacity at the East Chicago plant had increased 38% since 1952, and the pollution load was currently 6,076 pounds of BOD per day. Presently some 12 million gallons of water were pumped from the lake each day and about 10 million gallons were returned as cooling water. The 2 million gallons retained by the plant were treated in its waste abatement facilities before being discharged into the lake again. The water returned to Lake Michigan was chlorinated, and was sampled on a frequent basis seven days a week. A complete analysis was made each day of the samples taken. Capital expenditures by Mason Chemicals, Inc., for industrial waste control from 1940 through 1962 totaled approximately $14,327,000. The operating cost of the waste abatement program currently was about $1,225,000 annually.

Up to the early 1960's, the anti-pollution controls placed on firms such as Mason Chemicals were relatively lax. Only occasionally did either state or federal authorities take action to reduce water pollution. Such action typically was in the form of setting minimum standards of waste abatement to be achieved by individual firms by a certain date, with court action to be brought against those failing to comply. A shortcoming of this approach, however, was the fact that any *relative* improvement in the quality of each gallon of industrial water returned to Lake Michigan often was more than nullified by the fact that increased production required more and more water, hence increasing the *absolute* total of pollutants.

Although Mason Chemicals, Inc., did not find it a hardship to meet such standards as government imposed in the past, the company realized early in 1965 that the "good old days" were all but past regarding water pollution, and that the firm would have to devote serious attention to shaping new policies to meet new conditions. One aspect of the new situation, of course, was the Federal government's call for a public conference on water pollution in the Chicago area and the increasing likelihood of extensive federal activity in the future. A second aspect of the problem for the company was how to handle the growing volume of complaints by East Chicago residents about both the company's role in water pollution of the lake and the objectionable odors which originated in its waste treatment facilities and pervaded a considerable portion of the city.

If Mason Chemicals were forced to meet the water standards which some federal officials apparently had in mind for Lake Michigan, the company knew that it would be faced with a difficult problem both technically and financially. The cost could easily run in the neighborhood of $25 million, and, depending upon the time limit involved, such a requirement would have a profound effect on the future course of the company's business. In particular, management at Mason Chemicals had been giving serious consideration to a series of steps to modernize and expand production facilities at the East Chicago plant, and whatever position the company took in the proceedings at the federal anti-pollution conference would have to be made in this light.

MASON CHEMICALS' PLANNED EXPANSION

The firm's desire to modernize and expand had its origin in the prosperity of the early 1960's. Sales, profits, and tax considerations were favorable, and the prolonged period of prosperity was accompanied by an expanding demand for heavy industrial chemicals, especially in the Midwest, where steel producers, auto manufacturers, and other major industrial chemical users were experiencing rapid growth.

As a well-established firm with excellent access to this market, Mason Chemicals believed it would be desirable to modernize and expand the productive capacity of its East Chicago plant by about 30% over the next five years, provided suitable financing could be arranged. A variety of considerations precluded the issuance of additional common stock; thus any new capital investment would have to be financed by retained earnings and long-term borrowing. Depending upon the specific facilities to be included in such an expansion program, the cost was estimated at between $70 million and $85 million. These figures, when contrasted with the cost of previous major expansions in the company's history, emphasized the steady inflation which had occurred in the absolute dollar cost of expansion, but more troublesome than this observation was the fact that the cost of such major expansion would not fall evenly over the whole five-year period. The principal burden of the necessary capital expenditures would come in a 20-month period during the third and fourth years.

Furthermore, to achieve the desired increase in the capacity of the East Chicago plant, it would be necessary to utilize virtually all remaining vacant land at the site. As far as efficiency in production was concerned, this made good sense, but it presented two unattractive prospects with respect to waste abatement. First, it would prevent any additional land from being devoted to waste treatment facilities; second, it would increase the demand on existing waste treatment facilities by at least 30%, and Mason Chemicals was already being criticized by the Federal government and local residents for the inadequacy of its waste abatement program.

The only available alternatives for boosting the capacity of the present space devoted to waste abatement were: (1) to deepen the existing settling lagoons (an expensive process which promised diminishing returns in terms of keeping pace with the increased quantity of pollutants accompanying any plant expansion); (2) the development of some entirely new technology to cope with the company's particular pollution problems. The latter certainly was not inconceivable, but even if successful, the time and money required for a technological breakthrough were quite unpredictable.

Thus the spatial demands and the cost of more extensive waste treatment facilities seemed directly opposed to the spatial and financial requirements of plant modernization and expansion. And along this line, Mason Chemicals was troubled by some information concerning its strongest competitor in the heavy industrial chemical market in the Midwest.

This competitor also was known to be considering expansion to strengthen its position in the growing market, and while it had some financial problems of its own to contend with, it did not face any spatial problems, since its plant site in neighboring Hammond, Indiana, contained a substantial quantity of unused acreage. Furthermore, in reference to the forthcoming federal anti-pollution conference, at which this firm also was to appear, one of the firm's vice presidents said in a newspaper interview that the Public Health Service had "grossly misinterpreted the facts" about water pollution in the area, and that the company had no intention of disclosing the amounts and types of materials in its industrial wastes, since such information would aid its competitors.

Mason Chemicals recognized that to some extent their competitor was correct in suggesting that information about industrial wastes could be of assistance to a competitive firm. Set against this, however, was the fact that government officials and the public generally were likely to regard this viewpoint simply as a corporate refusal to admit guilt in the matter of water pollution and a rejection of any responsibility to help correct the situation.

As the date for the federal anti-pollution conference neared, the management of Mason Chemicals recognized that they faced two problems of differing magnitudes which called for some decisive action on the part of the company. The lesser of these was the problem of community relations involving the objections being raised by some residents of East Chicago. These complaints were regarded by the company as somewhat contradictory, since they criticized the company both for its contribution to water pollution in Lake Michigan and for the strong odors which emanated from the company's efforts to treat waste in its lagoon system. Nonetheless, they could not be lightly dismissed.

The greater problem facing management concerned the position the company should take at the forthcoming anti-pollution conference. The considerations here were: What water quality standards should the company support as a satisfactory compromise between its own interests and the public interest? How much information should the company make public regarding its past and present waste abatement program? How could the firm reconcile its desire to modernize and expand its East Chicago plant with its future policy in regard to waste abatement? and, finally, What type of public relations effort, if any, should accompany the decisions which the company reached in these matters?

27
CAMPAIGN GM

After General Motors Corporation's annual meeting in 1969, the *Detroit Free Press* reported:

> You could tell you were at the General Motors Corporation annual meeting. As usual, GM operatives made sure Ford's exhibit in Cobo Hall was draped, out of sight of stockholders.
> And the three pestiest gadflies who always make the GM meeting were on hand, picking away at GM Board Chairman James M. Roche. The three are New Yorkers Lewis D. Gilbert, Wilma Soss, and, the most vituperative, Evelyn Y. Davis . . .

The major items on which these three people continually challenged management were executive compensation, whether or not officers should receive additional fees for serving as directors, and the adequacy of information to stockholders in the annual report.

The following year, at the 1970 annual meeting, the three pesty gadflies were present again. But among the corporation's critics, most of the attention centered on a group of young men and women representing "The Campaign to Make General Motors Responsible." This was a subcommittee of a Washington-based organization called "The Project on Corporate Responsibility."

In January, 1970, the Project had purchased 12 shares of General Motors common stock. This was the initial step of its campaign to add nine resolutions to GM's proxy statement in hopes of making the giant corporation more responsive to public needs and concerns. At first glance, the thought that a block of 12 shares could force a corporation with 287.5 million shares of common stock outstanding to change its way of doing business appeared absurd. Yet within General Motors the challenge was not lightly dismissed, for management knew as well as everyone else that the guiding hand behind the Project was Ralph Nader.

General Motors and Nader had been protagonists since November, 1965, when the latter's book *Unsafe at Any Speed* was published. The substantive safety issues raised by the book were accompanied by a controversial episode in which Nader accused General Motors of using unethical and illegal tactics to try to silence him.

Following a Senate investigation, James M. Roche, then president of General Motors, acknowledged on March 22, 1966,[1] that representatives of the corporation had exceeded the boundaries of acceptable behavior, and he issued an extraordinary public apology to Nader. Nader was not fully satisfied, apparently feeling that the seriousness of the offense demanded additional remedies, and in November, 1966, he instituted a multi-million-dollar legal suit charging General Motors and certain individuals with "harassment and invasion of privacy." This suit was still pending and unresolved at the time of GM's 1970 annual meeting.

In addition, by 1970 Ralph Nader's standing as a consumer spokesman had expanded far beyond what anyone dreamed possible in 1965, when he originally tackled General Motors and the automobile industry. Aided and encouraged by sympathetic legislators, a favorable press, and a variety of other interests, Nader's consumer welfare activities had broadened from automobile safety to include unwholesome meat products, natural gas pipeline safety, radiation hazards, air and water pollution, misleading and deceptive packaging, abuses in the operation of nursing homes, and countless other matters.

Nader's single-minded dedication and zeal on behalf of consumer causes (plus his undeniable ability to get results) struck a responsive chord among college students, young intellectuals, and reform-minded groups during the late 1960's. One example of this response was the Project on Corporate Responsibility. Organized during the summer of 1968, it was composed of young lawyers who decided to devote their time and talents to investigating and publicizing corporate practices they believed to be unfair to the nation's consumers.

---

[1] *Newsweek*, April 4, 1966, p. 77.

Although one of the co-ordinators of Campaign GM, Mr. John Esposito, was employed by the Center for Responsive Law, an organization headed by Nader, Campaign GM's literature described its official relationship with Ralph Nader as follows:

> Mr. Nader was involved in the discussions leading up to the submission of the proposals, but he is not a member of Campaign GM or the Project on Corporate Responsibility, Inc., nor is he a financial contributor thereto.

Despite this statement, and Nader's own declaration that he had no official connection with the campaign and would continue to operate independently, the public found it difficult to disassociate Ralph Nader from Campaign GM. After all, it was Nader who originally announced the formation of the group to the press, and the nine proxy proposals appeared to reflect a good deal of Nader's consumer philosophy. Indeed, to many people the young lawyers in Campaign GM were simply another task force of "Nader's Raiders."

PROPOSALS MADE BY CAMPAIGN GM

Following the purchase of the 12 shares of stock, Campaign GM submitted to the corporation's management nine resolutions for inclusion in the proxy statement and presentation at the annual meeting to be held in Detroit on May 22, 1970. The nine proposals submitted were summarized in Campaign GM's own literature as follows:

1. Increasing the Board of Directors by three to permit the seating of new members who will insist that the Board take account of the many social consequences of its decisions. We have proposed three candidates to fill those seats. They are Betty Furness, former Special Presidential Assistant on Consumer Affairs; Rene DuBos, a biologist and one of the nation's most eminent environmental experts; and the Rev. Channing Phillips, a Democratic National Committeeman and the first black nominee for the President of the United States.
2. Establishing an independent committee to study past GM decisions and to recommend structural changes and substantive goals for the future.
3. Amending the corporate charter to forbid GM to undertake any activity that is inconsistent with the public interest.

4. Committing GM to specific policies in regard to air pollution, (5) minority employment, (6) auto warranties, (7) auto safety, (8) public mass transit, and (9) employee health and safety.

REACTION OF GENERAL MOTORS AND
THE SECURITIES AND EXCHANGE COMMISSION

When asked by the press about the nine proposals, a General Motors spokesman in Detroit said, "Our procedure is to review submissions from stockholders as they are received. We will follow procedures for handling these resolutions as specified by the Securities and Exchange Commission." [2]

About four weeks later, General Motors Corporation told the SEC that all nine proposals were being rejected, primarily because they did not specifically involve shareholder responsibilities. The company declared that inclusion of the proposals in the proxy statement was not required under SEC rules because they involved proxy solicitations and were made to promote social causes. [3]

Officials of the Project on Corporate Responsibility, Inc., said they planned legal action to press their demands, possibly even seeking an injunction to postpone GM's annual meeting. They retained a New York lawyer who previously had represented shareholders in fights with management, and also proceeded to petition the Securities and Exchange Commission to require General Motors to include the proposals in the company's proxy statement. [4]

To the considerable surprise of many knowledgeable parties, the SEC, after evaluating this request, decided that General Motors' proxy material must include Campaign GM's first two proposals. (The SEC indicated it would not take any adverse action if the other seven were omitted.) General Motors Corporation accepted this ruling and in their "Notice of Annual Meeting of Stockholders and Proxy Statement" included the full text of the first two proposals made by Campaign GM. (For the complete text of the proposals, see Appendix A.)

Of the total list of five shareholder proposals contained in General Motors' Proxy Statement, Campaign GM's proposals on corporate responsibility appeared as numbers 4 and 5. The accompanying recommendation by management to all shareholders was that they should

[2] *The Wall Street Journal,* February 9, 1970.
[3] *The Wall Street Journal,* March 6, 1970.
[4] *The Wall Street Journal,* March 6, 1970.

vote *against* both of these proposals. To support its recommendation management enclosed with the proxy statement a 21-page booklet entitled "GM's Record of Progress," which each shareholder was urged to read carefully. The booklet presented a rather glowing picture of the corporation's social concerns and accomplishments in those areas in which it was being criticized and which formed the essence of Shareholder Proposal No. 4.

Campaign GM prepared a proxy statement of its own, including a rather different notion of GM's "record of progress":

> We want to submit to the shareholders an opportunity to adopt various measures which, in the opinion of the Campaign Co-ordinators, are designed to make the Corporation more responsible to the community as a whole. It is the opinion of the Co-ordinators that all corporations must serve interests larger than their shareholders if the community and the corporations are to function effectively in the increasingly complex years ahead. Since the Co-ordinators believe this involves a reassessment and a change in the corporation's goals and priorities, the decision to change is properly made by the shareholders. Since General Motors is the largest corporation, it is felt that its responsibility and the responsibility of its shareholders are paramount. While General Motors has not ignored these concerns, it is the opinion of the Co-ordinators that its efforts have been inadequate.

GENERAL MOTORS CORPORATION'S BOARD OF DIRECTORS

With Proposal No. 5, calling for an increase in the size of General Motors' board of directors to 26 members, Campaign GM called attention both to the role of corporate boards of directors and to the make-up of GM's board. (For a list of all GM board members, including their age and business affiliation, see Appendix B.) In 1969 there were 24 men serving on General Motors' board. Their average age was just over 65. The youngest director was 54 and the oldest was 94. The latter was Charles S. Mott, whose 50 plus years as a director included four years on the board of General Motors Company from 1913 to 1917, and membership on the board of General Motors Corporation from 1917 to the present. Although Mott's age raised the over-all average of the board, only three of the 24 directors in 1969 were under 60 years old.

Two of the 1969 directors, Richard King Mellon (one of the richest men in the United States) and Albert L. Williams, were not standing for re-election in 1970 because of a government ruling on interlocking directorships. Management nominated only one individual as a replacement, Mr. Oscar A. Lundin, executive vice president in charge of finance of General Motors Corporation. Mr. Lundin was 59.

Assuming the election of these 23 men at the 1970 annual meeting, the directors' average age would be just under 65 and the average length of service on General Motors' board 11.5 years. (Two of the men were elected for the first time in 1970 and their period of service was not counted in the average.)

Of these 23 men, 11 either held or formerly held high positions in General Motors Corporation. The remaining 12 included the president of the Bechtel Corporation, the chairman of Eli Lilly and Company, the former chairman of the First National Bank of Boston, the chairman of the Southern Company, the chairman of the Allied Chemical Corporation, the chairman of the Massachusetts Institute of Technology, the chairman of the Mellon National Bank and Trust Company, the chairman of the Union Electric Company, the chairman and president of The Royal Bank of Canada, the president of The Procter & Gamble Company, the counsel to the law firm of Perkins, Daniels & McCormack, and the President of Marshall Field & Company. The board's composition indicated that General Motors followed the practice of having both inside and outside directors.

FUNCTIONS OF A BOARD OF DIRECTORS

The scope and character of a board's duties and the manner in which directors fulfill their responsibilities vary from company to company. Professor Harold Koontz of U.C.L.A., in his book *The Board of Directors and Effective Management*,[5] declares:

> In the business corporation, board members legally stand in the place of the real owners of the corporation, the stockholders. In this position, they are not legal agents in the sense that they must do the individual shareholder's bidding, but are rather representatives of the stockholders as a group. As representatives of the stockholders, therefore, the directors have the authority to exercise the powers of the corporation—subject only to restrictions imposed by the laws of the state and the Federal

[5] Harold Koontz, *The Board of Directors and Effective Management*, McGraw-Hill, New York, 1967, p. 19.

government—as such powers are conferred upon it by shareholders through the articles of incorporation (charter) or company by-laws.

Koontz says there are seven different kinds of boards and nine basic functions for a board to perform. The seven kinds of boards are: (*a*) dummy boards, (*b*) family boards, (*c*) owner-controlled boards, (*d*) insider-controlled boards with outside members, (*e*) outside-controlled but insider-led boards, (*f*) inside boards, and (*g*) outside boards.

The basic responsibility of any board is to see that the enterprise is well managed and that the interests of those it represents are faithfully followed. How is this done? Koontz breaks the job into nine parts: [6]

1. *Trusteeship*
   Safeguarding and husbanding the company's assets in the long-term interests of the shareholders.
2. *Determination of Enterprise Objectives*
   It is not enough to say that a business exists to make a profit. Although this must be a basic goal of any business, it must be translated into enterprise goals supportive of profit.
3. *Selection of Executives*
   Many boards select the president or chief executive officer and approve his nomination of other officers. They should know the characteristics of his key line subordinates, since the next president or chief executive officer will probably come from that group.
4. *Securing Long-Range Business Stability and Growth*
   The board must see to it that the company is in tune with the rapidly changing environment in which it operates. This is a particularly good reason for having outside directors.
5. *Assuring That Plans Are Designed to Meet Major Objectives*
6. *Approval of Major Company Decisions*
7. *Checking on Results*
8. *Disposition of Company Profits and Assets*
   What proportions of any earnings shall be distributed to owners as dividends, reinvested in the business, or used to reduce indebtedness?
9. *Approval of Mergers and Acquisitions*
   Transactions of this nature shape the nature and future of a company, and careful study is necessary before making a decision of this kind.

All of these matters for consideration typically come to a board from the operating management of a company. Board members may approve, disapprove, or modify proposals coming within their purview.

[6] Koontz, *op. cit.*, pp. 25–31.

More detailed, continuing supervision of management's activities often is provided by key board committees, particularly executive committees or finance committees.

THE SELECTION OF BOARD MEMBERS

Criteria for selecting board members differ from company to company. When Keith Funston was head of the New York Stock Exchange from 1951 to 1967, he instituted a regulation that every company newly listed on the exchange must have at least two outside directors. Yet there is considerable room for argument over the precise balance to be struck between outside directors and officer directors. Knowledge of a company's intricacies seems essential, but so does the need for the outside look at inside operations. Professor Stanley C. Vance of the University of Oregon reports: [7]

> In only the rarest instances do outside directors have even the faintest idea of technical processes, the competitive strains, or the real financial status of the host company. But from the pinnacles of industry we hear the rebuttal loud and clear: Our major corporations do not need or seek directors who are intimately conversant with the host company; they seek rather (or so it is said) men of character, sound judgment, intuition, poise, statesmanship, wisdom, sophistication, economic integrity, and similar lofty—but nonetheless intangible—traits.

Obviously, the world does not exactly abound with men and women who meet these standards.

In a study of what he calls "directorate dimensions," Professor Vance has concluded that there are seven factors or traits presently found in the boards of all large corporate enterprises. They are: [8]

1. Technical expertise
2. Managerial expertise
3. Access to lines of credit
4. Broad economic knowledge
5. Public image
6. Membership on other major boards
7. Owners' equity

[7] Stanley C. Vance, *The Corporate Director: A Critical Evaluation,* Dow Jones-Irwin, Inc., Homewood, Ill., 1968, p. 4.

[8] Vance, *op. cit.,* p. 36.

Vance emphasizes that not every member of every board possesses all of these characteristics, but that every good board has all of these features represented somewhere within its membership. Moreover, the more numerous the specific strengths of each board member, the more effective the board's guidance and leadership are likely to be.

Even if all of the above business considerations are well represented on a particular corporation's board, there remains the question of whether such a traditional list is sufficient to cover the full range of corporate needs and responsibilities, both current and future. To the participants in Campaign GM and the Project on Corporate Responsibility, the above list is strikingly incomplete, for it does not manifest adequate concern either for various constituent groups or for society as a whole, both of whose future welfare rests to a considerable extent in corporate hands.

THE COURTSHIP OF THE INSTITUTIONS

Once General Motors followed the SEC's ruling and included two of Campaign GM's resolutions as part of the official proxy statement, both sides began to seek support for their respective positions. With 287.5 million shares outstanding among some 1.4 million shareholders, the key to the outcome appeared to lie with institutional holders of large blocks of stock—foundations, universities, and mutual funds. Accordingly, both the management of General Motors Corporation and officials and sympathizers of Campaign GM made special appeals to these institutional shareholders.

One of the largest university holders was Massachusetts Institute of Technology, with 291,000 shares. In fact, the head of MIT, James R. Killian, Jr., was a member of General Motors' board. GM's management sent Roger B. Smith, treasurer, and Frederick W. Bowditch, director of emission control, to Cambridge in order to persuade MIT to vote its shares against Proposals 4 and 5. A student-faculty committee listened to their presentation for about half an hour. By coincidence, Ralph Nader was on the campus that day and strolled into the meeting just in time to hear Campaign GM and its proposals described as "simply a move to harass management." He made no full-scale rejoinder, but did offer a parting comment that GM's description of the part-time work of "four young lawyers pitted against GM's

2,000 to 3,000 lawyers as overextending the use of the word 'harassment.' " [9]

Other large universities holding General Motors stock in their portfolios were: University of Michigan—28,696 shares; University of Texas—66,500 shares; University of California—93,775 shares; Harvard University—287,000 shares; University of Pennsylvania—29,000 shares; and Yale University—85,686 shares. A dozen foundations held more than 5 million shares.

General Motors had an advantage in having more money and people at its disposal than the Project on Corporate Responsibility. The gathering of votes for Campaign GM had to be done almost entirely by mail and on a budget of only $30,000. On April 10, the *Wall Street Journal* reported that Campaign GM:

> . . . mailed 2,000 of its proxy statements this week to mutual funds, brokers, universities and other institutions that hold large blocks of stock. In some cases, a spokesman said, it wasn't known whether the institution owned GM stock.
> Campaign GM said it plans to set up regional distribution centers where individual stockholders may pick up proxy material. The group's proxy statement contains the two project proposals included in the GM proxy plus a third that would amend the company's certificate of incorporation. The amendment would declare that none of the purposes of the corporation can be implemented in a manner which is detrimental to the public health, safety or welfare or in a manner which violates any law of the U.S. or of any state in which the corporation does business.[10]

During the next six weeks, the press gave considerable coverage to how the institutional world was going to vote its stock at the GM meeting. The University of Michigan decided to vote its 28,696 shares in favor of management. President Robben Fleming's letter to the co-chairman of a campus environmental action group declared that the school had a commitment to help fight pollution and would continue to pursue such a goal. "But," Fleming added, "as to how stock proxies should be voted in order to express the university's concern for improving the environment, the regents have had a consistent policy of voting university shares with the recommendations of management or of withholding its proxy votes and disposing of its shares. It will con-

[9] *Business Week*, April 18, 1970.
[10] *The Wall Street Journal*, April 10, 1970.

tinue this policy for the next General Motors stockholders meeting and will vote for the recommendations of the management." [11]

When the *Wall Street Journal* reported that the Regents of the University of Texas had decided to vote their 66,500 shares in favor of management, it also noted that "GM has been personally contacting many of its larger shareholders urging them to vote in favor of management's recommendations. One Detroit banker, for example, says that GM 'has been putting tremendous pressure on bank trust departments here to make sure they vote their shares for management.' " [12]

The black dimension of the controversy was underscored at the end of April when five black members of the U.S. House of Representatives and eight white members of the House (the latter all Democrats from the New York City area) endorsed Campaign GM's drive to elect representatives of the public to the board of General Motors. The black members were particularly interested in the nomination of Channing Phillips. Their statement declared, "Of the top 25 U.S. corporations, not one has a black person on its board of directors." [13] They also charged that General Motors had been "unresponsive to the needs of black Americans."

By early May it became clear that Campaign GM had no serious hopes of capturing a majority of the 285 million outstanding shares. Instead, the Campaign's leadership believed that in the face of management's inherent advantages, a 10% vote for their proposals would represent a "victory." Even that figure appeared rather ambitious, for other than a few political endorsements and some 400 letters of support, the group had little tangible shareholder backing. Yet there was strong student support at places such as Stanford, MIT, Columbia, Harvard, and the University of Pennsylvania, all of whose trustees were about to vote on the matter. GM already had "won" the Universities of Southern California, Texas, Detroit, and Michigan.

On May 20, 1970, two days before GM's annual meeting, the *New York Times* reported that the 160,000 shares of General Motors stock held by City of New York pension funds would be voted against the corporation's management. The city's representative to the meeting said the vote against General Motors management would be a "sym-

[11] *The Chicago Sun-Times,* April 19, 1970.
[12] *The Wall Street Journal,* April 20, 1970.
[13] *The New York Times,* May 1, 1970.

bolic gesture" that would awaken people to the need to make one of the largest corporations of the country more socially responsible.

On the other hand, the Rockefeller Foundation, which held 195,532 shares, decided to support management in the belief that Campaign GM's proposals were essentially "unwieldy and impractical." In reaching this conclusion, however, the trustees of the Rockefeller Foundation acknowledged the validity of Campaign GM's social concerns, and declared that they were "not prepared to let the matter rest." In an explanation of the foundation's actions (the complete text of which may be found in Appendix C), President J. George Harrar commented:

> We do not share the view which was expressed by management that the Campaign GM proposals represent an attack on the Corporation. This is a defensive and negative attitude at a time when all leading American institutions of government, business, philanthropy, education and religion should be seeking fresh approaches to demands for change and reform. We believe the language of the Campaign GM proposals is more reasonable and temperate than the response of management. We also believe the goals of the proposals have been designed to serve the public good by increasing the Corporation's awareness of the major impact of its decisions and policies on society at large.
>
> The concerns expressed by Campaign GM represent far more than the aspirations of one group of private citizens and indeed go beyond the demand of the American consumer for safer, healthier and more durable products at reasonable cost. They are clearly pointed in the direction in which General Motors and every American corporation must move if they are to function effectively and responsibly in the difficult years ahead. As stockholders and citizens we urge that management respond affirmatively to the goals of the proposals and search for acceptable ways to realize them.

This kind of moral, if not proxy, support prompted Mrs. Susan Weiss Gross, Campaign GM's press secretary, to state on the eve of GM's annual meeting: "We've won, because we've started a great national debate on corporate responsibility and we have forced corporations and shareholders to re-examine their policies." [14]

GM'S ANNUAL MEETING

In addition to the direct challenge raised by Campaign GM, the corporation's annual meeting occurred in an atmosphere of national economic recession, a 34% decline in the corporation's first quarter

[14] *The New York Times*, May 20, 1970.

profits compared with 1969, widespread labor turmoil in both the public and the private sectors, and demonstrations and disruptions by college students and other activists at corporate annual meetings around the country.

Protests at the latter focused on environmental pollution and the war in Viet Nam and reached near-violent proportions in some instances. Honeywell, Inc.'s meeting in Minneapolis had to be adjourned only 14 minutes after it was called to order, while the same day Gulf Oil struggled through a two-hour meeting in Pittsburgh during which some 30 protesters repeatedly shouted their demands for the company to end all defense contracts. Commonwealth Edison's meeting in Chicago was picketed by several hundred people and about 70 of them staged a floor demonstration demanding an end to air pollution.

When Chairman James M. Roche called General Motors' annual meeting to order at 2:00 P.M. on May 22, 1970, no one knew exactly what to expect except that it was likely to be an extraordinary session. And no one was disappointed.

> The focus of the GM meeting on the two proposals [of Campaign GM] made the meeting unlike any other in GM history. For one thing, there were hardly any financial questions as such, even though GM is in a profit slump and recently cut its dividend. For another, hundreds of the more than 2900 who attended were college and university students, some bearded, others wearing shirts and Levis. Many arrived hours before the meeting and had never attended a corporate annual meeting before; some brought picnic lunches. Many either owned only a few GM shares, or none at all, using other holders' proxies to get into the meeting. From the start of the meeting, many of these issue-oriented holders were bidding for attention, often in hurly-burly conflict with the regular annual meeting goers, other small stockholders and others with special interests. As a result, the flow of questioning and comments from the floor often was disjointed and confusing, and it took an hour and 20 minutes just to get through board nominations. The two main proposals weren't introduced until the meeting was more than three hours old.[15]

Although Campaign GM spokesmen had declared previously they would regard backing by 10% of the outstanding shares a "win," their actual tally was only about 2.5% of the votes cast. The final tabulation of votes of all five shareholder proposals (Nos. 4 and 5 of which were sponsored by Campaign GM) was as follows:

[15] *The Wall Street Journal*, May 25, 1970.

Number, Description, and Management's Recommendations on Each Shareholder Proposal	*Number of Shares Voted*	*Per Cent of Votes Cast*
1. To Ratify the Selection of Independent Public Accounts FOR	237,646,082 FOR 897,315 AGAINST	99.62% FOR 0.38% AGAINST

	Stockholders Voting and Per Cent	
	849,492 FOR 10,073 AGAINST	98.83% 1.17%

	Number of Shares Voted	*Per Cent of Votes Cast*
2. To Limit Executive Compensation AGAINST	11,986,285 FOR 221,579,207 AGAINST	5.13% 94.87%

	Stockholders Voting and Per Cent	
	117,443 FOR 742,183 AGAINST	13.66% 86.34%

	Number of Shares Voted	*Per Cent of Votes Cast*
3. Cumulative Voting AGAINST	6,650,363 FOR 226,893,816 AGAINST	2.85% 97.15%

	Stockholders Voting and Per Cent	
	62,614 FOR 797,212 AGAINST	7.28% 92.72%

	Number of Shares Voted	*Per Cent of Votes Cast*
4. To Establish a GM Shareholders Committee AGAINST	6,361,299 FOR 227,052,866 AGAINST	2.73% 97.27%

	Stockholders Voting and Per Cent	
	61,794 FOR 798,078 AGAINST	7.19% 92.81%

	Number of Shares Voted	*Per Cent of Votes Cast*
5. To Increase the Number of Directors AGAINST	5,691,130 FOR 227,776,076 AGAINST	2.44% 97.56%

	Stockholders Voting and Per Cent	
	53,495 FOR 806,398 AGAINST	6.22% 93.78%

Source of these tabulated votes was GM's post-meeting report.

The above results meant that the two unsuccessful proposals sponsored by Campaign GM could be included in GM's 1971 proxy statement only with the approval of management. This is because, under SEC rules, proposals which fail to receive the support of at least 3 per cent of the votes cast cannot be put in a proxy statement for three years unless management grants its permission.

POST-MEETING CONCLUSIONS

Despite the overwhelming vote margins achieved by management, many participants and observers came away from GM's meeting with the feeling that the results were inconclusive. For example, as noted above, the Rockefeller Foundation had cast its votes for management with the caveat that it was "not prepared to let the matter rest there." Nor was Campaign GM, for its members remained in Detroit until the next week to hold the "First Annual Convention on Corporate Responsibility." *Time* magazine reported it was more a rally than a convention, with many members inclined to dismiss the General Motors outcome as only an initial test case.[16] Many supporters of Campaign GM also believed they would have had much greater success had it not been for the extension of the Viet Nam war into Cambodia and the death of four students at Kent State University during the uproar that followed. These events sparked unprecedented turmoil and violence on the nation's college campuses and occupied the attention of Campaign GM's principal backers—college students— during the weeks leading up to the annual meeting.

From management's point of view, the Campaign GM episode underscored the need to ponder some fundamental questions about what constitutes "the public interest" and how corporate activities can be reconciled with changing public objectives and expectations. There also was the matter of to what extent and in what manner corporations should be prepared to share their power with so-called public interest groups or spokesmen. The latter issue arose from the fact that some of General Motors' critics appeared to be more concerned about the apparent inability of outsiders to influence the corporation's decisions than about the specific policies adopted by management and the board of directors.

APPENDIX A

Proposal Number 4

Whereas the shareholders of General Motors are concerned that the present policies and priorities pursued by the management have failed

[16] *Time,* June 1, 1970, p. 55.

to take into account the possible adverse social impact of the Corporation's activities, it is

RESOLVED that:

1. There be established the General Motors Shareholders Committee for Corporate Responsibility.

2. The Committee for Corporate Responsibility shall consist of no less than fifteen and no more than twenty-five persons, to be appointed by a representative of the Campaign to Make General Motors Responsible, and a representative of United Auto Workers, and a representative of the Board of Directors, acting by majority vote. The members of the Committee for Corporate Responsibility shall be chosen to represent the following: General Motors management, the United Auto Workers, environmental and conservation groups, consumers, the academic community, civil rights organizations, labor, the scientific community, religious and social service organizations, and small shareholders.

3. The Committee for Corporate Responsibility shall prepare a report and make recommendations to the shareholders with respect to the role of the corporation in modern society and how to achieve a proper balance between the rights and interest of shareholders, employees, consumers and the general public. The Committee shall specifically examine, among other things:

   A. The Corporation's past and present efforts to produce an automobile which:
      (1) is non-polluting
      (2) reduces the potentiality for accidents
      (3) reduces personal injury resulting from accidents
      (4) reduces property damage resulting from accidents
      (5) reduces the costs of repair and maintenance whether from accidents or extended use

   B. The extent to which the Corporation's policies towards suppliers, employees, consumers and dealers are contributing to the goals of providing safe and reliable products.

   C. The extent to which the Corporation's past and present efforts have contributed to a sound national transportation policy and an effective low-cost mass transportation system.

   D. The manner in which the Corporation has used its vast economic power to contribute to the social welfare of the nation.

   E. The manner by which the participation of diverse sectors of society in corporate decision-making can be increased including nomination and election of directors and selection of members of the committees of the Board of Directors.

4. The Committee's report shall be distributed to the shareholders and to the public no later than March 31, 1971. The Committee shall be authorized to employ staff members in the performance of its duties. The Board of Directors shall allocate to the Committee

those funds the Board of Directors determines reasonably necessary for the Committee to accomplish its tasks. The Committee may obtain any information from the Corporation and its employees reasonably deemed relevant by the Committee, provided, however, that the Board of Directors may restrict the information to be made available to the Committee to information which the Board of Directors reasonably determines to be not privileged for business or competitive reasons.

Proposal Number 5
RESOLVED:

That Number 15 of the By-Laws of the Corporation be amended to read as follows:

15. The business of the Corporation shall be managed by a board of twenty-six members.

APPENDIX B
Nominees for General Motors Corporation's Board of Directors

Name of Candidate	*Business Affiliation*	*Age As of Annual Meeting*	*Year Elected to GM Board*
Stephen D. Bechtel, Jr.	Bechtel Corporation	69	1969
Eugene N. Beesley	Eli Lilly and Company	61	1965
Lloyd D. Brace	First National Bank of Boston	67	1959
Albert Bradley	Former Chairman of Board of GM	78	1933
Harllee Branch, Jr.	The Southern Company	63	1965
Edward N. Cole	President of GM	60	1961
John T. Connor[1]	Allied Chemical Corporation	55	1964
Frederic G. Donner	Former Chairman of Board of GM	67	1942
Richard C. Gerstenberg	Vice Chairman of Board of GM	60	1967
John F. Gordon	Former President of GM	70	1951
James R. Killian, Jr.	Chairman of M.I.T.	65	1959
Roger M. Kyes	Executive Vice President of GM	64	1954
Oscar A. Lundin	Executive Vice President of GM	59	1970
John A. Mayer	Mellon National Bank and Trust	60	1968
J. Wesley McAfee	Union Electric Company	67	1963
W. Earle McLaughlin	The Royal Bank of Canada	54	1967
Howard J. Morgens	The Procter & Gamble Company	59	1963
Charles S. Mott	Former Vice President of GM	94	1917
Thomas L. Perkins	Perkins, Daniels & McCormack	64	1965
James M. Roche	Chairman of the Board of GM	63	1962
George Russell	Former Vice Chairman of Board	65	1956
Gerald A. Sivage	Marshall Field & Company	60	1970
Harold G. Warner	Executive Vice President of GM	69	1968

[1] Mr. Connor did not serve as a director during the period January 5, 1965, through May 18, 1967, when he was Secretary of Commerce of the United States.

APPENDIX C

The following statement by The Rockefeller Foundation was made public on May 12, 1970, by its president, Dr. J. George Harrar. The Foundation held 195,532 shares of General Motors stock.

The trustees of The Rockefeller Foundation, which owns a substantial block of General Motors stock, believe with the organizers of Campaign GM that the corporations of America must assert an unprecedented order of leadership in helping to solve the social problems of our time. We realize that for corporations to exercise this leadership they must continue to prosper and to grow and to be profitable investments to their stockholders.

But to stop there is to stop short of the moral and civic response required of the leaders of industry by the present crisis in our social order. For there are constituents other than stockholders to whom corporations are also obligated. There are battles to be waged against racism, poverty, pollution, and urban blight which the government alone cannot win; they can be won only if the status and power of American corporate industry are fully and effectively committed to the struggle. Conventional responses to persistent problems will neither produce equality of opportunity for the victims of society nor achieve an acceptable quality of life for the nation as a whole. What is needed from business today is leadership which is courageous, wise and compassionate, which is enlightened in its own and the public's interest, and which greets change with an open mind.

In our judgment, the management of General Motors did not display this spirit in its response to the two proposals offered by Campaign GM. We recognize that these proposals are, from management's viewpoint, unwieldly and impractical; Campaign GM itself conceded the difficulty it encountered in trying to determine a method of selecting members of a Committee for Corporate Responsibility. Because of these inadequacies we are prepared, this time, to sign our proxy as requested by management.

But we are not prepared to let the matter rest there.

We do not share the view which was expressed by management that the Campaign GM proposals represent an attack on the Corporation. This is a defensive and negative attitude at a time when all leading American institutions of government, business, philanthropy, education, and religion should be seeking fresh approaches to demands for change and reform.

We believe the language of the Campaign GM proposals is more reasonable and temperate than the response of management. We also believe the goals of the proposals have been designed to serve the public good by increasing the Corporation's awareness of the major impact of its decisions and policies on society at large.

The concerns expressed by Campaign GM represent far more than the aspirations of one group of private citizens and indeed go beyond the demand of the American consumer for safer, healthier and more durable products at reasonable cost. They are clearly pointed in the direction in which General Motors and every American corporation must move if they are to function effectively and responsibly in the difficult years ahead. As stockholders and citizens we urge that management respond affirmatively to the goals of the proposals and search for acceptable ways to realize them.

One major obstacle, we recognize, is the difficulty any corporation faces in attempting to work toward these objectives in concert with others. The anti-trust laws prevent concerted action, yet separate action by firms in the same industry may be prohibitively costly. To resolve this dilemma, corporations should, we believe, take the lead in urging government to set standards or impose regulations that will apply equally to all. In that way, a principal objective of Campaign GM can be realized consistent with the continued financial well-being of the corporation in a competitive environment.

In studying the proposals of Campaign GM, the trustees of the Rockefeller Foundation realize that we must examine our overall investment philosophy. The responsibility of the Foundation as a stockholder requires us to consider the needs and problems of management. But the responsibility of the Foundation, committed in its charter to the mission of serving the well-being of mankind, requires us to recognize that more is at stake than our role as a stockholder. We shall maintain a continuous review of our investments with these considerations in mind.

APPENDIX D

Financial Statistics of General Motors Corporation

Time Period	Dollar Sales of All Products	Net Income	Earned Per Share of Common Stock	Dividend Per Share of Common Stock	World-wide Employment
1965	20,733,982,000	2,125,606,000	$7.41	$5.25	735,000
1966	20,208,505,000	1,793,392,000	$6.24	$4.25	745,000
1967	20,026,252,000	1,627,276,000	$5.66	$3.80	728,000
1968	22,755,403,000	1,731,915,000	$6.02	$4.30	757,000
1969	24,295,141,000	1,710,695,000	$5.95	$4.30	794,000
1st Quarter of 1970	5,579,000,000	348,000,000	$1.21	$0.85	776,281

Number of Shares Owned	Per Cent of Stockholders Owning Number of Shares
1– 25	41.7%
26– 50	17.7%
51–100	19.2%
101–200	10.6%
201 and over	10.8%
	100.0%

28

EASTMAN
KODAK
AND FIGHT

For Rochester, New York, the long, hot summer came in July of
1964. Four days of rioting and violence, set off by the arrest of a 17-
year-old Negro on charges of drunkenness, ended with four persons
dead, hundreds injured, a thousand arrested, and property damage
totaling $1 million.

Rochester is described as a proud city—"proud of its tradition of
abundant, locally provided social services, proud of its reputation as a
clean, progressive community"[1]—and so, for many Rochesterites, finding an answer to the question "Why?" was not easy. Some, of course,
had no difficulty at all spotting the source of the trouble. Said one civic
leader:

> This city seems to have become a victim of its own generosity. Rochester
> is known as a soft touch for welfare and relief chiselers. As a result, there
> has been a large influx of shiftless Negroes with no real desire to work for
> a living.
> In 1950, there were only about 6,500 Negroes in Rochester. Now there
> are 33,000. Many of the newcomers are ne'er-do-wells. They are the
> people who live in squalor, who won't try to better themselves, whose
> main interest seems to be where the next bottle of booze is coming from.[2]

Outsiders, on the other hand, tended to look for the seeds of violence in a complex of causes—the Negro's segregated and run-down

[1] Patrick Anderson, "Making Trouble is Alinsky's Business," *The New York Times
Magazine*, October 9, 1966.
[2] *U.S. News & World Report*, August 10, 1964, p. 38.

housing; his lack of education, lack of job skill, and lack of motivation; his frustration and sense of hopelessness in the face of poverty; his animus against the police—in general, the smoldering resentment which an alienated Negro felt toward a prosperous white community. But whatever the cause or causes of the racial explosion, the disastrous results left little doubt that there was a "new, angry, combustible force" in the city's midst.

Rochester is a thriving industrial area, with such firms as Eastman Kodak, Xerox, Bausch & Lomb, Taylor Instruments, and divisions of General Motors and General Dynamics offering well-paid jobs to highly skilled workers, and the city speaks of itself in glowing terms:

> A community of more than 700,000 people with the highest percentage of skilled, technical and professional employees of any major U.S. metropolitan area; more engineers than any one of 23 States; the highest median family income of any city in the State, sixth highest in the nation . . . 67 percent of the residents owning their own houses.[3]

Understandably, the scars have been erased from this public relations picture; for Rochester, along with the rest of urban America, is woefully afflicted with mounting "inner city" problems.

In 1964, Rochester's 35,000 Negroes accounted for about one-tenth of the city's population.[4] Living in a slum area, they worked at construction or low-pay service jobs or were on relief.[5] For, although the city's major industries adhered to equal-opportunity policies, Negroes, with their minimum skills and education, could not meet most job requirements. Eastman Kodak, the largest employer of all, had recently begun to actively recruit Negro workers; but, after the riot, its industrial relations director pointed out to a *New York Times* reporter: "We're not in the habit of hiring bodies. We need skills. We don't grow many peanuts in Eastman Kodak." [6]

Following the summer's outburst of violence, the Rochester Area Council of Churches (a Protestant group) had brought in two members of Dr. Martin Luther King's Southern Christian Leadership Con-

---

[3] From a full-page ad run in the February 5, 1967, issue of *The New York Times* and quoted in Raymond A. Schroth, "Self-Doubt and Black Pride," *America*, April 1, 1967, p. 503.

[4] The total population of Rochester decreased from 332,488 in 1950 to 318,611 in 1960, while its Negro population grew from 7,590 to 23,586.

[5] *Business Week*, August 1, 1964, p. 24.

[6] Quoted in *Newsweek*, August 10, 1964, p. 27.

ference to see what could be done about easing conditions in the poverty-stricken Negro areas. But after several weeks, and for reasons which have never been clearly explained, the SCLC representatives departed. The Council then invited Saul Alinsky, the "middle-aged deus ex machina of American slum agitation," [7] to Rochester. And, predictably, a cry of outrage went up. The city's two Gannet-owned newspapers immediately denounced the church leaders' move; a local radio station told the clergymen that in the future they would have to pay for their Sunday morning radio time, which, up to that point, had been free; and the Community Chest hastened to invite the Urban League to set up shop in Rochester.

SAUL ALINSKY AND "FIGHT"

Acid-tongued and voluble, Saul Alinsky makes good copy, but mention of his name alone is sufficient to set the teeth of dozens of American communities on edge. Alinsky, who believes that the poor (because they are not a power bloc) are cut off from any meaningful participation in the democratic process, has spent three decades organizing slum communities throughout the United States. In 1940, with the financial backing of Marshall Field III, he set up the Industrial Areas Foundation, "a kind of training school for agitators," in Chicago. Soon other philanthropists and foundations and several church groups (particularly the Catholic Archdiocese of Chicago) [8] were contributing money to IAF's work. Alinsky, who borrowed many of his techniques from the American labor movement, spent the 1940's and 1950's organizing Mexican-American slums in California and various other slum districts in Chicago, Detroit, and New York. He came into national prominence in the early 1960's when he put together the Woodlawn Organization on Chicago's south side.

The aim of an Alinsky project is to create a "disciplined, broad-based power organization capable of wringing concessions—better jobs, better schools, better garbage collection, better housing—from the local establishment." [9] Through organization, the IAF seeks to replace the slum resident's alienation with participation in the decision-making

[7] *The New York Times Magazine,* October 9, 1966, p. 28.

[8] Bishop Bernard Sheil of Chicago was a strong Alinsky supporter, and it was he who introduced Alinsky to Marshall Field.

[9] *The New York Times Magazine,* October 9, 1966.

process. "The hell with charity," says Alinsky. "It's self-determination that counts."

When invited to a community, the IAF sends in an organizer who scouts around churches, barbershops, and pool halls looking for potential slum leaders and for any existing organizations which might be welded into a power bloc. Once an effective combination has been set up, the IAF pulls out and the organization is on its own. This generally takes two or three years, and the Foundation charges $50,000 a year for its services.[10] "One thing we instill in all our organizations," Alinsky says, "is that old Spanish civil war slogan, 'Better to die on your feet than to live on your knees.' Social scientists don't like to think in these terms. They would rather talk about politics being a matter of accommodation, consensus—not this conflict business. This is typical academic drivel. How do you have a consensus before you have a conflict? There has to be a rearrangement of power and then you get consensus."[11] But Alinsky disclaims any interest in imposing values or political goals on slum residents—"We're just technicians trying to organize people" is Alinsky's approach to a project.

In Rochester, the IAF project became known as FIGHT (Freedom, Integration, God, Honor—Today).[12] Alinsky sent Edward Chambers, his top organizer, to the city in the spring of 1965, and in June of that year, FIGHT adopted a constitution and elected its first president, the Reverend Franklin Florence. Reverend Florence, a Church of Christ minister, is

> very much the New Negro. He is angry and articulate. He wears a "Black Power" button, reveres the memory of Malcolm X and is studiously rude to most whites. . . . Florence's relationship with Alinsky and Chambers is a delicate one. He clearly resents the fact that he needs their help. In Rochester, as elsewhere, the days are numbered when white men can lead the black man's revolt.[13]

But Alinsky believes that the Negro needs white allies, and so a "separate but not quite equal" group called "the Friends of FIGHT"

[10] Alinsky draws a $25,000-a-year salary from the Foundation; organizers are paid $15,000.

[11] *The New York Times Magazine,* October 9, 1966.

[12] This acronym prompted the publisher of the Gannett newspapers to offer a few "less offensive" names. "How about W-O-R-K instead of F-I-G-H-T, how about L-O-V-E, how about T-R-Y, how about D-E-E-D-S?" See the *New Republic,* January 21, 1967, pp. 11–13.

[13] *The New York Times Magazine,* October 9, 1966.

was organized to provide money, legal expertise, and tutors for various FIGHT programs.

FIGHT's biggest success since its founding involved the city's urban renewal plan; there, the Negro organization won provision for construction of new housing on vacant land before destruction of the old, low-rise public housing on scattered sites, nonprofit public housing corporations, and 250 units of public housing where only two units had been planned.

In its first efforts to tackle the unemployment problem, FIGHT had arranged an on-the-job training program with Xerox for 15 Negroes; but by September, 1966, it had broadened its sights considerably when it began negotiating with Eastman Kodak for the recruitment, training, and hiring of 600 Negroes. Taking on Kodak was something that just wasn't done in Rochester, Reverend Florence explained, "but we knew if we could get Kodak in line, every other business would follow." [14]

THE COMPANY

Rochester has often been called the Kodak City, for profitable Eastman Kodak, with 41,000 people on its local payroll, is by far the largest employer in the Rochester area and a dominant influence on community life.[15] Over the years, Kodak has projected a quality image— in product and in management—and the company has long been known as a good place to work. Its personnel turnover is one-fourth the national industrial average, and none of its U.S. plants has ever been unionized.

Much of "the Kodak way" is derivative of founder George Eastman's approach to company management; and at his death in 1932, "his three closest associates took over more or less as a team, with considerable commingling of responsibility and a singularity of purpose: to do as Mr. Eastman would have done." [16] A "philosopher-tinkerer," Kodak's founder pioneered in several areas of industrial relations.[17] By 1903,

[14] The Binghamton, New York, *Sunday Press*, April 23, 1967.

[15] Kodak employs about 13 percent of the area's labor force and about one out of three in industry.

[16] Robert Sheehan, "The Kodak Picture—Sunshine and Shadow," *Fortune*, May, 1965, p. 129.

[17] Mr. Eastman was also a philanthropist par excellence. In 1924, he gave away half of his fortune. His total gifts amounted to more than $75 million, with the University of Rochester and the Massachusetts Institute of Technology the leading

his company had worked out an employment stabilization program to overcome seasonal variations in labor needs and to cut down on layoffs; in 1911, it created a benefit, accident, and pension fund for employees; and in 1912, it established its unique wage-dividend policy whereby the rate of dividends to workers is scaled to the rate of cash dividends paid to stockholders. In 1966, for example, a wage dividend of $69.3 million was paid in cash to approximately 63,000 Kodak employees in the United States, or contributed for their benefit to the employees' savings and investment plan. This was $39.50 for each $1,000 earned over the previous five-year period.

George Eastman was also a firm believer in hiring the best brains available; and with nearly 450 of its employees holding doctorates, Kodak, it is said, appears to have more Ph.D.'s running around the shop than office boys.[18] A glance at the credentials of several of its executives quickly confirms the fact that Kodak has, for some time, stressed formal academic training and intellectual achievement. Albert Chapman, who joined Kodak in 1919 and who retired as chairman of the board at the end of 1966, was a Phi Beta Kappa, with a doctorate in physics from Princeton. William Vaughn, Chapman's successor, is a Phi Beta Kappa also. After receiving an "A" in every course he took at Vanderbilt University, Vaughn went on for a master's degree in mathematics at Rice Institute, received a second bachelor's degree at Oxford (where he studied as a Rhodes Scholar), and started to work for Kodak in 1928. Louis Eilers, who succeeded Vaughn as president, began his Kodak career as a research chemist in 1934 after receiving a Ph.D. from Northwestern University.[19]

Financially, too, Kodak is an impressive company. The world's largest supplier of photographic materials and a leading manufacturer of chemicals, plastics, and synthetic fibers, it ranked thirty-fifth in size among U.S. industrial corporations in 1966.

During the past decade, operations showed uninterrupted gains, sales growing at a 7.4% compound annual rate, while earnings advanced at

---

beneficiaries. Kodak has continued the philanthropic tradition. In the last decade, the company has given $22 million to Rochester's hospitals, schools, and Community Chest (of which Eastman was a founder).

[18] Philip A. Cavalier, "Kodak's Growth: Never Out of Focus," *The Magazine of Wall Street,* November 26, 1966, p. 246.

[19] Mr. Eilers returned to Rochester as an executive vice president in 1964, after serving five years in Kingsport, Tennessee, first as vice president and later as president of Kodak's Tennessee Eastman and Texas Eastman companies.

an 11.5% compound annual rate. Focusing on the period starting in 1962 to the present, the picture gets even better. Overall sales crossed the billion-dollar mark for the first time in 1962. But, with 1966 sales estimated at roughly $1.7 billion, we see a gain of almost 70%. . . . From a financial point of view, Kodak is extremely strong. It has no long-term debt, while cash and marketable securities exceed its current liabilities.[20]

KODAK UNDER FIRE

It was somewhat surprising, in the fall of 1966, to find seemingly imperturbable Eastman Kodak smack in the center of a mushrooming controversy. In September, the company was asked by FIGHT if it would consider setting up a training program (to include such fundamentals as reading and arithmetic) for some 500 to 600 Negroes. "We're not talking about the man who can compete," Reverend Florence pointed out to Kodak officials. "We're talking about the down-and-out, the man crushed by this evil system, the man emasculated, who can't make it on his own. He has a right to work."[21] And he went on to propose that FIGHT recruit and Kodak train these unemployables over an 18-month period for entry-level jobs with the company. When FIGHT approached Kodak, its main argument was that in the past the company had ignored Rochester's Negroes and had hired white workers from other cities—that now it should give favored treatment to local Negroes regardless of the expense. "If Kodak can take pictures of the moon," Florence contended, "it can create 500 jobs for our people."

"We were sympathetic and open-minded," said William Vaughn, who was president at the time. "We realize this is a civic problem and a national problem that has to be solved."[22] Therefore, Vaughn did not expressly turn down Florence's idea, but agreed to further talks. At a second meeting on September 14, FIGHT presented its proposal in writing, and Vaughn distributed a statement which outlined Kodak's plans for expanding training programs and invited FIGHT to refer possible applicants. After this meeting, Vaughn turned future discussions[23] over to Kenneth Howard of the industrial relations department.

[20] *The Magazine of Wall Street,* November 26, 1966, pp. 277, 278.
[21] *Business Week,* April 29, 1967, p. 38.
[22] *Ibid.,* pp. 38–39.
[23] Nonunion Kodak carefully avoided the use of the word "negotiations" in describing its dealings with FIGHT.

Representatives of Kodak and FIGHT met twice again in September, but the meetings never got off the ground. Back and forth went letters between Kodak and FIGHT, with neither side agreeing on what had taken place.[24] Reverend Florence refused to discuss anything but the FIGHT proposal, while Kodak continued to argue that FIGHT should co-operate, as other organizations were doing, by referring candidates for the company's expanding training programs for the unskilled and uneducated.

The previous spring, Kodak had issued a Management Letter setting forth a change in emphasis in the company's employment policies.

> . . . our policy had been simply to try to employ the person best fitted to do the work available without regard for his or her background. We have moved actively beyond that position. We now seek to help the individual who lacks the necessary qualications to become qualified. In other words, we are contributing to the training of the individual so that he or she can qualify for employment. . . .
> Overall, it appears that industry must look less critically at the individual's school record and work experience and more at his potential. Frustration and unfavorable circumstances in early life often result in a school record far below the person's actual potential.

The Letter went on to describe several special training programs which Kodak was already operating and those which were in the process of development. But FIGHT contended that these "limited" programs encompassed "neither the imagination nor boldness required to tackle the serious employment problems of Rochester."

Throughout the September meetings, both Kodak and FIGHT had refused to budge an inch, and

> the situation was aggravated by the fact that the FIGHT negotiators did not trust Howard. The formidable Rev. Florence is quick to sense when a white man is ill at ease in his presence, and he could not respect a man who seemed to be afraid of him. But perhaps nonunion Kodak was not accustomed to bargaining with another "power" organization.[25]

In television and newspaper conferences, Reverend Florence promised to keep pressuring Kodak until it "woke up and came into the twentieth century," while Saul Alinsky called Kodak's attitude "arro-

[24] For copies of two of the letters included in this correspondence, see Appendix A.
[25] *America*, April 1, 1967, p. 503.

gant" and typical of Rochester's "self-righteousness." Alinsky further accused the company of playing a public relations "con game" with FIGHT, when in October it announced the hiring of the Indiana-based Board of Fundamental Education to help expand its remedial education programs. The new programs were to have an initial enrollment of 100, but, as it turned out, the trainees had already been selected. Sixty had recently been hired by Kodak and 40 were regular employees.[26]

For its part, Kodak showed determination to stick by its position that FIGHT should cooperate with Kodak's plans, and in November it sent a letter to company supervisors explaining its stand on the FIGHT proposal:

> We [cannot] enter into an arrangement exclusively with any organization to recruit candidates for employment and still be fair to the thousands of people who apply on their own initiative or are referred by others.
> We [cannot] agree to a program which would commit Kodak to hire and train a specific and substantial number of people in a period which would extend so far into the future.
> . . . we responded by telling FIGHT that we would expand and broaden certain special training activities, and we expressed the hope that they would refer candidates to us. . . . At the same time, we have affirmed that we cannot delegate decisions on recruitment, selection, and training for KODAK jobs to any outside group. Other organizations with whom we have worked readily understand this.

Despite a background of deadlocks, discussions were eventually resumed in December as a result of a luncheon conversation between John G. Mulder, a Kodak assistant vice president,[27] and an acquaintance of his, the Rev. Marvin Chandler, who was an official of FIGHT. During the course of their talk about possible ways to resolve the dispute, Chandler told Mulder that FIGHT would prefer a new negotiating team. The two men next discussed the matter at an unannounced meeting in Kodak's board room on December 16, and Vaughn (who hoped "there was a new deal here") gave Mulder the go-ahead

---

[26] See the *Rochester Democrat*, October 26, 1966, and the *Rochester Times-Union*, October 24, 1966.

[27] Mr. Mulder, the assistant general manager of Kodak Park Works, the company's largest installation in the Rochester area, was also president of the city's Council of Social Agencies. His wife is a member of the Friends of FIGHT.

to meet with FIGHT representatives. Kodak had expected to deal with Chandler, but Reverend Florence attended the two-day meetings which followed; and on December 20, he and Mulder signed a joint statement to the effect that FIGHT and Kodak had agreed to "an objective of the recruitment and referral (to include screening and selection) of 600 unemployed people over a 24-month period, barring unforeseen economic changes affecting the Rochester community. FIGHT, at its own expense, would provide counseling for the employees selected by Kodak." (For the full text of the statement, see Appendix B.)

According to reports, Kodak's president-elect Louis Eilers [28] exploded when he heard of the signing. The next morning Kodak's executive committee voted to repudiate the agreement, and the following day the board of directors agreed. A statement was then drafted, and Eilers informed reporters that the agreement was invalid because Mulder had no authority to sign any document on Kodak's behalf. He told newsmen that Kodak had neither intended nor authorized such an arrangement and that when management heard about it, "We all expressed the greatest of displeasure at the signing." Asked why Mulder would sign the statement if he had no authority to do so, Eilers could only reply that the assistant vice president had "apparently not been informed of company policies." [29] He added, however, that he "didn't envision any change in Mulder's job." Mulder himself declined to comment on the dispute, saying he was "in no position to talk," but he personally had gone to Reverend Chandler's home to break the news that Kodak would not honor the agreement. As for FIGHT's president, he announced that his organization would demand that the agreement be put into effect. "They've shown they're no good and deceitful. Obviously, there are people in Kodak who know what such a program can mean, yet there are hard-line people who don't care a thing about partnership with the poor." Florence insisted that he had asked Mulder three times if he had authority to sign the agreement.

In the midst of the uproar that followed, Kodak ran a conciliatory two-page ad in the local morning and afternoon newspapers stating it

[28] In November, 1966, Kodak had announced Mr. Chapman's resignation as board chairman, eective January 1, 1967, Mr. Vaughn's election to the chairmanship, and Mr. Eilers' election to the presidency.

[29] *The New York Times*, January 7, 1967. While the public probably will never know what Vaughn's directions to Mulder were, Vaughn insists that the assistant vice president exceeded his instructions, feeling that "he got trapped, or rather trapped himself." See *Business Week*, April 29, 1967, p. 40.

"sincerely regret[ted] any misunderstanding," but it could not "discriminate by having an exclusive recruiting arrangement with any organization. Nor, owing to the uncertainties of economic conditions [could]
the company commit itself on a long-term basis to employ a specific
number of people." Kodak was "deeply concerned to do all that [it]
reasonably can to meet a pressing social need in this community,
namely, to try to develop employment opportunities," and management was taking "many positive steps" in this direction.

But the tone of remarks made by Kodak's president at a news conference on January 6 was decidedly bitter. Eilers took the occasion to
fire off a succession of charges against FIGHT. Its "talk about employment," he said, was "being used as a screen for making a power drive"
in the community, and its demands were "arbitrary and unreasonable."

> Since the Alinsky forces were brought to Rochester, FIGHT has run a
> continuing war against numerous Rochester institutions that help build
> Rochester—the school system, the community chest, the city govern-
> ment, and even organizations especially set up to help solve minority
> group problems.
> Kodak's turn came last September. A savage attack has been directed at
> us since that time.[30]

FIGHT, he charged, was trying to gain an exclusive hold on 600
jobs, and the training and hiring program which it insisted the company agree to would require Kodak management to surrender its
prerogative to determine whom to hire and when. This the company
neither could nor would do. Eilers pointed out that Kodak had some
1,200 to 1,500 Negroes among its Rochester employees, several hundred
of whom had been hired in the last few months,[31] and the company already had special training and employment programs for the unskilled
and uneducated, with which FIGHT had repeatedly refused to co-
operate. Later, Eilers was to say:

> To tell the truth, I don't know what they want. Certainly not jobs—
> they could have had those, and still can. Every one of the other 10
> referring agencies in Rochester has placed people in jobs at Kodak and
> none has asked for an exclusive deal.

[30] *The New York Times,* January 7, 1967.
[31] "Kodak's Vaughn grants that FIGHT pressure led Kodak to hire more Negroes,"
Business Week, April 29, 1967, pp. 39–40.

This year we'll have about 300 more in our training program. It's too bad FIGHT doesn't want to participate.[32]

A COMMUNITY DIVIDED

Between 1960 and 1967, Rochester had accomplished far more than the country as a whole in increasing Negro employment, but an unrelenting influx of unskilled and uneducated Southern Negroes had completely wiped out the city's gains. While Negro employment in the area had risen 43 per cent (more than four times the national average), there had been a 46 per cent increase in the Negro population of working age. Availability of jobs was not the problem. At the beginning of 1967, there were 10,000 job openings in the Rochester area, but 60 per cent of these openings required a high school education and more than 15 per cent required a college degree. Yet 54 per cent of Rochester's unemployed Negro males had less than a ninth-grade education.

The Rochester community, already confronted with an uphill situation and the specter of another racial explosion, was splintered in its reaction to the Kodak-FIGHT dispute. "Kodak made FIGHT look good," a University of Rochester professor said. "If I were Alinsky," said the acting president of Friends of FIGHT, "I would have bribed Eilers to repudiate the agreement."[33] To add to the tension, a number of Kodak employees were members of Friends of FIGHT and there were rumors of an ideological split within the company itself. For weeks following Kodak's repudiation of the agreement, sermons for and against FIGHT and the Council of Churches were heard at Sunday services. And the publisher of Rochester's newspapers excoriated the Council for widening the "gulf between pulpit and pew" by bringing in a divisive force which had attacked a "company famed the world over for its sometimes ponderous but ever humane approach to all things." The president (a Kodak employee) and two members of the board of directors of the Council resigned in protest against its continued support of FIGHT. Still, the Council gained an ally in Fulton J. Sheen, the newly appointed bishop of the Rochester Catholic diocese, who, in his first appointment, named a highly vocal FIGHT sup-

---

[32] The Binghamton *Sunday Press*, April 23, 1967.
[33] Barbara Carter, "The FIGHT against Kodak," *The Reporter*, April 20, 1967, p. 30. There was some feeling in Rochester that FIGHT would have been hard put to produce the 600 Negroes its proposal called for.

porter and Kodak critic as his special vicar to minister to the poor of the city. And representatives of the National Council of Churches, the United Presbyterian Church, and the United Church of Christ came out in support of FIGHT.

Within the Negro community itself, there was a mixed reaction to FIGHT's abrasive tactics. The head of the local Urban League attacked Reverend Florence's "irresponsibility" and questioned whether "FIGHT and only FIGHT should be the spokesman for the 'poor' black man in the Rochester community." A supporter of FIGHT ("Negroes must have a militant organization"), he objected to Florence's followers calling him a traitor to the cause because he did not "necessarily follow the FIGHT philosophy as projected by Minister Florence."[34] The Urban League also took strong exception to Florence's statement that it would be joining a "conspiracy" if it referred any applicants to Kodak's training programs.

On the whole, most Rochesterites seemed anxious to get Kodak and FIGHT "unhooked" from their dispute, and a group of industrial and religious leaders set about organizing Rochester Jobs, Inc., to provide work for 1,500 hard-core unemployed. The organization received commitments from 40 companies (including Kodak) to provide on-the-job training, remedial education, and counseling, with jobs to be divided on a quota basis.

Determined to hold Kodak to the signed agreement, however, Reverend Florence did nothing throughout the uneasy winter to lessen the mounting tension. In January, he invited Stokely Carmichael to speak to a FIGHT rally. Promising a national boycott which would bring Kodak to its knees, Carmichael predicted that "When we're through, Florence will say 'Jump,' and Kodak will ask 'How high?' "[35] Florence next fired off a telegram to Kodak's president, warning: "The cold of February will give way to the warm of spring, and eventually to the long hot summer. What will happen in Rochester in the summer of 1967 is at the doorstep of the Eastman Kodak Company. . . . You'll be hearing from us, and it won't be in black and white."[36]

And Kodak did hear from FIGHT—at its annual meeting on April 25. The entire two-and-three-quarters hour meeting (except for a brief review of operating results) was devoted to the Kodak-FIGHT dispute.

[34] *The Reporter*, April 20, 1967, p. 31.
[35] *Ibid.*, p. 28.
[36] *The Reporter*, April 20, 1967, p. 31.

Reverend Florence (the owner of one share of Kodak stock)[37] took the floor to demand that the company reinstate the December 20 agreement, and when Chairman Vaughn refused, Florence, together with 25 FIGHT supporters, walked out of the meeting, declaring, "This is war—and I state it again—war." Florence told 600 demonstrators waiting outside, "Racial war has been declared on American Negroes by Eastman Kodak. Kodak has shown American Negroes that powerful companies can't be trusted." He promised the crowd that FIGHT would conduct a national campaign against Kodak, including a "candlelight service" in Rochester on July 24, the third anniversary of the city's race riot.

To stockholders remaining in the meeting (including representatives of several church groups who had withheld their proxies from management),[38] Vaughn explained that Kodak refused to honor the December 20 agreement because it was unauthorized. "In his overzealousness to resolve the controversy, Mr. Mulder put his name to a document prepared by FIGHT," the Chairman said. "The incident was most unfortunate and regrettable. We have acknowledged it was a mistake and have apologized for it ever since." (Vaughn later told reporters that Mulder was still an assistant vice president and would not be penalized for his action.)

FIGHT, in the meantime, increased its request to Kodak and asked the company to provide 2,000 jobs, and Saul Alinsky gave Kodak warning of what to expect in the future. "The battle," said he, "will be in Eastman Kodak's arena—the nation from Harlem to Watts."

Looking back over the long-drawn-out dispute, Kodak's president opined: "I think we used too much patience."[39]

---

[37] In anticipation of the annual meeting, Florence and each of nine other FIGHT officials had purchased a share of Kodak stock, for a total of ten shares.

[38] FIGHT had succeeded in getting stockholders to withhold proxies for about 40,000 shares. At the meeting, 84 per cent of Kodak's 80,772,718 shares outstanding were voted for management. Reverend Florence had also filed suit to get the company to give him access to its list of stockholders, but a New York State court denied the request.

[39] *Business Week*, April 29, 1967, p. 41.

APPENDIX A

EASTMAN KODAK COMPANY
Rochester, New York 14650

September 28, 1966

Minister Franklin Florence, President
FIGHT
FIGHT Headquarters
86 Prospect Street
Rochester, New York 14608

Dear Minister Florence:

I have your letter of September 26 from which I note that apparently considerable misunderstandings still exist as to what we tried to convey to you and your associates in FIGHT at our meeting on September 14.

In the first place, Kodak's programs and plans described at that meeting, in response to your verbal proposal of September 2, were *not* simply " a repeat of your limited special training programs," as you state in your letter. If you will reread, closely and carefully, the second paragraph on page 2 of the statement handed to you at our meeting on September 14 you will see that we are talking of "an *expanded* concept of on-the-job training," which we go on to describe in general terms. We went on to say that we hoped "to benefit from suggestions which FIGHT may offer," as well as from those of other organizations interested in these matters.

Since the goals of "the FIGHT proposal" seemed to be so close to the aims of our programs, we assumed that you wanted to cooperate in making our efforts more successful.

We have indicated to you on several occasions that we cannot accept your "proposal," which is, quoting from your September 14 memorandum, as follows: "Kodak would train over an 18-month period between 500 and 600 persons so that they qualify for entry level positions across the board. FIGHT would recruit and counsel trainees and offer advice, consultation, and assistance in the project." Your memorandum also states that the project ". . . would be geared to individuals with limited education and skills . . ." and that ". . . areas to be worked out would include selection criteria, recruitment, training needs . . ." and that "programs should include remedial reading and arithmetic; industrial orientation and training to afford a basic understanding of industrial processes, tools, machinery, and work rules; basic skills training like material handling, blueprint reading, and mechanical principle; others." In addition, you have indicated that you expected this company to undertake all this exclusively in cooperation with FIGHT.

We have tried to make clear to you why we cannot accept the "FIGHT proposal." Apparently, it is necessary at this time for me to restate our position.

1. In light of the company's legal obligations and its responsibilities to Kodak customers, employees, stockholders, other applicants for employment, and the community, the company obviously cannot discriminate by granting any one organization an exclusive or monopolistic position in the recruitment, selection, or training of Kodak people.

2. We are not in a position to establish any statistical objective or quota for any special training programs which we undertake. Our ability to hire a person at Kodak depends first on the existence of a job opening and, second, on the availability of a person qualified to fill that opening.

During the last several months, we have hired a good many people, among whom were many Negroes. We hope we can continue to provide additional job opportunities in the future. But it is impossible for us to say how many, if any, such opportunities will be available at Kodak six months, a year, or 18 months hence. It would be an inexcusable deception on our part to promise something we cannot be sure of honoring.

You are quoted in this morning's paper as having said last evening, "I hate to believe a company of this stature would misguide poor people." We have no intention of misguiding anyone and it is precisely for this reason we cannot promise a given number of jobs at some future date when we do not control the economic and other factors which create the job opportunities.

I think both you and we are concerned with a problem to which no one has yet found a satisfactory solution—that is, how to motivate people to prepare themselves for job openings, and how to train people for industrial jobs who are lacking in such fundamental skills as reading, writing, and arithmetic. Certainly it would be dishonest and unfair to the people involved if we were to suggest that we have the knowledge or manpower to take on such a complete job where, so far as I know, no others have succeeded. However, as we have told you, we are planning to expand our special training efforts to see what further we can do. We are naturally anxious that any program we undertake have some reasonable chance of success.

What we are trying to do is to see what we can accomplish, by special training programs, to upgrade persons who are willing to try to improve themselves so they can qualify for the kinds of jobs we have. In doing this, we will seek the assistance of interested organizations which are willing to cooperate in constructive ways.

If FIGHT is interested in cooperating on this basis by making suggestions for the programs or referring applicants for them, I would again suggest that you resume discussions with Mr. Howard. If, on the other hand, your interest is solely in talking further about "the FIGHT proposal," I doubt that anything very useful could come from just going over the same ground that has been covered in the several talks that have already taken place.

Yours very truly,

/s/   W. S. Vaughn
President

WSVaughn:eml

F I G H T

October 7, 1966
Mr. W. L. Vaughn, President
Eastman Kodak Company
343 State Street
Rochester, New York 14650

Dear Mr. Vaughn:

I have your letter of September 28th and offer at this time the following observations.

An American economy which is in the first stages of inflation and which has shown an accompanying rising employment rate finds itself threatened by an alarming increase in unemployment among Negroes. The last figure issued by our government pointed to 8.3% of all employable Negroes were unemployed. It is clear to all students and observers of economic conditions among the Negroes of America that the employment rate in the various ghettos from Harlem to Watts are substantially higher. This dangerous condition not only for the Negro population but the general American public becomes particularly ominous since it follows on the heels of civil rights legislation, extensive job retraining programs, and a convergence of public opinion and government pressure upon private industry and organized labor to drop their discriminatory hiring practices and to open jobs for Negro fellow Americans. So, we are confronted with the strange and frightening anomaly of increasing employment for whites occurring simultaneously with decreasing employment for Negroes.

There are a number of reasons for this kind of economic sickness and one of the major ones is the fact that large industries such as Eastman Kodak persist in employing the same testing procedures for hiring eligibility to Negro applicants as they do with white applicants. The pursuit of this practice indicates an extraordinary insensitivity to the social and educational circumstances which have prevailed in our country for many years: circumstances of limited opportunities, economywise, education-wise, and in almost every other sector of our life which all Americans today are fully cognizant of and are moving toward their correction. It is clear that a Negro of the same age as that of a white has not had the academic opportunities to qualify for the same test. It is clear that if there is to be be an intelligent approach to this issue that those factors must be taken into consideration in terms of equity as well as the practical politics of keeping a healthy American way for all people. The obvious remedy lies in avoidance in the trap of this discriminatory test and hiring of Negroes for jobs where they will not only receive on-the-job training, but also special educational programs to bring them up to the point where they could then qualify under the test. Any employer who would regard this as discrimination in reverse would be guilty of an extraordinary shortsightedness and unawareness of the general situation prevailing in our nation today.

This has been the issue in our approach to Eastman Kodak. With it has gone our own feelings that if private industry does not meet this challenge that we will of necessity have to assume that there is no other recourse but massive governmental public projects and we have nowhere else to turn except to our government. Paradoxically, major industries in America, including Eastman Kodak, have always expressed concern for the ever expanding encroachment by government in various areas of our life. They have regarded this with a great deal of alarm. Some of the most conservative of them have denounced it as creeping socialism. We, ourselves, believe that the democratic way of life would hold to most problems being met and resolved on a local community basis and that there is that kind of free initiate in various sectors of our society: that government should not move in unless local communities are obviously unable, incapable, or unwilling, to meet their own problems. Eastman Kodak has the opportunity to make a significant contribution by co-operating with FIGHT's proposal. But, if FIGHT continues to be stalled and politely rejected as it has been to this date, then we must conclude that while industry talks about government encroaching upon all spheres of the American scene that in fact, it is just talk and that it is coming because industry refuses to act. We, like all other Americans, prefer to be employed by our government, to have our dignity, to have a job and to have an economic future rather than to have a basket full of empty generalities and unemployment by private industry which is immobilized by its own straightjacket by antiquated definitions of discrimination and by an astounding blindness to their own self-interest.

Use of terms like "exclusively," "monopolistic," "arbitrary demands," etc. in reference to the FIGHT proposal does an injustice to the careful thought and consideration that has gone into our suggestions. We have not even had the opportunity to discuss the details of our approach with Eastman Kodak.

Sincerely,

/s/   Franklin Florence
      Minister Franklin Florence

FF:ks

APPENDIX B

December 20, 1966

A special committee appointed by Eastman Kodak president, William Vaughn, has been meeting Monday and Tuesday with officers of the FIGHT organization.

Kodak representatives stated that they have not employed traditional standards of hiring for the last two years. FIGHT hailed this as a step in the right direction as well as Kodak officers' statement that they will deal with the problem of hard-core unemployed.

Job openings, specifications and hourly rates were discussed and agreed upon by the joint group.

January 15th was agreed upon as the date for a beginning of the referral of 600 employees, the bulk of which would be hard-core unemployed (unattached, uninvolved with traditional institutions).

Under the agreement, the FIGHT organization and Kodak agreed to an objective of the recruitment and referral (to include screening and selection) of 600 unemployed people over a 24-month period, barring unforeseen economic changes affecting the Rochester community. FIGHT, at its own expense, would provide counseling for the employees selected by Kodak.

Kodak agrees to the following: join with FIGHT in a firm agreement to

- A. Continue semi-monthly meetings between Kodak and FIGHT to increase the effectiveness of the program.
- B. Kodak will familiarize FIGHT counselors with the foremen and work skills required, and in turn FIGHT will familiarize Kodak foremen with the life and environment of poor people.
- C. Kodak and FIGHT will share information on the referrals.
- D. Kodak and FIGHT will issue a 60-day community progress report.

John Mulder
Asst. Vice President, Eastman Kodak
Asst. General Manager, Kodak Park Works
Franklin D.R. Florence
President of FIGHT

29
THE
CLOROX
CASE

The owners of Clorox Chemical Company, nearing retirement age and wanting to sell the company, approached Procter & Gamble with the idea of a merger.[1] At the time, Clorox was the nation's largest producer of household liquid bleach, and P & G the leading U.S. manufacturer of soap, detergent, and cleanser products. Liquid bleach, like Procter's product lines, was a low-priced, rapid-turnover household item sold mainly through grocery stores and supermarkets and presold through mass advertising and sales promotions. After studying the liquid bleach market for two years, Procter's promotion department recommended that the company buy Clorox rather than bring out a bleach of its own. Since a "very heavy investment" would be required to obtain a satisfactory market share for a new bleach, "taking over the Clorox business . . . could be a way of achieving a dominant position in the liquid bleach market quickly, which would pay out reasonably well." The promotion department's report predicted that P & G's sales, distributing, and manufacturing setup could up Clorox's market share in areas where it was low and make a number of savings which would increase the profits of the business considerably. Additionally, the department pointed out that P & G could make more effective use of Clorox's advertising budget and achieve substantial advertising economies.

[1] In argument before the United States Supreme Court, P & G's attorneys said that initiative for the merger rested solely with Clorox owners, who wanted to dispose of their business for estate purposes "in exchange for the marketable securities of a big company." See *Advertising Age,* February 20, 1967, p. 194.

Procter decided to go ahead with the merger, and on August 1, 1957, acquired the assets of Clorox in exchange for stock of Procter having a market value of approximately $30.3 million. Two months later, on October 7, 1957, the Federal Trade Commission filed a complaint charging that Procter's purchase of Clorox might substantially lessen competition, or tend to create a monopoly in the production and sale of household liquid bleaches, in violation of Section 7 of the Clayton Act.[2]

At the time of the acquisition, P & G had assests in excess of one-half billion dollars and annual sales of $1.15 billion. More than half ($514 million) of its total domestic sales were in the soap-detergent-cleanser field, and in packaged detergents alone its sales were $414 million. Procter held 54.4 per cent of the packaged detergent market, and, together with Colgate-Palmolive and Lever Brothers, accounted for more than 80 per cent of this market. In 1957, P & G's percentages of national sales lined up as follows: 54.4 per cent of packaged detergents; 31 per cent of toilet soap; 30 per cent of lard and shortening; and 19 per cent of shampoo. In addition, the company was a major producer of food and paper products. The giant soap company was also the nation's largest advertiser and in 1957 spent more than $80 million on advertising and an additional $47 million on sales promotion.

In the liquid bleach industry, Clorox, with almost 50 per cent of the market, was by far the leader. The company (which in the five years prior to the merger had experienced a steady and continuing growth in sales, profits, and net worth) had assets of over $12 million and annual sales of slightly less than $40 million. In 1957, Clorox spent nearly $3.7 million on advertising and $1.7 million for promotional activities. The company had no salesmen but sold its product through brokers and distributors.

Household liquid bleach (5¼ per cent sodium hypochlorite and 94¾ per cent water) was a relatively inexpensive item to manufacture, but because of high shipping costs and a low sales price, it was not profitable to sell the bleach more than 300 miles from the point of

[2] "No corporation engaged in commerce shall acquire, directly or indirectly, the whole or any part of the stock or other share capital and no corporation subject to the jurisdiction of the Federal Trade Commission shall acquire the whole or any part of the assets of another corporation engaged also in commerce, where in any line of commerce in any section of the country, the effect of such acquisition may be substantially to lessen competition, or to tend to create a monopoly."

manufacture. And Clorox, with 13 plants scattered throughout the United States, was the only company in the industry distributing its product nationally. Purex, its closest rival,[3] had as many plants, but its bleach was available on less than half the national market, and most other manufacturers, having but one plant, were limited to a regional market. In 1957, the six leading producers of household liquid bleach held the following market shares:

Brand	Per Cent of Total U. S. Sales
Clorox	48.8
Purex	15.7
Roman Cleanser	5.9
Fleecy White	4.0
Hilex	3.3
Linco	2.1
	79.8
All other brands (about 200 producers)	20.2

Only eight bleach manufacturers had assets in excess of $1 million; very few had assets of more than $75,000; and total industry sales were less than $100 million annually (less than 10 per cent of Procter's annual sales).

PROCEEDINGS BEFORE THE FEDERAL TRADE COMMISSION

The Procter-Clorox case became something of a football before the Federal Trade Commission.

June 7, 1960. Following a series of hearings which extended over a 14-month period, the hearing examiner issued his initial decision finding the acquisition violative of Section 7 and ordering divestiture.[4]

June 15, 1961. On appeal, the Commission set aside the initial decision and remanded the matter to the hearing examiner for the purpose of taking additional evidence on the post-merger situation in the liquid bleach industry.[5]

[3] While Clorox produced only liquid bleach, Purex manufactured other products, including abrasive cleaners, toilet soap, and detergents. Total sales of all Purex products were approximately $50 million in 1957.

[4] A brief description of the procedural steps involved in a Federal Trade Commission case is found in Appendix A.

[5] 58 F. T. C. 1203.

> As the hearing examiner has pointed out, this case involves a conglomerate acquisition and is therefore one of first impression. . . . [S]ince a conglomerate acquisition does not have the . . . "automatic" effects of a vertical or horizontal merger, . . . a consideration of post-acquisition factors is appropriate.

The record, as presently constituted, the Commission held, did not provide "an adequate basis for determining the legality" of the acquisition and a remand would provide "a more complete and detailed post-acquisition picture . . . allowing the Commission an informed hindsight upon which it can act rather than placing too strong a reliance upon treacherous conjecture."

February 28, 1962. The remand hearing took only two days, and the hearing examiner then rendered a second decision, again finding against P & G and ordering divestiture.

December 15, 1963. On a second appeal, the Commission affirmed the hearing examiner's decision and ordered divestiture.[6] In this second decision, the Commission held the post-merger evidence irrelevant. (In the interim between the two decisions, the personnel on the Commission had changed, so that only one Commissioner participated in both decisions.) The admission of post-acquisition data, the Commission wrote,

> is proper only in the unusual case in which the structure of the market has changed radically since the merger . . . or in the perhaps still more unusual case in which the adverse effects of the merger on competition have already become manifest in the behavior of the firms in the market. If post-acquisition data are to be allowed any broader role in Section 7 proceedings, a [company], so long as the merger is the subject of an investigation or proceeding, may deliberately refrain from anti-competitive conduct—may sheathe, as it were, the market power conferred by the merger—and build, instead a record of good behavior to be used in rebuttal in the proceeding.

But more important, said the Commission,

> if a market structure conducive to non-competitive practices or adverse competitive effects is shown to have been created or aggravated by a merger, it is surely immaterial that specific behavioral manifestations have not yet appeared.

[6] In ordering the divestiture, however, the Commission said that Procter might spin off the acquired assets to a new corporation owned by P & G stockholders but under separate management.

THE FINAL DECISION OF THE
FEDERAL TRADE COMMISSION

Keenly aware that the legality of Procter's purchase of Clorox was a question largely of first impression ("The absence of authoritative, specific precedents in this area compels us to look to basic principles in the interpretation and application of Section 7"), the Commission described the acquisition as a "product-extension" merger.[8] Packaged detergents and household liquid bleach are used complementarily, the Commission pointed out, and from the housewife's point of view are closely related products. Moreover, since detergents and bleach are low-cost, high-turnover consumer products, sold to the same customers, at the same stores, and by the same merchandising methods, the merger offered possibilities for significant integration at both marketing and distribution levels.

> By this acquisition, then, Proctor has not diversified its interests in the sense of expanding into a substantially different, unfamiliar market or industry. Rather, it has entered a market which adjoins, as it were, those markets in which it is already established, and which is virtually indistinguishable from them insofar as the problems and techniques of marketing the product to the ultimate consumer are concerned.

Taking a look at the pre-merger liquid bleach industry, the Commission called it highly concentrated, oligopolistic, strongly characterized by product differentiation through advertising, and barricaded to new entry, to a degree inconsistent with effectively competitive condi-

[7] *1963 Trade Cases* 16, 673.

[8] Here, the Commission wrote: "Another variant of the conventional horizontal merger is the merger of sellers of functionally closely related products which are not, however, close substitutes. This may be called a product-extension merger. The expression 'functionally closely related,' as used here, is not meant to carry any very precise connotation, but only to suggest the kind of merger that may enable significant integration in the production, distribution or marketing activities of the merging firms. . . . Only when the various subcategories of horizontal and vertical mergers have been exhausted do we reach the true diversification or conglomerate merger, involving firms which deal in unrelated products." But all mergers, said the Commission, "whether they be classified as horizontal, vertical or conglomerate, are within the reach of Section 7, and all are to be tested by the same standard." Definitional distinctions, the Commission continued, "import no legal distinctions under Section 7. The legal test of every merger, of whatever kind, is whether its effect may be substantially to lessen competition, or tend to create a monopoly, in any line of commerce in any section of the country."

tions. Between them, Clorox and Purex accounted for almost 65 per cent of liquid bleach sales and, together with four other firms, for almost 80 per cent—and of these six companies, a single one, Clorox, was dominant.[9] Only Purex could be considered to have been a significant competitor of Clorox, and its bleach was not sold in half of the country; in fact, in several areas, Clorox faced no competition whatever from the leading firms in the industry.

Since all liquid bleaches were chemically identical, the success of Clorox, a premium brand, was obviously due to the company's "long-continued mass advertising," whereby its name had become widely known to and preferred by the housewife, "notwithstanding its high price and lack of superior quality." Most bleach manufacturers, the Commission observed, could not afford to advertise extensively, and although Purex was a large advertiser, its advertising was "very possibly less effective" than Clorox's because of its geographically limited market. Thus, the chief effect of Clorox's "intensive" advertising had been to gain a large share of the market at a higher price to the consumer. Given the importance of product differentiation in the bleach industry, advertising outlays were a formidable barrier to entry even before the merger, because any outsider who hoped to capture a satisfactory share of the market would have to incur a very heavy initial investment to promote its brand.

Having described the liquid bleach industry in these terms, the Commission went on to find that the substitution of multi-product P & G, with its huge assets and enormous advertising power, for the dominant, but relatively small, single-product Clorox would lend further rigidity to an almost oligopolistic industry by scaring off potential competitors and inhibiting active competition from those firms already in the industry.

First, the Commission tried to ferret out the consequences for competition if P & G replaced Clorox in the bleach industry. Pinning much of its argument against the merger on P & G's advertising and promotional power and the cost savings and other advantages resulting therefrom, the Commission found that post-merger Clorox could ob-

[9] According to the Commission, Clorox's dominant position was "dramatically" shown by the fact that Procter "preferred to pay a very large premium for the good will of Clorox (the $17.7 million difference between the purchase price of Clorox, $30.3 million, and the valuation of Clorox's assets, $12.6 million, suggests the size of this premium), rather than enter the industry on its own."

tain 33⅓ per cent more network TV advertising for the same amount of money it had spent prior to the acquisition. This was due to the discounts which Procter received on its tremendous volume of TV advertising, and, the Commission noted, similar advertising discounts were available to P & G in the other media. But the advertising advantages of the merger were not limited to volume discounts. For example, P & G could afford to buy entire network TV programs on behalf of several of its products—something which pre-merger Clorox could not have done unless it were willing to put a disproportionate amount of its advertising budget into a single project. Also, if Procter felt that Clorox faced stiff competition in a particular locality, it could run a TV commercial in that area alone, while the rest of the country watched an ad for other Procter products. Thus Clorox, the Commission pointed out, could gain the advantage of association with network TV, while limiting its advertising outlays to selected regional markets. Additional competitive advantages could be gained by including Clorox in P & G's sales promotion campaigns, cutting down greatly on Clorox's processing and mailing costs. And joint advertising in newspapers and magazines offered further possibilities for considerable cost savings.

The Commission went on to speculate that P & G's sales force might be able to induce retailers to give Clorox more and better shelf space, and that, as a multiproduct firm operating in a market of single-product firms, Procter might engage in systematic underpricing, subsidizing such action with profits from its other markets. And, the Commission continued,

> the conditions which retard competition in an industry are to an important degree psychological. They stem from competitors' appraisal of each other's intentions, rather than from the intentions—or the actions taken upon them—themselves. The appropriate standpoint for appraising the impact of this merger is, then, that of Clorox's rivals and of the firms which might contemplate entering the liquid bleach industry. To such firms, it is probably a matter of relative indifference, in setting business policy, how actively a Procter-owned Clorox pursues its opportunities for aggressive, market-dominating conduct. The firm confined by the high costs of shipping liquid bleach, and the high costs of national or regional advertising, within a geographically small area, cannot ignore the ability of a firm of Procter's size and experience to drive it out of business (not necessarily deliberately) by a sustained local campaign of advertising, sales promotions and other efforts. . . . A small or medium-

sized firm contemplating entry cannot ignore the fact that Procter is a
billion-dollar corporation whose marketing experience extends far beyond the limited horizons of the liquid bleach industry and whose aggregate operations are several times greater than those of all firms in the
industry combined. Even a large firm contemplating entry into such an
industry must find itself loath to challenging a brand as well-established
as Clorox bleach, when that brand is backed by the powerful marketing
capacities of a firm such as Procter. If we consider, in other words, not
what Procter will in fact do to exploit the power conferred on it by the
merger, or has done, but what it can and is reasonably likely to do in
the event of a challenge to its dominant market position in the liquid
bleach industry, we are constrained to conclude that the merger has increased the power of Clorox, by dominating its competitors and discouraging new entry, to foreclose effective competition in the industry.

Turning next to the substantiality of the merger's anticompetitive
effects, the Commission said that five factors taken together persuaded
it that Procter's purchase of Clorox violated Section 7.[10]

1. The relative disparity in size and strength as between Procter and
the largest firms of the bleach industry;

2. The excessive concentration in the industry at the time of the
merger, and Clorox's dominant position in the industry;

3. The elimination, brought about by the merger, of Procter as
a potential competitor of Clorox;

4. The position of Procter in other markets; and

5. The nature of the "economies" made possible by the merger.

Procter's financial resources and scale of operations, the decision
pointed out, overshadowed the entire liquid bleach industry, and the
cost advantages made possible by the merger would substantially affect
competitive conditions in the market. And the barriers to entry, "already formidable, become virtually insurmountable when the prospective entrant must reckon not with Clorox, but with Procter."

By the merger, P & G obtained a protected market position. Clorox's
substantial market power might enable Procter to strengthen its position in other industries. And since Clorox and Procter manufacture
closely related products, P & G might use Clorox bleach as a tying
product, loss leader, or cross-coupon offering to promote other Procter
products.

Still another important factor to consider about the merger was

[10] Here, the Commission noted: "We need not, and do not, consider whether one
or more of these factors, taken separately, would be dispositive of the case."

that it eliminated the "salutary" effect of Procter as a potential competitor of Clorox. In the past, the Commission reasoned, P & G had frequently extended its product lines by going into industries in which it had not been active before; it was one of the very few manufacturers of household cleaning products powerful enough to successfully challenge Clorox's position; and it had actually thought about the possibility of going into the liquid bleach business on its own. Therefore, Procter "must have figured as a tangible influence on Clorox's policies," and was, though in absentia, "by reason of its proximity, size, and probable line of growth, a substantial competitive factor" in the bleach industry. Before the acquisition, Procter "was not only a likely prospect for new entry into the bleach market, it was virtually the only such prospect." Thus, the merger by eliminating Procter as a potential entrant removed "one of the last factors tending to preserve a modicum of competitive pricing and business policies" in the bleach industry.[11]

Moving on to P & G's strong market position in other product areas, the Commission asserted that Procter's manifest strength rebutted any inference that it could not bring the enormous financial resources to bear on the liquid bleach industry. If P & G were spread thin over its other markets, it might be a different story; but such was not the case. Procter was a highly profitable company with demonstrated ability to mobilize and use its financial strength.

> Just as ownership of Clorox may enable Procter to enhance its competitive edge in other markets, so Procter's position in other markets may enhance its dominance, through its acquisition of Clorox, of the liquid bleach industry. . . .
> The short of it is that a conglomerate merger involving firms which have dominant power in their respective markets tends to reinforce and augment such power.

And, finally, in answer to Procter's arguments that the merger should be upheld on grounds of "efficiencies" (cost savings in advertising and sales promotions), the Commission found that in the instant case this

---

[11] Here, the decision noted: "We have no occasion to speculate on such questions as whether or not Procter, had its acquisition of Clorox been blocked, would in fact have entered the bleach industry on its own, or whether or not had it done so, the result would have been to increase competition in the industry—although, with reference to the second question, we note the Supreme Court's recent observation that 'one premise of an antimerger statute such as § 7 is that corporate grown by internal expansion is socially preferable to growth by acquisition.'"

type of "efficiency . . . hurts, not helps, a competitive economy and burdens, not benefits, the consuming public." For while "marketing economies, including those of advertising and sales promotion, are as desirable as economies in production and physical distribution," the point had been reached in the liquid bleach industry where advertising had lost its informative aspect and merely entrenched the market leader.

> The undue emphasis on advertising which characterizes the liquid bleach industry is itself a symptom of and a contributing cause to the sickness of competition in the industry. Price competition, beneficial to the consumer, has given way to brand competition in a form beneficial only to the seller. In such an industry, cost advantages that enable still more extensive advertising only impair price competition further; they do not benefit the consumer.

Though the Commission rejected the post-merger evidence, it noted that Clorox's market share in 1961 was 51.5 per cent, compared with its 48.8 per cent share in 1957. And it concluded:

> Had Procter in fact fully integrated the marketing and other activities of Clorox in its overall organization, perhaps dramatic post-acquisition changes, directly traceable to the merger, would have occurred. But, save for taking advantage of certain advertising cost advantages and introducing sales promotions, Procter in the period covered by the post-acquisition evidence has carefully refrained from changing the nature of the operation; even the network of independent brokers has been retained. Such restraint appears to be motivated by a general Procter policy of moving slowly and cautiously in a new field until the Procter management feels totally acclimated to it. It is possible, as well, that the pendency of the instant proceeding has had a deterrent effect upon expansionist activities by Procter in the liquid bleach industry.

BEFORE THE U.S. COURT OF APPEALS FOR THE SIXTH CIRCUIT [12]

Procter appealed the Commission's order and, in a unanimous decision, the Circuit Court upheld the acquisition and directed dismissal of the complaint.

> The Commission recognized that complete guidelines for this type of merger have not yet been developed and that the case presented a chal-

[12] *Proctor & Gamble Company v. F.T.C.*, 358 F. 2d 74 (1966).

> lenge to it and to the courts "to devise tests more precisely adjusted to the special dangers to a competitive economy posed by the conglomerate merger." We do not believe these tests should involve application of a per se rule.
>
> The Supreme Court has not ruled that bigness is unlawful, or that a large company may not merge with a smaller one in a different market field. Yet the size of Procter and its legitimate, successful operations in related fields pervades the entire opinion of the Commission, and seems to be the motivating factor which influenced the Commission to rule that the acquisition was illegal.

Findings of illegality, the appellate court observed, "may not be based upon 'treacherous conjecture,' possibility, or suspicion. And yet this is exactly what the second Commission indulged in. . . ."

Noting the Commission's opinion that the liquid bleach industry was highly concentrated, with virtually insurmountable barriers to entry on a national scale, the three-judge panel said that, while it probably would be difficult to break into the market on a national basis without expending a large sum of money, there was no evidence that anyone had ever tried to do so. And, the court continued, the fact that, in addition to the six leading bleach manufacturers, there were 200 smaller companies, both before and after the merger, "would not seem to indicate anything unhealthy about the market conditions."

The justices gave short shrift to the Commission's lengthy discourse on P & G's advertising might:

> Doubtless Procter could advertise more extensively than Clorox, but there is such a thing as saturating the market. We find it difficult to base a finding of illegality on discounts in advertising. . . . the fact that a merger may result in some economies is no reason to condemn it.

Nor did the appellate court find any merit to the Commission's claim that multiproduct Procter might be able to obtain more shelf space for Clorox. The evidence was clear, the Court wrote, that pre-merger Clorox obtained very adequate shelf space.

Turning to the Commission's finding that the merger eliminated P & G as a potential competitor,[13] the judges held that there was no evidence tending to prove that Procter ever intended to enter the bleach business on its own; in fact, its promotion department had

---

[13] The Court noted that this issue had not been raised until after all the evidence was in and the appeal taken to the second Commission.

recommended against such a move. Therefore, the Commission's find-ing, the Court held, was based on "mere possibility and conjecture."

> Household liquid bleach is an old product; Procter is an old company. If Procter were on the brink [of entering the market on its own], it is surprising that it never lost its balance and fell in during the many years in which such bleach was on the market. It had never threatened to enter the market.

The reviewing court did not engage in any discussion as to the type of merger involved, but simply stated: "The merger in the present case was neither vertical nor horizontal, but conglomerate. The second Commission has characterized it as product extension." Under Section 7, the Court continued,

> it is necessary to determine whether there is a reasonable probability that the merger may result in a substantial lessening of competition. Amended Section 7 was intended to arrest anticompetitive tendencies in their incipiency. A mere possibility is not enough. [Citations omitted.]

P & G, according to the Court, "merely stepped into the shoes of Clorox," and whether it could do better than Clorox remained to be seen.

> The Nielsen tables . . . for a period of five years prior to the merger and four years after, do not reveal any significant change in the rate of growth of Clorox.
> . . . subsequent to the merger, competitors of Clorox sold substantially more bleach for more money than prior thereto. This evidence certainly does not prove anti-competitive effects of the merger. The Commission gave it no consideration.

The Sixth Circuit held the Commission in error in ruling that post-merger evidence was admissible only in unusual cases. Since a Section 7 proceeding involves the "drastic remedy of divestiture," said the justices, "any relevant evidence must be considered." The extent of the inquiry into post-merger conditions and the weight to be attached to the evidence may well depend on the circumstances of the case, they wrote, but where, as here, the evidence has been obtained, it should not be ignored. As for the contention that P & G's post-merger behavior may have been influenced by the pending litigation, this again, said the Court, was "pure conjecture." If, in the future, Procter engaged in predatory practices, the Federal Trade Commission had ample powers to deal with it.

And, finally, the Court observed, Clorox wanted to sell its assets. A small company could not qualify; it "had to sell to a larger company or not sell at all."

BEFORE THE SUPREME COURT OF THE UNITED STATES [14]

The Federal Trade Commission appealed the Sixth Circuit's ruling, and, with Mr. Justice Douglas delivering the opinion (dated April 11, 1967), the Supreme Court in a 7 to 0 decision reversed the judgment of the Court of Appeals and remanded, with instructions to affirm and enforce the Commission's order.[15]

In essence, the Court said "Amen" to the Federal Trade Commission's exhaustive opinion. It adopted the Commission's product-extension merger characterization,[16] agreeing that it did not "aid analysis to talk of this merger in conventional terms, namely, horizontal or vertical or conglomerate"; and it repeated the Commission's statement that "all mergers are within the reach of § 7, and all must be tested by the same standard, whether they are classified as horizontal, vertical, conglomerate or other."

The majority opinion declared: "The anticompetitive effects with which this product-extension merger is fraught can easily be seen: (1) the substitution of the powerful acquiring firm for the smaller, but already dominant, firm may substantially reduce the competitive structure of the industry by raising entry barriers and by dissuading the smaller firms from aggressively competing; (2) the acquisition eliminates the potential competition of the acquiring firm." The premerger liquid bleach industry, Justice Douglas wrote, was already oligopolistic. Clorox held a dominant position nationally, and in certain localities its position approached monopoly proportions. Thus,

---

[14] 35 LW 4329.

[15] Mr. Justice Stewart and Mr. Justice Fortas did not participate in the decision. Mr. Justice Harlan wrote a concurring opinion.

[16] The opinion noted: "Since the products of the acquired company are complementary to those of the acquiring company and may be produced with similar facilities, marketed through the same channels and in the same manner, and advertised by the same media, the Commission aptly called this acquisition a 'product-extension merger.' "

with P & G replacing Clorox, it was probable that Procter would become the price leader, causing the oligopoly to become more rigid, and smaller firms would probably become more cautious in competing because of a fear of P & G.

Additionally, the merger "may have the tendency" to raise the entry barriers, for Procter's tremendous advertising budget would enable it to divert advertising monies to meet the short-term threat of a newcomer. And the substantial advertising discounts which Procter enjoyed might put off potential competitors. Regarding this latter point, the opinion flatly stated: "Possible economies cannot be used as a defense to illegality."

In reversing the judgment of the Court of Appeals, the Court upheld the Federal Trade Commission's finding that the merger eliminated P & G as a potential competitor.

> The evidence . . . clearly shows that Procter was the most likely entrant. . . . Procter was engaged in a vigorous program of diversifying into product lines closely related to its basic products. Liquid bleach was a natural avenue of diversification since it is complementary to Procter's products, is sold to the same customers through the same channels, and is advertised and merchandized in the same manner.

In its reliance upon post-merger evidence, Justice Douglas wrote, the Court of Appeals "misapprehended" the standards applicable in a Section 7 proceeding.

> Section . . . was intended to arrest the anticompetitive effects of market power in their incipiency. The core question is whether a merger may substantially lessen competition, and necessarily requires a prediction of the merger's impact on competition, present and future. The section can deal only with probabilities, not certainties. And there is certainly no requirement that the anticompetitive power manifest itself in anticompetitive action before § 7 can be called into play. [Citations omitted.]

CONCURRING OPINION OF MR. JUSTICE HARLAN

While agreeing that the Federal Trade Commission's order should be sustained, Justice Harlan took issue with the majority opinion because it made no effort to formulate standards for the application of Section 7 to mergers "which are neither horizontal nor vertical and which previously have not been considered in depth by this Court."

It is regrettable to see this Court as it enters this comparatively new field of economic adjudication starting off with what has almost become a kind of *res ipsa loquitur* approach to antitrust cases.

The majority opinion "leaves the Commission, lawyers, and businessmen at large as to what is to be expected of them in future cases of this kind." And while the Court declares that all mergers (no matter what they are called) must be tested by the same standard, it is equally important, Justice Harlan wrote, "to recognize that different sets of circumstances may call for fundamentally different tests of substantial anticompetitive effect."

The Justice agreed with the Commission's finding that the post-merger evidence was irrelevant and that in conglomerate or product-extension merger cases inquiry "should be directed toward reasonably probable changes in market structure," for "only by focusing on market structure can we begin to formulate standards which will allow the responsible agencies to give proper consideration to such mergers and allow businessmen to plan their actions with a fair degree of certainty."

Justice Harlan gave the following summary of four guides for determining the legality of conglomerate or product-extension mergers:

First, the decision can rest on analysis of market structure without resort to evidence of post-merger anticompetitive behavior.

Second, the operation of the pre-merger market must be understood as the foundation of successful analysis. The responsible agency may presume that the market operates in accord with generally accepted principles of economic theory, but the presumption must be open to challenge of alternative operational formulations.

Third, if it is reasonably probable that there will be a change in market structure which will allow the exercise of substantially greater market power, then a prima facie case has been made out under § 7.

Fourth, where the case against the merger rests on the probability of increased market power, the merging companies may attempt to prove that there are countervailing economies reasonably probable which should be weighed against the adverse effects.

And he found that the Commission's opinion conformed to this analysis.

While agreeing that the Commission was justified in giving no weight to P & G's efficiency defense (because discounts on large advertising outlays are not "true efficiencies"), Justice Harlan felt that the

Commission's view on advertising economies was "overstated and over-simplified."

> Undeniably advertising may sometimes be used to create irrational brand preferences and mislead consumers as to the actual differences between products, but it is very difficult to discover at what point advertising ceases to be an aspect of healthy competition. It is not the Commission's function to decide which lawful elements of the "product" offered the consumer should be considered useful and which should be considered the symptoms of industrial "sickness." It is the consumer who must make that selection through the exercise of his purchasing power.

ADDENDUM

In February of 1967, nearly two months before the Supreme Court handed down its ruling on the Clorox merger, the Federal Trade Commission split 3 to 2 in accepting a consent settlement,[17] by which Procter & Gamble (in exchange for being allowed to keep the Folger Coffee Company, which it had purchased in 1963[18]) promised not to buy any domestic grocery products companies in the next seven years without prior FTC approval and further promised not to engage in any additional coffee mergers for the next ten years. P & G also agreed that during the next ten years it would report all incipient mergers involving any kind of product in the domestic market to the Commission.

The consent settlement further provided that P & G would not accept any media discounts or rate reductions on coffee advertising during the next five years when such discounts or reductions are based on advertising of other Procter products, and that it would not conduct

[17] Under the Commission's rules, a party against whom the FTC had decided to issue a complaint is served with notice of the Commission's intention and receives a copy of the intended complaint and order. The party served may file a reply indicating willingness to have the proceeding disposed of by entry of an agreement containing a consent order. When such a reply is received, the party served, its counsel, and members of the Commission's Division of Consent Orders participate in the preparation and execution of an agreement containing a consent order. If the Commission subsequently determines that the proposed agreement should be accepted, it issues its complaint and simultaneously enters its decision and order.

[18] In a ten-year period, P & G had acquired five grocery product companies: W. T. Young Foods, Inc. (peanut butter and peanut products), 1955; prepared mix division of Nebraska Consolidated Mills (cake mixes), 1956; Charmin Paper Mills (paper tissues and related products), 1957; Clorox, 1957; and J. A. Folger & Co. (coffee), 1963.

any coffee promotion in conjunction with its other products during the same period.

The majority, which included Commissioner Philip Elman, who had written the Commission's ruling against the Clorox merger, did not give any explanation for its acceptance of the settlement. But Commissioner Mary Gardiner Jones, who dissented on the grounds that regulation was inadequate and the FTC should have sought divestiture, said: "Instead of seeking divestiture, the order seeks to regulate, in a quite direct manner and for a five-year period, certain aspects of P & G's conduct of joint promotions involving coffee and its other products and P & G's ability to exact reductions in media rates because of the magnitude of its several expenditures on advertising." [19]

The text of the FTC's complaint, which was released publicly with the announcement of the consent settlement, contended that the merger between P & G and Folger, the nation's second largest non-retailer of regular coffee and fourth in soluble coffee, might substantially lessen competition in the coffee business. Like Clorox, Folger was a single-product company, and, as in the Clorox situation, P & G was entering a new product field with its purchase of Folger.

The Commission had notified P & G in June of 1966 that it intended to challenge the Folger purchase and to seek divestiture, and its complaint stressed P & G's advertising and promotional strength and its ability to "achieve significant cost reductions" in: the buying of green coffee; the procuring of financing; the buying and placement of advertising; the conducting of consumer and sales promotions; the buying of containers and packaging materials; and the procuring of warehousing and transportation.[20]

APPENDIX A

Under the Administrative Procedure Act and the Federal Trade Commission's rules, the initial decision of a hearing examiner becomes the decision of the Commission 30 days after it has been served upon the parties to the proceeding unless prior thereto (i) an appeal is made to the Commission; (ii) the Commission by order stays the effective date of the decision; or (iii) the Commission issues an order placing the case on its own docket for review. In rendering its decision on appeal

[19] *Advertising Age,* February 27, 1967, p. 36.
[20] *Ibid.*

or review, the Commission may adopt, modify, or set aside the findings, conclusions, and order of the initial decision.

A final decision by the Commission results in a dismissal or a cease and desist order. If the Commission issues a dismissal, the proceedings are at an end, for counsel supporting the complaint may not petition the courts for review. If the Commission issues a cease and desist order, this order may be appealed to a United States Court of Appeals, which may affirm, enforce, modify, or set aside the order. The judgment and decree of a Court of Appeals are subject to review by the United States Supreme Court upon certiorari.

PART SEVEN
THE
HUMAN FACTOR
IN
ADMINISTRATION

30

THE CASE
OF THE
MISSING TIME

It was 7:30 Tuesday morning when Chet Craig, general manager of the Norris Company's Central Plant, swung his car out of the driveway of his suburban home and headed toward the plant in Midvale, six miles away. The trip to the plant took about twenty minutes and gave Chet an opportunity to think about plant problems without interruption.

The Norris Company operated three printing plants and did a nation-wide business in quality color work. It had about 350 employees, nearly half of whom were employed at the Central Plant. The company's headquarters offices were also located in the Central Plant building.

Chet had started with the Norris Company as an expeditor in its Eastern Plant 10 years ago, after his graduation from Ohio State. After three years he was promoted to production supervisor, and two years later he was made assistant to the manager of the Eastern Plant. A year and a half ago he had been transferred to the Central Plant as assistant to the plant manager, and one month later, when the manager retired, Chet was promoted to general plant manager. (See Exhibit 1.)

Chet was in good spirits this morning. Various thoughts occurred to him as he said to himself, "This is going to be the day to really get things done." He thought of the day's work—first one project, then another—trying to establish priorities. He decided that the open-end unit scheduling was probably the most important—certainly the most urgent. He recalled that on Friday the vice president had casually

exhibit 1
Organization Chart of the Norris Company

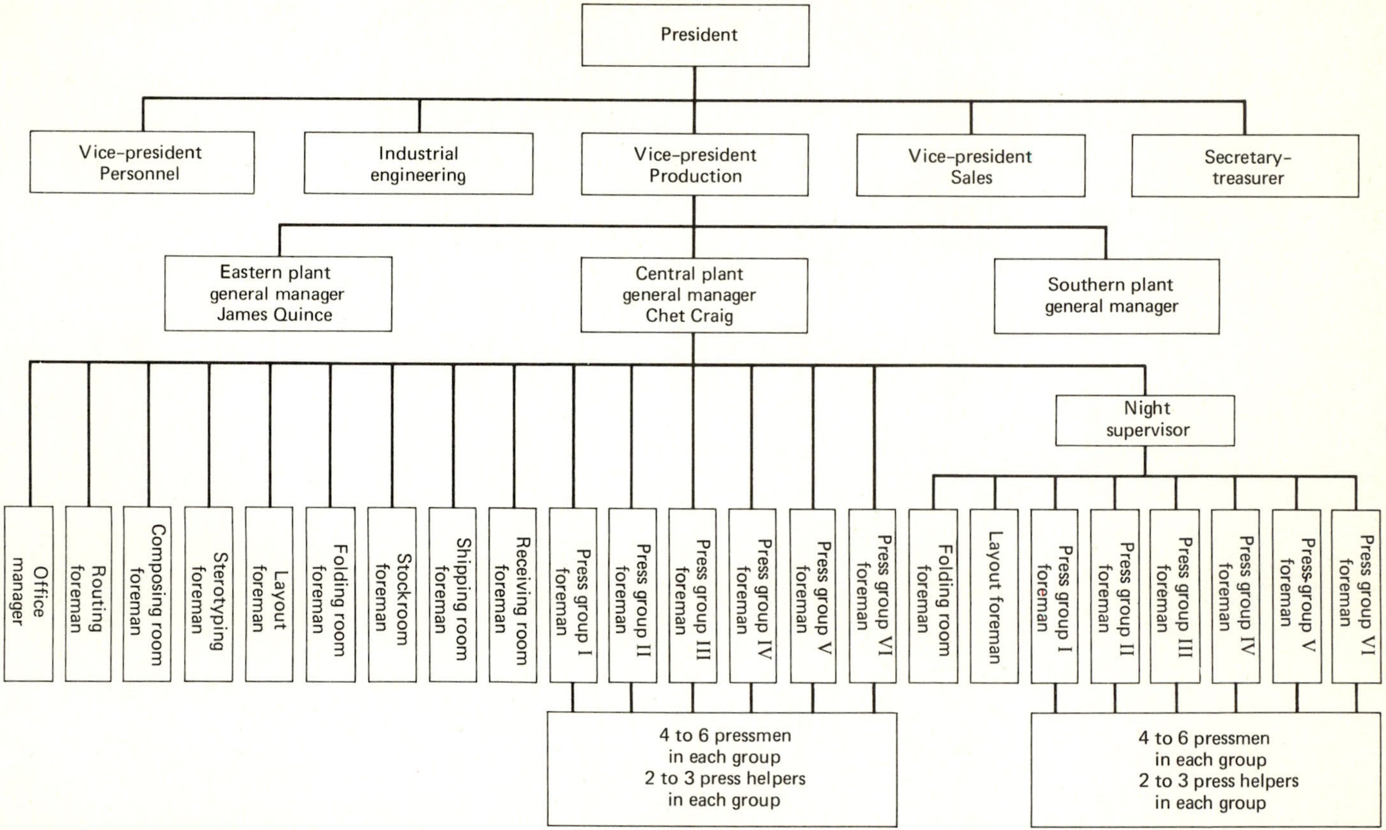

President

Vice-president Personnel

Industrial engineering

Vice-president Production

Vice-president Sales

Secretary–treasurer

Eastern plant general manager James Quince

Central plant general manager Chet Craig

Southern plant general manager

Night supervisor

Office manager

Routing foreman

Composing room foreman

Sterotyping foreman

Layout foreman

Folding room foreman

Stockroom foreman

Shipping room foreman

Receiving room foreman

Press group I foreman

Press group II foreman

Press group III foreman

Press group IV foreman

Press group V foreman

Press group VI foreman

4 to 6 pressmen in each group
2 to 3 press helpers in each group

Folding room foreman

Layout foreman

Press group I foreman

Press group II foreman

Press group III foreman

Press group IV foreman

Press group V foreman

Press group VI foreman

4 to 6 pressmen in each group
2 to 3 press helpers in each group

asked him if he had given the project any further thought. Chet realized that he had not been giving it any attention lately. He had been meaning to get to work on his idea for over three months, but something else always seemed to crop up.

"I haven't had time to really work it out," he said to himself. "I'd better get going and finish it off one of these days." He then began to break down the objectives, procedures, and installation steps in the project. It gave him a feeling of satisfaction as he calculated the anticipated cost savings. "It's high time," he told himself. "This idea should have been completed a long time ago."

Chet had first conceived the open-end unit scheduling idea almost two years ago just prior to leaving the Eastern Plant. He had talked it over with the general manager of the Eastern Plant, and both agreed that it was a good idea and worth developing. The idea was temporarily shelved when Chet had been transferred to the Central Plant a month later.

His thoughts returned to other plant projects he was determined to get under way. He started to think through a procedure for the simpler transport of dies to and from the Eastern Plant. He thought of the notes on his desk: the inventory analysis he needed to identify and eliminate some of the slow-moving stock items; the packing controls which needed revision; and the need to design a new special order form. He also decided that this was the day to settle on a job printer to do the outside printing of simple office forms. There were a few other projects he could not recall offhand, but he felt sure that he could tend to them sometime during the day. Again he said to himself: "This is the day to really get rolling."

When he entered the plant, Chet was met by Al Noren, the stockroom foreman, who appeared troubled. "A great morning, Al," said Chet, cheerfully.

"Well, I don't know, Chet; my new man isn't in this morning," said Noren morosely.

"Have you heard from him?" asked Chet.

"No, I haven't."

"These stock handlers take it for granted that if they're not here, they don't have to call in and report. Better ask Personnel to call him."

Al hesitated a moment. "Okay, Chet," he said, "but can you find me a man? I have two cars to unload today."

Making a note of the incident, Chet headed for his office. He greeted some workers discussing the day's work with Marilyn, the office manager. As the meeting broke up, Marilyn took some samples from a clasper and showed them to Chet, asking if they should be shipped that way or if it would be necessary to inspect them. Before he could answer, Marilyn went on to ask if he could suggest another clerical operator for the sealing machine to replace the regular operator, who was home ill. She also told him that Gene, the industrial engineer, had called and was waiting to hear from him.

Chet told Marilyn to ship the samples, and he made a note of the need for a sealer operator and then called Gene. He agreed to stop by Gene's office before lunch, and started on his routine morning tour of the plant. He asked each foreman the volumes and types of orders he was running, the number of people present, how the schedules were coming along, and the orders to be run next; he helped the folding-room foreman find temporary storage space for consolidating a carload shipment; discussed quality control with a pressman who had been running poor work; arranged to transfer four people temporarily to different departments, including two for Al in the stock room; and talked to the shipping foreman about pickups and special orders to be delivered that day. As he continued through the plant, he saw to it that reserve stock was moved out of the forward stock area; talked to another pressman about his requested change of vacation schedule; had a "heart-to-heart" talk with a press helper who seemed to need frequent assurance; and approved two type and one color okays for different pressmen.

Returning to his office, Chet reviewed the production reports on the larger orders against his initial projections and found that the plant was running slightly behind schedule. He called in the folding-room foreman, and together they went over the lineup of machines and made several changes.

During this discussion the composing-room foreman stepped in to cover several type changes and the routing foreman telephoned for approval of a revised printing schedule. The stockroom foreman called twice—first to inform him that two standard, fast-moving stock items were dangerously low, and later to advise him that the paper stock for the urgent Dillon job had finally arrived. Chet telephoned this information to the people concerned.

He then began to put delivery dates on important inquiries received from customers and salesmen. (The routine inquiries were handled by

Marilyn.) While he was doing this he was interrupted twice, once by a sales correspondent calling from the West Coast to ask for a better delivery date than originally scheduled, and once by the vice president of personnel, asking Chet to set a time when he could hold an initial induction interview with a new employee.

After dating the customer and salesman inquiries, Chet headed for his morning conference in the executive office. At this meeting he answered the vice president for sales' questions in connection with "hot" orders, complaints, the status of large-volume orders, and potential new orders. Then he met with the vice president and general production manager to answer "the old man's" questions on several production and personnel problems. Before leaving the executive offices, he stopped at the office of the purchasing agent to inquire about the delivery of some cartons, paper, and boxes and to place an order for some new paper.

On the way back to his own office Chet conferred with Gene about two current engineering projects. When he reached his desk, he lit a cigarette and looked at his watch. It was ten minutes before lunch— just time enough to make a few notes of the details he needed to check in order to answer knotty questions raised by the vice president for sales that morning.

After lunch Chet started again. He began by checking the previous day's production reports, did some rescheduling to get out urgent orders, placed delivery dates on new orders and inquiries received that morning, and consulted with a foreman about a personal problem. He spent about twenty minutes at the TWX [1] going over mutual problems with the Eastern plant.

By midafternoon Chet had made another tour of the plant, after which he met with the vice president of personnel to review with him a touchy personal problem raised by one of the clerical employees, the vacation schedules submitted by his foremen, and the pending job evaluation program. Following this conference, Chet hurried back to his office to complete the special statistical report for Universal Waxing Corporation, one of Norris's biggest customers. When he finished the report he discovered that it was ten after six and he was the only one left in the office. Chet was tired. He put on his coat and headed for the parking lot. On the way out he was stopped by the night super-

---

[1] Leased private telegram communication system using a teletypewriter.

visor and the night layout foreman for approval of type and layout changes.

As he drove home Chet reviewed the day he had just completed. "Busy?" he asked himself. "Too much so—but did I accomplish anything?" The answer seemed to be "Yes, and no." There was the usual routine, the same as any other day. The plant kept going and it was a good production day. "Any creative or special project work done?" Chet winced. "I guess not."

With a feeling of guilt Chet asked himself: "Am I an executive? I'm paid like one, and I have a responsible assignment and the authority to carry it out. My superiors at headquarters think I'm a good manager. Yet one of the greatest returns a company gets from an executive is his innovative thinking and accomplishments. What have I done about that? Today was just like other days, and I didn't do any creative work. The projects that I was so eager to work on this morning are no further ahead than they were yesterday. What's more, I can't say that tomorrow night or the next night they'll be any closer to completion. This is a real problem, and there must be some answer to it.

"Night work? Yes, sometimes. This is understood. But I've been doing too much night work lately. My wife and family deserve some of my time. After all, they are the people for whom I'm really working. If I spend much more time away from them, I'm not meeting my own personal objectives. I spend a lot of time on church work. Should I eliminate that? I feel I owe that as an obligation. Besides, I feel I'm making a worthwhile contribution in this work. Maybe I can squeeze a little time from my fraternal activities. But where does recreation fit in?"

Chet groped for the solution. "Maybe I'm just rationalizing because I schedule my own work poorly. But I don't think so. I've studied my work habits, and I think I plan intelligently and delegate authority. Do I need an assistant? Possibly, but that's a long-time project and I don't believe I could justify the additional overhead expense. Anyway, I doubt whether it would solve the problem."

By this time Chet had turned off the highway into the side street leading to him home. "I guess I really don't know the answer," he said to himself as he pulled into his driveway. "This morning everything seemed so simple, but now—"

31
SURENESS COMPANY

The Sureness Company produced and distributed nationally a complete line of large and small appliances, such as dishwashers, laundry units, dryers, refrigerators, home freezers, electric stoves, air conditioners, irons, toasters, blenders, beaters, and squeezers. Sureness was one of the largest in the industry and its sales had doubled in the past decade. The company employed a prominent consulting firm to study the productivity and efficiency of their executives and the results of a number of significant organization changes made to keep pace with expansion.

As part of its study approach, the consulting firm assigned one of its senior account executives, Phillip Harms, to interview all company executives to determine their views on how their productivity could be improved. Prior to interviewing each executive the consultant studied the man's personnel record, the general nature of his work, his position in the organizational structure, and the number and type of persons reporting to him. Following is an interview with the sales manager.

STALEY: I'm glad that top management has decided to study the productivity of its executives. This company can certainly use some help on this subject. We're all working too many hours—and I, for one, don't see any relief in sight. In my own case I know I work a lot longer than forty hours each week and so does my boss, the vice-president of marketing.

HARMS: How much time would you guess you put in each week? Could you break this down by type of work activity?

STALEY: Both of your questions are tough to answer, since some weeks I spend a majority of my time in the field. There's one stretch around the first of the year when I'm in the field for better than a solid month. That's the time when we introduce our new models.

HARMS: Well, I can see why your problem is a little different from some of the other executives I've talked to—but why not tell me what you did last week. You were here all last week, weren't you?

STALEY: Yes, I was here last week, but I'm not sure that it was a typical week. Well, O.K., let's try it on for size and see what happens. You'll want to make some notes, won't you? Should I have my secretary record our discussion?

HARMS: No, I'll just do a little scribbling from time to time. Go ahead.

STALEY: I usually get to the office about 8:00, which is a half hour before the bell rings. By the time my secretary gets in, I have her work pretty well lined up for the day. From about 8:30 or 8:45 to nearly 10 I'm dictating and handling papers. I feel that paper work is important in a big company like this and if I don't keep on top of it I'm really in trouble. Of course, I do a lot of my work over the telephone—especially with my district sales managers.

After 10 o'clock I don't have any prescribed routine. It all depends on where the fire is and what's going on in the vice-president's office. I'd guess I average an hour a day with him. He wants to know everything that goes on in this department so I find that I spend a lot of time briefing him on our activities. When I was new on this job I was glad that he was there with a net to bail me out, but I've had this job for almost two years and he still seems to worry about everything I do. Say, I assume that whatever I tell you is confidential. I have a note here from the president which says that I'm not to hold anything back.

HARMS: That's right. Nothing you tell me will ever be revealed. That's why I didn't want your secretary to take any minutes of this meeting.

STALEY: Well, don't misunderstand me—I've got a swell boss—but the company would be a lot better off if he spent more of his time working on over-all company problems instead of worrying about my operations. He does the same thing with the advertising manager and the sales engineering manager. I can't speak for them, but in my case it's like he was still running the department and I was the assistant manager.

HARMS: What kinds of matters do you discuss with him?

STALEY: Everything. About once a day he asks me to come up for a meeting. He then asks how things are going, and the first thing you know he's got me telling him about all my problems. Also, he remembers them and asks me later what I did about them. Of course, sometimes he tells me what to do—and how to do it. He's got a sharp memory and wants me to report back on the action I took. But heck, I'm a big boy now and can make most of my own decisions. Also, he gets a copy of all my sales analysis reports.

HARMS: What kinds of reports are these?

STALEY: These are reports which come out weekly from our sales analysis unit showing sales by product item, by distributor, by sales district, and so on. They show sales for the week, sales cumulated for the year, sales for the same period last year, and the quota. Boy, when I'm off quota he's really on my back. I suppose in some cases he's got a right to be. I'll say one thing, though; he's a guy you can talk to. He'll listen to me, and for the most part he'll let me do what I want. Of course, we've been working together for over ten years now.

One problem with trying to keep him fully informed is that I have to be on top of everything. This means that I do many of the things that probably should be left to some of my staff. I think one of the problems that this company has is delegation. My boss should delegate more, and if he would, then I could do more delegating.

HARMS: Could you be a little more specific about this matter of delegation?

STALEY: Well, delegation is an abstract subject, but take the matter of signatures. When I was assistant sales manager no one could sign a letter except the boss. When I took over, I studied the situation and found that four members of my staff wrote 80 per cent of the letters in this office. Therefore I told these people that they could sign for me, but that before the letters were mailed I would check them. I was told by the V.P. that it wouldn't work, but it's worked fine so far.

HARMS: If you check all the letters, then how does this save you any time?

STALEY: I don't really read them—I just glance at them. From this I can tell what's important—and these I read more carefully. It only takes me about 15 or 20 minutes a day to check these letters, but before I delegated responsibility it took me almost an hour. Also, I've noticed that I find fewer errors. People know they've got the responsibility, whereas before they could rely—or thought they could—on me to catch their mistakes. Now they have the responsibility.

HARMS: Do you have any other thoughts on delegation?

STALEY: Well, we have a tough situation here which prevents me from doing all the delegation I'd like. My assistant is an old-timer—been with the company for over 20 years. He's a nice guy and a real salesman. Trouble is he can't administer. He used to be a district manager, but his health went bad and the doctor said he'd have to get an office job with regular hours and no traveling. He knows all the salesmen and many of our big accounts. If I want any information about the history of a salesman or a big account, I just ask him and the chances are he'll give me a quick and accurate fill in.

But he's no administrator. I find that I have to do part of his job. He's terrible about answering correspondence or even routing things. About twice a week I sit down with him at his desk and go over the stuff in his "in" basket. He doesn't seem to mind. I don't know what he'd do if he had a really tough boss.

HARMS: Do you have any other people on your staff to whom you feel you can't delegate?

STALEY: Yes, I do. I have a research director who at times drives me nuts. He's a smart technologist who knows his statistics—but he can't see the forest for the trees. Research isn't any good unless it's problem-oriented.

It's got to help serve a marketing problem. Well, I have to practically tell this research specialist what the study objectives should be. What's more, I have to suggest the kinds of information he should get in order to solve the problem. But after that he's a good man. He does have difficulty writing a final report. Several times I've had to take his reports home and rewrite them so that my boss will be able to understand them.

HARMS: Can you tell me more about how you spend your day?

STALEY: Let's see—we were up to about 10 in the morning just after I'd finished dictating to my secretary. Well, as I said, I don't have a regular schedule after that. I spend about an hour a day with my boss and probably average about another hour a day working with our advertising manager and the head of our sales engineering department. Then there are always several long-distance phone calls from the field from salesmen or customers. Some of these I can turn over to my assistant, but usually I figure if it's important enough to warrant a long-distance call that it's important enough for me to answer. I always have some personal visitors —salesmen, product men, and so on. I like to talk with them if only for a few minutes since it gives me a feeling of knowing what's going on in the market. There are also plenty of committee meetings—production coordination, styling, incentives, and so on. The higher one gets in an organization, the more committees he's on. But I don't mind too much—I learn a lot. By the time 5 o'clock comes my "in" basket is filled up again and so I load a lot of things in my brief case and head for home. I do all my magazine reading at home—they'd think I was loafing if they caught me reading on the job. I know I'd feel that way if I found any of my men doing it. I never get a chance to do any really good reading. At times I worry about this, because if I ever get promoted I probably ought to know about such things as the tariff, the national debt, the important trends in business, and so on. I even come down here on Saturdays and work trying to get caught up. When we're planning our activities for the next year I find I'm head over heels in work—days, nights and week-ends. My wife hardly knows me and soon I'll need an introduction to my kids. Speaking of the time, I'm afraid I'll have to beg off for today. I've got to make a meeting date. I'm late now.

HARMS: You've been very cooperative. Would you object to my talking to any of your staff?

STALEY: No, just as long as you arrange a time which is convenient for them.

After Staley had left, Harms paid a visit to the company's research director, Don Hartwig. He explained who he was and what he wanted and asked when he could get together with Hartwig. The latter replied that now was as good a time as any.

HARMS: Delegation is always a big problem in a company as large as this. Still there are always ways in which it can be improved. Do you have any suggestions as to what can be done about it within this office? You probably got a note from the president saying I'd be around. Everything will be kept absolutely confidential.

HARTWIG: Gee, this is something I haven't thought about for quite some time. All in all, I think things run pretty smoothly around here. I have some problems with my boss, Mr. Staley, but they're not too serious. His biggest trouble is that he works too hard and expects everybody who works for him to do the same. Generally speaking he's a real good guy, but he insists at times on spelling things out too much. Sometimes he spells things out so much that I'm boxed in. Also, he tries to tell me how to make surveys. He's way out of touch with the latest research techniques. He hasn't been in research for ten years and a lot has happened since then. But I guess it's natural for a guy to be interested in a field he used to be pretty good in.

I have a relatively small section here—only about a half dozen people. We farm out any big stuff, and our advertising agency helps a lot. They have a research man full-time on this account. I don't really have many delegation problems. I'll tell you a guy you really ought to talk with who has this problem. He's Matt Keerney, Staley's assistant. He's a wonderful guy and in his day was probably the best salesman in the company. His health got bad and they gave him a desk job. He really knows his stuff and advises Staley on just about everything. In fact, I'm not sure he doesn't make most of his decisions. Staley treats him O.K., except he's always after him for not following company procedures. Matt isn't a paper hound, but he can get more done with a phone call than any of the rest of us could with a dozen letters. You ought to talk with him. Trouble is he's on vacation right now and won't be back for a couple of weeks.

HARMS: It's just about lunch time and I've a luncheon date with somebody from the advertising department. Can I come back sometime and talk again?

HARTWIG: You sure can. Any time.

Sometime later Harms talked at length with the vice-president of marketing, Fred Kroll. Part of the interview dealt with the problem of delegation. On this subject Kroll said:

In my job I don't have much of a problem of delegation. I have only about five people who report to me. Take my sales manager, for example. He's one of my boys. We've been together for a long time, but despite all this there are times, I'm sure, when he feels that I won't get off his back. But this is a "dog eat dog" business. You have to keep the pressure on day and night. I'm responsible for the total marketing operation which runs well over one hundred million dollars a year. If I'm not on top of the latest price cut, the latest merchandising gimmick, the latest "deal," I don't feel that I'm doing my job. You have to push your men—drive them, because if you don't you'll wake up some morning and find that some competitor has stolen part of your market. I'm considered by some people to be old-fashioned—I won't delegate my life away—but I get results and that's what counts.

Harms then asked what he thought about the delegation in the sales department. Kroll replied:

I don't pay much attention to whether Staley delegates or not. I figure that's his business. I don't tell him how to run his people. I never hear any complaints so I guess he's probably doing O.K. Staley has one problem though—he brings me too damn many problems. For example, yesterday he wanted my advice on what to do with a San Francisco department store which had refused delivery of their last order. How should I know what he should do. I know what I'd do because Bob Scope, the buyer in the Frisco store, is an old friend of mine. Another thing about Staley is that he's not out in the field enough. You don't sell appliances by sitting in the home office. He ought to be out there on the firing line. But Staley's a good man—we all have some faults. He's one of the best in the business. Sometimes I wish he knew just how good he really is.

32

BARRETT
TRUMBLE

Professor Floyd Hall of Bristol University was visiting his old friend Barrett Trumble, president of Green & Richards, the leading quality department store in Gulf City, one of the fastest-growing metropolitan centers of the South. Hall read at breakfast of Trumble's election as president of the Community Fund.

Trumble said, "You might wonder, Floyd, why I would accept this job. I've already done my stint as general campaign manager for the Fund. I guess most people consider this kind of work an important community responsibility but, at the same time, enough of a headache to expect others to take over after you've done your share. I feel differently about it. Unless business leaders continue to spearhead the private sponsorship of needed community agencies, their functions, which must be performed by someone, will more and more be taken over by the Federal, state, and municipal governments."

Trumble went on to say, "I played hard to get for quite a while. I told the boys I wouldn't take the job till we had firmed up our plans to raise funds for the next three years, including agreement on and acceptance by three executives who will take over successively as general campaign managers. Also, I insisted on the Fund setting up an advisory council of business executives, consisting of company presidents. I find that if we are going to get anything done around Gulf City, the way to do it is through the top brass. Now we have twenty business leaders on this council and I am sure there is nothing we want to have done that we can't swing through this group. Then again, I think it's good for G & R for me to be out front in this type of job. As you can see from the morning's paper, we get pretty good publicity. In addition, I intend to have all meetings of the council and some meetings of the more important committees in our executive dining room in the store. And I am sure it won't turn out to be too much work. A job like this is just a job of getting it organized."

TRUMBLE'S OUTSIDE ACTIVITIES

Professor Hall suggested, "It sounds as though you have it well organized. However, don't you think you will still be harassed by personal appeals and requests from all the other agencies in Gulf City and from others who are interested in community welfare?"

Trumble replied, "Frankly, Floyd, I wouldn't tell this to anyone else, but I must confess that if I didn't have these outside interests, I'd just be twiddling my thumbs down at the store."

Hall was surprised. He knew that Trumble served on the boards of five other businesses: the First Federal Savings and Loan Association, the Commercial National Bank, the Equitable Casualty Insurance Company, Intercontinental Textile Products Corporation, and National Laboratories. He was also a trustee of the Franklin Museum of Modern Art, the Gulf City Symphony Orchestra, Hambletonian College, and the National Retail Merchants Association. Barrett was also a member of the business advisory committee to the Department of Commerce and the treasurer of the Gulf States' Republican Committee.

Barrett explained, "But these other activities don't really take much of my time. Most of these boards have no more than one meeting per month, and they are not very active during the summer months. Of course, when I am on any board committees, it takes a little more time. Then, down at the store, we have things so well organized that the operation pretty well runs itself. Ever since I brought in Tom Jenkins as executive vice-president, I only find it necessary to get into things at the overall policy level."

TRUMBLE AND HIS VICE-PRESIDENTS

Hall recalled that when Jenkins joined Green & Richards, the vice-presidents in charge of customer relations and store operations had resigned to go with other merchandising firms. Trumble pointed out, "Of course, their resignations made it possible for us to promote two out-standing junior executives who were coming along so fast that we couldn't have kept them in the business if we hadn't been able to move them up the ladder. We now have eight vice-presidents reporting to Jenkins; one each for ready-to-wear merchandising, home-furnishings merchandising, store operations, personnel relations, cutomer relations, control, advertising, and research. Tom and his eight vice-presidents constitute an executive council which meets twice a week. I sit in on all the meetings and have an opportunity to keep in touch with major policy questions. Once in a while I find it necessary to step in where there is a strong difference of opinion, but I can usually rely on Tom to straighten things out without my intervention."

Hall asked, "Don't you find it necessary, as president, to meet with the heads of other businesses in town on questions which involve all the stores in town? For example, don't you have common problems like retaining the importance of the central business district as a shop-ping center or instituting charges for customer services which you can no longer render free of charge?"

"Yes, you have a point there. I could spend a lot of my time doing this, but the other boys are really better qualified than I am to make a contribution to joint meetings with other stores. For example, take the question of charging for deliveries, which is a hot subject right now. I think it is something all the stores must consider seriously. But why should I spend the time sitting in on the series of harangues among the other merchants in town when Jack Ogleby (vice-president for store operations) is really up to date on this question and can quote chapter and verse when they get down to brass tacks in their discussions? Any-way, before anybody does anything about this, the question will come before our executive council, and I will get in on it at that point."

HOW TRUMBLE SPENDS HIS TIME

Hall wondered how Trumble used the rest if his time in directing the operations of Green & Richards. "Well, I guess I spend a good 10 per cent of my time with the board of directors—in regular meetings of the board, in preparing for these meetings, and in individual confer-ences with some of the more interested members of the board. For exam-ple, Frederic Pellham (senior partner of the leading law firm in Gulf City) is on my neck now, pressing us to come up with a ten-year plan for our business. He thinks we should be looking to the future growth and development of G & R rather than concentrating on today's profits alone. However, the board as a whole now has enough confidence in me so that the others don't needle me the way Fred does.

"Also, the Green family is concerned with maintaining a good steady return on their investment. They aren't interested in spending the kind of money we would need over the next few years if we were going all out to become the largest department store in the South, which is what Fred would like to see.

"Then, I meet with the executive council twice a week. I have a regular meeting every Monday morning with Tom Jenkins. I am always available to talk with the other vice-presidents about any of their problems. They know that I won't make any decision on the matters they bring to me, but I am always glad to toss ideas around with them for whatever help that may be. But I guess I would have to say that most of my time in the store is spent just going through the business as much as I can. I spend between three and four hours a day walking through the store, particularly in the sales departments, just seeing how things are going, chatting with the people as I go, doing everything I can to help give people a lift. It helps keep me in touch with the way things are moving out on the selling floor, and I am sure that the people down the line feel better to see me around, because they know that I am not trying to run things from an ivory tower."

OPERATING RESULTS OF G & R

"How has the store been doing the last couple of years, Barrett?"

"I certainly can't complain, Floyd. I would say our sales and profits are excellent. Every quarter, for the last three years, we have done better than our budgeted dollar sales, gross profit, and net profit. By the way, I have always found it useful to present to the board of directors a highly conservative sales and profit plan so there won't be any unpleasant surprises when the final reports are in. Our reports are better than the Federal Reserve reports for Gulf City as a whole and better than the National Retail Merchants Association averages. Looking ahead, with defense spending the way it is, creeping inflation, population trends in general, and the growth curve for Gulf City, I don't see how we can miss. Sometimes I wonder if we might show even better results if I put a little more pressure on the boys or if I spent a little more time myself in some of our major problem areas. But here we are, the major downtown store, with three suburban stores (two of which we did not have six years ago) and with our sales increasing every year somewhere between 4 and 6 per cent. Our operating profits before income taxes have averaged 7.6 per cent of sales for the last five years."[1]

DELEGATION AND MANAGEMENT DEVELOPMENT

"And now I have built a team. As I see my job, it is to help select and develop competent people for our key jobs and then let them go ahead and do the things they are qualified to do and for which they are being well paid. It seems to me you either delegate responsibility and authority or you don't. The trouble with most store heads with whom I am familiar is that they talk a lot about delegation but they spend a lot of their own personal time going around and asking the department heads why they bought this, what they think of that, why don't they do so and so. One of our mutual friends, who runs a store up North, tells me that he thinks his job is one of constantly impressing department heads with the fact that he is thoroughly familiar with the way things are going in each department. He watches each department's figures like a hawk and calls people on the phone or on the carpet to discuss what they have in mind to correct things in the future. I don't see why we spend a lot of time developing people and pay them the money that we do if we don't rely on them to take the kind of action that is good for business and therefore for themselves."

Floyd asked Barrett if he was satisfied with his executive staff. "I would think you would have problems from time to time, humans being what they are."

Trumble replied, "Sure, like any other big happy family, we have our troubles from time to time. For example, Malcolm Donaldson (vice-president for personnel) gets himself steamed up on a special training course for executives and makes the mistake of bringing it up cold at the executive council meeting. The boys kick it around but finally decide that department heads have too many pressing problems confronting them; that it would be unwise to take them away from their operations for extended training sessions. Mal's idea gets voted down. Then, later in

[1] The National Industrial Conference Board had reported that the previous year's operating profits of large department stores averaged 5.6 per cent of sales.

the day, he comes to me to see if he can get my backing for the idea, knowing that I am all for more and more executive training.

"What Mal ought to do is talk with some of the other vice-presidents ahead of time and get them interested in the idea and at least briefed to the point where they understand thoroughly what Mal has in mind. Most things get settled in our business outside of council meetings; the interested executives are covered individually or in small groups ahead of time, so that when the issue comes to a vote at the council meeting, it is pretty much a matter of rubber-stamping the proposal.

"Mal really needs a lot of help, anyway. We have just employed a personnel consulting firm, with an annual retainer of $20,000. They keep us in touch with what is going on in other businesses, union trends, etc.; they work with Mal on employee training courses and do a lot of other things for us. For example, I learned the other day that one of their communications specialists is helping Mal write employee bulletins before they come to me for my signature."

BOARD RELATIONS

"You were saying, Barrett, that you don't have much trouble with the board of directors."

"No, except for Fred Pellham, who is a little troublesome from time to time. He has made it a point to dig into our business more deeply than the other directors. He gets his own industry figures direct from the Fed, National Retail Merchants, and Harvard Business School, so that he can compare our operations with what others are doing. As I told you, he is trying to get us to think further ahead and anticipate the changes that are likely to happen ten years from now, so that we will be able to make the necessary moves today in terms of what is going to happen then, instead of struggling year by year to keep abreast as things shift. Of course, most merchants realize that department store business is, at best, a ninety-day business; we have to be quick on our feet to meet day-to-day changes. No one has a good enough crystal ball to be able to forecast several years ahead.

"The other directors now accept almost anything I propose as a sound idea. Over the last five or six years, I have been careful to make sure that the things that I brought before the board were thoroughly explored and based on conservative projections. As a result, I no longer find it necessary to justify most of the things I want to do. Sometimes I wonder if they are a little too easy on me. However, I don't know; it is certainly a lot more comfortable this way. I can't say that I would like to repeat the struggles that I had in selling the board this idea or that idea during the first year or two I was in this job. I guess no president wants a board of directors that is as active in the business as their own stockholders expect them to be. From my own experience in serving as a director on these other boards, I find it pretty easy to put the management on the spot by raising questions which are not self-evident from the figures presented to the board. Before every board meeting in these other concerns, I spend a lot of time going over the material they send us ahead of time, because I think I have the responsibility, both legal and moral, as a director to serve as His Majesty's loyal opposition, so to speak."

OTHER ACTIVITIES

"By and large, it looks to me as though things are in pretty good shape at Green & Richards, but every once in a while I wonder where I am going. Here I am, close to fifty, doing well financially—my directorships alone give me a pretty good income. Of course, income is not important in my tax bracket, and I definitely feel that my serving on these outside boards is a good thing for the store. Too many of my retailer friends aren't in touch with the methods and viewpoints of other businessmen. I think I have the advantage over them as a result of these contacts outside our own trade.

"Apart from these business and community activities, I seem to have plenty of time for golf; I get in three rounds a week on the average, except when Jane and I are away on vacation. I guess I told you that we are leaving the middle of next month for a cruise around the world. In a way, this will combine business and vacation. It will give me an opportunity to touch base with some of our important resources from whom we import in the Far East and Europe. Our merchants are over there regularly, but I think it means something from time to time to have the head of the business pay them a visit. I get a real kick out of meeting their families, going through their operations, and talking about the problems they are up against. It seems to me that they get something out of it, too. In one sense, it does the same thing I try to do when I walk around the store each day—and maintaining good relations with our key resources, both domestic and foreign, is almost as important as good employee relations, I think. I also try to spend as much time as I can in our domestic markets—especially in New York and on the West Coast."

Since Trumble was thoroughly wound up, Hall continued to listen without comment.

SATISFACTION THROUGH CONTRIBUTION

"I get a good deal of satisfaction out of things I am doing. I thoroughly enjoy my regular job. I feel that Green & Richards is making an important contribution to our growing community.

"I am convinced we help raise the cultural standards of Gulf City through our emphasis on quality merchandise and good taste; through constantly making available to our customers exciting new items, many of them exclusive with us; through concerts, Christmas and Easter festivities, art shows, and many other events throughout the year. I think our reputation for courteous service (and there is nothing more important), for making good on all commitments, for integrity and fairness in all dealings with customers, resources, and employees, sets an example for others in the community. And I believe that my chief contribution to Green & Richards is to help other people understand, believe in, and apply these principles to their day-to-day problems. My job is to help our executives grow and develop to the full limit of their capacities, to the point where they can operate on their own, within our guiding policies and principles. To the extent I am successful in doing this, I not only improve the sales and profits of the store but also feel, in some degree, the kind of satisfaction you derive from your teaching—the satisfaction which one gets from helping others.

"I would hate to give up any of my outside business interests or directorships. As for the Community Fund, the Museum, and the other community service activities, I consider them too important to give up—they make it possible for me, in a small way, to repay the community for my own good fortune. You said you wanted to talk with me, Floyd, about the kind of problems I find most troublesome. I guess my problem is that I don't have any real problems at the present time. Of course, if we had a real recession, I would have my hands full down at the store without any of these outside interests. However, from the looks of things, there isn't going to be too much for me to sink my teeth into in the near future."

EARLIER PROBLEMS AS GENERAL MERCHANDISE MANAGER

"Sometimes I find it hard to look back to nine years ago with G & R. I'm sure you remember how Jane used to complain about the way I worked around the clock and never had any time for her or the youngsters. At that time, we were in really bad shape. During the preceding five years, the store had slipped from position to a shaky fourth in relation to the other stores in Gulf City. Someone had to get in and work closely with the buyers, one after another. I practically lived with each merchant, helping him get his department back on its feet. In some cases, we found it necessary to replace them with seasoned buyers from other stores. I hated to bring in so many executives from the outside, but we simply didn't have enough good people coming along at the lower levels to do much promoting from within.

"And the store had developed such a poor reputation in some markets that I was forced to work personally with many leading apparel, accessories, and home-furnishings resources before we were in a position to carry their lines again. With conditions as they were and with our competitors doing everything they could to keep us from regaining our No. 1 spot, this was a job I had to tackle myself, as general merchandise manager. The divisional supervisors and buyers just weren't strong enough to deal with the presidents and owners of some of the finest manufacturing establishments in this country and abroad. It was hard work, but it was also a lot of fun."

WHERE DO I GO FROM HERE?

"I can't help wondering what the next stop should be. Young Barrett and Sheila are well along in college and, except for summers, have flown the nest. The only way I can continue to grow is to keep on tackling new, challenging problems. I know that some of my friends think I'm already spreading myself too thin. From the look on your face, Floyd, it may be in your mind, too. I think I am pretty close to the boys down at the store, but it may be that they, too, think I am becoming an absentee president. However, as I have already said, I believe thoroughly in the significance of the causes for which I am working outside of the business, and I also believe each of them, in one way or another, helps contribute to the success of Green & Richards. Besides, I just can't see myself sitting in the office down at the store, reading a newspaper and waiting for someone to come in with a problem.

"Every so often, I have thought about trying a few years of government service. Through my work on the business advisory council of the Department of Commerce, I am in touch with a good many of the key people in the Administration. If they knew that I might be available, I suspect there would be an opportunity for me to move in at a level challenging enough to be more than just another bureaucratic job. Several of my friends have even had the temerity to suggest my name for governor, but in this state, a Republican candidate has lost the race before he starts. I think what I would really like to do is talk with you a little bit about your own experiences as a teacher. Perhaps, at this point in my career, I could get the greatest satisfaction from helping pass on to young people coming along some of the things I think I have learned in business. What do you think, Floyd?"

Hall arose as the two wives entered the room and said, "Why don't we let things soak a bit? You've given me so much to think about I hardly know where to begin."

TRUMBLE'S BACKGROUND

Floyd Hall recalled that Trumble had graduated from Hambletonian College. With business conditions as they were at the time, he had gone on to take his M.B.A. at the Tuck School of Business Administration at Dartmouth. All of his business life had been spent in retailing. Barrett had started as an assistant buyer of women's ready-to-wear at Fisk Brothers in Buffalo, New York. He progressed rapidly to the place where he was merchandising their entire ready-to-wear line. After eight years, he left Fisk to become divisional merchandise manager of a leading Southeast department store. Four years later, he became assistant general merchandise manager of a nationally known high-quality store on the East coast. He joined Green & Richards as vice-president and general merchandise manager and became president two years later. Hall recalled that Trumble had always been active in community affairs, wherever he worked. In the twenty-odd years Hall had known him, Trumble had never shown any evidence of being under pressure. Hall considered this unusual in an industry noted for heavy demands it made on its executives. Trumble had always had time for a full social life and an opportunity to take advantage of his consuming interest in golf. Barrett had been runner-up twice in the national intercollegiate golf championship while in college. He continued to play top-drawer golf after graduation, reaching the quarter finals of the National Amateur in his midforties. Two years earlier, he had been runner-up for the Gulf State Championship and had been club champion of the Jefferson Davis Country Club for six years running.

THE "SERMON"

Floyd Hall remembered that Trumble had sent him a copy of a talk he had given before the Parkville Presbyterian Church shortly after he became president of G & R. When he returned to Bristol, he found it was still in his files.

THE OPPORTUNITIES AND RESPONSIBILITIES
OF THE CHRISTIAN LAYMAN
IN THE COMMUNITY

Excerpts from Barrett Trumble's Talk

Parkville Presbyterian Church
Wednesday Evening—November 28

It is very good to be with you, and I am sure that you understand that I am not here to preach. . . . But I thought that perhaps we could all think out loud, in an informal way, about the subject at hand, namely, the layman's opportunity and responsibility in the community.

The first thing we should ask ourselves is: What is a Christian layman? Obviously, a Christian layman is a follower of Jesus Christ and, in essence, stands for and believes, with his heart, in the teachings of Jesus. In this conjunction, it might be interesting to point out that Jesus Himself was a layman. Although he was called Rabbi (that is to say, teacher), there is no record of His attending a theological school. Further, Jesus surrounded Himself with laymen from the common walks of life, and although the message came down out of Heaven through Christ into the church, it was carried out of the church into life by laymen who preached the Gospel. There was really no other way to do this. . . .

. . . We might stress the qualities Jesus stands for and the kind of person He wants the Christian layman to be.

Taking great liberties with Matthew: In Chapter 5, Verse 3, which begins, "Blessed are the poor in spirit for theirs is the kingdom of Heaven" and goes on through the various beatitudes that Jesus mentioned, it seems quite clear that (1) kindness and consideration for others—giving the other fellow a second chance, (2) aggressive courage —going the second mile for good causes, (3) courtesy—coming from the heart, (4) thoughtfulness and understanding, (5) fairness, (6) integrity and vision, and (7) faith are some of the vital qualities that we should strive to possess in our everyday living if we would measure up to Jesus' standards.

. . . These very same qualities that Christ taught us to strive and stand for are the ones that make for true success in everyday life. I think it important to emphasize here that I am talking about inner spiritual, rather than material, success—the sort which would lead a man such as Disraeli to want to be a great *man* rather than a great *lawyer*. These qualities make for true success in every walk of life, whether one is engaged in teaching, farming, a profession, business, or household duties. The old idea that to be successful one had to be ruthless, unscrupulous, and tough with people just doesn't stand up today and it is my honest opinion that the inability to handle, work with, and influence people is probably the cause of the greatest number of personal failures in life. Time and time again, I have—and I am sure you have—seen brilliant people who appeared to have just what it takes for success fail utterly because they overlooked the fact that one rarely succeeds alone but rather succeeds because others make one successful. . . .

I have been very fortunate in my life to have met and watched a great number of prominent people at work. I think you will agree with me when I say that a Charles Wilson or a George Marshall or a Dwight Eisenhower exemplifies fully these qualities that I have listed. I have never met a more humble, homespun, or thoughtful man than Charles Wilson; nor a more kind, considerate, and honest one than Marshall; nor a more thoughtful, fair, or courageous man than Eisenhower. As a matter of fact, it seems to me that the greater the man, the fewer the pretenses and the more down-to-Christian-fundamentals he is. . . .

Let me quote, again, from the text: Ephesians 4:32—"Be ye kind one to another, tender-hearted, forgiving." In Barrie's play, *Little White Bird,* a young husband is waiting at the hospital for his child to be born. He has never been unkind to his wife, but he wonders if he has been as kind as he might have been. "Let us make a new rule from tonight," he says, "always to be a little kinder than is necessary." . . . "Somehow, I never thought it paid," said Lincoln, when his friends urged him to make a stinging reply to a bitter, untrue word spoken about him. In the end, kindness, even to those who have been unkind to us, is never regretted. "A little kinder than is necessary" is the finest of the little arts of life, if not its final joy. The only things we are never sorry for are the kind things said and done to others. They make a soft pillow at the end.

. . . What are the obligations of the layman to his business or profession? In this regard, we have a great obligation to attempt to do the best possible job that we can in the field we are in, whatever that field might be. I believe it was Plato who said, "The source of the greatest happiness is in a job well done." Furthermore, by doing a good job in our field, whether it be as a mother in a home, a teacher in the school, a doctor in the hospital, or a businessman, we raise the standard of living and happiness of all those around us, and I am sure you will agree this is a most worthwhile goal.

Then there is the obligation of the layman to his fellow worker. To realize the dignity of man, to make his working and living conditions as pleasant as possible, to treat him with inner courtesy—coming from the heart. . . .

More directly and to the point of our subject, there is the obligation of the layman to his community, and I mean this in the large sense—the community being either local, national, or worldwide. Now, this interest in the obligation to the community can take the form of helping to improve the school system, of working with the sick and needy through the hospitals and in other ways helping to take care of the less fortunate. It can take the form of interest in striving for better, more enlightened, and honest government or in working for world peace. And finally, it can take the shape of interest in the church and in what the church stands for. Certainly, in some small way to help improve the lot of one or all of these five community efforts would be a most Christian thing to do—certainly something that Jesus urges us to pursue. Schools need better facilities, and teachers need more pay; the sick need care—the needy, relief from want; the government needs to understand and work for world peace and tolerance. And, certainly, the church, of all these community needs, should always be in our minds as an ever-present source of spiritual guidance, helping us to live every day a better and more Christian life. As I see it, going to church once a week isn't enough. We must also strive in our everyday living to *live* by the examples and teachings of Jesus. . . . It is not enough to just accept these teachings of Jesus. We must make these teachings work for us in our daily life.

. . . A Christian church is not a religion of monuments, but a religion of life. Of course, all of us must work for the physical needs of the church. But we must realize that the human race can never be saved by priests and monks and ministers alone, but rather by the Christian layman courageously setting a living example and aggressively selling, if you please, the teachings of Christ in his community. Every great idea must express itself in form. There must be an organization, but organization alone is not enough. Any religion worth having must demonstrate a power that makes changes in the lives of people who profess it. . . .

In conclusion—so many times I have heard people say that working for all these causes is fine, but what can I do about it—I am only one individual. . . . Of course, if everyone lived as Jesus taught us to live, there would probably not be need for helping other people. . . . If we solve our problems from a Christian and spiritual standpoint, we have taken a great step toward helping to solve the world's problems. Secondly, one doesn't have to head up organizations to be helpful. There are all levels of responsibility in community work for . . . anyone who wants to help. Finally, the argument that one is too busy would seem highly unjustified when the old expression, "When you want a job done, give it to a busy man," is so true.

PART EIGHT
THE
REFORMULATION PHASE:
RECYCLING AND
REAPPRAISING COURSES
OF ACTION

33

IRISH
ROPES
LIMITED

During 1969 Irish Ropes Ltd. suffered a work stoppage which resulted in a direct loss of £125,000 ($300,000). "Thereby," said Mr. Michael Rigby-Jones, chairman and managing director, "hangs the tale of our annual accounts."

"During the past three years we have met as wide a range of problems and difficulties as one would normally expect to incur in a ten-year period. Our task is now to overcome this setback by making our company more efficient in spite of further cost increases. The primary responsibility is with management, and we are aware of our task. We are now trading at a profit again, although at a lower rate than in previous years." In his 1970 Annual Report (see Exhibits 5 to 9), Mr. Rigby-Jones said:

The gross profit of £13,243 ($31,783) is an improvement over last year's loss of £52,673 (126,415), but is an unsatisfactory result for the year's trading. Changing in accounting methods and taxation adjust the net profit to £53,234 ($127,761), compared to a loss of £45,823 ($109,975). This does not give a satisfactory return on the capital employed of £1,727,694 ($4,146,465) nor a return on the sales volume of £3,359,151 ($8,061,962), nor a satisfactory result for the efforts of many people, nor the creation of sufficient funds to maintain and expand the business.

For the past three years I have specifically mentioned the effect of inflation on our business. This year costs increased at a greater rate than ever before and there is no definite sign of an abatement. Our income on the home market has been controlled by government price legislation for the past three years and income from exports has been lost as customers overseas are not willing to pay for Irish inflation. On the other hand, the expenses of running the business have continued to increase with the result that the cost of manufacture in this country now exceeds those of our nearest competitors. It is not yet clear what the government's recent actions will yield, as they fail to squarely tackle the real problem of incomes rising ahead of productivity. The increase and retrospective company taxation will reduce the means by which companies can expand and increase productivity through new investment. Rising standards of living will only be earned through efficiency and expanding industry.

Our company has a high labor content and must export over half of its output, so it is inevitable that profits are the first to decline and disappear under excessive inflation. However, we have to find our own solutions and this we are doing through a major investment in increasing factory efficiency, ceasing production of products which are no longer economic, improving management, and a determined effort to expand sales. The results will be significant, but unless the rate of inflation is substantially reduced, they will be swallowed up by further cost increases.

Irish Ropes' assets had expanded from £7,188 ($30,405) at the time of its founding in 1934 to £1,733,792 ($4,161,110) in 1970, and the expansion had come almost entirely from retained earnings. Since the end of World War II the company's sales had increased over twelvefold and the number of its employees had almost quadrupled. The company started as a producer for the Irish domestic market; in 1971 it was mainly an exporter, with over 50% of its tonnage and over 60% of its sales revenue from the export market. Abroad, Irish Ropes had achieved an excellent reputation for the quality of its sisal products, and in Ireland the company was lauded for setting an example in many fields, particularly in modern management and good labor relations (see Exhibit 1).

EARLY HISTORY OF THE COMPANY

Prior to 1933 Ireland's rope requirements had been imported, mostly from England. In 1933 the Irish Republic imposed a 33⅓% duty on the importation of cordage. At the time, Eric Rigby-Jones (father of Michael) was operating a rope factory in Liverpool, where his family had been ropemakers for six generations, specializing in high-quality ropes, such as mountain climbers' ropes and lariats. He also manufactured common ropes and twines for export to Ireland. Eric Rigby-

exhibit 1

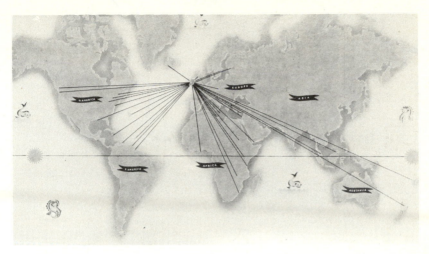

Jones had to choose between abandoning the Irish market and establishing a plant in Ireland. He decided to relocate within the Irish Republic. He found some abandoned century-old British cavalry barracks in Newbridge, a farm town of about 2,000 located 30 miles below Dublin on the River Liffey. He thought the roomy buildings were ideal; he bought a section of the garrison and with six employees began production in July, 1933. His firm already had a loyal customer following in Ireland, and his business quickly prospered. Within 10 years it had 300 employees and was supplying the bulk of Ireland's rope and twine requirements. Eric Rigby-Jones became a leader in Irish industry and took an active part in Irish civic affairs.

ROPE AND CORDAGE IN IRELAND [1]

The company's cordage products which were sold in Ireland fell into two categories: harvest twines, and ropes and parcel twines.

The harvest twine group consisted of binder twines, baler twines, and hayband. Binder twine was used to tie sheaves of grain as they came off the grain reapers. Binder twine sales had been declining for the past decade, as a result of the growing use of grain combines. The decline was offset by the growing demand for baler twine, used by hay

[1] See Appendix A.

and straw balers. Baler twine was very similar to binder twine except
that it was considerably stronger. Hayband was a very cheap twine,
made from sisal waste, which farmers used for tying down their
haycocks.

Irish Ropes was a monopoly supplier of harvest twines in Ireland,
where its market was protected by high import duties. While harvest
twines accounted for one-third of the company's total tonnage of production, they returned less than 15% of the company's total profit. The
profit might have been higher, especially in years in which delayed
harvests pushed up prices, but as a matter of policy Irish Ropes kept
its prices moderate to avoid any accusation of taking advantage of its
monopoly situation. In the late 1960's the price of harvest twines was
the lowest it had been in 10 years, and largely offset the benefit of
exceptionally high sales.

In 1966 the Irish Republic entered into a free trade agreement with
the United Kingdom. According to the terms of the agreement, the
duties on cordage would be reduced from year to year until they
reached zero in 1975. Mr. Rigby-Jones felt that the company's Irish
market was reasonably secure, but he had misgivings. "In England
there are four ropeworks," he said, "each larger than we. Each of them
would only have to sell a hundred tons in Ireland a year, which they
could do by marginal cost selling, and our home market would be
gone. Continental twine spinners can also compete with us very favorably."

The category of ropes and parcel twines contained a wide variety of
products. The output of this product group had been declining slowly,
but within the product group there were both major increases and
decreases. Within this category were some of the company's most
profitable products and some of the least profitable.

"We will probably not expand the cordage end of our business,"
said Mr. Rigby-Jones, "and as free trade comes about we may even
lose a share of our Irish market to larger English and Continental
ropemakers. By converting to polypropylene we will probably be able
to hold our home market, but we will be likely to lose some of our
export markets. We might even lose some of our home market to
dumpers, if antidumping regulations are not effective. We might withdraw from the production of some of the highly competitive mass
standard qualities, such as harvest twines, but we will remain in the

cordage business and specialize in the spinning of fine twines and make specialty short-run, high-quality ropes and twines."

TINTAWN SISAL CARPETING

Mr. Eric Rigby-Jones had originally intended to spin fine white sisal yarns to be sold to the carpet weavers. His inability to develop that market had persuaded him to have his own company weave carpeting. Rather than make cheap matting, he decided to use white, artificially dried sisal, which was more expensive but permitted dyeing in lighter colors, making a quality carpeting, which he called Tintawn.

After a number of years of experimenting with weaving, patterns, and styles, production began in earnest in 1952. Tintawn found ready consumer acceptance, and thereafter the company regularly added more looms. In 1969–1970, Tintawn represented over one-third of the total tonnage production and over 50% of the total profits of the company. It was the fastest-growing segment of the company's export sales.

"Our company has no natural advantage in the production of ropes," said Mr. Rigby-Jones. "Ropemaking has become standardized and static. Tintawn, however, lends itself to promotion and merchandising as a quality product. There is a great market potential and we are developing more. No one, so far, has duplicated the effort of Irish Ropes in producing a sisal matting of high quality and artistic coloring and pattern. Of all of Irish Ropes products, Tintawn has shown the most success."

During the 1960's, Irish Ropes sales of Tintawn increased several fold, with most of the growth occurring in England and Ireland, where Tintawn was advertised in national daily newspapers, Sunday supplements, and on radio and television. In Ireland, Tintawn was sold through some 70 home furnishings distributors. Sales in England were through a wholly owned subsidiary, Tintawn Limited, of Reading, England. The English business had grown to such an extent that Tintawn Limited had quadrupled the size of its original premises. The Tintawn brand name became well established in Ireland and the United Kingdom, which together accounted for 75% of total Tintawn sales. The British carpet market improved in 1970, and Irish Ropes looked forward to further expansion in 1971 and 1972.

In 1960 Irish Ropes had expected the two European free trade areas

to merge. In anticipation of this union it made a serious effort to introduce Tintawn into the Continental markets. To offset the 21% duty
in Germany, the Tintawn price was lowered by about 10%; dimensions were changed from yards to meters; designs were changed to
stripes and bolder patterns; brighter colors were used; and even the
name was Germanized by spelling it Tintaun.

There were a number of German firms which produced excellent-
quality sisal carpeting at prices Irish Ropes could not meet. They also
offered high-grade service and prompt delivery. One West German firm
was selling sisal carpeting of superior quality laid down in London at
prices which were 25% below those of Tintawn. When the combined
free trade area failed to materialize, Irish Ropes' management decided
to switch its efforts to other export areas, including the EFTA countries of Denmark, Sweden, and Norway.

Dutch sisal carpetings were lighter in weight than Tintawn but they
sold for about 25% less than Tintawn, and this price differential
pulled customers away from the superior-quality Tintawn. The Dutch
had also begun to imitate the colors and designs of Irish Ropes. "Copying our designs is a penalty we pay for being the leader in our field,"
said Mr. Rigby-Jones. "There is nothing we can do to stop it. We can
only try to keep originating new designs faster than the old ones are
copied, and hope to stay ahead of the field. We decided to pull out of
the Common Market countries, but we have the prospect well in mind,
and when Ireland does gain entrance, we will make a new attempt to
win a position in the Continental market."

In 1962 the Tintawn distributor in the United States ceased business
abruptly. Irish Ropes then organized a subsidiary, Tintawn, Inc., of
New York, to carry on the business. Tintawn, Inc., was managed for
Irish Ropes by SMA, the Scandinavian Marketing Association, a
Swedish organization, which did the actual selling. Irish Ropes maintained the inventories and granted credit up to 90 days for SMA
customers.

In the United States, Tintawn was cheaper than most other forms
of carpeting, but carpet layers were paid rates reaching as high as $5
an hour, which increased the final installed price of the Tintawn considerably. Although the United States was by far the largest carpet
market in the world, Tintawn had never achieved a significant volume
of sales in this market. The Irish Ropes management was investigating

to determine whether there was a market for Tintawn in the United States, at least in the large population centers.

CARPETING PRODUCTION AND SALES

In Ireland, during the 1960's, the sale of carpeting, particularly of the wall-to-wall type, had grown by as much as 20% per annum. Woven carpets accounted for about 70% of sales, Tintawn 10%, and tufted carpetings 10%, and the balance was in various types.

It was believed that the small market share of tufted carpets in Ireland was caused by lack of promotional effort, by high Irish import duties, and by the small size of the Irish market. Tufted carpeting was economical to make; a single loom turned out 300,000 square yards a year per shift, versus 50,000 square yards of woven carpet per three shifts. Most tufted carpeting was made of synthetics which had good wearability and cost only half as much as wool. Tufted carpeting represented over 80% of U.S. carpet sales—only 18% of this was woolen. In the United Kingdom woven carpeting sales were increasing 0.05% per year, while tufted sales increased 10% annually. United Kingdom tufted manufacturers were successfully exporting to Germany, France, and Holland, despite competent Continental tufters and import duties of 25%.

In Ireland, wool carpets had the largest share of the market, but Irish Ropes was late in entering the wool field. Ireland had plenty of native wool, but the best carpet wools came from the highlands of India and Tibet, and these were cut off by political action. Irish Ropes also assumed that Ireland would follow the experience of the U.S. and the U.K., with tufted carpeting rapidly taking over the market.

For its initial entry into the field of tufted carpeting, Irish Ropes organized a subsidiary, Irish Carpets, Ltd., to manufacture soft-pile carpets using the brand name Cushlawn. The carpets were made of Dutch nylon, which was the synthetic most used in the United States. Initial production was for the home market, making three weights. Weight made a difference in luxuriousness and price but not in wearability. Some U.S. firms made 20 weights.

As a result of production difficulties and sales promotion expenses, Irish Carpets lost money in its first years. In 1968 a new quality of carpet which was 80% wool and 20% nylon was introduced under the name Curragh. At that time, Irish Carpets UK, Ltd., was established as a separate company to market Cushlawn and Curragh carpets in Britain. Irish Carpets found development costs to be substantial, especially the cost of providing samples, and it also found that sales were slow in developing. While these products were being introduced, the volume of carpets imported into Ireland continued to increase.

In 1969 Irish Carpets continued to operate at a loss, because of overproduction and intense competition in the United Kingdom. Loom capacity had been expanded, but weaving was still in a bay of the Irish Ropes plant in Newbridge. Irish Carpets UK had not produced the desired results as a distribution system. Therefore, the sales and marketing of Tintawn and Cushlawn were integrated, and for marketing reasons the name Tintawn Carpeting Ltd. was changed to Curragh Carpets Ltd., which marketed all Irish Ropes' carpets except in the United Kingdom, where Tintawn Ltd. was well known. Curragh was the brand name of the soft-pile carpets which were being promoted throughout Ireland.

RAW MATERIALS

All of Irish Ropes' sisal[2] requirements were purchased through a single London broker, a leading firm with whom the company had had close connections since the day of its founding. The broker was in constant contact with many sisal estates in Tanzania, East Africa, and some of these plantations were owned and operated by the brokerage firm. "Buying from a single source," said Mr. Rigby-Jones, "means we have all our eggs in one basket, but we have made sure that it is a very good basket."

Shipments were received every four or five weeks on ships which sailed directly from Africa to the port of Dublin. Since the sources of its supplies were so distant, purchasing requirements were budgeted six months in advance, and a stock of over 1,500 tons of sisal fiber was kept on hand.

The buying of sisal had always been personally supervised by the managing director because the price of raw sisal had always been very volatile and the raw material made up a large percentage of the total factory cost of Irish Ropes' products. During 1962–1963, the price of sisal increased approximately 50%, from £99 ($277) to £148 ($414) per

[2] See Appendix B.

ton, the limited supply possibly being caused by spinning mills being established in sisal-growing countries, and by the imposition of an export tax by the new independent government of Tanzania. During 1964, the price fell to £110 ($308), and by October, 1965, it stood at £82 ($229.60). When British Ropes lowered its price of binder twine £28 ($78.40) a ton, Irish Ropes countered with a reduction of £30 ($84), but Irish Ropes made no reduction in the price of Tintawn. For the fiscal year ending in August, 1964, Irish Ropes' net profit increased by 47%; in 1965 it increased another 50%. It was generally conceded that this was the result of astute sisal-buying on the part of Mr. Rigby-Jones. Irish Ropes' competitors suffered substantial losses as a result of the large fall in raw material prices. In 1969–1970 the price of raw sisal increased again and it was possible to recover only some of the higher cost in higher prices charged for finished goods.

Throughout the history of Irish Ropes, sisal had been the company's predominant raw material, and with the rising popularity of man-made fibers the management gave serious consideration to the possible disappearance of sisal from the world markets. While synthetics were commanding an increasing share of world fiber markets, the consumption of natural fibers, including wool, cotton, and sisal, had continued to rise, and sisal consumption had been increasing annually at the rate of 2% per year. The economies of the East African states were so dependent upon sisal that it was believed that they would support its production by desperate measures, such as abolishing the present export duties and possibly eventually subsidizing sisal-growing. Productivity in sisal-growing was rising, having increased by 75% per man-hour during the past 10 years. The threat of substitution of artificial fibers was already seen to be acting as a brake on rising sisal prices. It was concluded that supplies and prices of sisal would continue to be economical for the foreseeable future. The management of Irish Ropes switched a portion of its production to synthetic fibers, but it believed that sisal would remain its predominant material for the immediate future.

"We are well aware in our everyday lives," said Mr. Rigby-Jones, "of the growing use of synthetic fibers, and it is of great concern to us that our company is not using synthetic fibers to the extent that it should. This is particularly true in the rope trade, where natural fibers have been altogether eliminated in some uses. One of the main factors in the recent drop in the price of raw sisal was the threat of competition from synthetic baler twine. The reason that we have not developed in this direction as much as other rope manufacturers is that up to July, 1966, the British market was closed to us by a high rate of duty, even when our synthetic raw fiber was purchased from that country."

Mr. Rigby-Jones was convinced that polypropylene had excellent possibilities in rope manufacture. It was twice as strong per unit of weight, which meant that ropes of considerably smaller diameter made of polypropylene would replace heavier ropes made from natural fibers. Polypropylene floated in water; it weighed less per length and it resisted deterioration from rotting. In addition, rope made of this synthetic material lasted an average of twice as long and was readily available from numerous sources at relatively stable prices.

In 1970 Irish Ropes invested £30,000 ($72,000) in a plant to extrude 250 tons of polypropylene a year. Polypropylene chips were available to all purchasers at the same price. The same year a new Tintawn Softcord carpet was successfully launched after test marketing in 1969. "We plan to increase production and sales of this unique product," said Mr. Rigby-Jones. "It is unique because as carpet manufacturers we manufacture the product from the basic raw material of polypropylene granules to fiber to finished carpet. Its production has involved considerable technology and development. The change from natural to synthetic fibers has continued in spite of the lowest cost of sisal in many years. Our synthetic fiber production has been expanded, as we must offset the decline in demand for other products. Additional ranges of tufted carpets have been introduced on the home market and we now offer the public a considerable range of carpets in design, quality, and cost."

THE PLYTAWN EXPERIENCE

"In view of the competitive vulnerability of cordages," said Mr. Rigby-Jones, "we considered diversifying into related products. We sought products in fields which would provide growth at the rate of 5% to 10% per annum." Irish Ropes intensively sought new products which might use its existing manufacturing capabilities and marketing facilities. Initially, the company gave attention to (1) Plytawn, and (2) extending the Irish Ropes line of carpeting. The management decided to first explore the possibilities in Plytawn.

In the plastics industry the principal material used for reinforcement was Fiberglas, which provided tremendous strength—often much more than was needed. Sisal-reinforced plastic was not as strong, but cost only one-third as much. However, sisal retained moisture and imparted a yellow color. Since 1960 Irish Ropes had been experimenting with a sisal-reinforced plastic, which it called Plytawn.

Sisal reinforcing was either chopped fibers, woven fibers, or a chemically bonded web. Irish Ropes chose to develop the bonded web, which required skill to produce. No one had ever made a bonded sisal mat before, and so the company invested £25,000 ($60,000) in machinery to enable it to produce samples. A subsidiary company, Plytawn Limited, was formed to separate accounting and tax matters. The original objective was to furnish manufacturers with the materials in rolls, as Owens-Corning did with its Fiberglas, but several years of intensive sales effort beamed at manufacturers in the United Kingdom and on the Continent failed to arouse interest. Most manufacturers clung to what the Plytawn salesmen called "the metal attitude."

Failing to sell the bonded web, Plytawn Limited became involved in the manufacturing of finished products. It made a baby-chair shell for high chairs and sought a manufacturer who would complete it. It made the shell of an adult lounging chair and sought an upholsterer to finish it. It developed Plytawn seat buckets, which it offered to British Motors Corporation at a marginal price, and BMC was ready to accept when its supplier of pulp-board frames cut its price 30%. "We always seemed," said Mr. Rigby-Jones, "to be in the position of almost catching the big one who somehow managed to get away from us."

Irish Ropes also considered making prefabricated units in standard sizes for small buildings, such as telephone booths, bus shelters, and public conveniences. Another possibility was a bottle crate made of plastic for firms such as Coca Cola; the plastic crates were lighter, lasted longer, were easy to clean, and required no maintenance. Also considered were office furniture, school desks, household hardware, kitchen tools, and other utensils. Most of these items required blow and injection molding, and the machine and die costs could be recovered only by very long runs. The gardening market offered such possibilities as flower pots, sprinkling cans, spray cans, and seeding boxes, but wood and galvanized iron were cheaper, and it was questionable whether a customer would pay 50% more for a plastic item, even though it lasted 150% longer.

Plytawn Limited never had a profitable year, and in many years it incurred losses of over £20,000 ($48,000) per year. In 1968 the decision was made to liquidate the Plytawn Division. "Plytawn had a potential," said Mr. Rigby-Jones, "but we were unable to develop it. We found, too, that the reinforced plastics industry was not experiencing an impressive growth."

THE NEWBRIDGE PLANT

In 1933 Irish Ropes started production with six employees, using one building of the old British cavalry barracks. Newbridge was then a farm town of 2,000. In 1971 the company had 1,035 employees. Its plant site had been expanded to a 13-acre parcel, surrounded by public roads, and there were 8 acres (350,000 square feet) of plant buildings (see Exhibit 2). The company also had 19 acres for future industrial development and 19 acres for staff houses and recreation.

From the beginning there had been a shortage of housing in Newbridge. In the company's early years a renovated British Army hospital had been used to house staff personnel. Since then the company had built nine modern residences, which it rented to senior staff executives at 60% of the average local rent level. In 1957 the company built a £9,000 ($21,600) hostel for staff on the plant premises. The company charged no rent to hostel residents, who lived there on a self-governing basis, sharing the cost of meals, which amounted to about £12 ($28.80) per man monthly. The hostel was modern and well appointed, but the residents felt some dissatisfaction at being forced into association with their fellow staff members outside of office hours. Table conversations tended to be dominated by rope and carpet themes.

"We are very concerned," said Mr. Rigby-Jones, "that any further expansion in our present locality may be limited unless there is an adequate local labor supply available. This means that more houses are immediately required in Newbridge, together with all the needed services, such as water, sewerage, schools, churches, and so on. If the local resources are not expanded, we shall be obliged to expand elsewhere. We find that the concepts of planning and priorities are sadly lacking in the local environment."

In April, 1970, a major reorganization was undertaken in Irish Ropes' hard fiber production. This consisted of constructing a new spinning mill of 48,780 square feet which would join other buildings to make 2½ acres under a single roof, supplanting a spread of sepa-

exhibit 2
The Newbridge Plant

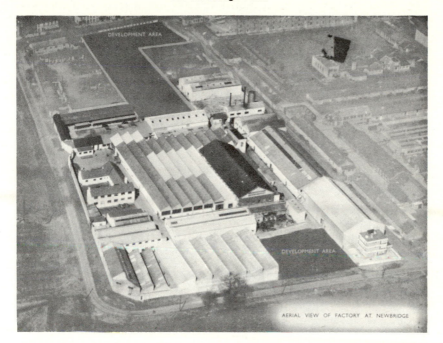

(a) Aerial View of Factory at Newbridge

(b) Preparing Sisal Fiber for Spinning

(c) New 12-foot Loom. This loom is the first of its kind in the world and is capable of weaving sisal carpet of superb quality up to 12 feet in width.

rate buildings which had been connected by in-company roadways. The work amounted to an almost rebuilding of the old factory. It involved the moving of some 250 machines and was expected to be completed in June, 1971, at a cost of about £250,000 ($600,000). This reconstruction replaced a factory which had been built up in piecemeal fashion over the years into one which would have a flowline production layout, lower operating costs, and improved working conditions. It was the largest construction undertaking which Irish Ropes had ever carried out, and the company attempted to minimize the considerable expense and loss of output involved by extremely detailed planning and control.

LABOR RELATIONS

In the spring of 1969, in common with most other Irish companies, Irish Ropes' production was totally halted for five weeks as the result of a nationwide strike of the maintenance workers and the refusal of other workers to pass the strikers' picket lines. Irish Ropes was a member of the Federated Union of Employers and supported the stand taken by the Federation because it believed that the demands made by the maintenance workers would have serious repercussions. The direct cost of the strike to Irish Ropes was put at about £125,000 ($360,000). The management believed that the loss was substantially more than this because at the time the company was in a totally oversold condition, working three shifts six days a week; there was no spare capacity to enable the company to catch up on lost production. Irish Ropes assumed that there were many customers, particularly overseas customers, who were disturbed by Irish Ropes' failure to deliver during that period and its inability to compensate later. After production was resumed it took several months to restore a reasonable inventory situation. "The five-week closure set us back in the short term," said Mr. Rigby-Jones, "but we will learn from this experience."

In the annual report for 1969 Mr. Rigby-Jones stated:

> The size of wage increments being granted nationally are much higher than the possible increase in productivity. In many cases the increases are in the public and service sectors, which do not have to meet export competition. This leads our employees into expectations which bear

little relationship to our competitive situation, and hence a very difficult position in which to reach agreement. We have been making extra
efforts to improve labor relations, particularly through better communications.

It is understandable that many people, particularly the lower paid, have
aspirations for higher incomes and make comparisons to other occupa-
tions in our small country. However, it is the price at which we can sell
our work abroad that really determines our incomes, and unless we solve
the problem of matching expectations with competition, this industry
cannot be viable. It must be possible to solve this problem constructively, and not permit unemployment to be the eventual outcome.

The rate of increase in costs has placed management in a position that
it is practically unable to increase production at a sufficiently high rate.
From 1966 to 1970 our basic wage rates have increased by 50% plus the
extra costs of fringe benefits and holidays. The average annual increase
in incomes in 1969–1970 is more than double the years 1964–1968 and
four and a half times greater than between 1956 and 1964.

At the time of the Maintenance Strike we were negotiating a new Wage
Agreement. We received a wage demand which was hardly negotiable,
and bore little relation to our business or concern for the future employment of many people dependent upon exports. Days of negotiation
and explanation of the company's position brought no agreement after
three secret ballots on the job and the largest wage offer ever made.
Strike notice was served and expired. We considered that a further closure of the factory would put all our exports in jeopardy, and a settlement was made to increase wages 13½% from March to December,
1969, and a further 6½% from January to December, 1970—a total increase of 20%. We are now paying wages and salaries equal or above
most of our competitors in Britain and have become a relatively high-
cost country for our industry.

Irish Ropes considered itself to be a labor-intensive company, selling
over 50% of its production in export markets. The rate of inflation in
Ireland in 1969–1970 was approximately twice that of the countries in
which Irish Ropes sold its products. A publication by the Irish Economic and Social Research Institution indicated that Irish unit labor
costs in the year 1969 increased 12%. Within Irish Ropes the unit
labor cost of production increased by over 50% during the period
1965–1970.

In the decade 1959 to 1969, average prices in Ireland increased by
50%, compared with 41% in the United Kingdom. In Ireland, weekly
earnings for male workers in manufacturing industries increased from

£9/10s ($26.60) per week in 1960 to £20/10s ($49.20) in 1969 with a reduction in working hours from 47.1 to 45.3. In the United Kingdom, in the same period, comparable male earnings increased from £15 ($42.60) to £24/10s ($58.80) while hours worked dropped from 47.4 to 45.7. The United Kingdom and Commonwealth countries were Irish Ropes' largest export markets.

In 1960, the Irish pay-packet was 67% of that of the United Kingdom, whereas in 1969–1970 it had risen to 85%. In Ireland, working days lost per 1,000 persons employed averaged 828 in the 10-year period 1959 to 1969, compared with 262 in the UK. The maintenance strike caused 31,000 men to be out of work for five weeks, causing a national loss of 600,000 work days and the loss of an estimated £20 million ($48 million) in exports.

"There has been a rapid change in the labor situation in Newbridge," said Mr. Rigby-Jones. "Labor turnover and absenteeism have become significant costs and problems to us during the past two years. The labor supply position in Newbridge has changed dramatically and we lost production during the year due to a shortage of workers. Our wage agreement ends this year and negotiations for a new agreement are in hand. Although our wage costs exceed those of our competitors in Britain over-all, we have received a claim to increase basic wages by £6/15s ($16.20) per week at an annual cost of £270,000 ($648,000)." In Ireland, in 1970, it was commonplace to have major negotiations taking place in which employees were asking for wage increases of £6 ($14.40) per week.

All Irish Ropes plant employees worked under a wage incentive plan, and despite current labor problems the management continued to have faith in its incentive program. Under the incentive system efficiency was measured in pounds per machine per hour, which was translated into standard minutes. Bonus payments began at 70% of standard and increased above that percentage. The average bonus payment for the factory was 105%; no one consistently earned under 90%. Bonus payments added about 25% to the company's annual payroll. After the inauguration of the bonus system it was estimated that productivity increased between 25% and 50%. Irish Ropes believed that it benefited from the incentive plan in several ways: Less close supervision was needed; Irish Ropes wages were good and a job there was attractive; the company obtained high production; labor turnover was low; and the quality of its production was high.

SALES

Total sales in 1970 were 4% greater than the previous year, but as 1969 was affected by the five weeks' maintenance workers' strike and there had been some price increases, sales declined. The export content of sales fell from 55% to 52% in terms of the real value of the pound. Cordage sales on the home market were satisfactory, but export sales were lost as a result of high costs and noncompetitiveness. Carpet sales were maintained on the home market, but export sales, including Britain, were lower, as the carpet trade was passing through a difficult period. Tufted carpeting operations were not expected to make a significant contribution to profits in the future. "We are directing our efforts to increasing our sales volume profitably," said Mr. Rigby-Jones, "because we must increase our income and re-establish our position overseas."

During the 1960's, Irish Ropes had increased its sales by 200%, partly because of price appreciation, but mainly because of increased tonnage. The company had sales in every part of the globe (see Exhibit 1), but its high-potenial markets were the United Kingdom, the United States, Australia, and Canada, where it sold high-performance cordages and Tintawn. Where the company had once tried to push into many markets, it was now concentrating on selected markets.

Ireland was not a member of the EEC or EFTA, and in these areas Irish Ropes competed with local producers who could sell duty-free throughout their trade area. Duties in Common Market countries were from 14% to 20%. Irish Rope had once exported a considerable volume of fishing lines to the EFTA countries of Scandinavia, but its position there had deteriorated.

Irish Ropes met severe price competition from local producers whose basic costs were lower. The Portuguese used West African sisal grown in their nearby colony of Angola; Irish Ropes' sisal, however, came the long route from Tanzania in East Africa. The Portuguese had both lower freight costs and lower wage costs. Henequin was a fiber plant which was native to Mexico; also, Mexican labor costs were so low that by comparison Irish labor costs were high. The United States levied no duty on agricultural twines, and the Mexicans, the Portuguese, and the Africans sold in the United States market at prices Irish Ropes could not match.

Most shipments from Ireland had to go to Liverpool on the west coast of England, to be transshipped from there, a fact which added heavily to shipping charges. The rate from Dublin direct to any port in the United States was the same as the rate from Liverpool, but direct sailings from Dublin were few. There was only one line which had one sailing a month from Dublin to the interior of the United States via the Great Lakes Seaway. Most Irish Ropes shipments went via Liverpool. It cost almost as much to ship to Glasgow, Scotland, 200 miles from Dublin, as to New York, 3,500 miles away.

ORGANIZATION STRUCTURE

In 1965 Irish Ropes engaged a consulting firm to make a thorough study of its organization structure. It was recommended that the organization, based on functional lines, be reorganized along product line divisions. (See Exhibits 3 and 4.)

The managing director was to be relieved of personally dispatching many of his previous responsibilities, while still retaining over-all control of the decentralized activities. In his early experience as managing director, Mr. Rigby-Jones admitted, it made him nervous to be away from the work even for limited periods. After the reorganization it was not unusual for him to be away two or three days a week, and to permit subordinates to act on his behalf.

Mr. Bernard Roche, formerly the company's sales director, was appointed deputy managing director, and while he increased the time he spent in general administration, he continued to personally direct all sales activities. Mr. Roche had been with the company since its establishment by Mr. Eric Rigby-Jones, and his experience was utilized for long-range planning and policy formulation.

Each product line became the responsibility of a division manager. The first product line divisions were Tintawn, Cordage, Plytawn, and Cushlawn. Each division manager was held responsible for his own production, sales, finances, and profitability.

Two service departments were established: (1) technical services, which was responsible for all technical and product development in all divisions; and (2) planning and administrative services, which was responsible for the headquarters office, clerical procedures, accounting, credit control, tax returns, inventory records, dividend payments, legal matters, insurance, payroll, pension fund, and personnel records.

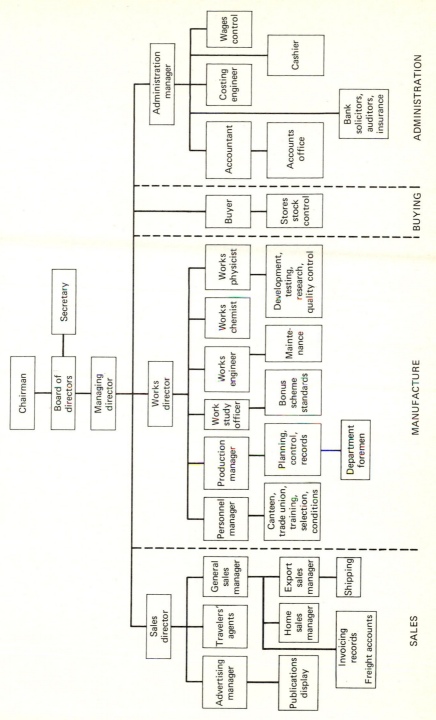

exhibit 3

Organization Chart of Irish Ropes, Ltd., before Reorganization in 1965

ADMINISTRATION

BUYING

MANUFACTURE

SALES

exhibit 4

Outline of Proposed Organization Structure of Irish Ropes, Ltd., after Reorganization in 1965

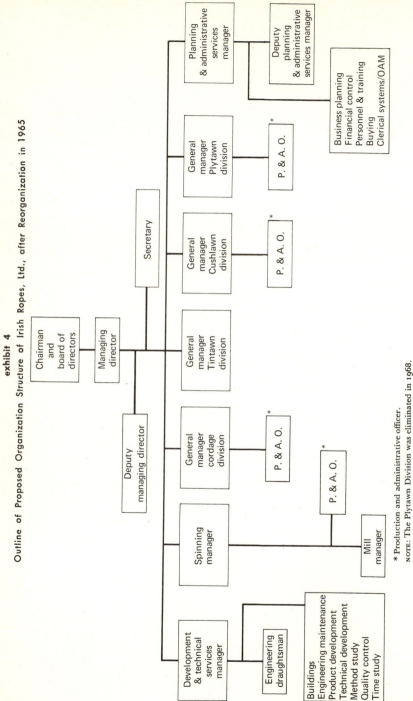

* Production and administrative officer.
NOTE: The Plytawn Division was eliminated in 1968.

With the reorganization of the company, Mr. Rigby-Jones was relieved of many of the activities which had been his personal duty. Shortly after the reorganization he stated: "I don't like the new organization; it seems so impersonal. I formerly managed people, and ran a business. Now I must learn a new job—dealing with a set of relationships. But I know that I ought to delegate more, and now I'll do a better job of developing new managers. Before there was only one business manager in the place. Now there will be a number of people keeping a closer eye on the profit ball."

For 30 years after its founding the chairman of Irish Ropes had been Arthur Cox, a wealthy and eminent Dublin attorney, who numbered among his clients Sir Winston Churchill and George Bernard Shaw. "Mr. Cox never imposed his opinions on us," said Mr. Michael Rigby-Jones ruefully. "This might have been a blessing, but it left the burden of critical decisions to me. There were times when I would have appreciated some positive guidance."

When Mr. Cox retired in 1962, Mr. Michael Rigby-Jones became chairman, and he continued to be managing director of the company. Mr. P. J. Doyle, an original shareholder of the company, and Mr. H. E. Guinness, a veteran merchant banker, retired in 1969. Mr. Bernard Roche, deputy managing director of the company, and Arthur Shiel, administration director and secretary of the company, both veteran executives, continued as board members. There were two newcomers: Mr. Joseph McCabe, managing director of Tintawn Limited and the youngest senior executive in the company, and Mr. D. S. A. Carroll, governor of the Bank of Ireland. Mr. Joseph McCabe was also appointed assistant managing director of Irish Ropes Ltd. It was generally recognized that the board and Mr. Rigby-Jones acted in harmony, and that Mr. Carroll proved to be a valuable addition. Mr. Carroll did not hesitate to introduce new ideas, and his judgment was valued on all matters.

Looking upon the 1965 reorganization in retrospect in 1970, Mr. Rigby-Jones said:

> I regret to say that our reorganization from a functional to a divisional basis did not succeed and we are now in the process of rebuilding a structural organization. I see the errors now as follows: the division of the company into divisions became divisive. Managers were told to run their divisions as separate businesses and they went so far as to forget that they worked for one company. There was a lot of "buck-passing" that developed.

With very few exceptions we did not have the caliber of people to fit a divisional management structure. Some positions we filled proved disastrous by putting existing staff into new positions. It was the "square peg into the round hole" problem. The service divisions, technical services and administration, were so large that they swamped some other divisions and caused considerable resentment.

Undue emphasis on job specifications, glorified management accounts, controls, and a neglect of simple line management was evident, particularly in the factory. Increased emphasis on selling caused the factory to become neglected.

I personally found that I had delegated so much that I had lost commercial contact with the business, and I am finding it quite difficult to get back into this aspect of the business. We are presently in the midst of an enormous reorganization.

I have always been keen on modern management methods, but my frame of mind at the moment is to cut out a lot of the jargon and techniques and get back to more simple and direct factory line management where the "buck" has to stop and satisfaction given or heads will roll. Too many of the management techniques stultify shop floor initiative and common sense if they are not properly used. The real answer is to have a balance. I think we had swung too far one way, and now we have to swing back a little to get into balance again.

BALANCE SHEET CHANGES

Since inflation had affected the value of money, the Irish Ropes management decided to make some major changes in its accounting. The balance sheet was simplified by placing all specific Revenue Reserves into a General Reserve. The basis for valuing stocks was revised to conform with modern accounting practices, which resulted in a surplus. The stocks of Irish Carpets Ltd. were written down, and the net effect of these changes was a surplus of £22,525 ($54,060).

The charge for depreciation had in previous years included amounts to provide for increased costs of renewal of assets; the original cost had already been fully provided and depreciation continued to be charged at existing rates. The board decided that henceforth depreciation to be charged for Plant and Machinery would be spread over its estimated life. The effect of this decision was to reduce the depreciation charge by £27,968 ($67,123). The cumulative amount of the replacement element of past depreciation was £262,087 ($629,009). Of this, £51,087 ($122,609) was applied to write down particular machinery and the balance of £211,000 ($506,400) was transferred to the General Reserve.

The board also decided that it was no longer necessary to depreciate Property and Buildings, because with inflation they increased in value. The effect in 1970 was to reduce the depreciation charge by £18,416 ($44,198). Buildings were now shown on the balance sheet at cost, and the cumulative depreciation of £178,363 ($428,071) was transferred to General Reserve. The Irish Ropes properties were known to be worth more than the £420,374 ($1,008,898) shown on the balance sheet, but it was recognized that their value depended upon cirmumstances which might change. An independent professional survey showed that for insurance purposes it would cost £1,670,000 ($4,008,000) to duplicate the premises in 1970.

The effect of these changes, plus additions made during the year, was to increase the Fixed Assets by £425,882 ($1,022,117) and the Net Current Assets by £61,647 ($147,953). The board of directors was satisfied that the total value of the company of £1,727,694 ($4,146,466), as shown on the balance sheet, continued to be conservative, but it was also of the opinion that it was necessary to obtain a satisfactory return on this capital.

MANAGEMENT'S VIEW OF THE FUTURE

Mr. Rigby-Jones was very much concerned with costs, which were rising substantially. "In this situation," he said, "we have to increase efficiency every year just to maintain profits, let alone to raise them. With the depreciating value of money, we shall eventually be forced to increase our prices, but the competitive situation of our products in many markets does not permit this. In addition, on the Home Market, the Government continues to maintain price control. We were in favor of this legislation when it was introduced, as it was hoped that it would have some effective control on costs. This has not proved to be the case and we now object most strongly to Government interference and the additional work involved in dealing with the price control system, which impedes commercial decisions. Our private enterprise view is that competition is an adequate price control and that efficiency and effort should be rewarded by profits and return on investments. We are very concerned to see price control being operated as profit control and, at the same time, wage and salary costs out of control.

"Our concern with increasing costs and severe competition in many areas makes unwise any forecast. But we have the abilities required for progress. Our company is now more involved in the carpet trade and we shall have to take more risks in marketing our products, with considerable promotional expenses. Demand continues to rise, but so does competition. Our future is closely tied to the national economies, both at home and in Britain. We plan for expansion, and there will be no letup in our efforts to increase our productivity. . . .

"I think we are going to have a very difficult time for two years, as already there is a high inflation rate built into wages in this country in 1971 and I expect that we shall see some hardship developing as companies retract or go out of business. I look forward to there being little more sense by 1972, but we must make sure that we survive and solve our own problems, many of which are of our own making. I believe that when we have completed the reorganization in which we are now involved we shall once again have an efficient factory, but it is going to be a real struggle to overcome the drift which we have permitted in the past few years.

"More opportunities for exporting in 1971 may be provided if we can regain our relative competitiveness. There are too many uncertainties to forecast the future, but we are reacting constructively to the adversities which we face and are confident that in time we shall overcome them. We have the ability to regain a satisfactory level of profits and to further expand the company if we are given a workable opportunity in a more stable economic environment."

APPENDIX A
ROPE MANUFACTURE

Ropemaking was an ancient art. Sailing ships had once been the principal users of rope, and in their day ropemaking had flourished. With their passing many ropemaking firms had gone out of existence. In 1970, the relatively few remaining ropemaking firms had standardized the ropemaking process, using machines which were virtually identical. These were textile machines which were capable of handling hard, heavy fibers.

Basically, the process of ropemaking was the same everywhere. The sisal fiber, as it was received in 560-pound bales, varied as to thickness and the individual length of the fibers. These were blended into a uniform distribution by passing them through a series of combing and carding machines which straightened the fibers, laid them parallel, and staggered the ends so that there was a continuous overlap. From its initial tangled state in the bale the fiber came out of these "goods" machines in a continuous ribbon known as a "sliver." The first goods machine produced a sliver as thick as a man's thigh. This was gradually reduced by successive combings through a series of goods machines culminating in a finished smooth, level ribbon less than an inch wide. During the process the fibers were sprayed with an oil-and-water emulsion which softened the fibers and made them more pliable, prevented damage to them during the fabricating process, and acted as a preservant in the later life of the rope, giving it water-repellency and making it resistant to rot and mildew.

From the goods machines the fibers went to the spinning machines. Here the finished sliver was once more attenuated to make it more slender, and by twisting it was converted from a ribbon into a cylindrical form in which the fibers were compressed against each other. This twisted assemblage of fibers, called "yarn," was the first basic component part of a rope. The compression of the fibers from the twisting resulted in a friction between the fiber surfaces which held each fiber in place when under tension.

The finished yarns were then twisted together to form a strand. Depending on the finished rope desired, a strand might require anywhere from two to several hundred yarns. The final operation, known as "laying" a rope, consisted of twisting three or four strands together. Three or four ropes laid together formed a cable. In each successive twisting operation the twists were in the opposite direction. Cordage, the ropes used for such purposes as clotheslines and lariats, was formed by braiding the strands together.

APPENDIX B
SISAL

Sisal was a fiber obtained from the plant Agave Sisalana, most of which was grown in East Africa. On the plantation the fibers were beaten out of the leaf tissues which contained them—a process known as "decortication"—and the hanks of fiber were hung in the sun to dry. Some of it was dried artificially by machines. For its rope and cordage requirements Irish Ropes bought sun-dried sisal from some sixty different estates, through a single agent.

A typical sisal yarn was spun by twisting together about fifty fibers, and the yarns in turn were twisted into strands. In the technology of ropemaking it was known that higher tensile strength and regularity could be achieved in the finished cordage if thinner fibers and thinner strands, and more of them, were used to form a cord. Thus, four thin yarns produced considerably higher performance qualities than two thick ones.

In the interest of securing high-quality materials, Mr. Eric Rigby-Jones in his day had visited Tanganyika,[3] and there he recognized the possibilities of spinning fine yarns from sisal. Sisal fibers varied in thickness depending on the age of the plant at the time of cutting, the first cutting of young sisal producing fibers which, although shorter, were much thinner. These fine fibers had previously been blended into the total mix. Mr. Eric Rigby-Jones made arrangements to purchase fine fibers as a separately graded classification. These fine fibers were used to produce light twine of high tensile strength and a few side products of Irish Ropes, such as fine, soft webbing and light sisal cloth used for buffing and filter cloths.

Sun-dried sisal varied considerably in natural color, in hues that ranged from white to golden buff. In rope production this had no significance, but for purposes of color control in the making of Tintawn carpeting, the delicate hues and brilliant shades required a natural color that was as white and as uniform as possible.

The fineness of the fiber also had a direct effect upon the dyeing. No dye penetrated into the sisal fibers, but the dye only spread itself upon the surface. Since coarse fibers had less total surface to receive the dye than the fine fibers, a heavier coating and a deeper shade would result from the application of the same amount of dye. The grade and the fineness of fiber, therefore, became a critical matter in color control.

[3] Now Tanzania.

exhibit 5   IRISH ROPES LIMITED
Balance sheet as at 31st August 1970

	Authorised	1970 Issued and Fully Paid £	Authorised	1969 Issued and Fully Paid £
Share Capital				
75,000 6% Cumulative Preference Shares of £1 each	75,000	60,000	75,000	60,000
3,000,000 Ordinary Shares of 5/– each	750,000	420,000	750,000	420,000
	825,000	480,000	825,000	480,000
Surplus and Reserves				
Capital Reserve. See Note 5		253,050		214,100
Revenue Reserves				
Reserve for Contingencies. See Note 7	—		313,000	
Stock Reserve See Note 7	—		66,000	
Replacement Reserve See Note 7	—		55,000	
Bad Debts Reserve See Note 7	—		10,000	
General Reserve See Note 7	833,363		—	
Profit and Loss Account	61,489	894,852	25,499	469,499
Future Taxation				
Estimated Income Tax Schedule D 1971/72	23,890		—	
Tax Equalisation. See Note 3	82,000	105,890	92,000	92,000
		£1,733,792		£1,255,599

	Cost	1970 Depreciation to Date £		Cost	1969 Depreciation to Date £	
Fixed Assets						
Property and Buildings. See Note 1	420,374	—	420,374	381,011	178,363	202,648
Plant, Machinery, and Motor Vehicles. See Note 2	992,594	629,912	362,682	932,824	781,289	151,535
	1,412,968	629,912	783,056	1,313,835	959,652	354,183
Interests in Subsidiaries						
Shareholdings at Cost		15,618			15,618	
Current Accounts		503,813	519,431		540,246	555,864
Current Assets						
Stock in Trade at Cost or Net Realisable value	481,525			403,418		
Sundry Debtors and Debit Balances	516,238			477,589		
Taxation Recoverable	2,916			—		
Cash in Hands	370,138	1,370,817		866	881,873	
Less: Current Liabilities						
Sundry Creditors and Accrued Charges	350,668			247,753		
Bank Overdraft	556,122			170,115		
Current Taxation	—			65,518		
Proposed Dividends (after deduction of Income Tax)	32,722	939,512		52,935	536,321	
Net Current Assets			431,305			345,552
			£1,733,792			£1,255,599

exhibit 6   IRISH ROPES LIMITED AND SUBSIDIARIES
Group balance sheet as at 31st August 1970

		1970 Issued and Fully Paid		1969 Issued and Fully Paid
	Authorised	£	Authorised	£
Share Capital				
75,000 6% Cumulative Preference Shares of £1 each	75,000	60,000	75,000	60,000
3,000,000 Ordinary Shares of 5/– each	750,000	420,000	750,000	420,000
	825,000	480,000	825,000	480,000
Surplus and Reserves				
Capital Reserve. See Note 5		253,050		214,100
Revenue Reserves				
Reserve for Contingencies. See Note 7	—		313,000	
Stock Reserve See Note 7	—		66,000	
Replacement Reserve See Note 7	—		55,000	
Bad Debts Reserve See Note 7	—		10,000	
General Reserve 'See Note 7	833,363		—	
Profit and Loss Account	51,543	884,906	32,497	476,497
Future Taxation				
Estimated Income Tax Schedule D 1971/72	27,738		—	
Tax Equalisation. See Note 3	82,000	109,738	92,000	92,000
		£1,727,694		£1,262,597

	Cost	1970 Depreciation to Date £		Cost	1969 Depreciation to Date £	
Fixed Assets						
Property and Buildings. See Note 1	420,374	—	420,374	381,011	178,363	202,648
Plant, Machinery, and Motor Vehicles. See Note 2	1,018,505	641,400	377,105	959,358	790,409	168,949
	1,438,879	641,400	797,479	1,340,369	968,772	371,597
Interest in Subsidiary			—			22,432
Current Assets						
Stock in Trade at Cost or Net Realisable value	733,955			749,645		
Sundry Debtors and Debit Balances	797,066			708,177		
Cash at Bank and in Hands	429,198	1,960,219		7,888	1,465,710	
Less: Current Liabilities						
Sundry Creditors and Accrued Charges	430,479			335,788		
Bank Overdraft	559,619			143,842		
Current Taxation	7,184			64,577		
Proposed Dividends (after deduction of Income Tax)	32,722	1,030,004		52,935	597,142	
Net Current Assets			930,215			868,568
			£1,727,694			£1,262,597

exhibit 7   IRISH ROPES LIMITED AND SUBSIDIARIES
Group profit and loss account for year ended 31st August 1970

	1970 £			1969 £	
Trading Profit/Loss Before Crediting	13,243			52,673	Loss
Decrease in Depreciation charge due to revised method of calculation. See Notes 1 and 2	46,384			—	
Trading Profit/Loss for the year	59,627			52,673	Loss

After Charging

	1970 £	1969 £
Directors' Emoluments:		
Fees	1,900	2,129
Other Emoluments	19,922	23,438
Provision of Pensions in respect of Executive Office	—	16,870
	21,822	42,437
Depreciation. See Notes 1 and 2	73,703	110,943
Auditors' Remuneration	2,400	2,400

Add: Net surplus on revision of basis of stock valuation		22,525		—	
		82,152		52,673	Loss
Deduct: Taxation on Profits for the year					
Income Tax	30,818		—		
Corporation Profits Tax	5,558		—		
U.K. Corporation Tax	2,542		—		
Taxation overprovided and Income Tax Recoverable	—		6,850		
Transfer from Tax Equalisation Reserve	(10,000)	28,918	—	6,850	
Group Profit/Loss after taxation, of which £70,178 (1969, £29,232 loss) is dealt with in the accounts of Irish Ropes Limited		53,234		45,823	Loss
Add: Balance forward from last year		32,497		74,860	
Transfer from Reserve for Contingencies		—		75,000	
Amount available for appropriation		£85,731		£104,037	
Appropriated as follows:					
Dividends for the year to date after deduction of Income Tax:					
6% Cumulative Preference Shares	2,688		2,940		
Ordinary Shares:					
Interim paid during the year	—		17,150		
Proposed final of 10%	31,500	34,188	51,450	71,540	
Balance Carried Forward to next year:					
Irish Ropes Limited	61,489		25,499		
Subsidiaries	(9,946)	51,543	6,998	32,497	
		£85,731		£104,037	

M Rigby-Jones
A Shiel
Directors

exhibit 8   GROUP STATISTICS

	1966	*1967*	*1968*	*1969*	*1970*
	£	£	£	£	£
Total sales	2,620,049	2,841,860	3,139,947	3,219,527	3,359,151
Home	1,085,587	1,209,087	1,202,446	1,442,535	1,613,661
Export	1,534,462	1,632,773	1,937,501	1,776,992	1,745,490
Trading Profit/Loss	237,874	262,209	278,737	(52,673)	13,243
Exceptional Items	—	—	—	—	68,909 (See 1)
Profit/Loss before taxation	237,874	262,209	278,737	(52,673)	82,152
Taxation	79,478	81,470	67,460	6,850 Cr.	28,918
Net profit/loss	158,396	180,739	211,277	(45,823)	53,234
Dividends	51,425	60,252	70,813	71,540	34,188
Retained profits	106,971	120,487	140,464	(117,363)	19,046 (See 2)
Total net assets	1,018,409	1,141,616	1,313,380	1,262,597	1,727,694
Net profit to total net assets employed	15.6%	15.8%	16.1%	—	3.1%
Number of employees	883	951	1,027	1,035	1,012

1. Exceptional items arise from:
    (*a*) change in basis for providing for depreciation,
    (*b*) change in methods of valuation of stock.

2. Changes in policy in relation to depreciation and provision for renewal have meant an accretion to net assets in 1970 of £389,363.

exhibit 9   NOTES ON ACCOUNTS

We have audited the annexed Balance Sheet and have obtained all the information and explanations which we considered necessary, except that owing to the closure of the banks we have been unable to obtain verification of the bank overdraft. Proper Books of Account have been kept and the Balance Sheet is in agreement therewith.

We have examined the annexed Group Balance Sheet and Group Profit and Loss Account. The Account of one of the Subsidiary Companies has been audited by another firm.

In our opinion the Balance Sheet and Group Accounts comply with the requirements of the Companies Act, 1963 and give respectively, in conjunction with the notes referred to, a true and fair view of the state of the Company's Affairs at the 31st August 1970 and a true and fair view of the State of Affairs and of the Profit of the Group.

Kennedy Crowley & Co
Chartered Accountants
69/71 St Stephen's Green
Dublin 2
16th November 1970

1. Property and Buildings were valued at 31st August 1970 on a reinstatement basis for insurance purposes at £1,670,000 by professional valuers. Arising from this valuation, no depreciation has been provided during the year (1969, £18,047). The cumulative depreciation on property and buildings to 31st August 1969 amounting to £178,363 has been transferred to General Reserve.

2. In previous years depreciation charges included amounts to provide for the increased cost of renewal of assets, the original cost of which had already been fully provided. No such provision has been included in the depreciation charge for the current year (1969, £28,117). The cumulative amount so provided to 31st August

exhibit 9   (continued)

1969 amounted to £262,087. Of this £51,087 has been utilised to write down particular assets the estimated useful lives of which have been revised and the balance
of £211,000 has been transferred to General Reserve.

3. Tax Equalisation represents estimated taxation deferred by initial allowances
on expenditure to 31st August 1970, at current rates of taxation.

4. Contracts for Capital Expenditure not provided for are estimated at £99,000
(1969, £26,500) for the Group.

5. Under Agreements between the Company and An Foras Tionscal, Grants of
£253,050 have been received or are receivable at 31st August 1970 (1969, £214,100).
There exists a contingent liability to repay in whole or in part the Grants received
if certain circumstances set out in the agreements occur before receipt of the final
instalment of the Grants or within ten years thereafter.

6. Overseas assets and liabilities have been converted at the middle rate of exchange at 31st August 1970.

7. Movements on Reserves

	£
General Reserve balance at 31st August 1969	
Transferred from:—	
Reserve for Contingencies	313,000
Stock Reserve	66,000
Replacement Reserve	55,000
Bad Debts Reserve	10,000
Depreciation on Property and Buildings to 31st August 1969	178,363
Excess depreciation on plant at 31st August 1969	211,000
General Reserve balance at 31st August 1970	833,363

34

ELGIN
NATIONAL
WATCH
COMPANY

INTRODUCTION

Elgin National Watch Company for the fiscal year ended February 28, 1962, experienced its most profitable year since 1957 and reported a net income of $1.4 million, equal to $1.52 per common share as contrasted with $114,000, or $.12 per share in the previous year. Net sales for the year amounted to $40.4 million, representing a gain of 21% over sales of $33.3 million for 1961. (See Exhibit 1.)

In reporting the improved performance of the company in the 1962 annual report, Mr. Margolis, chairman of the company and chief executive officer, stated that the improved earnings for the year reflected operating efficiencies, broadening of the product line, and profitable acquisitions. "Most of the increased income," he said, "came from the industrial group and other divisions in the consumer group." He continued:

> We have just completed the most successful year in the past six years of our long corporate history. The improved sales and profits picture reflects the beginning results of planned programs. Effective last March the company acquired the Welby Corporation and the Bradley Time Corporation, two clock companies with fine reputations and proved sales and earnings abilities. With the acquisition of Lohengrin Diamond Ring and its subsidiary, Syndicate Diamonds, last November, Elgin is provided with a prime source of diamonds for our watches as well as lines of diamond rings and related products that can be readily marketed through our present distributing channels.

exhibit 1 ELGIN NATIONAL WATCH COMPANY AND SUBSIDIARIES

Consolidated balance sheet

	2/28 1962	2/28 1961	2/28 1960	2/28 1959	2/28 1958	2/28 1957	2/28 1956	2/28 1955	2/28 1954	12/31 1953
Assets										
Cash	$ 1,029	$ 1,197	$ 1,626	$ 2,156	$ 2,490	$ 2,107	$ 2,357	$ 2,018	$ 2,119	$ 2,460
Marketable securities (+ accrued int.)	—	—	1,742	4,492	293	3,801	4,256	5,817	3,106	3,100
Accounts receivable (net)	9,163	8,513	7,948	5,505	6,621	9,114	9,681^b	6,926	8,036	15,051
Inventories, lower of cost (FIFO) or mkt.	13,132	11,149	10,288	8,475	12,418	14,343	15,471^b	14,679	18,094	16,380
Income tax refund	—	—	—	—	1,499	—	—^b	—	—	—
Invest. in govt. defense work (less prog. payments)	399	248	188	161	201	213	221	5,354	6,036	6,345
Prepaid insurance, etc.	—	—	—	—	—	—	—	217	173	220
Total current assets	$23,723	$21,107	$21,792	$20,789	$23,522	$29,578	$31,986	$35,011	$37,564	$43,556
Patents, less accum. amortization	—	—	—	—	10	99	114	106	—	—
Land, plant & equipment (cost)	13,516	12,956	12,577	—	16,061	17,526	17,109	16,362	15,293	15,191
Less accum. deprec. & amortization	8,304	7,816^c	7,613	—	9,892	9,340	8,488	8,031	7,444	7,340
Total capital assets	$ 5,212	$ 5,140	$ 4,964	$ 5,319	$ 6,169	$ 8,186	$ 8,621	$ 8,331	$ 7,849	$ 7,851
Total assets	$28,935	$26,247	$26,756	$26,108	$29,701	$37,863	$40,721	$43,448	$45,413	$51,407
Liabilities										
Accounts payable	$ 2,461	$ 1,251	$ 1,365	$ 929	$ 1,427	$ 1,170	$ 1,657	$ 1,946	$ 1,994	$ 1,902
Notes payable	600	600	600	500	500	500	500	300	3,850	10,250
Accruals (wages, etc.; pension contrib.)	2,279	1,643	1,663	1,437	1,656	2,001	2,247	2,726	3,112	2,174
Fed. inc. tax & other tax reserves	—	—	—	—	302	593	862	1,966	2,086	2,793
Dividends payable	—	—	—	—	—	137	137	502	137	—
Contractual price adjustment provs.	—	—	—	346	1,161	427	1,633	1,920	6	—
Provision for reloc. of operations	—	—	—	—	—	—	—	—	—	—
Total current liabilities	$ 5,340	$ 3,494	$ 3,628	$ 3,212	$ 5,064	$ 4,828	$ 7,128	$ 9,360	$11,185	$17,089
Reserve for casualty insurance	—	—	—	—	—	—	—	—	200	200
Long term notes payable	5,000^b	5,600^f	6,200^f	6,800	7,300	7,800	8,300	8,800	9,100	9,150
Capital stock	4,633	4,615	4,613	4,613	4,613	4,613	4,613	4,613	13,840	13,840
Paid-in surplus a	9,245	9,226	9,227	9,227	9,227	9,227	9,227	9,227^a	—	—
Earned surplus	4,717^e	3,309^e	3,196^e	2,370^e	3,629^e	11,509	11,567	11,562	11,214	11,257
Less treasury stock at cost	—	—	108	114	114	114	114	114	126	129
Total shareholders' equity	18,595	17,153	16,928	16,096	17,355	25,235	25,293	25,288	24,928	24,968
Total net worth & liability	28,935	26,247	26,756	26,108	29,701	37,863	40,721	43,448	45,413	51,407

a Paid-in capital arising from reduction in par value of capital stock (from $15 to $5).
b Includes Government defense operations.
c Includes provision for abandonment of machinery & equipment $523,505.
e Cash dividends restricted under long-term agreement. No dividends to be paid unless retained earnings exceed $5,153,400 after Dec. 30, 1954 plus $1,000,000 and working capital of at least $18,000,000.
f $600,000 due annually 1960–1964; $3,800,000 due in 1965.

ELGIN NATIONAL WATCH COMPANY AND SUBSIDIARIES
Consolidated Statement of Earnings

	3/1 1962	3/1 1961	3/1 1960	3/1 1959	2/28 1958	2/28 1957	2/28 1956	2/28 1955	2/28 1954	12/31 1953
Net sales	$40,429	$33,352	$30,973	$26,992	$31,123	$42,405	$51,477	$60,085	$7,012*	$56,721
Cost of goods sold	29,407	24,188	22,549	21,681	27,314	31,074	37,715	45,222	5,148*	39,958
Depreciation	580	516	487	471	760	828	822	668	115*	660
Advertis., selling & gen admin.	9,118	8,331	6,967	6,601	6,847	8,842	9,966	10,186	1,452*	10,752
Pension fund contribution	—[a]	—[a]	—[a]	—[a]	—[a]	—[a]	542	516	132*	807
Other income			76	148	127	92	138	185	16*	155
Interest expense & misc. chgs.	182	202	221	241	270	307	612	495	89*	720
Inc. before fed. inc. taxes	1,142	114	826	d1,761	d3,941	1,446	1,958	3,244	94*	3,979
Special charges/credits	265[b]				4,540[g]				—*	
Provision for fed. inco. taxes					cr.1,499	775	1,040	1,680		1,930
Net income (loss) after taxes	1,407[c]	114	826	d1,761	d6,982	671	918	1,564	94*	2,049
Special debit	—[e]	—[e]		cr.502[f]	578[h]			508[j]		
Earnings retained beginning of year	3,309[e]	3,196	2,370	3,629	11,507	11,567	11,562	11,414[k]	11,257*	10,383
Dividends (cash & stock)	—[e]	—[e]	—[e]	—[e]	319	730	913	909	137*	1,175[l]
Treasury stock at cost		108	108	114	114	114	114	114	126*	129
Retained earnings end of year	4,717[e]	3,309[e]	3,196[e]	2,370[e]	3,629	11,507	11,567	11,562	11,214*	11,257
Earnings per share	1.52	.12	.90	d1.93	d2.67	.74	1.01	1.71	.10*	1.76
Dividends per share					.35	.80	1.00	1.00	.15*	.60[l]

* Two months ending 2/28/54—Change in fiscal year ending from 12/31 to 2/28.
a No contribution made to the company's pension fund. Company states fund satisfactory.
b Recovery of costs and expenses charged to prior year's operation through settlement of contract claim.
c Tax-loss carry forward to 1964 amounted to $3,400,000 on 2/28/62; $5,000,000 on 2/28/61; $5,400,000 on 2/28/60.
e Cash dividends restricted under long-term debt agreement. No dividends to be paid unless consolidated retained earnings exceed $5,153,410 after Dec. 30, 1950 plus $1,000,000 and working capital of at least $18,000,000.
f Previous year's tax refund.
g Special charge. For relocation of operations $1,440,000; abandoned machinery & equipment $1,400,000; inventory write-off $1,200,000; liquidation of watch case & microphone operations $500,000.
h Provision for federal income taxes of previous years & for loss of future tax benefits applicable to vacation accruals.
j Provision for vacation pay earned prior to 3/1/54, net of applicable tax credit of $550,000.
k Includes $200,000 reserve for casualty insurance restored to retained earnings.
l Cash at the rate of $.60 per share ($541,000); stock-one share for twenty—42,287 shares at par value of $15 each ($634,000).

He stated further that the watch division historically had been plagued with the problem of high operating costs which stemmed in part from an outmoded plant built at the turn of the century, and in part from foreign competition. He pointed out that in order to meet this problem the board of directors had decided to sell the main Elgin plant contingent on "the appropriateness of the selling price" and to institute a pilot assembly watch plant somewhere in the South so as "to provide Elgin National Watch Company with greater flexibility in the marketplace to meet the severe international competition in the watch industry."

Mr. Margolis also voiced concern over President Kennedy's tariff program and its impact on the watch manufacturing industry. He conceded that "if the administration determined that lowered tariffs were best for the country, Elgin must go along." But he questioned the soundness of the program and urged that Congress and the President "reconsider the importance of watchmaking skills in the national defense."

In his report to the shareholders in 1961, Mr. Margolis stated:

> The American watch industry cannot operate any longer as an isolated force within the domestic market. In addition to the traditional competition of the Swiss, the American watch industry is now faced with intense competition from the French, the Germans, the Japanese and most recently, from the Russians. The rash of cheap products made abroad and domestically has confused the public, downgraded values, downgraded quality and the industry. After evaluating both the nature of the economy and of the competition, management of your company has embarked on a program of . . . aggressive marketing and diversifying into fields geared to the space age.

He emphasized also that the company would continue to adhere to two basic tenets: support of the jeweler, and dominance of quality over price. He closed his remarks by stating that "Elgin will seek to offset inordinately low wage costs of foreign nations through high productivity gained from efficient plant and equipment and cooperation of workers utilizing newer techniques and efficient planning."

Mr. Margolis, Elgin's chief executive officer, took over the day-to-day running of the company in May, 1962, when his appointment, Mr. Robert O. Fickes, resigned as president of the company over ". . . differences of policy as to the future direction the company will take." Mr. Fickes, who had served in various executive capacities with General Electric for more than thirty years, had been president of Elgin National Watch Company for thirteen months. In discussing Mr. Fickes' resignation, Mr. Margolis acknowledged that the latter had accelerated the long-range plans designed to cut costs and improve efficiency—including the automation of certain manufacturing operations at the Elgin, Illinois, watch plant. Mr. Margolis also remarked that at the time that Mr. Fickes had taken over the reins of the company, Elgin had been moving toward a "rather cumbersome decentralization of management" which he and Mr. Fickes felt had led the company to "slow decision-making" and an unnecessary "diffusion of responsibilities." Messrs. Fickes and Margolis reorganized the operations and established long-range objectives calling for the "expansion of industrial products sufficiently so that they would contribute about one-half of the sales volume."

CORPORATE DEVELOPMENT AND BACKGROUND

The company was originally incorporated in 1864 as the National Watch Company, but because the firm became so closely identified with the village of Elgin its name was changed shortly after 1900 to Elgin National Watch Company. Since its founding Elgin had been one of the best known watch manufacturers and had enjoyed the prestige of building the finest watch in America. The company produced its watch movements at a plant in Elgin, Illinois, and also at a plant in Lincoln, Nebraska, until the latter was sold in 1958. Elgin also produced its own fashion components up until 1958; watch cases were produced by its subsidiary, the Wadsworth Watch Case Company, Dayton, Kentucky; and watchbands by another subsidiary, the Hadley Company, Inc., Providence, Rhode Island.

Elgin had also operated an observatory where time was measured from the stars. This practice was discontinued in 1960 with the perfection of electronic timing devices. In addition, the company for many years ran the Elgin Watchmakers' College in order to provide its retail outlets with an assured supply of competent watch repairmen (known as watchmakers), and to train its retailers in jewelry repair, engraving, ordering of materials, and store management. This operation was also discontinued in 1960.

Elgin's market was greatly curtailed during World War II and the Korean War when the company devoted nearly all of its efforts to war production. During this period Swiss watches flooded the American market and gained acceptance. In an effort to alleviate this problem Elgin, along with other watchmakers, attempted during the 1950's to obtain relief from foreign competition by lobbying for protective tariffs on the basis that the watchmaking industry was essential for the national defense.

The company also recognized that another of its major problems stemmed from the fact that its watch sales were sensitive to changes in disposable income. For example, in the years in which personal income declined 10%, Elgin's sales often slipped 20% to 30%. Elgin's management attributed this to the fact that consumer expenditures for watches usually were considered a luxury and therefore postponable.

DIVERSIFICATION

Early in 1953, as the result of an intensive study made by management and aided by outside consultants, Elgin decided to undertake a program of diversification to offset its declining share of the watch market. Its stated objectives were to satisfy these corporate goals:

Expansion. The watch business had become essentially a replacement business. According to the consultants who advised Elgin, the average annual rate of growth for all firms in the watch industry from 1940 to 1951 was 5%. Elgin's rate was 4.38% and its share of the market was declining, due mainly to imports. As Elgin increased its import of watch movements, it created an additional problem of plant utilization. In 1953 watch production was only 75% of capacity; by 1961 it constituted less than 50%.

Improved Return on the Investment of Its Shareholders. The unit cost of watch movements rose from $5.10 in 1941 to $11.05 in 1951, and despite a substantial increase in manufacturing efficiency in the next decade, unit cost remained approximately at that level. The primary cause for the increased unit cost was labor, which rose from $.61 an hour in 1941 to $2.48 an hour in 1962. Elgin's average return (net income to net worth) was 7.7% for the period from 1946 to 1952, whereas the return from all manufacturing came to 15%.

Greater Stability in Long-term Operations. Since Elgin's watch sales were sensitive to changes in disposable income, the consultants advised the company to diversify into products less sensitive to disposable income or which moved in different or contrasting cycles. Following these principles, Elgin initially selected two fields which it believed were well adapted to the company's specialized talents—miniature electronics and precision production instruments. Later diversification brought the company into development of communications systems and equipment.

a. Miniature Electronics. This field included small specialized electronic components of a mechanical, electro-mechanical, and electronic nature. It also involved semi-conductors, capacitors, vibrators, resistors, printed circuits, and specialized batteries. Highly competitive radio parts were not included in the field. The consultants reported that electronics sales had risen from $600 million in 1946 to more than $4.3 billion in 1952. The industry had broad product markets in consumer, industrial, and governmental fields. Miniaturization was a basic trend in portable radios, hearing aids, guided missiles, ammunition, and communications equipment.

b. Precision Product Instruments. This field included mechanical, electrical, and electro-mechanical measuring and controlling instruments. The instruments measured, indicated, recorded, and controlled such factors as composition, optical properties, thickness and temperature, speed, fluid flow, and pressure. Elgin's interest was in instruments having high precision requirements. Elgin's consultants reported that the industry had enjoyed an annual growth rate of 21% during the 1946–1952 period, compared to an annual growth rate of 8% in gross national product and 6% growth in industrial plant and equipment. This increase had resulted from factors which had forced automatic production methods upon industry thereby increasing wage rates, demand for better quality, and production speeds surpassing human ability to control. The automatic instruments industry was generally considered to be on the threshold of major expansion. Members of Elgin's management believed that the company would make a special contribution in areas too intricate for manufacturers not experienced in highly precise operations which involved microscopic tolerances and the most complex assemblies.

c. Communications Systems and Equipment. This area included activities related to the design, development, production and installation of advanced communications equipment, such as advanced telephone and telegraph switching equipment, multiplex digital data handling, and other advanced communication equipment utilizing solid state and magnetic logic techniques.

After examining some 70 companies and 45 products, the first tangible results of Elgin's diversification program occurred with the cash acquisition in October, 1954, of Neomatic, Inc. (renamed Elgin-Neomatic, Inc.), Los Angeles, California, specialists in the design and manufacture of subminiature relays for guided missiles, aircraft, and mobile communications equipment. In March, 1955, Elgin acquired the American Microphone Company, Pasadena, California, manufacturers of microphones, phonograph pickups, cartridges, and related products, and the Advance Electric & Relay Company, Burbank, California, a leading relay producer.

With the purchase of these new companies Elgin's business fell into two main areas: *consumer products* manufactured and sold by the Elgin Watch Division, The Wadsworth-Hadley Division, and the Elgin Watch Company Ltd.; and *industrial products* manufactured by the Abrasives Division (later changed to Precision Products Division), the Electronics Division (later changed to the Controls Division), and the Micronics Division. With the successful bidding on a Navy high-speed teleprinter contract in 1961, a Communications Division was added to the industrial group. In 1961 the company purchased the Bradley Time Corporation, the Welby Corporation, and the Lohengrin Diamond Ring Company, each of which was added as a division to the consumer group, replacing the Wadsworth-Hadley Division. (See Exhibit 2.)

When the company undertook its diversification program in 1953, Mr. Joseph W. LaBine, Elgin's director of public relations, thought that shareholder and financial community relations were matters of first concern. "One of the basic jobs in our diversification program," he stated, "is that of improving the market value of our shares which currently sell for about half of their book value—a situation that presents a real problem should we ever be interested in diversifying through an exchange-of-stock transaction. The market price of our shares has been depressed in part by our record of low dividends and in part by unfavorable publicity incident to the tariff fight, in which we were in the unpleasant position of having to publicize a competitive problem that appeared to indicate financial insecurity." He noted that 62% of the shareholders, who owned 75% of the stock, lived in Elgin and the Chicago area; over 1,000 of these shareholders lived within the city of Elgin proper. The average holder had about 220 shares, and 645 employees owned 103,045 shares.

exhibit 2
ELGIN NATIONAL WATCH COMPANY
Organization Chart

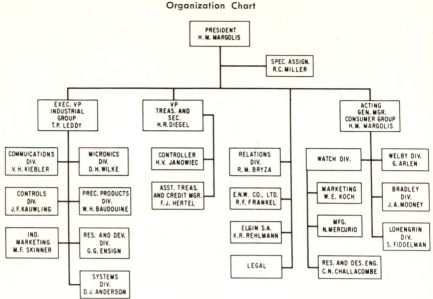

In June, 1954, the company reduced the par value of its shares from $15 to $5 and had received an authorization to issue 300,000 new shares on which shareholders waived their preemptive rights.

THE CHANGING WATCH MARKET

Management recognized the marked shift in the sale of watches over the years. Total watch sales had increased, but since 1932 there had been a shift away from pin-lever [1] watches to jewel watches. However, domestic watch manufacturers did not benefit from this increase. During and after World War II the added jeweled watch sales consisted mainly of large increases in imported Swiss watches. The switchover came as a result of World War II when the domestic watch manufacturers turned their facilities almost entirely to war work. The Swiss, who were neutral, made watches and were permitted by the Germans to export them. Swiss watches flooded the U.S. domestic

[1] A pin-lever watch is constructed without the use of jewels as bearings. This is the typical construction in watches retailing for less than $15.

market and acquired wide public approval and acceptance. Swiss watches were generally moderately priced, came in a large variety of case designs, and, with their more rapid turnover, brought larger profits to the retail jeweler. In 1944 total domestic watch sales of all kinds fell to an all-time low of 200,000 units, most of which came from prewar inventory.

SWISS COMPETITION AND TARIFFS

When the war was over the American jeweled manufacturers had no backlog of civilian orders and only three companies still manufactured most of their jeweled movements within the United States—Elgin, Hamilton, and Waltham. Bulova produced some movements domestically, but 70% of the watches sold under the Bulova name were manufactured in a plant owned and operated by the company in Switzerland. The three watch manufacturers formed the American Watch Manufacturers Association in an effort to obtain tariff protection on movements with 17 jewels or less. It was their contention that the human skills necessary for the making of precision instruments were essential for the country's defense.

In 1952 Elgin entered the low-priced watch field by importing Swiss movements, casing them, and selling them under the Wadsworth name, but was unable to capture more than 3% of the "under $30" market in any year. Prior to this time Elgin relied entirely on domestic watch production. But in 1954 it began importing for sale, under the Elgin name, certain Swiss specialty watches—mostly automatic or self-winding—which the management felt would round out the Elgin line but which, in its opinion, promised such low sales volume that it was not practical for the company to manufacture them in its own facilities.

Under the Tariff Act of 1930 the tariff on imported movements with 17 jewels or less ranged from $2.50 to $4.00; above 17 jewels the tariff was $10.75 per watch movement. In 1936 the United States signed a reciprocal trade agreement with Switzerland and lowered its tariffs on imports of watches. The new rates ranged from $1.80 to $2.70 on imported movements with 17 jewels or less, and no change in the rate on watches with movements above 17 jewels. The net effect of the reduced tariffs was that movements with 17 or fewer jewels, representing 99% of all movement imports, could be landed in the

U.S. at a duty-paid cost which was 25% less than the cost of making comparable watch movements in this country. The change in tariffs was followed by a further decline in the American manufacturers' participation in their own market, which had dropped from 52% of all jeweled timepieces sold in the United States in 1930 to approximately 38% of the market at the beginning of World War II, and to less than 20% during World War II. (See Exhibit 3.) Elgin, along with other American watchmakers, sought the protection of the higher tariffs by resorting to production of higher-jeweled and consequently higher-priced watches. Neither Elgin nor any other domestic watchmaker turned out a jeweled watch with fewer than 17 jewels after 1953.

Practically all watch movements imported in 1954 came from Switzerland. Moreover, the Swiss supplied 95% of the world market. Unlike many foreign industries which were inefficient by American standards, Swiss watchmakers were skilled craftsmen using efficient production techniques. Modern Swiss methods and machinery were adaptations of the so-called "American system." Late in the nineteenth century, American watchmaking machinery was freely exported to Switzerland and the Swiss horological industry was almost completely revamped.

The Swiss industry was rigidly regulated by Swiss federal legislation under which prices, the number of workers engaged in the industry, many aspects of trade relations, and even the right to engage in production were government controlled. There were restrictions on the exportation of watchmaking machinery and the furnishing of technical advice to foreign watchmaking enterprises. In addition, the Swiss government levied a tax of one franc against each jeweled watch movement exported. This tax produced a fund of about $15 million annually and was used for institutional advertising of Swiss watches.

The cost of a Swiss movement was about one-half that of an American-made movement, according to an Elgin official. One of the major reasons for this was the fact that the Swiss industry's labor rate was almost 60% lower than U.S. wage rates for comparable jobs, and labor constituted approximately 80% of the cost of making a watch movement. This differential had been increasing through the years. In 1936, when the reciprocal trade agreement with Switzerland had been negotiated, the Swiss advantage had been only 50%.

Until 1951 the trade agreement with Switzerland contained no

exhibit **3** **COMPARISON OF SALES OF DOMESTIC AND IMPORTED JEWELED-LEVER WATCHES IN THE UNITED STATES**
5-year moving average 1926–55, annual 1946–1961 (in thousands of units)

Period or Year	Total Domestic Jeweled-lever Watches		Total Imported Jeweled-lever Watches		Total Jeweled-lever Watches	
	Units	%	Units	%	Units	%
Average						
1926–1930	1,787	39.0	2,780	61.0	4,567	100.0
1931–1935	778	51.6	730	48.4	1,508	100.0
1936–1940	1,652	38.5	2,639	61.5	4,291	100.0
1941–1945	1,561	19.6	6,404	80.4	7,965	100.0
1946–1950	2,379	24.6	7,303	75.4	9,682	100.0
1951–1955	2,249	21.9	8,017	78.1	10,266	100.0
Annual						
1946	1,678	16.7	8,347	83.3	10,025	100.0
1947	2,280	24.9	6,873	75.1	9,153	100.0
1948	2,918	28.5	7,332	71.4	10,250	100.0
1949	2,620	29.1	6,367	70.9	8,987	100.0
1950	2,398	24.0	7,594	76.0	9,992	100.0
1951	3,093	26.1	8,759	73.9	11,852	100.0
1952	2,312	21.2	8,607	78.8	10,919	100.0
1953	2,301	19.3	9,613	80.7	11,914	100.0
1954	1,670	19.1	7,045	80.9	8,715	100.0
1955	1,871	23.6	6,062	76.4	7,933	100.0
1956	1,996	22.4	6,904	77.6	8,900	100.0
1957	1,453	17.4	6,910	82.6	8,363	100.0
1958	917	14.1	5,581	85.9	6,498	100.0
1959	1,574	18.2	7,068	81.8	8,642	100.0
1960	NA	—	6,846	—	NA	—
1961	NA	—	6,928	—	NA	—

SOURCE: U.S. Tariff Commission, *Reports on Watch Movements*, 1956 and 1962.

"escape clause" whereby either party nation could raise or lower tariffs on individual items without affecting the rates on all items in the trade agreement. The Trade Expansion Act of 1951 included an escape clause in connection with a year-to-year extension of the trade agreement to provide relief in the form of increased import duties if articles being imported into the United States seriously affected an industry. As a result of this provision several governmental agencies and investigating committees, including the Tariff Commission, recommended relief for the United States watch industry. President Eisenhower's action in raising tariffs 50% in July, 1954, climaxed a ten-year effort on the part of Elgin to secure protection for the jeweled watch industry. The 1954 increase in tariff ranged from $.09 on 1-jewel watches to $1.15 on 17-jewel watches and averaged about $1 per unit. There was no increase in tariffs on watches containing more than 17 jewels and in no instance did the new tariff schedule exceed the original rates set in the Tariff Act of 1930. (See Exhibit 4.)

The immediate impact of the 1954 increase in tariffs was a reduction in total import units, a decrease in market share of imported watches sold from approximately 59% in 1953 to 53% in 1955, and an increase in the retail price of such units. (See Exhibit 5.) A watch which formerly had been imported for a duty-paid cost of $8 sold to a dealer for

exhibit 4   RATES OF DUTY UNDER THE TARIFF ACTS OF 1930, 1936, AND 1954

	Tariff Rates		
Item	*1930*	*1936*	*1954*
Watch movements less than 1.77 inches wide:			
Having more than 17 jewels	$10.75	$10.75	$10.75
Having 2 to 17 jewels	1.25–2.50	0.90–1.80	1.25–2.50
Having no jewels or only 1 jewel	0.75–1.50	0.75–0.90	0.75–1.35
Additional duties on watches with 17 jewels or less:			
For each jewel in excess of 7	0.15	0.09	0.135
For each adjustment	1.00	0.50	0.50
Self-winding, or designed to operate in excess of 47 hours without rewinding	1.00	0.50	0.50

SOURCE: U.S. Tariff Commission, *Report on Watch Movements*, 1958, p. 21.

exhibit 5   COMPARISON OF SALES OF DOMESTIC AND IMPORTED WATCHES IN
THE UNITED STATES
5-year moving average 1926–55, annual 1946–1961 (in thousands of units)

Period or Year	Total Domestic Watches		Total Imported Watches		Total All Watches	
	Units	%	Units	%	Units	%
Average						
1926–1930	9,836	71.4	3,937	28.6	13,773	100.0
1931–1935	7,252	90.4	771	9.6	8,023	100.0
1936–1940	11,100	79.6	2,838	20.4	13,938	100.0
1941–1945	4,888	42.0	6,739	58.0	11,627	100.0
1946–1950	9,978	55.0	8,168	45.0	18,146	100.0
1951–1955	8,741	45.6	10,426	54.4	19,167	100.0
Annual						
1946	6,378	42.1	8,765	57.9	15,143	100.0
1947	11,104	60.8	7,173	39.2	18,277	100.0
1948	13,936	62.3	8,447	37.7	22,383	100.0
1949	8,810	53.9	7,527	46.1	16,337	100.0
1950	9,659	51.9	8,927	48.1	18,586	100.0
1951	11,422	50.9	11,007	49.1	22,429	100.0
1952	8,361	43.5	10,877	56.5	19,238	100.0
1953	8,337	41.2	11,875	58.8	20,212	100.0
1954	7,183	44.3	9,017	55.7	16,200	100.0
1955	8,358	47.2	9,355	52.8	17,713	100.0
1956	9,286	43.1	12,262	56.9	21,548	100.0
1957	7,782	38.9	12,243	61.1	20,025	100.0
1958	9,448	47.6	10,387	52.4	19,835	100.0
1959	11,282	45.6	13,472	54.4	24,754	100.0
1960	9,407	42.1	13,158	57.9	22,565	100.0
1961	9,689	43.4	12,627	56.6	22,316	100.0

SOURCE: U.S. Tariff Commission, *Reports on Watch Movements*, 1956 and 1962.

$12 and retailed for $23.95. A $1 increase in the tariff meant that the
import price increased to $9, the dealer price became $13.50, and the
watch retailed at $26.95.

In addition to the increased price and reduction in imported movements there was a significant shift in the composition of imports

away from the movements containing 16 and 17 jewels toward pin-lever movements containing no jewels, or movements containing but one jewel. (See Exhibit 6.) "The President's action is a boon to national security and to the business prospects of the American jeweled watch industry," said Mr. James G. Shennan, who was president of Elgin at the time. "So far as Elgin is concerned, we believe that the new tariff schedule will permit us to resume profitable operation of our domestic watchmaking facilities and to increase our sales by serving a larger segment of the jeweled watch market. This in turn will provide the broader mobilization base which the government believes to be essential for national security."

In 1957 imported watches regained their share of the U.S. market and constituted more than 61% of the watches sold in the United States. Although in the following year there was an increase in the number of domestic watches sold, the number of imported watches continued to increase and leveled off at approximately 57% of the U.S. market over the next four years.

INDUSTRY BACKGROUND

The American watch industry consisted of three types of firms. One manufactured jeweled-lever watches made wholly, or almost wholly, of domestic materials. These firms specialized in jeweled timepieces of quality. The second manufactured pin-lever or "clock-type" watches, most of which were non-jeweled and made primarily of domestic materials. Pin-lever watchmakers usually made clocks and other types of timing instruments. Firms of the third type were generally called assemblers. They imported movements, jeweled and non-jeweled, cased them in domestically manufactured cases, attached straps, and then packaged the watches for retail sale.

In the jeweled-lever watch field, in 1962, there were over 100 companies preparing finished watches. The major concerns were Elgin, Hamilton, Benrus, Bulova, Gruen, and Longines-Wittnauer. Of these, only two manufactured most of their jeweled movements within the United States—Elgin and Hamilton. Bulova produced some movements in this country but 70% of the watches sold under the Bulova name were manufactured in a plant owned and operated by the company in Switzerland. Elgin, Hamilton, and Bulova, as members of the American Watch Manufacturers' Association, consistently pushed for higher

exhibit 6 COMPARISON OF IMPORTED WATCH
MOVEMENTS, BY JEWEL COUNT
For the years 1946–1961 (in thousands of units)

Year	Movements Containing 0–1 Jewel	Movements Containing 16–17 Jewels
1946	618	6,226
1947	401	5,300
1948	1,215	5,577
1949	1,260	4,959
1950	1,433	5,868
1951	2,448	6,757
1952	2,470	7,060
1953	2,752	8,432
1954	2,532	6,217
1955	3,866	5,599
1956	5,986	6,177
1957	5,805	6,222
1958	5,294	4,692
1959	6,990	6,082
1960	7,085	5,971
1961	6,792	5,790

SOURCE: U.S. Tariff Commission, *Reports on Watch Movements*, 1956 and 1962.

protective tariffs. They consistently reaffirmed their stand that the industry was essential to the national defense. A second organization, The American Watch Association, was established by Longines-Wittnauer, Gruen, Benrus, and the other jeweled-lever watch companies who imported Swiss movements. This organization voiced opposition to higher tariffs and took the position that watchmaking skills were not essential to the national defense.

In the pin-lever watch field, in 1962, there were only four companies —U.S. Time Corporation, General Time Corporation, E. Ingraham Company, and The New Haven Clock and Watch Company. The New Haven Clock and Watch Company, which went into receivership in December, 1956, had all but eliminated its production of movements. By far the largest number of firms were engaged in watch assembly, i.e., in the casing, boxing, timing, and marketing of imported movements, mostly in jeweled counts of 17 or less.

DESIGN

At the time of the first World War, a revolution occurred in watch fashions—watches came out of the pocket and onto the wrist. Shortly thereafter women's wrist watches appeared. In the 1920's Elgin switched its production from 90% pocket to 90% wrist watches and gradually placed emphasis on styling. Watches grew smaller and thinner, and the old unwritten law that watches had to be round passed away. Except for the highly-jeweled pocket watches, the split-second accuracy of the older watch became unimportant, for anyone could learn the exact time by turning on the radio. No real merchandising program was initiated until the 1920's when Elgin began designing and producing its own cases and dials for its new line of wrist watches. Style was featured in national advertising.

"Our company is staking a large part of its future on the eye appeal of its products," stated Mr. William V. Judson, Elgin's director of design in 1947. "Elgin quality is well known. The performance of an Elgin watch is taken for granted. But today a watch must have something more than a fine and trusted movement. If a watch is to move from the jeweler's showcase to the customer's wrist, it must have good appearance. It must be well styled."

To regain and strengthen its market position, Elgin made four market surveys of the retail watch market in 1947 in the form of questionnaires in the *Saturday Evening Post*. From 136,000 responses received, the company was convinced that the American watch industry was failing to keep up with contemporary fashion designs. As it affected its own product, Elgin found that (1) its watches appealed to people over forty, (2) its watches had less allure to the growing younger market than others, (3) its lady's wrist watches were too big, and (4) the better grade Swiss watches with which Elgin competed had greater style acceptance.

Based on these findings, a campaign aimed at capturing more widespread consumer acceptance was launched. Elgin hired fifteen designers from the country's leading art schools and started its own design training school. The company broke with the tradition of following foreign leadership in design, chose six new designs through free-lance competition, and to keep its line fresh, thereafter introduced about 40 new models each year. In 1962 it had about 250 models in its entire line.

New design development and retooling were costly. Retooling costs for each new model ranged from $4,000 to $15,000. In 1950 Elgin spent approximately $350,000 on designing, and continued its expenditure at this rate for the next 12 years in an effort to assure its continued leadership in design. As one official remarked, "The company's aim was to achieve integrated design, which meant that everything having to do with the appearance of the watch had to harmonize. Case, dial, numerals and markers, hands, crystals, strap, cord, and even the package and the price tag had to belong together." He mentioned that price presented a real problem in design, and emphasized that the problem was one of designing a balanced line—a line including watches to be sold at different levels: Elgins, Elgin 19's, Lord and Lady Elgins, and diamond watches.

MARKETING

Prior to World War II the standard pattern of distribution for American jeweled watch manufacturers had been to sell to wholesale jewelers and to have several contact men call on large retailers. Elgin used these channels and had the same scale of markups as other leading jeweled lever producers—20% to 25% to the wholesaler, after which the retailer took 80% to 100%. This had been Elgin's sales pattern for 82 years. In 1946, however, after examining surveys which had shown that 90% of all Elgin watches had been purchased at jewelry stores, the company changed its distribution system by eliminating wholesalers and selling directly to jeweler retailers.

Under the new distribution system the country was divided into six geographical sales regions, each headed by a regional sales manager who reported to the general sales manager at Elgin. Where previously the company had only 72 wholesalers, it now sold to thousands of retailers. In 1946 Elgin had 31 "missionaries" who made goodwill calls. Six years later it had a nation-wide staff of trained salesmen. In 1962 its staff of 66 salesmen sold direct to about 17,000 active accounts. Each salesman had between 250 and 300 accounts. Salesmen called on the typical account four times a year; they called more frequently on the larger accounts, some as often as once a month. In areas where a small account was inconveniently located, a salesman might not call on it more than once a year.

Elgin consistently spent large amounts on its advertising. Initially, advertisements were carried in papers and magazines. When television became a national communication media, Elgin became a heavy user and ranked first or second in terms of dollars spent on TV advertising in the industry annually. In addition, the company consistently advertised in *Life, Look, Time, Sports Illustrated, Fortune,* and *National Geographic.* Lesser amounts were spent in radio advertising, mostly on a local basis. Elgin also had a full scale point of purchase program with displays and direct mail pieces for the jeweler.

Despite the severe foreign competition, Elgin's sales had increased significantly during the early 1950's and reached a peak of $60 million in 1955, with net income over $2 million in 1954. But when sales fell to $26 million in 1959, and when losses of $7 million and $1.8 million were suffered in 1958 and 1959, Elgin officials recognized that the company had lost a major share of the watch market, and instituted an evaluation of its product and distribution policies. It identified the major causes of its difficulties as (1) the general unrest and confusion existing in the watch market as a result of many "off brand" Swiss watches sold in the lower-priced field, and (2) the disruptive influence on conventional distribution channels and retail prices by discount houses which were at their peak in 1957.

Company officials admitted that Elgin had not completely kept abreast of changing trends such as the increased demand for round watches, sweep-second hands, shockproof, waterproof, and self-winding watches. Prior to 1958 the company had not produced a watch which could be retailed below $33.75 with the customary trade margin of 50%. Company policy had been positive and explicit in refusing to produce a watch under the Elgin name to retail for less than this amount. Management stated that selling a low-priced watch with Elgin's name would degrade the tradition of quality and craftsmanship built up by the company over many years. Some executives cited Packard automobile as an example of what would happen if a lower-priced watch were marketed. However, management agreed that the inexpensive "fashion" watches such as the Swiss timepiece in the $20 to $30 bracket, and the cheaper pin-lever watches—primarily American brands such as Timex—were gaining increasing acceptance. Although Elgin's Wadsworth line had been introduced a few years earlier to capture a share of this market, its failure to do so forced management to import certain Swiss specialty watches under the Elgin name—mostly automatic or self-winding watches—to round out its line.

In early 1958 Elgin was dealt a severe blow when the Office of Defense Mobilization ruled that the American watch industry was not essential to national defense. This decision precluded the possibility that higher tariffs might be imposed to restrict imports in the foreseeable future. During the next few months Elgin's management conducted a mail and personal interview survey among its dealers; 917 dealers answered the question, "Would an Elgin watch retailing at about $25 help your sales?" The results were:

	Personal Interviews	Mail Survey
Yes	76.5%	66.1%
No	23.5%	33.9%
Number answering	47	870

On the basis of this survey the marketing department in June, 1958, introduced its marketing plans for increasing Elgin's total watch sales with special emphasis on the "under $30" market. Consequently, the company eliminated the production and marketing of the Wadsworth watch, introduced a 19-jewel model in the medium-priced field to sell from $34.95 to $69.50, and began marketing a 17-jewel, low-priced Elgin, retailing from $19.95, which consisted of imported movements assembled in company-designed cases.

By the end of 1958 imports of watches by the company had increased substantially with the result that less than half of Elgin's watch manufacturing capacity was being used. Subsequently the company closed down and disposed of its Lincoln, Nebraska, plant; the Wadsworth Case Company plant at Dayton, Kentucky; and the Hadley Division plant at Providence, Rhode Island. To improve the reliability and reduce the costs of importing watches and watch movements, a subsidiary was established in Switzerland in 1959, and an important portion of the watch line was purchased from France.

Early in 1959 Elgin management instituted what it called "fresh marketing approaches" and made extensive changes in its distribution channels and methods. Although the company had always felt a great loyalty for the established legitimate local jeweler, who had distributed the product so successfully, and recognized that jewelry stores still dominated the retail sale of watches above the $30 price bracket which had been Elgin's strong field, management hesitated to break away from its traditional distribution policy. "Nevertheless," remarked an Elgin official, "because of the dynamic changes which are taking place in the watch market, we are determined to meet our competition, no matter how bizarre." Consequently, the Lord and Lady Elgin line was restricted to franchised jewelry outlets and marked with a suggested retail price that provided the retailer with the conventional 50% margin. The medium-priced line which was also restricted to retail jewelers carried a suggested retail price that provided a margin of 50% to 60%. Other watch lines were extended to selected catalogue and wholesale distributors and to premium houses, with suggested retail prices which provided margins of 40% to 45%.

EMPLOYEE RELATIONS

In November, 1961, Mr. Robert Bryza, formerly director of industrial relations of the Burton Rogers Company and a management consultant with the A. T. Kearney Company, was appointed general manager of the newly created Relations Division with specific responsibility for public relations, labor relations, and wage and salary administration.

Prior to this time these activities were handled by each division on a piece-meal basis. "When I accepted this position," remarked Mr. Bryza, "my major objective was to centralize and coordinate these scattered activities so as to insure uniform application of corporate policies and programs."

Within one year the insurance and benefits program was revamped. "Whereas previously each division developed, negotiated, and administered its own insurance plan," Mr. Bryza explained, "the new program was negotiated with a single insurance company and administered on a company-wide basis." He went on to say that similar arrangements were made in the labor relations area and culminated in a central industrial relations unit. Mr. Bryza also stated that his department planned company-wide labor-strategy six months in advance of negotiations. "However," he pointed out, "even though we develop over-all policy and plans in the home office, we have an employee relations manager at each plant conducting the negotiations on a local basis, subject to our approval. In addition, administration of the contract is handled at the plant level, except that grievances necessitating arbitration are handled in the home office."

In August, 1962, Elgin negotiated a new two-year agreement with the Elgin National Watch Workers' Union (affiliated with the American Watch Workers Union). The new contract provided for no change in wages in the first year and a 3% increase in the second year. Similar arrangements were negotiated with the International Association of Machinists. "Not all of our plants are unionized," remarked Mr. Bryza. "As a consequence we have had several unions attempting to take over our newer plants. Thus, in September, 1962, the I.B.E.W. and the I.A.M.[2] demanded recognition in our Chatsworth, California plant, claiming 30% representation of our employees. The NLRB held an election and fortunately 78% of the votes cast were for 'no union.' But less than 60 days later, as we were starting up operations in our Gadsden, Alabama plant, the I.B.E.W. began circulating membership cards to our employees in their homes. With our centralized policy and planning we were able to cope with this situation immediately and the organization drive fell through." According to Mr. Bryza, the labor relations picture was further complicated by the acquisitions of newer companies whose previous union contract agreements were often at variance with Elgin's labor policies. This was particularly true of the consumer products group.

As Elgin expanded into government contracts, Mr. Bryza established and headed an Industrial Security Division to enforce the security regulation required by the Defense Department.

Mr. Bryza pointed out that the company was confronted with a unique problem of planning for simultaneous contraction and expansion of operations. "Our industrial products are expanding at a rapid rate," he remarked, "while in our consumer products group we have been engaged in a steady retrenchment. Thus, we are faced with the problem of releasing skilled personnel in one area, while seeking skilled personnel in another area. Transfer of personnel between jobs is hampered not only by the differences in skill requirements, but also by the different locations of plants."

[2] International Brotherhood of Electrical Workers; International Association of Machinists.

MANAGEMENT AND ORGANIZATION

In a discussion on American business in general, and National Elgin Watch Company in particular, Mr. Margolis stated, "American industry is the most overmanaged in the world." At the time Mr. Margolis took over operating control of Elgin, the company had a complex decentralized organizational structure with ten committees functioning at the corporate level. When the resignation of Mr. James G. Shennan as president of Elgin in September, 1960, was followed shortly after by the resignations of three other key executives—Mr. George J. Daly, executive vice president and treasurer; Mr. S. D. Moorman, vice president for marketing, Watch Division; and Mr. Leroy A. Mote, secretary and general attorney, Mr. Margolis acted as president, financial vice president, and manager of the Watch Division while he scouted the country for a strong management team. For president he chose Mr. Robert O. Fickes, but when the latter resigned after thirteen months, Mr. Margolis again assumed the presidency of Elgin. For executive vice president and head of the industrial divisions he picked Mr. Thomas P. Leddy, a communications expert and former vice president with the Kellogg Division of International Telephone & Telegraph Corporation; Mr. Melvin Skinner, also of ITT Kellogg, was hired as marketing manager of the industrial group; and Mr. Harold F. Diegel, controller of Chrysler Corporation, was elected financial vice president and treasurer.

In his discussion of the previous organization Mr. Margolis remarked that in his opinion the Shennan management had been "too conservative" to grapple with what he called the "brutal" consumer market. Mr. Margolis also felt that the company had become too decentralized for its size and remarked that there were too many assistants around. An example of the unusual decentralized organization was the industrial group, whose four divisions were completely autonomous. Each division had its own accounting, marketing, advertising, sales personnel, and manufacturing departments. On many occasions salesmen for one division turned down orders for equipment from other divisions.

Streamlining of the organization was effected within a few months according to Mr. Margolis. More than 30 people from all administrative levels, including secretaries, were dropped as the new management consolidated and realigned the operations and put an end to the widespread decentralization. Mr. Margolis insisted that even though the management was being reduced, it was being strengthened. He estimated that his consolidations had reduced annual payroll and other outside fees by $500,000.

During 1961 the Industrial Products Group, under Mr. Leddy's guidance, was completely reorganized as the company stepped up its operations in the design, development, and production of precision miniaturized mechanisms, sophisticated communications devices and systems, electrical controls of high reliability, and special cutting and abrading tools. Three new executives with wide engineering backgrounds in the design and development of electronic requirements for the government's space, missile, and satellite programs, and formerly employed by ITT Kellogg, were added to key positions in the Industrial group. Each of the six industrial divisions maintained responsibility for manufacturing and reported directly to Mr. Leddy. All industrial marketing functions were grouped under a centralized marketing organization headed by Mr. Skinner, who also reported to Mr. Leddy. Financial matters were centralized under Mr. Diegel, who reported directly to Mr. Margolis.

By mid-1962 the Industrial Group had boosted its backlog to an all-time high of nearly $20 million as a result of Elgin's increased role in the nation's military and space programs.

The Consumer Products Group, which consisted entirely of the Elgin watch division, was also reorganized in 1961 into four divisions as a result of the acquisition of two clock companies—Welby and Bradley—and the purchase of Lohengrin Diamond Ring Company. (See Exhibit 2.)

NEW DEVELOPMENTS

In September, 1961, Elgin reentered the United States clock market with an extensive line of newly designed home, decorator, and travel timepieces. Elgin had withdrawn from the clock market in 1954, although it had never offered home and decorator clocks for sale under the Elgin name. All decorator and kitchen clocks contained self-starting, cordless, electric movements capable of operating for two years on one standard 1½-volt flashlight battery.

In 1960 the company introduced 72 new styles, including an electric watch. Two years later the Elgin Electronic, the thinnest, smallest

electronic wrist watch manufactured in the world, was introduced on
a national scale following three years of market testing.

In the industrial field Elgin was a leading source of safety and
arming devices for shells, rockets, and guided missiles. One of Elgin's
most important projects in 1961–1962 was the design and development
of an electronic communications system for the United States Navy
—a high-speed teletypewriter routing set capable of handling 20 different punches simultaneously and sending messages at the rate of 850
words per minute for a peak efficiency processing of 17,000 words per
minute. The company also produced components for the Skybolt missile, the F4H-1 Phantom fighter plane, the Bomarc missile, the Pershing
missile, the Minuteman missile, the Atlas missile, and the Apollo space
vehicle. In addition, Elgiloy, a cobalt-base alloy patented by Elgin,
was used in the manual control switch of Colonel John Glenn's Friendship VII space capsule. In 1959 industrial products contributed nearly
35% of the total sales volume. By 1961 the sales volume was split
50–50 between consumer and industrial goods. In mid-1962 an Elgin
official estimated that industrial goods would account for nearly 65%
of total sales volume for fiscal 1962.

In September, 1962, Mr. Margolis announced that Elgin had selected
Blaney, South Carolina, for the establishment of its pilot watch assembly plant as a "first step to provide Elgin National Watch with
greater flexibility to meet severe foreign competition" of watch sales.

35

RAILWAY
SUPPLY
CORPORATION

Early in 1959 Mr. John Mayer, president of Railway Supply Corporation, reviewed his company's current position with his executive group —George Jensen, Frank Noble, and Wilbert Bailey. He proposed that the next several months be spent in appraising the company's resources, markets, and growth potential. The changes within the organization and in its operation during the past few years had been many and drastic as the company struggled to regain the profitable position it formerly enjoyed. Mr. Mayer thought that the present activities of the company, although in some respects new to its experience, indicated a more promising future.

COMPANY OPERATIONS

Railway Supply conducted its operations under two principal divisions. The Fiber Division processed and fabricated insulation materials, mainly asbestos, operating a weaving plant at Nashville, Tennessee, and a fabricating plant at Aurora, Illinois. The Steel Division consisted of a Draft Gear Department which made hand brakes for railroad cars; the Railroad Car Parts Group which sold accessories to railroad refrigerator car manufacturers; and the Railroad Steel Parts Group which performed the manufacturing functions for the Railroad Car Parts Group. All steel fabricating was done in a single plant located in Harvey, Illinois. The Robust Rack operation, which produced an extensive line of adjustable storage racks, was purchased in March of 1958 and added to the Steel Division's product line.

EXECUTIVE GROUP

John Mayer was elected president of Railway Supply in 1948 when his father, Benjamin Mayer, assumed effective control of the company. The original holdings of the Mayer family were acquired from the estate of Charles Kahn who died in 1943. Mr. Kahn was one of the original founders and major stockholders of Railway Supply. Benjamin Mayer was the president and sole owner of Universal Rolling Mill Products Corporation. In 1959 Universal Rolling Mill owned 34.7% of Railway Supply, and the Mayer family owned an additional 6% of the outstanding stock. John Mayer was authorized to vote both blocks of stock.

All the major decisions of Railway Supply were made by John Mayer; however, he did not concern himself with day-to-day administration. He had many other interests in both business and the community.

Wilbert Bailey, a C.P.A., was the executive vice president and treasurer. He administered all of the accounting and financial matters of the company. He spent all of his time in the central office and made many of the detailed operating decisions. Mr. Kahn, the founder of the company, hired him in 1930 as an auditor; shortly thereafter he was elected treasurer, and in 1947 became executive vice president. Mr. Bailey worked closely with Mr. Mayer and executed the administrative policies set by him.

Frank Noble, vice president and general manager of the Steel Division, joined the company in 1952 at the invitation of Mr. King, who at that time served as chairman of the Board of Directors of Railway Supply. Mr. Noble had worked for ten years with Baldwin Locomotive where he had attained the position of assistant vice president and district sales manager. As a result of experience gained in Washington during the World War II period, he became a special Washington representative for a number of railway supply and equipment manufacturers. Through his work in this position he became acquainted with the management of Railway Supply and subsequently joined the company.

George Jensen, vice president and general manager of the Fiber

Division, was employed by Railway Supply in 1941. His prior experience included positions in financial control, sales, and production with several firms engaged in the manufacture of heavy machinery. Although Mr. Jensen was not formally trained as an engineer, he had acquired through experience a wealth of technical knowledge and manufacturing know-how. He was primarily concerned with the production activities of the Fiber Division and tended to allow his executive staff relatively free rein in other functions, particularly in sales and marketing. Mr. Jensen spent three or four days a week in the Aurora plant and each Monday in the Chicago central office. This day was reserved for conferences with Mr. Mayer, when he was available.

CORPORATE DEVELOPMENT

In 1910 Charles Kahn and Ralph Samuels organized a company to job miscellaneous supplies to railroads. Mr. Samuels had a talent for purchasing at bargain prices and Mr. Kahn, who was a highly competent salesman, marketed their supplies to the railway industry. In the early years of the company sales were confined mainly to asbestos products and rubber hose.

After World War I the partners bought an asbestos textile plant in Nashville, Tennessee, where they wove asbestos yarn, cloth, and tape. In 1936, through a license arrangement with a Dutch firm, Railway Supply became the American distributor for Tempbestos, a high-temperature asbestos. The distinguishing feature of this product was a long-fiber asbestos called Amosite which was found only in mines located in South Africa.

The partnership was dissolved and a corporation formed in 1918. Mr. Kahn acquired the bulk of the Railway Supply stock after the dissolution.

In 1940 the company bought an old factory in Wilmington, Delaware, which it converted to the manufacture of insulation materials for the Navy and for industry. In 1947, in its plant in Sherman, Texas, it began to produce pipe coverings for the oil refineries of the Southwest. In 1951 Railway Supply bought a large plant in Aurora, Illinois, which had once housed the repair shops of a railroad. This was adapted to the production of insulating blankets for the railroads.

In 1954 the company's general asbestos fabricating operations were moved to the Aurora plant.

Through the years Railway Supply had acquired several operations outside of the field of asbestos. In 1931 a small company, which manufactured draft gears marketed by Railway Supply, became insolvent and was acquired at an attractive price. In 1939 the company purchased the business and manufacturing facilities of a producer of railroad refrigerator car components. Railway Supply had served as the sales agent for this organization since 1925. The manufacturing facilities acquired in this transaction included a large plant in Harvey, Illinois. This unit became the central manufacturing facility for the Railroad Car Parts Group and all products fabricated out of steel and other metals.

Products of the Railroad Car Parts Group formed the backbone of the family of products which were consolidated into the Steel Division in 1956. The varied items manufactured and supplied to the railroads had, for the most part, been acquired or developed by Mr. Kahn. They had proven to be consistently profitable through the years. Although their profitability had declined in the post World War II period, they still formed an integral part of the company in 1959.

Prefabricated Housing. In 1950 Railway Supply entered the prefabricated steel building field. John Mayer believed that the market for buildings of this type was rapidly expanding and the company, by virtue of its plant and facilities for forming and stamping light steel, was well suited to compete in this industry. In an effort to take advantage of what was thought to be a lucrative market, Railway Supply rushed into the production of a line of low-cost residential dwelling units. In commenting on this venture Frank Noble, vice president of the Steel Division, remarked, "Apparently the company had difficulty from the start in producing these units. Large competitors in the industry were already pretty firmly entrenched when we entered the field. Their designs were standardized, much simpler, and much more functional than ours. The company moved too hastily in this operation. Too little thought went into the production and marketing problems."

After two years in the prefabricated housing field, Railway Supply's units were selling for less than 4% over the actual cost of producing the units. The selling, administrative, and erection costs produced a substantial loss on each unit which was sold. In 1953, after experiencing a loss of approximately $1.5 million, the company terminated the production and sale of its prefabricated housing units.

Heating and Cooling. In 1953 John Mayer became interested in the expanding market for air conditioning equipment. He decided that the manufacture and sale of air conditioning units would prove to be a profitable supplement to Railway Supply's business. After preliminary investigations of the market, he concluded that it would be necessary to combine the manufacture and sale of heating equipment with air conditioning units to keep pace with the current trend in the industry. A separate Heating and Cooling Division was organized for the administration, selling, and promotion of the new products and two plants were purchased to serve as the manufacturing units—one was located in North Carolina, and the other in South Chicago, Illinois.

The company's engineers designed and put into production a high quality thin-wall baseboard heating unit. At the same time Railway Supply's products were put on the market, competitors in the field introduced units constructed of copper tubing and aluminum fins. These products proved to have advantages of cost, design, and eye-appeal which rendered Railway Supply's steel radiators noncompetitive. John Parry, assistant general manager of the Steel Division, in commenting on the company's heating unit, stated, "We put a lot into our product. I think we would have done all right except for the fact that we were selling a Cadillac product for a Ford price."

After 18 months of losses and little success in penetrating the market, Railway Supply disposed of its assets in the heating and cooling business at a net loss of approximately $2 million.

Organizational Changes. When John Mayer was elected president in 1948, Louis Stern, a close friend of Mr. Kahn, was elected chairman of the board. Mr. Stern, through a long friendship with Mr. Kahn and an active interest in his company, had acquired an extensive knowledge of the railroad supply and asbestos business. As chairman of the board Mr. Stern assumed a very prominent role in policy-making. In an effort to relieve himself of an increasing administrative burden, Mr. Stern hired Norbert King as an administrative assistant. Organizational difficulties soon emerged mainly because of a lack of a clear-cut division between the functions of the chairman of the board and the president. Mr. Stern felt compelled to make an increasing number of significant operating decisions. Many of these decisions were critically questioned by Mr. Mayer. However, Mr. Mayer expressed great confidence in Mr. King, and in 1949 Mr. King replaced Mr. Stern as chairman of the board.

Late in 1949 Mr. King announced that the management was to be reorganized on a functional basis. He brought his friend, Frank Noble, into the company as vice president and general sales manager. George Jensen, who had been superintendent in the company's Aurora plant, was made vice president in charge of all manufacturing, including steel products. Wilbert Bailey, the treasurer, continued to be responsible for financial and accounting matters, and was given a new title of executive vice president and treasurer. (See Exhibit 1.)

Under the new arrangement Mr. Noble, who had little experience in selling asbestos, found himself depending upon Mr. Jensen for the direction of asbestos sales. Mr. Jensen, whose previous manufacturing experience had not included metal fabrication, continued to operate in the same way he had previously, except for reading and checking the weekly reports of the foremen to whom he left the active management of the steel fabricating plants. Neither Mr. Noble nor Mr. Jensen approved of the new management arrangement. After trying it for eighteen months with what he termed unsatisfactory results, John Mayer asked a management consulting firm to make a study of the company's organizational structure. As a result of their study and recommendations a reorganization was undertaken by the company. (See Exhibit 2.)

In the President's letter which accompanied the 1956 Annual Report of Railway Supply, Mr. John Mayer explained the reorganization in the following terms:

> The disposition of the former Heating and Cooling Division and the elimination of the problems attending it have permitted your management to concentrate its attention upon the development and promotion of other products.
>
> Based upon an intensive study made by a firm of management consultants during the past year, your board of directors has made several changes in the organizational structure of your company. Among other things, there was put into effect by your management a decentralization and integration program whereunder each of the two basic activities of the company would be under the guidance of an executive officer located at the division headquarters.

In discussing the results of the reorganization in early 1959 Mr. Bailey, the executive vice president, stated, "After two years we now

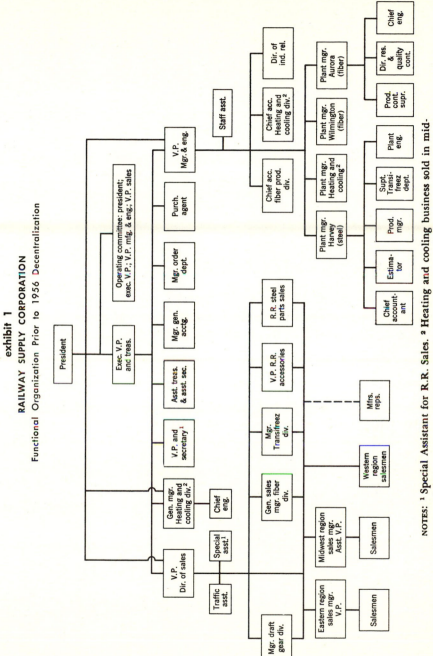

exhibit 1

RAILWAY SUPPLY CORPORATION

Functional Organization Prior to 1956 Decentralization

NOTES: [1] Special Assistant for R.R. Sales. [2] Heating and cooling business sold in mid-year 1956.

919

exhibit 2
RAILWAY SUPPLY CORPORATION
Organization After 1956 Decentralization

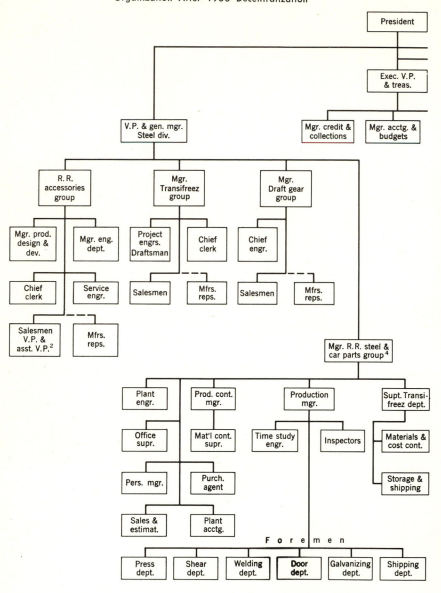

exhibit 2 (continued)

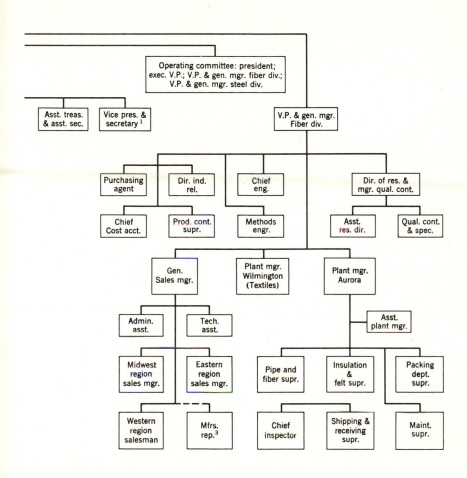

NOTES: [1] Also acted as Mgr. Draft Gear Div.   [2] Titles were holdovers from the early and prosperous era of selling R.R. equipment.   [3] Served as Mfrs. Reps. for both the Fiber Div. and the Draft Gear Div.   [4] Included the newly acquired and added products of the Robust Rack and Rectangular Tubing Groups.

feel that our two divisions are completely decentralized. We have reduced our central headquarters staff from about 100 to the present number of 25. Approximately 25 of this number were moved to the division offices in Aurora and Harvey. An additional 25 people were dropped when we eliminated the Heating and Cooling Division, and the remainder were determined to be excess personnel which had just been built up over the years.

"We are now able to operate much more effectively. Prior to the reorganization monthly reports and financial statements were frequently as much as one month late in arriving at the headquarters office. We traced most of this delay to the excess of information which passed between the cost accounting departments of the two plants to the general accounting department in headquarters. We have made many changes in our personnel and control functions. The following functions are now handled by the executive and office personnel of the headquarters organization.

General administration
Policy formulation
Long-range planning
Control over capital expenditures,
   operating expenditures, manpower,
   general wage levels, salaries,
   and product lines
Review and approval of major appropriations, budgets, appointments,
   and salary changes
Appraisal of divisional performance
General accounting
Internal auditing
Credit and collections
Accounts payable

Property ledgers
Insurance
Bank statements
Key punch operations
Consolidation and preparation
   of financial reports
Salaried payroll
Personnel records of headquarters
   personnel
Tax matters
Corporate secretarial duties
Receptionist-switchboard
Office secretarial duties

"In an effort to make our two divisions more self-contained operating units, we are now in the process of transferring the following functions:

General accounting for the divisions
Preparation of division financial statements
   and balance sheets
Accounts receivable
Accounts payable
Property records
Insurance records
Sales and expense reports now prepared at headquarters

"I would say we operate fairly effectively despite the separation of the headquarters and division offices. Our operating committee is made up of our president, John Mayer, myself, the two division vice presidents, and their general managers. The committee concerns itself mainly with the annual sales forecast, reviewing operating costs, and profit potentials. Of course, both George Jensen and Frank Noble spend at least one day a week at headquarters to review their operations. I take care of the day-to-day policy matters; however, Mr. Mayer is in on all of the major policy decisions—as a matter of fact, I would say he initiates most of them. This certainly has been true about our recent acquisitions. At the present time all members of the executive committee are vitally concerned about our future."

THE STEEL DIVISION

In 1956, when Mr. Frank Noble was placed in charge of the Steel Division, this unit of the business performed all of the fabricating operations except those involving insulating materials. The manufacturing processes consisted of forming, pressing, punching, welding, and hot dip galvanizing. Some machining was done, but foundry work was contracted to others. Most of the products were made from steel sheets, bars, rods, and shapes. (Exhibit 3 illustrates the major products of the Steel Division.) All of the division's manufacturing operations were centralized in the Harvey plant. The division's activities, however, were divided into product groups, each under the direction of a manager reporting to Mr. Noble. (See Exhibit 2.)

Draft Gear Group. The Draft Gear Group manufactured and sold three types of draft gears for railroad cars. A major factor in the manufacture of draft gears was the production of castings. Railway Supply purchased castings from independent foundries but did all of the required machining and processing for the gears in their own shops. The personnel of the group consisted of the manager, a chief engineer, and four salesmen who called on railroads. The group also sold through manufacturers' representatives (agents), in New York, Cleveland, St. Louis, New Orleans, and Louisville. These were the same sales agents who handled the company's fiber products. Sales volume was fairly steady, but profits depended upon the cost of purchased components. In 1958, when the railroads cut their maintenance activities, draft gear sales did not suffer as much as fiber products, but were sharply curtailed. (See Exhibit 6.)

Railroad Accessories Group. Railroad refrigerator car equipment, including steel floors and grates, racks, drain spouts, and hatch closures, made up the Railroad Accessories Group. Almost all of the manufacturing for these products was done in the Harvey plant; only minor components were purchased from outside sources. In addition to a manager, the personnel of the unit included a manager of Product Design and Development, a manager of Engineering, a chief clerk, a service engineer, a staff of nine draftsmen, and two salesmen. The group also used manufacturers' representatives in St. Louis and Toronto. The units were sold to refrigerator car manufacturers which comprised about ten principal accounts. Sales of the units fluctuated widely depending on the construction of refrigerator cars.

Management thought that the long-range future of this product group was clouded by the threat of mechanically refrigerated cars and the possibility that railroads might switch to carrying refrigerated truck trailers piggy-back on flat cars. Some of Railway Supply's customers considered the cost of mechanical refrigeration too high. The cost of a refrigerated car was approximately $25,000, and an iced bunker car about $13,000. However, the trend toward mechanically refrigerated cars was evident and several of the major companies, such as Carrier Corporation and Thermo-King, had installations in service. While the company did not view any significant market expansion for mechanically refrigerated cars in the near future, it entered the field in 1958 through a working arrangement with a noted inventor who held many patents on refrigerated car equipment. The system which the company acquired the right to manufacture and sell was based on circulating cool air around the walls of the car and not directly on the produce or perishable materials being transported. The company maintained that this provided for greater accuracy in temperature control. In October of 1959 the company had three units in service on a test basis with the three largest refrigerated car organizations. In the 1958 railroad maintenance recession, Railroad Accessories sales did not drop as sharply as the company's other products. (See Exhibit 6.)

Railway Steel and Car Parts Group. The Railroad Steel and Car Parts Group performed the manufacturing function for the Railroad Acces-

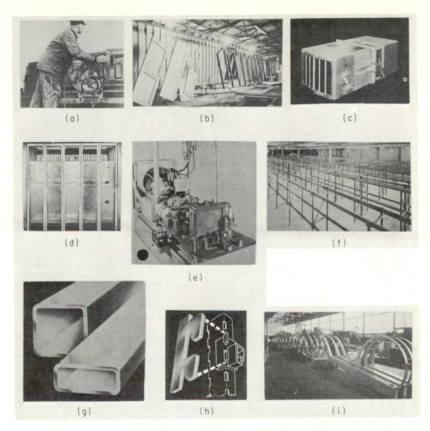

exhibit 3

Products of the Steel Division: (a) Draft Gears (hand brakes), (b) Custom Steel Fabrication, (c) Transifreez Units (truck refrigeration), (d) Refrigerator Car Specialties, (e) Mechanical Refrigeration (for R. R. refrig. cars), (f) Robust Racks Adjustable Storage Racks, (g) Square and Rectangular Tubing, (h) Adjustable "Snap-on" Units, and (i) Forming, Welding, Galvanizing.

sories and the Transifreez groups. It also did a sizable volume of contract steel fabricating and galvanizing for five key accounts:

Railco—Railroad car parts, principally refrigerator car parts. The Great Northern, Burlington, and St. Paul railroads were the principal customers because of a long-standing relationship established by the owner of Railco.

Concorp—A contractor's equipment company for which Railway Supply manufactured steel doors and frames. This operation was profitable for Railway Supply; however, it had expanded to such an extent that the management of Concorp was considering doing its own manufacturing.

Franklin—This company manufactured and sold a line of poles for lighting and advertising, and allied equipment. Railway Supply was able to produce electrically welded steel poles for Franklin because of its 40-foot shearing and forming press brake and the method the company had perfected of making a tight, smooth weld of that length.

Guard Grill—For which Railway Supply fabricated, by pressing and forming operations, steel grill guards for various machine tools such as punch presses, power saws, heavy duty grinders, and power shears.

Excel Door Hardware—A railroad equipment concern for which Railway Supply manufactured railroad car door parts, such as hinges, latches, rollers and glides, and bracings.

In selling to these contract customers, Railway Supply used a pricing formula that consisted of adding to its factory cost $2\frac{1}{2}\%$ for local administration and $6\frac{1}{2}\%$ for corporate expense, plus a markup for profit. In practice this had resulted in a profit of between 5% and 10% of the selling price. This formula had assured that sales would be profitable, but restricted the profit margin. The railroad equipment business from Railco and Excel Door was a significant portion of the Railroad Steel and Car Parts Group sales volume, but it fluctuated widely in keeping with the railroad equipment industry sales. The management of Railway Supply was aware that both of these accounts had frequently considered the possibility of doing their own manufacturing.

Robust Rack. Early in 1956 through Mr. John Mayer, the Steel Division secured a large subcontract from the Manufacturers' Equipment Company to fabricate a line of industrial heavy-duty steel shelves, racks, and bins. This patented line was sold under the trade name Robust Rack. Its distinguishing feature was an ingenious method of clips by which the parts, such as corner posts and shelves, could be hooked together quickly and simply without the use of nuts and bolts. The racks and shelving could be expanded into a wide variety of sizes. Robust Racks by Railway Supply had gained relatively widespread acceptance among manufacturers for storeroom and warehouse purposes.

Production of Robust Racks increased three-fold in the first four months of the contract. In view of the increased sales John Mayer made a proposal to the owners to buy their entire operation and, after six weeks of negotiations, succeeded in doing so. By October, 1958, the Robust Rack operation was the largest user of space in the Harvey plant. In December, 1958, the galvanizing department was sold to provide the Robust operation with more plant capacity.

Welded Steel Tubing. In March of 1958 Railway Supply began the production and sale of square and rectangular steel tubing in shapes up to 40″ in girth and ½″ in wall thickness. The company's entry into the field was preceded by a survey of the market made by a management consulting firm. The report of the consulting firm indicated that a promising market existed for certain sizes and types of tubing. Their survey indicated the following major conclusions:

1.   There was a growing market for square and rectangular welded steel tubing, but its exact size could not be calculated from the findings.

2.   Present suppliers of 3 x 3 to 4 x 4 inch squares (or comparable rectangular sizes) were fairly well entrenched and were apparently able to satisfy the current market demands for such sizes.

3.   For larger sizes, and for wall thicknesses in excess of ¼ inch, the market was smaller but was not satisfactorily supplied, either in quality or quantity, by present manufacturers.

4.   Distributors were generally receptive to a new entry into the field, and many of them would consider buying tubing from a new source, particularly in the sizes and wall thicknesses larger than those produced by such suppliers as Republic and Van Huffel.

5.   The building construction industry was the most promising single market for square and rectangular welded steel tubing, but this industry was unusually demanding with respect to product quality and would show definite resistance to two-piece construction in some instances, notably where surfaces were exposed.

6.   In order to make a successful entry into this field, a manufacturer would be required to produce competitively-priced tubing in 24-foot lengths with true dimensions and uniformly penetrating welds.

7.   In addition, a new manufacturer had to be prepared to incur some promotional expense in order to develop its brand acceptance and to create a more general recognition among distributors, architects, and end-users of the product features and practical applications of square and rectangular welded steel tubing.

8.   Geographically, a sizable portion of the total market could be reached by a tubing manufacturer located in the Chicago area.

Encouraged by this report, President Mayer requested the Steel Division to attempt to produce a smooth welded tube in excess of 1/4″ in wall thickness, up to 40″ in girth and 24′ in length. After much time and effort the company managed to produce satisfactory models. In commenting on this new venture John Parry, the assistant general manager of the Steel Division, stated, "We didn't have too much trouble producing a smooth welded tube in small sizes but we had great difficulty in producing tubing 24 feet in length. Until we accomplished this, as far as I know, no other company had been able to successfully produce a single-piece tubing unit of this size. This was because a copper follow bar, a holding back-up bar, had not been developed which was long enough and strong enough to perform the weld. We licked the problem in another way which we are now in the process of patenting.

"Our competition in tubing of this length is, outside of two-piece units, Seamless Steel Tubing which sells for as much as 60% more than our price. Although we still have production problems and our tubing needs to be perfected, we have sales of about $50,000 a month for our tubing."

Transifreez. During the 1940's Railway Supply manufactured ice bunkers for refrigerator trucks on a custom basis for the Donaldson Company of Cleveland. When Mr. Donaldson died in 1949, Mr. Mayer bought the assets of the business from the Donaldson estate. At that time iced trucks were already giving way to mechanical refrigeration. Realizing this, Mr. Mayer in February of 1951 purchased the assets of the Transifreez Corporation of Pittsburgh from its sole owner, Mr. Ray Reagan. The Transifreez refrigerating units had been designed by Mr. Reagan who was considered a very capable engineer. The product, however, had not been developed to the commercial stage due to the lack of capital. For this reason Mr. Reagan consented to sell to Railway Supply.

As part of the purchase agreement Mr. Reagan and the principal members of his technical staff were employed by Railway Supply. However, Mr. Reagan and Mr. Mayer became involved in a dispute over the development expenses and marketing plans for the Transifreez units. Aggravated by this and other disagreements, Mr. Reagan, after being in the employ of Railway Supply for six months, left the company. Six of his associates also resigned. Mr. Mayer then brought Mr. William Grimes, a Canadian refrigeration engineer, into the company as general manager of the Transifreez operation.

Mr. Reagan had designed three basic models of units for large truck trailers. These units (called the TR-15, the TR-20, and the TR-30) were expected to sell for $1,800, $2,200, and $2,900, respectively. Power units and compressors were purchased from the Omar Corporation of Akron, Ohio. Railway Supply fabricated the remainder of the unit and assembled it. In his first two years with Railway Supply, Mr. Grimes developed three additional truck trailer models: the TR-10 at $1,700; the TR-40 at $4,000; and the TR-50 at $5,000.

Mr. Grimes was convinced that there was a large potential market for a lighter unit, one capable of refrigerating small trucks which made store deliveries to retailers. This unit had to be light and compact, and capable of maintaining a temperature of 0° Fahrenheit under conditions which assumed the constant opening and closing of the truck doors. Early in 1956 Mr. Mayer consented to the development of such a light unit. By spring of 1957 Mr. Grimes was conducting breakdown tests of several hand-made models in his laboratory hot room. He made 35 models for tryout under field conditions. He was enthusiastic about the project in the testing stage; however, he doubted that a trouble-free unit could be put into production before 1959. The new unit was called the Runabout and was priced to sell for $500.

Sales of the Transifreez units varied from $65,000 in 1951, the first year of operation, to a high of $905,000 attained in 1957. (See Exhibit 6.) Four salesmen operating out of New York, Cleveland, Chicago, and Memphis worked out specifications and gave technical advice to prospective customers. Distribution was made through six manufacturers' representatives located in St. Paul, Detroit, San Antonio, New Orleans, San Diego, and St. Louis. Twenty-five distributors covered the entire country and had outlets in every major city. Mr. Grimes was not satisfied with the quality of these distributors. In his opinion four of them were good, six were fair, nine were worthless, and the remainder were too new to be judged. Within the next two years Mr. Grimes intended to replace six of the ineffective distributors and add sixteen new ones in the Pennsylvania-Ohio region, in the deep South, and the southwestern states. He planned to double the number of manufacturers' representatives and then to add another fifteen distributors to cover the West Coast.

Mr. Grimes eagerly looked forward to the introduction of the Runabout. He estimated that its unit sales for the next five years would be:

1959	500
1960	2,000
1961	3,000
1962	6,000
1963	well over 10,000

Mr. Grimes based his optimism on the trend toward the refrigerated trucking of such items as meat, produce, dairy products, fruits, and vegetables, and the rapidly growing consumption of milk, ice cream, and frozen foods. He pointed out that an increasing number of states and cities were passing laws requiring refrigerated trucks for milk deliveries. Mr. Grimes did not, however, expect his operation to be very profitable for some time. He thought that research and development expenditures should be increased and that an intensive advertising campaign would be necessary to properly promote the product.

When Mr. Reagan left Railway Supply at the end of 1951 the Transifreez operation was transferred from Pittsburgh to the Harvey plant of the company and became a part of the Steel Car Parts Group.

In discussing the Transifreez operation John Parry, the assistant general manager of the Steel Division, stated, "While we have the formal responsibility for the manufacture of the Transifreez units in our division, actually we have little to do with the whole operation. I would say Transifreez is still in the exploratory stages. It has produced about four or five models, none of which has worked well. No two units produced are alike. We still do not have a complete set of drawings for any model which could be considered standard. It seems to me that all models in production are really prototypes. This operation is losing about $3,000 a month currently."

Frank Noble, vice president and manager of the Steel Division, reinforced Parry's comments. "There are still a number of things wrong with the Transifreez units. The basic problem is that of a new unit designed by a new crew which has not had time to work out the bugs. You also have to remember that our shop is a poor place to manufacture a refrigeration unit. This type of operation requires precision work and clean facilities. Transifreez shares floor space with our heavy stamping, forming, and welding operations. Our shop is noisy and, because of the multipurpose, a dirty shop. We are accurate to only $\frac{1}{32}$ of an inch. While this is accurate enough for our basic operations, it does not measure up for refrigeration units.

"In addition to the problem of production facilities, our union relations are not right and we don't have the proper second-line supervision. Basically our Harvey workforce has little skill in precision fabrication. However, the shop union is strong and many employees have long years of service with the company. Many of the Transifreez positions pay higher rates than our other fabricating jobs. As openings occur in the Transifreez operation veteran employees insist their seniority rights entitle them to the higher paid positions which practically all of our workforce are unqualified to fill."

During 1957–1958 72% of the department's man-hours of labor had been spent on units which had special features and were not stocked as regular models. Mr. Grimes acted as chief engineer, but an increasing amount of his time was spent on administrative and promotional matters.

Sales of the Transifreez units were limited by Railway Supply's lack of service facilities. Only those distributors located in large cities operated service stations and carried repair parts. This limited Transifreez sales to homebased haulers who operated regularly scheduled runs. Railway Supply's principal competitor, the Kold King Corporation, had contractual arrangements with 92 service stations across the country for servicing long distance haulers. Transifreez had not organized a program for the service training of distributors. Parts lists, manuals, drawings, and instructions suitable for service were in the preliminary drafting stages.

Early in 1959 Mr. Mayer seriously considered liquidating the Transifreez operation. He said that he would like to sell it as a going business, or sell the assets. While he thought that market opportunities and prospects for the products were promising, he was concerned about the additional time and investment needed to make the Transifreez units competitive. As a result of a survey made by a management consulting organization Mr. Mayer had concluded that it would require an investment of approximately $300,000 to $400,000 and three to four years to rebuild the Transifreez operation to a point where it could take advantage of the market opportunities and prospects for refrigerated truck units.

In discussing the operations of the Steel Division and the future of the company, Frank Noble made the following statements:

"I'd like to emphasize that the character of our Harvey plant is changing rapidly. We acquired the Robust Rack Company in March of 1958. Our company was historically a manufacturer of refrigeration car ice bunkers. We had a reputation for high quality and good service. In recent years there had been a tendency toward mechanical refrigeration. Ice bunker manufacturing requires shearing, welding, and cutting, all of which we do well. We pretty much had a monopoly in the ice bunker field but now we have new competition in mechanical refrigeration and we are being forced into making a new product.

"There will be two major changes at our Harvey plant. The first will be the Robust Rack operation. We are now in the process of removing the galvanizing equipment. We need the space for the Robust Rack operation. It will cost us about $100,000 over the next several months to revamp the plant and to take some losses on conversion.

"The second major change is our entry into the manufacture of square and rectangular tubing. We are the only ones in the country that are now producing this type of tubing and currently we can sell more than we can make. Rand Mills can out-produce us in tubing up to 20 inches in girth and $\frac{1}{4}$-inch wall thickness but above those sizes we have the market pretty much to ourselves; however, we have to have long runs to turn out this seamless tubing efficiently. We make a smooth finish tubing on our press brakes and we have oversold our total production at practically no sales expense. This production operation sounds like a pretty simple thing but to produce a quality product requires quite a bit of know-how, and we're the only ones who have it so far.

"It is a vital necessity that we change our thinking from that of a job shop to that of a semiproduction shop. With the acquisition of the railroad refrigerator car parts operation many years ago we became pretty much a job shop. Making metal bulkheads was a feast or famine sort of business with production on the basis of large contracts from large railroads. In between we've tried to fill the holes with custom production for people like Concorp for whom we make metal doors which are a low-profit item. Our emphasis now will be on more proprietary products. In 1957 our railroad business was about 7 million dollars. We are nowhere close to that today. We probably will never achieve a General Motors type of mass production but we intend to standardize our items more so we can do at least some order filling from stock. There will be more standardization of products and much more standardization of parts. In the metal tubing end of the business small runs will be grouped to make longer runs."

John Parry, the assistant general manager, supported the opinion of Mr. Noble and added, "The railroad business just isn't what it used to be. There were times when our division made a 25 to 35% profit on certain products. But the railroad supply business seems to have gone dead altogether. From January to July of 1958 there was a 95% drop in the industry's purchases. Railway expenditures have declined drastically. (See Exhibit 4.) The outlook for 1959 might be better, but I doubt it."

exhibit 4 CLASS 1 RAILWAYS GROSS CAPITAL EXPENDITURES (IN MILLIONS OF DOLLARS)*

Year	Equipment	Roadways & Structures
1946	319,017	242,940
1947	565,901	298,788
1948	917,449	356,035
1949	981,320	330,880
1950	779,399	286,443
1951	1,050,849	363,146
1952	935,090	405,822
1953	857,893	401,904
1954	498,726	321,520
1955	568,202	341,319
1956	821,357	406,500
1957	1,007,749	386,956
1958	479,680	258,358

NOTE: When comparisons for outlays for previous years are made, consideration should be given to the increase in the average cost of all railway materials. In most cases, the prices of locomotives, freight and passenger cars, and other materials have more than doubled in the past ten years.

* Moody's *Transportation Manual*, 1959.

FIBER DIVISION

"Since the decline of the steam locomotive," stated George Jensen, vice president of the Fiber Division, "we have had our problems in seeking new markets for our products. Diesels don't need our long-fiber asbestos and they have knocked hell out of our market. We have tried a number of products in an effort to fill in the gap created by the loss of the railroad business."

Until 1950 the largest volume of product lines made by Railway Supply had been railroad insulation applications. After 1950 conversion to diesel locomotives by the major railroads was accelerated and requirements for asbestos were reduced to a relatively insignificant amount. Steam locomotives in service for Class 1 railways declined from 37.5 thousand in 1946 to approximately 2 thousand in 1958. The diesel units in service for this period increased from 4.4 thousand to 27.1 thousand.[1] During these years the railroads found themselves caught between rising operating costs and inflexible tariff rates. Threatened with insolvency, the industry reacted by drastically cutting expenditures for replacement and maintenance. After 1950 the company's railroad business dropped significantly, and by 1958 asbestos production for the railroads was almost at a standstill.

Product Line. Railway Supply processed and fabricated two types of asbestos.[2] It imported short-fiber, weaving-grade asbestos, called Chrysotile, from Canada, whose mines supplied 70% of the world's asbestos requirements. The balance of its material was the long-fiber asbestos called Amosite, obtainable only from South African mines. Railway's products were classified in two broad categories: (See Exhibit 5 for illustration of products.)

1. *Asbestos textiles* were produced by applying a layer of short-fiber asbestos upon cotton cloth or wire mesh. Asbestos textiles were fabricated into tapes and yarns used in construction work and flexible protective coverings. These products were typically used for low temperature applications—below 500–600° F.

2. *Insulation* was made from the long-fiber asbestos, which was pressed into rigid shapes, mostly pipe coverings, for high temperature applications (800 to 1200°F.). The Amosite pipe coverings were used

---

[1] Moody's *Transportation Manual,* 1959.

[2] Asbestos is a mineral which has all of the fibrous qualities of animal or vegetable fibers such as wool, cotton, or silk. It also has an extraordinary resistance to heat and rot. The heat and rot resistance properties are the basis of its industrial and commercial value. The crude asbestos fiber, as it is received from the mines, is processed in a manner similar to wool or cotton. These processes consisted of opening, carding, spinning, plying, weaving, and braiding. Also, by mixing the fiber with cohesive binding materials, it is possible to mold asbestos into hard, dense shapes, such as rigid pipe coverings and hard insulation blocks.

in power plants, in ships, and in various industrial applications. The division further classified its products into the following lines:

a. *Pipe covering*—rigid sectional pipes and block insulation molded from Amosite which could be formed into pipe sections 30″ in diameter and 5″ thick. This covering provided high thermal efficiency and unusual mechanical strength before and after ex-

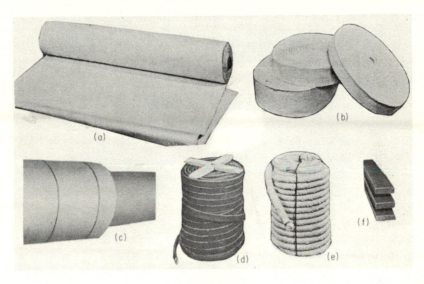

exhibit 5

Products of the Asbestos Division: (a) Asbestos Cloth, (b) Listing Tape, (c) Pipe Coverings, (d) Braided Tubing, (e) Asbestos Rope, (f) Block Insulation

posure to high temperatures. Amosite was also fabricated into a removable flexible blanket insulation, a woven sheathed felt used in marine, utility and refinery work. The pipe covering line made the largest sales and gross profit contribution of any line carried by the Fiber Division. (See Exhibit 7).

b. *Block insulation*—was molded from Amosite, as were pipe coverings, and was also used in high temperature applications. The blocks were rectangular in shape and included sizes from 1″ to 3″ in thickness, and from 6″ x 36″ to 36″ x 36″. The insulation block line had been unprofitable for some time and the management considered dropping the line but hesitated to do so because they thought pipe covering sales might suffer without a complementary line of blocks to sell to distributors.

c. *Flexible Insulation*—included asbestos in soft flexible forms such as blankets and tailored pads; Flexirock, a re-usable flexible pipe covering sheathed in a waterproof jacket which snapped open or shut by patented hooks; Asbesto-wrap, a sheathed flexible tape which was spiraled along steam pipes; Tempotube, a soft, flexible asbestos made in hollow pipe form and jacketed, and designed to slide over lengths of low temperature oil and heater lines. The flexible insulation line was second only to the pipe coverings in sales volume and percentage of gross profit. (See Exhibit 7.)

d. *Felt*—a soft rotproof and waterproof blanket which provided high thermal efficiency. Felt was sold in rolls 5' long and from ¾" to 1½" thick. This product returned the highest percentage of gross profit of any line in the company, but sales, which were principally to the Navy, were difficult to forecast and had shown a decline since 1952.

e. *Open Fiber*—carded asbestos fibers, furnished in 25- or 50-pound cartons were used as filtering mediums for processing liquids such as beers, wines, and acids, and were also used for electrical insulations and for packing the walls of home gas heaters. While this line required very little processing, the company recognized that it was a low-volume gross profit item.

f. *Jobbing Items*—called "trading items" by Railway Supply, were not manufactured by the company but were purchased and resold by the division to accommodate customers and round out the line. Volume was erratic, but the operation was usually profitable. (See Exhibit 7.)

g. *Packings and Gaskets*—included packings for pumps, either air, water, or high pressure steam; throttle, water heater, and stoker packings. Some packings were formed, some sold in coil lengths. Gaskets were stamped from sheet asbestos according to customers' specifications. Sales and profits of these lines were declining.

The first asbestos product Railway Supply manufactured in quantity was the woven tape which it had named Asbesto-wrap. This tape was spiraled around the steam lines of railroad locomotives to act both as an insulator and as a protective covering. Previous coverings used by the railroads had disintegrated when subjected to the abrasive impacts encountered in desert and mountain country. Asbesto-wrap was a new application of asbestos which had been designed and developed by a Mr. Tilley, a small manufacturer. Mr. Kahn purchased his patents and hired him. This new wrapping, a waterproof coated fabric, held together well under heavy usage and was quickly adopted by the railroad industry.

Other asbestos products for the railroads which the company manufactured included weatherproof tubing, pump packings, insulation jackets, and gaskets. Steam locomotives required large quantities of asbestos in a variety of forms and applications.

"We have a relatively broad line of asbestos products," stated Mr. Jensen, "however, we are very dependent upon our main raw material supplier. We have exclusive rights to produce Tempbestos in the United States. This is our trade name for the long-fiber asbestos called Amosite which is found only in South Africa. We are, of course, subject to the usual problems of price negotiations with a single supplier and we find competition from other kinds of asbestos, which use lower cost raw materials, to be very severe. In fact, we are almost ruled out of the lower temperature fields with our Amosite materials. The fine insulating properties of our Tempbestos in high temperature fields, however, has given our company the exclusive contract to supply the insulation requirements for the United States' fleet of atomic submarines.

"We gained our foothold in the Navy during World War II. Our insulation material became specified as standard for most of the United States naval vessels. The knowledge we picked up on our naval contracts aided in gaining an entry into the petroleum refiners and chemical plants. Supplying insulating materials for these industries constitutes a significant part of our business."

Sales. Fiber Division sales were made principally through distributors. Railway Supply was the only company in the industry which gave its distributors exclusive franchise rights within their sales territories. The sales manager of the Fiber Division considered distributor relations to be the key to a successful sales program and he emphasized this.

Fiber Division salesmen received a base salary plus a bonus based on quotas. The salesmen did not take orders. Their function was to supply customers with technical assistance in the determination of engineering specifications. They were also expected to promote the Railway Supply name in their territories. On occasions they worked with contractors directly on large-scale projects, such as the construction of power plants, oil refineries, and chemical plants. All customers sent their orders directly to the Aurora plant and each salesman was credited with sales emanating from his territory.

In 1957 there were sixteen salesmen in the Fiber Division. In November, 1958, eight salesmen were dismissed and two trainees were added to the staff. At the time the force was reduced, the salesmen's compensation was changed to a straight salary basis. The general sales manager explained that this action was necessary because of the many disputes over commissions on sales which overlapped several territories. He stated that in the future salesmen would be given a Christmas bonus whenever their performance and the income of the Division warranted it.

"We have been making a definite effort to sell, but on a smaller scale than we did three or four years ago. Our packing and textiles are perhaps receiving less attention from our salesmen than they should," said Mr. Jensen. "Our salesmen are basically pipe covering salesmen and that's where our primary effort is made. We have only one salesman for textiles in New York and one in Chicago. In comparison to our railroad business we are newcomers in the asbestos textile field. During the good years in the post-World War II period we oversold our production of insulation for railroads by 15% or more. With the decline of the railroad business we are now selling 80% of our production outside of this field.

"We use the Canadian asbestos, Chrysotile, a weaving grade asbestos, in our textile line. While it has definite cost advantages over our Amosite asbestos materials, price competition for asbestos textile materials is far greater. There is overcapacity in the asbestos textile business and we have great difficulty competing on a price basis. As a result we are proceeding cautiously in this field. The big margins we enjoyed in the railroad industry and on the jobs where specifications and know-how were important are definitely lacking in the asbestos textiles."

When the fiber operations became a separate division under Frank Jensen in 1956, the company had consolidated all of its asbestos manufacturing in two plants. The Aurora plant performed the bulk of the manufacturing operations and served as the headquarters for all personnel in the Division. The Nashville plant housed the weaving operation for asbestos textiles.

"The Aurora plant," stated Frank Jensen, "was converted from an old railroad shop into a facility for producing railroad insulating blankets. We acquired the plant in 1950 and by 1956 we had consolidated all of our fabricating operations in this facility. We have over 300,000 sq. ft. of manufacturing space at Aurora and we absorbed the operations of four smaller plants.

"While our Aurora plant is adequate and we made a good deal when we took over the property, it is not as efficient as the plant we lost to the Air Force through condemnation proceedings. We were sorry to lose this installation. It was located in Arkansas close to our markets and we enjoyed cheap gas fuel and a good labor situation. Before we were forced to give up this plant we had seriously considered enlarging it and making this location the center of our asbestos fabricating operations. Because of the necessity of finding a substitute for the Arkansas plant, and the need for consolidation and cost cutting caused by the drop in sales of insulation to the railroads, we decided to use the capacity we had available at Aurora.

"Our Nashville plant is really a weaving plant for our asbestos textile operations. The plant is in good condition and well maintained despite the fact that much of the weaving equipment dates back to the 1920's. However, we purchased four new cloth looms two years ago. We have about 140 employees at Nashville and plenty of room for expansion on our 20-acre site. While we are only in the asbestos business our Nashville plant is really a textile operation. Asbestos cloth and the varied related products are fabricated by overlaying asbestos on a fabric base. Our equipment is essentially the same as a textile plant. We have 14 cloth looms and 12 tape looms in the weaving department. Our yarn department, however, is not balanced with the weaving department and we are generally required to operate three shifts to keep pace with the two shifts of the weaving department. To obtain the needed equipment to assure a continuous production flow we would need to acquire additional equipment requiring an outlay of approximately $75,000.

"Currently one-half of the capacity of the Nashville plant is utilized for cloth and tape production. In order to save set-up time which requires 4 man days to change each loom to a cloth, looms are left with cloth standing so that they are ready for start-up when new orders are received. We would like to operate with a 30-day supply of yarn ahead of the weaving department. The backlog we had was absorbed by a hurry-up Navy order and we have not been able to build up an adequate reserve since that time.

"Our inventory level is affected by the amount of finished cloth and tape carried in stock and, of course, the yarn backlog ahead of the weaving department. Raw material also enters into the picture. It takes about 10 days in transit for a shipment of asbestos to reach Nashville from Canada. Taking all of these factors into account with the proper balance of backlogs, our inventory investment usually runs around $300,000. Because of the lack of proper backlogs, which affects our deliveries from time to time, we are running about $\frac{1}{3}$ less than this figure at present.

"Aurora directs and schedules all of Nashville's production. We feel we can get better coordination this way. A good part of the Nashville output, approximately 35% at standard manufacturing costs, is transferred to Aurora for further processing. This is mainly in the packing and insulation lines."

"The asbestos textile products present somewhat of a problem," said Mr. Jensen. "We really can't measure our share of the market very well. I'd guess in terms of all our line we probably have 2 to 3% of the total business. The figures of the American Textile Institute indicated that we acquired about 6% of the total business. Their figures, of course, include only the sales of member firms. Practically all of the firms sell essentially the same product lines. There is, of course, specialization in the industry; as a result we vary in terms of our share of the market for any particular product. The Institute's figures in recent years showed that we ranged from 0.3% of the lap asbestos business to as high as 38% of asbestos cloth sales. Asbestos cloth is the only item we sell in any volume. We definitely need new products and we have some we recently introduced to the market. It is too early to tell, however, what kind of reception they will get. For example, we are now taking orders for ironing-board cloth, Fortisan asbestos yarn for cables, a special insulation for electric cables, and a few other specialty items. I also believe some of the products we have on tap but have not yet marketed, may prove out. We now have an asbestos drapery material ready to market. We can produce it in a variety of colors and have put some style into it. We also have dishcloth material, a new type of overlapping insulating tape, and an absorbent brake lining yarn composed of asbestos and jute."

exhibit 6   RAILWAY SUPPLY CORPORATION

Steel division net sales and operating profits by product division, 1951–1958 (in thousands of dollars)

Year	Draft Gear			Railroad Accessories			Railroad Steel and Car Parts			Prefabricated Housing		
	Net Sales	Operating Profit		Net Sales	Operating Profit		Net Sales	Operating Profit		Net Sales	Operating Profit	
		Amount	% of Sales		Amount	% of Sales		Amount	% of Sales		Amount	% of Sales
1951	$547	$ (13)	(2.3)	$3,852	$520	13.5	$2,026	$468	23.1	$ 300	$(154)	(51.3)
1952	540	11	2.1	3,990	965	24.2	1,806	402	22.3	1,060	(440)	(41.5)
1953	629	35	5.5	2,331	469	20.1	1,661	302	18.1	740	(300)	(40.5)
1954	351	8	2.2	4,973	895	18.0	1,891	285	15.1	—	—	—
1955	573	44	7.7	3,088	422	14.0	3,600	332	9.2	—	—	—
1956	469	30	6.4	3,770	455	12.1	3,741	289	7.7	—	—	—
1957	475	45	9.5	4,371	692	15.8	4,441	600	13.5	—	—	—
1958	433	(22)	(5.1)	2,402	(90)	(3.7)	2,110	(94)	(4.4)	—	—	—

Year	Heating and Cooling			Transifreez			Robust Rack			Total Steel Division		
	Net Sales	Operating Profit		Net Sales	Operating Profit		Net Sales	Operating Profit		Net Sales	Operating Profit	
		Amount	% of Sales		Amount	% of Sales		Amount	% of Sales		Amount	% of Sales
1951	—	—	—	$ 65	$(10)	(15.4)	—	—	—	$ 6,790	$811	11.9
1952	—	—	—	260	(2)	(.8)	—	—	—	7,656	936	12.2
1953	$ 780	$ (150)	(19.2)	455	18	4.0	—	—	—	6,596	374	5.7
1954	4,160	(686)	(16.5)	585	30	5.1	—	—	—	11,960	532	4.4
1955	3,807	(1,349)	(35.4)	796	60	7.5	—	—	—	11,864	(491)	(4.1)
1956	1,747	(300)	(17.2)	910	15	1.6	—	—	—	10,637	489	4.6
1957	—	—	—	785	40	5.1	$1,790	—	—	10,072	1,377	13.7
1958	—	—	—	506	(35)	(6.9)		$(54)	(3.0)	7,241	(295)	(4.1)

exhibit 7 RAILWAY SUPPLY CORPORATION

Fiber division net sales and operating profits by product lines, 1951–1958 (in thousands of dollars)

Year	Pipe Covering			Asbestos Textiles			Flexible Insulation		
	Net Sales	Operating Profit		Net Sales	Operating Profit		Net Sales	Operating Profit	
		Amount	% of Sales		Amount	% of Sales		Amount	% of Sales
1951	$2,721	$541	19.9	$1,677	$ 33	2.0	$1,745	$285	16.3
1952	3,050	221	7.3	1,727	(34)	(6.9)	1,735	120	6.5
1953	2,920	161	5.5	1,319	(133)	(10.1)	1,751	79	4.5
1954	2,269	209	9.2	554	(50)	(9.0)	1,238	99	8.0
1955	2,113	43	2.0	860	(91)	(10.6)	1,182	8	.7
1956	2,350	188	8.0	872	(49)	(5.6)	1,193	72	6.0
1957	2,402	204	8.5	1,029	(41)	(4.0)	1,263	82	6.5
1958	1,807	27	1.5	723	(83)	(11.5)	918	(9)	1.0

exhibit 7 (continued)

Year	Felt			Block Insulation			Open Fiber		
1951	$862	$271	31.4	$287	$(23)	(8.0)	$144	$10	6.9
1952	521	114	22.0	373	(37)	(10.0)	137	3	2.2
1953	318	60	18.9	338	(39)	(11.5)	99	2	2.2
1954	290	55	19.0	150	(15)	(10.0)	81	2	2.5
1955	121	7	5.8	140	(27)	(19.3)	66	1	1.5
1956	130	13	10.0	111	(14)	(12.6)	47	1	2.1
1957	124	13	10.5	117	(12)	(10.3)	43	1	2.3
1958	90	4	4.05	68	(11)	(16.2)	32	(1)	(3.1)

Year	Packing and Gaskets			Jobbing Items			Total Fiber Division		
1951	$915	$23	2.5	$619	$95	15.3	$8,970	$1,235	13.8
1952	994	(30)	(3.0)	594	59	10.0	9,131	416	4.5
1953	931	(29)	(3.1)	549	46	8.4	8,225	147	1.8
1954	753	(120)	(16.0)	450	47	10.5	5,785	226	3.9
1955	716	(100)	(14.0)	361	22	6.1	5,559	(137)	(2.5)
1956	744	(60)	(8.1)	403	25	6.2	5,850	176	3.0
1957	788	(26)	(3.3)	394	25	6.4	6,160	246	4.0
1958	588	(61)	(10.4)	294	(1)	(.3)	4,520	(134)	(3.0)

exhibit 8 RAILWAY SUPPLY CORPORATION
Selected financial data 1951–1958

	1958	1957	1956	1955	1954	1953	1952	1951
As a per cent of sales:								
Gross profit	13.2%	22.8%	19.0%	12.7%	19.3%	18.2%	19.8%	24.9%
Selling and administration	16.8	12.8	15.0	16.3	15.0	14.7	11.7	11.9
Operating profit	(3.6)	10.0	4.0	(3.6)	4.3	3.5	8.1	13.0
Net income before nonrecurring items	(1.8)	5.0	3.3	(2.3)	1.8	1.6	3.8	6.2
Current ratio	8.5:1	7.5:1	2.7:1	2.1:1	2.1:1	2.3:1	3.3:1	2.4:1
Working capital (in thousands)	$5,903	$6,117	$4,833	$4,621	$5,038	$4,374	$4,645	$4,878
Book value (in thousands)	8,892	9,199	8,253	8,233	8,585	8,147	8,242	8,057
Market value (in thousands)	3,801	3,326	3,197	4,277	3,801	4,752	7,128	6,653
Earnings before nonrecurring items (in thousands)	(221)	812	547	(394)	318	232	632	984
Earnings including nonrecurring items (in thousands)	(306)	946	20	(352)	438	214	801	996
Dividends (in thousands)	—	—	—	—	—	309	617	617
Total capital employed (in thousands)	$9,482	$9,254	$8,320	$8,314	$8,677	$8,206	$8,242	$8,057
Earnings before nonrecurring items:								
As a per cent of total capital employed	(2.3)%	8.7%	6.6%	(4.7)%	3.7%	2.8%	7.7%	12.2%
As a per cent of book value	(2.5)	8.8	6.6	(4.8)	3.7	2.8	7.7	12.2
As a per cent of market value	(5.8)	24.4	17.1	(9.2)	8.3	4.9	8.9	14.8
Number of shares common stock outstanding	950,350	950,350	950,350	950,350	950,350	950,350	950,350	950,350
Per share:								
Working capital	$ 6.21	$ 6.43	$ 5.08	$ 4.86	$ 5.30	$ 4.60	$ 4.89	$ 5.13
Book value	9.36	9.68	8.68	8.67	9.04	8.58	8.68	8.48
Market value	4.00	3.50	3.37	4.50	4.00	5.00	7.50	7.00
Earnings before nonrecurring items	(.23)	.86	.57	.41	.33	.24	.67	1.04
Dividends	—	—	—	—	—	.33	.65	.65

944

exhibit 9 RAILWAY SUPPLY CORPORATION

Statement of income and retained earnings 1951–1958, years ending December 31 (in thousands of dollars)

	1958	1957	1956	1955	1954	1953	1952	1951
Net sales	$11,761	$16,232	$16,487	$17,423	$17,745	$14,821	$16,787	$15,760
Cost of sales	10,210	12,530	13,343	15,207	14,334	12,117	13,471	11,835
Gross profit	$ 1,551	$ 3,702	$ 3,144	$ 2,216	$ 3,411	$ 2,704	$ 3,316	$ 3,925
Selling and administrative expense	1,980	2,079	2,479	2,844	2,653	2,185	1,964	1,879
Operating profit (loss)	$ (429)	$ 1,623	$ 665	$ (628)	$ 758	$ 519	$ 1,352	$ 2,046
Interest expense (net)	—	5	118	116	108	33	33	5
Income before federal taxes and special items	$ (429)	$ 1,618	$ 547	$ (744)	$ 650	$ 486	$ 1,319	$ 2,041
Provision for federal taxes	cr.208	806	—	cr.350	332	254	687	1,057
Net income before special items	$ (221)	$ 812	$ 547	$ (394)	$ 318	$ 232	$ 632	$ 984
Add or deduct special items								
Gain or (loss) on sale, liquidation or abandonment of properties and relocation expense	(85)a	134b	(527)c	42	120d	(18)	169	12
Net income including special items	$ (306)	$ 946	$ 20	$ (352)	$ 438	$ 214	$ 801	$ 996
Earnings retained in business at beginning of year	5,517	4,571	4,551	4,903	4,465	4,560	4,376	3,977
	$ 5,211	$ 5,517	$ 4,571	$ 4,551	$ 4,903	$ 4,774	$ 5,177	$ 4,993
Dividends	—	—	—	—	—	309	617	617
Earnings retained in business at the end of year	$ 5,211	$ 5,517	$ 4,571	$ 4,551	$ 4,903	$ 4,465	$ 4,560	$ 4,376

a Loss on sale of property

b Gain on condemnation sale of property.

c Loss due to liquidation of cooling and heating division.

d $389,000 gain on sale of properties less $269,000 due to moving and other nonrecurring expense.

945

exhibit 10 **RAILWAY SUPPLY CORPORATION**

Consolidated balance sheets 1951–1958, years ending December 31 (in thousands of dollars)

Assets	1958	1957	1956	1955	1954	1953	1952	1951
Cash	$ 1,977	$ 1,997	$ 823	$ 454	$ 1,131	$ 780	$ 966	$ 1,104
Accounts and notes receivable	1,803a	1,693b	2,570c	2,759d	1,828	1,695	1,545	2,437
Inventories	3,910	3,368	4,203	5,520	6,782	5,179	4,167	4,948
Total current assets	$ 6,690	$ 7,058	$ 7,596	$ 8,733	$ 9,741	$ 7,654	$ 6,678	$ 8,489
Land, buildings and equipment	$ 5,420	$ 5,187	$ 5,218	$ 5,608	$ 5,309	$ 6,204	$ 5,916	$ 5,286
Less depreciation	2,545	2,330	2,134	2,123	1,876	2,563	2,490	2,295
Net property	$ 2,875	$ 2,857	$ 3,084	$ 3,485	$ 3,433	$ 3,641	$ 3,426	$ 2,991
Notes receivable	125	148	172	—	—	—	—	—
Deferred charges	579	132	231	276	263	270	252	269
Total assets	$10,269	$10,195	$11,083	$12,494	$13,437	$11,565	$10,356	$11,749

exhibit 9 (continued)

Liabilities

Notes payable	$ 40	$ 13	$ 1,638	$ 3,263	$ 3,263	$ 1,957	$ 325	$ 1,300
Accounts payable	521	716	936	655	876	1,134	1,436	2,044
Accruals	226	198	189	194	390	189	272	267
Federal income tax	—	14	—	—	174	—	—	—
Total current liabilities	$ 787	$ 941	$ 2,763	$ 4,112	$ 4,703	$ 3,280	$ 2,033	$ 3,611
Insurance reserve	—	—	—	68	57	79	81	81
Notes payable	26	33	40	46	52	59	—	—
Mortgage payable	16	22	27	35	40	—	—	—
Patents	548	—	—	—	—	—	—	—
Stockholders equity:								
Common stock	$ 3,220	$ 3,220	$ 3,220	$ 3,220	$ 3,220	$ 3,220	$ 3,220	$ 3,220
Capital surplus	798	798	798	798	798	798	798	798
Retained earnings	5,211	5,518	4,572	4,552	4,904	4,466	4,561	4,376
Less reacquired stock	337	337	337	337	337	337	337	337
Net common stock & surplus	$ 8,892	$ 9,199	$ 8,253	$ 8,233	$ 8,585	$ 8,147	$ 8,242	$ 8,957
Total	$10,269	$10,195	$11,083	$12,494	$13,437	$11,565	$10,356	$11,749

a Including claims for tax refund $299,000.
b Including notes receivable from heating and cooling division $280,000.
c Including receivable from heating and cooling division $621,000.
d Including advances to supplier $480,000 and tax refund claim $312,000.

RAILWAY EQUIPMENT INDUSTRY NOTES[3]

Few companies experience sharper ups and downs than railroad equipment builders, whose fortunes hinge to a great degree on the erratic changes in railroad earning power. With railroad purchases of rolling stock necessarily geared to changes in operating income, the "feast or famine" characteristics of the equipment market have forced most of the major equipment companies to widen sales opportunities through diversification. Some of these moves have been into heavy metal goods lines, which are also subject to considerable fluctuation from time to time.

In recognition of the railroads' major role in defense transportation, a provision of the 1950 tax law allowed five-year amortization of that portion of a purchase certified for wartime or emergency needs. Accordingly, equipment buying expanded sharply, reaching a peak late in 1955, when certifications of new purchases were discontinued. Since then, the decline in amortization tax deferment benefits, coupled with deterioration of railroad earnings and finances, resulted in a significant drop in new orders.

Permission by Federal authorities in 1956 and early in 1957 for several railroads to depreciate equipment over shorter life spans for tax purposes was conditioned on agreement by the carriers to replace rolling stock at the end of its depreciated life. Unfortunately, these agreements—which would provide larger depreciation cash flow for investment purposes—do not embrace a wide portion of the carrier group. The railroad industry presently is seeking broad changes in depreciation policies and initiation of a construction reserve fund. The latter would permit the industry to set aside tax-deductible reserves.

The railroad equipment industry is highly specialized, cumbersome, and inelastic. New techniques tending to check the rise in cost evolve slowly. Markets are limited and of such nature that volume usually cannot be stimulated by lowering prices; indeed, inflation of production costs, and hence selling prices, in postwar years has inhibited the railroads' ability to purchase more units. Necessary facilities involve large investment in plant and equipment. Accordingly, overhead burden is heavy. Labor costs are disproportionately high in dull periods because of the necessity of retaining minimum staffs of skilled workers and engineers.

[3] SOURCE: Standard & Poor's *Industry Surveys*, Standard & Poor's Corporation, Ephrata, Pa.

Reflecting the cyclical nature of orders, a fundamental condition of overcapacity exists except when demand is unusually strong. Overcapacity has been aggravated in some areas by the pressure of new competitors in the railroad equipment field. Thus, Timken Roller Bearing, primarily an automobile accessory maker, is aiming to increase its share of the railroad equipment market. The Budd Company, primarily a producer of automobile components, is a leading fabricator of railroad passenger cars.

To help offset the effects of wide cyclical fluctuations in sales and to attain fuller use of plant facilities, most railroad equipment concerns have pursued diversification programs in recent years, such as the pleasure boat business, dust and fume collecting fields, and electronics. Many diverse items are now manufactured, but most fall into the capital goods classifications. In some instances, sales of industrial goods exceed those of railroad products.

Under a war or armament economy, the industry's picture changes. The large plants and massive machinery are adaptable for production of large castings and various heavy tools of war, particularly aircraft components and tanks. Rising railroad traffic in such a period increases demand for primary products, so that the industry operates close to capacity. However, heavy taxes prevent corresponding gains in net income.

RAILROAD EQUIPMENT INDUSTRY
Employment and average earnings

Year	Production Workers (1,000)	Av. Hourly Earnings	Av. Weekly Earnings
1958	36.1	$2.65	$100.70
1957	54.7	2.52	100.80
1956	48.6	2.37	94.56
1955	41.7	2.25	90.45
1954	41.7	2.12	82.26
1953	62.4	2.03	80.39
1952	61.9	1.90	77.83
1951	59.0	1.87	76.48
1950	46.0	1.68	66.33
1949	59.1	1.62	63.54
1948	68.7	1.56	62.24
1947	66.6	1.41	57.06

SOURCE: U. S. Dept. of Labor.

Chart 1

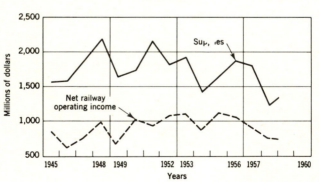

SOURCES: Association of American Railroads, Interstate Commerce Commission

SELECTED COMPANIES FINANCIAL DATA

Stanray Corp.

	Net Sales*	Oper. Inc.*	Net Bef. Taxes*	Net Income*	Net Wkg. Cap.*	Curr. Ratio Assets To Liabs.
1958	14.07	0.59	0.16	0.16	9.90	6.3–1
1957	30.70	6.95	6.24	2.92	11.06	3.3–1
1956	26.93	6.05	5.57	2.75	9.77	3.1–1
1955	19.82	3.43	2.82	1.41	8.67	4.0–1
1954	12.14	0.69	0.27	0.24	8.80	6.8–1
1953	25.14	4.31	3.92	1.92	8.94	3.9–1
1952	22.91	3.38	3.19	2.08	8.03	2.9–1
1951	35.16	7.94	7.84	3.20	9.84	2.6–1
1950	19.45	4.77	4.62	2.61	10.38	4.1–1
1949	17.29	4.26	3.98	2.31	7.49	10.2–1

American Brake Shoe Co.

	Net Sales*	Oper. Inc.*	Net Bef. Taxes*	Net Income*	Net Wkg. Cap.*	Curr. Ratio Assets To Liabs.
1958	138.00	16.41	9.68	4.78	42.8	4.1–1
1957	186.85	26.90	19.92	9.12	44.1	3.3–1
1956	186.14	24.50	19.16	8.96	32.4	2.2–1
1955	147.10	18.37	14.14	6.44	26.4	2.2–1
1954	109.92	12.68	9.20	4.30	19.4	2.3–1
1953	139.78	16.51	12.25	4.85	29.2	2.6–1
1952	135.38	14.77	11.34	4.64	25.8	2.5–1
1951	147.57	20.73	18.02	6.47	24.6	2.2–1
1950	106.58	14.07	12.34	5.94	22.5	2.6–1
1949	91.73	8.71	5.99	3.99	20.2	3.9–1

American Steel Foundries

	Net Sales*	Oper. Inc.*	Net Bef. Taxes*	Net Income*	Net Wkg. Cap.*	Curr. Ratio Assets To Liabs.
1958	94.54	12.02	8.92	4.52	27.95	3.4–1
1957	122.61	19.37	16.11	8.01	34.06	3.0–1
1956	117.13	20.15	17.47	8.37	33.24	2.8–1
1955	80.66	10.48	8.17	3.77	27.60	3.3–1
1954	89.01	9.55	8.01	3.63	30.40	3.8–1
1953	149.69	20.68	18.57	6.34	32.07	2.5–1
1952	139.56	19.32	17.03	6.04	29.76	2.2–1
1951	116.76	21.21	19.29	6.68	28.18	2.2–1
1950	54.40	7.35	6.32	3.72	29.11	4.3–1
1949	74.62	12.02	10.93	6.51	29.47	4.1–1

General Railway Signal Co.

	Net Sales*	Oper. Inc.*	Net Bef. Taxes*	Net Income*	Net Wkg. Cap.*	Curr. Ratio Assets To Liabs.
1958	18.44	3.13	3.22	1.62	11.86	4.8–1
1957	25.73	6.57	6.51	3.17	11.40	3.0–1
1956	25.71	6.62	6.48	3.14	9.21	2.7–1
1955	16.96	3.30	3.22	1.64	9.85	4.0–1
1954	15.99	2.36	2.32	1.21	11.51	5.4–1
1953	19.79	3.59	3.47	1.23	11.07	3.7–1
1952	21.62	5.06	4.91	1.44	10.85	2.9–1
1951	18.56	4.23	4.20	1.43	10.10	3.0–1
1950	13.61	2.98	2.90	1.50	9.38	4.1–1
1949	34.60	4.23	3.47	2.02	11.42	4.8–1

National Castings Co.

	Net Sales*	Oper. Inc.*	Net Bef. Taxes*	Net Income*	Net Wkg. Cap.*	Curr. Ratio Assets To Liabs.
1958	44.77	2.06	0.11	0.09	13.98	3.2–1
1957	64.89	8.03	6.32	3.12	15.80	2.9–1
1956	65.23	10.04	7.93	3.83	14.61	2.3–1
1955	58.96	7.48	5.49	2.38	11.96	2.4–1
1954	37.62	2.14	0.32	0.33	10.42	3.0–1
1953	57.73	7.55	5.25	2.25	12.90	3.2–1
1952	54.30	9.03	7.76	2.46	12.06	2.3–1
1951	63.92	13.54	12.83	4.13	12.27	2.0–1
1950	44.81	8.12	7.52	4.02	13.21	3.0–1
1949	34.60	4.23	3.47	2.02	11.42	4.8–1

Poor & Co.

	Net Sales*	Oper. Inc.*	Net Bef. Taxes*	Net Income*	Net Wkg. Cap.*	Curr. Ratio Assets To Liabs.
1958	26.6	1.47	1.48	0.87	10.13	6.0–1
1957	38.5	3.63	3.32	1.60	10.19	4.9–1
1956	42.3	4.53	4.33	2.05	9.97	3.4–1
1955	34.5	3.39	3.36	1.55	6.64	2.3–1
1954	28.1	2.29	2.29	1.07	7.13	3.6–1
1953	38.5	4.11	3.93	1.54	7.17	2.8–1
1952	34.4	3.77	3.56	1.27	6.99	2.6–1
1951	38.3	5.21	4.93	1.73	6.88	2.3–1
1950	26.0	2.87	2.70	1.44	6.60	2.9–1
1949	19.3	1.79	1.69	1.03	4.77	5.5–1

Youngstown Steel Door Co.

	Net Sales*	Oper. Inc.*	Net Bef. Taxes*	Net Income*	Net Wkg. Cap.*	Curr. Ratio Assets To Liabs.
1958	12.96	1.41	1.30	0.66	10.58	6.4–1
1957	31.05	5.82	5.63	2.70	10.56	5.1–1
1956	28.42	5.88	5.85	2.81	9.59	3.0–1
1955	20.19	3.36	3.32	1.51	8.83	3.5–1
1954	10.95	1.10	1.04	0.55	8.16	5.9–1
1953	17.36	3.08	3.04	1.17	8.18	3.8–1
1952	17.54	2.66	2.55	1.15	7.83	4.0–1
1951	24.56	4.99	4.83	1.67	7.66	2.9–1
1950	14.97	2.77	2.68	1.46	6.88	3.8–1
1949	9.64	1.36	1.16	0.70	6.25	7.4–1

Symington-Wayne Corp.

	Net Sales*	Oper. Inc.*	Net Bef. Taxes*	Net Income*	Net Wkg. Cap.*	Curr. Ratio Assets To Liabs.
1958	39.98	4.41	3.65	1.64	15.84	3.9–1
1957	43.64	3.61	3.08	1.68	15.00	3.3–1
1956	20.66	2.05	2.08	1.21	5.86	3.1–1
1955	15.37	1.66	1.64	0.92	5.69	3.3–1
1954	9.62	0.38	0.21	0.19	5.75	5.9–1
1953	19.24	2.67	2.43	0.85	6.53	3.0–1
1952	20.64	2.62	2.45	0.87	6.52	3.0–1
1951	18.59	2.40	2.36	0.91	4.73	2.5–1
1950	11.37	2.00	2.20	1.17	4.75	3.3–1
1949	10.07	1.21	1.10	0.67	6.45	8.2–1

SOURCE: Standard & Poor's *Industry Surveys* and Standard's *Listed Stock Reports*, Standard & Poor's Corporation, Ephrata, Pa.

* In millions of dollars.

36

OZARK
OIL
COMPANY

For the Ozark Oil Company the year 1963 resulted in a slightly higher total net income than the previous year and a modest increase in net income per share. Prior to this, there had been a reversal of a fairly steady downward trend in earnings that had begun in 1957. During this period Ozark's financial performance had not compared favorably with others in the industry. In 1963 Ozark's sales volume was $586 million; in 1953 it amounted to $358 million. However, income per common share in 1963 was only 98% of that in 1953, despite the higher sales volume (see Exhibits 1 through 4).

HISTORY

Ozark Oil Company had its origin in 1910 in the Kentucky Power Company, which operated electric generating stations in the Louisville area. Kentucky Power owned several coal fields in southern Illinois where natural gas fields were discovered, which led the company into the gas business, with St. Louis as one of its principal markets. Subsequent discovery of oil on its coal lands took the company into the oil business. Between 1910 and 1913 Kentucky Power acquired a number of petroleum operations, including various production leases in the Midwest and refineries in Ohio. A major acquisition of the period was a small, prospering, integrated oil company, the Ozark Oil Company, of Hannibal, Missouri, which had production and refining facilities and a chain of service stations. By 1914 the Kentucky Power Company had liquidated all of its gas and utility interests and had adopted the name Ozark Oil Company.

During the 25-year period which followed, Ozark grew through a series of mergers, acquisitions, and consolidations, which formed the basic geographic pattern of the company's future operations. After 1939 the company expanded by internal growth, developing an extensive network of production fields, pipelines, transport facilities, refineries, and service stations.

In 1948 the management embarked upon a major expansion program. It decided to allocate resources simultaneously to (1) increasing refining capacity; (2) expanding its marketing facilities; (3) increasing domestic expenditures for oil exploration. All three phases of the program were undertaken at the same time, management assuming that the discovery of new oil fields was almost a mathematical certainty, based upon its past experience and the expenditure of additional funds for exploration. The refining and marketing facilities were successfully enlarged according to plan, but discovery of significant new reserves of crude oil failed to materialize. The enlarged refining-marketing operations were retained without retrenchment from year to year, and increasing allocations were made to a stepped-up program of explorations which consistently failed to discover new sources of crude oil. Ozark Oil, since that period, existed with production facilities which supplied only about 40% of the crude oil necessary to supply its refinery and marketing capacities; it purchased remaining crude oil requirements at high cost from independent producers and from crude-rich integrated companies. "This situation is livable," said an Ozark executive, "when retail gasoline prices are high. When prices are low, we agonize."

Throughout its history the Ozark management had not attempted to expand marketing to a nationwide operation. Neither had it made any concentrated effort to align production, refining and marketing activities in the same geographic area.

THE MILLER ACQUISITION

Believing that its facilities would complement those which Ozark already owned, the Ozark management acquired the Miller Oil Company of Cleveland on August 1, 1959, for 955,100 shares of Ozark stock. Miller assets included crude oil and gas reserves, largely in Texas and British Columbia; undeveloped acreage in the United States and

Canada; an interest in a refinery near Cleveland; and an interest in oil pipelines in Ohio and Ontario. The acquisition added 3 million barrels annually to Ozark's crude production and about 75 million barrels of reserves.

THE COMPANY

In 1963 the Ozark Oil Company was considered a medium-sized integrated oil company engaged in exploration, production, transportation, refining, and marketing. It owned 3,492 oil and gas wells in the United States, Canada, Alaska, Latin America, and Africa. It was basically a domestic company; only in recent years had management ventured abroad.

Ozark had crude oil and condensate reserves estimated at 490 million barrels, of which 450 million were in the United States, 20 million in Canada, and 16 million in Venezuela. In addition, it had reserves of over two trillion cubic feet of gas in the United States. It held lease or option rights on the following acreage:

Locality	Undeveloped Acreage (Net)	Developed Acreage (Net)
United States and Canada	3,680,800	314,000
South and Central America	9,056,000	5,450
Other foreign	12,025,600	
Totals	24,762,400	319,450

Ozark had crude oil production in 21 states. Over 50% of its production was in the state of Texas, where production was restricted by Texas conservation regulations. It also produced in Illinois, Colorado, and Oklahoma.

Ozark owned an interest in 5,132 miles of crude oil pipelines; 2,700 miles of gathering lines; and 9,400 miles of product lines. It operated forty-five terminals for finished products, three tankers, four towboats, and nine barges. It had five refineries with a total daily capacity of 155,000 barrels. It sold its products in 15 North Central states through 13,046 retail gas stations (10,151 dealer-owned) (see Exhibit 5), 222 truck stops, and 825 bulk plants. It employed 240 scientists and technicians in its new research facility. It had over 8,000 employees. Since

1958 all activities were administered from a large new headquarters building it had erected at Ferguson, a suburb of St. Louis.

INDUSTRY TRENDS

From the end of World War II until 1958 domestic demand for oil increased steadily at a rate of about 6% annually. Overseas demand rose about 12% during the first postwar decade and continued to rise during the 1960's. After 1958 the United States rate of growth began to decline. In 1961 demand increased only 2.2%, the record postwar low. In the years which followed, the growth rate revived moderately, but forecasters agreed that the growth rate for the next several years would be only about 3%. Investment analysts no longer rated oil as a vigorous-growth industry.

During the 1950's additions to refinery capacity created a condition of excess capacity in the world petroleum industry. For the United States alone the excess was estimated to be over 20%. Refiners strove to keep their refining costs low by operating at as high a volume as possible. This brought pressure upon retail prices, and the result was intense price competition in every state. During 1963 15 out of 20 leading oil companies had profit margins which were lower than they had been during the declining-demand period from 1958 to 1961. "The oil industry," said an industry leader, "has achieved the singular distinction of being able to convert a sharply higher product demand into lower profits."

MANAGEMENT (SEE EXHIBIT 6)

Mr. Michael Randall, the president of Ozark, had joined the company in 1928 as an assistant treasurer. Thirty-one years old at the time, Mr. Randall had been an investment analyst with one of the largest banks in Houston, Texas. Mr. Randall progressed gradually through the financial departments of Ozark, became treasurer in 1950, and was elected president in 1954 to succeed Mr. Courtenay King, who had been elected chairman of the board.

Mr. King had spent his entire career with Ozark, having joined its predecessor, the Kentucky Power Company, on his graduation from college in 1910. Mr. King was a nephew of Mr. Myron Bullock, a distinguished Texas attorney and a major stockholder in Ozark, whose law firm had been legal counsel for the Ozark Oil Company almost from the inception of the business. Throughout his career Mr. King had been considered a protégé of "Judge" Bullock, consulting closely with him on any major move. Judge Bullock was a man of substantial means and was a director and major stockholder of the Houston bank where Randall had been employed. It was the Judge who had suggested to Courtenay King, then treasurer of Ozark, that he should invite young Randall to leave the bank and come to Ozark.

Judge Bullock's first introduction to Ozark had come from a family which dated back to prominence in the colonial period. This family had moved to Kentucky where it developed extensive business interests. Members of the family were large stockholders in Kentucky Power, and later, when the Ozark Oil Company's affairs came to center around its Texas oil fields and Galveston refining plant, the family looked to their Texas attorney, Judge Bullock, to represent their interests. As Ozark became a major oil company, Judge Bullock, on behalf of the family and later as a substantial stockholder himself, worked closely with Courtenay King and Michael Randall in directing the company's affairs. The Judge had never been an executive of the company. He had been a director for only a few years, and he had been an intermittent member of the executive committee. In 1964 Judge Bullock, then 91 years old, was still a major stockholder, as was the "colonial" family, and the Judge was still taking an active interest in Ozark affairs.

It was widely observed that, after his elevation to chairman of the board, Mr. King spent much of his time in Mr. Randall's office. Judge Bullock, then in retirement, never appeared at the Ozark headquarters office, but periodically Mr. King and Mr. Randall together visited him in his Galveston home. Announcements of major company events were made by Mr. King and Mr. Randall jointly. The board usually approved Mr. King's proposals. Mr. Randall had seldom disagreed with him in earlier years, but lately there had been rumors that Mr. Randall was no longer in agreement with Mr. King and the Judge because of their ultraconservatism.

Mr. Randall was a man of unquestionable good will who was zealous and eager to vitalize Ozark but was also indecisive, reluctant to take a determined stand against opposition, and a willing compromiser. As early as 1949 Mr. Randall had proposed that Ozark undertake a heavy exploration program, but Mr. King had not supported his proposals before the board. It was Mr. Randall who had sponsored such innovations as the Ozark Inns, truck stops, and Super Service Centers, projects which had been coolly received by Mr. King and certain veteran members of the Ozark board.

There were 17 members of the board in 1964, and they averaged 72 years in age. Board meetings had been tranquil and harmonious until 1959. In this year, as part of the Miller Oil merger, Mr. Barton Severe, former owner of Miller, came into a large block of Ozark stock, and the merger terms entitled him to two seats on the Ozark board. Mr. Severe declined a seat himself but nominated Wilbur Force, who had been president of Miller. Mr. Severe, then only 43, was known as a self-made man of great wealth and great force of personality. Mr. Force was equally aggressive. There was a growing awareness that at board meetings Mr. Force was found to be asking penetrating questions of Mr. King, who was no longer receiving the support of Mr. Randall.

In 1964 Mr. Severe asked that Mr. Force be made a member of the executive committee, which was composed of the chairman, the president, and the heads of each of the operating divisions. In making the request Mr. Severe pointed out that most major oil company executive committees met weekly; that Jersey Standard's met daily. Ozark's had been meeting once every two months.

EXPLORATION

In 1964 Ozark had still been unable to eliminate its poor "crude-sufficiency" ratio. The accelerated exploration program launched in 1949 had cost $412 million, an amount which was considerably above the industry average for a company of Ozark's size. During the first 10 years of the program, Ozark's discovery ratio, measured in terms of the value of reserves found per dollar expended in exploration, was 30% below the industry average. In 1952 Ozark produced 59,972 barrels of crude oil a day; in 1963 it was producing 58,881 barrels a day.

Although technicians in the oil industry claimed that the development of scientific equipment for locating new oil fields had taken most of the gamble out of exploration, it was generally conceded that Ozark had experienced incredibly bad luck in its explorations. In 1964 there was a joke circulating among oil men that Ozark had the dubious distinction of being the only company in the oil industry which could guarantee that every well it sank would result in a dry hole. That year Ozark outbid every major oil company to pay $19 million for an interest in several coveted offshore leases. After drilling eight dry holes, Ozark wrote off the tract as a total loss. An adjacent block, geographically less desirable, was leased by another major oil company, which brought in a heavy producing well on its first drilling.

In the period from 1955 to 1964 the cost of discovering additional oil reserves in the United States had increased significantly. During the five years ending with 1964 it had cost Ozark an average of $2.13 per barrel to discover new oil. Added to that were development, lifting, and administrative costs of $1.48 per barrel. This was a period when crude oil was generally selling for about $3 per barrel. However, a significant portion of the crude oil being produced by Ozark was from wells which the company had drilled over 20 years ago at a discovery cost of about 25¢ per barrel.

In the United States Ozark estimated that it cost $250,000 to drill an inland well and $1 million to $1.5 million to drill offshore. In both cases its recent experiences had resulted in less than one success in four attempts.

Over the years the Ozark management had consistently refrained from any foreign exploration and production because it feared the political instability abroad. In 1959 it decided to break with tradition and to venture abroad. By that time almost every major American oil company had extensive operations in various parts of the world, and generally prime land locations for exploration in the United States had been preempted. Therefore, in 1959 Ozark resorted to extensive explorations in the areas of the Gulf of Mexico offshore Louisiana and Texas, and in such areas as Alaska, Guatemala, Peru, Venezuela, and the Sahara Desert.

Ozark's search in Alaska, Peru, and the Sahara had been extremely disappointing. The Peruvian venture had produced no results and had been abandoned. The Sahara search was showing so little promise that the management was considering abandoning the project. Ozark's only activity in other areas of the Middle East consisted of a contribution toward the drilling of five wells in Arabia and some geologic seismatical studies.

Domestic wells had to be drilled deeper to tap new reserves; the flow from the deeper wells was diminishing; the cost of retrieving oil from the deeper wells was steadily increasing. Speaking of these costs, Mr. Randall said, "A barrel of domestic crude might cost somewhat more to produce than a barrel of foreign crude, but it costs twice as much per barrel to find foreign crude. Maybe we waited too long. If we don't find what we are looking for, we have only ourselves to blame."

In the years 1960 through 1963 Ozark spent $14 million in Alaskan explorations, $26 million in Guatemala, Peru, and the Sahara desert, and $9 million in the Arabian desert. During the period it spent a total of $238 million for exploration and discovered 68 million barrels of oil reserves. These 68 million barrels had cost Ozark $3.66 each to find at a time when crude could be purchased in the open market at about $3 above ground.

REFINING

The processes by which crude oil was converted into finished products were fairly uniform throughout the industry. Catalytic cracking was the same at most refineries, and most technical innovations were available to all refiners either free or by license. The size of refineries had been growing, while the number of refineries in the country had been diminishing. In 1934 600 United States refineries processed 3 million barrels of oil a day; in 1964 290 refineries processed 9 million barrels of oil a day.

In 1964 Ozark operated the following five refineries, none of which was considered large by industry standards:

	Capacity in Barrels per Day
East St. Louis, Illinois	20,000
Whiting, Indiana	40,000
Galveston, Texas	40,000
Houston, Texas	30,000
Cleveland, Ohio	25,000

In 1955 Ozark's refining capacity had been expanded abruptly by over 40% when it bought the Whiting refinery. This installation was purchased at what Ozark officials thought was a bargain price. The Cleveland refinery, which added another 12% to Ozark's capacity was obtained as a result of a corporate acquisition.

Technicians in the industry were of the opinion that Ozark had lagged in refinery modernization to such an extent that in terms of modern technology its refineries were obsolete. The Houston refinery had been built by Ozark in 1931. The East St. Louis refinery was 40 years old, and the management periodically considered dismantling or selling it. It was estimated that Ozark would need to spend $75 million to bring its refineries up to the efficiency level of modern plants. It cost Ozark 1¢ per gallon more to refine gasoline than it did other major oil companies, which resulted in about 9% higher cost per gallon.

"Using our own crude," said Mr. Randall, "we are able to net about $1 a barrel. But when we charge our refineries the $3 or so a barrel for the crude we have to buy on the open market, we lose money. There is no question about it. Our rate of profitability is riding on the amount of crude oil we can find."

TRANSPORTATION

The major portion of the crude oil which Ozark produced, purchased, and refined was transported through the company's own pipelines or ones in which Ozark owned an interest. Throughout the oil industry the over-all crude oil movements via pipeline were declining because of shrinking oil production in the older fields served by the pipelines and because of the increasing use of imported crude oil. Ozark's transportation operations, however, continued to be a profitable segment of the company's business. Especially profitable were the operations of certain segments of the network which continued to be fortunately located and which had been acquired decades ago at a fraction of their current value.

The management of Ozark felt that its transportation network was one of its strengths. Every year Ozark made additions to and improvements on the system. In 1963 it added a 73-mile wholly owned crude line in Wyoming and a 67-mile extension of an existing line in Texas to connect it with an existing line running to the company's Houston refinery. In addition, Ozark was one of seven owners of the 2,900-mile South States Pipeline being constructed between Houston, Texas, and Bayonne, New Jersey. The line would pass through the southern end of some of Ozark's marketing area, and spur lines were being added to reach some of the larger cities in the North Central states.

SERVICE STATIONS

"It is difficult to understand," said Mr. Randall, "why the industry continues to build stations on all four corners of an intersection with a market potential that can adequately support only one station. When a representation becomes more important than profitability as a means of determining a station-building program, we are bound to suffer the consequences in price fights between dealers, high rates of dealer turnover, and inadequate return on service station investment.

"Although there are fewer service stations today than for some years, there are still obviously more stations than the needed in most markets. Our company has been undertaking an extensive program of eliminating marginal stations. If the industry generally would adopt such a program, the results would be very beneficial to all of us. The economic health of every service station is directly affected by the health of every service station which is its neighbor."

Mr. Randall suggested certain guidelines which would direct Ozark's marketing efforts. There was to be restraint exercised in building more new service stations, and the locations of the new ones were to be determined by exhaustive traffic studies. Service station operations were to be profit-oriented rather than volume-producing. Ozark would make every effort to fully exploit the retail potential within its limited marketing area rather than to expand its market territory to additional states. This full exploitation was to be accomplished by eliminating marginal stations; by a program aimed at a smaller number of stations, each of which would be larger and more profitable; by introducing better merchandising practices; by intensive advertising; and by dealer training.

Ozark had already implemented this thinking as early as 1953, when it launched a determined drive to eliminate those stations which were hardly surviving. In the 10 years which followed, well over 1,000 marginal and uneconomical stations were liquidated, and over 500 unprofitable leases on service stations were terminated. The proceeds were used to build successful ones. In disposing of fee-owned stations, a studied effort was made to sell them to buyers who would convert them to non–service-station use. Many of them were remodeled to become gift shops, grills, realty offices, and even barber shops.

Studies indicated that a customer would trade, first of all, at whatever station was most convenient to him, provided that the brand was not unacceptable. In keeping with this, Ozark was highly selective in choosing new station sites. Preference was given to outlying sites in larger cities, to suburban locations, and to strategic locations on new highways.

A major feature in the program, introduced in 1959, was Ozark's Super Service Centers. These mammoth stations were positioned in central locations in certain fairly large cities, and wherever possible, they were located in new shopping centers. Two of these stations were opened in 1959; four in 1960; ten in 1961; twelve in 1962; eight in 1963; and nine in 1964. In each instance the opening of a new Super Service Center was introduced with a concentration of local advertising, and in some instances Ozark station attendants, clad in new Ozark uniforms, canvassed the entire local residential area in a doorbell-ringing campaign to solicit customers by telling them of the many services which would be offered at the new Super Service Center. Ozark's experience with the new super stations during the first few years indicated that they returned an exceptionally high volume of business, Furthermore, as a result of the Super Service advertising and merchandising programs, the business done by most of the old-line, smaller Ozark stations increased significantly.

In 1954 Ozark had 11,785 service stations. In 1964 it had 13,046 (see Exhibit 5). Statistics indicated that for the year 1964 the national average for gallons of gasoline pumped per station was 188,000. Most of Ozark's stations were selling over 300,000. The Ozark management felt that the appearance of its stations, as a result of its dealer-indoctrination program, was superior to that of any other major oil company.

A major phase of Ozark's marketing strategy was its development of a chain of commercial service stations. These large service stations were located along heavily traveled cross-country highway truck routes. Besides offering gasoline and diesel fuel at trucker discount prices, the commercial stations also furnished repair services, food, and lodging for the night. The grill-type restaurants offered hearty meals; lodging consisted of simple but clean and comfortable small rooms. These outlets were spaced out along the length of routes in such a way that a trucker could make a long trip through Ozark's territory and never be out of reach of an Ozark commercial station along the way.

In 1964 Ozark had 258 truck stops, one of the largest chains in the industry. The commercial outlet business had grown to such an extent that it accounted for 21% of Ozark's retail gasoline and diesel fuel sales. Every outlet had diesel fuel sales of over 100,000 gallons a month, and a number of them went over 500,000. Ozark planned to expand the system until it covered all of Ozark's market territory.

THE OZARK INNS

In 1963 Ozark's marketing executives conceived a new idea in travel units which would combine at a single convenient location a complete service station, a motel, and a restaurant. These units were to be located at strategic points along superhighways where there was likely to be a high incidence of travelers stopping for a night's rest. The units were intended to satisfy the three principal needs of most highway travelers: car service, meals, and lodging.

As a result of an extensive search, Ozark invited two nationally known companies to join it in the venture. Pierre's Pancake House, a well-known national restaurant chain, contracted to operate the restaurants on a concession basis. Their simple menu offered popular entrees, service was prompt and in good taste, prices were moderate, and the units, known as Ozark Inns, remained open around the clock. The motel units were leased out under franchise to the Homestead Hotel Corporation, an international hotel chain. Ozark leased the service stations to operators of proven performance and stipulated the extensive services which they were required to offer. At evening the traveler could leave his car at the service station while he stayed at the Inn. His car would be completely serviced, ready and waiting for him in the morning.

In 1963 Ozark opened its first three Ozark Inns on the Wisconsin freeway system. Initial acceptance of the Inns was good; management believed that they had far outdrawn any other service stations on the freeway. As far as the Ozark management knew, its Inns were unique in the industry, and no other major oil company was planning to duplicate them. Ozark opened six more in Illinois and Minnesota in 1964 and had plans to open fourteen more in other states in 1965.

PRICING

Gasoline price wars had been frequent throughout the industry during the postwar period, but Ozark had been especially plagued by competitive price-cutting in the 15 states which constituted its limited marketing area. Addressing stockholders in mid-1964, Mr. Randall said:

> Individual companies, and sometimes individual dealers, often trigger explosive price wars in their attempt to capture for themselves a larger share of the existing market. In the end such price competition is self-defeating; it inflicts damage upon everyone concerned, including the one who triggered the price war. These sporadic wars are entirely unconstructive; they do nothing to stimulate any over-all increase in the consumption of gasoline. Everyone in the oil industry would be better off if the energies and efforts dissipated in price wars would be applied to generating an enhanced public demand for more of our products—

in the form of increased motor travel and transport—and in the form of greater usage of heat and energy derived from petroleum sources.

Price wars come and go. There seems to be no relationship between them and the over-all condition of the industry. They vary in locale and in degree, are entirely erratic and unpredictable. It seems that there has always been an incidence of price-cutters in every market, some of whom believe that they have an inalienable right to indulge in cut-throat competition. There is no doubt that these marketing tactics have had a demoralizing effect upon the oil industry in recent years.

Price wars cannot achieve an enduring gain for anyone. Costs and expenses continue unabated during the period of the lower prices, and the only result is a struggle for higher volume on a lower profit basis. These axiomatic truths apply especially to the oil companies who use price as a sales tactic, for in recent years the cost of producing crude oil has grown progressively and wage rates have risen well over 25%.

Oversupply is generally blamed for our price troubles. This is by no means generally the case. Recently we have seen major oil companies extend the range of their products to lower-quality grades, which they introduce at lower prices. Several large oil companies also attempted to expand their retail distribution to a nationwide basis, using temporary price-cuts as a means of gaining a foothold in markets which had already been pre-empted. Furthermore, company suppliers who grant price protection to jobbers and dealers are often to blame for prolonging price wars.

We in the industry are the cause of our own price problems, and it is within our power to put our house in order. We believe that the petroleum industry can restore order in its own economy by (1) a reasonable regulation of supply and demand; (2) refraining from adding to the already excessive production capacity of the industry; (3) refraining from unreasonable additions to the existing marketing facilities by aiming for profitable operation rather than high volume and by taking a more statesmanlike attitude toward marketing policies to curb the existing malpractices. Oil companies expenses do not drop automatically with any drop in prices. During the price decline of recent years the cost of finding and producing crude oil has grown progressively. Also, industry wage rates rose about one third.

There is more to the price situation than oversupply. A factor in triggering many of the recent price wars was the introduction by some major oil companies of additional grades of lower-quality gasolines at lower prices. The recent moves of several large companies to expand their service station operations to nationwide coverage also caused product price-declines in a number of areas. Futhermore, price wars were prolonged as a result of price protection granted by supplier companies to jobbers and dealers.

Mr. Randall believed that an important factor in Ozark's declining profit level had been the abuse of the practice of providing marginal price protection on sales to unbranded marketers, allowances to dealers, and guaranteed margins to jobbers. He said:

> There might be some justification for help to dealers and other marketers when prices deteriorate. But when the profit margin guarantee is used to *beat* popular prices, rather than just matching them, then this does violence to the principle of the guarantee itself.
>
> Today we are witnessing the black-marketing of gasoline and the artful manipulation of inventories to enrich the unscrupulous at the expense of the supplier. In the interest of economy, ever-larger storage tanks are being placed in new service stations. In the hands of unscrupulous dealers, these large storage capacities can be used to juggle inventories by buying low and selling high. I know of one city where retail prices have been drastically below normal, where some dealers have been working on margins averaging up to 9¢ a gallon, and the dealer fills up just before the price restoration sets in. He will be selling his inventory of gasoline at the new price with a margin of 13½¢.

Mr. Randall also pointed out that 2.6 billion gallons of product sold by Ozark in 1964 brought the company about $36 million less than they would have brought at 1957 prices.

RESEARCH AND DEVELOPMENT

In 1955 Ozark built a new research center at Florissant, Missouri, which the Ozark management considered to be the most modern in the industry. The Ozark management paid premium salaries to attract accomplished scientists and technicians of superior skill. The research center was about 25 miles from Ozark's administrative headquarters at Ferguson. One reason this location had been chosen was that, as the research director put it, it was far enough removed from headquarters and from any operating facilities to discourage production and refining managers from foisting upon the laboratory their technical operating problems. Others in the industry commented that the considerable expense of Ozark's extensive new research facility could not be justified by the support which it gave to the company's sales promotion efforts and that pressure from headquarters caused the research center to give priority to the study of production and research problems. In 1964 its major projects were:

1. The development of a novel system for automatic processing of many types of exploration and oil field data

2. A simulation system, using scale models of terrain, to speed the analysis of exploration data developed on the actual search site

3. Improved methods for recovering additional crude oil from proven fields

4. An improved Ozark tire, which was undergoing extensive road tests

5. The development of electrochemical fluids for chucking industrial devices

6. A rustproofing compound which permitted Ozark dealers to under-coat heretofore inaccessible places on auto and truck bodies

7. The design of two new plant additions for the expansion of the petrochemical production facilities at Whiting

PETROCHEMICALS

The term *petrochemicals* was used to define any chemical which was made wholly or substantially from the hydrocarbon contents of petroleum or natural gas. Petrochemicals were finding acceptance in a wide variety of industrial usages, where they were replacing chemicals which had formerly been produced from more expensive animal and vegetable fats and oils. Almost every major oil company was engaging in the production of petrochemicals, which, as a class, were high-margin products. Many major oil company research programs were also being concentrated on the development of new petrochemicals.

Except for the manufacture of an extensive line of solvents and naphthas in conjunction with refinery operations, Ozark, until 1960, had not made any major investments in the petrochemical field. Between 1960 and 1964 Ozark made a series of petrochemical production additions to its Galveston and Whiting plants. The petrochemicals produced were used in the manufacture of decylic alcohol, plasticizers, and nylon and as lube additives. The marketing of petrochemicals was handled by the company's Midwest Mineral Oils division, which had advantageous marketing outlets. The Ozark management intended to continue to explore the possibility of expanding into other petrochemical projects. Management stated that manufacturing petrochemicals upgraded its simple oils into more refined products which yielded higher margins and were sold in less competitive markets. The expansion of the company's petrochemical activities was not, however, given priority in the company's over-all planning. Prior preference in the allocation of resources went to the exploration for new sources of crude oil.

FINANCIAL ACCOUNTING

"Oil industry accounting," said Mr. Randall, "is just about as comprehensible as the logic in Alice in Wonderland. Even C.P.A.'s are at times confounded by the intricacies of oil accounting. Some of the counterplays might look like a shell game, but the amazing thing about them is that they are perfectly legal." Mr. Randall was himself reputed to be as astute in matters of petroleum finance as anyone in the industry.

In 1961 Ozark began to include in its sales figures consumer taxes collected at the pump. This was a direct departure from previous practices and increased Ozark's already sharply rising sales volume figures.

Because of special tax regulations on depletion allowances, intangible developmental costs such as geologic surveys, and other considerations, oil companies were permitted to accumulate sizable revenues not subject to taxation. In spite of this, Ozark had by 1964 accumulated several years of tax credits, indicating that it had suffered operating losses. Ozark's 1964 report to stockholders had shown a profit of $31 million, while the report of the company made to the Internal Revenue Service showed a loss of $21 million after allowing $21 million for depletion.

Ozark used "carved-out production payments," which involved the sale of oil still in the ground on terms which entitled Ozark to repurchase rights. One effect of this was to enable Ozark to show its tax credit on its balance sheet as an account receivable. "What Ozark is actually doing," said a competitor, "is selling off corners of the farm to keep alive."

In 1961 Ozark switched its policy on exploration costs. Instead of charging off 100% of exploratory costs every year, it charged off 70% and capitalized 30%, reasoning that this was about in keeping with its current ratio of successful explorations. The result was a $2.6 million increase in income which was not explained by any note on the balance sheet.

In 1963 the management wrote off $24 million worth of nonproductive foreign properties. These write-offs were offset by reallocating a series of unused reserves which had been accumulated for refinery modernization. The end result was a $3 million addition to net income for that year. Mr. Randall became aware of the danger of loss years in 1962 when a Wall Street securities firm quietly bought over a million shares of Ozark during that year at prices ranging from $28 to $35, which were considerably lower than the book value. By 1963 adverse publicity had aroused in other financial interests an awareness of the plight of

Ozark. Several combines began to accumulate Ozark stock, and by mid-1964 Ozark stock was listed at $61 bid, $64 asked. By this time Mr. Randall was highly concerned at the imminent threat of a proxy fight, and he was fending off demands from several stockholder interests that they be given representation on the board.

PROSPECTS

Addressing a press conference in December, 1964, Mr. Randall read the following prepared statement to the assembled reporters:

> The Ozark Oil Company will observe its 50th birthday on May 24, 1965. During these 50 years the company earned over $600 million; it paid out over $300 million in dividends. We processed 1.2 billion barrels of crude oil into 60 billion gallons of products. Vehicles using our fuels drove half a trillion miles. Our other products heated countless homes, offices, and plants, powered jet planes, trains and vessels, and performed a myriad of other useful services.
>
> We at Ozark feel a justifiable pride in looking back over this creditable record of service to the nation. It is especially comforting to us at this time when prophets of doom have been indulging in dire predictions.
>
> We hear a lot of comments these days to the effect that the continuing weakness in product prices has taken all of the rose color out of the oil industry's outlook. I must admit that I have never seen such a fierce struggle for new markets and for added volume. I feel that this is a period of crucial trial, not only for the Ozark Oil Company, but for the industry as a whole.
>
> We are moving into an era of expanding demand caused by the population explosion of the sixties, the completion of our network of expressways, and by continuing record-breaking sales of new cars. But we are frustrated by many problems, both real and psychological. We need to thoroughly analyze these problems and to distinguish between policies and practices which have a real and lasting effect upon profits and those which pay in the short run but have detrimental long-run effects.
>
> I am convinced that our company is sound and that our industry is sound, and that we are a useful part of society. It would behoove us, therefore, as members of the oil industry, to make our company and the industry profitable and sound in every way. Furthermore, we have an obligation to the nation to keep the oil industry in such condition that it will stand ready to supply all forms of petroleum to the armed services in times of national emergency.
>
> We at Ozark feel that we are aware of our strengths and weaknesses. Our objectives are clearly defined and are aimed at capitalizing upon our strengths and correcting our deficiencies. We face the future with a sober degree of confidence. We have a feeling of urgency, and we are working to achieve our goals as soon as possible.

exhibit 1   FINANCIAL REVIEW

	Total Income*	Net Income	Net Income Per Common Share†‡	Dividends Per Common Share†	Book Value Per Common Share†	Net Working Capital	Long-term Debt	Capital Expenditures	Depreciation, Depletion, and Amortization	Motor Fuel and Oil Taxes Paid	Salaries, Wages, and Employee Benefits	Number of Employees
1963	$586,533,086	$23,813,880	$2.42	$1.28	$38.65	$ 83,844,800	$72,259,200	$49,111,200	$30,483,100	$102,136,800	$59,016,000	7,738
1962	557,345,700	23,160,000	2.34	1.28	37.50	85,775,200	75,360,000	67,067,200	28,082,100	98,264,800	57,608,000	7,831
1961	541,069,600	24,081,600	2.41	1.28	36.71	92,096,000	63,141,600	56,975,200	25,851,200	97,291,400	59,586,400	8,128
1960	523,560,000	26,044,000	2.63	1.28	35.35	103,446,400	64,620,000	48,020,800	26,496,000	99,452,800	58,706,400	8,086
1959	497,149,600	23,124,000	2.66	1.28	36.67	103,664,800	65,618,400	35,561,600	25,127,200	93,237,600	59,951,200	8,592
1958	468,146,400	23,057,600	2.68	1.28	35.29	95,461,600	69,106,400	37,501,600	23,967,200	85,509,600	58,451,200	8,785
1957	496,374,400	28,419,200	3.30	1.28	33.89	94,650,400	72,338,000	45,925,600	22,497,600	85,680,800	59,405,600	9,364
1956	474,238,400	29,248,000	3.42	1.28	31.86	84,788,800	68,832,800	46,504,800	22,335,600	82,331,200	58,920,800	9,682
1955	467,257,600	28,131,200	3.26	1.16	29.75	76,815,200	63,665,600	50,964,000	21,621,600	74,948,800	56,070,400	10,295
1954	376,852,800	24,930,400	2.85	1.20	27.96	71,263,200	24,962,400	41,792,800	19,086,400	63,409,600	50,536,000	9,738
1953	358,001,600	21,684,000	2.47	1.00	26.31	66,873,600	20,504,800	34,003,200	17,806,400	61,824,800	47,584,800	9,330

* Motor fuel and oil taxes paid are included in total income.

† For comparative purposes, data for years prior to 1955 have been restated to reflect the two-for-one stock split made in April, 1955.

‡ Based on the average number of shares outstanding during the year.

exhibit 2   OPERATING REVIEW

	Net Crude Oil Production, Barrels		Net Natural Gas Production MCF*	Natural Gasoline and LPG Produced, Gallons	Net Wells Completed—United States and Canada		
	United States and Canada	South America			Oil Wells	Gas Wells	Dry Holes
1963	21,090,400	1,419,200	82,545,600	62,868,800	65	7	38
1962	20,288,800	1,733,500	88,156,800	59,768,800	62	8	30
1961	20,266,400	2,012,000	89,698,400	57,080,000	77	14	61
1960	20,078,400	2,170,400	91,691,200	58,271,200	72	12	46
1959	17,300,000	1,865,600	85,544,800	58,396,000	112	15	43
1958	17,148,800	235,200	83,027,200	52,309,600	54	8	36
1957	19,220,800	....	75,098,400	57,386,400	86	14	46
1956	19,643,200	....	80,241,600	60,374,400	103	14	56
1955	19,747,200	....	78,587,200	56,302,400	158	13	46
1954	19,178,400	....	64,476,000	55,188,800	175	10	38
1953	20,618,400	....	51,339,200	59,230,000	78	6	26

* Thousands of cubic feet.

exhibit 2 (continued)

| | Undeveloped Acreage (Net) | | | Crude Oil Processed, Barrels | | | Sales of Gasoline, Gallons | Sales of Other Products, Gallons | Retail Outlets |
| | United States and Canada | South and Central America | Other Foreign | In Ozark Refineries | | By Others | | | |
				For Ozark	For Others	For Ozark			
1963	3,680,800	9,056,000	12,025,600	49,392,000	3,745,600	3,746,400	1,215,384,000	1,476,131,200	13,046
1962	4,560,800	8,980,800	12,008,800	48,196,800	3,606,400	3,878,400	1,164,181,600	1,417,413,600	12,552
1961	5,848,000	9,103,200	275,200	44,884,800	3,504,000	4,032,800	1,171,540,800	1,246,250,400	12,798
1960	3,919,200	606,400	275,200	45,245,600	3,513,600	4,025,600	1,203,073,600	1,142,421,600	12,532
1959	3,670,400	1,428,000	....	45,072,000	3,504,000	3,338,400	1,127,877,600	1,079,032,000	12,832
1958	3,473,600	4,862,400	....	44,393,600	3,679,200	820,000	1,113,818,400	944,607,200	12,763
1957	3,896,800	4,348,800	....	43,200,000	2,879,200	....	1,125,167,200	969,153,600	12,441
1956	3,924,000	....	....	44,405,600	3,459,400	....	1,105,824,800	985,025,600	12,790
1955	3,341,600	....	....	44,744,000	3,650,400	579,200	1,125,478,400	1,002,756,000	12,265
1954	2,679,200	....	....	36,212,000	1,539,400	3,631,200	925,834,400	860,529,600	11,650
1953	2,667,200	....	....	32,896,000	....	4,285,600	858,667,200	865,801,600	11,785

exhibit 3 CONSOLIDATED STATEMENTS OF INCOME AND SURPLUS
For the years ended December 31, 1963 and 1962

Statement of Income	*1963*	*1962*
Income:		
Gross operating income	$580,316,188	$552,717,522
Dividends, interest, etc.	6,216,898	4,628,170
	$586,533,086	$557,345,692
Costs and expenses:		
Costs, operating, selling, and general expenses	$356,063,211	$335,480,933
Taxes paid (including Federal income tax credit of		
$1,029,800 in 1963, and $2,080,000 in 1962)	112,558,571	108,665,113
Salaries, wages, and employee benefits	59,015,701	57,608,042
Provision for depreciation, depletion, and		
amortization	30,483,135	28,082,106
Interest expense	3,301,907	3,126,780
Cash discounts allowed	1,256,740	1,187,062
Income applicable to minority interests	39,941	36,050
	$562,719,206	$634,186,086
Net income for the year	$ 23,813,880	$ 23,159,606

Statement of Earned Surplus		
Balance at beginning of year	$295,749,679	$288,383,136
Undistributed earnings of subsidiary not previously		
consolidated	152,052	
	$295,901,731	$283,383,136
Add net income for the year	23,813,880	23,159,606
	$319,715,611	$311,542,742
Deduct cash dividends on common shares:		
Declared and paid during the year	$ 9,471,225	$ 12,636,882
Declared in 1963, payable March 1, 1964	3,158,646	
Declared in 1962, payable March 1, 1963	. . . .	3,156,181
	$ 12,629,871	$ 15,793,063
Balance at end of year	$307,085,740	$295,749,679

Statement of Paid-in Surplus		
Balance at beginning of year	$ 39,635,239	$ 39,635,239
Add excess of the option price received ($34.70 per		
share) in 1963 over par value ($4 per share) of		
common shares sold under the terms of the		
incentive stock ownership plan	176,251	
Excess of the amount received ($46.88 per share)		
in 1963 over par value ($4 per share) of common		
shares sold to the trustees of the employees'		
savings and stock bonus plan	9,013	
Balance at end of year	$ 39,820,503	$ 39,635,239

exhibit 4 CONSOLIDATED BALANCE SHEET
December 31, 1963 and 1962

Assets

	1963	1962
Current assets:		
Cash	$ 22,073,162	$ 25,401,435
United States government and other securities at cost, which approximates market	36,129,940	11,901,542
Accounts and notes receivable, less reserves of $1,081,659 in 1963 and $1,161,542 in 1962	53,497,716	52,390,566
Inventories		
Crude oil, refined oils, and merchandise	55,277,898	49,018,939
Materials and supplies, at latest cost, less allowance for condition	6,684,854	7,856,426
Total current assets	$173,663,570	$146,568,908
Investments, advances, etc.:		
Investments in and advances to subsidiaries not consolidated, at cost	$ 321,514	$ 425,517
Investments in securities of other companies, at cost	8,227,396	8,379,654
Receivables, etc., less reserves of $122,851 in 1963 and $360,002 in 1962	4,424,869	9,122,571
	$ 12,973,759	$ 17,927,742

Property, plant, and, equipment, at cost:

Classification	Gross	Reserve
Producing	$413,749,958	$175,798,365
Refining	109,925,544	80,533,486
Marketing	135,660,456	74,897,867
Transportation	34,624,301	14,393,947
Other	10,086,435	4,393,319
	$704,046,694	$350,016,984

	1963	1962
	$354,029,710	$346,197,933
Prepaid and deferred charges	2,401,734	3,326,626
Contracts, rights, patents, trade-marks, etc.	1	1
	$543,068,774	$514,021,210

Liabilities

	1963	1962
Current liabilities:		
Current portion of long-term debt	$ 9,174,143	$ 8,933,245
Accounts payable	39,184,455	38,740,761
Dividend payable March 1, 1964 and 1963	3,158,646	3,156,181
Accrued liabilities	9,501,633	9,963,576
Federal income taxes ($1,322,781 in 1963, less U.S. government securities in same amount; none in 1962)		
Total current liabilities	$ 61,018,877	$ 60,793,763
Long-term debt, excluding current portion:		
Promissory notes, $3\frac{3}{4}\%$, due semiannually, 1981 to 1990	$ 40,000,000	$ 40,000,000
Bank loan, $3\frac{3}{8}\%$, due annually to 1966	9,600,000	14,400,000
Pipeline mortgage sinking fund bonds, average interest 4.34%, due semiannually to 1976	8,448,800	9,154,400
Bank loan, $4\frac{1}{2}\%$ to July 1, 1967, variable 4 to 5% thereafter; $960,000 due annually July 1, 1967 to July 1, 1969, $1,920,000 due July 1, 1970	4,800,000	
Notes payable, $5\frac{1}{4}\%$, due quarterly to July 1, 1967	1,980,000	2,700,000
Serial notes, 2.95%, due semiannually to 1965	1,580,000	3,140,000
Purchase obligations, etc.	5,850,339	5,965,917
	$ 72,259,139	$ 75,360,317
Reserves and deferred credit:		
Reserve for replacement of inventories	$ 376,800	$ 601,600
Reserve for contingencies	3,195,931	3,171,228
Deferred income	24,369,417	3,873,511
	$ 27,942,148	$ 7,646,339
Minority interest in capital stock and surplus of subsidiaries	$ 342,361	$ 266,615

exhibit 4 (continued)

Liabilities

	1963	1962
Capital stock and surplus:		
Common stock authorized, 20,000,000 shares, par value $4 per share; 10,072,280 shares outstanding in 1963, and 10,064,593 shares outstanding in 1962, including treasury shares	$ 40,289,120	$ 40,258,372
Surplus (per accompanying statements)		
Paid-in surplus	39,820,503	39,635,239
Earned surplus	307,085,740	295,749,679
	$387,195,363	$375,643,290
Less treasury stock at cost, 200,000 shares	5,689,114	5,689,114
	$381,506,249	$369,954,176
	$543,068,774	$514,021,210

OZARK OIL COMPANY

exhibit 5 OZARK SERVICE STATIONS

	Number of Stations	Estimated % of Local Market
Kentucky	1,530	8.0
Ohio	1,040	6.1
Illinois	1,340	6.7
Michigan	766	4.3
Missouri	1,730	6.5
Nebraska	560	5.3
Iowa	1,520	5.7
Wiscosin	1,720	6.6
South Dakota	720	5.1
Montana	690	4.5
Wyoming	690	3.8
North Dakota	330	7.6
Tennessee	410	4.6
Total	13,046	

exhibit 6

OZARK OIL COMPANY ORGANIZATION

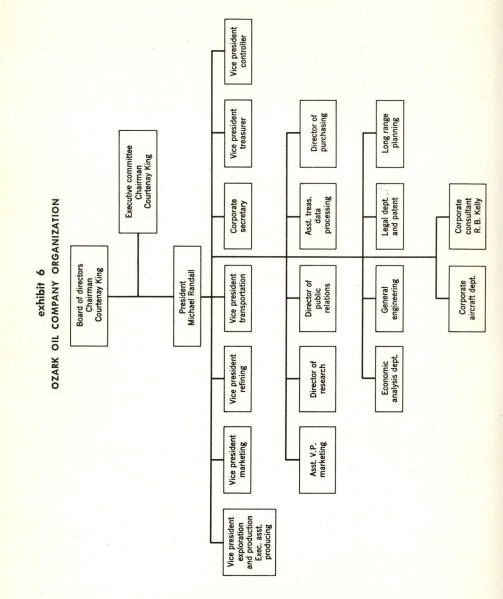